Franchise Opportunities Handbook

A Complete Guide for People Who Want to Start Their Own Franchise

by
The U.S. Department of Commerce
and
LaVerne L. Ludden, Ed.D.

The listing of franchisors in this book was originally published by the United States Department of Commerce, Minority Business Development Agency. It is one of the most comprehensive listings of franchise opportunities ever assembled. While the first several chapters and several appendices are new, the basic structure of the original listing of franchisors remains intact. It is our belief that making this book available through commercial channels will increase public access to this information.

An imprint of JIST Works, Inc.

Franchise Opportunities Handbook—*A Complete Guide for People Who Want to Start Their Own Franchise*

©1996, Park Avenue Publications

An Imprint of JIST Works, Inc.
720 North Park Avenue
Indianapolis, IN 46202-3431
Phone: 317-264-3720 Fax: 317-264-3709 E-mail: JIST Works@AOL.com

Printed in the United States of America

Order Code **P0734**

99 98 97 96 95   9 8 7 6 5 4 3 2 1

Library of Congress Cataloging-in-Publication Data Applied For

ISBN: 1-57112-073-4

TABLE OF CONTENTS

iv

INTRODUCTION

Franchising is an important part of the United States economy. Just how important is illustrated by the following statistics compiled by the International Franchise Association, a nonprofit trade association whose members are franchisors.

- Sales from franchisees in 1992 were $803 billion and are expected to reach $1 trillion by the year 2000.
- Franchise operations account for almost 41 percent of all retail sales.
- About 1 out of 12 businesses is a franchised operation—almost 600,000 businesses.
- Franchise establishments employ more than 8 million people.
- A franchised business has an average of 8 to 14 employees.
- A new franchise establishment is opened every 8 minutes of a business day.
- Studies have shown that 86 percent of franchise operations have the same owner five years after starting business and less than 3 percent failed over that same time.

These figures suggest why franchising is such a powerful economic force. What accounts for franchising's popularity? Perhaps this question can be answered by the results of a survey conducted by the Gallup Organization for the International Franchise Association. According to the poll, franchise owners had an average personal income of $124,290 in 1991, and 94 percent of the owners consider their operations to be successful. In addition, 75 percent of franchise owners indicated that their expectations for personal satisfaction in operating the franchise was met or exceeded.

Financial rewards and feelings of success experienced by franchise owners are attractive to potential business owners. People considering self-employment frequently regard a franchise as a practical option for starting a business. The purpose of this book is to help people who are thinking about buying a franchise. *Franchise Opportunities Handbook* is unique because of the resources it offers.

First and foremost, this book is a directory that lists more than 1,500 frachisors. However, it is far more than a directory. It provides valuable information about starting a business and selecting a franchise. You should find this guide to be a valuable reference in getting started on the road to self-employment.

Chapter 1 provides an introduction to self-employment. The chapter contains an assessment guide that helps you decide whether self-employment is an appropriate career choice. You also discover how to form your own business, write a business plan, finance the business, create a business team, and set up operations. This

chapter can be a useful resource even if you decide not to buy a franchise but to create an original business instead.

Chapter 2 provides basic information about franchising. It defines terms commonly used, explains the reasons that businesses franchise their operations, and describes the advantages and disadvantages of starting a franchised business. An important feature is the information it provides for evaluating and selecting a franchise. It identifies the materials that franchisors are required to give you. This information is essential to evaluate the data from the many franchisors listed in the *Handbook*.

Chapter 3 comprises the main body of the book. This chapter is a directory that lists more than 1,500 franchises. Each franchise listed contains a description of the operation, contact information, number of franchises, time in business, date began franchising, equity capital needed, franchise fee, royalty fee, financial assistance, managerial assistance, and training assistance. This information is updated periodically. For this reason, the date on which the franchisor submitted the data is included. It also demonstrates why it is necessary to verify the information when you first contact a franchisor.

There are several appendixes containing a directory of resources that can be used by aspiring entrepreneurs. Appendix A lists all offices of the Small Business Administration (SBA). This is the branch of government that provides support, resources, loans, and other assistance to small business owners. Appendix B contains a list of all Small Business Development Centers (SBDC). These organizations are funded by the SBA for the purpose of providing small business owners—or would-be owners—with technical assistance in the operation of their businesses. Appendix C provides an inventory of all Small Business Institutes (SBI) that are typically operated by universities and colleges under grants from the SBA. Appendix D includes a directory of Service Corps of Retired Executives (SCORE) offices. SCORE is a group of retired executives that volunteer their time to assist new and established entrepreneurs with business management and operational issues. All of these resources can prove valuable to the reader in investigating the potential for buying and operating a franchise. You can keep up-to-date on information about all of these resources—plus discover other useful information—through SBA Online. This is a toll-free bulletin board system (BBS). To access the BBS you need a 9,600 bps modem. The number to call is 800-697-INFO.

Information about franchisors included in chapter 3 is collected by the Department of Commerce's Minority Business Development Agency. It is published in the federal government's 23rd edition of the *Franchise Opportunities Handbook*. It is a major effort to collect this information and compile it in an organized fashion. We thank the agency and all personnel involved for their continued efforts and fine work in compiling this information.

CHAPTER 1
STARTING YOUR OWN BUSINESS

An entrepreneur looks for an opportunity for financial growth and seeks to achieve certain business goals. Entrepreneurs use different styles and methods in choosing and establishing a business. Some entrepreneurs prefer to institute their own business from the ground floor. Others feel more comfortable buying a business started by someone else. Still others find that it is more suitable to purchase a franchise and follow a model successfully used by many other business people. There are basics that all entrepreneurs, regardless of style, need to know when starting a business. The purpose of this chapter is to provide this essential information. This chapter is based on the information found in the book *Mind Your Own Business: Getting Started as an Entrepreneur.*[1] For more detailed information about starting your own business, you should read this book.

In this chapter, you learn how to create and operate a successful new enterprise. The subjects include deciding whether to start a business, selecting the right legal structure for your business, preparing a business plan, financing your business, and choosing a business team. As you read this chapter, you will learn whether starting your own business or buying a franchise is more suitable for you.

Entrepreneurship as a Career

Nearly one million individuals start their own businesses every year. This section helps you answer the important question, "Should I go into business for myself?" Whether the answer is yes, no, or maybe, you will be better prepared to make an important career decision after reading this section.

People decide to start their own business for a variety of reasons. A person seldom has just one reason for starting a business. Typically several motivational factors are at work. Here are a few common reasons for starting a business.

Independence. Many people become self-employed because they believe self-employment will offer them independence and control over their own work. This is limited by constraints placed on you by customers, suppliers, employees, and others. But these constraints affect all businesses. As a self-employed individual, you have the freedom to make decisions about how these forces will affect the operation of your business.

Job satisfaction. Entrepreneurs gain a great deal of satisfaction from their jobs. They know that they are responsible for their own success and failure.

Financial achievement. Most people become self-employed for financial gain. This may be accomplished through a high-paying salary or by a major accumulation of wealth.

Career opportunity. Some people start their own business because they find it a desirable career opportunity. They perceive it as a high-status career that is enjoyable and challenging.

Myths about Small Business

A realistic assessment of your interest in self-employment requires that you examine four common myths about entrepreneurship. In this section each myth is explained, and you are asked to develop conclusions about the impact each might have on the business you start.

Myth #1: Entrepreneurs are born, not made. Some people feel that they just aren't made to be entrepreneurs. Research on entrepreneurship has shown that experience and knowledge are far more critical to success than are personal characteristics. Your business knowledge and experience will contribute to your mastery of self-employment. You can increase your ability to have a successful small business by learning as much as you can about starting and managing small businesses.

Myth #2: The rate of small business failures is extremely high. Most people have read statistics that indicate a high rate of failure among new enterprises. Rates as high as 80 percent of businesses failing within the first five years have been reported. Recent statistics from the Department of Commerce indicate that fewer than 1 percent of all businesses were forced into bankruptcy during the period of 1972-1986. The number of new businesses that close within a five-year period may approach 50 percent, but the reasons for closure are not necessarily due to financial failures. The financial risk involved in starting a new business is therefore not as great as might be expected.

Myth #3: You need money to start your own business. Adequate financing is important for your new business. One of the major reasons that new businesses fail is poor financial planning for business needs. However, a wide variety of methods exist for obtaining financial resources and controlling costs. Not all funds have to come

---

1 LaVerne L. Ludden and Bonnie R. Maitlen, Mind Your Own Business: Getting Started as an Entrepreneur, Indianapolis, Ind.: JIST Works, Inc., 1994.

from your own pocket. Also, many service-related businesses can be started with little investment.

Myth #4: Most small businesses fail because of uncontrollable factors. A survey conducted by Minolta and reported in *USA Today* identified five major reasons for small business failure. These are (1) a lack of capital, (2) a lack of business knowledge, (3) poor management, (4) inadequate planning, and (5) inexperience. Such factors are controllable. To avoid potential problems that might affect your business, you must do adequate planning.

Why Self-Employment Is Easier Today

Self-employment today is easier than it has been in the past. This should be encouraging to those who are thinking about becoming entrepreneurs. Several reasons exist for this positive environment for self-employment, including resources that can help you start your business.

Capitalization. A number of sources currently exist for venture capital. Additionally, the home equity loan makes it possible for some individuals to invest in a small business opportunity using tax-deductible interest on their loans.

Lump-sum distributions. With a number of companies offering early retirement or the opportunity to sever employment, many individuals are given a severance package or pension benefit as a lump-sum distribution. This provides capital to invest in a business venture.

Computers and other electronic devices. Computers and other electronic devices, such as copiers, voice mail, and fax machines, make it easier for someone to conduct business. These computer and technical resources were unaffordable to small firms just a few short years ago.

Franchises. With the growing popularity of franchises, individuals can buy into an existing business without developing an original service or product. Some people prefer working with a tested idea instead of starting a business of their own.

State-wide programs for small business development. A number of state and national programs are designed to help small businesses. Some of these programs are described in the next section.

Help for Small Business Development

State economic development programs. Many state governments support small business development and have special programs to help small businesses. Those who make use of such resources will have a better chance of success in an adverse economy than those who do not. Check with your state Department of Commerce to see what programs are available in your geographic location. They can explain options such as training programs, incubator programs, and economic development incentives.

Small Business Administration. The federal government's Small Business Administration (SBA) has a variety of programs to assist small business owners. This includes special programs that provide management and technical assistance. In addition, loans and grants are available for qualified individuals. A list of SBA offices is contained in Appendix A.

Entrepreneurial Career Assessment

The Entrepreneurial Career Assessment Form is designed to introduce you to many of the characteristics of successful entrepreneurs. This self-evaluation can provide you with some guidance about the appropriateness of an entrepreneurial career for you. For the evaluation to be effective, you should respond to the questions in an honest and accurate manner.

Read the statements carefully, interpreting each one in the context of your personal experience. Determine how strongly you agree or disagree with the accuracy of the statement in describing yourself. Use the following scale to indicate your responses. Write the most appropriate number in the box before each statement.

Strongly Agree	5
	4
Somewhat Agree	3
	2
Strongly Disagree	1

_____ 1. I am willing to work 50 hours or more per week regularly.

_____ 2. My family will support my going into business.

_____ 3. I am willing to accept both financial and career risks when necessary.

_____ 4. I don't need all the fringe benefits provided by conventional employment.

_____ 5. I would like to take full responsibility for the successes and failures of my business.

_____ 6. I would experience more financial success by operating my own business.

_____ 7. I feel a great deal of pride when I complete a project successfully.

_____ 8. I have a high energy level that can be maintained over a long time.

_____ 9. I enjoy controlling my own work assignments and making all decisions that affect my work.

_____10. I believe that I am primarily responsible for my own successes and failures.

_____11. I have a strong desire to achieve positive results even when it requires a great deal of additional effort.

_____12. I have a good understanding of how to manage a business.

_____13. I can function in ambiguous situations.

_____14. One or both of my parents were entrepreneurs.

_____15. I believe that my abilities and skills are greater than those of most of my coworkers.

_____16. People trust me and consider me honest and reliable.

_____17. I always try to complete every project I start, regardless of obstacles and difficulties.

_____18. I am willing to do something even when other people laugh or belittle me for doing it.

_____19. I can make decisions quickly.

_____20. I have a good network of friends, professionals, and business acquaintances.

_____ **TOTAL**

Total the numbers you placed before the statements and enter the total in the space provided. Then refer to the following chart to determine a general assessment of your suitability for self-employment.

Score Assessment

80-100—You have outstanding ability to be an entrepreneur.

60-79—You have satisfactory ability to be an entrepreneur.

40-59—Self-employment may not be an appropriate career for you.

0-39—Probably you should avoid an entrepreneurial career.

Characteristics of an Entrepreneur

The following list describes some common characteristics of an entrepreneur. The number(s) after each characteristic indicates the related statement(s) in the assessment form you just used. This list interprets the form qualitatively and is based on research about entrepreneurs. Arriving at a conclusive portrait of a typical entrepreneur is very difficult. Therefore, you may score low on the assessment and still succeed as an entrepreneur.

Works hard (Statements I and 8). Self-employment requires a great deal of time and effort. The entrepreneur must perform a wide variety of time-consuming tasks. It is typical to put in 50- to 60-hour work weeks regularly.

Has family support (Statement 2). A successful entrepreneur needs family support. Stress caused by finances and time requirements can create disruptions in family relationships. The more positive support you receive from your family, the more you can concentrate on making the business a success.

Takes risks (Statement 3). Entrepreneurs are risk takers. They risk their careers, time, and money in order to make a success of their businesses. The entrepreneur typically sees a risk as a controllable situation. To be successful in self-employment, you should feel comfortable taking reasonable risks.

Sacrifices employment benefits (Statement 4). Benefits that you will find missing as an entrepreneur include a regular paycheck, fringe benefits, a nice office, secretarial assistance, equipment, and other features of employment you have grown to expect. These are no longer available unless you pay for them yourself.

Is independent (Statements 5 and 9). Entrepreneurs like being independent and in control of situations. Although being independent may not be a major concern for you, it is certainly an aspect of self-employment that you need to feel comfortable with.

Wants financial success (Statement 6). A primary reason that most entrepreneurs have for going into business is to achieve financial success. The desire for financial success provides motivational drive for the self-employed person.

Is energetic (Statements 1 and 8). Self-employment requires long work hours. The entrepreneur must have a high energy level to respond to the job's demands. In fact, an entrepreneur will often be energized by the work that is demanded and finds an energy loss when "relaxing." You will need stamina that allows you to work 12 to 16 hours per day, 6 to 7 days per week, and 52 weeks per year.

Has an internal locus of control (Statement 10). Successful entrepreneurs have an internal *locus of control,* or inner sense of responsibility for the outcome of a venture. To be an entrepreneur, you should have a strong sense of being a "victor" who is responsible for your actions.

Has a need to achieve (Statements 7 and 11). Entrepreneurs have a strong need for achievement. They strive to excel and accomplish objectives that are quite high. If you want to become an entrepreneur, you should be willing to set high goals for yourself and enjoy striving to achieve those goals.

Has business experience (Statement 12). An entrepreneur should have extensive business experience to be successful. General management experience is beneficial because an entrepreneur must know something about all types of management.

Has a self-employed parent as a role model (Statement 14). Entrepreneurs are more likely to have a parent—specially a father-who is self-employed. A parent's inspiration and knowledge about operating a business can contribute to an entrepreneur's success. If you have a parent who is self-employed, consider this a plus for your own success as an entrepreneur.

Has self-confidence (Statements 10, 15, and 18). An important characteristic of entrepreneurs is self-confidence. You need to believe in yourself. Your belief will help you overcome the problems that inevitably affect all self-employed persons at some point in their careers.

Has integrity (Statement 16). People often cite honesty and integrity as characteristics of entrepreneurs. Customers do not want to deal with business owners who are dishonest and unethical. You should feel positive about your ethical treatment of people and be committed to conducting your business with the utmost integrity.

Has determination (Statement 17). One of the most important characteristics of entrepreneurs is determination. This trait is closely related to self-confidence. The more you believe in yourself, the more likely you are to continue to struggle for success when faced with tremendous obstacles.

Adapts to change (Statements 13 and 19). A new business changes rapidly, so an entrepreneur must be able to adapt to change. The skills required for adaptation to change are the capacity to solve problems, the ability to make quick decisions, and the ability to learn from your experiences.

Has a good network of professionals (Statement 20). An entrepreneur has a good network of professionals. This network provides access to those who can be consulted for advice, information, and referrals. You should have an extensive network of professionals to whom you can turn for assistance.

Starting a Business

People often think of an entrepreneur as someone who has a new idea for a product or service and then creates a business to sell that new product or service. But being an entrepreneur doesn't always mean creating a new product or service. You can buy an existing business or purchase a franchise.

Starting Your Own Business

You might consider starting your own business if you have a new product or service or can add value to existing business concepts. Concepts for a new business may originate from your current employment, ideas refined from other people, hobbies, or spontaneously. Here is a list of advantages and disadvantage to starting your own business.

Advantages

- Starting your own business gives you more freedom in what you do and how you do it.

- Launching a new business avoids inheriting problems from a previous owner or facing restrictions from a franchisor.

- Starting your own business can usually be done with a smaller amount of capital.

- Owning the business you start and watching it grow can be very satisfying.

- Basing your own business on a new idea and a well-thought-out plan can be quite profitable.

Disadvantages

- It generally takes more time for a new business to become profitable.

- During the early stages of a new business, you may need to invest a great amount of time and money.

- A new business based on an innovative product or service may need additional capital during the start-up period to cover the time required to educate potential buyers about the new product or service.

- Starting a new business requires a number of business skills, such as time management, marketing, budgeting, goal setting and sometimes specific technical skills.

Buying a Business

You might consider buying an existing business if you want to be a business owner but don't want to go through the pains of starting your own business. Some individuals may be uncertain of how to do this, or they lack (or think they lack) the creativity, talent, or special skills to start their own business. This option may be quite practical for someone leaving a large corporation, a person seeking semi-retirement, and an owner of other businesses wanting to expand. There are a number of advantages and disadvantages to buying an existing business.

Advantages

- Purchasing a business usually takes much less time and effort than starting a business.

- An existing business already has a market and customer base.

- Such a business might have a staff and experts in place to work the plan.

- The business has a track record that can be reviewed and evaluated for future profitability.

- If the business is already profitable, it is possible to earn a profit from the beginning.

- If the established business is somewhat successful, the risk is considerably less.

- It is sometimes possible to get a real bargain by buying an existing business.

Disadvantages

- A business for sale may be on the market for internal problems known to the experienced seller, but not easily perceived by an inexperienced buyer.

- Even after you have done your homework to find out if an existing business has the right potential; there are no guarantees that the business will continue to be profitable.

- You buy the bad as well as the good about an existing business. It might not be structured the way you would like it to be and have workforce problems, a poor location, or accounts receivable that are high and largely uncollectible.

- Most small businesses are successful because of the talent and skills of their owners. You have no way of knowing what effect the owner's departure will have on the business.

- The inventory may have book value but be worthless.

- Buying an existing business might be more expensive than starting one of your own.

Buying a Franchise

To become self-employed, you might consider buying a franchise. A *franchise* is a product or idea that can be purchased from another person or company along with the expertise to start and operate the business. The buyer of a franchise is called a *franchisee,* and the seller is called a *franchisor.* Consider the following advantages and disadvantages to buying a franchise.

Advantages

- A franchise product or service has already been developed and field-tested.

- A franchise often has instant name recognition.

- The franchisor provides assistance in starting the franchise business.

- The franchisor can often assist the franchisee in obtaining financing for the new business.

- The franchisor can often provide support through consultants and trainers.

- Other franchisees can offer advice, feedback on their experience, and practical suggestions.

- A franchise business can get high-volume purchase prices for products.

Disadvantages

- You will pay a substantial fee for the franchise.

- As a business owner, you give up a great deal of control when you operate a franchise.

- You also have to maintain the business in accordance with standards set by the franchisor, and this can cost extra money.

- The franchisor might terminate your franchise if you don't abide by standards or might be able to buy back the franchise from you whenever the franchisor wants.

- You are dependent on the success of the franchisor. Some franchisees develop an extremely strong business, but when their franchisor

goes out of business, they find it impossible to continue operation.

Legal Forms of Organization

When you start a new business, you must determine its legal status. Each state has specific legal requirements you must meet to conduct business in the state. You will need to research what these requirements are for your state. You can get this information from the Secretary of State, a local attorney, or government organizations that consult with small businesses.

Legal Status of an Organization

To do business, an organization must have one of four basic types of legal status: sole proprietorship, partnership, limited partnership, or corporation. There are legal and tax issues to consider for each entity. These will be explained in this section.

Sole proprietorship. A sole proprietorship is the simplest legal status for a business and its taxes. When you start a sole proprietorship, you don't need to create a new entity or shift assets. You merely segregate a portion of your assets and dedicate them for business use.

Partnership. According to the IRS, a partnership may be a syndicate, group, pool, joint venture, or some other unincorporated organization that carries on a venture, business, or financial operation. The intentions of a partnership are joint ownership, mutual contribution of capital and services, shared control of the business, and a sharing of profits and losses.

Limited partnership. Two or more persons can form a limited partnership. Typically a certificate for a limited partnership must be filed with the Secretary of State or a state agency. A limited partnership has one or more general partners, who are involved in the daily management of the of the business, and at least one limited partner, who is involved as an investor.

Corporation. A corporation is a business entity created understate law. The corporation must have associates and a purpose for carrying on business. The corporation issues shares of stock to the partners. This provides the legal arrangement for stipulating how profits are divided. Corporations must follow specific state laws for corporations and file annual reports.

Subchapter S corporation. A Subchapter S Corporation (commonly called an "S Corporation") is a corporation that files for IRS status as an S Corporation. In this type of corporation, all income is taxed through the shareholders rather than the corporation.

Selecting a Legal Structure

You will need to choose the best legal status for your new business. In making this determination, you should consider the following questions:

1. What are your personal skills and preferences?

2. What kind of organization will your business be?

3. What taxes will you need to pay?

Personal Skills and Preferences

Your skills and preferences may influence your selection of a legal structure for your business. You may sense that they are more suitable for one type of legal structure than for another.

To operate a sole proprietorship, a person must have general management skills. You need to feel comfortable in the areas of marketing, sales, accounting, finance, human resource management, customer service, facility management, inventory control, and so on. Because a sole proprietor manages the entire operation, the person needs this broad range of expertise.

A partnership is suitable when you need others with more specialized skills. If you find partners with skills that complement your own skills, you will create a stronger business.

A corporation requires someone who works well in a team environment, You and other working members of the corporation will have to function as an effective work team.

Organizational Considerations

To determine the best structure for your business, you should consider the following organizational considerations.

Personal liability. Persons who start a business are often interested in how they can insulate their personal assets from the operation of the business. Corporate shareholders are usually not liable for the corporation's debts or liabilities. Statutes in many states provide that if a judgment is made against one member of a partnership, the assets of the sued partner can be tapped, but the assets of partners who have not been sued cannot be accessed. However, one partner may obligate another without the other's approval. A sole proprietorship is not a separate legal entity, and both an entrepreneur's and a spouse's assets can be at risk.

Separate legal entity. A second important consideration is whether the organization will be a separate legal entity from the individual owners. A corporation is a separate legal entity and may sue or be sued, hold and receive property, and enter into contracts in its own name. Partnerships can entangle personal and business matters and assets. A sole proprietorship is not a separate legal entity.

Formality of business conduct. A third point to consider is how formal you want the management of the operation to be. A corporation is managed through a board of directors. The directors must be elected by the corporation shareholders. The corporation must follow articles of incorporation and bylaws, hold regular meetings of its shareholders and directors, and keep accurate records and minutes of all proceedings. Management and control of the limited partnership are placed in the hands of the general partners. A partnership is like a sole proprietorship to the extent that there are few formal restrictions on how the business is managed. The partners, however, must comply with any partnership agreement they established. A sole proprietorship does not have to follow formalized procedures in its operation. The proprietor is free to make his or her own decisions and choose the businesses and locations in which he or she wants to operate.

Continuity of existence. A fourth consideration is how the business will continue if one of the principals of the business leaves the organization or dies. A corporation is a separate entity. Therefore, it continues to exist regardless of the resignation or death of a principal. The withdrawal or death of a partner may cause a limited partnership to cease and does cause a partnership to cease. If a sole proprietor dies, the business is terminated.

Transferability of interests. A fifth consideration is whether business interests can be transferred or sold, The corporation is the most flexible business form for transferring interests, because the property can be divided into any desired number of shares. Unless there is a different stipulation in an agreement, a general partner in a limited partnership—or a partner in a partnership—may transfer partnership interests and grant the rights to the transferee only with the consent of all other partners. A sole proprietor has complete freedom to sell or transfer any portion of his or her business assets. Legally, however, there is no business to sell because it doesn't exist without the proprietor.

Expense of organization. A sixth consideration is the amount of time and money you want to invest in forming a new business. Setting up a corporation can become expensive with the various required fees and start-up costs. Other possible expenses include fees to set up the formal structure, annual franchise taxes, costs to do business in other states, fees for preparing an annual tax return, and costs for reports required by the state. A limited partnership must follow statutory formalities, and compliance will incur certain expenses like filing fees and possible legal expenses. A general partnership can usually be organized with little formality or expense. A proprietorship usually has little or no expense.

Sources of operating capital. As you think about the right legal structure for your business, a seventh consideration is capital. You need to identify your capital needs, your resources, and other potential sources of capital. If you can provide all of the capital needed to start the business sucessfully, oucanselectwhateverlegalstructure meets your other needs and preferences. If, however, your financial resources are limited, you will need to consider your options for getting capital from other sources. The corporation is the most flexible structure for getting operating capital. A corporation can issue common or preferred stock and issue bonds to raise capital. A limited partnership can increase capital resources by using resources from all of the general partners and from limited partners who provide capital but do not manage the partnership. A partnership can only the capital available from only the partners. A sole proprietorship is usually limited to individual funds in combination with loans from various sources.

Tax considerations. You need to consider taxes before you determine your best form of business organization. The income earned by a corporation is taxed at a corporate rate rather than individual rate. The corporation's payment of corporate taxes and the shareholders' payment of individual taxes on dividends amount to double taxation. You can avoid double taxation by filing for Subchapter S status with the IRS. A certified public accountant (CPA) can advise how a tax is calculated for a Subchapter S corporation. Federal income tax is paid by the partners at individual tax rates. For tax purposes, the income a sole proprietorship earns is added to any other taxable income of the individual.

More than 70 percent of all businesses in the United States are sole proprietorships. This makes the sole proprietorship the most popular legal structure. Partnerships account for 10 percent, and corporations for a little over 19 percent of all businesses. Corporations, however, generate 90 percent of all American business revenues. This suggests that a corporation is the most successful form of legal structure because it provides the greatest opportunity for growth.

Writing a Business Plan

A business plan is a document that contains planning information about all aspects of a new enterprise. This section describes why and how to develop a business plan. You also learn the basics of a business plan and its main parts.

Goals of a Business Plan

New business owners tend to act with little thought about the need for planning. A reason is that planning can be hard and tedious work that produces no immediate response. A new venture needs a business plan for three basic reasons.

1. **Evaluate success.** Developing an entrepreneurial idea can generate much excitement and enthusiasm. With these emotions, you can overlook potential difficulties in starting a business. Creating a business plan forces you to look past the enthusiasm and examine carefully the business venture you are considering.

2. **Provide direction.** A business plan provides a blueprint for managing your new business. You can refer to the plan when you face critical decisions. This type of thoughtful management will help you be more effective in managing the growth of a new business.

3. **Obtain financing.** A business plan is an absolute requirement for getting outside financing for your business. Bankers, investors, government agencies, and venture capitalists expect to see a business plan before they will consider providing financial resources for your business.

Why Entrepreneurs Don't Plan

Knowing why entrepreneurs don't take time to develop a business plan or keep it updated might help you avoid failing into a similar pattern.

Lack of time. The hectic pace often found in a new business distracts a person from planning. This is one of the reasons for developing a business plan before you start a business.

Procrastination. Many business owners put off planning. To avoid this, make planning a priority and establish a schedule for periodic reviews. Then stick to the schedule.

Lack of expertise. A business plan can be a difficult document to create and may require broad expertise in management. A local Small Business Development Center or Small Business Institute can help you develop a business plan.

Lack of trust. Many entrepreneurs believe that they have a unique idea that must be kept secret for success. A nondisclosure agreement written by an attorney can avoid this situation from occurring. Ask any person reviewing your plan to sign a nondisclosure agreement.

Skepticism about value. Many business owners are skeptical about the value of planning. However, research indicates that this is one of the major reasons new businesses fail. The relationship between planning and success should provide some motivation to write a business plan.

Format for a Business Plan

No standard format exists for a business plan. A number of formats are available, and the Small Business Administration has a booklet that shows one suggested format. The 10 major sections of a business plan are explained in this section.

Executive summary. An executive summary provides an overview of a business plan. It should be informative and entice the reader to go further into the document. Avoid making the summary more than five pages.

Mission statement, goals, objectives, and strategies. Strategic planning principles should guide your business plan. It should include statements about four issues commonly associated with strategic planning: mission, goals, objectives, and strategies. The mission statement is a one-paragraph description of the reason or purpose of your business. A *goal* is a one-sentence statement of what you intend to accomplish with your business within three to five years. Limit yourself to no more than seven of the most important goals for your business. An *objective* is a one-sentence statement about a specific benchmark you intend to achieve with your business in the fulfillment of a goal. Each goal should contain three to five objectives. A *strategy* is a one-sentence statement that indicates how to achieve an objective. Each objective may have several strategies.

Marketing plan. When you develop the marketing section of your business plan, you should consider three issues: the industry, the market, and marketing strategy. In the industry analysis include its history, future trends, and how your business will fit into the industry. Analyze the market by describing potential customers for your product, reasons for buying your product or service, the geographic area of your market, and the market's size. Finally, you should consider market strategies, such as product price, sales management advertising, and credit policies.

Design and development plan. A product or service that requires design and development needs a plan for these tasks. Describe the status of the product or service. Indicate problems that could occur during the design or development stage. Discuss how these difficulties might impede design or development and increase costs. Focus on the degree of risk involved with the design or development phase. The budget should include detailed costs for the design and development phase.

Operations or manufacturing plan. This section of the plan shows how your business format will be conceived and operated. If your venture includes the manufacturing of a product, develop a manufacturing plan. This plan describes the facility needs, preferred plant location, space requirements, manufacturing process to be used, equipment requirements, and labor requirements.

If your business provides a service, you need to describe the service and how it is delivered. Your description should include the type of facility needed, methods that will be used to provide the service, equipment requirements, preferred location for the business, and labor force requirements.

Principal parties. The business plan should describe the principal parties involved in the business venture. This includes the experience, skills, and technical expertise of the management team. Provide a summary on each key individual. (You may use a resume for this purpose.) Describe the organizational structure of your business.

Work plan and schedule. Provide a general time line for the start-up of your business. For the work plan, specify a time frame for the completion of each task and indicate who will be responsible for completing each task. Include a milestone for each of the key activities described in the plan.

Potential problems and risks. A valuable exercise is to anticipate problems you may have during the start-up of your business. You should identify potential risks as well as possible problem areas. In your discussion, explain how you might resolve these problems or risks. Investors will want to know that you have anticipated such problems and are prepared to deal with them as they occur.

Benefits to the community. Discuss how your business will benefit the community in which you are living or working. Investors will want to see how your business will especially benefit them or their community. This will be an important issue if you seek government loans, grants, or tax deferments. Describe the potential economic or quality-of-life benefits you foresee.

Financial plan. The financial section is one of the most important parts of a business plan. The reason is that many businesses fail because of unrealistic financial projections. Make certain that the data you gather for this section of your business plan is both accurate and realistic. Investors will especially want to know how you plan to finance your new business and how realistic your projections are. The financial plan should cover a three- to five-year period. Include a detailed operating budget, profit and loss forecast, cash flow projections, and balance sheets for start-up, first year, and end of the forecast period. Many lending institutions will suggest specific formats for a financial plan.

A business plan is a key planning and financing instrument for a new business venture. The purpose of the plan is to generate information for the sake of developing the plan. The Small Business Administration has some excellent materials on how to develop a business plan. In your early research, find examples of business plans.

Financing Your Business

When you start a business, the most critical factor is the initial capitalization. A business plan is an important tool for financing your new business successfully. A plan helps you determine the financial needs of the business during its first few years of operation. You can thus avoid failure due to insufficient finances. Furthermore, the sources you approach financing your business usually require a business plan. In this section, you learn what sources of funds are available to begin a business.

Personal Resources

Many personal resources are usually a ailable to start a business. Relying on such resources is sometimes called *bootstrap financing.* A simple list includes the following sources:

1. Savings
2. Life insurance cash values
3. Investments
4. Home mortgages
5. Relatives and friends
6. Contract from former employer
7. Initial contracts with new customers
8. Credit from vendors

Equity

Another method for raising the necessary finances for your business is to give investors equity in the business in return for their cash investment. This approach can increase the amount of funds that can be raised. Most banks will back a strong group of investors more than a single individual. Disadvantages to this approach are a loss of control, increased legal requirements, less personal profit, and pressure to perform from shareholders.

Methods for Raising Equity Capital

There are many ways to raise capital through investors, but it is advisable to retain the services of an attorney when you use any of them. These methods for raising capital must be evaluated by balancing three factors. First, the amount of money raised is directly related to the number of available investors. Second, the more equity the shareholders purchase, the less profit and control you keep as the owner. Third, seeking investors from other states is complicated by increased laws and regulations at both the state and federal levels.

Intrastate stock sale. The sale of stocks in just one state limits the complexity of legal requirements. Stock sales require management to disclose information sufficient for investors to make informed decisions. Both private placement of stock and public offerings may take place in intrastate transactions.

Private placement. A private stock placement is usually limited to no more than 35 purchasers. This placement is regulated by state and federal laws. The number of investors limits the availability of funds through this type of offering.

Public offering. For a public offering, a company must demonstrate that it can provide investors with a good return on investment. It also requires an underwriter that will help in selling the stock. When the stock is sold to the public, the business has no control over who invests in the business.

Venture capital. A venture capital firm consists of individuals who invest funds in new or rapidly growing businesses. Because new ventures contain a high degree of risk, a venture capital firm expects a high rate of return, which can be as high as 50 percent.

Small Business Investment Corporations (SBICs). An SBIC is a venture capital firm that is licensed by the Small Business Administration. The SBIC must raise private money and can then use it to borrow additional funds from the SBA.

State and local governments. Some states and local governments invest in new businesses. Typically these promote specific types of business-for example, high-tech businesses, labor-intensive businesses, or businesses that will locate in economically depressed areas.

Obtaining Loans

Most lending institutions grant loans to a new business for specific purposes. In this section, you will read about the types of loans that may be obtained from a lending institution.

Secured loans. Lending institutions are likely to give a loan for the four purposes described here because the loan can be secured by the company's assets.

1. **Equipment purchase.** Obtaining equipment for an office, a store, or a manufacturing operation is often possible because the lending institution can place a lien against the equipment.

2. **Inventory.** A lending institution might be willing to give the credit necessary to purchase inventory When used by retailers, this credit is called *floor planning* In essence, the lending institution owns the inventory. As items are sold, the loan is repaid. This type of loan is usually a short-term loan.

3. **Buildings.** A bank might be willing to provide a loan for a building that it could secure with a mortgage. This type of loan would probably be for a long term (20+ years).

4. **Accounts receivable loan.** The accounts receivable of a business can often be used to get a loan. The lending institution speculates that most accounts will be paid and the business will be able to repay the loan.

Lending institution line of credit. A loan known as the line of credit establishes the maximum amount of money that may be borrowed from the lending institution. The borrower draws on the line of credit only as the money is needed.

Small Business Administration guaranteed loan programs. These programs provide guarantees to banks that lend to approved small businesses. The guarantees coverage of from 70 percent to 90 percent of a loan, depending on the amount. You can find out about these programs by contacting a local banker who works with or through the SBA.

Certified Development Company (CDC) loan program. The purpose of this loan program (503 Loan Program) is to help small businesses by providing longterm fixed asset financing, such as the purchase of land, buildings, new construction, expansion, or machinery and equipment. Contact the SBA for further information about this type of loan.

Federal farmers home administration. To promote economic development of small businesses in rural areas, the FHA provides loan guarantees of up to 90 percent of the value of a loan.

State and local government programs. Many state and local governments have loan programs. These often are designed to promote specific government goals and policies.

Lenders' Criteria for Business Loans

Lending institutions are usually conservative in their decisions. They expect a business to demonstrate a high probability that it will repay a loan. The following points are normally considered by lending institutions.

Business concept (business plan). Your business plan displays a well-planned approach to business.

Collateral. The lender might secure the loan by holding a lien against buildings, equipment, inventory, or other assets.

Down payment. The lender might require for the loan a down payment that must come from the principal(s) in the business.

Credit record. A new business does not have a credit record. Therefore, a lender will examine the credit history of the principals and may secure a loan through a lien on your personal assets.

Management ability. In deciding whether to grant you a loan, a lender will examine your management ability. This is evident in your work experience and business plan.

Considerations for a Financing Option

A decision about which financing option you will use must be based on the following considerations:

Availability. You might have a limited choice in financing options. The availability of capital from outside resources will vary with the general health of the economy, as well as that of your local area. Investors will be more likely to purchase stock when the economy **is** good. Government funds are usually more plentiful at the beginning and end of a fiscal year.

Repayment. A loan must be repaid with interest. You might be required to secure a loan with your personal assets, possibly taking on considerable financial risk. Shareholders do not have to be repaid.

Control. A lender will expect you to follow prudent management principles. Investors, however, will become more involved in decisions for the business. They will elect members to the board of directors and will serve as directors. An owner thus loses some control over the business when selling shares in it.

The Business Team

An entrepreneur should identify and build a team of key professionals who can help establish the business structure and operation. Every entrepreneur should seriously consider engaging an attorney, a certified public accountant, a banker an insurance agent, and consultants as needed. These professionals can provide expertise and advice for the new business. Don't avoid using these professionals because of the expense. You might pay far more monetarily and emotionally as your business grows.

Attorney

Initially, the attorney performs a critical function for your business by filing all the necessary legal documents and advising you on business licenses and zoning ordinances. The attorney thus helps you set up the legal foundation of your business. It is possible to find attorneys who will help you establish your business for a reasonable fee. You should expect legal assistance with the following matters.

Legal structure. An attorney will advise you on the best legal structure for your business. The attorney can prepare partnership agreements or incorporation papers. An attorney can also obtain stock certificates, a corporate seal, and a corporate record book, which are usually required by state law for a corporation.

Franchising and licensing. An attorney should review any type of licensing or franchise agreement that you sign. This should protect you from problems you cannot foresee.

Patents, trademarks, and copyrights. The protection of intellectual property is a vital part of business law in a competitive society. An invention is protected by a *patent. A trademark* is a word, name, symbol, or device used by a business to differentiate itself or a product from the rest of the market. A *copyright* protects written property and computer software. The practice of patent, trademark, and copyright law is highly technical. Your local attorney can identify reliable attorneys who specialize in this field of law.

Contracts and agreements. Frequently, you will enter into business agreements with other organizations. Such arrangements need to be formalized with a contract or agreement, which should be prepared or reviewed by an attorney.

Federal and state reports. It is advisable to have your attorney prepare or review reports that you must make to federal and state governments that affect the legal status of your business.

General legal matters. During the operation of a business, many issues arise that have legal implications. For example, terminating an employee, having an employee sign a noncomp etition agreement, and complying with city ordinances are matters for which you will need legal advice.

Establishing a professional relationship with an attorney at the start of your business helps ensure that you are in compliance with all laws and regulations. The attorney will become familiar with your business and will be prepared to offer informed advice should a legal issue arise that requires an attorney's assistance.

Accountant

A certified public accountant (CPA) can provide important advice about the operation of your business. This member of your business team is particularly important if you need help with accounting or tax preparation. You will find that an accountant is useful for the following reasons.

Legal structure. A CPA can help you choose the type of legal structure that will be most beneficial from a tax perspective.

Government forms and filings. A CPA can help you comply with many government requirements-for example, filing for Subchapter S status, obtaining an employer identification number from the IRS, and completing government tax and financial reports.

Accounting procedures. A CPA can help you choose the method of bookkeeping for your business. Many CPAS know of computer software programs that can maintain your financial records.

Tax preparation. A CPA can prepare the tax returns for your business. Tax regulations and tax court interpretations result in a complex system that requires an expert to keep abreast of changes.

Audits. A CPA can conduct an annual audit of your business if the volume of business is large in dollars. Publicly held corporations must obtain audits to disclose financial information to the shareholders. The audit protects business owners against misfeasance (unintentional violation of the law) or malfeasance (deliberate violation of the law) by employees who work with the finances for the business.

A CPA, therefore, can provide advice about a varietv of financial matters, such as loans and the issuance of stock. It is useful to receive advice also on tax planning, mergers and acquisitions, financial strategies, and related matters.

Banker

Many new entrepreneurs mistakenly think that a banker is an antagonist whom they must overcome to get a loan. A banker, however, serves a vital role in the financing of the organization. This professional can help you maintain a healthy financial outlook for your business. You need a banker who perceives the banker's role as a consultant and advisor that will contribute to the success of the business.

Banking services. You should find a bank that provides the banking services you need for your business. These include checking accounts, loans, lease programs, credit cards, electronic fund transfers, and financial planning.

Financial advice. A banker can provide you with advice about starting your business and arranging financings Usually, the banker will expect to see a business plan and will give you guidance on how to create and develop a plan if you don't have one.

Loans. A major service of a bank is the provision of business loans. Typical loans are for equipment and working capital. To help you meet your cash flow needs, seek a bank that is willing to provide a line of credit for your business.

Insurance Agent

A key element of any successful business is *risk management.* This refers to a plan for avoiding loss of business assets or earning capability. An insurance agent can show you how to manage your business risks by having several types of insurance.

Liability insurance. This insurance protects you from lawsuits that might result from injuries to other people or their property. Depending on your type of business, this might include premises insurance, product liability, officers and directors insurance, professional liability, and completed operations.

Property insurance. Your business will need this type of insurance for protection against damage or theft to facilities, equipment, office furniture, and vehicles.

Earnings insurance. This insurance protects you from severe financial loss for which you are not responsible. Three types of insurance fall into this category: business interruption insurance, bad-debt insurance, and business ownees life insurance.

Fidelity bonds. A fidelity bond protects your business against employee theft. This may be required by government or business to obtain a contract.

Workers' compensation. Many states require that a business with employees carry workers' compensation insurance. This insurance pays employees for losses due to accidents on the job

Health, life, and disability insurance. Business owners will typically need these insurance policies for protection against personal loss. You might also want to provide these types of insurance for employees so that you can be competitive when hiring.

A good insurance agent can advise you about which types of insurance are needed by your business. The agent can also recommend the coverage and deductible amounts that are most appropriate for your business.

Consultants

Consultants can often help a new business by providing expertise that an entrepreneur lacks. Some examples are described in the following paragraphs.

Business start-up. Some consultants specialize in starting new businesses. They can help you develop your business plan, get financing, and identify a location for the business.

Management. A person with technical expertise might need help from a consultant who can provide general management advice.

Human resources/Training. Personnel management is subject to many laws and technicalities. If you hire employees, you might need the services of a consultant who can advise you on the development and management of personnel systems and on employee training.

Technical expertise. You may need to hire a consultant who has technical expertise in the creation of a product or service that is integral to the operation of your company.

Consultants in the field. A valuable resource will be people who have gone into business for themselves and are working in the field or industry that interests you.

Selection of Your Business Team

Professionals who become part of your business team are important to the success of your business, but they can also have an adverse effect on your business. The following useful guidelines for choosing professionals for your business team are included to help you avoid adverse effects.

Time. The more time and effort that you expend in identifying professionals for your business team, the greater will be the likelihood of getting the right people.

Develop a comprehensive list. Contact friends, relatives, and business acquaintances about professionals they have used. You also should contact local professional associations and ask for referrals to professionals who are familiar with entrepreneurial enterprises.

Interview the professionals. Contact the professionals directly. Interview more than one in each specialty before making your selection.

Check references. Talk to clients whom the professionals list as references. Seek a competent individual with whom you feel comfortable.

Care and attention. You need to be assured that the professional has the time and willingness to work with your business. A professional may be good, but a lack of attention will not help you solve business problems.

Character. The professional you select must be trustworthy, honest, and reliable. The professional must place the interests of your business above personal interests, or at least maintain a balance between them.

Charges or fees. You must consider the professional's fees for services, but this should not be the most important factor in making a choice.

Reflect on the following questions when making your final decision about which professional to use for your business.

1. How much experience with small businesses does the person have?

2. Does the person appear enthusiastic about working with your business?

3. Did the professional offer advice you found useful?

4. Are the references from other clients positive?

5. Can you afford the fees the professional will charge?

6. Can the professional provide the services you might need as your business grows?

7. Will the person continue to assist your business?

Assembling a competent, reliable, and enthusiastic business team is important for your new business. You should therefore select your business team carefully.

Beginning Operations

An obstacle facing every new business is the start-up phase. This includes all of the detailed activities involved in opening your doors for customers. Every new business needs a facility, equipment, supplies, and record keeping system. This section examines how to organize these parts of your business.

Establishing an Office

To choose a facility, you need to consider its location, the type of facility that is best for your business, and the purchase of office equipment and supplies.

Choosing a Location. The first step in selecting a facility is to determine the best location for it. The following factors need to be considered.

Customers. A primary consideration is the location of your customers. Will they come often to your facility? If they will, you need to consider ease of access, parking, and visibility. Will you be manufacturing a product and shipping it to customers? If so, you need to consider ease of shipment to customers. Will you often go to your customers' locations? If that is true, you should consider the selection of a site near most of your customers and good transportation facilities.

Workforce. A business that will require a significant number of employees should be located near a workforce of a large number of people who possess the skills needed for your business. You will also want to consider locating near education resources that can provide continued training to keep the skills of your workforce current.

Preferences. Where would you enjoy working? You should consider your personal preferences as well as those of other principals in the business. You might prefer a location close to your home. You might want to move to a new part of the country. You might prefer a rural, urban, suburban, or metropolitan area.

Services. A business should be near the services and products that are necessary for its operation. Are there adequate utility supplies? Are there good telecommunication services available? Are there required suppliers nearby? Do you have access to support services, such as consultants, marketing firms, print shops, and temporary personnel agencies?

Costs. You must keep in mind the expenses for a particular location. What is the average pay and type of fringe benefits expected by the workforce in the area? What types of taxes must be paid? What are the costs of utilities? What will it cost to lease or buy a building? The costs for a location will affect the price of your product or service and the need for working capital.

Choosing a Facility

Once you have identified a location, you must select the facility. For this decision, you must determine the type of facility that will be most adequate for you. In selecting a facility, consider the following factors:

Number of employees needed. You should try to project the number of employees needed for the next two to three years. This will help you determine the total amount of space, the number and size of rest rooms, the number of parking places, and the square footage of office or production space for each employee.

Customer access and service. There should be adequate parking space for customers. They should be able to access your building easily from the parking area. Drivethrough services are important to many people who are busy. Likewise, your ability to deliver services to customers can be important.

Storage space. List all of the equipment, inventory, and supplies that will need to be stored. Determine the method for storage and how much space this will require.

Production space. Unless you have a great deal of experience in the type of production done by your business, you will probably need an expert to help you calculate the production space required.

Office space. The amount and type of office space needed will depend on the total number of employees who will need office space, and the amount of privacy they will require.

Shipment processing and distribution. If you will be marketing products, you will need adequate space for packaging them. You will also require space to store the products until they are shipped.

Utilities. You will need access to utilities. These may include water, electricity, and gas. Furthermore, you will need to be sure that the electrical wiring is adequate for all machinery and office equipment.

Type of Facility

You have three basic options for a facility for your business. The advantages and disadvantages of each are considered in the following paragraphs.

Working at home. Working at home is one inexpensive solution for a new business. American business is replete with legends of organizations that began in the owner's garage. Its advantages are low cost, convenience, relaxed environment, flexibility, and more family involvement. Disadvantages include distractions, feeling of isolation, lower customer esteem, zoning limitations, and merging your social and business life.

Renting an office or suite. An alternative to working at home is to rent or lease a single office or an office suite. It is often possible to find an executive suite where a receptionist, secretarial staff, and specialized office equipment can be shared with other professionals. Some communities have business incubation centers that provide these facilities and services. The advantages to this approach are reasonable costs, association with other professionals, improved image, business amenities, short-term commitment, and flexibility in office expansion. Its disadvantages are less control over facility, equipment, and personnel; reliance on another's facility management; competitors; and limited customer access.

Leasing or purchasing a building. Another alternative is to lease or purchase a building when more than one person works in your business, when its operations are too large for an office environment, and when it is a retail business. Advantages include a high level of facility control, flexibility in remodeling and expansion, and better parking. The disadvantages are higher expenses, cost of furnishings, maintenance, and complications when you outgrow the facility.

Setting Up an Office

This section serves as a guide to purchasing the basic equipment and supplies you need for setting up an efficient office.

Purchasing equipment. You will need equipment to outfit an office for your business. General equipment includes furniture, a phone system, a computer system, and various office machines.

1. **Furniture.** The amount and type of furniture you need depends on the need to impress customers and make them feel comfortable.

2. **Phone system.** Your phone system is one of your most important tools because it enables you to have good communication with customers. You would be well advised to hire a telecommunications consultant for one day to identify the most effective phone system for your business and to recommend the best vendors to supply and service the system.

3. **Computer system.** A computer system can help you make effective use of modern office tools. The software applications that you will most likely need are word processing, an electronic spreadsheet, a database, an accounting program, communications, and a graphics presentation package.

4. **Copier.** A copier is essential to most businesses. You will need to make copies of financial records, proposals to customers, letters, and many other kinds of documents.

5. **Fax.** A fax machine allows you to transmit images from one location to another. You must either have a dedicated phone line for the fax or buy a fax that senses when a fax message is incoming and switches from phone operation to fax operation. It is possible to install a fax or modem/fax board in your computer.

6. **Dictation unit.** Having a portable dictation unit is helpful for making notes to yourself or for dictating documents. This unit will be particularly useful if you do much traveling.

7. **Postage meter.** A business that mails a large volume of letters or packages through the U.S. Postal Service will find a postage meter quite useful.

Purchasing supplies. The best way to purchase office supplies is to get an office supply store catalog and go through it, making a list of the supplies you will need. You should consider also some special supplies.

1. **Printed materials.** You will want to have some special items printed. These should look attractive and project a professional image. Included in this category are letterheads, envelopes, business cards, invoices, shipping labels, and presentation folders.

2. **Time-appointment system.** An entrepreneur should manage time effectively. For this, you may need an appointment and time management system.

Keeping Records

An important task in starting a business is to develop a system for record keeping which will ensure that all important data is retained in a well-organized manner. Some legal requirements exist for record keeping, so you should make certain that you are aware of them. A personal computer provides inexpensive but highly effective ways to store, organize, and retrieve records. This section reviews items that you need to consider in record keeping.

Financial records. Many states require that a corporation use a double-entry bookkeeping system. if your business will be a proprietorship or partnership, you should consult with an accountant to determine the best bookkeeping system for your needs. You should keep a general ledger, general journal, accounts receivable, accounts payable, payroll records, depreciation records, cash receipts, cash payments, inventory, sales, and payroll tax forms.

Personnel records. You must keep accurate and complete records about any employees you hire. Federal and state governments have many laws and regulations you must meet in the hiring, promotion, and termination of employees. The forms you should keep for each employee include application, proof of citizenship, I-9 form, withholding forms, copy of professional license, appraisals, and disciplinary actions.

Customer data. Customers are one of the most important assets your business will possess. You should retain information about your customers. If this information is complete and well organized, your business will be more valuable to a prospective buyer of your business.

This section has indicated the types of records you must retain for your business. These records represent the minimum of record keeping for any organization. You will find that many other records are useful, such as those about suppliers, professional contacts, advertisers, consultants, and competitors' products.

Summary

This chapter demonstrates the complexity of starting your own business. The chapter raises points that help you consider whether self-employment is a feasible career for you. It may challenge you to start a new business venture, or it may result in a decision to remain an employee who has a steady paycheck. Those readers who have been encouraged to open a new business will want to read the next chapter. In chapter 2, you will discover how to pursue self-employment through the purchase of a franchise.

CHAPTER 2
A FRANCHISING PRIMER

According to *Webster's Encyclopedic Unabridged Dictionary, a franchise* is permission granted by a manufacturer to a distributor or retailer to sell his products and the territory to which such permission extends. The legal definition expands this meaning. A franchise may also extend the right to use a predetermined method for marketing products or services through outlets that use a known name or trademark. The International Franchise Association, the major trade association in franchising, defines the term as "a continuing relationship in which the franchisor provides a licensed privilege to do business, plus assistance in organizing, training, merchandising, and management in return for a consideration from the franchise." There are four basic types of franchises used by business in the United States.

Product franchise. Manufacturers use the product franchise to govern how a retailer distributes their product. The manufacturer grants a store owner the authority to distribute goods by the manufacturer and allows the owner to use the name and trademark owned by the manufacturer. The store owner must pay a fee or purchase a minimum inventory of stock in return for these rights. Some tire stores are good examples of this type of franchise.

Manufacturing franchises. These types of franchises provide an organization the right to manufacture a product and sell it to the public, using the franchisor's name and trademark. This type of franchise is found most often in the food and beverage industry. Most bottlers of soft drinks receive a franchise from a company and must use its ingredients to produce, bottle, and distribute the soft drinks.

Business opportunity ventures. These ventures typically require that a business owner purchase and distribute the products for one specific company. The company must provide customers or accounts to the business owner, and in return the business owner pays a fee or other consideration as compensation. Examples include vending machine routes and distributorships.

Business format franchises. This is the most popular form of franchising. In this approach, a company provides a business owner with a proven method for operating a business using the name and trademark of the company. The company will usually provide a significant amount of assistance to the business owner in starting and managing the company. The business owner pays a fee or royalty in return. Typically, a company also requires the owner to purchase supplies from the company.

This chapter introduces terms commonly used in franchising. It examines the reasons behind the decision of a business to sell franchises. The chapter contrasts the advantages and disadvantages involved in purchasing a franchise. A checklist to help you determine your fit as a franchisor is included. The chapter concludes with a detailed procedure for evaluating and selecting a franchise.

Terms and Definitions

Several terms are commonly used in association with the concept of franchising. A person interested in purchasing a franchise needs to be familiar with these terms. In this section you will find an explanation for the most important of these terms.

Franchise—A legal agreement that allows one organization with a product, idea, name, or trademark to grant certain rights and information about operating a business to an independent business owner. In return, the business owner (franchisee) pays a fee and royalties to the franchisor.

Franchisor—A company that owns a product, service, trademark, or business format and provides this to a business owner in return for a fee and possibly other considerations. A franchisor often establishes the conditions under which a business owner operates but does not control the business or have financial ownership. McDonalds® is an example of a franchisor.

Franchisee—A business owner who purchases a franchise from a franchisor and operates a business using the name, product, business format, and other items provided by the franchisor. For example, McDonalds® sells a franchise to a franchisee. This allows the franchisee to open and operate a McDonalds® fast-food restaurant.

Franchise fee—A one-time fee paid by the franchisee to the franchisor. The fee pays for the business concept, rights to use trademarks, management assistance, and other services from the franchisor. This fee gives the franchisee the right to open and operate a business using the franchisor's business ideas and products.

Royalty—A continuous fee paid by the franchisee to the franchisor. The royalty is usually a percent of the gross revenue earned by the franchisee.

Franchise trade rule—A law regulated by the Federal Trade Commission that places several legal requirements on franchisors. It requires that franchisors disclose all pertinent information to potential buyers of a franchise. These disclosures provide potential buyers with most information needed to make a wise purchasing decision.

Federal Trade Commission (FTC)—A commission authorized by the United States Congress to regulate the franchise business. The Federal Trade Commission oversees the implementation of the Franchise Trade Rule and monitors the activities of franchisors. You can register complaints about a franchisor with this agency. Contact the office of your local U.S. Representative or Senator for information about how to register a complaint with the FTC.

Disclosure statement—Sometimes called an offering circular, a document that provides information on 20 items required by the FTC. These items are described later in this chapter. The law requires that a franchisor provide a disclosure statement to a potential franchise buyer.

Trademark—A distinctive name or symbol used to distinguish a particular product or service from others. A trademark must be registered with the U.S. Patent and Trademark Office. It can be used exclusively by the owner, and no one else can use it without the owner's permission. Part of a franchise's value is the right to use a recognized trademark.

The Franchisor's Perspective

What motivates a business to offer a franchise? The answer to this question will help a potential franchisee become a more knowledgeable consumer. Understanding the franchisor's perspective can help the franchisee select a franchise and negotiate its purchase.

More rapid expansion. A primary reason for a business to become a franchisor is the capability to expand more rapidly. A lack of capital and a dearth of skilled employees can slow business expansion. The franchisee provides both when a new outlet is opened. A franchisor may assist a franchisee in obtaining financing for a new business, but the franchisee bears the liability for repayment of the funds. In addition, the franchise owner usually is selected because of business experience and management skills. Thus, a franchise operation is a mutually beneficial proposition for both the franchisor and franchisee.

Higher motivation. When a business franchises its operations, it acquires a motivated group of managers. Each manager is an owner and has a high level of motivation for success. A manager also is more accountable for actions because the manager as an owner is totally responsible for business outcomes. This means that a potential franchisee should ask why a franchisor wants the franchisee to purchase a franchise. If the only benefit a franchisee brings is money, the franchisee should be cautious about why the franchisor wants to do business.

Capital. There is another advantage to franchising a business. It allows a company to raise money without selling an interest in the business. The franchisor uses franchise fees for business expansion. Issuing stock often results in reduced control and less profits per shareholder. Loans are often given with certain provisions attached and cost a significant amount of money in the form of interest paid. Franchising is an alternative that overcomes these disadvantages. However, it is useful to explore some drawbacks faced by a frahchisor.

Image. The name and image of a company are at risk when it is sold to other individuals. Thus, a franchisor often is quite particular about quality and standards that franchisees are expected to meet. Franchisors therefore usually designate very specific business practices that franchisees must follow. The concern over image also helps explain why many franchisors reserve the right to buy back a franchise operation. Potential franchisees can take comfort in the fact that most franchisors want to see them succeed. This also motivates franchisors to provide the support necessary to help achieve success.

Less profitability for franchisor. Another disadvantage to a franchisor is the sacrifice of profits. A company-owned outlet is often more profitable than a franchise. In addition, the company owns the outlet's assets. A potential franchisee should consider future motivations of a franchisor when purchasing a franchise. Will the franchisor try to buy back a business after a franchisee invests the time and energy to make the operation profitable? A franchisor should view the success of a profitable operation as beneficial to both parties.

Potential competition. Franchising a business also has the liability of training competitors. Franchisees may learn how a business operates and then decide to replicate the operation under another name. This has happened to some franchisors, so it makes others cautious. A good franchisor will try to establish a positive relationship with franchisees to avoid this problem. The restrictions placed on franchisees are usually balanced by rewards in an attempt to retain their loyalty.

As you review a franchise agreement, keep in mind the franchisor's perspective. Look for an agreement that takes a balanced approach. A good franchisor is one that desires to create a relationship where both parties are winners.

The Franchisee's Perspective

It is important to consider the costs and benefits from the franchisee's perspective before deciding to buy a franchise. This section examines both costs and benefits for a franchisee. Many of these were presented earlier but are explained here in greater detail.

Benefits

The following benefits provide a good rationale for starting a business by purchasing a franchise. These must be balanced by the costs or disadvantages.

Lower risks. Most business experts agree that a franchise operation has a lower risk of failure than an independent business. The statistics on this vary depending on the definition of failure. Whatever statistics are used, they consistently suggest that a franchise is more likely to succeed than are independent businesses.

Established product or service. A franchisor offers a product or service that has sold successfully. An independent business is based on both an untried idea and operation. Three factors will help you predict the potential success of a franchise. The first is the number of franchises that are in operation. The second predictor is how long the franchisor and its franchisees have been in operation. A third factor is the number of franchises that have failed, including those bought back by the franchisor.

Experience of franchisor. The experience of the

franchisor's management team increases the potential for success. This experience is often conveyed through formal instruction and on-the-job training.

Group purchasing power. It is often possible to obtain lower-cost goods and supplies through the franchisor. Lower costs result from the group purchasing power of all franchises. To protect this benefit, most franchise agreements restrict the franchisee from purchasing goods and supplies through other sources.

Name recognition. Established franchisors can offer national or regional name recognition. This may not be true with a new franchisor. However, a benefit of starting with a new franchisor is the potential to grow as its business and name recognition grow.

Efficiency in operation. Franchisors discover operating and management efficiencies that benefit new franchisees. Operational standards set in place by the franchisor also control quality and uniformity among franchisees.

Management assistance. A franchisor provides management assistance to a franchisee. This includes accounting procedures, personnel management, facility management, etc. An individual with experience in these areas may not be familiar with how to apply them in a new business. The franchisor helps a franchisee overcome this lack of experience.

Business plan. The first chapter discussed the importance of a business plan. Most franchisors help franchisees develop a business plan. Many elements of the plan are standard operating procedures established by the franchisor. Other parts of the plan are customized to the needs of the franchisee.

Start-up assistance. The most difficult aspect of a new business is its start-up. Few experienced managers know about how to set up a new business because they only do it a few times. However, a franchisor has a great deal of experience accumulated from helping its franchisees with start-up. This experience will help reduce mistakes that are costly in both money and time.

Marketing assistance. A franchisor typically offers several marketing advantages. The franchisor can prepare and pay for the development of professional advertising campaigns. Regional or national marketing done by the franchisor benefits all franchisees. In addition, the franchisor can provide advice about how to develop effective marketing programs for a local area. This benefit usually has a cost because many franchisors require franchisees to contribute a percentage of their gross income to a co-operative marketing fund.

Assistance in financing. It is possible to receive assistance in financing a new franchise through the franchisor. A franchisor will often make arrangements with a lending institution to lend money to a franchisee. Lending institutions find that such arrangements can be quite profitable and relatively safe because of the high success rate of franchise operations. The franchisee must still accept personal responsibility for the loan, but the franchisor's involvement usually increases the likelihood that a loan will be approved.

Proven system of operation. An attractive feature of most franchises is that it has a proven system of operation. This system has been developed and refined by the franchisor. A franchisor with many franchisees will typically have a highly refined system based on the entire experience of all these operations.

Costs

The benefits to purchasing a franchise explain why more than 500,000 franchise operations exist in the United States. However, this compares to almost 14 million independent businesses. There are obviously reasons why not everyone chooses the franchise option.

Payment of franchise fee. A major drawback to starting a franchise is the initial franchise fee. This can range from a few thousand to several hundred thousand dollars. There are two critical matters that affect your decision about buying a franchise. These are whether you can afford the franchise fee and if you can expect a reasonable return on investment.

On-going royalty payments. Franchisors also will typically require a franchisee to make continuous royalty payments. The payments are a percentage of the gross income from the business. Usually the royalty payment is less than 10 percent. Some franchisees begin to resent the royalty payments after several years because they have developed experience and built a strong customer base. This success often results in a feeling that the business could continue without the assistance of the franchisor. Besides the royalty payment, franchisors often require a cooperative marketing payment that amounts to a small percentage of gross income.

Conformity to standard operating procedures. It is important to understand that for most franchisors, there is just one way to do things, and that is *their* way. Success results from proven methods of operation, so the franchisor does not want any variations. A franchisee can become frustrated when he or she believes that there is a better way to do things.

Inability to make changes readily. A franchisor may prohibit you from selling products or services other than those approved by the franchisor. These restrictions are difficult to follow when you believe that there is strong customer demand for a new or different product. There is often a method for making suggestions, but this can be cumbersome and time-consuming. The franchisee is subject to decisions made in the central office of the franchisor. As a franchisee, you must be willing to limit your independence as an entrepreneur.

Underfinanced, inexperienced, weak franchisor. It is important to realize that all franchisors are not equal. You may have more to offer the franchisor than the franchisor has to offer you. It is critical that you carefully check the credentials of the franchisor's management team and board of directors. However, do not ignore a franchisor just because the franchisor is new. Doing this may result in the loss of a great bargain. How many people wish they could have bought a McDonalds® franchise when Ray Kroc first began selling them?

Duration of relationship. There is typically no way to extricate yourself from a relationship with a franchisor other than to sell the business. Find out what restrictions exist on selling the franchise to another person. Also, determine what conditions must exist to force the franchisor to buy back the operation. Given the permanency of most franchise relationships, you need to ask yourself whether you want to be involved with the franchisor for the rest of your business career.

Dependent on franchisor's success. The success of a franchise is usually dependent on the franchisor's suclcess. Some well-known franchisors have failed such as Lums® and Arthur Treacher's Fish & Chips®. When this occurs, the franchisee usually fails. Carefully examine a franchisor's business plans and financial reports. This will help identify potential weaknesses. However, many problems occur when a franchisor is purchased by a larger corporation or when a new management team is brought in to run the business. When this occurs, the franchisees are unable to control the situation.

People who decide to purchase a franchise are typically happy with their decision. The introduction referred to a 1992 Gallup poll. This poll found that 73 percent of franchisees met or exceeded their expectations. The growth rate for franchise operations often outpaces the economy. Thus, franchising can be an excellent choice. But is it the right choice for you?

Personal Considerations

Franchising is obviously a good choice for many business owners. However, you need to consider several personal issues when deciding whether franchising is the best option for you. This section will help you explore whether buying a franchise is a good personal choice.

Compatibility

The following questions will help you explore how well you might fit into a franchise operation. Check each statement that you agree with.

_____ I prefer to limit my risk as much as possible.

_____ I am willing to operate the business in exact accordance with the instructions of a franchisor.

_____ I am willing to forgo sales on new ideas and products because of franchisor restrictions.

_____ I am comfortable with sharing my success, including profits, with a franchisor.

_____ I enjoy being part of a well-known organization.

_____ I feel that I need the management experience and assistance that a franchisor can provide.

_____ I need assistance in developing a business plan.

_____ I do not feel comfortable with establishing a business from the ground floor up.

_____ My experience in marketing is limited, and a franchisor would help overcome this weakness.

_____ The help a franchisor provides in financing might make the difference in my ability to start a business.

_____ I am willing to pay a franchise fee to obtain a proven business operation.

_____ I feel comfortable establishing a long-term relationship with a franchisor.

_____ I am comfortable linking my success with the success of the franchisor.

_____ I enjoy selling products and services created by someone else instead of creating my own.

_____ I am willing to purchase goods and services as directed from the franchisor.

Count the number of items that you have checked. Use the scores below to help you interpret the results.

0-6—Franchising is probably not a good alternative for you.

6-10—Franchising has some attraction, but you have some doubts that need to be carefully considered.

11-15—Franchising appears to be appealing and would probably fit your personal business needs.

Financial Resources

It is important to determine your financial capability to invest in a franchise. This can be more important than your compatibility with franchising. There are three tables that follow. Use the first table to evaluate your personal financial status. The second table will help determine the costs that are involved in starting a specific franchise operation. The third table will assist you in calculating the expenses that you need for operating capital during the first three months of operation.

TABLE I
PERSONAL FINANCIAL STATEMENT

ASSETS		LIABILITIES	
Cash on hand	$ _____	Accounts payable	$ _____
Savings account	_____	Loans payable	_____
Stocks or bonds	_____	Contracts payable	_____
Loans receivable	_____	Real estate loans	_____
Accounts receivable	_____	Taxes	_____
Real estate	_____	Other Liabilities	_____
Life insurance	_____		_____
Automobiles	_____		_____
Other assets	_____		_____
TOTAL ASSETS	$ _____	**TOTAL LIABILITIES**	$ _____

NET WORTH (ASSETS MINUS LIABILITIES) $ _____

TABLE2
START-UP COSTS ESTIMATE

Franchise fee	$ _____
Building cost (new or remodeling)	$ _____
Fixtures and equipment	$ _____
Installation of fixtures/equipment	$ _____
Telephone system/installation	$ _____
Utility deposits	$ _____
Insurance	$ _____
Attorney, account, and other professional fees	$ _____
Licenses, permits	$ _____
Supplies	$ _____
Initial inventory	$ _____
Advertising, promotions	$ _____
Signs	$ _____
Vehicles	$ _____
Other	$ _____
TOTAL START-UP COSTS	$ _____

TABLE 3
MONTHLY EXPENSES

Personal living expenses	$ _____
Employee wages	$ _____
Employee fringe benefits & payroll taxes	$ _____
Building payment/rent	$ _____
Maintenance	$ _____
Utilities	$ _____
Insurance	$ _____
Advertising	$ _____
Supplies	$ _____
Postage/Shipping	$ _____
Transportation	$ _____
Inventory replacement	$ _____
Taxes	$ _____
Royalty payments	$ _____
Other	$ _____
TOTAL	$ _____
TOTAL X 3	$ _____

Multiplying by 3 provides an estimate of the operating capital that you will need. This would be enough money to operate for three months without having any income. Some experts recommend that you also plan on six to 12 months for personal living expenses. The reason for this is that it may take that long before you can withdraw any money from the business.

Personal Assessment

As you review this section, you can assess both your interest in a franchise and financial ability to purchase one. You may find that there are many advantages for you to purchase a franchise. The reader who makes this discovery will find the next section quite useful. You will learn how to select a franchise.

Selecting a Franchise

Franchising has been around since the Middle Ages but reached its economic apex in the 1970s in the United States. It has been enjoying a resurgence that started in the late 1980s. The success of franchising has attracted some inexperienced and occasionally fraudulent franchisors. In 1979 the federal government implemented a law to protect consumers from fraudulent franchisors. However, the old Latin saying "caveat emptor," or "let the buyer beware," still applies to the purchase of a franchise.

This chapter describes a simple process to evaluate a franchise and protect your investment. The process is not foolproof, and misjudgments can still occur. However, following the process will help you avoid disastrous mistakes made by many other people. The steps that are explained will assist you in finding a franchise that is a suitable match for you and has the potential for financial success.

Process for Selecting a Franchise

There are five steps you can follow when selecting a franchise with the most potential. Each step is listed in a logical order. However, you may find that it is possible to carry out more than one step at a time. These steps represent a process based on models frequently proposed in books and articles about franchises.

Step 1—Examine opportunities. There are hundreds of franchises. In most types of businesses you will find several franchise opportunities. For example, if you have an interest about a particular type of business, like a donut shop, you will find 16 franchisors listed in this directory. There are other directories that you can use to expand your search along with some magazines that periodically publish lists of franchisors. You want to contact and compare all possible franchise choices. This gives you an opportunity to review the costs and benefits provided for each franchisor. You will probably want to narrow the possible alternatives to a finalist group of no more than five. This group of finalists should represent those that you want to consider seriously. You need to complete the next four steps with each franchisor.

Step 2—Examine the franchise and franchisor. It is important to obtain thorough information from each franchisor about the franchise. In fact, the federal government and several states have laws stipulating the information that a franchiser must provide. The document containing this information is called a disclosure statement or may be referred to as a Uniform Franchise Offering Circular (UFOC). The following list contains the twenty items of information that must be supplied by a franchisor.

1. Information identifying the franchiser and its affiliates and describing their business experience.

2. Information identifying and describing the business experience of each of the franchisor's officers, directors, and management personnel responsible for franchise services, training, and other aspects of the franchise program.

3. A description of the lawsuits in which the franchiser and its officers, directors, and management personnel have been involved.

4. Information about any previous bankruptcies in which the franchiser and its officer, directors, and management personnel have been involved.

5. Information about the initial franchise fee and other initial payments that are required to obtain the franchise.

6. A description of the continuing payments franchisees are required to make after the franchise opens.

7. Information about any restrictions on the quality of goods and services used in the franchise and where they may be purchased, including restrictions requiring purchases from the franchiser or its affiliates.

8. A description of any assistance available from the franchiser or its affiliates in financing the purchase of the franchise.

9. A description of restrictions on the goods or services franchisees are permitted to sell.

10. A description of any restrictions on the customers with whom franchisees may deal.

11. A description of any territorial protection that will be granted to the franchisees.

12. A description of the conditions under which the franchise may be repurchased or refused renewal by the franchisor, transferred to a third party by the franchisee, and terminated or modified by either party.

13. A description of the training programs provided to franchisees.

14. A description of the involvement of any celebrities or public figures in the franchise.

15. A description of any assistance in selecting a site for the franchise that will be provided by the franchisor.

16. Statistical information about the present number of franchises, the number of franchisees projected for the future, the number of franchises terminated, the number the franchisor has decided not to renew, and the number repurchased in the past.

17. The financial statements of the franchisors.

18. A description of the extent to which franchisees must personally participate in the operation of the franchise.

19. A complete statement of the basis for any earnings claims made to the franchisee, including the percentage of existing franchises that have actually achieved the results that are claimed.

20. A list of the names and addresses of other franchisees.

A franchisor may want to conduct a preliminary approval of you before providing this information. The law stipulates that the information must be provided before you sign a franchise agreement. Further, you must be given a chance to review this information without interference from the franchisor. The sooner you have this document, the sooner you can begin your screening process. Do not be reluctant to let a franchisor know that you are reviewing this information and comparing it with competitors. Franchisors that are upset with this approach and unwilling to do business in this manner are probably not the kind of organization with which you want to be associated. A strong franchisor is not afraid to compete directly with rivals.

Step 3—Analyze and evaluate the disclosure statement. Information contained in the disclosure statement provides a basis for thoroughly analyzing the potential for a franchise. However, it is also necessary to investigate the franchisor to ensure that all information is truthful and accurate. Note the following points about this step:

1. Points to consider about the franchisor.

   a) **Experience of the directors and management.** The experience of both management and directors can be critical to the franchisor's competence. These individuals should have sufficient experience that they can add significantly to your own business expertise. They should have special knowledge and understanding about the type of business operation that they are selling.

   b) **Number of franchises in operation.** The number of franchisees provides some measure of the stability and experience of the franchisor. It is possible that a new franchisor provides a great ground floor opportunity. However, your risk is reduced when you select a franchisor that has a large number of franchisees. Each franchisee provides the franchisor with added experience in starting new operations. This combined experience will prove highly beneficial in getting your business started.

   c) **Number of franchises no longer in operation.** You need to find the number of franchisees who have been closed or repurchased by the franchisor or gone out of business. This information can be even more important than the number of currently operating franchises. Franchisors will sometimes buy out or close unsuccessful franchisees in order to remove problems. It is important to know how many situations like this have occurred. The more franchisees that have experienced problems, the greater your risk becomes in purchasing a franchise.

   d) **Years franchisor has been in operation.** The length of experience often indicates stability and a higher potential for franchises to succeed in the future. However, there are some good opportunities with younger franchisors. Do not let this factor alone discourage you from considering an association with a franchisor.

   e) **Type and amount of training.** The type and amount of training the franchisor provides can prove critical to your success. The best training programs will include a combination of classroom training and on-the-job training. There should be a few weeks of training involved to be highly effective.

   f) **Type of management assistance provided.** There should be a large amount of assistance provided with the start-up of the business. This period of time is normally the most difficult and requires the greatest amount of assistance. However, there should be continued assistance offered regularly, as well as for unexpected crises.

   g) **Financial stability.** The certified financial statement provided by the franchisor should indicate a financially healthy organization. Any type of questionable financial problems should result in caution about developing an association with the franchisor.

   h) **Assistance in financing.** Determine the assistance that the franchisor can provide for financing your business. Will the financing include the franchise fee, equipment, building, supplies, and operating capital? A less reliable franchisor may not obtain financing that will be most beneficial to a franchisee. Be sure to examine carefully the interest rate and loan conditions and have them reviewed by a professional attorney or an accountant.

   i) **Site location assistance.** An old expression about retail establishments states that there are three critical elements to business success. These are location, location, and location. While this is an exaggeration, it illustrates the importance of site location. An experienced franchisor should be able to provide sophisticated techniques for accomplishing this task.

j) **Planning and constructing a building.** Assistance in constructing a building can help you save a great deal of money. Find out whether there is any additional fee for this assistance.

k) **Reputation among franchisees.** The franchisor's customers are its franchisees. The best way to determine how you will be treated as a customer and franchisee is to talk with other franchisees. If possible, try to talk with those who are no longer in business. They can offer a unique insight into franchisor treatment and services. More is said about this later on.

l) **Projected operating losses.** Determine how long a franchisee is expected to operate before revenue will be sufficient to cover expenses. This will help you calculate the amount of funds you will need to raise in order to cover this deficit.

m) **Potential profits.** A critical element in deciding about a franchise is the amount of annual profits that you can expect. Have a cost analysis done to determine whether the projected profit is enough to ensure a reasonable return on investment. You should ask other franchisees whether the profit they make each year is close to what the franchisor told them to expect. Project the length of time that it will take to recover your initial investment.

2. Points to consider about personal needs.

a) **Equity requirements.** The franchise fee and the capital investment requirements are the biggest obstacle for most potential franchisees. Use Table 1 in chapter 2 to calculate your net worth. Discuss this with a banker to determine an amount of money that you can borrow. (There are other ways to raise capital, but a loan is perhaps the most common way of financing a franchise.) This information can be used to eliminate quickly those franchisers whose equity requirement is more than the amount of money you can finance.

b) **Interest and enthusiasm.** A franchisee needs to be excited and enthusiastic about a franchisor's product or service. There are several reasons for this. You will be associated with the franchisor for many years and need enthusiasm for motivation. Another reason for excitement about the franchisor is that it will be sensed by your customers and employees. Your customers will be more likely to patronize your business when they observe your enthusiasm. Employees will work harder when they are inspired by your excitement.

c) **Business skills.** The franchise should match well your business experience and skills. The more you know about the business operation, the higher your potential for success. This does not mean you must have experience with the specific product or service. You should expect the franchisor to provide training and management assistance, but related skills and experience will enhance these.

3. Points to consider about market viability.

a) **Community fit.** Many products and services can be successful in one area but may not work well in another. Customs, tastes, traditions, wealth, and other factors affect the success of a product or service in a community. Franchisors will sometimes conduct a market survey to determine the franchise's viability for your community. However, you need to verify the accuracy of such a study. Less honest franchisors may attempt to modify the survey's outcome to use it as a selling point.

b) **Location availability.** The importance of location has already been noted. You need to consider how critical location would be to this particular business. Next, it is necessary to determine whether a location suitable for the business exists within your community. If you have doubts about available sites, you should reconsider your investment in the franchise.

c) **Longevity of product.** Ask yourself whether the product or service is faddish. To protect your investment, the franchise should have long-term staying power. To do this, it is often necessary to look past your enthusiasm and be objective. Read what business magazines have to say about the product or service. Ask the advice of experienced business people. Talk with friends who would be typical of your future customers. These combined opinions will help you predict the product's longevity.

d) **Population stability.** Find out the population projections for the community in which you plan to place the franchise. City government, chamber of commerce, Small Business Development Corporation, economic development commission, and other sources can help provide this information. The long-term growth of the population will have a significant affect on the franchise's potential success.

e) **Competition.** Study the competition that will compete directly against the franchise. Then study indirect competition. For example, a specialty coffee shop might compete against delis, gourmet shops, etc.

f) **Price.** The price for the product or service should be consistent with average incomes for people in your area. A high-price product will sell in an area where income is high but would probably be a loser in an area with low-income households.

g) **Advertising.** Find out how much advertising the franchisor does on a local, regional, and national basis. This is very important when you consider the value of a franchise. A franchisor with a less expensive franchise fee may lower operating costs by limiting its advertising. This may hurt your franchise sales and business growth.

h) **Advertising campaign effectiveness.** The franchisor's marketing expertise is very important to your success. You should expect the franchisor's help in generating sales. A franchisor should offer effective advertising tools that include the creation of newspaper, radio, and television advertisements. These should be professionally prepared along with a marketing strategy that will maximize their use.

i) **Cooperative advertising.** Most franchisors require the franchisee to pay cooperative marketing fees. This is typically a percentage of revenues. It is important to understand how this money will be used and what impact it should have on your franchise.

Step 4—Investigate the franchisor. It is important for you to investigate the franchisor thoroughly. You wouldn't want to become a partner with someone you didn't know or trust. Consider your relationship with the franchisor a partnership and check the franchisor out completely. There are three stages to this investigation. Beware of any franchisor that wants you to make a decision so quickly that you will not, have time to go through the following investigative process.

1. Investigate the credibility and reliability of the franchisor.

   This is particularly critical with franchisors that have been in operation for a short time. Information from sources such as the Better Business Bureau and Dunn and Bradstreet can tell you a great deal about the franchisor. Try to find a person or company who will run a credit check on the organization. If the franchisor is a smaller and less-well-known company, you may also want to conduct a background and credit check on the management and corporate officers.

   The disclosure statement must include information about lawsuits. If there are lawsuits pending against the franchisor, investigate these by contacting the attorney for the plaintiffs. Ask the attorney to explain anything he or she can about the lawsuit. Question the franchisor about what the attorney tells you. You should feel comfortable that the lawsuit is about an issue that would not affect you.

2. Talk with franchisees about their experience.

   The disclosure statement is required to have a list of franchisees. Pick a group of franchisees at random to contact. Your conversation with franchisees can provide important information. Some questions to ask are these:

   a) Did the franchisor follow through on its promises?

   b) Does the franchisor provide good management assistance?

   c) Does the franchisor provide good marketing and advertising programs?

   d) What are the strengths of the franchisor? What are the weaknesses?

   e) Do you consider your franchise to be a success? What has contributed the most to this success?

   f) Did the franchisor make any mistakes during the start-up? How could the mistakes have been avoided?

   g) Have there been management and operational mistakes? How could these have been avoided?

   h) How strict is the franchisor about business being conducted exactly as described in operating manuals?

   i) If you could do anything over again what would it be?

   j) Would you recommend that a person buy this franchise?

   Carefully review the answers that you get. Are there consistent problems or concerns raised by the franchisees? A consistency indicates a pattern that increases the probability that the problem will be repeated with your franchise. Likewise, positive answers should encourage you to seriously consider entering into an agreement with the franchisor.

3. Seek the advice of professionals about the franchisor and franchise agreement.

   Three professionals that you should definitely confer with are an attorney, an accountant, and a banker.

   a) An attorney is needed to review the franchise agreement. This is your contract with the franchiser and provides the only written commitment and promises that exist. Anything that has been verbally promised should be in this agreement. The attorney and you should review in the agreement the following items:

      • What is the contract length? It should be the same length discussed with the franchisor.

      • Does it provide an exclusive territory? If not, what protection is offered against other franchisees taking business away from you? Proliferation of franchisees can seriously erode your revenue. This is the reason that you need some protection.

- Are there restrictions on selling the franchise? The more limitations that exist, the more difficult it will be for you to recover your money. Many franchisors will offer to buy back the franchise, but there are often conditions. You need to have a clear understanding of what you must do in order to initiate the buy-back provision.

- What are the criteria you can use to cancel the contract? Likewise, what are the criteria the franchiser can use to cancel the contract? These criteria should be reasonable and provide a clear process for canceling the contract.

- Does the franchiser agree to buy back the franchise if it is canceled. This is absolutely necessary, or you risk loosing all of your initial investment in the company. Furthermore, determine whether the franchisor will compensate you for the goodwill built during your operation of the franchise. Goodwill is a valuable asset and takes a significant investment of time and effort to accumulate.

- Are there any franchise requirements that you believe are unwise, illegal, or unethical? Sections of a contract that make you uncomfortable at the start of a business relationship may result in problems at a later date. You will probably feel uncomfortable implementing a provision that you don't believe is right.

- Has the attorney identified any problems with the contract? There are a number of legal technicalities connected with most business contracts. An experienced attorney will be able to advise you about these provisions.

b) An accountant should review two primary items for you. First, the accountant should examine the corporation's financial information that is provided in the disclosure statement. Second, the accountant should review the financial potential of the business. You should ask the accountant the following questions:

- Is the initial investment for the franchise fee, equipment, and building reasonable? The accountant may be familiar with fair market value for these things or should be able to obtain this information.

- Are the royalties and cooperative advertising rates reasonable? There are ratio tables that illustrate typical expenditures for certain categories of business. The tables can be used to indicate whether these rates being charged by the franchiser are within a normal range.

- What will your financial situation during the first five years of operation? A form that is often used in a business plan is a financial proforma. The financial proforma is a five year financial plan. The plan includes projections for income, expenses, cash flow, and profits. Review this plan with your accountant and determine the potential return on investment for the franchise.

- Is the investment a reasonable risk? All new businesses are risky. However, you must balance out three key areas to determine the degree of personal risk. These include your personal assets, resources for financing the franchise, and the potential return on investment. You should be able to afford any loss to your personal assets. The financing should provide a monthly repayment schedule that is reasonable and affordable. Potential return on investment should directly correlate with the risk that is involved.

c) A banker should be contacted to review the franchise, the financial proforma, and your personal financial statement. The banker can provide insight into the financing issues that will be involved. The banker needs to answer the following question:

- Would the bank consider giving you a loan to finance your business? This question can be directed to your accountant to determine how affordable the purchase is for you. The banker's answers are given from a lender's viewpoint. When a bank turns you down for a loan, the loan officers have noted problems. Ask the loan officer to fully explain the reasons for not making the loan. This information will allow you to evaluate for yourself whether these are serious problems that could impede the franchise's success.

- Do the loan officers feel that the franchiser is credible? The bank will take more risk when your personal assets are sufficient to underwrite the loan. This doesn't give you any assurance that they have made a positive assessment about the franchiser or the franchise agreement. Make sure that the loan officer provides a complete explanation about the loan review board's evaluation of your potential for success. What strengths and weaknesses do they judge the franchiser to possess?

- What are the lending conditions? These conditions, including the interest rate, provide additional information that can be used to assess the viability of the franchise. More liberal conditions indicate a more positive evaluation of the franchise by the loan officers. Also, attractive conditions will increase your profit potential.

You should weigh the review and recommendations of all three professionals before you make your final decision about a franchise. These experts can provide important advice, and you should value their opinions.

Step 5-Make a decision. As with all decisions, this is usually easier said than done. This section contains dozens of questions that need to be investigated. Sometimes you will discover positive facts about the franchise, and sometimes negative facts. It is possible that the positive or negative facts will be so one-sided that it is simple to make a decision. However, it is more typical to find that the facts must be organized in a manner that facilitates the decision-making process.

A simple but effective decision-making approach is the T method. To follow this method, you make a T on a page. On the left side of the T, list all positive reasons for purchasing the franchise; and on the right side, all the negative reasons. Once the two lists are completed, assign each item a number to designate its importance. A simple scale of 1 for unimportant, 2 for somewhat important, and 3 for very important can be used. Total the numbers for both sides. The larger the numerical difference between these totals, the more sure you can be of your decision. Totals that are close will make it more difficult to decide. However, an investment of this importance should usually be one that makes you feel confident of success. After completing the T-method exercise, you should feel certain that your decision is correct. A decision to purchase a franchise should result in enthusiasm for the undertaking. Without dedication and enthusiasm, you may find it difficult to achieve success.

Summary

This chapter has provided a basic introduction to the concept of franchising. It also examined the advantages and disadvantages in purchasing a franchise. Finally, it helped guide you in the decision-making process about purchasing a franchise. In the next chapter, you will discover a directory containing hundreds of franchise opportunities. You can put into practice the advice contained in this chapter in reviewing and evaluating these opportunities.

CHAPTER 3
DIRECTORY OF FRANCHISE OPPORTUNITIES

Several directories of franchise opportunities are published in the United States. Each directory has features that make it unique. One thing that sets this directory apart from others is that it is an authoritative compilation of information collected by the Minority Business Development Agency of the U.S. Department of Commerce. This directory contains more information about financial, training, and managerial assistance than is typically found in other directories.

The directory organizes the franchises into 43 categories. This structure allows you to focus on the types of franchises in which you are most interested. The categories are in alphabetical order. The following list is shown to help you locate a category more quickly.

A category contains a list of several franchises. Each franchise is described using a standard format that includes 12 items about a franchise and franchisor. Understanding how to interpret this information will help you use this handbook more effectively. As an example, an entry from the *Handbook* is shown below. Each item in the example is labeled with a number that corresponds with the explanation about the item. The explanations provide tips on how to best use the information contained in each item.

Sample Entry

WILD BIRDS UNLIMITED
3003 E. 96th St., #201
Indianapolis, IN 46240
Telephone: (800) 326-4928 (317) 571-7100
Fax: (317) 571-7110
Mr. Paul E. Pickett, Director of Franchise Development

1

Number of Franchised Units: 152
Number of Company-Owned Units: 0
Number of Total Operating Units: 152

2

In Business Since: 1981 ← 3   **Franchising Since:** 1983 ← 4

Description of Operation: Wild Birds Unlimited is North America's original and largest group of retail stores catering to the backyard birdfeeding and nature enthusiast. We have over 150 stores in the US and Canada. Stores provide birdseed, feeders, houses, optics and nature-related gifts. Additionally, stores provide extensive educational programs to the public on backyard birdfeeding. Franchisees are provided with a full support system. **5**

Equity Capital Needed: $60,000 - $90,000 ← **6**

Franchise Fee: $15,000 ← **7**

Royalty Fee: 3% ← **8**

Financial Assistance: No. ← **9**

Managerial Assistance: Wild Birds Unlimited provides site selection and lease negotiation assistance. Franchisees attend an initial training session and are then given field training at their store. Support is given in all operational areas, including vendor discounts, business planning, marketing and advertising. **10**

Training Provided: The franchisor provides a 5-day initial training session, covering assorted topics, including customer service, employee training, store build-out, inventory and suppliers, marketing and advertising and detailed business operations. On-going training is given in the form of monthly newsletters, quarterly marketing guides, visits by field representatives and annual and regional meetings. **11**

Information Submitted: January 1994 ← **12**

1. Contact Information. This item includes the name of the franchisor and its address. It also includes telephone numbers. When you are interested in a franchise, make contact by phone, fax, or letter—the name of a company representative is given. Make it clear that you want some basic information about the franchise. The company representative may work with you directly or may have a sales representative contact you. Be prepared to ask some of the questions covered in chapter 2.

2. Number of Franchises. One important piece of information about a franchise is the number of franchisees that are in business. A franchisor with more franchises probably has a high level of experience and a good product that makes it attractive to other investors. Franchisors with fewer units may provide an opportunity to get in on the ground floor of a successful operation, but you should carefully investigate these franchisors.

A franchisor's ownership of operating units can be an indicator of both positive and negative factors. The number of company-owned units provides information about two important questions to investigate. First, does the company own the units because the franchisees failed and the franchisor had agreed to buy back the units? You can tell about the potential success of a franchise and by asking this question. Second, were franchisees forced to sell units back to the company? This question can help you determine whether the franchisor might be predatory. In other words, certain franchisors may use franchisees to

start a business, wait until operations are successful, then purchase it back for their own financial gain. It is also important to note franchisors that don't own any franchisees. They may become too removed from operations to relate to common problems encountered by franchisees.

3. In Business Since. This item tells you how long an organization has been in business. You can use this information, in combination with the number of franchisees, to evaluate the experience and stability of a franchisor. Many business experts feel that a business in operation for more than five years has a much higher chance of success. Look for experienced franchisors if you want to minimize your risk. Less experienced franchisors present a higher risk but offer the potential to get in on the ground floor of a what could become a booming franchise operation.

4. Franchising Since. It is interesting to note how long a span exists between the establishment of the business and the first franchise operation. A short time span probably indicates that the business started with the intent to develop franchise operations. On the positive side, the franchisor probably knows franchising and is interested in making this part of the business a success. On the other side, the franchise operation may not be based on a mature and well-tested business model. You could be one of the "guinea pigs" that provides the franchisor with valuable information about how to operate a franchise.

A franchisor with a large time span between the establishment of the business and the beginning of franchising is probably a very experienced business operator. This type of franchisor has a great deal of operational experience that can be useful to you. However, be aware that this operator may give a higher priority to operating his or her own business units at the expense of support for franchisees. In addition, the owners may know about operating a business unit but may not be proficient in managing a franchise operation. You may experience many frustrations because of such franchising inexperience.

5. Description of Operation. A brief description of the business concept is contained in this section. It provides information about the product or service and identifies some features that make the franchise unique. This is the most useful section for matching your business interests with franchise opportunities. Recognize that the limited space for the description means that you are reading an abbreviated explanation of the franchise concept. Therefore, you should consider further investigating those franchisors that appear to partially meet your interests. A more thorough examination of the franchisor may result in a better match with your business interests.

6. Equity Capital Needed. For most people, the money required to purchase a franchise and start operations is a critical element in identifying potential franchises. The stated equity capital typically represents an average that most franchisees spend to get their business started—it may even include initial operating costs needed prior to generating enough revenues to cover day-to-day expenses. You might be able to start a franchise for less or it may cost more depending on factors such as location and construction.

7. Franchise Fee. This is the amount of money that must be paid to the franchisor for the rights to operate a franchise. It normally pays for training and some managerial assistance. This money often cannot be recovered—unlike equipment that can be sold—and represents a significant part of the financial risk in purchasing a franchise. Check the conditions under which the fee may be recovered. For example, does the franchisor guarantee to buy back a failed franchise? Can the franchise be sold to another buyer? Under what conditions can the franchise be sold?

Carefully investigate whether the franchisor actually provides a concept and subsequent support system that warrants the fee it charges. A simple idea may be worth a great deal of money when the franchisor can provide a support system that has demonstrated the potential to help franchisees become successful. Conversely, a unique and exciting concept is worth little when there is insufficient support from the franchisor in implementing the business.

8. Royalty Fee. This is an extremely important piece of information. It tells you how much the franchisor expects you to pay as an on-going cost of business. A franchisor typically expects the franchisee to pay the royalty on gross sales. This means that the franchisor gets paid regardless of the operation's profitability. A small royalty fee may indicate little follow-up support is planned. A high royalty fee should ensure a significant amount of day-to-day support from the franchisor. Determine what you receive in return for the royalty. This assistance might include continued management assistance, advanced training, new marketing concepts, and continued product or service development.

9. Financial Assistance. Financial assistance refers to the programs the franchisor provides to aid a franchisee in financing an operation. This is an important consideration to investors that have a limited amount of capital or don't have enough money to finance all equity requirements. However, the franchisor may not be the only, or best, source of financing so don't let the lack of such assistance deter you from further investigation.

10. Managerial Assistance. Managerial assistance should be available during all phases of your company's life span. A franchisor should view your success as an integral part of its success. The amount of assistance provided is one indicator of the franchisor's commitment to help your business succeed. Operation start up is the most critical time for managerial assistance but continued guidance is important to long-term growth of your company.

11. Training Provided. An important service that a franchisor provides is training for the franchisee. You may want to be cautious in purchasing a franchise that provides a small amount of training. If the concept is so simple that you need little training, the franchisor's assistance to implement a new business may not be important enough to pay for. If the concept is more complex, you should expect a sufficient amount of training to gain the expertise needed to run a prosperous operation. The best training is a combination of classroom—or one-on-one training—at the franchisor's facility combined with field training at your own place of business.

12. Information Submitted. This is the date when the franchisor submitted information about the operation to the Department of Commerce. The information included in this *Handbook* will change over time. Verify the accuracy of the data when you contact the franchisor.

Use Data with Caution

Inclusion of a franchisor in this *Handbook* does not constitute an endorsement or recommendation, nor is the *Handbook* an exhaustive list of all franchisors. All reference books face the difficulty of being 100 percent accurate. It is possible that some inaccurate data has been inadvertently reported or compiled. Before making a decision, be sure to verify the data in this book by directly contacting the franchisor.

FRANCHISE COMPANY DATA

ART SUPPLIES

DECK THE WALLS
16825 Northchase Dr., # 910
Houston, TX 77060
Telephone: (800) 443-3325 (713) 874-3684
Fax: (713) 874-3650
Ms. Ann Nance, Franchise Development Co-ordinator

Number of Franchised Units: 196
Number of Company-Owned Units: 3
Number of Total Operating Units: 199

In Business Since: 1979   **Franchising Since:** 1980

Description of Operation: Art and custom framing retail stores located in regional malls.

Equity Capital Needed: $75,000

Franchise Fee: $35,000

Royalty Fee: 6%

Financial Assistance: SBA, through third party.

Managerial Assistance: Regional director offers complete assistance in all facets of business, including merchandising, employee relations, inventory control, selling, etc.

Training Provided: 2-week training class, plus in-store training.

Information Submitted: December 1993

FASTFRAME USA
1200 Lawrence Dr., # 300
Newbury Park, CA 91320
Telephone: (800) 521-3726 (805) 498-4463
Fax: (805) 498-8983
Mr. Brian J. Harper, Chief Operating Officer

Number of Franchised Units: 151
Number of Company-Owned Units: 1
Number of Total Operating Units: 152

In Business Since: 1986   **Franchising Since:** 1987

Description of Operation: Franchising of custom picture framing retail stores.

Equity Capital Needed: $150,000 - $200,000

Franchise Fee: $25,000

Royalty Fee: 7.5%

Financial Assistance: The leasing package ranges from $30,000 - $40,000.

Managerial Assistance: Assistance includes marketing, purchasing, operations and accounting.

Training Provided: We provide 2 weeks of training at the corporate training center in retail management and custom framing techniques.

Information Submitted: November 1993

GREAT FRAME UP SYSTEMS
9335 Belmont Ave.
Franklin Park, IL 60131

Telephone: (800) 55-FRAME (708) 671-2530
Fax: (708) 671-2580
Mr. Terry Bobroff, Director of Franchise Sales

Number of Franchised Units: 136
Number of Company-Owned Units: 0
Number of Total Operating Units: 136

In Business Since: 1971   **Franchising Since:** 1975

Description of Operation: Do-it-yourself and custom framing retail stores.

Equity Capital Needed: $140,000

Franchise Fee: $25,000

Royalty Fee: 6%

Financial Assistance: The franchisor will finance one half of franchise fee to qualified veterans through VetFran program. No other financing is offered, but assistance in obtaining conventional financing is available.

Managerial Assistance: Besides manuals, monthly newsletters, workshops, advertising promotional material and an annual conference, our directors of business development call on each franchise 5 - 6 times per year, providing guidance and assistance in every aspect of their business. Toll-free #s to our staff in Franklin Park, IL are provided.

Training Provided: An extensive 32-day training program in our Evanston, IL training center. All aspects of business and framing are covered, as well as hands-on training in actual store situation. Workshops and toll-free phone to training center are provided for on-going education.

Information Submitted: January 1994

KENNEDY STUDIOS
140 Tremont St.
Boston, MA 02111
Telephone: (800) 448-0027 (617) 542-0868
Fax: (617) 695-0957
Mr. Kevin G. Richard, General Manager

Number of Franchised Units: 38
Number of Company-Owned Units: 15
Number of Total Operating Units: 53

In Business Since: 1968   **Franchising Since:** 1984

Description of Operation: Kennedy Studios is the only art and framing franchise that provides site-specific artwork by nationally-renowned watercolor artist Robert Kennedy. Prints and posters are published specifically for your gallery, as well as original water colors. Custom framing is also a prominent aspect of your business. We locate mainly in urban and resort locations and target corporate and trade accounts, as well as tourism.

Equity Capital Needed: $40,000 - $80,000

Franchise Fee: $15,000 - $25,000

Royalty Fee: 3%

Financial Assistance: None.

Managerial Assistance: Assistance with site location, lease negotiations, construction, floor plans, store set-up and training at franchisee site, as well as on-going field support. A marketing plan is provided, as well as national vendor accounts, employee policy and an operations manual.

1

Training Provided: Training takes place at 1 of 3 training sites in Cape Cod, MA, Key West, FL or Rehoboth Beach, DE. Training continues on-site, both before and after opening. On-going field support is provided to assist with framing techniques, purchasing, merchandising and sales.

Information Submitted: January 1994

AUTOMOTIVE

AAMCO TRANSMISSIONS
One Presidential Blvd.
Bala Cynwyd, PA 19004
Telephone: (800) 223-8887 (215) 668-2900
Fax: (215) 664-4570
Mr. Gary Gray, Director of Franchise Development

Number of Franchised Units: 635
Number of Company-Owned Units: 0
Number of Total Operating Units: 635

In Business Since: 1963   **Franchising Since:** 1963

Description of Operation: AAMCO is the world's largest chain of transmission service centers, specializing in all types of automobile transmission and related repairs. Our Company philosophy is to continue to increase our competitive advantage and market share through technical expertise and customer satisfaction. AAMCO provides a complete A to Z training course at its corporate headquarters. No automotive experience is needed. Operational, technical and sales support is provided on an on-going basis.

Equity Capital Needed: $43,000 minimum.

Franchise Fee: $30,000

Royalty Fee: 7%

Financial Assistance: AAMCO will assist franchisees in securing necessary financing and/or leasing arrangements.

Managerial Assistance: AAMCO provides a proven business system, along with on-going operational and technical support.

Training Provided: AAMCO offers a comprehensive, 5-week operator's training program held at its home office in Bala Cynwyd, PA.

Information Submitted: November 1993

ACC-U-TUNE & BRAKE
2510 Old Middlefield Way
Mountain View, CA 94043
Telephone: (800) 400-8863 (415) 968-8863
Fax: (415) 968-1869
Mr. John Johnson, Director of Franchise Development

Number of Franchised Units: 21
Number of Company-Owned Units: 3
Number of Total Operating Units: 24

In Business Since: 1976   **Franchising Since:** 1980

Description of Operation: Tune-up, brakes, drive-thru oil change and maintenance. State-of-the-art buildings.

Equity Capital Needed: $125,000 - $225,000

Franchise Fee: $27,500

Royalty Fee: 7.5%

Financial Assistance: Some financing is available. We will assist in obtaining SBA or conventional financing.

Managerial Assistance: 3 weeks on-site with new franchisee. On-going support.

Training Provided: 3 weeks in home office and Company store.

Information Submitted: March 1994

AERO-COLOURS
8270 Belvedere Ave., # 100
Sacramento, CA 95826
Telephone: (800) 669-2376 (916) 451-2376
Fax: (916) 451-2378
Mr. Steven M. Mudd, Vice President/General Manager

Number of Franchised Units: 16
Number of Company-Owned Units: 8
Number of Total Operating Units: 24

In Business Since: 1985   **Franchising Since:** 1993

Description of Operation: Mobile paint touch-up process used to repair nicks, chips, scratches and other blemishes in painted surfaces. Service is provided to car dealers, fleet owners, insurance companies and retail customers. Aero-Colours employs a very sophisticated system for paint mixing, matching, application and blending. Each franchisee is granted the right to use the Aero-Colours process in an exclusive territory.

Equity Capital Needed: $25,000 - $40,000

Franchise Fee: $25,000

Royalty Fee: 7%, or less, declining scale.

Financial Assistance: Financing is extended to qualified franchisees on approved credit. Terms are negotiated depending on the size and price of the exclusive territory being purchased.

Managerial Assistance: After the initial 4-week training session, franchisees may take advantage of our toll-free service and technical line. In addition, a staff manager may be reached by a paging system any time Mon. - Fri. Annual follow-up visits are made to each franchise at no additional charge.

Training Provided: An extensive training program, lasting 160 hours over a 4-week period, is used to train franchise owners and their employees in all aspects of the Aero-Colours process, including technical, operating, sales, marketing, accounting and bookkeeping.

Information Submitted: March 1994

AID AUTO STORES
275 Grand Blvd., P. O. Box 281
Westbury, NY 11590
Telephone: (800) 432-9339 (516) 338-7889
Fax: (516) 338-7803
Ms. Randi Pincus, Director of Advertising

Number of Franchised Units: 79
Number of Company-Owned Units: 3
Number of Total Operating Units: 82

In Business Since: 1953   **Franchising Since:** 1953

Description of Operation: Franchisor, distributor and retailer of automotive parts and accessories in the NY, NJ and CT metro automotive aftermarkets. Aid Auto Stores sells automotive parts and accessories to the franchisees to re-sell to the retail customers. Aid Auto Stores operates Company-owned stores in a retail capacity.

Equity Capital Needed: $175,000 - $180,000

Franchise Fee: $22,500

Royalty Fee: $1,175 per month.

Financial Assistance: 30-day terms on merchandise.

Managerial Assistance: Each franchise opened receives assistance regarding location, information on product set-ups and actual product literature and information.

Training Provided: Store set-up and training is provided and is on-going. Initial merchandising, product knowledge, operations and training support the set-up of each franchise. Auto parts technical knowledge is provided.

Information Submitted: November 1993

ALL TUNE AND LUBE
407 Headquarters Dr., # 7
Millersville, MD 21108
Telephone: (800) 935-8863 (410) 987-1011
Fax: (410) 987-3060
Mr. Louis Kibler, Vice President of Franchise Development

Number of Franchised Units: 229
Number of Company-Owned Units: 0
Number of Total Operating Units: 229

In Business Since: 1985　　　　Franchising Since: 1986

Description of Operation: Automotive servicing. "One stop" total car care, including tune-ups, brakes, exhaust, engine replacement and more.

Equity Capital Needed: $7,500 initial deposit on franchise fee; approximate total investment -$119,000.

Franchise Fee: $22,500

Royalty Fee: 7%

Financial Assistance: Yes.

Managerial Assistance: Managerial assistance available. All Tune and Lube provides training manual, operations staff visits, toll-free telephone assistance, technical schools, newsletters and more. Continuing support in all areas of franchise operations, including marketing, research, management and administration.

Training Provided: All Tune and Lube provides extensive training, consisting of 2 weeks of franchise business management, training at the corporate training facility, 2 weeks of in-center training, 1 week of center management training and operational support.

Information Submitted: March 1994

ALTRACOLOR SYSTEMS
P. O. Box 2124
Kenner, LA 70063
Telephone: (800) 678-5220 (504) 454-7233
Fax: (504) 454-7233
Mr. Maurice M. Kahn, Director of Franchise Development

Number of Franchised Units: 88
Number of Company-Owned Units: 2
Number of Total Operating Units: 90

In Business Since: 1988　　　　Franchising Since: 1991

Description of Operation: Mobile automotive paint repair and touch-up system.

Equity Capital Needed: $25,000 - $40,000

Franchise Fee: $9,950

Royalty Fee: $80 per week.

Financial Assistance: Cash required is $9,950, plus $1,750 training fee. $13,500 opening inventory may be financed by franchisor for 36 months at 12% interest.

Managerial Assistance: Orientation training includes guidance in purchasing and expense control. Field training includes opening of new accounts and organizational counseling.

Training Provided: 3 days of in-house orientation in New Orleans, LA training center. 1 week in field includes setting up new accounts and technical advice.

Information Submitted: March 1994

AMERICAN BRAKE SERVICE
1 Battery March Park, # 105
Quincy, MA 02169
Telephone: (800) 227-7285 (617) 479-0017
Fax: (617) 479-2041
Mr. W. Craig Carter, President

Number of Franchised Units: 7
Number of Company-Owned Units: 0
Number of Total Operating Units: 7

In Business Since: 1991　　　　Franchising Since: 1991

Description of Operation: Automotive specialty brake service franchise, specializing in brakes, shocks, joints and front suspension. We utilize existing or converted 3 - 4 bay facilities, as well as build-to-suit locations and offer 1 hour or less brake service with a low price and lifetime guarantee.

Equity Capital Needed: $80,000 - $140,000

Franchise Fee: $19,500

Royalty Fee: 6%

Financial Assistance: We assist each franchisee or master franchisee with the preparation of his/her business plan and selection of lender.

Managerial Assistance: We assist the franchisee with pre-opening and post-opening advertising, as well as supplying him/her with the approved creative materials. Further assistance is provided in pre-construction and post-operational support, on-going technical assistance and new programs.

Training Provided: 2 weeks of training at our corporate headquarters is required. This consists of 1 week of classroom and 1 week of technical store training. On-going training in various areas is also provided.

Information Submitted: January 1994

AMERICAN FLUID TECHNOLOGY
239 Littleton Rd., # 4D
Westford, MA 01886
Telephone: (800) 245-6869 (508) 692-6700
Fax: (508) 692-0345
Mr. Ed Rosamilio, Sales Co-ordinator

Number of Franchised Units: 21
Number of Company-Owned Units: 0
Number of Total Operating Units: 21

In Business Since: 1990　　　　Franchising Since: 1991

Description of Operation: AFT's mobile on-site anti-freeze/coolant recycling services are wanted by industry to turn environmental expenses into profitable solutions. Featuring a combination of Prestone's recycling formula and AFT's patented technology, the AFT service is like a factory on wheels - totally self-contained and van powered. Recycled anti-freeze and coolant are verified by makers of Prestone and General Motors to exceed all ASTM standards. AFT comes to the work place and minimizes waste 99%.

Equity Capital Needed: $60,000 - $90,000

Franchise Fee: $25,000

Royalty Fee: 10%

Financial Assistance: SBA 10-year financing at approximately 8 3/4 %. Package includes equipment, working capital and franchise fees. 20% equity down.

Managerial Assistance: Technical assistance provided by Prestone Technology Systems, the makers of Prestone anti-freeze. This includes lab analysis and technical support, manufacturer's hotline and overnight parts delivery. AFT provides hotline and on-going consulting.

Training Provided: Two days of sales and computer training, one day at Prestone on chemistry of coolant and five days of training on equipment. Prestone anti-freeze/coolant will assist on technical data, chemical analysis and quality assurance.

Information Submitted: November 1993

ATLAS TRANSMISSION
4444 W. 147th St.
Midlothian, OH 60445

Telephone: (800) 377-9247 (708) 389-5922
Fax: (708) 389-9882
Mr. Jack E. Yost, Jr., Vice President of Franchise Development

Number of Franchised Units: 29
Number of Company-Owned Units: 0
Number of Total Operating Units: 29

In Business Since: 1964   Franchising Since: 1982

Description of Operation: Transmission and drive train service and repairs of trucks, cars, 4 x 4's and RV's. Foreign and domestic. Retail, wholesale and fleet.

Equity Capital Needed: $100,000 - $130,000

Franchise Fee: $27,500

Royalty Fee: 7%

Financial Assistance: Data not available.

Managerial Assistance: We provide operations, training, sales, owner's school and on-going assistance from operations, technical, legal and accounting departments. Assistance with national accounts and vendors.

Training Provided: We have a center manager's school for center training and owner's school. 800# service for operations and technical questions.

Information Submitted: January 1994

AUTO ACCENTS
6550 Pearl Rd.
Cleveland, OH 44130
Telephone: (216) 888-8886
Fax: (216) 888-4333
Mr. Joe McClelan, Franchise Director

Number of Franchised Units: 1
Number of Company-Owned Units: 4
Number of Total Operating Units: 5

In Business Since: 1979   Franchising Since: 1991

Description of Operation: Auto Accents is an automotive add-on center. We sell and install cellular phones, stereo systems, sun roofs, gold painting, alarms, running boards and accessories for making driving more fun. Auto Accents was voted in Top 30 Autosound Retailer of the Year nationwide and Cellular One's Agent of the Year for Ohio.

Equity Capital Needed: $80,000 - $120,000

Franchise Fee: $9,700

Royalty Fee: 5%

Financial Assistance: None.

Managerial Assistance: Full training on all aspects of opening, hiring, dealing with landlords, municipalities and paperwork, retaining and developing a good team and all aspects of managing the business.

Training Provided: Prior to opening, a full 3 weeks at headquarters is provided free to franchisee and a full week after opening at franchisee's site. Franchisee will be regularly trained and updated on procedures and techniques.

Information Submitted: November 1993

AUTO AMERICA / WESTERN AUTO
2107 Grand Ave.
Kansas City, MO 64108
Telephone: (800) 274-6733 (816) 346-4609
Fax: (816) 346-4188
Mr. Charles E. Hutchens, Vice President of Store Development

Number of Franchised Units: 987
Number of Company-Owned Units: 378
Number of Total Operating Units: 1365

In Business Since: 1909   Franchising Since: 1935

Description of Operation: Auto America is a discount automotive superstore, featuring tires, batteries, parts and accessories and automotive service - all under one roof. We offer more than 15,000 automotive products, including Michelin, Diehard, AC-Delco, Monroe, Craftsman and many more.

Equity Capital Needed: $130,000 - $180,000

Franchise Fee: $25,000

Royalty Fee: 5%

Financial Assistance: None.

Managerial Assistance: After completion of a comprehensive training program for new franchisees and employees, an experienced Auto America store manager will work in the franchisee's new store for 4 - 6 weeks, as needed. Much on-going follow-up assistance is provided.

Training Provided: The new franchisees must successfully complete a 5-week training program in an open/operating Auto America store. Auto America trainers go to franchisee's store to train employees (approximately 1 week).

Information Submitted: January 1994

AUTO LAB DIAGNOSTIC & TUNE-UP CENTER
15965 Jeanette St.
Southfield, MI 48075
Telephone: (810) 559-1415 (616) 966-0500
Fax: (810) 557-7931
Mr. Geoffrey Stebbins

Number of Franchised Units: 18
Number of Company-Owned Units: 0
Number of Total Operating Units: 18

In Business Since: 1984   Franchising Since: 1984

Description of Operation: Automotive diagnostic and tune center.

Equity Capital Needed: $115,000 - $145,000

Franchise Fee: $19,500

Royalty Fee: 7%

Financial Assistance: Indirect financing and leasing options are available.

Managerial Assistance: Data not available.

Training Provided: Yes.

Information Submitted: January 1994

AUTO ONE / SUN COUNTRY AUTO CENTERS
15965 Jeanette St.
Southfield, MI 48075
Telephone: (810) 559-1415
Fax: (810) 557-7931
Ms. Colleen McGaffey

Number of Franchised Units: 40
Number of Company-Owned Units: 0
Number of Total Operating Units: 40

In Business Since: 1988   Franchising Since: 1988

Description of Operation: Auto appearance and protective services.

Equity Capital Needed: $45,000 - $90,000

Franchise Fee: $20,000

Royalty Fee: 5%

Financial Assistance: Indirect financing and leasing options are available.

Managerial Assistance: Data not available.

Training Provided: Yes.

Information Submitted: January 1994

4

BATTERIES PLUS
2830 N. Grandview Blvd.
Pewaukee, WI 53072
Telephone: (800) 274-9155 (414) 548-9155
Fax: (414) 548-9175
Mr. Dale Hintz, Vice President of Marketing

Number of Franchised Units: 2
Number of Company-Owned Units: 8
Number of Total Operating Units: 10

In Business Since: 1988   Franchising Since: 1992

Description of Operation: Batteries Plus is "America's Battery Store," providing "1,000's of batteries for 1,000's of items," serving both retail and commercial customers. The $7 billion battery market, growing 5% annually, is driven by technology and lifestyles. Batteries Plus is a unique opportunity in this growth industry not yet saturated with competitors. Our program incorporates a unique and recognizable store design, coordinated graphics, color scheme, signage and product brands.

Equity Capital Needed: $85,000 - $150,000

Franchise Fee: $20,000

Royalty Fee: 3% of gross sales.

Financial Assistance: Guidance on preparing business plans and pro formas.

Managerial Assistance: Franchise managers are provided with comprehensive manuals on "how to" operate a Batteries Plus store. Documentation and checklists cover all areas of store operations.

Training Provided: 4 weeks of intensive training is done in our training center. Training covers technical product issues, store operations, customer service, commercial sales and custom battery assembly.

Information Submitted: November 1993

BIG O TIRES
11755 E. Peakview Ave.
Englewood, CO 80111
Telephone: (800) 622-2446 (303) 790-2800
Fax: (303) 790-0225
Ms. Nancy LaViolette, Franchise Qualifications Specialist

Number of Franchised Units: 361
Number of Company-Owned Units: 9
Number of Total Operating Units: 370

In Business Since: 1962   Franchising Since: 1967

Description of Operation: Retail tire and undercar service centers.

Equity Capital Needed: $300,000 net worth; $80,000 cash.

Franchise Fee: $21,000

Royalty Fee: 2%

Financial Assistance: Assistance will be provided in locating, financing and preparing loan and lease applications.

Managerial Assistance: Training is provided at the national training center.

Training Provided: Training consists of opening and closing procedures, merchandising and display and overall store management. Hands-on training with a 10-bay service area.

Information Submitted: January 1994

BRAKE SHOP, THE
44899 Centre Court, # 104
Clinton Township, MI 48038
Telephone: (800) 866-2725 (313) 228-9010
Fax: (313) 228-2111
Mr. Ken Rempel, Sr., Director of Franchise Development

Number of Franchised Units: 75
Number of Company-Owned Units: 3
Number of Total Operating Units: 78

In Business Since: 1987   Franchising Since: 1989

Description of Operation: The Brake Shop handles all automotive brake system repair needs. The Brake Shop, typically 1,500 - 4,000 square feet, is located in strip malls, automotive malls or free-standing units. Prior automotive experience not needed.

Equity Capital Needed: $50,000 - $80,000

Franchise Fee: $22,500

Royalty Fee: 8%

Financial Assistance: Equipment lease financing is available. The Brake Shop offers a special plan to veterans as a sponsor of VetFran.

Managerial Assistance: Franchisees are given extensive training and support in the operations and marketing of the business. In addition to a comprehensive operations manual and marketing tool kit, the operations support team provides on-going technical and sales seminars. A quarterly newsletter communicates new programs to the franchisees.

Training Provided: The new franchisee attends a 2-week training session at the corporate training facility, then an operations manager provides 2 additional weeks of training on-site during the shop opening.

Information Submitted: November 1993

BRAKE WORLD
300 NW 82nd Ave.
Plantation, FL 33324
Telephone: (800) 394-BRAKE (305) 472-3333
Fax: (305) 452-9885
Mr. Gerald D. Hopkins, Vice President

Number of Franchised Units: 31
Number of Company-Owned Units: 0
Number of Total Operating Units: 31

In Business Since: 1972   Franchising Since: 1975

Description of Operation: Automotive and light truck brake and auto repairs.

Equity Capital Needed: $40,000 - $45,000

Franchise Fee: $25,000

Royalty Fee: 5%

Financial Assistance: The franchisor may offer a financing arrangement to the franchisee for the initial franchise fee and/or for the purchase of the initial equipment, inventory, supplies and other materials solely for the establishment of the franchise. This is offered as an accommodation, so as to lessen the initial cash outlay of a franchisee.

Managerial Assistance: Data not available.

Training Provided: Mandatory initial on-the-job training is provided for the franchisee by the franchisor at no charge. The training is led by a person designated by the franchisor at the franchisor's facilities in Miami, FL or another site closer to the franchisee as designated by the franchisor. The franchisee will be responsible for travel, lodging and living expenses. The franchisor presently does not offer any other refresher courses. Any personnel the franchisee wants to be trained can be trained for $50/day.

Information Submitted: November 1993

BUDGET BRAKE & MUFFLER
422 - 4940 Canada Way
Burnaby, BC V5G 4K7 CAN
Telephone: (604) 294-6114
Fax: (604) 294-1648
Mr. Warren Swanson, President

Number of Franchised Units: 23
Number of Company-Owned Units: 2
Number of Total Operating Units: 25

In Business Since: 1969   **Franchising Since:** 1972

Description of Operation: Retail automotive service repairs - specializing in brakes and exhaust.

Equity Capital Needed: $175,000

Franchise Fee: $25,000

Royalty Fee: 4.5%

Financial Assistance: Bank financing is available to approved franchisees. Normal cash requirements are 40% of new store operations.

Managerial Assistance: Assistance is available at all times. Support staff in-store operations, accounting, computer and advertising is at head office.

Training Provided: Average training takes 60 days. 2 weeks of classroom and 6 weeks of in-store, hands-on training.

Information Submitted: December 1993

CAR-X MUFFLER & BRAKE SHOPS
8430 W. Bryn Mawr. Ave., # 400
Chicago, IL 60187
Telephone: (800) 359-2359 (312) 693-1000
Fax: (312) 693-0309
Mr. Bill Olsen, Director of Franchise Operations

Number of Franchised Units: 97
Number of Company-Owned Units: 54
Number of Total Operating Units: 151

In Business Since: 1973   **Franchising Since:** 1973

Description of Operation: Retail automotive repair shops that specialize in exhaust, suspension, front end and brake repairs.

Equity Capital Needed: $200,00 - $250,000

Franchise Fee: $18,500

Royalty Fee: 5%

Financial Assistance: Franchise assistance is provided through local sources and national SBA lenders.

Managerial Assistance: In-shop, hands-on training, coupled with 6 - 8 weeks of classroom training. Close supervision by operations manager for first 6 months, with semi-annual follow-up after initial period.

Training Provided: Data not available.

Information Submitted: January 1994

CARTEX LIMITED
42816 Mound Rd.
Sterling Heights, MI 48314
Telephone: (800) 421-7328 (810) 739-4330
Fax: (810) 739-4331
Mr. Lawrence P. Klukowski, Chief Executive Officer

Number of Franchised Units: 71
Number of Company-Owned Units: 3
Number of Total Operating Units: 74

In Business Since: 1980   **Franchising Since:** 1988

Description of Operation: Auto interior fabric repair, with national recognition, using the trademarked Fabrion system. This is a mobile business, servicing auto dealers, auction houses and rental car agencies with the Fabrion repair system for cloth and velour auto interiors.

Equity Capital Needed: $18,500

Franchise Fee: $13,500 - $19,500

Royalty Fee: $160 - $240. Not based on % of sales.

Financial Assistance: No financial assistance is available.

Managerial Assistance: Specific instructions on account billing and book records. Suggestions and contacts for employing contractors.

Training Provided: We will assist you in opening accounts and provide on-the-job training in franchisee's area. A support representative will visit whenever needed in your given area. The corporate office has a national recognition advertising campaign, with direct mail pieces going out every 60 days.

Information Submitted: February 1994

CHAMPION AUTO STORES
5520 N. Highway 169
New Hope, MN 55428
Telephone: (800) 279-9377 (612) 535-5984
Fax: (612) 535-5984
Mr. Mark Wold, Vice President Franchise Development

Number of Franchised Units: 125
Number of Company-Owned Units: 45
Number of Total Operating Units: 170

In Business Since: 1956   **Franchising Since:** 1961

Description of Operation: Retail sale of automotive parts, accessories and tires.

Equity Capital Needed: $75,000 - $100,000

Franchise Fee: $20,000

Royalty Fee: 0%

Financial Assistance: None.

Managerial Assistance: The franchisor gives assistance in advertising, inventory control, purchasing, sales, merchandising, expense control and employee management throughout the affiliation.

Training Provided: Sales and management training with a minimum of 20 days is required by the franchisor.

Information Submitted: April 1994

COTTMAN TRANSMISSION SYSTEMS
240 New York Dr.
Fort Washington, PA 19034
Telephone: (800) 394-6116 (215) 643-5885
Fax: (215) 643-2519
Mr. Fred Haas, Director of Franchise Development

Number of Franchised Units: 132
Number of Company-Owned Units: 4
Number of Total Operating Units: 136

In Business Since: 1962   **Franchising Since:** 1962

Description of Operation: Franchised repair centers, specializing in all types of transmission repair and related services. The Company's mission is to promote dynamic growth through integrity, professionalism and caring service.

Equity Capital Needed: $95,000 - $110,000

Franchise Fee: $22,500

Royalty Fee: 7.5%

Financial Assistance: Licensed franchisees are provided with the assistance necessary to obtain financing.

Managerial Assistance: Cottman Transmission provides both initial and continual operational, sales, management and technical support. Complete and professional advertising support services.

Training Provided: Cottman Transmission provides a comprehensive, initial 4 weeks of training at the national support headquarters in Fort Washington, PA, as well as continual training at the franchisee's location.

Information Submitted: November 1993

DENT DOCTOR
7708 Cantrell Rd.
Little Rock, AR 72207
Telephone: (800) 946-3368 (501) 224-0500
Fax: (501) 224-0507
Mr. Tom Harris, President

Number of Franchised Units: 32
Number of Company-Owned Units: 7
Number of Total Operating Units: 39

In Business Since: 1988   Franchising Since: 1990

Description of Operation: Paintless dent removal services for both wholesale and retail vehicle owners. Dent Doctor franchisees operated from both mobile and fixed locations. Dent Doctor franchisees remove minor dents, door dings and nail damage from vehicles with a special process that requires no painting for a fraction of the cost and time to repair it in the body shop.

Equity Capital Needed: $59,000 - $79,000

Franchise Fee: $29,500

Royalty Fee: 6%

Financial Assistance: We will assist you in business plan. No financing available.

Managerial Assistance: Dent Doctor franchisees receive a complete operations manual that specifies in detail all of the policies and procedures for operating the business. A toll-free management hotline is available for management issues.

Training Provided: An intensive 8-week training program is required to learn the Dent Doctor paintless dent removal system. Dent Doctor also offers on-going refresher training, as well as an annual meeting to keep all franchisees up to date on the latest technology.

Information Submitted: November 1993

DENTPRO
45 Quail Court, # 103
Walnut Creek, CA 94596
Telephone: (800) 868-DENT (510) 944-3323
Fax: (510) 944-1844
Mr. Mike Dumke, Director of Franchise Sales

Number of Franchised Units: 15
Number of Company-Owned Units: 0
Number of Total Operating Units: 15

In Business Since: 1991   Franchising Since: 1993

Description of Operation: DentPro specializes in removing dents and dings from vehicles without harming the paint. We offer a convenient and affordable way for people to repair and beautify their cars. The benefits to customers are enormous. Average repair time is minimized because DentPro is a mobile business. Repairs are made at the client's location. This significantly reduces costs over comparable body shop work and eliminates "down time." Specialized skills and techniques are used.

Equity Capital Needed: $35,000 - $100,000

Franchise Fee: $25,000 and up.

Royalty Fee: 7%

Financial Assistance: Financing is available.

Managerial Assistance: DentPro's on-going support program keeps franchisees abreast of new technical advances as they develop and provides tips on how to operate your business more successfully. We have a 24-hour support line for technical and business assistance, a newsletter, special conferences and advanced training sessions to update your knowledge and benefit from networking with your colleagues.

Training Provided: The key to your long-term success as a DentPro professional is the intensive training and apprenticeship you will receive. DentPro trains new franchisees in both the technical aspects of the business as well as thorough business management skills. The technical portion encompasses both dent removal skills and finishing techniques that are exclusive to DentPro. During the training, you will learn the ways of operating a successful dent repair business - advanced business systems, accounting, etc.

Information Submitted: February 1994

DORAN'S AUTOMOTIVE SERVICE CENTER
P. O. Box 83009
Baton Rouge, LA 70884
Telephone: (504) 767-3257
Fax: (504) 344-4848
Mr. Ronnie Doran, President

Number of Franchised Units: 2
Number of Company-Owned Units: 0
Number of Total Operating Units: 2

In Business Since: 1974   Franchising Since: 1991

Description of Operation: Full-service automotive center, providing tires, alignments, front end repairs, oil changes, tune ups and other minor mechanical repairs.

Equity Capital Needed: $100,900 - $154,600, excluding real estate.

Franchise Fee: $15,000

Royalty Fee: 5%, or $250 per week minimum.

Financial Assistance: Assistance with preparing SBA loan application.

Managerial Assistance: Assistance with site selection. Operations and training manuals provided.

Training Provided: 1 week of classroom training and 1 week of on-the-job training at franchisor headquarters.

Information Submitted: November 1993

DR. NICK'S TRANSMISSIONS
4444 W. 147th St.
Midlothian, IL 60445
Telephone: (800) 377-9247 (708) 389-5922
Fax: (708) 389-9882
Mr. Jack E. Yost, Jr., Vice President of Franchise Development

Number of Franchised Units: 19
Number of Company-Owned Units: 0
Number of Total Operating Units: 19

In Business Since: 1979   Franchising Since: 1979

Description of Operation: Transmission and drive train service and repairs of trucks, cars, 4 x 4's and RV's. Foreign and domestic. Retail, wholesale and fleet.

Equity Capital Needed: $100,000 - $130,000

Franchise Fee: $27,500

Royalty Fee: 7%

Financial Assistance: We provide referrals to third-party financing, based only on the prospect's credit.

Managerial Assistance: We provide operations, training, sales, owner's school and on-going assistance from operations, technical, legal and accounting departments. Assistance with national accounts and vendors.

Training Provided: We offer a center manager's school for center training and owner's school. 800# service for operations and technical questions.

Information Submitted: January 1994

ECONO LUBE N' TUNE
2402 Michelson Dr., # 200
Irvine, CA 92715
Telephone: (800) 628-0253 (714) 852-6630
Fax: (714) 852-6688
Mr. Robert Cradic, Director

Number of Franchised Units: 130
Number of Company-Owned Units: 65
Number of Total Operating Units: 195

In Business Since: 1977   **Franchising Since:** 1978

Description of Operation: Auto service, lube, tune and brakes.

Equity Capital Needed: $60,000 - $120,000

Franchise Fee: $29,500 - $79,500

Royalty Fee: 6%

Financial Assistance: None.

Managerial Assistance: 3-week training program. On-going support.

Training Provided: 1 week of classroom training, 1 week of training in shop and 1 week of training in franchisee's shop.

Information Submitted: November 1993

EXPRESS OIL CHANGE
P. O. Box 19968
Birmingham, AL 35219
Telephone: (205) 945-1771
Fax: (205) 940-6025
Mr. Julian Bell, Franchise Sales

Number of Franchised Units: 28
Number of Company-Owned Units: 11
Number of Total Operating Units: 39

In Business Since: 1979   **Franchising Since:** 1983

Description of Operation: Fast automotive service.

Equity Capital Needed: $175,000 - $375,000

Franchise Fee: $10,000

Royalty Fee: 5%

Financial Assistance: None available.

Managerial Assistance: We provide initial training, counsel and advice in evaluating prospective sites, provide initial and continuing advisory service in the operation, provide franchisee with an initial set of recommended accounting, inventory and inspection forms and provide an experienced manager for up to 5 days to assist in the opening of the outlet. Other services upon request.

Training Provided: The training program consists of an orientation and training program for the franchisee and/or franchisee's manager at such place and for such length of time as franchisor shall designate, usually in Birmingham, AL, for up to 2 weeks. The initial orientation and training program covers all aspects of the licensed business. The franchisor will also review the operating manual with the franchisee and provide on-the-job training in retail automotive business. An initial training program is mandatory.

Information Submitted: January 1994

FAIR MUFFLER & BRAKE SHOPS
4851 W. 115th St.
Alsip, IL 60658
Telephone: (800) MUFFLER (708) 489-0270
Fax: (708) 489-0276
Mr. Terrence M. Johannes, President

Number of Franchised Units: 19
Number of Company-Owned Units: 4
Number of Total Operating Units: 23

In Business Since: 1990   **Franchising Since:** 1991

Description of Operation: Automotive after-market undercar repair facility, including, but not limited to, exhaust, brakes, suspension, alignment and front end.

Equity Capital Needed: $120,000 - $250,000

Franchise Fee: $17,500

Royalty Fee: 6%

Financial Assistance: None.

Managerial Assistance: We provide constant communication between the home office and all of our franchisees. Personal visits are a big part of the program.

Training Provided: Training is for 4 weeks for both classroom and in-shop and includes the training of 1 owner/operator and 2 employees.

Information Submitted: March 1994

GAS TANK RENU-USA
12727 Greenfield St.
Detroit, MI 48227
Telephone: (800) 932-2766 (313) 837-6122
Fax: (313) 273-4759
Mr. Jim Dupuie, Sales Manager

Number of Franchised Units: 34
Number of Company-Owned Units: 0
Number of Total Operating Units: 34

In Business Since: 1986   **Franchising Since:** 1986

Description of Operation: Gas Tank Renu-USA has a patented process for the repair of fuel tanks for cars, trucks, boats and industrial applications. It is well suited for the antique and collector auto marketplace.

Equity Capital Needed: $20,000 - $30,000

Franchise Fee: $9,000

Royalty Fee: 0%

Financial Assistance: Data not available.

Managerial Assistance: Complete training for start-up on-site; site selection assistance; co-op advertising plan; site visits, newsletters and conferences.

Training Provided: Complete on-site training, usually 2 - 3 days.

Information Submitted: January 1994

GLASS DOCTOR
1550 Beaver Run Rd.
Norcross, GA 30093
Telephone: (800) 334-6509 (404) 925-0045
Fax: (404) 481-8542
Mr. Carl King, Franchise Marketing Director

Number of Franchised Units: 186
Number of Company-Owned Units: 8
Number of Total Operating Units: 194

In Business Since: 1974   **Franchising Since:** 1981

Description of Operation: We are in the business of replacing broken glass. The majority of this is replacing automobile windows and windshields and the balance is split between commercial and residential glass and mirrors. The largest percentage of our business is mobile. Our uniquely retro-fitted service vehicles allow us to service our customers at their site and at their convenience, at work or home. Our mobile operations format allows our franchisees to service large, multiple territories from one service center.

Equity Capital Needed: $95,000 - $250,000 (according to territory size).

Franchise Fee: $15,000 per territory.

Royalty Fee: 6%

Financial Assistance: The franchisor will finance franchise fees when the franchisee purchases a large number of multiple territories.

Managerial Assistance: We provide annual franchise meetings (national), regional meetings, an operations manual and assistance in hiring initial personnel.

Training Provided: We offer training at the corporate office for franchise owners and newly-hired staff. Agenda, workbook and hands-on experience are included.

Information Submitted: March 1994

GOODEAL DISCOUNT TRANSMISSIONS
P. O. Box 50
National Park, NJ 08063
Telephone: (800) 626-8695 (609) 848-1919
Fax: (609) 273-6913
Mr. John Mikulski, President

Number of Franchised Units: 30
Number of Company-Owned Units: 0
Number of Total Operating Units: 30

In Business Since: 1979   **Franchising Since:** 1984

Description of Operation: Transmission franchise.

Equity Capital Needed: $75,000

Franchise Fee: $22,500

Royalty Fee: Flat fee.

Financial Assistance: Equipment leasing to qualified operators.

Managerial Assistance: On-going training available throughout the term of the agreement.

Training Provided: On-going training available throughout the term of the agreement.

Information Submitted: January 1994

GOODYEAR TIRE CENTERS
1144 E. Market St.
Akron, OH 44316
Telephone: (216) 796-3467
Fax: (216) 796-1876
Mr. Hart M. Harding, Manager of Franchising

Number of Franchised Units: 301
Number of Company-Owned Units: 929
Number of Total Operating Units: 1230

In Business Since: 1900   **Franchising Since:** 1968

Description of Operation: Retail tires and automotive services.

Equity Capital Needed: $75,000 - $125,000

Franchise Fee: $15,000

Royalty Fee: 3%

Financial Assistance: Equipment leasing is available. Land, building and financial support are available.

Managerial Assistance: An assigned dealer development counselor assists in franchise operation.

Training Provided: Training includes 10 weeks of formal classroom and on-the-job training.

Information Submitted: November 1993

GREASE 'N GO (ATLANTIC)
6720 Curran St.
McLean, VA 22101
Telephone: (703) 556-6166
Fax: (703) 442-8671
Mr. James W. Reid, President

Number of Franchised Units: 11
Number of Company-Owned Units: 4
Number of Total Operating Units: 15

In Business Since: 1984   **Franchising Since:** 1990

Description of Operation: Automotive convenience oil change and lube centers, providing full fluid and filter services for all motor vehicles on a no-appointment, while-you-wait basis. The centers also provide ancillary maintenance services, such as fuel system tune-up, light bulb replacement, radiator and engine flushes, windshield wiper replacements, etc.

Equity Capital Needed: $100,000 liquid assets, $250,000 net worth.

Franchise Fee: $0

Royalty Fee: 2%

Financial Assistance: Little assistance is needed if the candidate meets capital requirements. The Company will offer advice and limited assistance if candidate wishes to build or own the operating premises.

Managerial Assistance: On-going operational and marketing consultation and assistance are available as needed on an expense reimbursed fee basis.

Training Provided: 2 weeks of hands-on training are available for the franchisee and manager training on an on-going basis.

Information Submitted: March 1994

GREASE MONKEY INTERNATIONAL
216 16th St., # 1100
Denver, CO 80202
Telephone: (800) 822-7706 (303) 534-1660
Fax: (303) 534-2906
Mr. Roger D. Auker, Director of Franchise Development

Number of Franchised Units: 156
Number of Company-Owned Units: 38
Number of Total Operating Units: 194

In Business Since: 1978   **Franchising Since:** 1979

Description of Operation: Grease Monkey International provides convenient, preventative maintenance services for motor vehicles. The basic preventative maintenance service, done in approximately 10 minutes, includes changing the oil and oil filter, lubricating the chassis, checking and replenishing all vital fluids, adjusting tire pressure, checking exterior lights, vacuuming the interior and cleaning the exterior windows.

Equity Capital Needed: $125,000

Franchise Fee: $28,000

Royalty Fee: 5%

Financial Assistance: Financial assistance may be available from third parties.

Managerial Assistance: Professional manager's workshops, assistance from corporate headquarters, as well as regional managers, video training program, complete with manager and employee workbooks and training of employees prior to opening.

Training Provided: 1-week training program in Denver, CO, covering operations, accounting, marketing and hands-on training on vehicles in GM Company-owned centers. National and regional workshops are provided on a regular basis by corporate personnel and regional managers.

Information Submitted: November 1993

GUARANTEED TUNE UP
89 Headquarters Plaza, N. Twr., 14th
Morristown, NJ 07960
Telephone: (800) 543-5829 (201) 539-7538
Fax: (201) 933-1757
Mr. Thomas J. Michaels, Director of Marketing

Number of Franchised Units: 5
Number of Company-Owned Units: 0
Number of Total Operating Units: 5

In Business Since: 1984   **Franchising Since:** 1984

Description of Operation: Automotive tune-up and automobile repair service business.

Equity Capital Needed: Turn-key operation approximately $90,000; $35,000 cash and balance financed for qualified investors.

Franchise Fee: $15,000

Royalty Fee: 6%

Financial Assistance: We will assist in securing outside financing.

Managerial Assistance: Continuous managerial assistance is provided in all phases of the operation to insure the proper operation of the business.

Training Provided: An intensive 1-week training program is provided for shop managers, mechanics or owners.

Information Submitted: March 1994

HOMETOWN AUTO SERVICE
2062 W. Main St.
Jeffersonville, PA 19403
Telephone: (800) 231-2254 (215) 539-1400
Fax: (215) 539-9011
Mr. Joseph DeWitt, Franchise Development Manager

Number of Franchised Units: 7
Number of Company-Owned Units: 4
Number of Total Operating Units: 11

In Business Since: 1990   **Franchising Since:** 1991

Description of Operation: Hometown is in the general automotive repair business. By providing outstanding customer service in a clean and friendly environment, Hometown seeks to re-establish the concept of the "Neighborhood Garage."

Equity Capital Needed: $35,000

Franchise Fee: $25,000

Royalty Fee: 6%

Financial Assistance: We provide assistance in business plan development, sources of bank financing and equipment leasing.

Managerial Assistance: On-going assistance in the following areas - technical, financial, marketing and advertising and research and development.

Training Provided: A comprehensive, 5-week training program, consisting of 2 weeks of classroom instruction and hands-on management in our pilot center, plus 3 weeks of on-site training. Detailed operations manuals and on-going trouble shooting are provided.

Information Submitted: November 1993

INDY LUBE 10-MINUTE OIL CHANGE
6505 East 82nd St., # 209
Indianapolis, IN 46250
Telephone: (800) 326-LUBE (317) 845-9444
Fax: (317) 577-3169
Mr. Jim R. Sapp, President

Number of Franchised Units: 6
Number of Company-Owned Units: 10
Number of Total Operating Units: 16

In Business Since: 1986   **Franchising Since:** 1989

Description of Operation: Indy Lube is a chain of 10-minute oil change centers which specialize in automotive fluid maintenance. Indy Lube sets itself apart from the competition by providing fast, quality service in a

pleasant setting. All Indy Lube stores have landscaped exteriors, brightly painted buildings and interior reception areas, complete with wallpaper, cloth chairs and a courtesy telephone.

Equity Capital Needed: $50,000 - $100,000

Franchise Fee: $18,000

Royalty Fee: 5%

Financial Assistance: No direct financial assistance; however, there is assistance available with business plan preparation for presentations to financial institutions.

Managerial Assistance: Indy Lube provides criteria and assistance in interviewing. Franchise store managers and/or owners are invited to train at a corporate store for 2 weeks prior to the opening of the franchise. There are on-going training meetings each month for managers, assistant managers, employees and franchise owners.

Training Provided: Same as above.

Information Submitted: January 1994

J. D. BYRIDER SYSTEMS
5680 W. 71st St.
Indianapolis, IN 46278
Telephone: (800) 947-4532 (317) 668-1554
Fax: (317) 668-1572
Mr. R. Keith Emerson, Vice President of Franchise Development

Number of Franchised Units: 68
Number of Company-Owned Units: 1
Number of Total Operating Units: 69

In Business Since: 1979   **Franchising Since:** 1989

Description of Operation: J. D. Byrider is a full-service franchisor, providing a complete package franchise for the sale and financing of 5-year and older cars to customers who cannot qualify for conventional financing.

Equity Capital Needed: $225,000 - $584,000

Franchise Fee: $29,000

Royalty Fee: 3%, or minimum of $1,000 per month.

Financial Assistance: None at this time.

Managerial Assistance: Thorough training in the methods, disciplines and controls to accompany the proprietary software. The variances are all designed to indicate where a small problem is prior to escalation.

Training Provided: Initial training is a 5 - 6 week process, conducted both in headquarters and in the field. The process includes basic presentation skills, credit scoring, management of sales counselors, how to buy the automobiles for profitable return and proper and productive collection methods.

Information Submitted: November 1993

JIFFY LUBE INTERNATIONAL
P. O. Box 2967
Houston, TX 77252
Telephone: (800) 327-9532 (713) 546-4100
Fax: (713) 546-8762
Ms. Brandi Carlile, Franchise Development

Number of Franchised Units: 667
Number of Company-Owned Units: 412
Number of Total Operating Units: 1079

In Business Since: 1979   **Franchising Since:** 1979

Description of Operation: Largest quick-lube system in the industry.

Equity Capital Needed: Approximate total investment - $200,000; initial cash needed - $100,000.

Franchise Fee: $35,000

Royalty Fee: 5%

Financial Assistance: None.

Managerial Assistance: Jiffy Lube International provides continual management services, for the life of the franchise, in such areas as accounting, advertising, policies, procedures and operations. Complete manuals are provided. Regional managers are available to work closely with franchisees and visit service centers regularly to assist in solving problems.

Training Provided: Jiffy Lube International provides a mandatory course to the franchisee or approved manager which consists of working at a Jiffy Lube Service Center for 4 weeks. You must also attend a standard operations training course for an additional 1 week at Jiffy Lube headquarters.

Information Submitted: March 1994

KENNEDY TRANSMISSION
410 Gateway Blvd.
Burnsville, MN 55337
Telephone: (612) 894-7020
Fax: (612) 894-1849
Mr. Andrew Hammond, President

Number of Franchised Units: 15
Number of Company-Owned Units: 1
Number of Total Operating Units: 16

In Business Since: 1962   **Franchising Since:** 1977

Description of Operation: Retail repair and service of automatic and manual transmissions and other driveline components in automobiles and light trucks.

Equity Capital Needed: $85,000 - $120,000

Franchise Fee: $17,500

Royalty Fee: 6%

Financial Assistance: No direct assistance. We can direct franchisee to sources of financing and we can assist in SBA financing. We have a working relationship with a major bank with preferred SBA status.

Managerial Assistance: Assistance in all aspects of store set-up, including hiring, office procedures, accounting, inventory management, goal setting and tracking. Full set of written policies and procedures manuals. Limited group buying agreements with critical vendors. Frequent store visits by franchise representatives.

Training Provided: 3 weeks of training included in initial franchise fee. Heavy sales emphasis - telephone skills, communicating repairs to customer, obtaining job approval and final vehicle delivery. Also, emphasis on shop workflow management.

Information Submitted: November 1993

KING BEAR
1390 Jerusalem Ave.
North Merrick, NY 11566
Telephone: (516) 483-3500
Fax: (516) 483-0615
Mr. Frank J. Garton, Director of Franchise Sales

Number of Franchised Units: 62
Number of Company-Owned Units: 0
Number of Total Operating Units: 62

In Business Since: 1972   **Franchising Since:** 1973

Description of Operation: Full-service automotive service centers, featuring quick lube, brake service, tune-ups, front-end alignment, ride control products and general automotive repair. Single, multiple and master license worldwide programs are available.

Equity Capital Needed: $45,000

Franchise Fee: $25,000

Royalty Fee: 5%

Financial Assistance: $45,000 start-up cash, with $140,000 total investment required. SBA loan program to qualified individuals.

Managerial Assistance: Back up for sales, service and administration on an on-going basis. Complete operations training manuals and sales aids. Franchise field personnel visit stores on a 10-day cycle.

Training Provided: An intensive 1-week of classroom and 1 week of in-field training. Complete training manual.

Information Submitted: November 1993

LEE MYLES TRANSMISSIONS
140 Rt. 17 N.
Paramus, NJ 07652
Telephone: (800) LEE-MYLE (201) 262-0555
Fax: (201) 262-5177
Mr. Sal Gargone, Marketing

Number of Franchised Units: 85
Number of Company-Owned Units: 0
Number of Total Operating Units: 85

In Business Since: 1947   **Franchising Since:** 1964

Description of Operation: Automotive transmission service and repair.

Equity Capital Needed: $40,000 - $60,000

Franchise Fee: $25,000

Royalty Fee: 6%

Financial Assistance: Some financing is available.

Managerial Assistance: Assistance includes in-class, on-site management training on all Lee Myles policies and procedures, various technical training seminars and the periodic on-site review and evaluation of center activities by home office professional personnel.

Training Provided: Training includes an intensive 2-week training period in our corporate office and in your center, as well as special follow-up seminars on technical, sales and marketing, operations and business planning. One of the most valuable tools you will receive is the Lee Myles operations and owner's manual. In it you will find explicit directions and methods on how to run your business. You will also receive on-going, in-center and operations support

Information Submitted: January 1994

LENTZ U.S.A. SERVICE CENTER
1001 Riverview Dr.
Kalamazoo, MI 49001
Telephone: (800) 354-2131 (616) 342-2200
Fax: (616) 342-9461
Mr. Gregory A. Lentz, Vice President of Franchise Sales

Number of Franchised Units: 12
Number of Company-Owned Units: 11
Number of Total Operating Units: 23

In Business Since: 1983   **Franchising Since:** 1989

Description of Operation: Automotive undercar repair facility. Lentz USA is a specialty shop, concentrating on exhaust, brakes and suspension services. It is a middle-end to high-end service store with 10,000 associated warranty locations nationwide.

Equity Capital Needed: $36,000 - $50,000

Franchise Fee: $18,500

Royalty Fee: 7% - 0%

Financial Assistance: The franchisor will assist signed franchisees with sources of financing. There are many alternatives available to those with a good credit rating. Although we do not finance our franchisees, we have many proven sources for our franchisees.

Managerial Assistance: Our franchisees are trained initially for 80 hours of both classroom and hands-on training before grand opening. Then, we have continuing support that includes site visits.

Training Provided: Our franchisees are trained initially for 80 hours of both classroom and hands-on training before grand opening. Then we have continuing support that includes site visits.

Information Submitted: November 1993

LUBEPRO'S INTERNATIONAL
1630 Colonial Pkwy.
Inverness, IL 60067
Telephone: (800) 654-5823 (708) 776-2500
Fax: (708) 776-2542
Mr. Philip L. Robinson, Chairman

Number of Franchised Units: 30
Number of Company-Owned Units: 4
Number of Total Operating Units: 34

In Business Since: 1978   **Franchising Since:** 1986

Description of Operation: LubePros service centers provide fast-service oil changes, lubrication, replacement of certain filters and fluids and certain related courtesy services for motor vehicles.

Equity Capital Needed: $160,000

Franchise Fee: $25,000

Royalty Fee: 5%

Financial Assistance: We direct the franchisee to third-party lenders and build-to-suit developers.

Managerial Assistance: Field service and seminars are provided periodically.

Training Provided: We provide 10 days of training, including on-site training.

Information Submitted: March 1994

MAACO AUTO PAINTING AND BODYWORKS
381 Brooks Rd.
King of Prussia, PA 19406
Telephone: (800) 296-2226 (215) 265-6606
Fax: (215) 337-6113
Ms. Linda E. Kemp, Manager

Number of Franchised Units: 435
Number of Company-Owned Units: 1
Number of Total Operating Units: 436

In Business Since: 1972   **Franchising Since:** 1972

Description of Operation: Since 1972, MAACO has been in the production auto painting and bodyworks industry. We have painted and repaired over 7 million automobiles. Our slogan, "Uh-oh, better get MAACO," has given MAACO national brand-name recognition.

Equity Capital Needed: $174,000 total investment, includes franchise fee.

Franchise Fee: $25,000

Royalty Fee: 8%

Financial Assistance: Third-party financial assistance is available to qualified applicants.

Managerial Assistance: MAACO provides on-going operational support, regional meetings, seminars and conventions.

Training Provided: We offer a comprehensive 4-week training program, concentrating on the management, systems and procedures of a MAACO center. Also, a center manager's training course is also available.

Information Submitted: February 1994

MAD HATTER CAR CARE CENTERS
1235 Styron St.
Charlotte, NC 28203

Telephone: (800) 523-1023 (704) 342-1023
Fax: (704) 342-6969
Mr. Jon Sink, President

Number of Franchised Units: 49
Number of Company-Owned Units: 0
Number of Total Operating Units: 49

In Business Since: 1986   **Franchising Since:** 1986

Description of Operation: Under-car service.

Equity Capital Needed: $50,000 - $200,000

Franchise Fee: $30,000

Royalty Fee: 8%

Financial Assistance: Plenty, to help find financing.

Managerial Assistance: 3 weeks of initial and on-going training.

Training Provided: Management for opening and operating a Mad Hatter Car Center. On-site training, computer training, estimating and much, much more.

Information Submitted: December 1993

MASTER MECHANIC, THE
1989 Dundas St. E.
Mississauga, ON M2L 1A2 CAN
Telephone: (905) 629-3773
Fax: (905) 629-3864
Mr. Andrew Wanie, President

Number of Franchised Units: 16
Number of Company-Owned Units: 0
Number of Total Operating Units: 16

In Business Since: 1981   **Franchising Since:** 1986

Description of Operation: Full-service automotive repair garages to the retail market. Professional service for imported and domestic cars and vans. Specializing in general repairs, tune-ups, alignments, engine performance and driveability.

Equity Capital Needed: $100,000 (Canadian).

Franchise Fee: $25,000 (Canadian).

Royalty Fee: 6%

Financial Assistance: Assistance with preparation of bank financing presentation. Franchisor will attend with franchisee to acquire bank and government-sponsored financing. Franchisee usually provided with "turnkey" operation.

Managerial Assistance: Training in existing locations, at head office and with manufacturers of equipment and product. Operations manual. Monthly management meetings for all franchisees. On-site assistance by franchisor.

Training Provided: Procedures and technical training are conducted on-site and at existing locations and head office. Management training courses provided by specialists in management and automotive servicing. Business training by franchisor accountants.

Information Submitted: December 1993

MCQUIK'S OILUBE
P. O. Box 46, 3861 N. Wheeling Ave.
Muncie, IN 47308
Telephone: (800) 445-6393 (317) 282-2183
Fax: (317) 747-8127
Mr. Alan Jackson, Director of Franchise Operations

Number of Franchised Units: 55
Number of Company-Owned Units: 34
Number of Total Operating Units: 89

In Business Since: 1980   **Franchising Since:** 1985

Description of Operation: McQuik's Oilube provides high-quality, reasonably-priced, fast-service oil change, lubrication and related automotive services through its centers to the general public. The services at the centers are provided by trained personnel who follow a detailed vehicle service system.

Equity Capital Needed: $300,000 - $650,000

Franchise Fee: $15,000

Royalty Fee: 4%

Financial Assistance: McQuik's Oilube does not offer any financial assistance. There are limited financial packages, however, through our parent company, Quaker State.

Managerial Assistance: In addition to our training program, we also provide on-going support in the form of scheduled visits to the store (approximately 9 per year), technical bulletins, certification programs, customer satisfaction surveys, fleet programs, advertising and other administrative areas.

Training Provided: The franchisee is required to participate in a 4-week training program. 2 weeks are spent at our Company training facility, the remaining 2 weeks at the franchisee's site.

Information Submitted: December 1993

MEINEKE DISCOUNT MUFFLER SHOPS
128 S. Tryon St., # 900
Charlotte, NC 28202
Telephone: (800) 634-6353 (704) 377-8855
Fax: (704) 377-1490
Ms. Amy Daniel, Franchise Sales

Number of Franchised Units: 917
Number of Company-Owned Units: 7
Number of Total Operating Units: 924

In Business Since: 1972   **Franchising Since:** 1972

Description of Operation: Meineke Discount Muffler Shops offers fast, courteous service in the merchandising of automotive exhaust systems, brakes, shock absorbers, struts, CV joints and oil changes. Unique inventory control and group purchasing power enable Meineke to adhere to a "Discount Concept" and deliver quality service. No mechanical skills required.

Equity Capital Needed: $91,000

Franchise Fee: $22,500

Royalty Fee: 7%

Financial Assistance: Third-party financing or leasing option is available to qualified individuals.

Managerial Assistance: Meineke provides an initial 4-week training program at its Charlotte, NC training center. Management, technical and sales training are all provided. Once a shop is open, franchisees receive on-going sales analysis and operational analysis, including personnel, facility, service and sales review. Dealers receive marketing, advertising, merchandising and promotion support. Dealers also receive customer service assistance in the form of counseling and mediation assistance.

Training Provided: We provide 4 weeks of schooling and on-the-job training at the Charlotte headquarters. In addition, Meineke provides continuous field supervision and group operational meetings.

Information Submitted: March 1994

MERLIN'S MUFFLER & BRAKE
1 N. River Ln., # 206
Geneva, IL 60134
Telephone: (800) 652-9900 (708) 208-9900
Fax: (708) 208-8601
Mr. Mark M. Hameister, Director of Franchise Development

Number of Franchised Units: 41
Number of Company-Owned Units: 4
Number of Total Operating Units: 45

In Business Since: 1975   **Franchising Since:** 1975

Description of Operation: Central to Merlin's retail concept is an upscale, 6-bay automotive service facility, designed and developed as an important result of Merlin's complete real estate program. Merlin's typical franchise business plan and working cash requirement facilitates first year cash flows appropriate to owner operation, as well as semi-absentee management.

Equity Capital Needed: $45,000

Franchise Fee: $26,000 - $30,000

Royalty Fee: 4.9%

Financial Assistance: Subject to individual qualifications, the franchise is readily financable by third parties, i.e. SBA, bank, equipment leasing, inventory vendor, etc. The franchisor provides extensive assistance to franchisees relative to securing financing.

Managerial Assistance: New franchisee assistance includes, but is not limited to, the following: 5 weeks of training, operations and personnel manuals, hotline phone service, grand opening, marketing, on-site corporate staff for at least 2 - 4 weeks, vendor assistance on product, video library in shop, etc.

Training Provided: Merlin's provides a comprehensive 5-week technical and management training program at the headquarter's training facility and operating service center. Topics include personnel, marketing, product and purchasing, customer service, bookkeeping and accounting, equipment use and maintenance, etc.

Information Submitted: December 1993

MIDAS
225 N. Michigan Ave.
Chicago, IL 60601
Telephone: (800) 621-0144 (312) 565-7500
Fax: (312) 565-7881
Mr. Richard C. Pope, National Director of Franchising

Number of Franchised Units: 2197
Number of Company-Owned Units: 328
Number of Total Operating Units: 2525

In Business Since: 1956   **Franchising Since:** 1956

Description of Operation: Midas Muffler and Brake Shops are the world's largest chain of under-the-car specialty automotive repair shops. Services include exhaust replacement, brake repair and suspension and front end. Lube, oil and filter service is also available at most locations.

Equity Capital Needed: $179,000 - $292,000

Franchise Fee: $20,000

Royalty Fee: 10%

Financial Assistance: Midas provides no direct financial assistance, but will put applicants in contact with a list of lending institutions experienced in financing Midas Muffler and Brake Shops.

Managerial Assistance: Site selection, design and construction, training, advertising and marketing, purchasing of both inventory and equipment. Research and development, Mystery Shopper Programs, national and local public relations and field support.

Training Provided: 3 weeks of classroom training, plus 1 week of in-shop training. On-going local and regional workshops and seminars, video and print programs for franchisee use in training personnel. Courses include technical, human resource and retailing.

Information Submitted: January 1994

MIDAS CANADA
105 Commander Blvd.
Agincourt, ON M1S 3X8 CAN

Telephone: (416) 291-4261
Fax: (416) 291-0635
Mr. Michael Claener, Vice President of Retail Operations

Number of Franchised Units: 207
Number of Company-Owned Units: 33
Number of Total Operating Units: 240

In Business Since: 1960   **Franchising Since:** 1961

Description of Operation: Total under-the-car service, specializing in exhaust, brakes, suspension and front end.

Equity Capital Needed: $225,000 total investment.

Franchise Fee: $25,000

Royalty Fee: 5% royalty; 5% advertising.

Financial Assistance: None. The franchisee must arrange his/her own financing.

Managerial Assistance: Each region has a Market Manager who is in touch with each shop by telephone and makes a visit at least once a month. Marketing, financial and real estate guidance are also available when required.

Training Provided: Our training is tailored to the needs of each individual. Everybody has a minimum of 1 month of training and some have 3 months.

Information Submitted: January 1994

MING AUTO BEAUTY CENTERS
346 E. 100 South
Salt Lake City, UT 84111
Telephone: (800) 443-3213 (801) 521-8799
Fax: (801) 521-4723
Mr. Eric Jergensen, Vice President of Operations

Number of Franchised Units: 39
Number of Company-Owned Units: 3
Number of Total Operating Units: 42

In Business Since: 1935   **Franchising Since:** 1972

Description of Operation: Ming provides the finest automotive protection and beautification processes to keep a vehicle shining for years. The legendary Ming "Mirror Finish" is a secret process which smoothes a vehicle's painted surface for a brilliant, guaranteed long-lasting shine. Other services include interior protection, sound deadening and undercoating, rust protection, trunk liner and a full range of detail products. Ming is the brilliant opportunity for enthusiastic individuals who enjoy owning their own business.

Equity Capital Needed: Varies.

Franchise Fee: $19,500

Royalty Fee: 6%

Financial Assistance: Ming assists potential franchisees identify potential financing sources and prepare submissions.

Managerial Assistance: Each franchisee is given a complete system of manuals, classroom training, on-site technical training and sales training. On-going training includes site visits, workshops and a monthly newsletter. Access to franchise operations personnel is constant.

Training Provided: Each franchisee is provided a 10-day new franchisee training session, involving both classroom and hands-on training. Training includes technical procedures, as well as day-to-day management and sales. A 5-day training session upon opening and a 2-day follow-up within 90 days is also provided. Ming also conducts annual site visits and inspections to assure quality adherence.

Information Submitted: March 1994

MINIT-TUNE & BRAKE AUTO CENTERS
398 W. Fifth Ave.
Vancouver, BC V5Y 1J5 CAN

Telephone: (604) 873-5551
Fax: (604) 873-5553
Mr. Sam Amlani, Vice President

Number of Franchised Units: 60
Number of Company-Owned Units: 0
Number of Total Operating Units: 60

In Business Since: 1976   **Franchising Since:** 1976

Description of Operation: Tune-ups, oil changes, brakes and minor engine repairs.

Equity Capital Needed: $95,000 - $105,000

Franchise Fee: $20,000

Royalty Fee: 5%

Financial Assistance: Leasing arrangements are provided on equipment purchase.

Managerial Assistance: The franchisor is available for consultation.

Training Provided: Training includes 10 days at the head office.

Information Submitted: January 1994

MIRACLE AUTO PAINTING & BODY REPAIR
3157 Corporate Place
Hayward, CA 94545
Telephone: (510) 887-2211
Fax: (510) 887-3092
Mr. Jim Jordan, Marketing Director

Number of Franchised Units: 37
Number of Company-Owned Units: 2
Number of Total Operating Units: 39

In Business Since: 1953   **Franchising Since:** 1964

Description of Operation: Production auto painting and collision repair.

Equity Capital Needed: $55,000 - $75,000

Franchise Fee: $35,000

Royalty Fee: 5%

Financial Assistance: Assistance with securing financing, including SBA, etc.

Managerial Assistance: Continues for term of contract.

Training Provided: 2 weeks of classroom training, 2 weeks of on-site training and as-needed for term of the contract.

Information Submitted: November 1993

MISTER FRONT END
192 N. Queen St.
Etobicoke, ON M9C 1A8 CAN
Telephone: (416) 622-9999
Fax: (416) 622-9999
Mr. Gerry R. Jones, President

Number of Franchised Units: 1
Number of Company-Owned Units: 1
Number of Total Operating Units: 2

In Business Since: 1973   **Franchising Since:** 1983

Description of Operation: Heavy duty spring, suspension, air conditioning and alignment specialist.

Equity Capital Needed: Data not available.

Franchise Fee: $15,000

Royalty Fee: 5%

Financial Assistance: Data not available.

Managerial Assistance: Complete support for as long as necessary.

Training Provided: We offer 3 months of training at the home base, followed by consultation at any time and for as long as necessary.

MISTER TRANSMISSION
30 Wertheim Ct., # 5
Richmond Hill, ON L4B 1B9 CAN
Telephone: (905) 886-1511
Fax: (905) 886-1545
Mr. Kevin Brillinger, Vice President of Corporate Development

Number of Franchised Units: 92
Number of Company-Owned Units: 0
Number of Total Operating Units: 92

In Business Since: 1963   Franchising Since: 1969

Description of Operation: Canada's largest transmission repair specialist. Our service is offered coast to coast. The Mister Transmission franchise system is a proven sales and marketing program, in business for over 30 years.

Equity Capital Needed: $100,000 - $125,000

Franchise Fee: $25,000

Royalty Fee: 7%

Financial Assistance: The financing program through a chartered bank is available to qualified applicants.

Managerial Assistance: We provide a management training course at the head office, on-going training sessions and in-store assistance, a complete training manual, advertising support, computer system, real estate support and operations support.

Training Provided: Training is available for owners, their managers and employees.

Information Submitted: March 1994

MR. TRANSMISSION
4444 W. 147th St.
Midlothian, IL 60445
Telephone: (800) 377-9247 (708) 389-5922
Fax: (708) 389-5922
Mr. Jack E. Yost, Jr., Vice President of Franchise Development

Number of Franchised Units: 88
Number of Company-Owned Units: 1
Number of Total Operating Units: 89

In Business Since: 1956   Franchising Since: 1976

Description of Operation: Mr. Transmission provides transmission and drive train service and repairs of trucks, cars, 4 x 4's and RV's. Foreign and domestic. Retail, wholesale and fleet.

Equity Capital Needed: $100,000 - $130,000

Franchise Fee: $27,500

Royalty Fee: 7%

Financial Assistance: We provide referrals to third-party financing, based only on the prospect's credit.

Managerial Assistance: We provide operations, training, sales, owner's school and on-going assistance from operations, technical, legal and accounting departments, as well as assistance with national accounts and vendors.

Training Provided: Center manager's school for center training and owner's school. 800# service for operations and technical questions.

Information Submitted: January 1994

MULTISTATE TRANSMISSIONS
4444 W. 147th St.
Midlothian, IL 60445
Telephone: (800) 377-9247 (708) 389-5922
Fax: (708) 389-9882
Mr. Jack E. Yost, Jr., Vice President of Franchise Development

Number of Franchised Units: 33
Number of Company-Owned Units: 1
Number of Total Operating Units: 34

In Business Since: 1973   Franchising Since: 1973

Description of Operation: Multistate Transmissions provides transmission and drive train service and repairs of trucks, cars, 4 x 4's and RV's. Foreign and domestic. Retail, wholesale and fleet.

Equity Capital Needed: $100,000 - $130,000

Franchise Fee: $27,500

Royalty Fee: 7%

Financial Assistance: We provide referrals to third-party financing, based only on the prospect's credit.

Managerial Assistance: We provide operations, training, sales, owner's school and on-going assistance from operations, technical, legal and accounting departments, as well as assistance with national accounts and vendors.

Training Provided: Center manager's school for center training and owner's school. 800# service for operations and technical questions.

Information Submitted: January 1994

NOVUS WINDSHIELD REPAIR
10425 Hampshire Ave. S.
Minneapolis, MN 55438
Telephone: (800) 328-1117 (612) 944-8000
Fax: (612) 944-2542
Mr. Robin Smith, President

Number of Franchised Units: 887
Number of Company-Owned Units: 1
Number of Total Operating Units: 888

In Business Since: 1972   Franchising Since: 1985

Description of Operation: NOVUS Windshield Repair is the #1 low-investment franchise in the United States. NOVUS franchisees offer customers a convenient, economical alternative to windshield replacement by repairing stone-damaged windshields with our patented process. NOVUS Windshield Repair is a high-potential, long-term, full-time franchise opportunity.

Equity Capital Needed: $21,000

Franchise Fee: $11,000

Royalty Fee: 6%

Financial Assistance: Not available.

Managerial Assistance: With our "Executive in the Field" program, you're sure to get your business off on the right foot. We offer national advertising programs and insurance programs. Our toll-free hotline allows you to order products 24 hours a day. One-on-one phone consultation is available with experienced support managers. Plus, you'll receive a monthly newsletter filled with information on technical procedures, sales tips, motivational profiles and product news.

Training Provided: NOVUS Windshield Repair gives you the on-going training and support needed to guide you from your first day of training and throughout your career as a franchise owner. We offer complete technical and business training at our Minneapolis, MN headquarters. We offer one-on-one consultation with our 8-day program and teach you how to offer a full-service windshield repair franchise.

Information Submitted: December 1993

OIL BUTLER INTERNATIONAL
1599 Route 22 W.
Union, NJ 07083
Telephone: (908) 687-3283
Fax: (908) 687-7617
Mr. Samuel Casternovia, President

Number of Franchised Units: 13
Number of Company-Owned Units: 1
Number of Total Operating Units: 14

In Business Since: 1987　　　　　**Franchising Since:** 1991

Description of Operation: Mobile oil change service. Oil Butler's uniquely-designed, high-tech vehicle provides the corporate image and service your customers will expect from the leader in the field of on-site oil changes. Fleet, employee and residential markets with repeat customers. Low investment. Low overhead. Complete training and on-going support.

Equity Capital Needed: $10,000 - $15,000

Franchise Fee: $7,000 +

Royalty Fee: 7%, or $50 weekly minimum.

Financial Assistance: We provide veteran and military discounts, as well as outside sources for financing.

Managerial Assistance: Assistance is provided in setting up suppliers, inventory control, account scheduling, promotion, bookkeeping and hiring.

Training Provided: We offer classroom and in-field training for mechanics of oil changes, marketing and sales and purchasing.

Information Submitted: March 1994

OIL CAN HENRY'S
1200 NW Front Ave., # 690
Portland, OR 97209
Telephone: (800) 765-6244 (503) 243-6311
Fax: (503) 228-5227
Mr. Carl Nelson, Director of Franchise Development

Number of Franchised Units: 27
Number of Company-Owned Units: 3
Number of Total Operating Units: 30

In Business Since: 1978　　　　　**Franchising Since:** 1988

Description of Operation: Fast oil, lube and fluid franchises.

Equity Capital Needed: $85,000

Franchise Fee: $25,000

Royalty Fee: 5.5%

Financial Assistance: Third-party financing.

Managerial Assistance: Complete 5-week franchise operation training course. On-going head office support.

Training Provided: 5 weeks of training.

Information Submitted: January 1994

OIL EXPRESS FAST LUBE SYSTEMS
15 Spinning Wheel Rd., # 428
Hinsdale, IL 60521
Telephone: (708) 325-8666
Fax: (708) 325-8683
Mr. Daniel R. Barnas, President

Number of Franchised Units: 33
Number of Company-Owned Units: 19
Number of Total Operating Units: 52

In Business Since: 1980　　　　　**Franchising Since:** 1981

Description of Operation: 10-minute oil change.

Equity Capital Needed: $75,000 - $100,000

Franchise Fee: $25,000

Royalty Fee: 5%

Financial Assistance: Independent bank financing is available, based upon the franchisor's reputation. Independent oil company. Equipment loan financing available. Total financing available - typically 80% - 85% of the total project costs.

Managerial Assistance: We provide a 30-hour management development school. A minimum of 10 days of on-the-job training. Training manuals and video tapes. On-going advice and assistance. Technical meetings.

Training Provided: Same as above.

Information Submitted: March 1994

PAINT SHUTTLE, THE
P. O. Box 478
Monee, IL 60449
Telephone: (708) 534-1419
Fax: (708) 534-9475
Ms. Jacqueline L. Miller, President

Number of Franchised Units: 13
Number of Company-Owned Units: 1
Number of Total Operating Units: 14

In Business Since: 1988　　　　　**Franchising Since:** 1992

Description of Operation: Complete auto paint restoration process for the repair of stone chips, scratches, minor rust spots, moldings, trim and urethane bumpers. All of the latest products and equipment are included. For men and women alike.

Equity Capital Needed: $50,000

Franchise Fee: $35,000

Royalty Fee: 10%

Financial Assistance: Financial assistance is available for qualified franchisees.

Managerial Assistance: On-going support through telephone, pagers, manuals and periodic refresher courses of new products and applications.

Training Provided: A 2-week, extensive training program, consisting of all hands-on training by qualified Paint Shuttle technicians in the franchisee's geographical area. All accounts are acquired. All products and their uses are thoroughly gone over.

Information Submitted: November 1993

PRECISION TUNE
748 Miller Dr., SE, P. O. Box 5000
Leesburg, VA 22075
Telephone: (800) 231-0588 (703) 777-9095
Fax: (703) 779-0137
Mr. Phil Trigg, Director of Franchise Recruitment

Number of Franchised Units: 538
Number of Company-Owned Units: 3
Number of Total Operating Units: 541

In Business Since: 1975　　　　　**Franchising Since:** 1978

Description of Operation: Precision Tune, America's largest engine performance car care company, offers a variety of services - tune-up, quick oil and lube, brake service, engine performance repair and maintenance. Franchisees are provided with comprehensive training programs, continuous operating support, marketing and advertising support and inventory and management support. Area franchise opportunities also available.

Equity Capital Needed: $137,100 - $194,600

Franchise Fee: $25,000

Royalty Fee: 7.5%

Financial Assistance: While Precision Tune does not provide direct financial assistance, equipment leasing is available to qualified prospects through a third party. Assistance is also provided in SBA loan applications through an outside party. Precision Tune participates in the VetFran program and will finance 50% of the franchisee fee for 12 months at 0% interest for qualified veterans.

Managerial Assistance: A 2-week management course is required for all franchisees. In addition, most franchisees are supported in their local market by an area sub-franchisor who owns and operates centers. Area sub-franchisors assist in business management, technical training and on-going support as needed. Those franchisees located in areas not covered by an area sub-franchisor are assisted by corporate operations and marketing staff members.

Training Provided: Training for each staff level: franchisee management training - 2 weeks, center manager - 1 week, engine performance technical training - 5 weeks, brake technician training - 1 week. We also offer classes in air conditioning, cooling system service, fuel injection service, lighting service, lube, oil and filter service and transmission service.

Information Submitted: January 1994

PROMPTO
13 Scott Dr.
Westbrook, ME 04092
Telephone: (207) 775-4016
Fax: (207) 775-4018
Mr. Kevin A. King, Franchise Director

Number of Franchised Units: 8
Number of Company-Owned Units: 6
Number of Total Operating Units: 14

In Business Since: 1984   **Franchising Since:** 1985

Description of Operation: Prompto operates a chain of drive-thru oil, filter and lube change facilities in New England. Prompto specializes in the basic fluid changes and focuses on high-volume, low-tech operations. Prompto enjoys a much higher customer count than industry averages.

Equity Capital Needed: $50,000

Franchise Fee: $17,500

Royalty Fee: 5%

Financial Assistance: While the Company does not provide financial assistance in all cases, the Company does assist in the preparation of documents to assist prospective franchisees seeking approval of their bank loans.

Managerial Assistance: Management assistance is provided through Prompto's training program, distribution program to assist in cost controls and its detailed operations manual.

Training Provided: Prompto trains new franchisees at its training operation in Portland, ME for a period of 3 weeks. Thereafter, Prompto inspects operations and is available for phone consultations during regular business hours.

Information Submitted: November 1993

RUST CHECK
1285 Britannia Rd. E.
Mississauga, ON L4W 1C7 CAN
Telephone: (800) 387-6743 (905) 670-7878
Fax: (905) 670-7539
Mr. Robert Wowk, National Sales Manager

Number of Franchised Units: 240
Number of Company-Owned Units: 2
Number of Total Operating Units: 242

In Business Since: 1981   **Franchising Since:** 1981

Description of Operation: Rust prevention franchise in the areas of industrial and automotive applications. Services involve the sale and distribution of leading corrosive prevention and protecting materials, chemicals and technology for all applications.

Equity Capital Needed: $25,000 - $75,000

Franchise Fee: $25,000

Royalty Fee: 0%

Financial Assistance: Terms available.

Managerial Assistance: Site selection assistance, computer, accounting, administration and sales assistance are available.

Training Provided: We offer complete technical training, installation assistance and on-going support.

Information Submitted: January 1994

SAF-T AUTO CENTERS
121 N. Plains Industrial Rd., Unit H
Wallingford, CT 06492
Telephone: (800) 382-7238 (203) 294-1094
Fax: (203) 269-2532
Mr. Richard Bilodeau, President

Number of Franchised Units: 13
Number of Company-Owned Units: 1
Number of Total Operating Units: 14

In Business Since: 1978   **Franchising Since:** 1985

Description of Operation: Saf-T Auto Centers is an owner-operated auto repair shop, offering steering, suspension, brakes, mufflers, lubrication and minor repair. Our main effort is to put good mechanics in a business opportunity where they can capitalize on their trade.

Equity Capital Needed: $65,000

Franchise Fee: $15,000

Royalty Fee: $400 per month.

Financial Assistance: Leasing and third-party assistance.

Managerial Assistance: 1 week of on-site administrative training, plus operations manual to include marketing assistance.

Training Provided: Must have experience in the auto repair industry. This is a pre-requisite.

Information Submitted: November 1993

SERVICE CENTER
7655 E. Gelding Dr., # A-3
Scottsdale, AZ 85260
Telephone: (800) 729-7424 (602) 998-1616
Fax: (602) 948-7308
Mr. Gerald Zukerman, President

Number of Franchised Units: 18
Number of Company-Owned Units: 3
Number of Total Operating Units: 21

In Business Since: 1991   **Franchising Since:** 1992

Description of Operation: Supply various services to both residential and commercial customers. Franchisee creates a shell or umbrella, within which various skilled trades people can perform services. The franchisee is the management head of the company and various trades are performed by independent service people. The franchisee essentially performs the business management expertise and provides the capital, while trained technicians actually perform the work.

Equity Capital Needed: $39,000 - $51,000

Franchise Fee: $25,000

Royalty Fee: 7%, plus $75 per month for software maintenance.

Financial Assistance: Service Center will carry 50% of the $25,000 franchise fee. Terms are 5 years at 8%, with no interest on repayments on the note during the first year of operation. The note is secured only by the franchise. No personal guarantee.

Managerial Assistance: Service Center will literally create a turn-key business, so that on the first day of operation there will be technicians to run the calls, staff to answer the phones and dispatch technicians and run the office. The advertising program will be in place and customers will be calling for service. In short, a complete operating business.

Training Provided: Each franchisee and his/her staff will be taught every function of the business operation. Should any staff member have to be replaced, each of the other people trained in the operation will be able to assume the duties of the missing person. In addition, we are tied to each franchise office via modem and can operate a remote site franchise from our corporate office.

Information Submitted: January 1994

SHINE FACTORY, THE
3519 14th St., SW, 2nd Fl.
Calgary, AB T2T 3W2 CAN
Telephone: (403) 243-3030
Fax: (403) 243-8137
Mr. Bruce Cousens, President

Number of Franchised Units: 26
Number of Company-Owned Units: 0
Number of Total Operating Units: 26

In Business Since: 1979   **Franchising Since:** 1979

Description of Operation: Canada's largest automotive and polishing franchise.

Equity Capital Needed: $90,000 - $150,000

Franchise Fee: $10,000 - $50,000

Royalty Fee: 8%

Financial Assistance: We assist in bank negotiations.

Managerial Assistance: Each franchisee receives assistance in location, sales, bookkeeping, employee relations, operations and advertising.

Training Provided: 2 weeks of hands-on and theory training, 1 week of marketing at the franchisee's location and on-going follow-up.

Information Submitted: December 1993

SPEEDEE OIL CHANGE & TUNE-UP
6660 Riverside Dr., # 101
Metairie, LA 70003
Telephone: (800) 451-7461 (504) 454-3783
Fax: (504) 454-3890
Mr. Kevin Bennett, Executive Vice President

Number of Franchised Units: 132
Number of Company-Owned Units: 2
Number of Total Operating Units: 134

In Business Since: 1980   **Franchising Since:** 1982

Description of Operation: Speedee specializes in a 17-point quick oil change, diagnostic tune-up and brake service while the customer waits. No appointment is necessary. Other preventative maintenance services performed are emission control system service, fuel systems cleaning, air conditioning recharges, radiator flushes, transmission service, differential service and replacement of filters, wiper blades, radiator cap, etc.

Equity Capital Needed: $80,000 - $150,000

Franchise Fee: $30,000 - $40,000

Royalty Fee: 6%

Financial Assistance: Not available.

Managerial Assistance: We provide a 3-day orientation at corporate headquarters, manuals, seminars, operations staff, field service representatives, newsletters and grand opening.

Training Provided: We offer 2 - 4 weeks of management review at a local office and 1 - 2 weeks of in-store training at open shop.

Information Submitted: January 1994

SPEEDY MUFFLER KING
8430 W. Bryn Mawr Ave., # 400
Chicago, IL 60187
Telephone: (800) 359-2359 (312) 693-1000
Fax: (312) 693-0309
Mr. Bill Olsen, Director of Franchise Operations

Number of Franchised Units: 107
Number of Company-Owned Units: 258
Number of Total Operating Units: 365

In Business Since: 1956   **Franchising Since:** 1986

Description of Operation: Retail automotive repair shops that specialize in exhaust, suspension, front end and brake repairs.

Equity Capital Needed: $226,000 (excluding land and building).

Franchise Fee: $18,500

Royalty Fee: 5%

Financial Assistance: Local sources and SBA.

Managerial Assistance: We provide 6 - 8 weeks of training, with field operations support. Management is by the dealer.

Training Provided: Same as above.

Information Submitted: January 1994

SPEEDY TRANSMISSION CENTERS
902 Clint Moore Rd., # 216
Boca Raton, FL 33487
Telephone: (800) 336-0310 (407) 995-8282
Fax: (407) 995-8005
Mr. D'Arcy J. Williams, President

Number of Franchised Units: 30
Number of Company-Owned Units: 0
Number of Total Operating Units: 30

In Business Since: 1983   **Franchising Since:** 1983

Description of Operation: Repair, replacement and servicing of components related to the automotive drive train, including transmission repair, both automatic and standard. Centers service automobiles, trucks and commercial vehicles. Units are self-contained and approximately 2,400 - 3,000 square feet.

Equity Capital Needed: $20,000 - $40,000

Franchise Fee: $19,500

Royalty Fee: 7%

Financial Assistance: The franchisor can provide financing for a portion of the initial fee to qualified candidates. A third-party equipment supplier provides financing for major equipment in the center - up to approximately $30,000 to qualified franchisees.

Managerial Assistance: The franchisor provides complete management manuals, as well as continuous consultation. Newsletters and local meetings are used to update management skills. An 800# is available for use by franchisees requiring assistance. The franchisor assists in the selection of real estate, the obtaining of necessary licenses and in obtaining skilled labor for the center.

Training Provided: Each franchisee attends a 3-week training course in either Atlanta, GA or Boca Raton, FL. Included in this period is 1 week of classroom operational training. Training can vary depending on the background and experience of the franchisee. On-going management training classes are provided by the franchisor in local areas.

Information Submitted: November 1993

SPOT-NOT CAR WASHES
2011 W. 4th St.
Joplin, MO 64801
Telephone: (800) 682-7629 (417) 781-2140
Fax: (417) 781-3906
Mr. Forrest Uppendahl, Vice President

Number of Franchised Units: 26
Number of Company-Owned Units: 0
Number of Total Operating Units: 26

In Business Since: 1968 **Franchising Since:** 1985

Description of Operation: High-pressure spray, frictionless automatic and self-service combination car washes.

Equity Capital Needed: $250,000 - $350,000

Franchise Fee: $25,000

Royalty Fee: 5%

Financial Assistance: SBA funding and leasing arrangements with approved sources.

Managerial Assistance: On-going operations and marketing. Assistance through periodic visits and field meetings.

Training Provided: We provide 7 days at the corporate office, plus 5 days of field training in an operating unit.

Information Submitted: November 1993

STOP BRAKE SHOPS
13844 Alton Parkway, # 132
Irvine, CA 92718
Telephone: (800) 244-2725 (714) 380-2601
Fax: (714) 380-0212
Mr. Don St. Ours, President

Number of Franchised Units: 17
Number of Company-Owned Units: 1
Number of Total Operating Units: 18

In Business Since: 1980 **Franchising Since:** 1981

Description of Operation: We specialize in brakes, tune-ups, smog service, fuel injector, ride control, shocks, struts and cooling system maintenance.

Equity Capital Needed: $92,000 - $125,000

Franchise Fee: $17,500

Royalty Fee: 6%

Financial Assistance: We will help in getting a loan from a third party.

Managerial Assistance: Data not available.

Training Provided: Classroom instruction in policies and procedures, customer relations, goods and services, performance evaluation, service and parts manuals. State requirements: video presentation discussion, repair order writing. Brake systems orientation: video presentation, discussion. In-shop, hands-on instruction: brake system review. Smog Service Orientation: video orientation, discussion. Hands-on instruction: smog service review. Tune-up service orientation: video presentation, discussion.

Information Submitted: March 1994

SUPERGLASS WINDSHIELD REPAIR
6090 McDonough Dr., # 0
Norcross, GA 30093
Telephone: (404) 409-1885
Fax: (404) 840-8182
Mr. David A. Casey, President

Number of Franchised Units: 94
Number of Company-Owned Units: 1
Number of Total Operating Units: 95

In Business Since: 1992 **Franchising Since:** 1993

Description of Operation: Mobile and fixed location repair of rock-damaged and cracked windshields for commercial fleets, auto dealerships, insurance companies and individual motorists.

Equity Capital Needed: $9,500 - $28,500

Franchise Fee: $5,617.

Royalty Fee: 3%

Financial Assistance: 3% - 0% financing on entire franchise cost. Typical—$9,500 total price; $6,500 down payment; 24 payments of $138.43 after 4-month grace period.

Managerial Assistance: 5 days of on-site marketing assistance in the franchisee's exclusive territory. On-going telemarketing assistance for term of franchise agreement, monthly newsletters, annual convention and national accounts.

Training Provided: We provide 5 days in Atlanta, GA for technical, marketing and bookkeeping training. All manuals are provided. 5 additional days of marketing assistance in franchisee's exclusive territory to establish regular commercial accounts.

Information Submitted: November 1993

TIRES PLUS AUTO SERVICE CENTERS
701 Lady Bird Ln.
Burnsville, MN 55337
Telephone: (612) 895-4927
Fax: (612) 895-4981
Mr. John Hyduke, Vice President of Development

Number of Franchised Units: 20
Number of Company-Owned Units: 35
Number of Total Operating Units: 55

In Business Since: 1976 **Franchising Since:** 1981

Description of Operation: Tires Plus is the largest independently-owned tire retailer in the Midwest. We are single and multi-store franchises in large and medium-sized markets. Our concept is unique and competitively aggressive. We seek to dominate the markets that we enter.

Equity Capital Needed: $100,000 - $200,000

Franchise Fee: $30,000

Royalty Fee: 3%

Financial Assistance: Yes.

Managerial Assistance: Tires Plus has tremendous buying power that can be used for the benefit of the franchisee. We provide site selection, construction drawings and design assistance. We also provide field operations support, computer training support, marketing support and financial analysis support.

Training Provided: We provide 2 weeks of classroom training. We provide in-store training and pay your salary for up to 6 months at one of our corporate stores. We also provide a comprehensive operations management manual.

Information Submitted: January 1994

TUFFY AUTO SERVICE CENTERS
1414 Baronial Plaza Dr.
Toledo, OH 43615
Telephone: (800) 228-8339 (419) 865-6900
Fax: (419) 865-7343
Mr. Jim McKay, Director of Franchise Sales

Number of Franchised Units: 142
Number of Company-Owned Units: 4
Number of Total Operating Units: 146

In Business Since: 1970 **Franchising Since:** 1971

Description of Operation: Sales and installation of exhaust systems, brakes, shocks, front-end alignment and suspension, oil changes, air conditioning service, etc.

Equity Capital Needed: $75,000 cash minimum.

Franchise Fee: $20,000

Royalty Fee: 5%

Financial Assistance: Equipment lease financing is available to qualified applicants.

Managerial Assistance: On-going training and supervision are provided by the operations and training departments. Marketing and advertising assistance are provided by the marketing department.

Training Provided: We offer 1 week of new franchisee training, 2 weeks of in-shop assistance at opening and on-going support.

Information Submitted: January 1994

TUNEX AUTOMOTIVE SPECIALISTS
556 East 2100 S.
Salt Lake City, UT 84106
Telephone: (800) HI-TUNEX (801) 486-8133
Fax: (801) 484-4740
Franchise Sales Department

Number of Franchised Units: 15
Number of Company-Owned Units: 4
Number of Total Operating Units: 19

In Business Since: 1974   **Franchising Since:** 1975

Description of Operation: Diagnostic "tune-up" services and repairs of engine-related systems (i.e. ignition, carburetion, fuel injection, emission, computer controls, cooling and air-conditioning) for maximum customer satisfaction. We analyze all systems for problems so that the customer can make service and repair decisions.

Equity Capital Needed: $105,000 - $120,000

Franchise Fee: $19,000

Royalty Fee: 5%

Financial Assistance: Some financing is provided, as well as equipment lease assistance.

Managerial Assistance: We provide quarterly training sessions, annual evaluations and a toll-free "assist-line."

Training Provided: Initial training: classroom - 1 week; grand opening - 1 week; follow-up - 1 week.

Information Submitted: March 1994

US1 AUTO PARTS
5 Dakota Dr., # 210
Lake Success, NY 11042
Telephone: (516) 358-5100
Fax: (516) 358-2717
Mr. Reuben Alcalay, President

Number of Franchised Units: 21
Number of Company-Owned Units: 2
Number of Total Operating Units: 23

In Business Since: 1983   **Franchising Since:** 1990

Description of Operation: Automotive discount supermarket.

Equity Capital Needed: $125,000 - $175,000

Franchise Fee: $25,000

Royalty Fee: 6%

Financial Assistance: All our franchisees received financial assistance of up to 85% on a turn-key operation.

Managerial Assistance: We offer training in stores that are already running for an unlimited time.

Training Provided: Same as above.

Information Submitted: March 1994

VALVOLINE INSTANT OIL CHANGE
301 E. Main St., # 1200
Lexington, KY 40507
Telephone: (800) 622-6846 (606) 264-7070
Fax: (606) 264-7049
Mr. W. Jeffrey Malicote, Franchise Sales

Number of Franchised Units: 66
Number of Company-Owned Units: 344
Number of Total Operating Units: 410

In Business Since: 1986   **Franchising Since:** 1988

Description of Operation: Fluid maintenance for passenger cars and light trucks.

Equity Capital Needed: $100,000 - $200,000

Franchise Fee: $15,000 - $25,000

Royalty Fee: 4% - 5% - 6%. Graduated royalty schedule to systems that attain certain set sales levels.

Financial Assistance: The licensor and/or its affiliates will offer (to qualified prospects) leasing programs for land, building, equipment, signage and POS systems.

Managerial Assistance: We provide support in all areas of franchise operations and marketing, site selection, construction, POS system and administration.

Training Provided: We offer a 4-stage training program, as well as proprietary manuals, videos, on-site support and training.

Information Submitted: January 1994

VEHICARE
290 Woodcliff Dr.
Fairport, NY 14450
Telephone: (800) 836-2468 (716) 248-0270
Fax: (716) 248-9404
Ms. Pamela Lloyd Tait, Director of Marketing Services

Number of Franchised Units: 3
Number of Company-Owned Units: 31
Number of Total Operating Units: 34

In Business Since: 1988   **Franchising Since:** 1989

Description of Operation: On-site mobile preventive maintenance for commercial fleets.

Equity Capital Needed: $200,000 - $400,000

Franchise Fee: $80,000 per million population.

Royalty Fee: 5%

Financial Assistance: Data not available.

Managerial Assistance: New operations are mostly joint ventures with Vehicare as managing general partner. Independent franchisees are invited to participate in all facility manager's training seminars.

Training Provided: We offer 1 week of initial training at the Company's headquarters, on-going sales training and facility manager seminars on a regular basis.

Information Submitted: March 1994

WOW / WASH ON WHEELS
5401 S. Bryant Ave.
Sanford, FL 32773
Telephone: (800) 345-1969 (407) 321-4010
Fax: (407) 321-3409
Mr. Jim B. Good, President

Number of Franchised Units: 102
Number of Company-Owned Units: 0
Number of Total Operating Units: 102

In Business Since: 1965   **Franchising Since:** 1987

Description of Operation: Mobile power cleaning franchise, providing cleaning services for a diverse market, including government, industrial and commercial buildings, residential homes and more.

Equity Capital Needed: $7,500 - $9,000

Franchise Fee: $7,500

Royalty Fee: $80

Financial Assistance: Financial assistance is available to qualified persons with good credit. The total investment is $23,000 - $33,000.

Managerial Assistance: On-going.

Training Provided: We offer 5 days of intensive training, then on-going, as well as manuals, seminars, newsletters, hotlines and direct mail.

Information Submitted: March 1994

ZIEBART TIDYCAR
1290 E. Maple Rd.
Troy, MI 48007
Telephone: (800) 877-1312 (810) 588-4100
Fax: (810) 588-1444
Mr. Dave Henderson, Assistant Manager for Franchising

Number of Franchised Units: 638
Number of Company-Owned Units: 23
Number of Total Operating Units: 661

In Business Since: 1954   **Franchising Since:** 1963

Description of Operation: Automotive application of detailing - accessories and protection services.

Equity Capital Needed: $99,000 - $161,000

Franchise Fee: $24,000

Royalty Fee: 8% - 5%

Financial Assistance: Leasing is available for equipment and decor, up to $25,000.

Managerial Assistance: We provide regional advertising support and regional sales support in the field.

Training Provided: All training is provided by the franchisor, including sales, management and all technical training.

Information Submitted: December 1993

BEAUTY SALONS AND SUPPLIES

ACCENT HAIR SALON
211 S. Main St., # 720
Dayton, OH 45402
Telephone: (513) 461-0394
Fax: (513) 223-3221
Mr. Claude Patmon, President

Number of Franchised Units: 9
Number of Company-Owned Units: 2
Number of Total Operating Units: 11

In Business Since: 1981   **Franchising Since:** 1987

Description of Operation: Hair salons located in major malls, focusing on hair care for the black family.

Equity Capital Needed: $40,000

Franchise Fee: $20,000

Royalty Fee: 5%

Financial Assistance: Data not available.

Managerial Assistance: Data not available.

Training Provided: Comprehensive 4 weeks of initial training in all aspects of the operating system.

Information Submitted: November 1993

COMMAND PERFORMANCE STYLING SALONS
P. O. Box 3000-266
Georgetown, TX 78628

Telephone: (800) 872-4247 (512) 869-1201
Fax: (512) 869-0366
Ms. Jackie Ellason, Franchise Relations

Number of Franchised Units: 110
Number of Company-Owned Units: 12
Number of Total Operating Units: 122

In Business Since: 1975   **Franchising Since:** 1976

Description of Operation: Full-service hair styling salons. Extensive educational program, national buying programs, salon design and real estate assistance. Computerized cash management, performance tracking and analysis, client record-keeping and inventory control. Other concepts will be offered in 1994.

Equity Capital Needed: $50,000 - $100,000

Franchise Fee: $25,000

Royalty Fee: 6%

Financial Assistance: Limited assistance is available for equipment leasing.

Managerial Assistance: The franchisor has 15 years in salon operations and operates Company-owned salons. On-site assistance is available, plus training at corporate headquarters in Company-owned salons.

Training Provided: Managerial and technical training, both on-site and in Company-owned salons.

Information Submitted: January 1994

COST CUTTERS FAMILY HAIR CARE
300 Industrial Blvd., NE
Minneapolis, MN 55413
Telephone: (800) 858-2266 (612) 331-8500
Fax: (612) 331-2821
Ms. Julie Langenbrunner, Development Administration

Number of Franchised Units: 499
Number of Company-Owned Units: 1
Number of Total Operating Units: 500

In Business Since: 1963   **Franchising Since:** 1967

Description of Operation: A value-priced, full-service salon concept that provides low-cost, no-frills hair services for the family. The franchisor created Cost Cutters to meet the demand for providing the public with quality hair services and products at a moderate price.

Equity Capital Needed: $6,600 - $13,800

Franchise Fee: $19,500

Royalty Fee: 6%

Financial Assistance: Loan programs are available for qualified start-up franchisees. Also, an equipment-lease program for existing (second store) franchisees is also available. There is also an SBA assistance program (paperwork assistance) for both start-up and existing operators.

Managerial Assistance: Managerial programs taught during training classes and during 10-day opening assistance.

Training Provided: 1 week at national headquarters and 10 days on-site. On-going training is available upon request. Continuing training available.

Information Submitted: November 1993

FANTASTIC SAM'S
3180 Old Getwell Rd.
Memphis, TN 38118
Telephone: (800) 844-7267 (901) 363-8624
Fax: (901) 363-8946
Mr. Rob Rutter, Vice President of Operations/Development

Number of Franchised Units: 1304
Number of Company-Owned Units: 6
Number of Total Operating Units: 1310

In Business Since: 1974　　　　**Franchising Since:** 1976

Description of Operation: Full-service family hair care centers.

Equity Capital Needed: $75,000 - $100,000

Franchise Fee: $25,000

Royalty Fee: $175.56 per week.

Financial Assistance: Some equipment leasing is available.

Managerial Assistance: Every region has a support center.

Training Provided: 1 week of intense training is provided at FSI in Memphis, TN. Also, on-going training in all regions.

Information Submitted: March 1994

FIRST CHOICE HAIRCUTTERS
6465 Millcreek Dr., # 210
Mississauga, ON L5N 5R6 CAN
Telephone: (800) 387-8335 (905) 821-8555
Fax: (905) 567-7000
Mr. Brian Tucker, President

Number of Franchised Units: 136
Number of Company-Owned Units: 73
Number of Total Operating Units: 209

In Business Since: 1980　　　　**Franchising Since:** 1981

Description of Operation: Value-priced family haircare centers. High-volume, low-cost, a la carte haircare for men, women and children.

Equity Capital Needed: $40,000

Franchise Fee: $25,000

Royalty Fee: 7%

Financial Assistance: Data not available.

Managerial Assistance: Annual seminar, annual "think tank," management training courses, semi-annual visits by operational consultants. Intense help is available by support office on an as-needed basis.

Training Provided: 1-week training program at support office. 2 weeks of training at franchisee's location. Annual training in franchisee's area.

Information Submitted: November 1993

GREAT CLIPS
3800 W. 80th St., # 400
Minneapolis, MN 55431
Telephone: (800) 999-5959 (612) 893-9088
Fax: (612) 844-3444
Ms. Kimberly MacDonald, Franchise Development

Number of Franchised Units: 368
Number of Company-Owned Units: 0
Number of Total Operating Units: 368

In Business Since: 1982　　　　**Franchising Since:** 1983

Description of Operation: High-volume, quality hair salons that specialize in cuts and perms for the entire family. Unique and attractive decor and quality advertising. Emphasis on strong, hands-on support to franchisees. Definite opportunity for growth in a fast-growing industry.

Equity Capital Needed: $72,000 - $98,400

Franchise Fee: $17,500

Royalty Fee: 6%

Financial Assistance: Bank presentation. We look for franchisees who are financially capable of pursuing this business or who have their own banking relationships established.

Managerial Assistance: In-house real estate assistance, advertising, construction and operations. Market field staff includes training and service reps, field consultants, trainers and regional directors.

Training Provided: New franchisee training and orientation lasts 3 days. Staff training for stylist, manager, assistant manager, receptionist, trend training and interaction management training.

Information Submitted: November 1993

GREAT EXPECTATIONS / HAIRCRAFTERS
125 S. Service Rd., P. O. Box 265
Jericho, NY 11753
Telephone: (800) 992-0139 (516) 334-8400
Fax: (516) 334-8575
Mr. Don vonLiebermann, President

Number of Franchised Units: 366
Number of Company-Owned Units: 38
Number of Total Operating Units: 404

In Business Since: 1955　　　　**Franchising Since:** 1961

Description of Operation: Full-service haircare salons with expanded retail operation. Salons offer complete hair and supplemental services to image and fashion-conscious individuals and entire families. Franchise package includes attractively-designed salons in a modern setting, utilizing newest hairstyling technology. Franchisor provides training, operational support, advertising material and assistance in site selection, lease negotiations, design and layout, equipment procurement, construction bids and personnel/recruitment.

Equity Capital Needed: $50,000 cash.

Franchise Fee: $20,000

Royalty Fee: 6%

Financial Assistance: The total investment range is from a low of $73,000 to a high of $176,500. Financial assistance is offered to qualified applicants. The franchisor identifies funding organizations and puts franchisees with a net worth of $100,000 plus in contact with such organizations.

Managerial Assistance: Area representatives and regional directors are available and make quarterly personal visits to franchisees. They are in contact with franchisees on an on-going basis by fax and letters, as well as meeting them at regional seminars and annual conventions.

Training Provided: Training is provided at headquarters or in a salon close to the franchisee's site for 5 - 7 days and at franchisee's unit for an additional 5 - 7 days. Assistance is also provided with operations and advertising manuals, video tapes and field representatives from national hair care manufacturers and distributors.

Information Submitted: March 1994

HAIR REPLACEMENT SYSTEMS/HRS
400 S. Dixie Highway
Hallandale, FL 33009
Telephone: (800) 327-7971 (305) 457-0050
Fax: (305) 457-0054
Mr. Kevin Maggs, Franchise Director

Number of Franchised Units: 45
Number of Company-Owned Units: 0
Number of Total Operating Units: 45

In Business Since: 1980　　　　**Franchising Since:** 1984

Description of Operation: Sales and service of non-surgical men and women's hair replacement systems.

Equity Capital Needed: $60,000 - $150,000

Franchise Fee: $6,500 for first 100,000 population; $1,000 for every additional 100,000 population.

Royalty Fee: 6%, or $100 per 100,000 population.

Financial Assistance: No financing.

Managerial Assistance: Site selection, office design, computer systems, assistance in staffing and contracts with new employees.

Training Provided: Training includes 1 week in the home office and a portion of a week in the new franchise location. Training covers tele-marketing, sales, styling, hair additions, computer use, marketing and receptionist.

Information Submitted: January 1994

HAIRLINE CREATIONS STUDIOS
5850-54 W. Montrose Ave.
Chicago, IL 60634
Telephone: (800) 424-7911 (312) 282-5454
Fax: (312) 282-5449
Mr. Paul V. Finamore, President

Number of Franchised Units: 3
Number of Company-Owned Units: 3
Number of Total Operating Units: 6

In Business Since: 1963   **Franchising Since:** 1992

Description of Operation: Specialists in sales and service of custom-made hair replacements and hair additions for hair loss clients. Full hair salon services for men and women. Custom-made hair replacements are protected under one or more of 6 US patents. One of America's fastest-growing industries. 1993 industry sales near $2 billion in product and service.

Equity Capital Needed: $100,000 - $175,000. (Regional sub-franchisor fee depending on geographical area).

Franchise Fee: $20,000 (individual studio franchise fee, outside of Illinois). Fee varies for special market areas.

Royalty Fee: 8%

Financial Assistance: Financial assistance is not available; however, we will assist in obtaining financing.

Managerial Assistance: We have created an intensive training program which every franchisee is required to attend and successfully complete. This program begins with classroom training, learning our system and philosophy, and continues in our existing operations learning day-to-day operational responsibilities and functions. The initial training is 8 - 12 weeks. Also, on-site training continues prior, during and after opening.

Training Provided: To help franchisees manage their business, detailed operations procedures and policy manuals are issued, providing every aspect of daily operations. On-going support from field reps provides guidance, periodic visits and evaluation. Regular phone contact also provided. Studios will assist the franchisees to train consultants, stylists and management. Our training is continuous. Guidance is provided in purchasing, supplier selection and marketing.

Information Submitted: January 1994

LEMON TREE, A UNISEX HAIRCUTTING ESTABLISHMENT
3301 Hempstead Tnpk.
Levittown, NY 11756
Telephone: (800) 345-9156 (516) 735-2828
Fax: (516) 735-1851
Mr. John L. Wagner, Vice President

Number of Franchised Units: 81
Number of Company-Owned Units: 0
Number of Total Operating Units: 81

In Business Since: 1976   **Franchising Since:** 1976

Description of Operation: Lemon Tree meets the hair care needs of all people, servicing the entire family at low, affordable prices, name-brand quality products and hours from early morning to late evening.

Equity Capital Needed: $35,000 - $50,000

Franchise Fee: $10,000

Royalty Fee: 6%

Financial Assistance: The franchisor may assist in obtaining financing for the franchise fee and equipment. The franchisor may agree to finance 1/2 of the franchisee's purchase of equipment and the franchise fee.

Managerial Assistance: The Lemon Tree management team will educate and guide the franchisee in market feasibility, site selection, techniques, lease negotiations, interior layout, personnel recruiting, insurance, merchandising, employee training, product sales, advertising and customer relations.

Training Provided: The franchisee will be trained 1 week at the franchisor's headquarters in the operation of the Lemon Tree. The franchisee will receive 1 week of in-shop training upon the salon's grand opening, including supplemental programs, seminars and workshops, as necessary.

Information Submitted: January 1994

PRO-CUTS
3716 Rufe Snow Dr.
Fort Worth, TX 76180
Telephone: (800) 542-2887 (817) 595-4171
Fax: (817) 595-3787
Mr. Donald H. Stone, President

Number of Franchised Units: 121
Number of Company-Owned Units: 17
Number of Total Operating Units: 138

In Business Since: 1982   **Franchising Since:** 1983

Description of Operation: Family hair care centers, providing quality haircuts for a low price. Also carrying a line of private-label, high-quality, hair care products exclusive to Pro-Cuts.

Equity Capital Needed: $50,000 - $60,000 (includes franchise fee).

Franchise Fee: $25,000

Royalty Fee: 4% - 6%

Financial Assistance: We have a third-party lender who will finance 70% of the cost of a new store, of which $25,000 would be collateralized by equipment and inventory and $45,000 would be leasehold improvements.

Managerial Assistance: Pro-Cuts has a computerized business operations system that ties the store, the franchise and the franchise support office together. Each franchisee is also assigned a support representative to assist with on-going operational challenges.

Training Provided: New franchisees attend a 3-day training session before their first store opens. Two workshops are conducted annually. Also, their support representatives provide additional training during the year, as needed.

Information Submitted: December 1993

SNIP N' CLIP HAIRCUT SHOPS
9300 Metcalf, Glenwood Pl., # 205
Overland Park, KS 66212
Telephone: (800) 622-6804 (913) 649-9303
Fax: (913) 649-0416
Mr. Dain R. Zinn, Vice President

Number of Franchised Units: 34
Number of Company-Owned Units: 41
Number of Total Operating Units: 75

In Business Since: 1976   **Franchising Since:** 1986

Description of Operation: Family hair care at budget prices. Snip n' Clip offers a complete shop for $39,500. Turn-key package includes franchise fee, equipment, decor and the initial supply of products.

Equity Capital Needed: $48,000 - $56,000

Franchise Fee: $10,000

Royalty Fee: 5%

Financial Assistance: None.

Managerial Assistance: Initial training for owner, manager and staff. On-going support on management and marketing.

Training Provided: We provide 2 days of opening training for new shops, including operations, customer service and personnel.

Information Submitted: November 1993

TRADE SECRET
130 Henry St., P. O. Box 58
Dousman, WI 53118
Telephone: (800) 462-6092 (414) 965-2196
Fax: (414) 965-3470
Mr. Bryan Patzkowski, Franchise Sales

Number of Franchised Units: 65
Number of Company-Owned Units: 25
Number of Total Operating Units: 90

In Business Since: 1983 **Franchising Since:** 1988

Description of Operation: Mall-based retail concept, specializing in "Salon-Only" professional hair care products. Trade Secret presents an exciting retail product environment to shoppers, while operating a compact, yet full-service, salon. Trade Secret is a division of Regis Corporation, which operates more than 1,200 salons worldwide.

Equity Capital Needed: $35,000 - $95,000

Franchise Fee: $27,500

Royalty Fee: 6.5%, discounted for timely payment.

Financial Assistance: None.

Managerial Assistance: We provide site-selection and lease negotiation, field consultant visits, operations manuals, customer manuals, customer service and product knowledge programs, annual franchisee convention, newsletters and numerous support programs.

Training Provided: Training consists of a comprehensive training program for franchisees at division headquarters. On-site assistance for grand opening. Financial statement review.

Information Submitted: January 1994

WE CARE HAIR
325 Bic Dr.
Milford, CT 06460
Telephone: (800) 888-4848 (203) 877-4281
Fax: (203) 876-6688
Mr. Keith Cross, Franchise Sales Manager

Number of Franchised Units: 132
Number of Company-Owned Units: 3
Number of Total Operating Units: 135

In Business Since: 1985 **Franchising Since:** 1986

Description of Operation: We Care Hair is a full-service salon designed for the entrepreneur, providing hair care, beauty supplies and tanning. No prior hair salon experience is needed or required. Multiple unit ownership encouraged.

Equity Capital Needed: $48,000 - $115,500

Franchise Fee: $7,500

Royalty Fee: 8%

Financial Assistance: Equipment leasing is available for qualified franchisees.

Managerial Assistance: A We Care Hair representative will make regular visits to your salon to inspect your operation and offer assistance, as needed.

Training Provided: A 2-week executive ownership training program covers all the fundamentals of establishing and operating a salon. The training takes place in the classroom and in an actual We Care Hair unit.

Information Submitted: November 1993

BUSINESS AIDS AND SERVICES

4-SQUARE ENTERPRISES
3060 Commerce Dr., # 4
Fort Gratiot, MI 48059
Telephone: (313) 385-8588
Fax: (313) 324-2911
Mr. Kay

Number of Franchised Units: 2
Number of Company-Owned Units: 1
Number of Total Operating Units: 3

In Business Since: 1993 **Franchising Since:** 1993

Description of Operation: 4-Square sells regional sub-franchises through which its independent regions individually sell and service local franchisees. Each franchise provides highly effective advertising for local merchants in co-operation with local non-profit organizations through community promotion.

Equity Capital Needed: Regional owner ($50,000 - $75,000); Local franchisee ($15,000 - $25,000) both include franchise fee.

Franchise Fee: $19,900

Royalty Fee: Data not available.

Financial Assistance: 4-Square may accept a note for 50% or less from an awarded owner/franchisee. The note is a cash substitute and must be paid off in installments and within 1 year.

Managerial Assistance: 4-Square produces complete training manuals, forms and sales aids. The regional owner is obligated to provide these materials, as well as continuing consultation, to the local franchisees for all aspects of the business.

Training Provided: The franchise includes basic and advanced management seminars. An extensive 3 weeks of classroom and in-field training are provided for all regional owners and franchisees.

Information Submitted: January 1994

ACCOUNTAX SERVICES (CANADA)
951 Wilson Ave., # 4
North York, ON M3K 2A7 CAN
Telephone: (416) 638-1303
Fax: (416) 638-1443
Mr. Vijay Kapur, Marketing Director

Number of Franchised Units: 10
Number of Company-Owned Units: 2
Number of Total Operating Units: 12

In Business Since: 1979 **Franchising Since:** 1981

Description of Operation: Accounting, bookkeeping, taxation and financial planning.

Equity Capital Needed: $25,000 - $35,000

Franchise Fee: $25,000

Royalty Fee: 4%

Financial Assistance: Yes, up to 50%.

Managerial Assistance: Yes, as well as on-going assistance.

Training Provided: Yes. A minimum of 2 weeks and a maximum of 6 months.

Information Submitted: January 1994

ACCOUNTING BUSINESS SYSTEMS
1355 Orange Ave., # 5
Winter Park, FL 32789
Telephone: (407) 644-5400
Fax: (407) 628-4160
Mr. Mark Silverberg, President

Number of Franchised Units: 22
Number of Company-Owned Units: 0
Number of Total Operating Units: 22

In Business Since: 1987   **Franchising Since:** 1989

Description of Operation: Complete accounting and tax franchise, including software, client marketing, training and support. Designed to put qualified individuals into public practice to serve small business.

Equity Capital Needed: $11,500

Franchise Fee: $9,500

Royalty Fee: $125 per month.

Financial Assistance: Financing is available.

Managerial Assistance: Initial management training and counseling. Full on-going telephone support.

Training Provided: An extensive 5 days of training in Orlando, FL covers client marketing, software operation, practice management and tax practice development.

Information Submitted: November 1993

AD SHOW NETWORK / ASN
3753 Howard Hughes Parkway, # 200
Las Vegas, NV 89109
Telephone: (800) 466-ASN/ (702) 366-7775
Mr. Kent Wyatt, President

Number of Franchised Units: 5
Number of Company-Owned Units: 0
Number of Total Operating Units: 5

In Business Since: 1992   **Franchising Since:** 1992

Description of Operation: ASN is a closed-circuit television show that provides advertisers the ability to focus exclusively on a specific target market. Contemporary display units are strategically placed (at local gathering places) in the heart of each business community. Each display contains a television monitor that shows brief 10 - 14 second commercials that are computer generated, with graphics, animation and special effects. Franchisee income is generated by the sale of advertising and production fees paid by advertisers.

Equity Capital Needed: $50,000 - 150,000

Franchise Fee: $25,000

Royalty Fee: Varies.

Financial Assistance: Approximately 50% financing is available to qualified, credit-worthy franchisees.

Managerial Assistance: After the initial training has been completed by the franchisee, in-house management and/or consultants are available on an on-going basis.

Training Provided: A 3 - 5 day, structured training session with applicable policy, management and sales manuals is provided to all franchisees at corporate offices.

Information Submitted: April 1994

ADVANCED BUSINESS CONCEPTS
145 N. Second Ave., # 5
Oakdale, CA 95361
Telephone: (800) 543-3976 (209) 848-9000
Fax: (209) 848-9009
Mr. Robert J. Farwell, Director of Operations

Number of Franchised Units: 7
Number of Company-Owned Units: 0
Number of Total Operating Units: 7

In Business Since: 1986   **Franchising Since:** 1990

Description of Operation: Advanced Business Concepts provides a unique business development program to business owners. The program helps these entrepreneurs to be more successful through the

implementation of systems, thereby solving problems and improving results. ABC franchisees offer the program to owners in their local area and get them started. Clients receive support for their programs by telephone from the corporate office.

Equity Capital Needed: $45,000 - $65,000 (includes franchise fee and first year's working capital).

Franchise Fee: $15,000

Royalty Fee: 0%

Financial Assistance: None.

Managerial Assistance: ABC provides a series of franchise operations manuals, videotapes and audiotapes to franchisees. Franchise support personnel are available by telephone on an unlimited basis. On-site assistance is also available.

Training Provided: Initial training consists of 30 days of intensive study by franchisee to learn the ABC systems. This is followed by on-site training by ABC training personnel. Extensive training materials, including manuals and training tapes, are provided.

Information Submitted: January 1994

ADVANCED ELECTRONIC TAX SERVICES
2616 W. 70th Ave.
Shreveport, LA 71108
Telephone: (800) 22-REFUND (318) 636-9751
Fax: (318) 636-9771
Mr. Jon David Murray, President

Number of Franchised Units: 6
Number of Company-Owned Units: 5
Number of Total Operating Units: 11

In Business Since: 1990   **Franchising Since:** 1992

Description of Operation: Advanced Electronic Tax Services offers franchised businesses for both single unit owner/operators and for multiple unit developers who will develop more than one store within a specific geographic area. Advanced Electronic Tax Services offices provide single-source convenience that enables qualified taxpayers to turn their tax refunds into cash within hours of filing their returns.

Equity Capital Needed: $26,250 - $39,250

Franchise Fee: $9,500

Royalty Fee: 10%

Financial Assistance: No financial assistance is available.

Managerial Assistance: As an Advanced Tax franchise owner, you will receive periodic visits from a trained field representative who will provide guidance and assistance and answer any questions you may have. In addition, you will receive, on loan, a copy of the confidential operations manual, which covers policies and procedures involved in running your business. As the manual is updated, revisions will be made available. And, we will be only a phone call away for answers to questions that arise during day-to-day operations.

Training Provided: The franchise includes an initial training and familiarization course of approximately 3 - 5 days. In addition, an Advanced Tax representative will assist with establishing and standardizing procedures and techniques essential to the operation of the franchised business.

Information Submitted: November 1993

ADVANTAGE PAYROLL SERVICES
126 Merrow Rd., P.O. Box 1330
Auburn, ME 04211
Telephone: (800) 876-0178 (207) 784-0178
Fax: (207) 786-0490
Mr. David J. Friedrich, President

Number of Franchised Units: 27
Number of Company-Owned Units: 1
Number of Total Operating Units: 28

In Business Since: 1967   **Franchising Since:** 1983

Description of Operation: Payroll and payroll tax filing. Franchisee computers are linked to franchisor's mainframe system. All tax deposits and quarterly reporting done by franchisor.

Equity Capital Needed: $20,000 - $40,000

Franchise Fee: $14,500

Royalty Fee: 0%

Financial Assistance: $5,000 note; 10% for 4 years.

Managerial Assistance: Data not available.

Training Provided: 2 weeks at home office. 10 days in field. On-going 800# support.

Information Submitted: January 1994

ADVENTURES IN ADVERTISING
2353 130th Ave. NE. # 110
Bellevue, WA 98005
Telephone: (800) 637-8668 (206) 885-9900
Fax: (206) 881-9200
Mr. Malcolm Alexander, Franchise Director

Number of Franchised Units: 0
Number of Company-Owned Units: 0
Number of Total Operating Units: 0

In Business Since: 1981   **Franchising Since:** 1994

Description of Operation: Adventures in Advertising provides medium to large companies with imprinted promotional products to be utilized in trade shows, product introductions, safety programs, service awards, incentive programs and recognition. Each franchisee provides local companies in their area with these items based upon national purchasing power. A custom-designed computer software program and total marketing support are provided.

Equity Capital Needed: $57,000 - $75,000

Franchise Fee: $17,500

Royalty Fee: 4% - 7%

Financial Assistance: None available.

Managerial Assistance: Each franchisee will be provided with a business operations manual and training in how to develop his/her office, sales force and market presence. Constant updates on product and market developments are provided.

Training Provided: Each franchisee receives 1 week of training and detailed manuals which include industry, sales development, client development and effective office management. 2 conferences per year and regular, on-going training programs are available for franchisees and their sales staff.

Information Submitted: March 1994

ADVISOR ONE
1097-C Irongate Ln.
Columbus, OH 43213
Telephone: (614) 864-1440
Mr. Raymond A. Strohl, President

Number of Franchised Units: 10
Number of Company-Owned Units: 1
Number of Total Operating Units: 11

In Business Since: 1986   **Franchising Since:** 1987

Description of Operation: Advising and consulting on investments. A related division, Broker One, is a stockbroker. Also, a related division, Money Broker One, is a loan broker.

Equity Capital Needed: $15,000

Franchise Fee: Varies.

Royalty Fee: Varies.

Financial Assistance: None.

Managerial Assistance: As much managerial assistance as needed is provided.

Training Provided: One month of training is provided, plus on-going training is provided for as long as needed or desired.

Information Submitted: November 1993

AIM MAIL CENTERS
20381 Lake Forest Dr., # B-2
Lake Forest, CA 92630
Telephone: (800) 969-0502 (714) 837-4151
Fax: (714) 837-4537
Mr. Michael Sawitz, Franchise Director

Number of Franchised Units: 18
Number of Company-Owned Units: 1
Number of Total Operating Units: 19

In Business Since: 1985   **Franchising Since:** 1989

Description of Operation: Aim Mail Centers take care of all your business service needs - from renting mailboxes, buying stamps, sending faxes and making copies to gift wrapping, greeting cards and passport photos, Aim Mail Centers offer it all, quickly and efficiently, without all the run-around. It's like having a post office, office supply store, gift shop and print shop all rolled into one!

Equity Capital Needed: $55,000 - $75,000

Franchise Fee: $17,500

Royalty Fee: 1% - 5%

Financial Assistance: SBA loans, FranVet, third-party financing.

Managerial Assistance: 2 weeks of training, 800# help-line, field support, workshops, newsletter (almost weekly), up-dates (both firmware and software at no charge), annual conventions and franchisee advisory committee.

Training Provided: Same as above.

Information Submitted: December 1993

AMERICAN INSTITUTE OF SMALL BUSINESS
7515 Wayzata Blvd., # 201
Minneapolis, MN 55426
Telephone: (800) 328-2906 (612) 545-7001
Fax: (612) 545-7020
Mr. Max Fallek, President

Number of Franchised Units: 4
Number of Company-Owned Units: 1
Number of Total Operating Units: 5

In Business Since: 1986   **Franchising Since:** 1989

Description of Operation: Publishers of educational materials, including books, software and videos on small business start-up, operation and entrepreneurship. Puts on seminars and workshops on small business start up and operations and on specific business subjects, such as advertising, public relations and writing a business plan.

Equity Capital Needed: $5,000 - $10,000

Franchise Fee: $2,000

Royalty Fee: 0%

Financial Assistance: Credit is extended on books, videos and software purchases sold by the franchisee.

Managerial Assistance: Complete training is provided on putting on a seminar or workshop, with the franchisor actually putting on the first workshop. Complete advertising materials, including literature, are provided.

Training Provided: Franchisees come to Minneapolis, MN for a 2-day training program or the Company will send a representative to the franchisee location and do the training on location. For the workshops, the Company will put on the first workshop for the franchisee and will provide complete workshop materials, which support the franchisee through the entire 1-day workshop, including videos, overhead transparencies and subject materials.

Information Submitted: November 1993

AMERICAN SIGN SHOPS
15965 Jeanette St.
Southfield, MI 48075
Telephone: (313) 557-2784
Ms. Colleen McGaffey

Number of Franchised Units: 33
Number of Company-Owned Units: 0
Number of Total Operating Units: 33

In Business Since: 1984   **Franchising Since:** 1987

Description of Operation: Computerized sign-making retail business.

Equity Capital Needed: $35,000 - $50,000 turn-key.

Franchise Fee: $15,000

Royalty Fee: 5%

Financial Assistance: The franchisor provides financial assistance in limited situations.

Managerial Assistance: On-going.

Training Provided: Yes.

Information Submitted: December 1993

ASSET ONE
1097 Irongate Ln., # C
Columbus, OH 43213
Telephone: (614) 864-1440
Mr. Raymond A. Strohl, President

Number of Franchised Units: 12
Number of Company-Owned Units: 1
Number of Total Operating Units: 13

In Business Since: 1985   **Franchising Since:** 1989

Description of Operation: Advising and consulting on financial planning and investments. A related division, Broker One, is a stockbroker and a second related division, Money Broker One, is a loan broker.

Equity Capital Needed: $15,000

Franchise Fee: Varies.

Royalty Fee: Varies.

Financial Assistance: None.

Managerial Assistance: As much managerial assistance as needed is provided.

Training Provided: 1 month of initial training is provided, plus on-going training is provided for as long as needed.

Information Submitted: January 1994

BINGO BUGLE NEWSPAPER
P. O. Box 51189
Seattle, WA 98115
Telephone: (800) 447-1958 (206) 527-4958
Fax: (206) 527-9756
Mr. Warren E. Kraft, Jr., President

Number of Franchised Units: 70
Number of Company-Owned Units: 0
Number of Total Operating Units: 70

In Business Since: 1982   **Franchising Since:** 1982

Description of Operation: Sell franchises for the Bingo Bugle Newspaper nationally. The Bingo Bugle is a monthly publication for bingo players. We also train and help the franchisees.

Equity Capital Needed: $5,500 - $9,000

Franchise Fee: $1,500 - $6,000

Royalty Fee: 10%

Financial Assistance: None.

Managerial Assistance: Data not available.

Training Provided: 2-day training session, tailored to prospect's experience in publishing and selling. Training subjects include checklist of everything franchisee needs to do at start-up, gathering research information on prospective buyers of advertising, preparation for selling ads, writing copy for ads, laying out ads, writing news stories, production of ads, production of news stories, photography, desktop publishing, typesetting and paste-up, bookkeeping and billing, distribution and multiple-edition advertising.

Information Submitted: November 1993

BRIDE'S DAY
750 Hamburg Tnpk., # 208
Pompton Lakes, NJ 07442
Telephone: (201) 835-6551
Fax: (201) 835-3639
Mr. David A. Gay, Publisher

Number of Franchised Units: 8
Number of Company-Owned Units: 2
Number of Total Operating Units: 10

In Business Since: 1987   **Franchising Since:** 1990

Description of Operation: Bride's Day is a free community magazine dedicated to assisting the bride with all aspects of wedding planning, while also offering an affordable, quality advertising vehicle for local wedding-related businesses. Franchisees work from home and have an excellent opportunity due to the recession-proof nature of the billion dollar wedding industry.

Equity Capital Needed: $5,000 - $10,000

Franchise Fee: $14,900

Royalty Fee: 6%

Financial Assistance: The franchise fee can be broken down into 2 installments of $7,450 each.

Managerial Assistance: Sales assistance, management training and day-to-day operations support are provided initially, as well as on an on-going basis.

Training Provided: Training involves 3 - 4 days at corporate, including both classroom and hands-on field work. In addition, a manager will travel to the franchise location and provide outside sales and management training.

Information Submitted: March 1994

BROKER ONE
1097-C Irongate Ln.
Columbus, OH 43213
Telephone: (614) 864-1440
Mr. Raymond A. Strohl, President

Number of Franchised Units: 9
Number of Company-Owned Units: 1
Number of Total Operating Units: 10

In Business Since: 1983   **Franchising Since:** 1984

Description of Operation: Stockbroker, discount stockbroker and investment advisor. A related division, Money Broker One, is a loan broker.

Equity Capital Needed: $20,000

Franchise Fee: Varies.

Royalty Fee: Varies.

Financial Assistance: None.

Managerial Assistance: As much managerial assistance as needed is provided.

Training Provided: 1 month of initial training is provided, plus on-going training is provided for as long as needed or desired.

Information Submitted: November 1993

BUYING & DINING GUIDE
80 Eighth Ave.
New York, NY 10011
Telephone: (212) 243-6800
Fax: (212) 243-7457
Mr. Allan Horwitz, President

Number of Franchised Units: 3
Number of Company-Owned Units: 0
Number of Total Operating Units: 3

In Business Since: 1979   **Franchising Since:** 1990

Description of Operation: Free distribution shopping guide.

Equity Capital Needed: $34,900 - $44,900

Franchise Fee: $29,900

Royalty Fee: $200 per month, plus.

Financial Assistance: The Company provides no direct financing; however, financial assistance is available to franchisees based upon adequate home equity through Company contacts in the financial community.

Managerial Assistance: The Company offers a franchisee 25 on-going revenue and support services. In-depth financial analysis is conducted on each issue of the franchisee's publication, plus free, unlimited consulting.

Training Provided: A minimum of 5 days of classroom training and a minimum of 5 days of on-site training are provided at the franchisee's location, at Company's expense.

Information Submitted: March 1994

CA$H PLUS
3572 Arlington Ave., # 2C
Riverside, CA 92506
Telephone: (800) 729-3142 (909) 682-2274
Fax: (909) 369-6806
Mr. John Collins, International Development Director

Number of Franchised Units: 15
Number of Company-Owned Units: 0
Number of Total Operating Units: 15

In Business Since: 1985   **Franchising Since:** 1989

Description of Operation: Check cashing service and related services. We are a first-class operation which offers check cashing and related services - money orders, wire transfers, cash advances, mailboxes, notary, UPS, fax, snacks, tax filing and other items. The list is growing all the time.

Equity Capital Needed: $30,000 - $45,000

Franchise Fee: $14,500

Royalty Fee: 6%

Financial Assistance: None.

Managerial Assistance: From beginning to end - site location, lease, start-up training, marketing, grand opening, etc. On-going support from corporate office.

Training Provided: Training is geared to each person. Usually 3 weeks of on-the-job training. Complete training on day-to-day operation, books, marketing, security, etc.

Information Submitted: November 1993

CATHEDRAL DIRECTORIES
1401 W. Girard Ave.
Madison Heights, MI 48071
Telephone: (800) 544-6903 (313) 545-1415
Fax: (313) 544-1611
Mr. Jack Frye, Franchise Sales Director

Number of Franchised Units: 2
Number of Company-Owned Units: 4
Number of Total Operating Units: 6

In Business Since: 1948   **Franchising Since:** 1993

Description of Operation: We publish church directories. Every directory is unique to the particular church. There is no charge to the church as the directory is advertising supported. Ads are sold on an annually renewed-basis to members of the community, such as funeral homes, florists, banks, etc. The directory is primarily a membership roster of the church members.

Equity Capital Needed: $20,000 - $30,000

Franchise Fee: $14,500

Royalty Fee: 0%

Financial Assistance: We design our assistance program to meet the needs of the franchisee. The franchisee would be expected to provide computer hardware and basic office equipment. We provide free training and on-going support.

Managerial Assistance: We provide 3 days of training at no charge. We also provide basic advice as to business set-up. We have on-going support and sales assistance in the field.

Training Provided: We provide, at no charge, 3 days of on-site training at Company headquarters - 1 day for marketing training and 2 days for computer software training. We schedule additional training in the field after the franchise is in operation.

Information Submitted: February 1994

CHECK EXPRESS USA
5201 W. Kennedy Blvd., # 750
Tampa, FL 33609
Telephone: (800) 521-8211 (813) 289-2888
Fax: (813) 289-2999
Mr. Michael Riordon, Director of Marketing

Number of Franchised Units: 143
Number of Company-Owned Units: 20
Number of Total Operating Units: 163

In Business Since: 1982   **Franchising Since:** 1988

Description of Operation: Cashing all types of checks for a fee, wire transfers, sale of money orders, mailboxes and small loans. Open 7 days a week for customer convenience.

Equity Capital Needed: $130,000

Franchise Fee: $24,500

Royalty Fee: 5% or $750 minimum.

Financial Assistance: Third-party leasing on equipment necessary to run store. Discounts are available to American veterans through the VetFran program.

Managerial Assistance: The franchisor provides manual for cashing checks, collections, marketing, managing the store and use of computer system. Support staff available 7 days a week.

Training Provided: 2 weeks in corporate training center - classroom and in-store training.

Information Submitted: November 1993

CHECK PATROL
1716 W. Main St.
Bozeman, MT 59715
Telephone: (406) 586-9944
Fax: (406) 586-7744
Mr. Raul Luciani, President/Chief Executive Officer

Number of Franchised Units: 2
Number of Company-Owned Units: 1
Number of Total Operating Units: 3

In Business Since: 1983   **Franchising Since:** 1990

Description of Operation: Check Patrol specializes in the collection of returned checks in all areas of retail and government where a check is accepted for payment. Check Patrol's unique method of operation provides a service very much needed by the business community.

Equity Capital Needed: $5,000 - $10,000

Franchise Fee: $5,000

Royalty Fee: 6%

Financial Assistance: Check Patrol will assist the prospective franchisee with information, steps and guidance to help obtain financing.

Managerial Assistance: Although management experience would be an asset, it is not necessary. Check Patrol will train the franchisee for the management and operation of his/her franchise before opening and through the life of the franchise, as needed.

Training Provided: Check Patrol will provide training at headquarters for one week for the operation of a Check Patrol check recovery franchise, in addition to one week on-site prior to opening. Training will consist of Check Patrol's method of operation, software operation and trade secrets.

Information Submitted: November 1993

CHECKCARE SYSTEMS
3907 Macon Rd., P. O. Box 9636
Columbus, GA 31908
Telephone: (706) 563-3660
Fax: (706) 563-3713
Mr. Mike Stalnaker, Executive Vice President

Number of Franchised Units: 52
Number of Company-Owned Units: 0
Number of Total Operating Units: 52

In Business Since: 1982   **Franchising Since:** 1984

Description of Operation: Electronic verification and guarantee of checks for retail business.

Equity Capital Needed: $80,000 - $100,000

Franchise Fee: $25,000 - $45,000

Royalty Fee: 5%

Financial Assistance: Half of franchise fee over a 3-year period.

Managerial Assistance: On-going management assistance, on-site training, computer support of custom software and training classes.

Training Provided: 2 weeks at franchisor headquarters.

Information Submitted: November 1993

COMMUNITY GRAPHICS
3495 Winton Pl., Bldg. A, # 4
Rochester, NY 14623
Telephone: (800) 398-3029 (716) 424-3350
Fax: (716) 271-2696
Mr. Robert J. Bartosiewicz, President

Number of Franchised Units: 12
Number of Company-Owned Units: 10
Number of Total Operating Units: 22

In Business Since: 1988   **Franchising Since:** 1992

Description of Operation: Advertising graphics company that works with planning director of cities to produce art rendering prints and maps of the community.

Equity Capital Needed: $20,000

Franchise Fee: $20,000

Royalty Fee: 6.5%

Financial Assistance: Most territories have to be paid in full.

Managerial Assistance: We provide a comprehensive, 1 week of fully-paid training, as well as 1 week of set-up in the territory purchased. Other assistance includes a full art staff, an 800 customer service line and on-call management consulting.

Training Provided: We provide a step-by-step process that will teach the person our system, including sales, paperwork, financial profit and loss and recruiting.

Information Submitted: March 1994

COMMWORLD
6025 S. Quebec St., # 300
Englewood, CO 80111
Telephone: (800) 525-3200 (303) 721-8200
Fax: (303) 721-8299
Mr. Tony Hildebrand, Vice President of Franchising

Number of Franchised Units: 51
Number of Company-Owned Units: 2
Number of Total Operating Units: 53

In Business Since: 1979   **Franchising Since:** 1983

Description of Operation: Conversion franchise. Franchisees sell and maintain commercial tele-communications systems. Potential franchisee is an existing company operating as an interconnect currently.

Equity Capital Needed: $8,200 - $154,200

Franchise Fee: $7,500 - $12,500

Royalty Fee: Varies.

Financial Assistance: We provide short-term financing of the initial franchise fee for qualified applicants.

Managerial Assistance: Data not available.

Training Provided: We offer 1 week of initial training. Additional business development, sales and technical training are available for a fee.

Information Submitted: March 1994

COMPREHENSIVE BUSINESS SERVICES
1925 Palomar Oaks Way, # 105
Carlsbad, CA 92008
Telephone: (800) 323-9000 (619) 431-2150
Fax: (619) 431-2156
Mr. Jack Frampton, Franchise Development Manager

Number of Franchised Units: 230
Number of Company-Owned Units: 0
Number of Total Operating Units: 230

In Business Since: 1949   **Franchising Since:** 1965

Description of Operation: Comprehensive offers the professional accountant an outstanding opportunity to own a practice serving the nation's growing small business marketplace. Comprehensive provides proven systems, including training in marketing, client processing and practice management. The Comprehensive method of doing business is designed to help franchisees attract and serve more clients and at higher fees than independent accountants. Franchisees benefit from a protected territory and national advertising.

Equity Capital Needed: $10,000 - $25,000

Franchise Fee: $25,000

Royalty Fee: 6%, plus 2%.

Financial Assistance: None at this time.

Managerial Assistance: 3 weeks of training covers marketing, client processing and practice management, as well as training for proprietary client write-up software.

Training Provided: Same as above.

Information Submitted: January 1994

CONTROL-O-FAX SYSTEMS
P. O. Box 5800, 3022 Airport Blvd.
Waterloo, IA 50704
Telephone: (800) 553-0070 (319) 234-4896
Fax: (319) 236-7350
Ms. Sandy Reicks, Franchise Director

Number of Franchised Units: 60
Number of Company-Owned Units: 0
Number of Total Operating Units: 60

In Business Since: 1969   **Franchising Since:** 1971

Description of Operation: Medical and dental office management systems and solutions.

Equity Capital Needed: $20,000 - $50,000

Franchise Fee: $11,895 - $26,395

Royalty Fee: 0%

Financial Assistance: $5,000 - $10,000 of the initial franchise fee can be financed on a 2 - 4 year note.

Managerial Assistance: Regional manager assigned to each franchise. Dealer forum held twice a year, in which 8 franchisees serve. 4 are selected by management and 4 are elected by franchisees. Dealer forum goals include dealer relations and problem solving.

Training Provided: Formal classroom training is provided. 1 week of initial, basic training. 3 days of advanced training. Regional learning seminars routinely held.

Information Submitted: November 1993

COUPON-CASH SAVER
925 N. Milwaukee Ave., # 108
Wheeling, IL 60090
Telephone: (708) 537-6420
Fax: (708) 537-6499
Mr. Joseph Nubie, Vice President

Number of Franchised Units: 10
Number of Company-Owned Units: 4
Number of Total Operating Units: 14

In Business Since: 1984   **Franchising Since:** 1990

Description of Operation: Coupon-Cash Saver provides its clients an affordable, highly-visible and very measurable direct mail advertising medium. We feature an attractive bound booklet form of distribution. This gives us greater shelf-life in the home and therefore additional name-awareness for our clients.

Equity Capital Needed: $26,500

Franchise Fee: Included above.

Royalty Fee: 8%

Financial Assistance: Not available.

Managerial Assistance: Each franchisee receives assistance in the development of an annual business plan and mid-year adjustments. On-going guidance in all phases of the business, with special emphasis on sales and effective ad development. Complete production management from

graphics to mailing. Monthly regional meetings. Operations manuals including updates. Regular field visits and emergency visits upon request.

Training Provided: We provide up to 3 weeks of initial training, 2 weeks of classroom training and up to 2 weeks in-field. On-going field training and regular phone assistance.

Information Submitted: March 1994

CRATERS AND FREIGHTERS
11861 E. 33rd Ave., # D
Aurora, CO 80010
Telephone: (800) 945-5682 (303) 361-6600
Fax: (303) 360-6472
Ms. Dianna S. Nordyke, President

Number of Franchised Units: 12
Number of Company-Owned Units: 0
Number of Total Operating Units: 12

In Business Since: 1990   **Franchising Since:** 1992

Description of Operation: As "specialty freight handlers," the Company serves an up-scale market of art galleries, museums, estate liquidators, interior decorators and a host of other clients to fulfill their specialized needs in moving a multitude of large, delicate and valuable freight shipments.

Equity Capital Needed: $40,000 - $50,000

Franchise Fee: $15,000

Royalty Fee: 5%

Financial Assistance: None on initial unit.

Managerial Assistance: Managerial assistance provided through continued support via a toll-free owner's hotline, regional meetings, newsletters and conventions.

Training Provided: Comprehensive training program, encompassing all facets of the business in classroom situations and hands-on training.

Information Submitted: January 1994

CREATIVE ASSET MANAGEMENT
120 Wood Ave. S., # 300
Iselin, NJ 08830
Telephone: (800) 245-0530 (908) 549-1011
Fax: (609) 259-1573
Mr. Christopher G. Kau, Executive Vice President

Number of Franchised Units: 52
Number of Company-Owned Units: 0
Number of Total Operating Units: 52

In Business Since: 1986   **Franchising Since:** 1988

Description of Operation: CAM is the nation's first and only registered investment advisory franchise. It utilizes the copyrighted and trademarked Start Now program of asset management. With complete training and on-going support, it is completely turn-key in all aspects of the business, including registration and licensing. The program is fee-based and income is not dependent on commissions. The program is the least-cost method for securing top-notch investment advice on an on-going basis.

Equity Capital Needed: $19,500

Franchise Fee: $17,500

Royalty Fee: $300 first year; second year minimum of $175+, based on services used from menu.

Financial Assistance: Yes.

Managerial Assistance: Creative Asset Management provides all the managerial support for the turn-key operation - complete training, product research and updates, a 12-technique marketing system, seminars, an efficient business system and continued on-going home office assistance.

Training Provided: Training begins with 3 days of intensive classroom instruction at the home office and includes marketing, presentation system, delivery and implementation of clients' diversified portfolios. All sessions are taped. This is followed by home study of 6 - 8 weeks, which helps you become a Registered Investment Advisor (RIA). Continuing education is done through home office support, with seminars, reading material and consultation with the franchisors.

Information Submitted: January 1994

DIRECT OPINIONS
23600 Mercantile Rd.
Beachwood, OH 44122
Telephone: (216) 831-7979
Fax: (214) 831-8868
Mr. Simon Cohen, Director of Franchise Development

Number of Franchised Units: 2
Number of Company-Owned Units: 1
Number of Total Operating Units: 3

In Business Since: 1983   **Franchising Since:** 1992

Description of Operation: Direct Opinions specializes primarily in customer satisfaction surveys for retail sales and service clients, market research surveys and lead generation services. Direct Opinions utilizes a system of home-based tele-marketers to conduct the actual phone interviews. The Direct Opinions business provides the franchisee with easy-to-operate systems. Reporting and record keeping are accomplished through the use of proprietary computer software programs.

Equity Capital Needed: $22,150 - $51,800

Franchise Fee: $10,000 - $25,000

Royalty Fee: 6% of first $100,000; 4% thereafter.

Financial Assistance: No royalties for first 6 months.

Managerial Assistance: Management training is provided during the initial training phase. Thereafter, management consultation is available by phone on a daily basis. Additionally, at franchisee's expense, franchisor will send representatives to franchisee's location for additional training.

Training Provided: Initial training is provided at franchisor's corporate headquarters in Cleveland, OH. Training is for a maximum period of 1 week, composed of 5 business days, 8-10 hours/day and a minimum period of 3 days depending on progress. Training is provided in sales, marketing, customer service, management techniques, computer operations, general accounting, bookkeeping and related business procedures.

Information Submitted: January 1994

DOLPHIN PUBLICATIONS
1235 Sunset Grove Rd.
Fallbrook, CA 92028
Telephone: (800) 343-1056 (619) 942-0472
Fax: (619) 728-3145
Mr. Robert Neral, National Sales Manager

Number of Franchised Units: 17
Number of Company-Owned Units: 85
Number of Total Operating Units: 102

In Business Since: 1984   **Franchising Since:** 1993

Description of Operation: We provide full production support (printing, labeling and mailing) and, in co-operation with our local franchisee, publish a high-gloss, 4-color magazine which is formatted for coupon and display advertising. Our franchises are ideal for individuals with sales backgrounds that are interested in a low-cost and stable business of their own.

Equity Capital Needed: $2,950

Franchise Fee: $2,950

Royalty Fee: 0%

Financial Assistance: Financing is available for part of the initial franchise fee.

Managerial Assistance: Continued assistance is available via our 800# help-lines and our inter-active fax.

Training Provided: Extensive training is provided, which includes both classroom and actual instructor-assisted ("on the street") client selling.

Information Submitted: April 1994

E. K. WILLIAMS & COMPANY
8774 Yates Dr., # 210
Westminster, CO 80030
Telephone: (800) 255-2359 (303) 427-4989
Fax: (303) 650-7286
Mr. O. B. Smith, Franchise Sales Manager

Number of Franchised Units: 309
Number of Company-Owned Units: 1
Number of Total Operating Units: 310

In Business Since: 1935   **Franchising Since:** 1947

Description of Operation: Franchised accounting, tax and consulting for small businesses. Monthly reports include profit and loss, balance sheet, cash flow, payroll check writing and other management tools. We develop our internal software as end-user software, allowing for regular modification and updates.

Equity Capital Needed: $38,000 - $95,000

Franchise Fee: $25,000

Royalty Fee: 8%, 6%, 4% - sliding scale.

Financial Assistance: None at present.

Managerial Assistance: We offer on-going training and assistance on-site. Semi-annual meetings and national conventions every other year. Toll-free phone assistance with hardware, software, marketing and other areas of needs.

Training Provided: We provide an intensive 2 weeks of classroom and in-field training. The first week is at the national support center, the second week is in a live office dealing with real situations. Training in all areas is covered.

Information Submitted: March 1994

ECONOTAX TAX SERVICES
P. O. Box 13829
Jackson, MS 39236
Telephone: (800) 748-9106 (601) 956-0500
Fax: (601) 956-0583
Mr. James T. Marsh, President

Number of Franchised Units: 46
Number of Company-Owned Units: 11
Number of Total Operating Units: 57

In Business Since: 1965   **Franchising Since:** 1968

Description of Operation: Econotax franchisees offer the public a complete range of tax services, including tax preparation, electronic return filing, refund loans, audit assistance and tax planning.

Equity Capital Needed: $2,500 - $10,000

Franchise Fee: $2,500

Royalty Fee: 15%

Financial Assistance: None.

Managerial Assistance: Support is provided for all aspects of conducting a successful tax practice.

Training Provided: A 1-week new owner workshop is held annually at Company headquarters. Regional seminars are held throughout the year. Self-study materials and 800# support available.

Information Submitted: November 1993

EFFECTIVE MAILERS
1151 Allen Dr.
Troy, MI 48083
Telephone: (800) 360-6360 (810) 588-9880
Fax: (810) 588-4299
Mr. Jai Gupta, President

Number of Franchised Units: 15
Number of Company-Owned Units: 1
Number of Total Operating Units: 16

In Business Since: 1982   Franchising Since: 1993

Description of Operation: EM offers direct mail advertising franchises. Direct mail advertising is an inexpensive, but very effective way for local businesses (retail, service and professionals) to advertise in their local markets. Each franchisee sells advertising to these local businesses in his/her franchised territory. Effective Mailers provides excellent support, including production of graphics, printing and mailing through the US Post Office.

Equity Capital Needed: $25,000 - $60,000

Franchise Fee: $22,000

Royalty Fee: Data not available.

Financial Assistance: None.

Managerial Assistance: Effective Mailers' corporate office sells advertising to one million homes itself. Whatever it learns from the field, it relays practical information through letters, updated manuals and aids.

Training Provided: 3 weeks of training includes 1 week in the classroom and 2 weeks in-field in the local territory.

Information Submitted: February 1994

EMPIRE BUSINESS BROKERS
4300 Seneca St., P. O. Box 622
Buffalo, NY 14224
Telephone: (716) 677-5229
Fax: (716) 643-2246
Mr. Nicholas R. Gugliuzza, President

Number of Franchised Units: 31
Number of Company-Owned Units: 2
Number of Total Operating Units: 33

In Business Since: 1981   Franchising Since: 1989

Description of Operation: The sale of existing businesses to qualified buyers.

Equity Capital Needed: $10,000 - $15,000

Franchise Fee: $8,900

Royalty Fee: 0%

Financial Assistance: We will finance half the fee for qualified individuals.

Managerial Assistance: Training is via mail, manuals and in person at the office of the franchisee.

Training Provided: Franchisees are lead through the listing and sale process of a business.

Information Submitted: March 1994

EQUALITY PLUS TELECOMMUNICATIONS
300 Church St.
Wallingford, CT 06492
Telephone: (800) 221-1511 (203) 284-1511
Fax: (203) 949-0097
Ms. Marie G. Meneo, Vice President of Franchise Development

Number of Franchised Units: 4
Number of Company-Owned Units: 1
Number of Total Operating Units: 5

In Business Since: 1992   Franchising Since: 1993

Description of Operation: EPT offers a circle of services developed and proven over thirty years to significantly reduce tele-communications expenses for businesses. We have saved clients as much as 59.6% of their tele-communications expenses. Tele-communications is one of the 5 unallocated operating expenses in most businesses. Our newest service includes long distance service with a unique billing application which provides a validation of savings. There is a service for all businesses. No previous experience necessary.

Equity Capital Needed: $3,000 - $5,000 and personal financial obligations.

Franchise Fee: $20,000 franchise; $80,000 master franchise.

Royalty Fee: Data not available.

Financial Assistance: None.

Managerial Assistance: Extensive training modules. On-going franchisee support via an 800# hotline. 5 volumes of operations manuals. On-going customer support to your client base through an experienced telecom staff, accounts receivable and billing service at no additional cost. As a franchisee, you sell the services and our customer service reps get the clients on our services and provide on-going support. A customer service number comes directly into the corporate office and all customers receive free consulting.

Training Provided: Comprehensive technical and sales training on all products and services. The training modules are designed to provide you with enough knowledge to understand and sell the circle of services. Sales training is performed by an expert who has sold the circle of services successfully for many years. Training does not end when the class is over. Franchisee's are encouraged to call the franchisee hotline for on-going assistance and support. Additional training is available on request.

Information Submitted: January 1994

EXECUTIVE, THE
1634-A Monterey Hwy., # 155
Birmingham, AL 35216
Telephone: (800) 264-3932 (205) 991-2970
Mr. Kevin A. Foote, President

Number of Franchised Units: 7
Number of Company-Owned Units: 1
Number of Total Operating Units: 8

In Business Since: 1987   Franchising Since: 1991

Description of Operation: Coupon magazine for executives.

Equity Capital Needed: $30,000

Franchise Fee: $22,000

Royalty Fee: Standard fee.

Financial Assistance: None.

Managerial Assistance: On-site training and toll-free hotline.

Training Provided: We provide sales, layout, distribution, printing and production training.

Information Submitted: January 1994

FASTSIGNS
2550 Midway Rd., # 150
Carrollton, TX 75006
Telephone: (800) 827-7446 (214) 702-0000
Fax: (214) 991-6058
Mr. Randy Marshall, Director of Franchise Development

Number of Franchised Units: 200
Number of Company-Owned Units: 1
Number of Total Operating Units: 201

In Business Since: 1985   Franchising Since: 1986

Description of Operation: #1 business-to-business franchise, Success '93; #1 sign franchise, Entrepreneur '90, '91, '92, '93, '94; ranked among the Inc. Magazine list of the 500 fastest-growing private companies for the past 3 years; founder of computer-generated quick-sign industry. Retail stores produce signs and graphics for business; unique systems include fully-documented operating procedures, order-based PO's with marketing support, proven sales and marketing techniques and national accounts programs.

Equity Capital Needed: $69,000

Franchise Fee: $20,000

Royalty Fee: 6%

Financial Assistance: Qualified franchisees may apply for SBA loans. FastSigns also has third-party financing available to qualified franchisees.

Managerial Assistance: Comprehensive training in financial management, operations management and marketing. Complete training manuals for every aspect of the business. Experienced field representatives provide on-site consultation in every area of the business.

Training Provided: An intensive 3 weeks of training covers complete FastSigns business system. No sign experience is needed; sales and marketing helpful. Comprehensive support includes site selection, store design, financing assistance, grand opening marketing package, on-site opening assistance, on-going store visits, toll-free hotline and more.

Information Submitted: January 1994

FINDERBINDER / SOURCEBOOK DIRECTORIES
8546 Chevy Chase Dr.
La Mesa, CA 91941
Telephone: (800) 255-2575 (619) 463-5050
Fax: (619) 463-5097
Mr. Gary Beals, President

Number of Franchised Units: 18
Number of Company-Owned Units: 2
Number of Total Operating Units: 20

In Business Since: 1974   Franchising Since: 1978

Description of Operation: These directories are add-on profit centers for small businesses in marketing, consulting, public relations, advertising, fund-raising, meeting planning or association management.

Equity Capital Needed: $15,000

Franchise Fee: $1,000

Royalty Fee: 15% down to 5%.

Financial Assistance: Not available.

Managerial Assistance: Detailed operations manual, training day and continued support by phone.

Training Provided: A full day of training is ample.

Information Submitted: November 1993

FORTUNE PRACTICE MANAGEMENT
9191 Towne Centre Dr., # 500
San Diego, CA 92122
Telephone: (800) 628-1052 (619) 535-1784
Fax: (619) 535-8254
Ms. Brenda Kaesler, Director of Franchise Support

Number of Franchised Units: 31
Number of Company-Owned Units: 0
Number of Total Operating Units: 31

In Business Since: 1990   Franchising Since: 1991

Description of Operation: Fortune Practice Management provides business consulting and seminar services to the health care industry, specializing in private practitioners in solo or group practice.

Equity Capital Needed: $35,000 - $55,000

Franchise Fee: $60,000

Royalty Fee: 15%

Financial Assistance: We will finance $30,000. Terms for 3 years.

Managerial Assistance: A complete operations manual is given to each franchisee and weekly coaching calls are made between the franchisee and the home office. There is a franchise support hotline available.

Training Provided: Initial training consists of 10 intensive classroom days at home office, plus 5 - 10 training days on-site.

Information Submitted: December 1993

FRANKLIN TRAFFIC SERVICE
5251 Shawnee Rd., P. O. Box 100
Ransomville, NY 14131
Telephone: (716) 731-3131
Fax: (716) 731-2705
Mr. Elliott A. Franklin, President

Number of Franchised Units: 5
Number of Company-Owned Units: 2
Number of Total Operating Units: 7

In Business Since: 1969   Franchising Since: 1986

Description of Operation: Franklin Traffic Service is a prominent company providing its nationwide clientele with audit and payment of freight bills, management reporting, management services and complete auditing and payment, customhouse brokerage audit and international logistics.

Equity Capital Needed: $25,000 +

Franchise Fee: $25,000 +

Royalty Fee: 0%

Financial Assistance: $11,000 - $14,000 is required in advance. Financing on balance to qualified applicants.

Managerial Assistance: Franklin Traffic Service maintains a bona fide interest in all franchisees. Manuals of operations, forms and directions are provided. In-the-field assistance is provided on a regular basis. The franchisees benefit from all new marketing concepts which are developed. Franklin Traffic encourages regular franchise contact and continually upgrades and maintains the highest level of quality possible.

Training Provided: We provide an intensive 3-week, mandatory training program for all new franchisees. Training consists of in-house programs and time in the field with Franklin Traffic training personnel.

Information Submitted: March 1994

GENERAL BUSINESS SERVICES
1020 N. University Parks Dr.
Waco, TX 76707
Telephone: (800) 583-6181 (817) 756-6181
Fax: (817) 756-0322
Mr. Dellray Lefevere, Senior Vice President

Number of Franchised Units: 339
Number of Company-Owned Units: 0
Number of Total Operating Units: 339

In Business Since: 1961   Franchising Since: 1961

Description of Operation: GBS offers tax counseling, business counseling, financial counseling, management counseling, personnel services, computer services, financial record keeping and wealth accumulation services to small and medium-sized companies.

Equity Capital Needed: 6 months of personal expenses.

Franchise Fee: $30,000

Royalty Fee: 10% - 2.5%, based on the volume and tenure with GBS.

Financial Assistance: None.

Managerial Assistance: A field support manager works with franchisees in the field and a marketing director works with them from the home office. Both are responsible for the building of the franchisee's business. The franchisees have a tax research department and business research department available to assist them in counseling their clients.

Training Provided: The first year the franchisee is in business, he/she completes a 50-week training period. The first 2 weeks are in Waco, TX, completing basic training, which consists of both technical and marketing training. A custom-designed, 28-week home-study course is next. After 90 days of business, there is 1-week of advanced training in Waco. Each year there are 8 different schools in their area. An annual convention is held in different locations yearly.

Information Submitted: January 1994

GOFAX PUBLIC PHONE/FAX
4101 SW 73rd Ave.
Miami, FL 33155
Telephone: (305) 264-6060
Fax: (305) 264-7312
Mr. Ralph F. Geronimo, President

Number of Franchised Units: 500
Number of Company-Owned Units: 0
Number of Total Operating Units: 500

In Business Since: 1988   **Franchising Since:** 1990

Description of Operation: Placing Gofax credit operated phone/fax machines in hotels, shopping centers (malls), libraries, car rental locations, etc.

Equity Capital Needed: $29,500 minimum.

Franchise Fee: Data not available.

Royalty Fee: Data not available.

Financial Assistance: Lease-purchase option plans are available for qualified investors. Fax or mail a business history and financial status today. Areas are limited!

Managerial Assistance: Gofax will assist all investors with site location, contract negotiations and more.

Training Provided: Prior to being "allowed" to invest, each prospect is required to visit the Gofax facilities in New England to gain a full understanding of the scope of his/her investment and the skills required. Operations guidance is available at all times from Gofax.

Information Submitted: November 1993

GOLFER'S DREAM MAGAZINE
9171 Eves Circle
Roswell, GA 30076
Telephone: (800) 733-8619 (404) 641-8619
Fax: (404) 641-8619
Mr. Michael Holder, President

Number of Franchised Units: 5
Number of Company-Owned Units: 1
Number of Total Operating Units: 6

In Business Since: 1992   **Franchising Since:** 1993

Description of Operation: Produces localized, full-color digest-sized golf magazines.

Equity Capital Needed: $10,650 - $29,400

Franchise Fee: $10,000 - $75,000

Royalty Fee: 0%; nominal fee added to production of magazine.

Financial Assistance: Payment plans available for most markets.

Managerial Assistance: 4 days of training included with franchise fee, which includes air and hotel accommodations. On-going support via 800#, quarterly updates, yearly meetings and personnel available to aid in training of franchisee's employees.

Training Provided: 4 days of training included with franchise fee, which includes air and hotel accommodations in Atlanta, GA.

Information Submitted: January 1994

GREETINGS
P. O. Box 25623
Lexington, KY 40524
Telephone: (606) 272-5624
Fax: (606) 273-2636
Mr. Larry Kargel, President

Number of Franchised Units: 4
Number of Company-Owned Units: 3
Number of Total Operating Units: 7

In Business Since: 1984   **Franchising Since:** 1990

Description of Operation: Target market advertising to new home owners, apartment residents, university and college residence hall students.

Equity Capital Needed: None.

Franchise Fee: $15,000

Royalty Fee: 5%

Financial Assistance: Yes, on franchise fee only.

Managerial Assistance: On-going assistance, as needed. Quarterly reviews. Franchisor assistance is as close as the phone.

Training Provided: 1 week of training at corporate office. 1 week at franchisee location.

Information Submitted: November 1993

HANDLE WITH CARE PACKAGING STORE
5675 DTC Blvd., # 280
Englewood, CO 80111
Telephone: (800) 525-6309 (303) 741-6626
Fax: (303) 741-6653
Mr. Richard T. Godwin, President/Chief Executive Officer

Number of Franchised Units: 380
Number of Company-Owned Units: 0
Number of Total Operating Units: 380

In Business Since: 1983   **Franchising Since:** 1983

Description of Operation: Custom packaging and shipping, from 1 - 1,000 pounds, domestically and internationally, with insurance available for any value. We are the small load specialist, shipping small, pre-packed items, as well as expertly packaging and shipping the FLAV (Fragile, Large, Awkward and Valuable) items that range from a teddy bear to an antique grandfather clock, original Picasso, room full of furniture and/or a mainframe computer.

Equity Capital Needed: $40,000

Franchise Fee: $17,500

Royalty Fee: 5%

Financial Assistance: Some financing is available.

Managerial Assistance: The Business Development Course teaches you to become a knowledgeable business professional and an effective store manager. It also teaches computer technology to reduce labor expenses and to maximize efficiency. It helps you with the first month of business, although 6 months of store experience is the best teacher. Reference books and manuals are also available.

Training Provided: A 10-day educational program has been designed to provide franchisees with classroom instruction, as well as hands-on experience. Standards of excellence are high-lighted throughout the program, not only in terms of packaging techniques, but business basics that include customer service, marketing, store management and operations.

Information Submitted: November 1993

HOMES & LAND MAGAZINE
1600 Capital Circle, SW
Tallahassee, FL 32310
Telephone: (800) 277-4357 (904) 574-2111
Fax: (904) 574-2525
Mr. Mike Flory, National Sales Manager

Number of Franchised Units: 215
Number of Company-Owned Units: 2
Number of Total Operating Units: 217

In Business Since: 1973   Franchising Since: 1984

Description of Operation: We are the nation's largest publisher of pictorial, community real estate advertising magazines, operating in 42 states and 14,000 communities. Free to consumers. Also available electronically via computer on-line service and facsimile. Franchisee handles promotion, sales, layout and distribution; franchisor offers production, printing, training and marketing support services.

Equity Capital Needed: $50,000 - $109,000

Franchise Fee: $20,000

Royalty Fee: 10.5%

Financial Assistance: The Company offers partial financing of initial fee to qualified veterans. Lease program available for street distribution racks.

Managerial Assistance: Assistance from regional managers and account executives. Training manuals, forms, sales aids, periodic newsletters and franchisee advisory council.

Training Provided: Initial 2-week classroom training in Tallahassee, FL. Regional and national meetings with seminars. Toll-free number for technical assistance. On-site production training available.

Information Submitted: December 1993

HQ BUSINESS CENTERS
120 Montgomery St., # 2350
San Francisco, CA 94104
Telephone: (800) 227-3004 (415) 781-7811
Fax: (415) 781-8034
Ms. Kitty McEntee, Manager of Development

Number of Franchised Units: 126
Number of Company-Owned Units: 0
Number of Total Operating Units: 126

In Business Since: 1967   Franchising Since: 1978

Description of Operation: HQ Business Centers are full-service executive suites which offer individual offices for lease and which include all business services.

Equity Capital Needed: $0 - $1,500,000

Franchise Fee: $0 - $100,000

Royalty Fee: 1.5%

Financial Assistance: None.

Managerial Assistance: A corporate staff provides consistent international support in the areas of standards, sales, advertising and marketing, new products, computer services, purchasing and expansion.

Training Provided: Although minimal training is provided by headquarters, we will supply the licensee with six manuals of operations and standards.

Information Submitted: November 1993

INTERFACE FINANCIAL GROUP
15965 Jeannette St.
Southfield, MI 48075
Telephone: (313) 557-2784
Fax: (313) 557-7931
Ms. Colleen McGaffey

Number of Franchised Units: 7
Number of Company-Owned Units: 0
Number of Total Operating Units: 7

In Business Since: 1991   Franchising Since: 1991

Description of Operation: Franchisee buys quality accounts receivable from client companies at a discount to provide short-term working capital to expanding businesses.

Equity Capital Needed: $50,000 - $100,000

Franchise Fee: $25,000

Royalty Fee: 8%

Financial Assistance: Data not available.

Managerial Assistance: Data not available.

Training Provided: 2 days at franchisor's corporate office. 3 days at franchise location.

Information Submitted: December 1993

INTERNATIONAL BUSINESS OPPORTUNITIES
P. O. Box 639
Pickering, ON L1V 3T3 CAN
Telephone: (905) 686-1152
Fax: (905) 686-0469
Mr. Kelly Rogers, Director

Number of Franchised Units: 35
Number of Company-Owned Units: 2
Number of Total Operating Units: 37

In Business Since: 1976   Franchising Since: 1980

Description of Operation: Business consultants. Worldwide networking.

Equity Capital Needed: $50,000

Franchise Fee: $20,000

Royalty Fee: 8%

Financial Assistance: Financial assistance is available.

Managerial Assistance: Yes. Training and support is provided.

Training Provided: On-going training programs.

Information Submitted: December 1993

INTERNATIONAL MERGERS & ACQUISITIONS
4300 N. Miller Rd., # 220
Scottsdale, AZ 85251
Telephone: (602) 990-3899
Fax: (602) 990-7480
Mr. Neil D. Lewis, President

Number of Franchised Units: 45
Number of Company-Owned Units: 0
Number of Total Operating Units: 45

In Business Since: 1969   Franchising Since: 1977

Description of Operation: IMA members are engaged in the profession of serving merger and acquisition-minded companies in the areas of consulting, financing, divestitures, mergers and acquisitions. In essence, we are a one-stop service for corporate needs.

Equity Capital Needed: $10,000 approximately.

Franchise Fee: $10,000

Royalty Fee: $375 per quarter, starting second year.

Financial Assistance: None.

Managerial Assistance: We offer a start-up program, which includes workshops, help-line and think tank and which utilizes other members' reservoir of talent.

Training Provided: It is very difficult to provide actual training for this type of business. We offer orientation sessions for new members to familiarize the franchisee with IMA and to determine "How To Make IMA Work For You." We have follow-up training sessions which vary with each member. We distribute a monthly hotline and have various creative work sessions throughout the year.

Information Submitted: January 1994

JACKSON HEWITT TAX SERVICE
4575 Bonney Rd.
Virginia Beach, VA 23462
Telephone: (800) 277-3278 (804) 473-3300
Fax: (804) 473-8409
Ms. Cynthia E. Peroe, Director of Franchise Development

Number of Franchised Units: 631
Number of Company-Owned Units: 83
Number of Total Operating Units: 714

In Business Since: 1960   **Franchising Since:** 1986

Description of Operation: Jackson Hewitt awards franchise territories to individuals who are dedicated to producing the highest-quality tax return possible. The Company utilizes a proprietary computerized tax interview system, designed to maximize deductions, reduce math errors and produce an accurate tax return for each and every customer. Our Superfast Refund is the trademark for a refund anticipation loan, which allows customers their refund minus fees in 24 hours or less. This provides an unparalleled advantage over others.

Equity Capital Needed: Data not available.

Franchise Fee: $15,000

Royalty Fee: 12% minus discounts; 6% advertising.

Financial Assistance: Yes. Jackson Hewitt provides in-house financing for people whom we feel are strong candidates for our franchise opportunities, but who cannot receive financing from banks.

Managerial Assistance: Over 40 field support members in place to help you develop your skills in getting and retaining customers. Our trainers will thoroughly teach you how to train your own staff so your preparers will be up-to-date on the latest tax laws. Jackson Hewitt provides franchisees with an 800# to help with any questions that may arise. We provide franchisees with a strong advertising support team. You will gain an immediate benefit from a national advertising and public relations campaign.

Training Provided: Jackson Hewitt School of Business Management is a 5-day, comprehensive training program designed to teach our business partners the skills necessary to launch a new franchise operation. This also includes workshops, seminars and group discussions. Extensive 2 days of training for Jackson Hewitt's electronic filing processing system. Plus a comprehensive operating manual, which has been designed to guide the franchisee through every facet of the business.

Information Submitted: December 1993

JAY ROBERTS & ASSOCIATES
81 N. Chicago St., # 105
Joliet, IL 60431
Telephone: (312) 236-6640 (815) 722-0683
Fax: (815) 722-4671
Mr. John S. Meers, President

Number of Franchised Units: 29
Number of Company-Owned Units: 2
Number of Total Operating Units: 31

In Business Since: 1965   **Franchising Since:** 1970

Description of Operation: Financial consulting - largest SBA loan packager and placer in USA. Accounts receivable, commercial loans, financial guarantees and other loan brokerage.

Equity Capital Needed: $5,000

Franchise Fee: $1,000

Royalty Fee: 10%

Financial Assistance: Data not available.

Managerial Assistance: 1 day of training - optional. Daily reports on loan progress.

Training Provided: Weekly newsletters. 400-page training manual (updated monthly).

Information Submitted: January 1994

LEDGERPLUS
401 St. Francis St.
Tallahassee, FL 32301
Telephone: (904) 681-1941
Fax: (904) 561-1374
Mr. Ronald L. Baker

Number of Franchised Units: 55
Number of Company-Owned Units: 1
Number of Total Operating Units: 56

In Business Since: 1989   **Franchising Since:** 1990

Description of Operation: The franchisor is offering a regional franchise program through which a regional owner solicits local franchisees. Local franchisees operate an accounting and tax practice, utilizing special marketing techniques, in addition to operational and computer systems, to provide tax, recordkeeping and other services to their clients.

Equity Capital Needed: $12,400 - $25,000

Franchise Fee: $12,000

Royalty Fee: 6%

Financial Assistance: None.

Managerial Assistance: On-going, continuing assistance from the home office and regional owner to the local franchisee.

Training Provided: 3 days of home office seminars and 2 days of in-the-field training.

Information Submitted: January 1994

MAIL BOXES ETC.
6060 Cornerstone Court West
San Diego, CA 92103
Telephone: (800) 456-0414 (619) 455-8800
Fax: (619) 546-7488
Ms. Jeanne Smith, Tele-Sales Representative

Number of Franchised Units: 2326
Number of Company-Owned Units: 1
Number of Total Operating Units: 2327

In Business Since: 1980   **Franchising Since:** 1981

Description of Operation: Mail Boxes Etc. (MBE) is the world's largest franchisor of postal, business and communication service centers. Among the many services offered at MBE Centers are packing and shipping anything, anywhere ("Big or small, we ship it all"), mail box rental, mail receiving and forwarding, package receiving, copying, printing, public fax network, telex and Western Union, office and packing supplies, notary public and national account programs for distribution and repair outlets for companies such as Xerox.

Equity Capital Needed: $30,000 - $50,000

Franchise Fee: $24,950

Royalty Fee: 5%, plus 2% advertising.

Financial Assistance: 70% financing through MBE's in-house finance program, which is easy to qualify for and does not require previous business experience or business credit history.

Managerial Assistance: Franchise owners get additional operating systems support through functional programs, such as programs regarding UPS and how to package properly. They receive management support operation reviews, which is an analysis of their centers. They also receive support through monthly newsletters and a national computer support network.

Training Provided: 3 weeks of management and operations training, often at the area franchisee's local pilot store. Franchise owners get continued training through ad association meetings, as well as at local and national conventions.

Information Submitted: November 1993

MAIL BOXES ETC. (CANADA)
505 Iroquois Shore Rd., # 4
Oakville, ON L6H 2R3 CAN
Telephone: (800) 661-MBEC (905) 338-9754
Fax: (905) 338-7491
Mr. Ronald E. Weston, Vice President Franchise Sales

Number of Franchised Units: 64
Number of Company-Owned Units: 1
Number of Total Operating Units: 65

In Business Since: 1990 **Franchising Since:** 1990

Description of Operation: Postal, business and communication services.

Equity Capital Needed: $95,000 - $100,000

Franchise Fee: $24,950

Royalty Fee: 6%

Financial Assistance: 50% financable through New Venture Business Loan and other similar programs with Canadian banks.

Managerial Assistance: An area franchisee provides managerial assistance to the center franchisee and management from the corporate office provides assistance to both area and center franchisees, as required.

Training Provided: Training includes 3 days in an operating center, before training at corporate, 1-week of classroom training at the corporate office and 1 week of training in an operating center, after training at corporate.

Information Submitted: February 1994

MANUFACTURING MANAGEMENT ASSOCIATES
1301 W. 22nd St., # 508
Oak Brook, IL 60521
Telephone: (708) 574-0300
Fax: (708) 574-0309
Mr. Roger Dykstra, Chairman

Number of Franchised Units: 3
Number of Company-Owned Units: 2
Number of Total Operating Units: 5

In Business Since: 1982 **Franchising Since:** 1992

Description of Operation: Manufacturing Management Associates has built its reputation providing small to mid-sized manufacturing and distribution companies with the technical and advisory services they need to achieve their individual business goals. Areas of expertise include manufacturing systems and network technology, process flow (JIT), quality (TQC), cost management, human resource change management, ISO 9000 certification preparation and work cell design/factory layout.

Equity Capital Needed: $25,000 - $35,000

Franchise Fee: $5,000 - $9,000

Royalty Fee: 7%

Financial Assistance: None available.

Managerial Assistance: Each new office will receive assistance regarding office location, necessary forms and office management. In addition, each office will receive 5 days of training in Chicago, IL. Manufacturing

Management Associates will also assist the franchisee in sales and marketing efforts to promote the success of the franchise. Other notable benefits include potential client leads, alliances with industry experts, project management methodologies, proprietary computer software systems, reference proposals and R & D.

Training Provided: An intensive 8-day seminar in Chicago, IL, where the franchisee will be exposed to a working office and receive extensive training in the policies of running a successful franchise. The franchisee will receive a thorough explanation of our proven methodologies, as well as training in our proprietary software and business systems. The training concludes with a study of effective ways to market yourself as a member of Manufacturing Management Associates.

Information Submitted: November 1993

MARTING FRANCHISE CORPORATION
504 S. Egbert St.
Monona, IA 52159
Telephone: (319) 539-2670
Fax: (319) 539-4271
Mr. Elmer L. Marting, President

Number of Franchised Units: 1
Number of Company-Owned Units: 1
Number of Total Operating Units: 2

In Business Since: 1987 **Franchising Since:** 1988

Description of Operation: Marting offers mobile 2-way and cellular phone sales and diagnostic services.

Equity Capital Needed: $35,000 - $50,000

Franchise Fee: $23,500

Royalty Fee: 7.5%

Financial Assistance: At present, no assistance is available.

Managerial Assistance: We provide sales training and diagnostic training.

Training Provided: We offer 2 weeks of in-house training at a Company location and 2 weeks in the field - on-site training in franchisee's area of operation.

Information Submitted: January 1994

MERCHANT ADVERTISING SYSTEMS
4115 Tiverton Rd.
Randallstown, MD 21133
Telephone: (410) 655-3201
Fax: (410) 655-0262
Mr. Donald A. Goldvarg, President

Number of Franchised Units: 0
Number of Company-Owned Units: 9
Number of Total Operating Units: 9

In Business Since: 1985 **Franchising Since:** 1987

Description of Operation: Provide major supermarkets and enclosed shopping malls with a free-standing advertising kiosk that gives them free advertising and a shopper reference and information center. We then sell local target market advertising to local merchants using custom-made signs and literature to attract shoppers in their respective areas.

Equity Capital Needed: $27,000 - $33,500

Franchise Fee: $23,500 - $29,500

Royalty Fee: 8%

Financial Assistance: We finance 15% of the franchise fee at 10% over the first 12 months. We can provide miscellaneous sources of other financing if needed.

Managerial Assistance: We drop-ship all necessary materials and signs. We also provide sales catalogs, training tapes (audio), demo signs and photo albums, complete business operations manuals testimonial (written) and the starting inventory of display centers.

Training Provided: Training includes 1 week each at our headquarters in Baltimore, MD and in-field at the franchisee's home territory. Full phone consultation, newsletters and annual follow-up training sessions are available.

Information Submitted: January 1994

MOBILE MONETARY SERVICES
148 19th St., NW
Canton, OH 44709
Telephone: (800) 755-6383 (216) 430-1900
Fax: (216) 430-1909
Mr. Joseph E. McClellan, President

Number of Franchised Units: 24
Number of Company-Owned Units: 2
Number of Total Operating Units: 26

In Business Since: 1989   **Franchising Since:** 1990

Description of Operation: Mobile check cashing service. Payroll checks only. By appointment only.

Equity Capital Needed: $75,000 - $125,000

Franchise Fee: $24,500

Royalty Fee: 5% of 1% of gross.

Financial Assistance: Vehicle can be leased or financed.

Managerial Assistance: The franchisor will assist in all aspects of running the business, from operations to accounting.

Training Provided: Training will consist of at least 1 week of field training prior to the opening, with an additional week of field training after the business is in operation.

Information Submitted: March 1994

MONEY BROKER ONE
1097-C Irongate Ln.
Columbus, OH 43213
Telephone: (614) 684-1440
Mr. Raymond A. Strohl, President

Number of Franchised Units: 5
Number of Company-Owned Units: 1
Number of Total Operating Units: 6

In Business Since: 1983   **Franchising Since:** 1985

Description of Operation: Loan broker, offering loans and financing to people, businesses and churches for financing almost any worthwhile project. A related division, Broker One, is a stockbroker.

Equity Capital Needed: $20,000

Franchise Fee: Varies.

Royalty Fee: Varies.

Financial Assistance: None.

Managerial Assistance: As much managerial assistance as needed is provided.

Training Provided: 1 month is provided, plus on-going training is provided for as long as needed or desired.

Information Submitted: November 1993

MONEY MAILER
14271 Corporate Dr.
Garden Grove, CA 92643
Telephone: (800) MAILER-1 (714) 265-4100
Fax: (714) 265-4091
Franchise Sales Department

Number of Franchised Units: 492
Number of Company-Owned Units: 0
Number of Total Operating Units: 492

In Business Since: 1979   **Franchising Since:** 1980

Description of Operation: Franchisees offer direct mail advertising services to local and national businesses and professionals, whose ads are combined and mailed in the same envelope to residences in the franchisee's exclusive market.

Equity Capital Needed: $10,000

Franchise Fee: $15,000 - $30,000

Royalty Fee: 10%

Financial Assistance: Direct and indirect financing are available for the initial franchise fee.

Managerial Assistance: Money Mailer produces complete training manuals, forms and sales aids. The regional owner provides these materials, as well as continuous consultation to the local franchisee for all aspects of the business. The regional and local franchise owners receive constant updates on the results of our product and market research. Money Mailer also sponsors an annual convention and aids communication between regions, local franchisees and the corporate office with regional conferences and newsletters.

Training Provided: An intensive 5 weeks of classroom and in-field training is provided for regional owners. Local franchisees receive a mandatory 2-week training course that includes 1 week of classroom training and 1 week of field training in their local areas.

Information Submitted: January 1994

NACOMEX, NATIONAL COMPUTER EXCHANGE
118 E. 25th St.
New York, NY 10010
Telephone: (800) 395-9006 (212) 777-0285
Fax: (212) 777-1290
Mr. Robert Zises, President

Number of Franchised Units: 2
Number of Company-Owned Units: 1
Number of Total Operating Units: 3

In Business Since: 1967   **Franchising Since:** 1992

Description of Operation: NACOMEX is a nationwide trading floor where corporations, resellers and the general public buy and sell new and used computer hardware systems and peripherals.

Equity Capital Needed: $34,000 - $90,000

Franchise Fee: $9,500 - $19,000

Royalty Fee: 3%

Financial Assistance: None.

Managerial Assistance: Comprehensive 3 - 5 day training program includes hands-on experience in brokering equipment, administrative management and sales techniques. A toll-free 800# is available for on-going marketing and technical support. Franchisees also receive a set of manuals which describe operations, management and marketing in detail.

Training Provided: Same as above.

Information Submitted: January 1994

NATIONAL CONSULTANT REFERRALS
8445 Camino Santa Fe, # 207
San Diego, CA 92121
Telephone: (800) 343-5200 (619) 552-0111
Fax: (619) 552-0854
Mr. Carl G. Kline, President

Number of Franchised Units: 0
Number of Company-Owned Units: 1
Number of Total Operating Units: 1

In Business Since: 1979   **Franchising Since:** 1993

Description of Operation: National Consultant Referrals is a referral service for independent consultants and experts. It provides a national marketing program to reach potential users of consulting services. Calls coming into its 800# are automatically routed to franchise offices located in the same area code as the caller. NCR maintains a free-form database of screened and reference-checked consultants who are matched by computer to client requests. Income is from referral fees paid by affiliated consultants.

Equity Capital Needed: $35,000 - $45,000

Franchise Fee: $25,000

Royalty Fee: 8%

Financial Assistance: None.

Managerial Assistance: Each new office will receive assistance regarding necessary forms and office management, as well as a fully-operational computer system. An extensive manual covers all operating procedures and includes a database of consultants and clients located in the franchisee's exclusive territory.

Training Provided: A 2-week training period is provided at the home office in San Diego, CA. This is a hands-on experience in an actual working office.

Information Submitted: November 1993

NATIONAL TELE-COMMUNICATIONS
300 Broadacres Dr., P. O. Box 8000
Bloomfield, NJ 07003
Telephone: (201) 338-1200
Fax: (201) 338-0222
Mr. Rocco Genova, Director of Operations

Number of Franchised Units: 134
Number of Company-Owned Units: 1
Number of Total Operating Units: 135

In Business Since: 1984   **Franchising Since:** 1990

Description of Operation: Tele-Communications consultants, providing discounted utilization of the AT&T, Sprint and MCI networks. Phone bill audit training, unlimited on-going support. Unlimited long-term residual income potential.

Equity Capital Needed: $15,000

Franchise Fee: $12,900

Royalty Fee: 0%

Financial Assistance: Not available.

Managerial Assistance: 4 days of initial intensive sales, marketing and analysis training. Follow-up courses for 5 additional management personnel to attend 4-day seminars. Unlimited on-going consultative support and tariff updates.

Training Provided: Complete telephone bill audit, tariff analysis, tariff reduction and bill audit overcharge recovery training in an intensive initial 4-day headquarter's indoctrination. Multiple return trainings for additional management personnel.

Information Submitted: November 1993

NATIONWIDE INCOME TAX SERVICE
14507 W. Warren
Dearborn, MI 48126
Telephone: (313) 584-7640
Fax: (313) 584-6829
Mr. Carl K. Gilbert, President

Number of Franchised Units: 32
Number of Company-Owned Units: 8
Number of Total Operating Units: 40

In Business Since: 1964   **Franchising Since:** 1966

Description of Operation: Preparation of federal, state and city income tax returns. Electronic filing and refund anticipation loans.

Equity Capital Needed: $10,000 - $30,000

Franchise Fee: $5,000

Royalty Fee: 7%

Financial Assistance: Data not available.

Managerial Assistance: Complete training and consultation.

Training Provided: 1 - 2 weeks of training at headquarters.

Information Submitted: November 1993

NEIGHBORHOOD CHECK CASHER, THE
1200 Travis, # 900
Houston, TX 77002
Telephone: (713) 659-6900
Fax: (713) 659-7400
Mr. Ed E. Hudson, Jr., President

Number of Franchised Units: 7
Number of Company-Owned Units: 7
Number of Total Operating Units: 14

In Business Since: 1989   **Franchising Since:** 1990

Description of Operation: Check cashing services, sale of money orders and other financial services, including USPS, notary, Western Union, lottery (where permitted by law), copies, faxes, lamination, postal box rentals and pagers.

Equity Capital Needed: $55,000 - $92,000

Franchise Fee: $20,000

Royalty Fee: 6%

Financial Assistance: None.

Managerial Assistance: After training, NCC offers on-going managerial assistance to franchisees in all aspects of the franchisee's operations. NCC's staff is always available to answer any questions that a franchisee may have. Technical support is provided to assist franchisees with all computer-related inquiries. NCC believes one of the keys to being a successful franchisee is support from the franchisor in all ways.

Training Provided: Each franchisee and 1 employee are provided with 1 week of training at the corporate office in Houston, TX. Prior to training, the franchisee is provided with an operations manual. Training includes a 2-hour video, plus several days of training on risk management, cash handling and our computer check cashing system. Training also includes an introduction to banking and other vendor relationships. A franchisee spends 1 day of on-the-job training at one of NCC's sister corporation centers.

Information Submitted: December 1993

NIX CHECK CASHING
17019 Kingsview Ave.
Carson, CA 90746
Telephone: (800) 325-1718 (310) 538-2242
Fax: (310) 538-3742
Mr. Dave Robinson, Director of Franchising

Number of Franchised Units: 1
Number of Company-Owned Units: 27
Number of Total Operating Units: 28

In Business Since: 1966   **Franchising Since:** 1991

Description of Operation: Check cashing and related financial services.

Equity Capital Needed: $30,000 - $70,000

Franchise Fee: $15,000 - $25,000

Royalty Fee: 6%, or $125 per week.

Financial Assistance: We provide no direct financing, but have identified sources interested in working on a case-by-case basis.

Managerial Assistance: Along with training, assistance is available upon request.

Training Provided: 2 weeks of classroom training, plus 150 hours of training in branch.

Information Submitted: December 1993

OFFICE ONE
1097-C Irongate Ln.
Columbus, OH 43213
Telephone: (614) 864-1440
Mr. Raymond A. Strohl, President

Number of Franchised Units: 7
Number of Company-Owned Units: 1
Number of Total Operating Units: 8

In Business Since: 1989   **Franchising Since:** 1989

Description of Operation: Sub-letting office space to sales representatives and small businesses. We furnish complete secretarial services, utilities, furniture and equipment rental, your own phone number, word processing, desktop publishing, photocopying, bookkeeping, fax services, notary services, messenger services and free parking.

Equity Capital Needed: $75,000

Franchise Fee: Varies.

Royalty Fee: Varies.

Financial Assistance: None.

Managerial Assistance: As much managerial assistance as needed is provided. Also, we can provide a complete turn-key operation.

Training Provided: 2 months of training are provided.

Information Submitted: November 1993

PACK 'N' MAIL MAILING CENTER
5701 Slide Rd., # C
Lubbock, TX 79414
Telephone: (800) 877-8884 (806) 797-3400
Fax: (806) 797-8142
Mr. Mike Gallagher, President

Number of Franchised Units: 200
Number of Company-Owned Units: 6
Number of Total Operating Units: 206

In Business Since: 1981   **Franchising Since:** 1989

Description of Operation: Complete business communications center, including shipping, packaging, fax service, complete copying service, mail box rentals and much more.

Equity Capital Needed: $25,000 - $65,000

Franchise Fee: $17,500

Royalty Fee: 0%

Financial Assistance: We offer $15,000 in a leased equipment program with another $15,000 in build-out allowance for a total of $30,000 of possible financing.

Managerial Assistance: We have 11 corporate officers and trainers with 30 years of combined experience.

Training Provided: We offer 2 weeks of training at one of 10 corporate centers located in the US.

Information Submitted: March 1994

PACKAGING PLUS SERVICES
20 S. Terminal Dr.
Plainview, NY 11803
Telephone: (800) 922-7225 (516) 349-1300
Fax: (516) 349-8036
Mr. Richard A. Altomare, President

Number of Franchised Units: 72
Number of Company-Owned Units: 6
Number of Total Operating Units: 78

In Business Since: 1986   **Franchising Since:** 1986

Description of Operation: The Company's primary goals are to provide consumers and small businesses with products and services efficiently and inexpensively. Packaging Plus Centers offer the convenient and cost-effective delivery of goods which are properly packaged, wrapped and shipped. In short, we ship just about anything, anywhere in the continental US and internationally. Packaging Plus Services uses a variety of packaging techniques and environmentally-friendly materials with reliable shippers. A one-stop convenience!

Equity Capital Needed: $30,000

Franchise Fee: $19,500

Royalty Fee: 3%

Financial Assistance: The franchisee will be given a $25,000 long-term note at 5% interest after the $30,000 equity capital down payment is made. The total turn-key cost of the entire store is $55,000.

Managerial Assistance: National and regional advertising programs provided by PPS. PPS will provide all of the technical knowledge, business and marketing support necessary for the operation of the business.

Training Provided: Hands-on training. PPS trainers spend several days in your new center with you. Marketing techniques, customer relations, positive attitude and general business operating skills are also covered. Plus an 800# hotline!

Information Submitted: November 1993

PADGETT BUSINESS SERVICES
160 Hawthorne Park
Athens, GA 30606
Telephone: (800) 323-7292 (706) 548-1040
Fax: (706) 543-8537
Mr. Greg Williams, Vice President of Sales

Number of Franchised Units: 254
Number of Company-Owned Units: 0
Number of Total Operating Units: 254

In Business Since: 1966   **Franchising Since:** 1975

Description of Operation: Monthly tax, accounting and consulting to the small business market represents 85% of all business.

Equity Capital Needed: $25,000 - $45,000

Franchise Fee: $34,500

Royalty Fee: 9%

Financial Assistance: A $20,000 note is available to qualified applicant from a third party.

Managerial Assistance: We provide 4 weeks of initial training, plus annual tax, operations and marketing seminars. Support in the areas of tax, IRS audit, accounting, marketing and practice management.

Training Provided: Same as above.

Information Submitted: January 1994

PAK MAIL CENTERS OF AMERICA
3033 S. Parker Rd., # 1200
Aurora, CO 80014
Telephone: (800) 833-2821 (303) 752-3500
Fax: (303) 755-9721
Mr. John H. Simon, Senior Vice President of Franchise Development

Number of Franchised Units: 219
Number of Company-Owned Units: 1
Number of Total Operating Units: 220

In Business Since: 1983   **Franchising Since:** 1984

Description of Operation: Pak Mail's one-stop shop offers the customer a convenient location to send packages, make copies, send or receive a fax or rent a private mailbox. However, it's the specialty services, such as bulk mail processing and packaging and crating, that have set Pak Mail ahead of the competition. Pak Mail's business format is a proven and reliable marketing, distribution and operating system that attracts and retains a loyal customer.

Equity Capital Needed: $50,000 - $80,000

Franchise Fee: $19,000

Royalty Fee: 5%

Financial Assistance: Fixture and equipment leasing is available.

Managerial Assistance: We provide site selection, lease negotiations, pre-training assistance, post-training assistance, bi-annual seminars and workshops, conventions and an 800# help-line. Regional support personnel and corporate experts.

Training Provided: We offer 1 week of training in the franchisor's facility in Denver, CO. 1 week following training in a Pak Mail facility. 3 days of set-up and opening assistance by corporate facility member. 3 - 4 months after opening, a 3-day Phase II training program is provided. Semi-annual workshops and regional training is provided thereafter.

Information Submitted: March 1994

PARCEL PLUS
2666 Riva Rd., # 120
Annapolis, MD 21401
Telephone: (800) 662-5553 (410) 266-3200
Fax: (410) 266-3266
Ms. Kristine Campbell, Director of Franchise Development

Number of Franchised Units: 80
Number of Company-Owned Units: 0
Number of Total Operating Units: 80

In Business Since: 1986   **Franchising Since:** 1988

Description of Operation: Packaging, shipping and business support services, including retailing UPS, Federal Express, AirBorne, Rodeway and other carriers. Business support services include photocopying, facsimile and computer support. "Big Cargo" profit center allows our system access to unique packaging and shipping techniques for unusual shipments.

Equity Capital Needed: $50,000 - $60,000

Franchise Fee: $17,500

Royalty Fee: 4%

Financial Assistance: Leasing companies are made available for equipment, which includes copiers, a computer, a cash register, scales, etc.

Managerial Assistance: 20-plus years of transportation management experience has been brought to bear on our franchised system.

Training Provided: 5 days of classroom and 5 days of in-store training, including goal setting, time management, business plan development, transportation consulting, computer, accounting and sales management techniques.

Information Submitted: November 1993

PARCELWAY COURIER SYSTEMS
3800 N. Central Ave., # 590
Phoenix, AZ 85012
Telephone: (800) 343-0200 (602) 263-0600
Fax: (602) 263-7404
Mr. George Siegel, Chief Executive Officer

Number of Franchised Units: 0
Number of Company-Owned Units: 4
Number of Total Operating Units: 4

In Business Since: 1990   **Franchising Since:** 1991

Description of Operation: On-demand, same-day messenger and courier service, transporting documents and parcels on an expedited basis.

Equity Capital Needed: $25,000

Franchise Fee: $15,000

Royalty Fee: 5%

Financial Assistance: We would consider financing franchise fee.

Managerial Assistance: Complete support at opening and continuing thereafter. Manuals and forms.

Training Provided: We provide 2 weeks of training.

Information Submitted: January 1994

PARSON-BISHOP SERVICES
7870 Camargo Rd.
Cincinnati, OH 45243
Telephone: (800) 543-0468 (513) 561-5560
Fax: (513) 527-8919
Mr. Lou Bishop, President

Number of Franchised Units: 62
Number of Company-Owned Units: 0
Number of Total Operating Units: 62

In Business Since: 1973   **Franchising Since:** 1987

Description of Operation: P-B's executive franchisees market P-B's guaranteed effective, low-cost accounts receivable management, collection and cash flow improvement plans. These exclusive plans provide solutions to an on-going, basic business need. More than 90% of businesses are prospects. Build equity from long-term, repeat customers. You must have a sales, marketing or management background and be qualified to call on upper-level management in corporations of all sizes.

Equity Capital Needed: $23,000 - $29,500

Franchise Fee: $18,000

Royalty Fee: 0%

Financial Assistance: None.

Managerial Assistance: We provide constant advertising, marketing and public relations support, plus videos and manuals. Computerized franchise management system.

Training Provided: We offer 1 week of classroom training at the home office, 2 training visits to the franchisee's area in the first 6 months and quarterly national and regional seminars. Continuous one-on-one support.

Information Submitted: March 1994

PENNYSAVER
80 Eighth Ave.
New York, NY 10011
Telephone: (212) 243-6800
Fax: (212) 243-7457
Mr. Allan Horwitz, President

Number of Franchised Units: 10
Number of Company-Owned Units: 0
Number of Total Operating Units: 10

In Business Since: 1979   **Franchising Since:** 1990

Description of Operation: Free distribution shopping guide.

Equity Capital Needed: $34,900 - $44,900

Franchise Fee: $29,900

Royalty Fee: $200 plus per month.

Financial Assistance: The Company provides no direct financing; however, financial assistance is available to franchisees based upon adequate home equity through Company contacts in the financial community.

Managerial Assistance: The Company offers a franchisee on-going revenue and support services. In-depth financial analysis is conducted on each issue of franchisee's publication, plus free, unlimited consulting.

Training Provided: We provide a minimum of 5 days of classroom training and a minimum of 5 days of on-site training at the franchisee's location, at the Company's expense.

Information Submitted: March 1994

PEYRON TAX SERVICE
3212 Preston St.
Louisville, KY 40213
Telephone: (800) 821-4965 (502) 637-7483
Mr. Dan Peyron, President

Number of Franchised Units: 500
Number of Company-Owned Units: 2
Number of Total Operating Units: 502

In Business Since: 1960   Franchising Since: 1965

Description of Operation: Peyron license others to operate tax preparation offices in stores, malls and storefront locations. Secured by Company, which also provides warranty package, electronic filing, refund loans, technical assistance, signs, flyers, tax newsletters and other materials and services. We also provide TV advertising for area operators.

Equity Capital Needed: $3,000 +

Franchise Fee: $3,000 +

Royalty Fee: 5%

Financial Assistance: None.

Managerial Assistance: Hire and train all personnel for area operators (minimum 10 locations) and supervise closely first year. No managerial assistance provided single location operators.

Training Provided: Basic tax preparation course, usually 10 weeks, if operator elects to prepare all tax returns and has had no experience.

Information Submitted: November 1993

PILOT AIR FREIGHT CORPORATION
Rte. 352, P. O. Box 97
Lima, PA 19037
Telephone: (800) 447-4568 (215) 891-8100
Fax: (215) 891-9341
Mr. Dick Morris, Senior Vice President/General Manager

Number of Franchised Units: 62
Number of Company-Owned Units: 2
Number of Total Operating Units: 64

In Business Since: 1970   Franchising Since: 1980

Description of Operation: Pilot provides the service of handling the air freight shipping requirements of their customers, both domestically and internationally.

Equity Capital Needed: $30,000 - $100,000, determined by market.

Franchise Fee: $50,000 - $150,000, varies.

Royalty Fee: 15%

Financial Assistance: None.

Managerial Assistance: We provide on-going communications with corporate headquarters and visits by Pilot's regional managers.

Training Provided: We offer 2 weeks of training in classroom, Pilot headquarters and visits by Pilot's regional managers.

Information Submitted: March 1994

PONY MAIL BOX & BUSINESS CENTER
13110 NE 177th Place
Woodinville, WA 98072

Telephone: (800) 767-7668 (206) 483-0360
Fax: (206) 486-6495
Mr. Robert E. Howell, President

Number of Franchised Units: 26
Number of Company-Owned Units: 1
Number of Total Operating Units: 27

In Business Since: 1983   Franchising Since: 1986

Description of Operation: Commercial mail receiving, shipping, fax, word processing, mail boxes, Western Union, mailing supplies, answering service, wedding announcements, business cards, stationery, stamps, rubber stamps, envelopes and packaging materials.

Equity Capital Needed: $50,000 - $65,000

Franchise Fee: $12,950

Royalty Fee: $1,400 a year.

Financial Assistance: Data not available.

Managerial Assistance: Highly-trained location assistance, specifications and drawings of build-out of offices, thorough training program, manual of operations, constant communications with each franchisee during term of contract. Expansion program in place.

Training Provided: Data not available.

Information Submitted: November 1993

POSTAL PLUS SERVICES
6465 Millcreek Dr., # 205
Mississauga, ON L5N 5R3 CAN
Telephone: (800) 387-8335 (905) 567-4180
Fax: (905) 567-5355
Mr. George Kostopoulos, Director of Franchise Development

Number of Franchised Units: 2
Number of Company-Owned Units: 0
Number of Total Operating Units: 2

In Business Since: 1991   Franchising Since: 1991

Description of Operation: Postal, packaging, courier, shipping and complete business support center.

Equity Capital Needed: $30,000 - $40,000

Franchise Fee: $20,000

Royalty Fee: 5%

Financial Assistance: Financing assistance through a lending institution.

Managerial Assistance: On-going management support.

Training Provided: We provide 3 weeks of on-site training.

Information Submitted: November 1993

POSTALANNEX+
9050 Friars Rd., # 400
San Diego, CA 92108
Telephone: (800) 456-1525 (619) 563-4800
Fax: (619) 563-9850
Mr. Carl J. Kosnar, Vice President of Development

Number of Franchised Units: 170
Number of Company-Owned Units: 1
Number of Total Operating Units: 171

In Business Since: 1985   Franchising Since: 1986

Description of Operation: Postal, parcel, copy shop, business and communications services. Complete postal, packaging and parcel shipping services. Copy and high-speed duplicating, facsimile. Electronic funds transfer, office and packaging supplies.

Equity Capital Needed: $55,000 - $80,000, including franchise fee.

Franchise Fee: $19,500

Royalty Fee: 5%

Financial Assistance: Financing of up to $56,000, for those who qualify, for equipment, signage, cabinetry and merchandise. PostalAnnex+ offers financing through various outside companies under a variety of terms and rates.

Managerial Assistance: Assistance is available 24 hours a day, 7 days a week, with store operation, marketing, accounting, legal, merchandising, promotions and advertising. An 800# is available to all franchisees.

Training Provided: 3 weeks of comprehensive training is available at the home office - 1 1/2 weeks in the classroom and 1 1/2 weeks in the corporate training store. During training, every aspect of our business is covered in detail.

Information Submitted: November 1993

POSTNET POSTAL & BUSINESS CENTERS
2225 E. Flamingo Rd., # 310
Las Vegas, NV 89119
Telephone: (800) 841-7171 (702) 792-7100
Fax: (702) 792-7115
Mr. Brian Spindel, Vice President

Number of Franchised Units: 107
Number of Company-Owned Units: 4
Number of Total Operating Units: 111

In Business Since: 1985   **Franchising Since:** 1992

Description of Operation: PostNet International Franchise Corporation, with a staff that has developed over 500 postal and business centers throughout the US, Alaska, Hawaii, Puerto Rico and Guam, began franchising in the spring of 1993 and currently has a network of over 130 franchisees. PostNet offers a turn-key operation that includes a complete store development package and provides assistance in the areas of site selection and store design, merchandising, marketing and daily store operations.

Equity Capital Needed: $57,000 - $85,000

Franchise Fee: $22,500

Royalty Fee: 3%

Financial Assistance: If required, PostNet assists new franchisees in obtaining financing by preparing a comprehensive business plan with financial projections to take to loan providers, including SBA affiliated banks.

Managerial Assistance: PostNet assists franchisees with managing their businesses by maintaining a constant line of communication with head-quarters through an 800# and through contact with PostNet Area Representatives. The development of the franchisee's business is monitored closely to assure that PostNet franchisees are growing according to plan. The Area Representative stays in contact with the franchisee and visits the store regularly. Regional meetings on business building and a 5-volume operations manual.

Training Provided: Each franchisee is trained up to 1 week in an area store and 5 - 7 days on-site. The corporate trainer leads the new business owner through set-up and merchandising, including pricing, interior signage and display. Training includes customer service techniques, staffing, record keeping, advertising, marketing and daily operations. The trainer assists the franchisee with the opening of the PostNet Center and insures that the franchisee feels comfortable in all aspects of business operation.

Information Submitted: January 1994

PREMIUM SHOPPING GUIDE
1235 Sunset Grove Rd.
Fallbrook, CA 92584
Telephone: (800) 343-1056 (619) 723-8133
Fax: (619) 728-3145
Mr. Robert Neral, National Sales Manager

Number of Franchised Units: 13
Number of Company-Owned Units: 76
Number of Total Operating Units: 89

In Business Since: 1984   **Franchising Since:** 1992

Description of Operation: Print, label and mail four-color direct mail coupon and display magazines for independent publishers in over 36 states.

Equity Capital Needed: $3,000 - $3,500

Franchise Fee: $2,950

Royalty Fee: 0%

Financial Assistance: Financing is available on franchise fee.

Managerial Assistance: Continuous 800# help-line provided.

Training Provided: In-house and field training provided.

Information Submitted: November 1993

RENTAL GUIDE
1600 Capital Circle, SW
Tallahassee, FL 32310
Telephone: (800) 277-4357 (904) 574-2111
Fax: (904) 574-2525
Mr. Tom Scardino, Vice President

Number of Franchised Units: 24
Number of Company-Owned Units: 5
Number of Total Operating Units: 29

In Business Since: 1973   **Franchising Since:** 1988

Description of Operation: Full-color magazines for apartment property advertising. Free to consumers. Franchisees handle promotion, sales, layout and distribution. Franchisor offers production, printing, training and marketing support services. Now in 17 states.

Equity Capital Needed: $44,750 - $105,000

Franchise Fee: $20,000

Royalty Fee: 10.5%

Financial Assistance: Partial financing of initial fee to qualified veterans. Lease program for distribution street racks.

Managerial Assistance: Assistance from regional managers and account executives. Training manuals, forms, sales aids, periodic newsletter, franchisee advisory council.

Training Provided: We provide an initial 2 weeks of classroom training in Tallahassee, FL. Regional and national meetings with seminars. Toll-free 800# for technical assistance.

Information Submitted: December 1993

RESORT MAPS
Rte. 100, Old High Sch., PO Box 726
Waitsfield, VT 05673
Telephone: (800) 788-5247 (802) 496-6277
Fax: (802) 496-6278
Mr. Chandler W. Weller, Executive Vice President

Number of Franchised Units: 0
Number of Company-Owned Units: 1
Number of Total Operating Units: 1

In Business Since: 1993   **Franchising Since:** 1993

Description of Operation: RMFI Maps is engaged in the sales, nurturing and support of franchised publishers of business and tourist information maps under the tradename of Resort Maps. It depends on and utilizes the business systems generated by Resort Maps, a company dedicated to providing a unique and creative method of alternative advertising media in the form of tourist and visitor information maps. Advertising space is supported by restaurants, resorts, retail stores, local attractions, etc.

Equity Capital Needed: $21,000 - $24,250 (includes $15,000 franchise fee).

Franchise Fee: $15,000

Royalty Fee: First year - 28% of gross advertising sales; second year and after - 25% of GAS.

Financial Assistance: No financing is available.

Managerial Assistance: We provide on-going 800# support, visits from a franchise coordinator and any other assistance and consultation as needed.

Training Provided: A comprehensive 5-day training program will be conducted in the home office in Waitsfield, VT and is designed to instruct the franchisee in how to operate and maintain a Resort Maps territory and will include an indoctrination into what a Resort Maps franchisee is required to do. Covered are basic principals of management skills, scheduling, cost control, ordering procedures, equipment, operation and sales skills.

Information Submitted: January 1994

SCORECARD PLUS
4150 Belden Village St., NW, # 303
Canton, OH 44718
Telephone: (800) 767-9273 (216) 493-9900
Fax: (216) 493-9274
Mr. Ed Kalail, Vice President of Operations

Number of Franchised Units: 3
Number of Company-Owned Units: 2
Number of Total Operating Units: 5

In Business Since: 1990   **Franchising Since:** 1992

Description of Operation: Scorecard Plus is a combination scorecard and full-color yardage book which replaces the traditional cardboard scorecard at public and semi-private golf courses throughput the US. The book also contains advertising which allows businesses to target the golfer, thereby reducing the cost of the program to the golf course.

Equity Capital Needed: Data not available.

Franchise Fee: $19,950

Royalty Fee: 8%

Financial Assistance: No financing is available on the franchise fee; however, we do help spread out operating costs in order to minimize the need for additional capital not generated from business sales.

Managerial Assistance: We provide assistance in the form of on-going consultation, sharing of specific forms or software programs and any other assistance we can provide to help insure the success of the franchisee.

Training Provided: A new franchisee receives up to 2 weeks of training at no additional cost, other than travel expenses. 1 week of training is at the franchisor's office with the second conducted in the franchisee's territory.

Information Submitted: January 1994

SERVING BY IRVING
233 Broadway, # 1036
New York, NY 10279
Telephone: (212) 233-3346
Fax: (212) 349-0338
Mr. Irving Botwinick, President

Number of Franchised Units: 4
Number of Company-Owned Units: 1
Number of Total Operating Units: 5

In Business Since: 1990   **Franchising Since:** 1990

Description of Operation: Experts at process serving and locating individuals.

Equity Capital Needed: $2,500 and up.

Franchise Fee: $25,000 +

Royalty Fee: To be determined.

Financial Assistance: Low interest rate financing is available.

Managerial Assistance: 4 weeks of training in New York and at the actual location.

Training Provided: Same as above.

Information Submitted: January 1994

SHIPPING CONNECTION
820 Simms St., # 12
Golden, CO 80401
Telephone: (800) 880-1995 (303) 331-6430
Fax: (303) 331-0960
Ms. Carol B. Green, Broker

Number of Franchised Units: 22
Number of Company-Owned Units: 1
Number of Total Operating Units: 23

In Business Since: 1982   **Franchising Since:** 1987

Description of Operation: Retail convenience centers that provide complete packaging and shipping services to the general public. Not limited to small parcels. Dealing with both businesses and individuals, you can literally ship any item, any size, to any place in the world. This business was founded by former UPS management personnel who will provide you with the latest techniques in packaging and shipping.

Equity Capital Needed: $30,000 - $35,000

Franchise Fee: $15,500

Royalty Fee: 5%

Financial Assistance: Not available.

Managerial Assistance: Operations manual, newsletters, annual seminars, co-operative advertising program, extensive follow-up and on-going support.

Training Provided: 2 weeks of training at national headquarters and 1 week on-site. Site selection and lease negotiation assistance. Franchisee is set up with negotiated discounts from suppliers and freight carriers, with whom he/she deals directly.

Information Submitted: November 1993

SHRED-IT
2359 Royal Windsor Dr., Unit 15
Mississauga, ON L5J 1K5 CAN
Telephone: (905) 855-2540
Fax: (905) 855-7732
Mr. John Prittie, Vice President of Franchise Development

Number of Franchised Units: 2
Number of Company-Owned Units: 2
Number of Total Operating Units: 4

In Business Since: 1989   **Franchising Since:** 1992

Description of Operation: Mobile paper shredding and recycling business, serving medical, financial, government and large and small business. Provide on-site shredding and recycling of shredded material. Business-to-business franchise.

Equity Capital Needed: $80,000 - $160,000

Franchise Fee: $35,000

Royalty Fee: 5%

Financial Assistance: Business plan development and introduction to banks and leasing companies.

Managerial Assistance: We provide market research, start-up assistance, training, proprietary accounting, operating and shredding systems, field support, managerial support, group purchasing, marketing, customer satisfaction, manuals, newsletters and public relations.

Training Provided: We provide 2 weeks in the head office and 1 week in the field at time of opening. 8 manuals on all aspects of the business.

Information Submitted: January 1994

SIGN EXPRESS
6 Clarke Circle, P. O. Box 309
Bethel, CT 06801
Telephone: (800) 525-7446 (203) 791-0004
Fax: (203) 743-7028
Ms. Laurie Wright, Executive Vice President

Number of Franchised Units: 75
Number of Company-Owned Units: 0
Number of Total Operating Units: 75

In Business Since: 1985   **Franchising Since:** 1988

Description of Operation: Full-service sign business. Using computer technology and-sign making expertise, you can provide a broad range of signs. Business-to-business service.

Equity Capital Needed: $50,000

Franchise Fee: $7,200

Royalty Fee: $1,600 annually.

Financial Assistance: Data not available.

Managerial Assistance: On-going support, 800#, pricing program and 20 years of sign-making experience.

Training Provided: Training in sign making, computer operation, sales, marketing, pricing, store operation and personnel.

Information Submitted: November 1993

SIGNERY, THE
1717 N. Naper Blvd., # 205
Naperville, IL 60563
Telephone: (800) 695-4257 (708) 955-0700
Fax: (708) 955-0704
Mr. Richard Gretz, President

Number of Franchised Units: 34
Number of Company-Owned Units: 2
Number of Total Operating Units: 36

In Business Since: 1986   **Franchising Since:** 1986

Description of Operation: Computer-generated, full-service sign shops. The Signery stores are located in heavy-traffic retail shopping centers.

Equity Capital Needed: $85,000 - $105,000

Franchise Fee: $22,500

Royalty Fee: 6%

Financial Assistance: Equipment leasing and financial assistance available.

Managerial Assistance: On-going training and support through field visits, regional seminars, newsletters and a toll-free telephone hotline.

Training Provided: A 3-week training program provides classroom instruction, combined with hands-on, in-store experience. Areas covered in initial 3-week training include equipment, operations, sales, customer service, safety, management, marketing, advertising, creative design, bookkeeping, accounting and cost analysis.

Information Submitted: November 1993

SIGNS & MORE IN 24
1739 St. Mary's Ave.
Parkersburg, WV 26101
Telephone: (800) 358-2358 (304) 422-SIGN
Fax: (304) 422-7449
Mr. Bruce Bronski, President

Number of Franchised Units: 2
Number of Company-Owned Units: 1
Number of Total Operating Units: 3

In Business Since: 1990   **Franchising Since:** 1992

Description of Operation: 24-hour sign franchise, offering all types of signs in 24 hours in a well-decorated retail store. In addition, custom-made residential and commercial awnings are offered, as well as flags, electrical and neon signage. Our variety allows for higher sales than similar companies and a total signage mix.

Equity Capital Needed: $45,000 - $99,000

Franchise Fee: $13,000

Royalty Fee: 3% - 6%

Financial Assistance: We help the potential franchisee prepare the business plans and marketing studies and help in finding the proper lending institutions.

Managerial Assistance: Signs and More in 24 provides 1 week of on-site assistance after opening, as well as 1 week of outside selling, along with 2 - 3 weeks of training at our headquarters. An 800# assistance hotline, constant news and product updates, along with operations, marketing, pricing and vendor manuals. In addition, on-site visits are available and a monthly newsletter, accounting and advertising systems are also provided.

Training Provided: Same as above.

Information Submitted: November 1993

SIGNS BY TOMORROW
6460 Dobbin Rd.
Columbia, MD 21045
Telephone: (800) 765-7446 (410) 992-7192
Fax: (410) 992-7675
Mr. Robert Nunn, Director of Franchise Development

Number of Franchised Units: 21
Number of Company-Owned Units: 1
Number of Total Operating Units: 22

In Business Since: 1986   **Franchising Since:** 1988

Description of Operation: One day computer-based sign shops. Signs By Tomorrow stores produce signs and graphics for virtually all sizes of businesses. The franchisee's role is to lead the sales and administrative areas in servicing a business-to-business clientele during regular working hours.

Equity Capital Needed: $85,000 - $95,000

Franchise Fee: $17,500

Royalty Fee: 5% - 3%

Financial Assistance: Equipment leasing plan is available.

Managerial Assistance: Signs By Tomorrow offers complete initial training and an on-going support program.

Training Provided: We offer 4 weeks of training - 1 week at SBT headquarters and 2 weeks at the franchisee's location.

Information Submitted: March 1994

SIGNS FIRST
813 Ridge Lake Blvd., # 390
Memphis, TN 38120
Telephone: (800) 852-2163 (901) 682-2264
Fax: (901) 682-2264
Ms. Linda Scammerhorn, Franchise Development Director

Number of Franchised Units: 19
Number of Company-Owned Units: 0
Number of Total Operating Units: 19

In Business Since: 1966   **Franchising Since:** 1989

Description of Operation: A computerized sign shop, marketed as the quickest sign company in town. A business package so complete that it requires no prior experience - We get you up and running. Enjoy the protection and support that 25 years of hands-on-experience offers.

Equity Capital Needed: $23,000 - $83,000

Franchise Fee: $10,000 - $15,000

Royalty Fee: 6%

Financial Assistance: Business plans, assistance with leasing, SBA or bank financing.

Managerial Assistance: On-going operational and marketing support, based on 25 years of hands-on experience.

Training Provided: A 2 - 3 day orientation program, 3 weeks of training, training manuals, videos, library and additional on-site training.

Information Submitted: December 1993

SIGNS NOW
4900 Manatee Ave. W., # 103
Bradenton, FL 34209
Telephone: (800) 356-3373 (813) 747-7747
Fax: (813) 747-5074
Mr. Dewey Eason, President

Number of Franchised Units: 124
Number of Company-Owned Units: 0
Number of Total Operating Units: 124

In Business Since: 1986   **Franchising Since:** 1986

Description of Operation: Computerized one-day sign shop, creating signs and graphics for business and retail.

Equity Capital Needed: $53,500 - $120,300

Franchise Fee: $19,800

Royalty Fee: 5%

Financial Assistance: Equipment leasing is available.

Managerial Assistance: We provide 2 - 4 weeks of training in a regional operating store. The complete corporate staff is trained in sign store operations. 20 regional managers in the field to assist.

Training Provided: Training includes 2 - 4 weeks in a regional operating store, 3 - 7 days on equipment and 1 week with regional manager in franchise store.

Information Submitted: December 1993

SPEEDY SIGN-A-RAMA, USA
1601 Belvedere Rd., # 402 E.
West Palm Beach, FL 33406
Telephone: (800) 776-8105 (407) 640-5570
Fax: (407) 640-5580
Mr. Tony Foley, Vice President

Number of Franchised Units: 150
Number of Company-Owned Units: 0
Number of Total Operating Units: 150

In Business Since: 1986   **Franchising Since:** 1987

Description of Operation: Full-service retail computerized sign franchise, utilizing the latest in computer software technology to produce custom signage quickly and inexpensively. No experience necessary. Full company training. A 2-week in-house training course with local back-up and support is provided on an on-going basis.

Equity Capital Needed: $35,000 - $75,000

Franchise Fee: $29,500

Royalty Fee: 6%

Financial Assistance: The Company provides financing for qualified applicants, as well as various programs to help the franchisee get started.

Managerial Assistance: After an intensive 2-week training course at national headquarters, assistance is provided on a local basis. This assistance includes complete support in all phases of running the franchise - from management to hiring to training personnel.

Training Provided: Training is a 2-week program that completely covers all phases of our franchise, from marketing techniques to complete training. Training is part of the franchise fee.

Information Submitted: November 1993

SUNBELT BUSINESS BROKERS
1 Poston Rd., # 190
Charleston, SC 29407
Telephone: (800) 771-7866 (803) 769-4363
Fax: (803) 766-8160
Mr. Edward T. Pendarvis, Chief Executive Officer

Number of Franchised Units: 21
Number of Company-Owned Units: 1
Number of Total Operating Units: 22

In Business Since: 1979   **Franchising Since:** 1992

Description of Operation: Sunbelt franchisees engage in general business brokerage. The downsizing of major companies has flooded the market with thousands of unemployed people looking for businesses to buy. Sunbelt franchisees use their executive talents to help people buy and sell businesses to benefit themselves and their families.

Equity Capital Needed: $7,000 - $50,000

Franchise Fee: $5,000 - $10,000

Royalty Fee: $3,000 - $5,000 per year.

Financial Assistance: None.

Managerial Assistance: Complete operating systems are provided, as well as on-site assistance with set-up and hiring brokers. Follow-up on-site visits insure a smooth start-up.

Training Provided: New broker training is held every month at regional training centers. Franchisees may send as many trainees as they wish, as often as they wish, at no additional cost. Follow-up and special training sessions are provided as needed at the franchisee's location. Advanced training sessions are available at the regional training sites.

Information Submitted: February 1994

SUPERCOUPS
180 Bodwell St.
Avon, MA 02322
Telephone: (800) 626-2620 (508) 580-4340
Fax: (508) 588-3347
Ms. Allison Botelho, Sales

Number of Franchised Units: 116
Number of Company-Owned Units: 0
Number of Total Operating Units: 116

In Business Since: 1983   **Franchising Since:** 1983

Description of Operation: SuperCoups is a co-operative direct mail advertising franchise. The head offices, located in Avon, MA, provide all production functions. The franchisee operates the sales office out of his/her home - no inventory to carry. No coupon printing or graphics experience necessary - just a sales person.

Equity Capital Needed: Franchise fee.

Franchise Fee: $22,900

Royalty Fee: $148 per mailing.

Financial Assistance: None.

Managerial Assistance: SuperCoups provides each franchisee with a complete set of managerial manuals, outlining everything from office supplies to sales techniques. Our large franchise system provides a network of managers to help any new franchisee get up and running.

Training Provided: Franchisees receive 1 week of in-house training and 1 week of in-field training at their franchise location. We provide 2 800#s for continual assistance, along with corporate-sponsored conferences, twice a year, featuring classes on new procedures and industry-related topics. Also, we offer the first 2 mailings free to help start your business off right!

Information Submitted: November 1993

TAXPRO ELECTRONIC FILING
P. O. Box 13829
Jackson, MS 39236
Telephone: (800) 748-9106 (601) 956-0500
Fax: (601) 956-0583
Mr. James T. Marsh, President

Number of Franchised Units: 142
Number of Company-Owned Units: 1
Number of Total Operating Units: 143

In Business Since: 1965   **Franchising Since:** 1968

Description of Operation: TaxPro provides software, training, 800#, technical support, specialized forms and supplies and advertising support for electronic tax refund loans. There are no up-front fees.

Equity Capital Needed: $0 - $5,000

Franchise Fee: $0

Royalty Fee: $5 per return.

Financial Assistance: None.

Managerial Assistance: 800# support provided for all aspects of the electronic filing operation.

Training Provided: 1 week of training is available at Company offices. Full procedures manuals and self-study material provided. 800# support all year.

Information Submitted: November 1993

TRADE LABOR
P. O. Box 70661
Nashville, TN 37207
Telephone: (800) 321-2825 (615) 824-2825
Fax: (615) 824-2825
Mr. Jim Shafer, President

Number of Franchised Units: 4
Number of Company-Owned Units: 1
Number of Total Operating Units: 5

In Business Since: 1991   **Franchising Since:** 1991

Description of Operation: Barter network system.

Equity Capital Needed: $999

Franchise Fee: $999

Royalty Fee: 5%

Financial Assistance: As needed.

Managerial Assistance: We will work with the new franchisee as needed.

Training Provided: Same as above.

Information Submitted: January 1994

TRIMARK
184 Quigley Blvd., P. O. Box 10530
New Castle, DE 19850
Telephone: (800) TRI-MARK (302) 322-2143
Fax: (302) 322-2163
Mr. Gilbert L. Kinch, Vice President of Sales and Marketing

Number of Franchised Units: 29
Number of Company-Owned Units: 3
Number of Total Operating Units: 32

In Business Since: 1969   **Franchising Since:** 1978

Description of Operation: TriMark is a co-op direct mail advertising and marketing franchise. Master and single franchise territories are available. Franchisee is responsible for retail sales and marketing for TriMark with local and national merchants, including professionals, in their exclusive territory. Franchisor provides the printing and mailing of the advertising packets from the publishing company.

Equity Capital Needed: Up to $5,000.

Franchise Fee: $7,000 - $29,000

Royalty Fee: $15 per ad.

Financial Assistance: TriMark will provide up to 100% financing of the initial franchise fee of both master and single territory franchises on an individual basis. If TriMark provides financing, the terms of the financing will be established in a separate agreement and not in the franchise agreement.

Managerial Assistance: TriMark provides new franchisees a confidential franchise operations manual and updates, training as described below, assistance in the master franchisee's respective state in the registration process of legal documents to sell sub-franchise territories, demographics/market structure, field assistance, as needed, bi-monthly newsletters and memos.

Training Provided: A 1-week training session at the corporate office, followed by a 1-week field training session at the franchisee's location is mandatory for both master and single territory franchisees. All master franchisees must successfully complete the TriMark master franchise training certification program in order to present the required training programs to their respective sub-franchisees. A national marketing meeting and an annual year-end meeting are held yearly at different locations.

Information Submitted: November 1993

TRIPLE CHECK INCOME TAX SERVICE
727 S. Main St.
Burbank, CA 91506
Telephone: (800) 283-1040 (818) 840-9077
Fax: (818) 840-9309
Mr. David W. Lieberman, President

Number of Franchised Units: 318
Number of Company-Owned Units: 2
Number of Total Operating Units: 320

In Business Since: 1941   **Franchising Since:** 1979

Description of Operation: Franchisor offers a full range of support services to independent tax practitioners, including training, technical (hotline), marketing (including group referral programs), proprietary worksheet schedule system and reduced computer costs. Through a sister company (Triple Check Financial Services), franchisees have an opportunity to engage in financial and investment planning services. The newest profit center - Triple Check Business Services - allows franchisees to offer sophisticated business counseling.

Equity Capital Needed: $500 - $8,000

Franchise Fee: None.

Royalty Fee: Varies.

Financial Assistance: Short-term loans are available through a local area bank.

Managerial Assistance: Assistance is in the form of written manuals and telephone communication with specialists in each area of managing a tax preparation, business services and financial services business.

Training Provided: We provide 80 hours of training each year to be done at a licensed location. Advanced tax preparation training to include audio cassette tapes, extensive manuals, form modules in the Triple Check worksheet system and a "sales and marketing" section to help the conservative-thinking accountant learn how you actually take advantage of our competitive advantages.

TV NEWS
80 Eighth Ave.
New York, NY 10011
Telephone: (212) 243-6800
Fax: (212) 243-7457
Mr. Allan Horwitz, President

Number of Franchised Units: 5
Number of Company-Owned Units: 1
Number of Total Operating Units: 6

In Business Since: 1979   Franchising Since: 1990

Description of Operation: Free distribution TV guide.

Equity Capital Needed: $15,500

Franchise Fee: $29,900

Royalty Fee: $150 per month.

Financial Assistance: The Company provides no direct financing; however, financial assistance is available to franchisees based upon adequate home equity through Company contacts in the financial community.

Managerial Assistance: The Company offers a franchisee on-going revenue and support services. In-depth financial analysis is conducted on each issue of franchisee's publication, plus free, unlimited consulting.

Training Provided: We offer a minimum of 5 days of classroom training and a minimum of 5 days of on-site training at the franchisee's location, at the Company's expense.

Information Submitted: March 1994

UNITED CHECK CASHING
325 Chestnut St., # 1005
Philadelphia, PA 19106
Telephone: (800) 626-0787 (215) 238-0300
Fax: (215) 238-9056
Mr. Seth N. Schonberg, Development Director

Number of Franchised Units: 20
Number of Company-Owned Units: 1
Number of Total Operating Units: 21

In Business Since: 1977   Franchising Since: 1991

Description of Operation: Convenience store of banking. Check cashing, money orders, wire transfers, authorized bill payments, fax, copies, notary, consumer loans, ATM's, lottery, credit card advances, tax service, photo ID systems and beeper sales.

Equity Capital Needed: $75,000 - $125,000

Franchise Fee: $17,500

Royalty Fee: .3% of 1% of check volume.

Financial Assistance: We can assist with $7,500 of the franchise fee. Equipment leasing.

Managerial Assistance: We provide classroom training at the corporate headquarters and hands-on training at our training store. Grand opening assistance and toll-free hotline for on-going daily assistance. We also offer computer programs for those with PC's.

Training Provided: Classroom training consists of everything from daily work processing to information on state and local laws, licensing, banking procedures and legal processes. The new franchisees also receive training in customer servicing, sales and human resources. One of the most important aspects of the training is the information provided on loss prevention and risk management.

Information Submitted: November 1993

UNITED COUPON CORPORATION
8380 Alban Rd.
Springfield, VA 22150
Telephone: (800) 368-3501 (703) 644-0200
Fax: (703) 569-2031
Mr. David N. Andersen, Director of Franchise Development

Number of Franchised Units: 86
Number of Company-Owned Units: 0
Number of Total Operating Units: 86

In Business Since: 1981   Franchising Since: 1982

Description of Operation: National corporation is expanding its operation. This is an excellent opportunity to join one of the leading companies involved in franchising in the direct mail advertising field. Strong repeat business potential. Sales and/or marketing experience is preferred.

Equity Capital Needed: 3 months of living expenses.

Franchise Fee: $18,900 - $21,900

Royalty Fee: 0%

Financial Assistance: Financing is available to qualified prospective franchisees.

Managerial Assistance: United provides production services such as art work, layout, typesetting, platemaking, printing, inserting, addressing, mailing, labeling, etc. Other assistance available through business management software, nationwide 800#, regional and national seminars.

Training Provided: We provide classroom and field training to new franchisees, training tapes on sales and business development, as well as sales force, time management, product knowledge and customer relations.

Information Submitted: November 1993

VAL-PAK DIRECT MARKETING
8605 Largo Lakes Dr.
Largo, FL 34643
Telephone: (800) 237-6266 (813) 393-1270
Fax: (813) 397-4968
Mr. Joseph H. Bourdow, Executive Vice President

Number of Franchised Units: 191
Number of Company-Owned Units: 0
Number of Total Operating Units: 191

In Business Since: 1968   Franchising Since: 1988

Description of Operation: The nation's largest local co-operative direct mail advertising company annually mails 310 million envelopes to consumers in all 50 states. 80,000+ businesses are clients. The franchise owner handles sales and clients. The franchisor handles graphics, printing and mailing.

Equity Capital Needed: $25,000 - $250,000

Franchise Fee: $500

Royalty Fee: 0%

Financial Assistance: The franchisor offers purchase financing in limited cases.

Managerial Assistance: V. P. Link office management software.

Training Provided: Training consists of a 3-day home study program, 5 days of classroom training and a 3-day on-site visit, plus 3-day annual training meetings 3 times a year.

Information Submitted: November 1993

VINYLGRAPHICS CUSTOM SIGN CENTRES
1733 Keele St.
Toronto, ON M6M 3W7 CAN
Telephone: (800) 265-7446 (416) 656-9988
Fax: (416) 656-3676
Mr. Tony Baxby, Director of Franchise Development

Number of Franchised Units: 8
Number of Company-Owned Units: 1
Number of Total Operating Units: 9

In Business Since: 1983 **Franchising Since:** 1990

Description of Operation: Vinylgraphics is a Canadian franchisor of custom sign centers that offers full-service interior and exterior signage, window lettering, vehicle and boat lettering, special event banners, magnetic signs, etc. to today's business community. The graphics are computer generated, utilizing state-of-the-art technology and proven vinyl films.

Equity Capital Needed: $40,000

Franchise Fee: $30,000

Royalty Fee: 6%, plus 2% co-operative advertising.

Financial Assistance: Financial assistance is provided - equipment rental and new venture loans.

Managerial Assistance: Data not available.

Training Provided: We offer 1 week of signmaking, 1 week on sign equipment, 1 week on business administration and 1 week on sales and marketing.

Information Submitted: March 1994

VOICE-TEL
23200 Chagrin Blvd., # 800
Cleveland, OH 44122
Telephone: (800) 333-5510 (216) 360-4400
Fax: (216) 360-4410
Ms. Nadia Gaster, Manager of Franchise Development

Number of Franchised Units: 129
Number of Company-Owned Units: 6
Number of Total Operating Units: 135

In Business Since: 1986 **Franchising Since:** 1986

Description of Operation: Voice-Tel is the leading provider of interactive voice messaging - a service that enables people to communicate without delay. Independent, locally-owned and managed service centers are strategically linked to form a superior international network. This network enables messages to be sent and serviced cost-effectively locally or long distance through all locations.

Equity Capital Needed: $100,000 - $150,000

Franchise Fee: $29,000 - $105,000

Royalty Fee: 6% - 10%

Financial Assistance: Third-party financing is available.

Managerial Assistance: Managerial support is provided in the form of manuals, weekly newsletters, seminars and a field representative program.

Training Provided: Initial training is provided at the corporate headquarters for 10 days, as well as on-site training at the franchisee's location. Also, regional trainings are provided on an on-going basis.

Information Submitted: November 1993

VR BUSINESS BROKERS
1151 Dove Street, Suite 100
Newport Beach, CA 92660
Telephone: (800) 377-8722
Fax: (714) 975-1940
Marci Rossi, Director of Franchise Sales

Number of Franchisee Units: 55
Number of Company-Owned Units: 0
Number of Total Operating Units: 55

In Business Since: 1979 **Franchising Since:** 1979

Description of Operation: VR Sells More Businesses in the USA than Anyone. Franchises are sold with a money back guarantee. Help buyers to buy and sellers to sell small to mid size businesses in many different industries.

Equity Capital Needed: Approximately $41,150 and up

Franchise Fee: 0

Royalty Fee: 0

Financial Assistance Available: No

Managerial Assistance: Yes. Ongoing support by office visits and telephone. Goal setting, action plan assistance, tracking system implementation are all a part of the ongoing assistance.

Traning Provided: Yes, 2 weeks and 5 phases of detailed training covering the many aspects of business brokerage including pricing a business, strategic targeted marketing, recruiting, servicing the listing, working with buyers, prospecting, etc.

Information Submitted: March 1995

WEDDING GUIDE, THE
44 Union Blvd., # 650
Lakewood, CO 80228
Telephone: (800) 530-8890 (303) 969-8094
Fax: (303) 969-8761
Mr. John Anderson, Vice President

Number of Franchised Units: 36
Number of Company-Owned Units: 2
Number of Total Operating Units: 38

In Business Since: 1985 **Franchising Since:** 1990

Description of Operation: The Wedding Guide is an internationally published bridal magazine, customized for each city and area. We reach over 1,000,000 engaged couples annually at the beginning of their planning and purchasing cycle. This lucrative advertising sales business offers a variety of marketing options, including monthly lists of engaged couples. The franchisor provides a license for exclusive territory, training and complete publishing support services.

Equity Capital Needed: $3,000

Franchise Fee: $10,000 - $30,000

Royalty Fee: 8%

Financial Assistance: $5,400 down and the Company will finance the balance.

Managerial Assistance: The Company handles all production and printing of books. Training is on-going through newsletters, 800#s and meetings.

Training Provided: We offer 1 week of training at the home office. Manuals, supplies, sales and business practices are covered in detail.

Information Submitted: March 1994

WEDDING PAGES, THE
11106 Mockingbird Dr.
Omaha, NE 68137
Telephone: (800) 843-4983 (402) 331-7755
Fax: (402) 331-2887
Mr. Doug S. Russell, Vice President of Marketing

Number of Franchised Units: 58
Number of Company-Owned Units: 28
Number of Total Operating Units: 86

In Business Since: 1982 **Franchising Since:** 1985

Description of Operation: Complete data base marketing system for wedding professionals to solicit business from brides and grooms. The system includes an ad and a mailing list.

Equity Capital Needed: $30,000 - $35,000

Franchise Fee: $15,000

Royalty Fee: 10%

Financial Assistance: Not available.

Managerial Assistance: We provide 2 1/2 days of in-house training and 2 1/2 days of field training, plus on-going assistance with a toll-free number, conventions and field visits.

Training Provided: Same as above.

Information Submitted: November 1993

WELCOME HOST OF AMERICA
13953 Perkins Rd.
Baton Rouge, LA 70810
Telephone: (800) 962-5431 (504) 769-3000
Fax: (504) 751-9039
Ms. Sing VanCleave, Franchise Director

Number of Franchised Units: 5
Number of Company-Owned Units: 2
Number of Total Operating Units: 7

In Business Since: 1987   **Franchising Since:** 1992

Description of Operation: Direct mail welcoming service for new neighbors or residents, parents of new babies and newlyweds.

Equity Capital Needed: $5,000 - $10,000

Franchise Fee: $6,000 - $8,000

Royalty Fee: 6%

Financial Assistance: 50% of franchise fee.

Managerial Assistance: We provide an intensive 5-day training - both classroom and field training. Welcome Host provides a complete operations and sales manual. Computer software is available. 800# for assistance.

Training Provided: Training includes office procedures, packing, mailings, sales and computer training.

Information Submitted: March 1994

WORLD TRADE NETWORK
580 Lincoln Park Blvd., # 255
Dayton, OH 45429
Telephone: (513) 298-3383
Fax: (513) 298-2550
Mr. Michael J. Wenzler, President/Chief Executive Officer

Number of Franchised Units: 17
Number of Company-Owned Units: 1
Number of Total Operating Units: 18

In Business Since: 1983   **Franchising Since:** 1993

Description of Operation: The World Trade Network is the first and only franchise and licensing entity to provide a global strategy linking trading partners worldwide. WTN offers both already established and new traders to the industry, the benefit of other offices to market and source products worldwide. WTN can efficiently represent a company in purchasing direct from foreign manufacturers and marketing directly to foreign distributors and retailers. WTN can provide a total turn-key import and export service.

Equity Capital Needed: $75,000

Franchise Fee: $15,000

Royalty Fee: 7% of gross profits or commissions.

Financial Assistance: Yes.

Managerial Assistance: WTN has produced a training manual, forms, contracts and many sales aids. After our one-week training course, assistance is only a phone call away. Convention seminars and a newsletter have produced help to each office on a continual basis.

Training Provided: An extensive 1-week training program at our home office in Dayton, OH is conducted to show each new office owner typical transactions from beginning to end. Your training for the import/export business includes letters of credit, shipping, documentation agreements, marketing methods and importing, along with many other aspects of the business.

Information Submitted: December 1993

WORLDWIDE INFORMATION SERVICES
P. O. Box 21261
Ft. Lauderdale, FL 33335
Telephone: (305) 764-7942
Mr. W. H. Bonneau, President

Number of Franchised Units: 6
Number of Company-Owned Units: 1
Number of Total Operating Units: 7

In Business Since: 1992   **Franchising Since:** 1993

Description of Operation: We offer consumer and business credit information from all credit bureaus, Social Security number tracing and verification, nationwide Kriss-Cross, referencing names and phone numbers, driving record and motor vehicle information, criminal history, death records, real property asset searches, professional license verification, worker compensation claims, employment and earning search, plus many other information searches. Skip tracing is our specialty, along with pre-employment screenings.

Equity Capital Needed: $4,995 - $9,995

Franchise Fee: $4,995

Royalty Fee: Data not available.

Financial Assistance: None.

Managerial Assistance: All services are provided by Worldwide Information Services via fax machines. We provide the proper legal and ethical techniques that are required to enjoy success and profitability.

Training Provided: Via mail, phone and fax, we provide training in direct mail and other advertising and marketing techniques that are needed to establish the client base.

Information Submitted: March 1994

X-BANKERS CHECK CASHING
809 Chapel St.
New Haven, CT 06510
Telephone: (800) 873-9226 (203) 495-8564
Fax: (203) 773-0418
Mr. Robert A. Swift, Jr., President

Number of Franchised Units: 3
Number of Company-Owned Units: 0
Number of Total Operating Units: 3

In Business Since: 1992   **Franchising Since:** 1992

Description of Operation: Check cashing and financial services. The primary business is check cashing, but other services, such as money wiring, money orders, tax preparation, photo ID's, fax, notary, photocopying and other services, are offered.

Equity Capital Needed: $83,500 - $97,900

Franchise Fee: $9,500

Royalty Fee: 3%, or $250 per month minimum.

Financial Assistance: None.

Managerial Assistance: Bookkeeping, advertising, marketing and supervisory skills training, as well as regulatory compliance training.

Training Provided: We provide 1 week of on-site training and 1 week at corporate headquarters, plus training manuals, construction specifications, design and decor specifications and daily operations training.

Information Submitted: November 1993

YELLOW JACKET DIRECT MAIL ADVERTISING
23101 Moulton Pkwy., # 110
Laguna Hills, CA 92653
Telephone: (800) 8-YELLOW (714) 951-9500
Fax: (714) 589-0899
Mr. Robert Philpott, Franchise Sales

Number of Franchised Units: 15
Number of Company-Owned Units: 0
Number of Total Operating Units: 15

In Business Since: 1988   **Franchising Since:** 1990

Description of Operation: Yellow Jacket Direct Mail Advertising sells franchises on a national level, with master franchises available. Yellow Jacket is a fast-growing franchise opportunity. It offers business owners a proven method of advertising that significantly improves their sales and profits. Complete production support, artwork, printing and mailing through the US mail is provided.

Equity Capital Needed: $17,000 - $26,000

Franchise Fee: $10,000 - $19,000

Royalty Fee: 6%

Financial Assistance: Financial assistance is available, depending upon the applicant's qualifications.

Managerial Assistance: We produce training manuals, sales aids and all applicable forms.

Training Provided: A complete 3-week training program includes classroom as well as field training. On-going field training support is also provided.

Information Submitted: March 1994

CAMPGROUNDS

KAMPGROUNDS OF AMERICA / KOA
550 N. 31st TWIII, P. O. Box 30558
Billings, MT 59114
Telephone: (800) 548-7239 (406) 248-7444
Fax: (406) 248-7414
Mr. David W. Johnson, Vice President of Licensing

Number of Franchised Units: 543
Number of Company-Owned Units: 11
Number of Total Operating Units: 554

In Business Since: 1961   **Franchising Since:** 1962

Description of Operation: Franchisor of campgrounds.

Equity Capital Needed: $85,000 minimum.

Franchise Fee: $20,000

Royalty Fee: 10% of campsite rental income.

Financial Assistance: None.

Managerial Assistance: Management schools, regional meetings, convention (annual) and consultants.

Training Provided: Orientation school, plus management schools, regional meeting, convention and consultants.

Information Submitted: December 1993

YOGI BEAR JELLYSTONE PARK CAMP/RESORTS
6201 Kellogg Ave.
Cincinnati, OH 45228

Telephone: (800) 626-3720 (513) 232-6800
Fax: (513) 231-1191
Mr. Robert E. Schutter, Jr., Vice President/General Manager

Number of Franchised Units: 73
Number of Company-Owned Units: 0
Number of Total Operating Units: 73

In Business Since: 1969   **Franchising Since:** 1970

Description of Operation: Leisure Systems, Inc. holds an exclusive license to franchise Yogi Bear's Jellystone Park Camp/Resorts in the US and Canada. Presently, there are 70 units in the US and 3 in Canada.

Equity Capital Needed: $28,000 +

Franchise Fee: $18,000

Royalty Fee: 6% operating and 1% advertising.

Financial Assistance: New franchisees are required to pay $7,000 of the franchise fee at the time of signing and the remaining $11,000 at the end of their first operating season.

Managerial Assistance: Leisure Systems, Inc. provides assistance in the areas of merchandising, accounting, operations and marketing. Operating manuals, forms and seminars are also provided. An annual symposium is conducted, centering on topics relevant to operations.

Training Provided: New franchisees are required to attend a 5-day training program held at the home office in Cincinnati, OH. Additional on-site training is also conducted for a period of 2 - 3 days.

Information Submitted: November 1993

CHILDRENS PRODUCTS AND SERVICES

A CHOICE NANNY
8950 Rte. 108, # 217
Columbia, MD 21045
Telephone: (800) 73-NANNY (410) 730-2356
Fax: (410) 964-5726
Ms. Jacqueline F. Clark, President

Number of Franchised Units: 14
Number of Company-Owned Units: 1
Number of Total Operating Units: 15

In Business Since: 1983   **Franchising Since:** 1989

Description of Operation: Nanny referral service. Computer-based. Quality training and background checking.

Equity Capital Needed: $12,000 - $50,000

Franchise Fee: $24,900

Royalty Fee: 6% - 10%

Financial Assistance: Financial assistance on resales. 25% cash down, balance financed.

Managerial Assistance: Help with lease negotiation, site selection, marketing, budgeting, recruiting, training, computer training and support.

Training Provided: 1-1/2 weeks of hands-on training at franchise headquarters, plus 1 - 2 days of additional training at franchise office. Help with business plan.

Information Submitted: March 1994

BABIES FIRST DIAPER SERVICE
5273 Hanson Ct.
Minneapolis, MN 55429
Telephone: (612) 533-1616
Fax: (612) 533-5915
Mr. James Dunlop, Vice President of Franchise Development

Number of Franchised Units: 1
Number of Company-Owned Units: 2
Number of Total Operating Units: 3

In Business Since: 1990   **Franchising Since:** 1991

Description of Operation: A home pickup and delivery service of laundered diapers for infants or incontinent adults. Markets of over 300,000 population may require laundry processing facilities as part of franchising package.

Equity Capital Needed: $90,000 - $300,000

Franchise Fee: $10,000 - $55,000

Royalty Fee: 6%

Financial Assistance: Not available at this time.

Managerial Assistance: Complete and on-going.

Training Provided: Complete in all phases and on-going as required.

Information Submitted: January 1994

BABY NEWS CHILDRENS STORES
23521 Foley St.
Hayward, CA 94545
Telephone: (510) 786-3460
Fax: (510) 785-1580
Mr. Roger O'Callaghan, President

Number of Franchised Units: 42
Number of Company-Owned Units: 1
Number of Total Operating Units: 43

In Business Since: 1962   **Franchising Since:** 1962

Description of Operation: Complete children's store, carrying juvenile furniture, clothing, pre-school toys, accessories and safety equipment.

Equity Capital Needed: $150,000

Franchise Fee: $15,000

Royalty Fee: 1% or $700 per month.

Financial Assistance: We will assist with paperwork and budgets to submit to lending institutions.

Managerial Assistance: We have a distribution center in Hayward, CA available to all stores.

Training Provided: Have continual training available. Recommend a minimum of 2 weeks.

Information Submitted: December 1993

BABY TOWN
7030 W. 105th St.
Overland Park, KS 66212
Telephone: (913) 649-8136
Fax: (913) 341-7263
Mr. Desmond Brivik, President

Number of Franchised Units: 0
Number of Company-Owned Units: 1
Number of Total Operating Units: 1

In Business Since: 1991   **Franchising Since:** 1993

Description of Operation: Complete baby and toddler retail store.

Equity Capital Needed: $100,000 - $200,000

Franchise Fee: $15,000

Royalty Fee: 3%

Financial Assistance: None.

Managerial Assistance: Support starts with the training program at the national headquarters and continues with on-site training. On-going support is just a telephone call away with the Baby Town USA support line. Franchise owners can talk to experts in inventory, marketing or business management. Also, representatives make periodic visits to assist the franchisee and to provide updates on new products.

Training Provided: Same as above.

Information Submitted: February 1994

CHILDREN'S ORCHARD
315 E. Eisenhower Pkwy., # 316
Ann Arbor, MI 48108
Telephone: (800) 999-KIDS (313) 994-9199
Fax: (313) 994-9323
Mr. Walter F. Hamilton, Jr., President

Number of Franchised Units: 54
Number of Company-Owned Units: 1
Number of Total Operating Units: 55

In Business Since: 1980   **Franchising Since:** 1985

Description of Operation: Up-scale children's products resale boutiques and large stores. These stores also feature brand new products. Children's Orchard emphasizes comprehensive training and franchisee support services. Locations from Maine to Hawaii.

Equity Capital Needed: $52,000 - $80,000

Franchise Fee: $14,500 - $19,500

Royalty Fee: Declining scale, starting at 6%.

Financial Assistance: We assist with SBA or other business financing.

Managerial Assistance: We provide regular shop evaluations, hotline, newsletters, individualized business consulting, management seminar by mail, published and custom statistical performance analysis.

Training Provided: We offer 2 weeks of basic training, all aspects of business system, general management and in-store practice. 5 or more additional days of on-site training includes grand opening assistance.

Information Submitted: November 1993

EXPLORATIONS
2650 N. Military Trail, # 140
Boca Raton, FL 33431
Telephone: (800) 55-SAMMY (407) 998-3435
Fax: (407) 998-3425
Mr. Fred C. Kriss, Chief Operating Officer

Number of Franchised Units: 8
Number of Company-Owned Units: 1
Number of Total Operating Units: 9

In Business Since: 1992   **Franchising Since:** 1993

Description of Operation: Explorations is a children's fitness and entertainment center. The naturally-themed indoor centers, designed for kids ages 1 - 12, are approximately 15,000 square feet and include proprietary play structures, licensed characters, a full-menu restaurant, birthday party rooms, adult and kiddie lounges, an electronic gameroom and a kiddie ride area.

Equity Capital Needed: $275,000 - $760,000

Franchise Fee: $30,000

Royalty Fee: 5%

Financial Assistance: We assist in the preparation of business plan.

Managerial Assistance: We provide full on-going support.

Training Provided: Training includes 2 weeks at headquarters and 1 week in store.

Information Submitted: February 1994

FUTUREKIDS
5777 W. Century Blvd., # 1555
Los Angeles, CA 90045

Telephone: (800) 765-8000 (310) 337-7006
Fax: (310) 337-0803
Mr. Jay Gillogly, Senior Vice President of Franchise Development

Number of Franchised Units: 305
Number of Company-Owned Units: 0
Number of Total Operating Units: 305

In Business Since: 1983   **Franchising Since:** 1989

Description of Operation: FutureKids, a privately-held company, is the world's largest chain of computer learning centers for children ages 3 - 13. Currently operating over 300 centers domestically and in 24 countries internationally, FutureKids' mission is to prepare young children for the future, where success will depend on the ability to work well with technology.

Equity Capital Needed: $64,000 - $89,400

Franchise Fee: $25,000

Royalty Fee: 10% + $360 per month.

Financial Assistance: None.

Managerial Assistance: Assigned regional managers offer field support and continuous support through telephone and computer network communications. Corporate newsletters, field seminars, annual convention and franchisee-lead committees lend sufficient assistance to all.

Training Provided: Training at FutureKids involves an extensive 2-week course at corporate headquarters in Los Angeles, CA, followed by 1 week of field training. On-going educational, technical, marketing and operational materials and telephone and computer network support are readily available and extended as routine corporate procedure.

Information Submitted: December 1993

GYM DANDY FOR TOTS+
3290 Tierney Pl.
New York, NY 10465
Telephone: (800) 831-6283 (718) 828-2399
Fax: (718) 828-2399
Ms. Diane Arenholz, President

Number of Franchised Units: 11
Number of Company-Owned Units: 2
Number of Total Operating Units: 13

In Business Since: 1983   **Franchising Since:** 1991

Description of Operation: Parent/child play, arts and crafts and party program. 4 months - 4 years.

Equity Capital Needed: $44,000 - $55,000

Franchise Fee: $20,000

Royalty Fee: $2,000 per year.

Financial Assistance: Some financing is possible.

Managerial Assistance: On-going support and updating of program. On-going training for franchisees at Company-owned locations.

Training Provided: 2 - 4 weeks of training at fully-operational franchise and classroom training until new franchisee is comfortable.

Information Submitted: November 1993

GYMBOREE
700 Airport Blvd., # 200
Burlingame, CA 94010
Telephone: (415) 579-0600
Fax: (415) 696-7452
Mr. Bob Campbell, Vice President of Franchise Sales

Number of Franchised Units: 409
Number of Company-Owned Units: 5
Number of Total Operating Units: 414

In Business Since: 1976   **Franchising Since:** 1978

Description of Operation: Parent and child participation play program. Specialized equipment, songs and games. Classes offered for children - newborn through 5 years of age.

Equity Capital Needed: $35,000 - $50,000

Franchise Fee: $27,000 for one site.

Royalty Fee: 6%

Financial Assistance: Not available.

Managerial Assistance: Data not available.

Training Provided: 10 days of training at the corporate offices covers all aspects of running a Gymboree program - management, hiring, office, computer and teaching classes. Bi-annual visits from consultants and annual seminar, with updates of business as a whole.

Information Submitted: November 1993

HEAD OVER HEELS
P. O. Box 530005
Birmingham, AL 35253
Telephone: (800) 850-FLIP (205) 879-6305
Fax: (205) 870-7330
Ms. Kim Bradshaw, Director of Franchise Sales

Number of Franchised Units: 2
Number of Company-Owned Units: 1
Number of Total Operating Units: 3

In Business Since: 1990   **Franchising Since:** 1993

Description of Operation: Gymnastics and motor skills development system for children.

Equity Capital Needed: $27,100 - $41,800

Franchise Fee: Aggregate registration fees and first month's tuition fees for each student collected by franchisee.

Royalty Fee: 6% - 10%

Financial Assistance: Financing is available for the initial equipment purchase and the computer software package.

Managerial Assistance: We provide pre-opening and opening assistance, direct assistance in the initial solicitation and development of the contract locations, assistance in purchasing equipment and other supplies, assistance in the establishment of administrative, bookkeeping and accounting procedures, an initial opening kit of forms, brochures and other necessary information and continued field support through monthly updates.

Training Provided: We offer 1 week of instruction and training in the operation of the franchise and continued training in sales, pre-opening and opening procedures in the franchisee's city.

Information Submitted: January 1994

KIDDIE ACADEMY INTERNATIONAL
108 Wheel Rd., # 200
Bel Air, MD 21015
Telephone: (800) 5-KIDDIE (410) 515-0788
Fax: (410) 569-9165
Ms. Britt Schroeter, Director of Franchise Development

Number of Franchised Units: 34
Number of Company-Owned Units: 9
Number of Total Operating Units: 43

In Business Since: 1979   **Franchising Since:** 1981

Description of Operation: Kiddie Academy has been a premier developer of Early Learning Centers since 1979. A strong focus in Northeast, Mid-Atlantic and Midwest areas. Kiddie Academy offers an advanced, tested, state-of-the-art curriculum incorporating traditional development milestones, with emphasis on reading skills, language development and social skills. Classes in computers and foreign languages. Infant through age 12.

Equity Capital Needed: $75,000 - $150,000

Franchise Fee: $20,000

Royalty Fee: 7%

Financial Assistance: Kiddie Academy has identified third-party lenders interested in providing financing to qualified franchisees and will assist in contacting lenders, developing loan packages and preparing business plans.

Managerial Assistance: Comprehensive training and support without additional cost. Kiddie Academy's step-by-step program assists with demographic and competitive surveys, site selection, lease negotiation, staff recruitment, training, licensing, grand-opening, accounting, marketing, advertising and curriculum. A true "turn-key" program that provides full support, so you can focus on running a successful business.

Training Provided: Kiddie Academy provides an intensive 2 weeks of classroom and on-site training for franchise owners in Baltimore, MD. A 1-week training session is provided for your center director, as well as on-site, hands-on training for your complete staff. Kiddie Academy has prepared a complete set of training manuals and understands that on-going support is one of the most important factors in a long and successful partnership.

Information Submitted: December 1993

KIDDIE KOBBLER
68 Robertson Rd., # 106
Nepean, ON K2H 8P5 CAN
Telephone: (800) 561-9762 (613) 820-0505
Fax: (613) 820-0505
Mr. Fred Norman, President

Number of Franchised Units: 35
Number of Company-Owned Units: 0
Number of Total Operating Units: 35

In Business Since: 1951   **Franchising Since:** 1968

Description of Operation: Children's shoe stores, located in major shopping centers. The extensive marketing program is designed to develop new and repeat business through intensive customer service, selection and value.

Equity Capital Needed: $150,000 - $170,000

Franchise Fee: $30,000 +

Royalty Fee: 4%

Financial Assistance: Assistance in the preparation of loan applications and possible SBA financing.

Managerial Assistance: Regular visits by field consultants, operations manual, buying assistance, regular information memos, head office personnel on call for advice, semi-annual franchise meetings, advertising assistance, new product advisory, leasing and store design services.

Training Provided: A minimum 3 months of in-store training with an established franchisee, covering all phases of customer service and record keeping, marketing, ordering, store maintenance, on-site assistance, both before and after grand opening.

Information Submitted: December 1993

KIDS KAB
2701 Troy Center Dr., # 291
Troy, MI 48084
Telephone: (810) 362-8280
Fax: (810) 362-8286
Ms. Heather Babcock, Franchise Licensing Specialist

Number of Franchised Units: 20
Number of Company-Owned Units: 0
Number of Total Operating Units: 20

In Business Since: 1991   **Franchising Since:** 1992

Description of Operation: Children's chartered transportation services.

Equity Capital Needed: $40,000 - $75,000

Franchise Fee: $26,000

Royalty Fee: 5%, plus 2% advertising.

Financial Assistance: Not available.

Managerial Assistance: Same as below.

Training Provided: 5 days of initial training, including marketing, advertising, computer operations, purchasing, accounting and risk management. In addition, on-site driver training and risk management, on-site training and assistance covering other areas of business, as well as continuous telephone support from all personnel.

Information Submitted: January 1994

KIDS' TIME
4 Ravinia Place
Bourbonnais, IL 60914
Telephone: (800) 922-0991 (815) 933-9091
Fax: (815) 937-1442
Mr. Greg Morse, President/Chief Executive Officer

Number of Franchised Units: 8
Number of Company-Owned Units: 2
Number of Total Operating Units: 10

In Business Since: 1981   **Franchising Since:** 1989

Description of Operation: Supervised play centers for kids ages 2 - 10 years. Parents drop off children for a maximum stay of 5 hours and pay an hourly fee per child. We provide pagers to parents when they leave the center.

Equity Capital Needed: $89,500 - $119,500

Franchise Fee: $19,500

Royalty Fee: 5%

Financial Assistance: We direct franchisees to financing source. We work with many lenders that will qualify and direct individuals to the proper source.

Managerial Assistance: We assign a franchise coordinator to each franchisee. Franchisees work with the coordinator on an on-going basis, as well as with our operations and management manuals.

Training Provided: 1 week of classroom training is included in the franchise fee. 1 week of on-site training is also provided. Training covers computer program, daily operations, marketing and employee relations.

Information Submitted: January 1994

KINDERDANCE INTERNATIONAL
268 N. Babcock St., # A
Melbourne, FL 32935
Telephone: (800) 666-1595 (407) 254-0590
Fax: (407) 254-3388
Mr. Bernard Friedman, Vice President

Number of Franchised Units: 68
Number of Company-Owned Units: 0
Number of Total Operating Units: 68

In Business Since: 1979   **Franchising Since:** 1985

Description of Operation: You don't have to be a dancer to be a Kinderdance franchisee. If you enjoy children and have high energy, you can qualify to join the nation's leader in quality pre-school education through dance, gymnastics and creative movement. No studio required. Our program has been taught to thousands of children in hundreds of child-care centers since 1979. Enjoy flexible hours, fulfilling work and adorable customers. Rated one of the top 15 franchises for women by Working Woman Magazine.

Equity Capital Needed: $4,000 - $6,000

Franchise Fee: $8,000 - $12,000

Royalty Fee: 10% - 15%

Financial Assistance: Kinderdance will finance (in-house) up to 50% of the initial franchise fee.

Managerial Assistance: We provide perpetual assistance, as needed, an 800# hotline available 24-hours a day, an operations manual, newsletters and active franchisee advisory counsel.

Training Provided: We offer an initial 7-day training session at the home office in Melbourne, FL. Follow-up on-site training within 90 days of start-up. Annual conferences (updated training material) are held at various locations in the US.

Information Submitted: November 1993

LITTLE GYM INTERNATIONAL, THE
150 Lake St. S., # 210
Kirkland, WA 98033
Telephone: (800) 352-4588 (206) 889-4588
Fax: (206) 828-0661
Mr. Tom Reid, National Sales Manager

Number of Franchised Units: 50
Number of Company-Owned Units: 0
Number of Total Operating Units: 50

In Business Since: 1992   **Franchising Since:** 1992

Description of Operation: Little Gym Fitness Centers for children offer a unique, integrated approach to child development. Our non-competitive classes are filled with fun and music, with instruction created especially for different age groups. Kids get a fun start on lifetime habits of fitness at the Little Gym.

Equity Capital Needed: $56,500 - $77,000

Franchise Fee: $27,500

Royalty Fee: 8%

Financial Assistance: None.

Managerial Assistance: W. Berry Fowler (Chmn. and CEO) founded Sylvan Learning Centers to offer individualized diagnostic testing and prescriptive basic skills to children and adults. Robin Wes (Founder and Vice Chmn.) founded the Little Gym 17 years ago and combined his years of experience as a physical education specialist, teacher and accomplished composer and musician. W. S. Butch Garrison (President and CEO) served as VP of Business Development for Sylvan Learning Centers.

Training Provided: The owner and key staff members attend a 2-week training program held at our corporate offices. Curriculum, program management, business systems and team building are covered. On-going training, seminars and workshops keep the franchisee on the leading edge of a dynamic business.

Information Submitted: December 1993

MISS LITTLE AMERICA
P. O. Box 1031
Jefner, FL 33584
Telephone: (813) 689-4308
Ms. Olga Knight, General Director

Number of Franchised Units: 1
Number of Company-Owned Units: 0
Number of Total Operating Units: 1

In Business Since: 1980   **Franchising Since:** 1992

Description of Operation: Beauty contest for children from infant - 18 years of age.

Equity Capital Needed: $6,000 maximum.

Franchise Fee: $3,900

Royalty Fee: 25% of net or $180 per month.

Financial Assistance: None.

Managerial Assistance: Data not available.

Training Provided: Training includes overseeing 2 beauty pageants arranged by the franchisee. A regional director will help and participate.

Information Submitted: January 1994

PEE WEE WORKOUT
34976 Aspenwood Ln.
Willoughby, OH 44094
Telephone: (800) 356-6261 (216) 946-7888
Ms. Margaret J. Carr, President

Number of Franchised Units: 27
Number of Company-Owned Units: 1
Number of Total Operating Units: 28

In Business Since: 1986   **Franchising Since:** 1987

Description of Operation: Fitness programs for children.

Equity Capital Needed: $2,000

Franchise Fee: $1,500

Royalty Fee: 10%

Financial Assistance: None.

Managerial Assistance: Marketing and administrative guidelines, toll-free hotline support and curriculum development for programming and nutrition.

Training Provided: Video-based training for all curricula.

Information Submitted: December 1993

PRE-FIT
10340 S. Western Ave.
Chicago, IL 60643
Telephone: (312) 233-7771
Fax: (708) 339-0302
Ms. Latrice Lee, Franchise Director

Number of Franchised Units: 19
Number of Company-Owned Units: 1
Number of Total Operating Units: 20

In Business Since: 1987   **Franchising Since:** 1992

Description of Operation: Pre-Fit is an Illinois-based franchise company that grants rights, trains, advises and assists franchisees in the establishment and operation of a pre-school fitness program known as PreFit. Our franchise business is a service engaged in teaching physical education classes to children 2 - 6 years. Our success-oriented sports and exercise program has been accepted as an elemental part of pre-school education. We are committed to the success of each and every franchisee.

Equity Capital Needed: $6,000 - $9,000

Franchise Fee: $500

Royalty Fee: 10%

Financial Assistance: Data not available.

Managerial Assistance: Our managerial training begins with our Franchisee Handbook of procedures and forms and continues with our Marketing Booklet and Instructor's Guide. All franchisees are provided with newsletters and health reports to help keep them abreast of educational trends and ideas. In addition, each franchisee is given detailed instructions for financial record keeping and personnel management.

Training Provided: All franchisees come into Chicago for a weekend training session. During this training session, each franchisee receives uniforms and a gym bag carrying the Pre-Fit logo, instructional training, lesson plans, workout routines, marketing tools, bookkeeping materials, start-up class equipment and an exclusive territory. Following this initial training, continuous training is provided through monthly video tapes, newsletters and an 800# for technical, teaching, marketing and motivational support.

Information Submitted: December 1993

PRIMROSE SCHOOLS
199 S. Erwin St.
Cartersville, GA 30120
Telephone: (800) 745-0728 (404) 606-9600
Fax: (404) 606-0020
Ms. Jo Kirchner, Executive Vice President

Number of Franchised Units: 21
Number of Company-Owned Units: 1
Number of Total Operating Units: 22

In Business Since: 1982   **Franchising Since:** 1988

Description of Operation: Quality educational childcare, with proven, traditional curriculum for infants through 4/5 kindergarten, after-school explorers club ages 5 - 12 years, Spanish, computer inter-generational program and strong parental communication. Programs develop positive self-esteem and a joy of learning.

Equity Capital Needed: $100,000 - $150,000

Franchise Fee: $48,500

Royalty Fee: 7%

Financial Assistance: Referral to consultants.

Managerial Assistance: Data not available.

Training Provided: We provide 2 weeks of corporate training and 1 week of on-site pre-opening support, 4 months of detailed, pre-opening operations and marketing plans monitored by management staff. Strong operations, programming and marketing support on-going after opening.

Information Submitted: February 1994

TEAM KIDS
8466 Colorado St.
Merrilville, IN 46410
Telephone: (800) 875-5439 (219) 942-2055
Fax: (219) 947-4507
Mr. Kevin Schmidt, President

Number of Franchised Units: 0
Number of Company-Owned Units: 3
Number of Total Operating Units: 3

In Business Since: 1972   **Franchising Since:** 1993

Description of Operation: Retailer of children's licensed products, featuring team logos of professional and collegiate apparel and novelty items. Girls' and boys' styles range from infant sizes to youth size 20.

Equity Capital Needed: $74,000 - $112,000

Franchise Fee: $20,000

Royalty Fee: 4%

Financial Assistance: Assistance with SBA programs is available.

Managerial Assistance: In addition to its operations manuals, Team Kids provides on-going assistance, as needed.

Training Provided: A 2-week training program is provided, which includes store operations, purchasing, merchandising, customer service, advertising and financial management. After a store is opened, the franchisee may phone the franchisor during business hours with questions. On-site visits are available at the franchisee's request.

Information Submitted: November 1993

TODDLIN' TIME
8084 Station Rd.
Manassas, VA 22111

Telephone: (703) 361-2945
Fax: (703) 361-2945
Ms. Tanya T. Wallace, President

Number of Franchised Units: 9
Number of Company-Owned Units: 0
Number of Total Operating Units: 9

In Business Since: 1991   **Franchising Since:** 1992

Description of Operation: A unique combination of exciting, colorful equipment and songs, games and activities. Weekly themes bring parents and their children together just for fun. A parent/toddler play-gym of the finest kind.

Equity Capital Needed: $3,500 - $5,000

Franchise Fee: $5,000

Royalty Fee: $450 annually.

Financial Assistance: We help provide assistance in obtaining start-up capital, offering suggestions that will enable the franchisee to become debt-free in a short period of time.

Managerial Assistance: Toddlin' Time operates 6 days a week, providing franchisees with help, feedback and assistance in maintaining a successful center. On-site visits, annual meetings and other means of communication are used often.

Training Provided: Toddlin' Time works diligently with franchisees as soon as the document signing is complete. A step-by-step procedures manual, as well as personalized assistance, is provided. A franchisee makes the decision as to when he or she is ready to operate on his/her own.

Information Submitted: November 1993

USA BABY
752 N. Larch Ave.
Elmhurst, IL 60126
Telephone: (800) 323-4108 (708) 832-9880
Fax: (708) 832-0139
Mr. Todd Levine, Franchise Coordinator

Number of Franchised Units: 42
Number of Company-Owned Units: 8
Number of Total Operating Units: 50

In Business Since: 1975   **Franchising Since:** 1986

Description of Operation: USA Baby is America's #1 chain of infant and juvenile furniture and accessories stores. Our stores offer one-stop shopping for parents and parents-to-be for all their babies' needs.

Equity Capital Needed: $75,000 - $150,000

Franchise Fee: $7,500 - $16,500

Royalty Fee: 3%

Financial Assistance: None.

Managerial Assistance: USA Baby offers assistance in site selection and lease negotiation, along with complete store layout plans. We provide owners with an operations manual, training manual, weekly newsletter and semi-annual owner's meetings.

Training Provided: We offer a 2-week training program at corporate offices and in-store training at opening.

Information Submitted: November 1993

WEE WATCH PRIVATE HOME DAY CARE
105 Main St.
Unionville, ON L3R 2G1 CAN
Telephone: (905) 479-4274
Fax: (905) 479-9047
Mr. Terry Fullerton, Vice President

Number of Franchised Units: 40
Number of Company-Owned Units: 0
Number of Total Operating Units: 40

In Business Since: 1984   **Franchising Since:** 1987

Description of Operation: Private home day-care agency, where a franchisee recruits, trains and supervises women to do day-care in their own homes. Parents needing care contact the agency for placement. A full day-care program is in place.

Equity Capital Needed: $15,000

Franchise Fee: $6,000

Royalty Fee: 8%

Financial Assistance: Not available.

Managerial Assistance: Complete manuals, field visits, convention, on-going training seminars and advertising campaigns are provided.

Training Provided: We offer 1 week at the home office and 3 days on-site.

Information Submitted: March 1994

CLEANING AND SANITATION

A-PRO SERVICES
P. O. Box 132, Harding Hwy.
Newfield, NJ 08344
Telephone: (800) 467-2776 (609) 697-1000
Fax: (609) 694-4433
Mr. Charles A. Simpson, President

Number of Franchised Units: 6
Number of Company-Owned Units: 1
Number of Total Operating Units: 7

In Business Since: 1987   **Franchising Since:** 1992

Description of Operation: A-Pro Services introduces you into a multi-billion dollar service industry with multiple profit centers, including carpet and upholstery dyeing/cleaning, tinting, fiber protection, carpet repair, flood/water restorations, odor control/removal and shop-at-home floor covering sales and installations. This home-based business offers a protected market area, on-going training and support, plus 0% financing if qualified. Call for a complete information package.

Equity Capital Needed: $6,000 - $7,000 ($10,700 total start-up).

Franchise Fee: $7,000

Royalty Fee: $200 per month.

Financial Assistance: The $7,000 franchise fee is payable as follows: down payment of $2,650, plus payments of $75 per month beginning with 3rd full month of business. The balance of $4,350 is financed by A-Pro Services at 0% interest.

Managerial Assistance: Each new franchisee is assigned his/her own personal marketing director to work individually with each franchisee to meet and achieve his/her own personal goals. Assistance is on-going in the start-up and building of the business. Periodic newsletters, 800# support line and updates readily available.

Training Provided: 5 days at our corporate center in Newfield, NJ. Training consists of video, classroom, on-the-job training, as well as office management, etc.

Information Submitted: December 1993

AEROWEST/WESTAIR SANITATION SERVICES
3882 Del Amo Blvd.
Torrance, CA 90503
Telephone: (310) 793-4242
Fax: (310) 793-2450
Mr. Graham H. Emery, President

Number of Franchised Units: 25
Number of Company-Owned Units: 0
Number of Total Operating Units: 25

In Business Since: 1984   **Franchising Since:** 1980

Description of Operation: Aerowest and Westair odor control and sanitation services for industrial and commercial washrooms.

Equity Capital Needed: $3,000 - $12,000

Franchise Fee: $2,000

Royalty Fee: Varies.

Financial Assistance: Up to 80% of any development fee may be financed with an interest rate of 10%, extending for up to a maximum term of 5 years. Financing for the franchise fee is not available.

Managerial Assistance: All administrative work is done by franchisor. This includes billing, collections, account tickets, report forms and various other service forms.

Training Provided: The franchisor provides franchisee with sales and service training conducted at a location designated by franchisor for a maximum of 2 weeks. Training is centered near residence of franchisee and at each of the franchisee's customers in order to instruct the trainee in the service work required. Follow-up training visits are conducted in subsequent months.

Information Submitted: February 1994

AIRE-MASTER OF AMERICA
P. O. Box 2310, Hwy. CC
Nixa, MO 65714
Telephone: (417) 725-2691
Fax: (417) 725-5737
Mr. Dave Burton, Franchise Director

Number of Franchised Units: 53
Number of Company-Owned Units: 5
Number of Total Operating Units: 58

In Business Since: 1958   **Franchising Since:** 1975

Description of Operation: Room deodorizing, restroom deodorizing and disinfecting service.

Equity Capital Needed: $25,000 - $75,000

Franchise Fee: $15,000

Royalty Fee: 5%

Financial Assistance: 50% of franchise fee to qualified applicants.

Managerial Assistance: Included with 5 days of in-house training.

Training Provided: An extensive 10-day training program - 5 days in-house and 5 days in territory.

Information Submitted: November 1993

AL-VIN SIDING CLEANING
1233 Main St., # 301
Buffalo, NY 14209
Telephone: (716) 883-2103
Mr. Keith Schaefer, President

Number of Franchised Units: 33
Number of Company-Owned Units: 1
Number of Total Operating Units: 34

In Business Since: 1987   **Franchising Since:** 1987

Description of Operation: Cleaning the exterior of homes and offices, etc., the franchisee will be supplied with a "turn-key" operation.

Equity Capital Needed: $15,000 - $25,000

Franchise Fee: $15,000

Royalty Fee: $1,000 - $2,000 per unit.

Financial Assistance: Data not available.

Managerial Assistance: You will receive 3 - 4 days of on-site training.

Training Provided: You will receive 3 - 4 days of on-site training.

Information Submitted: January 1994

AMERICAN ENTERPRISES
P. O. Box 2374
Kailua-Kona, HI 96745
Telephone: (800) 247-3001 (808) 329-2001
Mr. Ray E. Dille, President

Number of Franchised Units: 0
Number of Company-Owned Units: 1
Number of Total Operating Units: 1

In Business Since: 1985   **Franchising Since:** 1985

Description of Operation: A unique carpet and upholstery cleaning system. By using our very own (and basically the only chemical used), Rinse Out, an operator can remove 100% of almost any stain, as well as all shampoo and residue build-up. Thermal Rinse cleaning systems have been endorsed by major hotels, restaurants and real estate companies as the world's best cleaning system on the market, for reasons too numerous to count.

Equity Capital Needed: $5,000

Franchise Fee: $14,500

Royalty Fee: 8%

Financial Assistance: All equipment (carpet cleaning tools and machines) will be leased.

Managerial Assistance: 2 days in class. Perpetual assistance, as needed.

Training Provided: 1 week of on-the-job training at Company office. 2 weeks of field training in franchisee's local area.

Information Submitted: March 1994

AMERICAN LEAK DETECTION
888 Research Dr.,# 109
Palm Springs, CA 92262
Telephone: (800) 755-6697 (619) 320-9991
Fax: (619) 320-1288
Mr. Jim Tennell, Marketing Director

Number of Franchised Units: 166
Number of Company-Owned Units: 1
Number of Total Operating Units: 167

In Business Since: 1974   **Franchising Since:** 1985

Description of Operation: Pinpoint detection of water or sewer leaks under concrete slabs of homes, pools, spas, fountains, commercial buildings, etc., with electronic equipment manufactured by the Company.

Equity Capital Needed: $65,000

Franchise Fee: $29,500 +

Royalty Fee: 8% - 10%

Financial Assistance: Financing is available on approved credit for up to 50% of the franchise fee.

Managerial Assistance: Advertising, data processing, directory assistance, field technical consultant visitations, publicity, business group insurance and trade show booths.

Training Provided: 6 weeks of technical, hands-on training at corporate office in Palm Springs, CA, including marketing and sales training. On-going technical assistance available as needed to current and new franchisees. Annual convention to exchange and share technology and skills.

Information Submitted: December 1993

AMERICARE SERVICES
P. O. Box 2004
Elmhurst, IL 60126
Telephone: (800) 745-6191 (708) 595-6200
Mr. Michael Bruce, Vice President of Finance

Number of Franchised Units: 3
Number of Company-Owned Units: 7
Number of Total Operating Units: 10

In Business Since: 1991   **Franchising Since:** 1993

Description of Operation: Restroom sanitation, hygienic services, order control and janitorial supplies.

Equity Capital Needed: $4,750 - $24,000

Franchise Fee: $9,500

Royalty Fee: 30%

Financial Assistance: At our option, half the franchise fee may be financed.

Managerial Assistance: We basically do all office functions, including accounts receivable, weekly routes, scheduling and providing supplies.

Training Provided: 2 weeks of training, including how to run routes, sales and office procedures.

Information Submitted: January 1994

AMERICLEAN
6602 S. Frontage Rd.
Billings, MT 59101
Telephone: (800) 827-9111 (406) 652-1960
Fax: (406) 652-7710
Mr. Robert Pearson, President

Number of Franchised Units: 21
Number of Company-Owned Units: 1
Number of Total Operating Units: 22

In Business Since: 1979   **Franchising Since:** 1979

Description of Operation: Disaster restoration services and specialty cleaning.

Equity Capital Needed: $28,000 - $124,000

Franchise Fee: $15,000 - $45,000

Royalty Fee: 8.5% or less as volume grows.

Financial Assistance: Assistance with securing financing through third parties.

Managerial Assistance: 2 weeks of classroom and in-field training, plus installation and opening support. Operations manuals, support staff visits and toll-free support line. Certified restorer on staff.

Training Provided: Same as above.

Information Submitted: March 1994

BUCK-A-STALL PARKING LOT PAINTING
P. O. Box 1156
Madison, TN 37116
Telephone: (800) 321-BUCK (615) 824-2825
Fax: (615) 824-2825
Mr. Jim Shafer, President

Number of Franchised Units: 10
Number of Company-Owned Units: 1
Number of Total Operating Units: 11

In Business Since: 1988   **Franchising Since:** 1988

Description of Operation: Parking lot and factory floor paint marking.

Equity Capital Needed: $4,000

Franchise Fee: $3,999

Royalty Fee: 5%

Financial Assistance: As needed. Conversion franchise is $999.

Managerial Assistance: We will work with new franchisee at his/her location or ours.

Training Provided: Same as above, as needed.

Information Submitted: January 1994

BUDGET PEST CONTROL
One Parker Pl., Rt. 2, Box 37
Ponca City, OK 74604
Telephone: (800) 364-5739 (316) 522-3800
Fax: (405) 765-4613
Mr. J. Brad Parker, President

Number of Franchised Units: 5
Number of Company-Owned Units: 6
Number of Total Operating Units: 11

In Business Since: 1980   **Franchising Since:** 1981

Description of Operation: Residential and commercial pest control business, utilizing patented P.E.S.T. machine, along with proven marketing and management techniques.

Equity Capital Needed: $35,000 - $70,000

Franchise Fee: $25,000

Royalty Fee: 8% - first $100,000; 6% - second $100,000; 4% - third $100,000.

Financial Assistance: None.

Managerial Assistance: Can share mainframe computer system. On-site assistance and phone assistance.

Training Provided: 5 - 8 days of initial training in Ponca City, OK. Approximately 15 days of field training, then continuous, on-going training on-site and at corporate headquarters training facility.

Information Submitted: November 1993

BUILDING SERVICES OF AMERICA
36 S. State St., # 1200
Salt Lake City, UT 84111
Telephone: (800) 272-2741 (801) 364-3300
Fax: (801) 364-3322
Mr. Michael Jenkins, President

Number of Franchised Units: 2
Number of Company-Owned Units: 1
Number of Total Operating Units: 3

In Business Since: 1986   **Franchising Since:** 1990

Description of Operation: Building Services of America's "white glove" professional contract cleaning master franchise obtains janitorial contract accounts and business and provides these to associate franchisees that he/she sells. The master franchisee receives franchise fees, royalty fees, management fees, finder's fees, etc. from these associate franchises.

Equity Capital Needed: $15,000 - $50,000

Franchise Fee: $15,000

Royalty Fee: 4%

Financial Assistance: Because we have a low franchise fee, there is no financing available.

Managerial Assistance: The franchisor will support the franchisee by sending up-dated material pertaining to the franchisee's business. There will be a toll-free number for any questions the franchisee might have.

Training Provided: There will be a 2-week training program in a designated area by the franchisor and a 1-week training program in the franchisee's area. Training will include all aspects of running a Building Services of America master franchise, including both classroom and hands-on experience.

Information Submitted: November 1993

CEILING DOCTOR
5151 Beltline Rd., # 950
Dallas, TX 75240
Telephone: (214) 702-8046
Fax: (214) 702-9466
Mr. Jerry Sheaks, President

Number of Franchised Units: 118
Number of Company-Owned Units: 2
Number of Total Operating Units: 120

In Business Since: 1984   **Franchising Since:** 1986

Description of Operation: Industrial and commercial cleaning and restoration of ceiling and other specialty surfaces, both interior and exterior.

Equity Capital Needed: $25,000

Franchise Fee: $12,500

Royalty Fee: 8%, plus 2% national advertising.

Financial Assistance: Third-party financial assistance is available for the entire franchise fee and start-up package requirement, based on the credit history and assets of the new franchise prospect.

Managerial Assistance: 2 of the 7 days of training are spent in franchise business start-up - time management, account identification, telemarketing and sales. Monthly newsletters with "how to" tips and successes from organization.

Training Provided: Training is 7 days. We combine 1/3rd of the time in business set-up and management, along with 1/3rd in account development and 1/3rd in technical aspects and on-site, hands-on training.

Information Submitted: November 1993

CHEM-DRY CARPET, DRAPERY & UPHOLSTERY
451 North 1000 West
Logan, UT 84321
Telephone: (800) CHEM-DRY (801) 755-0099
Fax: (801) 755-0021
Mr. Mark S. Coon, National Franchise Director

Number of Franchised Units: 3547
Number of Company-Owned Units: 1
Number of Total Operating Units: 3548

In Business Since: 1977   **Franchising Since:** 1978

Description of Operation: Chem-Dry franchisees specialize in the care of carpet, drapery, upholstery and most fabrics. Our patented cleaner, The Natural, is 100% natural, removes almost all stains, is safe, non-toxic and dries within an hour. We also specialize in the removal of red dyes, pet stains and pet odors. With our various patented products, Chem-Dry franchisees can take out almost any stain their customer has.

Equity Capital Needed: $4,950 down.

Franchise Fee: $11,400

Royalty Fee: $175 per month.

Financial Assistance: $4,950 down payment. Remaining $10,000 is financed through Harris Research, Inc., at 0% interest, over a 60-month period.

Managerial Assistance: In the initial training, franchisees are trained on how to hire personnel and how to keep employees. They are given handbooks and manuals to refer to. They can call in at any time with any questions they may have.

Training Provided: Initial training can be done either at our location in Logan, UT or via our video tape system. All franchisees must complete the Chem-College tests. On-going training is provided, with conventions and mini-conventions throughout the year and around the US. A technician is on hand during business hours to answer all questions.

Information Submitted: November 1993

CHEM-DRY CLEANING (CANADA)
8361 B Noble Rd.
Chilliwack, BC V2P 7X7 CAN
Telephone: (800) 665-4090 (604) 795-9918
Fax: (604) 795-7071
Ms. Trudy V. Miller, Franchise Licensing/Sales

Number of Franchised Units: 90
Number of Company-Owned Units: 0
Number of Total Operating Units: 90

In Business Since: 1991   Franchising Since: 1991

Description of Operation: Jandor Enterprises (Canada) Ltd. is master franchisee and owns the exclusive right to offer Chem-Dry carpet and upholstery cleaning franchises in Canada. Jandor is the wholesale distributor of Chem-Dry cleaning products and equipment. As Chem-Dry headquarters for Canada, Jandor provides the independently-owned and operated franchises with the latest developments in innovative new products and state-of-the-art equipment, on-going technical support and updated training.

Equity Capital Needed: $12,950 plus goods/services tax (GST) down payment.

Franchise Fee: $9,500

Royalty Fee: $260 on-going each month with cost of living increases allowed in the 5-year term.

Financial Assistance: Interested parties may purchase a Chem-Dry franchise with a down payment of $12,950 + GST and pay the balance by making 48 payments of $280, interest included.

Managerial Assistance: The initial training includes written and verbal instruction regarding the successful management of the franchise business. Additional managerial assistance is provided through monthly newsletters, seminars and on a one-on-one basis by telephone or during personal visits to the franchise.

Training Provided: New franchises are provided with 1 week of extensive "on-the-job" training at a designated location within Canada (travel and accommodations not included), as well as manuals, video tapes and accompanying workbook tests. Training will include how to mix and apply cleaning solutions, use equipment, compute estimates, solicit and maintain business and the overall conduct of a Chem-Dry franchise. Up-dated training is provided at least once a year by seminars, video tapes and newsletters.

Information Submitted: January 1994

CHEMSTATION
3201 Encrete Ln.
Dayton, OH 45439
Telephone: (513) 294-8265
Fax: (513) 294-5360
Mr. Joseph Novostat, Director of Operations

Number of Franchised Units: 23
Number of Company-Owned Units: 2
Number of Total Operating Units: 25

In Business Since: 1965   Franchising Since: 1984

Description of Operation: Manufacture and distribute detergents in bulk.

Equity Capital Needed: $250,000

Franchise Fee: $20,000

Royalty Fee: 4%

Financial Assistance: None.

Managerial Assistance: Complete training manuals, as well as operations manual. Managerial support is provided on an on-going basis.

Training Provided: We provide an extensive 1-week training period at the home office in Dayton, OH. Sales, operations and administration training are on-going.

Information Submitted: January 1994

CLASSY MAIDS U.S.A.
P. O. Box 160879
Altamonte Springs, FL 32716
Telephone: (800) 445-5238 (407) 862-6868
Fax: (407) 862-4221
Mr. William K. Olday, President

Number of Franchised Units: 22
Number of Company-Owned Units: 0
Number of Total Operating Units: 22

In Business Since: 1984   Franchising Since: 1985

Description of Operation: Classy Maids USA offers to sell or grant franchises of 50,000 - 100,000 population in an exclusive geographic area, i.e. city, county or definable area. The franchise fee ranges from $2,950 - $9,500 for a metropolitan franchise. Franchisees can be operated from home to start. Our computer training program allows more time for management. High image logo and name encourages customer calls.

Equity Capital Needed: $3,000 - $15,000

Franchise Fee: $2,950 - $9,500

Royalty Fee: 6%: 4% net plus 2% local advertising allowance.

Financial Assistance: We will finance 50% of the franchise fee and 100% of the computer management program. 5-year pay-back on amount financed.

Managerial Assistance: A full week of intensive training of Classy Maids (the business). This training can be at our training centers in Florida or Wisconsin. For a nominal fee, training can take place at franchisee location. On-going 800# for constant consultation - franchisee hotline!

Training Provided: We offer state-of-the-art business training and support programs. The Classy Maids USA name and image are the finest in the industry. Training includes confidential business operating manual, recruiting and personnel development, customer identity and market, organization and operational structure, inventory, equipment training and supplies, accounting, taxes, licensing and reporting, scheduling jobs/maid crews, advertising and sales promotion programs, cleaning techniques, computer, etc.

Information Submitted: November 1993

CLEANING CONSULTANT SERVICES
1512 Western Ave., P. O. Box 1273
Seattle, WA 98111
Telephone: (800) 622-4221 (206) 682-9748
Fax: (206) 622-6876
Mr. William R. Griffin, President

Number of Franchised Units: 4
Number of Company-Owned Units: 2
Number of Total Operating Units: 6

In Business Since: 1976   Franchising Since: 1981

Description of Operation: In an effort to meet the growing demand for our services in the US and internationally, we have begun a licensing program to provide qualified professionals with an opportunity to become associate consultants in their local areas. Our sole purpose is to provide support services to those who own, manage and/or supervise cleaning operations. Our services include software support, books, videos and software sales, cleaning business magazine, temporary agency, seminars, inspections and consulting.

Equity Capital Needed: $3,000 - $10,000

Franchise Fee: $25,000

Royalty Fee: $50 per month.

Financial Assistance: Partial payments are available. Inventory on a time payment plan. Shipping service, brochures, catalogues and promotional material provided at no cost.

Managerial Assistance: We provide phone support and procedural guides.

Training Provided: We offer training manuals, on-site visits and 2 - 3 days at our training site in Seattle, WA.

Information Submitted: March 1994

CLEANING IDEAS
P. O. Box 7269
San Antonio, TX 78207
Telephone: (210) 227-9161
Fax: (210) 227-0002
Mr. Charles Davis, Vice President

Number of Franchised Units: 0
Number of Company-Owned Units: 12
Number of Total Operating Units: 12

In Business Since: 1979   **Franchising Since:** 1986

Description of Operation: Cleaning Ideas is a unique retail/wholesale store operation. Cleaning Ideas stores sell over 1,600 items and chemicals to be used for cleaning. All chemical items are manufactured by Cleaning Ideas, thus gross profits run as high as 60%. All products are sold with a money-back guarantee. Each store is 1,000 square feet.

Equity Capital Needed: $6,000 - $20,000

Franchise Fee: $1,000

Royalty Fee: 0%

Financial Assistance: Data not available.

Managerial Assistance: Cleaning Ideas provides on-going managerial and technical assistance for the duration of the franchise agreement.

Training Provided: An intensive 6-day, mandatory training course is scheduled for all new franchisees. All training is performed in Company-owned stores.

Information Submitted: March 1994

CLEANNET USA
9861 Broken Land Pkwy., # 208
Columbia, MD 21046
Telephone: (800) 735-8838 (410) 720-6444
Fax: (410) 720-5307
Mr. Dennis M. Urner, Vice President

Number of Franchised Units: 1125
Number of Company-Owned Units: 1400
Number of Total Operating Units: 1525

In Business Since: 1987   **Franchising Since:** 1988

Description of Operation: CleanNet provides professional building maintenance services to commercial properties and institutions throughout the US. CleanNet provides a complete turn-key system that provides the franchisee with business accounts, supplies, equipment and insurance.

Equity Capital Needed: $2,950 - $32,000

Franchise Fee: $2,950 - $32,000

Royalty Fee: 3%

Financial Assistance: CleanNet will finance approximately 50% of the franchise fee.

Managerial Assistance: CleanNet provides a complete program of managerial support, including training, quality control and customer support.

Training Provided: CleanNet's program provides intensive training, including classroom, video and on-the-job.

Information Submitted: January 1994

COIT SERVICES
897 Hinckley Rd.
Burlingame, CA 94010
Telephone: (800) 243-8797 (415) 697-5471
Fax: (415) 697-6117
Mr. Nick Granato, Franchise Director

Number of Franchised Units: 44
Number of Company-Owned Units: 7
Number of Total Operating Units: 51

In Business Since: 1950   **Franchising Since:** 1962

Description of Operation: Coit is a multi-service cleaning company, offering drapery cleaning, carpet cleaning, upholstery cleaning, area rug cleaning, air duct cleaning and more.

Equity Capital Needed: $20,000 - $70,000

Franchise Fee: $9,950

Royalty Fee: 6%

Financial Assistance: We will assist with third-party financing.

Managerial Assistance: Management assistance is available in all areas of the operation, including advertising, marketing, financial, operational, reporting procedures, information systems, sales, etc.

Training Provided: The initial training program will cover up to 2 weeks of basic training in all areas of the operation at any of the Company-owned operations.

Information Submitted: January 1994

CONTINENTAL CARPET CLEANING
2480 Walkey Rd.
Ottawa, ON K1G 3R8 CAN
Telephone: (800) 267-9749 (613) 521-8770
Fax: (613) 737-0530
Mr. Don Walsh, Vice President of Operations

Number of Franchised Units: 97
Number of Company-Owned Units: 0
Number of Total Operating Units: 97

In Business Since: 1984   **Franchising Since:** 1989

Description of Operation: Continental offers a unique opportunity for carpet cleaners or would-be carpet cleaners to operate as a nationally-recognized brand name. Access to the client card list of national US retail department stores.

Equity Capital Needed: $10,000

Franchise Fee: $15,000

Royalty Fee: 6%

Financial Assistance: May finance up to 75% of the franchise fee.

Managerial Assistance: Complete range of managerial assistance, including advertising support, computer support, field and office support, newsletter, 800 telephone line and technical support.

Training Provided: Depending on the range of experience, up to one week of on-site and/or head office training.

Information Submitted: November 1993

COTTAGECARE
7600 State Line Rd., # 230
Prairie Village, KS 66208
Telephone: (913) 383-1778
Fax: (913) 333-1166
Mr. Tom Schrader, Chief Operating Officer

Number of Franchised Units: 20
Number of Company-Owned Units: 5
Number of Total Operating Units: 25

In Business Since: 1989   **Franchising Since:** 1989

Description of Operation: Housecleaning service business - a big business approach in a "mom and pop" industry. Franchisor does all marketing (hands off "x" new customers weekly). Weekly operational analysis. Operates only in "jumbo territories" (very large and demographically defined). Extremely well-developed program.

Equity Capital Needed: $50,000 +

Franchise Fee: $12,500

Royalty Fee: 5%

Financial Assistance: The franchise fee may be financed at $5,000 down; $7,500 balance carried at 10% interest.

Managerial Assistance: Total marketing responsibility at headquarters. Systems development, weekly operational review, accountability, software and franchisee hotline.

Training Provided: 1 1/2 weeks of classroom and hands-on training in actual service center in Prairie Village, KS.

Information Submitted: November 1993

COUSTIC-GLO INTERNATIONAL
7111 Ohms Ln.
Minneapolis, MN 55439
Telephone: (800) 333-8523 (612) 835-1338
Fax: (612) 835-1395
Mr. Scott L. Smith, Vice President of Marketing

Number of Franchised Units: 160
Number of Company-Owned Units: 1
Number of Total Operating Units: 161

In Business Since: 1970   **Franchising Since:** 1980

Description of Operation: The Coustic-Glo concept offers a unique opportunity for an individual to pursue financial independence in a virtually untapped industry. The need for ceiling and wall cleaning and restoration is all around you in every structure you enter on a daily basis. As a Coustic-Glo franchisee, you will be provided with all of the equipment, products, cleaning solutions and the training necessary to prosper in the field.

Equity Capital Needed: $9,750 - $25,000, depending on the area assigned.

Franchise Fee: $37,500

Royalty Fee: 6%

Financial Assistance: Some Company financing is available.

Managerial Assistance: The home office of Coustic-Glo International provides continual support in all areas of this business. Toll-free phones are maintained to give direct and constant access to the home office and assistance with field problems, technical questions, etc. Complete test reports on all products are provided, with updating as necessary. A very aggressive national advertising campaign is pursued. Local ad mats and all product identification are provided.

Training Provided: Each new franchisee is provided with a very intensive 2 - 3 day training program that takes place in his/her respective exclusive area, under the direct supervision of an experienced franchisee that is brought in from his/her area to assist in the establishment of the new franchisee's business. Also available to the new franchisee is the option of a training course provided at the home office under the direct supervision of home office personnel.

Information Submitted: March 1994

COVERALL CLEANING CONCEPTS
3111 Camino Del Rio N., # 950
San Diego, CA 92108
Telephone: (800) 537-3371 (619) 584-1911
Fax: (619) 584-4923
Ms. Gerry Barlow, Vice President of Marketing

Number of Franchised Units: 2887
Number of Company-Owned Units: 0
Number of Total Operating Units: 2887

In Business Since: 1985   **Franchising Since:** 1985

Description of Operation: Turn-key commercial cleaning franchise. Initial fee includes training, equipment and supplies, customer accounts, on-going support in billing and accounts receivable, public relations and monitoring quality service. Insurance, additional business and additional training are also available. 9 different levels of business to choose from.

Equity Capital Needed: $2,050 - $30,100

Franchise Fee: $3,250 - $33,600

Royalty Fee: 5%

Financial Assistance: All packages financed over a period of 24 - 36 months, depending on package purchased. Down payment, ranging from $1,700 - $26,600, required.

Managerial Assistance: Billing and accounts receivable assistance, on-going quality assurance checks and assistance, insurance and equipment lease options available. Management advice.

Training Provided: Training is provided in business development and cleaning techniques. Various training and technical manuals supplied. On-going training seminars offered in product knowledge, usage, etc.

Information Submitted: November 1993

CUSTOM CARE FOR HOMES
1608 N. Miller Rd., # 5
Scottsdale, AZ 85257
Telephone: (602) 941-2993
Mr. Frank Hronek, President

Number of Franchised Units: 15
Number of Company-Owned Units: 1
Number of Total Operating Units: 16

In Business Since: 1986   **Franchising Since:** 1990

Description of Operation: Home cleaning, carpet cleaning and window cleaning for residential homes, plus some commercial cleaning.

Equity Capital Needed: $500 - $10,000

Franchise Fee: $2,900

Royalty Fee: $100 per month.

Financial Assistance: Data not available.

Managerial Assistance: Assistance is always at your fingertips - a phone call. Detailed documentation and manuals answer almost all of your management concerns. If not, speedy telephone assistance is immediately available.

Training Provided: Start your training with 4 hours of video tape instruction at your home. Then advance to a 190-page manual, which gives detailed instruction in every aspect of the business - marketing, advertising, sales, budgets and projections, accounting, record keeping, insurance, employee training, employee contracts and forms.

Information Submitted: November 1993

DURACLEAN INTERNATIONAL
3664 Duraclean Bldg., 2151 Waukegan
Deerfield, IL 60015
Telephone: (800) 251-7070 (708) 945-2000
Fax: (708) 945-2023
Mr. Michael Higgins, Director of Marketing

Number of Franchised Units: 663
Number of Company-Owned Units: 0
Number of Total Operating Units: 663

In Business Since: 1930   **Franchising Since:** 1945

Description of Operation: Distinct service markets and revenue center packages to fit your needs for independence and growth on own terms. Carpet cleaning, upholstery and drapery cleaning, ceiling and wall cleaning, water, fire and smoke damage restoration, janitorial, hard-surface floor care, ventilation and duct cleaning, pressure washing and ultrasonic blind cleaning.

Equity Capital Needed: $9,900 - $3,900 down.

Franchise Fee: $4,800

Royalty Fee: 10% - 2%

Financial Assistance: Financing arrangements are available from Duraclean International. Lease packages on vans are also available.

Managerial Assistance: Duraclean has specialists in all areas of this business - from technical, marketing, managerial to computer, assisting our franchisees on an on-going basis.

Training Provided: Duraclean puts an extraordinary amount of energy and attention into proper training techniques, so you will render a professional service, market effectively and manage efficiently. We provide training manuals, videotapes, schools, local hands-on assistance, our 800#, magazines, bulletins, conventions and area meetings.

Information Submitted: November 1993

ENVIROBATE
401 N. Third St., # 200
Minneapolis, MN 55401
Telephone: (800) 944-8095 (612) 349-9211
Fax: (612) 349-9167
Mr. Jeff Anlauf, President

Number of Franchised Units: 2
Number of Company-Owned Units: 0
Number of Total Operating Units: 2

In Business Since: 1989   **Franchising Since:** 1992

Description of Operation: The world's only environmental franchise. Provides environmental protection services to residential clients.

Equity Capital Needed: $90,000 - $130,000

Franchise Fee: $25,000

Royalty Fee: 6%

Financial Assistance: We will assist the franchisee with lending agencies. Provide financial information, pro formas and expected business volume.

Managerial Assistance: Complete training and assistance in the Envirobate system. On-going managerial assistance.

Training Provided: 2-week, comprehensive training system of Envirobate techniques. Outside EPA training required. No experience necessary.

Information Submitted: November 1993

ENVIRONMENTAL AIR SERVICES
1010 N. University Parks Dr.
Waco, TX 76707
Telephone: (800) 583-3828 (817) 752-5202
Fax: (817) 752-0661
Mr. Ray Adams, General Manager

Number of Franchised Units: 24
Number of Company-Owned Units: 1
Number of Total Operating Units: 25

In Business Since: 1992   **Franchising Since:** 1993

Description of Operation: Service franchise, offering health improvement with focus on indoor air quality. Assessment, consulting, air testing and comprehensive remediation services for the residential, commercial and insurance marketplace. Air washing; micro-filtration; tobacco smoke and soot removal; H.V.A.C. decontamination; biological, particulate and gaseous pollutant removal.

Equity Capital Needed: $32,000 - $59,000

Franchise Fee: $15,000

Royalty Fee: 7%

Financial Assistance: Equipment leasing; internal franchise fee financing; VetFran; now awarding international master licenses and regional director programs.

Managerial Assistance: Complete business plan and marketing plan, media placement, operations support, employee selection and management assistance, financial, accounting and administration assistance. Product knowledge and distribution assistant available.

Training Provided: Initial and on-going training modules, video and audio training, regional seminars, annual conventions, personal growth training, manuals for marketing, technical and management. Full indoor air quality training, utilizing the latest standards and procedures.

Information Submitted: December 1993

ENVIRONMENTAL BIOTECH
4404 N. Tamiami Trail
Sarasota, FL 34234
Telephone: (813) 358-9112
Fax: (813) 359-9744
Mr. Ray Charles, Director of Franchise Marketing

Number of Franchised Units: 68
Number of Company-Owned Units: 1
Number of Total Operating Units: 69

In Business Since: 1991   **Franchising Since:** 1991

Description of Operation: Our firm is in the business of finding solutions to environmental waste problems. Our bacterial systems are non-pathogenic, naturally-occurring bacteria, designed to eat grease, oil, sugar, starch and gelatin. The systems/products are sold only through our franchise network. We are a fully-integrated company, doing our own research and development, manufacturing and sales.

Equity Capital Needed: $50,000

Franchise Fee: $50,000

Royalty Fee: None.

Financial Assistance: The franchisor does not offer financial assistance.

Managerial Assistance: During our training school at world headquarters, there is 1 week of operations management curriculum given with full manuals. In addition, a field trainer goes for 1 week to the new franchisee's market and assists in hiring sales managers, etc. On-going managerial assistance is always available as needed or desired.

Training Provided: The franchisee training school ("Bug U") is 3 weeks in duration, with full manuals. The curriculum consists of 1 week of management training, 1 week of technical training and 1 week of hands-on installations of systems and field sales calls. Initial training is part of franchise package. Franchisees are welcome to come back to school for on-going training as needed or desired. We sponsor an "MBA" program of training.

Information Submitted: December 1993

FABRI-ZONE CLEANING SYSTEMS
3135 Universal Dr., # 6
Mississauga, ON L4X 2E2 CAN
Telephone: (905) 602-7691
Fax: (905) 602-7821
Mr. David S. Collier, President

Number of Franchised Units: 55
Number of Company-Owned Units: 1
Number of Total Operating Units: 56

In Business Since: 1981   **Franchising Since:** 1984

Description of Operation: Patented purification cleaning process for the cleaning of carpets, upholstery, ceilings, walls, blinds and drapes, plus smoke and damage restoration cleaning.

Equity Capital Needed: $3,000 - $10,000

Franchise Fee: $1,500

Royalty Fee: $100 monthly.

Financial Assistance: Business plan.

Managerial Assistance: Manager assistance.

Training Provided: 1 week of initial telephone support and regional seminars.

Information Submitted: December 1993

HEAVEN'S BEST CARPET & UPHOLSTERY CLEANING
247 N. 1st E., P. O. Box 607
Rexburg, ID 83440
Telephone: (800) 359-2095 (208) 359-1106
Fax: (208) 359-1236
Mr. Cody Howard, Chief Executive Officer

Number of Franchised Units: 113
Number of Company-Owned Units: 4
Number of Total Operating Units: 117

In Business Since: 1983   **Franchising Since:** 1983

Description of Operation: Heaven's Best is a unique, low-moisture cleaning process which provides a great alternative to the traditional total saturation methods of cleaning. Our customers love our dry-in-one-hour process. Our franchise is very affordable. Our business is one of quality and customer satisfaction.

Equity Capital Needed: $5,000 - $20,000

Franchise Fee: $9,500

Royalty Fee: $80 per month.

Financial Assistance: Some financial assistance may be available to qualified franchisees.

Managerial Assistance: The home office support is supplemented by a network of regional managers. An 800# hotline is available. Our procedures manual and regional seminars, coupled with our newsletter, keep each franchisee up-to-date on changes which occur within the industry. Our on-going support is tremendous.

Training Provided: We provide a complete and comprehensive 4-day training program at our corporate headquarters in Rexburg, ID. All aspects of the business are covered during the training. All franchisees must attend the training.

Information Submitted: November 1993

HOME CLEANING CENTERS OF AMERICA
11111 W. 95th St.
Overland Park, KS 66214
Telephone: (800) 767-1118 (913) 599-6453
Fax: (913) 599-6454
Mr. Mike Calhoon, President

Number of Franchised Units: 20
Number of Company-Owned Units: 0
Number of Total Operating Units: 20

In Business Since: 1981   **Franchising Since:** 1984

Description of Operation: Home cleaning service, with secondary emphasis on carpet cleaning, window cleaning and small office cleaning. Strong appeal to franchisees who want to manage people, not clean houses.

Equity Capital Needed: $20,000 - $30,000

Franchise Fee: $16,500

Royalty Fee: 4.5%

Financial Assistance: No.

Managerial Assistance: We have a 200-page operations manual. We have a 24-hour 800#. We do whatever it takes! Regular franchise visits.

Training Provided: 1 week of training in Kansas City, MO. On-going support. Annual seminar and training videos.

Information Submitted: November 1993

JAN-PRO CLEANING SYSTEMS
1500 Providence Hwy., # 39
Norwood, MA 02062
Telephone: (617) 762-2900
Fax: (617) 762-8557
Mr. Jack LaPointe, President

Number of Franchised Units: 150
Number of Company-Owned Units: 3
Number of Total Operating Units: 153

In Business Since: 1991   **Franchising Since:** 1991

Description of Operation: Jan-Pro Cleaning Systems is a franchisor in the commercial cleaning industry. We provide the resources that people need to establish themselves in their own cleaning business.

Equity Capital Needed: $2,800 - $26,000

Franchise Fee: $1,450

Royalty Fee: 8%

Financial Assistance: Financing is available for all of our franchise plans.

Managerial Assistance: Jan-Pro provides the franchisees with full support from the moment they start their business. This includes guidance from our operations staff, cash flow management, marketing assistance and customer relations.

Training Provided: Jan-Pro provides all franchisees with formal classroom and on-the-job, expert training in every aspect of proper cleaning techniques.

Information Submitted: November 1993

JANI-KING INTERNATIONAL
4950 Keller Springs Rd., # 190
Dallas, TX 75248
Telephone: (800) 552-5264 (214) 991-0900
Fax: (214) 991-5723
Mr. Jerry L. Crawford, President

Number of Franchised Units: 3860
Number of Company-Owned Units: 25
Number of Total Operating Units: 3885

In Business Since: 1969   **Franchising Since:** 1974

Description of Operation: Commercial cleaning franchisor, offering entrepreneurs a proven system for operating a business involved in the cleaning of office buildings, retail, medical and other facilities. Franchisees in this growth industry are owner/operators of their own businesses who also have access to regional support centers.

Equity Capital Needed: Under $25,000.

Franchise Fee: $6,500 - $14,000

Royalty Fee: 10%

Financial Assistance: Yes.

Managerial Assistance: A complete range of support services, from billings to business growth, are offered through regional support centers. More than 50 centers are located throughout North America and abroad.

Training Provided: The most comprehensive training course in the industry is available through regional support centers near the franchisee. Training covers cleaning, personnel, client relations, proposals and sales.

Information Submitted: March 1994

JANIBRITE
3045 Southcreek Rd., # 19
Mississauga, ON L4X 2X7 CAN
Telephone: (905) 624-4290
Fax: (905) 602-5383
Mr. Hossein Companieh, President

Number of Franchised Units: 25
Number of Company-Owned Units: 0
Number of Total Operating Units: 25

In Business Since: 1989   **Franchising Since:** 1990

Description of Operation: Building maintenance and janitorial service, franchised to individuals. Support is on an on-going basis to help the franchisee with his/her accounts, administration, etc.

Equity Capital Needed: $2,000 and up.

Franchise Fee: $2,000 - up.

Royalty Fee: 22.5%, all-inclusive (administrative, royalty and advertising).

Financial Assistance: Installment plan through our financing department.

Managerial Assistance: Accounting, customer services, problem solving, full support.

Training Provided: 1 - 2 weeks of training, video tape shows, free seminars and meetings.

Information Submitted: December 1993

JANTIZE AMERICA
15965 Jeanette
Southfield, MI 48075
Telephone: (810) 559-1415
Fax: (810) 557-2784
Ms. Colleen McGaffey

Number of Franchised Units: 19
Number of Company-Owned Units: 3
Number of Total Operating Units: 22

In Business Since: 1985   **Franchising Since:** 1988

Description of Operation: Commercial office cleaning.

Equity Capital Needed: $2,500 - $12,500

Franchise Fee: $3,200 - $16,000

Royalty Fee: 6% - 9%

Financial Assistance: Up to 50% of franchise fee.

Managerial Assistance: Data not available.

Training Provided: Yes.

Information Submitted: January 1994

JDI CLEANING SYSTEMS
646 Parkdale Ave. N., Unit 2
Hamilton, ON L8H 5Z4 CAN
Telephone: (905) 545-5886
Fax: (905) 545-5750
Franchise Director

Number of Franchised Units: 16
Number of Company-Owned Units: 2
Number of Total Operating Units: 18

In Business Since: 1969   **Franchising Since:** 1991

Description of Operation: Over 25 years of experience in the contract cleaning industry provides each franchisee with the know-how to operate a successful janitorial company. Our centralized system of accounting, customer service and marketing guarantees each franchise a professional image.

Equity Capital Needed: $20,000

Franchise Fee: $10,500

Royalty Fee: 13%

Financial Assistance: JDI works with each franchisee in securing financing. Through a host of government programs for small business and local banks, financing for the right individual is assured.

Managerial Assistance: JDI works through a centralized system of accounting for all franchisees. All invoicing and accounts receivables are managed at the home office. JDI's unique computerized customer service system also tracks and records all accounts.

Training Provided: Each franchisee must attend a 5-day, intensive training course at the home office. Also offered are sales and marketing training programs designed to fast track each franchisee in his/her sales efforts.

Information Submitted: March 1994

LANGENWALTER CARPET DYEING
1111 Richfield Rd.
Placentia, CA 92670
Telephone: (800) 422-4370 (714) 528-7610
Fax: (714) 528-7620
Mr. John Langenwalter, Vice President

Number of Franchised Units: 138
Number of Company-Owned Units: 2
Number of Total Operating Units: 140

In Business Since: 1975   **Franchising Since:** 1980

Description of Operation: Complete carpet color correction, including bleach spots, sun fading, pet stains, food stains, punch and other discolorations. Also, complete color changes and full wall-to-wall carpet dyeing.

Equity Capital Needed: $30,000

Franchise Fee: $17,500

Royalty Fee: $132 per month.

Financial Assistance: Limited to a case-by-case basis.

Managerial Assistance: A manual and an 800 toll-free technical support line.

Training Provided: 1 week of comprehensive training, with hands-on carpet and spot dyeing.

Information Submitted: November 1993

LASER CHEM
36 S. State St., # 1200
Salt Lake City, UT 84111
Telephone: (800) 272-2741 (801) 364-3300
Fax: (801) 364-3322
Mr. Michael Jenkins, President

Number of Franchised Units: 19
Number of Company-Owned Units: 1
Number of Total Operating Units: 20

In Business Since: 1978   **Franchising Since:** 1990

Description of Operation: Laser Chem offers the most advanced carpet and upholstery drycleaning system on the market. Carpets are restored to their original lustre and dry within minutes. It cleans 200% - 300% better than other systems. It cleans the entire fiber without any moisture going past the primary backing. The solutions are 100% environmentally safe.

Equity Capital Needed: $500 - $1,500, if you have your own vehicle.

Franchise Fee: $6,975

Royalty Fee: $125 per month - starts 6 months after franchise is purchased.

Financial Assistance: $4,675 down payment - $2,300 financed at 0% interest up to 60 months. First payment starts 6 months after franchise is purchased. $1,000 discount if franchise fee is paid up front.

Managerial Assistance: Receive a monthly newsletter that includes helpful information on business management, as well as advertising, marketing and any new discoveries in the carpet and upholstery field. A toll-free # is also available to call any time for assistance.

Training Provided: We fly you into our national headquarters for 3 - 4 days of hands-on and classroom training. We cover all aspects of carpet technology, advertising and even put together a personalized marketing plan for your area.

Information Submitted: November 1993

MAID BRIGADE
850 Indian Trail Rd.
Atlanta, GA 30247
Telephone: (800) 722-MAID (404) 564-2400
Fax: (404) 279-9668
Mr. Arthur F. Guyton, Director of Franchise Development

Number of Franchised Units: 238
Number of Company-Owned Units: 5
Number of Total Operating Units: 243

In Business Since: 1979   **Franchising Since:** 1980

Description of Operation: Residential maid service, using development teams of highly-trained maids who are insured and bonded. Maid Brigade services thousands of busy households throughout the US and Canada.

Equity Capital Needed: $25,000 - $30,000

Franchise Fee: $9,500 (included in equity capital).

Royalty Fee: 7% - 3%

Financial Assistance: No.

Managerial Assistance: Business plan development through diskette in start-up manual, maid training videos, micro-maid software, accounting and payroll software, confidential operations, advertising and marketing, personnel and pre-employment screening manuals are all included.

Training Provided: Study of the Company's start-up manual for several weeks as preparation for a formal week of training in Atlanta, GA. Each new franchisee is assigned a support specialist for several months. The specialist is usually an outstanding franchisee who is selected and trained to work very closely with all new franchisees. Continuous training occurs through quarterly regional meetings, an annual convention, newsletters and mail-outs.

Information Submitted: November 1993

MAID EASY
33 Pratt St.
Glastonbury, CT 06033
Telephone: (203) 659-2953
Ms. Patricia Brubaker, President

Number of Franchised Units: 1
Number of Company-Owned Units: 0
Number of Total Operating Units: 1

In Business Since: 1985   **Franchising Since:** 1987

Description of Operation: Maid Easy is a professional residential home cleaning service, supplying one maid per home for a personalized service.

Equity Capital Needed: $9,000 - $11,000

Franchise Fee: $3,000 - $5,000

Royalty Fee: None.

Financial Assistance: Because of the low franchise fee, no assistance is available. The equity capital needed may not be necessary all at once, but as the business grows, the franchisee can fund this him/herself by performing the actual cleaning work in the beginning, then stepping into a solely managerial position in the future.

Managerial Assistance: Each location will receive 1 week of training at the Maid Easy home office in Glastonbury, CT. A manual of instructions on office management, recruitment and marketing, plus training videos and computer programs, is included.

Training Provided: An extensive 1-week training period at home office, where franchisees can have hands-on training in all aspects of business operations.

Information Submitted: November 1993

MAID TO PERFECTION
2624-C Lord Baltimore Dr.
Baltimore, MD 21244
Telephone: (800) 648-6243 (410) 944-1900
Fax: (410) 944-5802
Ms. Gloria Goldstraw, Vice President

Number of Franchised Units: 24
Number of Company-Owned Units: 8
Number of Total Operating Units: 32

In Business Since: 1980   **Franchising Since:** 1990

Description of Operation: Maid to Perfection is an up-scale maid service, offering both residential and commercial cleaning. MTP appeals to today's sophisticated consumers by offering unique pricing, flexibility and diversified service. Our formatted system makes service easy to sell and, by combining both residential and commercial cleaning markets, MTP franchisees benefit from 2 separate multi-billion dollar industries.

Equity Capital Needed: $22,424 - $34,349

Franchise Fee: $8,995

Royalty Fee: 7%

Financial Assistance: Financial assistance is available to franchisees acquiring additional units and to regional developers.

Managerial Assistance: MTP provides a strong support system to franchisees on an on-going basis. Franchisees have immediate access to upper management for assistance and to receive individual attention. Also provided is an 800# hotline and a monthly newsletter.

Training Provided: Training is conducted at National Headquarters in Maryland for approximately 5 - 7 days. Franchisees learn all aspects of operating a cleaning business, using the Maid to Perfection's formatted system.

Information Submitted: November 1993

MAIDS INTERNATIONAL, THE
4820 Dodge St.
Omaha, NE 68132
Telephone: (800) THE-MAID (402) 558-5555
Fax: (402) 558-4112
Mr. Ron Schuller, Sales

Number of Franchised Units: 216
Number of Company-Owned Units: 0
Number of Total Operating Units: 216

In Business Since: 1979   **Franchising Since:** 1980

Description of Operation: Residential maid service franchise.

Equity Capital Needed: $13,500 - $23,500

Franchise Fee: $17,500

Royalty Fee: 5.5% - 7%

Financial Assistance: We will finance up to 50% of franchise fee.

Managerial Assistance: 6 weeks of pre-training counseling. 6 days of administrative corporate training, with complete hands-on computer training. 90-day post-training follow-up. Monthly newsletter, toll-free phone support, regional seminars, annual meetings and advertising and public relations programs.

Training Provided: 6 weeks of pre-training counseling. 6 days of technical corporate training. 90-day post-training follow-up. Toll-free technical phone support.

Information Submitted: November 1993

MAIDS PLUS
453 Beverly Ave.
Canal Fulton, OH 44614
Telephone: (800) 523-MAID (216) 854-3651
Fax: (216) 854-3001
Mr. Robert L. Pickens, Corporate Director

Number of Franchised Units: 2
Number of Company-Owned Units: 1
Number of Total Operating Units: 3

In Business Since: 1990   Franchising Since: 1992

Description of Operation: Residential, commercial and office cleaning service, specializing in cleaning, but also offering a variety of "PLUS" services.

Equity Capital Needed: $5,000

Franchise Fee: $10,000

Royalty Fee: 7%

Financial Assistance: Partial financing to qualified applicants.

Managerial Assistance: Guidance in ALL areas of operations, 800# for assistance, weekly bulletins, newsletters, field visits, products and supplies available at a substantial savings and more. The training never ends.

Training Provided: An intense 5 days of corporate office training in ALL areas of operations. Confidential operations manual. Start-up equipment and supplies.

Information Submitted: November 1993

MERRY MAIDS
11117 Mill Valley Rd.
Omaha, NE 68154
Telephone: (800) 798-8000 (402) 498-0331
Fax: (402) 498-0142
Mr. Robert E. Burdge, Franchise Sales Manager

Number of Franchised Units: 700
Number of Company-Owned Units: 1
Number of Total Operating Units: 701

In Business Since: 1980   Franchising Since: 1981

Description of Operation: Merry Maids is the largest and most successful maid service in the US. Money and Success Magazines have ranked Merry Maids a "Top 10 US Franchise." The Company's commitment to marketing, training and on-going support is unmatched. Merry Maids provides the most comprehensive software and equipment and supply package. Merry Maids is a member of the ServiceMaster quality service network.

Equity Capital Needed: $15,000 - $20,000

Franchise Fee: $12,500 - $20,500

Royalty Fee: 7% - 5%

Financial Assistance: Up to $11,500 is available towards the franchise fee for qualified buyers.

Managerial Assistance: Complete managerial focus and application, from initial training and extending through the Company's Advanced Performance Seminars for established franchise owners.

Training Provided: 5 days of headquarters training and all start-up equipment and supplies for 2 teams. On-going support includes 21 field regional coordinators, a "Buddy Program," weekly modem bulletin board, newsletters, regional meetings, national convention and an 800# for assistance. Products and supplies are available at savings up to 80%.

Information Submitted: November 1993

MOLLY MAID
540 Avis Dr., # B
Ann Arbor, MI 48108

Telephone: (800) MM-MOLLY (313) 996-1555
Fax: (313) 996-1906
Mr. Paul M. Wiljanen, Vice President - Sales/Marketing

Number of Franchised Units: 342
Number of Company-Owned Units: 3
Number of Total Operating Units: 345

In Business Since: 1979   Franchising Since: 1979

Description of Operation: Customers choose Molly Maid for their professional image and proven results world-wide. Inc. Magazine rated Molly Maid as one of the 500 fastest-growing companies for 3 years. Molly Maid has a proven system, with over 4 million cleanings performed.

Equity Capital Needed: $10,000 - $14,000

Franchise Fee: $9,900 - $24,900

Royalty Fee: 6% - 3%

Financial Assistance: Up to 50% of the initial franchise fee or $10,000, whichever sum is lesser, with an APR of 9.75% over 36 equal monthly installments.

Managerial Assistance: A 6-month "Right Start" program, which includes a business plan and marketing plan especially created for each franchisee, individually based on how quickly he/she wants to grow the business. A field representative will spend 2 days on-site with the franchisee at no charge after 45 - 60 days of operation.

Training Provided: 5 days of intense training in Ann Arbor, MI. Management, marketing, accounting, computer training and hands-on activities.

Information Submitted: December 1993

MR. ROOTER
P. O. Box 1309
Waco, TX 76703
Telephone: (800) 583-8003 (817) 755-0055
Fax: (817) 757-1667
Mr. Robert Tunmire, President

Number of Franchised Units: 182
Number of Company-Owned Units: 0
Number of Total Operating Units: 182

In Business Since: 1968   Franchising Since: 1974

Description of Operation: Franchise of full-service plumber and drain repair business.

Equity Capital Needed: $17,500

Franchise Fee: $17,500

Royalty Fee: 6%, declining on volume.

Financial Assistance: Up to 70% financing is available to credit-worthy applicants.

Managerial Assistance: Complete management and marketing assistance by home and field staff.

Training Provided: Mandatory 1 week of training at home office. Field training provided, as needed.

Information Submitted: December 1993

NATIONAL LEAK DETECTION
P. O. Box 3191
Palos Verdes Estate, CA 90274
Telephone: (800) 444-9421 (310) 377-2699
Fax: (310) 377-5363
Ms. Jeri Honda, Vice President of Marketing

Number of Franchised Units: 42
Number of Company-Owned Units: 6
Number of Total Operating Units: 48

In Business Since: 1989   Franchising Since: 1989

Description of Operation: Leak detection and repair on swimming pools, spas, fountains, ponds, domestic water supply lines, slabs, irrigation systems, walls and gas leaks.

Equity Capital Needed: $15,000

Franchise Fee: Varies.

Royalty Fee: 8%

Financial Assistance: In-house financing is available.

Managerial Assistance: On-going support and assistance available to all franchisees. Workshops and seminars on a continuing basis. New technology available to franchisee. Updated information given to franchisee through the "National Update." Corporate trainer will assist in helping new franchisee on technical knowledge.

Training Provided: Continued workshops and meetings on new technology and laws on industry. One-on-one training with corporate trainer. In-house workshop on administrative responsibilities.

Information Submitted: December 1993

NATIONAL MAINTENANCE CONTRACTORS
1801 130th Ave. NE
Bellevue, WA 98005
Telephone: (800) 347-7844 (206) 881-0500
Fax: (206) 883-4785
Mr. Lyle Graddon, President

Number of Franchised Units: 310
Number of Company-Owned Units: 2
Number of Total Operating Units: 312

In Business Since: 1970   **Franchising Since:** 1973

Description of Operation: Janitorial service business. Master franchise needed in major metro market, who in turn will generate janitorial accounts and sell them to unit franchisees who do the work. Complete training at home office and through manuals and videos. On-going support in the local markets.

Equity Capital Needed: Unit Franchise - $1,000; Master Franchise - $100,000.

Franchise Fee: Unit Franchise - $500; Master Franchise - $25,000.

Royalty Fee: Unit Franchise - 20%; Master Franchise - 4% - 3%, based on volume.

Financial Assistance: Financing is available through the Company and is interest-free for unit franchisees. Master franchise finance terms are flexible, based upon market cost and working capital needed.

Managerial Assistance: Support provided as needed - on-site visits, 800#, newsletters, letters, account pricing support, legal and accounting assistance.

Training Provided: Master franchise - 30 days of training, 3 manuals and videos, start-up support in local market, as needed. On-going meetings. Unit franchise - 5 days of training, manual and videos, on-going meetings and consultation.

Information Submitted: November 1993

NEXT GENERATION, INC.
C/O Kemplin Group
9891 Broken Land Parkway, Suite 405
Columbia, MD 21046
Telephone: (800) 381-8220 (410) 381-8271
Fax: (410) 381-8271
Mr. Michael Greenman, Director of Marketing

Number of Franchised Units: 5
Number of Company-Owned Units: 1
Number of Total Operating Units: 6

In Business Since: 1993   **Franchising Since:** 1993

Description of Operation: National commercial cleaning franchise (office buildings)—Maryland, Washington, D.C., Florida, and Ohio. Franchiser provides cleaning contracts based on size of franchise.

Equity Capital Needed: $1,400-$45,000

Franchise Fee: 0

Royalty Fee: 10%

Financial Assistance: Financing available.

Managerial Assistance: Unlimited assistance at no charge.

Training Provided: National certification training provided.

Information Submitted: August 1994

O.P.E.N. CLEANING SYSTEMS
2398 E. Camelback Rd., # 740
Phoenix, AZ 85016
Telephone: (800) 777-6736 (602) 224-0440
Fax: (602) 468-3788
Mr. Eric Roudi, President

Number of Franchised Units: 589
Number of Company-Owned Units: 3
Number of Total Operating Units: 592

In Business Since: 1983   **Franchising Since:** 1983

Description of Operation: Franchisor of office and commercial cleaning business. Franchisees are provided with guaranteed initial customers, training and equipment. In addition, franchisor provides on-going administrative and sales support to the franchisee. Ability to start part-time or full-time.

Equity Capital Needed: $2,500

Franchise Fee: $3,800

Royalty Fee: 15%

Financial Assistance: The franchisor generally finances up to 50% of the initial franchise fee.

Managerial Assistance: The franchisor's local office provides billing and collection services to all the franchisee's customers. It also assists the franchisees in customer service and acts as the contact person for all customer calls or inquiries. In addition, franchisees can utilize (free) bidding and proposal preparation service provided by the franchisor.

Training Provided: The initial training covers all areas of the janitorial industry, including efficiency, material usage and customer service. Later courses teach franchisees how to bid and secure additional clients and perform specialty work. Franchisor's local office provides on-going support.

Information Submitted: November 1993

OMNI-CLEAN
11111 Shady Tr., # 101
Dallas, TX 75229
Telephone: (214) 243-7883
Fax: (214) 243-5868
Mr. Rock Tapken, President

Number of Franchised Units: 17
Number of Company-Owned Units: 2
Number of Total Operating Units: 19

In Business Since: 1982   **Franchising Since:** 1982

Description of Operation: Franchised office cleaning is now available in Texas through Omni-Clean. Our program offers low start-up and guaranteed accounts. Full training and on-going support.

Equity Capital Needed: $3,000 - $30,000

Franchise Fee: $6,500

Royalty Fee: 10%

Financial Assistance: $6,500 franchise fee is 100% financed for 5 years. Only cost paid to start is for the accounts you wish to be guaranteed.

Managerial Assistance: Managerial assistance is available at all times. Through our network of regional offices, assistance is local and immediate.

Training Provided: Omni-Clean training is the most advanced in the industry. 1 week of our 2-week training program is on management and growth of the franchise.

Information Submitted: January 1994

PAUL W. DAVIS SYSTEMS
9000 Cypress Green Dr.
Jacksonville, FL 32256
Telephone: (800) 722-1818 (904) 730-0320
Fax: (904) 730-8972
Mr. David Freeman, Director of Franchise Sales

Number of Franchised Units: 207
Number of Company-Owned Units: 1
Number of Total Operating Units: 208

In Business Since: 1967   **Franchising Since:** 1970

Description of Operation: Paul W. Davis Systems is the world's largest international restoration company. We were founded in 1967 and have over 200 network franchises in the US, Canada and the UK. A Paul Davis Systems franchise is for the mature, entrepreneurial person who is service-oriented and who has the ability and patience to build and manage an organization. The demand for restoration is constant and not dependent on the economy, real estate or weather. We restore residential & commercial property with insurable losses.

Equity Capital Needed: $75,000 - $150,000

Franchise Fee: $19,900 - $46,000

Royalty Fee: 3.5% - 5%

Financial Assistance: None at this time.

Managerial Assistance: We have 1 week of field consulting for franchise start-ups, followed by 6 months of on-going telephone support for new owners. We also have 1 week of field consulting for job cost accounting.

Training Provided: We have a 5-week, mandatory new owner training class that includes franchise management, estimating, project management, job cost accounting, trades supervision and marketing. We also have an optional 2-week signature professional cleaning school. We provide 2 weeks of training for associates and contractors for a nominal fee.

Information Submitted: November 1993

PRECISION POWERWASH 2000
P. O. Box 463
W. Springfield, MA 01090
Telephone: (800) 633-3311 (413) 734-4384
Fax: (413) 736-1785
Mr. Mark Kraver, President

Number of Franchised Units: 1
Number of Company-Owned Units: 6
Number of Total Operating Units: 7

In Business Since: 1974   **Franchising Since:** 1993

Description of Operation: We specialize in cleaning the exterior of houses and cleaning truck fleets.

Equity Capital Needed: $35,000 - $49,000

Franchise Fee: $13,500

Royalty Fee: 5% - 3%

Financial Assistance: None.

Managerial Assistance: We will assist in all aspects of conducting a new business from A to Z.

Training Provided: We provide 2 weeks of training. Also, we will train as many new employees as needed.

Information Submitted: November 1993

PROFESSIONAL CARPET SYSTEMS
5182 Old Dixie Hwy.
Forest Park, GA 30050
Telephone: (800) 925-5055 (404) 362-2300
Fax: (404) 362-2888
Franchise Counselor

Number of Franchised Units: 222
Number of Company-Owned Units: 6
Number of Total Operating Units: 228

In Business Since: 1978   **Franchising Since:** 1981

Description of Operation: Professional Carpet Systems is the leader in "on-site" carpet redyeing, servicing thousands of apartment complexes, hotels and motels worldwide. Other PCS services include carpet cleaning, rejuvenation, repair, water and flood damage restoration and "guaranteed odor control." PCS has a total carpet care concept.

Equity Capital Needed: $9,700 +

Franchise Fee: $10,000

Royalty Fee: 6%

Financial Assistance: Some financing of initial franchise fee may be available to qualified applicants.

Managerial Assistance: Franchisees receive complete operations manuals, an accounting and bookkeeping system and on-going support from the franchisee's home office. PCS also offers on-going training that is provided quarterly. PCS' newsletter keeps franchisees up-dated on marketing and product information.

Training Provided: PCS franchisees attend a 2-week training program at the PCS home office. During the training program, franchisees gain hands-on experience.

Information Submitted: November 1993

PROFESSIONAL POLISH
2410 Gravel Rd.
Ft. Worth, TX 76118
Telephone: (800) 255-0488 (817) 589-0102
Fax: (817) 590-0240
Mr. Sid Cavanaugh, President

Number of Franchised Units: 31
Number of Company-Owned Units: 2
Number of Total Operating Units: 33

In Business Since: 1982   **Franchising Since:** 1986

Description of Operation: Janitorial, lawn, landscape and light building maintenance service at the local level. Master franchisor emphasis on marketing, training and management of local franchisees.

Equity Capital Needed: Local - $7,500; Master - $35,000.

Franchise Fee: $5,500 for a local franchise; $25,000 for a Master.

Royalty Fee: Local - 15%; Master - 5%.

Financial Assistance: PPI will finance balance of purchase at 12% interest.

Managerial Assistance: Local: minimum 30 days of training - up to 90 days, if needed: sales, public relations, all accounts receivable, bookkeeping, assistance with purchasing supplies, insurance and assistance with tax reports and expense record keeping. Master: marketing and accounting.

Training Provided: Local: minimum of 30 days. On-going support. Master: minimum of 90 days. On-going support.

PROPERTY DAMAGE APPRAISERS
6100 Western Pl., # 900
Fort Worth, TX 76107
Telephone: (800) 749-7324 (817) 731-5555
Fax: (817) 731-5550
Mr. Rick Cutler, Manager of Franchise Development

Number of Franchised Units: 198
Number of Company-Owned Units: 0
Number of Total Operating Units: 198

In Business Since: 1963   Franchising Since: 1963

Description of Operation: The industry's largest franchised appraising company. National marketing support, a computerized office management system, training and on-going management assistance are provided. Automobile damage appraising experience is a pre-requisite. PDA provides automobile and property appraisal services for insurance companies and the self-insured.

Equity Capital Needed: $9,250 - $23,450

Franchise Fee: $0

Royalty Fee: 15%

Financial Assistance: Not available.

Managerial Assistance: Perpetual assistance is provided, as needed, by regional managers.

Training Provided: Operational training is on site - 4 days in duration. A comprehensive operations manual and use guide for a computerized management system is provided.

Information Submitted: January 1994

RACS INTERNATIONAL
931 E. 86th St., # 102
Indianapolis, IN 46240
Telephone: (317) 259-7227
Fax: (317) 259-7014
Mr. Chuck Morrison, Regional Director

Number of Franchised Units: 95
Number of Company-Owned Units: 1
Number of Total Operating Units: 96

In Business Since: 1978   Franchising Since: 1991

Description of Operation: Commercial cleaning service that provides cleaning services for commercial, industrial and institutional facilities.

Equity Capital Needed: $4,000 - $30,000

Franchise Fee: $1,500

Royalty Fee: 10%

Financial Assistance: RACS will finance 50% of the franchise cost.

Managerial Assistance: The initial training includes sales, promotional techniques and management training.

Training Provided: The initial training program consists of 30 hours, or no less than 8 training sessions, including classroom instruction and daily exercises on commercial cleaning procedures and methods in office cleaning, restroom sanitizing and floor care.

Information Submitted: November 1993

RAINBOW INTERNATIONAL
1010 N. University Parks Dr.
Waco, TX 76707
Telephone: (800) 583-9100 (817) 756-2122
Fax: (817) 752-0661
Mr. John R. Appel, President

Number of Franchised Units: 750
Number of Company-Owned Units: 1
Number of Total Operating Units: 751

In Business Since: 1981   Franchising Since: 1981

Description of Operation: Rainbow franchisees offer services to commercial and residential clients. Services include disaster restoration - water, fire and smoke. Carpet care and cleaning, including services of carpet repair, pet decontamination and protective oversprays. Rainbow specializes in carpet dyeing and tinting. Other services offered are upholstery, drapery and ceiling cleaning.

Equity Capital Needed: $23,000

Franchise Fee: $15,000

Royalty Fee: 7%

Financial Assistance: Financing is available for qualified individuals.

Managerial Assistance: Rainbow provides extensive initial and on-going managerial assistance, including personnel management, financial management, administrative and marketing systems.

Training Provided: Rainbow provides extensive training for new franchisees that includes all phases of the Rainbow System. The initial training assists in launching a career for a new franchisee.

Information Submitted: December 1993

RESTORX
1135 Braddock Ave.
Braddock, PA 15104
Telephone: (800) 323-3278 (412) 351-8686
Fax: (412) 351-1394
Mr. Dick Davidson, Vice President of Marketing

Number of Franchised Units: 40
Number of Company-Owned Units: 1
Number of Total Operating Units: 41

In Business Since: 1982   Franchising Since: 1982

Description of Operation: Train franchisees to do restoration work for insurance company property losses. Areas of Restorx expertise are fire and smoke damage, water removal, electronic reclamation, fine arts and book reclamation, damage assessment, improvement of indoor air quality and deodorization.

Equity Capital Needed: $17,500 - $60,000

Franchise Fee: $17,500

Royalty Fee: $145 weekly.

Financial Assistance: Up to 60% financing is available at 1% above prime. Financing period for franchise fee is 24 months.

Managerial Assistance: Initially, 6 days of training at home office. Also, 3 days of marketing assistance in field. Seminars are conducted in the field to assist franchisees upon request. On-going marketing and advertising help is continually given to franchisee.

Training Provided: In addition to the above, a 24-hour a day, 7 days a week, 365 days a year hotline is available with technical assistance.

Information Submitted: November 1993

ROBO CLEAN
301 Howard St., 9th Fl.
San Francisco, CA 94105
Telephone: (800) 836-6762 (415) 543-2220
Fax: (415) 543-2224
Mr. Raymond Way, National Marketing Director

Number of Franchised Units: 125
Number of Company-Owned Units: 3
Number of Total Operating Units: 128

In Business Since: 1972   Franchising Since: 1992

Description of Operation: Robotic system for the inspection, cleaning and sanitation of air ducts (HVAC) in residential, commercial and industrial buildings.

Equity Capital Needed: $33,000

Franchise Fee: $29,500

Royalty Fee: 5%

Financial Assistance: Leasing program on $25,000.

Managerial Assistance: We provide on-site training, national advertising, national accounts and local marketing assistance.

Training Provided: Phase 1: 3 - 5 days of training on all technical and marketing aspects of the business in San Francisco, CA. Phase 2: Re-training and consultation 3 - 6 months into operation.

Information Submitted: March 1994

ROTO-ROOTER PLUMBING, SEWER & DRAIN SERVICE
300 Ashworth Rd.
West Des Moines, IA 50265
Telephone: (515) 223-1343
Fax: (515) 223-4220
Mr. Paul W. Carter, Director of Franchise Administration

Number of Franchised Units: 570
Number of Company-Owned Units: 84
Number of Total Operating Units: 654

In Business Since: 1935   **Franchising Since:** 1935

Description of Operation: Largest national provider of repair service plumbing and sewer-drain cleaning. Active in all 50 states, US Possessions, Canada and Japan.

Equity Capital Needed: $24,500 - $99,500

Franchise Fee: $1,000

Royalty Fee: Based on population.

Financial Assistance: None.

Managerial Assistance: Regional management conferences, annual plumbing symposium, traveling specialists in marketing, service and sales.

Training Provided: Provided as needed.

Information Submitted: November 1993

SERV U-1ST
10175 SW Barbur Blvd., Bldg.B.-100BA
Portland, OR 97219
Telephone: (503) 244-7628
Mr. Robert Rosenkranz, President

Number of Franchised Units: 10
Number of Company-Owned Units: 0
Number of Total Operating Units: 10

In Business Since: 1988   **Franchising Since:** 1988

Description of Operation: Complete janitorial service franchise, teaching complete janitorial management - financial control, getting started, production management, marketing, bidding and selling. On-going assistance in finding new accounts in your franchise area.

Equity Capital Needed: $3,000 - $12,000

Franchise Fee: $3,275

Royalty Fee: 3% - 15%

Financial Assistance: 75% of total initial fees to us if you have excellent credit and sufficient assets.

Managerial Assistance: On-the-job training. 8 annual group meetings and trainings. Open-door policy. Manuals.

Training Provided: Usually 8 initial trainings of 2 hours each in getting started and on-the-job training in production and production control.

Information Submitted: December 1993

SERVICE ONE COMMERCIAL CLEANING SYSTEMS
5104 N. Orange Blossom Tr., # 117
Orlando, FL 32810
Telephone: (800) 522-7111 (407) 293-7645
Fax: (407) 299-4306
Mr. Steve Rathel, President

Number of Franchised Units: 107
Number of Company-Owned Units: 0
Number of Total Operating Units: 107

In Business Since: 1964   **Franchising Since:** 1985

Description of Operation: Commercial janitorial business.

Equity Capital Needed: $200,000 - $1,800,000

Franchise Fee: $6,750 - $16,250

Royalty Fee: $175 per month.

Financial Assistance: Limited financing is available.

Managerial Assistance: Complete assistance in all phases.

Training Provided: 3-day training program, including all phases of cleaning, bidding, estimating and management.

Information Submitted: January 1994

SERVICE-TECH CORPORATION
21012 Aurora Rd.
Warrensville Hts., OH 44146
Telephone: (800) 992-9302 (216) 663-2600
Fax: (216) 663-8804
Mr. Alan J. Sutton, President

Number of Franchised Units: 3
Number of Company-Owned Units: 4
Number of Total Operating Units: 7

In Business Since: 1960   **Franchising Since:** 1989

Description of Operation: Indoor air quality remediation and industrial cleaning services. Opportunity to join 33 years of experience in solving the growing concerns associated with indoor air pollution. The list of cleaning services offered includes air duct systems, industrial exhaust systems, industrial ovens, overhead structural steel, restaurant hood exhaust systems, laboratory hood exhaust systems, computer room sub-floors, laundry and restroom exhaust systems. Wide range of customers.

Equity Capital Needed: $49,000

Franchise Fee: $19,000

Royalty Fee: 4% - 6%

Financial Assistance: Assistance in obtaining financing from outside sources.

Managerial Assistance: Franchisees receive assistance with office set-up, field preparation, business and accounting forms, reference manuals, advertising and marketing supplies, open line communication with main office, continual updates on industry-related matters and safety.

Training Provided: 14-day training schedule conducted at the corporate training center, with hands-on field instruction at job sites. Training in marketing, sales, field operations, accounting, personnel and management trainings.

Information Submitted: November 1993

SERVICEMASTER
855 Ridge Lake Blvd.
Memphis, TN 38120
Telephone: (800) 752-6688 (901) 684-7500
Fax: (901) 684-7580
Mr. Dan Kellow, Vice President of Market Expansion

Number of Franchised Units: 4149
Number of Company-Owned Units: 4
Number of Total Operating Units: 4153

In Business Since: 1947   **Franchising Since:** 1952

Description of Operation: ServiceMaster provides heavy cleaning services for homes, including carpet, upholstery, draperies, windows and disaster restoration. Janitorial services are also provided for the commercial market. As you would expect from a $2.5 billion company, we provide all the research, equipment, supplies, initial and continuous training you will need.

Equity Capital Needed: $7,500 - $12,500

Franchise Fee: $12,350 - $23,350

Royalty Fee: 4% - 10% or .5% - 1%.

Financial Assistance: We offer financing on the franchise fee, products and equipment. The term of financing is 5 years. We offer level and graduated payments.

Managerial Assistance: ServiceMaster has 78 different distributors in different regions around the US. These distributors serve as local support for the franchisees. Also, regional operations managers assist the franchisees in the growth and development of their business. All the departments within ServiceMaster have at least one person who handles franchise relations. Each distributor has owned and operated his/her own ServiceMaster for at least 5 years, as have the regional operations managers.

Training Provided: ServiceMaster has a 10-phase training program which includes manuals and videos, ServiceMaster orientation, self-study, on-the-job training, assistance with basic start-up tasks, 2 weeks spent with their distributor or own representative in actual on-the-job training, 1 week at the ServiceMaster Academy of Management which is held every other month, specific personalized training in marketing and sales, financial counseling, goal determination and personal review for future plans.

Information Submitted: December 1993

SHADE SHOWER
7950 E. Redfield Rd., # 120
Scottsdale, AZ 85260
Telephone: (602) 443-0432
Fax: (602) 991-1418
Mr. Brook Carey, President

Number of Franchised Units: 24
Number of Company-Owned Units: 0
Number of Total Operating Units: 24

In Business Since: 1988   **Franchising Since:** 1989

Description of Operation: Service commercial and residential customers at their locations. Hand wash mini-blinds, vertical blinds and pleated shades from a Shade Shower WashWagon (patents pending) mobile unit equipped with expandable hanging racks and a water treatment system. Also, clean interior windows and clean exterior windows and screens with pressure hot water system. Area franchises and protected territories.

Equity Capital Needed: $12,500 - $16,800

Franchise Fee: $0

Royalty Fee: 0%

Financial Assistance: Franchisee to arrange his/her own financing for purchase price, which includes all tools and equipment. An additional $5,000 of operating capital would be desirable to defray initial operating expenses and for adequate advertising to launch the business.

Managerial Assistance: Shade Shower provides continuing service in advertising, marketing, operations and financial management. 3 complete manuals are included. An initial supply of flyers, brochures, doorhangers, forms, stationery, envelopes, business cards, signage and ad slicks of the logo and display ad layouts are provided.

Training Provided: We offer 1 day of training in Scottsdale, AZ. Operational: one-on-one additional training in Scottsdale for as long as required.

Information Submitted: April 1994

SIGN WASHERS, THE / TSW
4278 Pacific Highway
Bellingham, WA 98226
Telephone: (206) 647-8545
Fax: (206) 647-8545
Mr. Doug Wilson, President

Number of Franchised Units: 14
Number of Company-Owned Units: 2
Number of Total Operating Units: 16

In Business Since: 1985   **Franchising Since:** 1986

Description of Operation: Awning maintenance franchise. Training on equipment and chemicals, brochures and on-going training. We specialize in the new generation of back-lite vinyl awning.

Equity Capital Needed: $25,000 - $65,000

Franchise Fee: $22,500

Royalty Fee: 7%

Financial Assistance: None.

Managerial Assistance: Sales training with sales professional. In-house management training. On-going support.

Training Provided: We provide manuals and videos, on-the-job training, 4 days of training at the head office, on-going support and networking with other TSW franchisees.

Information Submitted: January 1994

SPARKLE WASH
26851 Richmond Rd.
Cleveland, OH 44146
Telephone: (800) 321-0770 (216) 464-4212
Fax: (216) 464-8869
Mr. William Johnson, National Sales Manager

Number of Franchised Units: 206
Number of Company-Owned Units: 1
Number of Total Operating Units: 207

In Business Since: 1965   **Franchising Since:** 1967

Description of Operation: Mobile pressure cleaning and restoration.

Equity Capital Needed: $50,000 total investment.

Franchise Fee: Minimum $9,000.

Royalty Fee: 5% - 3%, decreasing % based upon sales.

Financial Assistance: Financial assistance is available for the vehicle and equipment. Sparkle Wash will finance up to a maximum of 50% of the fee (after the minimum fee).

Managerial Assistance: Both initial and on-going assistance are available. Assistance with initial marketing and advertising programs are emphasized. Also, on-going technical support and technical updates are provided. An annual convention and meeting provides further access to new products and market updates.

Training Provided: Complete training programs are included on the operation, maintenance, sales and marketing, business systems, advertising and estimating. This two-part training includes both headquarters and field training in the franchisee's territory.

Information Submitted: November 1993

STANLEY STEEMER CARPET CLEANER
5500 Stanley Steemer Pkwy.
Dublin, OH 43017

Telephone: (800) 848-7496 (614) 764-2007
Fax: (614) 764-1506
Mr. Philip P. Ryser, Vice President/General Counsel

Number of Franchised Units: 225
Number of Company-Owned Units: 22
Number of Total Operating Units: 247

In Business Since: 1947   **Franchising Since:** 1972

Description of Operation: Carpet and upholstery cleaning and related services.

Equity Capital Needed: $52,930 - $77,840

Franchise Fee: Based on population; $20,000 per 100,000.

Royalty Fee: 7% monthly.

Financial Assistance: Depending on credit worthiness, financial assistance is available.

Managerial Assistance: Initial training is provided. Assistance, as needed.

Training Provided: Initial training is provided. Assistance, as needed.

Information Submitted: March 1994

STEAM BROTHERS
933 1/2 Basin Ave., P. O. Box 2656
Bismarck, ND 58504
Telephone: (800) 767-5064 (701) 222-1263
Fax: (701) 258-9269
Mr. Adam Leier, President

Number of Franchised Units: 17
Number of Company-Owned Units: 0
Number of Total Operating Units: 17

In Business Since: 1977   **Franchising Since:** 1984

Description of Operation: Steam Brothers provides: carpet, drapery and upholstery cleaning; fire, smoke and water damage restoration; furnace and air-duct cleaning; and acoustical ceiling cleaning.

Equity Capital Needed: $11,000 - $55,000

Franchise Fee: $8,999

Royalty Fee: 5% - 6.5%

Financial Assistance: The initial franchise fee includes start-up equipment and inventory. The initial franchise fee of $8,999 can be financed with the franchisor with $4,995 down and $4,004 financed for 2 years at 10% interest.

Managerial Assistance: We provide manuals, seminars, field representatives, newsletters, troubleshooting hotlines, monthly advertising material and suggested uses, promotional recommendations, on-going new product and services packages and more.

Training Provided: We offer training at headquarters in Bismarck, ND for 5 days. Training at franchisee's location is for 2 days.

Information Submitted: March 1994

STEAMATIC
1320 S. University Dr., # 400
Fort Worth, TX 76262
Telephone: (800) 527-1295 (817) 332-1575
Fax: (817) 332-5349
Mr. Scott Bevier, Senior Vice President of Franchise Development

Number of Franchised Units: 327
Number of Company-Owned Units: 10
Number of Total Operating Units: 337

In Business Since: 1948   **Franchising Since:** 1968

Description of Operation: Steamatic provides water, fire and storm insurance restoration (disaster recovery services); indoor environmental services, air duct and coil cleaning; carpet cleaning; furniture cleaning; drapery cleaning; deodorizing; wood restoration; document restoration; corrosion control; ceiling and wall cleaning.

Equity Capital Needed: $40,000 - $75,000

Franchise Fee: $5,000 - $12,000 - $16,000 - $18,000, depending on the size of the territory.

Royalty Fee: 8% - 5%

Financial Assistance: Equipment, supplies, cleaning agents and chemicals can be financed.

Managerial Assistance: We provide continuous training and assistance in the franchisee's territory, regional and annual seminars, training and marketing tapes, TV, radio and print advertising provided. Direct mail and 24-hour toll-free numbers.

Training Provided: Initial training is 2 weeks. Advanced training is optional. The first week concentrates on the various cleaning and restoration services. The second week is a mini-business school session. Classes consist of advertising and marketing procedures, selling techniques, accounting methods, financial management, tele-marketing skill, commercial pricing, insurance, residential jobs, writing programs, maintenance contracts, brainstorming, role playing and much more.

Information Submitted: March 1994

SWISHER HYGIENE
6849 Fairview Rd., # 200
Charlotte, NC 28210
Telephone: (800) 444-4138 (704) 364-7707
Fax: (800) 444-4565
Mr. Jerry Allen, Vice President of Marketing

Number of Franchised Units: 60
Number of Company-Owned Units: 1
Number of Total Operating Units: 61

In Business Since: 1983   **Franchising Since:** 1990

Description of Operation: Commercial restroom hygiene company, providing once-a-week servicing to approximately 20,000 accounts nationally. In addition, we now offer 6 additional health-related services outside the restroom area to our customer base.

Equity Capital Needed: $45,000 - $75,000

Franchise Fee: $35,000 - $85,000

Royalty Fee: 6%

Financial Assistance: Partial financing may be available to a qualified candidate to provide him/her with a part of the initial franchisee fee at a reasonable rate over a 2 - 4 year period.

Managerial Assistance: We provide a total consolidated support system, involving accounting, receivables, customer service, 800# customer line, invoicing, data entry, field service and field sales support, etc. We are committed to a total support-oriented franchise.

Training Provided: We provide everything from initial training in our home office, to training on-site, to total on-going training and networking.

Information Submitted: November 1993

TOWN & COUNTRY OFFICE & CARPET CARE
2580 San Ramon Valley Blvd. # B-208
San Ramon, CA 94583
Telephone: (510) 867-3850
Fax: (510) 867-2756
Mr. Theodore F. Prince, President

Number of Franchised Units: 110
Number of Company-Owned Units: 0
Number of Total Operating Units: 110

In Business Since: 1971   **Franchising Since:** 1986

Description of Operation: Janitorial franchises.

Equity Capital Needed: $4,900 - $86,000

Franchise Fee: $3,500

Royalty Fee: 10% - 4%

Financial Assistance: We finance 2/3 of the franchise fee over 24 months by the franchisor.

Managerial Assistance: On-going.

Training Provided: 1 week, with refresher courses.

Information Submitted: November 1993

U. S. ROOTER
17025 Batesville Pike Rd.
North Little Rock, AR 72120
Telephone: (501) 835-1500
Ms. Maxine Ratliff, Secretary/Treasurer

Number of Franchised Units: 3
Number of Company-Owned Units: 0
Number of Total Operating Units: 3

In Business Since: 1965   **Franchising Since:** 1969

Description of Operation: We furnish patented sewer and drain cleaning equipment, a registered name and trademark, instruction and training, as well as help in any phase of the business to get the franchisee started in a business of his/her own.

Equity Capital Needed: $5,000 - $75,000

Franchise Fee: $20,000 - $25,000

Royalty Fee: Flat fee.

Financial Assistance: There is no financial assistance.

Managerial Assistance: Using our years of experience, we will instruct the new franchisee, using an instruction booklet and verbal communications.

Training Provided: We provide a 2-week training period to train the franchisee or whomever he/she chooses for us to train. Longer period, if required.

Information Submitted: January 1994

UNICLEAN SYSTEMS
212 Brooksbank Ave., # 460
N. Vancouver, BC V7J 2C1 CAN
Telephone: (604) 986-4750
Fax: (604) 987-6838
Mr. Jack B. Karpowicz, President

Number of Franchised Units: 289
Number of Company-Owned Units: 1
Number of Total Operating Units: 290

In Business Since: 1976   **Franchising Since:** 1981

Description of Operation: Professional office cleaning.

Equity Capital Needed: $6,500 +

Franchise Fee: $7,000 - $12,000

Royalty Fee: 10%

Financial Assistance: None.

Managerial Assistance: Telephone hotline.

Training Provided: We offer 1 week of training at the franchisee's home town location.

Information Submitted: March 1994

VALUE LINE MAINTENANCE SYSTEMS
P. O. Box 6450
Great Falls, MT 59406
Telephone: (800) 824-4838 (406) 761-4471
Fax: (406) 761-4486
Mr. Joseph P. Gilligan, General Counsel

Number of Franchised Units: 29
Number of Company-Owned Units: 0
Number of Total Operating Units: 29

In Business Since: 1959   **Franchising Since:** 1982

Description of Operation: Contract cleaning, providing janitorial services to large, single-floor retail outlets, such as supermarkets and general merchandise stores.

Equity Capital Needed: $50,800

Franchise Fee: $30,000

Royalty Fee: 10%

Financial Assistance: Financing of the franchise fee after an initial payment of $18,000. Financing is available on machine purchases through Company-owned supplier.

Managerial Assistance: We provide invoicing service, marketing assistance, up-dated training in new techniques and products, supply purchasing program, machine repair, other business, legal and technical assistance.

Training Provided: We provide a 2-week training course, plus additional site training in operations, financial control, marketing, service techniques, labor training, advertising and quality control.

Information Submitted: January 1994

CLOTHING AND SHOES

ATHLETE'S FOOT, THE
1950 Vaughn Rd.
Kennesaw, GA 30144
Telephone: (800) 524-6444 (404) 514-4719
Fax: (404) 514-4903
Mr. Joe DeMarco, Director of Franchise Development

Number of Franchised Units: 366
Number of Company-Owned Units: 279
Number of Total Operating Units: 645

In Business Since: 1971   **Franchising Since:** 1972

Description of Operation: The Athlete's Foot is the largest franchisor of specialty athletic footwear retail stores. We operate in 21 countries, including the US, Canada, Mexico, Australia, Europe and Asia. We sell name-brand athletic footwear and apparel, in a typical 2,000 SF store. Our stores are located in malls, strip centers and downtown locations.

Equity Capital Needed: $175,000 - $250,000

Franchise Fee: $25,000

Royalty Fee: 3.5%, plus .5% advertising fee.

Financial Assistance: None.

Managerial Assistance: New franchisees are assigned a New Owner Coordinator and a Franchise Coordinator who guides the franchisee through all the steps, from the training session to store opening. The Franchise Coordinator continues to work with the franchisee on an on-going basis. The Advertising Coordinator works with the new franchisee to develop a marketing plan for the grand opening and beyond.

Training Provided: New franchisees attend a 5-day training session in Atlanta. Training encompasses financial planning, inventory planning and control, open-to-buy inventory assortment, visual merchandising, store construction, operations, human resources and advertising. New franchisees certified in 2 other training programs, the Certified Sales Associate and Fit Technician. New franchisees also attend our Fit University in Naperville, IL for 3 days, becoming certified as a Master Fit Technician to certify their staff.

Information Submitted: November 1993

ATHLETIC ATTIC RETAIL CO.
P. O. Box 14503
Gainesville, FL 32604
Telephone: (904) 377-5289
Fax: (904) 377-7169
Mr. Jack Thompson, Executive Vice President

Number of Franchised Units: 60
Number of Company-Owned Units: 30
Number of Total Operating Units: 90

In Business Since: 1974   **Franchising Since:** 1974

Description of Operation: A retail sporting goods operation, specializing in the sale of active-wear apparel, athletic footwear and related sporting goods (racquetball, tennis, soccer, etc.).

Equity Capital Needed: $15,000 for franchise fee; $125,000 - $175,000 total investment. Minimum $45,000 cash required.

Franchise Fee: $15,000

Royalty Fee: 1.25%

Financial Assistance: No financial assistance is provided by the franchisor; however, all necessary information for loan applications is available.

Managerial Assistance: Assistance includes, but is not limited to, site selection, lease negotiations, store design, basic construction drawings, product mix assistance, opening supplier accounts, accounting systems, on-site opening assistance, complete operations manual, advertising manual, local advertising materials, monthly management and news-letters. Annual sales meetings.

Training Provided: The training program includes 1 week of classroom instruction in all aspects of store operations and 1 week of in-store instruction at the franchisor's training store.

Information Submitted: March 1994

FLEET FEET SPORTS
2407 J St.
Sacramento, CA 95816
Telephone: (916) 557-1000
Fax: (916) 557-1010
Mr. Tom Raynor, President

Number of Franchised Units: 37
Number of Company-Owned Units: 0
Number of Total Operating Units: 37

In Business Since: 1976   **Franchising Since:** 1978

Description of Operation: Retailer of specialty athletic footwear and apparel for lifetime sports (running, walking, cycling, swimming, aerobics and cross-training).

Equity Capital Needed: $125,000 - $175,000

Franchise Fee: $17,500

Royalty Fee: 4% - 2%

Financial Assistance: Financial planning, business planning, review and financing strategy.

Managerial Assistance: Operational expertise, financial training, retail sales expertise, computer networking and product exchange.

Training Provided: Depending on the status of the franchisee, training can range from 3 weeks - 6 months. Combination of classroom, store and research.

Information Submitted: November 1993

GABBRIELE
P. O. Box 158
Oakton, VA 22124
Telephone: (703) 934-4455
Fax: (703) 934-4459
Mr. F. Schmitt, Vice President of Franchising

Number of Franchised Units: 0
Number of Company-Owned Units: 6
Number of Total Operating Units: 6

In Business Since: 1982   **Franchising Since:** 1992

Description of Operation: Leather good retailers.

Equity Capital Needed: $60,000

Franchise Fee: $20,000

Royalty Fee: 5%, plus 1% advertising.

Financial Assistance: Not available.

Managerial Assistance: The training program is at the corporate head-quarters and corporate stores. During the training program, you will receive your copy of the Confidential Operations Manual for operating your store.

Training Provided: Pre-opening - Gabbriele staff will work with you on site selection, lease review, store set-up, inventory, personnel, advertis-ing and training. Gabbriele will guide you through your grand opening program. A member of the Gabbriele staff will also spend a week in your store prior to the grand opening.

Information Submitted: February 1994

JERSEY CITY
824 - 41st Ave., NE
Calgary, AB T2E 3R3 CAN
Telephone: (403) 230-5587
Fax: (403) 230-8370
Mr. Tim Walsh, Fran. Licensing Agent

Number of Franchised Units: 21
Number of Company-Owned Units: 7
Number of Total Operating Units: 28

In Business Since: 1983   **Franchising Since:** 1989

Description of Operation: Jersey City operates retail outlets, located in major shopping centers. We offer a wide variety of authentic replica league apparel and souvenir items. We carry merchandise licensed by the major professional and university sports leagues.

Equity Capital Needed: $130,000 - $180,000

Franchise Fee: $20,000

Royalty Fee: 5%

Financial Assistance: Assistance in sourcing financing from chartered banks is provided.

Managerial Assistance: We offer on-going training and support in pur-chasing, budgeting, merchandising, co-operative advertising and design of promotions, plus extensive professional assistance on daily oper-ations, as required.

Training Provided: We provide up to 2 weeks of head office and grand opening assistance, covering all aspects of store operations, including computers, sales, merchandising, budgets, supervision of staff and more.

Information Submitted: February 1994

MERLE HARMON'S FAN FAIR
424 Lamar Blvd. E., # 210
Arlington, TX 76011
Telephone: (800) 788-0983 (817) 277-0104
Fax: (817) 860-9160
Mr. Robert Ortegel, Vice President of Franchise Sales

Number of Franchised Units: 106
Number of Company-Owned Units: 40
Number of Total Operating Units: 146

In Business Since: 1977   **Franchising Since:** 1982

Description of Operation: Retail licensed sports apparel.

Equity Capital Needed: $128,000 - $199,000

Franchise Fee: $25,000

Royalty Fee: 5%

Financial Assistance: Not available.

Managerial Assistance: Fan Fair's field operations has Store Managers reporting to District Managers, who in turn report to Regional Managers, who in turn report to 2 National Sales Managers - both of whom report to our President. The emphasis is on daily execution and performance at the store level.

Training Provided: Fan Fair's training program will last somewhere between 7 - 10 days. Training includes an introductory session, an administrative session, construction, financial, purchasing, inventory control, merchandising, fixture planning, on-the-job training, advertising, store visits, etc.

Information Submitted: January 1994

PRO IMAGE, THE
563 West 500 South, # 330
Bountiful, UT 84010
Telephone: (800) 653-1991 (801) 292-8777
Fax: (801) 292-4603
Ms. Raylene Hendricks, Sales/Leasing

Number of Franchised Units: 209
Number of Company-Owned Units: 1
Number of Total Operating Units: 210

In Business Since: 1985   **Franchising Since:** 1985

Description of Operation: The Pro Image is a franchise selling licensed sportswear (jackets, jerseys, hats, T-shirts, sweats) and memorabilia (autographed balls and plaques, key chains, mugs, posters, etc.) of your favorite teams. MLB, NFL, NBA, NHL and NCAA. If you love sports, this is a fun business!

Equity Capital Needed: $200,000

Franchise Fee: $19,500

Royalty Fee: 4%

Financial Assistance: None.

Managerial Assistance: The Pro Image has a staff of knowledgeable and helpful people. Our warehouse is accessible to new franchisees to assist with merchandise orders. Each franchisee is assigned to a franchise manager who is available through our toll-free 800# and who makes a personal visit to each store on a yearly basis. Our merchandising manager is helpful with window displays and tips on making your store more attractive to the shopper. She writes articles for the Pro Image newsletter which is sent out monthly.

Training Provided: The new franchisees are given 4 days of training in the areas of employee management, accounting procedures, initial and on-going inventory purchases, merchandising and theft prevention.

Information Submitted: November 1993

SAY! FASHION SPREES
1365 Sixth Ave.
San Diego, CA 92101
Telephone: (800) 472-9669 (619) 238-1404
Fax: (619) 238-1558
Mr. Garrett C. Soule, Senior VP/Chief Financial Officer

Number of Franchised Units: 10
Number of Company-Owned Units: 1
Number of Total Operating Units: 11

In Business Since: 1990   **Franchising Since:** 1993

Description of Operation: Say! provides merchandise consisting of women's clothing and accessories, along with training and support services, to franchisees who will then sell such merchandise directly to consumers. Say is a "Boutique on Wheels." We take the international ladies' fashions and accessories directly to the consumer, when they want it and where they want it!

Equity Capital Needed: $13,000 - $18,000

Franchise Fee: $5,000 - $7,500

Royalty Fee: 6%

Financial Assistance: We are working on financing packages at this time.

Managerial Assistance: Our management team is available through weekend seminars, 2-day intensive trainings and actual field training programs. We accomplish this through "team work."

Training Provided: Our initial 2-day training program consists of introduction and goal setting, essentials of success, growth and development, bulk mail, networking, business forms, record keeping, fashion sprees, fashion coordinating, marketing, fashion and color.

Information Submitted: January 1994

SHOWCASE, THE / COMPLETE ATHLETE
1850 Delmar Dr.
Folcroft, PA 19032
Telephone: (800) 345-1485 (215) 532-7200
Fax: (215) 532-1833
Mr. Frank J. Miceli, Vice President of Marketing and Advertising

Number of Franchised Units: 50
Number of Company-Owned Units: 22
Number of Total Operating Units: 72

In Business Since: 1985   **Franchising Since:** 1987

Description of Operation: Retailer of authentic and replica sports team apparel and novelties.

Equity Capital Needed: $175,000 - $250,000

Franchise Fee: $30,000

Royalty Fee: 6%

Financial Assistance: Introductions can be made between qualified candidates and various lending institutions.

Managerial Assistance: We provide a 6-week training period with a district or regional manager. A 200-page manual "Rule Book" is provided, along with a 60-page "Play Book." Additionally, we provide on-going training seminars on a regional basis.

Training Provided: Same as above.

Information Submitted: November 1993

SOX APPEAL
6321 Bury Dr., # 1
Eden Prairie, MN 55346
Telephone: (800) 966-7699 (612) 937-6162
Fax: (612) 934-5665
Mr. Jack Abelson, Vice President of Franchise Development

Number of Franchised Units: 28
Number of Company-Owned Units: 0
Number of Total Operating Units: 28

In Business Since: 1984   **Franchising Since:** 1988

Description of Operation: Retail sale of men's, women's and children's shoes.

Equity Capital Needed: $90,000 - $130,000

Franchise Fee: $20,000

Royalty Fee: 5%

Financial Assistance: None.

Managerial Assistance: Aside from the initial training, franchisees may call our toll-free 800# for help and information on any subject at any time. We also provide detailed manuals to assist the franchisees.

Training Provided: 4 days of intensive, extensive training, including order writing, hiring and training the staff, back room operations, etc. Part of 1 day is spent in one of the local stores for hands-on training.

Information Submitted: November 1993

T-SHIRTS PLUS
4732 W. Waco Dr.
Waco, TX 76710
Telephone: (800) 880-0721 (817) 776-8872
Fax: (817) 776-6838
Ms. Vickie Watt, Director of Development

Number of Franchised Units: 113
Number of Company-Owned Units: 0
Number of Total Operating Units: 113

In Business Since: 1974   **Franchising Since:** 1976

Description of Operation: The sale and enhancement of athletic family apparel and customizing while the customer waits.

Equity Capital Needed: $100,000; $50,000 cash and $50,000 collateral.

Franchise Fee: $35,000

Royalty Fee: 6%, or flat $1,250 per month.

Financial Assistance: We will assist in SBA financing, helping to prepare the package and submit to a lender.

Managerial Assistance: We provide on-going support, monthly news and promotional packages, continuous software, support and assistance.

Training Provided: We provide a 7-day "college" training that is mandatory for all new franchise owners - providing training in all aspects of the business in Waco, TX.

Information Submitted: March 1994

CONSTRUCTION AND REMODELING

AIRE SERV
1010 University Parks Dr.
Waco, TX 76707
Telephone: (800) 583-2662 (817) 757-2662
Fax: (817) 757-1667
Mr. Matt Michel, Vice President/General Manager

Number of Franchised Units: 6
Number of Company-Owned Units: 0
Number of Total Operating Units: 6

In Business Since: 1993   **Franchising Since:** 1994

Description of Operation: National heating, ventilating and air conditioning franchise organization, focused on the residential and light commercial service and replacement market. Franchisees are typically progressive, professional, state-licensed HVAC contractors.

Equity Capital Needed: $20,000 - $100,000

Franchise Fee: $12,500 +

Royalty Fee: 6% - 3%

Financial Assistance: Financing is available.

Managerial Assistance: Aire Serv franchisees are provided with extensive sales, marketing, operations and management material, systems and support. On-going support is provided through national conferences, regional consultants and a toll-free hotline for immediate counseling and assistance.

Training Provided: Intensive sales, marketing and management training is provided for new franchisees (and their new hires). Additional training is provided throughout the year with 4 national conferences, each focused on a topic of concern to the HVAC contractor.

Information Submitted: December 1993

AMERICAN CONCRETE RAISING
918 Fairway Dr.
Bensenville, IL 60106
Telephone: (708) 595-5225
Fax: (708) 595-5366
Mr. John G. Meyers, President

Number of Franchised Units: 3
Number of Company-Owned Units: 1
Number of Total Operating Units: 4

In Business Since: 1983   **Franchising Since:** 1989

Description of Operation: Concrete restoration, slabjacking and pressure grouting. We save concrete rather than replace. This saves customers time and money. Clients include some of the leading corporations in the US.

Equity Capital Needed: $30,000 - $50,000

Franchise Fee: $15,000

Royalty Fee: 6% - 8%

Financial Assistance: None.

Managerial Assistance: 5 - 10 days of management training at home office and 5 days at franchisee's location. Also, extensive operations manual and continual field visits.

Training Provided: 5 - 10 days at home office - more if required. Continued field training and monthly published updates.

Information Submitted: November 1993

AMERICAN RESTORATION SERVICES
2061 Monongahela Ave.
Pittsburgh, PA 15218
Telephone: (800) 245-1617 (412) 351-7100
Fax: (412) 351-2544
Mr. Russell K. Case, President

Number of Franchised Units: 267
Number of Company-Owned Units: 1
Number of Total Operating Units: 268

In Business Since: 1970   **Franchising Since:** 1976

Description of Operation: General restoration of homes and commercial structures, using our unique line of cleaning and sealing products.

Equity Capital Needed: $30,000

Franchise Fee: $10,000

Royalty Fee: $1,500 per year.

Financial Assistance: Total cost paid to American Restoration is $22,500, of which $10,000 is through a lease and $5,000 is Company financed.

Managerial Assistance: Phone support, on-site visits and correspondence with master dealers.

Training Provided: A.R.S. trains dealers in marketing, sales, accounting and equipment operation.

Information Submitted: January 1994

AMERICAN ROOF-BRITE
3398 Sanford Dr.
Marietta, GA 30066
Telephone: (800) 476-9271 (404) 429-0232
Fax: (404) 424-1494
Mr. Larry Stevens, President

Number of Franchised Units: 11
Number of Company-Owned Units: 1
Number of Total Operating Units: 12

In Business Since: 1973   **Franchising Since:** 1990

Description of Operation: Clean ugly, stained asphalt roofing shingles. Work performed for roofing manufacturers and homeowners.

Equity Capital Needed: $5,995

Franchise Fee: $0

Royalty Fee: 6%

Financial Assistance: None.

Managerial Assistance: Data not available.

Training Provided: Phone consultation and manual with instructions.

Information Submitted: January 1994

ARCHADECK
2112 W. Laburnum Ave., # 109
Richmond, VA 23227
Telephone: (800) 882-7969 (804) 353-6999
Fax: (804) 358-1878
Ms. Julie West, Director of Business Development

Number of Franchised Units: 84
Number of Company-Owned Units: 0
Number of Total Operating Units: 84

In Business Since: 1980   **Franchising Since:** 1985

Description of Operation: Using photos, diagrams and videotapes, you will meet with customers. Back at your office, you will prepare 2 designs (pre-designs or custom designs) to present to the customer at a second meeting. Once the final design is chosen, you will send your preliminary sketches to the Company's drafting division which will supply full construction plans with complete material layouts and specifications. The sub-contract Archadeck-trained carpenters will usually build the deck in 2 - 3 days.

Equity Capital Needed: $35,000 - $75,000

Franchise Fee: $16,500 - $32,500

Royalty Fee: 7% - residential sales; 5% - commercial sales; 1% - advertising-residential sales.

Financial Assistance: Limited assistance.

Managerial Assistance: Marketing director will assist you in a marketing plan before you open your office. Step-by-step guidance in opening your business, starting with a business plan. Start-up field consultant will help in the first 3 months of operation. On-going field consultants in the areas of sales and construction. Toll-free numbers to all personnel at headquarters. Construction and drafting departments to assist you at anytime. Regional and national workshops and seminars all year round.

Training Provided: Archadeck would prefer that you have no experience in construction. We will teach you construction, design, product knowledge, computer software, marketing plan, sales and business operations in a 3-week training. Archadeck will train any employees that you hire later on. Before you arrive for the 3-week training, you will receive start-up materials, manuals, videotapes and audio tapes that will help prepare you for the sales and construction portions of the training.

Information Submitted: November 1993

B-DRY SYSTEM
1341 Copley Rd.
Akron, OH 44320
Telephone: (800) 321-0985 (216) 867-2576
Fax: (216) 867-7693
Mr. Joseph Garfinkel, Vice President

Number of Franchised Units: 69
Number of Company-Owned Units: 0
Number of Total Operating Units: 69

In Business Since: 1958   **Franchising Since:** 1978

Description of Operation: B-Dry System licensees receive territorial rights to their own area(s). Licensees are trained to install B-Dry's exclusive patented interior drainage system, designed to alleviate basement water leakage. The B-Dry system offers its customers a full life of the structure warranty on areas waterproofed. Transferable from owner to owner.

Equity Capital Needed: $25,000 - $45,000

Franchise Fee: $15,000 - $60,000 ($60,000 for area with 1,000,000 population).

Royalty Fee: 6%

Financial Assistance: B-Dry System will finance up to 75% of the franchise fee with no interest. The balance is payable at a rate of $150 per installed job.

Managerial Assistance: B-Dry licensees receive managerial assistance through regional seminars, workshops, audio and video tapes, on-site visits and tele-conferencing.

Training Provided: At B-Dry System's training center in Akron, OH, you will be taught technical basement waterproofing procedures, with the aid of one-on-one lessons, written manuals, audio tape and video tape presentations, classroom discussion and on-the-job instruction. On-going field training is also provided regularly and the monthly newsletters keep you further informed about refinements to the system. You will also receive B-Dry's advertising package/promotional materials, honed by 30 years' experience.

Information Submitted: March 1994

BATH FITTER
27 Berard Dr., # 2701
S. Burlington, VT 05403
Telephone: (800) 892-2847 (802) 860-2919
Fax: (802) 862-7976
Ms. Linda Brakel

Number of Franchised Units: 9
Number of Company-Owned Units: 1
Number of Total Operating Units: 10

In Business Since: 1984   **Franchising Since:** 1992

Description of Operation: Sales and installation of custom-molded acrylic bathtub liners, made-to-measure acrylic bath walls, shower bases, shower walls and related accessories.

Equity Capital Needed: $24,800 - $48,400

Franchise Fee: $12,500

Royalty Fee: 0%

Financial Assistance: Data not available.

Managerial Assistance: Direct assistance with preparation of a business plan; regular on-site visits by area representatives.; ad layouts, pre-printed full-color marketing materials; 800# hotline (24 hours).

Training Provided: Office and administration procedures (1 day); sales methods (1 day); installation techniques (3 days - owners and employees).

Information Submitted: November 1993

CALIFORNIA CLOSET COMPANY
1700 Montgomery St., # 249
San Francisco, CA 94111
Telephone: (415) 433-9999
Fax: (415) 433-2911
Ms. Megan Hall, Franchise Development Manager

Number of Franchised Units: 94
Number of Company-Owned Units: 3
Number of Total Operating Units: 97

In Business Since: 1978   **Franchising Since:** 1982

Description of Operation: California Closets sells and installs custom storage and organization systems for the home and office - closets, garages, entertainment centers, home offices and small business offices.

Equity Capital Needed: $75,000 - $200,000

Franchise Fee: $9,000 - $38,000

Royalty Fee: 6%

Financial Assistance: Outside financing for equipment purchases on start-up.

Managerial Assistance: Data not available.

Training Provided: 3-week training program for new franchisees. Site selection, site build-out assistance, equipment purchase assistance and on-site start-up assistance.

Information Submitted: November 1993

CERTA PROPAINTERS
1220 Valley Forge Rd.
Valley Forge, PA 19482
Telephone: (800) 462-3782
Fax: (215) 983-9884
Mr. Charles E. Chase, President

Number of Franchised Units: 39
Number of Company-Owned Units: 0
Number of Total Operating Units: 39

In Business Since: 1992   **Franchising Since:** 1993

Description of Operation: Full-service residential and commercial painting franchise. Training, on-going support, marketing and business development. Ideal franchisee has little or no painting experience, but has solid leadership and management abilities and skills. We are putting business men and women into the painting business.

Equity Capital Needed: $25,000 - $30,000

Franchise Fee: $15,000

Royalty Fee: $9,000 first year; $12,000 second year and thereafter.

Financial Assistance: The franchisor will finance up to 50% of the franchise fee and suppliers will finance other specific costs as well.

Managerial Assistance: Initial training - 2 weeks. Weekly follow-ups until year 3. 3-day annual conference, quarterly reviews and annual budgeting. Monthly newsletters, weekly meetings and monthly marketing planning.

Training Provided: 2 weeks of training prior to start-up; quarterly training in field. After year 1, advanced training is available to franchisees and their employees. Manuals, videos and one-on-one training.

Information Submitted: November 1993

CLOSET FACTORY, THE
12800 S. Broadway
Los Angeles, CA 90061
Telephone: (800) MY-CLOSET (310) 516-7000
Fax: (310) 538-2676
Mr. David Luoy, Vice President/Franchise Director

Number of Franchised Units: 29
Number of Company-Owned Units: 1
Number of Total Operating Units: 30

In Business Since: 1983   **Franchising Since:** 1985

Description of Operation: The Closet Factory markets, designs, manufactures, constructs and installs custom closets and storage systems for consumers and sells other related products and services.

Equity Capital Needed: Total investment approximately $185,000. Need $100,000 liquid.

Franchise Fee: $39,500

Royalty Fee: 5.75%

Financial Assistance: The franchisor does not provide any financing, but equipment and vans may be financed by franchisees through their sources.

Managerial Assistance: Closet Factory provides complete operations and sales manuals, collateral, advertising materials and sales aids. Franchise newsletter and meetings. Perpetual on-site and telephone assistance.

Training Provided: 2 weeks at our Los Angeles, CA headquarters. On-site, pre-opening training. Additional training is available, if necessary.

Information Submitted: November 1993

CLOSETTEC
55 Providence Hwy.
Norwood, MA 02062
Telephone: (800) 365-2021 (617) 769-9997
Fax: (617) 769-9996
Mr. David Rogers, President

Number of Franchised Units: 33
Number of Company-Owned Units: 0
Number of Total Operating Units: 33

In Business Since: 1985   **Franchising Since:** 1986

Description of Operation: Marketing, sales, design, manufacturing and installation of residential and commercial closet systems, storage systems, home/office/garage systems, etc.

Equity Capital Needed: $115,000 - $185,000

Franchise Fee: $30,000

Royalty Fee: 5.5%

Financial Assistance: None.

Managerial Assistance: Initial 7 - 10 days for opening of new operation. Continuing information via "Hottecs" and "Memotecs," annual conferences, franchisee interaction with 24-hour hotline.

Training Provided: A minimum 2 weeks of training at corporate training facility for owner and all staff. If desired, 7 - 10 days on site.

Information Submitted: November 1993

COMPREHENSIVE PAINTING
4723 N. Academy Blvd.
Colorado Springs, CO 80918
Telephone: (800) 374-8898 (719) 599-8983
Fax: (719) 599-7933
Mr. Michael H. Crawford, President

Number of Franchised Units: 1
Number of Company-Owned Units: 1
Number of Total Operating Units: 2

In Business Since: 1986   **Franchising Since:** 1992

Description of Operation: Comprehensive Painting provides residential home painting services and wood restoration, which includes treatment of decks, homes, wallpapering and painting services.

Equity Capital Needed: $11,500 - $30,000 (including fee).

Franchise Fee: $9,500

Royalty Fee: 6%

Financial Assistance: Royalty may be partially financed to qualified applicants. Equipment and signage financed by Sherwin Williams Paint Company to qualified applicants.

Managerial Assistance: Assistance includes customer newsletter, semi-annual advertising promotions, database and accounting services, as well as an 800# and on-going marketing with 4-color documentation and the use of videos for training and marketing.

Training Provided: 6 - 8 weeks of personal training in marketing, management, sales, estimating, applications and color recommending, as well as customer relations and personnel management.

EASI-SET INDUSTRIES
P. O. Box 300
Midland, VA 22728
Telephone: (703) 439-8911
Fax: (703) 439-1232
Mr. John G. Dallain, Vice President

Number of Franchised Units: 22
Number of Company-Owned Units: 7
Number of Total Operating Units: 29

In Business Since: 1978   Franchising Since: 1978

Description of Operation: ESI provides a service to concrete products producers who are seeking diversification and to persons interested in establishing a pre-cast concrete business. The approach is to supply them fully-developed, standard products which have been proven successful and profitable and to provide them with an on-going, comprehensive program of service.

Equity Capital Needed: Varies with product selected and franchisee's manufacturing capabilities. $35,000 - $215,000.

Franchise Fee: $15,000 - $25,000, varies.

Royalty Fee: 4% - 8%, varies.

Financial Assistance: None.

Managerial Assistance: We provide marketing consultation, production consultation, provide co-operative regional advertising and quarterly field visits.

Training Provided: Production training is for 1 - 2 weeks. Sales training is for 1 - 2 weeks.

Information Submitted: March 1994

ELDORADO STONE
P. O. Box 27
Carnation, WA 98014
Telephone: (800) 925-1491 (206) 883-1991
Fax: (206) 333-4755
Mr. Phil Pearlman, Vice President of Franchise Growth

Number of Franchised Units: 32
Number of Company-Owned Units: 0
Number of Total Operating Units: 32

In Business Since: 1969   Franchising Since: 1969

Description of Operation: Franchisee manufactures and sells Eldorado Stone's lightweight concrete, stone veneers and landscape stepping stones and pavers.

Equity Capital Needed: $65,000 - $175,000

Franchise Fee: $35,000, includes 400-mold start-up package.

Royalty Fee: 5%

Financial Assistance: None.

Managerial Assistance: On-going support is provided. Franchisee benefits from on-going product research and development and national sales leads for their manufacturing territory. Franchisee benefits by associating with a name known all over the world for quality. Eldorado Stone is the world's largest franchisor of products of this type.

Training Provided: The franchisee is trained for 1 week at training facility in Washington state. 1 week of opening assistance is provided at franchisee's facility when facility is ready. Operations manual and color formula books are provided.

Information Submitted: November 1993

FOUR SEASONS SUNROOMS
5005 Veterans Memorial Hwy.
Holbrook, NY 11741
Telephone: (800) 521-0179 (516) 563-4000
Fax: (516) 563-4010
Mr. Tony Russo, Vice President of Sales

Number of Franchised Units: 267
Number of Company-Owned Units: 5
Number of Total Operating Units: 272

In Business Since: 1975   Franchising Since: 1985

Description of Operation: Four Seasons offers an opportunity for qualified sales and marketing-oriented individuals to offer and sell the widest range of sunroom products available. No previous technical background or skills is required.

Equity Capital Needed: $25,000 - $40,000

Franchise Fee: $7,500 - $10,000 - $15,000, depending on level of dealer program.

Royalty Fee: None or 2.5% on non-Four Seasons products.

Financial Assistance: None.

Managerial Assistance: 3 - 5 days of initial training, training and operations manuals, videos and regional meetings and national convention.

Training Provided: General business (pro forma); advertising and marketing; sales and lead management; installation.

Information Submitted: November 1993

HANDYMAN CONNECTION
230 Northland Blvd., # 229
Cincinnati, OH 45246
Telephone: (800) 466-5530 (513) 771-1122
Fax: (513) 771-4975
Mr. Matthew Chimsky, Franchise Director

Number of Franchised Units: 8
Number of Company-Owned Units: 1
Number of Total Operating Units: 9

In Business Since: 1990   Franchising Since: 1991

Description of Operation: Handyman Connection provides small to medium-sized home repairs and remodeling.

Equity Capital Needed: $25,000 - $75,000

Franchise Fee: $25,000 - $75,000

Royalty Fee: 5%

Financial Assistance: 50% down and 50% in equal installments, paid monthly, with interest at 2 points over prime. For the first 6 months, no principal or interest payments are due.

Managerial Assistance: We completely train the franchisee for 2 weeks at our flagship operation in Cincinnati, OH and then spend the first week assisting the franchisee in opening the operation in his/her city. From then on, we supply the advertising copy and new marketing and recruiting concepts. The Franchise Director makes regular visits to all franchisees.

Training Provided: As described above, franchisees receive training at our home base and also receive an operations manual and video tapes that cover all the systems necessary to successfully operate one of our franchises.

Information Submitted: November 1993

HOLIDAY-PACIFIC HOMES
Box 851
Durham, ON N0G 1R0 CAN
Telephone: (519) 334-3532
Mr. Ken O'Brien, President

Number of Franchised Units: 2
Number of Company-Owned Units: 1
Number of Total Operating Units: 3

In Business Since: 1939   **Franchising Since:** 1988

Description of Operation: The franchisor will help you set up a local business selling and erecting pre-engineered homes. The Company guarantees an area to the franchisee. These kit homes are sold to interested buyers at a fixed price to assist with sales. The franchisee would also sell labor to erect the structure.

Equity Capital Needed: $0

Franchise Fee: $3,500

Royalty Fee: 3%

Financial Assistance: Data not available.

Managerial Assistance: We have a hotline phone # to the head office. We have had bankers lend assistance on managerial management techniques.

Training Provided: We will supply all related materials and manuals including catalogues, renderings and sales contracts.

Information Submitted: April 1994

INSULATED DRY-ROOF SYSTEM
152 SE 5th Ave.
Hillsboro, OR 97123
Telephone: (800) 779-1357 (503) 693-1619
Fax: (503) 693-1993
Mr. Todd C. Tawzer, President

Number of Franchised Units: 17
Number of Company-Owned Units: 0
Number of Total Operating Units: 17

In Business Since: 1989   **Franchising Since:** 1989

Description of Operation: Mobile and manufactured home roofing of a patented roofing system. Some commercial and non-mobile/manufactured residential sales.

Equity Capital Needed: $40,000 - $60,000

Franchise Fee: Varies with size of the exclusive territory.

Royalty Fee: 3%; minimum of $300 per month.

Financial Assistance: None.

Managerial Assistance: The franchisor provides initial training on business management and on-going support through non-mandatory training meetings. Annual review of business activities and updating business plan.

Training Provided: We train all franchisees on marketing, selling and installing the Insulated Dry-Roof System roof. Mandatory training prior to opening franchise territory and on-going training after opening.

Information Submitted: November 1993

JET-BLACK SEALCOATING & REPAIR
9033 Lyndale Ave. S.
Bloomington, MN 55420
Telephone: (612) 888-4444
Fax: (612) 888-4444
Mr. Douglas W. Hoiland, Vice President

Number of Franchised Units: 1
Number of Company-Owned Units: 1
Number of Total Operating Units: 2

In Business Since: 1988   **Franchising Since:** 1989

Description of Operation: Blacktop maintenance.

Equity Capital Needed: $30,000 - $40,000

Franchise Fee: $12,500

Royalty Fee: 8%

Financial Assistance: We will assist the franchisee in obtaining the best financing arrangements.

Managerial Assistance: The franchisee will receive 5 days of training at Jet-Black Sealcoating & Repair headquarters in Bloomington, MN.

Training Provided: Same as above.

Information Submitted: January 1994

KITCHEN SAVER OF CANADA
75 Bessemer Rd.
London, ON N0L 1T0 CAN
Telephone: (800) 265-0933 (519) 686-8888
Fax: (519) 658-7283
Mr. Craig Jones, President

Number of Franchised Units: 15
Number of Company-Owned Units: 1
Number of Total Operating Units: 16

In Business Since: 1986   **Franchising Since:** 1986

Description of Operation: Manufacturer of cabinet doors and drawerfronts for refacing purposes.

Equity Capital Needed: Varies.

Franchise Fee: Varies.

Royalty Fee: 0%

Financial Assistance: Not available.

Managerial Assistance: Set-up procedures, accounting package and on-site assistance.

Training Provided: Measuring, training and sales training.

Information Submitted: January 1994

KITCHEN SOLVERS
15965 Jeanette
Southfield, MI 48075
Telephone: (810) 559-1415
Fax: (810) 557-7931
Ms. Colleen McGaffey

Number of Franchised Units: 34
Number of Company-Owned Units: 1
Number of Total Operating Units: 35

In Business Since: 1982   **Franchising Since:** 1982

Description of Operation: Kitchen cabinet refacing, replacing doors and drawer fronts with new solid wood doors and covering framework with 1/8" wood panel.

Equity Capital Needed: $12,000 - $30,000

Franchise Fee: $12,500

Royalty Fee: 5%

Financial Assistance: None available.

Managerial Assistance: Data not available.

Training Provided: Director of marketing will assist you in developing a marketing and advertising plan, an advisory board council, 5 days of training includes sales, marketing, bookkeeping and installation, complete training manual, audio cassette, video cassette and presentation book, a toll-free 800#, guaranteed territory and bi-monthly newsletter.

Information Submitted: January 1994

KITCHEN TUNE-UP
131 N. Roosevelt
Aberdeen, SD 57401
Telephone: (800) 333-6385 (605) 225-4049
Fax: (605) 225-1371
Mr. Tony Haglund, Senior Vice President

Number of Franchised Units: 223
Number of Company-Owned Units: 0
Number of Total Operating Units: 223

In Business Since: 1986   **Franchising Since:** 1988

Description of Operation: Kitchen Tune-Up provides inexpensive wood care service to both the residential homeowner and the commercial property owner. This #1 rated franchise also offers door replacement materials. This is a home-based, no-inventory, high-profit margin business. Kitchen Tune-Up offers potential franchise owners the unique opportunity to attend training and evaluate the franchise before signing the franchise agreement.

Equity Capital Needed: $15,000 - $25,000

Franchise Fee: $11,500

Royalty Fee: 7%

Financial Assistance: None.

Managerial Assistance: On-going training programs, operations manuals and updates, national convention and monthly newsletters, along with advertising and promotional materials and substantial discounts. Perpetual assistance, as needed.

Training Provided: A 1-week pre-training program must be completed prior to attending a 1 week initial training seminar at franchisor's home office. Initial training then followed up with a 12-week training plan of action.

Information Submitted: November 1993

MAGNUM PIERING
13230 Ferguson Ln.
Bridgeton, MO 63044
Telephone: (800) 822-7437 (314) 291-7437
Fax: (314) 291-1115
Mr. Gregg A. Roby, Vice President/General Manager

Number of Franchised Units: 7
Number of Company-Owned Units: 0
Number of Total Operating Units: 7

In Business Since: 1984   **Franchising Since:** 1985

Description of Operation: Manufacturer and franchisor of products and processes used to raise and stabilize building foundations and flatwork.

Equity Capital Needed: $85,000 - $150,000

Franchise Fee: $20,000

Royalty Fee: 6% or $500.

Financial Assistance: Not available.

Managerial Assistance: Each new franchise is provided with 2 weeks of managerial training at a current franchise location.

Training Provided: The franchisee spends 1 week at a current franchise and 1 week at his own facility with one of our instructors.

Information Submitted: March 1994

NATIONAL INTERNATIONAL ROOFING CORP.
8411 Pyott Rd., # 102
Lake in the Hills, IL 60102
Telephone: (800) 221-7663 (815) 356-1155
Fax: (815) 356-1158
Ms. Christine Grechis, Director of Franchise Sales

Number of Franchised Units: 2
Number of Company-Owned Units: 12
Number of Total Operating Units: 14

In Business Since: 1991   **Franchising Since:** 1993

Description of Operation: Construction tradesman - make your roofing experience work for you! As part of the NIR Project Team, you'll own and operate your own roofing business, while sharing in the benefits of co-operative marketing, shared purchasing power, a managed referral network and more. The NIR franchise program has been designed as a way for qualified entrepreneurs to build their own business futures. Individual or master franchises are now available to qualified candidates.

Equity Capital Needed: $28,600 - $38,250

Franchise Fee: $17,500

Royalty Fee: 10%

Financial Assistance: No financing is provided through NIR; however, the franchisor will consult with and aid in presentation of loan package to lenders, investors or SBA.

Managerial Assistance: Data not available.

Training Provided: NIR provides a comprehensive, confidential operations manual, a 10-day training course, which includes sales and marketing techniques, administration and financial controls, skills in roofing applications and repairs and customer service procedures. In addition, NIR provides an 800# line, protected territories and on-going consulting support.

Information Submitted: November 1993

PERMA-DRY SYSTEMS
426 Caldwell Rd., P. O. Box 2697
Dartmouth, NS B2V 1A6 CAN
Telephone: (800) 565-5325 (902) 462-1500
Fax: (902) 462-2954
Mr. Dan Eddy, Director of Sales and Marketing

Number of Franchised Units: 17
Number of Company-Owned Units: 1
Number of Total Operating Units: 18

In Business Since: 1983   **Franchising Since:** 1990

Description of Operation: Permacrete and Perma-Dry Systems Limited provide our customers with a permanent solution to water control and shut-off problems through guaranteed concrete restoration services.

Equity Capital Needed: $35,000 - $40,000

Franchise Fee: $18,500 - $37,000

Royalty Fee: 4%, plus 2% advertising fee.

Financial Assistance: Not available.

Managerial Assistance: Managerial assistance to the franchisee includes reports of improvements in the Perma-Dry System, such as administrative, bookkeeping, accounting, inventory control and general operating procedures.

Training Provided: The training for new franchisees includes a minimum of 5 days of hands-on training, procedures, bookkeeping, personnel management, basic marketing and public relations techniques.

Information Submitted: January 1994

PROPERTY PROOF-IT SYSTEMS
8301 E. Prentice Ave., # 300
Englewood, CO 80111
Telephone: (800) 867-7663 (303) 773-9681
Fax: (303) 773-1332
Mr. David G. Law, President

Number of Franchised Units: 0
Number of Company-Owned Units: 2
Number of Total Operating Units: 2

In Business Since: 1993   **Franchising Since:** 1994

Description of Operation: Property Proof-It Systems offers franchisees environmentally-friendly, yet superior, products for fireproofing, waterproofing and concrete resurfacing. Each of these opportunities holds tremendous potential for profits. Decorative concrete resurfacing is fast becoming the thing to do for property owners of all kinds. We can help you build a waterproofing business that can save your customers thousands of dollars in concrete repair while putting thousands into your pockets.

Equity Capital Needed: $30,000 - $120,000; $12,000 individual franchise.

Franchise Fee: $35,000 area developer franchise.

Royalty Fee: 6%

Financial Assistance: No direct financial assistance is provided at this time. The franchisor does have a program for assistance with loan arrangements through SBA and local lending institutions.

Managerial Assistance: Property Proof-It Systems offers assistance with management issues on a perpetual basis, as needed.

Training Provided: Initial training is a 3-week process, including classroom instruction, hands-on instruction of application processes and techniques, trouble shooting, technical support discussions, writing bids and quotations, design and color instruction, advertising and marketing, as well as basic office and field policies and procedures. The third week is in the field, providing sales training and assistance in getting business and getting cash flow started.

Information Submitted: January 1994

SCREEN MACHINE, THE
19636 8th St. E.
Sonoma, CA 95476
Telephone: (707) 996-5551
Fax: (707) 996-0139
Mr. Wayne T. Wirick, President

Number of Franchised Units: 10
Number of Company-Owned Units: 1
Number of Total Operating Units: 11

In Business Since: 1986   Franchising Since: 1988

Description of Operation: Mobile unit doing job-site window and door screening (new or re-screen) and other related services.

Equity Capital Needed: $32,000 - $53,000

Franchise Fee: $15,000

Royalty Fee: 5%

Financial Assistance: None.

Managerial Assistance: Data not available.

Training Provided: Each prospective franchisee is thoroughly trained in the various aspects of conducting The Screen Machine business. This training includes marketing strategies, advertising techniques, basic accounting methods, operational procedures and hands-on technical instruction on how to custom fabricate screens and perform screen repair and other related work. To assure smooth operation, each franchisee is provided with advertising materials, audio/visual training and new products information.

Information Submitted: November 1993

SHOWERWALL INDUSTRIES
P. O. Box 215
Benson, MN 56215
Telephone: (612) 843-4353
Fax: (612) 843-4354
Mr. Craig Elliott, President

Number of Franchised Units: 0
Number of Company-Owned Units: 1
Number of Total Operating Units: 1

In Business Since: 1992   Franchising Since: 1992

Description of Operation: Bathroom renovation service/system that combines innovative, quality products with professional installation to offer a customized bathroom at an affordable price. Our signature product is the "One-Piece Masterpiece" seamless tub surround. The systematized Showerwall approach targets new construction and renovation markets in single-family and multi-family dwellings.

Equity Capital Needed: $53,000 - $98,500

Franchise Fee: $20,000

Royalty Fee: 5%

Financial Assistance: Equipment leasing and some assistance in securing third-party financing.

Managerial Assistance: Comprehensive 6-day training program in Company training center, plus pre-opening and grand opening assistance in your showroom with Company representative. We will also assist in site-selection, showroom layout and design, marketing and cross marketing with complimentary businesses.

Training Provided: Same as above.

Information Submitted: January 1994

STAR-VALLEY INSTALLATIONS
2253 Linda St.
Saginaw, MI 48603
Telephone: (517) 793-4484
Fax: (517) 752-7109
Mr. Monty Cazier, President

Number of Franchised Units: 0
Number of Company-Owned Units: 1
Number of Total Operating Units: 1

In Business Since: 1987   Franchising Since: 1993

Description of Operation: Star-Valley Installations offers a service of selling and installing products for homes and businesses. Franchisees will be trained to install mailboxes, flag poles, landscape lighting, above-ground swimming pools and other products after they have been test-marketed and approved by our sales department.

Equity Capital Needed: $3,000 - $6,000

Franchise Fee: $2,000

Royalty Fee: 8%

Financial Assistance: Due to the low cost for our franchise, no financial assistance is offered at the present time.

Managerial Assistance: We offer Company-prepared operations manuals, sales kits and prepared media advertising kits. All are based on our personal operation of a working business since 1987.

Training Provided: We offer 3 days of training at our home office. In addition, we will have on-going training by videos, newsletters and seminars.

Information Submitted: March 1994

COSMETICS AND TOILETRIES

ALOETTE COSMETICS
1301 Wright's Ln. E.
West Chester, PA 19380
Telephone: (800) 321-2563 (215) 692-0600
Fax: (215) 692-2334
Mr. Terry M. Wisdo, Director of Franchise Development/Operations

Number of Franchised Units: 102
Number of Company-Owned Units: 1
Number of Total Operating Units: 103

In Business Since: 1978   Franchising Since: 1978

Description of Operation: Aloette provides the customer with a unique line of Aloe-vera skin care products, as well as cosmetics. The Aloette family of products is primarily available through franchisees and are not typically sold in retail outlets. Beauty consultants market and sell Aloette products, primarily through home shows. Aloette is the only direct marketing franchise organization.

Equity Capital Needed: $35,000 - $65,000

Franchise Fee: $10,000 - $20,000

Royalty Fee: 5%

Financial Assistance: Financing available to qualified prospects.

Managerial Assistance: Each new franchisee is required to attend a 5-day new franchisee training. According to the agreement, each franchisee is entitled to a visit at least once a year. After 3 months, each new franchisee is visited by a member of the operations/sales team.

Training Provided: Throughout the 5 days of training, franchisees receive instruction in all areas of franchise management, including sales, recruiting, incentives, operations, business and financial management. They also have the opportunity to learn through the sharing and exchanging of ideas with franchisees from all across the country, as well as participate in interactive exercises to maximize learning.

Information Submitted: March 1994

BIOGIME SKIN CARE CENTER
1665 Townhurst, # 100
Houston, TX 77043
Telephone: (800) 338-8784 (713) 827-1972
Fax: (713) 461-3251
Mr. John C. Riemann, President

Number of Franchised Units: 8
Number of Company-Owned Units: 7
Number of Total Operating Units: 15

In Business Since: 1984   Franchising Since: 1990

Description of Operation: Retail specialty store, selling natural skin care products under the Biogime trade name. Located in regional shopping areas in major cities.

Equity Capital Needed: $8,000 - $125,000

Franchise Fee: $15,000

Royalty Fee: 2%

Financial Assistance: None.

Managerial Assistance: We provide manuals and field operations assistance.

Training Provided: Training consists of pre-opening training in the training store, post-opening training in the franchisee's location and on-going field training.

Information Submitted: March 1994

CARYL BAKER VISAGE COSMETICS
4732 W. Waco Dr.
Waco, TX 76710
Telephone: (817) 776-8872
Fax: (817) 776-6838
Ms. Vickie Watt, Director of Development/Leasing

Number of Franchised Units: 28
Number of Company-Owned Units: 2
Number of Total Operating Units: 30

In Business Since: 1969   Franchising Since: 1975

Description of Operation: A unique approach to skin care and cosmetics with an extremely high-quality line of cosmetics for the appearance-conscious woman.

Equity Capital Needed: $40,000

Franchise Fee: $25,000

Royalty Fee: 0%

Financial Assistance: Loan packaging and placement assistance is provided.

Managerial Assistance: We provide promotions, advertising, inventory control, security measures and simplified daily bookkeeping methods. We will back you every step of the way, so you can enjoy the exciting, successful future we have planned.

Training Provided: Site selection and lease negotiation. 2 - 3 weeks of intensive training at the home office in cosmetics, skin care, operations and accounting. Store opening and grand opening assistance by a representative (on location). Continued training through regional training seminars and store visits by representatives. A complete set of in-store training materials and manuals. Monthly merchandising assistance. On-going new product development.

Information Submitted: March 1994

CARYL BAKER VISAGE COSMETICS (CANADA)
801 Eglinton Ave., W.
Toronto, ON M5N 1E3 CAN
Telephone: (416) 789-7191
Fax: (416) 789-2594
Mr. Alan Baker, Vice President

Number of Franchised Units: 30
Number of Company-Owned Units: 1
Number of Total Operating Units: 31

In Business Since: 1969   Franchising Since: 1977

Description of Operation: Retail cosmetic and skin-care salons located in regional shopping malls.

Equity Capital Needed: Total investment of $90,000 - $95,000.

Franchise Fee: $25,000

Royalty Fee: 0%

Financial Assistance: Financial assistance is not available from the franchisor.

Managerial Assistance: We provide on-going assistance, covering an analysis of store performance, updates of computer programs used in the store, regular supervisor visits, as well as head office staff available at all times.

Training Provided: We offer 2 weeks of training at our school and Company store, covering product knowledge, marketing and all facets of store operations. In addition, 1 week by a supervisor at the new franchise store.

Information Submitted: March 1994

COSMETIC ISLAND
456 Main St.
Peniction, BC V2A 5C5 CAN
Telephone: (403) 277-6566
Fax: (403) 277-6566
Mr. Frank Webb, Franchise Director

Number of Franchised Units: 0
Number of Company-Owned Units: 1
Number of Total Operating Units: 1

In Business Since: 1993   Franchising Since: 1993

Description of Operation: Small kiosks, selling fine cosmetics and skin care products. Typically located in major shopping malls. Easy to learn and operate business, with low investment and high margins. Suits women with an interest in cosmetics and skin care.

Equity Capital Needed: $10,000 - $20,000

Franchise Fee: $0

Royalty Fee: 0%

Financial Assistance: None.

Managerial Assistance: Management assistance included covers topics such as general ledger accounting, purchasing, tax filing, payroll, etc.

Training Provided: Complete training in the use and application of the products being sold and in the operations of the store and customer selling techniques.

Information Submitted: March 1994

ELIZABETH GRADY FACE FIRST
200 Boston Ave.
Medford, MA 02155
Telephone: (800) FACIALS (617) 391-9380
Fax: (617) 391-4772
Mr. John P. Walsh, President

Number of Franchised Units: 15
Number of Company-Owned Units: 8
Number of Total Operating Units: 23

In Business Since: 1974   Franchising Since: 1982

Description of Operation: Skin care salons, with emphasis on individual consultation and clinical analysis, treatments by professional estheticians and a prescribed home care regime. Elizabeth Grady Face First's goal has always been to promote the healthiest skin for all people. Our commitment to serve the best interests of our customers is reflected in the quality of our complete line of products, many of which are specially developed for Elizabeth Grady salons.

Equity Capital Needed: $125,000

Franchise Fee: $25,000

Royalty Fee: 6%

Financial Assistance: Financial assistance is available to qualified applicants.

Managerial Assistance: Training includes periodic updates on all industry trends, new products and services, as well as new advertising and promotional techniques. In addition, franchisees will be provided with total on-going supervision and support in the form of periodic visits by our experienced staff to consult with your staff on all aspects of operations. Other assistance is provided on an as-needed basis.

Training Provided: Everything you need to know to operate is included in our training program. The tuition is included in your franchise fee. Furthermore, one of our representatives will work with you for one week during your first month of operation. Franchisees will also receive an operations manual covering all areas of importance.

Information Submitted: March 1994

H2O PLUS
676 N. Michigan Ave., # 3900
Chicago, IL 60614
Telephone: (800) 537-1119 (312) 642-1100
Fax: (312) 642-9207
Mr. James Gurke, Director of Franchising

Number of Franchised Units: 1
Number of Company-Owned Units: 54
Number of Total Operating Units: 55

In Business Since: 1989   Franchising Since: 1993

Description of Operation: Retailer of innovative and progressive cosmetic, skin-care, fragrance and bath products.

Equity Capital Needed: $240,000 - $380,000

Franchise Fee: $38,500

Royalty Fee: 4% - year 1; 5% - year 2; 5.5% - year 3.

Financial Assistance: None.

Managerial Assistance: Our franchisees participate in a weekly conference call with their regional field manager. They receive visits from their regional field manager a minimum of every 2 months. They have access to daily corporate contacts for support in marketing and promotions, human resources and training, finance and accounting, POS system and legal. They receive newsletters, training tips, new products, operational information from our corporate office weekly. Annual International Managers Meeting.

Training Provided: Training is in 4 parts: Part 1: 7-volume operating manual; Part 2: prior to store opening, franchisees participate in an intensive classroom/in-field training program that demonstrates "live" all

material in 7 volumes. Hands-on training in register and computer training; Part 3: 3 - 5 days in Company stores for orientation to customers, sales and store operations; Part 4: on-site training on store set-up and store-opening.

Information Submitted: March 1994

I NATURAL SKIN CARE & COSMETICS
355 Middlesex Ave.
Wilmington, MA 01887
Telephone: (800) 9-MAKEUP (508) 658-8921
Fax: (508) 988-9509
Ms. Sandra Cagnina, Franchise Co-ordinator

Number of Franchised Units: 0
Number of Company-Owned Units: 3
Number of Total Operating Units: 3

In Business Since: 1970   Franchising Since: 1970

Description of Operation: Operation of a retail shop that specializes in skin care, cosmetics and other related services. The franchisor offers private labeled and other products and accessories for sale to the shops.

Equity Capital Needed: $106,500 - $183,500

Franchise Fee: $15,000

Royalty Fee: 0-6 months - 1% of gross sales; 7-12 months-2% of gross sales; 13 months thru balance - 3% of gross.

Financial Assistance: No.

Managerial Assistance: Data not available.

Training Provided: Franchisor will provide an initial training program for the franchisee. The training is held at franchisor's corporate office. The program is approximately 1 week.

Information Submitted: December 1993

POTIONS & LOTIONS
10201 N. 21st Ave., # 8
Phoenix, AZ 85021
Telephone: (800) 456-3765 (602) 944-6642
Fax: (602) 395-9518
Mr. Jim Wellbeloved, Vice President of Franchising

Number of Franchised Units: 9
Number of Company-Owned Units: 8
Number of Total Operating Units: 17

In Business Since: 1974   Franchising Since: 1989

Description of Operation: Perfume and natural personal-care products retail store. Environmentally-friendly and cruelty-free.

Equity Capital Needed: $150,000 - $175,000

Franchise Fee: $25,000

Royalty Fee: 5%

Financial Assistance: Assistance in preparation of business plan and application for financing.

Managerial Assistance: Assistance during training period. On-site prior to store opening and during opening. Follow-up field visits for merchandising, store operation and maintenance of quality standards.

Training Provided: 10 days of intensive training covers all aspects of retail store operation, product knowledge and customer service.

Information Submitted: November 1993

ROSE VALENTI
135 Rockaway Ave.
Valley Stream, NY 11580
Telephone: (516) 825-0273
Fax: (516) 825-0285
Ms. Rose Valenti, Vice President

Number of Franchised Units: 0
Number of Company-Owned Units: 8
Number of Total Operating Units: 8

In Business Since: 1983   **Franchising Since:** 1992

Description of Operation: Fragrance and cosmetic retail sales.

Equity Capital Needed: $100,000 - $110,000

Franchise Fee: $25,000

Royalty Fee: 10%

Financial Assistance: None.

Managerial Assistance: Data not available.

Training Provided: We will train the franchisee for 4 weeks in our stores. We will then help to open store and generally help the franchisee. We will then be available for any further assistance by phone or fax and, if need be, in person.

Information Submitted: December 1993

TOP OF THE LINE COSMETICS & FRAGRANCES
1900 Military Rd., Box 11
Niagara Falls, NY 14304
Telephone: (716) 297-1761
Mr. Jamie Abraham, Director of Franchise Sales

Number of Franchised Units: 8
Number of Company-Owned Units: 17
Number of Total Operating Units: 25

In Business Since: 1983   **Franchising Since:** 1987

Description of Operation: Retail sales of prestigious, designer fragrances and brand-name cosmetics. Carry products for men, women and children. Bath lines, gift sets, make-up and facial treatments, as well as fragrances, are carried. Services provided are make-overs and color analysis.

Equity Capital Needed: $80,000 - $125,000

Franchise Fee: $23,900

Royalty Fee: 5%

Financial Assistance: We will not provide loans, but will assist in getting loans through the SBA.

Managerial Assistance: The franchisor provides set-up and training, on-going assistance through training tapes, promotional material and events and manuals. On-site training minimum of 1 week, plus training in a Company store for 1 week.

Training Provided: Training provided on-site and in the Company store totals 2 weeks. Store set-up and paperwork training, management training, personnel training, including product knowledge and color and make-over training, management and employee training manuals, videos and tapes. Training is on-going through the life of the franchise.

Information Submitted: January 1994

DRUG STORES

ARROW PRESCRIPTION CENTERS
40 East St.
Plainville, CT 06062
Telephone: (203) 747-4538
Fax: (203) 793-6813
Mr. Paul Gowern, Director of Franchise Development

Number of Franchised Units: 30
Number of Company-Owned Units: 6
Number of Total Operating Units: 36

In Business Since: 1987   **Franchising Since:** 1990

Description of Operation: Apothecary-style pharmacies, typically 2,000 square feet, specializing in dispensing prescriptions and health related over-the-counter medications. High emphasis on patient counseling and outcome analysis. The franchisee must be a registered pharmacist.

Equity Capital Needed: $30,000 - $50,000

Franchise Fee: $10,000

Royalty Fee: 6%

Financial Assistance: Yes. Franchisee financing facilities have been made available for the remaining capital cost of franchise. The terms are generally prime plus 2%, 5 years and require personal and corporate security.

Managerial Assistance: Managerial assistance is initially provided for demographics, site selection, remodeling, financing and grand openings. On-going assistance is provided with advertising, insurance, accounting services, pricing, vendor negotiations, contract coordination and regulatory updates.

Training Provided: Training is provided in accounting systems, concepts of the franchise, advertising, pharmacy systems, financial awareness, third-party contract administration, employee benefits and payroll. 1 week of training is provided at the headquarters office, plus field follow-up.

Information Submitted: February 1994

DRUG EMPORIUM
155 Hidden Ravines Dr.
Powell, OH 43065
Telephone: (614) 548-7080
Fax: (614) 548-6541
Mr. Terry D. Ruh, Director of Franchise Operations

Number of Franchised Units: 103
Number of Company-Owned Units: 133
Number of Total Operating Units: 236

In Business Since: 1977   **Franchising Since:** 1979

Description of Operation: Retail deep discount drug stores.

Equity Capital Needed: Data not available.

Franchise Fee: $25,000

Royalty Fee: 1% for $3.5 - $6.0 MM; 2% for $6.0 - $8.0 MM; 3% for $8.0 - $10.0 MM; 1.25% over $10.0 MM.

Financial Assistance: Not available.

Managerial Assistance: The complete corporate staff assists in servicing the franchise community. This process is coordinated through the franchise department.

Training Provided: We provide initial training of 6 weeks in various facets of the business, i.e. purchasing, receiving, accounting, cash management, operations, start-up, etc. Continual training on an as-needed basis.

Information Submitted: January 1994

MEDICAP PHARMACY
4700 Westown Pkwy, # 300, Regency W
West Des Moines, IA 50266
Telephone: (800) 445-2244 (515) 224-8400
Fax: (515) 224-8415
Mr. Calvin C. James, Vice President of Franchise Development

Number of Franchised Units: 100
Number of Company-Owned Units: 0
Number of Total Operating Units: 100

In Business Since: 1971   **Franchising Since:** 1974

Description of Operation: Medicap Pharmacy is a convenient, low-cost professional pharmacy. They typically operate in an 800 - 1,000 square foot location. 90% of the business is prescription and the remaining

10% consists of over-the-counter medications. New store start-ups and conversion of full-line drug stores and independent pharmacies to the Medicap concept.

Equity Capital Needed: $25,000 - $35,000 cash investment.

Franchise Fee: $15,000 for a new store; $8,500 for a conversion store.

Royalty Fee: New stores - 4% + 1% advertising; Conversion stores - 2% base receipts, 1% advert.-(4% on growth).

Financial Assistance: We help arrange financing.

Managerial Assistance: Complete support program for all stores - turn-key set-up and continued support.

Training Provided: 3 days of orientation at our corporate office. 3 days of on-site training, plus continued support.

Information Submitted: November 1993

MEDICINE SHOPPE, THE
1100 N. Lindbergh Blvd.
St. Louis, MO 63132
Telephone: (800) 325-1397 (314) 993-6000
Fax: (314) 569-9780
Ms. Elaine Cooper, Administrative Assistant

Number of Franchised Units: 968
Number of Company-Owned Units: 15
Number of Total Operating Units: 983

In Business Since: 1970   **Franchising Since:** 1970

Description of Operation: The Medicine Shoppe is a franchisor of professional pharmacies.

Equity Capital Needed: $63,000 - $111,800 (exclusive of origination fee).

Franchise Fee: $18,000 origination fee for new store.

Royalty Fee: 5.5%

Financial Assistance: $63,000 - $111,800 initial investment (exclusive of origination fee) includes remodeling of premises, purchase of equipment, fixtures, opening inventory, supplies and working capital. MSI will finance up to 90% upon loan approval. Loan is repaid on a schedule of up to 10 years.

Managerial Assistance: Operations personnel (district and regional managers) provide on-going support to franchisees. MSI also provides field marketing support; grand opening assistance, lease negotiation, leasehold improvement specifications and coordination, accounting system and third-party contract procurement.

Training Provided: Operations manuals are provided. New franchisees attend an intensive 6-day training school at MSI corporate offices. Thereafter, district and regional meetings and field seminars are conducted throughout the year at various locations within the various districts.

Information Submitted: March 1994

DRY CLEANING AND LAUNDRIES

APPARELMASTER
P. O. Box 62687
Cincinnati, OH 45262
Telephone: (800) 543-1678 (513) 772-7721
Fax: (513) 772-4117
Mr. George Beetz, Vice President

Number of Franchised Units: 175
Number of Company-Owned Units: 0
Number of Total Operating Units: 175

In Business Since: 1974   **Franchising Since:** 1974

Description of Operation: Apparelmaster enables drycleaners and/or launderers to establish an industrial uniform rental business.

Equity Capital Needed: $15,000 - $20,000

Franchise Fee: $8,200

Royalty Fee: 6%, 2%, 1%

Financial Assistance: Installment plan of $575 per month.

Managerial Assistance: We offer follow-up consultation visits through the life of the agreement, 800# hotline assistance, special reports, monthly information mailings, suppliers' corporate discount savings and large buying power.

Training Provided: We provide 2 weeks at the licensee's place of business, plus yearly visits.

Information Submitted: January 1994

AQUA CLEAN ECOLOGY CENTERS
3157 N. 34th Dr.
Phoenix, AZ 85017
Telephone: (800) 288-8685 (602) 269-0777
Fax: (602) 278-6463
Ms. Barbara DeRoma, President

Number of Franchised Units: 0
Number of Company-Owned Units: 0
Number of Total Operating Units: 0

In Business Since: 1993   **Franchising Since:** 1993

Description of Operation: Aqua Clean Ecology Centers is a professional, self-service coin laundry, combined with high-tech water purification units to sell pure drinking water and ice to the public. Services include large capacity washers, dryers, drop-off dry cleaning, wash, dry and fold, purified drinking water and ice.

Equity Capital Needed: $50,000 - $100,000

Franchise Fee: $15,000

Royalty Fee: 4%

Financial Assistance: Financing is available to qualified buyers. Financing for up to 7 years is available on all serialized equipment, which includes washers, dryers, coin changer, hot water heating system and water purification system.

Managerial Assistance: Aqua Clean provides complete training manuals, which include management, marketing and day-to-day operations, as well as a sales promotion information kit to enhance customer traffic flow into the store.

Training Provided: Training is mandatory. One week is spent in Phoenix, AZ in classroom and hands-on training. Company representative will also spend 5 days at franchisee's site training personnel.

Information Submitted: November 1993

AWC COMMERCIAL WINDOW COVERINGS
825 W. Williamson Ave.
Fullerton, CA 92632
Telephone: (800) 252-2280 (714) 879-3880
Fax: (714) 879-8419
Mr. Jim Wells, Vice President of Sales

Number of Franchised Units: 3
Number of Company-Owned Units: 1
Number of Total Operating Units: 4

In Business Since: 1963   **Franchising Since:** 1992

Description of Operation: Mobile dry cleaning services, provided on-location to commercial customers, as well as sales, installation and repair of all types of window coverings. AWC utilizes the customer base, references and reputation of the franchisor. Developed over the last 30 years.

Equity Capital Needed: $137,520 - $232,350 (including fee).

Franchise Fee: $50,000

Royalty Fee: 12.5%

Financial Assistance: Yes. Third party. Purchase to lease.

Managerial Assistance: We offer continuous consultation with franchisees on all aspects of the business by phone. Constant updates on product, market research and sales leads. Nationwide contracts are transferred to the franchisees. A well-coordinated marketing effort makes this an ideal growth opportunity.

Training Provided: 1 week of hands-on and classroom training is provided at the home office in Fullerton, CA, including operational techniques, manuals and product samples. 1 week of set-up and sales assistance at the franchisee's location. Continuous, open communication is maintained and encouraged.

Information Submitted: February 1994

CLEAN 'N' PRESS
655 Montgomery St., # 1200
San Francisco, CA 94111
Telephone: (800) 237-1711 (415) 362-1700
Fax: (415) 399-0886
Mr. Alan Block, President

Number of Franchised Units: 47
Number of Company-Owned Units: 0
Number of Total Operating Units: 47

In Business Since: 1991   **Franchising Since:** 1991

Description of Operation: Clean 'N' Press is a franchisor of dry cleaning and laundry stores and plants. We also offer the "Home Express" pick-up and delivery service. We provide franchisees with a complete turn-key system for everything from a single "Home Express" van to a multiple store/plant combination. Our plant with satellite stores is highly efficient. We also provide marketing assistance.

Equity Capital Needed: $22,000 - $200,000 +

Franchise Fee: $10,000 - $25,000 +

Royalty Fee: 9%

Financial Assistance: Third-party financing assistance is available.

Managerial Assistance: Each franchisee will receive assistance regarding Company-approved location, forms, management, accounting and marketing. All operational aspects are covered by the instruction manuals.

Training Provided: We provide an extensive, 1 - 2 week training period at an existing operation which varies depending on the background and experience of the franchisee. Complete operations manuals are provided.

Information Submitted: March 1994

COACHMAN DRY CLEANING & LAUNDRY
One Tower Bridge, # 800
W. Conshohocken, PA 19428
Telephone: (800) 841-8484 (215) 941-2789
Fax: (800) 841-8485
Mr. Jock M. Sommese, Chief Operating Officer

Number of Franchised Units: 14
Number of Company-Owned Units: 0
Number of Total Operating Units: 14

In Business Since: 1991   **Franchising Since:** 1992

Description of Operation: Pick-up and delivery service of dry cleaning and laundry from people's homes and offices.

Equity Capital Needed: $18,000 - $20,000

Franchise Fee: $18,000

Royalty Fee: Not applicable.

Financial Assistance: Up to 100% of franchise can be financed at competitive rates over a 5-year term.

Managerial Assistance: Perpetual assistance is available 24 hours per day, 7 days a week, with corporate officers, as well as management.

Training Provided: We offer an extensive 1-week program at the processor, on the truck and in the classroom. Initial review monthly and on-going afterwards.

Information Submitted: March 1994

COMET ONE-HOUR CLEANERS
406 W. Division St. (Hwy. 80)
Arlington, TX 76011
Telephone: (817) 461-3555
Fax: (817) 861-4779
Mr. Jack Godfrey, Jr., Sales Representative

Number of Franchised Units: 267
Number of Company-Owned Units: 11
Number of Total Operating Units: 278

In Business Since: 1955   **Franchising Since:** 1967

Description of Operation: Drycleaning and laundry packages. A complete turn-key operation. Our service includes site evaluation, market analyses, floor plan design and layout, 2-week training program, grand opening, advertising and on-hand consultation in-store after store opening. Parts, service and support for all equipment sold. All questions, parts and service are just a phone call away. Members of IFA, IFI, TLDA.

Equity Capital Needed: $135,000 - $200,000

Franchise Fee: $15,000

Royalty Fee: $1,000 per year.

Financial Assistance: Financing through Stephens Finance, Little Rock, AR. 5-year fixed rate.

Managerial Assistance: Part of training process. Consulting available as needed.

Training Provided: 2 weeks of comprehensive training in all facets of store operation - use of equipment, maintenance, marketing strategies, bookkeeping and customer service. Training provided in local store and in franchisee's store after opening.

Information Submitted: November 1993

DRY CLEANING STATION
4105 S. 84th St.
Omaha, NE 68127
Telephone: (800) 655-8134 (614) 369-8134
Fax: (800) 655-8134
Mr. Michael Coffee, Vice President of Franchise Development

Number of Franchised Units: 3
Number of Company-Owned Units: 2
Number of Total Operating Units: 5

In Business Since: 1987   **Franchising Since:** 1990

Description of Operation: Dry Cleaning Station is a new discount dry-cleaning concept that is revolutionizing the dry cleaning industry. Our format allows extremely attractive customer pricing while maintaining high quality and social responsibility on environmental issues. The Company's motto says it all - "The price brings them in, the quality keeps them coming back."

Equity Capital Needed: $40,000 - $50,000

Franchise Fee: $10,000

Royalty Fee: 5%

Financial Assistance: Dry Cleaning Station will assist qualified franchise owners to obtain third-party financing.

Managerial Assistance: Dry Cleaning Station provides extensive operations manuals to each new franchise owner, as well as significant on-going consultative field support. In addition, numerous forms, management aids and a state-of-the-art, point-of-sale computer/cash register system are provided.

Training Provided: Each new franchise owner receives a minimum of 1 week of intensive training in an existing location and 1 week of training at his/her own location from Company personnel and representatives of our equipment manufacturers and distributors. Also, numerous follow-up visits after he/she opens.

Information Submitted: March 1994

DUDS 'N SUDS
3000 Justin Dr., # G
Des Moines, IA 50322
Telephone: (800) 383-6421 (515) 270-3837
Fax: (515) 270-6656
Mr. John Aranowicz, Vice President

Number of Franchised Units: 80
Number of Company-Owned Units: 6
Number of Total Operating Units: 86

In Business Since: 1989   **Franchising Since:** 1989

Description of Operation: Coin-operated laundry with amenities. Large-screen TV, TV lounge, pool table, video arcade games, snack bar, drop-off dry cleaning and wash-dry-fold. Some locations have beer in snack bar.

Equity Capital Needed: $40,000

Franchise Fee: $20,000

Royalty Fee: 5%

Financial Assistance: We will help a franchisee locate financing. We construct a professional business plan and present the business plan to locate financial institutions. We also have leasing resources. SBA loans are very popular among previous franchisees of Duds' N Suds.

Managerial Assistance: On-going support both by telephone and visits to your location. A franchise advisory board is also part of our system. A yearly franchise/franchisee convention. Periodic training updates. At least 1 yearly visit from headquarters personnel.

Training Provided: Each new franchisee attends a 5-day training course at one of our educational facilities. They will learn all parts of the operation. Both classroom and store time. A 5-volume operations manual is at the heart of the system.

Information Submitted: November 1993

NU-LOOK 1-HOUR CLEANERS
15 SE Second Ave.
Deerfield Beach, FL 33441
Telephone: (305) 426-1111
Fax: (305) 570-6248
Mr. Karl N. Dickey, Jr., President

Number of Franchised Units: 52
Number of Company-Owned Units: 0
Number of Total Operating Units: 52

In Business Since: 1967   **Franchising Since:** 1967

Description of Operation: Retail dry cleaner.

Equity Capital Needed: $50,000 - $100,000

Franchise Fee: $5,000

Royalty Fee: 5%, including 3% advertising fee.

Financial Assistance: Yes.

Managerial Assistance: Perpetual assistance.

Training Provided: 4 weeks of training at our headquarters.

Information Submitted: January 1994

ONE HOUR MARTINIZING DRY CLEANING
2005 Ross Ave.
Cincinnati, OH 45212
Telephone: (800) 827-0207 (513) 351-5500
Fax: (513) 731-5513
Mr. Jerald E. Laesser, Vice President

Number of Franchised Units: 844
Number of Company-Owned Units: 0
Number of Total Operating Units: 844

In Business Since: 1949   **Franchising Since:** 1949

Description of Operation: New franchisees receive the full benefit of One Hour Martinizing's 40 plus years of experience in site-selection, training and marketing. Martinizing focuses totally on assisting its franchisees before, during and after opening. Martinizing offers instant brand awareness in any market for new franchisees.

Equity Capital Needed: $65,000 (minimum).

Franchise Fee: $25,000

Royalty Fee: 4%

Financial Assistance: Veterans of US Armed Forces are offered financing of the initial fee (VetFran). Others are assisted in locating funding sources, but direct financing is not provided.

Managerial Assistance: We provide complete start-up assistance, a comprehensive training program, location/site assistance with ads, computerized demographics capabilities, grand opening marketing package and on-going local store and marketwide promotional programs, field and operations assistance.

Training Provided: We offer a 3-week, comprehensive training program, which includes 1 week of classroom training and 2 weeks of in-store training, training manuals, operational and marketing ideas.

Information Submitted: January 1994

PRESSED 4 TIME
48 Mechanic St.
Newton, MA 02164
Telephone: (800) 423-8711 (617) 630-9026
Fax: (617) 630-9028
Mr. James J. Markson, President

Number of Franchised Units: 60
Number of Company-Owned Units: 1
Number of Total Operating Units: 61

In Business Since: 1987   **Franchising Since:** 1990

Description of Operation: Dry cleaning and shoe repair pick-up and delivery service, serving executives and staff at local businesses. A high repeat business, a low stress operation (5-day workweek, local cleaning plants do the actual cleaning) and incomparable training and support.

Equity Capital Needed: $12,000 - $14,500

Franchise Fee: $9,500

Royalty Fee: The greater of 3.5% or $200 per month per van for Year 1 and $300 per month per van for Year 2.

Financial Assistance: Not available.

Managerial Assistance: On-going support is available by telephone and in the territory by special request. All necessary supplies, forms and materials for the operation are available. Complete training, procedures and operations manual.

Training Provided: Training includes 2 days at the corporate offices, including 1 day of hands-on operations, the corporate vehicle and 1 day of intensive classroom training, covering start-up, record keeping, administration, dry cleaning, operations and sales. Also, 2 days of training in the franchisee's territory, consisting of marketing training in the field to establish initial accounts.

Information Submitted: January 1994

STAR CLEANERS
5858 Central Ave., 1st Fl.
St. Petersburg. FL 33707
Telephone: (800) 743-7827 (813) 343-8782
Fax: (813) 347-3449
Mr. S. D. Trip Camper, III, President

Number of Franchised Units: 9
Number of Company-Owned Units: 0
Number of Total Operating Units: 9

In Business Since: 1990   Franchising Since: 1991

Description of Operation: Full-service dry cleaning franchise.

Equity Capital Needed: $70,000

Franchise Fee: $20,000

Royalty Fee: $145 per week.

Financial Assistance: Through outside lenders and institutions, financing may be available to qualified franchisees, subject to capital requirements and credit approval.

Managerial Assistance: We provide complete training, marketing support and monthly follow-up.

Training Provided: Training consists of 2 - 3 weeks at headquarters in St. Petersburg, FL, 1 - 2 weeks at franchisee's location and 2 weeks at a regional office.

Information Submitted: December 1993

EDUCATIONAL PRODUCTS AND SERVICES

ACADEMY OF LEARNING
9011 Leslie St., # 205
Richmond Hill, ON L4B 3B6 CAN
Telephone: (905) 886-8973
Fax: (905) 886-8591
Mr. Les Prosser, Director of Franchising

Number of Franchised Units: 78
Number of Company-Owned Units: 2
Number of Total Operating Units: 80

In Business Since: 1987   Franchising Since: 1987

Description of Operation: Computer and business skills training centers, utilizing unique "Integrated Learning System." This system provides short, effective self-paced computer and related courses for the office, using a combination of audio tapes, computers, original software and workbooks. This method of training gives students full control over their attendance, pace and time of learning. Facilitators are on-site at all times, to assist, advise and motivate students.

Equity Capital Needed: $105,000 (includes franchise fee, working capital, furniture, equipment, start-up expenses).

Franchise Fee: $41,000

Royalty Fee: 0%

Financial Assistance: Assistance in obtaining bank financing.

Managerial Assistance: Full assistance in locating premises, lease negotiations, equipment purchases and miscellaneous applications as needed. Franchisee will receive a full "Administration Start-Up Kit," comprised of all forms needed in the day-to-day running of the business. Comprehensive operations manual provided, along with on-going newsletters and updates from home office.

Training Provided: Up to 3 weeks of in-house and on-site training in marketing and operations provided. On-site support in initial set-up of operation and on-going support. Both personal and home-office hotline.

Information Submitted: January 1994

ALAMO LEARNING SYSTEMS
3160 Crow Canyon Rd., # 335
San Ramon, CA 94583
Telephone: (800) 829-8081 (510) 277-1818
Fax: (510) 277-1919
Mr. Guy A. Hale, President

Number of Franchised Units: 6
Number of Company-Owned Units: 0
Number of Total Operating Units: 6

In Business Since: 1976   Franchising Since: 1993

Description of Operation: Alamo is an international leader in corporate education. We do business with 200 of the Fortune 500 companies. We specialize in TQM, rational thinking skills, innovation and fast-track ISO 9000 registration.

Equity Capital Needed: $50,000

Franchise Fee: $250,000

Royalty Fee: 10%

Financial Assistance: None.

Managerial Assistance: Alamo provides franchisee with complete turn-key operation, including modem for proposal writing, trained consultants and instructors, sales support, national marketing and telemarketing services.

Training Provided: Complete program for sales, product knowledge and train-the-trainer instruction. Also, on-going training support and client management systems.

Information Submitted: November 1993

AMRON SCHOOL OF THE FINE ARTS
1315 Medlin Rd.
Monroe, NC 28112
Telephone: (704) 283-4290
Fax: (704) 283-7274
Ms. Norma Williams, President

Number of Franchised Units: 0
Number of Company-Owned Units: 1
Number of Total Operating Units: 1

In Business Since: 1979   Franchising Since: 1986

Description of Operation: School to teach modeling, acting and cosmetics. Portfolios for models and actors. Franchise systems for sales in the US.

Equity Capital Needed: $20,000

Franchise Fee: $15,000

Royalty Fee: Sliding scale.

Financial Assistance: Owner will finance 1/2 of the franchise at 6% interest with monthly payments.

Managerial Assistance: We will assist in the first month of business.

Training Provided: Owner and teacher training at the home office. Franchisee pays his/her own hotel, travel and food expenses. 1 week of training for owner and 1 teacher.

Information Submitted: November 1993

BARBIZON SCHOOLS OF MODELING
1900 Glades Rd., # 300
Boca Raton, FL 33431
Telephone: (407) 362-8883
Fax: (407) 750-0999
Mr. Barry B. Wolff, President

Number of Franchised Units: 65
Number of Company-Owned Units: 0
Number of Total Operating Units: 65

In Business Since: 1939   Franchising Since: 1968

Description of Operation: Proprietary, private schools of modeling and related creative arts.

Equity Capital Needed: $45,900 - $89,000

Franchise Fee: $19,500 - $35,000

Royalty Fee: 7.5%

Financial Assistance: Up to 50% of the franchise fee.

Managerial Assistance: Initial training at home office, plus on-site training of franchisee and staff. On-going advice and assistance.

Training Provided: Data not available.

Information Submitted: November 1993

CITIZENS AGAINST CRIME
1022 S. Greenville Ave., # 280
Allen, TX 75002
Telephone: (800) 466-1010 (214) 390-7033
Fax: (214) 390-7606
Franchise Sales Department

Number of Franchised Units: 43
Number of Company-Owned Units: 3
Number of Total Operating Units: 46

In Business Since: 1980   **Franchising Since:** 1986

Description of Operation: CAC is a recognized leader in the field of safety education. Our professionally-trained speakers present the program "Living Safely in a Dangerous World" to businesses and organizations within each franchisee's protected geographic territory. The acclaimed program discusses ways to avoid, escape or survive crime. Profits are generated from the sale of high-quality safety items to seminar participants.

Equity Capital Needed: $20,000 (in addition to franchise fee).

Franchise Fee: $17,500 - $35,000, varies with population.

Royalty Fee: 0%

Financial Assistance: Up to 50% of the franchise fee may be financed.

Managerial Assistance: We provide phone support, a personal coach for each franchisee, 2 weeks of training when franchise purchased and a minimum of 2 trainings per year for management issues. Specialized retreats for improving sales skills and management skills.

Training Provided: We offer training in sales, marketing, operations, interviewing, hiring and training new employees, media, public relations, crime prevention and running a small business. Training is provided by video, audio and interaction with a corporate trainer. One week of training, held at corporate headquarters and one week in franchisee's office.

Information Submitted: March 1994

COM-CEP USA LEARNING CENTERS
9700 Rodney Parham Rd.
Little Rock, AR 72207
Telephone: (800) 874-1238 (501) 224-3050
Fax: (501) 227-6872
Mr. James E. Taylor, President

Number of Franchised Units: 18
Number of Company-Owned Units: 1
Number of Total Operating Units: 19

In Business Since: 1990   **Franchising Since:** 1990

Description of Operation: Retail adult learning center, using full-motion video instructors controlled by learners. Courseware includes computer skills (MS-DOS, Lotus, Excel, Word Perfect, etc.). People and management skills also included.

Equity Capital Needed: $84,500 - $100,000

Franchise Fee: $20,000 (included above).

Royalty Fee: 7%

Financial Assistance: We have no financing available - only counseling.

Managerial Assistance: 4 weeks of product and marketing training. Sales are usually to couples who use 1 - 2 part-time employees. Daily newsletters keep in touch. Goal setting. On-going sales and management courses.

Training Provided: Product knowledge and instruction in all offered courseware. Troubleshooting hardware. Management and sales training include identifying and targeting market, advertising and on-the-job center operation.

Information Submitted: November 1993

COMPUCOLLEGE SCHOOL OF BUSINESS
5650 Yonge St., # 1400
North York, ON M2M 4G3 CAN
Telephone: (800) 465-2700 (416) 733-4452
Fax: (416) 733-4627
Mr. Jerry H. Stessel, Vice President of Marketing

Number of Franchised Units: 28
Number of Company-Owned Units: 7
Number of Total Operating Units: 35

In Business Since: 1976   **Franchising Since:** 1982

Description of Operation: Private career school, specializing in business careers that include secretarial, hospitality, computers and business. 6 - 10 month programs.

Equity Capital Needed: $200,000 - $250,000

Franchise Fee: $75,000

Royalty Fee: 7%

Financial Assistance: None.

Managerial Assistance: We provide a turn-key operation, including help with site selection, lease negotiation, hiring and training of original staff and on-going head office support. Annual general meeting with franchisees and strategic planning meetings.

Training Provided: 1 month of training at head office is provided.

Information Submitted: January 1994

COMPUQUEST EDUCATIONAL SERVICES
6161 Busch Blvd., # 100
Columbus, OH 43229
Telephone: (800) 596-KIDS (614) 888-4900
Fax: (614) 888-4908
Mr. Stan Gebhardt, President

Number of Franchised Units: 59
Number of Company-Owned Units: 0
Number of Total Operating Units: 59

In Business Since: 1991   **Franchising Since:** 1991

Description of Operation: CompuQuest Educational Services provides educational instruction in the use of computers to children age 3 1/2 and older in licensed learning facilities through our CompuQuest for Kids program. Also, through our CompuQuest for Teens program, we provide SAT/ACT preparation courses to teenagers.

Equity Capital Needed: $18,500 - $28,500

Franchise Fee: $18,500 - CompuQuest for Kids; $10,500 - CompuQuest for Teens.

Royalty Fee: 12.5% - CompuQuest for Kids; 8% - CompuQuest for Teens.

Financial Assistance: Equipment leasing is available.

Managerial Assistance: On-going assistance and support from corporate staff and regional directors.

Training Provided: CompuQuest for Kids franchise - 2 days of training at corporate office in Columbus, OH. 2 days of on-site instructor training at franchisee's location, 5 days of field/marketing training on-site at franchisee's location.

Information Submitted: November 1993

COMPUTERTOTS
10132 Colvin Run Rd.
Great Falls, VA 22063
Telephone: (800) 531-5053 (703) 759-2556
Fax: (703) 759-1938
Ms. Carla Garbin, Vice President/Chief Operating Officer

Number of Franchised Units: 127
Number of Company-Owned Units: 0
Number of Total Operating Units: 127

In Business Since: 1983   **Franchising Since:** 1989

Description of Operation: Home-based franchise, offering early childhood computer education through day care centers, pre-schools and community centers.

Equity Capital Needed: $24,000 - $40,000

Franchise Fee: $15,900 - $23,900

Royalty Fee: 6% or $250.

Financial Assistance: Data not available.

Managerial Assistance: Thorough training and on-going assistance in marketing, human resources, program development (including curriculum) and financial management.

Training Provided: 6-day training in northern Virginia, encompassing all aspects of successful Computertots operations, including marketing, human resources, program development, teaching, financial management and hardware/software components.

Information Submitted: December 1993

CRESTCOM INTERNATIONAL
6900 E. Belleview Ave., 3rd Fl.
Englewood, CO 80111
Telephone: (303) 267-8200
Fax: (303) 267-8207
Mr. Kelly Allen, Marketing Director

Number of Franchised Units: 37
Number of Company-Owned Units: 3
Number of Total Operating Units: 40

In Business Since: 1987   **Franchising Since:** 1992

Description of Operation: The business centers around marketing and conducting video-based management and sales training. The training is a unique combination of video instruction, featuring renowned business and management personalities, combined with stimulating hands-on monthly seminars. Crestcom training is currently used by many leading organizations throughout the world.

Equity Capital Needed: $30,000 - $50,000

Franchise Fee: $52,500

Royalty Fee: 1.5%

Financial Assistance: Some financing of franchise fee is available.

Managerial Assistance: New franchisees go through 1 week of training (classroom and field), dealing with all aspects of the business. In addition, on-going training is available on a regular basis. Crestcom will attempt to provide assistance in finding financing. The Company also provides prospects with a lead referral program, telephone consultation, contests and incentives and training for franchisee's employees. A weekly newsletter & annual international meeting provide sales tips and input from other franchisees.

Training Provided: Crestcom offers initial classroom and field training. Additional training is available on an on-going basis.

Information Submitted: December 1993

ELS INTERNATIONAL
5761 Buckingham Parkway
Culver City, CA 90230
Telephone: (800) 468-8978 (310) 642-0982
Fax: (310) 649-5231
Mr. Richard Cheng, President

Number of Franchised Units: 42
Number of Company-Owned Units: 4
Number of Total Operating Units: 46

In Business Since: 1961   **Franchising Since:** 1978

Description of Operation: "English as a foreign language" schools abroad.

Equity Capital Needed: $150,000 - $300,000

Franchise Fee: $12,000 - $24,000

Royalty Fee: 3%

Financial Assistance: Not available.

Managerial Assistance: Complete operations manual and start-up guidance is provided prior to opening. On-going consultation and services, as needed.

Training Provided: 3 - 7 days of initial management training is provided prior to opening. Annual on-site visits and attendance at grand opening. On-going consultation.

Information Submitted: January 1994

EXECUTRAIN
1000 Abernathy Rd., # 400
Atlanta, GA 30328
Telephone: (800) 843-6984 (404) 396-9200
Fax: (404) 698-9180
Ms. Dawn Weiss, Franchise Sales Representative

Number of Franchised Units: 59
Number of Company-Owned Units: 3
Number of Total Operating Units: 62

In Business Since: 1984   **Franchising Since:** 1987

Description of Operation: Executrain is the worldwide computer training leader, specializing in the education of business professionals. We teach clients how to use popular business-related software through hands-on classroom training.

Equity Capital Needed: $150,000 - $200,000

Franchise Fee: $30,000 for a US franchise; $50,000 for a Master Franchise.

Royalty Fee: 6% - 9%

Financial Assistance: For US franchises, $20,000 of the $30,000 franchise fee is financed over a 2-year period.

Managerial Assistance: General management training is provided for all franchise owners, focusing on business planning. Continuous training and support is provided.

Training Provided: Sales training, instructor training, management information systems training and leadership training are all provided continuously for franchisees and their employees to attend, depending on the franchise growth stage.

Information Submitted: March 1994

FOURTH R, THE
1715 Market St., # 103
Kirkland, WA 98033
Telephone: (800) 821-8653 (206) 828-0336
Fax: (206) 828-0192
Mr. Robert L. McCauley, President

Information Submitted: December 1993

Number of Franchised Units: 36
Number of Company-Owned Units: 1
Number of Total Operating Units: 37

In Business Since: 1991   **Franchising Since:** 1992

Description of Operation: Franchisees teach computer skills to children 3-14 years old. Business can be conducted as home-based business or from commercial location. Broad curriculum includes ESL program and introductory classes for adults.

Equity Capital Needed: $17,000 - $20,000

Franchise Fee: $16,000 1st franchise; $7,500 each additional.Initial franchise fee includes 2 computers & software.

Royalty Fee: 5% - 9%

Financial Assistance: Franchisor-provided financing is available to qualified candidates.

Managerial Assistance: The franchisor provides continuing assistance and consultation to franchisee in all aspects of franchise operations, including continuing enhancements and additions to curriculum and product offerings.

Training Provided: Training is 40 - 60 hours, depending upon qualification and experience of franchisee, and covers all aspects of sales and operations.

Information Submitted: January 1994

GENIUS KID ACADEMY
404 Steeles Ave. W.. # 214
Thornhill. ON L4J 6X3 CAN
Telephone: (905) 886-1920
Fax: (905) 886-4919
Ms. Mira Aryev, President

Number of Franchised Units: 1
Number of Company-Owned Units: 1
Number of Total Operating Units: 2

In Business Since: 1992   **Franchising Since:** 1993

Description of Operation: Delivering high-quality computer education to children ages 3 - 12, as well as to adults. Nothing is more satisfying than preparing children for the future.

Equity Capital Needed: $60,000

Franchise Fee: $50,000

Royalty Fee: 15%

Financial Assistance: Data not available.

Managerial Assistance: Custom-made software will take care of all the aspects of running a computer learning center.

Training Provided: 1 month of training at the corporate location.

Information Submitted: January 1994

GODDARD SCHOOL. THE
381 Brooks Rd.
King of Prussia, PA 19406
Telephone: (800) 272-4901 (215) 337-6146
Fax: (215) 337-6113
Mr. Phil Schumacher, Director of Center Development

Number of Franchised Units: 11
Number of Company-Owned Units: 3
Number of Total Operating Units: 14

In Business Since: 1986   **Franchising Since:** 1988

Description of Operation: High-quality pre-school, offering day care hours. All Goddard teachers hold 4-year degrees in early childhood or elementary education.

Equity Capital Needed: $115,000

Franchise Fee: $25,000

Royalty Fee: 7%

Financial Assistance: The finance department will prepare pro formas and present them to at least 3 banks, including 1 SBA source.

Managerial Assistance: 5 full-time operations personnel (average experience in child care industry of 10 years) assist in ALL aspects of running the school and business.

Training Provided: We offer 2 weeks of formal training on the business aspects. Every school has a director to handle education.

Information Submitted: January 1994

GRADE EXPECTATIONS LEARNING CENTRES
105 Main St.
Unionville. ON L3R 2G1 CAN
Telephone: (905) 940-1944
Fax: (905) 479-9047
Mr. Terry Fullerton, President

Number of Franchised Units: 1
Number of Company-Owned Units: 0
Number of Total Operating Units: 1

In Business Since: 1993   **Franchising Since:** 1994

Description of Operation: Specializing in supplementary education, from grade 1 through 12. Enrichment and remedial programs use both traditional and computerized methods.

Equity Capital Needed: $35,000 - $50,000

Franchise Fee: $5,000

Royalty Fee: 10%

Financial Assistance: Not available.

Managerial Assistance: Complete manuals, field visits, advertising plans and seminars are provided.

Training Provided: Training includes 2 weeks in the founding franchise and 1 week on-site.

Information Submitted: March 1994

GWYNNE LEARNING ACADEMY
1432 W. Emerald, # 735
Mesa, AZ 85202
Telephone: (602) 644-1434
Fax: (602) 644-1434
Ms. Penny Gwynne, Treasurer

Number of Franchised Units: 14
Number of Company-Owned Units: 1
Number of Total Operating Units: 15

In Business Since: 1991   **Franchising Since:** 1991

Description of Operation: Video-based, interactive communications training, based on the latest scientific training technology for individuals and blue chip groups in business, government and education.

Equity Capital Needed: $45,000

Franchise Fee: $25,000

Royalty Fee: 7%

Financial Assistance: Indirect financial assistance is available.

Managerial Assistance: The franchisee is assisted with site selection, lease negotiations, record keeping materials and an initial training session.

Training Provided: A 7-day initial training session is provided to all new franchisees.

Information Submitted: January 1994

HONORS LEARNING CENTER, THE
5959 Shallowford Rd., # 517
Chattanooga, TN 37421
Telephone: (615) 892-1800
Ms. Margaret Craft, Director of Development

Number of Franchised Units: 1
Number of Company-Owned Units: 1
Number of Total Operating Units: 2

In Business Since: 1987   Franchising Since: 1992

Description of Operation: The Honors Learning Center is an educational facility, offering academic testing and individualized programs in reading, math, SAT/ACT prep, study skills, etc. for grades K - 12. These remedial and enrichment programs are offered during after-school hours and Saturdays. The educational programs are comprehension skill-based and the student success rate is fully documented.

Equity Capital Needed: $44,340 - $78,720 (includes fee).

Franchise Fee: $15,000

Royalty Fee: 8%

Financial Assistance: None.

Managerial Assistance: Each franchisee has a personal consultant at the home office available for answering questions and making suggestions about center operations on an on-going basis by telephone.

Training Provided: We provide up to 3 full weeks at the home office and 4 business days leading up to the grand opening.

Information Submitted: February 1994

JOHN CASABLANCAS MODELING & CAREER CENTER
111 E. 22nd St.
New York, NY 10010
Telephone: (212) 473-2725
Fax: (212) 420-0655
Ms. Charyn K. Parker, Director of Franchise Development

Number of Franchised Units: 50
Number of Company-Owned Units: 0
Number of Total Operating Units: 50

In Business Since: 1977   Franchising Since: 1977

Description of Operation: John Casablancas, Chairman of the Board of Elite Model Management Corporation, incorporates his modeling and personal development knowledge in Board of Education-approved curriculum.

Equity Capital Needed: $100,000 - $200,000

Franchise Fee: $6,500 - $27,000

Royalty Fee: 7%

Financial Assistance: Not available.

Managerial Assistance: Data not available.

Training Provided: 3 days of training, plus updated curriculum, operating and systems manuals.

Information Submitted: November 1993

KIP McGRATH EDUCATION CENTER
6465 Wayzata Blvd., # 940
St. Louis Park, MN 55426
Telephone: (800) 753-2571 (612) 593-1443
Fax: (612) 593-1684
Mr. James W. Sullivan, Chief Executive Officer

Number of Franchised Units: 9
Number of Company-Owned Units: 0
Number of Total Operating Units: 9

In Business Since: 1991   Franchising Since: 1992

Description of Operation: Supplemental tutoring services in reading, English language, spelling, math and study skills.

Equity Capital Needed: $18,000 - $20,000

Franchise Fee: $10,400

Royalty Fee: $150 per week.

Financial Assistance: Bank financing is available to those who qualify.

Managerial Assistance: We provide full training in curriculum and business systems. Marketing and advertising are centrally managed with full support to each franchisee.

Training Provided: We offer a 4-day introductory training in all aspects of the business, with quarterly updates and in-center training as required.

Information Submitted: January 1994

LEARNRIGHT
1315 W. College Ave., # 303
State College, PA 16801
Telephone: (800) 876-3450 (814) 234-9658
Fax: (814) 237-2030
Mr. Richard Catullo, Vice President of Franchise Operations

Number of Franchised Units: 0
Number of Company-Owned Units: 1
Number of Total Operating Units: 1

In Business Since: 1978   Franchising Since: 1993

Description of Operation: Founded in 1978 and incorporated in 1992, LearnRight Corporation is the parent company of LearnRight franchises, licensor of private schools dedicated to teaching people of all ages how to become more effective learners. LearnRight's specialized one-on-one instruction establishes a positive learning pattern, provides a foundation for improved academic performance, strengthens conceptual understanding and develops the student's confidence in learning. Also, thinking skills instruction.

Equity Capital Needed: $40,000 - $80,000

Franchise Fee: $15,000

Royalty Fee: 6%

Financial Assistance: Financing is available for the franchise fee only.

Managerial Assistance: Franchisees are provided with full educational and business support.

Training Provided: Franchisees attend LearnRight's 3-week franchise training program, consisting of classroom instruction and facility training.

Information Submitted: November 1993

NEW HORIZONS COMPUTER LEARNING CENTER
1231 E. Dyer Rd., # 140
Santa Ana, CA 92705
Telephone: (714) 438-9491
Fax: (714) 241-7836
Mr. Dean Gaston, Director

Number of Franchised Units: 39
Number of Company-Owned Units: 1
Number of Total Operating Units: 40

In Business Since: 1982   Franchising Since: 1992

Description of Operation: New Horizons Computer Learning Center is a complete PC, Macintosh, Novell and Unix training company. You provide one-day and two-day classes to businesses and individuals at your center or at the client's location.

Equity Capital Needed: $200,000 - $300,000

Franchise Fee: $30,000

Royalty Fee: 5%, or $1,000, whichever is higher.

Financial Assistance: We finance 50% of the franchise fee for 1 year with interest at 15% per annum.

Managerial Assistance: Franchisees are trained for 3 weeks at the headquarters and 1 week at their center on all aspects of running the business.

Training Provided: Same as above.

Information Submitted: December 1993

PRIORITY MANAGEMENT SYSTEMS
500 - 108th Ave. NE, # 1740
Bellevue, WA 98004
Telephone: (800) 221-9031 (206) 454-7686
Fax: (206) 454-5506
Mr. Todd Schmick, Vice President - Franchise Development

Number of Franchised Units: 270
Number of Company-Owned Units: 0
Number of Total Operating Units: 270

In Business Since: 1981   **Franchising Since:** 1984

Description of Operation: An international management training and human resources development organization, committed to providing clients with a curriculum of training programs designed to teach essential management skills. This is done through a series of group workshops and face-to-face consultations.

Equity Capital Needed: $35,000 - $45,000

Franchise Fee: $29,500

Royalty Fee: 9%

Financial Assistance: $9,500 down and a 3-year amortization of principal at 5% above the prime rate.

Managerial Assistance: Corporate support and development teams, as well as a regional coach, for each of our 10 regions. Newsletters, national public relations programs and participation in national trade shows.

Training Provided: Initial owner's training is 1 week. Owner training is one-on-one training with a regional coach in the field. Learning options are provided at the 2 regional meetings and the international conference.

Information Submitted: November 1993

SUCCESS MOTIVATION INSTITUTE
1600 Lake Air Dr., P. O. Box 2508
Waco, TX 76710
Telephone: (800) 678-5629 (817) 776-1230
Fax: (817) 757-9670
Mr. Willian Garner, President

Number of Franchised Units: 424
Number of Company-Owned Units: 0
Number of Total Operating Units: 424

In Business Since: 1960   **Franchising Since:** 1962

Description of Operation: We are the world leader in self-improvement programs, such as personal goal setting, sales management training, management training, sales training, time management and personal effectiveness. As an SMI franchisee, an individual receives the benefit of 32 years of experience, comprehensive training and on-going support.

Equity Capital Needed: $14,950

Franchise Fee: $14,950

Royalty Fee: 0%

Financial Assistance: Financing is available through Great Southwestern Acceptance Corporation.

Managerial Assistance: Data not available.

Training Provided: Comprehensive long-term training and support, including home office training conferences, regional training and field training. Our franchisee success system training program uses manuals, audio cassettes and videos. On-call support.

Information Submitted: December 1993

SYLVAN LEARNING SYSTEMS
9135 Guilford Rd.
Columbia, MD 21046
Telephone: (800) 284-8214 (410) 880-0889
Fax: (410) 880-8717
Ms. Flo Schell, Director of Franchise Systems Development

Number of Franchised Units: 476
Number of Company-Owned Units: 35
Number of Total Operating Units: 511

In Business Since: 1979   **Franchising Since:** 1980

Description of Operation: Sylvan is the leading private provider of supplemental education services in North America. Programs, directed at pre-school through adult, include reading, math, algebra, writing, study skills, SAT/ACT prep and more.

Equity Capital Needed: $45,000 - $75,000

Franchise Fee: $23,500 - $39,000

Royalty Fee: 8% - 9%

Financial Assistance: Some financing is available in selected locations.

Managerial Assistance: Complete start-up and on-going assistance is provided through highly-trained field consultants.

Training Provided: Comprehensive basic and on-going training are provided in all programs and operations.

Information Submitted: March 1994

VIDE-O-GO TAPE LEARNING CENTERS OF AMERICA
One Market Hall
Princeton, NJ 08540
Telephone: (800) 323-8433 (609) 520-9055
Fax: (609) 520-8468
Mr. Dean W. Stevens, Chief Executive Officer

Number of Franchised Units: 1
Number of Company-Owned Units: 1
Number of Total Operating Units: 2

In Business Since: 1989   **Franchising Since:** 1992

Description of Operation: Retail outlet of "How-To" cassette learning programs, specializing in the rental and sale of personal and professional development.

Equity Capital Needed: $32,500 - $72,500

Franchise Fee: $10,500

Royalty Fee: 4% - 6%

Financial Assistance: A business plan template is available for financial institution perusal.

Managerial Assistance: We provide an extensive operations manual, with a comprehensive supplier list, award-winning advertising and promotional campaigns and assistance. On-going publicity support and product evaluation.

Training Provided: Training consists of up to 10 days at a Company-owned outlet and up to 5 days of assistance during the franchisee's grand opening.

Information Submitted: November 1993

WONDERS OF WISDOM CHILDREN'S CENTERS
3114 Golansky Blvd., # 201
Prince William, VA 22192

Telephone: (800) 424-0550 (703) 670-9344
Fax: (703) 670-2851
Ms. E. Gail Scott, Vice President

Number of Franchised Units: 5
Number of Company-Owned Units: 1
Number of Total Operating Units: 6

In Business Since: 1989   **Franchising Since:** 1989

Description of Operation: Quality childcare, together with a developmental educational approach to early education, emphasizing language and social development, motor skills and reading. Infant through age 12. Programs developed over 25 years.

Equity Capital Needed: $112,325 - $195,500

Franchise Fee: $20,000

Royalty Fee: 6%, plus 1% advertising.

Financial Assistance: The franchisor will help locate financing. The SBA may be available to qualified applicants.

Managerial Assistance: Wonders of Wisdom provides all needed forms, handbooks and manuals, location assistance and state licensing package preparation. In addition, we design your facility and provide a list of approved suppliers and complete inventory. Monthly newsletters for franchisees and for parents.

Training Provided: We offer an extensive 3-week training period at the home office in basic business skills, computer skills, education and child care systems and marketing. Thereafter, we provide 1 week of training per year at your site for your employees and 1 week per year at our home office for the franchisee.

Information Submitted: January 1994

EMPLOYMENT SERVICES

1ST AGENCY PROFESSIONALS
511 Wilson NW
Grand Rapids, MI 49504
Telephone: (616) 791-4260
Fax: (616) 791-7039
Ms. Michele Sobczak, President

Number of Franchised Units: 0
Number of Company-Owned Units: 1
Number of Total Operating Units: 1

In Business Since: 1990   **Franchising Since:** 1992

Description of Operation: Provides nurses and nurse aides on a temporary basis to hospitals, nursing homes and other health care facilities.

Equity Capital Needed: $23,500 - $110,500

Franchise Fee: $25,000

Royalty Fee: 6.5%

Financial Assistance: Not available.

Managerial Assistance: Training at the home office and at the franchise office. On-call, 24-hour assistance.

Training Provided: Home office and franchise office.

Information Submitted: November 1993

AAA EMPLOYMENT
4908-C Creekside Dr.
Clearwater, FL 34620
Telephone: (800) 237-2853 (813) 573-0202
Fax: (813) 573-8709
Mr. Joseph M. Kotow, President

Number of Franchised Units: 22
Number of Company-Owned Units: 24
Number of Total Operating Units: 46

In Business Since: 1957   **Franchising Since:** 1977

Description of Operation: Emphasizes a full-service, general employment agency, specializing in placement at all levels of employment. Applicant-paid and employer-paid positions are handled. Low placement fee with convenient terms sets AAA Employment apart from other agencies.

Equity Capital Needed: $7,500 - $20,000

Franchise Fee: $10,000

Royalty Fee: 9%

Financial Assistance: No financial assistance is available.

Managerial Assistance: Support in all phases of the operation is an on-going commitment. Seminars and annual conventions are held and a weekly newsletter is provided, as well as an operations and training manual.

Training Provided: 2 - 4 weeks.

Information Submitted: November 1993

ACCOUNTANTS ON CALL
Park 80 West, Plaza II, 9th Fl.
Saddle Brook, NJ 07662
Telephone: (201) 843-0006
Fax: (201) 843-4936
Ms. Linda E. Krutzsch, Vice President of Operations

Number of Franchised Units: 13
Number of Company-Owned Units: 40
Number of Total Operating Units: 53

In Business Since: 1979   **Franchising Since:** 1981

Description of Operation: Temporary and permanent placement of accounting, bookkeeping and financial personnel.

Equity Capital Needed: $90,000 - $110,000

Franchise Fee: $25,000

Royalty Fee: 7%

Financial Assistance: Accounts receivable financing.

Managerial Assistance: Advise on site selection and staff hiring. Manuals and consulting assistance always available.

Training Provided: Approximately 2 - 3 weeks in corporate office and in a branch location. On-going training and seminars.

Information Submitted: January 1994

ADIA PERSONNEL SERVICES
100 Redwood Shores Pkwy.
Redwood City, CA 94065
Telephone: (800) 827-8928 (415) 610-1000
Fax: (404) 396-0813
Ms. Barbara M. Richardson, Franchise Development

Number of Franchised Units: 114
Number of Company-Owned Units: 154
Number of Total Operating Units: 268

In Business Since: 1957   **Franchising Since:** 1976

Description of Operation: Adia Personnel Services is principally engaged in providing a full-service temporary help franchise to franchisees who furnish office, clerical, word processing, sales, marketing, industrial and light technical personnel on a temporary, as-needed basis. The franchise is offered to qualified start-up and existing temporary help business owners.

Equity Capital Needed: $95,900, including initial franchise fee.

Franchise Fee: $17,500

Royalty Fee: Varies.

Financial Assistance: ADIA finances 100% of the temporary employees' payroll and accounts receivable financing for 90 days. In addition, Adia participates in the franchisee's local advertising through a co-operative advertising plan which funds up to 50% of local costs for pre-approved programs up to a determined amount, based on the franchisee's business. Adia may assist applicants in locating other sources of financing for capitalization.

Managerial Assistance: On-going consulting services and managerial guidance are provided on a regular basis. In addition to initial training, Adia maintains headquarters and field staff proficient in the entire industry spectrum. These resources are provided to each franchisee, offering advice and assistance in such areas as management, marketing, sales, operations, administration, computer information, training, office layout and design, legal affairs, insurance, government regulations, finance and purchasing.

Training Provided: Adia provides initial training to the franchisee in 3 phases, coinciding with the opening of the franchisee's office and after the opening. Initial orientation in operations is provided through manuals, branch observation, video training programs and computer training on Adia's office software system. The second phase is 2 training classes in sales and management, conducted at our international headquarters in the San Francisco area. Each class involves 5 days of intensive instruction in Adia sales.

Information Submitted: April 1994

ATWORK PERSONNEL SERVICES
1470 Main St., P. O. Box 989
White Pine, TN 37890
Telephone: (800) 233-6846 (615) 674-7666
Fax: (615) 674-8778
Ms. Diane Shelton, Sales

Number of Franchised Units: 16
Number of Company-Owned Units: 0
Number of Total Operating Units: 16

In Business Since: 1990   **Franchising Since:** 1992

Description of Operation: Personnel franchise, offering complete professional services, support and some accounts receivable financing for qualified applicants.

Equity Capital Needed: Up to $39,500.

Franchise Fee: $1

Royalty Fee: 7% on sliding scale, based on volume.

Financial Assistance: In addition to helping qualified franchisees acquire financing for their payroll, Atwork has consultants on staff to assist with problems, financial planning and to teach the franchisee's entire staff to sell and service accounts.

Managerial Assistance: Atwork has a staff of qualified personnel with degrees and/or specialized training in business management, accounting, clerical and computer technology.

Training Provided: All new franchisees are given up to 5 days of free training. Training is also provided for the franchisee's employees.

Information Submitted: March 1994

CAREER ADVANCEMENT SCIENCES
Six Market Square
Pittsburgh, PA 15222
Telephone: (412) 281-2005
Fax: (412) 281-2057
Mr. Richard D. Hindman, President

Number of Franchised Units: 7
Number of Company-Owned Units: 1
Number of Total Operating Units: 8

In Business Since: 1989   **Franchising Since:** 1993

Description of Operation: We provide comprehensive, custom personal marketing and corporate outplacement services for corporate, governmental and individual clientele. The CAS centralized support center provides all writing, research and production functions, while the field office is responsible for client development and project management activities.

Equity Capital Needed: $0 - $1,000

Franchise Fee: None.

Royalty Fee: 0%

Financial Assistance: None.

Managerial Assistance: Continuing managerial assistance is provided by headquarters staff and support personnel on an as-needed or requested basis. Supplemented by detailed operational procedures manuals, operating control records and financial control records analyses. Marketing, advertising and promotional assistance is provided.

Training Provided: Complete hands-on training program is conducted at the headquarter's offices prior to opening, with continuing training provided as needed on a situational basis. Detailed training manuals provided.

Information Submitted: November 1993

CHECKMATE SYSTEMS
P. O. Box 32034
Charleston, SC 29417
Telephone: (800) 964-6298 (803) 763-9393
Fax: (803) 763-9393
Mr. Ed Arrington, Vice President of Marketing

Number of Franchised Units: 4
Number of Company-Owned Units: 0
Number of Total Operating Units: 4

In Business Since: 1992   **Franchising Since:** 1993

Description of Operation: Checkmate provides total personnel administrative services to small business owners through the new technique of employee leasing. Business owners are completely relieved of all payroll, employee benefit and other personnel administrative duties when Checkmate assumes their employer duties and leases the employees back to them. Small business owners gain the purchasing power and tax advantages usually only available to large companies in providing employee benefits.

Equity Capital Needed: $25,000 - $50,000

Franchise Fee: $15,000

Royalty Fee: 3/10 of 1% of gross payroll processed.

Financial Assistance: Checkmate does not provide financing, but will assist the franchisee in finding adequate funding.

Managerial Assistance: The franchisee is provided comprehensive software as a part of the franchise fee. The Company provides back-up support for all of the functions the franchisee is required to perform for clients. The Company also provides professional marketing materials and support on an on-going basis.

Training Provided: The franchisee receives a minimum of 1 week of training in an operating franchise location, covering the principles of employee leasing, software operation and marketing.

Information Submitted: March 1994

COMPUTEMP
4401 N. Federal Hwy., # 202
Boca Raton, FL 33431
Telephone: (800) ASK-COMP (407) 362-9104
Fax: (407) 367-9802
Ms. Barbara D. Fleming, President/Chief Executive Officer

Number of Franchised Units: 4
Number of Company-Owned Units: 3
Number of Total Operating Units: 7

In Business Since: 1984   **Franchising Since:** 1991

Description of Operation: Computemp is a national temporary staffing service, specializing in providing information processing personnel. Our base of services includes data processing, micro/PC support and programming and systems support. All of our internal operations are completely automated, which translates into quality service.

Equity Capital Needed: $80,000 - $140,000

Franchise Fee: $30,000

Royalty Fee: 7%

Financial Assistance: Receivables-based financing is available.

Managerial Assistance: Back-up support and assistance is on-going.

Training Provided: Comprehensive training includes 2 weeks at one of our sites, plus follow-up at franchisee's site.

Information Submitted: November 1993

EXPRESS PERSONNEL SERVICES
6300 Northwest Expy.
Oklahoma City, OK 73132
Telephone: (800) 652-6400 (405) 840-5000
Fax: (405) 720-1040
Mr. C. Thomas Gunderson, Vice President of Franchising

Number of Franchised Units: 193
Number of Company-Owned Units: 0
Number of Total Operating Units: 193

In Business Since: 1983   **Franchising Since:** 1985

Description of Operation: Full-service temporary help service. Permanent and executive search divisions for recruiting also.

Equity Capital Needed: $55,000 - $95,000

Franchise Fee: $12,000 - $15,000

Royalty Fee: 6% - 9%

Financial Assistance: 100% financing of the temporary payroll and indirect financing for selected items, such as yellow page advertising, signage, computer software and industrial testing packages.

Managerial Assistance: Comprehensive assistance with site selection, help in negotiating leases, manuals and video training aids, testing and selection materials for temporary staffing. Continuous updates. An assigned field representative.

Training Provided: 2 full weeks of training at the corporate headquarters, followed with 1 full week in the new office as it opens with the assigned field representative. Continuous follow-up training in the field and in annual and regular seminars and workshops.

Information Submitted: November 1993

F-O-R-T-U-N-E FRANCHISE CORPORATION
655 Third Ave., # 1805
New York, NY 10017
Telephone: (800) 886-7839 (212) 697-4314
Fax: (212) 286-1877
Mr. Dennis Inzinna, Vice President

Number of Franchised Units: 64
Number of Company-Owned Units: 0
Number of Total Operating Units: 64

In Business Since: 1959   **Franchising Since:** 1969

Description of Operation: F-O-R-T-U-N-E Personnel Consultants is a national network of executive recruiting firms, specializing in the placement of middle management and executive level personnel with client companies throughout the US.

Equity Capital Needed: $50,000 - $70,000

Franchise Fee: $35,000

Royalty Fee: 7%

Financial Assistance: A portion of the franchise fee may be financed. Franchisor will give assistance in developing a business plan for presentation to other capital sources.

Managerial Assistance: Each new office receives assistance regarding licensing, office space, lease negotiations, insurance policies, telephone systems, office supplies, equipment and furniture. We provide comprehensive materials and manuals.

Training Provided: An intensive, 2-week training session at our headquarters in New York City. Included in this training is classroom and actual role playing on the telephone. Additional training takes place at franchisee's office and at periodic regional seminars.

Information Submitted: November 1993

FIRSTAT NURSING SERVICES
1645 Palm Beach Lakes Blvd., # 480
West Palm Beach, FL 33401
Telephone: (800) 845-7828 (407) 689-7100
Fax: (407) 684-9008
Mr. Dennis R. Allen, Vice President of Market Development

Number of Franchised Units: 13
Number of Company-Owned Units: 2
Number of Total Operating Units: 15

In Business Since: 1989   **Franchising Since:** 1990

Description of Operation: Home health care services, specializing in providing nursing care to patients in their homes on a continuous basis. Also, providing intensive care supplemental staffing to selected hospitals.

Equity Capital Needed: $175,000 - $195,000

Franchise Fee: $25,000

Royalty Fee: 5%

Financial Assistance: None.

Managerial Assistance: Once the franchise agreement has been executed, Firstat of America's STATstart program begins with site selection, lease negotiation, recommendations for office layout, furniture and equipment, insurance assistance, advertising contracts & campaign, recruiting/interviewing/hiring of staff, preparation of business development brochures, sales promotion, computer assistance, recommendations for signage and assistance with home health licensure and city and occupational licenses.

Training Provided: We offer a 5-day, intensive STATschool at corporate headquarters, followed by 5 days of on-site operational guidance before and after opening date. Additional on-site training and guidance are provided thereafter on an on-going basis.

Information Submitted: March 1994

FLEX-STAFF / PRO-TEM
214 N. Main St., # 202
Natick, MA 01760
Telephone: (508) 650-0026
Fax: (508) 650-0035
Mr. Giles A. Powers, President

Number of Franchised Units: 8
Number of Company-Owned Units: 1
Number of Total Operating Units: 9

In Business Since: 1970   **Franchising Since:** 1975

Description of Operation: Eligibility for our franchise opportunity is restricted to those individuals having substantial prior experience in the temporary services industry. We require a minimum of 2 years of successful, hands-on experience at the level of branch manager or above. By eliminating the need to train and closely supervise franchisees lacking temporary services experience, we are able to offer our services at a significantly lower cost.

Equity Capital Needed: $15,000 - $40,000

Franchise Fee: $1,000

Royalty Fee: Varies by market.

Financial Assistance: Financing of the temporary employee payroll and related payroll taxes is an integral part of our service to franchisees. We may also make available financing of Worker's Compensation deposit premiums.

Managerial Assistance: We provide substantial assistance in the back-office work of the franchisee, including payroll, invoicing, accounts receivable control, credit and collection and remittances.

Training Provided: Because we restrict our opportunity to individuals with substantial industry experience, our training program is limited to a brief training in our operating methods and systems.

Information Submitted: March 1994

HEALTH FORCE
177 Crossways Park Dr.
Woodbury, NY 11797
Telephone: (800) 967-1001 (516) 496-2300
Fax: (516) 496-3283
Ms. Pat Hiller, Director of Franchise Development

Number of Franchised Units: 50
Number of Company-Owned Units: 19
Number of Total Operating Units: 69

In Business Since: 1975   **Franchising Since:** 1982

Description of Operation: A national temporary health care service, specializing in home health care and supplemental staffing. We offer payroll funding, computer management, financing of receivables, training, site selections, office layout and national advertising program. Health Force allows you to become involved in all aspects of the temporary health care business quickly and easily.

Equity Capital Needed: $100,000 - $125,000

Franchise Fee: $39,500

Royalty Fee: 12% - 6%

Financial Assistance: We finance up to half the franchise fee ($19,750) in 24 notes. First note does not begin until 9 months after unit becomes operational.

Managerial Assistance: We do everything from initial business plan to on-going support through field service and operations.

Training Provided: 2 weeks of intensive training at corporate headquarters and 1 week in office. On-going regional training throughout the life of the contract.

Information Submitted: November 1993

HOMEWATCH
2865 S. Colorado Blvd.
Denver, CO 80222
Telephone: (800) 777-9770 (303) 758-7290
Fax: (303) 758-1724
Mr. Paul A. Sauer, President

Number of Franchised Units: 24
Number of Company-Owned Units: 4
Number of Total Operating Units: 28

In Business Since: 1973   **Franchising Since:** 1986

Description of Operation: Total home services. Pet and home services, while people are away on business or vacation. Elderly services - non-medical assistance for the elderly living in their own homes. Maintenance, repair and total remodeling services.

Equity Capital Needed: $25,000 - $30,000

Franchise Fee: $18,500

Royalty Fee: 6%

Financial Assistance: Multiple units only.

Managerial Assistance: Monthly calls, 800#, newsletters - quarterly and all service newsletter; videos on services and training; development of national accounts; advertising blitz at grand opening; national conventions; computer updates and faxes.

Training Provided: 1 full week at Homewatch headquarters. 3 full days at franchisee's locale for grand opening. Manuals, videos, development of business and marketing plans, all material and ads and role playing and OJT computer software. All insurance bonding for 1 year.

Information Submitted: November 1993

HOSTESS HELPER
20 Whittlesey Rd.
Newton Centre, MA 02159
Telephone: (617) 332-3516
Fax: (617) 630-1744
Ms. Ellen Hochberger, President

Number of Franchised Units: 0
Number of Company-Owned Units: 1
Number of Total Operating Units: 1

In Business Since: 1973   **Franchising Since:** 1990

Description of Operation: A temporary waitstaff and party-planning service. Hostess Helper provides waiters, waitresses and bartenders for functions of all sizes and can arrange for food, decorations, entertainment, etc.

Equity Capital Needed: $17,000 - $25,000, including franchise fee.

Franchise Fee: $10,000

Royalty Fee: 7%

Financial Assistance: Data not available.

Managerial Assistance: On-going assistance is always available by telephone. If location allows, on-site assistance is available.

Training Provided: Initial training takes 5 days at the head office in Massachusetts. On-going assistance is available after that.

Information Submitted: November 1993

JOBMATE
216 St. Paul St.
Pearl, MS 39208
Telephone: (601) 939-3333
Fax: (601) 936-2400
Mr. Harold Crawford, President

Number of Franchised Units: 5
Number of Company-Owned Units: 1
Number of Total Operating Units: 6

In Business Since: 1986   **Franchising Since:** 1989

Description of Operation: Staff leasing - client employers lease their current employees back from JobMate, which becomes responsible for writing payroll checks, making Federal and State deposits for withholding taxes and FICA, Workers' Compensation and benefits such as health, 401(k), employee assistance programs, etc.

Equity Capital Needed: $50,000

Franchise Fee: $30,000

Royalty Fee: 8%

Financial Assistance: $5,000 discount for minorities, veterans and women.

Managerial Assistance: JobMate will assist in setting up accounting systems and bank accounts in order to comply with the law. Advice and counsel will be provided to maintain accountability and compliance.

Training Provided: JobMate will train franchisee and staff in the concepts of staff leasing, marketing techniques and in payroll operations. Some familiarity with personal computers is necessary for the operators.

Information Submitted: December 1993

LABOR FORCE
5225 Katy Fwy., # 600
Houston, TX 77007
Telephone: (800) 299-4312 (713) 802-1284
Fax: (713) 802-1288
Mr. A. F. Nagel, President

Number of Franchised Units: 20
Number of Company-Owned Units: 0
Number of Total Operating Units: 20

In Business Since: 1970   **Franchising Since:** 1991

Description of Operation: We supply temporary personnel to almost every type of business or industry. The following are a few of the job classes we fill - clerical, electrical assembly, drivers, carpenters, plumbers, electricians, furniture manufacturing, carpet manufacturing, food processing, inventory crews, retail store helpers, recycling helpers, warehouse workers and many more.

Equity Capital Needed: $125,000 - $130,000

Franchise Fee: $25,000

Royalty Fee: 4.5% - 2%, depending on volume.

Financial Assistance: 60-day accounts receivable funding with affiliate company.

Managerial Assistance: Help with site selection, office set-up, manuals, forms, promotional material, bulk mailing and consulting on an as-needed basis. Periodic visits and an annual meeting with all franchisees.

Training Provided: 2 weeks of classroom and actual office training in a working environment. Personnel support available for travel expense charge.

Information Submitted: January 1994

LABOR WORLD
8000 N. Federal Hwy.
Boca Raton, FL 33487
Telephone: (800) 275-5000 (407) 997-5000
Fax: (407) 241-5589
Mr. Ed Secaul, Director of Franchise Development

Number of Franchised Units: 32
Number of Company-Owned Units: 6
Number of Total Operating Units: 38

In Business Since: 1974   **Franchising Since:** 1988

Description of Operation: Labor World is the market leader in light industrial temporary help. We provide the "blue collar" worker to most American industries. High-growth field with a very high profit margin. Low investment. Excellent training and support. INC. magazine rated Labor World in October, 1993 as the #19 fastest-growing private company in the US.

Equity Capital Needed: $50,000

Franchise Fee: $12,000 - $20,000

Royalty Fee: 3.5%

Financial Assistance: Payroll funding and Workers' Compensation funding.

Managerial Assistance: Extensive training - complete computer support program, plus field support. Additionally, we provide risk management, credit and personnel support.

Training Provided: 3 weeks in the field - hands on. 1 week or more at your location.

Information Submitted: November 1993

LINK STAFFING SERVICES
One West Loop, South. # 590
Houston, TX 77027
Telephone: (800) 848-5465 (713) 622-7488
Fax: (713) 622-7588
Mr. Ike Steele, Vice President of Franchising

Number of Franchised Units: 0
Number of Company-Owned Units: 8
Number of Total Operating Units: 8

In Business Since: 1976   **Franchising Since:** 1993

Description of Operation: Temporary service, supplying light industrial and industrial personnel to a variety of retail, commercial and manufacturing companies.

Equity Capital Needed: $95,000 - $195,000

Franchise Fee: $15,000

Royalty Fee: 32% - 40% of gross margin.

Financial Assistance: None, except Link finances the payroll for franchisee's temporary employees.

Managerial Assistance: Operations, risk management, sales, accounting and on-going field support as required.

Training Provided: 10 days of pre-opening training at Houston Support Center, followed by post-opening field training. On-going training, as needed.

Information Submitted: January 1994

MANAGEMENT RECRUITERS
1127 Euclid Ave., # 1400
Cleveland, OH 44115
Telephone: (800) 875-4000 (216) 696-1122
Fax: (216) 696-3221
Mr. Robert A. Angell, Vice President of Franchise Marketing

Number of Franchised Units: 402
Number of Company-Owned Units: 25
Number of Total Operating Units: 427

In Business Since: 1957   **Franchising Since:** 1965

Description of Operation: Management level and general personnel placement, search and recruiting service on an employer-paid, contingency fee basis.

Equity Capital Needed: $30,000 - $50,000

Franchise Fee: $40,000

Royalty Fee: 7%

Financial Assistance: None.

Managerial Assistance: The licensee is provided with a detailed operations manual, containing information, procedures and know-how for operating the business, computer hardware and software, an account executive, accounting and administrative assistant's manuals. Also receives a VCR/color TV, plus 38 video training films and a 90-day supply of all necessary operating forms, brochures, etc. Continuing advice, guidance and assistance through national meetings, seminars, training films, etc.

Training Provided: An intensive initial training program of approximately 3 weeks at headquarters, plus an additional on-the-job training program of approximately 3 additional weeks in licensee's first office. Training thereafter as needed. Staff will also assist and advise the licensee in securing suitable office space, lease negotiations, design and layout, office furniture, equipment, telephone systems, etc.

Information Submitted: November 1993

NORRELL SERVICES
3535 Piedmont Rd. NE
Atlanta, GA 30305
Telephone: (800) 765-6342 (404) 240-3000
Fax: (404) 240-3084
Mr. Mark Guyette, Regional VP of Franchise Development

Number of Franchised Units: 110
Number of Company-Owned Units: 98
Number of Total Operating Units: 208

In Business Since: 1961   Franchising Since: 1966

Description of Operation: A national temporary service with a 32-year track record of growth and profitability. Norrell is committed to providing the highest quality of service available to clients and temporary employees in the temporary help industry.

Equity Capital Needed: $60,000 - $95,000

Franchise Fee: None.

Royalty Fee: Varies with volume.

Financial Assistance: None.

Managerial Assistance: Extensive field support, automation of office functions through our BOSS system, comprehensive training programs and innovative support system. Finance temporary payroll and accounts receivable management (invoicing and collections).

Training Provided: Training - initial in-depth sales and service skills training to franchisees and their staff, followed by continual on-going training by Norrell field managers in local markets and through our comprehensive career development program.

Information Submitted: January 1994

NURSEFINDERS
1200 Copeland Rd., # 200
Arlington, TX 76011
Telephone: (800) 445-0459 (817) 460-1181
Fax: (817) 460-1969
Mr. Ed McGuinness, Vice President of Franchising

Number of Franchised Units: 58
Number of Company-Owned Units: 43
Number of Total Operating Units: 101

In Business Since: 1974   Franchising Since: 1978

Description of Operation: Nursefinders is a national provider of nurses and other health care professionals for home health care services and supplemental staffing to hospitals and other health care facilities.

Equity Capital Needed: $110,000 - $145,000

Franchise Fee: $19,600

Royalty Fee: 7%

Financial Assistance: Partial financing is available to qualified prospects.

Managerial Assistance: The franchisor assists the franchisee with site analysis and selection and office layout and design. Regional representatives visit the franchise sites at least annually to consult with franchisees about business operations and to offer suggestions for implementing Nursefinders' policies and procedures.

Training Provided: The franchisor provides 1 week of training at one of its established offices, 2 weeks at its corporate headquarters in Arlington, TX (or other locations designated by franchisor) and 1 week at the franchisee's site. Additional training includes on-site training visits and periodic management workshops.

Information Submitted: March 1994

REMEDY TEMPORARY SERVICES
32122 Camino Capistrano
San Juan Capistrano, CA 92675

Telephone: (800) 722-8367 (714) 661-1211
Fax: (714) 248-0813
Mr. Gerry Rhydderch, Vice President of Franchise Development

Number of Franchised Units: 38
Number of Company-Owned Units: 56
Number of Total Operating Units: 94

In Business Since: 1968   Franchising Since: 1987

Description of Operation: A full-service staffing franchise, specializing in office automation, clerical, legal and accounting positions, as well as light industrial business. Fully automated office.

Equity Capital Needed: $75,000 - $130,000

Franchise Fee: $15,000

Royalty Fee: Varies with gross margin.

Financial Assistance: Remedy provides funding of the temporary payroll.

Managerial Assistance: Help and advice with site location, lease and space planning. Regular visits by operations department to help in sales, recruiting, problem solving, national accounts, workmans comp issues, regular seminars and national meeting.

Training Provided: 2 weeks of pre-opening training, covering all aspects of operating and promoting a successful office. 1 week of classroom and 1 week of hands-on training in a Remedy office.

Information Submitted: January 1994

RETIREE SKILLS, INC.
1475 W. Prince Rd.
Tucson, AZ 85705
Telephone: (602) 888-8310
Fax: (602) 292-1147
Mr. Robert Rheinhart, President

Number of Franchised Units: 0
Number of Company-Owned Units: 1
Number of Total Operating Units: 1

In Business Since: 1978   Franchising Since: 1990

Description of Operation: Private temporary help service, specializing in the "over 50" worker. Designed for men and women.

Equity Capital Needed: $15,000 - $30,000

Franchise Fee: $9,500 - $15,000

Royalty Fee: 4%

Financial Assistance: None.

Managerial Assistance: On-going support. Site selection and lease negotiation assistance.

Training Provided: We provide 5 days at headquarters and 5 days on-site. On-going support.

Information Submitted: January 1994

ROTH YOUNG PERSONNEL
535 5th Ave., # 701
New York, NY 10017
Telephone: (800) 343-8518 (212) 557-4900
Fax: (212) 972-5367
Mr. William Beck, Director

Number of Franchised Units: 19
Number of Company-Owned Units: 0
Number of Total Operating Units: 19

In Business Since: 1963   Franchising Since: 1964

Description of Operation: Full-service executive and interim search and recruiting, specialization in the hospitality, food and food manufacturing, retail, health care and supermarket industries.

Equity Capital Needed: $38,000 - $56,000

Franchise Fee: $25,000

Royalty Fee: 3% - 8%

Financial Assistance: 50% of franchise fee.

Managerial Assistance: We provide a full manual, training videos, on-line support from headquarters and mentor office support.

Training Provided: We offer 1 - 2 weeks in headquarters, 1 week in an existing franchise and 1 week in our office.

Information Submitted: January 1994

SALES CONSULTANTS
1127 Euclid Ave., # 1400
Cleveland, OH 44115
Telephone: (800) 875-4000 (216) 696-1122
Fax: (216) 696-3221
Mr. Robert A. Angell, Vice President of Franchise Marketing

Number of Franchised Units: 127
Number of Company-Owned Units: 23
Number of Total Operating Units: 150

In Business Since: 1957   **Franchising Since:** 1966

Description of Operation: Specialized sales, sales management and marketing personnel placement, search and recruiting service on an employer-paid, contingency fee basis.

Equity Capital Needed: $30,000 - $50,000

Franchise Fee: $40,000

Royalty Fee: 7%

Financial Assistance: None.

Managerial Assistance: The licensee is provided with a detailed operations manual, containing information, procedures and know-how for operating the business, computer hardware and software, account executive, accounting and administrative assistant's manuals. Also receives a VCR/color TV plus 38 video training films and a 90-day supply of all necessary operating forms, brochures, etc. Continuing advice, guidance and assistance through national meetings, seminars, training films, etc.

Training Provided: An intensive initial training program of approximately 3 weeks at headquarters, plus an additional on-the-job training program of approximately 3 additional weeks in licensee's first office. Training thereafter as needed. Staff will also assist and advise the licensee in securing suitable office space, lease negotiation, design and layout, office furniture and equipment, telephone systems, etc.

Information Submitted: November 1993

SANFORD ROSE ASSOCIATES
265 S. Main St.
Akron, OH 44308
Telephone: (800) 837-9468 (216) 762-7162
Fax: (216) 762-1007
Mr. Douglas R. Ellertson, Vice President

Number of Franchised Units: 50
Number of Company-Owned Units: 0
Number of Total Operating Units: 50

In Business Since: 1957   **Franchising Since:** 1970

Description of Operation: A responsive search service, which is effective at virtually all levels in an organization. Uses data base of candidates and custom computer software to allow each office to make glove-fit matches with client openings without sacrificing personal relationships.

Equity Capital Needed: Additional $20,000 - $40,000.

Franchise Fee: $32,000

Royalty Fee: 7% - 3%

Financial Assistance: A portion of the franchise fee may be financed for qualified buyers.

Managerial Assistance: SRA's assistance begins during the investigation process through careful screening of franchisees. Each potential franchisee is given a clear understanding of what will be required to build the type of business envisioned at start-up. SRA provides market analysis and site-selection assistance. SRA training staff provides hands-on support during the early stages of business development. For the first 6 - 9 months, the franchisee interacts with a complement of staff members in strategic planning.

Training Provided: We provide a minimum of 10 days of training at corporate headquarters and an additional 5 days of training in the franchisee's office.

Information Submitted: January 1994

SITTERS UNLIMITED
23015 Del Lago, # D2-118
Laguna Hills, CA 92653
Telephone: (800) 328-1191 (714) 643-8133
Fax: (714) 472-8885
Ms. Sharon Gastel, President

Number of Franchised Units: 6
Number of Company-Owned Units: 0
Number of Total Operating Units: 6

In Business Since: 1979   **Franchising Since:** 1981

Description of Operation: Sitting service, full or part-time, for children, pets and elderly in homes or hotels and conventions.

Equity Capital Needed: $8,000 - $15,000

Franchise Fee: $8,000

Royalty Fee: 5%; percentage goes down as gross goes up.

Financial Assistance: We will personally finance up to 1/3.

Managerial Assistance: We offer 5 days of training on how to run the business, on-going support, meetings with other franchisees every 6 - 8 weeks and group advertising.

Training Provided: Data not available.

Information Submitted: March 1994

SNELLING PERSONNEL SERVICES
12801 N. Central Expy., # 700
Dallas, TX 75243
Telephone: (800) 766-5556 (214) 239-7575
Fax: (214) 239-6881
Mr. Richard H. Spragins, Senior VP of Marketing/Development

Number of Franchised Units: 259
Number of Company-Owned Units: 0
Number of Total Operating Units: 259

In Business Since: 1951   **Franchising Since:** 1956

Description of Operation: Full-service temporary and permanent personnel service franchise. Computerized national matching network. Specialties include, but are not limited to, sales and marketing, accounting and finance, data processing, engineering, health care and office support.

Equity Capital Needed: $35,000 - $146,000

Franchise Fee: $5,000

Royalty Fee: 8% for permanent; 40% of gross margin for temporary.

Financial Assistance: Payroll funding provided on temporary help.

Managerial Assistance: We provide 2 weeks of training at corporate offices and up to 2 weeks of on-site training. Support and field training provided.

Training Provided: Same as above.

Information Submitted: November 1993

STAFF BUILDERS
1981 Marcus Ave., # C-115
Lake Success, NY 11042
Telephone: (800) 342-5782 (516) 358-1000
Fax: (516) 358-3678
Mr. Ed Teixeira, Senior Vice President of Franchise Operations

Number of Franchised Units: 100
Number of Company-Owned Units: 30
Number of Total Operating Units: 130

In Business Since: 1961　　　Franchising Since: 1987

Description of Operation: Staff Builders provides home health services, including non-skilled and high-skilled nursing services, to patients in their homes. We are the third largest home health care provider in the US. We are a publicly-held company.

Equity Capital Needed: $105,000 - $150,000

Franchise Fee: $25,000

Royalty Fee: Split of gross margin.

Financial Assistance: Data not available.

Managerial Assistance: We provide fully-staffed field operations, clinical support, business development, national accounts, contracts, administrative department, financial services and a health care licensing department.

Training Provided: We provide 1 week of corporate training and 1 week of on-site training. Pre-opening start-up training prior to operation start-up.

Information Submitted: November 1993

TEMPS & CO.
245 Peachtree Center Ave., # 2500
Atlanta, GA 30303
Telephone: (800) 438-6086 (404) 659-5236
Fax: (404) 659-7139
Mr. Joe Haney, Director of Franchise Development

Number of Franchised Units: 9
Number of Company-Owned Units: 12
Number of Total Operating Units: 21

In Business Since: 1968　　　Franchising Since: 1988

Description of Operation: Temps & Co. is a temporary help service, specializing in office automation, technical and light industrial personnel. Our unique office automation and technical departments provide an outstanding service to our customers.

Equity Capital Needed: $100,000 (includes fee).

Franchise Fee: $12,500

Royalty Fee: 40%

Financial Assistance: We provide 100% financing of temporary payroll and accounts receivable. Indirect financing is provided through banking relationships and client referrals, marketing support, start-up, plans and support.

Managerial Assistance: As required to insure success of approved franchise prospects.

Training Provided: Training consists of 2 weeks of classroom training prior to opening, 1 week of on-site, start-up training and continuous on-site and field support. A national network of established clients is available for business development.

Information Submitted: November 1993

TODAYS TEMPORARY
18111 Preston Rd., # 700
Dallas, TX 75252
Telephone: (800) 822-7868 (214) 380-9380
Fax: (214) 713-4198
Ms. Janis Domino, Franchise Development Co-ordinator

Number of Franchised Units: 24
Number of Company-Owned Units: 59
Number of Total Operating Units: 83

In Business Since: 1982　　　Franchising Since: 1983

Description of Operation: A full-service, high-quality office clerical temporary employment service, utilizing a distinctive sales, service, promotional, quality control and accounting procedure known as the "Todays Way Method" of operations.

Equity Capital Needed: $90,000 - $145,000

Franchise Fee: Varies ($8,000 - $18,000).

Royalty Fee: Percentage varies with volume.

Financial Assistance: Payroll, receivables, insurance, credit and collections.

Managerial Assistance: Start-up, grand-opening assistance, site selection, initial and on-going systems, procedures, sales and operations support and training, manuals, customer satisfaction programs, technical and computer support, human resources, payroll and receivables.

Training Provided: Classroom and on-going field support in business operations, sales, operations and management, field sales development support and operations field development. All support is on-going.

Information Submitted: January 1994

TRC STAFFING SERVICES
100 Ashford Center N., # 500
Atlanta, GA 30338
Telephone: (800) 488-8008 (404) 392-1411
Fax: (404) 393-2742
Mr. Michael R. Baer, Vice President - Franchise Division

Number of Franchised Units: 20
Number of Company-Owned Units: 18
Number of Total Operating Units: 38

In Business Since: 1980　　　Franchising Since: 1984

Description of Operation: A national staffing services company, providing office support, clerical, word processing, data processing, marketing and light industrial personnel.

Equity Capital Needed: $75,000 - $100,000

Franchise Fee: No fee.

Royalty Fee: 9.5% or a 40/60 gross margin split.

Financial Assistance: None available.

Managerial Assistance: Each franchisee will be visited by his/her franchise support manager multiple times throughout the year. Also, our corporate offices provide marketing, payroll, credit and human resources support on a continuous basis.

Training Provided: The Atlanta, GA corporate offices provide formal training for operations, sales and branch management, as well as owner's training, which is provided for first-time franchise owners. Also, our franchise support managers will provide on-site training prior to opening and throughout the life of the franchise.

Information Submitted: November 1993

UNIFORCE SERVICES
1335 Jericho Tpk.
New Hyde Park, NY 11040
Telephone: (516) 437-3300
Fax: (516) 437-3392
Ms. Rosemary Maniscalco, Chief Operating Officer

Number of Franchised Units: 47
Number of Company-Owned Units: 13
Number of Total Operating Units: 60

In Business Since: 1961　　　Franchising Since: 1969

Description of Operation: Uniforce Temporary Services grants exclusive licenses to operate offices which provide temporary personnel with a wide variety of skills to employers in business, industry and government. Uniforce provides temporary personnel in the following skill categories: general office, automated office, medical office support, MIS, technical, accounting, marketing and light industrial services.

Equity Capital Needed: $75,000 - $100,000

Franchise Fee: $15,000

Royalty Fee: Varies.

Financial Assistance: Data not available.

Managerial Assistance: We provide full training, site selection assistance, a video newsletter, financing, preparation of temporary payroll and on-going operational back-up.

Training Provided: Same as above.

Information Submitted: March 1994

WE CARE HEALTH SERVICES
601 - 1011 Rosser Ave.
Brandon, MB R7A OL5 CAN
Telephone: (204) 725-4222
Fax: (204) 728-8146
Ms. Joan Plante, Director of Franchise Sales

Number of Franchised Units: 29
Number of Company-Owned Units: 0
Number of Total Operating Units: 29

In Business Since: 1984   **Franchising Since:** 1988

Description of Operation: Private duty nursing, companion sitters, palliative care, homemaking, house cleaning, para-medicals, staff relief and transportation.

Equity Capital Needed: $25,000

Franchise Fee: $25,000

Royalty Fee: 5%

Financial Assistance: None.

Managerial Assistance: We provide complete training at the corporate office with manuals, followed up by training and on-going support on-site.

Training Provided: We offer 1 week of intensive training at the home office, followed up by training on-site and on-going support and training visits. All training, computer software and manuals are included.

Information Submitted: January 1994

WESTERN MEDICAL SERVICES
220 N. Widget Ln.
Walnut Creek, CA 94598
Telephone: (800) 872-8367 (510) 930-5345
Fax: (510) 256-1515
Mr. A. Terry Slocum, President, Franchising Division

Number of Franchised Units: 17
Number of Company-Owned Units: 23
Number of Total Operating Units: 40

In Business Since: 1967   **Franchising Since:** 1967

Description of Operation: With over 40 offices, Western offers a full range of health care personnel services, including home health care. A program for Medicare certification is available. Franchise includes intensive training, computerized caregiver payroll and accounts receivable financing, professional risk management, credit and legal expertise, optional office automation systems and much more.

Equity Capital Needed: $50,000 - $100,000

Franchise Fee: $10,000 - $50,000

Royalty Fee: 0%; share of gross profit varies depending upon sales volume.

Financial Assistance: Western provides complete financing of the caregiver payroll and accounts receivable. Financing of a portion of the franchise fee is available to applicants with at least 2 years of management experience in the health care or staffing industries.

Managerial Assistance: Western handles all payrolling and invoicing through our computerized corporate payroll facility and offers professional advertising and public relations materials and support, risk management, legal and credit assistance, video orientation and training resources, sales leads, office automation systems and more.

Training Provided: Western provides 5 days of intensive classroom instruction at the corporate offices, 2 days of field office training in the San Francisco Bay Area and a 3-day, on-site training completion visit by a Western training representative. In addition, Western offers on-going, shared-cost affiliate workshops, peer groups and seminars.

Information Submitted: November 1993

WESTERN TEMPORARY SERVICES
301 Lennon Ln.
Walnut Creek, CA 94598
Telephone: (800) USA-TEMP (510) 930-5345
Fax: (510) 256-1515
Mr. A. Terry Slocum, President, Franchising Division

Number of Franchised Units: 98
Number of Company-Owned Units: 207
Number of Total Operating Units: 305

In Business Since: 1948   **Franchising Since:** 1957

Description of Operation: Western Temporary Services is a privately-held international temporary help firm. Founded in San Francisco in 1948, Western today has over 350 offices in 8 countries and is widely recognized as a leader in the temporary help industry. Western provides office, light industrial, medical, technical, accounting, outsourcing, marketing and Santa/photo personnel. Exclusive-territory franchises are still available in prime markets.

Equity Capital Needed: $50,000 - $100,000

Franchise Fee: $10,000 - $50,000

Royalty Fee: 0%; gross profit is divided based on sales volume.

Financial Assistance: Western provides unlimited financing of the temporary payroll and accounts receivable. Financing of a portion of the franchise fee is available to applicants with at least 2 years of management experience in the industry.

Managerial Assistance: Western handles all payrolling and invoicing through our computerized corporate payroll facility and offers professional advertising and public relations materials and support, risk management, legal and credit assistance, video orientation and training resources, QWIZ testing and tutorial software and support, national accounts, sales leads, office automation systems and more.

Training Provided: Western provides 5 days of intensive classroom instruction at the corporate offices, 2 days of field office training in the San Francisco Bay Area and a 3-day, on-site training completion visit by a Western training representative. In addition, Western offers on-going, shared-cost affiliate workshops, peer groups and seminars.

Information Submitted: November 1993

FLORISTS

BOTANICAL ENVIRONMENTS SYSTEMS
8915 Sherbrook Ct.
Owings, MD 20736
Telephone: (800) 334-2731 (301) 855-3722
Fax: (301) 855-0309
Mr. Mark N. Fisher, Chief Executive Officer

Number of Franchised Units: 2
Number of Company-Owned Units: 1
Number of Total Operating Units: 3

In Business Since: 1989   Franchising Since: 1989

Description of Operation: Indoor plant care and indoor plant design. Sales and installation in offices, hotels, restaurants and residences, etc.

Equity Capital Needed: $37,500 - $45,000

Franchise Fee: $25,000

Royalty Fee: 10%

Financial Assistance: Provided in the form of initial accounts and financed over the term of the agreement. Tangible items provided as part of franchise fee are mini-van/cargo van and equipment.

Managerial Assistance: Assistance primarily in the areas of marketing, new techniques, products and suppliers who provide unique items.

Training Provided: 2 weeks in total - 1 week of classroom and 1 week in field. Includes instruction in marketing, sales, installation, care and business administration.

Information Submitted: November 1993

BUNING THE FLORIST
3860 W. Commercial Blvd.
Ft. Lauderdale, FL 33309
Telephone: (800) 940-1778 (305) 488-3000
Fax: (305) 486-0622
Mr. R. Demerest, Vice President

Number of Franchised Units: 4
Number of Company-Owned Units: 16
Number of Total Operating Units: 20

In Business Since: 1925   Franchising Since: 1960

Description of Operation: Buning The Florist offers unique retail florist shops. The franchise package includes assistance in site selection, store layout and a complete training program at headquarters in Fort Lauderdale, FL.

Equity Capital Needed: $50,000

Franchise Fee: $15,000

Royalty Fee: 4%

Financial Assistance: No financial assistance is provided by the franchisor.

Managerial Assistance: The franchisor assists the franchisee in all aspects of shop operation, recordkeeping, advertising, promotion and selling techniques. Manuals of operations and counseling are provided. Home office personnel are available for periodic visits.

Training Provided: 2 weeks of training are provided at Company headquarters in Ft. Lauderdale, FL, plus continuing training in-store under Company supervision.

Information Submitted: March 1994

CONROY'S FLOWERS
6621 E. Pacific Coast Hwy., # 280
Long Beach, CA 90803
Telephone: (800) 435-6937 (310) 594-4484
Fax: (310) 596-2342
Ms. Barbara Lucci, Vice President of Franchising/Real Estate

Number of Franchised Units: 101
Number of Company-Owned Units: 0
Number of Total Operating Units: 101

In Business Since: 1960   Franchising Since: 1974

Description of Operation: Franchisor for full-service florist and mass merchandiser of quality cut flowers, floral arrangements and blooming plants. Facilities are 2,000 - 2,300 square foot locations at high-exposure intersections and shopping center end caps.

Equity Capital Needed: $125,000 minimum.

Franchise Fee: $75,000

Royalty Fee: 7.75%, with 3% advertising contribution.

Financial Assistance: None.

Managerial Assistance: Conroy's provides accounting assistance and operational support and coordinates local and regional advertising programs in electronic and print media.

Training Provided: Conroy's provides an extensive 6-week training program, with on-going training seminars.

Information Submitted: November 1993

FOLIAGE DESIGN SYSTEMS
1553 SE Fort King Ave.
Ocala, FL 34471
Telephone: (800) 933-7351 (904) 629-7351
Fax: (904) 629-0355
Mr. John S. Hagood, President

Number of Franchised Units: 42
Number of Company-Owned Units: 3
Number of Total Operating Units: 45

In Business Since: 1971   Franchising Since: 1980

Description of Operation: Sale, lease and short-term rental of live, artificial and preserved interior foliage and decorative containers. Related products include seasonal decorative items, etc. Design, install and maintain interior foliage in office buildings, hotels, residences, restaurants, etc. Weekly professional plant care and maintenance by uniformed technicians.

Equity Capital Needed: $35,000 - $150,000

Franchise Fee: $20,000 - $100,000

Royalty Fee: 6%

Financial Assistance: None.

Managerial Assistance: On-site training, on-going phone support (800#), assistance with design and bidding, monthly information and educational internal newsletter, network of leads and sources, annual meetings, marketing materials and complete operating manuals.

Training Provided: Initial 8 - 10 weekdays at corporate office, followed up by on-site training. Training covers all facets of business from plant care, plant identification, to sales and marketing to office procedures. Complete operations manuals provided.

Information Submitted: November 1993

GROWER DIRECT FRESH CUT FLOWERS
4220 - 98 St., # 301
Edmonton, AB T5B 1R3 CAN
Telephone: (403) 436-7774
Fax: (403) 436-3336
Mr. Bill Hustler, Senior Vice President

Number of Franchised Units: 127
Number of Company-Owned Units: 0
Number of Total Operating Units: 127

In Business Since: 1990   Franchising Since: 1991

Description of Operation: Low-cost, cash and carry flower stores. Operate from a walk-in cooler. Roses are featured. Low inventory, high turn-over. One of Canada's fastest-growing franchises.

Equity Capital Needed: $60,000

Franchise Fee: $20,000

Royalty Fee: $40 per box.

Financial Assistance: None.

Managerial Assistance: Data not available.

Training Provided: We offer 1 week of store training and 3 days of schoolroom training.

Information Submitted: January 1994

NATURE INDOORS
3000 Graystone Dr.
Semmes, AL 36575
Telephone: (205) 649-8001
Fax: (205) 649-8871
Mr. William Wyers, Vice President

Number of Franchised Units: 8
Number of Company-Owned Units: 0
Number of Total Operating Units: 8

In Business Since: 1985   Franchising Since: 1986

Description of Operation: Interior plant leasing and maintenance.

Equity Capital Needed: $15,000

Franchise Fee: $10,000 - $20,000

Royalty Fee: 5%

Financial Assistance: None.

Managerial Assistance: On-site assistance in setting up office, sales and installations. 400-page procedures manual.

Training Provided: 40 hours of training at home office. On-site training in sales, installations and maintenance.

Information Submitted: March 1994

PARKER INTERIOR PLANTSCAPE
1325 Terrill Rd.
Scotch Plains, NJ 07076
Telephone: (800) 526-3672 (908) 322-5552
Fax: (908) 322-4818
Mr. Richard Parker, President

Number of Franchised Units: 2
Number of Company-Owned Units: 1
Number of Total Operating Units: 3

In Business Since: 1948   Franchising Since: 1980

Description of Operation: Sell or rent live plants, flowers, trees, containers, etc. to Fortune 500 corporations. We also guarantee and maintain them.

Equity Capital Needed: $1,000

Franchise Fee: $15,000

Royalty Fee: 0%

Financial Assistance: None.

Managerial Assistance: We train in all aspects of the business and help the franchisee get started.

Training Provided: Same as above.

Information Submitted: January 1994

SILK PLANT FOREST
2108 South Blvd.
Charlotte, NC 28203

Telephone: (704) 332-8733
Fax: (704) 332-8790
Mr. David Elden, Director of Franchising

Number of Franchised Units: 0
Number of Company-Owned Units: 10
Number of Total Operating Units: 10

In Business Since: 1987   Franchising Since: 1993

Description of Operation: A specialty retailer of artificial silk plants, trees and floral arrangements and other related home furnishings. The merchandise is offered at reasonable and competitive prices, while being of the highest quality. The stores display the products as an accessory and a premier ornamental accent. The modern store design offers accents to complement and display the merchandise. SPF locates its leased retail stores in regional strip or power centers. Operations include commercial and wholesale services.

Equity Capital Needed: $83,000 - $110,000

Franchise Fee: $25,000

Royalty Fee: 5%

Financial Assistance: No.

Managerial Assistance: We will assist with site location, lease negotiations, accounting procedures and systems and inventory control. Hands-on training.

Training Provided: We offer an extensive, 4-week training period - in-field training, either in the corporate headquarters or a mix of locations, including the franchisee's own store after opening. On-going training and seminars are also provided.

Information Submitted: March 1994

FOOD—DONUTS

COFFEE TIME DONUTS
477 Ellesmere Rd.
Scarborough, ON M1R 4E5 CAN
Telephone: (416) 288-8515
Fax: (416) 288-8895
Mr. Danny Grammenopoulos, Executive Vice President

Number of Franchised Units: 120
Number of Company-Owned Units: 2
Number of Total Operating Units: 122

In Business Since: 1982   Franchising Since: 1989

Description of Operation: Coffee Time Donuts is one of the largest franchisors of stores which sell coffee and donuts in Ontario. Coffee Time Donut stores offer a wide variety of menu items and are open 24 hours a day to attract customers for an "any time" of the day "mini-meal." In addition to a wide variety of donuts, muffins, croissants, pastries and a gourmet blend coffee as snack foods, the menu expands to include soups, chili, salads, sandwiches and choices of various hot and cold beverages.

Equity Capital Needed: Data not available.

Franchise Fee: $15,000

Royalty Fee: 4.75%

Financial Assistance: Coffee Time Donuts does not, in the normal course of business, provide financing directly to a potential franchisee. What Coffee Time Donuts has done is to arrange financial assistance packages with various chartered banks experienced in franchising matters.

Managerial Assistance: Outside of the initial training program covered below, Coffee Time supports the franchise network by providing on-going store visitations by qualified field representatives. Franchisees are encouraged to view their opinions during the council meeting held every 2 months, or at the regional meeting held semi-annually.

Training Provided: Coffee Time's training program covers all facets of the coffee and donut selling business. There is particular emphasis on those aspects of the business and store which make for a successful franchisee. Coffee Time goes beyond the simple operating aspects of the business to include maintaining a clean, attractive store, serving customers in a warm and efficient manner and fostering good employee relationships.

Information Submitted: December 1993

DIXIE CREAM DONUT SHOP
P. O. Box 30130
Bowling Green, KY 42102
Telephone: (800) 788-1042 (502) 782-6109
Fax: (502) 782-6109
Mr. Michael G. Catlett, Vice President of Sales

Number of Franchised Units: 31
Number of Company-Owned Units: 0
Number of Total Operating Units: 31

In Business Since: 1929   **Franchising Since:** 1946

Description of Operation: Franchisor of donut shops, offering retail and wholesale sales opportunities. Qualified franchisees are supplied proprietary ingredient flours which produce donuts that are unique and appealing. Simple and cost efficient program has proven successful since 1929. No royalties means a higher profit potential. Protected individual and area franchises are available for immediate development. Packages tailored to meet individual plans and market potential.

Equity Capital Needed: $5,500 - $85,000

Franchise Fee: $5,000, plus $3,000 for training.

Royalty Fee: Data not available.

Financial Assistance: We will assist franchisee in procuring bank financing.

Managerial Assistance: The franchisee will be assisted in pre-opening and post-opening process by corporate management staff.

Training Provided: On-site training, involving production, sales, scheduling, etc. Operations manual provided.

Information Submitted: November 1993

DONUT DELITE CAFE
77 Bessemer Rd., # 19
London, ON N6E 1P9 CAN
Telephone: (519) 668-6868
Fax: (519) 668-1127
Mr. Joe Garagozzo, President

Number of Franchised Units: 23
Number of Company-Owned Units: 7
Number of Total Operating Units: 30

In Business Since: 1984   **Franchising Since:** 1985

Description of Operation: Donuts, muffins, cookies, soups, sandwiches, breads, etc.

Equity Capital Needed: $25,000

Franchise Fee: $20,000

Royalty Fee: 5%, plus 2% advertising.

Financial Assistance: Bank financing. Franchisor assistance is available, if needed.

Managerial Assistance: The head office, with 7 well-trained employees, assists in every area.

Training Provided: Total turn-key training.

Information Submitted: March 1994

DONUT INN
22120 Clarendon St., # 110
Woodland Hills, CA 91367
Telephone: (800) 4 BAKERY (818) 888-2220
Fax: (818) 888-2893
Franchise Development Director

Number of Franchised Units: 116
Number of Company-Owned Units: 3
Number of Total Operating Units: 119

In Business Since: 1975   **Franchising Since:** 1982

Description of Operation: Up-scale California-style donut, pastry, muffin, scone, cookie, croissant and bagel shops.

Equity Capital Needed: Equipment package approximately $45,000 - $65,000.

Franchise Fee: $23,750 - $95,000, varies with area.

Royalty Fee: 5.5%

Financial Assistance: SBA approved.

Managerial Assistance: We provide a comprehensive recipe and procedures manual that guides the franchisee in the everyday operation relating to product and quality control, service, sales, bookkeeping, inventory, ordering, marketing, etc. Whenever the franchisee has a question or needs advice on anything relating to his/her Donut Inn shop, there is a 24-hour a day, 7-day a week, hotline.

Training Provided: We provide 3 - 4 weeks of concentrated training in all phases of the business in our training facility. Continuous updating and re-training, as needed, on the newest and most innovative concepts and equipment. 1 week of training in your store upon opening.

Information Submitted: March 1994

KRISPY KREME DOUGHNUT
P. O. Box 83
Winston-Salem, NC 27102
Telephone: (919) 725-2981
Fax: (919) 725-2506
Mr. Philip R. S. Waugh, Director of Franchise Development

Number of Franchised Units: 50
Number of Company-Owned Units: 45
Number of Total Operating Units: 95

In Business Since: 1937   **Franchising Since:** 1960

Description of Operation: Krispy Kreme franchises a unique system for the production, marketing, distribution and sale of doughnuts and related products to the public from Krispy Kreme Doughnut shops. Currently, Krispy Kreme franchisees operate doughnut shops primarily in the Southeast US. The Company is granting franchises for the Midwest and Northeastern US. Krispy Kreme is the world's leading producer of doughnuts, selling more than 3 million doughnuts and related products per day. Largest maker of yeast-raised doughnuts.

Equity Capital Needed: $225,000 per store.

Franchise Fee: $25,000

Royalty Fee: 6%

Financial Assistance: No assistance at this time, only guidance in securing financing.

Managerial Assistance: We provide assistance in site selection, operational support, equipment maintenance and openings.

Training Provided: We offer an intense 6-week training course for owners and managers.

Information Submitted: November 1993

ROBIN'S DONUTS
725 Hewitson St.
Thunder Bay, ON P7B 6B5 CAN

Telephone: (807) 623-4453
Fax: (807) 623-4682
Mr. Ron Whitehead, Franchise Sales

Number of Franchised Units: 185
Number of Company-Owned Units: 5
Number of Total Operating Units: 190

In Business Since: 1975   Franchising Since: 1977

Description of Operation: Coffee, donuts, submarine sandwiches, soups, salads, etc. Fast-food restaurant.

Equity Capital Needed: $100,000

Franchise Fee: $35,000

Royalty Fee: 4%

Financial Assistance: Financing is provided through major banks. Guidance provided.

Managerial Assistance: We assist in accounting, costing, staffing, sales/marketing, advertising, purchasing, operations, research and development and construction.

Training Provided: 5-weeks of hands-on training at our national training center. 2 additional weeks with training team on-site.

Information Submitted: December 1993

SOUTHERN MAID DONUTS
3615 Cavalier Dr.
Garland, TX 75042
Telephone: (800) 9-DONUTS (214) 272-6425
Fax: (214) 276-3549
Mr. Lon Hargrove, President

Number of Franchised Units: 54
Number of Company-Owned Units: 0
Number of Total Operating Units: 54

In Business Since: 1937   Franchising Since: 1939

Description of Operation: Produce and sell varieties of donuts, muffins, kolaches and other delicious items, as well as coffee, juices and soda drinks.

Equity Capital Needed: $20,000 - $100,000

Franchise Fee: $5,000, payable $500 per year.

Royalty Fee: 0%

Financial Assistance: We provide no formal financing plan; however, we provide franchisees with valuable information for obtaining financing from lenders and/or leasing companies.

Managerial Assistance: The Company provides location selection assistance, floor planning, equipment selection and procurement, financing advice, employee selection criteria, forms management and on-the-job training.

Training Provided: The Company sends its personnel to the franchisee's location to train the owner, manager and employees in all phases of successful operation, with follow-ups as needed.

Information Submitted: January 1994

TIM HORTON
874 Sinclair Rd.
Oakville, ON L6K 2Y1 CAN
Telephone: (905) 845-6511
Fax: (905) 845-0265
Ms. Lilian Longdo, Franchise Co-ordinator

Number of Franchised Units: 825
Number of Company-Owned Units: 25
Number of Total Operating Units: 700

In Business Since: 1964   Franchising Since: 1965

Description of Operation: Tim Horton's is Canada's largest franchised retail coffee, donut and specialty baked goods chain, with over 800 stores across Canada and the US. The franchisee purchases a turn-key operation, the right to use Tim Horton's trademarks and tradenames, as well as a comprehensive 7 - 8 week training program and on-going operational and marketing support.

Equity Capital Needed: Minimum $85,000.

Franchise Fee: $15,000 - $50,000

Royalty Fee: 4.5%

Financial Assistance: Financing packages are available through major chartered banks in Canada.

Managerial Assistance: We offer the assistance of the operations staff with the initial store opening and the on-going support and guidance of the head office personnel, who are experienced in all aspects of this business.

Training Provided: A 7 - 8 week training program is conducted at the franchisor's principal offices in Oakville, ON, Canada. Costs incurred while in training (accommodations, meals, etc.) are the responsibility of the franchisee.

Information Submitted: March 1994

WINCHELL'S DONUT
1800 E. 16th St.
Santa Ana, CA 92701
Telephone: (800) 347-9347 (714) 565-1800
Fax: (714) 565-1801
Mr. Mel Allison, Franchise Representative

Number of Franchised Units: 75
Number of Company-Owned Units: 300
Number of Total Operating Units: 375

In Business Since: 1948   Franchising Since: 1950

Description of Operation: Winchell's offers coffee, soft drinks, muffins, donuts and other bakery products.

Equity Capital Needed: $85,000

Franchise Fee: $20,000

Royalty Fee: 5%

Financial Assistance: None.

Managerial Assistance: Store visits by a Winchell's representative, plus marketing support.

Training Provided: Complete donut training is conducted at a designated training store, normally taking 3 - 4 weeks.

Information Submitted: January 1994

YUM YUM DONUT SHOPS
18830 E. San Jose Ave.
City of Industry, CA 91748
Telephone: (818) 964-1478
Fax: (818) 912-2779
Mr. Lincoln Watase, President

Number of Franchised Units: 80
Number of Company-Owned Units: 1
Number of Total Operating Units: 81

In Business Since: 1971   Franchising Since: 1992

Description of Operation: Retail donut shops.

Equity Capital Needed: None.

Franchise Fee: Data not available.

Royalty Fee: 3%

Financial Assistance: Due to the low start-up costs, financial assistance is not necessary.

Managerial Assistance: Managerial assistance is available. However, we are looking for individuals with current retail donut shop managerial experience.

Training Provided: Training is available. However, we are looking for individuals with current retail donut shop managerial experience.

Information Submitted: March 1994

FOODS—ICE CREAM, YOGURT, CANDY, POPCORN AND PRETZELS

2001 FLAVORS CAFE
6924 Canby Ave., # 115
Reseda, CA 91335
Telephone: (800) 426-8584 (818) 881-4072
Fax: (818) 881-6734
Mr. Mike Whitman, President

Number of Franchised Units: 15
Number of Company-Owned Units: 0
Number of Total Operating Units: 15

In Business Since: 1983   **Franchising Since:** 1992

Description of Operation: 2001 Flavors of both yogurt and ice cream, smoothies, shakes, etc. We also serve 12 flavors of instantly-brewed coffee, along with espresso, cappuccino, etc. Our food concept, along with yogurt, ice cream and coffees, features incredibly delicious stuffed potato creations.

Equity Capital Needed: $23,000 - $130,000

Franchise Fee: $2,500 - $15,000

Royalty Fee: 5%

Financial Assistance: Equipment leasing - a total of around $60,000.

Managerial Assistance: Basic instruction manuals, operations, marketing and management. Continuing education in all facets of retailing.

Training Provided: Initial training in franchisee location, along with hands-on help at opening and beyond.

Information Submitted: November 1993

ABBOTT'S FROZEN CUSTARD
4791 Lake Ave.
Rochester, NY 14612
Telephone: (716) 865-7400
Fax: (716) 865-6034
Mr. Jack Perry, Director of Franchise Development

Number of Franchised Units: 15
Number of Company-Owned Units: 6
Number of Total Operating Units: 21

In Business Since: 1903   **Franchising Since:** 1954

Description of Operation: Abbott's Frozen Custard is an ice cream business, offering to sell the franchisee the right to operate one or more retail frozen custard stands where the public may purchase frozen custard, frozen yogurt, sherbet, soft drinks and other desserts and related food products. The franchise includes equipment package, installation and the right to use Abbott's name and product line (including Abbott's frozen custard mix) and methods of operation.

Equity Capital Needed: $60,000 - $70,000

Franchise Fee: $24,500

Royalty Fee: 3.25%

Financial Assistance: We do not provide any financing ourselves; however, we do work with a regional bank in the upstate New York area.

Managerial Assistance: Four weeks of intensive training and regular visits on a permanent basis.

Training Provided: Four weeks, consisting of two weeks at a Company location and at least two weeks at the franchisee's location. Training continues until we determine that it is no longer needed.

Information Submitted: November 1993

ALL AMERICAN FROZEN YOGURT & ICE CREAM SHOPS
4800 SW Macadam Ave., # 301
Portland, OR 97201
Telephone: (503) 224-6199
Fax: (503) 224-5042
Mr. C. R. Duffie, Jr., President

Number of Franchised Units: 11
Number of Company-Owned Units: 6
Number of Total Operating Units: 17

In Business Since: 1986   **Franchising Since:** 1988

Description of Operation: Retail shop, selling frozen yogurt and ice cream. Majority of shops are in enclosed shopping centers. Up-scale design.

Equity Capital Needed: $45,000

Franchise Fee: $20,000

Royalty Fee: 5%

Financial Assistance: The Company offers no direct financing arrangements. Company has financial contacts with lenders.

Managerial Assistance: Comprehensive training program. 1 week at corporate office and 1 week in store. Complete operations training, including manuals, accounting, menu items, personnel and day-to-day operations.

Training Provided: Data not available.

Information Submitted: March 1994

AMERICANDY COMPANY
1401 Lexington Rd.
Louisville, KY 40206
Telephone: (800) 822-6392 (502) 583-1776
Fax: (502) 583-1776
Mr. Omar L. Tatum, President

Number of Franchised Units: 0
Number of Company-Owned Units: 1
Number of Total Operating Units: 1

In Business Since: 1980   **Franchising Since:** 1993

Description of Operation: The marketing of confections and chocolates representing 50 states in beautiful red/gold AmeriCandy presentation boxes. The Company owns retail stores and also distributes its products through specialty shops and catalogs. Currently developing an overseas market in Asia.

Equity Capital Needed: $85,000

Franchise Fee: $25,000

Royalty Fee: 6%

Financial Assistance: There is currently no financial assistance.

Managerial Assistance: On-site training in the Company-owned store in Louisville, KY - accounting, packaging and marketing. Special emphasis on direct response.

Training Provided: The franchisee will spend 2 weeks at Company headquarters and learn all management procedures.

Information Submitted: November 1993

AUNTIE ANNE'S
P. O. Box 529
Gap, PA 17527

Telephone: (717) 442-4766
Fax: (717) 442-4139
Mr. David Hood, Director of Franchising

Number of Franchised Units: 144
Number of Company-Owned Units: 6
Number of Total Operating Units: 150

In Business Since: 1988   **Franchising Since:** 1989

Description of Operation: Auntie Anne's stores sell fresh, hand-rolled, soft pretzels in a variety of flavors, hand-squeezed lemonade and assorted dips for the pretzels. Mainly located in enclosed malls, our stores can also be found in airports and farmers' markets across the US.

Equity Capital Needed: $110,000 - $150,000

Franchise Fee: $21,000

Royalty Fee: 5%, plus 1% advertising fee.

Financial Assistance: Data not available.

Managerial Assistance: Auntie Anne's has developed a confidential operations manual for franchisees that addresses all aspects of owning an Auntie Anne's. There is also a store support department that provides continual support and consulting. Franchisees receive constant updates on new procedures. Our marketing department is available to help each franchisee individually, as well as the entire system. Auntie Anne's sponsors bi-annual seminars and workshops and a monthly newsletter for franchisees and managers.

Training Provided: We offer extensive training for both store owners and their managers. An intensive, 9 days of training at the home office will enable new owners to learn every aspect of running a store and give them hands-on training. There is also a 3-day training program for managers and employees who are new to Auntie Anne's or who need "refresher" training.

Information Submitted: November 1993

BASKIN 31 ROBBINS ICE CREAM
50 Ronson Dr., # 131
Etobicoke, ON M9W 1B3 CAN
Telephone: (416) 245-3131
Fax: (416) 245-3040
Ms. Kavita Hildenbrand, National Franchise Director

Number of Franchised Units: 197
Number of Company-Owned Units: 0
Number of Total Operating Units: 197

In Business Since: 1940   **Franchising Since:** 1971

Description of Operation: Retail sale of hard and soft ice cream and frozen desserts.

Equity Capital Needed: $45,000 - $50,000

Franchise Fee: $25,000

Royalty Fee: .5% of 1%.

Financial Assistance: We have packages set up with banks that detail our operation, but it will be dependent on the franchisee's application and his/her relationship with the bank.

Managerial Assistance: A district manager is assigned to every location, operating as the franchisee's business advisor and operational consultant.

Training Provided: An extensive 3-week training program in California is a mandatory requirement.

Information Submitted: February 1994

BEN AND JERRY'S HOMEMADE
P. O. Box 240
Waterbury, VT 05676

Telephone: (802) 244-6957
Fax: (802) 244-1629
Ms. Carol Hedenberg, Real Estate Manager

Number of Franchised Units: 97
Number of Company-Owned Units: 4
Number of Total Operating Units: 101

In Business Since: 1976   **Franchising Since:** 1981

Description of Operation: Franchised ice cream parlors.

Equity Capital Needed: $150,000 - $200,000

Franchise Fee: $25,000

Royalty Fee: 0% royalty, 4% advertising.

Financial Assistance: None available.

Managerial Assistance: We provide on-going managerial assistance and representative visits quarterly. Manuals and guidelines are updated as needed.

Training Provided: We offer 14 days of training prior to store opening, 4 to 5 days of on-site assistance during store opening, on-going training seminars and specialized training as needed by the franchisee.

Information Submitted: January 1994

BOURBON STREET CANDY COMPANY
266 Elmwood Ave., # 287
Buffalo, NY 14222
Telephone: (905) 994-0440
Fax: (905) 871-4223
Mr. Blaine McGrath, President

Number of Franchised Units: 20
Number of Company-Owned Units: 0
Number of Total Operating Units: 20

In Business Since: 1990   **Franchising Since:** 1991

Description of Operation: Candy and related gift items. Self-serve concept.

Equity Capital Needed: $60,000 (kiosk to $150,000 + (in-line).

Franchise Fee: $20,000

Royalty Fee: 5%

Financial Assistance: Yes.

Managerial Assistance: The franchise includes on-going support, as requested or required.

Training Provided: Each new franchisee receives operations manuals, in addition to having 1 week of training at an operating location and the assistance of a representative of the franchisor's staff in the opening of the franchisee's store for up to 1 week.

Information Submitted: April 1994

BRESLER'S ICE CREAM & YOGURT
999 E. Touhy Ave., # 333
Des Plaines, IL 60018
Telephone: (800) 535-3333 (708) 298-1100
Fax: (708) 298-0697
Mr. Howard Marks, VP, Director of Franchise Development

Number of Franchised Units: 242
Number of Company-Owned Units: 8
Number of Total Operating Units: 250

In Business Since: 1963   **Franchising Since:** 1968

Description of Operation: A treat shop for the entire family, featuring our private recipes of premium ice cream and soft-serve yogurts. Specialty items include no-fat "ice creams" and lite yogurt made without sugar, fat or cholesterol. Other menu items include assorted fresh fruits and candy toppings, sundaes, shakes, soft drinks, coffee and specially-prepared cakes and pies for all occasions.

Equity Capital Needed: $125,000 - $160,000

Franchise Fee: $15,000

Royalty Fee: 6%

Financial Assistance: The franchisor does not offer financing, but will assist in securing third-party financing.

Managerial Assistance: Besides the comprehensive 12-day training program and grand opening assistance, we'll continue to be there for you with on-going guidance and field support for as long as you're a franchise owner. Our territory managers will visit your shop to consult with you and advise you in the areas of sales forecasts, sales and operational objectives, as well as on the plans to meet your goals.

Training Provided: Comprehensive 12-day training program in Company training facility, plus 8 days of pre-opening and grand opening assistance at your shop with Company representative. Also included is assistance in site selection, store layout and design, equipment purchasing and marketing.

Information Submitted: December 1993

CANDY BLOSSOMS
7511 Lemont Rd., # 152
Darien, IL 60561
Telephone: (800) 572-5931 (708) 985-9406
Fax: (708) 985-6469
Mr. Sam Norton, Vice President

Number of Franchised Units: 12
Number of Company-Owned Units: 1
Number of Total Operating Units: 13

In Business Since: 1991   **Franchising Since:** 1992

Description of Operation: We make unique candy arrangements resembling floral arrangements.

Equity Capital Needed: $65,000

Franchise Fee: $15,000

Royalty Fee: 5%

Financial Assistance: None.

Managerial Assistance: Data not available.

Training Provided: 2 weeks of hands-on training in headquarters store.

Information Submitted: January 1994

CANDY EXPRESS
10480 Little Patuxent Pkwy, # 320
Columbia, MD 21044
Telephone: (410) 964-5500
Fax: (410) 964-6404
Mr. Joel Rosenberg, President

Number of Franchised Units: 51
Number of Company-Owned Units: 4
Number of Total Operating Units: 55

In Business Since: 1988   **Franchising Since:** 1989

Description of Operation: America's leading retail candy franchise, operating in regional shopping malls throughout the US. Easy to operate, self-serve format includes the largest variety of candies and confections anywhere. Over 1,000 items carried.

Equity Capital Needed: $150,000 - $190,000

Franchise Fee: $25,000

Royalty Fee: 6%, plus 1%, or 7%.

Financial Assistance: We provide a referral service to a finance company that provides financing at reasonable rates to our franchisees.

Managerial Assistance: We provide our franchisees with a total turn-key opportunity. Included are site selection, lease negotiations, store design, store construction, a 2-week training course, grand opening services and a 600-page operations manual.

Training Provided: We provide classroom and in-store training in all phases of store operations. Included are merchandising, accounting, sales, staffing, buying, managing, etc. 600-page operations manual.

Information Submitted: March 1994

CANDY HQers
3522 Charlotte St.
Pittsburgh, PA 15201
Telephone: (412) 687-4441
Fax: (412) 687-4506
Mr. Mark R. Lando, President

Number of Franchised Units: 7
Number of Company-Owned Units: 7
Number of Total Operating Units: 14

In Business Since: 1991   **Franchising Since:** 1992

Description of Operation: Help-yourself bulk candy retail operation. Typical store is 900 square feet in malls. We specialize in candy (90%) and related gift items. No popcorn, nuts or coffee beans. This allows our own stores to be smaller and maintain higher margins due to reduced markdowns due to spoilage.

Equity Capital Needed: $110,000 - $200,000

Franchise Fee: $30,000

Royalty Fee: 6%

Financial Assistance: None.

Managerial Assistance: Bankers "loan" package, field visits, financial planning, landlord package, assigned franchise coordinator, complete training manuals, newsletter, vendor contacts, product procurement and discount programs.

Training Provided: Initial training of 5 - 7 days at home office, supported by 350 pages of manuals, including all necessary forms. Grand opening training for 1 week at franchisee's store. Re-training available.

Information Submitted: January 1994

CARBERRY'S HOMEMADE ICE CREAM PARLORS
42 Rose St.
Merritt Island, FL 32953
Telephone: (407) 452-8900
Fax: (407) 454-4785
Mr. Steven R. Carberry, President

Number of Franchised Units: 3
Number of Company-Owned Units: 3
Number of Total Operating Units: 6

In Business Since: 1980   **Franchising Since:** 1983

Description of Operation: Full-service ice cream parlor, featuring delicious homemade ice cream and yogurt. Our program is unique, developing both a successful retail business and a wholesale business selling to restaurants, hotels, etc. Each store is set up as a complete ice cream and yogurt manufacturing operation.

Equity Capital Needed: $60,000

Franchise Fee: Data not available.

Royalty Fee: None.

Financial Assistance: None.

Managerial Assistance: Carberry's provides a monthly newsletter, updating the trends in the ice cream and yogurt industry.

Training Provided: Carberry's provides complete training in all phases of ice cream parlor operations. Program provides numerous recipes for Carberry's famous ice cream, yogurt, ice cream cakes and pies.

CARVEL ICE CREAM BAKERY
20 Batterson Park Rd.
Farmington. CT 06032
Telephone: (800) 322-4848 (203) 677-6811
Fax: (203) 677-8211
Mr. Wayne King, Manager of Business Development

Number of Franchised Units: 553
Number of Company-Owned Units: 22
Number of Total Operating Units: 575

In Business Since: 1934   Franchising Since: 1947

Description of Operation: Carvel Ice Cream Bakery, the third largest retail ice cream chain in the US, is positioned to provide high-quality, custom ice cream dessert and novelties, professionally prepared from scratch. In addition to full-service retail outlets, unit opportunities include kiosks, mini-stores and vending carts. Carvel offers qualified operators the opportunity to participate in a Branded Products Program in supermarkets and convenience stores. Convenience and value are #1 priority to consumers.

Equity Capital Needed: $80,000 - $100,000

Franchise Fee: $10,000

Royalty Fee: Minimum of $10,960.

Financial Assistance: None.

Managerial Assistance: Carvel requires 2 weeks of comprehensive training, including field training, accompanied by operations and product preparation manuals to use as a reference.

Training Provided: Marketing support, as well as on-going consultation services by District Managers and Area General Managers, is provided.

Information Submitted: November 1993

EMACK & BOLIO'S ICE CREAM AND YOGURT
P. O. Box 703
Brookline Village, MA 02140
Telephone: (617) 739-7995
Fax: (617) 232-1102
Mr. Robert Rook, President

Number of Franchised Units: 30
Number of Company-Owned Units: 0
Number of Total Operating Units: 30

In Business Since: 1975   Franchising Since: 1977

Description of Operation: Super-premium ice cream and non-fat yogurt, specialty coffees and pastries.

Equity Capital Needed: $50,000 - $75,000

Franchise Fee: $0

Royalty Fee: 0%

Financial Assistance: None.

Managerial Assistance: We provide training manuals, training in marketing and manuals for store construction, marketing, ad slick books, as well as TV commercials.

Training Provided: Training manuals, videos and in-store training are provided.

Information Submitted: January 1994

FUDGE COMPANY, THE
103 Belvedere Ave.
Charlevoix, MI 49720
Telephone: (616) 547-4612
Fax: (616) 547-4612
Mr. Robert L. Hoffman, President

Number of Franchised Units: 4
Number of Company-Owned Units: 0
Number of Total Operating Units: 4

In Business Since: 1977   Franchising Since: 1983

Description of Operation: All-natural homemade fudge. Our candy is cooked in copper kettles and "creamed" on marble slabs, in full view of the public. The showmanship of making fudge provides a unique, enjoyable and profitable operation. The Fudge Company provides the equipment, the franchisee provides the building and location.

Equity Capital Needed: $15,000 - $35,000

Franchise Fee: $12,000 - $15,000

Royalty Fee: 3%

Financial Assistance: Not available.

Managerial Assistance: Data not available.

Training Provided: The franchisor trains and educates the franchisee for 2 - 3 weeks in one of its stores.

Information Submitted: January 1994

GELATO AMARE
11504 Hyde Pl.
Raleigh, NC 27614
Telephone: (919) 847-4435
Fax: (919) 870-1090
Mr. John Franklin, President

Number of Franchised Units: 4
Number of Company-Owned Units: 1
Number of Total Operating Units: 5

In Business Since: 1983   Franchising Since: 1986

Description of Operation: Gelato Amare stores feature products that appeal to the total frozen dessert market! We serve delicious Italian-style super-premium, low-fat, low-calorie ice cream easily made right in the store, with several flavors. Lactose-free! We also feature all-natural, sugar-free frozen yogurt. In addition, we serve espresso, cappuccino, cookies, light soups, salads and sandwiches.

Equity Capital Needed: $75,000 - $130,000

Franchise Fee: $18,900

Royalty Fee: 5%

Financial Assistance: We provide cash flow and break-even analyses and all relevant data to lending institutions.

Managerial Assistance: We provide on-going personnel, pricing, marketing, advertising, public relations, promotion, merchandising and operations assistance.

Training Provided: We provide complete small business management training and all training specific to our business to help insure franchisee success.

Information Submitted: November 1993

GOOD FOR YOU FRUIT & YOGURT
6 W. 17th Ave.
Vancouver, BC V5Y 1Z4 CAN
Telephone: (604) 875-1029
Fax: (604) 873-6899
Mr. Amir Hemani, Controller General

Number of Franchised Units: 21
Number of Company-Owned Units: 0
Number of Total Operating Units: 21

In Business Since: 1983   Franchising Since: 1983

Description of Operation: Our stores feature our uniquely reciped frozen yogurt in a multitude of flavors. Unlike other frozen yogurts, we do not add any artificial colors or flavors - just fresh, frozen fruit of your choice.

Equity Capital Needed: $50,000 - $100,000 (Canadian).

Franchise Fee: $25,000 (Canadian).

Royalty Fee: 5%

Financial Assistance: Per individual situation, financial assistance can be reviewed and considered.

Managerial Assistance: Training and on-going support is available.

Training Provided: All training is done in Vancouver, BC. In some cases, training is done on-site in individual cities.

Information Submitted: March 1994

GORIN'S HOMEMADE ICE CREAM
158 Oak St.
Avondale Estates, GA 30002
Telephone: (404) 292-0043
Fax: (404) 292-0081
Mr. Marvin B. Young, Franchise Development

Number of Franchised Units: 29
Number of Company-Owned Units: 5
Number of Total Operating Units: 34

In Business Since: 1980   **Franchising Since:** 1981

Description of Operation: Up-scale homemade ice cream and sandwich shop, featuring gourmet ice cream and a wide selection of grilled deli sandwiches.

Equity Capital Needed: $35,000-$50,000, total investment of $100,000-$150,000.

Franchise Fee: $21,500

Royalty Fee: 5%

Financial Assistance: Equipment lease assistance is available.

Managerial Assistance: We provide site selection, equipment lists, preliminary store drawings, inventory lists and specifications and on-going supervision for the operation of the business.

Training Provided: We offer 3 - 4 weeks of comprehensive training in all aspects of the operation for 3 management personnel per store.

Information Submitted: March 1994

HAAGEN-DAZS SHOPPE COMPANY, THE
Glenpointe Centre E.
Teaneck, NJ 07666
Telephone: (800) 793-6872 (201) 907-6705
Fax: (201) 907-6701
Mr. Alan Guinn, Franchise Development Manager

Number of Franchised Units: 257
Number of Company-Owned Units: 2
Number of Total Operating Units: 259

In Business Since: 1961   **Franchising Since:** 1978

Description of Operation: Haagen-Dazs operates retail shops which represent excellent sampling and marketing opportunities for entrepreneurs. The Company seeks motivated entrepreneurs who recognize quality in products and services and who will represent the undisputed leader in the super-premium ice cream segment with distinction.

Equity Capital Needed: $119,500 - $297,500

Franchise Fee: $35,000

Royalty Fee: $1.16 per gallon of ice cream purchased.

Financial Assistance: None.

Managerial Assistance: Franchisees receive assistance with site selection and negotiation, attend an 11-day training school and receive on-going operations consulting and advice from Company representatives. Company franchise area managers are trained professionals.

Training Provided: Potential franchisees must attend and successfully complete an 11-day training school, located in Fairfield, NJ. This school offers training development in the day-to-day operation of the business.

Information Submitted: January 1994

HIGH WHEELER ICE CREAM PARLOUR AND RESTAURANT
P. O. Box 141
Kalamazoo, MI 49004
Telephone: (616) 345-0950
Fax: (616) 345-6887
Mr. Roger W. Buchholtz, President

Number of Franchised Units: 2
Number of Company-Owned Units: 1
Number of Total Operating Units: 3

In Business Since: 1975   **Franchising Since:** 1986

Description of Operation: Large turn-of-the-century, family-oriented ice cream parlour restaurants, featuring an extensive ice cream creation menu and over 45 flavors of ice cream, gourmet hamburgers, lunches and dinners. Further enhanced by an old-fashioned candy and bake shop, where fudge, chocolates, candies, brownies, cookies and breads are made in view of the customers.

Equity Capital Needed: $100,000, total investment $1,000,000.

Franchise Fee: $35,000 minimum.

Royalty Fee: 4%

Financial Assistance: Available to qualified prospects.

Managerial Assistance: We provide complete on-going managerial support.

Training Provided: We offer 8 weeks of full training in all aspects of the operation at Company headquarters.

Information Submitted: March 1994

I CAN'T BELIEVE IT'S YOGURT!
3361 Boyington Dr., # 200
Carrollton, TX 75006
Telephone: (800) 269-4374 (214) 392-3012
Fax: (214) 788-5036
Mr. Fred Addington, Director of Franchise Development

Number of Franchised Units: 275
Number of Company-Owned Units: 3
Number of Total Operating Units: 278

In Business Since: 1977   **Franchising Since:** 1977

Description of Operation: Our business is serving soft-serve frozen yogurt in cones, sundaes, parfaits and shakes. Our ICBIY "softie" frozen yogurt is a special recipe we manufacture ourselves to insure the highest of quality and innovation.

Equity Capital Needed: Total investment approximately $150,000. Equity capital varies due to location & financial strength.

Franchise Fee: $15,000

Royalty Fee: 5%

Financial Assistance: Not available at this time.

Managerial Assistance: Our Company has an ICBIY franchise consultant who is a resource for trouble shooting in all areas of store operations and is readily available for managerial and technical assistance. Such assistance and supervision will be provided in the following ways: mail, phone contacts, visits, conferences, newsletters, clinics and seminars. These methods will remain in effect for the duration of the business partnership between the Brice Group and its franchise owners.

Training Provided: Shortly before the opening of a franchise store, a 10-day training session will be conducted. A maximum of 2 people representing each franchise store can attend. This school will cover our success formula, accounting and bookkeeping procedures, operations, staffing, cost control and the basics of management.

ICE CREAM CHURN
P. O. Box 1569
Byron, GA 31008
Telephone: (800) 822-2967 (912) 956-5880
Fax: (912) 956-1864
Mr. Lee Anderson, Vice President of Sales

Number of Franchised Units: 542
Number of Company-Owned Units: 0
Number of Total Operating Units: 542

In Business Since: 1973   Franchising Since: 1981

Description of Operation: Ice Cream Churn establishes ice cream parlors, offering 32 flavors of ice cream and yogurt, within another business, such as delis, bakeries, video stores, convenience stores, donut shops, truckstops, etc. Churn's regional agents assist in setting up the locations, signs, train employees and then support the location with on-going promotional support. Kiosks for malls and drive-thru are also available.

Equity Capital Needed: $5,000 - $15,000

Franchise Fee: $5,000

Royalty Fee: $1.00 per tub.

Financial Assistance: Financing is available for equipment and sign packages in most areas.

Managerial Assistance: Regional agents train managers and all employees upon the opening of locations and on regular monthly visits. Additional training is available as needed. ICC also provides promotions to increase sales and works with managers to implement these programs.

Training Provided: ICC provides training and training manuals to each location which cover all phases of the operation. This training is performed at the actual location prior to and after opening of the Churn.

Information Submitted: November 1993

ISLAND FREEZE
2330 Kalakava Ave., # 204
Honolulu, HI 96815
Telephone: (808) 922-0030
Fax: (808) 923-3054
Mr. Ronald Scelza, President

Number of Franchised Units: 1
Number of Company-Owned Units: 2
Number of Total Operating Units: 3

In Business Since: 1986   Franchising Since: 1988

Description of Operation: Sale of Dolewhip frozen dessert in cones, cups, shakes and smoothies.

Equity Capital Needed: $39,500 - $114,000

Franchise Fee: $18,500

Royalty Fee: 5%

Financial Assistance: We will assist in obtaining financing.

Managerial Assistance: We will assist on an on-going basis in all aspects of business.

Training Provided: 1 week on-site in Honolulu, HI and pre-opening training and assistance at your site.

Information Submitted: December 1993

KERNELS POPCORN
40 Eglinton Ave. E., # 250
Toronto, ON M4P 3A2 CAN
Telephone: (416) 487-4194
Fax: (416) 487-3920
Ms. Bernice Sinopoli, Operations Administration

Number of Franchised Units: 54
Number of Company-Owned Units: 18
Number of Total Operating Units: 72

In Business Since: 1983   Franchising Since: 1984

Description of Operation: Retail popcorn stores - gourmet popcorn sold in a variety of bag sizes and specialty gift packaging.

Equity Capital Needed: $110,000 - $150,000 (Canadian).

Franchise Fee: $25,000

Royalty Fee: 8%

Financial Assistance: We provide the applicant with a prospectus for his/her bank. No other financial assistance is available.

Managerial Assistance: Assistance is provided during the store opening and there is on-going assistance available via the telephone, memos, correspondence and supervisory visits.

Training Provided: Training is provided at the head office and at a designated location. Training is also extended to the store opening. Training period is approximately 7 - 10 days.

Information Submitted: January 1994

KILWIN'S CHOCOLATES AND ICE CREAM
355 N. Division Rd.
Petoskey, MI 49770
Telephone: (616) 347-3800
Fax: (616) 347-6951
Mr. Don McCarty, Vice President

Number of Franchised Units: 24
Number of Company-Owned Units: 1
Number of Total Operating Units: 25

In Business Since: 1947   Franchising Since: 1982

Description of Operation: Full-line confectionery shops, featuring Kilwin's hand-made chocolates, fudge and Kilwin's own original-recipe ice cream.

Equity Capital Needed: $90,000 - $175,000

Franchise Fee: $20,000

Royalty Fee: 5%

Financial Assistance: None.

Managerial Assistance: Interviewing, hiring, training and employee supervision guides, as well as on-going training, are provided. 140-page operations manual.

Training Provided: 10 days of initial training at headquarters and store. On-going training as needed.

Information Submitted: November 1993

LARRY'S ICE CREAM & YOGURT PARLOURS
999 E. Touhy Ave., # 333
Des Plaines, IL 60018
Telephone: (800) 424-6285 (708) 298-1135
Fax: (708) 298-0697
Mr. Howard B. Marks, Vice President of Franchise Development

Number of Franchised Units: 38
Number of Company-Owned Units: 2
Number of Total Operating Units: 40

In Business Since: 1982   Franchising Since: 1983

Description of Operation: A frozen dessert shop for the entire family, featuring the traditional ice cream parlor experience and "Florida's Favorite." Larry's homemade-style ice cream and yogurt, specialty items include non-fat ice cream and yogurt that is custom-blended to order. Other menu items include fresh fruits and candy toppings, sundaes, shakes, banana splits, soft drinks and coffee.

Equity Capital Needed: $80,000 - $130,000

Franchise Fee: $15,000

Royalty Fee: 3%

Financial Assistance: The franchisor will assist in securing third-party financing.

Managerial Assistance: Besides assisting you in your pre-opening and grand opening training, we will continue to be there for you with on-going guidance and field support. Our territory managers will visit your shop to consult with you and advise you in the areas of sales forecasts and sales and operational objectives, as well as the plans to meet your objectives.

Training Provided: Our operations department provides pre-opening training, which teaches all facets of our system. This includes menu preparation, equipment preparation, employee training, personnel policies, internal control systems, sales techniques and the basic elements to local shop marketing and advertising. In short, all the tools needed to operate your business on a day-to-day basis.

Information Submitted: December 1993

MAISON DU POPCORN
188 Washington St.
Norwich, CT 06360
Telephone: (203) 886-0360
Fax: (203) 886-7966
Mr. William A. Abate, Vice President

Number of Franchised Units: 10
Number of Company-Owned Units: 1
Number of Total Operating Units: 11

In Business Since: 1986   **Franchising Since:** 1990

Description of Operation: Maison Du Popcorn offers gourmet popcorn in 24 different flavors, snow cones in all flavors, hot pretzels and gift tins.

Equity Capital Needed: $100,000

Franchise Fee: $20,000

Royalty Fee: 6%

Financial Assistance: No financial assistance is available from the franchisor.

Managerial Assistance: We provide 2 weeks of training at opening, plus help at anytime for any problem occurring while in business. We work with the franchisee until opening of the store.

Training Provided: We offer training in inventory, sales, payroll and accounting and every aspect of the business, including training of employees, training of manager, making and selling of a quality product, etc.

Information Submitted: January 1994

MARBLE SLAB CREAMERY
3100 S. Gessner, # 305
Houston, TX 77063
Telephone: (713) 780-3601
Fax: (713) 780-0264
Mr. Ronald J. Hankamer, Jr., Franchise Development

Number of Franchised Units: 26
Number of Company-Owned Units: 2
Number of Total Operating Units: 28

In Business Since: 1983   **Franchising Since:** 1984

Description of Operation: Retail ice cream stores, featuring super-premium, quality ice cream, cones baked fresh daily, fresh-frozen yogurt, cookies and brownies and frozen pies and cakes. Ice cream is custom-designed for customers on frozen marble slabs and made daily in each store. Open 7 days a week.

Equity Capital Needed: $35,000 - $45,000

Franchise Fee: $19,000 - $25,000

Royalty Fee: 5% in year 1; 6% thereafter.

Financial Assistance: None; however, the franchisor will provide assistance in locating financing through independent financial institutions.

Managerial Assistance: Marble Slab Creamery maintains an on-going business relationship with its franchisees, with assistance available in all phases of store operations. A complete operations manual is provided to all franchisees. Company field personnel visit stores on a regular basis to insure the consistency of operations throughout the franchise system. Marble Slab Creamery constantly updates advertising programs and evaluates new products for its franchised locations.

Training Provided: 10 days of training in the Company's training facilities in Houston, TX. 6 additional days of training at franchisee's store (3 days before opening and 3 days after opening).

Information Submitted: November 1993

NIELSEN'S FROZEN CUSTARD
P. O. Box 731
Bountiful, UT 84010
Telephone: (800) 322-6324 (801) 484-7500
Fax: (801) 484-8768
Mr. Dave Russell, Chief Executive Officer

Number of Franchised Units: 2
Number of Company-Owned Units: 7
Number of Total Operating Units: 9

In Business Since: 1981   **Franchising Since:** 1984

Description of Operation: Nielsen's Frozen Custard and grinder sandwiches is proud to bring back the goodness and taste of a by-gone era. Using our specially-designed, patented freezing machine and secret recipes, we can teach you how to make the finest frozen dairy product available. We are also looking for Area Franchise Developers to share in franchise fees and royalties.

Equity Capital Needed: $10,000

Franchise Fee: $10,000

Royalty Fee: 8%

Financial Assistance: We finance equipment or can put you in touch with leasing companies familiar with us.

Managerial Assistance: Initial and on-going managerial assistance, including helpful "forms" in our manual.

Training Provided: Nielsen's training personnel will instruct you and your people during the build-out of your store at our training facility. You will receive a Nielsen's "Know-How Book," which covers everything from the design and operation of the machine to the recipes and finished products. During the training school, the hands-on "know-how" will flow to you. We also cover accounting procedures, employee management, customer relations and much more.

Information Submitted: December 1993

PHILLY'S FAMOUS SOFT PRETZEL COMPANY
2000 W. Glades Rd., # 200
Boca Raton, FL 33431
Telephone: (800) 262-1567 (407) 338-5575
Fax: (407) 338-5650
Mr. Troy Turkin, Executive Vice President

Number of Franchised Units: 0
Number of Company-Owned Units: 0
Number of Total Operating Units: 0

In Business Since: 1991   **Franchising Since:** 1993

Description of Operation: Gourmet soft pretzel distributorship program. Our full-funded, extensive training program will train the franchisee how to become a food distributor. Our unique opportunity and low start-up costs put the franchisee on the path to success. No other soft pretzel company makes a variety of flavored soft pretzels which are no-fat, no-cholesterol and all-natural. It is the fastest-growing snack food in this country.

Equity Capital Needed: $14,900, plus working capital ($5,000 - $10,000).

Franchise Fee: $14,900

Royalty Fee: 0%

Financial Assistance: As a corporation, we do not provide financing. We can, however, supply the prospective franchisee with information needed to obtain financing.

Managerial Assistance: The franchisee is provided with an extensive training program in Florida at corporate headquarters. He/she receives an operations manual, sales scripts, 90-minute training videos, 800# hotline and continuous support through phone, fax and mail.

Training Provided: One-on-one training discusses Company and industry background, new Company set-up, sales, operations, role playing, account and distributor interviews, product preparation, equipment education and much, much more.

Information Submitted: December 1993

PRETZEL GOURMET
15 Engle St., # 302
Englewood, NJ 07631
Telephone: (800) 332-2229 (201) 871-0370
Fax: (201) 871-7168
Ms. Stacey Sommers, Marketing Director

Number of Franchised Units: 1
Number of Company-Owned Units: 3
Number of Total Operating Units: 4

In Business Since: 1990   **Franchising Since:** 1993

Description of Operation: Gourmet freshly-baked, hand-rolled, soft pretzels and homemade lemonade slush.

Equity Capital Needed: $40,000 - $60,000

Franchise Fee: $18,500

Royalty Fee: 5%

Financial Assistance: Financing assistance available to new franchisees consists of assistance in preparing a business plan narrative with pro forma operating statements and cash flows. In addition, the franchisor will assist in making introductions to potential lenders.

Managerial Assistance: Data not available.

Training Provided: We provide approximately 2 weeks of training program in Company headquarters and retail unit. Instruction covers a full range of baking techniques and services, operation of equipment, record keeping, advertising, publicity, marketing and basic techniques of management.

Information Submitted: December 1993

PRETZEL TIME
5285 Devonshire Rd.
Harrisburg, PA 17112
Telephone: (717) 540-8163
Fax: (717) 540-8179
Mr. Rich Hankins, Senior Vice President

Number of Franchised Units: 80
Number of Company-Owned Units: 7
Number of Total Operating Units: 87

In Business Since: 1991   **Franchising Since:** 1992

Description of Operation: Pretzel Time specializes in the sale of fresh, hot, soft pretzels, hand-rolled and baked in view of customers, plus specialty toppings and beverages.

Equity Capital Needed: $115,000

Franchise Fee: $10,000

Royalty Fee: 7%, plus 1% advertising fee.

Financial Assistance: Not available.

Managerial Assistance: Pretzel Time provides on-going field support through regular corporate communications. The Directors of Franchise Operations contacts franchisees at least twice monthly to discuss unit operations and concerns, visits each unit at least once a month and provides extensive training.

Training Provided: Corporate officials provide an in-depth, three-level training program, wherein franchisees and managers learn operational skills ranging from dough preparation to customer service, supervisory skills to recruit, train and maintain quality employees and financial skills to understand paperwork and boost unit sales. The training process includes 5 days at the corporate training facility and test kitchen and 5 days on-site at opening.

Information Submitted: January 1994

PRETZEL TWISTER, THE
4196 Corporate Sq.
Naples, FL 33942
Telephone: (800) 745-0214 (813) 643-2075
Fax: (813) 643-5639
Mr. Keith Johnson, President

Number of Franchised Units: 1
Number of Company-Owned Units: 1
Number of Total Operating Units: 2

In Business Since: 1992   **Franchising Since:** 1993

Description of Operation: Hand-rolled, soft gourmet pretzels and healthy fruit shakes.

Equity Capital Needed: $86,000 - $125,000

Franchise Fee: $12,500

Royalty Fee: 4%

Financial Assistance: Data not available.

Managerial Assistance: Training in accounting and payroll. Operations manual. Business start-up assistance, including site selection.

Training Provided: 1 week at our training facilities and 1 week of training on location.

Information Submitted: November 1993

P. S. I LOVE YOU - CANDY BOUQUETS
7101 Woodrow Ave.
Austin, TX 78758
Telephone: (800) 727-9338 (512) 452-0202
Fax: (512) 452-0224
Ms. Suzie Bush, President

Number of Franchised Units: 4
Number of Company-Owned Units: 1
Number of Total Operating Units: 5

In Business Since: 1989   **Franchising Since:** 1991

Description of Operation: Floral candy bouquets. Retail store that operate like a florist.

Equity Capital Needed: $25,000

Franchise Fee: $15,000

Royalty Fee: 5% of net.

Financial Assistance: None.

Managerial Assistance: 2 weeks of formal training. On-going support.

Training Provided: 2 weeks of formal training. Training to assemble bouquets, operations and procedures manual, management of retail and mall locations.

Information Submitted: January 1994

RITA'S WATER ICE/RITA'S ITALIAN ICE
1251 Byberry Rd., # 1
Philadelphia, PA 19116
Telephone: (800) 677-RITA (215) 698-1215
Fax: (215) 698-9860
Mr. Stephen J. Izzi, Franchise Director

Number of Franchised Units: 20
Number of Company-Owned Units: 3
Number of Total Operating Units: 23

In Business Since: 1984   **Franchising Since:** 1989

Description of Operation: Italian ice franchise, serving gelato and Italian ices.

Equity Capital Needed: $69,300 - $82,000

Franchise Fee: $20,000

Royalty Fee: 6.5%

Financial Assistance: None.

Managerial Assistance: On-going support in all aspects of shop operations.

Training Provided: The training program touches on all aspects of store operations, from manufacturing the product, ordering supplies and storefront operations to tallying receipts and making bank deposits.

Information Submitted: November 1993

ROCKY MOUNTAIN CHOCOLATE FACTORY
P. O. Box 2408, 265 Turner Dr.
Durango, CO 81301
Telephone: (800) 438-7623 (303) 259-0554
Fax: (303) 259-5895
Ms. Sheila Thompson, Franchising Sales Assistant

Number of Franchised Units: 92
Number of Company-Owned Units: 14
Number of Total Operating Units: 106

In Business Since: 1981   **Franchising Since:** 1982

Description of Operation: Retail sale of packaged and bulk gourmet chocolates, brittles, truffles, sauces, cocoas, coffees, assorted hard candies and related chocolate and non-chocolate items. In-store preparation of fudges, caramel apples and dipped fruits via interactive cooking demonstrations. Complete line of gift and holiday items. Supplemental retail sale of soft drinks, ice cream, cookies and brewed coffee.

Equity Capital Needed: $200,000 - $250,000 net worth; $25,000 - $50,000 cash.

Franchise Fee: $19,500

Royalty Fee: 5%, plus 1% marketing and promotional fee = 6% all together.

Financial Assistance: None at this time.

Managerial Assistance: On-going support and training provided by field staff. Annual national meetings and bi-annual regional meetings.

Training Provided: Complete training provided in customer service, record keeping, merchandising, inventory control and marketing during 10-day program at corporate headquarters, in addition to several days on-site for store opening.

Information Submitted: November 1993

SCOOPERS ICE CREAM
22 Woodrow Ave.
Youngstown, OH 44512
Telephone: (216) 793-9049 (216) 758-3857
Mr. Norman J. Hughes, Jr., President

Number of Franchised Units: 5
Number of Company-Owned Units: 2
Number of Total Operating Units: 7

In Business Since: 1981   **Franchising Since:** 1991

Description of Operation: Homemade ice cream store. Made fresh daily.

Equity Capital Needed: $35,000 - $50,000

Franchise Fee: $15,000

Royalty Fee: 5%

Financial Assistance: Data not available.

Managerial Assistance: Site selection, technical know-how, recipes, operation of units and store design.

Training Provided: We provide a 40-hour training period at the main store, as well as training at the franchisee's location. On-going support provided.

Information Submitted: November 1993

SWEET CITY
1604 Hilltop West, # 204-A
Virginia Beach, VA 23451
Telephone: (804) 422-3061
Fax: (804) 491-5543
Mr. Joseph L. Caffrey, Director of Franchise Development

Number of Franchised Units: 9
Number of Company-Owned Units: 0
Number of Total Operating Units: 9

In Business Since: 1991   **Franchising Since:** 1992

Description of Operation: A Sweet City system store offers a visually-stunning appearance, between 500 - 750 different sweets, nuts and confections, a large inventory of sugar-free, salt-free and low-calorie products and visible on-site fudge making. Simple operation (95% of the products are sold by weight), full service and self-service operation.

Equity Capital Needed: $45,000 - $135,000

Franchise Fee: $15,000 (to increase to $20,000 mid-1994).

Royalty Fee: 6%

Financial Assistance: Sweet City offers limited direct financing. Specifically, direct financing is available to Veterans (not dishonorably discharged) to the extent of 40% of the franchise fee for 2 years at market rates. (All potential franchisees must meet all usual and customary qualifications prior to being accepted as a franchisee.) Otherwise, Sweet City works closely with several financial sources that specialize in franchises, as well as the SBA. Company will assist in business plan development.

Managerial Assistance: Experienced Sweet City managers will be at each new store to insure that the merchandising and displays are perfect for the grand opening.

Training Provided: We conduct comprehensive classroom training at our headquarters, field training (for an actual "hands-on, in-the-trenches" experience) in one of our existing stores and on-site training for the franchisee and his/her staff in the franchisee's store prior to the grand opening. During this training period, every aspect of operating a Sweet City store is thoroughly covered.

Information Submitted: November 1993

TCBY SYSTEMS
1100 TCBY Tower, 425 W. Capitol Ave.
Little Rock, AR 72201
Telephone: (501) 688-8229
Fax: (501) 688-8251
Ms. Evelyn Simone, Director of Franchise Sales

Number of Franchised Units: 2187
Number of Company-Owned Units: 132
Number of Total Operating Units: 2319

In Business Since: 1981   Franchising Since: 1982

Description of Operation: Frozen yogurt, served in a variety of specialty desserts.

Equity Capital Needed: $105,000 - $190,000

Franchise Fee: $20,000

Royalty Fee: 4%

Financial Assistance: No financial assistance is available.

Managerial Assistance: You will receive operations manuals, a library of training tapes (which are updated regularly) and a trained division manager will be present to guide you through your first 5 days of operation to insure a smooth, efficient and successfully opening period. The division manager will evaluate your operation and advise you on a regular basis.

Training Provided: A 10-day training program at corporate headquarters in Little Rock, AR is provided to you and your manager. This program has been designed to cover vital areas of importance in your success as a franchise owner. It covers the operations manual, library of training tapes, equipment layout, methods of inventory control, bookkeeping and accounting, equipment maintenance, advertising, promotion methods, standards of quality, personnel policies, training of your employees and operational techniques.

Information Submitted: November 1993

WHITE MOUNTAIN CREAMERY
1576 Bardstown Rd.
Louisville, KY 40205
Telephone: (502) 456-2663
Fax: (502) 456-2056
Mr. Charles G. Ducas, Vice President

Number of Franchised Units: 38
Number of Company-Owned Units: 1
Number of Total Operating Units: 39

In Business Since: 1985   Franchising Since: 1987

Description of Operation: White Mountain Creamery is a unique concept, featuring the on-site production of super-premium ice cream, frozen yogurt and bakery goods. We appeal to a wide market niche by offering products for the entire family, everything from fat-free, sugar-free diet desserts and bakery products to rich, award-winning ice cream. We also offer frozen cakes and pies, as well as specialty coffees in a friendly, family atmosphere. Our locations include strip centers, some with a drive-thru window, and enclosed malls.

Equity Capital Needed: $50,000 - $65,000

Franchise Fee: $20,000

Royalty Fee: 4%

Financial Assistance: We assist in the evaluation of your business plan for submission to commercial leaders and/or SBA personnel. We do not offer internal financing at this time.

Managerial Assistance: We offer floor plan and store layout, site selection and lease negotiation, construction assistance, pre-opening equipment planning, pre-opening crew training and product production assistance and grand opening planning assistance. Post-opening service continues throughout the term of the franchise to help you manage your store's growth and profitability. There is a 1% co-operative marketing and advertising fund.

Training Provided: Training consists of a 14-day combination classroom and in-store training at headquarters for profit making knowledge - includes philosophy and sales strategy, customer sales and service, promotional marketing and inventory control, accounting, profitability and cash control management, merchandising, hiring and training. Confidential and comprehensive training manuals. Extensive continuing education programs. Special training sessions available.

Information Submitted: November 1993

YOGEN FRUZ
7500 Woodbine Ave., Main Fl.
Markham, ON L3R 1A8 CAN
Telephone: (905) 479-8762
Fax: (905) 479-5235
Mr. Michael Serruya, President

Number of Franchised Units: 230
Number of Company-Owned Units: 5
Number of Total Operating Units: 235

In Business Since: 1986   Franchising Since: 1987

Description of Operation: Frozen yogurt and frozen dairy-related treats.

Equity Capital Needed: $25,000

Franchise Fee: $25,000

Royalty Fee: 6%

Financial Assistance: Data not available.

Managerial Assistance: The franchisor negotiates the lease, handles the preparation of plans, contracts the construction, equips the entire store, sets up suppliers and arranges distribution.

Training Provided: Training includes 1 week at a corporate store and 1 week of training at the franchisee's store. Operations manual, marketing manual and manager's manual.

Information Submitted: January 1994

YOGURT & SUCH
438 Woodbury Rd.
Plainview, NY 11803
Telephone: (800) YOG-SUCH (516) 624-7100
Fax: (516) 624-7108
Mr. Bill Reichert, Franchise Development

Number of Franchised Units: 7
Number of Company-Owned Units: 5
Number of Total Operating Units: 12

In Business Since: 1982   Franchising Since: 1989

Description of Operation: America's healthy fast-food restaurants, featuring our own frozen non-fat yogurt and guilt-free glace (dietary frozen dessert), along with a full menu of natural, healthy food, such as salads, pastas, sandwiches, soups and beverages. Dynamic state-of-the-art units feature seating for 48+ along with take-out facilities.

Equity Capital Needed: $125,000 - $248,000

Franchise Fee: $25,000

Royalty Fee: 5%, plus 1% advertising.

Financial Assistance: We provide indirect contacts with SBA and equipment leasing companies.

Managerial Assistance: Continuous, on-going support includes hotline and periodic visits.

Training Provided: We offer a 14-day training program at Company stores and assistance through grand opening.

Information Submitted: March 1994

YOGURTERIA
14 Great Neck Rd.
Great Neck, NY 11021
Telephone: (516) 829-7480
Fax: (516) 829-0490
Mr. Dominic Maggiore, President

Number of Franchised Units: 5
Number of Company-Owned Units: 4
Number of Total Operating Units: 9

In Business Since: 1987   Franchising Since: 1989

Description of Operation: Yogurteria is a yogurt and food restaurant operation with 35 - 50 seats. Customers are offered a variety of freshly-prepared foods, such as pasta, vegetables, lasagna, rice dishes, garden salads, sandwiches and soups. Each Yogurteria has 4 yogurt machines serving 8 varieties of frozen yogurt and frozen desserts.

Equity Capital Needed: $185,000 - $250,000

Franchise Fee: $25,000

Royalty Fee: 5%

Financial Assistance: Yogurteria is affiliated with a restaurant equipment leasing company which offers financing on yogurt machines to franchisees.

Managerial Assistance: Yogurteria provides complete operations manuals and guidelines to assist franchisees in day-to-day operations. Franchisees receive consistent support by Yogurteria franchise operations personnel.

Training Provided: Yogurteria has a 4-week training program at its training store. A combination of classroom training and hands-on training is used. On-site training is also provided for at least 30 days at the franchisee's location.

Information Submitted: November 1993

GENERAL MERCHANDISING STORES

BEN FRANKLIN CRAFTS
500 E. North Ave.
Carol Stream, IL 60188
Telephone: (800) 669-6413 (708) 462-6201
Fax: (708) 690-1356
Mr. C. Wayne Pyrant, Vice President of Franchise Sales

Number of Franchised Units: 929
Number of Company-Owned Units: 10
Number of Total Operating Units: 939

In Business Since: 1977   Franchising Since: 1920

Description of Operation: Retail crafts and variety stores. Ben Franklin Crafts is a full-service craft superstore, including in-store craft classes, knowledgeable staff and fast, efficient checkouts. Merchandise includes an extensive line of craft products - florals, wearable art, custom framing, art supplies, yarns, needlework and sewing supplies.

Equity Capital Needed: $600,000 - $1,000,000 (30% - 40% of total investment).

Franchise Fee: $30,000

Royalty Fee: 2% - 5%

Financial Assistance: The Company will assist the franchisee in obtaining bank financing and/or third-party financing.

Managerial Assistance: We provide the following services: customer demographics; direct site selection and lease negotiations; store design; on-going marketing programs/advertising; accounting systems; inventory and quality control systems; group health, medical, auto, etc., insurance;

on-site and regional assistance; written operations, sales and marketing manuals; communications publications; and a national advisory committee made up of 10 franchise owners.

Training Provided: 4 weeks in total - 2 weeks at corporate headquarters; 2 weeks in store and on-going, semi-annual training sessions at Company conventions.

Information Submitted: December 1993

DOLLAR DISCOUNT STORES OF AMERICA
1362 Naamans Creek Rd.
Boothwyn, PA 19061
Telephone: (800) 227-5314 (215) 497-1991
Fax: (215) 485-6439
Mr. Mitchell Insel, Franchise Director

Number of Franchised Units: 29
Number of Company-Owned Units: 0
Number of Total Operating Units: 29

In Business Since: 1983   Franchising Since: 1985

Description of Operation: Retail franchise - dollar stores and variety discount stores.

Equity Capital Needed: $96,750 - $126,925

Franchise Fee: $18,000

Royalty Fee: 3%

Financial Assistance: The franchisor will assist prospective franchise owner in preparing loan application, as well as referring prospective franchise owner to potential institutions which provide loans to qualified applicants.

Managerial Assistance: We assist the new owner in ordering fixtures and merchandise. Provide minimum of 7 day field rep assistance in preparing store for opening. New franchise owner will get extensive support and assistance during opening period.

Training Provided: 1-week training class, where all facets of the business are discussed and new owners are trained on how to run the business and how to strive for the maximum profit potential.

Information Submitted: November 1993

TERRI'S CONSIGNMENT WORLD
1826 W. Broadway Rd., # 3
Mesa, AZ 85202
Telephone: (800) 455-0400 (602) 461-0400
Fax: (602) 969-5052
Mr. Marcus Curtis, President/Chief Operating Officer

Number of Franchised Units: 0
Number of Company-Owned Units: 3
Number of Total Operating Units: 3

In Business Since: 1979   Franchising Since: 1993

Description of Operation: Consignment home furnishings. The retailer deals in "Gently Used" home furnishings and accessories, appliances, sight and sound, from the public, model homes, liquidations and estates. Consignors receive top dollar when their quality furnishings sell. The buying public benefits by receiving name-brand merchandise at 50 to 70% below retail.

Equity Capital Needed: $140,000 + (includes fee and is a turn-key operation).

Franchise Fee: $20,000

Royalty Fee: 5%, plus 2% national advertising.

Financial Assistance: A comprehensive business plan is included with the franchise fee. TCW will assist the franchisee in completing the necessary applications for financing with a third-party lender. TCW does not determine if and how financing will be granted.

Managerial Assistance: TCW produces and updates its complete training manuals, training audio and video tapes, as well as all operations, training and management handbooks, forms and sales aids. TCW also an provides 800# support and help line, professional advertising and marketing, a yearly franchisee forum round table and much more.

Training Provided: We provide an intensive, 1-week training program in the TCW business system. Topics include acquiring and evaluating gently-used products, buying and pricing strategies, organization and merchandising, bookkeeping, accounting, staffing, marketing and advertising and consignment computer operations.

Information Submitted: November 1993

GROCERY AND SPECIALTY STORES

7-ELEVEN STORES
2711 N. Haskell Ave., 22nd Fl.
Dallas, TX 75221
Telephone: (800) 255-0711 (214) 828-7764
Fax: (214) 841-6776
Franchise Department

Number of Franchised Units: 10606
Number of Company-Owned Units: 2986
Number of Total Operating Units: 13592

In Business Since: 1927   **Franchising Since:** 1964

Description of Operation: Convenience store.

Equity Capital Needed: Varies by store.

Franchise Fee: Varies by store.

Royalty Fee: 0%

Financial Assistance: Financing is available through the Company for a portion of the cost of the business licenses, cash register fund and/or investment in the inventory, as well as franchisee's continuing purchases and operating expenses.

Managerial Assistance: Field training, in-store support, local meetings, central purchasing, central data processing, newsletters and administration, including bookkeeping, physical audits of the inventory and preparation of financial summaries.

Training Provided: Prospective franchisee is required to work in a 7-Eleven store for a total of 100 hours. In addition, prospective franchisees receive instruction in the actual operation of a 7-Eleven through approximately 15 days of training in a store, followed by 5 days of classroom training in Dallas, TX.

Information Submitted: January 1994

AHH-SOME GOURMET COFFEE
84 Hanover St.
Manchester, NH 03101
Telephone: (800) AHH-SOME (603) 624-7600
Fax: (603) 624-2544
Mr. George B. Metivier, President

Number of Franchised Units: 1
Number of Company-Owned Units: 1
Number of Total Operating Units: 2

In Business Since: 1992   **Franchising Since:** 1993

Description of Operation: Gourmet coffee, wholesale and retail. Espresso bar.

Equity Capital Needed: $75,000 - $125,000

Franchise Fee: $15,500

Royalty Fee: 5%

Financial Assistance: Not at this time.

Managerial Assistance: On-site training in both existing units, as well as the new franchise unit. On-going operational and managerial support.

Training Provided: Training in all operations is on-going. We work on location, as well as through use of the manual. New operators are taken step-by-step through all phases of operation.

Information Submitted: January 1994

BAGEL BUILDERS FAMOUS BAKERY-CAFE
1460 Blackwood-Clementon Rd.
Clementon, NJ 08021
Telephone: (609) 232-BAKE
Fax: (609) 228-9322
Mr. Rocco Fiorentino, Franchise Development

Number of Franchised Units: 10
Number of Company-Owned Units: 6
Number of Total Operating Units: 16

In Business Since: 1985   **Franchising Since:** 1992

Description of Operation: Bagel bakery-cafe, featuring grilled items, eggs, omelets, salads, soups, deli-meats, spreads, espresso, cappuccino and specialty items.

Equity Capital Needed: $140,000 - $220,000

Franchise Fee: $22,500

Royalty Fee: 4%

Financial Assistance: Not available.

Managerial Assistance: 3 weeks of in-store training. 1 week in new store with training staff before opening. 2 weeks in store after opening with training.

Training Provided: Same as above.

Information Submitted: January 1994

BAGEL CONNECTION, THE
1408 Whalley Ave.
New Haven, CT 06515
Telephone: (203) 387-0595
Fax: (203) 387-6611
Mr. Mark Merrill, Franchise Sales Agent

Number of Franchised Units: 10
Number of Company-Owned Units: 2
Number of Total Operating Units: 12

In Business Since: 1983   **Franchising Since:** 1990

Description of Operation: TBC is a 50 - 75 seat fast-food restaurant, serving 36 varieties of New York-style bagels, appetizers, sandwiches, salads, desserts, beverages, gourmet coffee and more. Stores vary in size from 1,800 - 2,600 square feet.

Equity Capital Needed: $150,000 - $300,000

Franchise Fee: $30,000

Royalty Fee: 5%

Financial Assistance: Qualified franchisees will be provided with a combination of at least 10 traditional and non-traditional financing sources which have either previously provided existing franchisees with financing or expressed an interest to do so. In some cases, TBC may self-finance a portion of the franchise fee.

Managerial Assistance: Franchisees are provided with business plans, record keeping and administrative control forms, operations and employee manuals, multi-media advertising programs, approved product, equipment and vendor lists, insurance specifications, quality assurance and guideline checklists, build-out specifications and recommended contractors.

Training Provided: Franchisees are provided with 30 days of pre-opening training, grand opening assistance and on-going training for franchisees and their staff.

Information Submitted: December 1993

BAGELSMITH RESTAURANTS & FOOD STORES
37 Van Syckel Rd.
Hampton, NJ 08827
Telephone: (908) 730-8600
Fax: (908) 730-8165
Mr. Wayne Smith, President

Number of Franchised Units: 21
Number of Company-Owned Units: 1
Number of Total Operating Units: 22

In Business Since: 1979   Franchising Since: 1982

Description of Operation: What makes us special is, of course, our Bagelsmith Bagel. But, we are also famous for our delicatessen, featuring only high-quality products. Whether in our restaurants or in our convenience food stores, we provide our customers with high-quality products, friendly, knowledgeable service, in a clean, pleasant, family-oriented environment.

Equity Capital Needed: Data not available.

Franchise Fee: $25,000

Royalty Fee: 1% - 3%, depending on annual gross sales.

Financial Assistance: None.

Managerial Assistance: The General Manager stays with the new franchisee for at least 2 weeks after grand opening.

Training Provided: Training is provided in our Company-owned store and at our corporate office for a minimum of 120 hours prior to grand opening.

Information Submitted: February 1994

BAHAMA BUCK'S ORIGINAL SHAVED ICE COMPANY
310 S. Mill Ave., # A-102
Tempe, AZ 85281
Telephone: (602) 649-3453
Mr. Blake Buchanan, President

Number of Franchised Units: 0
Number of Company-Owned Units: 2
Number of Total Operating Units: 2

In Business Since: 1989   Franchising Since: 1992

Description of Operation: Bahama Buck's serves gourmet shaved ice in over 70 different flavors and combinations. We also serve fresh-squeezed lemonades, limeades and many other refreshing drinks in a fun, exciting tropic atmosphere.

Equity Capital Needed: $40,000 - $60,000

Franchise Fee: $15,000

Royalty Fee: $250 - $500 per month.

Financial Assistance: Bahama Buck's will help find financial assistance for the franchise owner.

Managerial Assistance: Bahama Buck's provides site selection, marketing and managerial manuals, as well as sales forms, menus and other assistance. Annual meetings may be held and franchise owners will be updated on new product information and technology. "Open Door" policy is practiced between franchisee and franchise owners.

Training Provided: Bahama Buck's offers a 5-day training program that covers all aspects of the business. Franchise owners or managers will participate in a store currently in operation. Operations manuals are also provided.

Information Submitted: November 1993

*See Benny's Bagels, Inc. on page 281

BEST BAGELS IN TOWN
480-19 Patchogue Holbrook Rd.
Holbrook, NY 11741
Telephone: (516) 472-4104
Mr. Jay Squatriglia, President

Number of Franchised Units: 5
Number of Company-Owned Units: 1
Number of Total Operating Units: 6

In Business Since: 1988   Franchising Since: 1990

Description of Operation: Quick-service bagel and bakery restaurant. Eat-in or take-out fresh bagels, rolls, breads and pastries. Hot and cold drinks.

Equity Capital Needed: $50,000 - $90,000

Franchise Fee: $12,500

Royalty Fee: 4%

Financial Assistance: Yes.

Managerial Assistance: Assistance provided as needed through the duration of contract term of 10 years.

Training Provided: Yes. Periods vary at both new owner's location and at home office.

Information Submitted: December 1993

BLACK TIE EXPRESS
1 Bridge Plaza, # 400
Ft. Lee, NJ 07024
Telephone: (800) 69B-LACK (201) 592-5050
Fax: (201) 592-4773
Mr. Steven Beagelman, Director of Franchise Development

Number of Franchised Units: 6
Number of Company-Owned Units: 1
Number of Total Operating Units: 7

In Business Since: 1991   Franchising Since: 1993

Description of Operation: BTE is a home and office food delivery service. BTE offers restaurants the opportunity to multiply their profits with no cost. Each operation typically delivers food from 15 - 20 participating restaurants in their area. The menus are the same as in the restaurants themselves and the franchisee receives a 30% discount from each restaurant.

Equity Capital Needed: $30,000 - $40,000

Franchise Fee: $7,500

Royalty Fee: $250 per month.

Financial Assistance: Financing is available to those who qualify for all of the hard assets, such as computer hardware, 2-way radios, phone systems and credit card machine. A potential franchisee must have $18,000 - $20,000 cash available. The balance can be financed.

Managerial Assistance: Use of 800# for consultation and advice, field visits by operations personnel, corporate franchise meetings, group advertising and marketing seminars. Additional training and consultation for employees and managers.

Training Provided: There is a 1-week training program, which includes the solicitation of restaurant accounts, order taking, dispatching, routing, billing, accounting and working with the Foodware software program.

Information Submitted: January 1994

BLUE CHIP COOKIES
124 Beale St., # 401
San Francisco, CA 94510
Telephone: (800) 888-9866 (415) 546-3840
Fax: (415) 546-9717
Mr. Ivan Steeves, President

Number of Franchised Units: 32
Number of Company-Owned Units: 13
Number of Total Operating Units: 45

In Business Since: 1983   **Franchising Since:** 1984

Description of Operation: Gourmet bakery products, produced from scratch and baked fresh daily. Our menu includes cookies, brownies, muffins, cinnamon rolls, fruit bars and espresso drinks, as well as coffee, tea, sodas, juice, bottled waters, yogurt and/or ice cream.

Equity Capital Needed: $170,000 - $195,000 (includes fee).

Franchise Fee: $29,500

Royalty Fee: 4%

Financial Assistance: We refer the franchisee to an outside lender.

Managerial Assistance: Site selection assistance is provided upon request. Review of construction plans and equipment. Operational, marketing and financial analysis is provided.

Training Provided: An extensive 2-week training period prior to store opening at a home-based Company store will give you hands-on training. Operations representatives will be present at your store location for 3 - 5 days at the opening to assist in opening your store. Continued support is available via bi-annual operational visits and telephone consultations.

Information Submitted: March 1994

BOARDWALK PEANUTS
P. O. Box 749, 10th St. & Boardwalk
Ocean City, NJ 08226
Telephone: (800) 527-2430 (609) 399-3359
Fax: (609) 398-3546
Mr. Leo Yeager, III, President

Number of Franchised Units: 1
Number of Company-Owned Units: 4
Number of Total Operating Units: 5

In Business Since: 1971   **Franchising Since:** 1987

Description of Operation: Retail nuts, chocolates, popcorn and seasonal items.

Equity Capital Needed: $60,000 - $100,000

Franchise Fee: $12,000

Royalty Fee: 5%

Financial Assistance: Assistance with bank loans. Loan package.

Managerial Assistance: We provide an operations manual and 2 days of on-site opening assistance.

Training Provided: We offer a 7-day training program. 800# for instant response to problems.

Information Submitted: March 1994

BODACIOUS BUNS
4676 Admiralty Way
Santa Monica, CA 90292
Telephone: (800) 324-8801 (310) 574-5350
Fax: (310) 574-5355
Mr. Sean Richardson, President

Number of Franchised Units: 6
Number of Company-Owned Units: 1
Number of Total Operating Units: 7

In Business Since: 1986   **Franchising Since:** 1990

Description of Operation: Retail specialty bakery and coffee bar, specializing in cinnamon rolls, muffins, scones, croissants, gourmet coffees and teas. Customized or standard gift baskets. Requested items, like mugs, stuffed animals, T-shirts, etc. are also offered. Any item on the menu can be shipped anywhere in the country.

Equity Capital Needed: $150,000 - $250,000

Franchise Fee: $25,000

Royalty Fee: 5%

Financial Assistance: None.

Managerial Assistance: The Company provides purchasing, marketing, long-term business planning and on-going operational support.

Training Provided: The Company provides 10 days of training prior to opening. Training and support during grand opening week is also provided, followed up with additional training on an as-needed basis.

Information Submitted: March 1994

BUNS MASTER BAKERY SYSTEMS
6505E Mississauga Rd. N.
Mississauga, ON L5N 1A6 CAN
Telephone: (905) 858-1336
Fax: (905) 567-1299
Mr. Richard L. Bensette, Vice President

Number of Franchised Units: 112
Number of Company-Owned Units: 3
Number of Total Operating Units: 115

In Business Since: 1972   **Franchising Since:** 1977

Description of Operation: Distinctive quality breads, buns, rolls and other bakery products are merchandised on a self-serve basis.

Equity Capital Needed: $75,000 - $100,000

Franchise Fee: $25,000

Royalty Fee: 4% - 5%

Financial Assistance: The franchisee is assisted in putting together a business plan for presentation to his/her banker or a bank offering a franchise package for Buns Master Bakery franchisees.

Managerial Assistance: On-going assistance is provided to franchisees in baking, merchandising, employee relations, bookkeeping, security, wholesale business development, equipment maintenance, inventory control and labor productivity.

Training Provided: 2 - 3 weeks of training at head office and corporate store locations is provided prior to opening; 2 - 3 weeks of additional training is provided at the franchisee's bakery after opening. Thereafter, on-going technical, merchandising and management assistance is provided as required.

Information Submitted: November 1993

CAROLE'S CHEESECAKE COMPANY
1272 Castlefield Ave.
Toronto, ON M6B 1G3 CAN
Telephone: (416) 256-0000
Mr. Michael C. Ogus, Executive Vice President

Number of Franchised Units: 8
Number of Company-Owned Units: 1
Number of Total Operating Units: 9

In Business Since: 1979   **Franchising Since:** 1980

Description of Operation: Manufacturer and retailer of a line of 100 flavors of premium-brand cheesecakes and 20 baked gourmet cake dessert items.

Equity Capital Needed: $8,500 - $125,000 (of which 65% may be borrowed).

Franchise Fee: $15,000 - $25,000

Royalty Fee: 0%

Financial Assistance: Major Canadian banks may provide up to 65% or more of required total capital expenditures, depending on the credit rating of the applicant.

Managerial Assistance: Full training is offered at a Company-owned outlet. On-going assistance. No prior knowledge or experience is required.

Training Provided: Full training is offered at a Company-owned unit. On-site supervision and assistance is given at the franchisee's location during opening stage.

Information Submitted: March 1994

CHESAPEAKE BAGEL BAKERY
1360 Beverly Rd., # 104
McLean, VA 22101
Telephone: (703) 893-2600
Fax: (703) 893-8048
Mr. Arnold R. Salus, Director of Franchising

Number of Franchised Units: 23
Number of Company-Owned Units: 7
Number of Total Operating Units: 30

In Business Since: 1981   **Franchising Since:** 1985

Description of Operation: 30 stores open and operating in Metro DC, VA and MD area. Sales on a national basis are under way.

Equity Capital Needed: $120,000 - $150,000

Franchise Fee: $22,500

Royalty Fee: 4%

Financial Assistance: We help with securing bank loans, SBA loans (Title 7) and equipment leasing.

Managerial Assistance: Yes.

Training Provided: Yes.

Information Submitted: March 1994

CINDY'S CINNAMON ROLLS
1432 S. Mission Rd., # A
Fallbrook, CA 92028
Telephone: (800) 428-7655 (619) 723-1121
Fax: (619) 723-4143
Mr. Tom Harris, President

Number of Franchised Units: 30
Number of Company-Owned Units: 0
Number of Total Operating Units: 30

In Business Since: 1985   **Franchising Since:** 1986

Description of Operation: Hot cinnamon rolls in major regional malls.

Equity Capital Needed: $120,000 - $150,000

Franchise Fee: $25,000

Royalty Fee: 5%

Financial Assistance: We provide help in leasing equipment.

Managerial Assistance: 1 week of training at a training center and 1 week of training at store when opening. After store is open, we provide newsletters and personal visits

Training Provided: Same as above.

Information Submitted: January 1994

COFFEE BEANERY, THE
G-3429 Pierson Pl.
Flushing, MI 48451
Telephone: (800) 728-2326 (313) 733-1020
Fax: (313) 733-1536
Mr. Kevin Shaw, Director of Franchise Development

Number of Franchised Units: 78
Number of Company-Owned Units: 25
Number of Total Operating Units: 103

In Business Since: 1976   **Franchising Since:** 1985

Description of Operation: The Coffee Beanery retails whole bean coffees and beverages, espresso and cappuccino in a variety of styles in carts, kiosks, in-line mall stores and streetfront cafes.

Equity Capital Needed: $250,000

Franchise Fee: $25,000

Royalty Fee: 6%

Financial Assistance: We have third-party financing available to those who qualify.

Managerial Assistance: Assistance with all business matters, hiring and firing, inventory control, marketing, merchandising, product knowledge and on-going in-store training.

Training Provided: Training is a 4-week program broken into 3 parts - 1 week of classroom, 1 week of in-store training and 2 weeks in the unit when it opens.

Information Submitted: December 1993

COMPANY'S COMING BAKERY CAFE
1121 Centre St. N., # 440
Calgary, AB T2E 7K6 CAN
Telephone: (800) 361-1151 (403) 230-1151
Fax: (403) 230-2182
Ms. Janine Hunka, Franchise Sales Manager

Number of Franchised Units: 22
Number of Company-Owned Units: 0
Number of Total Operating Units: 22

In Business Since: 1988   **Franchising Since:** 1989

Description of Operation: Building upon the reputation of Company's Coming Cookbooks, a familiar and trusted name with millions of households, the idea of a Bakery Cafe was born. Featuring over 65 varieties of freshly-baked goods, including mini loaves, brownies, carrot cakes and over 20 varieties of gourmet coffees.

Equity Capital Needed: $100,000 - $200,000

Franchise Fee: $25,000

Royalty Fee: 8%

Financial Assistance: Royal Bank of Canada.

Managerial Assistance: Day-to-day operations, marketing and promotions, administrative functions, supplier requirements, staff training, quality control analysis done every quarter.

Training Provided: Hands-on training of approximately 14 days in every aspect of the business.

Information Submitted: November 1993

COOKIE BOUQUET / COOKIES BY DESIGN
6757 Arapaho Rd., # 761
Dallas, TX 75248
Telephone: (800) 945-2665 (214) 239-7474
Fax: (214) 239-1144
Mr. David Patterson, Vice President of Franchise Development

Number of Franchised Units: 72
Number of Company-Owned Units: 1
Number of Total Operating Units: 73

In Business Since: 1983   **Franchising Since:** 1987

Description of Operation: Unique retail opportunity! Gift bakery, specializing in hand-decorated cookie arrangements and gourmet cookies created for special events, holidays, centerpieces, etc. Clientele include both individual and corporate customers. A wonderful, delicious alternative to flowers or balloons.

Equity Capital Needed: $43,500 - $98,000

Franchise Fee: $18,500

Royalty Fee: 6%

Financial Assistance: None.

Managerial Assistance: Cookie Bouquet produces complete training, operations, design, decorating and employee manuals. Stores receive periodic visits from corporation representatives. The corporation publishes a monthly newsletter and holiday bulletins and also holds an annual convention.

Training Provided: An extensive 2-week "Cookie College" at the corporate headquarters in Dallas, TX will show new franchise owners a working store, where they can have hands-on training in every aspect of the business.

Information Submitted: November 1993

COOKIES IN BLOOM
5429 N. MacArthur Blvd.
Irving, TX 75038
Telephone: (800) 222-3104 (214) 518-1749
Fax: (214) 580-1831
Ms. Mary Pinac, Owner

Number of Franchised Units: 5
Number of Company-Owned Units: 0
Number of Total Operating Units: 5

In Business Since: 1988   **Franchising Since:** 1992

Description of Operation: Decorated cookies arranged in floral bouquet pattern.

Equity Capital Needed: $25,000 - $70,000

Franchise Fee: $9,500

Royalty Fee: 5%

Financial Assistance: None.

Managerial Assistance: Cookies In Bloom personnel are trained completely in all areas of the managerial skills needed to operate a Cookies In Bloom shop - everything from employee hiring to tax report preparation.

Training Provided: Each Cookies In Bloom franchisee is fully trained in all areas of the preparation of the cookie arrangements, as well as sales training.

Information Submitted: January 1994

CREATIVE CROISSANTS
2712 Transportation Ave., # F
National City, CA 91950
Telephone: (800) 735-3182 (619) 474-3388
Fax: (619) 474-3390
Mr. Michael Epstein, Manager of Marketing Relations

Number of Franchised Units: 30
Number of Company-Owned Units: 3
Number of Total Operating Units: 33

In Business Since: 1981   **Franchising Since:** 1986

Description of Operation: Up-scale restaurant, featuring gourmet coffees, espresso and cappuccino drinks, freshly-tossed salads, gourmet sandwiches, baked potatoes and unique hot meal croissants. Also, featuring baked goods, freshly-baked on the premises - complete bakery line of croissants - dessert croissants, danish, puff pastry and muffins.

Equity Capital Needed: $99,000 - $145,000

Franchise Fee: $17,500

Royalty Fee: 4.5%

Financial Assistance: Not available.

Managerial Assistance: On-going business planning, site selection assistance, lease negotiations, promotional support, marketing support, national contracts with food and beverage vendors.

Training Provided: 2 weeks of training in operational store, as well as classroom training. Opening week help and staff support, as well as assistance with promotional items for grand opening.

Information Submitted: November 1993

EDELWEISS DELI EXPRESS
Unit 7 - 3331 Viking Way
Richmond, BC V6V 1X7 CAN
Telephone: (604) 270-2360 (604) 275-DELI
Fax: (604) 270-6560
Mr. Duncan Williams, President

Number of Franchised Units: 20
Number of Company-Owned Units: 1
Number of Total Operating Units: 21

In Business Since: 1973   **Franchising Since:** 1988

Description of Operation: We find the location. We build turn-key. We help hire people and train the new employees. We help order all food and work with the food distribution. We stay with the franchisee for 1 - 2 weeks at opening. We will do bi-weekly checks and can be called any time for assistance.

Equity Capital Needed: $85,000 - $115,000

Franchise Fee: $30,000

Royalty Fee: 5%, plus 2% advertising.

Financial Assistance: We will work with banks or any other financial institution.

Managerial Assistance: Director of Marketing; Director of Franchising; Director of Food Services; Training Supervisor.

Training Provided: We train new franchisees for 4 or more weeks or whatever it takes. We give on-going assistance for 10 years. We have training manuals, forms, sales aids, franchise meetings every second month and also product seminars.

Information Submitted: January 1994

EXPRESS MART
6567 Kinne Rd.
Dewitt, NY 13214
Telephone: (315) 446-0125
Fax: (315) 446-1355
Mr. Mark E. Maher, Director of Franchising

Number of Franchised Units: 10
Number of Company-Owned Units: 45
Number of Total Operating Units: 55

In Business Since: 1989   **Franchising Since:** 1990

Description of Operation: Convenience stores - the franchise is a license to utilize the franchisor's service name "Express Mart," related service mark and logotype, as well as the franchisor's system for identification, layout and operation of convenience stores. These stores feature the sale of pre-packaged and prepared foods, beverages, sundries, motor fuels and convenience store goods at a single approved location.

Equity Capital Needed: $20,000 - $50,000 start-up cash; $136,750 - $461,600 total investment.

Franchise Fee: $15,000

Royalty Fee: 3%

Financial Assistance: Express Mart will assist the franchisee in securing financing through the franchisee's bank or other sources. They will also assist in negotiating leasing arrangements on equipment.

Managerial Assistance: Express Mart uses proven methods, provides co-ordination and counsel from highly-skilled professional managers with considerable experience in convenience store and petroleum marketing. It provides tested programs, a comprehensive procedures manual and a strong field support network.

124

Training Provided: We provide comprehensive training: 1 week of classroom training in Phase I, and 1 week of in-store training in Phase II. Phase I deals with gasoline merchandising, convenient-store merchandising, alcohol management, inventory and loss control, recruiting, hiring, interviewing and customer relations. Phase II is on-site training on all applications.

Information Submitted: January 1994

GLENDALE SYSTEMS
127-25 Metropolitan Ave.
Kew Gardens, NY 11415
Telephone: (718) 441-9300
Fax: (718) 441-2200
Mr. Arthur J. Winston, Franchising Manager

Number of Franchised Units: 21
Number of Company-Owned Units: 3
Number of Total Operating Units: 24

In Business Since: 1954   **Franchising Since:** 1980

Description of Operation: Full-fledged bakery manufacturer - 300 items, 55 frozen items - from donuts to wedding cakes.

Equity Capital Needed: $150,000

Franchise Fee: $24,000

Royalty Fee: 6%

Financial Assistance: We will take notes for 3 - 5 years at percentage after at least 50 - 60% down payment.

Managerial Assistance: We train all of our new franchisees for 4 weeks. Subjects include how to bake off in store and how to run a successful retail operation from A to Z. Have supervisor to guide every week of the year.

Training Provided: Training is inclusive with baking off and running retail business, with supervision.

Information Submitted: January 1994

GLORIA JEAN'S GOURMET COFFEES
1001 Asbury Dr.
Buffalo Grove, IL 60089
Telephone: (800) 333-0050 (708) 808-0580
Fax: (708) 808-0593
Mr. Cecil Johnson, Franchise Development

Number of Franchised Units: 153
Number of Company-Owned Units: 25
Number of Total Operating Units: 178

In Business Since: 1979   **Franchising Since:** 1986

Description of Operation: America's largest retail gourmet coffee franchisor offers the highest-quality gourmet coffees, teas and accessories. Our unique store design and exclusive coffee bean counter are the focal point of our nationally-honored company. Each store offers up to 64 varieties of coffee, plus a complete line of signature teas, along with a complete line of state-of-the-art coffee and tea accessories.

Equity Capital Needed: $75,000 - $125,000

Franchise Fee: $25,000

Royalty Fee: 6%

Financial Assistance: Assistance in locating third-party financing.

Managerial Assistance: Complete on-going support and training through district managers and training department staff. Extensive video tape training available, along with complete operations manual.

Training Provided: 10-day "Coffee 101" classes are held in our new corporate training center and corporate stores. Corporate staff at store for 11 days during the grand opening, plus on-going monthly visits, annual convention and extensive training manual.

Information Submitted: November 1993

GOURMET CUP COFFEE
11 N. Skokie Hwy.
Lake Bluff, IL 60044
Telephone: (708) 735-0200
Fax: (708) 735-0244
Mr. Tony Piwowarczyk, Director of Operations

Number of Franchised Units: 49
Number of Company-Owned Units: 3
Number of Total Operating Units: 52

In Business Since: 1985   **Franchising Since:** 1985

Description of Operation: Gourmet Cup Coffee is the master US franchisor for Canada's second-largest gourmet coffee chain. Gourmet Cup Coffee franchisees capitalize on high-profit espresso-based beverages and the proven experience of 54 successful stores. We train franchisees to generate maximum revenue from a product that half of all Americans use every day, often several times a day.

Equity Capital Needed: $91,300 - $280,250

Franchise Fee: $15,000

Royalty Fee: 8%

Financial Assistance: The franchisor has developed relationships with various sources to assist potential franchisees in securing third-party financing.

Managerial Assistance: Gourmet Cup Coffee's finely-tuned system provides invaluable competitive advantages for our franchisees. Gourmet Cup Coffee provides franchisees with proven, successful business systems (including sophisticated site selection and award-winning store design expertise), high-quality product, proprietary methods, processes and procedures and the Gourmet Cup trademarks, logos and signs.

Training Provided: Our training and support are unsurpassed in the industry. New franchisees receive 7 weeks of training - 3 days at our corporate offices, 12 days at an established store and 4 weeks at the franchisee's store. Support and instruction continue through formal seminars and informal contact with the corporate staff.

Information Submitted: March 1994

GRABBAJABBA
1121 Centre St. N., # 440
Calgary, AB T2E 7K6 CAN
Telephone: (800) 361-1151 (403) 230-1151
Fax: (403) 230-2182
Ms. Janine Hunka, Franchise Sales Manager

Number of Franchised Units: 26
Number of Company-Owned Units: 0
Number of Total Operating Units: 26

In Business Since: 1988   **Franchising Since:** 1990

Description of Operation: Up-scale European coffee house, featuring specialty coffees (cappuccino), over 45 varieties of gourmet coffees, decadent desserts and pastries, European-style sandwiches, soups, salads, Italian gelato and ice cream.

Equity Capital Needed: $125,000 - $200,000

Franchise Fee: $25,000

Royalty Fee: 8%

Financial Assistance: Royal Bank of Canada.

Managerial Assistance: Day-to-day operations, marketing and promotions, administration functions, supplier requirements, staff training. Quality control analysis done every quarter.

Training Provided: Hands-on training of approximately 14 days in every aspect of the business.

Information Submitted: November 1993

GREAT AMERICAN COOKIE COMPANY
4685 Frederick Dr., SW
Atlanta, GA 30336
Telephone: (800) 336-2447 (404) 696-1700
Fax: (404) 699-0887
Ms. Betty W. Ansley, Vice President

Number of Franchised Units: 260
Number of Company-Owned Units: 74
Number of Total Operating Units: 334

In Business Since: 1977   Franchising Since: 1978

Description of Operation: Retail cookie stores, primarily in major regional malls nationwide.

Equity Capital Needed: $30,000 - total investment is between $140,000 - $160,000.

Franchise Fee: $25,000

Royalty Fee: 7%

Financial Assistance: None.

Managerial Assistance: Complete training is provided in all operations of a cookie store.

Training Provided: Managerial assistance is provided for as long as necessary.

Information Submitted: March 1994

GREAT DAY COFFEE COMPANY
960 S. Third St.
Louisville, KY 40203
Telephone: (800) 705-9100 (502) 581-9100
Fax: (502) 581-9137
Mr. Toni Conti, Vice President

Number of Franchised Units: 3
Number of Company-Owned Units: 1
Number of Total Operating Units: 4

In Business Since: 1992   Franchising Since: 1993

Description of Operation: Specializing in selling gourmet coffees to offices, deli's and up-scale restaurants.

Equity Capital Needed: $5,000 - $15,000

Franchise Fee: $5,000

Royalty Fee: 6%

Financial Assistance: Equipment programs and purchasing programs are available.

Managerial Assistance: We offer total managerial assistance from the beginning. Managers are constantly available to answer any questions a franchisee may have. An extensive training manual is provided.

Training Provided: We provide 1 week of training at the corporate office, consisting of coffee knowledge, paper work and actual riding with a local Great Day representative on delivery stops. Also, 1 week of training at franchisee's site is provided.

Information Submitted: January 1994

GREAT EARTH COMPANIES
8981 Sunset Blvd., # 307
West Hollywood, CA 90069
Telephone: (800) 374-7328 (310) 777-0400
Fax: (310) 777-0460
Mr. Carl Nassif, Vice President of Operations

Number of Franchised Units: 120
Number of Company-Owned Units: 5
Number of Total Operating Units: 125

In Business Since: 1971   Franchising Since: 1988

Description of Operation: Retail vitamin stores.

Equity Capital Needed: $75,000 - $125,000

Franchise Fee: $30,000

Royalty Fee: 6%

Financial Assistance: 80% of initial fee of $22,500.

Managerial Assistance: Assistance includes site selection, lease negotiations and operating procedures.

Training Provided: We offer a 4-week course at Vita-U, the Company's California training facility, that covers product knowledge, sales training, store operations and the new store opening.

Information Submitted: March 1994

GREAT HARVEST BREAD COMPANY
28 S. Montana St., P. O. Box 488
Dillon, MT 59725
Telephone: (800) 442-0424 (406) 683-6842
Fax: (406) 683-6842
Mr. John Poundstone, Development

Number of Franchised Units: 63
Number of Company-Owned Units: 1
Number of Total Operating Units: 64

In Business Since: 1969   Franchising Since: 1978

Description of Operation: Retail premium bread bakeries, specializing in whole wheat products.

Equity Capital Needed: $100,000 - $200,000, at least $50,000 liquid, unincumbered cash on hand or obtainable.

Franchise Fee: $24,000

Royalty Fee: 7%

Financial Assistance: No direct financial assistance is available. Franchisee/lender technical and negotiation assistance offered.

Managerial Assistance: In addition to access to the world's best baking wheat, Great Harvest provides strong managerial assistance in all areas of business start-up, opening and post-opening business operations. On-going support.

Training Provided: In addition to close, thorough on-going training and assistance throughout the start-up phase, franchisee participates in 3 intensive 1-week trainings: 1 week on-site at new unit, 1 week at franchise headquarters training facility and 1 week at host bakery(ies).

Information Submitted: December 1993

HEAVENLY HAM
20 Mansell Ct. E., # 500
Roswell, GA 30076
Telephone: (800) 899-2228 (404) 993-2232
Fax: (404) 587-3529
Ms. Anne Conner, Franchise Sales

Number of Franchised Units: 75
Number of Company-Owned Units: 1
Number of Total Operating Units: 76

In Business Since: 1984   Franchising Since: 1984

Description of Operation: Our franchised retail stores specialize in selling spiral-sliced honey and spiced, fully-baked, hardwood-smoked hams. Stores also sell smoked turkey, ribs, delicious condiments and take-out ham and turkey sandwiches. A true specialty food store, selling quality products and offering outstanding service to our customers.

Equity Capital Needed: $90,200 - $166,400

Franchise Fee: $25,000

Royalty Fee: 5%

Financial Assistance: Not available.

Managerial Assistance: We provide site selection, lease negotiation, standard floor plan and equipment layout, specifications, full pre-opening, operations, marketing and accounting manuals and full training. On-going planning after help with business plan.

Training Provided: We offer a full week in Atlanta, GA in store and classroom. Pre-opening and during store start-up training.

Information Submitted: March 1994

JAKE'S TAKE N' BAKE PIZZA
620 High St.
San Luis Obispo, CA 93401
Telephone: (805) 543-3339
Mr. Willis E. Reeser, President

Number of Franchised Units: 10
Number of Company-Owned Units: 0
Number of Total Operating Units: 10

In Business Since: 1984   **Franchising Since:** 1986

Description of Operation: Sell un-baked pizzas. Also sell salads, ice cream, cookie dough and cold drinks.

Equity Capital Needed: $40,000 - $50,000

Franchise Fee: $10,000

Royalty Fee: 3%

Financial Assistance: None.

Managerial Assistance: In store at least once a week.

Training Provided: Training includes 2 weeks in an operating store and 1 week in the new store when opening.

Information Submitted: March 1994

JAVA CENTRALE
1610 Arden Way, # 299
Sacramento, CA 95815
Telephone: (800) 551-5282 (916) 568-2310
Fax: (916) 568-1240
Mr. Thomas A. Craig, Vice President of Marketing

Number of Franchised Units: 6
Number of Company-Owned Units: 1
Number of Total Operating Units: 7

In Business Since: 1992   **Franchising Since:** 1992

Description of Operation: European-style gourmet coffee cafe, offering over 40 fine roasted coffees, available by the pound, fresh-brewed and specialty beverages, including espresso, cappuccino, latte, mocha...hot or iced. Fresh morning baked goods, deli sandwiches, salads and desserts. Nothing is baked or cooked on the premises. Site selection assistance, extensive training, on-going field support and aggressive marketing are provided.

Equity Capital Needed: $175,000 - $250,000 total investment. $75,000-$85,000 cash required.

Franchise Fee: $25,000

Royalty Fee: 6%

Financial Assistance: No financial assistance is available through the franchisor.

Managerial Assistance: We provide operational training at a Company-owned facility and on-site training before the cafe opens. Manuals for operation and marketing. Field representatives to cafes monthly. Newsletters and continuing promotion ideas.

Training Provided: We offer 2 weeks of franchisee and manager training, covering all aspects of cafe operations with on-the-job experience in the Company operational/training cafe. Then, the training crew spends 2 weeks at the new cafe prior to the opening to assist in employee training and final cafe preparation.

Information Submitted: January 1994

JOFFREY'S COFFEE & TEA CO.
4517 W. Ohio Ave.
Tampa, FL 33614
Telephone: (800) 458-5282 (813) 875-5198
Fax: (813) 873-1403
Mr. Scott D. Campbell, Vice President of Franchising

Number of Franchised Units: 3
Number of Company-Owned Units: 2
Number of Total Operating Units: 5

In Business Since: 1984   **Franchising Since:** 1994

Description of Operation: Specialty gourmet coffee house and retail store, specializing in in-house, roasted coffees and specialty desserts. Over 50 gourmet and flavored coffees are offered by the pound, as well as a wide range of coffee-related merchandise, such as espresso machines, coffee makers, cups, coffee grinders, etc. Over 80% of Joffrey's sales are comprised of in-house consumption of coffee drinks, desserts and baked goods.

Equity Capital Needed: $218,000 - $385,000

Franchise Fee: $20,000

Royalty Fee: First year 3%; second year 4%; remainder 5%.

Financial Assistance: Not available.

Managerial Assistance: We provide initial training and support through on-going clinics and workshops, point-of-sale and accounting system set-up assistance, marketing assistance and on-going research and development.

Training Provided: We offer an intensive 4-week training program, broken into 3 phases, using demonstrations, videos, hands-on practice, homework assignments and certification in each phase. Phase 1: roasting plant training, clinics and cuppings; Phase 2: staff positions (in-store); and Phase 3: shift management and administration.

Information Submitted: March 1994

JUICE CLUB
17 Chorro St., # C
San Luis Obispo, CA 93405
Telephone: (800) 545-9972 (805) 549-0232
Fax: (805) 549-0343
Ms. Linda Ozawa, Vice President of Marketing

Number of Franchised Units: 2
Number of Company-Owned Units: 1
Number of Total Operating Units: 3

In Business Since: 1990   **Franchising Since:** 1991

Description of Operation: Convenient health food restaurant, specializing in blended-to-order smoothies, fresh juices and healthy snacks.

Equity Capital Needed: $158,000 - $202,000

Franchise Fee: $20,000

Royalty Fee: 4%

Financial Assistance: Juice Club cannot provide in-house financing, but work with the SBA in gaining financing.

Managerial Assistance: The home office supports the franchisees through hotlines, seminars and annual conventions. The home office supplies the franchisees with motivational information, accounting support and on-going training.

Training Provided: The home office thoroughly trains the franchisee in all areas of store operation for a 30-day (non-consecutive) minimum at the home office training center. The home office also assists in training the initial crew on-site in the franchisee's store.

Information Submitted: November 1993

KATIE MCGUIRE'S PIE & BAKE SHOPPE
17682 Sampson Ln.
Huntington Beach, CA 92647

Telephone: (714) 847-0325
Fax: (714) 842-2060
Ms. Kaye Bass, President

Number of Franchised Units: 18
Number of Company-Owned Units: 0
Number of Total Operating Units: 18

In Business Since: 1983   Franchising Since: 1984

Description of Operation: Retail sale of Katie McGuire's home-style pies, cakes, cookies, quiche, muffins, croissants and other quality bakery products.

Equity Capital Needed: $85,000 - $150,000

Franchise Fee: $22,500

Royalty Fee: 6%

Financial Assistance: We assist in arranging equipment and tenant improvement leasing to qualified franchisees.

Managerial Assistance: Marketing and operational support provided on an on-going basis.

Training Provided: Baking class, bookkeeping and business operations. Training in operating shops.

Information Submitted: December 1993

LE MUFFIN PLUS
675 W. Peachtree St., NE
Atlanta, GA 30308
Telephone: (404) 876-3858
Fax: (404) 394-5527
Mr. Albert Brull, President

Number of Franchised Units: 21
Number of Company-Owned Units: 7
Number of Total Operating Units: 28

In Business Since: 1985   Franchising Since: 1985

Description of Operation: Gourmet muffin, cookie and coffee shop, catering to the high-volume foot traffic market.

Equity Capital Needed: Varies according to size, scope and location.

Franchise Fee: $25,000

Royalty Fee: 8%

Financial Assistance: None.

Managerial Assistance: We provide complete site selection, lease negotiation, design service, continual management assistance and product development.

Training Provided: We offer a comprehensive training program in the franchisee's shop, including, but not limited to, shop opening, detailed baking and preparation instruction, materials acquisition, personnel and systems management.

Information Submitted: March 1994

LI'L PEACH
101 Billerica Ave.
N. Billerica, MA 01862
Telephone: (617) 721-0000
Fax: (508) 663-9622
Mr. Kevin M. Lydon, Director of Franchising

Number of Franchised Units: 62
Number of Company-Owned Units: 0
Number of Total Operating Units: 62

In Business Since: 1971   Franchising Since: 1972

Description of Operation: Li'l Peach offers fully-equipped and stocked convenience food stores, averaging approximately 1,800 - 2,400 square feet. All stores are open 7 days a week, most from 6 AM to midnight.

Equity Capital Needed: $50,000 - $60,000

Franchise Fee: $15,000 - $25,000

Royalty Fee: 11% - 18%

Financial Assistance: Financial assistance is available to qualified candidates.

Managerial Assistance: Data not available.

Training Provided: We provide 3 weeks of intensive in-store training.

Information Submitted: April 1994

LISA'S TEA TREASURES
1151 Minnesota Ave.
San Jose, CA 95125
Telephone: (800) 500-4TEA (408) 947-8734
Fax: (408) 947-8419
Ms. Melissa Dyrdahl, Vice President of Sales

Number of Franchised Units: 5
Number of Company-Owned Units: 1
Number of Total Operating Units: 6

In Business Since: 1988   Franchising Since: 1992

Description of Operation: Lisa's Tea Treasures Tea Room and Gift Parlour is a specialty purveyor of the finest quality teas and tea-related accessories. Tea is served in an elegant, sophisticated Victorian setting. The menu offers 15 afternoon teas from around the world, as well as finger sandwiches, tea cakes, cookies, scones, savories and beautifully-decorated sweets. We also offer fine bulk teas and gourmet foods, as well as tea ware and Victorian-era gift items.

Equity Capital Needed: $130,000 - $190,000

Franchise Fee: $25,000

Royalty Fee: 6%

Financial Assistance: We provide assistance in locating third-party financing.

Managerial Assistance: We provide a detailed operations manual, initial ordering guide, on-site assistance at grand opening, newsletters and monthly promotional events and national and regional meetings.

Training Provided: Each franchisee attends 10 days of training at our corporate location. This includes approximately 30% of classroom training on the history of tea, how to conduct a tea tasting, the proper etiquette of serving tea, etc. In-depth training is also provided on business management, purchasing, inventory control, marketing and merchandising.

Information Submitted: March 1994

LOGAN FARMS HONEY GLAZED HAMS
10001 Westheimer Rd., # 1040
Houston, TX 77042
Telephone: (800) 833-4267 (713) 781-3773
Fax: (713) 977-0532
Mr. Pink Logan, President

Number of Franchised Units: 17
Number of Company-Owned Units: 1
Number of Total Operating Units: 18

In Business Since: 1984   Franchising Since: 1984

Description of Operation: Gourmet meat stores, specializing in the sale of honey-glazed, spiral-sliced hams. Also sell gourmet rib eye roast, pork loins, chicken breast, smoked turkeys, spiral-sliced boneless hams, spiral-sliced honey-glazed turkey breast, smoked sausage, bacons, cheesecakes and a variety of honey mustard and preserves. Stores also have a deli department making a variety of subway sandwiches and poor-boys.

Equity Capital Needed: $250,000

Franchise Fee: $25,000

Royalty Fee: 3%

Financial Assistance: None.

Managerial Assistance: During the first week of the franchise opening, the franchisor or an employee is on-location for opening assistance. The franchisor offers continuing services relative to the conduct of the franchisee's business.

Training Provided: We offer 2 weeks on procedures and techniques in manufacturing and marketing the products, manuals for advertising and market programs, record-keeping and inventory control.

Information Submitted: March 1994

M & M MEAT SHOPS
640 Trillium Dr., P. O. Box 2488
Kitchener, ON N2H 6M3 CAN
Telephone: (519) 895-1075
Fax: (519) 895-0762
Ms. Christine Freeman, Administration Assistant

Number of Franchised Units: 117
Number of Company-Owned Units: 3
Number of Total Operating Units: 120

In Business Since: 1980   **Franchising Since:** 1981

Description of Operation: Sale of specialty flash-frozen foods, including beef, pork, poultry, seafood, party foods, vegetables, desserts, etc. Primarily heat-and-serve convenience foods. Most portions are controlled.

Equity Capital Needed: $150,000 unencumbered.

Franchise Fee: $30,000

Royalty Fee: 3%

Financial Assistance: Turn-key cost approximately $300,000. Financing through a chartered bank. Bank package provided.

Managerial Assistance: Complete training. Field consultant on site at store for 2 weeks after grand opening with regular visits and monitoring thereafter.

Training Provided: 2 - 3 weeks of corporate store training. Site selection, lease negotiations and advisory council provided.

Information Submitted: December 1993

MANHATTAN BAGEL COMPANY
15 Meridian Rd.
Eatontown, NJ 07724
Telephone: (908) 544-0155
Fax: (908) 544-1315
Mr. Glenn D. Slovenko, Director of Franchise Development

Number of Franchised Units: 28
Number of Company-Owned Units: 0
Number of Total Operating Units: 28

In Business Since: 1987   **Franchising Since:** 1988

Description of Operation: Up-scale bagel eateries, offering deli items, soups and full breakfast fare. Operations are configured 100% turn-key, with site selection and lease negotiation.

Equity Capital Needed: $75,000 - $100,000

Franchise Fee: $30,000

Royalty Fee: 5%

Financial Assistance: Assistance with SBA loan processing.

Managerial Assistance: Comprehensive, hands-on training, with detailed operations manual and regular field assistance in marketing, merchandising, food preparation and other business facets.

Training Provided: 1 week of managerial and administrative training, classroom, plus 2 weeks of hands-on, in-store training required. Refresher courses are also given, as needed.

Information Submitted: November 1993

MICHEL'S BAKERY & CAFE
17 W 705 Butterfield Rd., # E
Oakbrook Terrace, IL 60181
Telephone: (800) 968-0359 (708) 629-0800
Fax: (708) 629-0823
Mr. Robert E. Tischler, Vice President - Corporate Development

Number of Franchised Units: 4
Number of Company-Owned Units: 1
Number of Total Operating Units: 5

In Business Since: 1988   **Franchising Since:** 1991

Description of Operation: Bakery and cafe stores located in regional malls, strip centers and office complexes, offering muffins, cinnamon rolls, cookies and treats, along with a quality deli offering a unique array of sandwiches, soups and salads.

Equity Capital Needed: $120,000 - $175,000

Franchise Fee: $25,000

Royalty Fee: 6%

Financial Assistance: None.

Managerial Assistance: Extensive training program at both an operating unit and the corporate headquarters, outlining the business format and operation of a store. On-going assistance after the unit is open for business.

Training Provided: We provide a 3-week training program in an operating unit prior to the opening of the store and 1 week in store after opening. On-going support from a field operations staff.

Information Submitted: November 1993

MMMARVELOUS MMMUFFINS
3300 Bloor St. W., # 2900, Box 54
Etobicoke, ON M8X 2X3 CAN
Telephone: (416) 236-0055
Fax: (416) 236-0054
Ms. Robyn Paikin, Franchise Assistant

Number of Franchised Units: 106
Number of Company-Owned Units: 5
Number of Total Operating Units: 111

In Business Since: 1979   **Franchising Since:** 1980

Description of Operation: Muffins, baked on the premises.

Equity Capital Needed: $40,000 - $60,000

Franchise Fee: $25,000

Royalty Fee: 7%

Financial Assistance: We provide guidance in preparing the business plan for bank submission as well as bank introductions, if required.

Managerial Assistance: A store services representative provides continuing assistance in all areas of store operations. Field consultants provide leadership and support, assist in implementing standards of operations, consult and identify profitability opportunities to achieve maximum potential. Regular store visits. Marketing programs are set up to assist the franchisee in marketing and promotions necessary in his/her business.

Training Provided: We have an intensive 10-day training program for new franchisees. This program has been designed to provide all students with the knowledge, tools and equipment necessary to maximize the potential of their stores.

Information Submitted: January 1994

MOM'S BAKE AT HOME PIZZA
4457 Main St.
Philadelphia, PA 19127
Telephone: (215) 482-1044
Mr. Nicholas Castellucci, President

Number of Franchised Units: 20
Number of Company-Owned Units: 0
Number of Total Operating Units: 20

In Business Since: 1961 **Franchising Since:** 1981

Description of Operation: Mom's Pizza franchises "Bake at Home" pizza stores. The franchisee purchases his/her supplies from the main office. The franchisee then retails a fresh, hand-made gourmet pizza, which is baked at the customer's convenience in his/her home.

Equity Capital Needed: $55,000

Franchise Fee: Included in $55,000

Royalty Fee: None.

Financial Assistance: Not available.

Managerial Assistance: 1 week of training in an existing Mom's Bake at Home Store. Continual training, as needed.

Training Provided: 1 week of training in an existing Mom's Bake at Home Store. On-site training at the new location with Mom's personnel.

Information Submitted: November 1993

MONSIEUR FELIX & MR. NORTON COOKIES
729 Yonge St.
Toronto, ON M4Y 2B5 CAN
Telephone: (800) 463-7055 (416) 929-2250
Fax: (416) 929-7649
Ms. Jan Findley, Director of Franchise Development

Number of Franchised Units: 14
Number of Company-Owned Units: 11
Number of Total Operating Units: 25

In Business Since: 1985 **Franchising Since:** 1990

Description of Operation: 100% natural, freshly-baked gourmet cookies in 12 decadent flavors, made from the finest ingredients, including European chocolate. Innovative, exclusive gift packaging has been designed and trademarked for retail sale or home or office delivery. Corporate gift programs are also available.

Equity Capital Needed: $150,000 - $180,000 (includes $25,000 franchise fee).

Franchise Fee: $25,000

Royalty Fee: 5%

Financial Assistance: We will provide guidance in preparing a business plan for various banking institutions who have dealt with Monsieur Felix and Mr. Norton cookies.

Managerial Assistance: Monsieur Felix and Mr. Norton Cookies provides comprehensive manuals as well as financial, accounting, administrative, computer and realty assistance. On-going operations support in all areas, in addition to an annual convention. An advisory council and a quarterly newsletter are also part of the program.

Training Provided: A comprehensive 2 weeks of training is provided at the home office in Montreal, PQ. In addition, 1 week is spent working in an actual store. Operations personnel are present for 1 week to assist with training of employees and to insure a smooth opening. Manuals are also provided.

Information Submitted: December 1993

MOXIE JAVA INTERNATIONAL
199 E. 52nd St.
Boise, ID 83702

Telephone: (800) 659-6963 (208) 322-7773
Fax: (208) 322-6226
Mr. Jerome Eberharter, Chief Executive Officer

Number of Franchised Units: 14
Number of Company-Owned Units: 4
Number of Total Operating Units: 18

In Business Since: 1988 **Franchising Since:** 1991

Description of Operation: Espresso bar and cafe, serving espresso drinks, specialty coffees and pastries. Coffee accessories are also sold.

Equity Capital Needed: $27,500

Franchise Fee: $3,500 - $17,500

Royalty Fee: 5.5%

Financial Assistance: Moxie Java International does not provide financial assistance to new franchisees.

Managerial Assistance: Assistance is provided in the operation of a cafe, inventory controls, ordering, vendor and supplier information, financial information, weekly reports, daily shift reports, staffing, promotions and advertising.

Training Provided: We provide training in espresso machine operation, drinks, maintenance and troubleshooting, coffee brewing operation, maintenance and troubleshooting, coffee information, brewing, blends, flavored, decaf, growing, processing, etc. Customer service, merchandising and promotions.

Information Submitted: March 1994

MR. BULKY TREATS AND GIFTS
755 W. Big Beaver Rd., # 1600
Troy, MI 48084
Telephone: (313) 244-9000
Fax: (313) 244-9365
Mr. Gerard C. Ales, Director of Franchise Sales

Number of Franchised Units: 102
Number of Company-Owned Units: 106
Number of Total Operating Units: 208

In Business Since: 1983 **Franchising Since:** 1985

Description of Operation: Nation's largest bulk candy retailer, with over 20 retail stores in major malls, coast to coast. Our existing, self-service merchandise centers feature a dazzling array of quality foods sold by the ounce or pound, including domestic and international candies and snacks, plus consumable gifts and treats. Mr. Bulky Treats and Gifts offers discriminating investors the opportunity for significant growth in one of the fastest-growing segments of the specialty food industry.

Equity Capital Needed: $70,000 - $75,000

Franchise Fee: $45,000

Royalty Fee: 6%

Financial Assistance: Mr. Bulky Treats and Gifts will assist new franchisees in obtaining third-party financing.

Managerial Assistance: Franchisees will receive on-site assistance on a rotational or as-needed basis. Comprehensive business assessment will be conducted yearly. National meetings, regional meetings, buying assistance, national account negotiations, bi-weekly merchandising newsletters. Constant updates on the results of our product and market research.

Training Provided: An extensive 1-week training period at the home office. Extensive, 1-week training period held on-site, including final construction supervision, store merchandising and computer installation and training.

Information Submitted: November 1993

MR. MUGS
P. O. Box 20019
Brantford, ON N3P 2A4 CAN

Telephone: (519) 752-9890
Fax: (519) 752-0978
Mr. Ron Hewitt, Franchise Director

Number of Franchised Units: 19
Number of Company-Owned Units: 2
Number of Total Operating Units: 21

In Business Since: 1984   Franchising Since: 1986

Description of Operation: A very active coffee and donut chain with a deli bar, combined with homemade soups and chili. A complete line of fresh-baked muffins is offered, along with freshly-baked bread.

Equity Capital Needed: $60,000 - $70,000

Franchise Fee: $20,000

Royalty Fee: 4%

Financial Assistance: Support with loan applications and sources of funding. Partial financing available in Canada only.

Managerial Assistance: On-site head office staff available for assistance whenever necessary in all aspects of business.

Training Provided: Extensive training in baking, marketing, advertising and all aspects of successfully running a franchise.

Information Submitted: November 1993

MURPHY'S PIZZA / PAPA ALDO'S
775 Baywood Dr., # 316
Petaluma, CA 94954
Telephone: (707) 769-1200
Fax: (707) 769-8100
Mr. Robert Graham, President

Number of Franchised Units: 110
Number of Company-Owned Units: 5
Number of Total Operating Units: 115

In Business Since: 1984   Franchising Since: 1986

Description of Operation: High-quality products (pizza, calzone and lasagna), made from scratch for the customer to bake at home. We offer the highest-quality products and sell them to the consumer at a great value.

Equity Capital Needed: $80,000 - $100,000

Franchise Fee: $17,500

Royalty Fee: 5%, plus 1% marketing.

Financial Assistance: None.

Managerial Assistance: The franchisee must be the owner/operator. No investors. Managerial skills are taught during training program. On-site representative assists franchisee in developing management skills.

Training Provided: 1 week of training at corporate headquarters. 3 weeks at other franchise stores. Field representative works with you for the first week at your store and during your grand opening promotions.

Information Submitted: November 1993

MY FAVORITE MUFFIN
15 Engle St., # 302
Englewood, NJ 07631
Telephone: (800) 332-2229 (201) 871-0370
Fax: (201) 871-7168
Mr. Ronald Sommers, President

Number of Franchised Units: 47
Number of Company-Owned Units: 3
Number of Total Operating Units: 50

In Business Since: 1987   Franchising Since: 1991

Description of Operation: Over 100 varieties of freshly-baked muffins, gift baskets, bagels and gourmet coffees in a variety of locations.

Equity Capital Needed: $60,000 - $70,000

Franchise Fee: $25,000

Royalty Fee: 5%

Financial Assistance: Financing assistance available to new franchisees consists of assistance in preparing a business plan narrative with pro forma operating statements and cash flows. In addition, the franchisor will assist in making introductions to potential lenders.

Managerial Assistance: Data not available.

Training Provided: We provide 2 weeks of training in Company-owned units and 1 week in the franchised store. Training topics cover baking techniques and services, ordering of supplies, on-going operations, hiring and other practical operational aspects of operating the franchised facility.

Information Submitted: December 1993

NUTTER'S BULK & NATURAL FOODS
1601 Dunmore Rd., SE, # 107
Medicine Hat, AB T1A 1Z8 CAN
Telephone: (800) 665-5122 (403) 529-1664
Fax: (403) 529-6507
Mr. Bruce Champion, Franchise Licensing Director

Number of Franchised Units: 23
Number of Company-Owned Units: 5
Number of Total Operating Units: 28

In Business Since: 1982   Franchising Since: 1983

Description of Operation: Nutter's offers a huge selection of products, ranging from exotic tea and coffee, natural and organic products, aromatic spices, pastas, grains, beans and deli products, to everyday, fine-quality baking needs. All this is offered in a clean, healthy, friendly store atmosphere. No messy containers or bins, but rather a brightly-decorated store with attractive dispensing containers.

Equity Capital Needed: $100,000 - $150,000

Franchise Fee: $30,000

Royalty Fee: 4%

Financial Assistance: No financing is available at this time.

Managerial Assistance: New franchisees are provided with location analysis, including site selection and lease negotiations. We provide complete store layouts and store equipment packages. Also provided are complete operating packages, from accounting systems to extensive merchandising to promotional programs and staff training. We offer capital and operating budgets, coordinated franchise-wide promotional programs, sample advertising layouts and on-going advertising assistance.

Training Provided: We provide a 30-day training program at our head office. The program includes all aspects of day-to-day business. On-site training is also provided at the time of opening.

Information Submitted: January 1994

OKY DOKY FOODS
1250 Iowa St.
Dubuque, IA 52001
Telephone: (319) 556-8050
Fax: (319) 582-6334
Mr. John F. Thompson, General Manager

Number of Franchised Units: 8
Number of Company-Owned Units: 8
Number of Total Operating Units: 16

In Business Since: 1916   Franchising Since: 1964

Description of Operation: Convenience stores.

Equity Capital Needed: $25,000

Franchise Fee: $0

Royalty Fee: 2%

Financial Assistance: Depends upon applicant.

Managerial Assistance: As much as required.

Training Provided: On-the-job training.

Information Submitted: January 1994

PAPA ALDO'S INTERNATIONAL
4356 SW Multnomah Blvd.
Portland, OR 97219
Telephone: (800) 257-7272 (503) 246-7272
Fax: (503) 245-3654
Mr. Jerry Kenney, President

Number of Franchised Units: 62
Number of Company-Owned Units: 4
Number of Total Operating Units: 66

In Business Since: 1981   **Franchising Since:** 1982

Description of Operation: Papa Aldo's is the leader in the take-and-bake pizza business. Papa Aldo's is only currently interested in opening new locations in Oregon, Washington and Idaho. Papa Aldo's franchisees are owner-operators who work the business. We feature take-and-bake pizza, calzones and lasagna. No customer seating.

Equity Capital Needed: $70,000 - $100,000

Franchise Fee: $17,500

Royalty Fee: 5%

Financial Assistance: None available from franchisor.

Managerial Assistance: Operations representatives visit stores at least once each month and call each week. Franchisor assists with site selection, store design and purchasing.

Training Provided: 1 week at our corporate offices in Portland, OR for as many people as franchisee cares to send, then 1 week on-the-job at the new store opening.

Information Submitted: November 1993

PERFECT PORTIONS FROZEN FOODS
15 Burgar St., 2nd Fl.
Welland, ON L3B 2S6 CAN
Telephone: (905) 735-2000
Fax: (905) 735-5825
Mr. Andre J. Champagne, President

Number of Franchised Units: 11
Number of Company-Owned Units: 1
Number of Total Operating Units: 12

In Business Since: 1985   **Franchising Since:** 1986

Description of Operation: Portion-controlled retailer of frozen foods.

Equity Capital Needed: $225,000

Franchise Fee: $30,000

Royalty Fee: 4%

Financial Assistance: Not available.

Managerial Assistance: Data not available.

Training Provided: We offer 1 full week of training at the head office and corporate store, plus on-site start-up, set-up and staff training for 2 weeks. On-going assistance, business plans and marketing meetings.

Information Submitted: January 1994

QUICKWAY CONVENIENCE STORE
44 Grand St.
Sidney, NY 13838
Telephone: (607) 561-2700
Fax: (607) 563-1460
Mr. Thomas J. Mirabito, Jr., Vice President of Marketing

Number of Franchised Units: 3
Number of Company-Owned Units: 35
Number of Total Operating Units: 38

In Business Since: 1952   **Franchising Since:** 1992

Description of Operation: Gasoline station and convenience store, featuring the sale of groceries, tobacco products, candy, made-to-order sandwiches, snacks, soda, beer and gasoline.

Equity Capital Needed: $75,000 - $400,000

Franchise Fee: $7,500

Royalty Fee: 3%

Financial Assistance: None.

Managerial Assistance: We will train store management and personnel and our store supervisors will make a minimum of 2 visits per month.

Training Provided: The owners will be given the opportunity to work in a Company-owned outlet for 2 - 3 weeks, along with any personnel hired by the franchisee. Franchisees will also be given the opportunity to attend all Company-owned store meetings and training sessions.

Information Submitted: November 1993

QUIX SYSTEMS
4 N. Third St.
Temple, TX 76501
Telephone: (817) 778-3547
Fax: (817) 778-0910
Mr. George Dejewski, Director of Franchising

Number of Franchised Units: 3
Number of Company-Owned Units: 29
Number of Total Operating Units: 32

In Business Since: 1958   **Franchising Since:** 1992

Description of Operation: Quix Convenience Food Stores with fuel installations. Standard franchise offering is on existing locations in Texas. Quix Systems also has a dealer franchise program geared toward the development of new sites.

Equity Capital Needed: $75,000 (approximately).

Franchise Fee: $25,000

Royalty Fee: 5%

Financial Assistance: Quix Systems does not offer any financing, but will provide assistance in obtaining financing.

Managerial Assistance: On-going operations support provided by franchise advisor. Other marketing assistance includes manuals, newsletters, vendor negotiations, promotional programs, bulletins and signage, layouts, schematics, advertising media and grand opening support.

Training Provided: An intensive 2 weeks of classroom and in-field training is provided. An additional 80 hours of on-site training is provided within the first 3 weeks of operation.

Information Submitted: November 1993

QUIZNO'S
7555 E. Hampden Ave., # 601
Denver, CO 80231
Telephone: (303) 368-9424
Fax: (303) 368-9454
Mr. Scott K. Adams, Director of Franchising

Number of Franchised Units: 32
Number of Company-Owned Units: 6
Number of Total Operating Units: 38

In Business Since: 1981   **Franchising Since:** 1986

Description of Operation: Up-scale Italian deli theme, specializing in subs, soups, salads and pasta.

Equity Capital Needed: $150,000 - $200,000

Franchise Fee: $15,000

Royalty Fee: 5%

Financial Assistance: We will assist with financing.

Managerial Assistance: We provide a 17-day training program that includes all aspects of running the day-to-day operations.

Training Provided: Same as above.

Information Submitted: November 1993

SAINT CINNAMON BAKE SHOPPE
7181 Woodbine Ave., # 222
Markham, ON L3R 1A3 CAN
Telephone: (905) 470-1518
Fax: (905) 470-8112
Mr. Robert Hassell, Vice President

Number of Franchised Units: 71
Number of Company-Owned Units: 1
Number of Total Operating Units: 72

In Business Since: 1986   Franchising Since: 1986

Description of Operation: Freshly-baked cinnamon rolls made in front of the customer and served immediately from the oven. The cinnamon rolls are served with quality coffees in a kiosk or in-line concept.

Equity Capital Needed: $40,000 - $75,000

Franchise Fee: $25,000

Royalty Fee: 6%

Financial Assistance: The franchisor will assist in arranging various options for purchaser lease.

Managerial Assistance: The franchisor is involved from the beginning (finding location) to the opening and continued assistance. This is worked through the master franchisee of each territory who maintains a link from the franchisee to the franchisor.

Training Provided: The franchisee receives 2 weeks of training in all aspects of the operation. On-going assistance is provided to the individual owner through the master franchisee of the area.

Information Submitted: January 1994

SAMMI'S DELI
114 Wilton Hill Rd.
Columbia, SC 29212
Telephone: (803) 781-7977
Mr. Hassan Addahoumi, President

Number of Franchised Units: 2
Number of Company-Owned Units: 1
Number of Total Operating Units: 3

In Business Since: 1984   Franchising Since: 1991

Description of Operation: Fast food.

Equity Capital Needed: $60,000 - $80,000

Franchise Fee: $9,500

Royalty Fee: 5% or $350, whichever is higher.

Financial Assistance: None available at this time.

Managerial Assistance: 5 days of training in the new location.

Training Provided: A 2-week training course, comprised of hands-on instruction at our training store and classroom orientation at our headquarters. At opening, our staff remains for at least 5 days, assisting in all aspects of the opening.

Information Submitted: January 1994

SANGSTER'S HEALTH CENTRE
P. O. Box 996
Yorkton, SK S3N 2X3 CAN

Telephone: (306) 783-9177
Fax: (306) 783-3331
Mr. R. Sangster, President

Number of Franchised Units: 15
Number of Company-Owned Units: 4
Number of Total Operating Units: 19

In Business Since: 1971   Franchising Since: 1978

Description of Operation: Retail sale of vitamins, herbs, natural cosmetics, natural foods, body building and supplies, specializing in our own name-brand products and also national company brands.

Equity Capital Needed: $10,000 - $15,000

Franchise Fee: $15,000

Royalty Fee: 5%

Financial Assistance: We help arrange bank financing with business plans and projections.

Managerial Assistance: Franchisees are trained in supervision, accounting and the various things that managers need.

Training Provided: Franchisees will train in an existing operation, as well as be trained in their own location.

Information Submitted: January 1994

SCHLOTZSKY'S DELI
200 W. Fourth St.
Austin, TX 78701
Telephone: (800) 846-2867 (512) 449-7500
Fax: (512) 477-2897
Mr. Kelly R. Arnold, Franchise Sales Director

Number of Franchised Units: 273
Number of Company-Owned Units: 1
Number of Total Operating Units: 274

In Business Since: 1971   Franchising Since: 1977

Description of Operation: Sandwich, soup, salad and pizza. Quick service. A proprietary product that is different from other sandwiches. All products are served hot - no cold sandwiches.

Equity Capital Needed: $60,000 - $80,000

Franchise Fee: $15,000

Royalty Fee: 6%

Financial Assistance: Equipment leasing and direct assistance with regional lenders.

Managerial Assistance: Local developers, who act as service representatives, provide as much hands-on assistance as is required to insure success.

Training Provided: Training consists of 2 weeks in a restaurant. In addition, a 3-person opening team will be on location for the first week of operation.

Information Submitted: January 1994

SECOND CUP COFFEE
3300 Bloor St. W., # 2900, Box 54
Etobicoke, ON M8X 2X3 CAN
Telephone: (416) 236-0053
Fax: (416) 236-0054
Ms. Robyn Paikin, Franchise Assistant

Number of Franchised Units: 173
Number of Company-Owned Units: 9
Number of Total Operating Units: 182

In Business Since: 1975   Franchising Since: 1979

Description of Operation: Specialty gourmet coffees and teas.

Equity Capital Needed: $60,000 - $80,000

Franchise Fee: $20,000

Royalty Fee: 9%

Financial Assistance: We provide guidance in preparing the business plan for bank submission. Bank introduction if required.

Managerial Assistance: Store service representatives give continuing assistance in all areas of store operations by phone. Field consultants provide leadership and support, assist with standards of operation, consult and identify profitability. Regular store visits by a field consultant. Marketing programs are set up on a yearly basis to assist franchisee in all marketing and promotions. Monthly marketing manual is included.

Training Provided: Second Cup Coffee Co.'s "Coffee College" is an intensive, 2-week program for new franchisees. This program has been designed to provide all students with the knowledge, tools and equipment necessary to maximize the potential of their store.

Information Submitted: December 1993

STAN EVANS BAKERIES
2280 W. Henderson Rd., # 206
Columbus, OH 43220
Telephone: (614) 459-1251
Fax: (614) 459-0780
Mr. Stan Evans, President

Number of Franchised Units: 0
Number of Company-Owned Units: 4
Number of Total Operating Units: 4

In Business Since: 1987   **Franchising Since:** 1993

Description of Operation: Bakers of a wide variety of stone-ground, whole wheat breads, dinner rolls, buns, sweets, etc.

Equity Capital Needed: $150,000 - $217,000

Franchise Fee: $25,000

Royalty Fee: 6%

Financial Assistance: Not available.

Managerial Assistance: Each franchisee will receive manuals containing the necessary forms for internal reporting, food and labor cost control. Assistance with promotions and advertising, site location, build-out, equipment, equipment purchases, equipment installation, etc.

Training Provided: We offer extensive training in a Company bakery for owner and bakers for 3 - 4 weeks and additional training in the franchisee's bakery. On-site training for counter help and baker's helpers. Training for setting up new accounts and daily operational training.

Information Submitted: January 1994

STUFF 'N TURKEY
9199 Reistertown Rd., # 212C
Owings Mills, MD 21170
Telephone: (410) 581-9393
Fax: (410) 363-3308
Mr. Alan Morstein, President

Number of Franchised Units: 14
Number of Company-Owned Units: 7
Number of Total Operating Units: 21

In Business Since: 1986   **Franchising Since:** 1989

Description of Operation: Stuff 'N Turkey is a specialty deli operation, featuring home-cooked turkey and glazed ham. A unique, healthy and home-cooked approach.

Equity Capital Needed: $60,000 - $175,000

Franchise Fee: $25,000

Royalty Fee: 5%

Financial Assistance: We will assist in obtaining financing.

Managerial Assistance: On-going.

Training Provided: We offer 2 weeks of training at a Company store and 1 week on-site.

Information Submitted: April 1994

TOPSY'S INTERNATIONAL
221 W. 74th Terrace
Kansas City, MO 64114
Telephone: (816) 523-5555
Fax: (816) 523-4747
Mr. Robert Ramm, President

Number of Franchised Units: 16
Number of Company-Owned Units: 1
Number of Total Operating Units: 17

In Business Since: 1950   **Franchising Since:** 1967

Description of Operation: Retail popcorn and ice cream shop. Regional malls provide the best location. Topsy's is the leader in the popcorn gift canister business. Topsy's enhances its store volumes by its corporate and mail order canister program.

Equity Capital Needed: $100,000 - $150,000

Franchise Fee: $20,000

Royalty Fee: 5%

Financial Assistance: Due to the number of years the Company has been in business and the success on most of its franchisees, this franchise concept has been approved for many levels of SBA financing.

Managerial Assistance: Managerial and marketing programs are on-going throughout the term of the franchise.

Training Provided: The franchisee is required to train in Kansas City, MO in an existing shop and commissary for at least 1 week. The franchisor provides a representative for a period of approximately 3 - 5 days during the opening of each franchised location. These periods can be extended, depending upon the franchisee's background and expertise.

Information Submitted: January 1994

TREATS
418 Preston St.
Ottawa, ON K1S 4N2 CAN
Telephone: (613) 563-4073
Fax: (613) 563-1982
Mr. John A. Deknatel, Chief Operating Officer

Number of Franchised Units: 157
Number of Company-Owned Units: 5
Number of Total Operating Units: 162

In Business Since: 1977   **Franchising Since:** 1980

Description of Operation: Treats is a retail bakery concept that offers consumers fresh, "hot from the oven" baked muffins, cookies, cinnamon swirls, brownies, crumbles and other similar high-quality baked products. In addition to fresh-baked goods and gourmet coffee, some locations serve soups, salads, made-to-order sandwiches, hot luncheon specials and frozen yogurt.

Equity Capital Needed: $30,000 - $90,000

Franchise Fee: $25,000

Royalty Fee: 8%; 2% advertising.

Financial Assistance: We will assist the franchisee by introducing him/her to various lending institutions.

Managerial Assistance: We provide on-going assistance, as required. District managers are available throughout Canada and the US. Confidential operations and recipe manuals are provided.

Training Provided: You will be required to attend a 2-week Treats training course, where all aspects of operation, administration and management will be taught. During your training program, you will actively participate in all aspects of operating and managing a Treats franchise.

TROPIK SUN FRUIT & NUT
37 Sherwood Terrace, # 101
Lake Bluff, IL 60044
Telephone: (708) 234-3407
Fax: (708) 234-3856
Ms. Barbara Wellard, President

Number of Franchised Units: 73
Number of Company-Owned Units: 10
Number of Total Operating Units: 83

In Business Since: 1980   Franchising Since: 1980

Description of Operation: "Fun Munchies" - neat things to nibble on - great gifts, drinks and popcorn.

Equity Capital Needed: $50,000 - $80,000

Franchise Fee: $20,000

Royalty Fee: 6%

Financial Assistance: Data not available.

Managerial Assistance: We provide training in operations and business procedures. We are on-site at time of opening. Regular memos about new products, policies, merchandising, manual up-dates and semi-annual franchise conferences.

Training Provided: On-site training at time of transfer of existing store or opening of a new store. Covers all aspects, from merchandising to payroll.

Information Submitted: December 1993

WEE-BAG-IT QUICK DINING & DELIVERY
2200 Corporate Blvd., NW. # 317
Boca Raton, FL 33431
Telephone: (800) 533-7161 (407) 994-3994
Fax: (407) 994-4334
Ms. Allegra A. Owens, Vice President of Corporate Development

Number of Franchised Units: 1
Number of Company-Owned Units: 4
Number of Total Operating Units: 5

In Business Since: 1989   Franchising Since: 1991

Description of Operation: Unique restaurant franchise prepares up-scale, quality entrees for breakfast and lunch and delivers them to the customer within 45 minutes. Specializing in tailored corporate catering and home entertaining. We feature healthy foods prepared fresh - gourmet soups, sandwiches, salads, stuffed potatoes and specialty entrees.

Equity Capital Needed: $74,000 - $139,000 total estimated investment.

Franchise Fee: $15,000

Royalty Fee: 5%

Financial Assistance: Not available.

Managerial Assistance: We provide architectural renderings, site selection, lease negotiations, equipment and supplier contacts, comprehensive marketing plans, advertising campaigns, operations, supplies, restaurant management training and grand opening assistance.

Training Provided: Our comprehensive 3-week training program includes hands-on, in-store food preparation, daily opening and closing procedures, cost and inventory controls, point of sale computer system training, employee recruitment and training, marketing and sales and on-going promotional support reviews, evaluations, menu and product updates and new customer sales strategies.

Information Submitted: November 1993

WHITE HEN PANTRY
660 Industrial Dr.
Elmhurst, IL 60126
Telephone: (800) 726-8791 (708) 833-3100
Fax: (708) 833-0292
Mr. Richard L. Paszylk

Number of Franchised Units: 344
Number of Company-Owned Units: 2
Number of Total Operating Units: 346

In Business Since: 1965   Franchising Since: 1965

Description of Operation: A White Hen Pantry is a convenience food store of approximately 2,500 square feet. There is generally up-front parking for 10 - 15 cars. Stores are usually open 24 hours (some operate a lesser number of hours) for 365 days a year. The product line includes a service deli, fresh bakery, fresh produce and a wide variety of staples. White Hen Pantry stores are franchised to local residents who become operators of this "family business."

Equity Capital Needed: $20,000 - $25,000 (varies by location).

Franchise Fee: $20,000

Royalty Fee: Base weekly fee plus 7%.

Financial Assistance: The total minimum investment averages $56,800 - $60,000. The investment includes approximately $27,000 in merchandise, $5,000 in security deposit, $3,000 in supplies, $200 in a cash register fund and $20,000 as a training and processing fee. Financial assistance is available.

Managerial Assistance: This is a well-organized and comprehensive program. Other services provided include merchandising, accounting, promotions, advertising and business insurance (group health and plate glass insurance are optional). Store counselor visits are regular and frequent.

Training Provided: Classroom and in-store training precede store opening. Follow-up training is provided after taking over the store. Detailed operations manuals are provided.

Information Submitted: March 1994

HEALTH AND FITNESS

AMERICARE / DENTAL CENTERS U.S.A.
3233 W. Peoria Ave., # 112
Phoenix, AZ 85029
Telephone: (602) 548-9178
Fax: (602) 548-9472
Dr. Bernard Serbin, President/Chief Executive Officer

Number of Franchised Units: 0
Number of Company-Owned Units: 4
Number of Total Operating Units: 4

In Business Since: 1978   Franchising Since: 1987

Description of Operation: Dental centers in Sears Roebuck and Co., Montgomery Ward and strip shopping centers.

Equity Capital Needed: $250,000 - $350,000

Franchise Fee: $20,000

Royalty Fee: 3%

Financial Assistance: No.

Managerial Assistance: Perpetual assistance, as needed.

Training Provided: Varies, depending on the background and experience of the franchisee.

Information Submitted: January 1994

135

AMIGO MOBILITY CENTER
6693 Dixie Hwy.
Bridgeport, MI 48722
Telephone: (800) 821-2710 (517) 777-6537
Fax: (517) 777-8184
Mr. Richard E. Zimmer, Franchise Operations

Number of Franchised Units: 11
Number of Company-Owned Units: 3
Number of Total Operating Units: 14

In Business Since: 1968   **Franchising Since:** 1984

Description of Operation: Amigo Mobility Centers sell and service mobility products to individuals with walking disabilities. The centers operate in protected territories throughout the US. They sell and service mobility products, such as electric scooters, lift chairs, wheelchairs and other adaptive equipment. Sold to individuals whose mobility is affected by an illness such as stroke, MS, joint replacement or older aged people to maintain their independence.

Equity Capital Needed: $59,000 - $90,000

Franchise Fee: $20,000

Royalty Fee: 3% - 5%

Financial Assistance: We assist franchisees in proposals to lending institutions and in the development of their business plans.

Managerial Assistance: The franchisee receives operations manuals, advertising manuals and service manuals. Assistance also includes site selection, lease negotiation, store set-up and grand opening staffing. On-site visits and a step-by-step operational system to follow.

Training Provided: An intensive 3-week classroom/in-field initial training program that includes 1 week of classroom on operations, advertising, sales and service and 1 week of in-store training at a Company-owned unit and 1 week in the franchisee's area. On-going training includes phone, written and on-site instruction on all aspects of the business.

Information Submitted: November 1993

AMPLEX MEDICAL SUPPLIES
2930 E. Washington St.
Phoenix, AZ 85034
Telephone: (800) 284-2878 (602) 231-0202
Fax: (602) 231-0232
Mr. Gregory L. Foutz, President

Number of Franchised Units: 1
Number of Company-Owned Units: 0
Number of Total Operating Units: 1

In Business Since: 1990   **Franchising Since:** 1992

Description of Operation: Home medical supplies - oxygen and durable medical equipment. Rental and sales.

Equity Capital Needed: $50,000 - $1,000,000

Franchise Fee: $25,000

Royalty Fee: 5%

Financial Assistance: The franchisee is solely responsible for all financing arrangements. We cannot estimate if you will be able to obtain financing or, if so, the terms of such financing. We have not established standard or uniform financing arrangements. At the franchisee's request, however, we may refer the franchisee to independent leasing companies that may consider providing equipment lease arrangements, at varying terms, to credit-worthy applicants. We do not benefit financially from any such arrangements.

Managerial Assistance: Before opening, the franchise agreement obligates Medical Services Franchise Corp. to do the following before your Amplex Medical Supplies facility opens: provide checklists and guidance in all aspects of opening, provide operating manuals, software, catalogs, etc., establish administrative, billing, accounting, etc. procedures, provide telephone support and maintain a distribution warehouse.

Training Provided: After payment of the franchise fee, the initial training program of approximately 10 days must be successfully completed. Instruction includes recruiting, training and managing employees, advertising, marketing and sales methods, technical operations, computerized billing system operations, equipment training, etc. The franchisee is responsible for food, lodging and transportation costs. Respiratory therapist training also required.

Information Submitted: November 1993

BEVERLY HILLS WEIGHT LOSS CLINIC
200 Highpoint Ave., # B-5
Portsmouth, RI 02878
Telephone: (800) 825-4500 (401) 683-6620
Fax: (401) 683-6885
Mr. O. J. Mulkey, President

Number of Franchised Units: 97
Number of Company-Owned Units: 0
Number of Total Operating Units: 97

In Business Since: 1986   **Franchising Since:** 1989

Description of Operation: Beverly Hills Weight Loss Clinics are medically supervised. Patients must have lab work performed and doctor approval before starting the program. Our patients are taught to modify their eating habits and eat regular store-bought food from the start. The Company takes pride in its success with weight loss and especially with maintaining the loss.

Equity Capital Needed: $45,000

Franchise Fee: $15,000

Royalty Fee: 8%

Financial Assistance: Not available.

Managerial Assistance: Area supervisors are available to assist with on-site training, advertising, site location and general problem solving.

Training Provided: 2 weeks of classroom training is provided.

Information Submitted: January 1994

CALORIE SHOP WEIGHT LOSS CENTERS, THE
395 Springside Dr.
Akron, OH 44333
Telephone: (216) 666-7952
Fax: (216) 666-6180
Ms. Dianne Riffle, Franchise Development

Number of Franchised Units: 22
Number of Company-Owned Units: 4
Number of Total Operating Units: 26

In Business Since: 1992   **Franchising Since:** 1993

Description of Operation: Supervised weight reduction business, offering the consumer a comprehensive program utilizing individual treatment, pre-planned meals, personal care counseling and weight maintenance.

Equity Capital Needed: $58,000 - $115,000

Franchise Fee: $9,950

Royalty Fee: Varies.

Financial Assistance: None.

Managerial Assistance: Site location assistance, marketing and advertising.

Training Provided: Initial 4 weeks of training prior to grand opening. 2 additional weeks within the first 6 months. On-going training seminars, meetings and conventions.

Information Submitted: January 1994

CAROL BLOCK
1403 S. Belden St.
McHenry, IL 60050

Telephone: (800) 424-7537 (815) 344-0488
Fax: (815) 344-2503
Mr. Neal Rohr, Executive Vice President

Number of Franchised Units: 0
Number of Company-Owned Units: 14
Number of Total Operating Units: 14

In Business Since: 1937   **Franchising Since:** 1985

Description of Operation: Permanent hair removal.

Equity Capital Needed: $70,000

Franchise Fee: $28,000

Royalty Fee: 7%

Financial Assistance: None.

Managerial Assistance: On-going.

Training Provided: 2 weeks.

Information Submitted: December 1993

DIET CENTER
921 Penn Ave., 9th Fl.
Pittsburgh, PA 15222
Telephone: (800) 333-2581 (412) 338-8700
Fax: (412) 338-8743
Mr. Paul J. Modzelewski, Vice President of Franchise Development

Number of Franchised Units: 942
Number of Company-Owned Units: 0
Number of Total Operating Units: 942

In Business Since: 1970   **Franchising Since:** 1972

Description of Operation: Diet Center counselors work one-on-one with clients, helping them develop a personalized, low-fat eating style and a more active lifestyle. With the aid of a new behavior-management program, clients design their own practical solutions for losing and maintaining weight. Diet Center clients learn to improve their health and appearance by focusing on reducing body fat, instead of obsessing over some "ideal" number on scale.

Equity Capital Needed: $25,000 - $50,000

Franchise Fee: $12,000 - $18,000

Royalty Fee: 8%

Financial Assistance: The franchisor will assist qualified applicants by financing 1/3 of the initial franchise fee.

Managerial Assistance: Diet Center provides marketing, advertising, real estate and lease negotiations, as well as a complete nutritional staff. 800# assistance is also available to all owners.

Training Provided: Diet Center assists in all training aspects, from grand opening assistance to program and nutritional training. Training is provided both at our home office and in regional areas.

Information Submitted: November 1993

DIET LIGHT
300 Market St., # 101
Lebanon, OR 97355
Telephone: (800) 248-7712 (503) 259-3573
Fax: (503) 259-3506
Ms. Kathy Bengston, President

Number of Franchised Units: 6
Number of Company-Owned Units: 12
Number of Total Operating Units: 18

In Business Since: 1983   **Franchising Since:** 1988

Description of Operation: Individual weight-loss counseling with our portion-controlled meals and optional fitness facilities with toning tables and cardio-vascular equipment.

Equity Capital Needed: $25,000 - $30,000

Franchise Fee: $15,000

Royalty Fee: 0%

Financial Assistance: Diet Light will carry the contract for franchise fee. There will be no interest if it is paid off within a 12-month period.

Managerial Assistance: Training at headquarters. On-going support from main office. Training manuals are also given.

Training Provided: Training time will vary, depending on the background and experience of the franchisee. Normal time is 3 days - 1 week at corporate office, going over counseling and sales. Also, on-going training 4 times a year at headquarters.

Information Submitted: November 1993

DIET WORKSHOP, THE
Ten Brookline Pl. W., # 107
Brookline, MA 02146
Telephone: (800) 366-DIET (617) 739-2222
Fax: (617) 739-0107
Ms. Lois L. Lindauer, Founder

Number of Franchised Units: 18
Number of Company-Owned Units: 3
Number of Total Operating Units: 21

In Business Since: 1965   **Franchising Since:** 1967

Description of Operation: Weight control and diet counseling service.

Equity Capital Needed: $75,000 - $100,000

Franchise Fee: $12,500

Royalty Fee: 5%

Financial Assistance: None.

Managerial Assistance: Data not available.

Training Provided: We provide training in all aspects of the business, including financial, marketing, recruiting, training and motivating staff, site selection, center layouts, etc.

Information Submitted: January 1994

FORM-YOU-3 WEIGHT CONTROL & AEROBICS
4790 Douglas Circle NW
Canton, OH 44718
Telephone: (800) 525-6315 (216) 499-3334
Fax: (216) 499-8231
Mr. Walter E. Poston, Vice President of Franchise Development

Number of Franchised Units: 157
Number of Company-Owned Units: 15
Number of Total Operating Units: 172

In Business Since: 1982   **Franchising Since:** 1984

Description of Operation: Form-You-3 offers weight control and aerobics, as well as other secondary services - food products, clothing, convenience items related to services. Structured diet and aerobics program that meet almost all of the guidelines set and approved by regulatory agencies. Requires 800 - 3,000 square feet, depending on market. Trained counselors and aerobics instructors.

Equity Capital Needed: $39,000 - $89,000

Franchise Fee: $9,800 - $13,300

Royalty Fee: 6% or $500.

Financial Assistance: Some assistance offered.

Managerial Assistance: Support in the areas of advertising and training. Seminars on hiring, recruiting, sales, service, basic business operations and financial guidance. On-going support through visits, video and newsletter.

Training Provided: Marketing, sales and service training, as well as owner's and manager's training. Training is comprehensive and on-going.

Information Submitted: November 1993

GLORIA MARSHALL FIGURE SALONS
P. O. Box 3299
Seal Beach, CA 90740
Telephone: (310) 493-9527
Fax: (310) 493-1947
Ms. Laina Sullivan, Vice President of Franchising

Number of Franchised Units: 0
Number of Company-Owned Units: 65
Number of Total Operating Units: 65

In Business Since: 1965   **Franchising Since:** 1994

Description of Operation: Weight loss, nutrition and exercise. We provide personalized programs for our women-only clientele to insure and guarantee inches and weight loss. Moderate, low-impact exercise, combined with a sensible, low-fat, healthy eating plan with supermarket-purchased foods delivers toned, proportioned figure to our patrons. We provide more than just weight loss - we reshape a woman's figure through a figure correction personalized program.

Equity Capital Needed: $49,150 - $145,950

Franchise Fee: $25,000

Royalty Fee: 10%

Financial Assistance: We provide recommendations to third-party financial institutions.

Managerial Assistance: To make sure you maximize the potential of every salon location, you will receive guidance and detailed instructions on site selection, tenant improvements, construction and lease negotiations. We will also provide you with assistance in all aspects of salon operations to insure high productivity. 2 key components include grand opening teams with hands-on training; customized business operations and administration computer systems; administrative support for off-site and on-site management.

Training Provided: Training is broken into three phases: 1) franchisee training - franchise ownership & administration, salon management, selection and training of employees; 2) manager and employee training - salon operations, structure of patron's program, common problems and solutions, sales and service for a direct response business; and 3) on-going classes - salon management skills, updated information on nutrition and exercise physiology.

Information Submitted: March 1994

GNC FRANCHISING
921 Penn Ave.
Pittsburgh, PA 15222
Telephone: (800) 766-7099 (412) 338-8931
Fax: (412) 288-2033
Director of Franchising

Number of Franchised Units: 425
Number of Company-Owned Units: 977
Number of Total Operating Units: 1402

In Business Since: 1935   **Franchising Since:** 1988

Description of Operation: GNC franchising offers the opportunity to operate General Nutrition stores. GNC is a national specialty retailer of vitamins, minerals and sports nutrition supplements for the self-care and personal health enhancement markets.

Equity Capital Needed: $50,000

Franchise Fee: $20,000

Royalty Fee: 5% - 6%

Financial Assistance: GNC offers direct financing on a 5-year note.

Managerial Assistance: GNC has a staff of franchise consultants who operate exclusively in the field to support our franchisees in all aspects of business operations.

Training Provided: New franchisees receive 3 weeks of initial training, including an intensive 1-week training class at corporate headquarters. On-site assistance is provided prior to opening, with continuous, unparalleled retail support.

Information Submitted: November 1993

HEALTH SYSTEMS PLUS WELLNESS & WEIGHT MANAGEMENT
P. O. Box 1150
Orem, UT 84058
Telephone: (801) 225-2739
Fax: (801) 225-7759
Mr. Arthur E. Hansen, Director of Franchise Sales

Number of Franchised Units: 46
Number of Company-Owned Units: 5
Number of Total Operating Units: 51

In Business Since: 1990   **Franchising Since:** 1991

Description of Operation: Health Systems Plus Wellness & Weight Management is a holistic and comprehensive, lifelong wellness and weight management program. Services include training and support, monitoring of metabolic rates, body composition analysis, individual counseling and motivation, nutritional guidance, weekly behavior modification classes, individualized exercise programs, personal fitness trainers, individualized menu plans with well-balanced meals, medical risk analysis and life management.

Equity Capital Needed: $30,000 - $80,000

Franchise Fee: $9,000

Royalty Fee: 6%

Financial Assistance: None.

Managerial Assistance: Health Systems Plus provides all the necessary tools to start a business from the ground floor. Health Systems Plus can assist in developing a business plan and can help with all the start-up details with site location and demographics. There are in-field area managers that work with the franchisees on a regular basis to teach, motivate and train. We also provide reporting systems for accurate accounting of day-to-day operations and pro formas. There is also advanced business training.

Training Provided: Training is the key to any successful franchise operation. At Health Systems Plus, we are committed to training as the critical factor for operating a prosperous franchise. With thoroughly-trained franchisees, managers and employees, we can insure the continuing growth of successful franchises. The Health Systems Plus training program consists of 5 key areas - basic training, training in an operating center, training in new center, advanced center and regional and yearly conventions.

Information Submitted: March 1994

HOLLYWOOD WEIGHT LOSS CLINICS INTERNATIONAL
P. O. Box 1070 College Station
Fredericksburg, VA 22402
Telephone: (703) 372-6700
Fax: (703) 372-7593
Mr. Johnny Ventura, Franchise Director

Number of Franchised Units: 33
Number of Company-Owned Units: 2
Number of Total Operating Units: 35

In Business Since: 1989   **Franchising Since:** 1990

Description of Operation: Weight loss clinics.

Equity Capital Needed: $8,500 - $45,000

Franchise Fee: $5,000

Royalty Fee: 8%

Financial Assistance: Financial assistance is available if needed and on an approved basis only - no finance fees or charges.

138

Managerial Assistance: Each area has an area supervisor responsible for on-going training and center evaluations.

Training Provided: An initial 3 days of training is included in the franchise fee. Optional weekly area meetings and mandatory area monthly meetings are conducted by the franchisor or the franchisor's assistant.

Information Submitted: January 1994

INCHES-A-WEIGH
P. O. Box 59346
Birmingham, AL 35259
Telephone: (800) 241-8663 (205) 879-8663
Fax: (205) 879-2106
Mr. Scott Simcik, Franchise Director

Number of Franchised Units: 30
Number of Company-Owned Units: 3
Number of Total Operating Units: 33

In Business Since: 1986   **Franchising Since:** 1991

Description of Operation: Inches-A-Weigh is a unique blend of nutrition and on-site exercise, for women only. Specifically targeted to accommodate the needs of the 40+ market. A semi-absentee investment with high profit margins in an industry that sizzles! Our nutritional program endorses real supermarket foods, supported by a computer dietary analysis. Isokinetic exercise with specifically designed equipment is combined with a complete cardiovascular program.

Equity Capital Needed: $40,000 - $60,000

Franchise Fee: $29,500

Royalty Fee: 4%

Financial Assistance: The franchise fee is deferred, in part, for qualified investors with industry experience. Financing is available on some master territories or regions.

Managerial Assistance: We provide site selection assistance, lease negotiation, lease review, pre-grand opening marketing and 90-day media placement.

Training Provided: The owner's orientation in Birmingham, AL covers all aspects of marketing, management, operations and accounting (6 days). Pre-grand opening employee training on nutrition, sales conversion and telephone.

Information Submitted: March 1994

INTERNATIONAL BIOKINETICS CORPORATION
1372 W. Center
Orem, UT 84057
Telephone: (800) 657-4000 (801) 221-0510
Fax: (801) 221-0606
Mr. DeLoy M. Sallenback, Chairman

Number of Franchised Units: 7
Number of Company-Owned Units: 0
Number of Total Operating Units: 7

In Business Since: 1989   **Franchising Since:** 1991

Description of Operation: Health products - marketing and selling Super NutriVita formula, time-released vitamin mineral, enzyme, amino acid product and Nutriway nutritional mix, milk replacement made of soy and whey with vitamins and minerals added to it. It's not milk, it's better. We also sell many other products created by Dr. Anthony Pescetti.

Equity Capital Needed: $2,000 - $3,500

Franchise Fee: $1,000 plus 2.5 cents per person in defined franchise area.

Royalty Fee: $39 per month.

Financial Assistance: Franchisee financial assistance is not applicable to our Company.

Managerial Assistance: Assistance is available as needed. A manual of instructions is available covering aspects of operational and product information.

Training Provided: An extensive 3-day training period at the home office in Orem, UT will show new owners how to present and sell products and health and nutrition ideas to customers and potential franchisees.

Information Submitted: November 1993

JAZZERCISE
2808 Roosevelt St.
Carlsbad, CA 92008
Telephone: (800) FIT IS IT (619) 434-2101
Fax: (619) 434-8958
Mrs. JoAnn Kocyk

Number of Franchised Units: 5200
Number of Company-Owned Units: 0
Number of Total Operating Units: 5200

In Business Since: 1974   **Franchising Since:** 1983

Description of Operation: Jazzercize is a dance fitness program using choreographed dance fitness routines to music. The franchisee must successfully complete a training workshop and be proficient in dance and exercise in order to qualify for a franchise.

Equity Capital Needed: Approximately $3,000.

Franchise Fee: $650 - US; $325 - foreign.

Royalty Fee: 20%

Financial Assistance: None.

Managerial Assistance: Jazzercize provides the services of agents who supervise and assist franchisees in all facets of their business on an on-going basis.

Training Provided: Training includes a 4-day workshop.

Information Submitted: April 1994

JERRYANN ELECTROLYSIS INTERNATIONAL
1097 Old Country Rd., # 102
Plainview, NY 11803
Telephone: (516) 931-9400
Fax: (516) 692-7178
Ms. Ann Paduano, President

Number of Franchised Units: 2
Number of Company-Owned Units: 3
Number of Total Operating Units: 5

In Business Since: 1986   **Franchising Since:** 1991

Description of Operation: A complete electrolysis center. All JerryAnn electrologists use the patented JerryAnn method of electrolysis. Medical atmosphere - sterilized equipment. Up to 4 treatment rooms per office.

Equity Capital Needed: $17,000 - $35,000

Franchise Fee: $25,000

Royalty Fee: $200 - $400 per week.

Financial Assistance: None.

Managerial Assistance: JerryAnn provides training manuals, printed literature, site selection assistance, sales aides and advertising strategies. Back-up support in all areas of the franchise, including visits by JerryAnn personnel to franchisees.

Training Provided: The training period lasts approximately 3 weeks. Franchisees learn the electrolysis method, business skills, sales techniques and human interaction skills. Training groups consist of less than 4 people to facilitate a more "one-on-one" approach to learning.

Information Submitted: November 1993

LORRAINE'S TROPI-TAN
G-4290 Miller Rd.
Flint, MI 48507
Telephone: (800) 642-4826 (810) 230-0090
Fax: (810) 230-0090
Mr. Vince Lorraine, President

Number of Franchised Units: 3
Number of Company-Owned Units: 5
Number of Total Operating Units: 8

In Business Since: 1979   Franchising Since: 1985

Description of Operation: Indoor sun-tanning salon and related sales and services.

Equity Capital Needed: $30,000 - $70,000

Franchise Fee: $7,000

Royalty Fee: 3.5% or $4,200.

Financial Assistance: While TropiTan does not provide actual monetary financial assistance, we do provide help in securing bank loans, i.e. preparation of any required documents, forms, etc.

Managerial Assistance: Managers of Company-owned salons can be reached at a toll-free # 7 days a week. Upper management can be consulted by appointment.

Training Provided: Franchise management is required to complete a 2-week training program at a corporate salon prior to opening the franchised store. Also included in the franchise fee is 1 week of on-site training, during which time Tropi-Tan management will assist in preparation for store opening at the franchise location.

Information Submitted: December 1993

MIRACLE-EAR
4101 Dahlberg Dr.
Golden Valley, MN 55422
Telephone: (800) 234-7714 (612) 520-9749
Fax: (612) 520-9520
Mr. Jim Darland, Director of Franchise Licensing

Number of Franchised Units: 284
Number of Company-Owned Units: 2
Number of Total Operating Units: 286

In Business Since: 1948   Franchising Since: 1984

Description of Operation: Manufacturer and retail sales of hearing aids.

Equity Capital Needed: $65,000 - $100,000

Franchise Fee: $20,000

Royalty Fee: 5%

Financial Assistance: None.

Managerial Assistance: We provide direct and hands-on training. National support.

Training Provided: We offer 6 weeks of initial training and on-going support.

Information Submitted: January 1994

NAILS 'N' LASHES STUDIO
Box 340, 18817 Kennedy Rd.
Sharon, ON LOG 1V0 CAN
Telephone: (905) 473-5774
Fax: (905) 473-5774
Mr. Irving Fine, President

Number of Franchised Units: 19
Number of Company-Owned Units: 0
Number of Total Operating Units: 19

In Business Since: 1970   Franchising Since: 1972

Description of Operation: Application of artificial fingernails and eye-lashes, using a unique product for the nails that is exclusive only to our studio.

Equity Capital Needed: $15,000 - $25,000

Franchise Fee: $5,000 - $15,000

Royalty Fee: 0%

Financial Assistance: Subject to approved credit - up to 75% assistance.

Managerial Assistance: We provide full assistance in seeking and leasing a location, opening directions, back-up support on an on-going basis.

Training Provided: We offer 6 weeks of training, including on-site support and training manual.

Information Submitted: March 1994

O2 EMERGENCY MEDICAL CARE SERVICE
5950 Pinetree Dr.
W. Bloomfield, MI 48322
Telephone: (313) 661-0581
Fax: (313) 661-0581
Mr. Donald M. Stern, President

Number of Franchised Units: 16
Number of Company-Owned Units: 1
Number of Total Operating Units: 17

In Business Since: 1987   Franchising Since: 1989

Description of Operation: Placement of portable emergency oxygen units and first-aid kits. First-aid and CPR training are provided to all business to comply with state and federal regulations (OSHA).

Equity Capital Needed: $35,000

Franchise Fee: $12,000

Royalty Fee: Varies.

Financial Assistance: None by Company. Third-party leasing companies for required inventory.

Managerial Assistance: Full in-house support and guidance.

Training Provided: 5 working days at Michigan headquarters.

Information Submitted: November 1993

OUR WEIGH
3340 Poplar Ave., # 136
Memphis, TN 38111
Telephone: (901) 458-7546
Ms. Helen K. Seale, President

Number of Franchised Units: 4
Number of Company-Owned Units: 9
Number of Total Operating Units: 13

In Business Since: 1974   Franchising Since: 1974

Description of Operation: A unique weight-control group, consisting of 30-minute meetings, behavior modification, exercise and, most importantly, a nutritional diet that allows members to eat what they like and not have to eat foods they don't like. First in the field to introduce "food rewards." Free weekly weigh-ins upon reaching desired weight.

Equity Capital Needed: $1,000 - $25,000

Franchise Fee: $1,500

Royalty Fee: 0%

Financial Assistance: None.

Managerial Assistance: 2 weeks at headquarters in Memphis, TN.

Training Provided: Managerial classes, advertising, etc.

Information Submitted: January 1994

PHYSICIANS WEIGHT LOSS CENTERS
395 Springside Dr.
Akron, OH 44333
Telephone: (216) 666-7952
Fax: (216) 666-6180
Ms. Dianne Riffle, Franchise Development

Number of Franchised Units: 104
Number of Company-Owned Units: 0
Number of Total Operating Units: 104

In Business Since: 1979 **Franchising Since:** 1980

Description of Operation: Supervised weight reduction business, offering the consumer a comprehensive program, by utilizing individual treatment, personal care, counseling and weight maintenance.

Equity Capital Needed: $40,000 - $100,000

Franchise Fee: $7,500

Royalty Fee: 10%, or $150 per week minimum.

Financial Assistance: None.

Managerial Assistance: Site location assistance, marketing and advertising support.

Training Provided: Initially, 4 weeks of training prior to grand opening. 2 additional weeks within the first 6 months. On-going training seminars, meetings and conventions.

Information Submitted: January 1994

PHYSICIANS WEIGHT LOSS CENTRES (CANADA)
2 Bloor St. W., # 700
Toronto, ON M4W 3R1 CAN
Telephone: (416) 921-7952
Fax: (416) 923-2071
Ms. Jeannie Butler, Director of Canadian Operations

Number of Franchised Units: 8
Number of Company-Owned Units: 4
Number of Total Operating Units: 12

In Business Since: 1987 **Franchising Since:** 1987

Description of Operation: Out-patient weight loss clinics.

Equity Capital Needed: $40,000 - $70,000

Franchise Fee: $10,000

Royalty Fee: 10% on service, not on products.

Financial Assistance: Data not available.

Managerial Assistance: We provide site location, lease negotiation, legal and medical advice, as well as marketing and distribution assistance.

Training Provided: We offer a minimum of 6 weeks of training.

Information Submitted: March 1994

SLENDER CENTER
6515 Grand Teton Plaza, # 241
Madison, WI 53719
Telephone: (608) 833-1477
Fax: (608) 833-4402
Ms. Jean C. Geurink, President

Number of Franchised Units: 18
Number of Company-Owned Units: 2
Number of Total Operating Units: 20

In Business Since: 1979 **Franchising Since:** 1981

Description of Operation: Individualized weight management education. No pre-packaged foods. Use of 3-step breakthrough program which increases intake at 3 stages using normal, regular foods. Behavior system training (Breakthrough Thinking), which personalizes behavior change. Appropriate for career/lifestyle/weight/etc. modification. No

drugs or products. Comprehensive program manual provided all clients. Programs for men, women, adolescents, nursing mothers, vegetarians. Audio cassette on affirmations/relaxation/self-esteem.

Equity Capital Needed: $8,000 - $22,000, plus franchise fee.

Franchise Fee: $12,000 - $27,000

Royalty Fee: 6%

Financial Assistance: None.

Managerial Assistance: We provide grand opening assistance for 5 days, support phone staff available on-going, all print copy, TV commercials and radio scripts, monthly newsletter and regional meetings.

Training Provided: We offer an initial 5 days of training at corporate headquarters. Procedure and policy manuals are provided.

Information Submitted: March 1994

VOLPE NAILS
213 Tracy Creek Rd.
Vestal, NY 13850
Telephone: (800) 848-6573 (607) 786-5051
Fax: (607) 786-9023
Mr. Gary Donson, Vice President

Number of Franchised Units: 56
Number of Company-Owned Units: 1
Number of Total Operating Units: 57

In Business Since: 1981 **Franchising Since:** 1990

Description of Operation: Volpe Nails offers a full-service nail care salon, including pedicure systems and related retail products.

Equity Capital Needed: $16,000 - $100,000

Franchise Fee: $4,000 - $8,000 - $12,000; variable.

Royalty Fee: 4%

Financial Assistance: No direct financing is available; however, we will assist in preparing business loan applications.

Managerial Assistance: A complete policy manual is provided. 800# phone support is available 5 days a week. 1 - 2 days of initial management training, plus 2 - 3 days of computer training. On-going management training provided.

Training Provided: We offer a 3 - 4 week initial training program for all nail technicians. Training fee is included in the franchise fee.

Information Submitted: November 1993

HOME FURNISHINGS

A SHADE BETTER
3615 Superior Ave.
Cleveland, OH 44144
Telephone: (800) 722-8676 (216) 391-0200
Fax: (216) 391-8118
Mr. James P. Prexta, President

Number of Franchised Units: 0
Number of Company-Owned Units: 4
Number of Total Operating Units: 4

In Business Since: 1989 **Franchising Since:** 1993

Description of Operation: A Shade Better is a franchisor of a niche-oriented retail business system that is comprised of lampshades, lamps and other lighting accessories. A Shade Better provides its franchisees with an exclusive territory, complete store designs and thorough training in A Shade Better merchandising.

Equity Capital Needed: $115,500 - $147,000

Franchise Fee: $35,000

Royalty Fee: 6%

Financial Assistance: Data not available.

Managerial Assistance: Each new store will receive assistance regarding site selection, merchandise and marketing assistance and access to the A Shade Better operating systems. Each store will receive continuing guidance and complete training.

Training Provided: An extensive 5-day training period at the home office in Cleveland, OH, will provide instruction in the A Shade Better sales and administrative techniques, financial controls and customer service procedures. A representative from a Shade Better will also spend 10 - 14 days at your store for the grand opening.

Information Submitted: January 1994

A WORLD OF DECORATING
2240 Woolbright Rd.
Boynton Beach, FL 33426
Telephone: (800) 952-4570 (407) 738-1278
Fax: (407) 369-2180
Franchise Director

Number of Franchised Units: 3
Number of Company-Owned Units: 0
Number of Total Operating Units: 3

In Business Since: 1993   **Franchising Since:** 1993

Description of Operation: Decorating center, offering all types of home and office decorating products. For example: window treatments, carpet, wood floors, tile floors, wallpaper, fabrics and more. Option to fabricate some products.

Equity Capital Needed: $47,300 - $56,300

Franchise Fee: $19,500

Royalty Fee: 5%

Financial Assistance: None.

Managerial Assistance: Complete and thorough training manuals are issued for every category of operation. Video tapes are supplied as supplemental instructions. Hands-on demonstrations are provided by the training instructors.

Training Provided: A World of Decorating offers 3 categories of franchise participation. Complete, on-going training is tailored to each category. Teaching is offered at the national headquarters and/or the individual centers. Training includes measuring and calculation of materials and labor needed for window treatments, carpeting, floor tile, wallpaper and installation. Instruction is provided for selling skills, advertising, center management, hiring personnel and basic decorating principles.

Information Submitted: March 1994

ALMOST HEAVEN, LTD.
Rt. 5-FS
Renick, WV 24966
Telephone: (304) 497-3163
Fax: (304) 497-2698
Ms. Stephanie Cleghon, Vice President of Franchise Sales

Number of Franchised Units: 1953
Number of Company-Owned Units: 0
Number of Total Operating Units: 1953

In Business Since: 1971   **Franchising Since:** 1976

Description of Operation: The most complete line of hot water, health and leisure products made today. Almost Heaven, Ltd. manufactures wooden hot tubs in several shapes and sizes in California redwood, Honduras mahogany, American white oak and Burmese teak; and spas, whirlpool bathtubs and steamrooms in all ceramic tile in an infinite assortment of styles and sizes. Hot tub and spa systems include genuine Jacuzzi-brand whirlpool equipment. Almost Heaven also manufactures acrylic portable spas, acrylic bathtubs and steamrooms.

Equity Capital Needed: $5,000 - $10,000

Franchise Fee: $0

Royalty Fee: 0%

Financial Assistance: We provide help in securing bank financing.

Managerial Assistance: On-going assistance via telephone and fax after initial training at factory.

Training Provided: Complete factory training, video and free consulting.

Information Submitted: November 1993

BATH GENIE
1 Brigham St.
Marlboro, MA 01752
Telephone: (800) 255-8827 (508) 481-8827
Fax: (508) 624-6444
Mr. John Foley, General Manager

Number of Franchised Units: 26
Number of Company-Owned Units: 1
Number of Total Operating Units: 27

In Business Since: 1974   **Franchising Since:** 1984

Description of Operation: Bathtub repair and resurfacing.

Equity Capital Needed: $10,000 - $50,000

Franchise Fee: $24,500

Royalty Fee: 0%

Financial Assistance: None.

Managerial Assistance: Total training to start up the business. A complete package is provided.

Training Provided: Both in-field and at corporate headquarters.

Information Submitted: March 1994

BATHCREST
2425 S. Progress Dr.
Salt Lake City, UT 84119
Telephone: (800) 826-6790 (801) 972-1110
Fax: (801) 977-0328
Mr. Lloyd Peterson, Vice President of Sales

Number of Franchised Units: 163
Number of Company-Owned Units: 1
Number of Total Operating Units: 164

In Business Since: 1979   **Franchising Since:** 1985

Description of Operation: Bathroom refinishing. With the bathroom being the #1 refinished room in the home, Bathcrest is in a unique position to make money by saving the homeowner up to 80% of replacement costs. Our proven process and product is used in commercial and residential homes. Now you can cash in on the refinishing trend. With our "No Royalties" philosophy, you earn it, then you keep it.

Equity Capital Needed: $24,500 - $41,000

Franchise Fee: $3,500

Royalty Fee: $1,200 annual renewal fee.

Financial Assistance: None.

Managerial Assistance: Comprehensive operations manual. On-the-job training of marketing, advertising, daily operation procedures, estimating and sales. Newsletters, ad slicks and manuals to help in all phases of the business. 2 toll-free watts lines for support and ordering.

Training Provided: To help insure your success, we offer 1 week of on-the-job training with paid airfare, room and board. Complete equipment, printing and enough material to recoup your investment. National and regional conferences. Two toll-free watts lines for technical support.

Information Submitted: November 1993

CARPET NETWORK
109 Gaither Dr., # 302
Mt. Laurel, NJ 08054
Telephone: (800) 428-1067 (609) 273-9393
Fax: (404) 273-0160
Mr. Leonard Rankin, President

Number of Franchised Units: 20
Number of Company-Owned Units: 1
Number of Total Operating Units: 21

In Business Since: 1991   Franchising Since: 1992

Description of Operation: Mobile carpet and window treatment business. Our franchisees go directly to the home or business with over 3,000 carpet choices and a complete line of window treatments. Our franchisees purchase directly from leading mills and are therefore able to offer the consumers great values, convenience and service.

Equity Capital Needed: $2,000 - $4,000

Franchise Fee: $13,500

Royalty Fee: 5% on gross sales.

Financial Assistance: None.

Managerial Assistance: In addition to extensive training, we offer a 24-hour support line, monthly newsletter, on-going training, field visits and a marketing program, including, but not limited to, ad slicks and a complete image package.

Training Provided: After a franchisee signs up, we send him/her an in-home training package, consisting of audio tapes, video tapes and workbooks, providing general knowledge of the carpet and window treatment business. Then the franchisee comes to corporate head-quarters for 5 days of training, where we cover product, color and design, marketing, organizational skills, measuring, sales techniques, etc.

Information Submitted: November 1993

CARPETERIA
28159 Ave. Stanford, P. O. Box 5902
Valencia, CA 91355
Telephone: (800) 356-6763 (805) 295-1000
Fax: (805) 257-4958
Ms. Natalie Wooldridge, Franchise Co-ordinator

Number of Franchised Units: 40
Number of Company-Owned Units: 30
Number of Total Operating Units: 70

In Business Since: 1960   Franchising Since: 1972

Description of Operation: Carpeteria is the West Coast's largest carpet-specialty retailer, with 70 stores in 6 states and a 15-vehicle shop-at-home service. Carpeteria stores also feature vinyl and hardwood flooring, ceramic tile and a huge assortment of area rugs. Some stores feature an extensive custom window treatment and drapery department.

Equity Capital Needed: $250,000

Franchise Fee: $25,000 - $150,000

Royalty Fee: 3% - 4%

Financial Assistance: Limited financial assistance is available to new franchisees.

Managerial Assistance: Among the many benefits Carpeteria franchisees enjoy are volume purchase agreements - a result of the system's tremendous buying clout and experienced negotiating abilities; integrated co-operative advertising opportunities; industry-renowned marketing and merchandising services; site selection, lease negotiation, market development and financial assistance; a co-operatively funded business research and development program; training programs; and access to Carpeteria's 30 + years of experience.

Training Provided: The Carpeteria system also conducts regular roundtable planning and discussion meetings, as well as individual and market conferences.

Information Submitted: November 1993

COLOR TILE & CARPET
515 Houston St.
Ft. Worth, TX 76102
Telephone: (800) 688-8063 (817) 870-9400
Fax: (817) 870-9589
Mr. Gary T. Lomax, Vice President of Franchising

Number of Franchised Units: 146
Number of Company-Owned Units: 805
Number of Total Operating Units: 951

In Business Since: 1953   Franchising Since: 1989

Description of Operation: Home furnishings, specialty flooring, wallcovering and window treatment store.

Equity Capital Needed: $165,000 - $241,000

Franchise Fee: $22,500

Royalty Fee: 4.25%, plus advertising fee of 9%.

Financial Assistance: Friendly lenders, assistance with business plan preparation.

Managerial Assistance: 4 - 6 weeks of training; corporate region manager program; operations department under the responsibility of vice-president of operations.

Training Provided: Home-study course, 4 - 6 weeks of on-site training in a corporate store, on-going training and regional seminars.

Information Submitted: January 1994

COLOR YOUR CARPET
2465 Ridgecrest Ave.
Orange Park, FL 32065
Telephone: (800) 321-6567 (904) 272-6567
Fax: (904) 272-6750
Ms. Connie D'Imperio, President

Number of Franchised Units: 108
Number of Company-Owned Units: 1
Number of Total Operating Units: 109

In Business Since: 1979   Franchising Since: 1989

Description of Operation: Carpet-dyeing on-site - color restoration, tinting, color repair, color designing, spot dyeing, fade/bleach/stain removal and complete color changes. Extraordinary customer satisfaction and referral sales. Consumer convenient, recession-friendly, safe and intelligent alternative to costly carpet replacement. Royalty of 3%. Total investment of $39,000 includes franchise fee, protected territory, inventory, equipment, training, van and more.

Equity Capital Needed: $39,000 total investment.

Franchise Fee: $15,000

Royalty Fee: 3% - 5%

Financial Assistance: Business plan provides for third-party financing of single units. SBA qualified. Special programs for women, minorities and/or first franchisee in a state or country. Master franchise financing up to 50% of master franchise fee for qualified investors.

Managerial Assistance: We offer dye master certification, comprehensive technical and business training program. 1 week of classroom and workshop in Florida and 3 weeks of field training in your area. Toll-free hotline, news release ads, executive marketing newsletters and technical updates.

Training Provided: Same as above.

Information Submitted: March 1994

CREATIVE COLORS INTERNATIONAL
5550 W. 175th St.
Tinley Park, IL 60477
Telephone: (800) 933-2656 (708) 614-7786
Fax: (708) 614-9685
Ms. JoAnn Foster, President

Number of Franchised Units: 11
Number of Company-Owned Units: 1
Number of Total Operating Units: 12

In Business Since: 1980   Franchising Since: 1991

Description of Operation: Creative Colors International franchisees offer convenient, on-site repairs to leather, vinyl, velour, plastics, carpeting and other materials at a cost far less than replacement parts.

Equity Capital Needed: $19,500 +

Franchise Fee: $19,500

Royalty Fee: 6%, or $40 per week.

Financial Assistance: Financing is available on supplies and equipment. An entire financing package should be available by March, 1994.

Managerial Assistance: Each franchisee receives periodic visits from a field representative, who will provide guidance and quality control and answer as many questions as possible. A toll-free number is available for day-to-day questions and answers. An operations manual is available for instructions covering all aspects of the business.

Training Provided: Franchisees and all their employees or contractors must participate in an initial training and familiarization course of about 2 weeks in duration at world headquarters. They'll learn sales and marketing techniques, financial controls, upholstery coloring, restoration and repair methods and other administrative and operational aspects of the business. At the grand opening of the business, a field representative will spend 1 - 2 weeks with the owner.

Information Submitted: November 1993

DECOR DISTINCTION
1122 Finch Ave. W., # 7
Downsview, ON M3J 3J5 CAN
Telephone: (416) 736-0003
Fax: (416) 736-6135
Mr. Serge Belanger, Vice President

Number of Franchised Units: 10
Number of Company-Owned Units: 1
Number of Total Operating Units: 11

In Business Since: 1989   Franchising Since: 1989

Description of Operation: We provide a complete interior design service in the comfort of your home.

Equity Capital Needed: $15,000 - $18,000

Franchise Fee: $15,000 - $25,000

Royalty Fee: 9.5% - 8%

Financial Assistance: We will finance up to $12,500. The terms are either 2 or 3 years. Open loan.

Managerial Assistance: We provide an accounting program with training, on-going support from in-house staff and a management seminar provided by outside consultant on topics such as sales, time management and accounting.

Training Provided: We offer 10 days of training at the head-office, followed by a complete correspondence course in interior design.

Information Submitted: March 1994

DECORATING DEN SYSTEMS
7910 Woodmont Ave., # 200
Bethesda, MD 20814

Telephone: (800) 428-1366 (301) 652-6393
Fax: (301) 652-9017
Mr. Jim Bugg, Jr., Chief Operating Officer

Number of Franchised Units: 1307
Number of Company-Owned Units: 2
Number of Total Operating Units: 1309

In Business Since: 1969   Franchising Since: 1970

Description of Operation: The first affordable, international, shop-at-home interior decorating service. Each franchise is operated by a professionally-trained decorator who brings thousands of samples of drapery, furniture, carpet and wall coverings to their customer in a specially-equipped ColorVan. The customer enjoys the convenience of reviewing generous samples in the lighting conditions which exist in his/her home or office. The Decorating Den guarantee of satisfaction is most important!

Equity Capital Needed: $8,000 - $12,000

Franchise Fee: $8,900 - $23,900

Royalty Fee: 7% - 15%

Financial Assistance: Financing is available for up to $10,000 of the initial franchise fee.

Managerial Assistance: Managerial assistance comes from the regional offices, with strong support from the corporate headquarters. Each regional office is equipped with a coordinator who keeps franchisees trained in the fields of decorating, retail sales, bookkeeping, etc. Franchisees are also given manuals which cover all aspects of the business. Monthly training classes.

Training Provided: Decorating Den's initial training takes approximately 6 months. It combines classroom work, home study, meetings, seminars and on-the-job experience, including working with an experienced decorator. Secondary, advanced and graduate training continue throughout the franchise owner's career with Decorating Den. Franchise owners and decorators are trained to identify lifestyle, personality, color preferences - and to work within a customer's budget. Emphasis is on the "feeling" and the way people live.

Information Submitted: December 1993

DIAL-A-FLOOR
P. O. Box 157
Convent Station, NJ 07961
Telephone: (800) 4-FLOORS (201) 625-2206
Fax: (201) 625-1615
Mr. Richard Pinto, President

Number of Franchised Units: 1
Number of Company-Owned Units: 1
Number of Total Operating Units: 2

In Business Since: 1991   Franchising Since: 1993

Description of Operation: The Dial-A-Floor concept was designed to bring all of the customer's floor covering needs directly to their doors. The ideal way to sell home fashions is to show them in the home. Since customers cannot take their homes to a store, you do the next best thing, you take the store to them. It enables you to coordinate and show floor covering products in the rooms or areas of the home where they will be used.

Equity Capital Needed: $11,000 - $16,000

Franchise Fee: $6,500

Royalty Fee: 5%

Financial Assistance: None available at this time.

Managerial Assistance: Help is just a telephone call or fax away. We are always ready to answer operational or general business questions or to assist with estimates. We continue to seek new products to update our selections. We keep our franchisees informed about what's new in our industry, current trends, etc. We also continually evaluate and update advertising to create consumer demand for our products.

Training Provided: Dial-A-Floor's comprehensive training program, in our modern facility, uses state-of-the-art videotapes and training sessions presented by mill, fiber, accounting, advertising and sales professionals about product and fiber knowledge, sales approach, closing techniques, measuring and estimating mechanics, office management, bookkeeping and advertising. At the end of the training, you will be equipped with a Dial-A-Floor tech kit with all materials to get started.

Information Submitted: January 1994

DIP 'N' STRIP
2141 S. Platte River Dr.
Denver, CO 80223
Telephone: (303) 781-8300
Mr. E. Roger Schuyler, President

Number of Franchised Units: 248
Number of Company-Owned Units: 1
Number of Total Operating Units: 249

In Business Since: 1970   **Franchising Since:** 1972

Description of Operation: Franchised operations assisting the household, community antique dealers, furniture refinishers, industrial and commercial accounts in the removal of finishes from wood and metal. Operation requires about 2,000 square feet of warehouse space with concrete floor, drain, cold water tap, 220-volt power, overhead door and small office space. Removals accomplished with a cold stripping formula in chemical solutions, with 3 large tanks. All equipment is supplied.

Equity Capital Needed: $12,500 - $16,000

Franchise Fee: None.

Royalty Fee: 6% (3% returned for co-op advertising).

Financial Assistance: Up to $3,000 at 6% for 3 years for those who qualify.

Managerial Assistance: Staff is available Monday - Friday and every day by phone. After training and grand opening, operations manuals are furnished, as well as all advertising layout materials and slicks.

Training Provided: 1 week at the franchisee's location at the time of the grand opening.

Information Submitted: November 1993

DR. VINYL & ASSOCIATES
13665 E. 42nd Terrace South, # H
Independence, MO 64055
Telephone: (800) 531-6600 (816) 478-0800
Fax: (816) 478-3065
Mr. Tom Rafter, Vice President of Operations

Number of Franchised Units: 109
Number of Company-Owned Units: 5
Number of Total Operating Units: 114

In Business Since: 1972   **Franchising Since:** 1981

Description of Operation: Dr. Vinyl franchisees provide mobile repair, reconditioning and after-market sales and services to auto dealers and other commercial accounts, such as vinyl, leather, velour, fabric, bumper, windshield, plastic and paintless dent repair, application of striping, body moldings, deck racks, graphics, gold plating, etc.

Equity Capital Needed: $19,500

Franchise Fee: $19,500

Royalty Fee: 4% - 7%

Financial Assistance: Data not available.

Managerial Assistance: Dr. Vinyl provides franchisees an 800# for ordering supplies, technical and accounting assistance, a monthly newsletter, field assistance, an annual technical and awards convention, advertising programs and a recently implemented industry first - a Company-sponsored IRA investment program!

Training Provided: Dr. Vinyl initially provides 3 weeks of training for new franchisees, (2 weeks in Kansas City, MO for combined classroom and field training and 4 - 5 days in franchisee's territory). On-going technical assistance via newsletter, conventions and telephone. Franchisees may return at any time for update and instruction. Training is also available for all franchisees' employees or sub-contractors.

Information Submitted: November 1993

DRAPERY WORKS SYSTEMS
4640 Western Ave.
Lisle, IL 60532
Telephone: (800) 353-7273 (708) 963-2820
Fax: (708) 963-1370
Ms. Sheila Muehling, President

Number of Franchised Units: 0
Number of Company-Owned Units: 1
Number of Total Operating Units: 1

In Business Since: 1978   **Franchising Since:** 1993

Description of Operation: Custom drapery and soft bedding accessories mobile business. Offers franchise owners the opportunity to own a business, work flexible hours and have the potential to earn substantial money. Designed for people who like to work with people, you do not need to be a designer, interior decorator or seamstress. On-going training, assistance, proven systems and corporate marketing support.

Equity Capital Needed: $5,000

Franchise Fee: $7,500

Royalty Fee: 5%

Financial Assistance: None available at this time.

Managerial Assistance: Owner/management support is available by telephone.

Training Provided: We teach independent business owners the selling techniques necessary to succeed in the custom window treatment industry. Strongest emphasis in selling, measuring and calculating each treatment.

Information Submitted: December 1993

EXPRESSIONS CUSTOM FURNITURE
3636 S. I-10 Service Rd. S., # 103
Metairie, LA 70001
Telephone: (800) 544-4519 (504) 834-9222
Fax: (504) 837-7613
Mr. B. Daniel Bish, Vice President of Franchise Development

Number of Franchised Units: 56
Number of Company-Owned Units: 5
Number of Total Operating Units: 61

In Business Since: 1978   **Franchising Since:** 1983

Description of Operation: Expressions is a manufacturer and retailer of fine, designer custom upholstery. Stores are dramatically arranged and displayed with unique accessories, appealing to affluent and fashion-oriented individuals.

Equity Capital Needed: $70,000 - $80,000

Franchise Fee: $15,000 - $30,000

Royalty Fee: 3.5%

Financial Assistance: The Company provides no direct financing, but has relationships established with financial firms.

Managerial Assistance: Grand opening, as well as on-going, assistance in all facets of its business.

Training Provided: Training for 3 weeks prior to opening, as well as on-going on-site training provided by regional managers.

Information Submitted: December 1993

FLOOR COVERINGS INTERNATIONAL
5182 Old Dixie Hwy.
Forest Park, GA 30050
Telephone: (800) 955-4324 (404) 361-5047
Fax: (404) 366-4606
Franchise Counselor

Number of Franchised Units: 340
Number of Company-Owned Units: 0
Number of Total Operating Units: 340

In Business Since: 1985   **Franchising Since:** 1988

Description of Operation: Floor Coverings International is a mobile floor covering retailer that brings the carpet store to the customer's front door. FCI's mobile service concept means that there are no high overhead costs. Our CarpetVan is loaded with a store full of colorful, name-brand styles that customers coordinate with the existing decor and lighting of their home or office.

Equity Capital Needed: $6,100 - $12,600

Franchise Fee: $14,000 - $29,000

Royalty Fee: 5%

Financial Assistance: Not available.

Managerial Assistance: Franchisees receive complete operations and marketing manuals. Regional directors meet with franchisees regularly to offer product and training updates and encourage information exchange. FCI's operations are low overhead. No inventory, rent or receivables are required. FCI is recognized by major manufacturers as a volume purchaser of carpet and enjoys discounts on nationally-known products, which allows competitive pricing at high gross profits. Monthly newsletter and annual convention.

Training Provided: FCI provides a comprehensive training program with 2 weeks of training at the home office in Atlanta, GA. After attending FCI's training program, franchisees have the product and sales knowledge needed to help their customers make informed purchase decisions that yield customer satisfaction.

Information Submitted: November 1993

FURNITURE MEDIC
277 Southfield Pkwy., # 130
Forest Park, GA 30050
Telephone: (800) 877-9933 (404) 361-9933
Fax: (404) 363-9797
Franchise Counselor

Number of Franchised Units: 112
Number of Company-Owned Units: 0
Number of Total Operating Units: 112

In Business Since: 1992   **Franchising Since:** 1993

Description of Operation: Furniture Medic is an on-site furniture restoration and repair franchise. Everyone has furniture - hotels, restaurants, homes, etc. Wood furniture is easily damaged during manufacturing, warehousing, transporting and by daily wear and tear. Furniture Medic restoration techniques can save this furniture for a fraction of replacement or refinishing costs. Furniture Medic provides franchisees with specialized equipment and territory.

Equity Capital Needed: $5,600 - $10,000

Franchise Fee: $7,000

Royalty Fee: $200 per month.

Financial Assistance: Not available.

Managerial Assistance: Franchisees receive complete operations, training and marketing manuals. Furniture Medic provides on-going support and has a toll-free telephone hotline that franchisees use to reach the home office. Franchisees receive newsletters and product updates. Training updates, marketing information and other important information is provided through Furniture Medic's annual convention.

Training Provided: The 3-week comprehensive training program that Furniture Medic provides includes a 1-week home study course and 2 weeks of training and hands-on experience at Furniture Medic's home office in Atlanta, GA. Furniture Medic's training program is designed to turn out well-rounded business people. Along with teaching our systems and products, high priority is given to teaching customer service, time management, monitoring sales and profit, motivation, discipline and people skills.

Information Submitted: November 1993

FURNITURE WEEKEND
21 W. Main St.
Malone, NY 12953
Telephone: (800) 562-1606 (518) 483-1328
Fax: (518) 483-4091
Mr. Larry Kriff, President

Number of Franchised Units: 4
Number of Company-Owned Units: 4
Number of Total Operating Units: 8

In Business Since: 1981   **Franchising Since:** 1990

Description of Operation: Limited hours retail furniture business.

Equity Capital Needed: $89,000 - $145,500

Franchise Fee: $15,000

Royalty Fee: 5%

Financial Assistance: None available at this time.

Managerial Assistance: On-going assistance is provided for advertising, merchandising, buying, employee relations, sales and store performance analysis. Periodic on-site evaluations. 24-hour hotline for problem solving.

Training Provided: 6 days of training in Company store. 6 days of on-site training and assistance in sales and operations.

Information Submitted: November 1993

GUARDSMEN WOODPRO
2960 Lucerne, SE
Grand Rapids, MI 49546
Telephone: (800) 253-3957 (616) 940-2900
Fax: (616) 285-7870
Mr. Tony Ziegler, Franchise Development Manager

Number of Franchised Units: 0
Number of Company-Owned Units: 1
Number of Total Operating Units: 1

In Business Since: 1915   **Franchising Since:** 1993

Description of Operation: On-site, mobile, wood touch-up and repair service.

Equity Capital Needed: $35,000 - $50,000

Franchise Fee: $25,000 - $35,000

Royalty Fee: Varies.

Financial Assistance: Third-party assistance.

Managerial Assistance: Guardsmen Woodpro provides its franchise partners with on-going support, such as initial promotional assistance programs, continuing education courses, research and development on new products and financial management assistance.

Training Provided: Guardsmen Woodpro offers 2 weeks of training, concentrating on the enhancement of managerial marketing and accounting skills, as well as a thorough program on touch-up and repair procedures and techniques.

Information Submitted: December 1993

146

HOUSE OF BLINDS & MORE
2300 W. 8 Mile Rd.
Southfield, MI 48034
Telephone: (313) 357-4710
Fax: (313) 357-4777
Mr. Barry Balbes, President

Number of Franchised Units: 2
Number of Company-Owned Units: 11
Number of Total Operating Units: 13

In Business Since: 1983   Franchising Since: 1993

Description of Operation: Franchisor offers a retail business, featuring the sale and installation of window treatments such as vertical blinds, mini-blinds, shades, shutters, draperies and related products and services. 3 franchises are offered: 1) showroom stores; 2) showroom factory outlet stores, enabling the franchisee to fabricate vertical blinds at its location; and 3) a mobile van program. Because franchisor's affiliated company manufactures vertical and mini-blinds, franchise owner has access to product at big savings.

Equity Capital Needed: $54,000 - $117,000 (retail store); $26,000 - $86,500 (mobile van).

Franchise Fee: $15,000

Royalty Fee: 5%

Financial Assistance: The franchisor may accept a promissory note for up to $10,000 of the initial franchise fee. The note is payable in 12 installments and is due in 1 year. Interest is at prime plus 1%.

Managerial Assistance: Each franchise owner receives training, an operations manual, forms, sales aids, product samples and updates, marketing and advertising samples and continuous consultation with technical and support staff. An annual meeting of franchise owners is anticipated.

Training Provided: The franchisor has an extensive training program, including instruction in vertical blind fabrication, window treatment installation, sales and marketing, inventory control and general store operations. The franchisor will provide a Company representative to assist the franchise owner prior to and after the franchise opening.

Information Submitted: January 1994

KOTT KOATINGS
27161 Burbank St.
Foothill Ranch, CA 92610
Telephone: (800) 452-6161 (714) 770-5055
Fax: (714) 770-5101
Mr. John M. Kott, Vice President

Number of Franchised Units: 333
Number of Company-Owned Units: 1
Number of Total Operating Units: 334

In Business Since: 1953   Franchising Since: 1973

Description of Operation: With over 40 years of experience, Kott Koatings is the world's largest and most knowledgeable bathtub, tile and fiberglass refinishing company. The franchise fee of US $19,995 includes accommodations and airfare to and from our training center, 1 week of hands-on training, along with all the supplies and equipment necessary to begin your franchised operation.

Equity Capital Needed: $19,995

Franchise Fee: $19,995

Royalty Fee: Data not available.

Financial Assistance: Data not available.

Managerial Assistance: Kott Koatings' highest priority is the success of its individual franchisees. We offer on-going technical support to our franchise network, along with advertising advice and ideas. These and more are all advantages to being part of the Kott Koatings' family of authorized franchisees.

Training Provided: Training takes place at Kott Koatings' international headquarters in Southern California. 1 - 2 weeks of instruction will include detailed demonstrations, along with hands-on training working with the most advanced, state-of-the-art refinishing system and products. Training manuals and sales presentation books are also provided.

Information Submitted: March 1994

LIFESTYLE MOBILE CARPET SHOWROOM
P. O. Box 3876
Dalton, GA 30721
Telephone: (800) 346-4531 (706) 673-6252
Fax: (706) 673-6390
Mr. Dewey Moss, President

Number of Franchised Units: 5
Number of Company-Owned Units: 0
Number of Total Operating Units: 5

In Business Since: 1991   Franchising Since: 1992

Description of Operation: Mobile showroom which sells carpet directly to the homeowner in his/her home.

Equity Capital Needed: $9,000 - $12,000

Franchise Fee: $9,000

Royalty Fee: 5%

Financial Assistance: None.

Managerial Assistance: 1-week training program at the home office. On-going field training during the initial start-up phase.

Training Provided: 1-week training program plus on-going training in the field as the program starts up.

Information Submitted: November 1993

LIVING LIGHTING
4699 Keele St., # 1
Downsview, ON M3J 2N8 CAN
Telephone: (416) 661-9916
Fax: (416) 661-9706
Mr. Michael Mayerson, Vice President of Franchising

Number of Franchised Units: 32
Number of Company-Owned Units: 0
Number of Total Operating Units: 32

In Business Since: 1971   Franchising Since: 1971

Description of Operation: Living Lighting provides retail and residential lighting.

Equity Capital Needed: $250,000 - $350,000

Franchise Fee: $30,000

Royalty Fee: 6%

Financial Assistance: None.

Managerial Assistance: On-going visits by operations supervisors, on-going advice, lease advice, advertising materials, buying assistance, etc. are all supported by home office specialists.

Training Provided: Training is on-site at other locations. Theory training seminars.

Information Submitted: March 1994

MARBLE RENEWAL
P. O. Box 56011
Little Rock, AR 72215
Telephone: (501) 663-2080
Fax: (501) 663-2401
Mr. Trey Whatley, Franchise Development

Number of Franchised Units: 22
Number of Company-Owned Units: 1
Number of Total Operating Units: 23

In Business Since: 1988   **Franchising Since:** 1989

Description of Operation: Marble Renewal provides restoration and maintenance services for marble, terrazzo, granite, slate, hardwood and other natural surfaces.

Equity Capital Needed: $29,000 - $72,000

Franchise Fee: $17,500

Royalty Fee: 8% - 5%

Financial Assistance: Individual.

Managerial Assistance: Full-service support.

Training Provided: 1 week of on-site training and 2 weeks at corporate office. Manuals, newsletters, seminars and field representatives. On-going training.

Information Submitted: January 1994

MIRACLE METHOD BATHROOM RESTORATION
3732 W. Century Blvd., # 6
Inglewood, CA 90303
Telephone: (800) 444-8827 (310) 671-4995
Fax: (310) 671-1146
Mr. Richard Crites, President

Number of Franchised Units: 123
Number of Company-Owned Units: 0
Number of Total Operating Units: 123

In Business Since: 1978   **Franchising Since:** 1980

Description of Operation: Highest-quality and longest-lasting bathtub and tile refinishing available. We do spot repairs and full refinishing on porcelain and fiberglass bathtubs, repairs and refinishing of wall and counter and floor tile, repairs on fiberglass and acrylic spas and refinishing of cultured marble and formica.

Equity Capital Needed: $10,000 - $15,000

Franchise Fee: $16,500

Royalty Fee: 5% - 7.5%, or minimum $300 per month.

Financial Assistance: We make introductions to outside providers of financing for local franchises. Company financing is possible for qualified purchases of regional area development franchises.

Managerial Assistance: 1 week of on-site start-up assistance is provided to establish promotion, advertisements, office establishment and sales training. Further assistance is available by 800# hotline during business hours.

Training Provided: We provide 2 weeks of intensive technical training in the franchise headquarters, complete training in refinishing porcelain, ceramic, fiberglass, formica and acrylic, as well as spot repairs, color matching and fiberglass repairs. An 800# hotline available during business hours.

Information Submitted: January 1994

NAKED FURNITURE
P. O. Box F, 799 Northern Blvd.
Clarks Summit, PA 18411
Telephone: (800) 352-2522 (717) 587-7800
Fax: (717) 586-8587
Mr. Bruce C. MacGowan, President

Number of Franchised Units: 42
Number of Company-Owned Units: 1
Number of Total Operating Units: 43

In Business Since: 1972   **Franchising Since:** 1976

Description of Operation: Naked Furniture is the nation's largest retailer of custom-finished and ready-to-finish solid wood home furnishings, offering a wide range of innovative and affordable choices. We serve

our markets with attractive, professionally-run stores and a diverse selection of quality products that allow our store owners to maintain their leadership position in the rapidly-growing specialty furniture market.

Equity Capital Needed: $71,500 - $122,500 start-up; cash, ability to borrow.

Franchise Fee: $19,500

Royalty Fee: 4%

Financial Assistance: The franchisor will assist in preparing a financial proposal for lenders.

Managerial Assistance: The franchisor assists with merchandising, site selection, lease negotiation, interior display, accounting, advertising, customer service, office procedures, product knowledge and selection. Computer-linked distribution center.

Training Provided: We offer 2 weeks of training at the corporate offices and prototype store, as well as on-going field support, as needed by individual franchisee.

Information Submitted: March 1994

NORWALK - THE FURNITURE IDEA
100 Furniture Pkwy.
Norwalk, OH 44857
Telephone: (800) 837-2565 (419) 668-4461
Fax: (419) 663-0021
Mr. Bob Young, Vice President of Franchising

Number of Franchised Units: 27
Number of Company-Owned Units: 6
Number of Total Operating Units: 33

In Business Since: 1902   **Franchising Since:** 1987

Description of Operation: Custom living room furniture specialty stores, offering 2,000 fabrics and leathers available on over 500 styles, with delivery in just 35 days.

Equity Capital Needed: $100,000 - $175,000

Franchise Fee: $30,000

Royalty Fee: 0%

Financial Assistance: Third-party financing assistance is available. Inventory financing is available.

Managerial Assistance: Multiple training sessions and seminars are required before franchise opens.

Training Provided: Management training, video tape program, on-site sales staff training and service manager training. On-going seminars.

Information Submitted: January 1994

PERMA CERAM ENTERPRISES
65 Smithtown Blvd.
Smithtown, NY 11788
Telephone: (800) 645-5039 (516) 724-1205
Fax: (516) 724-9626
Mr. Joseph A. Tumolo, President

Number of Franchised Units: 181
Number of Company-Owned Units: 1
Number of Total Operating Units: 182

In Business Since: 1975   **Franchising Since:** 1976

Description of Operation: Resurfacing and repair of porcelain and fiberglass bathroom fixtures, such as tubs, sinks and wall tile with Perma Ceram's Porcelaincote. The process is used in private homes, apartments, hotels/motels, institutions, etc., and is available in white and all colors. Established national accounts.

Equity Capital Needed: $19,500 total investment, includes all equipment, materials, supplies and training.

Franchise Fee: Data not available.

Royalty Fee: 0%

Financial Assistance: Data not available.

Managerial Assistance: Advertising, sales and promotional materials, on-going managerial and technical assistance are provided. Continual updating of information is provided through bulletins, newsletters and personal contact. Return visits to the training facility are available, if necessary.

Training Provided: We offer 5 days of training at an established location with all expenses included in the cost of the dealership. Technical training, sales training, management, marketing, etc. Operations manual provided.

Information Submitted: March 1994

PERMA-GLAZE
1638 S. Research Loop Rd., # 160
Tucson, AZ 85710
Telephone: (800) 332-7397 (602) 722-9718
Fax: (602) 296-4393
Mr. Dale R. Young, President

Number of Franchised Units: 168
Number of Company-Owned Units: 0
Number of Total Operating Units: 168

In Business Since: 1978   **Franchising Since:** 1981

Description of Operation: Perma-Glaze specializes in the restoration and refinishing of bathroom and kitchen fixtures, such as bathtubs, sinks and ceramic tiles. Materials to be refinished include porcelain, fiberglass, acrylic, cultured marble, formica, kitchen appliances, shower enclosures and most building materials. Services include chip repair, fiberglass and acrylic repairs, restoration and reglazing of fixtures. Available in any color. All work has warranty.

Equity Capital Needed: $2,000 - $3,000

Franchise Fee: $27,500

Royalty Fee: 0%

Financial Assistance: Data not available.

Managerial Assistance: Due to the nature of the business operation, most managerial services are handled by the franchisee within his/her home.

Training Provided: A 5-week training course is provided at the international headquarters located in Tucson, AZ. An additional 3 days of on-site training is provided about 6 - 8 weeks after the franchisee's return from Tucson. Training includes all technical and application processes, marketing and financial direction.

Information Submitted: January 1994

PRECIOUS PLACES
8321 Linden Oaks Ct.
Lorton, VA 22079
Telephone: (800) 937-6880 (703) 690-0854
Fax: (703) 690-7143
Ms. Debbie Hobar, President

Number of Franchised Units: 2
Number of Company-Owned Units: 1
Number of Total Operating Units: 3

In Business Since: 1988   **Franchising Since:** 1993

Description of Operation: Precious Places offers a unique and innovative shop-at-home or office service for decorating children's rooms. This home-based business specializes in creative decor for infant to pre-teen rooms and offers specialty furniture, bed linens, accessories, wallcoverings, window treatments and more at affordable prices. Exclusive concentration on the juvenile market, residential and commercial, with an emphasis on customer service, creativity and innovative merchandise, has catered to an untapped niche.

Equity Capital Needed: $2,600 - $8,600

Franchise Fee: $9,000

Royalty Fee: 7%

Financial Assistance: Precious Places offers no financing at this time. We will, however, assist qualified prospective franchisees in locating financial assistance.

Managerial Assistance: Complete operations manual to new franchisees. Details of office location, equipment, workrooms, contractors and necessary forms are included. Business stationery is provided. On-site assistance is available if Regional Manager is established. Franchises receive continual updates on products, services, workrooms and trade shows.

Training Provided: Initial training provided at franchisor's headquarters. Training, operations and other franchise-related manuals provided. On-going training, seminars and workshops held throughout the fiscal year. Regional Managers in certain areas will provide frequent support meetings and additional training sessions. Monthly newsletters inform franchisees of current issues. Trade show attendance encouraged.

Information Submitted: November 1993

PROFUSION SYSTEMS
2851 S. Parker Rd., # 650
Aurora, CO 80014
Telephone: (800) 777-3873 (303) 337-1949
Fax: (303) 337-0790
Mr. David F. Lowe, Director of Franchising

Number of Franchised Units: 218
Number of Company-Owned Units: 2
Number of Total Operating Units: 220

In Business Since: 1980   **Franchising Since:** 1982

Description of Operation: Plastic, vinyl, leather and laminate repair. Servicing commercial businesses such as restaurants, hotels, airports, hospitals, etc. Franchisees can offer lifetime repairs on tears, rips, cuts and burns. Mobile repair ability - almost all work performed on-site.

Equity Capital Needed: $15,000 - $30,000

Franchise Fee: $20,500 +

Royalty Fee: 6%

Financial Assistance: Upon qualification, the franchisor may finance up to 50% of the franchise fee.

Managerial Assistance: Franchisees receive operations, technical and field supervision manuals, plus 800# telephone assistance.

Training Provided: 9 days at headquarters includes technical, management, sales and accounting training. 4 days of field supervision follows approximately 6 weeks after completion of initial training.

Information Submitted: January 1994

PTR TUB & TILE RESTORATION
3398 Sanford Dr.
Marietta, GA 30066
Telephone: (800) 476-9271 (404) 429-0232
Fax: (404) 429-0232
Mr. Larry Stevens, President

Number of Franchised Units: 75
Number of Company-Owned Units: 1
Number of Total Operating Units: 76

In Business Since: 1973   **Franchising Since:** 1990

Description of Operation: Restore the beauty to old, dull, hard-to-clean bathtubs and tile. No painting or mess. Can be used the same day.

Equity Capital Needed: $5,995

Franchise Fee: Data not available.

Royalty Fee: 20%

Financial Assistance: Varies.

Managerial Assistance: Data not available.

Training Provided: Hands-on training and computer use for office. Manual.

Information Submitted: November 1993

RE-BATH
1055 S. Country Club Dr., Bldg. 2
Mesa, AZ 85210
Telephone: (800) 426-4573 (602) 844-1575
Fax: (602) 964-8365
Mr. David Andow, Director of Franchise Development

Number of Franchised Units: 26
Number of Company-Owned Units: 1
Number of Total Operating Units: 27

In Business Since: 1979   **Franchising Since:** 1991

Description of Operation: Re-Bath offers custom-manufactured, high-impact acrylic bathtub liners, wall systems and shower liners designed to go over existing bathtubs, ceramic tile walls and shower bases. Re-Bath offers a permanent solution at a fraction of the cost of replacement.

Equity Capital Needed: $22,500 - $30,000

Franchise Fee: $10,000 plus $5,000 start-up kit.

Royalty Fee: $25 per unit.

Financial Assistance: Re-Bath offers no financial assistance for the franchise fee. However, Re-Bath, under certain circumstances, will finance a required start-up package for a period of up to 6 months.

Managerial Assistance: Re-Bath Corporation provides its franchisees with complete training manuals, forms and marketing materials. On-going support is available in all areas of operation, installation, marketing and sales. Monthly operational and marketing updates and informational newsletters keep the network informed. Annual conventions provide training updates.

Training Provided: The new franchise owners attend a 5 - 6 day mandatory training program prior to opening. Training takes place at Re-Bath National Headquarters in Mesa, AZ and covers all phases of installation, operations, sales and marketing. Both classroom and hands-on training are provided.

Information Submitted: November 1993

SLUMBERLAND
3060 Centerville Rd.
Little Canada, MN 55117
Telephone: (612) 482-7500
Fax: (612) 482-0027
Mr. Kenneth R. Larson, President

Number of Franchised Units: 20
Number of Company-Owned Units: 11
Number of Total Operating Units: 31

In Business Since: 1967   **Franchising Since:** 1968

Description of Operation: Retail furniture.

Equity Capital Needed: $112,500 - $295,000

Franchise Fee: $10,000

Royalty Fee: 3%

Financial Assistance: None.

Managerial Assistance: A complete management package is available to all franchisees. The assistance includes marketing, advertising, sales training and office set-up.

Training Provided: Training is provided at the corporate headquarters in St. Paul, MN. It includes a thorough explanation of product knowledge, sales training and hands-on management assistance. On-going training is also provided, as well as conference call training twice a month.

Information Submitted: January 1994

SPR CHIP REPAIR
3398 Sanford Dr.
Marietta, GA 30066
Telephone: (800) 476-9271 (404) 429-0232
Fax: (404) 424-1494
Mr. Larry Stevens, Sr., President

Number of Franchised Units: 20
Number of Company-Owned Units: 1
Number of Total Operating Units: 21

In Business Since: 1973   **Franchising Since:** 1973

Description of Operation: Repair chips, cracks, burns, holes, porcelain, fiberglass, acrylic and cultured marble. National accounts.

Equity Capital Needed: $1,295

Franchise Fee: Data not available.

Royalty Fee: 20%

Financial Assistance: None.

Managerial Assistance: Data not available.

Training Provided: Hands-on training. Manual with instructions.

Information Submitted: November 1993

SPRING CREST DRAPERY CENTERS
505 W. Lambert Rd.
Brea, CA 92621
Telephone: (800) 552-5523 (714) 529-9993
Fax: (714) 529-2093
Mr. Jack W. Long, President

Number of Franchised Units: 153
Number of Company-Owned Units: 1
Number of Total Operating Units: 154

In Business Since: 1955   **Franchising Since:** 1968

Description of Operation: Retail stores selling custom window coverings and related decorating accessories. The franchisor is the manufacturer of an exclusive drapery system sold only through franchised stores.

Equity Capital Needed: $25,000 - $70,000

Franchise Fee: $15,000

Royalty Fee: 5% - 3%

Financial Assistance: Financing assistance is available.

Managerial Assistance: Spring Crest provides assistance with site location, design and set-up, operations manual, forms, supplier arrangement, newsletter, meetings, home office and regional support.

Training Provided: We provide a combination of classroom and in-field training over a 3 - 4 week period. On-going training through regional meetings and conferences.

Information Submitted: December 1993

STAINED GLASS OVERLAY
1827 N. Case St.
Orange, CA 92665
Telephone: (800) 944-4746 (714) 974-6124
Fax: (714) 974-6529
Mr. William A. Slippy, Jr., Vice President of Franchising

Number of Franchised Units: 351
Number of Company-Owned Units: 0
Number of Total Operating Units: 351

In Business Since: 1974   **Franchising Since:** 1981

Description of Operation: Stained Glass Overlay is the world's largest franchisor of decorative glass products, with locations in 32 countries. The exclusive SGO-patented process can decorate any glass or acrylic surface, adding incomparable beauty to homes, churches, restaurants, hotels, etc. We are looking for industrious, motivated individuals who have the desire to own their own successful business.

Equity Capital Needed: $45,000 - $80,000

Franchise Fee: $34,000

Royalty Fee: 5%

Financial Assistance: SGO is currently offering financing, in the US only, for up to $20,000 of the purchase price ($45,000), payable over a period of up to 3 years and at an interest rate of 10% per year. In as much as SGO has introduced this financing program on a trial basis only, there is no certainty as to how long it will continue to be offered.

Managerial Assistance: In addition to the comprehensive training program, we offer new franchisees a follow-up visit by one of our management team to their SGO studio between 3 - 6 months after opening. The purpose is to help them overcome any sort of difficulties in operating their business by hands-on, field training.

Training Provided: Training includes all aspects of operating a successful SGO franchise, with emphasis on the SGO process, marketing, sales and management of the business.

Information Submitted: March 1994

STENCIL HOME GALLERY
2300 Pilgrim Rd.
Brookfield, WI 53005
Telephone: (414) 797-9974
Ms. Sandra Barker, President

Number of Franchised Units: 0
Number of Company-Owned Units: 2
Number of Total Operating Units: 2

In Business Since: 1988   **Franchising Since:** 1993

Description of Operation: Retail franchise, specializing in decorative border stencils for the home and also featuring gifts and home furnishings.

Equity Capital Needed: $47,800 - $98,800

Franchise Fee: $15,000

Royalty Fee: 5%

Financial Assistance: None.

Managerial Assistance: The franchisor will provide initial training to one manager for each store developed.

Training Provided: The initial training program will include, but is not limited to, advice and guidelines with respect to merchandising, advertising, store decoration and store operation.

Information Submitted: January 1994

SURFACE SPECIALISTS SYSTEMS
2362 175th Ln., NW
Andover, MN 55304
Telephone: (612) 753-3717
Fax: (612) 753-6360
Mr. Wayne McClosky, President

Number of Franchised Units: 23
Number of Company-Owned Units: 1
Number of Total Operating Units: 24

In Business Since: 1931   **Franchising Since:** 1982

Description of Operation: Repair and refinish acrylic spas, porcelain tubs and sinks, fiberglass tubs and showers, cultured marble and plastic laminates. We also repair PVC and ABS showers and tubs and treat tubs, tile and showers with a skid-resistant bottom surface. Factory authorized warranty from 34 plumbingware manufacturers. Excellent opportunity.

Equity Capital Needed: $15,000 - $20,500

Franchise Fee: $9,500 - $14,500

Royalty Fee: 5%, or $50 per month minimum.

Financial Assistance: We finance $4,500 for 3 years at 10% interest.

Managerial Assistance: Unlimited phone consultation after training.

Training Provided: 3 weeks of training in Minneapolis, MN. Manual, video training, films, newsletters and phone consultation.

Information Submitted: January 1994

TUB & TILE
8808 Jolly Dr.
Ft. Washington, MD 20744
Telephone: (800) 938-8453 (301) 630-4400
Fax: (301) 630-0359
Mr. Wayne Stegeman, President

Number of Franchised Units: 0
Number of Company-Owned Units: 1
Number of Total Operating Units: 1

In Business Since: 1986   **Franchising Since:** 1991

Description of Operation: Bathtub reglazing and ceramic tile installation.

Equity Capital Needed: $19,900

Franchise Fee: $12,900

Royalty Fee: 0%

Financial Assistance: None.

Managerial Assistance: We provide marketing, sales and business management training.

Training Provided: 7 days of classroom and on-the-job training is provided.

Information Submitted: November 1993

WALLPAPERS TO GO
16825 N. Chase
Houston, TX 77060
Telephone: (800) 843-7094 (713) 874-0800
Fax: (713) 874-3655
Ms. Denise Hudson, Franchise Development Assistant

Number of Franchised Units: 61
Number of Company-Owned Units: 16
Number of Total Operating Units: 77

In Business Since: 1986   **Franchising Since:** 1986

Description of Operation: The nation's largest franchisor of in-stock specialty wallpaper stores, offering extensive selection of coordinating products, including window coverings, fabrics, decorative accessories, paint, along with thousands of rolls of wallcovering.

Equity Capital Needed: $129,000 - $155,000 (includes franchise fee).

Franchise Fee: $15,000 - $25,000

Royalty Fee: 6%

Financial Assistance: We provide a finance package - assistance with preparing a proposal for the bank and/or SBA. We participate in the VetFran program (finance up to 50% of the franchise fee.)

Managerial Assistance: We provide on-going merchandising support and programs, promotions, on-going store visits by operations field directors, lease negotiations, legal comments, site selection, national convention, store layout and design.

Training Provided: Training consists of 1 week of comprehensive training at corporate office. 1 - 2 weeks or more of in-store training prior to and during opening of store.

Information Submitted: December 1993

WATERBED EMPORIUM
7120 Krick Rd.
Walton Hills, OH 44146
Telephone: (800) 443-1163 (216) 786-8800
Fax: (216) 786-8807
Mr. Bruce G. Davis, President

Number of Franchised Units: 19
Number of Company-Owned Units: 0
Number of Total Operating Units: 19

In Business Since: 1985   **Franchising Since:** 1986

Description of Operation: The franchisee sells waterbeds and bedroom furniture at the retail level and buys all his/her products through Pacific Waterbed at the wholesale level, so a large investment in inventory is not required.

Equity Capital Needed: $50,000 - $80,000

Franchise Fee: $10,000

Royalty Fee: 3%

Financial Assistance: We would finance some of the inventory to help get the franchisee started.

Managerial Assistance: We go on-location to help the franchisee with hands-on assistance, as well as a management manual.

Training Provided: A training manual is provided, as well as on-the-job training in the store.

Information Submitted: November 1993

WINDOW-OLOGY
770-B N. Main St.
Orange, CA 92668
Telephone: (800) 303-2300 (714) 997-9675
Fax: (714) 771-0120
Mr. Jim Nichols, Vice President

Number of Franchised Units: 8
Number of Company-Owned Units: 1
Number of Total Operating Units: 9

In Business Since: 1987   **Franchising Since:** 1991

Description of Operation: Sales and installation of window coverings. We are a mobile shop-at-home concept.

Equity Capital Needed: $3,000 - $5,000

Franchise Fee: $20,000

Royalty Fee: 5%

Financial Assistance: Yes.

Managerial Assistance: Hotline assistance is available during normal business hours. Fax support is available 24 hours a day. All assistance is perpetual.

Training Provided: 2 - 3 weeks of classroom and in-field training is included, during which time there will be a factory tour and product presentations.

Information Submitted: December 1993

WINDOWEAR
770-B N. Main St.
Orange, CA 92688
Telephone: (800) 303-2300 (714) 997-9675
Fax: (714) 771-0120
Mr. Jim Nichols, Vice President

Number of Franchised Units: 4
Number of Company-Owned Units: 1
Number of Total Operating Units: 5

In Business Since: 1989   **Franchising Since:** 1991

Description of Operation: Mobility and in-house service is the driving force behind this window covering sales concept. A Windowear franchise makes you your own boss. You're in control of your future and you have the support of a successful corporation behind you. There is no costly store front overhead. You operate this business out of your own home.

Equity Capital Needed: $15,000 - $25,000

Franchise Fee: $20,000

Royalty Fee: 5%

Financial Assistance: Yes.

Managerial Assistance: In addition to the 2 weeks of formal training, we will support on-going, day-to-day operations over the phone. Also, we make occasional visits to the location for hands-on assistance.

Training Provided: We provide 2 weeks of training at our corporate office. This training is both classroom and hands-on in the field. We also provide an operations training manual.

Information Submitted: January 1994

WORLDWIDE REFINISHING SYSTEMS
1020 University Parks Dr.
Waco, TX 76707
Telephone: (800) 583-9099 (817) 756-2122
Fax: (817) 756-2938
Mr. Charles H. Wallis, Executive Vice President

Number of Franchised Units: 485
Number of Company-Owned Units: 0
Number of Total Operating Units: 485

In Business Since: 1971   **Franchising Since:** 1988

Description of Operation: Refinishing of bathtubs, ceramic tile, countertops, fiberglass showers, appliances, sinks and lavatories.

Equity Capital Needed: $15,000 - $45,000

Franchise Fee: $9,500 - $19,000

Royalty Fee: 5% - 7%

Financial Assistance: We finance half of the franchise fee for about 25% of our franchises. The decision to finance is made for deserving candidates only after all other options have been fully explored.

Managerial Assistance: We provide separate 800#'s for technical and marketing assistance, regional meetings and an annual convention. Marketing and management goals are set periodically with the marketing department.

Training Provided: Training is for 12 days. The training is for a turn-key operation in both technical matters and marketing, management and administration issues. No prior experience is necessary.

Information Submitted: December 1993

HOTELS AND MOTELS

AMERICAN MOTEL/HOTEL BROKERS
5333 N. Seventh St., # 300
Phoenix, AZ 85014
Telephone: (800) 999-2642 (602) 230-2110
Fax: (602) 230-9272
Mr. Robert Fitzgerald, President

Number of Franchised Units: 12
Number of Company-Owned Units: 0
Number of Total Operating Units: 12

In Business Since: 1972   **Franchising Since:** 1992

Description of Operation: Lodging real estate brokerage lists and sells hotels, motels, resorts and golf courses throughout North America.

Equity Capital Needed: $150,000 - $200,000

Franchise Fee: $25,000

Royalty Fee: 8%

Financial Assistance: Data not available.

Managerial Assistance: Offer training, set-up of office and business systems, advertising and new listings.

Training Provided: 1 - 2 weeks, depending on the experience of the franchisee.

Information Submitted: January 1994

AMERICINN MOTEL
18202 Minnetonka Blvd.
Deephaven, MN 55391
Telephone: (800) 634-3444 (612) 476-9020
Fax: (612) 476-7601
Mr. John R. Whisnant, President

Number of Franchised Units: 36
Number of Company-Owned Units: 0
Number of Total Operating Units: 36

In Business Since: 1987   **Franchising Since:** 1987

Description of Operation: Upper and economy lodging.

Equity Capital Needed: $350,000 - $500,000

Franchise Fee: $20,000

Royalty Fee: 4.5%

Financial Assistance: None.

Managerial Assistance: AmericInn provides complete training manuals, as well as on-going, continuous consultation with the local franchisees, in addition to an annual convention and regional workshops.

Training Provided: AmericInn provides complete training for managers, front-desk personnel and housekeepers.

Information Submitted: January 1994

BEST INN OF AMERICA
1205 Skyline Dr., P. O. Box 1719
Marion, IL 62959
Telephone: (800) TELL-US5 (618) 997-5454
Fax: (618) 993-5974
Ms. Lynn Brewer, Vice President Real Estate/Franchise Development

Number of Franchised Units: 4
Number of Company-Owned Units: 18
Number of Total Operating Units: 22

In Business Since: 1968   **Franchising Since:** 1983

Description of Operation: Limited service, up-scale motel. All suites and regular motels with a 100% satisfaction program.

Equity Capital Needed: $400,000 - $500,000

Franchise Fee: $10,000 for 75 units and under.

Royalty Fee: 2% of total sales.

Financial Assistance: Assistance is available through several services.

Managerial Assistance: Complete training for all new franchisees on management level.

Training Provided: Total training program and update training.

Information Submitted: January 1994

CHOICE HOTELS INTERNATIONAL
10750 Columbia Pike
Silver Spring, MD 20901
Telephone: (800) 547-0007 (301) 593-5600
Fax: (301) 681-4563
Mr. Jeffrey T. Williams, Senior Vice President - Development

Number of Franchised Units: 3005
Number of Company-Owned Units: 21
Number of Total Operating Units: 3026

In Business Since: 1934   **Franchising Since:** 1939

Description of Operation: Hotel/motel franchise. Products range from economy to mid-price to up-scale.

Equity Capital Needed: $350,000

Franchise Fee: Varies by brand: $15,000 - $40,000 minimum.

Royalty Fee: 4% - 8%

Financial Assistance: Choice will help prepare financing requests.

Managerial Assistance: Includes national and worldwide marketing ($40 million annual budget), worldwide reservations, advertising, public relations, monthly newsletter, product purchasing, renovation, guest relations, employee training and more.

Training Provided: Data not available.

Information Submitted: November 1993

CONDOTELS INTERNATIONAL
2703 Hwy. 17 S.
N. Myrtle Beach, SC 29582
Telephone: (800) 845-0631 (803) 272-8400
Fax: (803) 272-6556
Mr. Raymond L. Mann, Jr., Franchise Analyst

Number of Franchised Units: 4
Number of Company-Owned Units: 1
Number of Total Operating Units: 5

In Business Since: 1982   **Franchising Since:** 1989

Description of Operation: Operates as a hotel franchisor, except that the accommodations provided are condominium homes rather than hotel rooms. Franchisees manage rentals of resort condos for the condo homeowners and provide check-in and daily maid service.

Equity Capital Needed: $45,200 - $192,500

Franchise Fee: $35,000

Royalty Fee: 4%

Financial Assistance: None.

Managerial Assistance: On-going support.

Training Provided: 10 days at corporate headquarters. 2 days on-site.

Information Submitted: November 1993

COUNTRY LODGING BY CARLSON
P. O. Box 59159, Carlson Pkwy.
Minneapolis, MN 55459
Telephone: (800) 477-4200 (612) 449-1326
Fax: (612) 449-1338
Ms. Nancy Johnson, Senior Director of Development

Number of Franchised Units: 38
Number of Company-Owned Units: 0
Number of Total Operating Units: 38

In Business Since: 1987   **Franchising Since:** 1987

Description of Operation: Limited-service lodging facilities (inns, suites, resorts). Old-world charm, exterior architecture and interior decor.

Equity Capital Needed: $300,000

Franchise Fee: $20,000

Royalty Fee: Year 1: 2% gross room revenue; year 2: 2.5% gross room revenue; years 3 - 15: 3% gross room revenue.

Financial Assistance: Introduction to potential lenders.

Managerial Assistance: Complete operations manual, assistance with opening, training, operation set-up, teach PICI hiring (passion, intelligence, compassion, intensity), philosophical and technical training programs for easy application by manager, sales and marketing tools, graphic design and advertising support.

Training Provided: Guest service training, technical departmental training, management skills training, housekeeping skills seminar, sales training, 10-day on-site opening support.

Information Submitted: December 1993

COURTYARD BY MARRIOTT
1 Marriott Dr.
Washington, DC 20058
Telephone: (800) 638-8108 (301) 380-8521
Fax: (301) 380-6699
Ms. Maureen McEnerney, Hotel Development

Number of Franchised Units: 20
Number of Company-Owned Units: 196
Number of Total Operating Units: 216

In Business Since: 1983   **Franchising Since:** 1991

Description of Operation: Moderate-priced hotel chain with 220+ hotels throughout the United States and 4 in the United Kingdom.

Equity Capital Needed: Data not available.

Franchise Fee: $400 per room.

Royalty Fee: 4% / 4% / 5%

Financial Assistance: Data not available.

Managerial Assistance: Each hotel has a direct representative to assist with marketing, sales, operations and training. In addition, each hotel receives division support for systems, procurement and operations.

Training Provided: We provide classroom and on-site operation training, ranging from 2 - 6 weeks, manual and videos included. Other classroom training is offered in marketing and sales, guest services and financial.

Information Submitted: January 1994

DAYS INNS OF AMERICA
339 Jefferson Rd.
Parsippany, NJ 07054
Telephone: (800) 932-6726 (201) 428-9700
Fax: (201) 428-0526
Mr. John Osborne, Executive Vice President-Franchise Development

Number of Franchised Units: 1450
Number of Company-Owned Units: 0
Number of Total Operating Units: 1450

In Business Since: 1970   **Franchising Since:** 1970

Description of Operation: Days Inn of America is the licensor of Days Inn guest lodging facilities.

Equity Capital Needed: Estimate of initial investment required to construct and open ranges from $1.6 - $20.2 million.

Franchise Fee: $26,000 or $300 per room.

Royalty Fee: 5%

Financial Assistance: Mortgage financing, assistance in processing SBA loans and preferred vendor leasing are available.

Managerial Assistance: Full services are available, including site selection, design and construction, opening and other operational support, along with sales and marketing support.

Training Provided: Complete hotel/motel management and operations training are available, including classroom instruction, videos and on-site.

Information Submitted: April 1994

DOUBLETREE CLUB HOTEL SYSTEMS
410 N. 44th St., # 700
Phoenix, AZ 85008
Telephone: (800) 222-TREE (602) 220-6666
Fax: (602) 220-6753
Mr. David A. Sherf, Senior Vice President for Development

Number of Franchised Units: 11
Number of Company-Owned Units: 3
Number of Total Operating Units: 14

In Business Since: 1984   **Franchising Since:** 1985

Description of Operation: Limited-service lodging concept, combining 4-star quality accommodations, an airline-style "club" room and an affordable room rate. Targeted primarily toward the commercial business traveler, families on weekends and small groups. Doubletree Club Hotels offer the guest an exceptional price/value relationship.

Equity Capital Needed: $3,000,000 - $5,000,000

Franchise Fee: $30,000

Royalty Fee: 3%

Financial Assistance: None.

Managerial Assistance: Franchisor offers marketing and operations support, which are provided on an on-going basis from the corporate office in Phoenix, AZ. In addition, Doubletree has a regional manager of operations responsible for overseeing all Doubletree Club Hotels in the system.

Training Provided: A minimum 5-day training program, including system management, management techniques, personnel policies, etc. Periodically, training courses, conferences and seminars are also offered. Additional training programs are implemented as needed.

Information Submitted: January 1994

DOWNTOWNER INNS
1726 Montreal Circle
Tucker, GA 30084
Telephone: (800) 247-4677 (404) 270-1180
Fax: (404) 270-1077
Mr. Richard A. Johnson, Director of Franchise Development

Number of Franchised Units: 5
Number of Company-Owned Units: 0
Number of Total Operating Units: 5

In Business Since: 1973   **Franchising Since:** 1991

Description of Operation: Moderately-priced accommodations with all amenities.

Equity Capital Needed: Varies with size and complexity of project.

Franchise Fee: $100 per room. $10,000 minimum.

Royalty Fee: 4% or $395.

Financial Assistance: We assist in locating potential lenders and in the preparation of the loan package.

Managerial Assistance: A mandatory management seminar is conducted semi-annually.

Training Provided: On-site training for front desk and housekeeping staff is provided.

Information Submitted: January 1994

EMBASSY SUITES
6800 Poplar Ave., # 200
Memphis, TN 38138

Telephone: (800) EMBASSY (901) 758-3100
Fax: (901) 756-9479
Mr. Thomas L. Keltner, Senior Vice President of Development

Number of Franchised Units: 52
Number of Company-Owned Units: 55
Number of Total Operating Units: 107

In Business Since: 1983   Franchising Since: 1984

Description of Operation: Franchising and operation of Embassy Suites hotels.

Equity Capital Needed: $5,000,000 - $10,000,000

Franchise Fee: $500 per room, with a minimum of $100,000.

Royalty Fee: 4%

Financial Assistance: No.

Managerial Assistance: Yes.

Training Provided: Numerous programs are available.

Information Submitted: March 1994

FAIRFIELD INN BY MARRIOTT
1 Marriott Dr.
Washington, DC 20058
Telephone: (301) 380-5237
Fax: (301) 380-6699
Ms. Maureen McEnerney, Manager of Franchise Development

Number of Franchised Units: 52
Number of Company-Owned Units: 80
Number of Total Operating Units: 132

In Business Since: 1987   Franchising Since: 1990

Description of Operation: Economy lodging with a rooms-only concept.

Equity Capital Needed: Varies by project.

Franchise Fee: $200 - $375 per room.

Royalty Fee: 4% of room sales.

Financial Assistance: Standard programs are not currently available. Financial assistance is considered on a case-by-case basis, limited to labor, multi-unit, multi-product franchise partners or strategically important conversions.

Managerial Assistance: Each franchised hotel is managed in conjunction with the franchise partner's management team by the Fairfield Inn area management team.

Training Provided: Data not available.

Information Submitted: January 1994

HAMPTON INN & SUITES
6800 Poplar Ave., # 200
Memphis, TN 38138
Telephone: (800) HAMPTON (901) 758-3100
Fax: (901) 756-9479
Mr. Thomas L. Keltner, Senior Vice President of Development

Number of Franchised Units: 0
Number of Company-Owned Units: 0
Number of Total Operating Units: 0

In Business Since: 1983   Franchising Since: 1994

Description of Operation: Franchising and operation of Hampton Inn & Suites.

Equity Capital Needed: $1,000,000 - $2,500,000

Franchise Fee: $400 per room, with a minimum of $40,000.

Royalty Fee: 4%

Financial Assistance: Second mortgage financing is available.

Managerial Assistance: Yes.

Training Provided: Numerous programs are available.

Information Submitted: March 1994

HAMPTON INN HOTEL DIVISION
6800 Poplar Ave., # 200
Memphis, TN 38138
Telephone: (800) HAMPTON (901) 758-3100
Fax: (901) 756-9479
Mr. Thomas L. Keltner, Senior Vice President of Development

Number of Franchised Units: 339
Number of Company-Owned Units: 39
Number of Total Operating Units: 378

In Business Since: 1983   Franchising Since: 1983

Description of Operation: Franchising and operation of Hampton Inn Hotels.

Equity Capital Needed: $500,000 - $2,500,000

Franchise Fee: $400 per room, with a minimum of $40,000.

Royalty Fee: 4%

Financial Assistance: Lender referrals.

Managerial Assistance: Yes.

Training Provided: Numerous programs are available.

Information Submitted: March 1994

HAWTHORN SUITES HOTELS
400 Fifth Ave.
Waltham, MA 02154
Telephone: (617) 290-0175
Fax: (617) 290-0471
Mr. Paul T. White, Executive Vice President

Number of Franchised Units: 10
Number of Company-Owned Units: 5
Number of Total Operating Units: 15

In Business Since: 1986   Franchising Since: 1986

Description of Operation: Hawthorn Suites are limited service, all-suite hotels, geared to meet the needs of upper and mid-scale extended stay customers and the small meetings market.

Equity Capital Needed: Construction cost of hotel varies from $40,000 - $60,000 per suite. The cost of land is additional.

Franchise Fee: $400 per room or $50,000.

Royalty Fee: 2.5% - 4%

Financial Assistance: Limited financial assistance is possible on an individual basis.

Managerial Assistance: Full assistance is provided in site selection, architectural plans and FF & E review. Guidance is provided for pre-opening planning, staffing, training and marketing. Continuing operational consultation is provided. Every property receives a series of manuals on all phases of the operation. Our marketing suite program consists of a state-of-the-art 800#, computerized reservations system, consumer research, advertising campaigns and our Marketing Plus Program.

Training Provided: Operational seminars are offered in the areas of housekeeping and maintenance, front office, management techniques, marketing and sales throughout the year.

Information Submitted: March 1994

HOLIDAY INN WORLDWIDE
3 Ravinia Dr., # 2000
Atlanta, GA 30346
Telephone: (404) 604-2100
Fax: (404) 604-2107
Mr. Jimmy Thomas, Director of Franchise Marketing

Number of Franchised Units: 1608
Number of Company-Owned Units: 175
Number of Total Operating Units: 1783

In Business Since: 1951   **Franchising Since:** 1952

Description of Operation: Franchisor of hotel/motel properties, which include Holiday Inn Hotel, Holiday Inn Crown Plaza, Holiday Inn Crown Plaza Resorts, Holiday Inn Express, Holiday Inn Garden Court and Holiday Inn SunSpree Resorts.

Equity Capital Needed: 5% - 30%

Franchise Fee: $300 per room.

Royalty Fee: 5%

Financial Assistance: Through an in-house agency, GIAC, loans for refurbishment and development are available to qualified applicants.

Managerial Assistance: The franchise development team coordinates the application until just prior to opening. Our Road Scholars will open the hotel and provide instant training to the hotel personnel. Our field representatives will offer continuous on-site training programs to hotel personnel, including workshops. In-house representatives dedicated to specific hotels are available via a toll-free line to any answering questions the hotel or franchisee may have.

Training Provided: Same as above.

Information Submitted: January 1994

HOMEWOOD SUITES
6800 Poplar Ave., # 200
Memphis, TN 38138
Telephone: (800) CALL HOME (901) 758-3100
Fax: (901) 756-9479
Mr. Thomas L. Keltner, Senior Vice President of Development

Number of Franchised Units: 18
Number of Company-Owned Units: 8
Number of Total Operating Units: 26

In Business Since: 1988   **Franchising Since:** 1988

Description of Operation: Franchising and operation of Homewood Suites.

Equity Capital Needed: $1,500,000 - $3,500,000

Franchise Fee: $400 per room, with a minimum of $40,000.

Royalty Fee: 4%

Financial Assistance: Second mortgage financing is available.

Managerial Assistance: Yes.

Training Provided: Numerous programs are available.

Information Submitted: March 1994

HOSPITALITY FRANCHISE SYSTEMS
339 Jefferson Rd., P. O. Box 278
Parsippany, NJ 07054
Telephone: (800) 932-4677 (201) 428-9700
Fax: (201) 428-6057
Mr. John D. Snodgrass, President

Number of Franchised Units: 3790
Number of Company-Owned Units: 0
Number of Total Operating Units: 3790

In Business Since: 1990   **Franchising Since:** 1990

Description of Operation: HFS is the world's largest hotel franchisor, with over 3,700 Days Inn, Howard Johnson, Park Inns, Ramada and Super 8 hotels and over 370,000 rooms. A pure franchisor, HFS does not own or operate any of the hotel properties. Through royalty payments and reservation and marketing fees, HFS franchisees are entitled to not only use the brand names but the support services the Company offers, including marketing/advertising campaigns, training programs, central reservation systems and financial expertise.

Equity Capital Needed: Data not available.

Franchise Fee: $350 per room.

Royalty Fee: Days Inn - 6.5%; Howard Johnson - 4%; Park Inn 2.67% - 4%; Ramada - 4%.

Financial Assistance: HFS franchisees can now access financial resources for refinancing, acquisitions, new construction, renovation and leasing by simply calling a toll-free number. We have lenders that will provide competitive rates for qualifying franchisees and who are sensitive to the needs of our industry.

Managerial Assistance: An extensive 3 - 4 day orientation for new general managers, conducted at our home office. This is a mandatory program for all general managers new to the system within 6 months of taking over the position. This program trains managers on how to use the resources from Hospitality Franchise Systems. If further assistance is needed, the general managers from each property have a franchise service manager who is assigned to help them with any questions or anything else needed.

Training Provided: Several training seminars and sessions are available in housekeeping, front office, sales, food and beverage, management and supervisory skills, guest service, safety and security.

Information Submitted: March 1994

HOSPITALITY INTERNATIONAL
1726 Montreal Circle
Tucker, GA 30084
Telephone: (800) 247-4677 (404) 270-1180
Fax: (404) 270-1077
Mr. Richard A. Johnson, Director of Franchise Development

Number of Franchised Units: 348
Number of Company-Owned Units: 0
Number of Total Operating Units: 348

In Business Since: 1982   **Franchising Since:** 1982

Description of Operation: Hotel franchisor of Master Hosts Inns and Resorts, Red Carpet Inns, Scottish Inns, Passport Inns and Downtowner Inns, has over 375 franchised properties in 32 states, the Bahamas, Canada and South America. Hospitality Intl. is one of the fastest-growing hotel systems in the industry, providing tremendous support services - 24-hour reservation "ReservaHost" system, group sales and marketing, housekeeping and management training, creative services, reasonable fees and interest in the franchisee's success.

Equity Capital Needed: Varies.

Franchise Fee: $100 - $150 per room; $10,000 - $15,000 minimum.

Royalty Fee: 2.5% - 4.5%, or $350 - $435, whichever is greater.

Financial Assistance: We assist the franchisee in contacting potential lenders.

Managerial Assistance: Mandatory management seminar conducted semi-annually.

Training Provided: On-site training for front desk and housekeeping staff.

Information Submitted: November 1993

HOWARD JOHNSON FRANCHISE SYSTEMS
339 Jefferson Rd.
Parsippany, NJ 07054
Telephone: (800) 932-6726 (201) 428-9700
Fax: (201) 428-9700
Mr. John Osborne, Executive Vice President-Franchise Development

Number of Franchised Units: 600
Number of Company-Owned Units: 0
Number of Total Operating Units: 600

In Business Since: 1954   **Franchising Since:** 1954

Description of Operation: Howard Johnson Franchise Systems is the licensor of Howard Johnson guest lodging facilities.

Equity Capital Needed: An estimate of initial investment required to construct and open ranges from $1.6 - $20.2 million.

Franchise Fee: Data not available.

Royalty Fee: 5%

Financial Assistance: Mortgage financing, assistance in processing SBA loans and preferred vendor leasing are available.

Managerial Assistance: Full services available, including site selection, design and construction, opening and other operational support, as well as sales and marketing support.

Training Provided: Complete hotel/motel management and operations training is available, including classroom instruction, videos and on-site training.

Information Submitted: April 1994

INNSUITES HOTELS
P. O. Box 26907
Phoenix, AZ 85068
Telephone: (800) 842-4242
Fax: (602) 491-1008
Mr. Kelly Robinson

Number of Franchised Units: 4
Number of Company-Owned Units: 6
Number of Total Operating Units: 10

In Business Since: 1980   **Franchising Since:** 1984

Description of Operation: As a successful long-time owner/operator and franchisor in the all-suite hospitality industry, we offer the new property assistance in all phases of conversion through opening to include daily operations and accounting procedures. For property conversions, we work with the franchisee in developing a plan to align the property with the Company and all-suite industry standards. Our goal is to improve the bottom line of your business without sacrificing the quality of service.

Equity Capital Needed: Varies with size of operation. Hotel conversion suggested.

Franchise Fee: $15,000 deferred.

Royalty Fee: 1.5% or per cent of business sent.

Financial Assistance: None.

Managerial Assistance: We provide continuous managerial and technical assistance, as needed.

Training Provided: Management is required to attend a 2-week program at a designated corporate facility for classroom and hands-on management training. The designated person representing the owner must complete a 2-day seminar at the corporate office. Training is available for all positions of employment if desired.

Information Submitted: March 1994

KNIGHTS LODGING
26650 Emery Pkwy.
Cleveland, OH 44128
Telephone: (800) 843-5644 (216) 464-5055
Fax: (216) 464-2210
Mr. Roger J. Bloss, Executive VP Franchising/Development

Number of Franchised Units: 150
Number of Company-Owned Units: 29
Number of Total Operating Units: 179

In Business Since: 1991   **Franchising Since:** 1992

Description of Operation: Hotel/motel franchise and management company.

Equity Capital Needed: $100,000 +

Franchise Fee: $15,000

Royalty Fee: 8%

Financial Assistance: We provide access to co-operating financial institutions.

Managerial Assistance: Initial training at national business and education conference, then property managers can obtain daily support through 800# and manuals supplied by franchisor.

Training Provided: American Hotel/Motel Association Educational Institution provides training and video support, as well as a corporate team twice yearly. Regional training classes.

Information Submitted: January 1994

MASTER HOSTS INNS AND RESORTS
1726 Montreal Circle
Tucker, GA 30084
Telephone: (800) 247-4677 (404) 270-1180
Fax: (404) 270-1077
Mr. Richard A. Johnson, Director of Franchise Development

Number of Franchised Units: 40
Number of Company-Owned Units: 0
Number of Total Operating Units: 40

In Business Since: 1973   **Franchising Since:** 1982

Description of Operation: Moderately-priced accommodations with all amenities.

Equity Capital Needed: Varies with size and complexity of project.

Franchise Fee: $150 per room. $15,000 minimum.

Royalty Fee: 4.5% or $435.

Financial Assistance: We assist in locating potential lenders and in the preparation of the loan package.

Managerial Assistance: A mandatory management seminar is conducted semi-annually.

Training Provided: We offer on-site training for front desk and housekeeping staff.

Information Submitted: January 1994

MICROTEL
One Airport Way, # 200
Rochester, NY 14624
Telephone: (716) 436-6000
Fax: (716) 436-1865
Mr. George Justus, Senior Vice President of Franchise Development

Number of Franchised Units: 14
Number of Company-Owned Units: 0
Number of Total Operating Units: 14

In Business Since: 1986   **Franchising Since:** 1987

Description of Operation: Budget sector hotel chain.

Equity Capital Needed: $600,000

Franchise Fee: $25,000

Royalty Fee: 2.5%

Financial Assistance: Assistance is limited to providing introductions to potential lenders.

Managerial Assistance: In-house "consultants" available to work with franchisees as problem solvers and program developers.

Training Provided: Training programs are tailored to meet the franchisee's specific needs.

Information Submitted: January 1994

PARK INNS INTERNATIONAL
339 Jefferson Rd.
Parsippany, NJ 07054

Telephone: (800) 932-6726 (201) 428-9700
Fax: (201) 428-0526
Mr. John Osborne, Executive Vice President-Franchise Development

Number of Franchised Units: 108
Number of Company-Owned Units: 0
Number of Total Operating Units: 108

In Business Since: 1986   **Franchising Since:** 1986

Description of Operation: Park Inns International is the licensor of Park Inn International and Park Plaza guest lodging facilities. From 5-star Park Plaza to Park Inn International - full and/or limited service hotels.

Equity Capital Needed: Estimates of the initial investment required to construct and open range from $1.6 - $20.2 million.

Franchise Fee: $100 per room.

Royalty Fee: 1.9%

Financial Assistance: Mortgage financing, assistance in processing SBA loans and preferred vendor leasing are available.

Managerial Assistance: Full services available, including site selection, design and construction, opening and other operational support, along with sales and marketing support.

Training Provided: Complete hotel/motel management and operations training is available, including classroom instruction, videos and on-site training.

Information Submitted: April 1994

PASSPORT INN
1726 Montreal Circle
Tucker, GA 30084
Telephone: (800) 247-4677 (404) 270-1180
Fax: (404) 270-1077
Mr. Richard A. Johnson, Director of Franchise Development

Number of Franchised Units: 20
Number of Company-Owned Units: 0
Number of Total Operating Units: 20

In Business Since: 1973   **Franchising Since:** 1982

Description of Operation: Budget motels. Limited amenity lodging.

Equity Capital Needed: Varies with size and complexity of project.

Franchise Fee: $100 per room. $10,000 minimum.

Royalty Fee: 3.5% or $350.

Financial Assistance: We assist in locating potential lenders and in the preparation of the loan package.

Managerial Assistance: A mandatory management seminar is conducted semi-annually.

Training Provided: We provide on-site training for front desk and housekeeping staff.

Information Submitted: January 1994

RAMADA INNS
339 Jefferson Rd.
Parsippany, NJ 07054
Telephone: (800) 932-6726 (201) 428-9700
Fax: (201) 428-0526
Mr. John Osborne, Executive Vice President-Franchise Development

Number of Franchised Units: 650
Number of Company-Owned Units: 0
Number of Total Operating Units: 650

In Business Since: 1959   **Franchising Since:** 1959

Description of Operation: Ramada Franchise Systems is the licensor of Ramada guest lodging facilities.

Equity Capital Needed: Estimate of initial investment required to construct and open ranges from $1.6 - $20.2 million.

Franchise Fee: $30,000 or $300 per room.

Royalty Fee: 4%

Financial Assistance: Mortgage financing, assistance in processing SBA loans and preferred vendor leasing are available.

Managerial Assistance: Full services are available, including site selection, design and construction, opening and other operational support, along with sales and marketing support.

Training Provided: Complete hotel/motel management and operations training is available, including classroom instruction, videos and on-site.

Information Submitted: March 1994

RED CARPET INN
1726 Montreal Circle
Tucker, GA 30084
Telephone: (800) 247-4677 (404) 270-1180
Fax: (404) 270-1077
Mr. Richard A. Johnson, Director of Franchise Development

Number of Franchised Units: 140
Number of Company-Owned Units: 0
Number of Total Operating Units: 140

In Business Since: 1969   **Franchising Since:** 1982

Description of Operation: Moderately-priced accommodations with all amenities.

Equity Capital Needed: Varies with size and complexity of project.

Franchise Fee: $150 per room. $15,000 minimum.

Royalty Fee: 4% or $395.

Financial Assistance: We assist in locating potential lenders and in the preparation of the loan package.

Managerial Assistance: A mandatory management seminar is conducted semi-annually.

Training Provided: We provide on-site training for front desk and housekeeping staff.

Information Submitted: January 1994

SCOTTISH INNS
1726 Montreal Circle
Tucker, GA 30084
Telephone: (800) 247-4677 (404) 270-1180
Fax: (404) 270-1077
Mr. Richard A. Johnson, Director of Franchise Development

Number of Franchised Units: 140
Number of Company-Owned Units: 0
Number of Total Operating Units: 140

In Business Since: 1973   **Franchising Since:** 1982

Description of Operation: Budget motels. Limited amenity lodging.

Equity Capital Needed: Varies with size and complexity of project.

Franchise Fee: $100 per room. $10,000 minimum.

Royalty Fee: 3.5% or $350.

Financial Assistance: We assist in locating potential lenders and in the preparation of the loan package.

Managerial Assistance: A mandatory management seminar is conducted semi-annually.

Training Provided: We offer on-site training for front desk and housekeeping staff.

Information Submitted: January 1994

SUPER 8 MOTELS
1910 Eighth Ave., NE
Aberdeen, SD 57402

Telephone: (800) 843-1960 (605) 225-2272
Fax: (605) 225-5060
Mr. Dale Aasen, Executive Vice President of Sales and Marketing

Number of Franchised Units: 1083
Number of Company-Owned Units: 0
Number of Total Operating Units: 1083

In Business Since: 1972   **Franchising Since:** 1972

Description of Operation: Super 8 Motels is the franchisor of "Economy Motels," which offer a full-size room with color TV, direct dial phones, attractive decor and VIP Frequent Traveler Club.

Equity Capital Needed: An estimate of initial investment required to construct and open ranges from $450,000 - $3,000,000.

Franchise Fee: $20,000

Royalty Fee: 4%

Financial Assistance: Mortgage financing, assistance in processing SBA loans and preferred vendor leasing are available.

Managerial Assistance: Full services are available, including site selection, design and construction, opening and other operational support, along with sales and marketing support.

Training Provided: Complete hotel and motel management and operations training are available, including classroom instruction, videos and on-site training.

Information Submitted: April 1994

INSURANCE

ISU INTERNATIONAL
100 Pine St., # 1700
San Francisco, CA 94111
Telephone: (415) 788-9810
Fax: (415) 397-5530
Ms. Nyla Starr, Senior Vice President

Number of Franchised Units: 85
Number of Company-Owned Units: 0
Number of Total Operating Units: 85

In Business Since: 1979   **Franchising Since:** 1980

Description of Operation: Conversion franchises for independent insurance agencies.

Equity Capital Needed: Not applicable.

Franchise Fee: $12,500

Royalty Fee: Flat fee plus 3%.

Financial Assistance: None.

Managerial Assistance: Regional office staffs.

Training Provided: 3 days for new franchisee principals; 5 days for CSR's and producers in agencies.

Information Submitted: January 1994

LAWN AND GARDEN

BAREFOOT GRASS LAWN SERVICE
450 W. Wilson Bridge Rd.
Worthington, OH 43085
Telephone: (614) 846-1800
Fax: (614) 846-5431
Mr. David Kuhlman, Franchise Co-ordinator

Number of Franchised Units: 36
Number of Company-Owned Units: 48
Number of Total Operating Units: 84

In Business Since: 1976   **Franchising Since:** 1976

Description of Operation: Barefoot Grass provides professional, granular lawn care to residential and commercial lawns. Fertilizers, weed controls, insect controls and disease controls are applied on a scheduled basis, following prescribed programs. Enjoyable outdoor work environment.

Equity Capital Needed: Minimum $25,000.

Franchise Fee: $25,000

Royalty Fee: 10%

Financial Assistance: None.

Managerial Assistance: Barefoot Grass provides continuing management services for the duration of the franchise in such areas as computer services, including customer records; bookkeeping, including accounts receivable, payroll; marketing and advertising; purchasing and inventory control. Operating and technical manuals and updates are provided. Forms and supplies are available. Regional managers are available to work closely with franchisees and visit regularly to assist with problem solving and quality control.

Training Provided: Technical agronomic training, sales training and business training are provided. Training is conducted at the franchisee's site or at the franchisor's headquarters in Worthington, OH, a Columbus suburb. Formal introductory programs last at least 4 days, with follow-up provided as needed.

Information Submitted: March 1994

CLINTAR GROUNDSKEEPING SERVICES
4210 Midland Ave.
Scarborough, ON M1V 4S6 CAN
Telephone: (800) 361-3542 (416) 291-1611
Fax: (416) 291-6792
Mr. Bob Goodwin, Vice President

Number of Franchised Units: 10
Number of Company-Owned Units: 2
Number of Total Operating Units: 12

In Business Since: 1973   **Franchising Since:** 1986

Description of Operation: Clintar provides commercial groundskeeping services year round - landscape maintenance, snow and ice control, power sweeping, light construction, tree care and irrigation maintenance.

Equity Capital Needed: $50,000 - $100,000

Franchise Fee: $30,000

Royalty Fee: 8%

Financial Assistance: Assistance includes the development of budgets and cash flows, as well as bank presentation.

Managerial Assistance: As needed. We provide minimum monthly financial and business review.

Training Provided: Training is provided for the first full year, classroom and on-site. On-going, as needed.

Information Submitted: January 1994

EMERALD GREEN LAWN CARE
9333 N. Meridian St.
Indianapolis, IN 46260
Telephone: (800) 783-0981 (317) 846-9940
Fax: (317) 846-1696
Mr. Rick Knepper, Chief Executive Officer

Number of Franchised Units: 12
Number of Company-Owned Units: 1
Number of Total Operating Units: 13

In Business Since: 1984   **Franchising Since:** 1985

Description of Operation: Full-service residential lawn, tree and shrub care program.

Equity Capital Needed: $60,000 - $90,000

Franchise Fee: $15,000

Royalty Fee: 8.5% - 6.5%

Financial Assistance: Not available.

Managerial Assistance: We provide an initial 12 days of training, on-going field service, technical support, marketing, administration, staff training, financial planning and safety. Operations and technical manuals provided. Annual seminars and regional meetings.

Training Provided: The initial training, 12 days at the Company head-quarters, and in-field experience, cover all phases of the business.

Information Submitted: March 1994

ENVIRO MASTERS LAWN CARE
Box 178
Caledon East, ON LON 1E0 CAN
Telephone: (905) 584-9592
Fax: (905) 584-0402
Mr. Martin Fielding, President

Number of Franchised Units: 24
Number of Company-Owned Units: 2
Number of Total Operating Units: 26

In Business Since: 1987   **Franchising Since:** 1991

Description of Operation: Lawn care company, specializing in organic products and environmentally-considerate applications. We provide seasonal programs throughout the growing season.

Equity Capital Needed: $15,000 - $20,000

Franchise Fee: $15,000 - $20,000

Royalty Fee: 5%

Financial Assistance: Data not available.

Managerial Assistance: Enviro Masters provides a complete manual with continuous consultation and on-going support. Franchisees receive regular newsletters and attend regular meetings and seminars.

Training Provided: Our training program is on-going thorough the first year of business. This includes in-field training, as well as marketing, sales, administration and turf management.

Information Submitted: January 1994

LAWN DOCTOR
142 Hwy. 34, Box 512
Matawan, NJ 07747
Telephone: (800) 631-5660 (908) 583-4700
Fax: (908) 583-8254
Mr. Edward L. Reid, National Franchise Director

Number of Franchised Units: 292
Number of Company-Owned Units: 1
Number of Total Operating Units: 293

In Business Since: 1967   **Franchising Since:** 1967

Description of Operation: Offering an automated lawn-care service, Lawn Doctor provides all-natural and regular fertilization, plus control applications using the exclusive Turf Tamer equipment manufactured and used only by Lawn Doctor. Additionally, a broad range of cultural care practices, utilizing Integrated Pest Management to develop the health and beauty of turf and landscape areas with environmentally-balanced care.

Equity Capital Needed: $20,000

Franchise Fee: None.

Royalty Fee: 10%

Financial Assistance: Up to $12,000 - 6 years at 12% interest.

Managerial Assistance: On-going operations support, seminars and group meetings. 2-year new dealer support assistance.

Training Provided: 2-week intensive training program. 2-year concentrated new dealer support assistance.

Information Submitted: November 1993

LIQUI-GREEN LAWN CARE
9601 N. Allen Rd.
Peoria, IL 61615
Telephone: (800) 747-5211 (309) 243-5211
Fax: (309) 243-5247
Mr. C. Millard Dailey, Director

Number of Franchised Units: 25
Number of Company-Owned Units: 1
Number of Total Operating Units: 26

In Business Since: 1953   **Franchising Since:** 1971

Description of Operation: Lawn-care maintenance and sales.

Equity Capital Needed: $5,000 - $6,000

Franchise Fee: $5,000

Royalty Fee: $2,500 to start and graduated up to cap of $6,000.

Financial Assistance: To qualified buyers, we can put you in business for as low as $2,500, but you must have at least another $2,500 to purchase phone, insurance, advertising and working capital.

Managerial Assistance: Purchasing power, agronomics, technical assistance, an 800#, availability to answer any and all questions, monthly newsletter and annual seminars.

Training Provided: All training will be in the assigned territory with a hands-on sales representative.

Information Submitted: January 1994

MR. TREES
P. O. Box 1609
San Anselmo, CA 94960
Telephone: (415) 485-1180
Fax: (415) 485-1837
Mr. Tripp Curtis, President

Number of Franchised Units: 1
Number of Company-Owned Units: 1
Number of Total Operating Units: 2

In Business Since: 1983   **Franchising Since:** 1993

Description of Operation: Mr. Trees provides environmentally-sound holistic tree and shrub care.

Equity Capital Needed: $100,000

Franchise Fee: $28,500

Royalty Fee: 6%

Financial Assistance: None.

Managerial Assistance: We provide training in all areas of the operation and back-up support in all areas of the operation.

Training Provided: We offer 3 weeks of total training - 1 week of training as a technical arborist, 1 week of technical, operational and sales training and 1 week of sales and operational training during the franchisee's first week of operation.

Information Submitted: March 1994

NITRO-GREEN PROFESSIONAL LAWN & TREE CARE
2791 F. N. Texas St., # 300
Fairfield, CA 94533

Telephone: (800) 982-5296 (707) 428-4281
Fax: (707) 428-5297
Mr. Roger Albrecht, President/Chief Executive Officer

Number of Franchised Units: 38
Number of Company-Owned Units: 2
Number of Total Operating Units: 40

In Business Since: 1977   **Franchising Since:** 1979

Description of Operation: Automated professional lawn and tree care services.

Equity Capital Needed: $40,000 - $45,000

Franchise Fee: $17,400

Royalty Fee: 7%

Financial Assistance: Financing of equipment and a portion of franchise fee is available.

Managerial Assistance: We provide a toll-free hotline, complete business planning, market planning and guidance, as well as periodic on-site visits.

Training Provided: We offer 1 week of training at the corporate headquarters and 1 week of on-site opening.

Information Submitted: January 1994

NUTRITE
P. O. Box 1000
Brossard, PQ J4Z 3N2 CAN
Telephone: (800) 561-7449 (514) 462-2555
Fax: (514) 462-3634
M. Jacques Cardinal, Director

Number of Franchised Units: 40
Number of Company-Owned Units: 0
Number of Total Operating Units: 40

In Business Since: 1964   **Franchising Since:** 1984

Description of Operation: Lawn care.

Equity Capital Needed: $40,000

Franchise Fee: $15,000

Royalty Fee: $3,500.

Financial Assistance: None.

Managerial Assistance: Courses are given during the season to all franchisees.

Training Provided: Training is provided all year for franchisees and employee of franchisees. There are 3 major meetings per year for training with our specialists.

Information Submitted: January 1994

SERVISTAR HOME & GARDEN SHOWPLACE
P. O. Box 1510
Butler, PA 16003
Telephone: (412) 283-4567
Fax: (412) 284-6623
Mr. Dave Meder, General Manager

Number of Franchised Units: 172
Number of Company-Owned Units: 0
Number of Total Operating Units: 172

In Business Since: 1988   **Franchising Since:** 1988

Description of Operation: A full-line retail garden center, featuring nursery stock, soil, fertilizer, gift department, crafts, outdoor equipment and much more.

Equity Capital Needed: $75,000 +

Franchise Fee: $1,500

Royalty Fee: $4,800 a year.

Financial Assistance: SBA and National Co-operative Bank.

Managerial Assistance: We provide store design, layout, set-up, ordering, advertising, supplies and agricultural guidance.

Training Provided: We offer owner clinics, along with field sales support.

Information Submitted: March 1994

SPRING-GREEN LAWN AND TREE CARE
11927 Spaulding School Dr.
Plainfield, IL 60544
Telephone: (800) 435-4051 (815) 436-8777
Fax: (815) 436-9056
Mr. Bill Ticknor, Director of Franchise Development

Number of Franchised Units: 119
Number of Company-Owned Units: 11
Number of Total Operating Units: 130

In Business Since: 1977   **Franchising Since:** 1977

Description of Operation: A national network of lawn and tree care businesses committed to beautifying our earth.

Equity Capital Needed: $50,000 - $60,000

Franchise Fee: $30,000

Royalty Fee: 9% - 6%

Financial Assistance: Data not available.

Managerial Assistance: We offer a thorough 1-week initial training program. This program is classroom and practical training, consisting of goal setting and planning, lawn-care theory and technology, field operations, equipment operation and maintenance, computerized and bookkeeping management, sales and promotion. This is all backed with customized reference and audio/video tools that become part of your personal reference library.

Training Provided: Data not available.

Information Submitted: March 1994

TERRA SYSTEMS
P. O. Box 220706
Charlotte, NC 28222
Telephone: (704) 522-0310
Mr. Bill Jones, President

Number of Franchised Units: 0
Number of Company-Owned Units: 1
Number of Total Operating Units: 1

In Business Since: 1992   **Franchising Since:** 1994

Description of Operation: Organic and organic-based lawn care services, integrated pest management-based tree and shrub care.

Equity Capital Needed: $35,000

Franchise Fee: $22,000

Royalty Fee: 7%

Financial Assistance: None.

Managerial Assistance: The Company owner and 1 other individual are required to attend training at Terra Systems' main office.

Training Provided: Training includes all aspects of organic lawn care and tree and shrub care, sales, management, soil types, grasses and all associated problems (i.e. weeds, diseases), tree and shrub identification and associated concerns (i.e. disease, insects, etc.), plus methods of care. 2 weeks of in-house training at Company premises, then a minimum of 3 field visits at the franchisee's location.

Information Submitted: April 1994

WEED MAN
2399 Royal Windsor Dr.
Mississauga, ON L5J 1K9 CAN

161

Telephone: (905) 823-8550
Fax: (905) 823-4594
Mr. Michael Kernaghan, Director of Franchise Development

Number of Franchised Units: 110
Number of Company-Owned Units: 3
Number of Total Operating Units: 113

In Business Since: 1970   Franchising Since: 1977

Description of Operation: Residential lawn care services.

Equity Capital Needed: $25,000 - $750,000

Franchise Fee: $25,000

Royalty Fee: $7,600 per production truck per year.

Financial Assistance: None.

Managerial Assistance: Complete support in technical, administration, marketing and sales is provided.

Training Provided: We offer 1 week of orientation, followed by on-going seminars.

Information Submitted: February 1994

OPTICAL

AMERICAN VISION CENTERS
90 John St., 26th Fl.
New York, NY 10038
Telephone: (800) 232-5558 (212) 385-1000
Fax: (212) 385-1149
Mr. Seth Poppel, President

Number of Franchised Units: 51
Number of Company-Owned Units: 5
Number of Total Operating Units: 56

In Business Since: 1977   Franchising Since: 1979

Description of Operation: Franchisor of optical stores, providing eyecare (optometric services) and eyewear (frames, lenses, contact lenses and sunglasses). Featuring name brands. Note: All franchisees must have optical background as an optometrist, optician or store manager.

Equity Capital Needed: $15,000 - $25,000 down payment. $20,000 - $30,000 working capital.

Franchise Fee: $10,000

Royalty Fee: 8.5%

Financial Assistance: The Company directly provides up to 90% financing and arranges accounts with key product and equipment vendors. Company will also support franchisee in obtaining SBA and/or bank financing.

Managerial Assistance: Franchisees must have significant prior optical background. Support provided for purchasing, advertising, legal, operations, etc. on an "as-needed" basis. Detailed operating manual provided.

Training Provided: "As-needed" training, which should be minimal.

Information Submitted: November 1993

EVER VISION
235 Hunters View
Roswell, GA 30075
Telephone: (800) 925-0194 (404) 594-0974
Fax: (404) 518-1894
Ms. Cheryl Keeter, President

Number of Franchised Units: 0
Number of Company-Owned Units: 2
Number of Total Operating Units: 2

In Business Since: 1992   Franchising Since: 1993

Description of Operation: Manufacture and distribution of bulk windshield washer fluid and dispensers (coin-op)

Equity Capital Needed: $100,000

Franchise Fee: $27,000

Royalty Fee: 6%

Financial Assistance: Assistance in applying for funding.

Managerial Assistance: At start-up - 2 weeks before and 2 weeks after opening. On-going - field visits, 800# support line, newsletters.

Training Provided: Training includes 1 week at our facility, 1 week at a chosen location and 2 weeks after start-up to work out any "bugs."

Information Submitted: January 1994

FIRST OPTOMETRY EYECARE CENTERS
32600 Gratiot Ave.
Roseville, MI 48066
Telephone: (313) 296-7800
Fax: (313) 294-2623
Mr. D. M. Borsand, Chief Executive Officer

Number of Franchised Units: 18
Number of Company-Owned Units: 20
Number of Total Operating Units: 38

In Business Since: 1980   Franchising Since: 1981

Description of Operation: Sale of eyecare services, eyeglasses and contact lenses.

Equity Capital Needed: $150,000 - $250,000

Franchise Fee: $10,000

Royalty Fee: 7%

Financial Assistance: Not available.

Managerial Assistance: Field assistant, initial training course, on-going training courses and weekly manager's meetings.

Training Provided: All aspects of how to deliver services and products and make people who buy them happy.

Information Submitted: January 1994

NUVISION
2284 S. Ballenger Hwy., Box 2600
Flint, MI 48501
Telephone: (800) 733-5468 (313) 767-0900
Fax: (313) 767-6390
Ms. Joanne Holmquist, Manager of Franchise Operations

Number of Franchised Units: 38
Number of Company-Owned Units: 73
Number of Total Operating Units: 111

In Business Since: 1949   Franchising Since: 1983

Description of Operation: Retailer of eyeglasses, contact lenses, accessories and supplies, with complete optometric facilities.

Equity Capital Needed: $75,000 - $500,000

Franchise Fee: $15,000

Royalty Fee: 8.5% and 7% advertising.

Financial Assistance: Yes, to qualifying applicants.

Managerial Assistance: Complete corporate staff support.

Training Provided: On-going.

Information Submitted: January 1994

PROCARE VISION CENTERS
926 N. 21st St.
Newark, OH 43055

Telephone: (800) 837-5569 (614) 366-7341
Fax: (614) 366-5453
Dr. Eva K. Pound-Bickle, Vice President

Number of Franchised Units: 18
Number of Company-Owned Units: 1
Number of Total Operating Units: 19

In Business Since: 1981   **Franchising Since:** 1985

Description of Operation: ProCare provides vision care products and services through franchises owned and operated by licensed vision care professionals. The success of each and every franchisee has always been a high priority. That success is achieved through the constant support and assistance of a strong and experienced corporate staff. ProCare Vision Centers help caring vision professionals compete through franchising.

Equity Capital Needed: $30,000 - $200,000

Franchise Fee: $8,000

Royalty Fee: 5%

Financial Assistance: Relationships with lending and leasing institutions have been established that allow the franchisee the opportunity to acquire funds.

Managerial Assistance: Each prospective and current franchisee receives extensive on-going information on merchandise, supplies, products, equipment, location, construction and marketing, as well as on-going computer support. Complete training manuals and weekly communications, as well as monthly newsletters, are used to further enhance the on-going support of the franchisor.

Training Provided: Training for the franchisee, managers and staff is available at the corporate headquarters and at the franchisee's office. The prescribed training at the corporate headquarters takes place 1 - 2 weeks prior to the opening of the office and for a period of 3 - 8 business days. On-site training is available at the franchisee's office for 1 week prior to opening. Additional training for new staff members is available on an on-going basis.

Information Submitted: March 1994

READING GLASSES-TO-GO
9131 King Arthur Dr.
Dallas, TX 75247
Telephone: (214) 631-6082
Fax: (214) 688-1046
Mr. Robert Granoff, President

Number of Franchised Units: 4
Number of Company-Owned Units: 6
Number of Total Operating Units: 10

In Business Since: 1987   **Franchising Since:** 1992

Description of Operation: Retail stores selling optical-quality, designer-style reading glasses at affordable prices. Instant gratification.

Equity Capital Needed: $71,900 - $102,900

Franchise Fee: $19,000 (included in equity range).

Royalty Fee: 6%

Financial Assistance: None.

Managerial Assistance: Approximately 10 - 12 days at the Dallas, TX training center and approximately 7 additional days when store opens. Periodic visits to stores.

Training Provided: Same as above.

Information Submitted: November 1993

SINGER / SPECS
1235 Westlakes Dr., # 160
Berwyn, PA 19312

Telephone: (800) 343-4786 (215) 875-8814
Fax: (215) 695-0886
Ms. Karen Culp, Franchise Director

Number of Franchised Units: 29
Number of Company-Owned Units: 7
Number of Total Operating Units: 36

In Business Since: 1946   **Franchising Since:** 1986

Description of Operation: Singer / Specs offers the franchising option that allows professionals to compete with the large optical chains and superstores. Our philosophy allows the owner/operator to retain the commitment to quality eyecare, while Singer / Specs provides a comprehensive practice management system, including everything from site selection and power buying to proven merchandising and traffic generating techniques.

Equity Capital Needed: $15,000 - $159,000

Franchise Fee: $15,000

Royalty Fee: 7%

Financial Assistance: Singer / Specs has a 90% financing program available for qualified franchisees.

Managerial Assistance: Singer / Specs offers continual assistance through regional support manager visits, personal meetings with the president of the Company, a direct 800# hotline, quarterly management seminars, a complete policies and procedures manual, along with employee, marketing and sales handbooks.

Training Provided: Singer / Specs provides in-depth training on technical developments in the optical industry, as well as new ways to manage and improve the business. This training begins with an intensive classroom and in-store instruction 7 - 30 days prior to grand opening (depending on the background and experience of the individual). An additional 3 days of on-site training during grand opening. The training process continues throughout the relationship with on-going training and seminars.

Information Submitted: December 1993

PET SHOPS

CANINE COUNSELORS
1660 Southern Blvd.
West Palm Beach, FL 33406
Telephone: (800) 456-DOGS (407) 640-3970
Fax: (407) 640-3973
Mr. Robert Ward, President

Number of Franchised Units: 4
Number of Company-Owned Units: 3
Number of Total Operating Units: 7

In Business Since: 1982   **Franchising Since:** 1987

Description of Operation: Professional dog training and behavior problem-solving. Schools provide services on location, in client's home or business, with lifetime training warranty.

Equity Capital Needed: $39,000

Franchise Fee: $29,000

Royalty Fee: 7%, or $100 per week minimum.

Financial Assistance: On-going training and support of franchisees and their employees. Sale and training services provided by franchisor. Operations manual, all data entry provided by franchisor, monthly report and newsletter.

Managerial Assistance: Franchise meetings provide various workshops on business and employee management skills. Individual assistance quarterly on location by franchisor provides franchisee with local support.

Training Provided: 2 weeks at home office in West Palm Beach, FL, followed by 2 weeks on location in franchisee's new territory.

Information Submitted: November 1993

CAT'S PAJAMAS, THE
P. O. Box 48
Lincolnville, ME 04849
Telephone: (207) 789-5139
Ms. Toni R. Miele, President

Number of Franchised Units: 1
Number of Company-Owned Units: 1
Number of Total Operating Units: 2

In Business Since: 1989   **Franchising Since:** 1991

Description of Operation: Unique boarding and grooming facility that caters to felines and their owners.

Equity Capital Needed: $30,000 - $40,000

Franchise Fee: $10,000

Royalty Fee: 5% of annual gross revenues.

Financial Assistance: We do not finance. We refer to state and federally-funded programs targeted for women entrepreneurs.

Managerial Assistance: Continuous managerial training and assistance provided on an as-needed basis, including public relations, advertising, marketing, analysis and bookkeeping.

Training Provided: 1 week of on-site training and comprehensive operations manual. On-going consultation and support for the life of the contract.

Information Submitted: November 1993

CHERRYBROOK
P. O. Box 15, Rte. 57
Broadway, NJ 08808
Telephone: (800) 524-0820 (908) 689-7979
Fax: (908) 689-7988
Mr. Wayne Ferguson, President

Number of Franchised Units: 8
Number of Company-Owned Units: 1
Number of Total Operating Units: 9

In Business Since: 1968   **Franchising Since:** 1990

Description of Operation: Full-service dog and cat supplies - with retail convenience, at wholesale prices.

Equity Capital Needed: $70,000 - $100,000

Franchise Fee: $16,000

Royalty Fee: None.

Financial Assistance: The franchisee provides his/her own financing.

Managerial Assistance: Representatives from franchisor visit franchise locations monthly to help with promotions, merchandising, etc.

Training Provided: 1 week of training provided at Company headquarters prior to franchise opening.

Information Submitted: November 1993

PAWS & CLAWS PET NUTRITION CENTERS
6465 Millcreek Dr., # 205
Mississauga, ON L5N 5R3 CAN
Telephone: (800) 387-8335 (905) 567-4180
Fax: (905) 567-5355
Mr. George Kostopoulos, Director of Franchise Development

Number of Franchised Units: 4
Number of Company-Owned Units: 2
Number of Total Operating Units: 6

In Business Since: 1986   **Franchising Since:** 1990

Description of Operation: Specialty retailer, dedicated to providing for the total nutritional needs of pets by offering a complete line of quality pet foods and supplies. Knowledgeable staff which is extensively trained on animal care and maintenance.

Equity Capital Needed: $35,000

Franchise Fee: $25,000

Royalty Fee: 6%

Financial Assistance: Financial assistance through lending institution.

Managerial Assistance: On-going management support, store visits, newsletter and central purchasing.

Training Provided: 2 weeks of on-site training, educating the franchisee on the day-to-day procedures necessary for the successful operation of the business.

Information Submitted: November 1993

PET NANNY OF AMERICA
1000 Long Blvd., # 9
Lansing, MI 48911
Telephone: (517) 694-4400
Ms. Rebecca A. Brevitz, President

Number of Franchised Units: 16
Number of Company-Owned Units: 1
Number of Total Operating Units: 17

In Business Since: 1983   **Franchising Since:** 1986

Description of Operation: Franchisees provide professional, personalized in-home pet care when owners are away or otherwise unable to provide the needed care. Additional home-watch services are provided free of charge, i.e. mail and newspaper pick-up, plants, lights on and off, trash set-out, etc.

Equity Capital Needed: $1,500 - $4,500

Franchise Fee: $8,700

Royalty Fee: 5%, or $25 per week minimum.

Financial Assistance: Based on the application and personal interview, Pet Nanny of America will provide in-house financing, covering up to 50% of the initial franchise fee.

Managerial Assistance: Included in training program. Corporate principals are always available for consultation and will, if possible, visit the new location to assist in initial marketing.

Training Provided: We provide a training program of 4 days in duration, covering all aspects of business operation (marketing, office management and client interaction), as well as hands-on animal handling. Video tapes developed by veterinarian are included in package for use by franchisee in training future representatives.

Information Submitted: November 1993

PET PALS
8301 E. Prentice Ave., # 300
Englewood, CO 80111
Telephone: (800) 275-9000 (303) 771-8251
Fax: (303) 773-1332
Mr. Johnny M. Wilson, Franchise Development

Number of Franchised Units: 0
Number of Company-Owned Units: 11
Number of Total Operating Units: 11

In Business Since: 1983   **Franchising Since:** 1993

Description of Operation: Boutique strip center retail site, offering accessories to the public for pet products, including a proprietary line of foods and other products.

Equity Capital Needed: $95,000 - $100,000

Franchise Fee: $22,500

Royalty Fee: 6%

Financial Assistance: In special cases, the franchisor may provide up to 50% financing. The franchisor gives assistance in obtaining financing.

Managerial Assistance: We provide operational on-site learning, manuals, merchandising, annual meeting, promotional program, newsletters, continuous support and an 800# support line.

Training Provided: Training includes 6 days of training in the home office and 1 week of on-site training. Opening support.

Information Submitted: March 1994

PET VALU
7300 Warden Ave., # 400
Markham, ON L3R 9Z6 CAN
Telephone: (905) 946-1200
Fax: (905) 946-0659
Mr. David J. Wheat, Director of Franchise Development

Number of Franchised Units: 143
Number of Company-Owned Units: 23
Number of Total Operating Units: 166

In Business Since: 1976   **Franchising Since:** 1987

Description of Operation: Sale of pet foods and pet supplies.

Equity Capital Needed: $35,000 - $135,000

Franchise Fee: $12,000

Royalty Fee: 6%

Financial Assistance: None.

Managerial Assistance: Dedicated franchise field consultant.

Training Provided: 3 weeks of total training provided - 1 week of classroom training and 2 weeks of store training.

Information Submitted: November 1993

PET XTRA
7805 Arjons Dr.
San Diego, CA 92126
Telephone: (800) 748-5577 (619) 693-3639
Fax: (619) 693-1120
Ms. Cyndi Etnyre, Director of Franchise Development

Number of Franchised Units: 21
Number of Company-Owned Units: 6
Number of Total Operating Units: 27

In Business Since: 1973   **Franchising Since:** 1982

Description of Operation: Pet Xtra/PetMart is a petless pet store concept. The focus is on selling pet food and supplies within the community. We are a service-driven organization that provides our customers with top-quality pet products by friendly, knowledgeable owners.

Equity Capital Needed: $75,000

Franchise Fee: $125,000 - total turn-key package.

Royalty Fee: 6%

Financial Assistance: We can put prospective franchisees in touch with several financial institutions that specialize in franchise financing.

Managerial Assistance: Our operations department is extremely thorough in assisting new franchisees throughout their term as a franchisee within the system. Support includes business goals, local marketing efforts, employee financial guidance and overall operational support. A training manager is specifically hired for continuous on-site and off-site support. The operations department will make periodic store reviews to help improve any areas in need of assistance and make sure the system is working effectively.

Training Provided: We have an extensive 2-week training program which incorporates both in-store operations and training at the corporate office. Training is covered in the following areas - management, product knowledge, merchandising, inventory control, record keeping, advertising, public relations and basic animal care.

Information Submitted: March 1994

PET-TENDERS
P. O. Box 23622
San Diego, CA 92193
Telephone: (800) PET-TENDERS(619) 298-3033
Ms. Cheryl Dagostaro, President

Number of Franchised Units: 3
Number of Company-Owned Units: 1
Number of Total Operating Units: 4

In Business Since: 1983   **Franchising Since:** 1990

Description of Operation: Pet-Tenders is an in-home pet and housesitting service that cares for pets in the comfort of their own home.

Equity Capital Needed: $2,000 - $5,400

Franchise Fee: $8,500

Royalty Fee: 5%, plus 2% advertising fee.

Financial Assistance: To qualified applicants.

Managerial Assistance: On-going assistance, as needed.

Training Provided: 5 days of training at Company headquarters.

Information Submitted: December 1993

PETENTIAL
22201 DuPont, # 400
Irvine, CA 92715
Telephone: (714) 675-9546
Fax: (714) 673-8225
Mr. Mike Farley, President

Number of Franchised Units: 0
Number of Company-Owned Units: 0
Number of Total Operating Units: 0

In Business Since: 1993   **Franchising Since:** 1993

Description of Operation: Free home-delivery vehicles supply pet owners quality nutritional pet food and products. Each franchisee is trained to be a pet care consultant, providing pet owners expert advise on pet care and maintenance.

Equity Capital Needed: $25,000 - $38,000

Franchise Fee: $12,500

Royalty Fee: 6%

Financial Assistance: No financing is available on franchisee fee or inventory needs. Lease financing on approved credit for home delivery van. Fleet rates available.

Managerial Assistance: All management is hands-on. Expert advice available. Advisory committee. 14 years of experience as President/CEO with one of the country's largest pet food companies.

Training Provided: Comprehensive home study course to train each franchisee as a pet care consultant. 10 lessons, each requiring 5 - 6 hours of study. Followed by 3 days of classroom training on marketing and all aspects of business, followed by workshops.

Information Submitted: November 1993

PETLAND
195 N. Hickory St.
Chillicothe, OH 45601
Telephone: (800) 221-5935 (614) 775-2464
Fax: (614) 775-2464
Mr. James L. Whitman, Executive Vice President

Number of Franchised Units: 134
Number of Company-Owned Units: 1
Number of Total Operating Units: 135

In Business Since: 1967   **Franchising Since:** 1972

Description of Operation: Full-service pet retail store, offering expert pet counseling to consumers and offering over 3,000 merchandise items. 50% of merchandise is proprietary, exclusive to Petland franchisees. Primary retail focus is on the "hobby pets," such as tropical fish, pet birds, reptiles, amphibians, small mammals such as rabbits, guinea pigs and hamsters. Comprehensive animal husbandry systems, employee-training programs and proprietary animal fixtures focus consumer attention to tropical fish and pet sales .

Equity Capital Needed: $50,000 - $125,000

Franchise Fee: $25,000

Royalty Fee: 4.5%

Financial Assistance: Petland will provide assistance with the loan request package and assist the franchisee with bank presentation and the on-going banking relationship.

Managerial Assistance: Petland will assist the new franchisee with site location, lease negotiations, construction and grand opening marketing. Petland will assist the new franchisee with the development of a comprehensive business plan. Petland requires the production of monthly financial statements and executive-level management monitors actual results as compared to plan with the new franchisee.

Training Provided: Petland requires all franchisees to attend 4 weeks of training. The 4 weeks are comprised of 1 week of classroom training, 1 week of hands-on training in a corporate training store, 1 week in the new store prior to opening and 1 week of post-opening training. Video and audio training tapes and comprehensive operating manuals are provided, in addition to field service representative visits to the retail store. Bi-annual franchise meetings are held for idea exchanges. Monthly marketing guides.

Information Submitted: January 1994

PETS ARE INN
7723 Tanglewood Court, # 150
Minneapolis, MN 55439
Telephone: (800) 248-PETS (612) 944-8298
Fax: (612) 941-4919
Mr. Jim Platt, Director of Operations

Number of Franchised Units: 18
Number of Company-Owned Units: 0
Number of Total Operating Units: 18

In Business Since: 1982   **Franchising Since:** 1987

Description of Operation: Finally, pet boarding without cages! When most people go on vacation, they must impose on friends or family or look to a kennel facility for the care of their pet. How special is your pet? Today's pet has become the "Yuppie Puppy" or "Yuppie Kitty." Pets Are Inn boards pets in private homes, thereby providing a loving home environment. Both pet and owner prefer the "piece of mind" and "worry free" services provided. This business is designed to be run from the home.

Equity Capital Needed: $25,000 - $35,000

Franchise Fee: $12,000

Royalty Fee: 10% or monthly minimums.

Financial Assistance: Prepare business plan. SBA micro loan program.

Managerial Assistance: Territory selection and initial business set up. Our training session covers operations, sales, marketing, pricing and computerized accounting and data base systems. An industry leader, franchise owners benefit from our Master Insurance Program, national and regional meetings, 800# referral network and on-going support.

Training Provided: Territory selection and initial business set up. Our training session covers operations, sales, marketing, pricing and computerized accounting and data base systems. An industry leader, franchise owners benefit from our Master Insurance Program, national and regional meetings, 800# referral network and on-going support.

Information Submitted: November 1993

PUPPY HUT
5201 Monroe St.
Toledo, OH 43623
Telephone: (419) 843-FIDO
Fax: (419) 478-BARK
Ms. Jacqueline M. Zajac, Director of Franchising

Number of Franchised Units: 0
Number of Company-Owned Units: 1
Number of Total Operating Units: 1

In Business Since: 1991   **Franchising Since:** 1992

Description of Operation: "America's #1 drive-thru and fun place for pets!" The Puppy Hut is a restaurant for pets, featuring nutritious and delicious treats for your best friend, your dog.

Equity Capital Needed: $50,000

Franchise Fee: $5,000

Royalty Fee: 5%

Financial Assistance: Franchisees needs to arrange their own financing.

Managerial Assistance: Each new location will receive managerial assistance.

Training Provided: An intensive classroom and in-field training at your own Puppy Hut location is provided. On-going training is also provided to assist all Puppy Hut restaurant owners.

Information Submitted: December 1993

SHAMPOO CHEZ
1380 Soquel Ave.
Santa Cruz, CA 95062
Telephone: (800) 888-BATH (408) 427-BATH
Fax: (408) 457-2845
Ms. Anne Singer, President

Number of Franchised Units: 1
Number of Company-Owned Units: 1
Number of Total Operating Units: 2

In Business Since: 1983   **Franchising Since:** 1986

Description of Operation: Self-service dog wash - natural, non-toxic pet supplies and professional dog and cat grooming.

Equity Capital Needed: $25,000

Franchise Fee: $15,000

Royalty Fee: 3.5% for first 6 months; 5% thereafter.

Financial Assistance: None.

Managerial Assistance: Custom computer software program, product seminars, assistance in site selection, lease negotiations, central data processing and purchasing, field training and evaluation of field operations, inventory control, operations manual, monthly operational and marketing ideas, bi-monthly customer newsletter and pricing guide.

Training Provided: On-the-job training at Company headquarters in Santa Cruz, CA, for 5 days during the month prior to opening to familiarize the franchisee with the proven business practices and procedures of operation, assistance in setting up store and opening for business. A minimum of 1 on-site visit per month during first 6 months of operation. Personal visits to store periodically throughout the term of franchise.

Information Submitted: November 1993

PRINTING

ALPHAGRAPHICS PRINTSHOPS OF THE FUTURE
3760 N. Commerce Dr.
Tucson, AZ 85705
Telephone: (800) 955-6246 (602) 293-9200
Fax: (602) 887-2850
Mr. B. A. Mitchell-Chavez, Vice President - Franchise Development

Number of Franchised Units: 328
Number of Company-Owned Units: 2
Number of Total Operating Units: 330

In Business Since: 1970   Franchising Since: 1980

Description of Operation: AlphaGraphics' high-tech rapid response printing stores offer a complete line of reprographic services which include high-speed duplication, single and multi-color printing, desktop design and publishing, custom presentation materials and an international satellite computer network that transmits camera-ready text and graphics in minutes to any AlphaGraphics store worldwide.

Equity Capital Needed: $70,000 - $100,000, plus living expenses for 1 year.

Franchise Fee: $25,900

Royalty Fee: 8% - 5% - 3%

Financial Assistance: The franchisor supplies sources of financing to franchisee and at the franchisee's request, the franchisor will assist in completing necessary applications.

Managerial Assistance: The franchisor provides a minimum of 48 hours of support in the form of consultation by telephone or in person or through meetings and seminars.

Training Provided: 3 weeks of training are provided at the corporate training center. 2 weeks of training are provided in the franchisee's store, as well as 1 week of advanced franchisee training 9 - 12 months after store's opening.

Information Submitted: December 1993

AMERICAN SPEEDY PRINTING CENTERS
2555 S. Telegraph Rd., # 400
Bloomfield Hills, MI 48302
Telephone: (800) 726-9050 (313) 335-6200
Fax: (313) 335-9499
Mr. Jerry Bergler, Executive Vice President

Number of Franchised Units: 520
Number of Company-Owned Units: 0
Number of Total Operating Units: 520

In Business Since: 1976   Franchising Since: 1977

Description of Operation: American Speedy provides printing, copying, desktop publishing and related services to businesses and organizations.

Equity Capital Needed: $50,000 - $100,000

Franchise Fee: $42,500

Royalty Fee: 6%

Financial Assistance: Leasing of equipment through several established third-party leasing companies.

Managerial Assistance: 3 weeks of comprehensive classroom training, followed by 2 weeks of on-site training.

Training Provided: Same as above.

Information Submitted: January 1994

AMERICAN WHOLESALE THERMOGRAPHERS / AWT
12715 Telge Rd.
Cypress, TX 77429

Telephone: (800) 942-9526 (713) 373-9142
Fax: (800) 542-8539
Mr. Kevin Camp, President

Number of Franchised Units: 20
Number of Company-Owned Units: 0
Number of Total Operating Units: 20

In Business Since: 1980   Franchising Since: 1980

Description of Operation: AWT is wholesale printer servicing the needs of the printing retailer with quality raised letter printing. AWT satisfies the soaring demand for professional business cards, stationery, announcements and invitations. 25-hour turn-around on orders.

Equity Capital Needed: $137,000 - $147,000

Franchise Fee: $38,500

Royalty Fee: 5%

Financial Assistance: Interest-free financing for a portion of the franchise fee. Third-party financing available, including equipment financing.

Managerial Assistance: Support system unequaled in the industry.

Training Provided: AWT support begins with market research, site evaluation, hands-on and classroom training (currently 2 weeks), field training (2 weeks) and on-site training (1 week).

Information Submitted: March 1994

BUSINESS CARDS TOMORROW / BCT
3000 NE 30th Place, 5th Fl.
Ft. Lauderdale, FL 33306
Telephone: (800) 627-9998 (305) 563-1224
Fax: (305) 565-0742
Mr. Gene Graves, Franchise Development

Number of Franchised Units: 95
Number of Company-Owned Units: 1
Number of Total Operating Units: 96

In Business Since: 1975   Franchising Since: 1977

Description of Operation: World's largest wholesale printing chain, specializing in next-day delivery of thermographed business products (business cards, stationery, teledex cards and promotional items), 2-day delivery of thermographed social products (wedding invitations and social stationery) and next-day delivery of custom-made marking devices (standard and self-inking rubber stamps). Also, distributors of Spinks Inks and Pelican Paper products.

Equity Capital Needed: $145,000 minimum cash required, including franchise fee.

Franchise Fee: $35,000

Royalty Fee: 6% of monthly gross sales.

Financial Assistance: Outside sourcing for 5-year/60-month equipment lease program.

Managerial Assistance: 2 weeks of classroom and hands-on training at the Ft. Lauderdale, FL headquarters, followed by 2 weeks of on-site training and opening assistance by operations field representatives.

Training Provided: Operations manuals, proprietary computer software package, management information systems department and R & D. Franchisee seminars, conventions, regular plant visits by operations field representatives, special training classes and newsletter, monthly advertising, marketing campaigns and mailing programs. Annual Dealer Appreciation Program. Dealer catalog training videos. Corporate Print Shop provides product catalogs, price lists, display items and technical advice and assistance.

Information Submitted: November 1993

COPIES NOW, A FRANCHISE OF SIR SPEEDY
23131 Verdugo Dr.
Laguna Hills, CA 92653

Telephone: (800) 752-7537 (714) 472-0330
Fax: (714) 458-1297
Mr. Dave Collins, Vice President of Franchising

Number of Franchised Units: 95
Number of Company-Owned Units: 0
Number of Total Operating Units: 95

In Business Since: 1983   **Franchising Since:** 1984

Description of Operation: Full-service business communications center, providing high-speed copying, electronic publishing, color reproduction, engineering, copying, bindery and fax services for small to mid-sized businesses.

Equity Capital Needed: $135,500, including franchise fee.

Franchise Fee: $45,500

Royalty Fee: 4% - 6%

Financial Assistance: 100% financing is available for the franchise fee and equipment. Minimum cash $40,000.

Managerial Assistance: Financing, site selection and market survey, floor planning and design of store, complete starting inventory, monthly mailers, newsletter and advertising repros, resident business management consultant for store, systemwide advertising, print media and direct mail, regional roundtable training sessions and all pro seminars, national convention and vendor show, on-going research and development and complete operations, marketing and administrative manuals.

Training Provided: We offer 2 weeks in our University in Laguna Hills, CA, for 2 people. Airfare and hotel are included. 2 weeks on-site during opening with a field representative.

Information Submitted: March 1994

FRANKLIN'S PRINTING, COPYING & GRAPHICS
135 International Blvd. NW
Atlanta, GA 30303
Telephone: (800) 554-5699 (404) 522-7100
Fax: (404) 522-0492
Mr. Bob Dolan, Vice President - Support & Development

Number of Franchised Units: 76
Number of Company-Owned Units: 0
Number of Total Operating Units: 76

In Business Since: 1971   **Franchising Since:** 1977

Description of Operation: Franklin's is a commercial quick printing, high-speed, high-tech copying franchise, providing complete communication and imaging services to both the business community and the public. Franklin's marketing program includes a unique and aggressive direct program and an outside salesperson from day one, using a proprietary software program to identify and follow up on prospects. Franklin's is one of the most consistently successful franchises in the industry.

Equity Capital Needed: $55,000

Franchise Fee: $25,000

Royalty Fee: 5%

Financial Assistance: Assistance in the preparation of the loan package and with presentation to lending institutions to secure loan.

Managerial Assistance: Market research, site selection and lease negotiation. Set-up of shop, grand opening sales blitz and 3 additional visits to the site in the first 6 months. System-wide annual operating and ratio studies to be used as a teaching and management tool, weekly newsletter to keep store owners up to the minute on the latest news relating to them, conventions, seminars and workshops. Regional owners' roundtable meetings. National contract pricing.

Training Provided: Our business partners receive 1 week of pre-training class in store training, 2 weeks of classroom training and 3 weeks of on-site support within the first 2 months of operation. Toll-free assistance via fax and phone is on-going to all locations.

168

Information Submitted: November 1993

INK WELL PRINTING
12715 Telge Rd.
Cypress, TX 77429
Telephone: (800) 942-9526 (713) 373-9142
Fax: (713) 542-8539
Ms. LaDonna Meadows Allen, Vice President

Number of Franchised Units: 58
Number of Company-Owned Units: 0
Number of Total Operating Units: 58

In Business Since: 1972   **Franchising Since:** 1972

Description of Operation: Ink Well printing centers are positioned to provide high-quality, commercial printing, typesetting and high-speed copying to the business community.

Equity Capital Needed: $138,000 - $146,000

Franchise Fee: $25,000

Royalty Fee: 6%

Financial Assistance: Partial financing is available to qualified applicants. Minimum cash required is $65,000, including working capital.

Managerial Assistance: Our support system is unequaled in the industry.

Training Provided: We provide 5 weeks of classroom and hands-on training, research and development and owner-to-owner participation.

Information Submitted: March 1994

INSTY-PRINTS
1010 S. Seventh St., # 450
Minneapolis, MN 55415
Telephone: (800) 779-1000 (612) 337-9800
Fax: (800) 369-1234
Mr. David C. Oswald, Vice President of Development

Number of Franchised Units: 277
Number of Company-Owned Units: 2
Number of Total Operating Units: 279

In Business Since: 1965   **Franchising Since:** 1967

Description of Operation: Insty-Prints Centers are the businessperson's choice for computerized graphic design, volume copying and commercial printing services. Franchise partners receive guidance, training and support in market analysis, sales and advertising, operations and bottom-line business management. Previous experience in printing is not necessary. However, a strong desire to succeed, the ability to market aggressively and a passion for superior customer service are required.

Equity Capital Needed: $60,000 - $90,000

Franchise Fee: $29,500

Royalty Fee: 4.5%

Financial Assistance: Financially-qualified individuals may finance the cost of the fixtures, equipment and signage necessary to open an Insty-Prints business through a lease plan arranged by the franchisor. FBS Business Finance Corporation offers a 7-year lease at very competitive rates.

Managerial Assistance: Insty-Prints' professional field support teams are on-call business consultants that advise franchisees in all phases of business planning, financial analysis, operations, human resource development and marketing. Proven sales-building marketing programs and the industry's best automated direct mail program are available to all Insty-Prints franchise partners.

Training Provided: From the signing of the franchise agreement, training never ends. Market and site evaluation, pre-training assistance, 4 weeks of classroom and hands-on training, on-site opening support, specialized video and audio programs and regional and national conferences are all part of Insty-Prints' commitment to success.

Information Submitted: November 1993

KWIK-KOPY PRINTING
One Kwik-Kopy Ln.
Cypress, TX 77429
Telephone: (800) 942-9526 (713) 373-9142
Fax: (800) 542-8539
Ms. LaDonna Meadows Allen, Vice President

Number of Franchised Units: 516
Number of Company-Owned Units: 0
Number of Total Operating Units: 516

In Business Since: 1967   Franchising Since: 1967

Description of Operation: Centers offer fine printing, quality copied materials, design, typesetting and other services, primarily to the business community.

Equity Capital Needed: $138,500 - $146,000, plus $45,000 working capital.

Franchise Fee: $25,000

Royalty Fee: Maximum of 8%.

Financial Assistance: Financing is available to qualified applicants for balance.

Managerial Assistance: Our support system is unequaled in the industry.

Training Provided: We provide 5 weeks of hands-on classroom and field training. Training continues with an annual conference and trade show. Custom software, public relations and direct mail programs.

Information Submitted: March 1994

KWIK-KOPY PRINTING (CANADA)
15900 Yonge St.
Aurora, ON L4G 3G8 CAN
Telephone: (800) 387-9725 (905) 798-7007
Fax: (905) 727-1952
Mr. John B. Johnson, Vice President of Sales

Number of Franchised Units: 94
Number of Company-Owned Units: 0
Number of Total Operating Units: 94

In Business Since: 1978   Franchising Since: 1979

Description of Operation: Kwik-Kopy Printing is a full-service, quick-print shop, specializing in quality products and service excellence. Our shops provide outstanding reproduction services such as printing, copying, bindery, design, fax service and much more for the business community around the center. All our shops are franchised and proudly owner-operated.

Equity Capital Needed: $70,000 - $80,000

Franchise Fee: $20,000

Royalty Fee: 6%

Financial Assistance: For qualified prospects, Kwik-Kopy Canada will provide financing for up to $15,000 of the franchise fee. We also assist in preparing a 2-year business plan for new franchisees.

Managerial Assistance: Kwik-Kopy Canada provides assistance to franchisees in sales and promotion programs, on-going seminars for staff, production and technical assistance and administrative and financial planning. Bi-weekly and monthly communications and annual conferences.

Training Provided: Training is conducted at Kwik-Kopy's International Training Center in Cypress, TX. Training includes all facets of running the business and monitoring the franchisee's progress. Kwik-Kopy provides its own software programs for the business.

Information Submitted: January 1994

LAZERQUICK COPIES
27375 SW Parkway Ave.
Wilsonville, OR 97070
Telephone: (800) 477-2679 (503) 682-1322
Fax: (503) 682-1670
Mr. Michael Hart, Director of Franchising

Number of Franchised Units: 9
Number of Company-Owned Units: 34
Number of Total Operating Units: 43

In Business Since: 1968   Franchising Since: 1990

Description of Operation: Lazerquick Copies centers are complete, one-stop, printing and copying centers. All centers feature state-of-the-art electronic publishing and electronic graphics and imaging services that support our wide-range of quality, fast-service offset printing, high-speed copying, color laser copying and related bindery and finishing services. The Lazerquick franchise is based on value and performance. Affiliates benefit from our unique and innovative programs.

Equity Capital Needed: $135,000 - $190,000 (inclusive of franchise fee).

Franchise Fee: $20,000

Royalty Fee: 5% during first 5 years; 2.5% of increased sales in year 6.

Financial Assistance: Financing is offered through indirect sources only. Lazerquick does not carry financing for franchise operations.

Managerial Assistance: Assistance is on-going and on an as-needed basis. The assistance is preferably offered via telephone, fax, modem and mail.

Training Provided: Franchise affiliates receive 5 weeks of intensive, hands-on training in our training facility, with additional optional weeks of training in a working location, plus on-site assistance during the first week of operation. Regular field visits, manuals, bulletins and an 800# hotline provide on-going support.

Information Submitted: November 1993

PIP PRINTING
27001 Agoura Rd., # 200
Agoura Hills, CA 91301
Telephone: (800) 292-4747 (818) 880-3800
Fax: (818) 880-3857
Ms. Jaime Vane, Manager of Business Development

Number of Franchised Units: 768
Number of Company-Owned Units: 0
Number of Total Operating Units: 768

In Business Since: 1943   Franchising Since: 1968

Description of Operation: PIP Printing locations offer a full range of business communications, from initial concept to finished printed product. PIP's services include short-run, full-run, multi-color printing, high-volume copying, desktop publishing, layout, design and finishing on an array of products, including newsletters, brochures, bound presentations, business stationery and forms. PIP works to meet the needs of small and medium-sized businesses.

Equity Capital Needed: $189,000 - $297,500

Franchise Fee: $40,000

Royalty Fee: 1% - 7% (sliding scale).

Financial Assistance: We do not offer financing, but we will assist potential franchisees through the review process with their financial institution.

Managerial Assistance: PIP's franchisees get on-going assistance from our staff. After the initial 2 weeks of training, the owners may request a visit from business consultants trained in sales, marketing, operations and finance. This service is free of charge. We also conduct workshops, regional meetings and biennial conclaves that are held nationwide and cover a wide range of topics, from customer service to the future of the printing industry. We also supply owners with training, operations and safety manuals.

Training Provided: A 2-week business printing management course is offered in our corporate offices for new franchise owners. On-going training workshops offered nationwide. Specialized field visits from business consultants on marketing, sales, operations and finance.

Information Submitted: November 1993

PRINTHOUSE EXPRESS, THE
222 Catoctin Circle, SE, # 201
Leesburg, VA 22075
Telephone: (800) 779-0029 (703) 777-0020
Fax: (703) 777-3551
Mr. Bruce Chamberlin, Director of Marketing

Number of Franchised Units: 18
Number of Company-Owned Units: 1
Number of Total Operating Units: 19

In Business Since: 1982   **Franchising Since:** 1987

Description of Operation: A regional printing, copying and desktop publishing business, providing full service printing to the business community.

Equity Capital Needed: $65,000

Franchise Fee: $42,000

Royalty Fee: 6%, declining to 3.5%

Financial Assistance: The franchisor will provide financing of up to $17,000 of the franchise fee and 100% of equipment to qualified franchisees.

Managerial Assistance: Yearly business and marketing planning, plus a minimum of 4 training classes per year for owners and/or employees. The Printhouse Express provides "on-call" management assistance to all franchise owners.

Training Provided: We train in business techniques, such as basic management, financial planning, financing, customer relations, employee management and equipment output expectations. Marketing training is a major part of our training.

Information Submitted: November 1993

QUIK PRINT
3445 N. Webb Rd.
Wichita, KS 67226
Telephone: (800) 825-COPY (316) 636-5666
Fax: (316) 636-5678
Mr. Johnny Tarrant, Senior Vice President

Number of Franchised Units: 142
Number of Company-Owned Units: 63
Number of Total Operating Units: 205

In Business Since: 1963   **Franchising Since:** 1967

Description of Operation: Quik Print is a full-service printing and copying center, offering a full range of service, from desktop publishing to bindery. Complete training and support, including site selection, improvements, bookkeeping, advertising and sales assistance, etc.

Equity Capital Needed: $150,000

Franchise Fee: $35,000

Royalty Fee: 5%

Financial Assistance: Up to $100,000 SBA loan to qualified buyers.

Managerial Assistance: We provide site selection, lease negotiation, overseeing of leasehold improvements, marketing and sales programs.

Training Provided: Training includes 4 weeks at corporate headquarters, plus 2 weeks at location.

Information Submitted: March 1994

SIGNAL GRAPHICS PRINTING
6789 S. Yosemite St.
Englewood, CO 80112
Telephone: (800) 852-6336 (303) 779-6789
Fax: (303) 779-8445
Mr. Bob Mitchell, Director of Franchise Sales

Number of Franchised Units: 40
Number of Company-Owned Units: 0
Number of Total Operating Units: 40

In Business Since: 1974   **Franchising Since:** 1982

Description of Operation: Full-service printing centers, offering high-speed copying, fax, typesetting, quick-printing and a special emphasis on quality commercial printing. Comprehensive training, a proven system of operations and a state-of-the-art equipment package can help newcomers to the field quickly dominate their marketplace. On-going franchise support is a specialty, with management and technical help always on call from headquarters.

Equity Capital Needed: $65,000 - $90,000

Franchise Fee: $18,000

Royalty Fee: 5%, declining to 0%.

Financial Assistance: The franchisee is required to have a minimum of $18,000 for the franchise fee and $45,000 in working capital in liquid funds. Franchisor will assist franchisee in locating third-party financing for the equipment package of $104,000.

Managerial Assistance: In addition to the initial training and start-up assistance, 2 on-site follow-up visits are provided during the first year of operation. A toll-free 800# hotline, Signal-grams and newsletters are provided for on-going management assistance.

Training Provided: A member of the top management team assists owners with site procurement, lease negotiation and store layout. Operations and management training consists of 3 weeks at headquarters, followed by 1 week on-site during opening.

Information Submitted: November 1993

SIR SPEEDY PRINTING CENTERS
23131 Verdugo Dr.
Laguna Hills, CA 92653
Telephone: (800) 854-3321 (714) 472-0330
Fax: (714) 472-3444
Mr. Dave Collins, Vice President of Franchising

Number of Franchised Units: 858
Number of Company-Owned Units: 1
Number of Total Operating Units: 859

In Business Since: 1968   **Franchising Since:** 1968

Description of Operation: Sir Speedy, the business printer, provides computer graphics and page layout, high-speed copying, printing and bindery services in black and white or full color. We are a customer service-oriented, market-driven company.

Equity Capital Needed: $40,000 - $65,000

Franchise Fee: $17,500

Royalty Fee: 6% (4% first year).

Financial Assistance: Sir Speedy provides assistance to franchise applicants in obtaining financing from either a leasing company, which finances equipment only; a non-bank lender, which finances equipment and soft costs; or with an SBA national underwriter, which will do either. A franchisee may use his/her own local sources.

Managerial Assistance: Sir Speedy provides operations manuals, toll-free hotlines, regional business management consultants, local franchisee associations, an audio and video resource library, seminars at regional roundtables and annual conventions.

Training Provided: Training provided includes an intense 2-week classroom session at corporate, a 1 1/2 week on-site session with a corporate representative and a 1-week session with a franchisee consultant on-site. Including a 3-day follow-up visit, 5 weeks of training are provided.

Information Submitted: March 1994

TEMPTCO
733-F Lakeview Plaza Blvd.
Worthington, OH 43085
Telephone: (800) 827-2679 (614) 846-4510
Fax: (614) 846-4512
Mr. Chuck Young, President

Number of Franchised Units: 3
Number of Company-Owned Units: 1
Number of Total Operating Units: 4

In Business Since: 1986   **Franchising Since:** 1992

Description of Operation: Temptco is a franchisor of wholesale copy and bindery service franchises. By pooling the sales efforts of local printers and retail copy centers, we are able to provide high-speed and color copies at wholesale prices.

Equity Capital Needed: $55,000

Franchise Fee: $25,000

Royalty Fee: 5%

Financial Assistance: Temptco will assist prospective franchisees in securing the proper financing.

Managerial Assistance: Temptco provides a complete support system to franchise owners. The support system includes, but is not limited to, training manuals, marketing manuals, seminars, meetings, monthly communications, financial analysis and on-site visits.

Training Provided: The Temptco training program consists of a 4-week program - 2 weeks are spent at the corporate office and production facility, while the second 2 weeks are spent on-site at the franchise location. The training program is designed to teach new owners not only how to operate their center, but also to successfully manage their business.

Information Submitted: November 1993

UNITED PRINTING UNLIMITED
P. O. Box 616249
Orlando, FL 32861
Telephone: (407) 246-0207
Mr. Jack Swat, General Manager/Chief Executive Officer

Number of Franchised Units: 12
Number of Company-Owned Units: 2
Number of Total Operating Units: 14

In Business Since: 1985   **Franchising Since:** 1986

Description of Operation: Printing center. Offset printing.

Equity Capital Needed: $25,000

Franchise Fee: $25,000

Royalty Fee: 5% of gross profit.

Financial Assistance: 80% - 90% financial assistance.

Managerial Assistance: We provide accounting, sales and promotion assistance.

Training Provided: Training consists of 3 weeks in the classroom and 1 week on-site. On-going support. In-shop training.

Information Submitted: December 1993

REAL ESTATE

4-SALE HOTLINE, THE
5921 S. Middlefield Rd., # 200
Littleton, CO 80123
Telephone: (800) 869-1995 (303) 730-3100
Fax: (303) 730-8346
Mr. Chris Petty, President

Number of Franchised Units: 4
Number of Company-Owned Units: 4
Number of Total Operating Units: 8

In Business Since: 1991   **Franchising Since:** 1993

Description of Operation: Real estate information services built around inter-active communications technologies (touchtone phone, fax, etc.) We help real estate agents take their advertising, marketing and information management into the next century. We help consumers interact with the data and more efficiently connect to the appropriate agent.

Equity Capital Needed: $70,000 - $100,000

Franchise Fee: $15,000 - $25,000

Royalty Fee: 7%

Financial Assistance: Assistance possible on franchise fee.

Managerial Assistance: Full support, including manuals, instructions and sample materials, plus toll-free support line.

Training Provided: 1 full week of training at proto-type franchise in Denver, CO, plus 1 week of sales training and coaching at your location.

Information Submitted: January 1994

ADVANTAGE RADON CONTROL CENTERS
804 Second St. Pike
Southampton, PA 18966
Telephone: (800) 535-8378 (215) 953-9200
Fax: (215) 953-8837
Mr. Perry S. Ecksel, Chief Executive Officer

Number of Franchised Units: 1
Number of Company-Owned Units: 5
Number of Total Operating Units: 6

In Business Since: 1984   **Franchising Since:** 1991

Description of Operation: Environmental testing, with emphasis placed upon those services attached to the transfer of real estate. We are actively pursuing trained home inspectors who wish to expand their services to include environmental inspections. Specializing in radon testing and mitigation, we can improve performance and/or increase sales.

Equity Capital Needed: $15,000 - $25,000

Franchise Fee: $17,500

Royalty Fee: 8%

Financial Assistance: 65 - 80% financing for qualified individuals.

Managerial Assistance: Excellent training and on-going assistance for all franchisees.

Training Provided: In-house and on-the-job training program. Assistance in obtaining federal and state licensing. Development of QA/QC plans. Periodic updating during course of year as prescribed by EPA.

Information Submitted: January 1994

AMBIC BUILDING INSPECTION CONSULTANTS
1200 Rt. 130
Robbinsville, NJ 08691
Telephone: (800) 88-AMBIC (609) 448-3900
Fax: (609) 426-1230
Mr. W. David Goldstein, President

Number of Franchised Units: 20
Number of Company-Owned Units: 0
Number of Total Operating Units: 20

In Business Since: 1987   **Franchising Since:** 1988

Description of Operation: Home and building inspections and related environmental tests of residential, commercial and industrial properties.

Equity Capital Needed: $5,000 - $10,000

Franchise Fee: $10,000 - $16,500

Royalty Fee: 6% on-going; 3% advertising.

Financial Assistance: Ambic will assist in locating financing.

Managerial Assistance: Toll-free "HelpLine," marketing assistance, technical support, computer software updates, public relations and marketing material, business operations, site visits.

Training Provided: Approximately 4 weeks, including inspector training, hands-on and classroom experience, business operations, computer, public relations and marketing, customer response and initial marketing campaign.

Information Submitted: January 1994

AMERISPEC HOME INSPECTIONS
1855 W. Katella Ave., # 330
Orange, CA 92667
Telephone: (800) 426-2270 (714) 744-8360
Fax: (714) 744-4602
Mr. John Harrison, National Sales Manager

Number of Franchised Units: 178
Number of Company-Owned Units: 0
Number of Total Operating Units: 178

In Business Since: 1987   **Franchising Since:** 1988

Description of Operation: A national home inspection franchise which sells independently-owned and operated businesses to entrepreneurs in exclusive territories. We provide extensive marketing programs, professional training and a complete referral network. Our owners use a proprietary software program to generate a unique narrative report and/or an on-site report to clients. Large or small area franchises available - priced accordingly.

Equity Capital Needed: $19,500 - $49,500, including franchise fee.

Franchise Fee: $9,950 - $20,900, depending on size of territory.

Royalty Fee: 7%, or $250 per month ($125 per month for smaller areas).

Financial Assistance: We directly provide financing of up to 50% of the initial franchise fee on large franchised areas. We also assist in finding outside financing.

Managerial Assistance: We provide an operations manual as a guide and provide extensive training during our initial 2-week course. We provide a formal 2 - 3 day follow-up (one-on-one, on-site at the owners office), which includes all aspects of the business, monthly telephone contact with owners, twice annually regional training and annual national training. All include management review.

Training Provided: The standard training is described above. We additionally provide a monthly technical update program and supplement this training with personalized training where called for. The agenda items for regional training are set by owners' requests. Finally, we certify additional inspectors through an approved field training program.

Information Submitted: November 1993

APARTMENT SEARCH INTERNATIONAL
7900 Xerxes Ave. S., # 2250
Minneapolis, MN 55431
Telephone: (800) 989-3764 (612) 830-0509
Fax: (612) 830-9019
Mr. John Appert, Executive Vice President

Number of Franchised Units: 1
Number of Company-Owned Units: 22
Number of Total Operating Units: 23

In Business Since: 1965   **Franchising Since:** 1992

Description of Operation: You're probably aware of how a travel agency or a real estate brokerage firm works. Imagine a similar type of business helping renters find apartments and you'll have a basic understanding of Apartment Search. We link the right renters with the right apartments. The properties are listed with Apartment Search as a form of advertising. The service is paid for by the apartment owner and is free to renters.

Equity Capital Needed: $50,000 - $80,000

Franchise Fee: $40,000

Royalty Fee: 15%

Financial Assistance: Financing is usually obtained by local sources for furniture, fixtures and equipment.

Managerial Assistance: The franchisor provides in-store opening assistance and advanced managerial training programs. The franchisor also provides administrative support for invoicing, collections, inventory management and accounting programs.

Training Provided: All franchisees must attend and successfully complete the week-long training program provided by the Company. The cost is included in your franchisee fee; however, travel and lodging are at your expense.

Information Submitted: November 1993

APARTMENT SELECTOR
P. O. Box 8355
Dallas, TX 75205
Telephone: (800) 324-FREE (214) 361-4420
Fax: (214) 361-8677
Mr. Kendall A. Laughlin, Chairman

Number of Franchised Units: 20
Number of Company-Owned Units: 0
Number of Total Operating Units: 20

In Business Since: 1959   **Franchising Since:** 1987

Description of Operation: A rental referral agency (apartment locator). We assist renters for free. All fees are paid by property owner. Founded in 1959. Extensive training. Computer programs included.

Equity Capital Needed: $5,000 - $20,000

Franchise Fee: $1,000

Royalty Fee: 5%

Financial Assistance: None.

Managerial Assistance: Management will visit location, at franchisee's expense, during year. Complete telephone and computer support.

Training Provided: Video, tapes, computer and extensive manuals cover prospecting and listings.

Information Submitted: November 1993

BETTER HOMES & GARDENS REAL ESTATE SERVICE
2000 Grand Ave.
Des Moines, IA 50312
Telephone: (800) 274-7653 (515) 284-2355
Fax: (515) 284-3801
Mr. Randy Schwager, Vice President of Member Development

Number of Franchised Units: 658
Number of Company-Owned Units: 0
Number of Total Operating Units: 658

In Business Since: 1902   **Franchising Since:** 1978

Description of Operation: The Better Homes and Gardens Real Estate service is a national residential real estate marketing service which licenses selected real estate firms to an exclusive territory. Members and affiliates total 652 in the United States and 6 in Canada. The real estate service typically receives a joining fee from new member firms and thereafter a franchise fee based on a percentage of the member's gross commission income on residential housing sales. Member firms may purchase marketing programs/materials.

Equity Capital Needed: $40,000 - $200,000

Franchise Fee: Sliding scale.

Royalty Fee: 5% maximum.

Financial Assistance: Deferred payment program on identity materials - 50% down, 18 installment payments with no interest. Initial franchise, if required, may also be paid on a deferred payment plan.

Managerial Assistance: Better Homes and Gardens Management Training Institute, Better Homes and Gardens Management Orientation Session, Better Homes and Gardens Management Operating System, Better Homes and Gardens Recruiting System, Better Homes and Gardens In-Touch Service Program.

Training Provided: Better Homes and Gardens Sales Associate Orientation Program, Better Homes and Gardens Advantage Training Program, Better Homes and Gardens Medallion Club Summit Program, Better Homes and Gardens International Business Conference and Convention, Better Homes and Gardens In-Touch Service Program.

Information Submitted: November 1993

BUYER'S RESOURCE
6950 E. Belleview Ave., # 100
Englewood, CO 80111
Telephone: (800) 359-4092 (303) 843-9100
Fax: (303) 843-9258
Ms. Deana L. Martinez, Franchise Sales

Number of Franchised Units: 58
Number of Company-Owned Units: 0
Number of Total Operating Units: 58

In Business Since: 1989   Franchising Since: 1989

Description of Operation: Franchisor of exclusive buyer-broker real estate firms, representing buyers exclusively in real estate transactions.

Equity Capital Needed: $35,000 - $65,000

Franchise Fee: $9,000 - rural/resort; $12,500 - metropolitan.

Royalty Fee: 5%, plus 2% advertising fee.

Financial Assistance: No standards - done on case-by-case basis.

Managerial Assistance: Corporate officers bring their strong and deep personal commitment to Buyer Agency and to each Buyer's Resource franchise office. Direct support and consulting services are provided by all.

Training Provided: 5 days of initial training, on-going seminars, annual conventions, telephone training and in-house training.

Information Submitted: November 1993

BY OWNER REALITY NETWORK
501 W. Appleway, Appleway Sq. Mall
Coeur d'Alene, ID 83814
Telephone: (208) 667-6184
Fax: (208) 664-4539
Ms. Ann Wall, Vice President

Number of Franchised Units: 7
Number of Company-Owned Units: 1
Number of Total Operating Units: 8

In Business Since: 1985   Franchising Since: 1986

Description of Operation: Real estate centers in retail locations, offering sellers money-saving marketing and services, in addition to full broker and realtor services.

Equity Capital Needed: $14,850

Franchise Fee: $16,500

Royalty Fee: 10%, including advertising fees.

Financial Assistance: Owner does not currently offer financing for franchisees.

Managerial Assistance: Franchise locations within the existing master franchise areas receive on-going and hands-on support from the master (sub) franchisor. Franchise locations in other areas will be managed directly from the corporate headquarters of franchisor. On-going support is considered a top priority for network success.

Training Provided: Initial: a minimum of 3 days training at corporate headquarters. Prior to opening - hands-on training and preparation for opening. On-site at new location. Grand opening - franchisor representative on hand for grand opening. On-going: on-going training and education is encouraged by all parties - franchisees and franchisor representatives.

Information Submitted: January 1994

CENTURY 21 REAL ESTATE
2601 SE Main St., Century Centre
Irvine, CA 92713
Telephone: (800) 826-8083 (714) 553-2100
Fax: (714) 553-2133
Mr. Duane Mora, Vice President of Franchise Marketing

Number of Franchised Units: 6000
Number of Company-Owned Units: 0
Number of Total Operating Units: 6000

In Business Since: 1972   Franchising Since: 1972

Description of Operation: World's largest real estate franchising organization, established to provide a marketing support system for independently-owned and operated real estate brokerage offices. We offer international advertising, VIP referral system, residential and commercial sales training, management training, national accounts center, client follow-up and other real estate-related services. Subsidiary of Metropolitan Life Insurance Company.

Equity Capital Needed: $15,000 - $30,000

Franchise Fee: $15,000 - $30,000

Royalty Fee: Determined by region, usually 6%.

Financial Assistance: Some financing may be available.

Managerial Assistance: New members attend the International Management Academy, a 5-day orientation/management training seminar held in Irvine, CA. Other courses in sales management, business management, leadership, relocation and commercial brokerage are offered at the regional level. A performance-based program, Operation Orbit, is delivered at a variety of locations throughout the organization and helps attendees use the various elements of the Century 21 office management system.

Training Provided: Performance-based training is available to Century 21 sales associates, covering a wide range of topics. The 21 Plus program sets the standard for customer-oriented real estate sales and epitomizes a quality service approach. Programs in relocation, investment, career management, finance and quality service are also offered.

Information Submitted: April 1994

CRITERIUM ENGINEERS
650 Brighton Ave.
Portland, ME 04102
Telephone: (800) 242-1969 (207) 828-1969
Fax: (207) 775-4405
Mr. Peter E. Hollander, Director of Marketing/Development

Number of Franchised Units: 63
Number of Company-Owned Units: 0
Number of Total Operating Units: 63

In Business Since: 1957   **Franchising Since:** 1959

Description of Operation: Criterium Engineers is a nationwide franchise network of registered professional engineers, specializing in buildings and related consulting services. Services include residential and commercial inspections, insurance investigations, environmental assessments, capital reserve studies, design and related services. Clients include buyers, building owners and managers, lenders, attorneys, insurance companies and government agencies.

Equity Capital Needed: $2,500

Franchise Fee: $22,500

Royalty Fee: 6%

Financial Assistance: A down payment of $10,000 is required. Franchisor will finance the balance of the franchise fee.

Managerial Assistance: 1 week of initial training is provided at the franchisor's main office. Annual business workshops are held in the Fall with several business sessions. Customized software and unlimited toll-free phone support is provided to all franchisees.

Training Provided: Data not available.

Information Submitted: November 1993

EGAL - "AMERICA'S HOME INSPECTION SERVICE"
P. O. Box 226
Paola, KS 66071
Telephone: (800) 368-9201 (913) 294-3945
Mr. Timothy J. Warkins, President

Number of Franchised Units: 11
Number of Company-Owned Units: 0
Number of Total Operating Units: 11

In Business Since: 1987   **Franchising Since:** 1988

Description of Operation: Home inspection and radon screening.

Equity Capital Needed: $3,000 - $10,000

Franchise Fee: $7,900

Royalty Fee: 5%

Financial Assistance: None.

Managerial Assistance: There is an 800# for all franchisees to ask questions and 7 years of experience.

Training Provided: 1 week of training at the home office in all phases of operation.

Information Submitted: November 1993

ELECTRONIC REALTY ASSOCIATES / ERA
4900 College Blvd.
Overland Park, KS 66211
Telephone: (800) 728-0999 (913) 491-1000
Fax: (913) 491-9133
Mr. Tom Schmitt

Number of Franchised Units: 3096
Number of Company-Owned Units: 0
Number of Total Operating Units: 3096

In Business Since: 1971   **Franchising Since:** 1972

Description of Operation: Electronic Realty Associates (ERA) is a membership organization for licensed real estate brokerage firms, offering its services and programs for use by its members. ERA grants the use of its registered trademarks and service marks and designs, logos, colors and color patterns and business methods to its members to promote identification with the products and marketing services of ERA and to permit co-ordination of advertising programs. ERA members participate in a national referral program.

Equity Capital Needed: The initial franchise fee is $18,900, plus $690 for each branch office.

Franchise Fee: $16,900 - $18,900

Royalty Fee: Varies.

Financial Assistance: ERA does have a financial assistance program to aid new members in the payment of the initial membership fees. New members who qualify may, upon payment of $5,000, finance $13,000 by payment $3,500 within 60 days, $3,500 within 90 days and $6,000 within 120 days. Other financing arrangements may be available from time to time, at the sole option of ERA.

Managerial Assistance: ERA provides continuing management service to members in many areas, including training, advertising, insurance and residential · service contract administration. Complete manuals of operations, forms and directions. We work closely with members and assist in problem solving. ERA sponsors brokers councils in each locality and conducts marketing and product research to maintain high ERA consumer acceptance.

Training Provided: A new member must participate in an orientation training program to familiarize the broker with the ERA services and programs. Other training programs believed by ERA to be beneficial to members and to be important for full and effective implementation are provided.

Information Submitted: March 1994

GROUP TRANS-ACTION BROKERAGE SERVICES
550 Sherbrooke, W., # 775
Montreal, PQ H3A 1B9 CAN
Telephone: (514) 288-6777
Fax: (514) 288-7543
Mr. Jean-Louis Bernard, General Manager

Number of Franchised Units: 48
Number of Company-Owned Units: 0
Number of Total Operating Units: 48

In Business Since: 1978   **Franchising Since:** 1982

Description of Operation: Complete real estate services - purchase, sale, relocation, homefinding, etc.

Equity Capital Needed: $50,000

Franchise Fee: $16,500

Royalty Fee: $130 per agent per month.

Financial Assistance: 25% minimum down payment - balance can be repaid in 12 consecutive months without interest.

Managerial Assistance: Back-up support in all areas of franchise operations.

Training Provided: The franchise includes basic and advanced seminars. Other training is available as required.

Information Submitted: November 1993

HELP-U-SELL
102 West 500 South, # 600
Salt Lake City, UT 84101
Telephone: (800) 366-1177 (801) 355-1177
Fax: (801) 521-6018
Mr. Marv Hoffman, Executive Vice President

Number of Franchised Units: 312
Number of Company-Owned Units: 3
Number of Total Operating Units: 315

In Business Since: 1976   **Franchising Since:** 1978

Description of Operation: Help-U-Sell, established in 1976, has recently expanded the menu of services that is offered to buyers and sellers. The Help-U-Sell method provides specific services to the seller for a set fee. In addition, sellers can choose to place their property into the Multiple Listing Service. Buyers can view properties on their own, but are encouraged to be shown by an agent and/or be represented by a buyer's agent. The marketing system can generate hundreds of buyer and seller leads without the need to cold-call.

Equity Capital Needed: Varies, depending on existing or start-up office.

Franchise Fee: $4,500 +

Royalty Fee: 8.5%, or 2% of population.

Financial Assistance: Terms are available in most areas.

Managerial Assistance: A management consultant assigned to each office.

Training Provided: We offer 5 days of intensive initial training at corporate headquarters in Salt Lake City, UT. On-going support and training through a personal operations consultant, as well as regional and national conventions.

Information Submitted: March 1994

HER REAL ESTATE
4656 Executive Dr.
Columbus, OH 43220
Telephone: (800) 848-7400 (614) 459-7400
Fax: (614) 457-6807
Ms. Karen S. Workman, President

Number of Franchised Units: 12
Number of Company-Owned Units: 25
Number of Total Operating Units: 37

In Business Since: 1976   **Franchising Since:** 1981

Description of Operation: Personalized approach to real estate franchising. Brokers keep their own identity and marks of franchisor do not detract or dominate. On-location educational opportunities. Franchisees offered exclusive territories. Also provided are test-marketed, award-winning marketing tools and techniques.

Equity Capital Needed: $6,800 - $23,000

Franchise Fee: $2,500 - $80,000

Royalty Fee: 5%, plus 1% advertising.

Financial Assistance: A portion of the initial franchisee fee is used for conversion of office.

Managerial Assistance: Support programs through field representation, continuing education and other unique educational opportunities.

Training Provided: Initial 2 weeks of training for anyone new to the Company. On-going follow-up programs, along with monthly continuing education.

Information Submitted: December 1993

HOMETEAM INSPECTION SERVICE
4010 Executive Park Dr., # 420
Cincinnati, OH 45241
Telephone: (800) 598-5297 (513) 733-9300
Fax: (513) 563-7416
Mr. Paul Spires, President

Number of Franchised Units: 52
Number of Company-Owned Units: 0
Number of Total Operating Units: 52

In Business Since: 1991   **Franchising Since:** 1993

Description of Operation: National franchisor of home inspections. The HomeTeam is unique and approaches this rapidly-growing business in a different way - and this way is the reason we've grown into one of the fastest-growing companies in this industry.

Equity Capital Needed: $4,050 - $12,750

Franchise Fee: $8,950 - $20,900

Royalty Fee: 6%

Financial Assistance: We will finance up to 50% of the initial franchise fee.

Managerial Assistance: The franchisee will be trained in all aspects of operating the business. Marketing, accounting and management will all be included. On-going assistance will be available throughout the franchise term.

Training Provided: Each franchisee will receive a 14-day, comprehensive training program at the corporate office.

Information Submitted: March 1994

HOUSEMASTER - "THE HOME INSPECTION PROFESSIONALS"
421 W. Union Ave.
Bound Brook, NJ 08805
Telephone: (800) 526-3939 (908) 469-6565
Fax: (908) 469-7405
Ms. Kathleen A. Kuhn, Director of Marketing

Number of Franchised Units: 148
Number of Company-Owned Units: 0
Number of Total Operating Units: 148

In Business Since: 1979   **Franchising Since:** 1979

Description of Operation: Home inspections for home buyers and sellers. With the high price of housing and the growing need for full disclosure, a home inspection is becoming a must in the course of real estate transactions.

Equity Capital Needed: $15,000 - $40,000

Franchise Fee: $4,800 - $35,000

Royalty Fee: 7.5% plus 2.5% advertising.

Financial Assistance: None.

Managerial Assistance: Data not available.

Training Provided: 5 days of marketing and operations training and 5 days of technical training. All training is performed at the Company's 2,000 square foot training facility in Bound Brook, NJ. On-going marketing and technical training for employees is included in the initial franchise fee.

Information Submitted: December 1993

MORTGAGE SERVICE ASSOCIATES
21 Brock St.
North Haven, CT 06473
Telephone: (800) 767-3004 (203) 773-3001
Fax: (203) 787-0114
Mr. Joseph D. Raffone, President

Number of Franchised Units: 3
Number of Company-Owned Units: 1
Number of Total Operating Units: 4

In Business Since: 1946   **Franchising Since:** 1990

Description of Operation: Computerized field services, used nationwide by banks, S & L's, mortgage bankers and State and Federal agencies. Commercial and residential property inspections (required by VA, FHA & PMI's). Appraisals, market analyses, pre-purchase inspections, monthly inspections, area trend reports, homeowner interviews, damage repair estimates, property securing-repair-renovation and REO sale make-ready. Construction supervision and coordination. No licensing. On-going revenue and national clients.

Equity Capital Needed: $15,000 - $50,000

Franchise Fee: $15,000 - $50,000

Royalty Fee: 2.5% - 15%

Financial Assistance: Negotiable.

Managerial Assistance: Staff support, on-site help with start-up, procedural updates and guides.

Training Provided: 40 hours of structured training at franchisor's location, 30 hours of structured training at franchisee's location and on-going support thereafter.

Information Submitted: December 1993

NATIONAL TENANT NETWORK
P. O. Box 1664
Lake Grove, OR 97034
Telephone: (800) 228-0989 (503) 635-1118
Fax: (503) 635-9392
Mr. Edward F. Byczynski, President

Number of Franchised Units: 12
Number of Company-Owned Units: 4
Number of Total Operating Units: 16

In Business Since: 1980   **Franchising Since:** 1987

Description of Operation: Residential and commercial tenant performance reporting. Analysis of retail credit and tenant performance data maintained on a nationally-networked mainframe computer. Low-overhead, high cash flow, turn-key opportunity. All equipment provided by franchisor. National accounts may be provided to business at start-up.

Equity Capital Needed: $30,000 - $50,000

Franchise Fee: $30,000

Royalty Fee: 10%

Financial Assistance: Up to 50% financing is available on the purchase of developed territories.

Managerial Assistance: All that is required of a new NTN operation.

Training Provided: Initially, 1 full week at franchisee's site. Operational training and marketing manuals. On-going, close working relationship among all NTN offices, 6 days a week.

Information Submitted: November 1993

PROFESSIONAL HOUSE DOCTORS
1406 E. 14th St.
Des Moines, IA 50316
Telephone: (800) 288-7437 (515) 265-6667
Fax: (515) 265-7032
Mr. Dane J. Shearer, President

Number of Franchised Units: 4
Number of Company-Owned Units: 1
Number of Total Operating Units: 5

In Business Since: 1982   **Franchising Since:** 1991

Description of Operation: Providers of environmental and building science services to residential and commercial clients. Services include radon testing and mitigation, building inspections, indoor air quality analysis, asbestos and lead analysis, energy analysis and consultation, structural moisture analysis, healthy house investigations, environmental do-it-yourself test kits and much more.

Equity Capital Needed: $50,000

Franchise Fee: $25,000

Royalty Fee: 6%, or $100 minimum.

Financial Assistance: We can help to secure financing.

Managerial Assistance: All phases of managerial assistance are included, such as marketing, record keeping, training, media files, sample letters and forms, as well as continuous support from our staff.

Training Provided: Training begins at the corporate headquarters for 2 weeks and continues with on-site training as the franchisee's needs dictate.

Information Submitted: November 1993

PRUDENTIAL REAL ESTATE AFFILIATES, THE
3200 Park Center Dr., # 1500
Costa Mesa, CA 92626
Telephone: (800) 666-6634 (714) 966-7900
Fax: (714) 434-3735
Mr. Steven A. Ozonian, Executive Vice President

Number of Franchised Units: 434
Number of Company-Owned Units: 0
Number of Total Operating Units: 434

In Business Since: 1988   **Franchising Since:** 1988

Description of Operation: Offer and sale of franchises for the operation of real estate brokerage to selected real estate brokers throughout the US and certain foreign countries.

Equity Capital Needed: $25,565 - $45,900 (excluding franchise fee).

Franchise Fee: $25,000 - $73,000 and up.

Royalty Fee: 1.25% - 6%

Financial Assistance: The franchisor may allow the franchisee to defer payment of all or a portion of the initial franchise fee and may permit financing of other obligations owed to the franchisor. The annual rate of interest ranges from 9% - 15% for up to 36 months or equal to the highest rate permitted by law, whichever is lower.

Managerial Assistance: Each location manager is required to attend the franchisor's Management Academy. An initial orientation program is provided by the franchisor for managers.

Training Provided: Optional staff training seminars are available.

Information Submitted: February 1994

RE/MAX INTERNATIONAL
5445 DTC Parkway, # 1200
Englewood, CO 80111
Telephone: (800) 525-7452 (303) 770-5531
Fax: (303) 796-3599
Ms. Maureen Lawrence, Public Relations Co-ordinator

Number of Franchised Units: 2273
Number of Company-Owned Units: 0
Number of Total Operating Units: 2273

In Business Since: 1973   **Franchising Since:** 1975

Description of Operation: RE/MAX is an international real estate franchise network. The franchise offered is set up to allow sales associates who join a RE/MAX franchise to receive the highest possible compensation in return for sharing common overhead expenses and certain other fees. RE/MAX offers its franchisees training programs, a full-service relocation company, an R.E.O. (asset management) company, awards banquets, referral network, advertising research, company publications, educational seminars and an annual convention

Equity Capital Needed: $10,000 - $25,000, varies from region to region.

Franchise Fee: $10,000 - $25,000

Royalty Fee: $100 per sales associate.

Financial Assistance: Yes.

Managerial Assistance: An intensive 2 days of individual instruction is given by national staff, teaching new owners how to operate the Realty Executives 100% concept, using methods with over 20 years of proven success. A comprehensive operations manual, coupled with the instant accessibility of a national staff, who also administer Company-owned offices, provide on-going assistance. New accounting software is available at additional expense.

Training Provided: Unlimited consultation in proven, successful accounting procedures, recruiting techniques, clerical hiring and advertising methods is provided. National and regional meetings cover topics of vital interest to owners. Operation of national referral network and volume purchasing to our brokers and associates.

Information Submitted: April 1994

REALTY ONE
7310 Potomac Dr.
Boise, ID 83704
Telephone: (800) REALTY-1 (208) 322-2700
Fax: (208) 322-2756
Mr. David W. Dildine, President

Number of Franchised Units: 2
Number of Company-Owned Units: 1
Number of Total Operating Units: 3

In Business Since: 1985   Franchising Since: 1987

Description of Operation: Full-service real estate franchise company, offering a new concept in real estate brokerage. Featuring "Real 100%" commissions - the Realty One concept. A method of real estate business operation uniquely different from conventional-type real estate offices.

Equity Capital Needed: $75,000 - $100,000

Franchise Fee: $15,000

Royalty Fee: Fixed monthly fee.

Financial Assistance: None.

Managerial Assistance: We provide on-site managerial assistance for the start-up of a new franchise, as well as corporate office staff assistance.

Training Provided: We offer on-site training in the franchisee's local board of realtors and realtor community, including site location, start-up assistance, operations and recruitment of realtors.

Information Submitted: March 1994

REALTY WORLD
3030 Old Ranch Pkwy., # 190
Seal Beach, CA 90740
Telephone: (800) 777-5565 (310) 430-9050
Fax: (310) 431-4008
Ms. Yvonne M. Corrigan-Carr, Executive Vice President

Number of Franchised Units: 702
Number of Company-Owned Units: 0
Number of Total Operating Units: 702

In Business Since: 1974   Franchising Since: 1974

Description of Operation: Realty World Corporation has developed a plan designed to enable independent real estate brokerage offices to benefit from broad name identification and to enable such offices to compete more effectively in the real estate industry. The Realty World System is one of the largest real estate franchise organizations in North America, with independently-owned and operated offices throughout the US, Canada, Mexico and Israel.

Equity Capital Needed: $27,000 - $38,000 (start up).

Franchise Fee: $15,900

Royalty Fee: 1% - 5%

Financial Assistance: Realty World Corporation makes financing available to new franchisees.

Managerial Assistance: The Realty World System includes the common use and promotion of the service mark Realty World and other marks, the production of commercials for use in radio and TV and other media advertising, sales training programs, educational programs, training manuals, a program for referral of real estate listings and various forms, procedures and systems to assist in the operation and management of a real estate office.

Training Provided: RWC holds the RealStart Management Training Academy for new franchisee broker/owners. It is a 5-day orientation and business planning session, highlighting Realty World programs and services.

Information Submitted: February 1994

ROOM-MATE REFERRAL SERVICE CENTERS
P. O. Box 890575
Oklahoma City, OK 73189
Telephone: (405) 692-0947
Fax: (405) 634-3096
Ms. Florence S. Cook, Chief Executive Officer

Number of Franchised Units: 22
Number of Company-Owned Units: 2
Number of Total Operating Units: 24

In Business Since: 1979   Franchising Since: 1984

Description of Operation: A service company that handles the placement of persons as roommates, for economic and a variety of other needs.

Equity Capital Needed: $6,500 - $15,000

Franchise Fee: $4,500 - $11,000

Royalty Fee: 5%

Financial Assistance: 25% of the franchise fee is carried personally at no interest.

Managerial Assistance: After initial training, we are always available by phone. Once a year, we go back into the area at our expense for additional training or whatever help is needed.

Training Provided: A manual and enough forms to last at least 3 months are provided. We go into the area of the new franchisee to train. We are there 2 1/2 - 3 days. Besides training, we help locate the site needed for the business. We do the training at our own expense.

Information Submitted: March 1994

TERMINIX INTERNATIONAL
855 Ridge Lake Blvd.
Memphis, TN 38120
Telephone: (800) 654-7848 (901) 766-1351
Fax: (901) 766-1107
Mr. Bob Morris, Director of Franchise Recruitment

Number of Franchised Units: 224
Number of Company-Owned Units: 401
Number of Total Operating Units: 625

In Business Since: 1927   Franchising Since: 1927

Description of Operation: World's largest structural pest control company, with over 600 service centers nationwide and in several foreign countries, offering termite and pest control services to residential, commercial and industrial customers.

Equity Capital Needed: $29,500 - $49,900

Franchise Fee: $25,000 - $50,000

Royalty Fee: 7%

Financial Assistance: With approved credit, Terminix will finance up to 70% of the initial franchise fee.

Managerial Assistance: On-going technical, operational, sales and marketing support.

Training Provided: Training for new franchisees covers a wide variety of disciplines, including technical aspects of termite and pest control, operations management and production, general business procedures, sales and sales management and personnel administration.

Information Submitted: November 1993

WORLD INSPECTION NETWORK INTERNATIONAL
10220 SW Greenburg Rd., N. Twr. 345
Portland, OR 97223
Telephone: (800) 30-WORLD (503) 246-9505
Fax: (503) 246-9663
Ms. Dianne Knapp, President

Number of Franchised Units: 9
Number of Company-Owned Units: 2
Number of Total Operating Units: 11

In Business Since: 1993   **Franchising Since:** 1993

Description of Operation: A national home inspection and property condition analysis franchise company that offers complete services for the home buyer, seller and real estate agent. World targets market areas and awards a specific number of franchisees in that area to achieve strategic market share goals. World provides a complete business operating system from start to inspections and beyond in this fast-growing market.

Equity Capital Needed: $28,000 - $120,000, includes franchise fee and varies based on # of vans and inspectors in service.

Franchise Fee: $13,950 urban area; $10,500 rural area (population 150,000 or less).

Royalty Fee: 7.5%, plus 2.5% to national advertising fund.

Financial Assistance: Yes.

Managerial Assistance: Each new franchisee receives assistance regarding business procedures and management skills. A complete operations and procedures manual is provided, covering all aspects of the operation. On-going back-up support in all areas of franchise operation. Sales, marketing and administration is provided with available field representative support on request.

Training Provided: A very complete 14 days of classroom and in-field, hands-on instruction is provided at the Corporate Service Center. The training includes all aspects of technical and administrative details of the home inspection industry. Franchisees are trained on the use of the "Home Condition Analysis" software system and the professional reporting format that is used by 200 home inspectors nationwide. Marketing strategy support and instruction provided. Environmental hazard inspection training is provided as well.

Information Submitted: February 1994

RECREATION—ENTERTAINMENT—TRAVEL

ADMIRAL OF THE FLEET CRUISE CENTERS
3430 Pacific Ave. SE. # A-5
Olympia, WA 98501
Telephone: (800) 877-7447 (206) 438-1191
Fax: (206) 438-2618
Mr. Bob L. Lovely, Vice President

Number of Franchised Units: 2
Number of Company-Owned Units: 5
Number of Total Operating Units: 7

In Business Since: 1986   **Franchising Since:** 1986

Description of Operation: Cruise-only travel agency.

Equity Capital Needed: $100,000 - $150,000

Franchise Fee: $25,000

Royalty Fee: .7% of 1%.

Financial Assistance: None.

Managerial Assistance: Training in all aspects of the business. The best computer software in the business. On-going training and marketing assistance. Special purchasing assistance.

Training Provided: Pre-opening training for manager/owner and staff. On-going sales, marketing and operations.

Information Submitted: March 1994

ALGONQUIN TRAVEL
657 Bronson Ave.
Ottawa, ON K1S 4E7 CAN

Telephone: (800) 668-1743 (613) 233-7713
Fax: (613) 233-7805
Ms. Katrina Rourke, Franchise Development

Number of Franchised Units: 50
Number of Company-Owned Units: 1
Number of Total Operating Units: 51

In Business Since: 1964   **Franchising Since:** 1978

Description of Operation: Full-service travel agency. Mission - to develop a team of successful travel agencies working together to exceed the expectations of the traveling consumer. Goal - to be the dominant, best quality, best service and best value travel chain in each market in which we are active.

Equity Capital Needed: $75,000 - $150,000

Franchise Fee: $35,000

Royalty Fee: 6% - 10%

Financial Assistance: Government small business loans, full assistance in loan applications, including business plan writing and financial forecasts.

Managerial Assistance: 3 weeks of training in Ottawa, ON: 1 week on-site; staff recruiting and agency set-up; franchisee buddy system; automation training; 6 months of complimentary automation for new locations; toll-free phone and E-mail; experienced field support staff.

Training Provided: Full training curriculum.

Information Submitted: December 1993

AMERICAN DARTERS ASSOCIATION
1000 Lake St. Louis Blvd., # 325
Lake St. Louis, MO 63367
Telephone: (314) 625-8621
Fax: (314) 625-2975
Mr. Glenn Remick, President

Number of Franchised Units: 74
Number of Company-Owned Units: 0
Number of Total Operating Units: 74

In Business Since: 1991   **Franchising Since:** 1991

Description of Operation: The American Darters Association is distinguished by its multi-year contract with Anheuser-Busch to promote nationwide dart leagues. Franchisees organize and maintain dart teams under the Bud Light/American Dart League name. A copyrighted league management program and handicap system allows players of all abilities to compete evenly, players are attracted by large national tournaments and member discounts with national companies.

Equity Capital Needed: $1,250, plus franchise fee.

Franchise Fee: Based on population.

Royalty Fee: 20%; $3 of weekly team fee.

Financial Assistance: Not available.

Managerial Assistance: Initial training, on-going training and support. A full-time support representative is assigned to each franchisee. Monthly correspondence is provided for all franchisees.

Training Provided: Initial 3-day training seminar, as well as on-going training and updates.

Information Submitted: December 1993

AMERICAN MILLIONAIRES
2922 E. Chapman Ave., # 100
Orange, CA 92669
Telephone: (714) 967-6378
Mr. Mark Tomaino, General Manager

Number of Franchised Units: 2
Number of Company-Owned Units: 0
Number of Total Operating Units: 2

In Business Since: 1979   **Franchising Since:** 1982

Description of Operation: Singles club/computer singles network. Date from home.

Equity Capital Needed: $20,000

Franchise Fee: $5,000

Royalty Fee: 3%, negotiable.

Financial Assistance: Data not available.

Managerial Assistance: Full training, on-site assistance, corporate training and scripted sales presentations. Corporation provides leads.

Training Provided: 2 months in main office learning trade, formulas, measures and modes of performance.

Information Submitted: January 1994

AMERICAN POOLPLAYERS ASSOCIATION
1000 Lake St. Louis Blvd., # 325
Lake St. Louis, MO 63367
Telephone: (314) 625-8611
Fax: (314) 625-2975
Ms. Kelly A. Wilmes, Franchise Licensing Representative

Number of Franchised Units: 206
Number of Company-Owned Units: 0
Number of Total Operating Units: 206

In Business Since: 1981   **Franchising Since:** 1982

Description of Operation: The American Poolplayers Association is the governing body of amateur pool. It sanctions weekly league play for over 120,000 members through a nationwide franchising network.

Equity Capital Needed: 90 days of cash reserve. No income generated until teams are playing.

Franchise Fee: $4,100

Royalty Fee: 20% of weekly fees.

Financial Assistance: We will finance up to $3,000. There are 4 different payment plans to choose from.

Managerial Assistance: Each franchisee is assigned to a support representative who will be in touch with him/her on a weekly basis. The support representative is available during all business hours to assist with daily league operations.

Training Provided: Each prospective franchisee is required to attend a 5-day training program in suburban St. Louis, MO. Covered in the training is our unique handicapping system, computer software program training, national and local advertising, local marketing strategies and all concepts of league activity.

Information Submitted: January 1994

ATEC GRAND SLAM U.S.A.
11320 Trade Center Dr., # C
Rancho Cordova, CA 95742
Telephone: (800) 775-2607 (916) 851-8330
Fax: (916) 851-1899
Mr. Bruce Carlyle, Executive Vice President - Sales

Number of Franchised Units: 87
Number of Company-Owned Units: 1
Number of Total Operating Units: 88

In Business Since: 1976   **Franchising Since:** 1984

Description of Operation: ATEC Grand Slam U.S.A. provides a fun, exciting and profitable business opportunity for the entrepreneur interested in owning a sports-related franchise. We are America's premiere business devoted to baseball and softball - providing quality, family entertainment. Revenue areas include batting ranges, academy, pro shop, facility rental, slam-ball basketball, parties, summer camps, video games and concessions.

Equity Capital Needed: $150,000 - $250,000 (including franchise fee), 30% from non-borrowed personal resources.

Franchise Fee: $15,000

Royalty Fee: 3.5% or yearly minimum. $6,000 year 1, $9,000 year 2 and $12,000 every year thereafter.

Financial Assistance: ATEC Grand Slam does not provide direct financing; however, we will provide assistance in suggesting a third party to work with. We will also provide assistance in the preparation of your business plan, which a lending institution will require.

Managerial Assistance: ATEC Grand Slam provides assistance in site selection and exclusive territories. We also provide on-going assistance in pro shop buying, franchise support, customer service support, marketing and advertising, research and development of equipment and a coaching certification program. National meeting in August at a resort location. Franchisees bring their families and have the opportunity to learn more about their business in a very professional atmosphere, as well as informal social gatherings.

Training Provided: ATEC Grand Slam provides a comprehensive training session at our National Training Center in Sacramento, CA. Our training staff will cover all revenue centers of the business in the classroom and you will receive actual "hands-on" experience in our Company store next to our headquarters.

Information Submitted: November 1993

CALCULATED COUPLES
3370 N. Hayden Rd., # 123-296
Scottsdale, AZ 85251
Telephone: (800) 44-MATCH (602) 494-7783
Mr. David E. Gorman, President

Number of Franchised Units: 7
Number of Company-Owned Units: 6
Number of Total Operating Units: 13

In Business Since: 1983   **Franchising Since:** 1987

Description of Operation: Singles matchmaking party service. Patent-pending system matches hundreds of singles each week at Calculated Couples matchmaking parties. Replaces dating services. Fun, unique, part-time, all-cash singles business.

Equity Capital Needed: $5,000 - $9,000

Franchise Fee: $4,995 - $6,995

Royalty Fee: $100 per month.

Financial Assistance: $4,995 down. Balance, if any, financed over 6-month period.

Managerial Assistance: Operations handbook describes operating procedures, toll-free 800# if assistance is needed. Consultants may also be hired from home office if necessary.

Training Provided: Operations handbook plus new training videotape. Headquarters visit is optional, but not required.

Information Submitted: December 1993

CANADIAN POOL LEAGUE
Box 722
Walkerton, ON N0G 2V0 CAN
Telephone: (519) 881-2196
Fax: (519) 881-2520
Mr. Lindsay Dobson, President

Number of Franchised Units: 7
Number of Company-Owned Units: 0
Number of Total Operating Units: 7

In Business Since: 1989   **Franchising Since:** 1989

Description of Operation: Solicit and administer pool leagues through taverns, billiard halls, etc. Providing weekly play year-round with updated material on a weekly basis.

Equity Capital Needed: $6,000

Franchise Fee: $0

Royalty Fee: 20% or $5 per team.

Financial Assistance: We do not offer financial support.

Managerial Assistance: On-going telephone support is available. Actual in-field assistance available if necessary.

Training Provided: A 5-day training seminar held in St. Louis, MO. This covers everything from software training to financial reports.

Information Submitted: December 1993

CINEMA 'N' DRAFTHOUSE / CINEMA GRILL
P. O. Box 28467
Atlanta, GA 30358
Telephone: (404) 250-9536
Fax: (404) 250-9536
Mr. John J. Duffy, Vice President

Number of Franchised Units: 20
Number of Company-Owned Units: 2
Number of Total Operating Units: 22

In Business Since: 1975   **Franchising Since:** 1980

Description of Operation: Cinema Grill is a theater/restaurant format that is universally appealing and distinctive. We start with a proven recession-proof product - food, drink and film - combined in a stylish, art deco theater. Then we enhance its value by offering space for business seminars, sports telecasts and private parties. For daytime use.

Equity Capital Needed: $100,000 - $450,000

Franchise Fee: $20,000

Royalty Fee: 3%

Financial Assistance: Assistance provided in putting together business plans, landlord/developer negotiation and direction in SBA and various other programs.

Managerial Assistance: Initially, you and your theater manager will be required to attend a 3-day training program, providing step-by-step operational techniques, in addition to pre-opening, on-site training.

Training Provided: Regular visits from regional managers insure that the operations of the theater are kept up to standards. Also, assistance is provided with new products, accounting controls, promotions and personnel guidance.

Information Submitted: November 1993

CLUB NAUTICO
850 NE 3rd St., # 204
Dania, FL 33004
Telephone: (800) NAUTICO (305) 927-9800
Fax: (305) 927-1300
Ms. Gina A. Durnak, Vice President of Marketing

Number of Franchised Units: 55
Number of Company-Owned Units: 7
Number of Total Operating Units: 62

In Business Since: 1984   **Franchising Since:** 1986

Description of Operation: Each Club Nautico retail center rents superior-quality powerboats to the qualified general public and sells memberships. The Club Nautico network focuses on providing the consumer with an easy, convenient and affordable alternative to boat ownership, allowing members to enjoy highly preferential rates at any Club in the world. The Company's service mark "Love Work," actually originated when a franchisee suggested the epithet to accurately describe the business. Club Nautico sells entertainment!

Equity Capital Needed: $100,000

Franchise Fee: $25,000

Royalty Fee: 10%

Financial Assistance: Equipment leasing available through franchisor.

Managerial Assistance: On-site training on request and toll-free number (800) BOATRENT.

Training Provided: Franchisees must successfully complete a comprehensive, 2 weeks of training at the Club Nautico boot camp in Ft. Lauderdale, FL for classroom and "on the water" training. Technical training related to fleet and engine management is available free and is held at OMC regional training facilities on an on-going basis. 5 days of training at your Club Nautico is available by request. Toll-free assistance and 24-hour paging service is also available.

Information Submitted: November 1993

COMPLETE MUSIC
7877 L St.
Omaha, NE 68127
Telephone: (800) 843-3866 (402) 339-0001
Fax: (402) 339-1285
Mr. Ken Matthews, Director of Franchising

Number of Franchised Units: 112
Number of Company-Owned Units: 1
Number of Total Operating Units: 113

In Business Since: 1972   **Franchising Since:** 1984

Description of Operation: Complete Music, the nation's largest franchised mobile entertainment service, provides entertainment for special events. Franchise owners hire and train a staff of D.J.'s to perform at these events.

Equity Capital Needed: $15,000 - $20,000

Franchise Fee: $9,500 for major market.

Royalty Fee: 8%

Financial Assistance: Partial assistance is available to qualified individuals.

Managerial Assistance: Complete Music provides on-going support, in addition to initial training. The support team would include in-office managerial staff, as well as experienced owners' support in other cities.

Training Provided: Training includes 10 days at Complete Music's corporate office, covering all aspects of day-to-day operations, including marketing, training of staff, hiring procedures, etc. Initial training also includes a 4-day visit to the franchisee's city.

Information Submitted: March 1994

CRUISE HOLIDAYS INTERNATIONAL
9665 Chesapeake Dr., # 401
San Diego, CA 92123
Telephone: (800) 866-7245 (619) 279-4780
Fax: (619) 279-4788
Franchise Development Department

Number of Franchised Units: 160
Number of Company-Owned Units: 0
Number of Total Operating Units: 160

In Business Since: 1984   **Franchising Since:** 1984

Description of Operation: Cruise Holidays International is the oldest and largest chain of cruise-only agencies in the world, specializing in the sale of cruise vacations to the general public. Cruising has become the fastest-growing and most profitable segment of the travel industry. Cruise Holidays offers comprehensive training, national advertising and no inventory. Cruise Holidays represents all the major cruise lines.

Equity Capital Needed: $84,000 - $130,000

Franchise Fee: $29,500

Royalty Fee: 1% or $525.50.

Financial Assistance: Financial assistance to veterans who qualify under the VetFran program. Franchisor will finance up to 50% of the franchise fee through a small interest note.

Managerial Assistance: We provide 2 weeks of comprehensive training in marketing, advertising, sales, customer service, product knowledge, business operations and accounting. A free cruise is included as part of the training. On-site visits and assistance. Group and convention sales and advanced training available.

Training Provided: Same as above.

Information Submitted: March 1994

CRUISE LINES RESERVATION CENTER
9229 Kaufman Place
Brooklyn, NY 11236
Telephone: (718) 763-4259
Mr. Bernard Korn, President

Number of Franchised Units: 24
Number of Company-Owned Units: 1
Number of Total Operating Units: 25

In Business Since: 1989   Franchising Since: 1990

Description of Operation: Cruise-only travel agency.

Equity Capital Needed: $1,000 - $2,000

Franchise Fee: $500

Royalty Fee: 1%

Financial Assistance: None.

Managerial Assistance: Unlimited consultation.

Training Provided: Training is provided through comprehensive manuals and nationwide training seminars.

Information Submitted: January 1994

DEK STAR DEK & ROLLER HOCKEY CENTERS
1106 Reedsdale St., # 201
Pittsburgh, PA 15233
Telephone: (412) 231-1660
Fax: (412) 323-1399
Mr. Larry A. Gaus, President

Number of Franchised Units: 1
Number of Company-Owned Units: 2
Number of Total Operating Units: 3

In Business Since: 1990   Franchising Since: 1992

Description of Operation: Manufacturer and manager of indoor and outdoor recreational facilities, including deckhockey, rollerhockey, soccer, volleyball, etc. We offer complete construction, design, financial and management assistance. Start-up and business planning assistance also provided.

Equity Capital Needed: $150,000 +

Franchise Fee: $5,000

Royalty Fee: 0%; negotiated consulting fee after time.

Financial Assistance: We provide a leasing finance program on selected components of our package to credit-worthy clients.

Managerial Assistance: Operational training, on-site manuals, monthly operational and marketing assistance. Field assistance is on-going at owner's facilities.

Training Provided: DekStar provides a complete training program (2 weeks) and manuals. Classroom and on-the-job (actual facility management) training provided to all owners.

Information Submitted: January 1994

DUFFERIN GAME ROOM STORE
52 Titan Rd.
Toronto, ON M8Z 2J8 CAN
Telephone: (800) 268-2597 (416) 239-2761
Fax: (416) 239-2218
Mr. Mark W. Wells, President

Number of Franchised Units: 14
Number of Company-Owned Units: 33
Number of Total Operating Units: 47

In Business Since: 1986   Franchising Since: 1986

Description of Operation: Dufferin specializes in billiards. Products manufactured in Canada by "Dufferin." It is a "family fun" store that carries a full range of games, puzzles, darts, shuffleboard, casino, chess, bar equipment, ping-pong, air-hockey, foosball. "Having Fun - Selling Fun" - That's a Dufferin Game Room Store.

Equity Capital Needed: $150,000 - $200,000

Franchise Fee: $30,000

Royalty Fee: 5%

Financial Assistance: None.

Managerial Assistance: Included in training program.

Training Provided: Training takes 2 - 4 weeks, as required.

Information Submitted: March 1994

EMPRESS TRAVEL
465 Smith St.
Farmingdale, NY 11735
Telephone: (516) 420-9200
Fax: (516) 420-4752
Mr. Arnold R. Tolkin, Chairman

Number of Franchised Units: 63
Number of Company-Owned Units: 0
Number of Total Operating Units: 63

In Business Since: 1958   Franchising Since: 1970

Description of Operation: East Coast retail travel agency network. Affiliated with one of the country's largest travel wholesalers. Franchisee enjoys the benefits of massive advertising, including weekly full-page advertisements in the New York Times and other papers such as Newark Star Ledger, The Washington Post, The Philadelphia Inquirer, The Albany Times Union, The New York Post, Newsday and others.

Equity Capital Needed: $2,500 - $100,000

Franchise Fee: $20,000

Royalty Fee: From $7,500 per year.

Financial Assistance: None from franchisor.

Managerial Assistance: Weekly communication via Company newsletter. Monthly seminars on sales techniques, marketing ideas and operational know-how. Telephone support is 5 days a week, 52 weeks a year.

Training Provided: We offer an extensive, 2-week training course, plus on-going assistance, as described above. In addition, training for each employee on an airline reservation system is completed by either American Airlines Sabre System or Continental on System One at no additional cost to the franchisee.

Information Submitted: January 1994

FUN SERVICES
3815 S. Ashland Ave.
Chicago, IL 60609
Telephone: (800) 926-1223 (312) 847-2600
Fax: (312) 847-6127
Mr. Jay Holt, Business Development

Number of Franchised Units: 120
Number of Company-Owned Units: 1
Number of Total Operating Units: 121

In Business Since: 1965   Franchising Since: 1965

Description of Operation: Fun Services provides a wide range of community entertainment and fund raising programs. Some of these are the original "Santa's Secret Shop" program; the "Fun Fair" school carnival program; and employee and company events, such as picnics and conventions. The fund raising areas are designed for school children in small groups or whole school projects. Some of the programs are "Great American Gift Wrap" and "Gifts for All Seasons," as well as the incentive prize program "Just for Fun."

Equity Capital Needed: $25,000

Franchise Fee: $75,000 - $100,000

Royalty Fee: $150 per month.

Financial Assistance: Some franchise financing may be available upon credit application.

Managerial Assistance: 3-day, on-site start-up training school at an existing franchise location. Annual conventions and sales meetings are held throughout the year. The cost of the first training school is included in the franchise fee, which includes hotel and transportation.

Training Provided: Same as above, plus on-site visits by franchisor staff continues throughout the franchise term.

Information Submitted: January 1994

FUN WORKS
3216 Power Blvd.
Metairie, LA 70003
Telephone: (504) 887-5678
Fax: (504) 887-5437
Mr. Frank M. Scurlock, President

Number of Franchised Units: 1
Number of Company-Owned Units: 1
Number of Total Operating Units: 2

In Business Since: 1986   **Franchising Since:** 1992

Description of Operation: An indoor "soft play" amusement center, specializing in participating play for children ages 2 - 12. Play area consists of child play toys such as Space Pillow, Sea of Balls, Cargo Net, Cheese Maze, etc. Business consists of general admission birthday parties and groups. Play area is complimented with game area and concession stand.

Equity Capital Needed: $100,000

Franchise Fee: $25,000

Royalty Fee: 6%

Financial Assistance: None.

Managerial Assistance: Site selection assistance, installation of operational procedures for this type of business and necessary forms. 1 week of hands-on training at home office prior to opening. Operations manual and advertising material provided.

Training Provided: 1 week of hands-on training at home office and 1 week of hands-on training at new site during opening. Additional follow-up training available on request for additional fee.

Information Submitted: December 1993

GALAXSEA CRUISES
1400 E. Oakland Park Blvd., # 103
Ft. Lauderdale, FL 33334
Telephone: (800) 821-1072 (305) 564-7072
Fax: (305) 564-7049
Ms. Lois Jean Utt, Vice President of Marketing and Operations

Number of Franchised Units: 54
Number of Company-Owned Units: 1
Number of Total Operating Units: 55

In Business Since: 1988   **Franchising Since:** 1989

Description of Operation: Cruise-only travel franchise network, with programs in place that help franchisees corner the cruise market - a $50 billion industry. Franchise owners can take advantage of the most rapidly-growing, profitable segment of the travel industry - and enjoy an exciting lifestyle. Extensive product and sales training, monthly marketing strategies and volume buying power are a part of the GalaxSea system.

Equity Capital Needed: $80,000 - $120,000 (includes franchise fee).

Franchise Fee: $25,000

Royalty Fee: 1%

Financial Assistance: We will finance up to $10,000 of initial franchise fee.

Managerial Assistance: The regional support staff provides assistance in central data processing, field operations evaluation, regional training, regionalized marketing programs, outside sales training programs, business and finance management and product knowledge training.

Training Provided: We provide an initial 10-day product knowledge/marketing/operations training, followed by 3 days on-site during the first month, with quarterly on-site visits thereafter. National and regional seminars and conferences, seminars-at-sea and other field training.

Information Submitted: January 1994

GLAMOUR GIRL & BOY BEAUTY CONTEST
P. O. Box 1031
Jefner, FL 33584
Telephone: (800) 829-8723 (813) 689-4308
Fax: (904) 767-2194
Ms. Olga Knight, General Director

Number of Franchised Units: 1
Number of Company-Owned Units: 0
Number of Total Operating Units: 1

In Business Since: 1980   **Franchising Since:** 1992

Description of Operation: Beauty contest for children.

Equity Capital Needed: $6,000

Franchise Fee: $3,900

Royalty Fee: 25% of net or $180 monthly.

Financial Assistance: 50% down; balance over 60 months.

Managerial Assistance: We will operate 2 shows with franchisee.

Training Provided: Same as above.

Information Submitted: January 1994

GREAT EXPECTATIONS
16830 Ventura Blvd., # P
Encino, CA 91436
Telephone: (818) 788-5200
Fax: (818) 788-5304
Mr. Jeffrey Ullman, President/Chief Executive Officer

Number of Franchised Units: 42
Number of Company-Owned Units: 5
Number of Total Operating Units: 47

In Business Since: 1976   **Franchising Since:** 1977

Description of Operation: Great Expectations is the oldest and largest singles relationship service in the world. In 1976, it created "video dating," so that singles could meet each offer for a committed romantic relationship. Currently, video dating is only one of several unique services offered to its singles membership.

Equity Capital Needed: $162,000 - $377,000

Franchise Fee: $55,000

Royalty Fee: 8%

Financial Assistance: Negotiable.

Managerial Assistance: Besides training at the franchisee's home center and the franchisor's headquarters, frequent communication is maintained through telephone and letter correspondence. The franchisee is encouraged to pick up the phone and call the franchisor or fellow franchisees.

Training Provided: We offer an intensive and comprehensive 2 weeks of training at the Los Angeles headquarters, followed by a 4-week training visit to the franchisee's center. Additional training visits to the franchisee, as well as at main headquarters, are scheduled. Training includes a 500-page operations manual.

Information Submitted: March 1994

HAUNTED HAYRIDES
135 Old Cove Rd., Ste. 210
Liverpool, NY 13090
Telephone: (800) 344-2868 (315) 453-6009
Fax: (315) 453-3820
Mr. Matthew M. Jacob, Sr., Chief Executive Officer

Number of Franchised Units: 21
Number of Company-Owned Units: 3
Number of Total Operating Units: 24

In Business Since: 1985   **Franchising Since:** 1989

Description of Operation: Haunted Hayrides is an entertainment concept operated during the month of October with a Halloween theme. Acts and actors are scheduled on a trail or road that in and of itself could be considered scary. These "haunts" increase that aspect. We consider a Haunted Hayride to be good old-fashioned, All-American fun.

Equity Capital Needed: $30,000 - $45,000

Franchise Fee: $15,000

Royalty Fee: 10% ($5,000 minimum).

Financial Assistance: The franchisor does not provide any financial assistance.

Managerial Assistance: Franchisor actively participates and must approve the future site of a Haunted Hayrides. The franchisor will advise the prospective franchisee as to zoning, leasing and sources of supply for equipment. The franchisor must approve every phase of the operation before the season starts and visit each site during the season. The franchisee is responsible to the franchisor for all charges except the first visit.

Training Provided: The franchisor provides 2 days of intensive training, generally at the home office in Liverpool, NY. A confidential manual is provided to each franchisee for study and reference. The manual is the focus of the 2-day training, but all phases of operating a hayride are studied by means of video tape, etc. and one-on-one discussions with other franchisees that are already in business.

Information Submitted: January 1994

MANDY'S MATCHING SERVICE
6500 Jericho Tpke., # 206A
Commack, NY 11725
Telephone: (800) 626-3971 (516) 462-1847
Fax: (516) 462-6137
Mr. Paul Schlanger, President

Number of Franchised Units: 4
Number of Company-Owned Units: 0
Number of Total Operating Units: 4

In Business Since: 1987   **Franchising Since:** 1990

Description of Operation: Personal dating service.

Equity Capital Needed: $28,000 - $50,000

Franchise Fee: $15,000

Rcyalty Fee: 7%

Financial Assistance: A portion of the initial franchise fee may be financed through the franchisor.

Managerial Assistance: 1 month of training at franchisor's location.

Training Provided: 1 month of training at franchisor's location and 5 days at franchisee's location.

Information Submitted: November 1993

MEGA 900 COMMUNICATIONS
P. O. Box 562
Mystic Island, NJ 08087
Telephone: (800) 316-MEGA (302) 654-0829
Fax: (609) 294-2120
Mr. Thomas P. Clay, President

Number of Franchised Units: 4
Number of Company-Owned Units: 1
Number of Total Operating Units: 5

In Business Since: 1989   **Franchising Since:** 1990

Description of Operation: Turn-key 900/800 audiotext application. Dating magazine with territorial rights available for franchisees. $750 for 5,000 copies. Typed and shipped.

Equity Capital Needed: $750 - $2,000

Franchise Fee: $750 - magazine.

Royalty Fee: 50% or $1 on 1.95.

Financial Assistance: Due to the delayed pay-out interval at the end of the beginning month, advanced copies of the dating magazine will be granted to those franchisors who do the required minutes for one month.

Managerial Assistance: Data not available.

Training Provided: Training will be provided to all franchisees in the form of recognizing the premium markets for joint ventures, ad placement and magazine placement.

Information Submitted: December 1993

MISS ARISTA PAGEANT, USA
P. O. Box 55181
Hayward, CA 94545
Telephone: (800) 973-3333 (510) 888-2300
Fax: (510) 538-1997
Ms. Maggie-Judith Fluker, Director

Number of Franchised Units: 0
Number of Company-Owned Units: 4
Number of Total Operating Units: 4

In Business Since: 1983   **Franchising Since:** 1994

Description of Operation: National entertainment competition pageants for women, men, teens and children. Support the performing arts categories of: acting, dance, vocal music, instrumental music, models, producers, directors and writers. Awards, prizes, scholarships and many other opportunities.

Equity Capital Needed: $10,000 - $50,000

Franchise Fee: $2,500 - $10,000 range.

Royalty Fee: 15%, negotiable.

Financial Assistance: Yearly training sessions, seminars and classroom-type instruction. Assistance with the production and music for the first pageant. Limited volunteer training of the volunteers in local and state franchises.

Managerial Assistance: We provide yearly training sessions for managers, continuous support, advice and help and recommendations of other professionals to assist or train if available.

Training Provided: We offer on-location training of administration, operations, production, volunteer support, staffing, policies, procedures and details and areas pertaining to the success of the local and state pageants.

Information Submitted: April 1994

OUTDOOR CONNECTION
1001 E. Cliff Rd.
Burnsville, MN 55124
Telephone: (708) 351-4060 (612) 890-0407
Mr. Robert Laddusaw, President

Number of Franchised Units: 36
Number of Company-Owned Units: 0
Number of Total Operating Units: 36

In Business Since: 1988   Franchising Since: 1988

Description of Operation: Outdoor Connection arranges and promotes fishing and hunting trips. The network of lodges and outfitters is located throughout North America. The franchisees represent those lodges to customers in their local area.

Equity Capital Needed: $1,100 - $5,600

Franchise Fee: $5,800 - $7,800

Royalty Fee: 3% - 4%

Financial Assistance: The franchisor will provide a promissory note for a portion for 1 year.

Managerial Assistance: The franchisor helps with and suggests plans for planning 6 month and 1 year objectives. Also, a plan to reach those objectives is suggested.

Training Provided: A well-organized, 1 1/2 day training program includes product knowledge, paperwork for bookings, bookkeeping, advertising, trade show knowledge, sales hints and more.

Information Submitted: January 1994

PARTY ANIMALS
180 Allen Rd., # 118
Atlanta, GA 30328
Telephone: (404) 303-7789
Fax: (404) 303-9839
Ms. Cheryl Carter, President

Number of Franchised Units: 10
Number of Company-Owned Units: 0
Number of Total Operating Units: 10

In Business Since: 1987   Franchising Since: 1992

Description of Operation: Party Animals offers unique, costumed characters and entertainers, specializing in corporate parties, trade shows, holiday events, grand openings and birthday parties. All our characters face paint, perform magic, make animal balloons and add life to any event.

Equity Capital Needed: Approximately $6,000, after the initial fee.

Franchise Fee: $12,500

Royalty Fee: 6%

Financial Assistance: Yes.

Managerial Assistance: Operational training at corporate office. On-site manuals, monthly updates, marketing pieces and ideas, yearly convention and on-going phone and fax support.

Training Provided: Party Animals offers 2 - 3 days at the corporate office, training in a busy location. Then we go to the new location and go on sales calls, place advertising, etc., for 2 - 3 days. Training includes 3 manuals, a monthly update, yearly convention and on-going telephone support.

Information Submitted: November 1993

PUTT-PUTT GOLF COURSES OF AMERICA
P. O. Box 35237, 3007 Ft. Bragg Rd.
Fayetteville, NC 28303
Telephone: (910) 485-7131
Fax: (910) 485-1122
Mr. Jim Evans, National Director of Franchising

Number of Franchised Units: 266
Number of Company-Owned Units: 10
Number of Total Operating Units: 276

In Business Since: 1954   Franchising Since: 1954

Description of Operation: Family fun centers, including Putt-Putt Golf, game rooms, bumper boats, batting cages, Formula K raceways and TotalPlay. Also, independent design.

Equity Capital Needed: $100,000 +

Franchise Fee: $20,000 - golf & games; $25,000 - fun center.

Royalty Fee: 5% Golf; 3% Games.

Financial Assistance: Not available.

Managerial Assistance: We provide regional training schools, a video training tape series, training manuals and certificates, as well as on-site training.

Training Provided: Same as above.

Information Submitted: January 1994

RECORDS ON WHEELS
255 Shields Ct.
Markham, ON L3R 8V2 CAN
Telephone: (905) 475-3550
Fax: (905) 475-4163
Ms. Rosie Knapp, Franchise Director

Number of Franchised Units: 24
Number of Company-Owned Units: 18
Number of Total Operating Units: 42

In Business Since: 1974   Franchising Since: 1975

Description of Operation: Retail stores, offering compact discs, cassettes, video and music accessories. Retail operations across Canada. Stores which are successful tend to have managers with a general interest in music trends.

Equity Capital Needed: $75,000 +

Franchise Fee: $7,500

Royalty Fee: 0%

Financial Assistance: No financing.

Managerial Assistance: In most locations, stores are owner-operated. General guidelines from head office are enforced with every location.

Training Provided: Where possible, hands-on training is held in another location.

Information Submitted: January 1994

TOGETHER DATING SERVICE
161 Worchester Rd., 2nd Fl.
Framingham, MA 01701
Telephone: (800) 635-3836 (508) 620-1115
Fax: (508) 872-7679
Mr. John Byron, Vice President of Franchise Development

Number of Franchised Units: 112
Number of Company-Owned Units: 8
Number of Total Operating Units: 120

In Business Since: 1974   Franchising Since: 1981

Description of Operation: Personalized introduction service.

Equity Capital Needed: $75,000 - $232,000

Franchise Fee: Depends on market size.

Royalty Fee: 8%

Financial Assistance: To be evaluated in accordance with the franchisee's application.

Managerial Assistance: We supply training at a corporate facility and on-going assistance, as needed, through the use of our corporate marketing department, accounting department, etc.

Training Provided: Training is provided in all aspects of our business; i.e. sales, marketing and promotions.

Information Submitted: November 1993

TPI TRAVEL SERVICES
3030 N. Rocky Point Rd., W., # 100
Tampa, FL 33607
Telephone: (800) 393-7767 (813) 281-5670
Fax: (813) 281-2304
Mr. Bernhard Benet, President

Number of Franchised Units: 345
Number of Company-Owned Units: 1
Number of Total Operating Units: 346

In Business Since: 1987   **Franchising Since:** 1987

Description of Operation: Full-service travel agency. Set-up includes training, automation, computers, software, on-site assistance, ticket processing, higher commissions, support and assistance.

Equity Capital Needed: $15,000 - $20,000

Franchise Fee: $10,995

Royalty Fee: $95

Financial Assistance: We can finance a portion of the franchise fee.

Managerial Assistance: We provide full support through toll-free numbers and by communication through software.

Training Provided: Training consists of 5 days at corporate office and includes airfare and hotel.

Information Submitted: January 1994

TRAVEL AGENTS INTERNATIONAL
111 Second Ave. NE, 15th Fl.
St. Petersburg, FL 33701
Telephone: (800) 678-8241 (813) 894-1537
Fax: (813) 894-6318
Ms. Lori Langenhahn, Franchise Co-ordinator

Number of Franchised Units: 368
Number of Company-Owned Units: 3
Number of Total Operating Units: 371

In Business Since: 1980   **Franchising Since:** 1982

Description of Operation: Complete start-up assistance, including site selection, lease negotiations, staffing, industry accreditation, bonding, extensive training, furniture package, accounting service, office design, sales and marketing programs. Proprietary publications, 24-hour emergency service, field service consultants, national promotions and a high commission earnings program. Also available is a program to assist in the purchase of an existing agency.

Equity Capital Needed: $81,500 - $131,000

Franchise Fee: $30,000

Royalty Fee: $500 per month flat fee.

Financial Assistance: From time to time, services are available to finance $15,000 of the franchise fee.

Managerial Assistance: Operational specialists work with the franchisee from the time the agreement is signed to complete the necessary steps to open the agency. Extensive flow charts are used to assure timely completion of each task. On-site, 2-day visit at opening the office, plus 6 additional visits the first year to assist with budget, planning, marketing, personnel and "entrepreneurship" topics.

Training Provided: We offer an initial 2 weeks of training for owners and 1 week for managers, as well as 1 week of optional training for travel consultants. Training topics include travel industry information, TAI procedures and programs, salesmanship techniques, marketing ideas, budget and business sessions.

Information Submitted: March 1994

TRAVEL NETWORK
560 Sylvan Ave.
Englewood Cliffs, NJ 07632
Telephone: (800) 872-8638 (201) 567-8500
Fax: (201) 567-1838
Ms. Stephanie Abrams, Vice President of Marketing

Number of Franchised Units: 310
Number of Company-Owned Units: 1
Number of Total Operating Units: 311

In Business Since: 1982   **Franchising Since:** 1983

Description of Operation: We provide complete start-up assistance (site selection, lease negotiations, staffing, industry accreditation, bonding, furnishings package, 5-week intensive front-end training), accounting package, complete computerization, on-going, continuous support and training, both locally and on-site, in-field, plus regional and national meetings, saturated marketing program and a high commissions earning program.

Equity Capital Needed: $80,000 - $100,000

Franchise Fee: $29,900

Royalty Fee: $350 per month - year 1; $550 per month - year 2; $750 per month - year 3.

Financial Assistance: 90% financing of turn-key store furnishings package.

Managerial Assistance: We provide automated accounting training, computer training, on-site field management training and toll-free hotline. Inside support structure for assistance, on-going, targeted trainings on each aspect of travel agency management.

Training Provided: 1 week each training for business development and marketing; agency operations (budgeting, pre-opening) and agency management; airline computer training; on-site at store level for pre-opening; automated accounting and post-opening budgeting.

Information Submitted: November 1993

TRAVEL PROFESSIONALS INTERNATIONAL
10172 Linn Station Rd., # 360
Louisville, KY 40223
Telephone: (800) 626-2469 (502) 423-9966
Fax: (502) 423-9914
Mr. John E. Boyce, Vice President of Franchising

Number of Franchised Units: 62
Number of Company-Owned Units: 1
Number of Total Operating Units: 63

In Business Since: 1983   **Franchising Since:** 1984

Description of Operation: Travel Professionals International is a franchisor of full-service travel agencies. A related company is a franchisor of travel schools.

Equity Capital Needed: $100,000 - $150,000

Franchise Fee: $33,000

Royalty Fee: 5%

Financial Assistance: No financing is available; however, information will be provided to lending institutions.

Managerial Assistance: We provide site-selection assistance and employee recruiting assistance. Marketing programs developed and manuals provided. On-going consulting services are available from staff of travel industry professionals.

Training Provided: Basic training includes 10 days in travel agency management and computer orientation. On-going training is provided in management, marketing and sales techniques.

Information Submitted: December 1993

TRAVELPLEX INTERNATIONAL
655 Metro Pl. S., # 250
Dublin, OH 43017
Telephone: (800) 221-9581 (614) 766-6315
Fax: (614) 766-0540
Mr. Darryl E. Warner, President

Number of Franchised Units: 17
Number of Company-Owned Units: 0
Number of Total Operating Units: 17

In Business Since: 1984   **Franchising Since:** 1989

Description of Operation: Retail travel agency franchise organization, specializing in business and vacation travel arrangements. This unique franchise has been created by working agency owner-managers. A comprehensive training program is provided for all staff levels. TravelPlex International provides recruitment services and productive office procedures. Franchisees receive sales and marketing programs, operational support and effective networking with member agencies.

Equity Capital Needed: $50,000

Franchise Fee: $30,900

Royalty Fee: $400 per month.

Financial Assistance: We will finance 24% of the franchise fee for 24 months.

Managerial Assistance: All manager applicants are screened, interviewed, rated and tested by the TravelPlex International management team.

Training Provided: 1 to 2 weeks at headquarters in Columbus, OH and 3 to 4 weeks on-site. Additional time as needed.

Information Submitted: November 1993

U.S.A. TOURIST SAVINGS CENTERS
4479 W. Irlo Bronson Hwy.
Kissimmee, FL 34746
Telephone: (800) 484-4499 (407) 396-4877
Fax: (407) 396-2938
Mr. Dean Chase, President

Number of Franchised Units: 0
Number of Company-Owned Units: 1
Number of Total Operating Units: 1

In Business Since: 1992   **Franchising Since:** 1994

Description of Operation: Sale of attraction tickets, timeshare tours (not timeshare sales), hotel and motel reservations locally, nationwide and worldwide, as well as retail merchandise.

Equity Capital Needed: $35,000 - $50,000

Franchise Fee: $35,000

Royalty Fee: 1% - 5%

Financial Assistance: Almost any finance plan is available to a qualified, potential franchisee.

Managerial Assistance: The owner/founder of the franchise has 35 years of retail sales experience. VP and controller has 34 years of retail sales experience and executive duties covering over 300 retail stores.

Training Provided: Training is provided by a comprehensive 2 weeks at Orlando, FL, where all franchisees are given 40 hours of on-premises schooling, then a like period of work-studies each evening. Training continues with 20 hours of hands-on training in a franchisor retail outlet. For the initial 2 months, training will be provided on an as-needed basis. Following this time, training will be provided continually by phone, for as long as is necessary.

Information Submitted: February 1994

ULTRAZONE
1700 E. Desert Inn Rd., # 305
Las Vegas, NV 89109
Telephone: (800) 628-2829 (702) 734-3617
Fax: (702) 734-3618
Mr. Drew Pawlak, Vice President

Number of Franchised Units: 4
Number of Company-Owned Units: 1
Number of Total Operating Units: 5

In Business Since: 1993   **Franchising Since:** 1993

Description of Operation: Ultrazone, the ultimate laser adventure. The most exciting investment in franchising's newest industry - live-action laser games. An American company, offering the most advanced laser game technology on the planet, backed by 7 years of research, development and operations. Ultrazone offers franchise owners service and support unequaled in the industry. Investment ranges from $320,000 - $480,000.

Equity Capital Needed: $290,000 - $400,000

Franchise Fee: $15,000

Royalty Fee: 5% of gross, or $2,000 per month.

Financial Assistance: No financing is currently available.

Managerial Assistance: On-going business support, from date of signing, through pre-opening and daily operations.

Training Provided: We offer 5 days of on-site training, plus 10 days of pre-opening training.

Information Submitted: February 1994

UNIGLOBE TRAVEL (INTERNATIONAL)
1199 W. Pender St., # 900
Vancouver, BC V6E 2R1 CAN
Telephone: (604) 662-3800
Fax: (604) 662-3878
Mr. Martin Charlwood

Number of Franchised Units: 1065
Number of Company-Owned Units: 0
Number of Total Operating Units: 1065

In Business Since: 1980   **Franchising Since:** 1980

Description of Operation: Uniglobe is the largest travel franchisor in the world. Its franchisees receive a vast array of services, including national TV advertising, consumer-recognized brand image, profitability software programs, one-on-one travel agency business consultation, franchise operator and manager forums, preferred supplier override programs and unparalleled training in all facets of the travel industry. Entrepreneur Magazine awarded Uniglobe #1 in Travel Agency Franchising.

Equity Capital Needed: $3,000 - $150,000

Franchise Fee: $47,500

Royalty Fee: .5% - 1%

Financial Assistance: Financial assistance includes a bonding program for ARC approval, on-going financial consultation, business plan and financing assistance in helping to secure a loan.

Managerial Assistance: The travel industry's most in-depth support program from front and back office to sales and marketing. A partial list of support programs includes software for agency management, Uniglobe's own back office system, management reports, productivity reports, corporate client reports, financial reports, commission tracking and billing reports. Budget and finance programs also.

Training Provided: Uniglobe offers the industry's most in-depth training courses - international management academy, advanced international management academy, Uniglobe orientation, commercial sales, vacation sales, group and incentive sales, video-based training, financial manage-ment and standardized operating procedures for the entire Uniglobe system.

Information Submitted: January 1994

VIP BOAT CLUB
P. O. Box 1344
Dunedin, FL 34697
Telephone: (800) 352-2169 (813) 734-5969
Fax: (813) 736-0839
Mr. Franklin C. Reinke, President

Number of Franchised Units: 4
Number of Company-Owned Units: 1
Number of Total Operating Units: 5

In Business Since: 1990   **Franchising Since:** 1992

Description of Operation: VIP Boat Clubs are located in beautiful marinas and resort areas, providing an alternative to boat ownership. Each club offers a variety of boats for fishing, cruising, island hopping, swimming and skiing to members, based on a reservation system. Members join for 1 - 2 years, or part of a year. Daily rental also available. VIP Boat Club "Puts the fun back into boating."

Equity Capital Needed: $80,000 - $100,000 (includes franchise fee).

Franchise Fee: $25,000

Royalty Fee: 5%

Financial Assistance: For qualified buyers, we will finance 50% or less of the franchise fee. We will also assist qualified buyers in applying for financing of boats, if needed.

Managerial Assistance: VIP Boat Club provides a complete operations manual, forms and sales aids. We assist in site selection, lease negotia-tions, licenses and setting up the business as a turn-key operation. We offer the franchisees assistance in purchasing their boats, motors, equipment and supplies at discount rates. All our franchisees purchase business insurance at group rates. We do joint advertising, shows and promotions. We provide continuous consultation to the franchisees by telephone and by periodic visits.

Training Provided: We offer 2 weeks of training at an existing franchise, 2 weeks of training at the franchisee's site and periodic follow-up training, as needed.

Information Submitted: January 1994

WORLD GYM
3110 Main St., # 205
Santa Monica, CA 90405
Telephone: (310) 450-0080
Fax: (310) 450-3455
Mr. Thomas P. Vitacco, President

Number of Franchised Units: 175
Number of Company-Owned Units: 0
Number of Total Operating Units: 175

In Business Since: 1980   **Franchising Since:** 1986

Description of Operation: World Gym grants licenses for health fitness centers, offering a full range of services, including free weights, selectorized equipment, cardio-vascular equipment, aerobics, child care, pro-shop, food and beverage, wellness, etc.

Equity Capital Needed: $350,000 - $750,000

Franchise Fee: $15,000

Royalty Fee: Flat rate.

Financial Assistance: Not available.

Managerial Assistance: We provide on-going training seminars and own-ers meetings, training and operations manuals covering all aspects of the business.

Training Provided: Same as above.

Information Submitted: December 1993

RENTALS—AUTO AND TRAILER

AFFORDABLE USED CAR RENTAL SYSTEM
96 Freneau Ave., # 2
Matawan, NJ 07747
Telephone: (800) 631-2290 (908) 290-8300
Fax: (908) 290-8305
Mr. Charles A. Vitale, General Manager

Number of Franchised Units: 100
Number of Company-Owned Units: 0
Number of Total Operating Units: 100

In Business Since: 1981   **Franchising Since:** 1981

Description of Operation: We provide training, insurance and manage-ment support for a car rental profit center.

Equity Capital Needed: $15,000 - $30,000

Franchise Fee: $3,500 - $6,000

Royalty Fee: $10 - $15 per car per month, depending on number of cars.

Financial Assistance: The franchise fee can be financed at 0% interest.

Managerial Assistance: 2-day training school, manual and forms, per-sonal on-site visits and reinforcement tapes.

Training Provided: 2 days at our corporate office - customer screening, vehicle selection, advertising and telephone techniques.

Information Submitted: January 1994

AIRWAYS RENT A CAR
4025 N. Mannheim Rd.
Schiller Park, IL 60176
Telephone: (708) 678-2300
Fax: (708) 678-2600
Ms. Gail Lazzara, Director of Operations

Number of Franchised Units: 35
Number of Company-Owned Units: 5
Number of Total Operating Units: 40

In Business Since: 1967   **Franchising Since:** 1981

Description of Operation: Worldwide reservation system for daily car rental locations. Reservation systems operated by division of American Airlines.

Equity Capital Needed: $100,000 - $350,000

Franchise Fee: $5,000 - $40,000

Royalty Fee: $11.00 per reservation.

Financial Assistance: Introduction to auto finance companies.

Managerial Assistance: Data not available.

Training Provided: 1 week at Airways headquarters and complete operations manual.

Information Submitted: November 1993

BUDGET RENT A CAR
4225 Naperville Rd.
Lisle, IL 60532
Telephone: (800) 621-2844 (708) 955-1900
Fax: (708) 955-7799
Mr. Larry Lanham, Director of Franchise Development

Number of Franchised Units: 2772
Number of Company-Owned Units: 387
Number of Total Operating Units: 3159

In Business Since: 1958   **Franchising Since:** 1960

Description of Operation: Car and truck rental, both in airport and local markets.

Equity Capital Needed: Varies.

Franchise Fee: $15,000 minimum.

Royalty Fee: 7.5%

Financial Assistance: 80% of the initial franchise fee may be financed over 12 months at reasonable interest rates.

Managerial Assistance: Assistance is available through routinely scheduled operational visits to discuss franchisee's performance. Also, regional meetings, workshops and profit groups are held on a periodic basis.

Training Provided: Training classes are conducted on an as-needed basis in both corporate headquarters and in the franchisee's city(ies).

Information Submitted: December 1993

DOLLAR RENT A CAR
100 N. Sepulveda Blvd., 6th Fl.
El Segundo, CA 90245
Telephone: (310) 535-7574
Fax: (310) 535-7495
Mr. Mario E. Nargi, Vice President of Franchise Development

Number of Franchised Units: 1300
Number of Company-Owned Units: 40
Number of Total Operating Units: 1340

In Business Since: 1965   **Franchising Since:** 1967

Description of Operation: Daily rental car.

Equity Capital Needed: $7,000 - $1,000,000

Franchise Fee: Depends on type of operation. Minimum of $7,500.

Royalty Fee: 8%

Financial Assistance: A portion of the initial franchise fee may be financed under certain circumstances.

Managerial Assistance: Initial training includes all facets of managing the rental car business.

Training Provided: New licensees receive on-site training in operations, fleet management, customer service, record keeping, local marketing and sales. Additional training given on an on-going basis.

Information Submitted: November 1993

DOLLAR RENT A CAR (CANADA)
1580 Yonge St.
Toronto, ON M4T 1Z8 CAN
Telephone: (416) 969-1190
Fax: (416) 969-9582
Mr. Richard Pett, Director of Franchising

Number of Franchised Units: 11
Number of Company-Owned Units: 3
Number of Total Operating Units: 14

In Business Since: 1993   **Franchising Since:** 1993

Description of Operation: As part of the worldwide Dollar Rent A Car system, we offer our franchisees a full support package, including fleet and insurance programs, a reservation system, marketing, advertising, training and on-going assistance.

Equity Capital Needed: $150,000 (minimum).

Franchise Fee: $25,000 (minimum).

Royalty Fee: 7%, plus 2% national advertising.

Financial Assistance: Extended payment terms for the franchise fee may be negotiated in some cases. Assistance and advice are provided for fleet and business financing.

Managerial Assistance: We provide assistance with rental location, lease negotiation, leasehold improvements, staff recruitment, local marketing and advertising, administration and accounting set-up.

Training Provided: We offer a combination of classroom and on-site training, a minimum of 1 week in each case, plus on-going courses at all staff levels.

Information Submitted: March 1994

PAYLESS CAR RENTAL
2350 34th St., N.
St. Petersburg, FL 33713
Telephone: (800) 729-5255 (813) 321-6352
Fax: (813) 321-1715
Ms. Kathleen Gassner, Director of Franchise Development

Number of Franchised Units: 150
Number of Company-Owned Units: 0
Number of Total Operating Units: 150

In Business Since: 1971   **Franchising Since:** 1971

Description of Operation: Automobile rental.

Equity Capital Needed: Varies according to the number of vehicles in the fleet and site selection.

Franchise Fee: Varies according to location: airport or non-airport. Range is $6,000 - $250,000.

Royalty Fee: 8%

Financial Assistance: None.

Managerial Assistance: Assistance is available for new and existing locations in operations, reservations, fleet, marketing, management information systems and supplies. Assistance is offered and implemented in on-going system bulletins, manual updates and newsletters. Departments are available via 800# for assistance.

Training Provided: New locations receive a 3-day orientation session at Payless headquarters, 1 week of on-site training at opening by an operations manager and 1 week of computer training by an approved computer vendor. On-going support is available as needed by all departments. Operations visits are made as deemed necessary, with a minimum of 2 per year.

Information Submitted: January 1994

PRACTICAL RENT A CAR
3763 Las Vegas Blvd. S.
Las Vegas, NV 89109
Telephone: (800) 424-7722 (702) 798-0025
Fax: (702) 798-4739
Mr. Elliott Smoler, Managing Director

Number of Franchised Units: 115
Number of Company-Owned Units: 0
Number of Total Operating Units: 115

In Business Since: 1989   **Franchising Since:** 1989

Description of Operation: Practical Rent a Car is a daily rental, short-term leasing, automobile and truck franchise system. The operators of Practical have reservation systems, fleet programs, handicapped vehicle programs, insurance programs, national advertising, promotional items and printing contracts.

Equity Capital Needed: $100,000 - $500,000

Franchise Fee: Varies by location.

Royalty Fee: $20 per vehicle.

Financial Assistance: None at this time.

Managerial Assistance: On-going training at corporate headquarters. Regional meetings and annual conventions. Quarterly newsletters. New employees may attend training at the Practical Academy.

Training Provided: Each new office will receive assistance regarding office location, rate setting, fleet mix, necessary forms and office management, including hands-on experience, at a 5-day training program at the home office.

RENT A VETTE
1025 W. Laurel, # 102
San Diego, CA 92101
Telephone: (800) 627-0808 (619) 238-3883
Fax: (619) 238-4279
Mr. John Pounds, President

Number of Franchised Units: 3
Number of Company-Owned Units: 1
Number of Total Operating Units: 4

In Business Since: 1981   Franchising Since: 1992

Description of Operation: Sports car rentals, requiring a minimum of 50% Corvettes; the balance can be any type of sports car from Mustang to Mercedes Benz. Criteria for franchisee: population of at least 1,000,000, airport arrivals of 7,500,000 and year-round good weather.

Equity Capital Needed: $300,000 - $1,000,000

Franchise Fee: $12,500

Royalty Fee: 3% - first year; 4% - second year; 5% - on-going.

Financial Assistance: The Company will guide the franchisee in the right direction, but provides no direct financing.

Managerial Assistance: We provide a 12-week countdown from site selection to opening, home office training and on-site training. On-going support for the length of the agreement.

Training Provided: We offer software and computer training, advertising, accounting and day-by-day answers to any problems that might occur.

Information Submitted: February 1994

RENT-A-WRECK OF AMERICA
11460 Cronridge Dr., # 118
Owings Mills, MD 21117
Telephone: (800) 421-7253 (410) 581-5755
Fax: (410) 581-1566
Mr. Gene Blum, Director of Public Relations

Number of Franchised Units: 400
Number of Company-Owned Units: 0
Number of Total Operating Units: 400

In Business Since: 1973   Franchising Since: 1978

Description of Operation: Rent and lease new and used cars, trucks and vans to the public and businesses.

Equity Capital Needed: $60,000 - $100,000 if stand alone. $25,000 - $40,000 if add-on.

Franchise Fee: $5,000 - $22,500; average $12,500.

Royalty Fee: 6%, plus 2% advertising.

Financial Assistance: Rent-A-Wreck will finance up to 75% of the franchise fee (not including cars). We will finance cars after an initial 6 month period, if in good standing.

Managerial Assistance: Managerial assistance is readily available to new franchisees, as is the assistance of the franchisee advisor council. Also available are seminars at the annual convention and the annual regional conferences.

Training Provided: All new franchisees are required to attend a 5-day Company school for which there is no cost, other than hotel and meals. The school provides all instructional material and manuals required.

Information Submitted: April 1994

SENSIBLE CAR RENTAL
96 Freneau Ave., # 2
Matawan, NJ 07747

Telephone: (800) 367-5159 (908) 583-8500
Fax: (908) 290-8305
Mr. Charles A. Vitale, General Manager

Number of Franchised Units: 110
Number of Company-Owned Units: 0
Number of Total Operating Units: 110

In Business Since: 1986   Franchising Since: 1986

Description of Operation: We provide training, insurance and management support for a car rental profit center.

Equity Capital Needed: $15,000 - $30,000

Franchise Fee: $3,500 - $6,000

Royalty Fee: $10 - $15 per car.

Financial Assistance: The franchise fee can be financed at zero interest.

Managerial Assistance: We provide a 2-day training school, manual and forms, personal on-site visits and reinforcement audio cassettes.

Training Provided: 2 days at our corporate offices cover customer screening, vehicle selection, advertising, telephone techniques, etc.

Information Submitted: January 1994

THRIFTY CAR RENTAL SYSTEM
6050 Indian Line
Mississauga, ON L4V 1G5 CAN
Telephone: (905) 612-1881
Fax: (905) 612-1893
Mr. Bill J. McNiece, Vice President

Number of Franchised Units: 159
Number of Company-Owned Units: 6
Number of Total Operating Units: 165

In Business Since: 1968   Franchising Since: 1972

Description of Operation: Provide car and truck rental and leasing services.

Equity Capital Needed: Varies.

Franchise Fee: Varies.

Royalty Fee: 8%

Financial Assistance: We provide vehicle financing, computer financing and franchise fee financing.

Managerial Assistance: Data not available.

Training Provided: We provide pre-opening in-store training, opening on-site training and on-going on-site training. Areas covered are operations, accounting, computers and fleet control.

Information Submitted: January 1994

THRIFTY RENT-A-CAR SYSTEM
5330 E. 31st St.
Tulsa, OK 74135
Telephone: (918) 665-3930
Fax: (918) 669-2213
Mr. Ted Williams, Executive Director

Number of Franchised Units: 913
Number of Company-Owned Units: 18
Number of Total Operating Units: 931

In Business Since: 1950   Franchising Since: 1962

Description of Operation: More than 90% of our retail outlets are owned by independent businesses who are licensed to use our trade name. Thrifty has a significant presence both in the airport and local car rental markets.

Equity Capital Needed: Varies on size.

Franchise Fee: $8,500 and up.

Royalty Fee: 8%

Financial Assistance: Special financing packages may be made available in certain cases to assist in the purchase of the franchise itself.

Managerial Assistance: Thrifty believes we provide our owners with the tools necessary to be successful. With that in mind, Thrifty has optional programs available for fleet, insurance, counter automation software and continuing training for all levels of employees, from initial orientation, field visits for operational check-ups, on-site training, on-site start-up assistance, operational reviews, financial analysis with comparison to similarly situated owners, market analysis, policy guidelines and an 800#.

Training Provided: Same as above.

Information Submitted: March 1994

U-SAVE AUTO RENTAL OF AMERICA
7525 Connelley Dr., # A
Hanover, MD 21076
Telephone: (800) 272-8728 (301) 760-8727
Fax: (410) 760-4452
Ms. Sandy Frankton, Qualifications Specialist

Number of Franchised Units: 510
Number of Company-Owned Units: 2
Number of Total Operating Units: 512

In Business Since: 1978   **Franchising Since:** 1979

Description of Operation: U-Save Auto Rental rents cars, vans and light-duty trucks to neighborhood and leisure customers, local businesses and people in need of temporary replacement vehicles. We also service commercial and government travelers in selected off-airport locations.

Equity Capital Needed: Net worth of at least $250,000, of which $60,000 is liquid.

Franchise Fee: $7,500 - $15,000

Royalty Fee: Based on fleet size.

Financial Assistance: Partial fleet leasing assistance is available.

Managerial Assistance: U-Save Rental provides support services to help franchisees operate and build their rental business. Some of these services include operating manuals, field support, marketing materials and supplies, fleet leasing programs, vehicle insurance programs, nationwide reservation systems and a president's advisory council.

Training Provided: We offer initial classroom guidance from experienced instructors about how a U-Save Auto Rental business operates and how to function as a franchisee. On-going training through national conventions, regional meetings and annual operational reviews. Also, a toll-free telephone connection to the U-Save Rental National Support Center for assistance.

Information Submitted: March 1994

UGLY DUCKLING RENT-A-CAR
2525 E. Camelback Rd., # 510
Phoenix, AZ 85016
Telephone: (800) 843-3825 (602) 381-8459
Fax: (602) 553-7070
Mr. Kevin W. Holt, President

Number of Franchised Units: 130
Number of Company-Owned Units: 1
Number of Total Operating Units: 131

In Business Since: 1977   **Franchising Since:** 1977

Description of Operation: Ugly Duckling rents used cars, trucks and vans. The vehicles are typically 3 - 5 years old, with between 40,000 - 60,000 miles. Rates are as much as half those of the majors. Our primary target is people who need a car to temporarily replace a car which has been stolen or damaged or is being repaired. We also rent to businesses and leisure travelers.

Equity Capital Needed: $25,000 - $150,000

Franchise Fee: $7,500 - $25,000

Royalty Fee: 6%

Financial Assistance: None.

Managerial Assistance: The franchise includes on-going consulting in all areas of car rental operations and marketing and free use of a sophisticated car rental software program.

Training Provided: All franchisees are required to attend a 4-day training program. Comprehensive operations and software.

Information Submitted: March 1994

WHEELCHAIR GETAWAYS
P. O. Box 605
Versailles, KY 40383
Telephone: (800) 642-2042 (606) 873-4973
Fax: (606) 873-4973
Mr. Stewart Gatewood, President

Number of Franchised Units: 67
Number of Company-Owned Units: 0
Number of Total Operating Units: 67

In Business Since: 1988   **Franchising Since:** 1989

Description of Operation: Wheelchair Getaways provides rental of specially-converted vans on a daily basis to people using wheelchairs. Customers include people who use wheelchairs.

Equity Capital Needed: $85,000 - $95,000

Franchise Fee: $15,000 for population of 200,000 - 500,000.

Royalty Fee: $525 per van per year, plus advertising fee..

Financial Assistance: For qualified franchisees, financing is available to purchase the 2 new vans required to start the business.

Managerial Assistance: We provide meetings on a regular basis, as well as back-up support in all areas of franchise operations on an on-going basis.

Training Provided: Basic training is for 2 days. Additional training is provided by phone. Back-up support, as needed. Training includes business and administration, operations, customer relations and marketing approaches.

Information Submitted: March 1994

RENTALS—MISCELLANEOUS

AARON'S RENTAL PURCHASE
3001 N. Fulton Dr., NE
Atlanta, GA 30363
Telephone: (800) 551-6015 (404) 237-4016
Fax: (404) 240-6594
Mr. Todd Evans, Director of Franchise Development

Number of Franchised Units: 10
Number of Company-Owned Units: 60
Number of Total Operating Units: 70

In Business Since: 1955   **Franchising Since:** 1992

Description of Operation: Provides electronics, appliances, furniture and jewelry on a "cash and carry" basis or on a monthly rental program.

Equity Capital Needed: $120,000 - $150,000

Franchise Fee: $14,500

Royalty Fee: 5%

Financial Assistance: Aaron's Rental Purchase does not offer direct financial assistance, but can provide sources for inventory financing.

Managerial Assistance: Provides support and assistance in all areas of franchise operations on an on-going basis. A set of instruction manuals is also provided which covers all aspects of operation.

Training Provided: All franchisees are invited to attend a comprehensive training course held at the corporate office in Atlanta, GA to supplement classroom training. Franchisees spend an average of about 4 weeks in an Aaron's Rental Purchase showroom for on-the-job training.

Information Submitted: December 1993

BABY'S AWAY INTERNATIONAL
846 S. Vance St., # B
Lakewood, CO 80226
Telephone: (800) 571-0077 (303) 936-7151
Fax: (303) 727-8828
Mr. Steve Hoodecheck, Vice President of Business Development

Number of Franchised Units: 0
Number of Company-Owned Units: 9
Number of Total Operating Units: 9

In Business Since: 1990   **Franchising Since:** 1993

Description of Operation: Rental of baby supplies, ranging from cribs to toys to VCR's and more.

Equity Capital Needed: $5,000 - $8,000

Franchise Fee: $7,000

Royalty Fee: 9%, plus 5% advertising.

Financial Assistance: 50% down and 50% payable over 12 months.

Managerial Assistance: We offer complete assistance in getting the franchisee operational. We also provide a program for identifying and establishing contact with prospective clients, including advertising programs.

Training Provided: We provide 3 days of training at the franchisee's location, as well as manuals, newsletters, a national 800# referral service and on-going consulting.

Information Submitted: January 1994

COLORTYME
8700 Stemmons, # 180
Dallas, TX 75247
Telephone: (214) 634-2266
Fax: (214) 631-7343
Mr. Ken Glascow, Director of Franchise Development

Number of Franchised Units: 355
Number of Company-Owned Units: 56
Number of Total Operating Units: 411

In Business Since: 1979   **Franchising Since:** 1981

Description of Operation: ColorTyme provides a specialized inventory of rental products, such as televisions, audio-video equipment, appliances, furniture, jewelry, pagers and computers - offered to consumers under a "Rent-To-Own" program.

Equity Capital Needed: $62,816 - $125,600

Franchise Fee: $10,000 - $25,000

Royalty Fee: 3%

Financial Assistance: ColorTyme Financial Services has contracted with NationsCredit Commercial Corporation (NCC) to provide funding to CFS for financing offered by CFS to ColorTyme franchisees. CFS offers financing for all approved products purchased by the franchisee from the franchisor or any other supplier.

Managerial Assistance: The duration of the initial training program will be approximately 3 weeks, prior to the opening of the ColorTyme Rental Store. The franchisor will provide 2 weeks of classroom instruction in Dallas, Texas, and an additional 1 week of on-the-job training in Dallas or, at the franchisor's option, at an existing training store selected by the franchisor and acceptable to the franchisee.

Training Provided: Data not available.

Information Submitted: December 1993

FORMALS ETC.
1634 Hyland Park Dr.
Pineville, LA 71360
Telephone: (318) 640-3766
Fax: (318) 640-8191
Mr. Sam Brimer, President

Number of Franchised Units: 16
Number of Company-Owned Units: 5
Number of Total Operating Units: 21

In Business Since: 1984   **Franchising Since:** 1990

Description of Operation: Formals Etc. offers ladies' formal wear rental at the retail level. Ladies can rent bridal, bridesmaid, prom, party and pageant gowns for a fraction of the retail price, without sacrificing style, quality, service or selection.

Equity Capital Needed: $60,000 - $90,000

Franchise Fee: $15,000

Royalty Fee: 6%

Financial Assistance: None.

Managerial Assistance: Formals Etc. provides software, manuals, inventory selection assistance and a manufacturing facility that is dedicated to the support of the Formals Etc. organization.

Training Provided: 1 week of training at the home office, with supplemental manuals.

Information Submitted: November 1993

GINGISS FORMALWEAR CENTER
180 N. LaSalle St., # 1111
Chicago, IL 60601
Telephone: (800) 621-7125 (312) 236-2333
Fax: (312) 580-7170
Mr. Jerrold A. Sutlin, Director of Franchise Development

Number of Franchised Units: 213
Number of Company-Owned Units: 32
Number of Total Operating Units: 245

In Business Since: 1936   **Franchising Since:** 1968

Description of Operation: Gingiss Formalwear specializes in the rental and sale of men's formalwear and related accessories. Gingiss is the leader in this highly recession-proof industry and the only national formalwear chain. Gingiss manufactures its own proprietary line of formalwear exclusively for its franchisees.

Equity Capital Needed: $59,00 - $180,000

Franchise Fee: $15,000

Royalty Fee: 0% - 10%

Financial Assistance: Up to $65,000 is available to whose who qualify for a merchandise loan.

Managerial Assistance: Gingiss provides on-going, on-site managerial assistance through its Regional Franchise Advisors. Assistance is provided in merchandising, advertising, hiring, training and financial matters. Additional assistance is available at regional and national meetings.

Training Provided: 2 weeks of intensive training is provided in Company-owned stores and at the corporate headquarters. 1 week of training is provided on-site at the new store at opening. On-going training is provided in-store and at regional and national meetings.

Information Submitted: November 1993

GRAND RENTAL STATION / TAYLOR RENTAL CENTERS
P. O. Box 1510
Butler, PA 16003

Telephone: (412) 284-6427
Fax: (412) 284-1782
Mr. Tom Hazel, General Manager

Number of Franchised Units: 540
Number of Company-Owned Units: 0
Number of Total Operating Units: 540

In Business Since: 1957   Franchising Since: 1957

Description of Operation: General rental store. Grand Rental Station/Taylor Rental Centers is the largest general rental store in the USA.

Equity Capital Needed: $200,000 +

Franchise Fee: $2,300

Royalty Fee: 1.3%

Financial Assistance: Data not available.

Managerial Assistance: Store design, inventory space, inventory supply, advertising, computerization and operational guidance are provided.

Training Provided: We offer 1 week of training school, plus field support.

Information Submitted: March 1994

JOE RENT ALL
28, rue Vanier
Chateauguay, PQ J6J 3W8 CAN
Telephone: (514) 692-6268
Fax: (514) 692-2848
Mr. J. M. Bissonnette, President

Number of Franchised Units: 65
Number of Company-Owned Units: 0
Number of Total Operating Units: 65

In Business Since: 1979   Franchising Since: 1982

Description of Operation: Renting tools, equipment, party goods, recreational vehicles, boats, etc.

Equity Capital Needed: $40,000

Franchise Fee: $15,000 or $20,000.

Royalty Fee: 4%, plus 3% publicity.

Financial Assistance: This assistance is provided through banks.

Managerial Assistance: Each franchisee receives manuals and necessary forms for office management (computer) on all aspects of controls and operation. Seminars on products, leadership, research and development, etc.

Training Provided: An extensive week of training at the head office and about 2 weeks of training at franchisee's location. Necessary forms to control renting on all aspects of operations and services to customers.

Information Submitted: November 1993

MILITARY RENT-ALL
3545 Motor Ave., # 200
Los Angeles, CA 90034
Telephone: (800) 669-2221 (310) 204-2220
Fax: (310) 204-0148
Mr. Matt Feinstein, Director or Franchise Development

Number of Franchised Units: 12
Number of Company-Owned Units: 6
Number of Total Operating Units: 18

In Business Since: 1969   Franchising Since: 1988

Description of Operation: Located on or near military bases, these stores rent washers, dryers, refrigerators, freezers, automotive and garden equipment, TV's, VCR's and furniture.

Equity Capital Needed: $40,000 - $200,000

Franchise Fee: $20,000

Royalty Fee: 6%

Financial Assistance: Financing is available when taking over an established store and converting it into a Military Rent-All. Existing locations available nationwide. SBA and VetFran.

Managerial Assistance: Location assistance, store set-up and layout, consultation, business development manuals, buying power, bookkeeping services, advertising and marketing services are all included.

Training Provided: Initial in-store training in all aspects of running a successful rental store, plus on-going training, as necessary. No previous rental business experience is needed.

Information Submitted: November 1993

YARD CARDS
2940 West Main St.
Belleville, IL 62223
Telephone: (618) 233-0491
Fax: (618) 277-1594
Mr. Michael Hoepfinger, President

Number of Franchised Units: 12
Number of Company-Owned Units: 1
Number of Total Operating Units: 13

In Business Since: 1983   Franchising Since: 1986

Description of Operation: Rental of 8-foot greeting cards for any and all occasions - graduation, Valentine's Day, birthday, retirement, Mother's and Father's Day, anniversary cards, etc. Even storks to announce births! Can be operated as a home-based business or added on to an existing business.

Equity Capital Needed: $5,000 - $15,000

Franchise Fee: $1,000 minimum.

Royalty Fee: 5%

Financial Assistance: None.

Managerial Assistance: Constant communications and operations manual.

Training Provided: Optional training is a maximum of 3 days.

Information Submitted: November 1993

RESTAURANTS, DRIVE-INS AND CARRY OUTS

1 POTATO 2
5640 International Pkwy.
New Hope, MN 55428
Telephone: (800) 333-8034 (612) 537-3833
Fax: (612) 537-4241
Mr. Todd D. King, Vice President of Franchising

Number of Franchised Units: 45
Number of Company-Owned Units: 24
Number of Total Operating Units: 69

In Business Since: 1977   Franchising Since: 1985

Description of Operation: Fast-food restaurant chain, featuring baked potato entrees, with a variety of toppings, plus many other potato products (fresh-cut fries, mashed potatoes, double-baked supremes, country skillet combos). 1 Potato 2 offers a healthy alternative to fast foods. Located in major mall food courts with its Lite Potatoes. Franchise features quarterly visits by field staff, monthly publications, weekly informal mailings, annual conference and a comprehensive training program.

Equity Capital Needed: $90,000 - $130,000

Franchise Fee: $20,000

Royalty Fee: 4.5%

Financial Assistance: The Company does not offer financial assistance.

Managerial Assistance: The franchise offers complete operations manuals, training manuals, recipe books, etc.

Training Provided: An extensive 2-week training period at a corporate training location, where franchisees have "hands-on" training, followed by in-store assistance when the location opens.

Information Submitted: November 1993

A & W RESTAURANTS
17197 N. Laurel Park Dr., # 500
Livonia, MI 48152
Telephone: (800) 222-2337 (313) 462-0029
Fax: (313) 462-1017
Mr. J. Bryon Stephens, Director of Franchise Development

Number of Franchised Units: 695
Number of Company-Owned Units: 10
Number of Total Operating Units: 705

In Business Since: 1919   **Franchising Since:** 1925

Description of Operation: Restaurants, serving hamburgers, hot dogs and the world's #1-selling root beer.

Equity Capital Needed: $20,000 - $80,000

Franchise Fee: $15,000 - $75,000

Royalty Fee: 4%

Financial Assistance: Not available.

Managerial Assistance: A & W provides operational, marketing and facilities management support to the franchisees.

Training Provided: 2 - 6 weeks of training, depending on previous experience, combining both classroom and on-the-job training.

Information Submitted: February 1994

A. G. HERO
730 2nd Ave. South, # 800
Minneapolis, MN 55402
Telephone: (612) 371-9557
Fax: (612) 332-6946
Mr. Dwight A. Bonewell, Corporate Development

Number of Franchised Units: 0
Number of Company-Owned Units: 3
Number of Total Operating Units: 3

In Business Since: 1990   **Franchising Since:** 1993

Description of Operation: A. G. Hero restaurants combine 3 popular food items - the hero or sub sandwich, made on bread baked daily in each restaurant, fresh-baked cookies and high-quality, non-fat frozen yogurt with a fresh fruit topping bar. The unique combination of these 3 foods creates a well-balanced menu for all tastes.

Equity Capital Needed: $71,650 - $119,400

Franchise Fee: $9,900

Royalty Fee: 6%

Financial Assistance: No financial assistance is currently available.

Managerial Assistance: After the franchisee and the franchisee's manager have successfully completed the franchisor's training program, the franchisor will furnish 1 representative of the franchisor for not less than 5 days (2 days prior to opening, opening day and 2 days following opening day), who will provide opening assistance. Within 4 weeks following the opening, the franchisor will furnish I representative of the franchisor for follow-up assistance.

Training Provided: The franchisor will provide a training program for the franchisee and the franchisee's manager in Minneapolis to familiarize them with the business system and the operations of A. G. Hero. The training will include classroom and on-the-job instruction on basic business procedures, equipment operation, employee training, hiring and

firing, basic accounting, customer relations, advertising and promotion, food preparation, food presentation, purchasing, housekeeping, security and other business topics.

Information Submitted: November 1993

AL'S DINER
8230 Calumet Ave.
Munster, IN 46321
Telephone: (219) 836-0009 (708) 333-0009
Fax: (219) 836-0009
Mr. David Estrada, Franchise Director

Number of Franchised Units: 10
Number of Company-Owned Units: 0
Number of Total Operating Units: 10

In Business Since: 1986   **Franchising Since:** 1990

Description of Operation: Al's Diner was founded in 1986 with the idea of taking a daring step backward to the 50's - an era of good food, good service and great music. With that in mind, each Al's Diner contains memorabilia from the 50's. We display signs and posters, both inside and outside. Each location captures the spirit of the 50's. In addition, each location has a Wurlitzer juke box amply stocked with songs from the 50's. Waiters and waitresses dress in the style of the 50's. Good food, great service and atmosphere.

Equity Capital Needed: $70,000 +

Franchise Fee: $15,000

Royalty Fee: 3.5% - first year; 4% - thereafter.

Financial Assistance: None.

Managerial Assistance: The Al's Diner franchise program will provide you with the experience you'll need to start your Al's Diner restaurant. We will assist you with site selection, lease negotiations, layout and design, construction supervision, recommended equipment and suppliers.

Training Provided: The Al's Diner franchise program will provide you with the experience you'll need to start your Al's Diner restaurant. We will provide you with a training program, operations manual, recipes and on-going support.

Information Submitted: March 1994

APPLEBEE'S INTERNATIONAL
4551 W. 107th St., # 100
Overland Park, KS 66207
Telephone: (913) 967-4000
Fax: (913) 341-1695
Mr. Larry M. Bader, Director of Franchise Development

Number of Franchised Units: 310
Number of Company-Owned Units: 65
Number of Total Operating Units: 375

In Business Since: 1983   **Franchising Since:** 1983

Description of Operation: Applebee's is positioned as a neighborhood grill and bar, where consumers can obtain a high-value experience through attractively-priced food and alcoholic beverages. The principles of fast food (convenience, quality and service, coupled with limited time and money) can be applied to an adult consumer.

Equity Capital Needed: $4,000,000 net worth and $500,000 in liquid assets.

Franchise Fee: $35,000

Royalty Fee: 4%

Financial Assistance: Outside lenders.

Managerial Assistance: Training is provided for the general manager, the kitchen manager and the franchisee's restaurant managers in our operations training facility for such period as the franchisor shall deem reasonably necessary. Franchisee personnel shall complete the course to the franchisor's reasonable satisfaction.

Training Provided: Applebee's basically provides management training, pre-opening assistance, on-going and follow-up assistance. Additionally, they help find site locations and offer assistance with purveyors for purchasing. Marketing programs and format assistance are provided.

Information Submitted: April 1994

ARBY'S
1000 Corporate Dr.
Ft. Lauderdale, FL 33334
Telephone: (800) 487-2729 (305) 351-5100
Fax: (305) 351-5190
Mr. Anthony G. Foster, Vice President of Franchising

Number of Franchised Units: 2406
Number of Company-Owned Units: 263
Number of Total Operating Units: 2669

In Business Since: 1964   **Franchising Since:** 1964

Description of Operation: Fast-food restaurant, specializing in roast beef sandwiches.

Equity Capital Needed: $250,000 liquid; $500,000 net worth.

Franchise Fee: $37,500

Royalty Fee: 4%

Financial Assistance: No direct assistance; however, Arby's will guide franchisees in obtaining financing.

Managerial Assistance: Manuals, advice and counseling are available, covering all aspects of Arby's operation.

Training Provided: Training includes classroom and in-store training - 1 week of training for the owner and 5 weeks for the operator.

Information Submitted: March 1994

ARMAND'S CHICAGO PIZZERIA
4231 Wisconsin Ave., NW
Wahington, DC 20016
Telephone: (202) 363-6268
Fax: (202) 363-3461
Mr. Calvin Everett, Operations Director

Number of Franchised Units: 5
Number of Company-Owned Units: 4
Number of Total Operating Units: 9

In Business Since: 1969   **Franchising Since:** 1978

Description of Operation: Casual-theme restaurant, specializing in deep-dish pizza. For 14 years, we were voted "Best Pizza" award in Washington, DC area. Considered a local institution. Flexible franchise concepts available in 3 styles - full service with bar, express delivery and campus carry-out.

Equity Capital Needed: $150,000 +

Franchise Fee: $25,000

Royalty Fee: 3.5% or $2,500 minimum.

Financial Assistance: Not available.

Managerial Assistance: Full training and orientation. Operations manual and recipe manual included. All forms, computer programs and preferred vendors list available.

Training Provided: 6 - 10 week training period required of at least 3 principal individuals, preferably on location at existing stores in Washington, DC. 2 - 4 weeks of on-site follow-up training and assistance at franchisee's site.

Information Submitted: November 1993

ARTHUR TREACHER'S FISH & CHIPS
7400 Baymeadows Way, # 300
Jacksonville, FL 32256

Telephone: (800) 321-3113 (904) 739-1200
Fax: (904) 739-2500
Mr. Michael D. Proulx, Director of Franchise Development

Number of Franchised Units: 130
Number of Company-Owned Units: 20
Number of Total Operating Units: 150

In Business Since: 1969   **Franchising Since:** 1969

Description of Operation: The franchisor develops, owns, operates and licenses others to own and operate a unique fast-food restaurant with a limited menu and system. This system includes a method of operation, customer service, quality control, trade secrets, technical knowledge, specially-designed decor, equipment, lay-out plans, signs, food distribution programs and accounting systems.

Equity Capital Needed: $72,500 - $157,500

Franchise Fee: $19,500

Royalty Fee: 6%

Financial Assistance: The franchisor does not offer financing to franchisees either directly or through affiliates. The franchisor receives no revenues or other commissions from anyone who offers or arranges financing for franchisees.

Managerial Assistance: Management assistance covers all facets of the operation.

Training Provided: The initial training program is 3 weeks in duration and takes place at the national headquarters in Jacksonville, FL and at a designated restaurant location. Training covers all facets of the restaurant operation.

Information Submitted: January 1994

BACK YARD BURGERS
2768 Colony Park Dr.
Memphis, TN 38118
Telephone: (901) 367-0888
Fax: (901) 367-0999
Mr. Barry Pitts, Director of Franchise Development

Number of Franchised Units: 40
Number of Company-Owned Units: 9
Number of Total Operating Units: 49

In Business Since: 1986   **Franchising Since:** 1988

Description of Operation: Back Yard Burgers operates and franchises quick-service, predominantly double drive-through, restaurants under the name Back Yard Burgers. The restaurants are designed to project a backyard theme that emphasizes charbroiling fresh, great-tasting food (including hamburgers, gourmet hamburgers, chicken filet sandwiches and other sandwich items), as customers would cook in their own back yards.

Equity Capital Needed: $350,000

Franchise Fee: $25,000

Royalty Fee: 4%

Financial Assistance: None.

Managerial Assistance: Monthly visits to franchisee's restaurant by district managers to assist with operations, accounting, marketing, training of new personnel or any other areas of need.

Training Provided: 4 weeks of training provided at the corporate office in Memphis, TN. 70% hands-on training in BYB Restaurant and 30% classroom training. Administration manual, operations manual, new store opening manual and marketing manual provided. At least 3 management personnel must be certified.

Information Submitted: November 1993

BALDINOS GIANT JERSEY SUBS
760 Elaine St.
Hinesville, GA 31313

Telephone: (912) 368-2822
Fax: (912) 369-3923
Ms. Mary Forsythe, Office Manager

Number of Franchised Units: 10
Number of Company-Owned Units: 6
Number of Total Operating Units: 16

In Business Since: 1975   **Franchising Since:** 1982

Description of Operation: Submarine sandwich shop. In-store baking.

Equity Capital Needed: $75,000

Franchise Fee: $10,000

Royalty Fee: 4.5%

Financial Assistance: None.

Managerial Assistance: Manuals, seminars, field representatives, hotlines and grand opening assistance available.

Training Provided: Training is provided to franchisees at a Company store in Hinesville, GA. Also, 1 - 2 weeks of on-site training provided.

Information Submitted: January 1994

BASSETT'S ORIGINAL TURKEY
P. O. Box 40016
Philadelphia, PA 19106
Telephone: (800) 282-8875 (215) 922-4614
Fax: (215) 922-7182
Mr. Roger Bassett, President

Number of Franchised Units: 11
Number of Company-Owned Units: 2
Number of Total Operating Units: 13

In Business Since: 1983   **Franchising Since:** 1989

Description of Operation: Bassett's is a fast-food, family restaurant, featuring fresh-roasted, real turkey breast sandwiches, Thanksgiving-style dinners and made-to-order salads.

Equity Capital Needed: $50,000 - $100,000

Franchise Fee: $21,000

Royalty Fee: 5%

Financial Assistance: Third party.

Managerial Assistance: We provide managerial assistance on an on-going basis as part of the training and after opening. It includes all aspects of operations.

Training Provided: The training is 3 - 2 weeks at a training store and least 1 week after opening. It includes everything to operate a successful store.

Information Submitted: March 1994

BEEFY'S
112 D. Shivel Dr.
Hendersonville, TN 37075
Telephone: (615) 822-6430
Fax: (615) 822-6111
Mr. Daniel Montgomery, President

Number of Franchised Units: 22
Number of Company-Owned Units: 0
Number of Total Operating Units: 22

In Business Since: 1984   **Franchising Since:** 1985

Description of Operation: Fast-food double drive-thru, featuring hamburgers, chicken sandwiches, fries, onion rings, soft drinks and desserts. Quality food, fast service and economical prices make the operation attractive to a wide variety of customers.

Equity Capital Needed: $40,000 - $250,000

Franchise Fee: $17,000

Royalty Fee: 4%

Financial Assistance: Beefy's will give referrals, but does not give hands-on financial assistance.

Managerial Assistance: We offer a complete training program, on-going operational support and periodic operation visits to individual units

Training Provided: A minimum of 15 work days, includes classroom and in-store training. Inventory control, labor control, service operations, ordering, hiring and training are among topics covered.

Information Submitted: January 1994

BENIHANA OF TOKYO
8685 NW 53rd Terrace
Miami, FL 33166
Telephone: (305) 593-0770
Fax: (305) 592-6371
Mr. Michael W. Kata, Vice President

Number of Franchised Units: 11
Number of Company-Owned Units: 39
Number of Total Operating Units: 50

In Business Since: 1964   **Franchising Since:** 1970

Description of Operation: The Benihana Steakhouse chain is known throughout the world for its top-quality food and service. Each guest's meal is prepared right before his/her eyes by an entertaining chef who introduces all the ingredients before he/she masterfully cooks. Twice recognized as America's most popular full-service restaurant.

Equity Capital Needed: $1,500

Franchise Fee: $50,000

Royalty Fee: 6%

Financial Assistance: None.

Managerial Assistance: Benihana will provide both pre-opening and post-opening support for the duration of the franchise. Also provided are forms, training manuals, posters, newsletters and point-of-sale material.

Training Provided: Prior to the opening of the restaurant, Benihana will provide training for both chefs and managers alike. Such training programs require each trainee to work in a Benihana restaurant for a period of 12 - 16 weeks until properly trained in general restaurant management and food preparation.

Information Submitted: November 1993

BENNETT'S PIT BAR-B-QUE
6551 S. Revere Pkwy., # 285
Englewood, CO 80111
Telephone: (303) 792-3088
Fax: (303) 792-5801
Mr. James A. Silbaugh, Vice President of Marketing

Number of Franchised Units: 12
Number of Company-Owned Units: 3
Number of Total Operating Units: 15

In Business Since: 1984   **Franchising Since:** 1989

Description of Operation: Full-service and limited-service bar-b-que restaurants, featuring real hickory-smoked barbeque in a fast-paced, friendly, family atmosphere.

Equity Capital Needed: $250,000 net worth and $100,000 liquid.

Franchise Fee: $25,000

Royalty Fee: 3.5%

Financial Assistance: None.

Managerial Assistance: Site approval, lease negotiations and construction management are available on a fee basis.

Training Provided: Training consists of 4 - 8 weeks at the training center, plus 1 - 2 weeks of initial on-site training.

Information Submitted: March 1994

BIG BOY INTERNATIONAL
4199 Marcy Dr.
Warren, Mi 48091
Telephone: (810) 755-8583
Fax: (810) 757-4737
Mr. Ronald E. Johnston, Senior Executive Vice President

Number of Franchised Units: 728
Number of Company-Owned Units: 141
Number of Total Operating Units: 869

In Business Since: 1938   **Franchising Since:** 1952

Description of Operation: Full-service family restaurant, featuring in-store bakery, breakfast, dinner, soup, salad and fruit bar.

Equity Capital Needed: $150,000

Franchise Fee: $25,000

Royalty Fee: 3%

Financial Assistance: The franchisor will provide a list of lenders.

Managerial Assistance: The franchisor will train all levels of the management team, including hourly personnel.

Training Provided: 8 weeks of training is provided to new franchisees.

Information Submitted: March 1994

BIG TOWN HERO
405 Court St. NE, # 201
Salem, OR 97301
Telephone: (503) 371-9564
Fax: (503) 371-9584
Mr. Fred Lindhe, President

Number of Franchised Units: 12
Number of Company-Owned Units: 0
Number of Total Operating Units: 12

In Business Since: 1989   **Franchising Since:** 1990

Description of Operation: Sandwiches, salads, soups, fresh bread and baked goods from scratch. Fast and friendly.

Equity Capital Needed: $36,100 - $81,000

Franchise Fee: $15,000

Royalty Fee: 5%

Financial Assistance: No assistance is given (references).

Managerial Assistance: Assistance available 24 hours a day. Our job is to use our skills and experience to help each franchise owner achieve his/her goals.

Training Provided: Each franchise owner is given 2 weeks of pre-opening training and 10 days after opening. Training is provided to operate, diagnose and rectify or remedy any part of the store or operation.

Information Submitted: December 1993

BIRD CALLS
2200 Corporate Blvd., # 305
Boca Raton, FL 33431
Telephone: (800) 598-3557 (407) 995-9003
Fax: (407) 995-9008
Mr. William Manseau, Director of Franchising

Number of Franchised Units: 0
Number of Company-Owned Units: 1
Number of Total Operating Units: 1

In Business Since: 1990   **Franchising Since:** 1992

Description of Operation: Double drive-thru chicken and turkey restaurant.

Equity Capital Needed: $300,000 - $400,000

Franchise Fee: $25,000

Royalty Fee: 5%

Financial Assistance: None at the present time.

Managerial Assistance: Bird Calls will provide adequate staff and upper management to assist in the opening and on-going support of a Bird Calls franchisee. Bird Calls will have district managers always available to aid in any and all problems that might arise.

Training Provided: Bird Calls has a 14-day training program. In these 14 days, you will be able to run a Bird Calls restaurant. All franchisees get complete reference manuals to aid in their training.

Information Submitted: January 1994

BJ'S KOUNTRY KITCHEN
4325 N. Golden State Blvd., # 102
Fresno, CA 93722
Telephone: (209) 275-1981
Fax: (209) 275-8786
Mr. Gary Honeycutt, Chairman

Number of Franchised Units: 8
Number of Company-Owned Units: 0
Number of Total Operating Units: 8

In Business Since: 1981   **Franchising Since:** 1989

Description of Operation: Kountry Coffee Shop, operating 6 a.m. to 2 p.m., that bustles! Shorter hours and a single shift give you more time to do it right, as well as monitor the performance of others. Breakfast and lunch (especially breakfast) mean lower food cost with biscuits and gravy, omelets, hamburgers and sandwiches. Good ol' basic food served quickly, simply and economically with real hustle and bustle!

Equity Capital Needed: $65,000 - $130,000

Franchise Fee: $25,000

Royalty Fee: 5%

Financial Assistance: Partial financing of the lease is available, subject to credit approval. Cost includes franchise fee and site acquisition.

Managerial Assistance: The franchise office is staffed with full-time management for assistance.

Training Provided: We train the beginner to become a pro by keeping our operation simple. The franchisee, plus 2 employees, get a 2-week classroom and on-site program which offers the techniques and training to BUSTLE, including full operations, advertising, record keeping, personnel and management. Full manuals and follow-up support.

Information Submitted: March 1994

BLAZERS ALL AMERICAN BARBEQUE
13610 N. Scottsdale Rd., # 10-352
Scottsdale, AZ 85254
Telephone: (800) 655-7319
Fax: (602) 951-8534
Mr. Michael Ruby, Director of Franchise Development

Number of Franchised Units: 1
Number of Company-Owned Units: 1
Number of Total Operating Units: 2

In Business Since: 1992   **Franchising Since:** 1992

Description of Operation: 1,000 - 1,500 square feet of limited seating, pick-up and delivery, gourmet, barbeque restaurant.

Equity Capital Needed: $22,850 - $38,850

Franchise Fee: $20,000 + $5,000 franchise training fee.

Royalty Fee: 5%

Financial Assistance: Available - WAC.

Managerial Assistance: Constant contact with a regional opening advisor.

Training Provided: Week-long executive management training class. Classroom and hands-on instruction provided.

Information Submitted: December 1993

BLIMPIE
1775 The Exchange, # 215
Atlanta, GA 30339
Telephone: (800) 447-6256 (404) 984-2707
Fax: (404) 980-9176
Mr. Dennis G. Fuller, Vice President

Number of Franchised Units: 630
Number of Company-Owned Units: 0
Number of Total Operating Units: 630

In Business Since: 1964   **Franchising Since:** 1971

Description of Operation: National quick-service restaurant, serving fresh-sliced submarine sandwiches and salads

Equity Capital Needed: $90,000 - $120,000

Franchise Fee: $18,000

Royalty Fee: 6%

Financial Assistance: Financing is available through third-party sources.

Managerial Assistance: Corporate assistance from all departments, including District Manager. Area development assistance on a local level. Assistance provided - real estate selection, lease negotiations, construction, bids, equipment, signage, pre-opening and grand opening training, marketing and operational assistance.

Training Provided: 80 hours of intensive training prior to attending a week-long Blimpie Business School in Atlanta, GA. 40 hours of additional training in store prior to opening. A Blimpie representative will spend the first 2 weeks with franchisees when they open the restaurant.

Information Submitted: November 1993

BOARDWALK FRIES
8307 Main St.
Ellicott City, MD 21043
Telephone: (410) 465-5020
Fax: (410) 465-5213
Mr. Jack Csicsek, Vice President of Franchising and Leasing

Number of Franchised Units: 69
Number of Company-Owned Units: 11
Number of Total Operating Units: 80

In Business Since: 1981   **Franchising Since:** 1983

Description of Operation: Fast-food restaurants, located in regional malls, street locations and free standing buildings. Specialty concept of fresh-cut french fries, hot dogs, fresh-squeezed lemonade and soda products.

Equity Capital Needed: $90,000 - $200,000

Franchise Fee: $25,000

Royalty Fee: 7%; 2% advertising.

Financial Assistance: None.

Managerial Assistance: Data not available.

Training Provided: 12-day training program at corporate headquarters. 5 days with representative from home office at opening of store.

Information Submitted: January 1994

BOBBY RUBINO'S PLACE FOR RIBS
1900 E. Sunrise Blvd.
Ft. Lauderdale, FL 33304

Telephone: (305) 763-1478
Fax: (305) 467-1192
Mr. Jerry Moniz, Director of Operations

Number of Franchised Units: 7
Number of Company-Owned Units: 9
Number of Total Operating Units: 16

In Business Since: 1978   **Franchising Since:** 1980

Description of Operation: Full-service BBQ restaurant, specializing in ribs, chicken and shrimp. All units have full-service lounges and take-out facilities. Open for lunch and dinner, serving steaks, prime-rib and other popular items.

Equity Capital Needed: $400,000 - $650,000

Franchise Fee: $35,000

Royalty Fee: 4%

Financial Assistance: None.

Managerial Assistance: Bobby Rubino's USA provides management material, training manuals and on-going assistance for the term of the franchise. Visits to the franchisee occur on a regular basis. Assistance is offered in all areas of the business.

Training Provided: Training provided for franchisee's management personnel in Florida for 4 weeks. Up to 5 people may attend. Provides a training team for store openings for up to 3 weeks. On-going training is provided for the franchisee.

Information Submitted: March 1994

BOJANGLES' FAMOUS CHICKEN 'N BISCUITS
P. O. Box 240239
Charlotte, NC 28224
Telephone: (800) 366-9921 (704) 527-2675
Fax: (704) 523-6803
Ms. Linda S. Guthrie, Franchise Co-ordinator

Number of Franchised Units: 80
Number of Company-Owned Units: 121
Number of Total Operating Units: 201

In Business Since: 1977   **Franchising Since:** 1978

Description of Operation: Fast-service chicken and biscuits restaurant.

Equity Capital Needed: Minimum net worth of $400,000 for first store, plus $100,000 for each additional store.

Franchise Fee: $20,000 for first store, $15,000 for each additional store.

Royalty Fee: 4%

Financial Assistance: None.

Managerial Assistance: A franchise field service representative is available on a continuing basis for franchisee support.

Training Provided: We offer an 8-week training program at Bojangles' University and restaurants.

Information Submitted: March 1994

BONJOUR BAGEL CAFE
225 S. Lake Ave., # M-153
Pasadena, CA 91101
Telephone: (818) 304-9023
Fax: (818) 792-8756
Mr. Stephan A. Metz, President

Number of Franchised Units: 0
Number of Company-Owned Units: 1
Number of Total Operating Units: 1

In Business Since: 1992   **Franchising Since:** 1993

Description of Operation: Bonjour Bagel Cafe is an ambient, up-scale bagel bakery cafe, offering a wide variety of freshly-baked bagels, wholesome bagel sandwiches, delicious soups and salads, fresh juices and beverages, specialty baked goods and a complete selection of aromatic, gourmet coffees. All bagels are baked fresh daily at each Bonjour Bagel Cafe location and all menu items are carefully selected and prepared to insure their freshness, good taste and nutritional value. Children's menu available.

Equity Capital Needed: $200,000 - $346,000

Franchise Fee: $35,000

Royalty Fee: 5%

Financial Assistance: The franchisor does not offer the franchisee any financing, either directly or indirectly. However, the franchisor will assist the franchisee in securing financing for furniture, fixtures and equipment required in the operation of the franchisee's business.

Managerial Assistance: Bonjour Bagel Cafe provides management training, pre-opening assistance, on-site opening assistance, food preparation training, marketing and sales training, advertising programs, bakery consultation, lease and site consultation, research and development of new food and retail products, assistance in equipment leasing and purchasing and will provide periodic nutritional and health news releases. Franchisor will loan the franchisee operations, training, marketing and employee manuals.

Training Provided: Pre-opening training of 10 business days is provided to franchisee and one other designated employee or representative of franchisee. An additional 5 days of training will take place, commencing on the first day the cafe is opened for business. Initial training will include all aspects of operating a Bonjour Bagel Cafe, including, but not limited to, on-site food preparation, proper baking procedures, customer service procedures, management techniques, equipment operation, purchasing and scheduling.

Information Submitted: December 1993

BOSTON BEANERY RESTAURANT & TAVERN
265 High St., # 600
Morgantown, WV 26505
Telephone: (304) 292-2035
Fax: (304) 292-2057
Mr. Steve Jones, Vice President of Administration

Number of Franchised Units: 3
Number of Company-Owned Units: 2
Number of Total Operating Units: 5

In Business Since: 1984   **Franchising Since:** 1988

Description of Operation: Mid-scale restaurant and tavern - casual, old-Boston theme.

Equity Capital Needed: $378,500 - $552,500

Franchise Fee: $25,000

Royalty Fee: 4% of gross.

Financial Assistance: None.

Managerial Assistance: We provide full management assistance until store opening. On-going consultation and follow-up in the areas of operations, people development, marketing and profit control.

Training Provided: We offer an 8-week training program for the General Manager, a 6-week training program for the Assistant Manager, assistance in staff pre-opening training and 1 week of support staff assistance after opening.

Information Submitted: February 1994

BOX LUNCH, THE
P. O. Box 666
Truro, MA 02666

Telephone: (508) 349-3509
Fax: (508) 349-3661
Mr. Owen MacNutt, President

Number of Franchised Units: 9
Number of Company-Owned Units: 0
Number of Total Operating Units: 9

In Business Since: 1977   **Franchising Since:** 1981

Description of Operation: The Box Lunch sandwich shops produce rolled pita sandwiches of a very high quality to the broad lunch market. Young and old marvel at our speed, quality and cleanliness. The rolled sandwiches are made to order in seconds from fresh ingredients.

Equity Capital Needed: $70,000 - $85,000

Franchise Fee: $15,000

Royalty Fee: 4.5%

Financial Assistance: Not available.

Managerial Assistance: Daily conversation and reporting forces the operator to keep records and be on top of business. Marketing techniques are discussed and implemented.

Training Provided: Training includes 6 - 10 weeks of on-the-job training and 2 weeks on-site. Complete training on how to run our business, plus weekly supervision visits and monthly owners meetings. Unit will not open until operator is capable.

Information Submitted: January 1994

BOXIES
3361 Boyington
Carrollton, TX 75006
Telephone: (800) 269-4374 (214) 392-3012
Fax: (214) 788-5036
Mr. Fred Addington, Jr., Director of Franchising

Number of Franchised Units: 0
Number of Company-Owned Units: 0
Number of Total Operating Units: 0

In Business Since: 1993   **Franchising Since:** 1993

Description of Operation: Retail shop, selling yogurt, Java Coast gourmet coffee, sandwiches, soup, bakeries, etc. Boxies Cafe represents a flexible franchising approach. TrendMatch Marketing allows for future shifts in consumer dining trends. Modules can be combined with existing I Can't Believe It's Yogurt, Java Coast Fine Coffees and bakery modules. Other modules can be added later.

Equity Capital Needed: $180,000 - $220,000

Franchise Fee: $15,000

Royalty Fee: 5% royalty and 2% marketing.

Financial Assistance: None.

Managerial Assistance: Data not available.

Training Provided: Extensive training in Dallas, TX at the corporate office. On-site support at opening of store. Periodic inspections and field consultants. Telephone hotline, newsletters, etc.

Information Submitted: November 1993

BREADEAUX PISA
Frederick Ave. at 23rd St.
St. Joseph, MO 64506
Telephone: (816) 364-1088
Fax: (816) 364-3739
Mr. Larry Mark, Director of Franchise Development

Number of Franchised Units: 70
Number of Company-Owned Units: 1
Number of Total Operating Units: 71

In Business Since: 1985   **Franchising Since:** 1985

Description of Operation: Fast pizza operation; fresh dough daily; 100% dairy products; 100% meat toppings, no extenders.

Equity Capital Needed: $75,000 - $125,000

Franchise Fee: $15,000

Royalty Fee: 5%

Financial Assistance: Referral to franchise financing company.

Managerial Assistance: We provide site selection, store layout and floor plan, policies and standards manuals, advertising manuals and grand opening support.

Training Provided: We offer a minimum of 30 hours of training, covering 200 methods of operating the franchised bakery - no charge to franchisee.

Information Submitted: January 1994

BRIDGEMAN'S RESTAURANTS
6009 Wayzata Blvd., # 113
St. Louis Park, MN 55416
Telephone: (800) 297-5050 (612) 593-1455
Fax: (612) 541-1101
Ms. Mary C. McKee, Franchising/Market Development

Number of Franchised Units: 24
Number of Company-Owned Units: 6
Number of Total Operating Units: 30

In Business Since: 1936   **Franchising Since:** 1967

Description of Operation: A full-service, family-style restaurant, featuring our famous ice cream specialty treats. Bridgeman's also awards franchise opportunities for Dip Shoppe concept, offering ice cream treats and limited sandwich menu or the soda fountain concept with the full line of ice cream treats and, finally, the Dip Station, which allows the franchisee to dispense all of our 22 natural rich and creamy flavors of ice cream.

Equity Capital Needed: We list no requirements.

Franchise Fee: $750 - $25,000

Royalty Fee: 2%

Financial Assistance: Bridgeman's furnishes no financial assistance.

Managerial Assistance: District managers offer on-going programs to provide better customer service and improve profitability. The Company gives continual supervision and evaluation of service, cleanliness and food quality. The district managers are on-site for several days each quarter and are also available on-call.

Training Provided: Operational, training and menu manuals are given to each new franchisee. The hands-on training program consists of 4 - 6 weeks at a corporate site. The length of the training will depend upon the experience of the trainee.

Information Submitted: January 1994

BURGER KING CORPORATION
17777 Old Cutler Rd.
Miami, FL 33157
Telephone: (800) 394-0940 (305) 378-7011
Fax: (305) 378-7262
Mr. John R. Blackerby, Director of Franchise Administration

Number of Franchised Units: 6163
Number of Company-Owned Units: 958
Number of Total Operating Units: 7121

In Business Since: 1954   **Franchising Since:** 1954

Description of Operation: Burger King is a highly-recognized, world-wide brand, with over 6,800 points of distribution. New lower cost facility design and flexible ownership guidelines continue to make Burger King an attractive franchise investment.

Equity Capital Needed: 35% of non-real estate investment on range of $73,000 - $511,000.

Franchise Fee: $40,000

Royalty Fee: 3.5%

Financial Assistance: Data not available.

Managerial Assistance: Burger King franchisees have available to them a group of support personnel who specialize in all phases of business activities, including operations, training, marketing, profit and loss control, real estate and construction.

Training Provided: Burger King offers a full range of training to its franchisees, including basic and advanced operations courses, equipment seminars, human relations training, franchisee business courses, etc.

Information Submitted: January 1994

BW-3 FRANCHISE SYSTEMS
2634 Vine St.
Cincinnati, OH 45219
Telephone: (800) 688-2932 (513) 961-1847
Fax: (513) 751-7170
Mr. Arthur L. Bowman, Franchise Sales Director

Number of Franchised Units: 8
Number of Company-Owned Units: 8
Number of Total Operating Units: 16

In Business Since: 1982   **Franchising Since:** 1991

Description of Operation: BW-3 (Buffalo Wild Wings and Weck) feature buffalo-style chicken wings, ranging from mild to wild. They have an extensive menu, with burgers, chicken breasts and beef, all featured on the Weck roll. All BW-3 restaurants have full bars with 12 beers on tap and 42 offered. Most restaurants feature 100" screen televisions and NTN, the National Trivia Sports game. 12 are campus locations and 4 in busy traffic areas.

Equity Capital Needed: $200,000 - $350,000

Franchise Fee: $19,500

Royalty Fee: 5%

Financial Assistance: Not available.

Managerial Assistance: There is a thorough 2-week training program in Cincinnati, OH. An opening team will be at the location for at least 1 week. A team leader will visit once a month to evaluate the franchise and management.

Training Provided: Same as above.

Information Submitted: November 1993

CAFE BRESLER'S
999 E. Touhy Ave., # 333
Des Plaines, IL 60018
Telephone: (800) 535-3333 (708) 298-1100
Fax: (708) 298-0697
Mr. Howard Marks, VP, Director of Franchise Development

Number of Franchised Units: 1
Number of Company-Owned Units: 1
Number of Total Operating Units: 2

In Business Since: 1992   **Franchising Since:** 1993

Description of Operation: A cafe serving unique and healthy food. Our day starts with fresh pastries, served along side our gourmet coffee, espresso and cappuccino. For lunch and dinner, our salad selections can't be beat and we have great pastas, sandwiches, quiche and our signature focaccia. Each meal is perfectly complemented with Bresler's famous ice cream and yogurts. Cafe Bresler's equals quality, variety, value and success.

Equity Capital Needed: $225,000 - $300,000

Franchise Fee: $25,000

Royalty Fee: 4%

Financial Assistance: The franchisor will assist in securing third-party financing.

Managerial Assistance: Besides assisting in the pre-opening and grand opening training, our operations department will continue to be there for you with on-going guidance and field support for as long as you're a franchise owner. Our territory managers will visit your shop to consult with you and advise you in the areas of sales forecasts and sales and operational objectives, as well as on the plans to meet your goals.

Training Provided: A full training program is provided. Support begins with location selection, construction planning and opening assistance. Operations personnel visit units on a regular basis.

Information Submitted: December 1993

CAFE SALADS ETC.
4300 N. Miller Rd., # 143
Scottsdale, AZ 85251
Telephone: (800) 472-5170 (602) 946-2939
Fax: (602) 946-1061
Mr. James L. Courtney, Vice President of Franchise Development

Number of Franchised Units: 1
Number of Company-Owned Units: 1
Number of Total Operating Units: 2

In Business Since: 1992   **Franchising Since:** 1993

Description of Operation: Step into an indoor rose garden at Cafe Salads Etc., featuring fresh, healthy salads, pastas, sandwiches, soups and desserts at reasonable prices. Customers enjoy table service, pick-up or delivery. Food is easily prepared, requiring no costly cooks or grills. Developed by Robert Drake (founder of Drake's Salad Bar Restaurants) for single or multi-unit operators. Low investment, simple to run, with complete training and support.

Equity Capital Needed: $25,000 - $70,000

Franchise Fee: $10,000

Royalty Fee: 5%

Financial Assistance: The franchisor will assist franchisees in obtaining financing through banks, the SBA and/or equipment-leasing companies. We provide our loan proposal and business plan to franchisees, which includes pro forma profit and loss, cash flow projections, specifications and general information.

Managerial Assistance: Cafe Salads Etc. provides site selection assistance, lease negotiation assistance, site development/construction monitoring, staff recruitment help, initial inventory planning, grand opening plan, advertising plan and on-going training and support.

Training Provided: 2 weeks at headquarters and in training restaurant, plus 2 more weeks in franchisee's restaurant.

Information Submitted: November 1993

CAP'N TACO
P. O. Box 415
North Olmsted, OH 44070
Telephone: (216) 676-9100
Mr. Raymond Brown, Director of Franchise Sales

Number of Franchised Units: 1
Number of Company-Owned Units: 2
Number of Total Operating Units: 3

In Business Since: 1976   **Franchising Since:** 1986

Description of Operation: We are a Mexican quick-service restaurant, featuring fresh-made, on-premises food. Our production system can produce up to 3,000 products per hour with minimum labor. Double drive-thru, strip center, mall or free-standing stores, with beer and margarita options will be offered.

Equity Capital Needed: $85,000 - $130,000

Franchise Fee: $15,000

Royalty Fee: 5%

Financial Assistance: None available.

Managerial Assistance: We assist with site selection, build-out, equipment, inventory, grand opening, hiring and on-going support.

Training Provided: A minimum of 2 weeks at our headquarters for owner and manager. Yearly seminar. Pre-opening and 2 weeks of post-opening assistance. On-going training throughout the year, as required or requested.

Information Submitted: November 1993

CAPTAIN D'S
1717 Elm Hill Pike, # A-10
Nashville, TN 37210
Telephone: (800) 346-2790 (615) 231-2066
Fax: (615) 231-2790
Mr. Chip Maxwell, Director of Development

Number of Franchised Units: 307
Number of Company-Owned Units: 347
Number of Total Operating Units: 654

In Business Since: 1969   **Franchising Since:** 1969

Description of Operation: Quick-service, dine-in or take-out seafood restaurant, serving baked, broiled and fried fish, shrimp and chicken entrees and a variety of vegetables and desserts.

Equity Capital Needed: $150,000

Franchise Fee: $15,000

Royalty Fee: 3%

Financial Assistance: None.

Managerial Assistance: On-site opening assistance

Training Provided: We offer 6 - 8 weeks of in-store training.

Information Submitted: January 1994

CAPTAIN TONY'S PIZZA & PASTA EMPORIUM
2990 Culver Rd.
Rochester, NY 14622
Telephone: (800) 332-8669 (716) 467-2250
Fax: (716) 467-0784
Mr. Michael J. Martella, President

Number of Franchised Units: 19
Number of Company-Owned Units: 0
Number of Total Operating Units: 19

In Business Since: 1972   **Franchising Since:** 1986

Description of Operation: Pizza franchise.

Equity Capital Needed: $95,000 - $125,000

Franchise Fee: $9,500

Royalty Fee: 4% - 5%

Financial Assistance: Not available.

Managerial Assistance: Data not available.

Training Provided: 1 week at Company-designated training facility and 2 weeks on-site.

Information Submitted: November 1993

CARL'S JR. RESTAURANTS
1200 N. Harbor Blvd.
Anaheim, CA 92803
Telephone: (800) 422-4141 (714) 520-4452
Fax: (714) 520-4409
Ms. Renea Hutchings

Number of Franchised Units: 256
Number of Company-Owned Units: 394
Number of Total Operating Units: 650

In Business Since: 1956   **Franchising Since:** 1984

Description of Operation: Carl Karcher Enterprises operates a chain of fast-food restaurants that offers moderately-priced, high-quality food in attractive and comfortable surroundings. A diversified menu features hamburgers, specialty sandwiches, salad bar, dessert items and breakfasts.

Equity Capital Needed: $250,000 net worth, of which $175,000 must be liquid assets from non-borrowed funds.

Franchise Fee: $35,000

Royalty Fee: 4%

Financial Assistance: Interim financing for land and construction, with third-party commitment to assume the franchisor's position.

Managerial Assistance: We provide site selection, real estate construction and an orientation course prior to opening. Opening assistance. Thereafter, CKE will provide franchise operations personnel to assist the franchise operator during the entire term of the franchise.

Training Provided: Training includes 1 week of classroom and an additional 9 weeks of in-restaurant training at corporate headquarters in Anaheim, CA.

Information Submitted: April 1994

CASA OLE MEXICAN RESTAURANT
1135 Edgebrook Dr.
Houston, TX 77034
Telephone: (713) 943-7574
Fax: (713) 943-9554
Mr. Glen Rex, Director of Franchise Services

Number of Franchised Units: 21
Number of Company-Owned Units: 19
Number of Total Operating Units: 40

In Business Since: 1973   **Franchising Since:** 1979

Description of Operation: Full-service, freshly-prepared Mexican food served in our friendly, casual dining room. Menu price range: appetizers $3.35 - $5.95, entrees $3.45 - $7.95, children's menu $2.25 - $2.95, margaritas, beer and wine.

Equity Capital Needed: $325,000 - $1,000,000

Franchise Fee: $25,000

Royalty Fee: 5%

Financial Assistance: None available.

Managerial Assistance: 4-6 weeks' training in advance of opening for each manager and assistant manager. 15 days of training for the chef. Advice, assistance and training manuals for staff positions. Franchisor representatives on hand during first 2 weeks of new store opening. We also provide advice and guidance to the franchisee, beginning with site selection, through construction and grand opening. We utilize a comprehensive store development guidelines manual to aid the new franchisee throughout the development phase.

Training Provided: Data not available.

Information Submitted: January 1994

CASSANO'S PIZZA & SUBS
1700 E. Stroop Rd.
Dayton, OH 45429
Telephone: (513) 294-8400
Fax: (513) 294-8107
Mr. Richard O. Soehner, Senior Vice President

Number of Franchised Units: 14
Number of Company-Owned Units: 47
Number of Total Operating Units: 61

In Business Since: 1953   **Franchising Since:** 1957

Description of Operation: Cassano's grants franchises to operate Cassano's Pizza & Subs restaurants. The menu features pizza prepared to customer's orders from a selection of ingredients and including our crust, the formulation and preparation of which is a trade secret. Cassano's also offers specially-prepared sandwiches, salads, garlic bread, potato chips and beverages, including beer and wine where available. Cassano's restaurants provides on-premises dining, take-out service and delivery.

Equity Capital Needed: $141,000 - $390,000

Franchise Fee: $10,000

Royalty Fee: 4%

Financial Assistance: Currently, Cassano's does not provide financial assistance. There are, however, lending institutions who are willing to provide financing, based on the strength of the franchisee.

Managerial Assistance: Cassano's will furnish operating assistance to the franchisee as often as Cassano's deems necessary. This includes guidance in methods of food preparation, packaging and sales; sale of additional authorized products and services; hiring and training of employees; advertising and promotion programs; establishment and maintenance of administrative, inventory control and general operating procedures.

Training Provided: Before opening, the franchisee or manager of the restaurant is required to satisfactorily complete a minimum 4-week training program given by Cassano's in Dayton, OH. Cassano's will also provide training for up to 2 additional employees. Training is free of charge, but franchisee is responsible for travel, room and living expenses while at training. The training program consists of lectures, demonstrations, discussions and participation in the operation of Cassano's restaurants in the Dayton area.

Information Submitted: March 1994

CATERINA'S
415 Avenida Pico, # N2, PO Box 5587
San Clemente, CA 92672
Telephone: (800) 252-7431 (714) 492-7431
Fax: (714) 492-9585
Ms. Josie Rietkerk, President

Number of Franchised Units: 2
Number of Company-Owned Units: 1
Number of Total Operating Units: 3

In Business Since: 1990   **Franchising Since:** 1993

Description of Operation: Caterina's is a business format franchisor, providing franchisees complete "turn-key" start-up and on-going assistance in the retail sales of fine chocolates, candy, self-serve yogurt and ice cream, gourmet coffee and cookies and related gift items.

Equity Capital Needed: $99,900 - $185,900 (includes franchise fee).

Franchise Fee: $15,000 - $25,000

Royalty Fee: 5%

Financial Assistance: Assistance in obtaining financing on approved credit.

Managerial Assistance: Continuous consultation and assistance to franchisees in all aspects of running a small business. Assistance in site location and lease negotiations at start-up.

Training Provided: Complete training manuals provided. 3 - 4 of weeks formal training to include day-to-day operations, personnel issues, customer service, marketing, financial controls, merchandising and product knowledge.

Information Submitted: November 1993

CENTRAL PARK U.S.A.
300 High St.
Chattanooga, TN 37403
Telephone: (615) 267-5646
Fax: (615) 267-2384
Mr. Robert M. Davenport, Jr., President

Number of Franchised Units: 55
Number of Company-Owned Units: 16
Number of Total Operating Units: 71

In Business Since: 1982   Franchising Since: 1987

Description of Operation: Double drive-thru, limited menu food service. Central Park is the low-cost provider of high-quality products.

Equity Capital Needed: $250,000 per unit.

Franchise Fee: $15,000

Royalty Fee: 4%

Financial Assistance: None.

Managerial Assistance: We provide a management training program, pre-opening support, on-going field support and training, accounting systems, real estate acquisition and site negotiation support. Modular building program through third party.

Training Provided: Data not available.

Information Submitted: February 1994

CHARLEY'S STEAKERY
1912 N. High St.
Columbus, OH 43201
Telephone: (614) 291-7122
Fax: (614) 291-7133
Mr. Thomas H. Hoover, Jr., Director of Development

Number of Franchised Units: 18
Number of Company-Owned Units: 4
Number of Total Operating Units: 22

In Business Since: 1986   Franchising Since: 1991

Description of Operation: We specialize in grilled sandwiches, salads and fries. Open kitchen concept, with exhibition-style cooking. Mainly located in regional malls, airports, college campuses and downtown.

Equity Capital Needed: $100,000 - $150,000

Franchise Fee: $15,000

Royalty Fee: 5%

Financial Assistance: None.

Managerial Assistance: We provide a minimum of 4 visits a year, covering all operations and management areas. Quarterly marketing support. Periodic newsletter to inform franchisees of changes and improvements.

Training Provided: We offer a comprehensive 2-week training course, consisting of classroom and field operations. Opening specialist will offer further training and troubleshooting on opening.

Information Submitted: January 1994

CHEDDAR'S
616 Six Flags Dr., # 116
Arlington, TX 76011
Telephone: (817) 640-4344
Fax: (817) 633-4452
Mr. Robert N. Bruff, Franchise Sales/Development

Number of Franchised Units: 9
Number of Company-Owned Units: 8
Number of Total Operating Units: 17

In Business Since: 1978   Franchising Since: 1984

Description of Operation: Full-service, casual dining restaurant, with alcoholic beverage service. Cheddar's is based on mainstream, traditional concepts, serving high-quality food, frequently prepared fresh from scratch, served in bountiful portions at low prices with a very high perceived price/value ratio. The environment is casual, with natural colors and materials.

Equity Capital Needed: $100,000 - $150,000

Franchise Fee: $30,000

Royalty Fee: 3%

Financial Assistance: None.

Managerial Assistance: Management training for 10 - 12 weeks for every manager and director of operations. Opening and training team for 2 - 3 weeks. Field consultant visits monthly. Assistance on all development. New product research and development. Full accounting systems and services. Design and construction assistance.

Training Provided: Same as above.

Information Submitted: January 1994

CHEF'S FRIED CHICKEN
20 Audobon Oaks Blvd.
Lafayette, LA 70506
Telephone: (318) 233-1621
Fax: (318) 233-9038
Mr. Lee Shelton, President

Number of Franchised Units: 9
Number of Company-Owned Units: 0
Number of Total Operating Units: 9

In Business Since: 1970   Franchising Since: 1971

Description of Operation: Fast-food fried chicken, with a touch of Cajun.

Equity Capital Needed: $75,000

Franchise Fee: $20,000, except for members of Vetfran, who are charged $5,000.

Royalty Fee: 4%

Financial Assistance: None.

Managerial Assistance: Assistance is provided during the opening until the franchisee is able to manage the operation. Then, when he/she has a problem, he/she can call in for assistance.

Training Provided: Franchisees are trained in operations until they are satisfied that they know the complete operation.

Information Submitted: November 1993

CHELSEA STREET PUB & GRILL
P. O. Box 9989
Austin, TX 78766
Telephone: (512) 454-7739
Fax: (512) 454-1801
Mr. Norman Crohn, President

Number of Franchised Units: 5
Number of Company-Owned Units: 14
Number of Total Operating Units: 19

In Business Since: 1973   Franchising Since: 1983

Description of Operation: Restaurant and pub, located in regional malls in Texas, Louisiana, Colorado, Oklahoma or New Mexico. Live entertainment after 9:00 PM. Serves hamburgers to steaks - over 75 menu items - liquor, beer and wine served. Table service. Giant TV screen.

Equity Capital Needed: $375,000 - $400,000

Franchise Fee: $30,000

Royalty Fee: 5%

Financial Assistance: None.

Managerial Assistance: We provide training, advertising, purchasing, bookkeeping, band booking, on-line E Mail and computer assistance, market research, construction supervision and day and night on-call.

Training Provided: We offer an extensive (6 weeks) of in-store training and 2 weeks in general office. Management assists in franchisee's unit for first 2 weeks when opened.

Information Submitted: March 1994

CHICAGO'S PIZZA
1111 N. Broadway
Greenfield, IN 46140
Telephone: (317) 462-9878
Mr. Robert L. McDonald, Chief Executive Officer

Number of Franchised Units: 9
Number of Company-Owned Units: 1
Number of Total Operating Units: 10

In Business Since: 1979   Franchising Since: 1982

Description of Operation: Pizza, salads and sandwiches, made from scratch. Inside dining, carry-out and delivery.

Equity Capital Needed: $100,000 - $325,000

Franchise Fee: $10,000

Royalty Fee: 4%

Financial Assistance: None.

Managerial Assistance: We provide management training in existing stores.

Training Provided: Management and hourly employees are trained in existing stores. Opening training (open to close) is provided the first 2 weeks after opening.

Information Submitted: November 1993

CHICKEN DELIGHT
395 Berry St.
Winnipeg, MB R3J 1N6 CAN
Telephone: (204) 885-7570
Fax: (204) 831-6176
Mr. Gary Thompson, Director of Franchise Development

Number of Franchised Units: 45
Number of Company-Owned Units: 18
Number of Total Operating Units: 63

In Business Since: 1952   Franchising Since: 1952

Description of Operation: Chicken Delight has been in business for over 40 years, featuring our famous pressure-fried chicken and fresh-dough pizza, plus other tasty selections. We cater to the fast-food market with dine-in, take-out, delivery and drive-thru.

Equity Capital Needed: $75,000

Franchise Fee: $20,000

Royalty Fee: 5%

Financial Assistance: Yes.

Managerial Assistance: We provide on-site operational training, manuals and marketing ideas. We also monitor the progress of all franchisees on a monthly basis.

Training Provided: We offer an intensive 4-week, in-field training program at our corporate stores. During the course of the training, the operational manager periodically checks the new franchisee's progress.

Information Submitted: January 1994

CHICKS NATURAL
12520 High Bluff Dr., # 315
San Diego, CA 92130

Telephone: (619) 793-0310
Fax: (619) 793-0042
Mr. Randy White, President

Number of Franchised Units: 7
Number of Company-Owned Units: 3
Number of Total Operating Units: 10

In Business Since: 1989   Franchising Since: 1991

Description of Operation: Develop and operate Chicks Natural rotisserie-cooked chicken restaurants.

Equity Capital Needed: $175,000 - $275,000

Franchise Fee: $25,000

Royalty Fee: 4%

Financial Assistance: Bank and SBA contacts.

Managerial Assistance: Site selection, assistance with construction plans, build rotisserie, attend grand opening and remain for 2 weeks, invitation to attend Company store's manager meetings.

Training Provided: Site selection, preparation of menu items, personnel policies, 2-week training on running restaurant. Manual provided for unit opening assistance.

Information Submitted: January 1994

CHICO'S
P. O. Box 890144
Temecula, CA 92589
Telephone: (800) 772-4426
Mr. Terry Shores, President

Number of Franchised Units: 3
Number of Company-Owned Units: 1
Number of Total Operating Units: 4

In Business Since: 1988   Franchising Since: 1993

Description of Operation: Chico's serves dinnerhouse-quality Mexican food in a fast-food setting. Authentic Mexican food products are made from scratch daily and topped with offerings from the salsa bar.

Equity Capital Needed: $95,000 - $250,000

Franchise Fee: $15,000

Royalty Fee: 5%

Financial Assistance: Assistance is provided in obtaining third-party financing.

Managerial Assistance: Operational training is on-site. Operating and training manuals. Marketing ideas.

Training Provided: We provide full training in all aspects of the business for one month - classroom and on-site.

Information Submitted: March 1994

CHICO'S 2 IN 1
584 Voutrait Rd., RR # 2
Mill Bay, BC V0R 2P0 CAN
Telephone: (800) 688-5371 (604) 743-9609
Fax: (604) 338-7234
Mr. Michael Moisson, Franchise Director

Number of Franchised Units: 2
Number of Company-Owned Units: 1
Number of Total Operating Units: 3

In Business Since: 1988   Franchising Since: 1993

Description of Operation: Fast-food restaurants, mainly take-out and delivery, specializing in fried chicken and pizza. Other menu items include pasta, ribs, burgers and salads.

Equity Capital Needed: Starting at $90,000, with $25,000 down payment O.A.C.

Franchise Fee: $10,000

Royalty Fee: 3%

Financial Assistance: The Company will help arrange bank financing and/or assist with financing with minimum down payment and approved credit.

Managerial Assistance: We provide full training manuals, videos, marketing assistance and annual meetings. Full support in all areas of franchise operations on an on-going basis.

Training Provided: Training includes 4 weeks at an established location, plus an additional 2 weeks in the new location.

Information Submitted: February 1994

CHINA GATE DELIVERY
3950 Lyman Dr.
Hilliard, OH 43026
Telephone: (614) 876-1188
Fax: (614) 876-9746
Mr. Bill Dolan, Executive Vice President

Number of Franchised Units: 2
Number of Company-Owned Units: 0
Number of Total Operating Units: 2

In Business Since: 1993   **Franchising Since:** 1993

Description of Operation: Delivery service.

Equity Capital Needed: $175,300 - $285,500

Franchise Fee: $9,500

Royalty Fee: $0 - $30,000 = 2%; $30,001 - $40,000 = 3%.

Financial Assistance: Not available.

Managerial Assistance: We provide real estate, construction, marketing, purchasing, training and operations assistance.

Training Provided: 2-week training program for restaurant manager and owner. 5 days of new unit opening assistance.

Information Submitted: November 1993

CHUBBY'S DINER
11638 Fair Oaks Blvd., # 210
Fair Oaks, CA 95628
Telephone: (800) 892-2749 (916) 966-7773
Fax: (916) 863-6778
Mr. David Miry, President

Number of Franchised Units: 38
Number of Company-Owned Units: 0
Number of Total Operating Units: 38

In Business Since: 1990   **Franchising Since:** 1990

Description of Operation: Our Chubby's Diners are simple, efficient, low-cost restaurant operations, where bread is baked fresh daily and hamburgers, chicken, fries, fabulous shakes and sundaes, breakfast, dinner and other convenient food items are served. We offer great food at excellent prices. Great fun for the entire family in a traditional, nostalgic 50's atmosphere.

Equity Capital Needed: $69,900 - $114,900

Franchise Fee: $8,000

Royalty Fee: 6%

Financial Assistance: Partial leasing of equipment through third party on approved credit.

Managerial Assistance: We provide on-going corporate support. Territory development representatives are assigned to advise and assist franchisees with operations. Aggressive marketing programs.

Training Provided: Training includes a full 10 days (minimum) of training at an operating unit. Upon opening, the development representative is on site for a minimum of 7 days to insure a smooth opening and to

assist with operations. Intensive training seminars, quarterly national advertising meetings and monthly regional advertising meetings to assist with promotions.

Information Submitted: January 1994

CHURCH'S CHICKEN
Six Concourse Pkwy., # 1700
Atlanta, GA 30328
Telephone: (800) 848-8248 (404) 353-3187
Fax: (404) 353-3170
Ms. Balencia Walker, Communications Manager

Number of Franchised Units: 473
Number of Company-Owned Units: 606
Number of Total Operating Units: 1079

In Business Since: 1952   **Franchising Since:** 1972

Description of Operation: Church's is a fast-food chicken restaurant, specializing in Southern-style dishes. Church's serves up authentically Southern fried chicken and mashed potatoes with the option of spicy jalepenos on the side. Church's chicken is the nation's second largest fast-food chicken chain, with approximately 1,079 units throughout the US and abroad.

Equity Capital Needed: $200,000 - $300,000

Franchise Fee: $25,000

Royalty Fee: 5% of gross sales.

Financial Assistance: Indirect assistance available to obtain financing. No direct assistance available. It is recommended that franchising prospects have $150,000 in liquid assets and a $300,000 new worth.

Managerial Assistance: Church's is absolutely committed to providing the operational support needed to produce the highest-quality product and satisfied customers. This support extends to thorough training on procedures, procurement of equipment and supplies as well as on-going field support.

Training Provided: The training department at Church's has programs that will help you understand every aspect of the business - from day-to-day operations and accounting to inventory and managing your staff.

Information Submitted: December 1993

CICI'S PIZZA
1620 Rafe St., # 114
Carrollton, TX 75006
Telephone: (214) 466-2424
Fax: (214) 466-2425
Mr. Michael O. Karns, Real Estate Department

Number of Franchised Units: 90
Number of Company-Owned Units: 10
Number of Total Operating Units: 100

In Business Since: 1985   **Franchising Since:** 1989

Description of Operation: Cici's Pizza provides its guests with delicious pizza, pasta, salad bar and dessert on an all-you-can-eat lunch and dinner buffet for only $2.99! Cici's Pizza also offers a value-priced take-out menu. Our low price, combined with great service and sparkling clean restaurants is making Cici's among the fastest-growing franchises in America!

Equity Capital Needed: $100,000 approximately.

Franchise Fee: $25,000

Royalty Fee: 0%

Financial Assistance: Cici's provides no corporate funding.

Managerial Assistance: Full training program.

Training Provided: Full training program.

Information Submitted: April 1994

CLUB SANDWICH
107 Cherry St.
New Canaan, CT 06840
Telephone: (800) 428-2675 (203) 972-6714
Fax: (203) 849-0405
Mr. Michael G. DeVito, President

Number of Franchised Units: 4
Number of Company-Owned Units: 0
Number of Total Operating Units: 4

In Business Since: 1988   Franchising Since: 1988

Description of Operation: Gourmet sandwich shop. Up-scale sandwiches, breakfasts, and desserts.

Equity Capital Needed: $60,000

Franchise Fee: $15,000

Royalty Fee: 5% plus 1%.

Financial Assistance: Equipment leasing.

Managerial Assistance: Complete manual with customer relations - recipe portions control. Open consultation at any time. Meeting every 2 months.

Training Provided: 4 weeks in home office; 2 weeks at franchisee's shop.

Information Submitted: January 1994

CONEY'S "WORLD FAMOUS HOT DOGS"
102 Dunlap St., P. O. Box 1137
Batesville, MS 38606
Telephone: (800) 826-6397 (601) 563-5822
Fax: (601) 563-8586
Mr. Robert L. Crites, President

Number of Franchised Units: 7
Number of Company-Owned Units: 1
Number of Total Operating Units: 8

In Business Since: 1991   Franchising Since: 1992

Description of Operation: Step right up to the most exciting franchise of the decade - Coney's "World Famous Hot Dogs" - featuring the Coney's all-beef hot dog on a steamed bun with your choice of many toppings. The Company's menu also includes sausages, foot longs, chicken, hamburgers, fries, steak, ham sandwiches and a delicious array of desserts, fat-free yogurts, cookies, apple pie and a variety of beverages.

Equity Capital Needed: $100,000

Franchise Fee: $7,500

Royalty Fee: 8%

Financial Assistance: None.

Managerial Assistance: At Coney's, we recognize that your success and our extensive franchise support system is designed to produce positive results for both of us. It includes expert assistance in site selection, operations, training programs, marketing and advertising.

Training Provided: Our field staff will provide hands-on assistance in the critical phases of managing your Coney's. A Coney's franchise consultant will advise you on a broad range of business concerns, including inventory control, accounting, personnel and purchasing. Before your Coney's opens, a Field Marketing Representative will help pinpoint your advertising opportunities necessary for high customer traffic and sales.

Information Submitted: November 1993

COUNTRY KITCHEN RESTAURANTS
P. O. Box 59159, Carlson Pkwy.
Minneapolis, MN 55459
Telephone: (800) 477-4200 (612) 449-1300
Fax: (612) 449-1338
Mr. Kim O. Andereck, Senior Director of Development

Number of Franchised Units: 235
Number of Company-Owned Units: 0
Number of Total Operating Units: 235

In Business Since: 1939   Franchising Since: 1977

Description of Operation: Sit-down, full-service family dining restaurant. Breakfast, lunch and dinner menu served 6 AM - 11 PM. Non-traditional sites in hotels, airports and truckstops will be considered.

Equity Capital Needed: $125,000 - $750,000

Franchise Fee: $25,000

Royalty Fee: 4%

Financial Assistance: Introduction to potential lenders.

Managerial Assistance: Full management training (8 weeks) included in initial franchise fee. Corporate trainers in new store for 4 weeks to help manager hire and train a staff.

Training Provided: On-going management support, operational support and re-training throughout the term of the agreement.

Information Submitted: December 1993

COUSINS SUBS
N83 W13400 Leon Rd.
Menomonee Falls, WI 53051
Telephone: (800) 238-9736 (414) 253-7700
Fax: (414) 253-7710
Mr. David K. Kilby, Vice President of Franchise Development

Number of Franchised Units: 28
Number of Company-Owned Units: 41
Number of Total Operating Units: 69

In Business Since: 1972   Franchising Since: 1985

Description of Operation: Uniquely developed submarine sandwich operation, with over 20 years of expertise. Volume-oriented, fast-service concept in an up-scale, in-line, strip or free-standing location, some with drive-up windows. Outstanding fresh-baked bread and the finest quality ingredients go into our hot and cold subs, delicious soups and garden-fresh salads. Franchising opportunities are available for a select group of single, multi-unit and area developer franchisees.

Equity Capital Needed: $50,000 - $100,000 liquid.

Franchise Fee: $10,000

Royalty Fee: 6% - 4%.

Financial Assistance: SBA source, equipment package leasing sources.

Managerial Assistance: Initially, Cousins provides design criteria and resource manual, franchise manual, operations manual, real estate site selection manual, sandwich making manual, modular video training program and recommended supplier list. Additionally, Cousins provides on-going seminars and training classes. A corporate area representative meets with each franchise location management 3 times per month to maintain communications and assist in problem solving.

Training Provided: Training includes a store building seminar for site selection, lease negotiation and construction, 24 days of hands-on training, plus 10 days of opening assistance and training. National and local store marketing support.

Information Submitted: March 1994

CULTURES
20 Bay St., Waterpark Pl., # 1605
Toronto, ON M5J 2N8 CAN
Telephone: (416) 368-1440
Fax: (416) 368-0804
Mr. John G. Beauparlant, General Manager

Number of Franchised Units: 33
Number of Company-Owned Units: 11
Number of Total Operating Units: 44

In Business Since: 1978   **Franchising Since:** 1980

Description of Operation: Cultures is a "fresh food" concept, in which all products are prepared on the premises every day. Salad, soup, sandwiches, a wide variety of baked goods and frozen yogurt specialties make up a healthy menu. We are dedicated to providing a "Better for You" customer experience, by offering great tasting, fresh food F.A.S.T. Friendly, Attentive, Speedy, Thoughtful.

Equity Capital Needed: $175,000 - $225,000 (Canadian).

Franchise Fee: $35,000 (Canadian).

Royalty Fee: 5%

Financial Assistance: We are currently investigating financial assistance programs by institutional banks.

Managerial Assistance: We provide the franchisees with central purchasing, field operations evaluation, field training, inventory control, newsletters and regional/national meetings.

Training Provided: We offer a comprehensive, 6-week in-store training program and on-going support from field representatives.

Information Submitted: January 1994

DAIRY BELLE FREEZE
832 N. Hillview Dr.
Milpitas, CA 95035
Telephone: (408) 263-2612
Fax: (408) 262-1218
Mr. Steven H. Goodere, Executive Vice President

Number of Franchised Units: 16
Number of Company-Owned Units: 1
Number of Total Operating Units: 17

In Business Since: 1957   **Franchising Since:** 1957

Description of Operation: A Dairy Belle restaurant is a place where the menu is large and diverse, with soft-serve ice cream desserts, hamburgers, hot dogs, hot sandwiches, Mexican food, several types of french fries and much more. We do not think of ourselves as a fast-food restaurant - more quick-service, because our food is "cooked to order," the way our customer would like it.

Equity Capital Needed: $51,000 - $180,000

Franchise Fee: $12,500

Royalty Fee: 5%

Financial Assistance: None.

Managerial Assistance: In addition to our intensive training program, the Company will have staff available to help new franchisees in their restaurant. We will continually assist our franchisees in all aspects of operations - from promotions through menu pricing, purchasing and customer relations.

Training Provided: We offer a complete restaurant management training program of 3 - 5 weeks. We also train our franchisees in bookkeeping and personal growth and development through understanding relationships and customer service.

Information Submitted: November 1993

DAIRY QUEEN CANADA
5245 Harvester Rd., P.O. Box 430
Burlington, ON L7R 3Y3 CAN
Telephone: (905) 639-1492
Fax: (905) 681-3623
Mr. Larry Carver, Franchise Development Manager

Number of Franchised Units: 438
Number of Company-Owned Units: 0
Number of Total Operating Units: 438

In Business Since: 1940   **Franchising Since:** 1950

Description of Operation: Franchising of quick-service restaurants. Fast food and frozen dairy treats.

Equity Capital Needed: $150,000 average.

Franchise Fee: $30,000

Royalty Fee: 4%

Financial Assistance: DQC will finance 50% of the initial franchise fee of $30,000.

Managerial Assistance: Assistance from all departments, as required - accounting, lease negotiation, operations, building plans, etc.

Training Provided: 2-week training period at head office in Minneapolis, MN for owners and managers. Training team at store opening.

Information Submitted: January 1994

DEL TACO
345 Baker St.
Costa Mesa, CA 92626
Telephone: (714) 540-8914
Fax: (714) 641-3612
Franchise Development

Number of Franchised Units: 90
Number of Company-Owned Units: 189
Number of Total Operating Units: 279

In Business Since: 1964   **Franchising Since:** 1967

Description of Operation: Quick-service Mexican/American restaurants.

Equity Capital Needed: Approximately $150,000

Franchise Fee: $25,000

Royalty Fee: 5%

Financial Assistance: Not available.

Managerial Assistance: The Del Taco system provides a method of restaurant operations and management, including site selection and layout criteria; designs for standardized Del Taco buildings; signs, graphics, names, logos and other decorative features; recipes and menus; furniture, fixtures and equipment specifications; marketing and advertising materials; operating procedures; training procedures and materials, specifications for food products and supplies.

Training Provided: Del Taco provides 12 weeks of in-restaurant and classroom training for instruction on basic restaurant management. Additional training and training aides are available on an on-going basis.

Information Submitted: December 1993

DEL'S LEMONADE & REFRESHMENTS
1260 Oaklawn Ave.
Cranston, RI 02920
Telephone: (401) 463-6190
Fax: (401) 463-7931
Mr. Joseph J. N. Padula, Executive Vice President

Number of Franchised Units: 27
Number of Company-Owned Units: 3
Number of Total Operating Units: 30

In Business Since: 1948   **Franchising Since:** 1965

Description of Operation: Soft frozen lemonade, pretzels, nachos, popcorn, pizza, candy and hot dogs. 16 ounce bottle of beverage line.

Equity Capital Needed: $50,000 - $80,000 minimum.

Franchise Fee: $15,000 and up.

Royalty Fee: Data not available.

Financial Assistance: Del's provides no financial assistance, but we will work with franchisee to put the business plan together.

Managerial Assistance: Del's has top-quality people working in the organization to assist and train all new franchises.

Training Provided: Assistance includes Del's manuals and on-the-job training.

Information Submitted: January 1994

DENNY'S
203 E. Main St.
Spartanburg, SC 29319
Telephone: (800) 733-6697 (803) 597-8403
Fax: (803) 597-8112
Ms. Joan Harrison, Manager

Number of Franchised Units: 423
Number of Company-Owned Units: 1020
Number of Total Operating Units: 1443

In Business Since: 1953   **Franchising Since:** 1984

Description of Operation: Full-service family restaurant - 24-hour operation.

Equity Capital Needed: Net worth requirement - $750,000; Liquid - $250,000.

Franchise Fee: $35,000

Royalty Fee: 4%

Financial Assistance: Not available at this date. May change.

Managerial Assistance: Data not available.

Training Provided: Currently a 30-day training program in a Denny's restaurant, plus a training crew in the restaurant 1 week prior to opening and 2 weeks after opening.

Information Submitted: December 1993

DESPERADO'S SALOON AND WESTERN EATERY
P. O. Box 20019
Brantford, ON N3P 2A4 CAN
Telephone: (519) 752-2945
Fax: (519) 752-0978
Mr. Ron Hewitt, Director of Franchising

Number of Franchised Units: 1
Number of Company-Owned Units: 1
Number of Total Operating Units: 2

In Business Since: 1993   **Franchising Since:** 1993

Description of Operation: Western atmosphere eatery and neighborhood saloon, featuring full kitchen with ribs, steak and chili.

Equity Capital Needed: $30,000 - $60,000

Franchise Fee: $20,000

Royalty Fee: 3%

Financial Assistance: Partial Company financing possible, along with assistance in securing funding from standard financial institutions.

Managerial Assistance: Assistance with marketing, store layout, entertainment policies, bookkeeping and on-going help from head office operations department.

Training Provided: An extensive 5 weeks of training, with head office help on opening. Assistance with ordering, scheduling and training of staff.

Information Submitted: November 1993

DIAMOND DAVE'S TACO COMPANY
201 S. Clinton St., # 281
Iowa City, IA 52240
Telephone: (319) 337-7690
Fax: (319) 337-4707
Mr. Stanley J. White, President

Number of Franchised Units: 33
Number of Company-Owned Units: 3
Number of Total Operating Units: 36

In Business Since: 1979   **Franchising Since:** 1981

Description of Operation: Diamond Dave's is a casual theme, sit-down Mexican/American restaurant with a lounge. Family dining, predominantly located in regional shopping malls. Fun and festive atmosphere with family prices.

Equity Capital Needed: $125,000 - $275,000

Franchise Fee: $15,000

Royalty Fee: 4%

Financial Assistance: In general, Diamond Dave's usually negotiates some cash contribution to construction from landlord. Equipment financing is available to qualified persons.

Managerial Assistance: Pre-training of owner/manager is required for 3 - 6 weeks before opening. Initial crew training for opening is provided. After opening, unit visits are performed; Spring and Fall franchise seminars are given.

Training Provided: Pre-opening training of key employees is provided in our Company-owned units. At opening, our trainers will be on-site to train the complete opening staff. Our people continue to train for up to a week afterwards.

Information Submitted: November 1993

DIDGERIDOOS ROTISSERIE CHICKEN
505 Consumers Rd.
Willowdale, ON M2J 4V8 CAN
Telephone: (416) 493-3900
Fax: (416) 493-3889
Mr. W. W. (Bill) Hood, President

Number of Franchised Units: 0
Number of Company-Owned Units: 0
Number of Total Operating Units: 0

In Business Since: 1994   **Franchising Since:** 1994

Description of Operation: Quick-service restaurant, with 40 - 60 seats. Service at counter, eat-in or take-out. No fried foods. No smoking. Not licensed to sell beer/wine. Fresh food prepared daily.

Equity Capital Needed: $75,000 - $100,000

Franchise Fee: $25,000

Royalty Fee: 5%

Financial Assistance: No financial assistance. We will assist in developing bank presentation.

Managerial Assistance: We provide site selection, lease negotiation, construction planning, training, grand opening, marketing and on-going consultation.

Training Provided: At corporate office, 3 weeks of on-site and office training. On location, 1 - 2 weeks of pre-opening and post-opening training.

Information Submitted: January 1994

DOMINO'S PIZZA
30 Frank Lloyd Wright Dr., Box 997
Ann Arbor, MI 48106
Telephone: (313) 930-3030
Fax: (313) 663-7922
Ms. Linda Popevich, Division Vice President

Number of Franchised Units: 4521
Number of Company-Owned Units: 500
Number of Total Operating Units: 5021

In Business Since: 1960   **Franchising Since:** 1967

Description of Operation: Pizza carry-out and delivery service.

Equity Capital Needed: $83,000 - $194,000

Franchise Fee: $0 - $6,000, varies.

Royalty Fee: 5.5%

Financial Assistance: Domino's Pizza does not directly provide financing, but we can refer the franchisee to lending institutions who will consider providing financing to qualified franchisees.

Managerial Assistance: Domino's Pizza only franchises to internal people and the kinds and duration of managerial and technical assistance provided by the Company are set forth in the franchise agreement.

Training Provided: Potential franchisees must complete the Company's current training program, which consists of both in-store training and classroom instruction.

Information Submitted: March 1994

DON CHERRY'S GRAPEVINE RESTAURANTS
88 Wilson St. W., # 2A
Ancaster, ON L9G 1N2 CAN
Telephone: (905) 648-7717
Fax: (905) 648-7723
Mr. Richard J. Scully, President

Number of Franchised Units: 24
Number of Company-Owned Units: 2
Number of Total Operating Units: 26

In Business Since: 1985   **Franchising Since:** 1987

Description of Operation: A full-service restaurant with a sports theme. Fully licensed, with average seating between 180 - 250 seats.

Equity Capital Needed: $250,000 - $400,000

Franchise Fee: $50,000

Royalty Fee: 6%

Financial Assistance: No assistance is available. The franchisee must not have financial encumbrances.

Managerial Assistance: Full training for 4 key position managers, plus 4 weeks training after opening. Help with accounting, inventory, hiring, etc.

Training Provided: An 8 - 10 week training program for all key personnel is provided.

Information Submitted: January 1994

DONATOS PIZZA
935 Taylor Station Rd.
Blacklick, OH 43004
Telephone: (800) 366-2867 (614) 864-2444
Fax: (614) 575-4466
Mr. Kevin King, Director of Franchising

Number of Franchised Units: 13
Number of Company-Owned Units: 43
Number of Total Operating Units: 56

In Business Since: 1963   **Franchising Since:** 1991

Description of Operation: High-quality pizza, subs and salads for dine-in, pick-up and delivery.

Equity Capital Needed: $300,000 - $350,000

Franchise Fee: $15,000

Royalty Fee: 4%

Financial Assistance: Not available.

Managerial Assistance: Each new franchisee is provided assistance in developing a business plan, securing financing, store development, site selection, on-going training and on-going business consultation.

Training Provided: The training period lasts between 4 - 8 weeks, depending upon the franchisee's prior experience. In addition, a field trainer is provided for the first 28 days. Additional assistance is available.

Information Submitted: November 1993

EDO JAPAN
602 Manitou Rd., SE
Calgary, AB T2G 4C5 CAN
Telephone: (403) 287-3822
Fax: (403) 243-6143
Mr. S. K. Ikuta, President

Number of Franchised Units: 62
Number of Company-Owned Units: 10
Number of Total Operating Units: 72

In Business Since: 1977   **Franchising Since:** 1986

Description of Operation: We are the original teppan/teriyaki-style, fast-food outlet that places emphasis on nutrition, high-quality food and the availability of vegetarian-style dishes. All menu items are prepared fresh, in full view of the customers. The teppan-style menu brings customers back again and again. Edo Japan has a highly successful, very profitable, fast-food concept. In the food courts, where we are located, we are generally in the top 3, often #1 in sales. There are 70+ Edo Japan restaurants in US and Canada.

Equity Capital Needed: $170,000 - $250,000

Franchise Fee: $20,000

Royalty Fee: 6%

Financial Assistance: The franchisee is responsible for his or her own financing.

Managerial Assistance: Scheduling of staff for busy and slow periods; cash register training; ordering of supplies and product; training of staff; introduction to new equipment; training in new menu items; and basic control of the store.

Training Provided: 2 weeks at head office includes food and sauce preparation, cooking, store procedures and training in accounting.

Information Submitted: December 1993

EDWARDO'S NATURAL PIZZA RESTAURANTS
205 W. Wacker Dr., # 1400
Chicago, IL 60606
Telephone: (800) 944-3393 (312) 345-8500
Fax: (312) 345-8522
Mr. Don Scatena, Vice President

Number of Franchised Units: 17
Number of Company-Owned Units: 12
Number of Total Operating Units: 29

In Business Since: 1978   **Franchising Since:** 1988

Description of Operation: Chicago-style stuffed pizza and more.

Equity Capital Needed: $270,000 - $500,000

Franchise Fee: $25,000

Royalty Fee: 5%

Financial Assistance: None.

Managerial Assistance: We provide on-site training and operational manuals.

Training Provided: Training includes 8 week sessions in the Chicago training center and 4 training supervisors at the site for 2 weeks on opening of new store.

Information Submitted: March 1994

EL CHICO RESTAURANTS
12200 Stemmons Fwy., # 100
Dallas, TX 75234
Telephone: (214) 241-5500
Fax: (214) 888-8198
Ms. Elizabeth Clark, Franchise Administration

Number of Franchised Units: 29
Number of Company-Owned Units: 56
Number of Total Operating Units: 85

In Business Since: 1940   **Franchising Since:** 1969

Description of Operation: Full-service Mexican food restaurant.

Equity Capital Needed: Data not available.

Franchise Fee: $35,000

Royalty Fee: 4%

Financial Assistance: We do not provide financial assistance.

Managerial Assistance: 2 regional managers for on-going field support.

Training Provided: A 12-week training program is required before opening. On-going training provided as needed. Training seminars provided throughout the year.

Information Submitted: January 1994

EL PASO MEXICAN KITCHENS
6070 S. Eastern Ave., # 300
Las Vegas, NV 89119
Telephone: (702) 597-2858
Fax: (702) 597-0743
Mr. Sean M. Collins, Vice President of Franchising

Number of Franchised Units: 4
Number of Company-Owned Units: 3
Number of Total Operating Units: 7

In Business Since: 1990   **Franchising Since:** 1993

Description of Operation: El Paso Mexican Kitchens offers a tremendous opportunity for success in free-standing, new or conversion, mall and shopping locations. Freshest products made daily in store, limited menu, affordable prices and open kitchen concept, express emphasis on highest quality and value - within a casual atmosphere, at a high-volume restaurant. Limited franchising and exclusive area development opportunities are now available for a select group of single and multi-unit franchises.

Equity Capital Needed: $48,500 - $65,000

Franchise Fee: $30,000

Royalty Fee: 6%

Financial Assistance: SBA approved. Lease package available.

Managerial Assistance: Data not available.

Training Provided: The franchise is a turn-key operation and requires limited experience. We offer a training program in our kitchen training center, which is comprehensive and on-going, including site selection, complete store set-up, grand opening, marketing, advertising and field support. Franchisees benefit from our proven successes.

Information Submitted: January 1994

ELMER'S PANCAKE & STEAK HOUSE
11802 SE Stark St., P. O. Box 16595
Portland, OR 97216
Telephone: (800) 325-5188 (503) 252-1485
Fax: (503) 257-7448
Ms. Anita Goldberg, Director of Franchising

Number of Franchised Units: 16
Number of Company-Owned Units: 11
Number of Total Operating Units: 27

In Business Since: 1960   **Franchising Since:** 1966

Description of Operation: Full services - breakfast, lunch and dinner. Special feature is breakfast, as well as all other menu items (unless special note), served all day. Banquet facilities, extensive menu. Some locations have lounges.

Equity Capital Needed: Minimum of $200,000 +; ability to finance the rest.

Franchise Fee: $25,000

Royalty Fee: 4%

Financial Assistance: None.

Managerial Assistance: We provide approximately 3 months of initial training. The opening crew provides training to new employees. We stay in close touch, especially first 2 years. Annual seminar.

Training Provided: Training takes place in Portland, OR and is one-on-one rather than classroom. All aspects of operating a restaurant are taught.

Information Submitted: January 1994

ERBERT & GERBERT'S SUBS & CLUBS
408 Riverside Ave.
Eau Claire, WI 54703
Telephone: (800) 283-5241 (715) 833-1375
Fax: (715) 833-8523
Mr. Kevin Schippers, President/Chief Executive Officer

Number of Franchised Units: 5
Number of Company-Owned Units: 1
Number of Total Operating Units: 6

In Business Since: 1988   **Franchising Since:** 1992

Description of Operation: Erbert and Gerbert's stores offer top-quality, gourmet submarine and club sandwiches on bread baked fresh on-site. A delivery service complements eat-in and carry-out services.

Equity Capital Needed: $72,600 - $119,400

Franchise Fee: $9,500

Royalty Fee: 6.5%

Financial Assistance: None available.

Managerial Assistance: Semi-monthly franchisee meetings cover advertising, labor and scheduling, cost control, quality control and other key management issues. Annual conventions focus more intensely on those same issues over 2-day periods. Newsletters supplement the face-to-face communication and training.

Training Provided: A 2-week training program involves 1 week of in-store, hands-on training in a Company store. Scheduling, food preparation, cash control and quality standards are covered in this weekly section. The second week involves administrative and management training required for cost control, payroll, financial management, etc. This is followed by 1 week of training at the time of start-up in the franchisee's store.

Information Submitted: November 1993

EVERYTHING YOGURT AND SALAD CAFE
1000 South Ave.
Staten Island, NY 10314
Telephone: (718) 494-8888
Fax: (718) 494-8776
Mr. Raymond C. Habib, Director of Franchising

Number of Franchised Units: 280
Number of Company-Owned Units: 7
Number of Total Operating Units: 287

In Business Since: 1976   **Franchising Since:** 1981

Description of Operation: Our concept is a healthy, quick-service restaurant, featuring frozen yogurt, sundaes and shakes, made-to-order salads, soups and sandwiches. We also serve a full line of fruit shakes and fresh-baked pretzels within our tandem unit called "Bananas."

Equity Capital Needed: $200,000 - $250,000

Franchise Fee: $25,000

Royalty Fee: 5%

Financial Assistance: Our Company will assist a new franchisee in obtaining either an SBA loan or do an equipment lease loan. We do not finance the candidate directly.

Managerial Assistance: All franchisees will complete a 2 - 4 week training program. Training is a hands-on program in a Company-owned store. We also are on-site for 1 week at the time the store opens.

Training Provided: All franchisees receive a full set of training, marketing and bookkeeping manuals. In addition, each location has a regional service manager with a 24-hour line when questions arise.

Information Submitted: November 1993

FAT BOY'S BAR-B-Q
1550 W. King St.
Cocoa, FL 32926
Telephone: (407) 636-1000
Fax: (407) 632-2964
Mr. Glenn A. Summers, President/Chief Executive Officer

Number of Franchised Units: 23
Number of Company-Owned Units: 0
Number of Total Operating Units: 23

In Business Since: 1958   **Franchising Since:** 1969

Description of Operation: Full-service restaurant, specializing in Bar-B-Que beef, pork, chicken, ribs and turkey prepared using a slow-smoked wood process. Steaks and seafood are also available. Serving breakfast, lunch and dinner, 7 days a week. Image unit seats 167, with banquet room option.

Equity Capital Needed: $75,000 - Up.

Franchise Fee: $35,000

Royalty Fee: 4%

Financial Assistance: The franchisor assists in the preparation of historical data, projections and packages which are submitted to various lenders. Equipment, as well as real estate, financing is available through the SBA or other local lenders. We also provide assistance in remodeling and negotiating leases or existing buildings which are acceptable.

Managerial Assistance: The Company prefers the franchisee and at least one managerial person to attend required training at the Company offices. On-going monitoring of monthly P & L's and all operations functions. Pre-opening and post-opening crew available.

Training Provided: A minimum of 400 hours is conducted in corporate offices and various operating restaurants. Training includes classroom, instruction manuals, standards and specifications, as well as hands-on food preparation during all day parts and at several locations.

Information Submitted: March 1994

FATBURGER
11110 W. Ohio Ave., # 208
Los Angeles, CA 90025
Telephone: (310) 914-1830
Fax: (310) 914-1838
Mr. Ali Nekumanesh, Franchise Director

Number of Franchised Units: 13
Number of Company-Owned Units: 6
Number of Total Operating Units: 19

In Business Since: 1952   **Franchising Since:** 1983

Description of Operation: Up-scale, quick-service restaurant.

Equity Capital Needed: $200,000

Franchise Fee: $25,000

Royalty Fee: 5%

Financial Assistance: Data not available.

Managerial Assistance: Full operational, technical and management support.

Training Provided: Initial and on-going monthly seminars.

Information Submitted: March 1994

FATSO'S HOMEMADE HAMBURGERS, ETC.
1446 Don Mills Rd., # 200
North York, ON M3B 3N3 CAN
Telephone: (416) 447-4584
Fax: (416) 444-0001
Mr. Steve Georgopoulos, President

Number of Franchised Units: 4
Number of Company-Owned Units: 1
Number of Total Operating Units: 5

In Business Since: 1984   **Franchising Since:** 1989

Description of Operation: Specializing in homemade hamburgers and salads, with self-serve toppings, in a fast-food concept.

Equity Capital Needed: $30,000

Franchise Fee: $20,000

Royalty Fee: 5%

Financial Assistance: We assist in the development of business plans and bank negotiations.

Managerial Assistance: We offer all aspects of day-to-day marketing, product development, accounting, real estate, legal and complete developmental operations from the start.

Training Provided: 6 - 8 weeks is spent between theory and actual site and off-premises locations.

Information Submitted: January 1994

FAZOLI'S SYSTEMS
836 E. Euclid Ave.
Lexington, KY 40502
Telephone: (606) 268-1668
Fax: (606) 268-2263
Mr. Gordon R. Doyle, Vice President of Franchising

Number of Franchised Units: 5
Number of Company-Owned Units: 38
Number of Total Operating Units: 43

In Business Since: 1988   **Franchising Since:** 1991

Description of Operation: Italian food - fast. A walk-up, take-out and drive-thru operation with approximately 100 seats.

Equity Capital Needed: $400,000 - $800,000

Franchise Fee: $20,000

Royalty Fee: 4%

Financial Assistance: None.

Managerial Assistance: A 5-week training program is required for a minimum of 3 persons per unit. Opening assistance is provided by Company personnel. Monthly supervision. Semi-annual meetings.

Training Provided: Same as above.

Information Submitted: March 1994

FLAMERS CHARBROILED HAMBURGERS
8761 Perimeter Park Blvd., # 201
Jacksonville, FL 32216
Telephone: (904) 641-7171
Fax: (904) 641-1140
Mr. Paul Martinez, Vice President of Marketing

Number of Franchised Units: 48
Number of Company-Owned Units: 12
Number of Total Operating Units: 60

In Business Since: 1987   **Franchising Since:** 1988

Description of Operation: Fast-food gourmet hamburger and chicken chain, located primarily in regional malls across the country. All food is cooked to order in plain view of the consumer. The food is cooked on a gas grill using lava rocks.

Equity Capital Needed: $130,000 - $185,000

Franchise Fee: $25,000

Royalty Fee: 5%

Financial Assistance: Third party and SBA.

Managerial Assistance: Regional management from parent company oversees the store after the grand opening crew has left.

Training Provided: 2 weeks of training in Orlando, FL.

Information Submitted: January 1994

FOSTERS FREEZE INTERNATIONAL
1052 Grand Ave., # C, P.O. Box 266
Arroyo Grande, CA 93420
Telephone: (800) 628-5600 (805) 481-9577
Fax: (805) 481-3791
Mr. Dennis G. Poletti, Director of Franchise Licensing

Number of Franchised Units: 146
Number of Company-Owned Units: 2
Number of Total Operating Units: 148

In Business Since: 1946   **Franchising Since:** 1946

Description of Operation: Fosters Freeze International is a franchisor of the unexcelled Fosters Freeze soft-serve desserts, plus a variety of high-quality food items.

Equity Capital Needed: $340,000 - $750,000, which includes the initial franchise fee of $40,000.

Franchise Fee: $25,000

Royalty Fee: 4%, and 3% sales promotion fee.

Financial Assistance: Fosters Freeze International's support team will assist in the location of financing for the franchisee.

Managerial Assistance: Assistance is provided in the areas of menu, private-label products, advertising, store openings, operations manuals, regular systemwide meetings, on-going communications and support staff to give continued support to the franchisee.

Training Provided: Training for the franchisee and his/her managers is provided at corporate headquarters located in Arroyo Grande, CA and at Company stores.

Information Submitted: March 1994

FOX'S PIZZA DEN
3243 Old Frankstown Rd.
Pittsburgh, PA 15239
Telephone: (412) 733-7888
Mr. James R. Fox, President

Number of Franchised Units: 140
Number of Company-Owned Units: 0
Number of Total Operating Units: 140

In Business Since: 1971   **Franchising Since:** 1974

Description of Operation: A complete pizza and sandwich operation, offering both fresh dough and shell pizza. Six different size pizzas, plus a large variety of sandwiches and Fox's famous Wedgies (a sandwich made on a pizza shell). Franchisee may expand his or her menu as desired. Franchisee may choose a sit-down store or a take-out and delivery only. We have our own commissary to service all your franchise needs.

Equity Capital Needed: $50,000 - $60,000

Franchise Fee: $8,000

Royalty Fee: $200 per month.

Financial Assistance: We assist with the business plan and work with prospective franchisee and local banks.

Managerial Assistance: Complete assistance with business plan, site location, assistance with lease, financing, equipment set-up, supervise renovation and on-site training of franchisee and employees. Assistance with bookkeeping and inventory control. We hold their hand from beginning to end.

Training Provided: 10 days of on-site training at franchisee's own unit. No need to attend out-of-state training schools.

Information Submitted: November 1993

FRIENDLY BANNERS RESTAURANTS
1965 W. 4th Ave., # 203
Vancouver, BC V6J 1M8 CAN
Telephone: (604) 737-7748
Fax: (604) 737-7993
Mr. Irwin Woodrow, President

Number of Franchised Units: 7
Number of Company-Owned Units: 0
Number of Total Operating Units: 7

In Business Since: 1969   **Franchising Since:** 1969

Description of Operation: Family-style restaurant, featuring big-scoop ice cream desserts. Restaurants strategically located in neighborhood areas—usually part of a strip mall.

Equity Capital Needed: $200,000

Franchise Fee: $30,000

Royalty Fee: 4%, plus 2% advertising.

Financial Assistance: Assistance will be given to acquire bank financing on behalf of the franchisee. This includes providing pro forma statements, cash flow projections, capital costs and attending meetings.

Managerial Assistance: Published manuals are available, as well as a requirement that the franchisee work and train in an existing franchise. Assistance will be given to hiring practices, accounting systems and controls required to minimize labor and food costs. Site location and set-up requirements will be provided.

Training Provided: On-site training is required at an existing franchise store. Opening advertising program is provided. Training team to assist with opening.

Information Submitted: December 1993

FRONT PAGE CAFE, THE
1101 S. Caraway Rd.
Jonesboro, AR 72401
Telephone: (501) 932-6343
Fax: (501) 931-9831
Mr. Mike Felts, Treasurer

Number of Franchised Units: 1
Number of Company-Owned Units: 2
Number of Total Operating Units: 3

In Business Since: 1989   **Franchising Since:** 1992

Description of Operation: Family-style (home cooking), full-service restaurant. Specializing in chicken, pork, beef and catfish. Unique atmosphere playing 50's and 60's music, antiques, old front pages on the walls, birthday board. All meals include our free pass-arounds, which includes our "flying rolls."

Equity Capital Needed: $80,000 - $200,000

Franchise Fee: $20,000

Royalty Fee: 5%

Financial Assistance: Not available.

Managerial Assistance: Data not available.

Training Provided: 2 weeks of training in Jonesboro, AR for up to 5 employees. Further training assistance in store at time of opening. Additional training as deemed necessary.

Information Submitted: January 1994

FUDDRUCKERS
One Corporate Pl., 55 Ferncroft Rd.
Danvers, MA 01923
Telephone: (800) 437-5474 (508) 774-9115
Fax: (508) 774-8485
Mr. Leo H. Skellchock, Vice President of Franchise Development

Number of Franchised Units: 81
Number of Company-Owned Units: 62
Number of Total Operating Units: 143

In Business Since: 1980   **Franchising Since:** 1983

Description of Operation: Fuddruckers is an up-scale restaurant, serving fresh ground beef patties from our on-premises butcher shop on our freshly-baked buns from our on-premises bakery. Breast of chicken, fish filet, hot dogs, a variety of salads, fries, onion rings, fresh cookies, brownies, pies, milk shakes and beverages with unlimited refills are also available. Garnish your selection with your choices from our bountiful produce bar. Fuddruckers is where you get the world's greatest hamburger and you do your own thing.

Equity Capital Needed: $350,000 - $1,200,000

Franchise Fee: $50,000

Royalty Fee: 5%

Financial Assistance: None. We have some lenders who have asked to be referred to any potential franchisees if the franchisee requests it.

Managerial Assistance: We have full-time operations consultants who make weekly contact and who visit a minimum of 2 times per year. Secret shopper surveys are also conducted regularly. Help is a phone call away.

Training Provided: 3 - 4 management people will be trained for 6 weeks in a Fuddruckers Company restaurant. All positions in the restaurant will be learned. Testing is weekly. Profile tests are available to compare with successful management profiles of Fuddruckers personnel.

Information Submitted: November 1993

FUNTIME INTERNATIONAL
2911 Turtle Creek Blvd., # 1250
Dallas, TX 75219
Telephone: (214) 740-0000
Fax: (214) 740-0011
Ms. Natasha Lombardo, International Franchise Co-ordinator

Number of Franchised Units: 10
Number of Company-Owned Units: 3
Number of Total Operating Units: 13

In Business Since: 1987   **Franchising Since:** 1992

Description of Operation: The children's and family entertainment industry is one of the fastest-growing markets worldwide. Rising young family populations have created a demand for exceptional and quality family entertainment. Fun Time Pizza answers this demand by combining the concepts of redemption gaming with exciting, life-like robotic performances and the universal appeal for quality pizza, resulting in the ultimate family entertainment facility. Based on the philosophy of "Food, Fun and a Whole Lot More."

Equity Capital Needed: $800,000 - $1,000,000

Franchise Fee: $30,000 for a single unit; $100,000+ for a Master Franchise.

Royalty Fee: Single unit 6%.

Financial Assistance: Various outside programs recommended.

Managerial Assistance: When you invest in a FunTime Pizza International franchise, you are joining the FunTime Pizza family. The members of this family have the same goals and ambitions that you have. Together, we work to build sales, image and profitability by sharing ideas that are common. You gain from years of expertise in site location, lease negotiations, construction and operations. FunTime Pizza franchisees are given detailed operations manuals, quality assurance visits and a willing corporate staff always available.

Training Provided: FunTime Pizza provides a complete and comprehensive 30-day training program prior to store opening. An experienced FunTime Pizza manager, from our corporate stores, will assist in final set-up and work with your newly-trained manager during grand opening, 2 weeks following. As part of the FunTime Pizza 30-day training program, new managers will work with experienced managers, observing customer service techniques and employee management systems. Franchisees may request additional training at any time.

Information Submitted: March 1994

GIFF'S SUB SHOP
634 N. Eglin Pkwy.
Ft. Walton Beach, FL 32548
Telephone: (904) 863-9011
Mr. Rick Arnette, Director of Operations

Number of Franchised Units: 5
Number of Company-Owned Units: 1
Number of Total Operating Units: 6

In Business Since: 1977   **Franchising Since:** 1985

Description of Operation: Subs and salads - featuring steaksubs. Home of the famous "Fighter Pilot Sub." Some stores offer breakfast, subs and biscuits. Average store employees 3 - 5 people.

Equity Capital Needed: $25,000 - $30,000

Franchise Fee: $7,500

Royalty Fee: 4%

Financial Assistance: Giff's offers no financial assistance.

Managerial Assistance: Data not available.

Training Provided: The new franchisee is trained for 1 week at home office and in the field as long as needed to operate successfully. They are also taught public relations, hiring practices, bookkeeping and food management. Our training manual covers everything needed to successfully operate a Giff's Sub Shop.

Information Submitted: November 1993

GIORGIO RESTAURANTS
222 St. Lawrence Blvd.
Montreal, PQ H2Y 2Y3 CAN
Telephone: (514) 845-4221
Fax: (514) 844-0071
Ms. Sylvie Paradis, Franchise Director

Number of Franchised Units: 18
Number of Company-Owned Units: 13
Number of Total Operating Units: 31

In Business Since: 1977   **Franchising Since:** 1985

Description of Operation: Chain of Italian restaurants - pastas and pizza.

Equity Capital Needed: $300,000

Franchise Fee: $30,000

Royalty Fee: 5%

Financial Assistance: No financial assistance.

Managerial Assistance: We assist in site location, architectural, training, staff, management, supplies, purchasing, advertising and marketing.

Training Provided: We provide a full theoretical and practical training program for 3 months. A support staff of 5 monitors for a 3-week period from the day the franchisee takes over his/her restaurant. A training manager is also on the premises 1 week before the opening and 7 weeks thereafter.

Information Submitted: January 1994

GODFATHER'S PIZZA
9140 W. Dodge Rd., # 300
Omaha, NE 68114
Telephone: (800) 456-8347 (402) 391-1452
Fax: (402) 392-2357
Mr. Bruce N. Cannon, Vice President of Sales

Number of Franchised Units: 376
Number of Company-Owned Units: 148
Number of Total Operating Units: 524

In Business Since: 1973   **Franchising Since:** 1974

Description of Operation: Pizza restaurant, serving 2 types of pizza crust, salads, beverages and sandwiches.

Equity Capital Needed: $136,500 - $291,000

Franchise Fee: $15,000

Royalty Fee: 5%

Financial Assistance: Not available.

Managerial Assistance: Regional Franchise Managers (RFM's) are assigned to all new franchisees to assist in getting their restaurant opened and operational. Additionally, the RFM's provide support in financial performance, business development, communications and on-going training.

Training Provided: A 4-week training program in Omaha, NE at GPI's corporate headquarters, which includes the research and development center and our flagship restaurant. This training is mandatory for the owners and their key operators. The franchisee is responsible for the cost.

Information Submitted: November 1993

GOLDEN CORRAL RESTAURANTS
5151 Glenwood Ave., # 300
Raleigh, NC 27612
Telephone: (800) 284-5673 (919) 781-9310
Fax: (919) 881-4485
Mr. Peter J. Charland, Vice President of Franchise Development

Number of Franchised Units: 137
Number of Company-Owned Units: 288
Number of Total Operating Units: 425

In Business Since: 1973   **Franchising Since:** 1987

Description of Operation: Steaks, buffet and bakery restaurant.

Equity Capital Needed: $1,200,000 - $2,400,000

Franchise Fee: $30,000 or $40,000.

Royalty Fee: 4%

Financial Assistance: Not available.

Managerial Assistance: Full assistance from site selection, training, opening assistance and on-going operations support.

Training Provided: 12-week program in 3 phases: 10 weeks in certified training restaurant and 2 weeks of classroom training.

Information Submitted: December 1993

GOLDEN FRIED CHICKEN
4835 LBJ Freeway, # 525
Dallas, TX 75244

Telephone: (214) 458-9555
Fax: (214) 458-9872
Mr. Victor F. Erwin, Executive Vice President

Number of Franchised Units: 88
Number of Company-Owned Units: 3
Number of Total Operating Units: 91

In Business Since: 1967   **Franchising Since:** 1972

Description of Operation: Franchisor of Golden Fried Chicken fast-food restaurants, specializing in quality fried chicken and appropriate side orders. A typical restaurant requires 2,000 square feet and a drive-thru window.

Equity Capital Needed: $25,000 - $125,000

Franchise Fee: $10,000

Royalty Fee: 4%

Financial Assistance: None.

Managerial Assistance: GFC provides continuous support for the life of the franchise, including pre-opening assistance, marketing programs, negotiation of national purchase contracts, operations manuals, regular visits by field personnel and product, equipment and market research.

Training Provided: 2 weeks of pre-opening training at a Company location, plus on-site opening assistance.

Information Submitted: November 1993

GOLDEN GRIDDLE FAMILY RESTAURANTS
505 Consumers Rd., # 1000
Willowdale, ON M2J 4V8 CAN
Telephone: (416) 493-3800
Fax: (416) 493-3889
Mr. W. W. (Bill) Hood, Executive Vice President

Number of Franchised Units: 48
Number of Company-Owned Units: 1
Number of Total Operating Units: 49

In Business Since: 1964   **Franchising Since:** 1976

Description of Operation: Full-service, sit-down, licensed family restaurant, featuring pancakes, waffles, eggs and an all you-can-eat lunch buffet.

Equity Capital Needed: $160,000 - $200,000

Franchise Fee: $10,000

Royalty Fee: 5%

Financial Assistance: No financial assistance, but will assist in putting bank presentation together.

Managerial Assistance: We provide site selection, lease negotiation, training, marketing and on-going consultation.

Training Provided: Training at corporate office - restaurant and office - 6 weeks. On location training - pre-opening - 3 weeks; post-opening - 1 - 2 weeks.

Information Submitted: January 1994

GOOMBA'S PASTA
770 E. Shaw Ave., # 222
Fresno, CA 93710
Telephone: (209) 229-4073
Fax: (209) 229-4074
Mr. Chris White, Manager of Franchise Development

Number of Franchised Units: 1
Number of Company-Owned Units: 3
Number of Total Operating Units: 4

In Business Since: 1991   **Franchising Since:** 1992

Description of Operation: Fast-food pasta! Goomba's Pasta combines the most popular ethnic food in America with speed and the low prices people look for today. Take-out, dine-in and drive-thru are available with a Goomba's Pasta franchise. The Goomba's Pasta operation is a streamlined system that is clean, sharp and efficient.

Equity Capital Needed: $90,000 - $180,000

Franchise Fee: $18,500

Royalty Fee: 4%

Financial Assistance: None.

Managerial Assistance: On-site operations training, manuals, scheduled visits and local marketing assistance.

Training Provided: Goomba's Pasta offers a comprehensive 20-day training program. The franchise owners will be trained in every aspect of the operation and will receive scheduled visits to support individual needs.

Information Submitted: January 1994

GREAT WRAPS!
158 Oak St.
Avondale Estates, GA 30002
Telephone: (404) 299-5081
Fax: (404) 292-0081
Mr. Marvin Young, Manager of Franchise Development

Number of Franchised Units: 45
Number of Company-Owned Units: 2
Number of Total Operating Units: 47

In Business Since: 1974   **Franchising Since:** 1981

Description of Operation: Fast-food franchisor - 50 + units open in 12 states. Operates in major regional mall food courts. Serves hot, grilled, pita-wrapped sandwiches with beef and lamb, steak and cheese, fresh vegetables and strips of chicken breast, plus fresh salads, such as Greek and caesar, kurly fries and soft drinks.

Equity Capital Needed: $180,000 - $250,000

Franchise Fee: $25,000

Royalty Fee: 5%

Financial Assistance: We will assist in finding financing, but make no claims to guarantee any loans.

Managerial Assistance: On-going field support, audits and 3 weeks of up-front training at the corporate training store. Store opening team (3 - 5 people) for up to 1 week after opening. Thorough pre-opening training manual and post-opening operations manual.

Training Provided: Same as above.

Information Submitted: November 1993

GRECO PIZZA DONAIR
105 Walker St., P. O. Box 1040
Truro, NS B2N 5G9 CAN
Telephone: (800) 565-4389 (902) 893-4141
Fax: (902) 895-1396
Mr. Chris MacDougall, Director of Development

Number of Franchised Units: 48
Number of Company-Owned Units: 6
Number of Total Operating Units: 54

In Business Since: 1977   **Franchising Since:** 1981

Description of Operation: The largest home-delivery chain of pizza, donair and oven-sub sandwiches in Atlantic Canada. Specializing in fast, free delivery.

Equity Capital Needed: $150,000 - $180,000 (Canadian).

Franchise Fee: $15,000 (Canadian).

Royalty Fee: 5%

Financial Assistance: Not available.

Managerial Assistance: 4-week correspondence test prior to 5-week training program, both on and off site. On-going managerial assistance available on an "as required" basis.

Training Provided: Same as above.

Information Submitted: November 1993

GREEK'S PIZZERIA
1600 University Ave.
Muncie, IN 47303
Telephone: (317) 284-4900
Mr. A. Chris Karamesines, Planning and Development

Number of Franchised Units: 20
Number of Company-Owned Units: 34
Number of Total Operating Units: 54

In Business Since: 1969   **Franchising Since:** 1978

Description of Operation: European dining and sports theme, with an enclosed or open kitchen concept, using wood or gas-fired ovens. Carry-out and free delivery services are available. Specialties are New York-style and Chicago deep-dish pizzas, calzones, pastas, gyros, subs. Imported and domestic beers and wines.

Equity Capital Needed: Limited dining - $73,000; Full dining - $158,000.

Franchise Fee: $12,000

Royalty Fee: 4% weekly.

Financial Assistance: Consultation is offered regarding banks, lease sources and financing on second units. Available to qualified applicants.

Managerial Assistance: Greek's Pizzeria offers professional assistance in marketing, real estate, construction, purchasing, advertising and accounting. Field consultants trained in restaurant operations continue valuable management assistance in advanced training, cost control and other pertinent subjects as the need may arise. Corporate testing of new products and equipment in Company stores by Research, Development and Standards Department assures the highest quality throughout the system.

Training Provided: The franchisor provides an intensive 2 weeks of on-the-job training in operations, theory and management. In addition, trained personnel are provided for 2 weeks during the grand opening to assist the franchisee.

Information Submitted: January 1994

GREEN BURRITO, THE
2831 E. Miraloma Ave.
Anaheim, CA 92806
Telephone: (714) 632-1672
Fax: (714) 632-2783
Ms. Kimberly Vengrow, Franchise Co-ordinator

Number of Franchised Units: 53
Number of Company-Owned Units: 9
Number of Total Operating Units: 62

In Business Since: 1980   **Franchising Since:** 1988

Description of Operation: A Mexican fast-food franchise, serving quality, restaurant-style food, in a fast-food atmosphere.

Equity Capital Needed: Data not available.

Franchise Fee: $25,000

Royalty Fee: 5%

Financial Assistance: None.

Managerial Assistance: We help in developing a plan for manager and employee-level needs. On-going support from an operations consultant assigned to each restaurant. Comprehensive training program for managers and employees. All manuals, etc. provided.

Training Provided: We offer a comprehensive 4-week training program, followed up by 2 weeks of in-store training after opening. Training is provided by the franchise trainer and the franchisee's operations consultant.

Information Submitted: March 1994

GROUND ROUND, THE
PO Box 9078, Braintree Hill Off. Pk.
Braintree, MA 02184
Telephone: (617) 380-3116
Fax: (617) 380-3233
Mr. Ed Daly, Director of Franchise Development

Number of Franchised Units: 44
Number of Company-Owned Units: 166
Number of Total Operating Units: 210

In Business Since: 1969   **Franchising Since:** 1970

Description of Operation: Full-service, casual theme, family restaurant with liquor.

Equity Capital Needed: Suggested net worth - $1,000,000; cash available of $400,000.

Franchise Fee: $40,000

Royalty Fee: 3%

Financial Assistance: None available.

Managerial Assistance: Ground Round's district franchise manager will consult with and discuss all aspects of operating a Ground Round restaurant.

Training Provided: We provide complete, comprehensive training and certification of the restaurant's management team, as well as employee training prior to and during the first weeks of operation.

Information Submitted: January 1994

HAPPI HOUSE RESTAURANTS
2901 Moorpark Ave., # 255
San Jose, CA 95128
Telephone: (800) SO-HAPPI (408) 244-0665
Fax: (408) 244-9262
Mr. Carlo Besio, President/Chief Executive Officer

Number of Franchised Units: 2
Number of Company-Owned Units: 7
Number of Total Operating Units: 9

In Business Since: 1976   **Franchising Since:** 1991

Description of Operation: Asian fast-food restaurant (primarily Japanese).

Equity Capital Needed: $200,000 - $240,000

Franchise Fee: $25,000

Royalty Fee: 5%

Financial Assistance: None.

Managerial Assistance: On-going managerial assistance program. Additional assistance available on request.

Training Provided: An intensive 2-week training program. Larger training program available at no extra cost when necessary. Excellent manuals and training materials.

Information Submitted: January 1994

HEID'S OF LIVERPOOL
130 Atlantic Ave., P. O. Box 711
Cohasset, MA 02025
Telephone: (800) 531-7655 (617) 383-6383
Fax: (617) 383-3124
Mr. Ron Blain, Vice President of Franchising

Number of Franchised Units: 4
Number of Company-Owned Units: 0
Number of Total Operating Units: 4

In Business Since: 1917   **Franchising Since:** 1993

Description of Operation: 50's and 60's diner decor, serving hot dogs, ice cream and more. Seating capacity ranges from 50 - 119.

Equity Capital Needed: $50,000 - $100,000 cash.

Franchise Fee: $25,000

Royalty Fee: 5%

Financial Assistance: Data not available.

Managerial Assistance: We provide assistance in site procurement, financing, presentations, construction and equipment. We assist in store opening and on-going operational, marketing and profitability analyses.

Training Provided: The training program consists of 4 days of financial management and 10 days of operational management.

Information Submitted: January 1994

HO-LEE-CHOW (CANADA)
320 Danforth Ave., # 202
Toronto, ON M4K 1N8 CAN
Telephone: (416) 778-6660
Fax: (416) 778-6694
Mr. Jake Cappiello, General Manager

Number of Franchised Units: 15
Number of Company-Owned Units: 3
Number of Total Operating Units: 18

In Business Since: 1989   **Franchising Since:** 1989

Description of Operation: Great Chinese food, delivered fast and fresh. Pick-up also available. No sit-down. Each dish cooked to order. No MSG added. Clean, bright, open kitchen concept.

Equity Capital Needed: $50,000 - $75,000

Franchise Fee: $25,000

Royalty Fee: 6%

Financial Assistance: We will aid in the preparation of required bank documents.

Managerial Assistance: We provide operational assistance for the general manager, group supervisor, corporate chef, corporate managers, corporate cooks, central order processing department and the accounting department.

Training Provided: We offer a minimum 5 weeks of training - 2 weeks of theory (maximum) and 3 weeks (minimum) of practical, in-store training.

Information Submitted: March 1994

HOBEE'S
4224 El Camino Real
Palo Alto, CA 94306
Telephone: (800) 462-3376 (415) 493-7117
Fax: (415) 493-0756
Mr. Edward Fike, Vice President

Number of Franchised Units: 6
Number of Company-Owned Units: 4
Number of Total Operating Units: 10

In Business Since: 1974   **Franchising Since:** 1986

Description of Operation: Hobee's franchises sit-down restaurants, serving healthy, California cuisine in a casual atmosphere. The chain is well known throughout Northern California and has won over 15 awards in 1993, which recognized Hobee's achievements in the areas of food quality, customer service and community involvement. Franchisees receive extensive support from the corporate office in the form of legal guidelines, a Company newsletter for customers and assistance with advertising promotions.

Equity Capital Needed: $200,000 - $400,000

Franchise Fee: $35,000

Royalty Fee: 5%

Financial Assistance: The franchisor does not provide financial assistance.

Managerial Assistance: Franchisees are free to enter Hobee's management program, provided space is available. Prior work experience at the restaurants is encouraged.

Training Provided: The franchisee receives extensive pre-opening training at a designated training store. Length of training depends upon restaurant experience. A special team assists franchisee at his or her site for several weeks during post-opening.

Information Submitted: January 1994

HOULIHAN'S
2 Brush Creek Blvd., P. O. Box 16000
Kansas City, MO 64112
Telephone: (800) 753-3675 (816) 756-2200
Fax: (816) 561-2842
Mr. Andrew C. Gunkler, Vice President of Franchising

Number of Franchised Units: 10
Number of Company-Owned Units: 50
Number of Total Operating Units: 60

In Business Since: 1972   **Franchising Since:** 1987

Description of Operation: Houlihan's has been one of the most successful casual dining concepts in the country for the past 20 years. The restaurant has broad appeal with its unique, relaxed atmosphere and ambiance. The menu consists of a wide selection of items cutting across many ethnic cuisines. Our commitment is to make every guest a repeat guest.

Equity Capital Needed: $300,000 - $450,000

Franchise Fee: $40,000

Royalty Fee: 4%

Financial Assistance: Financial assistance is available through third-party financial vendors that have approved the Houlihan's concept.

Managerial Assistance: On-site operational training, manuals, videos, on-going training sessions, quarterly owners meetings and annual conference.

Training Provided: An intensive 60-day "hands-on" training program in the restaurant for all General Managers. Training is conducted in the corporate restaurants. All training materials are provided, including manuals and videos. An abbreviated training program is available for the franchisee.

Information Submitted: January 1994

HUBB'S PUB
1535 Cogswell St., # A-3
Rockledge, FL 32955
Telephone: (407) 639-5080
Fax: (407) 639-8050
Mr. Kenneth Shifflett, Marketing Director

Number of Franchised Units: 1
Number of Company-Owned Units: 3
Number of Total Operating Units: 4

In Business Since: 1982   **Franchising Since:** 1992

Description of Operation: Licensed and operated as family restaurants, Hubb's offers a wide assortment of foods. From "Colossal Sandwiches" to non-fried finger foods, Hubb's has something for everyone. In addition, Hubb's offers 39 draft and over 200 bottled beers from around the world.

Equity Capital Needed: $30,000 - $400,000

Franchise Fee: $50,000

Royalty Fee: $1,000 per month after 26 months.

Financial Assistance: No direct financing is available, but we do assist qualified applicants in locating and applying to lenders. Investor/manager positions are also available to qualified applicants.

Managerial Assistance: Hubb's operational manuals are the guide to action for all franchisees. Periodic meetings in person or by telephone with franchisees aid in the review of each operation.

Training Provided: Full training including instruction with regard to Hubb's standards, methods, procedures and techniques. Complete individual instruction with all franchisees and up to 2 employees at an operating Hubb's Pub.

Information Submitted: November 1993

HUMPTY'S RESTAURANTS INTERNATIONAL
2505 MacLeod Trail S.
Calgary, AB T2G 5J4 CAN
Telephone: (800) 661-7589 (403) 269-4675
Fax: (403) 266-1973
Mr. Don Koenig, President

Number of Franchised Units: 29
Number of Company-Owned Units: 2
Number of Total Operating Units: 31

In Business Since: 1977   **Franchising Since:** 1986

Description of Operation: 24-hour, full-service family-type restaurant. Generous portions at very competitive prices. Very unique breakfast section of the menu. We promote children's meals and activities. Special promotions throughout the year, such as "2 for 1 Omelette Month."

Equity Capital Needed: $200,000 - $350,000 (Canadian).

Franchise Fee: $25,000

Royalty Fee: 5%

Financial Assistance: Financial assistance is not available; however, business plans are provided by the Company to assist the franchisee in approaching financial institutions.

Managerial Assistance: 4 weeks of training during the opening of the business. On-going monthly visits after opening. 800# for franchisees to call.

Training Provided: We offer 3 weeks of training prior to the opening for 2 people and 4 weeks during the opening period. Total of 7 weeks maximum.

Information Submitted: March 1994

HUNGRY HOWIE'S PIZZA & SUBS
35301 Schoolcraft Rd.
Livonia, MI 48150
Telephone: (800) 624-8122 (313) 422-1717
Fax: (313) 427-2713
Mr. Anthony P. Noga, Director of Franchise Development

Number of Franchised Units: 250
Number of Company-Owned Units: 0
Number of Total Operating Units: 250

In Business Since: 1973   **Franchising Since:** 1982

Description of Operation: Hungry Howie's Pizza & Subs offers a successful carry-out, delivery and 2-for-1 pizza franchise. The menu features unique, award-winning Flavored Crust Pizzas in 8 varieties, a selection of mouth-watering subs, fresh salads and Fruzza dessert pizzas. Hungry Howie's has over 260 locations in 9 states, including California, Georgia, Florida, Illinois, Kansas, Michigan, Nevada, North Carolina and Ohio and Windsor, Ontario.

Equity Capital Needed: $40,000 - $80,000

Franchise Fee: $9,500

Royalty Fee: 3% - first year; 4% - second year; 5% - third - 20th year.

Financial Assistance: We assist by referral to lending sources only.

Managerial Assistance: Hungry Howie's utilizes innovative management procedures and imaginative strategies to support the day-to-day operations of your store. We provide a variety of services and programs to help you increase your market share and enhance your financial position. From the start, you will benefit from the expertise of our franchise development team. We offer pre-opening/on-going support, site selection, lease negotiation, leasehold construction, operations, product specifications, construction and more.

Training Provided: Our unique strategies and techniques are introduced to you at our 4-week training program at our franchise training center. Both classroom and in-store training in food service management are offered - administration and daily operations, accounting, tax and inventory control, product specifications and product preparation, delivery operations, labor cost control, employee training, quality control and customer service.

Information Submitted: January 1994

INTERNATIONAL DAIRY QUEEN
P. O. Box 35286
Minneapolis, MN 55435
Telephone: (800) 285-8515 (612) 830-0294
Fax: (612) 830-0450
Mr. Eric Lavanger, Vice President of Franchise Development

Number of Franchised Units: 5449
Number of Company-Owned Units: 1
Number of Total Operating Units: 5450

In Business Since: 1940   **Franchising Since:** 1940

Description of Operation: Quick-service food restaurant.

Equity Capital Needed: $150,000 net worth, plus $85,000 liquid assets.

Franchise Fee: $30,000

Royalty Fee: 4%

Financial Assistance: 50% of franchise fee. We will assist in locating additional financing.

Managerial Assistance: Complete on-going operations assistance.

Training Provided: Comprehensive training.

Information Submitted: November 1993

INTERNATIONAL HOUSE OF PANCAKES / IHOP
525 N. Brand Blvd., 3rd Fl.
Glendale, CA 91203
Telephone: (818) 240-6055
Fax: (818) 240-0270
Ms. Anna Ulvan, Vice President of Franchising

Number of Franchised Units: 521
Number of Company-Owned Units: 51
Number of Total Operating Units: 572

In Business Since: 1958   **Franchising Since:** 1960

Description of Operation: Full-service family restaurant, serving breakfast, lunch, dinner, snacks and desserts, including a variety of pancake specialties and featuring the cook's Daily Special. Wine and beer are served in some locations.

Equity Capital Needed: Varies, depending on location.

Franchise Fee: Varies.

Royalty Fee: Varies.

Financial Assistance: None.

Managerial Assistance: The franchisor provides opening supervision, regular visits and assistance from field coordinators. A complete manual of operations specifies how each menu item is prepared and served and how the business is to be operated profitably.

Training Provided: We provide 6 weeks of classroom and on-the-job instruction. Continued training is available.

Information Submitted: March 1994

INTERNATIONAL POULTRY COMPANY
432 Sixth Ave.
New York, NY 10011
Telephone: (800) 410-1555 (212) 228-6800
Fax: (212) 228-8008
Ms. Linda D. Biciocchi, Vice President

Number of Franchised Units: 3
Number of Company-Owned Units: 1
Number of Total Operating Units: 4

In Business Since: 1988   **Franchising Since:** 1993

Description of Operation: Quick-service restaurant, featuring over 12 varieties of 100%-natural chicken, turkey and other poultry items, plus award-winning soups, salads and pastas. Eat-in, take-out, catering and delivery available.

Equity Capital Needed: $275,000 - $350,000

Franchise Fee: $25,000

Royalty Fee: 4.5%, service and royalty fee and 5.5% of monthly sales, advertising fee.

Financial Assistance: The Company provides no financing; however, we work with several lending agencies.

Managerial Assistance: IPC provides training to franchise owners and their managers in the operational and managerial aspects of the business. Training includes classroom instruction and on-the-job training. Follow-up courses and seminars are offered periodically or on an as-needed basis.

Training Provided: In addition to the initial training described above, new franchisees will receive IPC's system manuals, periodic updates on new products, suppliers, control procedures, advertising, promotions, etc. and Company newsletters. Our entire support staff is available for consultations on all aspects of IPC's business and its operations.

Information Submitted: January 1994

INTERSTATE DAIRY QUEEN
4601 Willard Ave.
Chevy Chase, MD 20815
Telephone: (800) 546-5923 (301) 913-5923
Fax: (301) 913-5424
Mr. Walt Tellegen, President

Number of Franchised Units: 99
Number of Company-Owned Units: 3
Number of Total Operating Units: 102

In Business Since: 1977   **Franchising Since:** 1977

Description of Operation: Fast-food and treat franchisor on inter-state highways. Specialists in marketing to the highway traveler.

Equity Capital Needed: $50,000 - $150,000

Franchise Fee: $25,000

Royalty Fee: 4%

Financial Assistance: None.

Managerial Assistance: Full-time professional field force consultants. 2 week training school. Financial management analysis and recommendations.

Training Provided: 2 weeks of school and pre-opening assistance from opening team covering 4 people weeks.

Information Submitted: November 1993

IRVINGS FOR RED HOT LOVERS
3330 Old Glenview Rd., # 3
Wilmette, IL 60091
Telephone: (708) 256-8855
Fax: (708) 256-8860
Mr. Andrew Greensphan, President

Number of Franchised Units: 12
Number of Company-Owned Units: 1
Number of Total Operating Units: 13

In Business Since: 1975   **Franchising Since:** 1990

Description of Operation: Irvings for Red Hot Lovers specializes in top-quality food, quick service and a friendly atmosphere at competitive prices. Our new menu includes our world-famous hot dogs, char-burgers, Italian beets, char-chicken, specialty fries, turkey burgers and "a whole lot more." A highly-effective operations format, our comprehensive menu and unique approach to advertising add to our recipe for success.

Equity Capital Needed: Data not available.

Franchise Fee: $20,000

Royalty Fee: 4%

Financial Assistance: Yes.

Managerial Assistance: Irvings produces complete training manuals, forms and sales aids. Monthly visits to franchisee locations include inspection reports, updates on operations forms and consultation with management. Also semi-annual owner meetings.

Training Provided: Comprehensive training lasts a total of 4 weeks. 1 week of classroom and 3 weeks at operation. Also includes 1 week of on-site assistance at franchisee's new location.

Information Submitted: November 1993

ITALO'S PIZZA SHOP
3560 Middlebranch Rd., N.E.
Canton, OH 44705
Telephone: (216) 455-7443
Mr. Italo P. Ventura, President

Number of Franchised Units: 13
Number of Company-Owned Units: 3
Number of Total Operating Units: 16

In Business Since: 1966   **Franchising Since:** 1975

Description of Operation: Italo's Pizza franchises are a carry-out operation with limited dining, specializing in pizza, chicken, pasta and other Italian dishes. Delivery is optional to franchisee. Our motto, Qualita e Abbondanza (quality and quantity), say everything. Italo's stresses quality, quantity, personal service and value.

Equity Capital Needed: $75,000 - $110,000

Franchise Fee: $12,000

Royalty Fee: 5%

Financial Assistance: Financing is not available. Franchisee must provide his/her own financial resources.

Managerial Assistance: Italo's Pizza provides continual assistance and support, along with recommendations, in all aspects of the business. Forms, manuals and detailed instructions are provided for smooth performance and operation. Periodic visits by franchisor allow for rapport and problem solution and assistance.

Training Provided: An intensive 3 weeks of training at corporate headquarters is provided, with additional assistance, if necessary, at the franchisee's location. Continual assistance, if needed, is available as well.

Information Submitted: November 1993

J. BRENNER'S CHICKEN & CHEESESTEAKS
158 Oak St.
Avondale Estates, GA 30002
Telephone: (404) 299-5081
Fax: (404) 292-0081
Mr. Marvin Young, Manager of Franchise Development

Number of Franchised Units: 5
Number of Company-Owned Units: 0
Number of Total Operating Units: 5

In Business Since: 1974   **Franchising Since:** 1981

Description of Operation: Fast-food franchisor, specializing in regional mall food courts. We have combined the traditional cheesesteak concept with a comprehensive "chicken menu." Our operation utilizes both a flat-top grill and an open-flame grill. We serve breast of chicken (boneless and marinated), chicken wings, chicken fryers and "Phillys," such as steak and cheese, chicken, veggie, etc., plus baked potatoes, salads, fries and soft drinks.

Equity Capital Needed: $185,000 - $250,000

Franchise Fee: $25,000

Royalty Fee: 5%

Financial Assistance: No direct financial assistance. We will assist in finding financing, but make no claims to guarantee the loans.

Managerial Assistance: On-going field support by corporate staff. Periodic seminars and an annual meeting.

Training Provided: Pre-opening training at corporate training store (3 weeks). Comprehensive training manual and operations manual.

Information Submitted: November 1993

JAKE'S PIZZA
16 Official Rd.
Addison, IL 60101
Telephone: (800) 4 A-JAKES (708) 543-0022
Fax: (708) 543-2220
Mr. James J. Banks, President/Chief Executive Officer

Number of Franchised Units: 38
Number of Company-Owned Units: 1
Number of Total Operating Units: 39

In Business Since: 1961   **Franchising Since:** 1965

Description of Operation: Jake's Pizza specializes in the sale of premium, thin crust, pan and stuffed pizzas. Eat-in, pick-up and delivery service is provided. Each store has an open "display" kitchen, open to the customers' view. Proprietary raw ingredients are used to insure consistency and quality of product.

Equity Capital Needed: $30,000 - $50,000

Franchise Fee: $15,000

Royalty Fee: 4% - 5%

Financial Assistance: There is no direct financing assistance available from the Company; however, we can suggest various outside lenders and leasing companies.

Managerial Assistance: We will aid the opening and on-going management of the franchise through a "start-up" team and an on-going support team.

Training Provided: The training course is for a total of 4 weeks - 2 weeks at headquarters and 2 weeks in the field at a corporate store. After the franchise opens, the corporate staff aids in training the franchisee's staff.

Information Submitted: March 1994

JB'S RESTAURANTS
1010 W. 2610 South
Salt Lake City, UT 84119
Telephone: (801) 974-4320
Fax: (801) 974-4385
Mr. George H. Gehling, Vice President

Number of Franchised Units: 14
Number of Company-Owned Units: 97
Number of Total Operating Units: 111

In Business Since: 1961   Franchising Since: 1990

Description of Operation: JB's is a leader in the family restaurant segment, serving breakfast, lunch and dinner to millions of guests each year. JB's appeals to a wide range of consumers, from the affluent "baby boomers" to children and seniors alike. Our success is founded on good food, reasonable prices, pleasant surroundings and a friendly staff. JB's broad menu is complemented by our fresh-food buffet and our bakery, enhancing our guest's perception of quality, variety and value.

Equity Capital Needed: $100,000 - $300,000

Franchise Fee: $25,000

Royalty Fee: 4%

Financial Assistance: None.

Managerial Assistance: JB's experienced staff is committed to providing support to our franchisees, including 1) comprehensive initial and on-going support; 2) on-going site visits by operations management; 3) marketing support; 4) product research and development; 5) purchasing support in negotiating programs with vendors; and 6) construction support during construction of your restaurant.

Training Provided: (1) Management training for franchisee and management team at Salt Lake City, UT corporate headquarters or other agreed upon location, (2) a special training team to assist during the crucial time immediately before and after your restaurant opens and (3) on-going, periodic management workshops on important operational and management topics.

Information Submitted: November 1993

JERRY'S SUBS - PIZZA
15942 Shady Grove Rd.
Gaithersburg, MD 20877
Telephone: (301) 921-8777
Fax: (301) 948-3508
Ms. Kathleen McDonald, Director of Franchise Development

Number of Franchised Units: 82
Number of Company-Owned Units: 1
Number of Total Operating Units: 83

In Business Since: 1954   Franchising Since: 1980

Description of Operation: Fresh-dough pizza and over-stuffed submarine sandwiches, served in up-scale retail outlets, featuring take-out service and self-service dining.

Equity Capital Needed: $60,000 - $90,000

Franchise Fee: $25,000

Royalty Fee: 5%

Financial Assistance: Jerry's meets SBA loan requirements.

Managerial Assistance: All franchisees receive on-going management assistance, which includes on-site visits and evaluations designed to maintain the integrity of the franchise. New franchisees receive as much as 10 days of full-time support to assist in their grand opening.

Training Provided: All franchisees must satisfactorily complete a 9-week training program. Training, which is full-time during this period, is competency-based and includes both practical and classroom instruction. Franchisees will be certified as managers upon completion.

Information Submitted: November 1993

JIMMY JOHN'S
1500 Executive Drive
Elgin, IL 60123
Telephone: (708) 888-7222
Fax: (708) 888-7327
Mr. Scott M. Nichols, President

Number of Franchised Units: 0
Number of Company-Owned Units: 11
Number of Total Operating Units: 11

In Business Since: 1983   Franchising Since: 1993

Description of Operation: Franchisor of Jimmy John's gourmet sandwich shops, which make, sell and deliver an up-scale signature line of french bread subs and wheat club sandwiches. Stores require small investment and can be located in strip centers, downtown store frontages and food courts in malls.

Equity Capital Needed: $55,000 - $127,000

Franchise Fee: $25,000

Royalty Fee: 5.5%

Financial Assistance: No direct financing assistance is available; however, we will provide necessary financial information to potential lending entities.

Managerial Assistance: 6 weeks of training is provided at corporate store location. This includes both operational and marketing assistance. Pre-opening assistance includes construction plans, site location and lease management.

Training Provided: Same as above.

Information Submitted: December 1993

JOEY'S ONLY
514 - 42 Ave., SE
Calgary, AB T2G 1Y6 CAN
Telephone: (800) 661-2123 (403) 243-4584
Fax: (403) 243-8989
Mr. David J. Mossey, Vice President

Number of Franchised Units: 32
Number of Company-Owned Units: 1
Number of Total Operating Units: 33

In Business Since: 1985   Franchising Since: 1992

Description of Operation: Family-style, seafood sit-down restaurant, specializing in fish and chips. Licensed for beer and wine.

Equity Capital Needed: $150,000 - $180,000

Franchise Fee: $25,000

Royalty Fee: 4.5%, plus 2% advertising.

Financial Assistance: We assist with arrangements with banks.

Managerial Assistance: The District Manager assists in the pre-opening and opening of the location (2 weeks). Continuous monthly visits to assist in better operating procedures.

Training Provided: We offer a 5-week training program, from dishwashing to cooking procedures, food handling and customer service.

Information Submitted: January 1994

JOHNNY ROCKETS - THE ORIGINAL HAMBURGER
1888 Century Park E., # 224
Los Angeles, CA 90067
Telephone: (310) 556-8811
Fax: (310) 556-3039
Mr. W. Robert Host, Vice President of Franchising

Number of Franchised Units: 44
Number of Company-Owned Units: 10
Number of Total Operating Units: 54

In Business Since: 1986   Franchising Since: 1988

Description of Operation: An old-fashioned malt shop, serving hamburgers, fries, shakes and malts, flavored cokes, sandwiches and pie. A simple, efficient operation with a limited menu, yet unlimited appeal.

Equity Capital Needed: $200,000

Franchise Fee: $39,000

Royalty Fee: 7%

Financial Assistance: None.

Managerial Assistance: Johnny Rockets will send one of its trained representatives to work with you at your facility for a period of up to 10 working days one week prior to opening through the first week of operation.

Training Provided: You and 2 managers and/or assistant managers will attend an initial training and familiarization course of up to 5 weeks at an operating Johnny Rockets' restaurant.

Information Submitted: March 1994

JUICY LUCY'S
2235 First St., # 206
Ft. Myers, FL 33901
Telephone: (800) 654-6817 (813) 332-0022
Fax: (813) 332-1262
Ms. Suzanne M. Grady, President

Number of Franchised Units: 7
Number of Company-Owned Units: 6
Number of Total Operating Units: 13

In Business Since: 1988   **Franchising Since:** 1990

Description of Operation: A fast-service, double drive-thru restaurant, serving hamburgers, freshly-made specialty sandwiches, fries and breakfast. Voted best hamburger in Southwest Florida 4 years in a row.

Equity Capital Needed: $250,000

Franchise Fee: $25,000

Royalty Fee: 5%

Financial Assistance: None.

Managerial Assistance: On-going supervisory support on a regular basis for the length of the franchise agreement.

Training Provided: Juicy Lucy's provides an extensive training program, which includes both classroom and on-site instruction, covering business procedures, food preparation and presentation, quality and cost control, purchasing, marketing, housekeeping and personnel management.

Information Submitted: March 1994

K-BOB'S USA
800 Rankin Rd. NE
Albuquerque, NM 87107
Telephone: (800) 225-8403 (505) 345-8403
Fax: (505) 345-0492
Mr. Edward R. Tinsley, III, President

Number of Franchised Units: 45
Number of Company-Owned Units: 2
Number of Total Operating Units: 47

In Business Since: 1966   **Franchising Since:** 1991

Description of Operation: Franchisor of restaurants.

Equity Capital Needed: $250,000 +

Franchise Fee: $25,000

Royalty Fee: 3%

Financial Assistance: K-Bob's Capital Resource Group, Ltd. was founded in 1992 to finance land and building construction and to serve as a financial vehicle to assist both new and existing franchisees with a lease-purchase program.

Managerial Assistance: K-Bob's USA's new store opening team is sent to a new unit 2 weeks prior to opening and spends a total of 1,272 man-hours assisting new franchisees with the opening and operation of their unit opening. Opening team cost of $13,000 is included in the franchise fee.

Training Provided: All new franchisees are required to attend our Company-owned and operated unit training facility in Truth or Consequences, NM for a period of 4 weeks, learning all aspects of operations, marketing, procurement and administration of a restaurant to K-Bob's USA standards.

Information Submitted: January 1994

KELSEY'S RESTAURANTS
450 S. Service Rd. W.
Oakville, ON L6K 2H4 CAN
Telephone: (905) 842-5510
Fax: (905) 842-5603
Mr. Toby Singlehurst, Director of Development

Number of Franchised Units: 17
Number of Company-Owned Units: 20
Number of Total Operating Units: 37

In Business Since: 1977   **Franchising Since:** 1981

Description of Operation: Licensed, full-service, casual dining, offering lunch, dinner and late-night menu with a wide variety of food items. Offering great value with large portions. The atmosphere is warm and the service is fast, friendly and efficient. We also cater to family dining. Stand-up bar available.

Equity Capital Needed: $200,000 +

Franchise Fee: $20,000

Royalty Fee: 5%

Financial Assistance: Varies.

Managerial Assistance: We will assist the franchisee in hiring and training a management team. We will also assist with a "hands-on" support team for the first 30 days of operation.

Training Provided: A 12-week, in-store training program is mandatory to learn Kelsey's operations and systems.

Information Submitted: January 1994

KETTLE RESTAURANTS
3131 Argonne
Houston, TX 77098
Telephone: (800) 929-2391 (713) 524-3464
Fax: (713) 524-7956
Mr. George Harris, Franchise Development

Number of Franchised Units: 95
Number of Company-Owned Units: 60
Number of Total Operating Units: 155

In Business Since: 1968   **Franchising Since:** 1968

Description of Operation: Full-service 24-hour family restaurant.

Equity Capital Needed: $150,000 - $500,000

Franchise Fee: $20,000

Royalty Fee: 5%

Financial Assistance: None.

Managerial Assistance: Managerial instruction is given during the normal on-the-job training. Technical assistance is given by the franchisor to key personnel prior to opening for business and after opening until the operation stabilizes. Periodic visits thereafter, approximately every quarter, or more often, if deemed necessary or requested.

Training Provided: We provide training for 4 - 10 weeks at our training center in Houston, TX.

Information Submitted: March 1994

KFC / KENTUCKY FRIED CHICKEN
1441 Gardiner Ln.
Louisville, KY 40213
Telephone: (800) 544-5774 (502) 456-8300
Fax: (502) 456-8255
Mr. Walter J. Simon, Vice President of Business Development

Number of Franchised Units: 3079
Number of Company-Owned Units: 2121
Number of Total Operating Units: 5200

In Business Since: 1954   Franchising Since: 1957

Description of Operation: Quick-service restaurant with a chicken-dominant menu.

Equity Capital Needed: $125,000 - $150,000

Franchise Fee: $25,000

Royalty Fee: 4%

Financial Assistance: Data not available.

Managerial Assistance: Site selection assistance, engineering and construction advice, equipment, materials and supplies advice, operating and training advice, product and equipment refinement, methods of quality control, meetings and seminars for methods in processing and marketing approved products. Periodic inspections to insure franchisee compliance with standards and specifications.

Training Provided: 7-week training course prior to opening outlet. Classes average 8 hours per day. 3 days are spent in a classroom and 30 days are spent in an outlet. In addition to initial training, KFC offers continual assistance in the areas of customer service, general outlet management, quality control and employee training. All courses are optional and free of charge, with the exception of out-of-pocket expenses.

Information Submitted: November 1993

KRYSTAL COMPANY, THE
One Union Square, 10th Fl.
Chattanooga, TN 37402
Telephone: (800) 458-5912 (615) 757-5652
Fax: (615) 757-5610
Mr. Tom Adams, Director of Franchise Development

Number of Franchised Units: 38
Number of Company-Owned Units: 240
Number of Total Operating Units: 278

In Business Since: 1932   Franchising Since: 1989

Description of Operation: Fast food hamburger concept, offering proven, destination-oriented products. Restaurants are open 24 hours.

Equity Capital Needed: 20% of total project costs.

Franchise Fee: $32,500

Royalty Fee: 4.5% of weekly gross receipts.

Financial Assistance: Krystal provides no financing; however, the Company does provide a list of financing sources and a suggested format for loan packages.

Managerial Assistance: Franchisee receives managerial assistance through a network of Krystal field consultants.

Training Provided: Franchisees and their management teams receive up to 8 weeks of classroom and on-the-job training.

Information Submitted: November 1993

L. A. SMOOTHIE HEALTHMART & CAFE
700 Canal St.
New Orleans, LA 70130
Telephone: (800) 643-3910 (504) 522-5588
Fax: (504) 522-0101
Mr. A. Albert Gardes, Chief Operating Officer

Number of Franchised Units: 3
Number of Company-Owned Units: 2
Number of Total Operating Units: 5

In Business Since: 1991   Franchising Since: 1992

Description of Operation: L. A. Smoothie is a unique franchise, geared to today's health-conscious consumer. A total health concept, featuring smoothies (all natural frosty fruit-based beverages, mostly with no fat or cholesterol, yet low in calories), a menu of healthy soups, salads, sandwiches, fresh juices, a line of vitamins/supplements, activewear, natural and healthy beauty aids, health books, etc. in 100 - 1,200 square foot, up-scale stores.

Equity Capital Needed: $57,500 - $87,000 (includes fee).

Franchise Fee: $12,500

Royalty Fee: 5%

Financial Assistance: We offer no financial assistance; however, we do offer guidance when applying for SBA loans and other types of loans.

Managerial Assistance: We provide both an operations manual and an employee manual. Managers are also trained by the corporate operations staff. Corporate operations staff aids management through store visits, newsletters, weekly phone contact, promotion and advertising assistance.

Training Provided: A 2-week training period is provided. All aspects of the business operation are covered, including food and smoothie preparation, inventory ordering and control, employee relations, accounting, marketing and promotion, overview of health industry and more. Training is done at both the corporate store and the franchise location for hands-on training. Also, classroom training with video and audio.

Information Submitted: December 1993

LA PIZZA LOCA
7920 Orangethorpe Ave., # 202
Buena Park, CA 90620
Telephone: (714) 670-0934
Fax: (714) 670-7849
Mr. Stanley F. Oliveira, Vice President of Franchise Development

Number of Franchised Units: 7
Number of Company-Owned Units: 29
Number of Total Operating Units: 36

In Business Since: 1986   Franchising Since: 1991

Description of Operation: Pizza delivery and carry-out company, whose La Pizza Loca restaurants cater to the tastes and customs of the Hispanic community. Unique Latin-flavored pizzas, competitively promoted price/value strategy, plus guaranteed free delivery in 30 minutes, provides La Pizza Loca customers outstanding quality, value and service.

Equity Capital Needed: $125,000 total investment (cash $40,000).

Franchise Fee: $15,000

Royalty Fee: 5%

Financial Assistance: La Pizza Loca will assist franchisees to secure their own independent financing.

Managerial Assistance: In addition to 4 weeks of formal training and 2 weeks on on-site opening assistance, La Pizza Loca will also provide grand opening and local store marketing planning assistance, as well as on-going, periodic visits from a La Pizza Loca Franchise Operations Consultant, who will provide guidance and consultation regarding the operation of a La Pizza Loca restaurant.

Training Provided: An initial training and familiarization course of about 4 weeks in duration is provided to the franchisee and his management team at La Pizza Loca's training school in Buena Park, CA. In addition to the initial training, a La Pizza Loca representative will also provide up to 2 weeks of on-site assistance at the commencement of restaurant operations.

LA ROSA MEXICAN RESTAURANTS
2210 E. 11th St.
Davenport, IA 52803
Telephone: (319) 322-4242
Fax: (319) 326-4097
Mr. Walter Newport

Number of Franchised Units: 8
Number of Company-Owned Units: 2
Number of Total Operating Units: 10

In Business Since: 1974   Franchising Since: 1979

Description of Operation: Family-style restaurants, specializing in unique recipes and methods for the preparation, display and service of premium-quality tacos, tostadas, enchiladas, burritos and other Mexican foods.

Equity Capital Needed: $25,000 - $50,000

Franchise Fee: $10,000

Royalty Fee: 4%

Financial Assistance: Data not available.

Managerial Assistance: 2 weeks of training at headquarters, plus assistance at site for restaurant opening. Operations manual. On-going consultation, as required or requested.

Training Provided: Same as above.

Information Submitted: December 1993

LA SALSA
11601 Santa Monica Blvd.
West Los Angeles, CA 90025
Telephone: (800) LA SALSA (310) 575-4233
Fax: (310) 575-9794
Mr. Larry Sarokin, Vice President of Franchising

Number of Franchised Units: 16
Number of Company-Owned Units: 25
Number of Total Operating Units: 41

In Business Since: 1979   Franchising Since: 1988

Description of Operation: Fresh and healthy Mexican quick-service restaurant.

Equity Capital Needed: $103,300

Franchise Fee: $29,500

Royalty Fee: 5%

Financial Assistance: None.

Managerial Assistance: Complete managerial training. Field service representative.

Training Provided: 5 - 8 weeks of in-store and classroom training. 1 week of new store training.

Information Submitted: December 1993

LARRY'S GIANT SUBS
8616 Baymeadows Rd.
Jacksonville, FL 32256
Telephone: (800) 358-6870 (904) 739-2498
Fax: (904) 739-2502
Mr. Mitch Raikes, Vice President

Number of Franchised Units: 28
Number of Company-Owned Units: 2
Number of Total Operating Units: 30

In Business Since: 1982   Franchising Since: 1986

Description of Operation: Own your own sandwich shop. Larry's Giant Subs is an up-scale, New York-style submarine sandwich shop, featuring 50 varieties of subs and numerous salads. Franchise features easy operation, no experience necessary, non-cooking environment and low royalty. Full training in corporate shop. Additional training at your franchise location. Affordable investment, as low as $45,000.

Equity Capital Needed: $45,000 - $55,000

Franchise Fee: $11,000

Royalty Fee: 5%

Financial Assistance: None.

Managerial Assistance: 24-hour hotline and problem assistance. Accounting systems.

Training Provided: Site selection, complete demographics, equipment purchases, 30 days of training at franchise headquarters and training of key employees. First week opening assistance so things run smoothly. Advertising programs.

Information Submitted: November 1993

LE CROISSANT SHOP
227 W. 40th St.
New York, NY 10018
Telephone: (212) 719-5940
Fax: (212) 944-0269
Mr. Jacques J. Pelletier, Vice President

Number of Franchised Units: 23
Number of Company-Owned Units: 3
Number of Total Operating Units: 26

In Business Since: 1981   Franchising Since: 1984

Description of Operation: French bakery cafe, serving croissants, sandwiches, salads, soups, muffins and bread.

Equity Capital Needed: $200,000 - $300,000

Franchise Fee: $22,500

Royalty Fee: 5%

Financial Assistance: No financial assistance.

Managerial Assistance: On-going visits and support by franchisor.

Training Provided: 4 weeks of training at Company headquarters. 1 week of support by franchise company crew at store opening.

Information Submitted: November 1993

LEE'S FAMOUS RECIPE CHICKEN
1727 Elm Hill Pike, # B-9
Nashville, TN 37210
Telephone: (800) 346-9637 (615) 231-2486
Fax: (615) 231-3453
Mr. Dave Bogart, Vice President of Franchise Operations

Number of Franchised Units: 225
Number of Company-Owned Units: 59
Number of Total Operating Units: 284

In Business Since: 1966   Franchising Since: 1966

Description of Operation: Sit-down and take-out chicken restaurant.

Equity Capital Needed: $578,000 - $778,000 average investment required.

Franchise Fee: $15,000

Royalty Fee: 3%

Financial Assistance: Finance sources are provided.

Managerial Assistance: Each franchisee attends an extensive 4 - 8 week training program in Nashville, TN in a Company-operated Lee's Famous Recipe training restaurant. Training includes crew training and scheduling, equipment use and maintenance, service and product standards, accounting, inventory and cost control procedures. An experienced restaurant training team will train all employees on site before the opening.

Training Provided: Same as above.

Information Submitted: March 1994

LITTLE CAESARS PIZZA
2211 Woodward Ave., Fox Office Ctr.
Detroit, MI 48201
Telephone: (800) 553-5776 (313) 983-6000
Fax: (313) 983-6390
Mr. Gary S. Jensen, Director of Franchise Sales

Number of Franchised Units: 3400
Number of Company-Owned Units: 1200
Number of Total Operating Units: 4600

In Business Since: 1959   **Franchising Since:** 1961

Description of Operation: The world's largest carry-out only pizza chain.

Equity Capital Needed: Data not available.

Franchise Fee: $20,000

Royalty Fee: 5%

Financial Assistance: Third-party financing is available in Canada and the US.

Managerial Assistance: Each franchisee is assigned personnel qualified in marketing, operations, finance, real estate, architecture and design.

Training Provided: The initial training school is 7 weeks in duration and covers every aspect of the business. There are continuing, on-going classes as well.

Information Submitted: March 1994

LONG JOHN SILVER'S RESTAURANTS
P. O. Box 11988, 101 Jerrico Dr.
Lexington, KY 40579
Telephone: (800) 545-8360 (606) 263-6371
Fax: (606) 263-6190
Vice President of Franchise Development

Number of Franchised Units: 470
Number of Company-Owned Units: 995
Number of Total Operating Units: 1465

In Business Since: 1969   **Franchising Since:** 1969

Description of Operation: Long John Silver's Restaurants is the largest seafood chain in the fish and seafood segment. We are approximately 1,500 units strong and are aggressively developing. We offer a menu of fish, seafood and chicken. Eat-in, take-out and drive-thru.

Equity Capital Needed: $300,000 net worth.

Franchise Fee: $12,500

Royalty Fee: 4%

Financial Assistance: Data not available.

Managerial Assistance: Directors of Franchise Operations work directly with new franchisees during the establishment and opening of new stores. Along with field marketing directors, the DFO's continue to maintain support. The franchise director acts as a liaison between the Company and the franchisee.

Training Provided: We provide an initial 5 1/2 weeks of training. Continual training is offered through workshops, seminars, conferences, etc.

Information Submitted: March 1994

LOS RIOS MEXICAN FOODS
835 Supertest Rd., # 200
North York, ON M3J 2M9 CAN

Telephone: (416) 665-4077
Fax: (416) 665-1483
Mr. Nick Lattanzio, Director of Franchising

Number of Franchised Units: 12
Number of Company-Owned Units: 0
Number of Total Operating Units: 12

In Business Since: 1983   **Franchising Since:** 1985

Description of Operation: Quick-service, Mexican-style food products operation for food court locations only, i.e. shopping centers, multi-use complexes and office towers.

Equity Capital Needed: $35,000 - $50,000

Franchise Fee: $20,000

Royalty Fee: 6%

Financial Assistance: Introduction to financial institutions, with preparation of financial proposal package provided.

Managerial Assistance: On-going assistance with product and operations development. Initial training is 4 weeks in total.

Training Provided: 4 weeks of total training - 2 weeks of theory and 2 weeks at store level.

Information Submitted: December 1993

MADE IN JAPAN - A TERIYAKI EXPERIENCE
2133 Royal Windsor Dr., # 23
Mississauga, ON L5J 1K5 CAN
Telephone: (905) 823-8883
Fax: (905) 823-5255
Mr. Nik Jurkovic, Director of Franchising/Development

Number of Franchised Units: 39
Number of Company-Owned Units: 1
Number of Total Operating Units: 40

In Business Since: 1985   **Franchising Since:** 1987

Description of Operation: Japanese teriyaki-style fast food, operating in food courts of shopping centers.

Equity Capital Needed: $80,000 - $150,000

Franchise Fee: $25,000

Royalty Fee: 6%

Financial Assistance: We will assist in the financial presentation.

Managerial Assistance: We provide on-going operational and marketing support with periodic visits.

Training Provided: We offer 2 weeks of training prior to opening - theoretical and on-site training. 2 weeks of training during opening is required.

Information Submitted: March 1994

MAGIC WOK
2060 W. Laskey Rd.
Toledo, OH 43613
Telephone: (800) 447-8998 (419) 471-0696
Fax: (419) 471-0405
Mr. Tony M. Stachurski, Vice President/General Manager

Number of Franchised Units: 17
Number of Company-Owned Units: 5
Number of Total Operating Units: 22

In Business Since: 1983   **Franchising Since:** 1990

Description of Operation: Magic Wok is the 10-year old Toledo, OH based, express Chinese cuisine restaurant franchise that offers sit-down, carry-out and, in some cases, drive-thru service. Stores are located in food courts, free-standing buildings or strip malls. Magic Wok's mission "keep it simple and make it fast," coupled with their "good food, good

223

service, good value" philosophy, establishes this 23-unit chain as a leader in the competitive Chinese fast-food franchise segment. Meals range from $3.50 - $4.00.

Equity Capital Needed: $100,000

Franchise Fee: $12,500

Royalty Fee: 5%

Financial Assistance: None at the present time.

Managerial Assistance: The Magic Wok management team aids in the entire process of developing the new franchisee store. Site selection, layout, plans, equipment, distribution and all other duties required.

Training Provided: The training program consists of 1 week in Toledo, OH at the training center. After the store opens, our staff will be on-site for 10 days - 2 weeks.

Information Submitted: November 1993

MAMMA ILARDO'S PIZZERIAS
9505 Reisterstown Rd., # 100 N
Owings Mills, MD 21117
Telephone: (410) 356-1405
Fax: (410) 356-9668
Mr. Joseph R. Simone, President

Number of Franchised Units: 50
Number of Company-Owned Units: 4
Number of Total Operating Units: 54

In Business Since: 1976   **Franchising Since:** 1985

Description of Operation: Quick-service pizza by the slice, whole pizza and calzone. In food courts, in-line and express units.

Equity Capital Needed: $30,000 - $100,000

Franchise Fee: $25,000 standard; $15,000 express.

Royalty Fee: 6% or 4% express.

Financial Assistance: No.

Managerial Assistance: 8 weeks of training in operations - marketing, design support and in-depth review of all phases of unit operation. Also work 3 weeks on-site with approved extensions. Managerial support is limited except through training! Franchisee is responsible for all hiring and management.

Training Provided: Data not available.

Information Submitted: November 1993

MANCHU WOK
400 Fairway Dr., # 106
Deerfield Beach, FL 33441
Telephone: (800) 423-4009 (305) 481-9555
Fax: (305) 481-9670
Mr. Gavin Swartzman, Vice President of Franchise Development

Number of Franchised Units: 105
Number of Company-Owned Units: 142
Number of Total Operating Units: 247

In Business Since: 1980   **Franchising Since:** 1980

Description of Operation: Chinese fast food.

Equity Capital Needed: $200,000 - $230,000

Franchise Fee: $30,000

Royalty Fee: 6%, plus 2% advertising.

Financial Assistance: Yes.

Managerial Assistance: On-going.

Training Provided: Training is provided in all operations of franchise.

Information Submitted: March 1994

MARCO'S PIZZA
5254 Monroe St.
Toledo, OH 43623
Telephone: (800) 262-7267 (419) 885-4844
Fax: (419) 882-4730
Mr. Kenneth R. Switzer, Director of Administration

Number of Franchised Units: 46
Number of Company-Owned Units: 19
Number of Total Operating Units: 65

In Business Since: 1978   **Franchising Since:** 1979

Description of Operation: Marco's Pizza stores offer pizza, hot sub sandwiches and cheese bread for carry-out and delivery. The Company was established in Toledo, OH in 1978 and has grown steadily to over 65 stores in Ohio, Michigan and Indiana. Marco's Pizza has built its business on a strong foundation of excellent quality products, superb customer service and great value.

Equity Capital Needed: $30,000 - $50,000

Franchise Fee: $12,000

Royalty Fee: 5%

Financial Assistance: No direct financing from Marco's is available. Marco's assists its new franchisees in obtaining bank financing or equipment leasing, depending on the franchisee's financial strength.

Managerial Assistance: Marco's Pizza franchisees are well-supported by the Marco's Franchise Department. Each franchisee is assigned an expert franchise representative to help insure his/her success. Each store is visited a minimum of twice a month by the franchise representative to help the franchisee and consult with him/her on any necessary matters. Marco's Pizza provides its franchisees a complete set of training, operations and administrative manuals.

Training Provided: Each new Marco's Pizza franchisee is trained in each and every aspect of the Marco's Pizza system, including marketing, advertising and administration. The training program is approximately 6 weeks in duration, 2 of which are held at the corporate training center. Prior food service or related experience is required.

Information Submitted: November 1993

MARK PI'S CHINA GATE
3950 Lyman Dr.
Hilliard, OH 43026
Telephone: (614) 876-1188
Fax: (614) 876-9746
Mr. Bill Dolan, Executive Vice President

Number of Franchised Units: 22
Number of Company-Owned Units: 0
Number of Total Operating Units: 22

In Business Since: 1978   **Franchising Since:** 1992

Description of Operation: Gourmet Chinese restaurant.

Equity Capital Needed: $201,800 - $1,061,000

Franchise Fee: $30,000

Royalty Fee: $0 - $150,000 = 2%; $150,001 - $200,000 = 3%; $200,001 + = 2%.

Financial Assistance: Not available.

Managerial Assistance: We provide real estate, construction, marketing, purchasing, training and operations assistance.

Training Provided: 2-week training program for restaurant manager and owner. 5 days of new unit opening assistance.

Information Submitted: November 1993

MARK PI'S EXPRESS
3950 Lyman Dr.
Hilliard, OH 43026

Telephone: (614) 876-1188
Fax: (614) 876-9746
Mr. William J. Dolan, Executive Vice President

Number of Franchised Units: 46
Number of Company-Owned Units: 0
Number of Total Operating Units: 46

In Business Since: 1992   **Franchising Since:** 1992

Description of Operation: Chinese fast-food restaurant.

Equity Capital Needed: $109,600 - $479,600

Franchise Fee: $20,000

Royalty Fee: 4%

Financial Assistance: Not available.

Managerial Assistance: We provide real estate, construction, marketing, purchasing, training and operations assistance.

Training Provided: 2-week training program for restaurant manager and owner. 5 days of new unit opening assistance.

Information Submitted: November 1993

MARK PI'S FEAST OF CHINA BUFFET
3950 Lyman Dr.
Hilliard, OH 43026
Telephone: (614) 876-1188
Fax: (614) 876-9746
Mr. William J. Dolan, Executive Vice President

Number of Franchised Units: 4
Number of Company-Owned Units: 0
Number of Total Operating Units: 4

In Business Since: 1993   **Franchising Since:** 1992

Description of Operation: Chinese menu buffet restaurant.

Equity Capital Needed: $301,800 - $1,246,000

Franchise Fee: $30,000

Royalty Fee: $0 - $150,000 = 2%; $150,001 - $200,000 = 3%; $200,001 + = 2%.

Financial Assistance: Not available.

Managerial Assistance: We provide real estate, construction, marketing, purchasing, training and operations assistance.

Training Provided: 2-week training program for restaurant manager and owner. 5 days of new unit opening assistance.

Information Submitted: November 1993

MARY'S PIZZA SHACK
P. O. Box 1049
Boyes Hot Springs. CA 95416
Telephone: (707) 938-3602
Fax: (707) 938-5976
Mr. Cullen Williamson, President

Number of Franchised Units: 2
Number of Company-Owned Units: 9
Number of Total Operating Units: 11

In Business Since: 1959   **Franchising Since:** 1990

Description of Operation: Full-service restaurant, serving pizza and Italian dishes developed by our founder Mary Fazio. We have successfully created a niche between typical pizza parlors and high-end Italian restaurants. We also have developed delivery systems in many of our locations.

Equity Capital Needed: $250,000

Franchise Fee: $30,000

Royalty Fee: 5%

Financial Assistance: Data not available.

Managerial Assistance: Each franchisee has the on-going support of a district supervisor for overall restaurant operations and a kitchen supervisor for quality control and assistance of food preparation procedures. Also available is advertising and local marketing assistance from the corporate office.

Training Provided: 6 - 8 weeks of in-field and classroom training is provided to the owner and manager. Also included is restaurant staff training one week prior to the opening and two weeks after the opening.

Information Submitted: March 1994

MAURICE'S GOURMET BARBEQUE
1600 Charleston Hwy., P. O. Box 6847
West Columbia, SC 29171
Telephone: (800) 628-7423 (803) 791-5887
Fax: (803) 791-8707
Mr. Julian Bosworth, National Director of Marketing

Number of Franchised Units: 1
Number of Company-Owned Units: 7
Number of Total Operating Units: 8

In Business Since: 1939   **Franchising Since:** 1990

Description of Operation: Maurice is offering the most unique barbeque concept in the world today, featuring real old-fashioned, pit-cooked barbeque as cooked in the colonial days, in addition to a high-quality product. We have improvised a high-tech system. The Company will sell franchises to an individual or to investor groups. We do have a business management plan to aid investor-owned franchises. 55 years of experience.

Equity Capital Needed: $150,000 - $250,000

Franchise Fee: $48,500

Royalty Fee: 5%

Financial Assistance: A Piggie Park reserves the right to permit deferred payment of a portion of any fee when individual circumstances warrant. These circumstances are based on considerations such as the number of restaurants to be constructed, the total time for constructing the restaurants and the franchise owner's ability to pay the entire development fee in one lump sum.

Managerial Assistance: The franchisor will provide back-up support in all areas of franchise operations. If the franchisee does not wish to participate in the day-to-day management of the franchise, the franchisee may elect Piggie Park to manage the franchise under specific terms.

Training Provided: The franchisee will be trained in our system and methodology, including standards, methods, procedures and techniques. This includes assistance in purchasing, advertising, marketing, promotions, operations and human resources.

Information Submitted: March 1994

MAZZIO'S PIZZA
4441 S. 72nd E. Ave.
Tulsa, OK 74145
Telephone: (918) 663-8880
Fax: (918) 664-2518
Mr. Steve Davis, Director or Franchise Operations/Development

Number of Franchised Units: 144
Number of Company-Owned Units: 103
Number of Total Operating Units: 247

In Business Since: 1961   **Franchising Since:** 1969

Description of Operation: Up-scale pizza restaurants.

Equity Capital Needed: $250,000 - $1,250,000

Franchise Fee: $25,000

Royalty Fee: 3%

Financial Assistance: None.

Managerial Assistance: Data not available.

Training Provided: 16 weeks of in-store training for franchise owner and management; 4 days of pre-opening training for all employees; 3 weeks of post-opening training support.

Information Submitted: January 1994

MCDONALD'S CORPORATION
One McDonald's Plaza, Kroc Dr.
Oak Brook, IL 60521
Telephone: (708) 575-6196
Fax: (708) 575-5645
Franchising Deptartment

Number of Franchised Units: 10229
Number of Company-Owned Units: 3768
Number of Total Operating Units: 13997

In Business Since: 1955   **Franchising Since:** 1955

Description of Operation: McDonald's is the world's leading food-service retailer in the global consumer market place, with nearly 14,000 restaurants in 70 countries. 85% of McDonald's restaurant businesses in the US are locally-owned and operated by independent entrepreneurs.

Equity Capital Needed: Minimum of $75,000 in non-borrowed personal resources to consider an individual for a franchise.

Franchise Fee: $22,500, plus $15,000 non-interest bearing franchise security deposit paid to McDonalds.

Royalty Fee: A monthly service fee of 3.5% of sales, plus the greater of monthly base rent or % rent of sales

Financial Assistance: McDonald's does not provide financing or loan guarantees.

Managerial Assistance: Operations, training, maintenance, accounting and equipment manuals are provided. McDonald's makes available promotional advertising material, plus field operations support.

Training Provided: Prospective franchisees are required to participate in a training and evaluation program which may, on a part-time basis, take 2 years or longer to complete.

Information Submitted: April 1994

MELLOW MUSHROOM PIZZA
695 North Ave., NE
Atlanta, GA 30308
Telephone: (404) 524-6133
Fax: (404) 223-5419
Mr. Marc Weinstein, Vice President

Number of Franchised Units: 16
Number of Company-Owned Units: 0
Number of Total Operating Units: 16

In Business Since: 1974   **Franchising Since:** 1985

Description of Operation: Pizza and sandwich restaurants.

Equity Capital Needed: $100,000

Franchise Fee: $25,000

Royalty Fee: 5%

Financial Assistance: Lease negotiations, equipment consulting and build-out consulting.

Managerial Assistance: We provide hands-on training in the operating location.

Training Provided: Hands-on training in operating location.

Information Submitted: January 1994

226

MELTING POT RESTAURANTS, THE
8406-G Benjamin Rd.
Tampa, FL 33634
Telephone: (813) 881-0055
Fax: (813) 889-9361
Mr. Matthew M. Jordan, Executive Assistant

Number of Franchised Units: 26
Number of Company-Owned Units: 4
Number of Total Operating Units: 30

In Business Since: 1975   **Franchising Since:** 1984

Description of Operation: Rated the #1 specialty restaurant franchise system by Entrepreneur Magazine in 1993. The Melting Pot offers a unique opportunity to stand apart from the competition. Select the franchise system that offers a unique concept, coupled with training, education and outstanding support. To become a part of our 1994 expansion plans, call now for a "quick fax" package.

Equity Capital Needed: $50,000 - $80,000

Franchise Fee: $15,600

Royalty Fee: 4.5%

Financial Assistance: This is the responsibility of the new franchisee.

Managerial Assistance: Melting Pot field representatives will be on hand prior to and during your restaurant opening to assist in employee orientation meetings and to conduct on-site training.

Training Provided: All franchisees and their managers must attend and successfully complete a comprehensive training program conducted at the Melting Pot Restaurants' headquarters in Tampa, FL. The cost of this program is included in the initial franchise fee. Franchisees and their managers pay their own costs of lodging, meals and transportation during training.

Information Submitted: January 1994

MICKEY FINN'S SPORTS CAFE
2211 Peoples Rd., # A
Bellevue, NE 68005
Telephone: (402) 292-2056
Fax: (402) 292-9712
Mr. John Vonnas, Vice President

Number of Franchised Units: 8
Number of Company-Owned Units: 0
Number of Total Operating Units: 8

In Business Since: 1989   **Franchising Since:** 1989

Description of Operation: Full-service, full-menu, sports-oriented, neighborhood bar and grill. Menu includes a variety of sandwiches, appetizers and Mexican specialty items.

Equity Capital Needed: $125,000 - $175,000

Franchise Fee: $15,000

Royalty Fee: 5%

Financial Assistance: None.

Managerial Assistance: The corporation provides a full staff of trained professionals to help with all aspects of operations.

Training Provided: Training is provided in existing positions and locations. Pre-opening and opening training. On-going and on-site training available.

Information Submitted: November 1993

MIKE SCHMIDT'S PHILADELPHIA HOAGIES
800 Bustleton Pike
Richboro, PA 18954
Telephone: (215) 322-6806
Fax: (215) 322-8472
Mr. Richard Speeney, President

Number of Franchised Units: 1
Number of Company-Owned Units: 2
Number of Total Operating Units: 3

In Business Since: 1990   **Franchising Since:** 1991

Description of Operation: Hoagie and steak restaurant.

Equity Capital Needed: $69,000 - $99,000

Franchise Fee: $10,000

Royalty Fee: 6%

Financial Assistance: None.

Managerial Assistance: Inventory control, food costs and weekly financial statements.

Training Provided: 2 weeks of training prior to opening and 1 week of training after opening.

Information Submitted: November 1993

MIKES RESTAURANTS
8250 Decarie Blvd.
Montreal, PQ H4P 2P5 CAN
Telephone: (514) 341-5544
Fax: (514) 341-6236
Mr. Neil Zeidel, Senior Vice President

Number of Franchised Units: 123
Number of Company-Owned Units: 11
Number of Total Operating Units: 134

In Business Since: 1968   **Franchising Since:** 1968

Description of Operation: M-Corp Inc., is a full-support franchise management company, currently operating a network of 134 Mikes Restaurant, which is the dominant purveyor of Italian food in Quebec - featuring pizzas, pastas and Italian sandwiches. Full table service in a family setting. Mikes' 30-minute delivery division oversees the home delivery of Mikes food.

Equity Capital Needed: $125,000 - $175,000

Franchise Fee: $45,000

Royalty Fee: 8%

Financial Assistance: Franchise financing programs are negotiated with major financial institutions on behalf of franchisees, offering excellent terms and conditions.

Managerial Assistance: We provide complete set-up of operating manuals, with on-going assistance offered by trained field consultants to assist franchisees in the maintenance of efficient employee working schedules, food costs, etc.

Training Provided: We offer pre-opening and takeover assistance. 6 - 8 weeks of full-time, in depth training by consultant in all aspects of franchise operations, plus 2 weeks of hands-on training team following opening.

Information Submitted: January 1994

MOUNTAIN MIKE'S PIZZA
1014 Second St., 3rd Fl.
Old Sacramento, CA 95814
Telephone: (800) 982-MIKE (916) 441-4493
Fax: (916) 441-0293
Mr. Ted Fumia, Chief Operating Officer

Number of Franchised Units: 70
Number of Company-Owned Units: 0
Number of Total Operating Units: 70

In Business Since: 1978   **Franchising Since:** 1978

Description of Operation: Pizza restaurant with oven-baked sandwiches, salad bar, beer and wine. Rustic theme and decor. Family-style, all-you-can-eat lunch. Franchise buy-back program.

Equity Capital Needed: $70,000

Franchise Fee: $20,000

Royalty Fee: 5%, or $1,000 minimum.

Financial Assistance: SBA.

Managerial Assistance: We provide on-going operational and advertising assistance. A franchise representative is on hand for 10 days at the opening of the restaurant.

Training Provided: We offer 5 weeks of in-store training.

Information Submitted: March 1994

MR. GOODCENTS FRANCHISE SYSTEMS
10100 Santa Fe Dr., # 202
Overland Park, KS 66212
Telephone: (800) 648-2368 (913) 648-2440
Fax: (913) 648-2497
Mr. Joe Santaniello, Vice President

Number of Franchised Units: 24
Number of Company-Owned Units: 2
Number of Total Operating Units: 26

In Business Since: 1988   **Franchising Since:** 1990

Description of Operation: Quick-service - dine-in, carry out or delivery. Serving submarine sandwiches and pasta.

Equity Capital Needed: $67,000 - $120,000

Franchise Fee: $12,500

Royalty Fee: 5%

Financial Assistance: Not available.

Managerial Assistance: Operations management, field service for consultation, marketing, administration, real estate and lease negotiating assistance.

Training Provided: A minimum of 30 days of training for new owners on operations and administration. Operations and training manuals, site selecting and sales building.

Information Submitted: November 1993

MR. JIM'S PIZZA
2995 LBJ Freeway, # 104
Dallas, TX 75234
Telephone: (800) 583-5960 (214) 241-9293
Fax: (214) 241-9296
Mr. Chris Bowman, Executive Director

Number of Franchised Units: 48
Number of Company-Owned Units: 2
Number of Total Operating Units: 50

In Business Since: 1977   **Franchising Since:** 1981

Description of Operation: Pizza carry out and delivery.

Equity Capital Needed: $50,000

Franchise Fee: $10,000

Royalty Fee: 4%

Financial Assistance: None.

Managerial Assistance: Business courses available.

Training Provided: 300 hours in store for pre-opening. First 10 days at your location for pre-opening. Yearly seminars and meetings.

Information Submitted: November 1993

MR. MIKE'S STEAKHOUSE
8765 Ash St., # 5
Vancouver, BC V6P 6T3 CAN

Telephone: (800) 668-MIKE (604) 322-7044
Fax: (604) 322-3143
Mr. Roger Newton, President

Number of Franchised Units: 24
Number of Company-Owned Units: 1
Number of Total Operating Units: 25

In Business Since: 1962   **Franchising Since:** 1963

Description of Operation: Family steakhouse, offering a 60+ item hot food, salad and dessert bar. Menu offers burgers, steak, chicken and seafood. Limited service.

Equity Capital Needed: $100,000 - $200,000

Franchise Fee: $25,000

Royalty Fee: 4%

Financial Assistance: Presentation package prepared for bank.

Managerial Assistance: On-site training minimum of 2 weeks. Off-site training for management. On-going head office support for marketing and advertising. Field representatives available for store use.

Training Provided: Franchisees are exposed to existing store policies and procedures. In-store training for all staff.

Information Submitted: December 1993

MR. STEAK
1401 17th St., # 800
Denver, CO 80202
Telephone: (800) 727-8325 (303) 293-0200
Fax: (303) 293-0299
Mr. Robert Hoadley, Vice President

Number of Franchised Units: 31
Number of Company-Owned Units: 0
Number of Total Operating Units: 31

In Business Since: 1962   **Franchising Since:** 1962

Description of Operation: Mr. Steak is a full-service steak restaurant, serving the highest-quality USDA choice steaks in a visually exciting, subtly-Western atmosphere. The Company enjoys an excellent price/value correlation. Full beverage service is an integral element of the Mr. Steak concept. We have earned the right to be called "America's steak expert."

Equity Capital Needed: $800,000 - $1,400,000 ($240,000 must be liquid).

Franchise Fee: $35,000

Royalty Fee: 4%

Financial Assistance: The franchisee is responsible for obtaining his/her own financing, with assistance from the franchisor.

Managerial Assistance: Opening and continuing assistance is provided by the Company. Site approval, lease assistance, building plans with specifications, construction inspection and opening assistance in marketing and advertising planning is also available. The franchisor also has regional franchise directors in the field. Restaurant accounting, equipment and many food items can be purchased with franchisor assistance. The Company provides operational assistance in new techniques developed by the Company.

Training Provided: A comprehensive 7 weeks of mandatory training is provided with the franchise fee. Travel, food and lodging are the responsibility of the trainee while in training.

Information Submitted: January 1994

MR. SUB
720 Spadina Ave., # 300
Toronto, ON M5S 2T9 CAN
Telephone: (800) 668-SUBS (416) 962-6232
Fax: (416) 962-9995
Mr. Kerry Shirakawa, Vice President of Business Development

Number of Franchised Units: 387
Number of Company-Owned Units: 13
Number of Total Operating Units: 400

In Business Since: 1968   **Franchising Since:** 1970

Description of Operation: Fast food - submarines, salad and soups.

Equity Capital Needed: $40,000

Franchise Fee: $15,000

Royalty Fee: 5%

Financial Assistance: Making contact with respective banks and preparing bank presentations on behalf of prospective franchisees.

Managerial Assistance: On-going field assistance, national advertising, local marketing and design development.

Training Provided: Comprehensive training program. Classroom and in-store practical training.

Information Submitted: January 1994

MRS. VANELLI'S PIZZA & ITALIAN FOODS
2133 Royal Windsor Dr., # 23
Mississauga, ON L5J 1K5 CAN
Telephone: (905) 823-8883
Fax: (905) 823-5255
Mr. Nik Jurkovic, Director of Franchising

Number of Franchised Units: 76
Number of Company-Owned Units: 4
Number of Total Operating Units: 80

In Business Since: 1981   **Franchising Since:** 1983

Description of Operation: Italian fast-food restaurant, operating in food courts of major shopping centers.

Equity Capital Needed: $40,000 - $60,000

Franchise Fee: $25,000

Royalty Fee: 6%

Financial Assistance: We will assist in the financial presentation.

Managerial Assistance: We provide on-going support. Operational and marketing support with periodic visits.

Training Provided: We offer 2 weeks of theoretical and on-site training prior to the opening, as well as 2 weeks of training during opening, if required.

Information Submitted: March 1994

MY FRIEND'S PLACE
106 Hammond Dr.
Atlanta, GA 30328
Telephone: (404) 843-2803
Fax: (404) 843-0371
Ms. Rosalind C. Katz, Vice President

Number of Franchised Units: 4
Number of Company-Owned Units: 3
Number of Total Operating Units: 7

In Business Since: 1980   **Franchising Since:** 1990

Description of Operation: Sandwich shops, catering to quality-oriented customers interested in a quick, light and healthy lunch, specializing in sandwiches, salads, soups, quiches and homemade desserts. We are a "Fresh Food Express."

Equity Capital Needed: $57,000 - $107,000

Franchise Fee: $15,000

Royalty Fee: Fixed service fees: 1st yr -$150/mo.,2nd-5th yr 200/mo., 6th-10th yr $250/mo., 11th-15th yr $300/mo.

Financial Assistance: Not available.

Managerial Assistance: Data not available.

Training Provided: Extensive training for a 3-week period. Additional training when and if required. On-going training seminars for new products, equipment and techniques.

Information Submitted: November 1993

NACHO NANA'S
7349 Via Paseo Del Sur, # 515-453
Scottsdale, AZ 85258
Telephone: (800) 316-2627 (602) 443-9338
Fax: (602) 443-5667
Mr. Dave Dorland, Director of Operations

Number of Franchised Units: 1
Number of Company-Owned Units: 0
Number of Total Operating Units: 1

In Business Since: 1993   **Franchising Since:** 1993

Description of Operation: Mexican fast food, catering to the up-scale market, with a menu designed for the "lite" food conscious.

Equity Capital Needed: $35,700 - $45,900

Franchise Fee: $9,500

Royalty Fee: 2%

Financial Assistance: Nacho Nana's does not directly provide financing; however, we can provide approved equipment financing sources who can deal directly with the franchisees.

Managerial Assistance: 6-day training school in Scottsdale, AZ, plus 5 days of training at the store to assist in new store opening.

Training Provided: 6-day training school in Scottsdale, AZ, plus 5 days of training at the store to assist in new store opening.

Information Submitted: November 1993

NATHAN'S FAMOUS
1400 Old Country Rd., # 400
Westbury, NY 11590
Telephone: (800) NATHANS (516) 338-8500
Fax: (516) 338-7220
Mr. Carl Paley, Senior Vice President

Number of Franchised Units: 163
Number of Company-Owned Units: 16
Number of Total Operating Units: 179

In Business Since: 1916   **Franchising Since:** 1979

Description of Operation: Nathan's Famous offers a large variety of menu items, featuring our world-famous, all-beef frankfurter and fresh-cut french fries in a contemporary atmosphere. Nathan's Famous offers 8 different prototypes, ranging from countertop modulars to free-standing restaurants - adaptable to all market considerations.

Equity Capital Needed: $150,000 - $200,000

Franchise Fee: $30,000

Royalty Fee: 4.5%

Financial Assistance: Yes.

Managerial Assistance: The Company offers site selection, lease negotiations and on-going support.

Training Provided: We provide comprehensive training to principals, managers and crew.

Information Submitted: March 1994

NUMERO UNO
15414 Cabrito Ave., # A
Van Nuys, CA 91406
Telephone: (800) 310-5377 (818) 779-8600
Fax: (818) 779-8626
Mr. Ron Gelet, President/Chief Executive Officer

Number of Franchised Units: 67
Number of Company-Owned Units: 6
Number of Total Operating Units: 73

In Business Since: 1973   **Franchising Since:** 1974

Description of Operation: Numero Uno is a premium pizza restaurant, featuring deep-dish pan pizza. The menu includes a variety of pastas, sandwiches, salads and desserts. Delivery is featured at all restaurants, which vary in size from 800 - 2,000 square feet.

Equity Capital Needed: $60,000 - $100,000

Franchise Fee: $6,000

Royalty Fee: $1,250 per month—take-out restaurant; $1,800 per month—dine-in restaurant.

Financial Assistance: We do not provide financial assistance, but will assist in obtaining lease financing to qualified applicants.

Managerial Assistance: Managerial assistance is on-going, with on-site operational and marketing reviews monthly.

Training Provided: Our 3 1/2 week training program includes job position training, food preparation, sanitation, basic management and accounting fundamentals.

Information Submitted: November 1993

OLIVE'S GOURMET PIZZA
3249 Scott St.
San Francisco, CA 94123
Telephone: (415) 921-6579
Fax: (415) 921-6579
Mr. Craig Cooper, President

Number of Franchised Units: 3
Number of Company-Owned Units: 2
Number of Total Operating Units: 5

In Business Since: 1986   **Franchising Since:** 1989

Description of Operation: Gourmet-style pizza and pasta restaurant, with wine and beer. Take-out or delivery.

Equity Capital Needed: $85,000 - $300,000

Franchise Fee: $20,000

Royalty Fee: 5%

Financial Assistance: None.

Managerial Assistance: Full-time managerial advice and consultation.

Training Provided: 30 days of training in San Francisco, CA for up to 2 people. 2 - 3 weeks of training at your store opening.

Information Submitted: December 1993

ORANGE JULIUS OF AMERICA
P. O. Box 39286
Minneapolis, MN 55439
Telephone: (800) 285-8515 (612) 830-0200
Fax: (612) 830-0450
Mr. Mark W. Lowder, Vice President - International Division

Number of Franchised Units: 493
Number of Company-Owned Units: 0
Number of Total Operating Units: 493

In Business Since: 1926   **Franchising Since:** 1930

Description of Operation: Franchising of specialty drink and hot dog shops.

Equity Capital Needed: $150,000 net worth; $70,000 liquid assets.

Franchise Fee: $15,000

Royalty Fee: 6%

Financial Assistance: OJA will finance 50% of the initial franchise fee.

Managerial Assistance: We provide complete, on-going operations assistance.

Training Provided: We offer a comprehensive training program.

Information Submitted: February 1994

PACINI
910 rue Belanger Est, # 204
Montreal, PQ H2S 3P4 CAN
Telephone: (514) 276-5818
Fax: (514) 276-8147
Mr. Gilles Pepin, President

Number of Franchised Units: 16
Number of Company-Owned Units: 18
Number of Total Operating Units: 34

In Business Since: 1980   **Franchising Since:** 1986

Description of Operation: Pacini is an Italian family restaurant, specializing in pasta and pizza under $10.

Equity Capital Needed: $250,000

Franchise Fee: $50,000

Royalty Fee: 5%

Financial Assistance: None.

Managerial Assistance: We provide operations, marketing and construction manuals.

Training Provided: We offer 3 months of full training for 3 operators, covering human resources, financial, marketing, operations and purchasing.

Information Submitted: March 1994

PANCAKE COTTAGE FAMILY RESTAURANTS
200 Broadhollow Rd., # 207
Melville, NY 11758
Telephone: (516) 271-0221
Fax: (516) 271-0449
Mr. Chris Levano, Vice President of Franchise Development

Number of Franchised Units: 22
Number of Company-Owned Units: 0
Number of Total Operating Units: 22

In Business Since: 1964   **Franchising Since:** 1967

Description of Operation: Full-service restaurant, offering over 200+ items for breakfast (served all day), lunch, full-course dinner and dessert.

Equity Capital Needed: $100,000

Franchise Fee: $35,000

Royalty Fee: 5%

Financial Assistance: Data not available.

Managerial Assistance: The Company will provide continued R & D information to franchisees, as well as regular store visits and regional meetings.

Training Provided: A minimum of 3 - 6 weeks in a Company training restaurant. Training will vary depending upon the prior experience of the candidate.

Information Submitted: November 1993

PASTA TO GO
2780 Rochester
Troy, MI 48083
Telephone: (313) 652-0796
Fax: (313) 689-9876
Mr. Mark A. Gunn, President

Number of Franchised Units: 4
Number of Company-Owned Units: 1
Number of Total Operating Units: 5

In Business Since: 1987   **Franchising Since:** 1991

Description of Operation: Fast-food Italian pasta. We serve pasta, along with a variety of sauces, salads and sandwiches.

Equity Capital Needed: $45,000 - $90,000

Franchise Fee: $10,000

Royalty Fee: 2%, plus 2% advertising.

Financial Assistance: We have third-party financing for equipment for qualified applicants.

Managerial Assistance: Operations training, operations manual, monthly inspections which in turn are formed into an action plan for marketing and operations, ideas, newsletter, hotline and meetings.

Training Provided: An extensive 2-week training program is provided in one of our stores. This will be followed by 2 weeks at the new franchisee's store. Additional training is available beyond that.

Information Submitted: January 1994

PASTEL'S CAFE
1121 Centre St. N., # 440
Calgary, AB T2E 7K6 CAN
Telephone: (800) 361-1151 (403) 230-1151
Fax: (403) 230-2182
Ms. Janine Hunka, Franchise Sales Manager

Number of Franchised Units: 18
Number of Company-Owned Units: 0
Number of Total Operating Units: 18

In Business Since: 1980   **Franchising Since:** 1981

Description of Operation: Pastel's, founded in 1980, features a full menu of the finest-quality gourmet sandwiches, a mouth watering array of specialty salads and hearty home-made soups, all prepared with fresh, healthy ingredients and presented with style.

Equity Capital Needed: $125,000 - $200,000

Franchise Fee: $25,000

Royalty Fee: 5%

Financial Assistance: Royal Bank of Canada.

Managerial Assistance: Day-to-day operations, marketing and promotions, administrative functions, supplier requirements, staff training and quality control analysis done every quarter.

Training Provided: Up to 21 days of hands-on training in every facet of the business.

Information Submitted: November 1993

PAUL REVERE'S PIZZA
1570 - 42nd St. NE
Cedar Rapids, IA 52402
Telephone: (800) 995-9437 (319) 395-9113
Fax: (319) 395-9115
Mr. Tom Mueller, Vice President

Number of Franchised Units: 37
Number of Company-Owned Units: 5
Number of Total Operating Units: 42

In Business Since: 1975   **Franchising Since:** 1981

Description of Operation: Pizza delivery, take-out and sit-down.

Equity Capital Needed: $40,000 - $70,000

Franchise Fee: $10,000

Royalty Fee: 4%

Financial Assistance: None.

Managerial Assistance: We provide site selection, equipment, accounting and store layout.

Training Provided: We offer 4 weeks of in-store training.

Information Submitted: February 1994

PEDRO'S TACOS OF CALIFORNIA
2313 S. El Camino Real
San Clemente, CA 92672
Telephone: (714) 498-5904
Fax: (714) 493-0562
Mr. Edward McNary, Owner

Number of Franchised Units: 1
Number of Company-Owned Units: 1
Number of Total Operating Units: 2

In Business Since: 1985   **Franchising Since:** 1991

Description of Operation: Mexican fast-food with low, value-oriented prices and a very limited, fast-service menu. Drive-thru optional, but recommended. A unique and very profitable concept.

Equity Capital Needed: $30,000

Franchise Fee: $15,000, returnable after 10 years.

Royalty Fee: 5%

Financial Assistance: On approved credit, Pedro's and an affiliate will finance up to 50% of the equipment, start-up and construction costs, excluding land, above and beyond any SBA, local bank or landlord financed costs which the franchisee may have already secured. This offer is quite unique in the industry.

Managerial Assistance: Data not available.

Training Provided: We offer a comprehensive, hands-on and intensive 2-week training period for approved franchisees at our prototype unit in San Clemente, CA.

Information Submitted: January 1994

PENN STATION STEAK & SUB
8510 Morningcalm Dr.
Cincinnati, OH 45255
Telephone: (513) 474-5957
Fax: (513) 474-5957
Mr. Jeff Osterfeld, President

Number of Franchised Units: 16
Number of Company-Owned Units: 0
Number of Total Operating Units: 16

In Business Since: 1985   **Franchising Since:** 1988

Description of Operation: Retail sale of various cheesecake and submarine sandwiches, fresh-cut fries and fresh-squeezed lemonade.

Equity Capital Needed: $140,000 - $180,000

Franchise Fee: $17,500

Royalty Fee: 6%

Financial Assistance: We will assist in the loan application process only.

Managerial Assistance: We have area representatives responsible for supervision of franchisees in a given area.

Training Provided: We offer 7 - 10 days of training prior to opening and 7 - 10 days of training after opening.

Information Submitted: January 1994

PEPE'S MEXICAN RESTAURANTS
1325 W. 15th St.
Chicago, IL 60608
Telephone: (312) 733-2500
Fax: (312) 733-2564
Mr. Edwin A. Ptak, Corporate Counsel

Number of Franchised Units: 55
Number of Company-Owned Units: 1
Number of Total Operating Units: 56

In Business Since: 1967   **Franchising Since:** 1967

Description of Operation: Full-service Mexican restaurant franchise, featuring a full range of Mexican items, including beer, wine and liquor.

Equity Capital Needed: $50,000 - $150,000

Franchise Fee: $15,000

Royalty Fee: 4%

Financial Assistance: The franchisor helps the franchisee find financing and will consider some financing on a case-by-case basis.

Managerial Assistance: We train new franchisees for up to 1 month prior to opening. After opening, we spend 1 - 2 weeks at the restaurant helping to operate.

Training Provided: Training includes instruction in operating restaurant, preparation of food, training of employees, record keeping and ordering of inventory.

Information Submitted: November 1993

PERKINS FAMILY RESTAURANTS
6075 Poplar Ave., # 800
Memphis, TN 38119
Telephone: (800) 877-7375 (901) 766-6400
Fax: (901) 766-6445
Mr. Robert J. Winters, Senior Franchise Director

Number of Franchised Units: 296
Number of Company-Owned Units: 126
Number of Total Operating Units: 422

In Business Since: 1958   **Franchising Since:** 1958

Description of Operation: Perkins Family Restaurants are full-service, family-style restaurants, offering a broad menu base, including breakfast, lunch and dinner entrees. More than half of the restaurants feature our signature bakery.

Equity Capital Needed: 20% of the total investment.

Franchise Fee: $35,000 (US) or $40,000 (Canadian).

Royalty Fee: 4%

Financial Assistance: We structured a Franchise Finance Program in conjunction with Bell Atlantic Tricon's Franchise Lending Division. The program is supported by Perkins with a limited guaranty of funds borrowed by the franchise.

Managerial Assistance: On-going supervision is provided for both pre-opening and post-opening activities. Support programs include training, marketing, purchasing, operations, site selection, construction, finance and equipment purchasing.

Training Provided: Licensee orientation and operations training. Management training and development. New store opening training assistance. Restaurant personnel training program and assistance.

Information Submitted: November 1993

PETER PIPER PIZZA
2321 W. Royal Palm Rd., # 101
Phoenix, AZ 85021
Telephone: (800) 899-3425 (602) 995-1975
Fax: (602) 995-8857
Mr. John F. Baillon, Director of Franchise Sales

Number of Franchised Units: 65
Number of Company-Owned Units: 27
Number of Total Operating Units: 92

In Business Since: 1972   **Franchising Since:** 1976

Description of Operation: Quality, value-priced, family-fun pizza restaurants. Large facilities make us the favorite place for teams, large groups and parties. Our casual, fun atmosphere of videos and redemption games, bawl crawl and tubes and pin balls appeals to the entire family.

Equity Capital Needed: $250,000 - $300,000

Franchise Fee: $25,000

Royalty Fee: 5%

Financial Assistance: We will provide sources for SBA and other lending organizations.

Managerial Assistance: 6 weeks of manager training and 3 weeks of opening team assistance. On-going operational visits at the facility.

Training Provided: 6 weeks of training, as needed. Manuals for operations and marketing provided. Training videos available.

Information Submitted: November 1993

PHILADELPHIA BAR & GRILL
2211 Peoples Rd., # A
Bellevue, NE 68005
Telephone: (402) 292-2056
Fax: (402) 292-9712
Mr. John Vonnas, Vice President

Number of Franchised Units: 8
Number of Company-Owned Units: 0
Number of Total Operating Units: 8

In Business Since: 1985   **Franchising Since:** 1985

Description of Operation: Full-service, full-menu, family-oriented neighborhood bar and grill. Menu concept is based around Philadelphia steak sandwiches (15 varieties).

Equity Capital Needed: $125,000 - $175,000

Franchise Fee: $15,000

Royalty Fee: 5%

Financial Assistance: None.

Managerial Assistance: The corporation provides a full staff of trained professionals to help with all aspects of operations.

Training Provided: Training is provided in existing positions and locations. Pre-opening and opening training. On-going and on-site training available.

Information Submitted: November 1993

PHILLY CONNECTION
120 Interstate N. Pkwy., E., # 112
Atlanta, GA 30339
Telephone: (800) 886-8826 (404) 952-6152
Fax: (404) 952-3168
Ms. Delphine Gaspart, Office Manager

Number of Franchised Units: 23
Number of Company-Owned Units: 0
Number of Total Operating Units: 23

In Business Since: 1985   **Franchising Since:** 1987

Description of Operation: Fast-food franchise, specializing in Philly cheesesteaks, hoagies and salads.

Equity Capital Needed: $100,000

Franchise Fee: $20,000

Royalty Fee: 5%, plus 2% co-op advertising fee.

Financial Assistance: None.

Managerial Assistance: Each new franchisee will receive assistance for the construction of his/her store, manuals will be provided for the operation, marketing ideas and accounting services will be offered.

Training Provided: New franchisees will train in Atlanta, GA with other franchisees prior to the opening of their store. For the first week of opening, the corporate office will provide full time on-site assistance. The corporate office periodically offers assistance to all franchisees.

Information Submitted: March 1994

PIZZA CHEF GOURMET PIZZA
13610 N. Scottsdale Rd., # 10-352
Scottsdale, AZ 85254
Telephone: (800) 655-7319 (602) 443-4221
Fax: (602) 951-8534
Mr. Michael Ruby, Director of Franchise Development

Number of Franchised Units: 160
Number of Company-Owned Units: 4
Number of Total Operating Units: 164

In Business Since: 1990   **Franchising Since:** 1991

Description of Operation: 1,000 - 1,500 square foot, limited seating, pick-up and delivery, gourmet pizza.

Equity Capital Needed: $41,900 - $54,400

Franchise Fee: $20,000 + $5,000 training fee.

Royalty Fee: 5%

Financial Assistance: Available - WAC.

Managerial Assistance: Constant contact with a regional opening advisor.

Training Provided: Week-long executive management training class. Classroom and hands-on instruction provided.

Information Submitted: December 1993

PIZZA DELIGHT
Box 2070, Station A
Moncton, NB E1A 6S8 CAN
Telephone: (506) 853-0990
Fax: (506) 853-4131
Mr. Malcolm Houser, Executive Vice President

Number of Franchised Units: 151
Number of Company-Owned Units: 2
Number of Total Operating Units: 153

In Business Since: 1968   **Franchising Since:** 1969

Description of Operation: Pizza, pasta, casual dining restaurants, also offering take-out and delivery. Recently opened a combination of Pizza Delight and Rooster's B.B.Q. (rotisserie chicken) units.

Equity Capital Needed: $60,000 - $120,000

Franchise Fee: $30,000

Royalty Fee: 6%

Financial Assistance: We will assist in the preparation of market studies and business plans. No direct involvement in franchise is provided.

Managerial Assistance: We provide site selection, lease/purchase negotiations, budgets, P & L's, financial, on-going operations and marketing support, purchasing and construction assistance.

Training Provided: We offer 2 weeks of training in a restaurant, plus 3 weeks at opening and on-going seminars.

Information Submitted: March 1994

PIZZA FACTORY
P. O. Box 989, 49430 Road 426
Oakhurst, CA 93644
Telephone: (209) 683-3377
Fax: (209) 683-6879
Mr. Ron Willey, Vice President

Number of Franchised Units: 75
Number of Company-Owned Units: 3
Number of Total Operating Units: 78

In Business Since: 1979 **Franchising Since:** 1985

Description of Operation: Family-oriented pizza restaurant, serving pizza, pasta, sandwiches and salad bar. Specializing in communities of 15,000 or less.

Equity Capital Needed: $100,000 - $175,000

Franchise Fee: $20,000, plus $2,500 training fee.

Royalty Fee: 3%, plus 1% advertising.

Financial Assistance: Partial financing on equipment.

Managerial Assistance: Corporate staff and officers are available at all times. Employee handbooks, owners manuals, regional meetings and conventions.

Training Provided: The minimum training time is 325 hours at a Pizza Factory training facility, covers all aspects of the business, including recipes, owner's manual, bookkeeping, customer service, ordering, employee management, etc.

Information Submitted: January 1994

PIZZA INN
5050 Quorum Dr., # 500
Dallas, TX 75240
Telephone: (800) 880-9955 (214) 701-9955
Fax: (214) 934-2314
Mr. Monty Whitehurst, Vice President of Franchise Sales

Number of Franchised Units: 422
Number of Company-Owned Units: 8
Number of Total Operating Units: 430

In Business Since: 1961 **Franchising Since:** 1963

Description of Operation: With over 30 years of franchising experience, Pizza Inn supports 430 full-service restaurants and delivery units in 20 states and 12 countries. Pizza Inn was named "America's #1 Choice in Pizza" in a recent annual survey by Restaurants and Institutions. Nation's Restaurant News rated us the leader in their Top 100 Chains.

Equity Capital Needed: $113,000 - $600,000

Franchise Fee: $7,500 - $20,000

Royalty Fee: 4%

Financial Assistance: None.

Managerial Assistance: Data not available.

Training Provided: Training includes 4 weeks in a Company store in Dallas, TX and 1 week of classroom in Dallas, TX.

Information Submitted: March 1994

PIZZA ONE
200 Montego Bay, P. O. Box 727
Mt. Clemens, MI 48043
Telephone: (313) 468-1200
Fax: (313) 468-8940
Mr. Mike Bischoff, President

Number of Franchised Units: 18
Number of Company-Owned Units: 37
Number of Total Operating Units: 55

In Business Since: 1984 **Franchising Since:** 1984

Description of Operation: Carry-out pizzeria with delivery available. Specializes in round or deep dish pizzas. Our "Big 1 and Little 1" submarines (8 varieties), 3 salads. 1 full-time manager, 1 assistant manager, 6 part-time drivers.

Equity Capital Needed: $50,000 - $65,000

Franchise Fee: $5,000

Royalty Fee: 3% - 5%, or $300 - $500.

Financial Assistance: Financial assistance will be available in 1994.

Managerial Assistance: Free training course of 400 hours. Monthly updates and on-going training for any future changes.

Training Provided: In-store operations, product making, accounting, recordkeeping and advertising.

Information Submitted: December 1993

PIZZA PIT
4253 Argosy Court
Madison, WI 53714
Telephone: (608) 221-6777
Fax: (608) 221-6771
Mr. Kerry P. Cook, Vice President

Number of Franchised Units: 26
Number of Company-Owned Units: 10
Number of Total Operating Units: 36

In Business Since: 1969 **Franchising Since:** 1984

Description of Operation: Free home delivery and carry-out of hand-crafted pizzas, specialty sandwiches, pasta and salads. The units are also adaptable to inside seating. Single and multiple-unit programs are available. Merged business concepts with family fun centers, bowling centers and convenience stores.

Equity Capital Needed: $125,280 - $264,740

Franchise Fee: $16,000 - $17,500

Royalty Fee: 5.5% - 6.5%, plus on-going advertising fee of 1%.

Financial Assistance: None.

Managerial Assistance: Pizza Pit offers on-going assistance to all franchise locations. We have operations advisors that make routine visits to assist management in the operation of their Pizza Pit.

Training Provided: We provide a comprehensive training program that covers all aspects of the operation of a Pizza Pit Restaurant, from order taking to profit planning.

Information Submitted: January 1994

PIZZA PIZZA
580 Jarvis St.
Toronto, ON M4Y 2H9 CAN
Telephone: (800) 263-5556 (416) 967-1010
Fax: (416) 967-0891
Mr. Sebastian Fuschini, Vice President of Franchising

Number of Franchised Units: 239
Number of Company-Owned Units: 13
Number of Total Operating Units: 252

In Business Since: 1968 **Franchising Since:** 1972

Description of Operation: Pizza Pizza Limited is Canada's leading pizza chain, consisting mainly of take-out and delivery stores with a menu that includes pizza, salads, wings, subs and Italian dinners. Pizza Pizza recently began an international expansion program, with the first restaurant opening in Costa Rica. Even after 25 years in business, Pizza Pizza continues to be a fast-paced, entrepreneurial corporation.

Equity Capital Needed: $100,000 - $150,000 (to purchase a turn-key operation).

Franchise Fee: $20,000 (included in above price).

Royalty Fee: 6%

Financial Assistance: Yes.

Managerial Assistance: Each store is assigned an area market representative who provides assistance on an on-going basis. In addition, the franchisor provides various service departments, such as accounting, real estate and marketing, which franchisees can access as needed.

233

Training Provided: An intensive 10-week program combines classroom and test kitchen training with in-store practical experience. A new franchisee who successfully completes this course should understand all aspects of operating and managing a Pizza Pizza outlet.

Information Submitted: December 1993

PIZZAS BY MARCHELLONI
1051 Essington Rd., # 130
Joliet, IL 60435
Telephone: (800) HOTPIE 4 (815) 729-4494
Fax: (815) 729-4508
Mr. Eric C. Alling, Vice President

Number of Franchised Units: 40
Number of Company-Owned Units: 4
Number of Total Operating Units: 44

In Business Since: 1986   **Franchising Since:** 1989

Description of Operation: Pizza delivery and carry-out restaurant. Dine-in concept available. Limited menu of pizza, soda and garlic bread. Extra items available.

Equity Capital Needed: $50,000 - $150,000

Franchise Fee: $18,500

Royalty Fee: 5%

Financial Assistance: None.

Managerial Assistance: Opening assistance for franchisees, including site selection, lease negotiations and help with layout of unit. On-going visits during construction and after opening. A member of our staff is on-site 4 days during the opening month. Open lines of communication to corporate office for questions.

Training Provided: 2 weeks of training at corporate store for owner and manager. Intensive course, covering all aspects of the pizza business, including hands-on training. On-going seminars on various topics. Additional training provided, if necessary, for owner, manager and employees at Company store.

Information Submitted: November 1993

PLUS 1 PIZZA
P. O. Box 516, 9100 Jeffrey Dr.
Cambridge, OH 43725
Telephone: (614) 432-6066
Fax: (614) 439-1331
Mr. Michael Waris, General Manager

Number of Franchised Units: 3
Number of Company-Owned Units: 11
Number of Total Operating Units: 14

In Business Since: 1977   **Franchising Since:** 1988

Description of Operation: 2 for 1 pizza. Carry-out and delivery.

Equity Capital Needed: $15,000 - $75,000

Franchise Fee: $15,000

Royalty Fee: 5%

Financial Assistance: None.

Managerial Assistance: Opening the franchise store with a corporate team of managers from Company stores has been extremely successful for our franchisees.

Training Provided: 2 weeks of management training at a corporate store.

Information Submitted: November 1993

POFOLKS
P. O. Box 20
Mt. Sterling, KY 40353

Telephone: (800) 876-3655 (606) 498-2200
Fax: (606) 498-7619
Ms. Regina Ingram

Number of Franchised Units: 79
Number of Company-Owned Units: 44
Number of Total Operating Units: 123

In Business Since: 1975   **Franchising Since:** 1983

Description of Operation: Full-service family restaurants with country cooking and down-home atmosphere.

Equity Capital Needed: $500,000 plus.

Franchise Fee: $25,000

Royalty Fee: 2.5%

Financial Assistance: None.

Managerial Assistance: We provide inspection and advice during the term of the franchise agreement. Co-operative purchasing is available through distributors. Regular meeting with franchise advisory committee. Annual franchise meeting.

Training Provided: We offer a 4-month manager training program in restaurants that also includes a 2-week classroom training course at corporate headquarters, as well as 4 days prior and 2 weeks after the opening of each restaurant.

Information Submitted: March 1994

PONDEROSA
P. O. Box 578
Dayton, OH 45401
Telephone: (800) 543-9670 (513) 454-2543
Fax: (513) 454-2525
Mr. Edward J. Day, Director of Franchise Sales

Number of Franchised Units: 407
Number of Company-Owned Units: 354
Number of Total Operating Units: 761

In Business Since: 1965   **Franchising Since:** 1966

Description of Operation: America's family steakhouse. A modified full-service, affordable family steakhouse restaurant, open 7 days a week for lunch and dinner. Menu features approximately 10 beef entrees, 4 seafood entrees, 3 chicken entrees and the Grand Buffet.

Equity Capital Needed: $500,000 net worth, $125,000 liquid.

Franchise Fee: $30,000

Royalty Fee: 4.8%

Financial Assistance: The franchisor assists in identifying sources.

Managerial Assistance: Real estate, architecture and construction, training, marketing, purchasing and product distribution, product development, franchise field consultant and unit operating team.

Training Provided: Training includes 5 weeks in field, then 1 week at headquarters, then 3 additional weeks in field. Follow-up training in steakhouse, as required.

Information Submitted: January 1994

POPEYES FAMOUS FRIED CHICKEN AND BISCUITS
Six Concourse Pkwy., # 1700
Atlanta, GA 30328
Telephone: (800) 848-8248 (404) 353-3107
Fax: (404) 353-3170
Ms. Balencia Walker, Communications Director

Number of Franchised Units: 700
Number of Company-Owned Units: 113
Number of Total Operating Units: 813

In Business Since: 1972   **Franchising Since:** 1976

Description of Operation: Popeyes Famous Fried Chicken and Biscuits is a fast-food chicken restaurant, specializing in cajun-style dishes. They serve authentic red beans and rice, spicy chicken, mashed potatoes and gravy and many other cajun-style side dishes. Popeyes Famous Fried Chicken and Biscuits is the nation's third largest fast-food chicken chain, with approximately 819 units throughout the US and abroad.

Equity Capital Needed: $200,000 - $300,000

Franchise Fee: $25,000

Royalty Fee: 5% of gross sales

Financial Assistance: Indirect assistance available to obtain financing. No direct assistance available. It is recommended that franchising prospects have $150,000 liquid and a $300,000 net worth.

Managerial Assistance: Popeyes is absolutely committed to providing the operational support needed to produce the highest-quality product and satisfied customers. This support extends to thorough training on procedures, procurement of equipment and supplies as well as on-going field support.

Training Provided: The training department at Popeyes has programs that will help you to understand every aspect of the business, from day-to-day operations and accounting to inventory and managing your staff.

Information Submitted: December 1993

PORT OF SUBS
5365 Mae Anne Ave., # A-29
Reno, NV 89523
Telephone: (702) 747-0555
Fax: (702) 747-1510
Ms. Patricia Larson, President

Number of Franchised Units: 52
Number of Company-Owned Units: 12
Number of Total Operating Units: 64

In Business Since: 1972   **Franchising Since:** 1986

Description of Operation: Submarine sandwich franchise, featuring unique front-line method of preparing specialty sandwiches, soups, salads and party platters. Bread is baked fresh daily on premises.

Equity Capital Needed: $50,000 - $70,000

Franchise Fee: $16,000

Royalty Fee: 5.5%

Financial Assistance: No direct financing is available, but we will assist qualified franchisees in finding lenders. Many operators have secured SBA loans.

Managerial Assistance: We provide assistance in site selection, construction, coordination and equipment ordering. We provide guidance with establishing the business from governmental process to administrative organization, as well as business forms, reference manuals, approved suppliers and operations assistance.

Training Provided: We offer 2 1/2 weeks of intensive training, plus 2 weeks in the franchisee's unit during initial opening.

Information Submitted: March 1994

POTTS HOT DOGS
P. O. Box 08195
Ft. Myers, FL 33908
Telephone: (813) 482-5432
Fax: (813) 768-5533
Mr. Bill Potts, President

Number of Franchised Units: 4
Number of Company-Owned Units: 5
Number of Total Operating Units: 9

In Business Since: 1984   **Franchising Since:** 1984

Description of Operation: Retail sales of hot dogs.

Equity Capital Needed: $25,000 - $40,000

Franchise Fee: $15,000

Royalty Fee: 4%

Financial Assistance: None.

Managerial Assistance: We will train the franchisee for at least 100 hours in one of our Company stores.

Training Provided: We will train the franchisee for at least 100 hours in one of our Company stores.

Information Submitted: November 1993

PRO*PORTION CAFE
999 E. Touhy Ave., # 333
Des Plaines, IL 60018
Telephone: (800) 257-4058 (708) 298-8330
Fax: (708) 298-0697
Mr. Howard B. Marks, Vice President of Franchise Development

Number of Franchised Units: 12
Number of Company-Owned Units: 0
Number of Total Operating Units: 12

In Business Since: 1975   **Franchising Since:** 1979

Description of Operation: A cafe that offers delicious, light lunches and dinners and incredible, low-calorie desserts. Variety and value are the keys. From our signature shredded salads and pitas to stuffed baked potatoes, quiches and pasta dishes to or own soft "ice cream" and cheesecake, to a full line of take-out items, there's something for virtually everyone. Not only is every item health-consciously prepared, but each is accompanied by the calorie count and substitution ("exchanges") for those on a diet program.

Equity Capital Needed: $214,000 - $278,000

Franchise Fee: $25,000

Royalty Fee: 5%

Financial Assistance: The franchisor will assist in securing third-party financing.

Managerial Assistance: Our operations department provides pre-opening training, which teaches all facets of our system. This includes menu preparation, equipment operation, employee training, personnel policies, international systems, sales techniques and the basic elements of local shop marketing and advertising. Our territory managers will visit your Cafe to consult with you and advise you in the areas of sales forecasts and sales and operational objectives, as well as on the plans to meet your goals.

Training Provided: A full training program is provided. Support begins with location selection, construction planning and opening assistance. We will provide and train you with all the tools needed to operate your business comfortably and confidently on a day-to-day basis.

Information Submitted: December 1993

RED BOY PIZZA
1000 Fifth Ave., # 5
San Rafael, CA 94901
Telephone: (415) 459-4271
Fax: (415) 485-0590
Mr. Peter Forstner, President

Number of Franchised Units: 8
Number of Company-Owned Units: 1
Number of Total Operating Units: 9

In Business Since: 1969   **Franchising Since:** 1984

Description of Operation: Pizza is the main item on the menu. In-house stores have pasta, soup and salad. To-go stores have only pizza and salad. Depending on location, the stores are open for lunch and dinner, 7 days a week. Beer and wine is served in-house, as well as soft drinks, coffee, tea, etc.

Equity Capital Needed: $55,000 - $130,000

Franchise Fee: $25,000

Royalty Fee: 5%

Financial Assistance: None.

Managerial Assistance: We provide on-going franchisee meetings, field visits and continuous consultation to the local franchisees for all aspects of the business.

Training Provided: We offer 10 days of training at the franchisee's store. Up to 2 months of training at a Company-owned store is available.

Information Submitted: March 1994

RED RIVER BAR-B-QUE
P. O. Box 306
Ingomar, PA 15127
Telephone: (412) 369-2888
Fax: (412) 369-2891
Mr. Ronald A. Sofranko, President

Number of Franchised Units: 0
Number of Company-Owned Units: 2
Number of Total Operating Units: 2

In Business Since: 1987   **Franchising Since:** 1987

Description of Operation: Authentic Southwestern-style bar-b-que, featuring sliced beef brisket, slow-cooked ham, ribs, chicken, wings, home-made Texas-style chili, homemade salads and signature side orders. Units are free-standing as of 8/1/94, with liquor licenses and signature label beers. Homemade pecan pie and peach cobbler are also featured.

Equity Capital Needed: $300,000 - $450,000

Franchise Fee: $29,500

Royalty Fee: 4%

Financial Assistance: The Company seeks qualified owner/operators with financial resources and restaurant experience. The Company cannot provide financial assistance at this time.

Managerial Assistance: The Company has 7 years of experience and of testing the concept, as well as testing new menu items and marketing processes.

Training Provided: We offer in-store training for a minimum of 6 - 8 weeks. Training crew for grand opening. Weekly operations assistance for first 6 - 12 months, as needed.

Information Submitted: March 1994

RED ROBIN INTERNATIONAL
28 Executive Park, # 200
Irvine, CA 92714
Telephone: (714) 756-2121
Fax: (714) 756-2540
Mr. Douglas N. Luebbe, Director of Franchise Development

Number of Franchised Units: 65
Number of Company-Owned Units: 44
Number of Total Operating Units: 109

In Business Since: 1969   **Franchising Since:** 1979

Description of Operation: Red Robin is a casual dining, full-service restaurant, appealing to couples, singles and families with an extensive food and beverage selection. Red Robin is decorated to entertain the young and young-at-heart. The interior is a mix of old and new, with bright colors against polished oak and brass, live plants, classic movie posters and decorative neon signs.

Equity Capital Needed: $400,000 - $500,000

Franchise Fee: $35,000

Royalty Fee: 4.5%

Financial Assistance: We do not have financial assistance available through our corporate headquarters. We do have outside financial companies that may help.

Managerial Assistance: Most new franchisees bring in their own staff when they open their new restaurant. Occasionally, if we hear that a manager is interested in the franchise location, we might be able to match the manager up with the franchisee.

Training Provided: The new franchisee will train for 10 weeks at one of our restaurants, starting in the back of the house, then on up to management. Our corporate office is fully staffed from construction department to marketing to assist new franchisees.

Information Submitted: January 1994

RENZIOS
701 W. Hampden Ave., # B-109
Englewood, CO 80110
Telephone: (800) 892-3441 (303) 781-3441
Fax: (303) 781-6611
Mr. Bill Grinstead, Franchise Director

Number of Franchised Units: 14
Number of Company-Owned Units: 8
Number of Total Operating Units: 22

In Business Since: 1975   **Franchising Since:** 1989

Description of Operation: Unique and impressive fast-food Greek restaurants, operating in regional malls, strip centers and free-standing units. Renzios fills the space between the typical fast-food restaurants and the full-service restaurant. Renzios offers traditional Greek recipes, featuring the nutritious beef and chicken Gyros sandwiches. For those who want more, there are meat platters, beef and chicken salads and platters. Authentic Greek pastries round off an exciting menu that is tempting to today's appetite.

Equity Capital Needed: $90,000 - $140,000 (including franchise fee).

Franchise Fee: 30% of capital requirement.

Royalty Fee: 5%

Financial Assistance: The franchisor will assist in locating available financing and equipment leasing.

Managerial Assistance: The franchisor will assist in site selection, lease negotiations and in developing the business plan for the franchisee. Franchisee will receive a 350-page, comprehensive operations manual.

Training Provided: The franchisee will receive up to 3 weeks of training in Denver, CO and up to 7 days of grand opening assistance.

Information Submitted: November 1993

RICKSHAW CHINESE RESTAURANT
1230 El Camino Real, # D-4
San Bruno, CA 94066
Telephone: (800) 952-8666 (415) 952-8666
Fax: (415) 952-8668
Ms. Anna Laveria May, Franchise Director

Number of Franchised Units: 3
Number of Company-Owned Units: 5
Number of Total Operating Units: 8

In Business Since: 1981   **Franchising Since:** 1992

Description of Operation: Fast-food restaurants, specializing in food-to-go. Freshly-cooked Chinese food.

Equity Capital Needed: Data not available.

Franchise Fee: $14,000 - $28,000

Royalty Fee: 4%

Financial Assistance: For qualified franchisees, we'll be able to help finance a portion of certain existing outlets, or we may assist with equipment.

Managerial Assistance: Franchisees will be trained in customer service, cooking methods, bookkeeping and personnel.

Training Provided: Training will be conducted in an actual restaurant. The on-the-job training will include everything a franchisee needs to know about running the business.

Information Submitted: November 1993

ROCKY ROCOCO PAN STYLE PIZZA
105 E. Wisconsin Ave., # 204
Oconomowoc, WI 53066
Telephone: (800) 888-7625 (414) 569-5580
Fax: (414) 569-5591
Mr. Thomas R. Hester, President

Number of Franchised Units: 30
Number of Company-Owned Units: 20
Number of Total Operating Units: 50

In Business Since: 1974   **Franchising Since:** 1974

Description of Operation: Pizza restaurant, providing full dining, carry-out, drive-thru, delivery service and featuring pizza by the slice.

Equity Capital Needed: $50,000 - $150,000

Franchise Fee: $15,000

Royalty Fee: 4%

Financial Assistance: None.

Managerial Assistance: We provide continuous business assistance in areas such as real estate, construction, operations (from restaurant opening to regular visits), marketing, finance and quality assurance.

Training Provided: We offer a 6-week manager training program, combination of classroom and in-restaurant, as well as various 1 - 2 day seminars.

Information Submitted: March 1994

ROCKY'S CAFE
4900 Blazer Pkwy.
Dublin, OH 43017
Telephone: (614) 766-3696
Fax: (614) 766-3605
Mr. Jeffrey D. Seaton, President

Number of Franchised Units: 0
Number of Company-Owned Units: 1
Number of Total Operating Units: 1

In Business Since: 1980   **Franchising Since:** 1993

Description of Operation: Rocky's cafe is a full-service, casual theme restaurant, specializing in high-quality food and legal beverages. There are 100 food items on the menu, featuring our famous fondues and 22 different varieties of Long Island Iced Tea. Fun atmosphere with dining for the general public, banquet facilities, private party rooms, catering services and an elevated 50-seat bar.

Equity Capital Needed: $300,000 - $1,800,000

Franchise Fee: $35,000

Royalty Fee: 4%

Financial Assistance: None.

Managerial Assistance: Support includes site review and approval, comprehensive training programs, complete start-up assistance, menu, manuals, recipes, prototype building plans, exclusive franchised area and on-going operational support.

Training Provided: We offer 5 weeks of comprehensive training in Columbus, OH and on-site pre-opening training.

Information Submitted: January 1994

ROLLO POLLO ROTISSERIE CHICKEN
4801 Sherborn Ln., B-1
Louisville, KY 40207
Telephone: (502) 896-6181
Fax: (502) 896-1534
Mr. Edward C. Binzel, Director of Franchising

Number of Franchised Units: 3
Number of Company-Owned Units: 3
Number of Total Operating Units: 6

In Business Since: 1991   **Franchising Since:** 1992

Description of Operation: Rotisserie chicken restaurant, with 13+ premium side dishes. Menu also features salads, sandwiches and kids' meals.

Equity Capital Needed: $100,000 - $300,000

Franchise Fee: $15,000 per store.

Royalty Fee: 4%

Financial Assistance: None at this time.

Managerial Assistance: Support is a standard part of the training program.

Training Provided: Training includes an extensive 4 - 6 week, in-store program for all franchisees and management trainees. Additional support is provided during grand opening.

Information Submitted: February 1994

ROSATI'S PIZZA
33 W. Higgins Rd., # 1010
S. Barrington, IL 60010
Telephone: (708) 836-0400
Fax: (708) 836-0429
Mr. Ronald Stockman, President

Number of Franchised Units: 13
Number of Company-Owned Units: 37
Number of Total Operating Units: 50

In Business Since: 1964   **Franchising Since:** 1988

Description of Operation: Specialized carry-out and delivery concept, featuring premier Chicago-style pizza and authentic Italian cuisine.

Equity Capital Needed: Total investment $100,000 - $125,000.

Franchise Fee: $15,000

Royalty Fee: 5%

Financial Assistance: None.

Managerial Assistance: We provide full-service franchise support, including assistance in site selection, lease negotiations and construction. Training includes management and on-site opening support. On-going marketing and operations assistance from field consultants.

Training Provided: Same as above.

Information Submitted: January 1994

ROUND TABLE PIZZA
655 Montgomery St., 7th Fl.
San Francisco, CA 94111
Telephone: (800) 866-5866 (415) 392-7500
Fax: (415) 627-3946
Mr. Jake Brown, Director of Franchise Sales

Number of Franchised Units: 564
Number of Company-Owned Units: 1
Number of Total Operating Units: 565

In Business Since: 1959   **Franchising Since:** 1961

Description of Operation: Family pizza restaurant - take-out and delivery.

Equity Capital Needed: $100,000 cash and $200,000 equity.

Franchise Fee: $25,000

Royalty Fee: 4%

Financial Assistance: We offer third-party lending assistance.

Managerial Assistance: We provide our franchisees with on-going operational and marketing assistance, updating management and operational materials.

Training Provided: Each franchisee attends 5 weeks of training - 2 weeks of operational training in a restaurant setting and 3 weeks of management training at our headquarters. The management training covers food, labor, employee hire, laws and local advertising.

Information Submitted: November 1993

S. P. UNLIMITED
1515 N. Federal Hwy., # 300
Boca Raton, FL 33432
Telephone: (800) 940-2134
Fax: (407) 394-2195
Mr. Donald Ryan, President

Number of Franchised Units: 70
Number of Company-Owned Units: 39
Number of Total Operating Units: 109

In Business Since: 1958   **Franchising Since:** 1979

Description of Operation: A full-service or take-out and delivery pizza chain, offering pizza, pasta, sandwiches, salads and dessert. A video tape is available, detailing operations and support.

Equity Capital Needed: $150,000 - $220,000

Franchise Fee: $20,000

Royalty Fee: 5%

Financial Assistance: We will provide assistance in securing financing.

Managerial Assistance: A complete on-the-job training program is provided. Training covers all aspects of the business - operational procedures, bookkeeping, employee training, advertising and promotion, menu selection and management techniques.

Training Provided: Comprehensive support for all franchisees includes assistance in site selection, store layout and design, equipment specifications, marketing, training, on-going support and research and development.

Information Submitted: April 1994

SALSA'S GOURMET MEXICAN
13610 N. Scottsdale Rd., # 10-352
Scottsdale, AZ 85254
Telephone: (800) 655-7319 (602) 443-4221
Fax: (602) 951-8534
Mr. Michael Ruby, Director of Franchise Development

Number of Franchised Units: 40
Number of Company-Owned Units: 1
Number of Total Operating Units: 41

In Business Since: 1992   **Franchising Since:** 1992

Description of Operation: 1,000 - 1,500 square foot, limited seating, pick-up and delivery gourmet Mexican restaurant.

Equity Capital Needed: $16,000 - $28,500

Franchise Fee: $20,000 + $5,000 training fee.

Royalty Fee: 5%

Financial Assistance: Available - WAC.

Managerial Assistance: Constant contact with a regional opening advisor.

Training Provided: Week-long executive management training class. Classroom and hands-on instruction provided.

Information Submitted: December 1993

SALVATORE SCALLOPINI
27190 Dequindre Rd.
Warren, MI 48092
Telephone: (313) 573-8960
Fax: (313) 573-0327
Mr. John Scott, Director of Franchising

Number of Franchised Units: 6
Number of Company-Owned Units: 6
Number of Total Operating Units: 12

In Business Since: 1982   **Franchising Since:** 1986

Description of Operation: Full-service Italian restaurants, ranging in size from 2,200 - 40,000 square feet.

Equity Capital Needed: Data not available.

Franchise Fee: $25,000

Royalty Fee: 4%

Financial Assistance: SBA, plus 7 lending programs.

Managerial Assistance: As a commission-based business, our management assistance is continuously provided.

Training Provided: 225 hours of intensive training, including all facets of our business.

Information Submitted: December 1993

SANDWICH BOARD, THE
10 Plastics Ave.
Etobicoke, ON M8Z 4B7 CAN
Telephone: (416) 255-0898
Fax: (416) 255-8086
Mr. Rudolph Dieter Hoefel, President

Number of Franchised Units: 21
Number of Company-Owned Units: 2
Number of Total Operating Units: 23

In Business Since: 1981   **Franchising Since:** 1985

Description of Operation: The Sandwich Board is a first-class, gourmet-style fast-food restaurant of up to 1,000 square feet in size, serving a wide variety of custom-made sandwiches, salads and daily hot specials, including soups. Beverages consist of juices, soft drinks and coffee (and, in some instances, beer and wine). Ice cream, yogurt and baked goods complete the menu. Office catering is a key ingredient in our operations.

Equity Capital Needed: $50,000 - $75,000

Franchise Fee: $25,000

Royalty Fee: 5%

Financial Assistance: Financial assistance (if necessary) from the franchisor is available for up to $40,000, secured by a greater mortgage.

Managerial Assistance: Throughout the term, the franchisor will continuously assist its franchisees in all areas of the business, placing special emphasis on the managerial aspect of the operation.

Training Provided: New franchisees are trained a minimum of 4 - 6 weeks on average during the initial training period. A pre-training period of at least 3 days is required prior to approval to determine the suitability of the applicant.

Information Submitted: January 1994

SBARRO
763 Larkfield Rd.
Commack, NY 11725
Telephone: (800) 766-4949 (516) 864-0200
Fax: (516) 462-9058
Mr. Larry Feierstein, Vice President of Franchising

Number of Franchised Units: 140
Number of Company-Owned Units: 540
Number of Total Operating Units: 680

In Business Since: 1955   **Franchising Since:** 1992

Description of Operation: Italian eateries.

Equity Capital Needed: $300,000 +

Franchise Fee: $35,000

Royalty Fee: 5%

Financial Assistance: None.

Managerial Assistance: Full training and on-going field support.

Training Provided: 5 weeks (at 40 hours per week) of in-store training.

Information Submitted: January 1994

SEAFOOD AMERICA
645 Mearns Rd.
Warminster, PA 18974
Telephone: (215) 672-2211
Fax: (215) 675-8324
Mr. Robert J. Brennan, President

Number of Franchised Units: 17
Number of Company-Owned Units: 0
Number of Total Operating Units: 17

In Business Since: 1976   **Franchising Since:** 1980

Description of Operation: Retail sale of seafood and related items.

Equity Capital Needed: $200,000 - $250,000

Franchise Fee: $15,000

Royalty Fee: 2%

Financial Assistance: No financing is available.

Managerial Assistance: We will provide total training and initial assistance upon opening the store.

Training Provided: Training is provided in an existing store for a period of 4 weeks.

Information Submitted: March 1994

SHOOTERS WATERFRONT CAFE U.S.A.
3033 NE 32nd Ave.
Ft. Lauderdale, FL 33308
Telephone: (305) 566-3044
Fax: (305) 566-2953
Mr. Melvin A. Burge, Executive Vice President

Number of Franchised Units: 4
Number of Company-Owned Units: 2
Number of Total Operating Units: 6

In Business Since: 1982   **Franchising Since:** 1985

Description of Operation: Full-service, up-scale waterfront restaurant, serving American-style cuisine. Docking for boats and patio dining.

Equity Capital Needed: $1,200,000 - $1,600,000

Franchise Fee: $100,000

Royalty Fee: 4%

Financial Assistance: None.

Managerial Assistance: We provide a minimum of 1 month and up to 3 months of training during the initial 6 months of the operation. At the franchisee's expense, the franchisor will provide a representative to assist in all phases of opening and the operation.

Training Provided: We offer training for the general manager and up to 6 additional employees for a minimum of 6 weeks.

Information Submitted: March 1994

SHORTSTOP
10777 Westheimer Rd., # 1030
Houston, TX 77477
Telephone: (800) 324-0067 (713) 783-0500
Fax: (713) 783-4608
Mr. Faisal H. Farooqui, Director of Franchising

Number of Franchised Units: 33
Number of Company-Owned Units: 4
Number of Total Operating Units: 37

In Business Since: 1986   **Franchising Since:** 1986

Description of Operation: Double drive-thru hamburgers, fries and drinks, specializing in $.99 deluxe burgers in 30 seconds, any way the customer wants. Delicious, seasoned burgers.

Equity Capital Needed: $60,000 - $80,000

Franchise Fee: $10,000

Royalty Fee: 4%

Financial Assistance: None.

Managerial Assistance: We provide a 2-week operations and management training program in corporate stores. We assist with site selection, manuals, national purchasing, new product information and methods of implementing, and restaurant visits to evaluate operations.

Training Provided: 2 weeks of rigorous operations training are provided in order to teach all the positions in the restaurant.

Information Submitted: March 1994

SIRLOIN STOCKADE: BUFFET - STEAKS - BAKERY
2908 N. Plum St.
Hutchinson, KS 67502
Telephone: (316) 669-9372
Fax: (316) 669-0531
Ms. Judy Froese, Director of Franchise Development

Number of Franchised Units: 74
Number of Company-Owned Units: 12
Number of Total Operating Units: 86

In Business Since: 1984   **Franchising Since:** 1984

Description of Operation: Sirloin Stockade restaurants feature top-quality steaks, chicken and fish entrees. A scatter-bar includes a deli/salad bar, a hot buffet and a dessert bar, at family prices. Restaurant facilities are free-standing buildings of 8,700 - 10,000 square feet, seating 300 - 400 people. A minimum of 60,000 square feet of land is required.

Equity Capital Needed: $200,000 - $250,000

Franchise Fee: $15,000

Royalty Fee: 3%

Financial Assistance: The franchisee must obtain financing through his/her personal resources.

Managerial Assistance: In addition to pre-opening assistance, SSI provides on-going training, education and assistance during the lifetime of the franchise agreement. Regular visits by SSI operation field consultants offer assistance in solving field problems, conducting quality control surveys and evaluating store operations. Franchisees are informed of new developments in the Company and the industry, as well as techniques to improve productivity and profitability. A system-wide marketing program is administered.

Training Provided: A comprehensive, 12-week training program in all phases of the operation is provided for store management at a Company training facility. The franchisee receives a complete set of confidential operations manuals, including recipes and food procedures, employee training, marketing and equipment manuals.

Information Submitted: March 1994

SIZZLER RESTAURANTS INTERNATIONAL
12655 W. Jefferson Blvd.
Los Angeles, CA 90066
Telephone: (310) 827-2300
Fax: (310) 822-5786
Mr. James S. McGinnis, Vice President of Franchise Development

Number of Franchised Units: 406
Number of Company-Owned Units: 275
Number of Total Operating Units: 681

In Business Since: 1959   **Franchising Since:** 1968

Description of Operation: Casual, family-style restaurant, specializing in steak, seafood and salads.

Equity Capital Needed: $1,500,000

Franchise Fee: $30,000

Royalty Fee: 4.5%

Financial Assistance: None.

Managerial Assistance: We provide manuals, seminars, field representatives, newsletters, grand openings, local marketing reps, co-ops and promotion kits.

Training Provided: 10 weeks in a certified training store, plus classroom instruction.

Information Submitted: March 1994

SKOLNIKS BAGEL BAKERY RESTAURANT
100 N. Broadway, # 2800
Oklahoma City, OK 73102
Telephone: (800) 820-0155 (405) 235-6124
Fax: (405) 232-2030
Mr. Roy S. Lemaire, Vice President of Development

Number of Franchised Units: 11
Number of Company-Owned Units: 15
Number of Total Operating Units: 26

In Business Since: 1981   **Franchising Since:** 1988

Description of Operation: Fast-food restaurant, featuring fresh-baked bagels and deli-style bagel sandwiches.

Equity Capital Needed: $75,000 - $90,000

Franchise Fee: $25,000

Royalty Fee: 4%

Financial Assistance: There is no financial assistance offered by Skolniks at this time.

Managerial Assistance: New franchisees are provided pre-opening assistance in the areas of site selection, lease negotiation and store design. An opening crew is provided and on-going operational unit visits take place on a regular basis.

Training Provided: We provide a comprehensive, 4-week training program in a designated Company-owned unit.

Information Submitted: November 1993

SMITTY'S
501 18th Ave. SW, # 600
Calgary, AB T2S 0C7 CAN
Telephone: (403) 229-3838
Fax: (403) 229-3899
Mr. Walter Chan, President

Number of Franchised Units: 93
Number of Company-Owned Units: 17
Number of Total Operating Units: 110

In Business Since: 1959   **Franchising Since:** 1960

Description of Operation: Family restaurant operator and franchisor for over 30 years in Canada and Hawaii. Concept originated as a pancake house and has developed into a full-menu, complementing breakfast, lunch and evening dining. Franchisee committees assist in design and implementation of menu and marketing programs.

Equity Capital Needed: $100,000 - $150,000

Franchise Fee: $35,000

Royalty Fee: 5%

Financial Assistance: Franchisee financing program is in place with a major chartered bank. This program permits lending at a higher debt-to-equity ratio.

Managerial Assistance: We provide an extensive 3-week training program in all aspects of running a restaurant. Restaurant opening assistance and on-going assistance is available.

Training Provided: In-depth food handling and preparation, front of the house operations, accounting, management, human resource, marketing, inventory and food cost control.

Information Submitted: December 1993

SNEAKY PETE'S HOT DOGS
1905 Indian Lake Dr.
Birmingham, AL 35244
Telephone: (404) 993-5393
Fax: (404) 992-9333
Mr. Tony Bastio, Franchise Sales Manager

Number of Franchised Units: 35
Number of Company-Owned Units: 1
Number of Total Operating Units: 36

In Business Since: 1966   **Franchising Since:** 1972

Description of Operation: Fast-food restaurant, specializing in hot dogs and featuring our own secret sauces. We also serve hamburgers, specialty sandwiches and breakfast. Great food at reasonable prices!

Equity Capital Needed: $50,000 - $150,000

Franchise Fee: $17,500

Royalty Fee: 4%

Financial Assistance: We will assist qualified candidates in securing bank loans.

Managerial Assistance: We assist in site selection, store design, management systems, personnel assistance, purchases of kitchen equipment and set-up with food distribution.

Training Provided: Our training is very comprehensive and covers all aspects of operations.

Information Submitted: December 1993

SOBIK'S SUBS
807 S. Orlando Ave., # T
Winter Park, FL 32789
Telephone: (407) 645-5007
Fax: (407) 647-2502
Mr. Norn Kaufman, Franchise Consultant

Number of Franchised Units: 41
Number of Company-Owned Units: 0
Number of Total Operating Units: 41

In Business Since: 1969   **Franchising Since:** 1981

Description of Operation: Our primary business is submarine sandwiches. Shops also sell salads, spaghetti and soups. Both free-standing and shopping center locations are acceptable.

Equity Capital Needed: $25,000 - $100,000

Franchise Fee: $7,500

Royalty Fee: 4%

Financial Assistance: Commercial market, SBA, etc.

Managerial Assistance: We provide shop visits by employees of the franchisor on a frequent basis. Additional help is available at the request of the franchisee.

Training Provided: A 2-week (100 hours) program of in-shop, as well as classroom, training is conducted before shop opening. Follow-up assistance is available when requested by the franchisee.

Information Submitted: November 1993

SONIC DRIVE INS
120 Robert S. Kerr Ave.
Oklahoma City, OK 73102
Telephone: (800) 569-6656 (405) 232-4334
Fax: (405) 272-8298
Mr. Stanley S. Jeska, Vice President of Franchising

Number of Franchised Units: 1194
Number of Company-Owned Units: 145
Number of Total Operating Units: 1339

In Business Since: 1953   **Franchising Since:** 1959

Description of Operation: 50's concept, drive-in fast-food restaurant, serving hamburgers, hot dogs, french fries and onion rings.

Equity Capital Needed: $250,000 - $300,000

Franchise Fee: $15,000

Royalty Fee: 4%

Financial Assistance: Sonic has an affiliation with several major financing sources that are well established in the business community. Financing is available for real estate and equipment through these financial sources.

Managerial Assistance: Management school (1 week), videos, field representatives, etc.

Training Provided: Same as above.

Information Submitted: December 1993

SONNY'S REAL PIT BAR-B-Q
217 N. Westmonte Dr., # 3019
Altamonte Springs, FL 32714
Telephone: (407) 862-4444
Fax: (407) 862-8707
Mr. C. Michael Turner, Director of Franchise Services

Number of Franchised Units: 71
Number of Company-Owned Units: 8
Number of Total Operating Units: 79

In Business Since: 1968   **Franchising Since:** 1976

Description of Operation: Sonny's Real Pit Bar-B-Q was founded in Gainesville, FL, featuring choice cuts of beef, pork, chicken and ribs, smoked over a hardwood fire and served at a great value in a full-service, sit-down restaurant. While every store features waitress service, the speed of service approximates or equals that of many fast-food restaurants. A significant portion of the business is through a take-out/walk-up window, while a drive-thru window is an option. Sonny's restaurants also offer catering.

Equity Capital Needed: $234,500 - $1,335,000

Franchise Fee: $25,000

Royalty Fee: 2.5%

Financial Assistance: Introductions and assistance will be provided between SBA programs and certain independent sale and leaseback programs for franchise development.

Managerial Assistance: Each franchisee receives a package of operations, training and accounting materials to guide in management. Manual revisions are updated. Sonny's representatives visit restaurants offering advice on many aspects of the business. Periodic franchisee

meetings are held on various aspects of restaurant ownership. An advertising/sales promotion package is available. 1% of monthly revenue is paid into advertising fund that promotes Sonny's system. Corporate purchasing maintains quality control.

Training Provided: The franchisee or operating manager will be required to take 400 hours of on-the-job training in one of Sonny's corporate restaurants. In addition, the assistant manager or head cook will be required to take 150 hours of training in kitchen operations. In the beginning, Sonny's will provide a complete training guide and operations manual in order to maintain consistency within the system.

Information Submitted: December 1993

SPAD'S PIZZA
2420 E. Grand River, P. O. Box 239
Williamston, MI 48169
Telephone: (517) 655-3944
Fax: (517) 655-5567
Mr. Mark Tithof, Director of Marketing

Number of Franchised Units: 16
Number of Company-Owned Units: 1
Number of Total Operating Units: 17

In Business Since: 1991   **Franchising Since:** 1992

Description of Operation: Drive-thru pizza-by-the-slice.

Equity Capital Needed: $300,000 - $500,000

Franchise Fee: $15,000

Royalty Fee: 4%

Financial Assistance: Not available.

Managerial Assistance: We provide a 4-week training program.

Training Provided: We provide a 4-week training program.

Information Submitted: March 1994

SPAGHETTI SHOP, THE
7301 Ohms Ln., # 300
Edina, MN 55439
Telephone: (612) 831-8191
Fax: (612) 831-9293
Mr. Brian D. Lynch, Director of Franchising

Number of Franchised Units: 40
Number of Company-Owned Units: 1
Number of Total Operating Units: 41

In Business Since: 1985   **Franchising Since:** 1985

Description of Operation: We provide authentic, fresh-cooked Italian food, served quickly and inexpensively. We have low start-up and operating costs, allowing for tremendous potential. Food experience is not necessary, but highly recommended.

Equity Capital Needed: $75,000 - $300,000

Franchise Fee: $20,000

Royalty Fee: 4%

Financial Assistance: The Spaghetti Shop is providing financial assistance. We will put the financing sources in contact with the franchisee.

Managerial Assistance: The Spaghetti Shop will be present at the opening of the franchised restaurant. Our training team will train the newly-hired employees and insure that the restaurant is operationally fit prior to opening to the public.

Training Provided: The initial period of training is 3 weeks. This is made up of on-site (restaurant) training and classroom training in marketing, financial controls and planning.

Information Submitted: November 1993

SPOONER'S SNAPPY TOMATO PIZZA COMPANY
P. O. Box 336
Florence, KY 41022
Telephone: (606) 283-2770
Fax: (606) 283-2849
Mr. David Meenach, President

Number of Franchised Units: 29
Number of Company-Owned Units: 0
Number of Total Operating Units: 29

In Business Since: 1993   Franchising Since: 1993

Description of Operation: Spooner's Snappy Tomato Pizza Company is a delivery, dine-in and carry-out pizzeria that offers the highest-quality pizza available. Our menu also includes hoagies, salads and our award-winning "Ranch Pizza." As a Spooner's franchisee, you will take part in the preparation of dough and other products on a daily basis for maximum freshness, without paying over-inflated commissary prices. Franchise owners also enjoy multiple store buying power discounts.

Equity Capital Needed: $70,000

Franchise Fee: $15,000

Royalty Fee: 5% royalty, plus 2.25% advertising.

Financial Assistance: Financing is not available; however, we will assist in obtaining financing on equipment packages.

Managerial Assistance: Corporate representatives will assist in opening of the store.

Training Provided: A 4-week training program covers every aspect of the business, including actual time in stores getting hands-on experience.

Information Submitted: November 1993

ST-HUBERT BAR-B-Q
2 Place Laval, # 500
Laval, PQ H7N 5N6 CAN
Telephone: (514) 668-4500
Fax: (514) 668-9037
Mr. Jacques Guilbert, Franchising and Real Estate Director

Number of Franchised Units: 76
Number of Company-Owned Units: 18
Number of Total Operating Units: 94

In Business Since: 1951   Franchising Since: 1967

Description of Operation: Restaurants (dining rooms, counters and delivery) of spit-roasted chicken and ribs. Units are located mainly in the province of Quebec, but also Ontario and New Brunswick (Canada).

Equity Capital Needed: $200,000 - $350,000

Franchise Fee: $40,000 (Canadian).

Royalty Fee: 4%, plus 3% for national advertising.

Financial Assistance: None.

Managerial Assistance: Management and marketing advisors are responsible for 10 - 15 units, plus head office support for human resources, real estate, accounting, data and supply.

Training Provided: We provide a 7-week training session, partly in restaurants.

Information Submitted: January 1994

STEAK 'N SHAKE
36 S. Pennsylvania St., 500 Century
Indianapolis, IN 46204
Telephone: (317) 633-4100
Fax: (317) 633-4105
Mr. James E. Richmond, Vice President

Number of Franchised Units: 108
Number of Company-Owned Units: 19
Number of Total Operating Units: 127

In Business Since: 1934   Franchising Since: 1939

Description of Operation: Steak 'n Shake is a unique restaurant concept, serving quick-seared steak burgers, thin french fries, genuine chili and hand-dipped milk shakes. Steak 'n Shake offers full waitress service, with food served on china, as well as drive-thru and take-out service, in a casual environment reminiscent of the 50's.

Equity Capital Needed: $500,000 +

Franchise Fee: $30,000

Royalty Fee: 4%

Financial Assistance: None.

Managerial Assistance: Steak 'n Shake will provide an opening crew to assist with the opening of the new restaurant. Complete building plans and consultation during construction of the restaurant are provided.

Training Provided: All new franchise employees, including restaurant management personnel, are given a comprehensive, on-the-job training program, utilizing personal instructions, training videos and workbooks.

Information Submitted: March 1994

STEAK-OUT
8210 Stephanie Dr.
Huntsville, AL 35802
Telephone: (205) 883-2300
Fax: (205) 883-4300
Ms. Shannon Belew, Franchise Licensing Manager

Number of Franchised Units: 48
Number of Company-Owned Units: 4
Number of Total Operating Units: 52

In Business Since: 1986   Franchising Since: 1987

Description of Operation: Steak-Out specializes in the delivery and carry-out of steaks, burgers and chicken. Salads, sandwiches, baked potatoes and desserts round out the menu of this quality and customer-oriented concept.

Equity Capital Needed: $174,250 - $247,000

Franchise Fee: $21,500 (included in start-up estimate).

Royalty Fee: 4%, plus 2% advertising.

Financial Assistance: None available.

Managerial Assistance: Field training and support is provided on an on-going basis by a field consultant and the home office.

Training Provided: A 6-week training program is provided to franchisees and their operational managers. This program prepares them to run any facet of the business, with a good comprehension of the industry and how Steak-Out relates to it.

Information Submitted: January 1994

STRAW HAT PIZZA
6400 Village Pkwy.
Dublin, CA 94568
Telephone: (510) 829-1500
Fax: (510) 829-9533
Mr. Jack T. Wood, President/Chief Executive Officer

Number of Franchised Units: 94
Number of Company-Owned Units: 0
Number of Total Operating Units: 94

In Business Since: 1987   Franchising Since: 1987

Description of Operation: Pizza restaurant.

Equity Capital Needed: $90,000 - $462,000

Franchise Fee: $10,000

Royalty Fee: 1.75%

Financial Assistance: None available.

Managerial Assistance: Included as part of our 4-week training program.

Training Provided: A 4-week training program is provided to all new franchisees. Follow-up visits by Regional VP (approximately 6 per year), monthly calendars from cooperative office, regional marketing meetings (twice per year) and annual member's convention.

Information Submitted: January 1994

STUFT PIZZA
1040 Calle Cordillera, # 103
San Clemente, CA 92673
Telephone: (714) 361-2522
Fax: (714) 361-2501
Mr. Jack Bertram, President

Number of Franchised Units: 32
Number of Company-Owned Units: 3
Number of Total Operating Units: 35

In Business Since: 1976   **Franchising Since:** 1985

Description of Operation: Award-winning pizza - from take-out to restaurant.

Equity Capital Needed: $100,000 - $300,000

Franchise Fee: $25,000

Royalty Fee: 3%

Financial Assistance: No Company financing is available.

Managerial Assistance: Training and follow-up meetings.

Training Provided: Data not available.

Information Submitted: November 1993

SUB STATION II
425 N. Main St., P. O. Drawer 2260
Sumter, SC 29150
Telephone: (803) 773-4711
Fax: (803) 775-2220
Ms. Susan H. Vaden, Vice President

Number of Franchised Units: 93
Number of Company-Owned Units: 3
Number of Total Operating Units: 96

In Business Since: 1975   **Franchising Since:** 1976

Description of Operation: Sub Station II is one of the fastest-growing submarine sandwich franchises in the country today. Our sandwich shops offer a variety of over 25 submarine sandwiches. We have developed an efficient method of preparing each sandwich to the customer's specifications. Emphasis is on high-quality food and cleanliness. No experience is necessary. We provide our franchisees with a thorough training program, including an operations manual, site selection, lease negotiations, store design and layout, etc.

Equity Capital Needed: $50,000 - $75,000

Franchise Fee: $10,500

Royalty Fee: 4%

Financial Assistance: Indirect financing is available through a third party.

Managerial Assistance: Our training program provides you with the systems, knowledge, know-how, support and support materials to get your business off to a successful running start. Our support continues with regular store visits, regional meetings, a national convention and regular newsletters. On-going help is as close as your telephone.

Training Provided: The franchisee is provided 1 week of intensive training at our corporate-owned location and 1 week at the franchisee's individual store location.

Information Submitted: November 1993

SUBMARINA SUBS AND SANDWICHES
12396 World Trade Dr., # 214
San Diego, CA 92128
Telephone: (619) 576-0155
Fax: (619) 576-0478
Mr. Patrick J. Rea, Director of Operations

Number of Franchised Units: 15
Number of Company-Owned Units: 0
Number of Total Operating Units: 15

In Business Since: 1977   **Franchising Since:** 1988

Description of Operation: A high-quality submarine sandwich shop. We also serve deli sandwiches, soup, garden salads and dessert items. All sandwiches are prepared in front of the customer.

Equity Capital Needed: $109,500 total opening cost.

Franchise Fee: $12,000

Royalty Fee: 6%

Financial Assistance: No financing is provided by Submarina; however, we can introduce franchisees to sources of financing who have worked with us in the past.

Managerial Assistance: Franchisees spend 2 weeks learning operations and management prior to opening. Their employees are trained in an operating Submarina prior to opening also. Then a Submarina representative will be at the store from opening to closing for the first 10 days of business.

Training Provided: Same as above.

Information Submitted: December 1993

SUBWAY
325 Bic Dr.
Milford, CT 06460
Telephone: (800) 888-4848 (203) 877-4281
Fax: (203) 876-6688
Mr. Donald Fertman, Director of Franchise Sales

Number of Franchised Units: 8191
Number of Company-Owned Units: 1
Number of Total Operating Units: 8192

In Business Since: 1965   **Franchising Since:** 1974

Description of Operation: World's largest submarine sandwich and salad chain. Open in all 50 states and 15 countries. Rated the #1 franchise five times by Entrepreneur Magazine. National TV advertising.

Equity Capital Needed: $48,900 - $90,700

Franchise Fee: $10,000

Royalty Fee: 8%

Financial Assistance: Equipment leasing is available for qualified franchisees.

Managerial Assistance: Subway provides field assistance in site selection, lease negotiations and opening week, plus a monthly unit inspection and evaluation.

Training Provided: An intensive 2-week training program covers the fundamentals of establishing and operating a Subway store. The training takes place in the classroom and in an actual Subway unit.

Information Submitted: November 1993

TACO CASA
P. O. Box 4542
Topeka, KS 66604
Telephone: (913) 267-2548
Fax: (913) 267-2652
Mr. James F. Reiter, President

Number of Franchised Units: 20
Number of Company-Owned Units: 1
Number of Total Operating Units: 21

In Business Since: 1963   **Franchising Since:** 1976

Description of Operation: Fast-food Mexican restaurants. Extensive menu, offering a wide variety of items from $.59 - $3.50.

Equity Capital Needed: $50,000 - $150,000

Franchise Fee: $15,000

Royalty Fee: 4%

Financial Assistance: No direct financial assistance is provided. Assistance in providing lending sources.

Managerial Assistance: We provide site inspections, hotline assistance available at all times, seminars, training programs, operations manuals, headquarters staff at site with 10 days' notice, newsletter and legal updates.

Training Provided: 2 weeks of training at headquarters is provided.

Information Submitted: November 1993

TACO GRANDE
P. O. Box 780066
Wichita, KS 67278
Telephone: (316) 744-0200
Fax: (316) 744-0299
Mr. John G. Wylie, President

Number of Franchised Units: 14
Number of Company-Owned Units: 10
Number of Total Operating Units: 24

In Business Since: 1960   **Franchising Since:** 1966

Description of Operation: Taco Grande offers a limited-menu Mexican restaurant, featuring drive-thru service. Our recipes are authentic Mexican recipes. We have been in successful operation for over 34 years. We offer excellent products, training and a cost-efficient and labor-saving building design.

Equity Capital Needed: $45,000 cash minimum. Total investment of $250,000 - $450,000.

Franchise Fee: $20,000

Royalty Fee: 3%

Financial Assistance: None is available at this time.

Managerial Assistance: We provide headquarters and on-site training, manuals, a monthly newsletter, Company-wide marketing fund provides POP materials, radio and TV ads, kids premiums, suggested reader board specials, etc.

Training Provided: We offer 3 - 4 weeks of training at a Company store in Wichita, KS, operations and training manuals and up to 2 weeks of on-site training at the store opening.

Information Submitted: March 1994

TACO MAKER, THE
P. O. Box 9519
Ogden, UT 84401
Telephone: (801) 621-7486
Fax: (801) 621-0139
Mr. Gil L. Craig, Sales

Number of Franchised Units: 80
Number of Company-Owned Units: 0
Number of Total Operating Units: 80

In Business Since: 1978   **Franchising Since:** 1978

Description of Operation: Mexican fast-food franchise, available in both single outlet, multi-outlet and master license with a variety of site options, including free-standing, mall, kiosk, double drive-thru and cart.

Equity Capital Needed: $75,000 - $100,000

Franchise Fee: $22,500

Royalty Fee: 5%

Financial Assistance: The franchisee obtains his/her own financing package.

Managerial Assistance: We help with the negotiation of the lease after assistance with site selection. Operations manuals and on-going marketing through national co-operative are available.

Training Provided: 30 days of extensive training in operations, personnel management and accounting procedures at corporate office. On-site training is provided to new owners by corporate trainers during opening period.

Information Submitted: January 1994

TACO MAYO
10405 Greenbriar Pl., # B
Oklahoma City, OK 73159
Telephone: (405) 691-8226
Fax: (405) 691-2572
Mr. Kurt W. Dinnes, Vice President

Number of Franchised Units: 65
Number of Company-Owned Units: 13
Number of Total Operating Units: 78

In Business Since: 1978   **Franchising Since:** 1980

Description of Operation: Taco Mayo restaurants are quick-service restaurants, specializing in Mexican-style food. All restaurants feature a uniform limited menu. The restaurants are primarily free-standing facilities with drive-thru and inside dining service. The restaurants produce a high-quality, large portion product, fast, at a very affordable pricing structure and in a clean and friendly atmosphere.

Equity Capital Needed: $50,000 - $99,000

Franchise Fee: $12,500

Royalty Fee: 3.5%

Financial Assistance: We offer assistance with business plan packages for presentation to lending institutions. Taco Mayo Franchise Systems does not provide any monetary assistance to new franchisees at the present time.

Managerial Assistance: The training programs cover initial training and continued education for crew members, shift leaders, assistant managers, managers and supervisors. In addition, we hold 2 educational conferences a year.

Training Provided: A 5-week training program includes a comprehensive 3-week training course conducted in store and in classroom by our certified franchise and management trainers, as well as 2 weeks of training assistance during the opening of the new franchise.

Information Submitted: March 1994

TACOTIME
3880 W. 11th Ave.
Eugene, OR 97402
Telephone: (800) 547-8907 (503) 687-8222
Fax: (503) 343-5208
Mr. Jim Thomas, Senior Vice President - Franchise Development

Number of Franchised Units: 295
Number of Company-Owned Units: 1
Number of Total Operating Units: 296

In Business Since: 1959   **Franchising Since:** 1961

Description of Operation: Mexican fast-food restaurant chain.

Equity Capital Needed: $300,000

Franchise Fee: $18,000 - first unit; $10,000 second + unit.

Royalty Fee: 5%

Financial Assistance: No direct financial assistance, but both the Money Store and Phoenix Leasing are actively supporting our franchising program.

Managerial Assistance: Franchisees are encouraged to send a person(s) to the TacoTime training class. This class is for management to learn, in a classroom setting, the theories of managing a TacoTime restaurant. Managerial assistance by a franchise consultant also takes place during the new opening and after the unit has been opened.

Training Provided: Training consists of Phase 1, which involves working in a facility similar to the one being opened. Operations are taught with an emphasis on sanitation and product quality. Phase 2 is taught in a classroom setting and is a basic small business management course lasting about 2 weeks. On-going training through manuals, videos and seminars is provided to keep each unit informed of events, methods and updates to the system. On-site training is provided during the opening process by experienced personnel.

Information Submitted: December 1993

TASTEE-FREEZ INTERNATIONAL
48380 Van Dyke, P. O. Box 180162
Utica, MI 48318
Telephone: (810) 739-5520
Fax: (810) 739-8351
Mr. Roger Johnson, Franchise Development

Number of Franchised Units: 301
Number of Company-Owned Units: 0
Number of Total Operating Units: 301

In Business Since: 1950   **Franchising Since:** 1950

Description of Operation: Fast food, including soft-serve ice cream and desserts. Plans available for free-standing building/food court/seasonal stores considered.

Equity Capital Needed: $35,000 - $65,000

Franchise Fee: $10,000

Royalty Fee: 4%

Financial Assistance: Third party to qualified persons.

Managerial Assistance: We provide on-going field support, marketing support, product development, area meetings, equipment advisor and store lay-out assistance.

Training Provided: Training consists of 2 weeks at the corporate office - total operation and business training given.

Information Submitted: January 1994

TASTY TACOS
1420 E. Grand Ave.
Des Moines, IA 50316
Telephone: (515) 262-3940
Fax: (515) 262-9821
Mr. Richard Mosqueda, President

Number of Franchised Units: 1
Number of Company-Owned Units: 5
Number of Total Operating Units: 6

In Business Since: 1961   **Franchising Since:** 1992

Description of Operation: Quick-service restaurant.

Equity Capital Needed: $30,000 - $45,000

Franchise Fee: $7,500

Royalty Fee: 4%

Financial Assistance: We are working with an equipment leasing company.

Managerial Assistance: We provide on-site assistance and on-going phone consultation.

Training Provided: We offer 1 month of training at a Company-owned restaurant and 2 weeks of on-site assistance.

Information Submitted: January 1994

TEXAS LOOSEY'S CHILI PARLOR & SALOON
P. O. Box 1697
Temecula, CA 92590
Telephone: (909) 677-3345
Fax: (909) 698-6643
Mr. Ron Walton, President

Number of Franchised Units: 2
Number of Company-Owned Units: 3
Number of Total Operating Units: 5

In Business Since: 1982   **Franchising Since:** 1987

Description of Operation: Sit-down dinner house and lounge, featuring ribs, steaks, chicken, burgers and Southwest specialties.

Equity Capital Needed: $450,000 - $500,000

Franchise Fee: $30,000

Royalty Fee: 5%

Financial Assistance: Possible SBA financing with 35% franchisee capital.

Managerial Assistance: On-going supervision after 5 weeks of training for 3 person management team at Company training center in California.

Training Provided: We provide 5 weeks of hands-on training, covering all aspects of the day-to-day operation, including menu management, accounting and employee training.

Information Submitted: January 1994

THIS IS IT! BAR-B-Q & SEAFOOD
4405 Mall Blvd., # 320
Union City, GA 30291
Telephone: (404) 964-1668
Fax: (404) 964-8539
Ms. Kimberly Crowder, Marketing Representative

Number of Franchised Units: 5
Number of Company-Owned Units: 3
Number of Total Operating Units: 8

In Business Since: 1983   **Franchising Since:** 1992

Description of Operation: This Is It! specializes in barbecue, seafood and hot buffalo wings, all prepared in our own private-label barbecue sauces and dry mixes and batters. This Is It! also features fresh vegetables and homemade desserts. We offer the freshest products, made daily in the store, at an affordable price.

Equity Capital Needed: $100,000 - $110,000

Franchise Fee: $12,500

Royalty Fee: $350 per week.

Financial Assistance: The franchisor may provide financing for an ongoing store, depending on credit approval and assets. Franchisor will assist franchise owner in locating outside financing, i.e. SBA.

Managerial Assistance: A pre-opening and daily operations manual is provided, covering all aspects of the operation. We offer newsletters, Company meetings and on-going marketing support.

Training Provided: Franchisees will undergo an extensive 3-week training period at a field location, as well as 1 week of training in their new unit.

Information Submitted: November 1993

THUNDERCLOUD SUBS
1102 W. 6th St.
Austin, TX 78703
Telephone: (512) 479-8805
Fax: (512) 479-8806
Mr. Rip Rowan, Franchise Director

Number of Franchised Units: 26
Number of Company-Owned Units: 6
Number of Total Operating Units: 32

In Business Since: 1975 **Franchising Since:** 1981

Description of Operation: Thundercloud prepares fresh submarine sandwiches, salads and soups. The concept is based on a combination of unique character and fast, healthy food. The units occupy 800 - 1,200 square feet in retail strip centers and free-standing sites. Full seating, limited seating, drive-thru or drive-thru only.

Equity Capital Needed: $50,000 - $100,000

Franchise Fee: $10,000

Royalty Fee: 4%

Financial Assistance: Not available.

Managerial Assistance: We provide hands-on, in-store assistance during the initial operating period, as well as periodic evaluations and in-store assistance, as required.

Training Provided: Training is tailored to the needs of the franchisee. Training is conducted in advance of opening in a Company-owned store and on-site following opening.

Information Submitted: January 1994

TIPPY'S TACO HOUSE
Box 665
Winnsboro, TX 75494
Telephone: (903) 629-7800
Fax: (903) 342-6001
Mr. W. L. "Jack" Locklier, Chief Executive Officer

Number of Franchised Units: 17
Number of Company-Owned Units: 0
Number of Total Operating Units: 17

In Business Since: 1958 **Franchising Since:** 1968

Description of Operation: Complete line of Tex-Mex food. Orders to be served, drive-thru and take-out. Some units deliver.

Equity Capital Needed: $30,000

Franchise Fee: $25,000

Royalty Fee: 3%

Financial Assistance: Advice on funding.

Managerial Assistance: We provide training, operations manual, opening assistance and on-going contact through telephone, letter or visits.

Training Provided: Training in an operating unit. Home office personnel open the unit with the franchisee and/or qualified field personnel.

Information Submitted: November 1993

TOBY'S GOODEATS
83 Bloor St. W., 2nd Fl.
Toronto, ON M5S 1M1 CAN
Telephone: (416) 927-0323
Fax: (416) 927-7678
Mr. Jody Ortved, Managing Partner

Number of Franchised Units: 0
Number of Company-Owned Units: 11
Number of Total Operating Units: 11

In Business Since: 1973 **Franchising Since:** 1990

Description of Operation: A chain of 11 electric 50's-flavor gourmet hamburger joints, which also serve salads, chicken, sandwiches, soups and desserts. Licensed for beer and wine. Decor is a comfortable combination of formica tables, funky posters, cute kitsch and music to bring back memories.

Equity Capital Needed: $350,000 - $550,000

Franchise Fee: $45,000

Royalty Fee: 5%, plus 2% advertising.

Financial Assistance: We can suggest possible sources for financing.

Managerial Assistance: Toby's will provide such supervision, assistance and consultation as Toby's deems necessary and advisable in the circumstances. Toby's representatives will visit the franchise on a regular basis to review progress and to provide advice and assistance.

Training Provided: Toby's will provide an extensive training program of 10 weeks at one of their corporate stores, covering all aspects of successful store operations, including food preparation procedures, operating policies, selling and merchandising and management control.

Information Submitted: December 1993

TOGO'S EATERY
900 E. Campbell Ave., # 1
Campbell, CA 95008
Telephone: (800) 698-6467 (408) 377-1754
Fax: (408) 377-4130
Ms. Valerie Konomos, Franchise Co-ordinator

Number of Franchised Units: 150
Number of Company-Owned Units: 9
Number of Total Operating Units: 159

In Business Since: 1977 **Franchising Since:** 1977

Description of Operation: Fast-food sandwiches.

Equity Capital Needed: $140,000 - $180,000

Franchise Fee: $12,500 - $35,000

Royalty Fee: 5%

Financial Assistance: None.

Managerial Assistance: We provide purchasing, cost control, sanitation, product development, promotion and general assistance for the life of the franchise.

Training Provided: We offer 2 weeks of on-site training, with periodic follow-up.

Information Submitted: March 1994

TOM'S HOUSE OF PIZZA
7730 Macleod Tr. S.
Calgary, AB T2H 0L9 CAN
Telephone: (403) 252-0111
Mr. John H. Windle, Vice President

Number of Franchised Units: 1
Number of Company-Owned Units: 2
Number of Total Operating Units: 3

In Business Since: 1963 **Franchising Since:** 1963

Description of Operation: Restaurant and lounge operation, specializing in thin-crust pizza. Family atmosphere.

Equity Capital Needed: $130,000

Franchise Fee: $5,000

Royalty Fee: $500 per month.

Financial Assistance: Assistance is available with either the head company, participating in ownership for first 3 years, or as a straight loan. 25% down payment.

Managerial Assistance: Data not available.

Training Provided: Training is provided at the head office location for about 4 - 6 weeks.

Information Submitted: January 1994

TONY ROMA'S - A PLACE FOR RIBS
10,000 North Central Expy., # 900
Dallas, TX 75231

Telephone: (214) 891-7600
Fax: (214) 696-6321
Mr. Larry D. Zimmerman, Vice President - Restaurant Development

Number of Franchised Units: 130
Number of Company-Owned Units: 28
Number of Total Operating Units: 158

In Business Since: 1972   **Franchising Since:** 1978

Description of Operation: Full-service restaurant with alcoholic beverages, specializing in ribs and chicken.

Equity Capital Needed: $300,000 liquid; $800,000 estimated total investment.

Franchise Fee: $50,000

Royalty Fee: 4%

Financial Assistance: Referrals only to those firms that have expressed an interest in providing capital to franchisees.

Managerial Assistance: We provide a training program for all managers. Manuals for operations, purchasing, marketing, recipes, building plans, visits to units and opening team are also provided.

Training Provided: Training is for 3 or more unit managers and lasts 4 - 6 weeks, depending on experience. Training manuals. Opening teams sent to units prior to openings.

Information Submitted: November 1993

TUBBY'S SUB SHOPS
6029 East 14 Mile Rd.
Sterling Heights, MI 48312
Telephone: (800) 752-0644 (313) 978-8829
Fax: (313) 977-8083
Ms. Amy B. Jones, Vice President of Franchise Development

Number of Franchised Units: 57
Number of Company-Owned Units: 3
Number of Total Operating Units: 60

In Business Since: 1968   **Franchising Since:** 1978

Description of Operation: Specialty submarine sandwich shop, featuring grilled sandwiches, soups, salads and ice cream.

Equity Capital Needed: $45,000 - $100,000

Franchise Fee: $15,000

Royalty Fee: 4%

Financial Assistance: We have relationships with third-party financiers.

Managerial Assistance: Every aspect of managing your business is addressed, from marketing to customer service classes to "how to structure your company and how to manage it financially." We also assist in site selection, lease negotiations and provide construction drawings from our engineers. Complete equipment packages are available from subsidiary company, Subline, Inc. On-going advertising and local store marketing support is given, along with frequent visits to your site from our experts. Complete grand opening package.

Training Provided: We provide a comprehensive 4-week training program - both in-store and classroom sessions. Every facet of your business is covered. Additional on-site assistance is given just prior to opening and during your first few weeks of operation.

Information Submitted: November 1993

UNCLE TONY'S PIZZA & PASTA RESTAURANTS
1800 Post Rd., 27 Airport Plaza
Warwick, RI 02886
Telephone: (401) 738-1321
Fax: (401) 732-1936
Mr. Edward A. Carosi, President

Number of Franchised Units: 6
Number of Company-Owned Units: 1
Number of Total Operating Units: 7

In Business Since: 1970   **Franchising Since:** 1976

Description of Operation: 150 - 180 seat, family-style Italian-theme restaurants, specializing in old world pizza, serving beer, wine and various cocktails.

Equity Capital Needed: $300,000

Franchise Fee: $35,000

Royalty Fee: 4%

Financial Assistance: We assist in loan packaging, SBA presentation and restaurant supply house financing.

Managerial Assistance: We provide every phase of management assistance, including on-site Company staff for an indefinite period of time.

Training Provided: We offer 12 weeks of on-the-job and classroom training.

Information Submitted: January 1994

WALLYBURGER EXPRESS DRIVE-THRU
4305 N. State Line Ave.
Texarkana, TX 75503
Telephone: (903) 784-1503 (903) 793-8307
Mr. Walter A. Hughes, Executive VP Operations/Development

Number of Franchised Units: 1
Number of Company-Owned Units: 1
Number of Total Operating Units: 2

In Business Since: 1990   **Franchising Since:** 1992

Description of Operation: Wallyburger sells flamebroiled hamburgers, cheeseburgers, bacon cheeseburgers, chicken sandwiches, fish sandwiches, BLT's and a secret recipe cutlet-on-a-bun sandwich. Spicy fries, shakes, apple sticks, hot dogs and chili. Wallyburger offers 5 value meals for customers to choose from.

Equity Capital Needed: $40,000 - $60,000

Franchise Fee: $7,500

Royalty Fee: 4%

Financial Assistance: Wallyburger will assist the franchisee in preparing an SBA loan package. Either 504 or 7A program or both together. Proper structure of the loan is essential for approval. Wallyburger can help speed this process, thus saving time and money.

Managerial Assistance: The franchisee will receive continued assistance and support from Wallyburger by a representative that will be assigned to the franchisee. Wallyburger will set up initial office management procedures. We will also provide all forms used by Wally Burger.

Training Provided: The store owner and manager will receive an intensive 2-week on-the-job training program, covering many areas, such as customer service process, kitchen, production system, facilities management and maintenance, personnel management, management fundamentals of restaurant operations, selecting food vendors and other suppliers, accounting and reporting requirements, office management procedures and other functions, as needed.

Information Submitted: January 1994

WARD'S RESTAURANTS
7 Professional Pkwy., # 103
Hattiesburg, MS 39402
Telephone: (800) 748-9273 (601) 584-9273
Fax: (601) 268-9273
Mr. Kenneth R. Hrdlica, President

Number of Franchised Units: 36
Number of Company-Owned Units: 10
Number of Total Operating Units: 46

In Business Since: 1978   **Franchising Since:** 1981

Description of Operation: Fast-food restaurant chain, featuring chili-dogs, chili-burgers and homemade root beer served in frosted mugs. The menu also includes a complete breakfast line, featuring homemade buttermilk biscuits and a variety of sandwiches. Restaurants have inside seating, as well as drive-thru service.

Equity Capital Needed: $90,000 - $120,000

Franchise Fee: $15,000

Royalty Fee: 3% - 5%

Financial Assistance: None available.

Managerial Assistance: The franchisor provides site selection, building, equipment, recruiting and training assistance prior to opening. Special opening support crew is provided during opening week. After opening, a franchise consultant makes periodic contacts and visits to the store.

Training Provided: A 4-week training program is provided for the owner and manager at Company headquarters. The owner must pay for transportation and living expenses while attending the training program.

Information Submitted: November 1993

WENDY'S INTERNATIONAL
P. O. Box 256
Dublin, OH 43017
Telephone: (614) 764-3094
Fax: (614) 764-6894
Ms. Barbara Langsdon, Director of Franchise Administration

Number of Franchised Units: 2644
Number of Company-Owned Units: 1129
Number of Total Operating Units: 3773

In Business Since: 1969   **Franchising Since:** 1971

Description of Operation: Wendy's is a quick-service hamburger restaurant.

Equity Capital Needed: $250,000

Franchise Fee: $30,000

Royalty Fee: 4%

Financial Assistance: None.

Managerial Assistance: We offer a 2-day corporate business orientation in conjunction with on-going regional support.

Training Provided: We provide 16 weeks of in-store and classroom training, conducted in a certified training store.

Information Submitted: January 1994

WESTERN SIZZLIN
P. O. Box 291509
Nashville, TN 37229
Telephone: (800) 247-8325 (615) 251-0023
Fax: (615) 251-3115
Mr. Jerry Miner

Number of Franchised Units: 315
Number of Company-Owned Units: 1
Number of Total Operating Units: 316

In Business Since: 1962   **Franchising Since:** 1968

Description of Operation: Semi-cafeteria style family steak house.

Equity Capital Needed: $250,000 liquid assets and $750,000 total net worth.

Franchise Fee: $25,000

Royalty Fee: 2%

Financial Assistance: No direct financial assistance is provided.

Managerial Assistance: Regional management consultants visit the franchise restaurants on a frequent basis.

Training Provided: Training for new franchisees is an intensive 8-week training program, followed by a 1 week classroom course.

Information Submitted: March 1994

WESTERN STEER FAMILY STEAKHOUSE / WSMP
WSMP Dr., P. O. Box 399
Claremont, NC 28610
Telephone: (800) 438-9207 (704) 459-5374
Fax: (704) 459-5375
Mr. Kenneth L. Moser, Vice President of Franchising

Number of Franchised Units: 70
Number of Company-Owned Units: 19
Number of Total Operating Units: 89

In Business Since: 1967   **Franchising Since:** 1975

Description of Operation: Economy family steakhouse, serving steaks, chicken, seafood, buffet and a free bakery with all entrees.

Equity Capital Needed: $165,000 - $250,000

Franchise Fee: $25,000

Royalty Fee: 3%

Financial Assistance: None.

Managerial Assistance: We offer operational training, periodic seminars, pre-opening and on-site training, weekly mail-outs, manuals, supervisor visit every 6 - 8 weeks and more, if needed.

Training Provided: We provide 4 weeks of training for managers and assistant managers. 1 week of pre-opening and opening assistance, more often, if needed.

Information Submitted: November 1993

WIENERSCHNITZEL
4440 Von Karman Ave.
Newport Beach, CA 92692
Telephone: (800) 432-3316 (714) 752-5800
Fax: (714) 851-2618
Mr. Alan F. Gallup, Director of Franchise Sales

Number of Franchised Units: 208
Number of Company-Owned Units: 87
Number of Total Operating Units: 295

In Business Since: 1964   **Franchising Since:** 1965

Description of Operation: Fast-food, hot dog segment leader.

Equity Capital Needed: $60,000 - $100,000

Franchise Fee: $30,000

Royalty Fee: 5%

Financial Assistance: Data not available.

Managerial Assistance: We provide 7 weeks of in-store and classroom training, as well as on-going training in a classroom after ownership, field supervision, an operations manual, training aids and video tapes.

Training Provided: Data not available.

Information Submitted: January 1994

WINGS TO GO
1256 S. Little Creek Rd.
Dover, DE 19901
Telephone: (302) 734-5512
Fax: (302) 734-5812
Mr. James F. Tisack, Executive Vice President

Number of Franchised Units: 48
Number of Company-Owned Units: 2
Number of Total Operating Units: 50

In Business Since: 1987   **Franchising Since:** 1990

Description of Operation: Retail restaurants, specializing in authentic buffalo-style chicken wings.

Equity Capital Needed: $40,000 - $65,000

Franchise Fee: $15,000

Royalty Fee: 3%

Financial Assistance: We will help prepare business plans to submit to lending institutions to secure financing. Direct financing is not available from the corporation at this time.

Managerial Assistance: Training consists of 1 week at the home office or other corporate facility. 2 weeks of on-site, hands-on training, with monthly follow-up visits or contact with a regional manager. Complete training manuals, forms and advertising aids.

Training Provided: We offer 1 week of training in corporate store and 2 weeks of on-site training.

Information Submitted: November 1993

YAYA'S FLAME BROILED CHICKEN
521 S. Dort Hwy.
Flint, MI 48503
Telephone: (313) 235-6550
Fax: (313) 235-5210
Mr. John D. Chinonis, President

Number of Franchised Units: 20
Number of Company-Owned Units: 1
Number of Total Operating Units: 21

In Business Since: 1985   **Franchising Since:** 1988

Description of Operation: Flame-broiled chicken, marinated with Yaya's special blend of herbs and spices. Side dishes include baked beans, mashed potatoes, rice pilaf, cole slaw and potato salad. No fried or frozen products. We specialize in flavor and nutrition.

Equity Capital Needed: $200,000 - $250,000

Franchise Fee: $20,000

Royalty Fee: 4%

Financial Assistance: None.

Managerial Assistance: We provide periodic inspections with operational evaluation and financial review and recommendations.

Training Provided: Complete operational and management training is provided.

Information Submitted: November 1993

ZERO'S MR. SUBMARINE
2106 Pacific Ave.
Virginia Beach, VA 23451
Telephone: (800) 588-0782 (804) 425-8306
Fax: (804) 422-9157
Mr. Martin A. Palacios, President

Number of Franchised Units: 9
Number of Company-Owned Units: 11
Number of Total Operating Units: 20

In Business Since: 1967   **Franchising Since:** 1987

Description of Operation: Zero's Mr. Submarine is a fast-food, sit-down and to-go restaurant, serving Italian submarine sandwiches and pizzas.

Equity Capital Needed: $30,000 - $60,000

Franchise Fee: $7,500

Royalty Fee: 5%, plus 2% advertising.

Financial Assistance: Data not available.

Managerial Assistance: Data not available.

Training Provided: Extensive training is provided for franchisees and managers at the corporate headquarters and also at the franchised location.

Information Submitted: January 1994

ZUZU HANDMADE MEXICAN FOOD
2651 N. Harwood, # 200
Dallas, TX 75201
Telephone: (800) 824-8830 (214) 922-8226
Fax: (214) 720-1332
Ms. Nicole Walker, Franchise Co-ordinator

Number of Franchised Units: 6
Number of Company-Owned Units: 6
Number of Total Operating Units: 12

In Business Since: 1989   **Franchising Since:** 1992

Description of Operation: Quick-service restaurant, serving consistent, fresh, healthful, regional and handmade Mexican food in a modern, clean, convenient facility.

Equity Capital Needed: $130,000 - $245,000

Franchise Fee: $20,000

Royalty Fee: 4%

Financial Assistance: ZuZu does not provide direct financing, but will assist in acquiring financing.

Managerial Assistance: Fully-supervised certification training for general managers, kitchen manager or chef is provided at the corporate training center. State-of-the-art point-of-sales control equipment, plus the leading food service cost control inventory accounting package. As part of our commitment to the success of our franchisees, we offer friendly, knowledgeable field support for any operational issues or questions that management may have.

Training Provided: We offer a comprehensive 8-week training program in the Dallas, TX area. The training program covers restaurant operations, product preparation and presentation, customer service, equipment maintenance and sanitation, marketing, management theory application and communication skills.

Information Submitted: November 1993

RETAIL—NOT ELSEWHERE CLASSIFIED

#1 SELLERS
266 Elmwood Ave., # 287
Buffalo, NY 14222
Telephone: (905) 871-5668
Fax: (905) 871-4223
Mr. Blaine McGrath, President

Number of Franchised Units: 0
Number of Company-Owned Units: 0
Number of Total Operating Units: 0

In Business Since: 1994   **Franchising Since:** 1994

Description of Operation: The retail sale of top selling books, video tapes and pre-recorded audio products, including cassettes and compact discs, magazines, newspapers, seasonal calendars and home video game cartridges. Other related entertainment products may be introduced from time to time.

Equity Capital Needed: $60,000 - $150,000

Franchise Fee: $20,000

Royalty Fee: 5%

Financial Assistance: Yes.

Managerial Assistance: The franchise includes on-going support, as requested or required.

Training Provided: Each new franchisee receives operations manuals, in addition to having 1 week of training at an operating location, and the assistance of a representative of the franchisor's staff in the opening of the franchisee's store for up to 1 week.

Information Submitted: April 1994

. . . .IT STORE
122 Cambridge Ave.
Toronto, ON M4K 2L6 CAN
Telephone: (416) IT-STORE (416) 778-6288
Fax: (416) 778-6293
Ms. Faye LeRoy, Franchise Director

Number of Franchised Units: 34
Number of Company-Owned Units: 20
Number of Total Operating Units: 54

In Business Since: 1981   **Franchising Since:** 1982

Description of Operation: Sales of gifts, cards and novelty items.

Equity Capital Needed: $150,000

Franchise Fee: $25,000

Royalty Fee: 6%

Financial Assistance: Franchisees to arrange own financing.

Managerial Assistance: Services of supervisor for up to 1 week at opening. Semi-annual meetings. Regular visits to all locations to offer merchandising and sales assistance. On-going head office support.

Training Provided: Initial 2 days of training in Toronto, ON. Training manuals.

Information Submitted: March 1994

ACTION SPORTS PHOTOS
4526 NW 1st
Oklahoma City, OK 73127
Telephone: (405) 942-0770
Fax: (405) 942-0555
Mr. Kim Bostick, Marketing Director

Number of Franchised Units: 0
Number of Company-Owned Units: 1
Number of Total Operating Units: 1

In Business Since: 1985   **Franchising Since:** 1992

Description of Operation: Sports photography business. Production, promotion and marketing of specialty photographic products within a geographic territory. Products include group and individual athletic photographs in folders, plaques, buttons, magnets, trading cards, etc. 3 plans offered (Hometown, Metro and Major Metro). Not restricted to athletics.

Equity Capital Needed: $14,560 - $40,058

Franchise Fee: $9,000 - $13,650

Royalty Fee: 0%

Financial Assistance: None available.

Managerial Assistance: Detailed business plan. Order entry, completion, packaging and shipping of products.

Training Provided: A minimum 3 days of intensive training in marketing and photography. Follow-up training as needed to insure product uniformity.

Information Submitted: November 1993

ALTERATIONS EXPRESS
2710 Belmont Ave.
Youngstown, OH 44505
Telephone: (800) 221-1198 (216) 629-9464
Fax: (216) 629-9465
Mr. George Rondinelli, Vice President

Number of Franchised Units: 3
Number of Company-Owned Units: 3
Number of Total Operating Units: 6

In Business Since: 1990   **Franchising Since:** 1994

Description of Operation: Quality clothing alterations at reasonable prices and fast service.

Equity Capital Needed: Negotiable.

Franchise Fee: $5,000 - $10,000

Royalty Fee: 4%

Financial Assistance: Data not available.

Managerial Assistance: We have start-up manuals for a complete turn-key operation, as well as marketing and advertising manuals. Our management manuals include weekly production, weekly budgeting, supply ordering and goal setting, plus our on-going support.

Training Provided: We begin every market with a talent search. We provide guidelines for management and assist them with the evaluation of prospective employees.

Information Submitted: March 1994

ASHLEY AVERY'S COLLECTABLES
3304 LaBranch St.
Houston, TX 77004
Telephone: (800) 324-3485 (713) 529-0190
Fax: (713) 529-9270
Mr. Craig Anderson, Franchise Sales

Number of Franchised Units: 5
Number of Company-Owned Units: 0
Number of Total Operating Units: 5

In Business Since: 1991   **Franchising Since:** 1992

Description of Operation: Retail sale of gifts and collectables in regional malls.

Equity Capital Needed: $84,750 - $259,750

Franchise Fee: $20,000 - $30,000

Royalty Fee: 4%

Financial Assistance: None.

Managerial Assistance: Through customer newsletters, periodic training, continuous consultation, monthly inventory, sale review, yearly visits and continuous collectable research, we provide both a "Board of Directors" and advisor.

Training Provided: We provide in-store training in all areas from book-keeping to sales. Classroom training - including concept fundamentals of operation, sales training, product education, personnel management and bookkeeping procedures. Manuals.

Information Submitted: March 1994

BALLOONS AND BEARS
1801 NE 23 Ave., # D-2
Gainesville, FL 32609
Telephone: (800) 771-2327 (904) 378-0955
Fax: (904) 378-5230
Mr. Brad Daniel, President/Chief Executive Officer

Number of Franchised Units: 0
Number of Company-Owned Units: 4
Number of Total Operating Units: 4

In Business Since: 1989   **Franchising Since:** 1993

Description of Operation: Balloons, gift store and florist - like none other. We are #1 in our industry. A combination of balloons, gift baskets, flowers and singing telegrams make us unique. High profit margins and low overhead make us profitable.

Equity Capital Needed: $45,000 - $60,000

Franchise Fee: $19,500

Royalty Fee: 6%

Financial Assistance: Assistance in obtaining SBA or conventional loans. Our director of operations is president of a national bank and provides the insight into the financing process.

Managerial Assistance: 2 - 3 weeks of training at headquarters. One week on-site and on-going visits and support. Management effective seminars and T.Q.M.

Training Provided: 2 - 3 weeks of intense training includes all operations, bookkeeping, accounting, management and operations.

Information Submitted: November 1993

BESTSELLERS
1 Dundas Court, Box 37,Toronto Eaton
Toronto, ON M5G 1Z3 CAN
Telephone: (800) 361-3181 (416) 593-8857
Fax: (416) 975-8392
Ms. Mary Kalogirou, President

Number of Franchised Units: 24
Number of Company-Owned Units: 2
Number of Total Operating Units: 26

In Business Since: 1989   **Franchising Since:** 1991

Description of Operation: A specialty retail environment, selling the best in entertainment. Top 20 - 40 books, music, video, audio, classified by number, in a stunning 400 - 500 square foot store.

Equity Capital Needed: $60,000 - $120,000

Franchise Fee: $20,000

Royalty Fee: 5%

Financial Assistance: A bank introduction is provided. They have the file and are well acquainted with the Company. Franchisees must show they are credit-worthy.

Managerial Assistance: All aspects of leasing, design, construction, training and on-going support are provided.

Training Provided: We assume the potential franchisee knows nothing of retailing, product knowledge, accounting, marketing, merchandising or personnel activities. We provide extensive 2-week training program, supervision and on-going support.

Information Submitted: December 1993

BIKE LINE
1035 Andrew Dr.
West Chester, PA 19380
Telephone: (800) 537-2654 (215) 429-4370
Fax: (215) 429-4295
Mr. Howard Lowman, Franchise Recruiter

Number of Franchised Units: 28
Number of Company-Owned Units: 19
Number of Total Operating Units: 47

In Business Since: 1983   **Franchising Since:** 1991

Description of Operation: Retail sales and service of bicycle and fitness equipment.

Equity Capital Needed: $105,400 - $150,500

Franchise Fee: $24,500

Royalty Fee: 4%

Financial Assistance: We will assist with third-party financing.

Managerial Assistance: We assist with site location and lease negotiating. We also provide a turn-key store and will work closely with our contractors through the build-out. We provide a full training program, as well as on-going support, monthly newsletters and bi-monthly meetings.

Training Provided: 2 weeks of on-site training, covering all aspects of running a bike shop. 5 days of support during grand opening.

Information Submitted: November 1993

BOOK RACK
2715 E. Commercial Blvd.
Ft. Lauderdale, FL 33308
Telephone: (305) 771-4310
Mr. Fred M. Darnell, President

Number of Franchised Units: 234
Number of Company-Owned Units: 1
Number of Total Operating Units: 235

In Business Since: 1963   **Franchising Since:** 1963

Description of Operation: The selling and trading of used and new paperback books.

Equity Capital Needed: $18,000 - $35,000

Franchise Fee: $6,000

Royalty Fee: $75 per month.

Financial Assistance: No financial assistance is available.

Managerial Assistance: We offer on-going newsletters, an annual meeting and 24-hour store support.

Training Provided: All new franchisees train for 1 week or longer. All store owners are welcome to retrain at any time.

Information Submitted: March 1994

BUTTERFIELDS, ETC.
1040 Wm. Hilton Pkwy., Circle Bldg.
Hilton Head, SC 29928
Telephone: (803) 842-6000
Fax: (803) 842-6999
Mr. Jim Lunceford, President

Number of Franchised Units: 22
Number of Company-Owned Units: 0
Number of Total Operating Units: 22

In Business Since: 1979   **Franchising Since:** 1986

Description of Operation: Retail gourmet kitchen store, located in up-scale malls. Our merchandise mix includes high-quality cookware, a large assortment of kitchen gadgets, cookbooks, decorative ceramics, linens, cutlery and fresh-roasted gourmet coffee beans.

Equity Capital Needed: $130,000 - $185,000

Franchise Fee: $20,000

Royalty Fee: 5% - 4%, based on units.

Financial Assistance: We do not offer a financing plan, but we can offer suggestions and referrals to various sources of financing. We can assist you in preparing a business plan, along with pro formas for your banker, once you become a franchisee.

Managerial Assistance: The Butterfields Operations Manual contains procedures, policies and practices essential for each step of your business development. This confidential guide is a valuable reference and excellent tool for training new employees. You will receive periodic visits by our field representatives, who will consult with you and offer useful advice on all facets of your operation.

Training Provided: Butterfields provides you with extensive training before, during and after your grand opening. We teach you the operational and management techniques necessary to provide consistent, high-quality merchandising and customer service. We provide training in personnel development, buying, merchandising, advertising and inventory control.

Information Submitted: February 1994

CANDLEMAN
P. O. Box 731, 424 NW Third St.
Brainerd, MN 56401
Telephone: (800) 328-3453 (218) 829-0592
Fax: (218) 829-0929
Ms. Sara Wise, Vice President

Number of Franchised Units: 21
Number of Company-Owned Units: 1
Number of Total Operating Units: 22

In Business Since: 1991   Franchising Since: 1992

Description of Operation: Sale of retail specialty stores, located in regional shopping malls, offering the widest selection of candles and accessories anywhere.

Equity Capital Needed: $50,000 - $75,000

Franchise Fee: $25,000

Royalty Fee: 6%

Financial Assistance: Assistance in preparing loan presentations to third-party lenders, such as the SBA.

Managerial Assistance: Complete start-up assistance, beginning with financing, site location, lease and remodeling negotiation to training in an operating store, various manuals, videos, promotions, proprietary computerized operating system, on-site support, 800#, newsletters, monthly reports, new products and more.

Training Provided: Data not available.

Information Submitted: November 1993

CATHOLIC STORE
3441 S. Broadway
Englewood, CO 80110
Telephone: (800) 776-6979 (303) 762-8385
Mr. Richard Weigang, President

Number of Franchised Units: 0
Number of Company-Owned Units: 1
Number of Total Operating Units: 1

In Business Since: 1981   Franchising Since: 1993

Description of Operation: The Catholic Store sells Bibles, books and religious gifts to the Catholic/Christian market. Catholic Store is the first franchise specializing in serving the unique Catholic market niche. Our computerized system and management program will help a motivated individual serve the Catholic community with on-going help and support.

Equity Capital Needed: $100,000 - $180,000 (includes fee).

Franchise Fee: $15,500

Royalty Fee: 6%, plus 2% advertising.

Financial Assistance: Not at the present time.

Managerial Assistance: Catholic store provides support for all areas of franchise operations and management. Catholic Store desires franchisees who want assistance to develop and exercise leadership in providing the best in Catholic books and gifts.

Training Provided: Catholic Store provides an intensive 2-week training program at our home store and on-going support and assistance. Catholic Store is highly motivated to do all it can to help a franchisee be successful in serving Catholic market needs.

Information Submitted: March 1994

CD EXCHANGE
2830 Ramada Way, # 200
Green Bay, WI 54304
Telephone: (800) 562-8785 (414) 592-9660
Fax: (414) 592-9664
Mr. Robert J. Weyers, Sales Vice President

Number of Franchised Units: 21
Number of Company-Owned Units: 4
Number of Total Operating Units: 25

In Business Since: 1992   Franchising Since: 1992

Description of Operation: Retail music store, engaged in the buying and selling of pre-owned compact discs and accessories. CD Exchange offers a complete turn-key operation and marketing system, allowing franchisees an effective way to participate in this high-growth industry.

Equity Capital Needed: $60,000 - $80,000

Franchise Fee: $10,000

Royalty Fee: 4%

Financial Assistance: Not offered at this time.

Managerial Assistance: Each new franchisee receives managerial assistance in site selection and lease negotiation. Also, a manual of instruction is provided covering all aspects of the operation. Additional on-site consultation is offered on an on-going basis.

Training Provided: 5-day training program at corporate office. Program encompasses both classroom and hands-on, in-store training. Additional training is provided at franchisee's location, if required.

Information Submitted: November 1993

CHESAPEAKE KNIFE & TOOL CO.
9385 G Gerwig Ln.
Columbia, MD 21046
Telephone: (703) 506-1016
Mr. Jack Herman, Executive VP, Director of Franchising

Number of Franchised Units: 3
Number of Company-Owned Units: 12
Number of Total Operating Units: 15

In Business Since: 1980   Franchising Since: 1993

Description of Operation: Chesapeake Knife & Tool operates retail cutlery and gift shops in regional and super regional shopping centers and in festival markets. We carry an extensive line of kitchen cutlery, sporting, hunting, camping knives and tools, as well as related gift items.

Equity Capital Needed: $160,800 - $250,000, includes franchise fee, complete buildout, opening inventory and fixtures.

Franchise Fee: $25,000

Royalty Fee: 6.5%

Financial Assistance: Depending on the franchisee's individual financial condition, banks may loan up to 65% of the total capital needed.

Managerial Assistance: Chesapeake Knife & Tool produces complete training manuals for all facets of our business. These manuals and subsequent updates, along with our merchandise and operations managers, will provide on-going managerial support.

Training Provided: An extensive 3-week training program is provided, consisting of 1 week of classroom training at our headquarters in Columbia, MD and 2 weeks of on-the-job training at one of our operating stores in the Washington, DC area.

Information Submitted: January 1994

CLUBHOUSE GOLF
P. O. Box 1280
Edmond, OK 73083
Telephone: (800) 580-2582 (405) 330-8484
Fax: (405) 330-8499
Mr. R. Kevin Leonard, Chief Executive Officer

Number of Franchised Units: 12
Number of Company-Owned Units: 0
Number of Total Operating Units: 12

In Business Since: 1989   Franchising Since: 1989

Description of Operation: Clubhouse Golf offers franchises for off-course retail golf stores with an up-scale pro shop look, emphasizing competitively-priced pro line golf equipment, quality men's and women's attire and attractive gifts and accessories. The stores offer custom club fitting, computerized swing analysis and club repair.

Equity Capital Needed: $250,000

Franchise Fee: $35,000

Royalty Fee: 2.5%, plus 1% advertising fund.

Financial Assistance: No financing is offered; however, Clubhouse Golf's management will provide extensive assistance in obtaining financing if needed.

Managerial Assistance: Each franchisee receives 3 weeks of extensive training: 1 week at Clubhouse headquarters, where day-to-day business decisions are discussed, i.e., insurance, forms, payroll, etc.; another week is spent in an existing franchise store, where each new franchisee experiences actually working in a retail golf store. Also, 1 week is spent at a specialty school for club repair, clubmaking and other shop repair specialties. Finally, representatives will be at the store opening for as long as needed.

Training Provided: Same as above.

Information Submitted: December 1993

COBBLESTONE QUALITY SHOE REPAIR
5944 Luther Ln., # 402
Dallas, TX 75225
Telephone: (800) 735-6231 (214) 696-4436
Fax: (214) 696-2483
Mr. David Wehner, Vice President of Franchising

Number of Franchised Units: 66
Number of Company-Owned Units: 39
Number of Total Operating Units: 105

In Business Since: 1906   **Franchising Since:** 1987

Description of Operation: The Cobblestone retail shoe repair business is an unprecedented opportunity for today's entrepreneur. It capitalizes on a growing market, steadily increasing consumer demand and the limited number of trained shoe repair craftsmen that exist today. Cobblestone Quality Shoe Repair takes the craftsmen and materials and puts them in centralized, state-of-the-art repair facilities. The Cobblestone franchisee moves out to a selling position, rather than behind the repair bench. High-traffic locations.

Equity Capital Needed: $49,800

Franchise Fee: $13,900

Royalty Fee: 6%

Financial Assistance: Applicants are directed to SBA financing.

Managerial Assistance: Cobblestone produces complete training and operations manuals. The local area developer is obligated to provide continuous consultation to the local franchisees. The area developer and franchisee receive constant updates on products and market research.

Training Provided: It is Cobblestone's task to see that you have the very latest information about shoe and luggage repair. To do this, 2 separate training courses have been established. Each uses 3 elements: classroom study with manuals, hands-on in-store training and hands-on factory training. 2 people per franchise receive the training that lasts about 14 days. You will receive manuals and reference guides. Customer service, counter sales, repair basics and operations training are taught.

Information Submitted: March 1994

CONTEMPO PORTRAITS
1235 S. Gilbert Rd., # 16
Mesa, AZ 85204

Telephone: (602) 926-2216
Fax: (602) 926-2382
Mr. Patrick Silard, President

Number of Franchised Units: 0
Number of Company-Owned Units: 0
Number of Total Operating Units: 0

In Business Since: 1987   **Franchising Since:** 1993

Description of Operation: Contempo Portraits franchise is a contemporary portrait studio, offering a new concept in portraiture. A unique blend of creative photography and effective marketing techniques distinguishes Contempo Portrait as a "first of its kind" in the industry.

Equity Capital Needed: $75,000

Franchise Fee: $25,000

Royalty Fee: 7%, plus 1% advertising.

Financial Assistance: The franchisor will assist the franchisee in obtaining financing through a third party.

Managerial Assistance: Contempo Portrait provides complete training manuals and forms, as well as continuous support and consultation. Seminars, newsletters and workshops will be scheduled on a regular basis.

Training Provided: Training will be conducted in an actual franchise with classroom-type sessions. The training will be supervised by the founder of Contempo Portraits.

Information Submitted: January 1994

COUNTRY CLUTTER
3333 Vaca Valley Pkwy., # 900
Vacaville, CA 95688
Telephone: (800) 4-CLUTTER (707) 451-6890
Fax: (707) 451-0410
Mr. Ken Petersen, President

Number of Franchised Units: 2
Number of Company-Owned Units: 2
Number of Total Operating Units: 4

In Business Since: 1991   **Franchising Since:** 1992

Description of Operation: A charming store for gifts, collectibles and home decor. A unique business that offers old-fashioned quality, selection and customer service. A complete franchise program that is professionally designed, computerized and planned to sell a perfected blend of country merchandise, made up of primarily American manufacturers and crafters. Rich arrangements and displays of textures, colors and aromas make shopping at Country Clutter a true sensory delight.

Equity Capital Needed: $151,000 - $251,000

Franchise Fee: $25,000

Royalty Fee: 4%

Financial Assistance: Country Visions (franchisor) does not directly assist in financing; however, we have established relationships with SBA and other financial sources.

Managerial Assistance: Graduate from our own Franchise Business Degree program! A complete home study course covers all business systems and operations. Also, enjoy a 3-day training seminar at our corporate offices in California. On-going support will be provided which includes 5 days of on-site training before you open.

Training Provided: Same as above.

Information Submitted: April 1994

CURTIS MATHES CORPORATION
2855 Marquis Dr., # 110
Garland, TX 75042
Telephone: (214) 494-6411
Fax: (214) 205-1103
Ms. Elena Roberts, Director of Marketing

Number of Franchised Units: 200
Number of Company-Owned Units: 0
Number of Total Operating Units: 200

In Business Since: 1920   **Franchising Since:** 1969

Description of Operation: Curtis Mathes markets the premier American brand of home electronics. The Company has extremely high name recognition nationally and a strong reputation for quality products (all covered by a 4-year warranty).

Equity Capital Needed: $50,000

Franchise Fee: $25,000

Royalty Fee: Data not available.

Financial Assistance: Financing may be arranged through Curtis Mathes with ITT.

Managerial Assistance: Varies, depending on needs and experience of the franchisee.

Training Provided: Operational, technical, legal and marketing training and/or manuals are provided as needed and at annual dealer conferences.

Information Submitted: February 1994

CYCLEPATH, THE
6465 Millcreek Dr., # 205
Mississauga, ON L5N 5R3 CAN
Telephone: (800) 387-8335 (905) 567-4180
Fax: (905) 567-5355
Mr. George Kostopoulos, President

Number of Franchised Units: 38
Number of Company-Owned Units: 2
Number of Total Operating Units: 40

In Business Since: 1981   **Franchising Since:** 1988

Description of Operation: The Cyclepath is Canada's foremost retail specialty bicycle franchise, with a successful chain of franchised stores operating coast to coast. We carry an extensive selection of brand-name and private-label bicycles, parts and accessories, catering to the needs of all cyclists, from the racing enthusiast to the recreational cyclist.

Equity Capital Needed: $50,000 - $100,000

Franchise Fee: $40,000

Royalty Fee: 0%

Financial Assistance: Financial assistance through a lending institution.

Managerial Assistance: On-going management support, marketing and promotion, central purchasing, inventory control, an 800# telephone hotline and regional meetings.

Training Provided: 1 - 2 weeks of training at head office. 1 - 2 weeks of on-site training.

Information Submitted: November 1993

DISCOUNT PARTY WAREHOUSE
538 Larkfield Rd.
East Northport, NY 11731
Telephone: (516) 368-5200
Fax: (516) 368-5213
Mr. Ed Rosenberg, President

Number of Franchised Units: 11
Number of Company-Owned Units: 22
Number of Total Operating Units: 33

In Business Since: 1976   **Franchising Since:** 1984

Description of Operation: Retail store of paper and plastic party supplies, decorations, greeting cards and balloons. We are a warehouse concept that features a wide selection of merchandise that is deeply discounted. We are the pioneers of the party goods business.

Equity Capital Needed: $250,000 - $300,000

Franchise Fee: $25,000

Royalty Fee: 5%

Financial Assistance: None.

Managerial Assistance: Company provides experienced personnel to assist in the set-up of the store and for the initial opening week of business. Constant and continual communication is performed via telephone, fax and mail.

Training Provided: Franchisees receive a professional 2-week training program at the franchisor's corporate offices in NY.

Information Submitted: November 1993

ELEGANT IMAGES
1019 Wilson Dr.
Baltimore, MD 21223
Telephone: (800) 445-1191 (410) 525-1700
Fax: (410) 646-0620
Ms. Martha Simons, Vice President

Number of Franchised Units: 9
Number of Company-Owned Units: 3
Number of Total Operating Units: 12

In Business Since: 1989   **Franchising Since:** 1991

Description of Operation: Elegant Images is a fantastic new concept that combines the skills of a make-up artist, hair stylist and accessory and wardrobe coordinator to create the most stunning, transformations imaginable. The fun and excitement continues with a high-fashion photography session which promises and delivers the star treatment. The entire session is guaranteed to pamper the client and create a unique and memorable event.

Equity Capital Needed: $136,000 - $215,000, including fee.

Franchise Fee: $25,000

Royalty Fee: 5%

Financial Assistance: Elegant Images does not directly provide financing; however, we will assist you in obtaining financing through a financial institution of your choice.

Managerial Assistance: You'll get pre-opening assistance, site selection and lease negotiations, store design and layout assistance, operations guidance and manuals, manpower recruitment techniques, professional finishing lab, purchasing guidelines and recommendations, marketing and advertising tools, access to our training facility and personnel as you expand, legal protection of the Elegant Images trademark, corporate visits and consultations.

Training Provided: The fundamental key to your success is the training that you and your management staff receive. During a 2-week training session, you will learn photographic make-up techniques, flattering hair design, lighting for glamour, background styling, high-fashion modeling techniques, more, more and more!

Information Submitted: November 1993

FLAG SHOP, THE
1755 West 4th Ave.
Vancouver, BC V6J 1M2 CAN
Telephone: (800) 663-8681 (604) 736-8161
Fax: (604) 736-6439
Ms. Doreen Braverman, President

Number of Franchised Units: 4
Number of Company-Owned Units: 2
Number of Total Operating Units: 6

In Business Since: 1975   **Franchising Since:** 1988

Description of Operation: Merchants and manufacturers of flags, banners, flag poles, pins, crests and other related flag paraphernalia. Rentals, design services and vexillogical information.

Equity Capital Needed: $30,000 - $80,000

Franchise Fee: $20,000

Royalty Fee: 17.5% surcharge on purchases.

Financial Assistance: The franchisor will contact franchisee's bank to assist with a line of credit and render financial statements to financial institutions.

Managerial Assistance: Daily by phone, fax and mail. Quarterly visits for advice and re-training; weekly mail packages with updated procedures, forms, ideas, monthly sales analyses; annual owners' meetings.

Training Provided: 3 weeks in Vancouver, BC and 1 week at franchisee's location. Training includes executive procedures, administrative procedures, financial control systems, production methodology, marketing (sales and local) and personnel procedures.

Information Submitted: December 1993

FORGET ME KNOT
575 8th Ave., 21st Fl.
New York, NY 10018
Telephone: (212) 714-0595
Ms. Sharon L. Mitzman, President

Number of Franchised Units: 1
Number of Company-Owned Units: 1
Number of Total Operating Units: 2

In Business Since: 1984   **Franchising Since:** 1993

Description of Operation: Custom-created gift baskets, which are generally ordered by telephone. Business can be home based or operated from a warehouse location. Ideal for sales and marketing-oriented persons. Computerized order-taking program.

Equity Capital Needed: $35,000 - $42,000

Franchise Fee: $17,500

Royalty Fee: 5%

Financial Assistance: None.

Managerial Assistance: Each regional location will receive customization of its product line and a portion of their color catalog to its area's particular requirements. After training, franchisees receive a complete operations manual as a reference and refresher. Management provides unlimited, on-going support to franchisees and continuously attends national trade shows to seek out new merchandise and develop new techniques in the gift basket industry. It provides up to 4 seasonal color catalogues per year as a sales tool.

Training Provided: 2 weeks of intensive training at FMK headquarters in New York City. Training emphasizes role playing, interaction and hands-on training in a working office atmosphere. 3 - 5 days of set-up and personal training at their location. Training covers overall business knowledge, as well as sales, marketing, basic accounting and a focus on FMK's unique system of operating a gift basket company.

Information Submitted: January 1994

GAME POWER HEADQUARTERS
9990 Global Rd.
Philadelphia, PA 19115
Telephone: (215) 969-5000
Fax: (215) 969-4550
Mr. Michael Flannery, Director of Franchise Sales

Number of Franchised Units: 0
Number of Company-Owned Units: 1
Number of Total Operating Units: 1

In Business Since: 1993   **Franchising Since:** 1993

Description of Operation: Game Power Headquarters is a full-service, one-stop shopping experience for lovers of interactive entertainment, an exploding $6 billion industry. Our exclusive interactive store design

outstrips everything the industry has seen before! The newest software and hardware and accessories are presented in a dynamic, user-friendly environment that will keep your customers flocking in.

Equity Capital Needed: $102,000 - $220,000

Franchise Fee: $10,000

Royalty Fee: 5%

Financial Assistance: Third party.

Managerial Assistance: Data not available.

Training Provided: Formal training program at corporate headquarters, site selection assistance, using the most sophisticated computerized geographical information system and on-going seminars and training programs for you and your staff. Complete, professional marketing and advertising.

Information Submitted: November 1993

GATEWAY NEWSTANDS
30 E. Beaver Creek Rd., # 206
Richmond Hill, ON L4B 1J2 CAN
Telephone: (800) 942-5351 (905) 886-8900
Fax: (905) 886-8904
Mr. Michael Aychental, Chief Executive Officer

Number of Franchised Units: 88
Number of Company-Owned Units: 1
Number of Total Operating Units: 89

In Business Since: 1983   **Franchising Since:** 1983

Description of Operation: Gift shops and light food and coffee take-out stores, located in shopping centers and office towers.

Equity Capital Needed: $55,000 - $125,000

Franchise Fee: $25,000 - $75,00

Royalty Fee: 3% of gross sales.

Financial Assistance: In-house financing is available for up to 50% of franchise fees to qualified applicants.

Managerial Assistance: Complete set-up, planning and on-site training, as well as lease negotiations and merchandising operations]during terms of lease.

Training Provided: Complete set-up, planning and on-site training, as well as lease negotiations and merchandising operations during terms of lease.

Information Submitted: November 1993

GOLF USA
1801 S. Broadway
Edmond, OK 73013
Telephone: (800) 488-1107 (405) 341-0009
Fax: (405) 340-8716
Mr. Jim Gould, Director of Franchising and Marketing

Number of Franchised Units: 75
Number of Company-Owned Units: 1
Number of Total Operating Units: 76

In Business Since: 1986   **Franchising Since:** 1989

Description of Operation: Franchise of retail golf stores.

Equity Capital Needed: $75,000 - $100,000

Franchise Fee: $30,000 - $40,000

Royalty Fee: 2%

Financial Assistance: Assistance in business plan operation.

Managerial Assistance: On-site training by qualified Golf USA staff member in all phases of retail store operations. An operations manual is provided to use for daily operations.

Training Provided: 1 week of training in all aspects of the operation of a retail store, i.e., hands-on computer training, basic accounting, merchandising, etc. at the international headquarters in Edmond, OK. Professional speakers and manufacturer's representatives are invited to the training classes.

Information Submitted: January 1994

HAKKY INSTANT SHOE REPAIR
1739 Sands Place, # F
Marietta, GA 30067
Telephone: (404) 956-8651
Fax: (404) 951-0355
Mr. Patrick Harper, Executive Manager

Number of Franchised Units: 65
Number of Company-Owned Units: 1
Number of Total Operating Units: 66

In Business Since: 1983   **Franchising Since:** 1989

Description of Operation: European, instant shoe repair.

Equity Capital Needed: $15,000 and up.

Franchise Fee: $9,000 - $12,000

Royalty Fee: 4%

Financial Assistance: We will help gain financial assistance with SBA loans and leasing on equipment.

Managerial Assistance: We provide monthly financial statements, mall reports, sales tax reports and various additional reports required by local, city, state governments, full-time marketing director, inventory control and machinery maintenance assistance.

Training Provided: We offer an initial 3 weeks of training in the training center. Grand opening support in store. On-going support with materials and machinery. A quarterly newsletter offers support with customer service and merchandising assistance.

Information Submitted: March 1994

HEEL QUIK / SEW QUIK
6425 Powers Ferry Rd., # 250
Atlanta, GA 30339
Telephone: (800) 255-8145 (404) 951-9440
Fax: (404) 933-8268
Ms. Pat Abbott, Franchise Co-ordinator

Number of Franchised Units: 384
Number of Company-Owned Units: 2
Number of Total Operating Units: 386

In Business Since: 1984   **Franchising Since:** 1985

Description of Operation: Heel/Sew Quik! - instant shoe repair, clothing alterations and monogramming.

Equity Capital Needed: $5,000 - $35,000

Franchise Fee: $2,500 - $17,500

Royalty Fee: 4%

Financial Assistance: We have several leasing companies that will work with new franchisees. We also have put together a formal SBA or business loan package.

Managerial Assistance: 2 weeks of training at our international training center in Atlanta, GA; store opening coordination and support in the field; manuals; videos; on-going support via toll-free 800#s; and field support.

Training Provided: Training is done at our training facility for 2 intensive weeks; video courses are also presented, following training in the field, along with manuals. Assistance in the field is provided during opening and on an on-going basis.

Information Submitted: November 1993

HOBBYTOWN USA
5930 S. 58th St., # P
Lincoln, NE 68516
Telephone: (402) 434-5052
Fax: (402) 434-5055
Mr. Marty Juarez, Director of Franchising

Number of Franchised Units: 88
Number of Company-Owned Units: 3
Number of Total Operating Units: 91

In Business Since: 1969   **Franchising Since:** 1986

Description of Operation: Hobbytown USA allows the rare opportunity to work and play at the same time. Hobbytown USA carries radio-controlled vehicles of all types - model trains, adventure games, models, sports cards and more! Hobbytown USA is the country's largest chain of hobby stores.

Equity Capital Needed: $70,000 - $80,000

Franchise Fee: $17,500

Royalty Fee: 3%

Financial Assistance: None.

Managerial Assistance: The Company will furnish timely computer updates, an evaluation of sales, an annual inventory and sales analysis, operations and pre-opening manuals and a monthly Company newsletter.

Training Provided: The Company requires a 1 week training program at the home office in Lincoln, NE. In addition, a field manager will assist the franchisee at the new store location, including the grand opening.

Information Submitted: January 1994

HOT LOOKS!
724 Old York Rd.
Jenkintown, PA 19046
Telephone: (800) 92-LOOKS (215) 572-8900
Fax: (215) 572-7054
Mr. Barry Fineman, President

Number of Franchised Units: 2
Number of Company-Owned Units: 8
Number of Total Operating Units: 10

In Business Since: 1946   **Franchising Since:** 1992

Description of Operation: High-fashion glamour portraits, wedding and special event photography.

Equity Capital Needed: $60,000 - $138,500

Franchise Fee: $19,500

Royalty Fee: 7%

Financial Assistance: None.

Managerial Assistance: Lease negotiations, marketing, merchandising, meetings and advertising assistance included.

Training Provided: Classroom and in-store training is an extensive 4-week experience.

Information Submitted: December 1993

HOW TO VIDEO SOURCE, THE
953 3rd Ave.
New York, NY 10022
Telephone: (212) 832-7429
Fax: (212) 832-7834
Mr. Joseph Meyersdorf, Vice President

Number of Franchised Units: 2
Number of Company-Owned Units: 1
Number of Total Operating Units: 3

In Business Since: 1991   **Franchising Since:** 1992

Description of Operation: The How To Video Source offers the world's largest selection of instructional videotapes. Each store carries approximately 1,500 - 2,000 separate titles, covering every educational subject imaginable. Topics include music, art, dance, crafts, travel, language, photography, beauty, fashion, auto care, home improvement, kitchen, gardening, parenting, sexuality, health and fitness, sports, business, education, computers and more.

Equity Capital Needed: $100,000 - $150,000

Franchise Fee: $15,000

Royalty Fee: 6%

Financial Assistance: The How To Video Source purchases products from hundreds of individual video producers. The How To Video Source may be able to establish credit terms for franchisees with many vendors prior to opening. This can save a large portion of the start-up costs necessary for inventory.

Managerial Assistance: The How To Video Source provides assistance in all aspects of the operation. Assistance includes site selection, format for store design, inventory customization, advertising and promotional materials, store catalog, constant updates of new videos, products available and much more.

Training Provided: An intensive 1-week training period. Hands-on training covers every detail and aspect of store operations. Training manuals are also provided.

Information Submitted: January 1994

INTERNATIONAL GOLF
9101 N. Thornydale Rd.
Tucson, AZ 85741
Telephone: (602) 744-1840
Fax: (602) 744-2076
Ms. Sheila J. White, Franchising Assistant

Number of Franchised Units: 47
Number of Company-Owned Units: 4
Number of Total Operating Units: 51

In Business Since: 1977   **Franchising Since:** 1981

Description of Operation: Off-course retail golf store. May add tennis and/or ski lines.

Equity Capital Needed: $275,000 - $300,000

Franchise Fee: $42,000

Royalty Fee: 2%

Financial Assistance: International Golf does not provide financing; however, help is provided in acquiring funds from financial institutions, including preparing the business plan.

Managerial Assistance: International Golf's support team is constantly available for advice and assistance, constantly updating franchisees on new merchandise, advertising and marketing programs, as well as improvements for daily operations.

Training Provided: We provide 2 weeks of training in all facets of the business for the franchise owner and key employee(s) at International Golf headquarters in Oklahoma City, OK with the Vice President of Operations.

Information Submitted: March 1994

JEWELRY REPAIR ENTERPRISES
1501 Decker Ave., # 107
Stuart, FL 34994
Telephone: (800) 359-0407 (407) 221-9207
Fax: (407) 221-9209
Mr. Robert Goldstein, Senior Advisor

Number of Franchised Units: 50
Number of Company-Owned Units: 3
Number of Total Operating Units: 53

In Business Since: 1985   **Franchising Since:** 1987

Description of Operation: Jewelry and watch repairs while you wait. Located in regional malls throughout the country.

Equity Capital Needed: $70,000

Franchise Fee: $13,000

Royalty Fee: 5%

Financial Assistance: Some financial assistance for qualified persons.

Managerial Assistance: Home office personnel are available to assist in completing forms and setting up record keeping.

Training Provided: On-site training in sales techniques and completion of forms and reports for a period of 1 week and longer if necessary.

Information Submitted: November 1993

JOHN SIMMONS
36 W. Calhoun Ave.
Memphis, TN 38103
Telephone: (800) 737-5567 (901) 526-5567
Fax: (901) 526-5605
Ms. Frances Cianciolo, President

Number of Franchised Units: 4
Number of Company-Owned Units: 1
Number of Total Operating Units: 5

In Business Since: 1985   **Franchising Since:** 1985

Description of Operation: General gifts.

Equity Capital Needed: $100,000 - $150,000

Franchise Fee: $15,000

Royalty Fee: 4.5%

Financial Assistance: Not available.

Managerial Assistance: Data not available.

Training Provided: We offer a 2 - 4 day training period.

Information Submitted: January 1994

JOHN T'S - GIFTS FOR HIM
362 Pacific St., # 4
Monterrey, CA 93940
Telephone: (800) 782-8988 (408) 375-4674
Fax: (408) 375-4675
Mr. George J. Antonaros, President

Number of Franchised Units: 0
Number of Company-Owned Units: 5
Number of Total Operating Units: 5

In Business Since: 1967   **Franchising Since:** 1991

Description of Operation: John T's is a retail men's gift shop, selling games, gifts, pipes and tobaccos in mall locations.

Equity Capital Needed: $120,000 - $250,000

Franchise Fee: $20,000

Royalty Fee: 5%

Financial Assistance: None

Managerial Assistance: We provide 2 weeks of training in a corporate store before the franchise unit opens, then 1 week in the new franchise unit upon grand opening. We'll visit the unit once per month thereafter.

Training Provided: We offer 2 weeks of in-store training (in one of the corporate stores) and 1 week in the new store for grand opening. Initially, visit once every month. In-store training at corporate store can be longer, depending on the need.

Information Submitted: January 1994

JUST-A-BUCK
15 Engle St., # 302
Englewood, NJ 07631
Telephone: (800) 332-2229 (201) 871-0370
Fax: (201) 871-7168
Ms. Stacey Sommers, Marketing Director

Number of Franchised Units: 4
Number of Company-Owned Units: 8
Number of Total Operating Units: 12

In Business Since: 1980   Franchising Since: 1992

Description of Operation: Diverse selection of quality merchandise for Just-A-Buck. This is a retail operation that caters to the ever-evolving low price-point marketplace. We pay close attention to quality in customer service, merchandising, operations and store design.

Equity Capital Needed: $70,000

Franchise Fee: $25,000

Royalty Fee: 3%

Financial Assistance: Financial assistance available to new franchisees consists of assistance in preparing a business plan, narrative with pro forma operating statements and cash flows. In addition, the franchisor will assist in making introductions to potential lenders.

Managerial Assistance: Just-A-Buck provides on-going support in re-ordering merchandise, inventory control, store appearance and seasonal merchandising (planning, projections and ordering). Our franchise office provides accounting assistance in analyzing sales figures, customer counts, average customer sale, cash sheets, office systems and payroll percent. Just-A-Buck will also advise and help to set guidelines for personnel, as well as loss prevention measures, and assist in equipment purchasing and repairs.

Training Provided: We provide a 15-day training program - 5 days of pre-opening assistance in Company units and 10 days on-site in a franchised unit. We will consult and advise with regard to initial inventory, merchandising and retailing display, design, store layout, sales techniques, personnel development and other business operational and advertising matters that directly relate to the franchise operation.

Information Submitted: December 1993

LAS VEGAS DISCOUNT GOLF & TENNIS
5325 S. Valley View Blvd., # 10
Las Vegas, NV 89118
Telephone: (800) 873-5110 (702) 798-7777
Fax: (702) 798-6847
Franchise Development

Number of Franchised Units: 57
Number of Company-Owned Units: 2
Number of Total Operating Units: 59

In Business Since: 1974   Franchising Since: 1984

Description of Operation: Las Vegas Discount Golf & Tennis franchises are retail stores specializing in golf and tennis equipment and apparel at discounted prices. The franchise program provides market analysis, site selection assistance, a proprietary computer system, exceptional training and all other services necessary to open and operate a store. Each franchisee is given an exclusive protected territory.

Equity Capital Needed: $300,000

Franchise Fee: $40,000

Royalty Fee: 3%

Financial Assistance: Franchisees must have a net worth of $300,000, but only $100,000 in liquid assets is necessary. The remaining $200,000 can be financed through an SBA loan. Assistance with business plans and pro formas are available.

Managerial Assistance: All aspects of management are covered in the initial training - how to be a good manager, how to hire and train employees, etc.

Training Provided: LVDG&T provides the industry's leading training and operational support. Each franchisee must complete an intensive 2-week class that includes classroom and in-store training. Continual training and operational support is available throughout the term of the franchise agreement.

Information Submitted: March 1994

LE CLUB INTERNATIONAL VIDEO FILM
301 Elaine
Fabreville (Laval), PQ H7P 2R1 CAN
Telephone: (800) 361-9156 (514) 628-1910
Fax: (514) 628-1034
Mr. Jules A. Menard

Number of Franchised Units: 63
Number of Company-Owned Units: 2
Number of Total Operating Units: 65

In Business Since: 1980   Franchising Since: 1981

Description of Operation: Video stores. Rental and sale of video cassettes.

Equity Capital Needed: $75,000 - $100,000

Franchise Fee: $25,000

Royalty Fee: 5%

Financial Assistance: Data not available.

Managerial Assistance: We provide financial assistance, site selection and market study assistance, lease negotiation, design and construction of the new store assistance, co-operative advertising and video cassette buying assistance.

Training Provided: The program consists of 2 days at the head office, 1 week in a corporate store and 1 week on-site starting the day of the opening of the new store.

Information Submitted: January 1994

LEMSTONE BOOKS
1123 Wheaton Oaks Court
Wheaton, IL 60187
Telephone: (708) 682-1400
Fax: (708) 682-1828
Mr. Jim Doyle, Sales Manager

Number of Franchised Units: 53
Number of Company-Owned Units: 1
Number of Total Operating Units: 54

In Business Since: 1981   Franchising Since: 1982

Description of Operation: "America's Christian Bookstore Franchise." Lemstone specializes in high-volume mall retailing. Our franchisees come from a wide range of professions. Our stores retail Christ-centered and family-oriented retail products. Product categories include Christian books, Bibles, recorded music, videos, stationery products, t-shirts and gift products.

Equity Capital Needed: Total investment: $140,000 - $200,000; Owner equity: $60,000 - $90,000.

Franchise Fee: $30,000

Royalty Fee: 4%, plus 1% advertising.

Financial Assistance: We assist the franchisee in preparing and obtaining local bank financing.

Managerial Assistance: We offer a complete turn-key operation, including site-selection, lease negotiations, construction, inventory selection, store set-up, operating systems and on-going promotional support and training. National seminars and an annual convention are also offered. On-site operational support, as required.

Training Provided: Initial training includes 1 week at the corporate headquarters and training store. On-going includes convention, seminars, employee training materials, newsletters and promotional training.

LITTLE PROFESSOR BOOK CENTERS
130 S. First St., # 300
Ann Arbor, MI 48104
Telephone: (800) 899-6232 (313) 994-1212
Fax: (313) 994-9009
Ms. Christi Shaw, Franchise Sales Co-ordinator

Number of Franchised Units: 118
Number of Company-Owned Units: 1
Number of Total Operating Units: 119

In Business Since: 1964   Franchising Since: 1969

Description of Operation: General full-service, community-oriented book stores.

Equity Capital Needed: $80,000

Franchise Fee: $29,000

Royalty Fee: 3.5%

Financial Assistance: Assistance in the loan application process.

Managerial Assistance: We provide support in all areas of franchised book store operations on an on-going basis.

Training Provided: We offer an extensive 10-day training period at the home office in Ann Arbor, MI in all areas related to running and managing book store daily operations, including bookselling, personnel, daily operations, financial, computer operations, etc. Also, on-site training of 5 - 7 days. More for a superstore.

Information Submitted: January 1994

MAC BIRDIE GOLF GIFTS
5250 W. 73rd St., # H
Minneapolis, MN 55439
Telephone: (800) 343-1033 (612) 830-1033
Fax: (612) 830-1055
Ms. Susan E. Schwartz, Director of Franchise Operations

Number of Franchised Units: 0
Number of Company-Owned Units: 8
Number of Total Operating Units: 8

In Business Since: 1989   Franchising Since: 1994

Description of Operation: Mac Birdie offers a wide variety of flexible, year-round and seasonal opportunities. Our exclusive Mac Birdie apparel line is supported by a variety of accessories, novelties and executive gifts. Options for selling Mac Birdie merchandise, such as kiosks, carts, catalog sales, gift racks and/or leased departments, depends on location and personal interests.

Equity Capital Needed: $30,000 - $100,000

Franchise Fee: $5,000 - $50,000

Royalty Fee: 5%

Financial Assistance: None.

Managerial Assistance: Business planning, site selection, lease negotiation and grand opening assistance. An extensive operations manual is distributed and up-dated regularly. A franchise newsletter will be distributed regularly and a franchise advisory committee will be approved as the network grows.

Training Provided: 1 week of professional training at the corporate headquarters is provided in merchandising, set-ups, product information, advertising, inventory, purchasing, personnel, customer service and sales. On-going training is provided. You will leave with your individual plan in hand.

Information Submitted: January 1994

MARBLES MUSIC & VIDEO
3545 Motor Ave., # 200
Los Angeles, CA 90034
Telephone: (800) 669-2221 (310) 204-2220
Fax: (310) 204-0148
Mr. Matt Feinstein, Director or Franchise Development

Number of Franchised Units: 12
Number of Company-Owned Units: 6
Number of Total Operating Units: 18

In Business Since: 1969   Franchising Since: 1988

Description of Operation: Total home entertainment centers, which include videos, movies, laserdiscs, video games, compact discs, cassette tapes, VCR's and accessories.

Equity Capital Needed: $40,000 - $200,000

Franchise Fee: $20,000

Royalty Fee: 6%

Financial Assistance: Financing is available when taking over an established video store and converting it into a Marbles Music & Video. Existing locations available nationwide. SBA and VetFran.

Managerial Assistance: Location assistance, store set-up and layout, consultation, business development manuals, buying power, bookkeeping services, advertising and marketing services are all included.

Training Provided: Initial in-store training in all aspects of running a successful retail store, plus on-going training, as necessary. No previous retail business experience is needed.

Information Submitted: November 1993

MICROPLAY VIDEO GAMES
2555 Dixie Rd., # 3
Mississauga, ON L4Y 2A1 CAN
Telephone: (800) 265-PLAY (905) 949-2580
Fax: (905) 949-0627
Mr. Todd Sturgeon, Controller

Number of Franchised Units: 60
Number of Company-Owned Units: 0
Number of Total Operating Units: 60

In Business Since: 1987   Franchising Since: 1993

Description of Operation: Microplay stores offer the consumer the ability to purchase, rent and trade from a large selection of new and used video games. The specialty stores have one product line, video games, and because of this focus, are able to provide better prices, service and selection to the video game customer. Microplay provides full training, on-going support and proprietary software for store operations.

Equity Capital Needed: $30,000 - $60,000

Franchise Fee: $29,500

Royalty Fee: 0% - 8%

Financial Assistance: Microplay offers business plans and cash flows for presentations to local and national franchise lenders.

Managerial Assistance: Support personnel are in regular contact with franchisees. All of the support staff are experienced game players that know the industry, the business and the customer. The Microplay M.O.S.T., an incredible point-of-sale computer system, handles up to the minute daily, weekly and monthly reports for sales, rentals and purchases. The M.O.S.T. provides inventory control, accounting, communication and tele-communication functions. The head office provides full computer support.

Training Provided: Franchisees participate in a full week of hands-on interactive training at the head office. Courses include advertising, marketing, hiring, product knowledge and general business procedures. This training is supplemented with 1 week of in-store training for owners and staff. Operations manuals and grand opening support are provided.

Information Submitted: March 1994

NATIONAL PROPERTY REGISTRY
P. O. Box 72376
Marietta, GA 30007
Telephone: (800) 971-5201 (404) 971-5200
Fax: (404) 977-7810
Mr. Robert J. Heller, President/Chief Executive Officer

Number of Franchised Units: 8
Number of Company-Owned Units: 0
Number of Total Operating Units: 8

In Business Since: 1993   Franchising Since: 1994

Description of Operation: A nationwide video inventory system for business and home owners, together with high security safekeeping and documentation. Only one exclusive franchisee is appointed in any one trading area. The Company provides full training. No inventory. No receivables. Can be operated from residence. The Company unconditionally guarantees the franchise investment until training is finished and the franchisee is prepared to commence business.

Equity Capital Needed: Less than $25,000.

Franchise Fee: $19,950

Royalty Fee: $500 per annum association fee.

Financial Assistance: The Company may extend financing of up to 50% to any new franchisee, repayable over 36 months at prime plus 4%.

Managerial Assistance: National Property Registry (NPR) offers complete training, including advertising, marketing, public relations, promotional guides, training in general management, video techniques, insurance policies and offers direct on-line support via a special 800# for use by franchisees only. The daily or weekly referral of leads to franchisee is provided by fax.

Training Provided: A 3 - 4 day classroom session covers all aspects of the business, office management, equipment operation and selection, employee recruitment and supervision, advertising and promotion, security and financial management. A complete training manual is provided to the franchisee. Hands-on training with equipment is provided.

Information Submitted: March 1994

NEVADA BOB'S PRO SHOP
3333 E. Flamingo Rd.
Las Vegas, NV 89121
Telephone: (800) 348-2627 (702) 451-3333
Fax: (702) 451-9378
Mr. Bob Hulley, Franchise Director

Number of Franchised Units: 275
Number of Company-Owned Units: 6
Number of Total Operating Units: 281

In Business Since: 1974   Franchising Since: 1978

Description of Operation: Selling discount golf equipment in an attractive atmosphere, specializing in top-of-the-line products by major manufacturers.

Equity Capital Needed: $275,000

Franchise Fee: $47,500 - $57,500

Royalty Fee: 3%

Financial Assistance: We assist in directing where and to whom to apply for financial assistance.

Managerial Assistance: Assistance in advertising, opening store and ordering products for inventory. Assistance in accounting and obtaining product information and availability.

Training Provided: We assist with a week of intensive training in Las Vegas, NV. Assist in site selection, lease negotiation and design of the store lay-out. A WATTS line is available for daily communication and support.

Information Submitted: November 1993

ONE HOUR MOTO PHOTO & PORTRAIT STUDIO
4444 Lake Center Dr.
Dayton, OH 45426
Telephone: (800) 733-6686 (513) 854-6686
Fax: (513) 854-0140
Mr. Dan Curtis, Director of Franchise Administration

Number of Franchised Units: 325
Number of Company-Owned Units: 60
Number of Total Operating Units: 385

In Business Since: 1981   Franchising Since: 1982

Description of Operation: Founded in 1981, Moto Photo is the world's largest franchisor of 1-hour photo processing and portrait stores, with 416 stores open and under development (331 franchised units, 61 company-owned units and 24 under development in 26 states and 3 countries). Moto Photo offers on-site processing, with a portrait studio, featuring the unique opportunity to return proofs in 1 hour and finished portrait packages in 5 days. Moto is ranked #31 in Success Magazine's Franchise Gold 100 and in Entrepreneur's Best 500.

Equity Capital Needed: $150,000

Franchise Fee: $35,000

Royalty Fee: 6%

Financial Assistance: Several sources are available, thus allowing the franchisee to make a minimum down payment of $50,000 and finance the balance.

Managerial Assistance: Site selection, design and construction, marketing (both grand opening and on-going) and training. On-going assistance is offered through a franchise business consultant network, regional meetings and conventions.

Training Provided: 3 weeks in the corporate offices, 1 week on-site and 2 weeks in a store.

Information Submitted: November 1993

PAPER FIRST
6900 Folger Dr.
Charlotte, NC 28270
Telephone: (704) 364-1785
Fax: (704) 366-0334
Mr. Mel Frank, President

Number of Franchised Units: 10
Number of Company-Owned Units: 1
Number of Total Operating Units: 11

In Business Since: 1980   Franchising Since: 1988

Description of Operation: Paper First stores are store-front distributors of paper and plastic supplies and related products and services. We inventory approximately 6,000 SKU's for party decorating, catering, food-service disposables, maintenance supplies, basic office papers, greeting cards and custom invitation services. We sell to walk-in retail customers and commercial contract accounts.

Equity Capital Needed: Data not available.

Franchise Fee: $15,000

Royalty Fee: Sliding scale: 2.5% - .5%.

Financial Assistance: Available on a case-by-case basis, as required.

Managerial Assistance: 7 operational manuals from pre-opening to marketing; proprietary cash and inventory control, profit management system; regular franchisee meetings; regular scheduled visits to franchisee locations, as requested.

Training Provided: 100 hours in existing store for sales training before opening; 40 hours of field training for commercial accounts before opening; 40 hours of clerical and administrative before opening; at least 4 days at new site before opening and 4 days after opening. On-going training for new employees.

Information Submitted: January 1994

PAPER WAREHOUSE
7634 Golden Traingle Dr.
Eden Prairie, MN 55344
Telephone: (800) 229-1792 (612) 829-5467
Fax: (612) 829-0247
Mr. Vernon Lewis, Director of Franchising

Number of Franchised Units: 21
Number of Company-Owned Units: 40
Number of Total Operating Units: 61

In Business Since: 1983   Franchising Since: 1987

Description of Operation: Retail party stores.

Equity Capital Needed: $101,000 - $195,000

Franchise Fee: $19,000

Royalty Fee: 3% - 5%

Financial Assistance: None.

Managerial Assistance: Daily assistance, as needed, in finance operations, human resources, advertising and merchandising.

Training Provided: We provide 1 week of training.

Information Submitted: January 1994

PAPYRUS
954 60th St.
Oakland, CA 94608
Telephone: (800) 872-7978 (510) 428-0166
Fax: (510) 428-0615
Ms. Kathleen A. Low, Director of Franchise Development

Number of Franchised Units: 33
Number of Company-Owned Units: 11
Number of Total Operating Units: 44

In Business Since: 1973   Franchising Since: 1988

Description of Operation: A Papyrus store offers the finest in greeting cards, paper accessories, gifts and custom-printed invitations, announcements and stationery. Sophisticated and up-scale, the stores are an exciting alternative to the traditional card store.

Equity Capital Needed: $75,000 - $100,000

Franchise Fee: $29,500

Royalty Fee: 6%

Financial Assistance: We provide third-party referrals.

Managerial Assistance: Data not available.

Training Provided: We offer 18 days of training - 12 days of initial training and 6 days during store set-up and opening. On-going regional training seminars and meetings, plus frequent on-site visits.

Information Submitted: March 1994

PARTY LAND
44 Second St. Pike
Southampton, PA 18966
Telephone: (800) PRTY-LND (215) 364-9500
Fax: (215) 364-4511
Mr. John L. Barry, Vice President of Sales

Number of Franchised Units: 25
Number of Company-Owned Units: 2
Number of Total Operating Units: 27

In Business Since: 1986   Franchising Since: 1988

Description of Operation: Retail party supplies, balloons and party favors. America's only international party supply franchise retailer.

Equity Capital Needed: $80,000 - $150,000

Franchise Fee: $25,000

Royalty Fee: 4%, or $150 per week (first year).

Financial Assistance: None.

Managerial Assistance: 8 years of professional party supply retail experience, with no failures - ever. Location assistance, merchandising, marketing, promotion, buying power, etc.

Training Provided: 1 week at corporate headquarters and 1 week at store - the most comprehensive and in-depth training in the industry today.

Information Submitted: December 1993

PARTY WORLD
10701 Vanowen St.
North Hollywood, CA 91605
Telephone: (818) 762-7717
Fax: (800) 905-8676
Mr. Stanley M. Tauber, President

Number of Franchised Units: 5
Number of Company-Owned Units: 15
Number of Total Operating Units: 20

In Business Since: 1978   Franchising Since: 1987

Description of Operation: Party World is a company that specializes in the sale of party supplies, utilizing one of the most unique marketing strategies in the industry. By offering a large selection, along with depth of merchandise and heavily discounted prices, we "bring the customer to us." In other words, the buying public seeks us out and we become the destination stop for party supplies.

Equity Capital Needed: $250,000

Franchise Fee: $20,000

Royalty Fee: 4% of gross.

Financial Assistance: The franchisor will assist the franchisee in obtaining financing.

Managerial Assistance: Continual management service in such areas as site selection, lease negotiations, store design, national buying programs, record keeping, advertising, inventory control and store operations. A complete manual of operations, forms, directions, hotline and advertising is provided. Field support managers are available to work closely with franchisees and visit stores regularly to assist in solving problems.

Training Provided: 3 weeks of intensive training at headquarters' store. On-going training and counseling at your store through field representatives. Complete operations manual and hotline.

Information Submitted: January 1994

PHOTO PRO PHOTOGRAPHY
1311 W. Hudson Rd.
Rogers, AR 72756
Telephone: (800) 950-1880 (501) 621-8881
Fax: (501) 621-8883
Mr. James E. Kitchel, President

Number of Franchised Units: 15
Number of Company-Owned Units: 2
Number of Total Operating Units: 17

In Business Since: 1992   Franchising Since: 1992

Description of Operation: The Company's goal is to capture a small share of the $4.5 billion youth picture market. Our mission statement is to out perform our customer's expectations in the areas of price, quality and reliability, while providing the maximum opportunities for individual achievement and financial security for our franchisees.

Equity Capital Needed: $3,500 - $6,500

Franchise Fee: $9,995

Royalty Fee: 0% royalty fee; 3% national advertising and promotional fund.

Financial Assistance: The franchisor offers financing arrangements to qualified franchisees in certain circumstances.

Managerial Assistance: As required.

Training Provided: The Company trains each franchisee in the effective utilization of its specific marketing approach as a way of gaining a larger market share. The Company offers training and support in two areas of photographer expertise, each defined according to the choice of equipment and training desired. Training is held in Rogers, AR.

Information Submitted: January 1994

POT POURRI
4699 Keele St., # 3
Downsview, ON M3J 2N8 CAN
Telephone: (416) 661-9916
Fax: (416) 661-9706
Mr. Michael Mayerson, Vice President of Franchising

Number of Franchised Units: 27
Number of Company-Owned Units: 1
Number of Total Operating Units: 28

In Business Since: 1991   **Franchising Since:** 1991

Description of Operation: Pot Pourri operates franchised kitchen and giftware retail stores.

Equity Capital Needed: $100,000 - $300,000

Franchise Fee: $25,000

Royalty Fee: 6%

Financial Assistance: We do not provide financial assistance.

Managerial Assistance: We provide on-going visits by operations specialists, financial advice by home office specialists, lease negotiations and advice by home office specialists, advertising preparation and materials, advice by headquarters specialists, buying assistance and training seminars.

Training Provided: Same as above.

Information Submitted: March 1994

PRO GOLF DISCOUNT
32751 Middlebelt Rd.
Farmington Hills, MI 48334
Telephone: (800) 776-4653 (313) 737-0553
Fax: (313) 737-9077
Mr. Steve Gossard, Director of Franchise Development

Number of Franchised Units: 166
Number of Company-Owned Units: 4
Number of Total Operating Units: 170

In Business Since: 1963   **Franchising Since:** 1975

Description of Operation: Pro Golf of America is the franchisor of Pro Golf Discount stores. With Pro Golf, you benefit from our 30 years of experience to give you every opportunity to succeed in the retail golf business. We provide you with instant name recognition, comprehensive training, tremendous buying power, exclusive merchandise program, national programs for advertising, yellow pages and credit cards. We also provide toll-free 800# for our franchisees to use for on-going assistance in their daily operations.

Equity Capital Needed: $350,000 - $400,000

Franchise Fee: $45,000

Royalty Fee: 2%

Financial Assistance: None.

Managerial Assistance: We provide a 2-week training program that covers all aspects of the business from staffing the store to ordering and merchandising. We also provide our franchisee with training manuals

in each of these areas. We have a toll-free number to put our franchises in touch with an experienced problem solver in any phase of the golf business.

Training Provided: Training is provided at our corporate offices. It is for 2 weeks and it covers all major areas required to get the store up and running - from store lay-out to staffing and ordering of inventories to grand opening sales.

Information Submitted: January 1994

RADIO SHACK
1600 One Tandy Center
Fort Worth, TX 76102
Telephone: (817) 390-3381
Fax: (817) 878-6845
Mr. Robert Owens, Vice President

Number of Franchised Units: 1800
Number of Company-Owned Units: 4600
Number of Total Operating Units: 6400

In Business Since: 1921   **Franchising Since:** 1969

Description of Operation: Retail electronics.

Equity Capital Needed: $50,000 - $60,000

Franchise Fee: $5,000

Royalty Fee: 0%

Financial Assistance: None, since our program is being offered only to existing retailers in specific markets. Since the applicants are already in business, they have developed their own financial contacts.

Managerial Assistance: We conduct annual meetings and workshops throughout the year. Frequent visits from experienced management people, offering suggestions and ideas. We make available many of the programs that have been successful at Radio Shack over the years. Frequent in-store visits by experienced representatives. Various training workshops throughout the year.

Training Provided: Data not available.

Information Submitted: January 1994

RAFTERS & PANHANDLER
4699 Keele St., # 1
Downsview, ON M3J 2N8 CAN
Telephone: (905) 661-9916
Fax: (905) 661-9706
Mr. Michael Mayerson, Vice President of Franchising

Number of Franchised Units: 59
Number of Company-Owned Units: 20
Number of Total Operating Units: 79

In Business Since: 1968   **Franchising Since:** 1968

Description of Operation: Franchised kitchenware and giftware retail stores.

Equity Capital Needed: $100,000 - $300,000

Franchise Fee: $25,000

Royalty Fee: 6%

Financial Assistance: None.

Managerial Assistance: We provide on-going support from our operations staff. On-site training includes theory and practical. Opening support, materials for advertising and advice by support staff are provided.

Training Provided: Same as above.

Information Submitted: March 1994

RED GIRAFFE VIDEO
10444 Bluegrass Pkwy.
Louisville, KY 40299

Telephone: (502) 499-0072
Fax: (502) 499-9683
Mr. James L. Cannon, Corporate Controller

Number of Franchised Units: 1
Number of Company-Owned Units: 18
Number of Total Operating Units: 19

In Business Since: 1986   **Franchising Since:** 1992

Description of Operation: Rental/retail sales of audio and video materials and related concessions.

Equity Capital Needed: $215,000 - $413,000

Franchise Fee: $15,000

Royalty Fee: 6%

Financial Assistance: None.

Managerial Assistance: On-going managerial assistance is available at no cost to the franchisee.

Training Provided: An intensive 2-week training period at the home office is required, along with 1 week of training at the franchisee's store.

Information Submitted: January 1994

RELAX THE BACK
5417 N. Lamar Blvd.
Austin, TX 78751
Telephone: (800) 451-5168 (512) 451-9842
Fax: (512) 452-8421
Ms. Virginia Rogers, President/Chief Executive Officer

Number of Franchised Units: 14
Number of Company-Owned Units: 1
Number of Total Operating Units: 15

In Business Since: 1984   **Franchising Since:** 1989

Description of Operation: Franchisor of specialty retail stores, featuring over 300 products for prevention and relief of back pain and related conditions. Products include ergonomically-designed office chairs and workstation accessories, specially-designed home furniture, car seats, specialty sleep products, tools and equipment, travel items and massage devices.

Equity Capital Needed: $55,000 - $150,000

Franchise Fee: $19,500

Royalty Fee: 5%

Financial Assistance: None available.

Managerial Assistance: 2 weeks of training at franchise headquarters in Austin, TX. 1 week on-site.

Training Provided: Same as above.

Information Submitted: December 1993

RODAN JEWELERS / SIMPLY CHARMING
13379B 72nd Ave.
Surrey, BC V3W 2N5 CAN
Telephone: (604) 572-3883
Fax: (604) 572-3993
Mr. Rob Davidson, President

Number of Franchised Units: 10
Number of Company-Owned Units: 4
Number of Total Operating Units: 14

In Business Since: 1976   **Franchising Since:** 1982

Description of Operation: Fine jewelry stores in key corner locations in major regional shopping centers. Turn-key established locations in BC, Canada, with proven track records and profits. No experience necessary. Stores specialize in diamonds, gold, watches, fine giftware, many exclusive lines, full in-store workshop and services at all stores.

Equity Capital Needed: $25,000 - $75,000

Franchise Fee: Rodan Jewelers - $75,000. Simply Charming - $50,000

Royalty Fee: 3% - 5%

Financial Assistance: The franchisor provides assistance by way of preparation and presentation of your plan and pertinent information to lending instructions, as well as offering in-house finance packages.

Managerial Assistance: We provide a manager's meeting every 6 weeks, on-going on-site inspections, constant access to advice and guidance through head office support staff, staff newsletters and full manual.

Training Provided: We offer an extensive in-house classroom training for 2 weeks, followed by a 2 - 3 month training program in-store at the franchisee's location, as well as on-going support, including regular attendance at franchised location for first 6 months.

Information Submitted: January 1994

SHAVER CENTER / CENTRE DU RASOIR
3151 rue Joseph Dubreuil
Lachine, PQ H8T 3H6 CAN
Telephone: (514) 636-4512
Fax: (514) 636-8356
Mr. Paul S. Cooper, President

Number of Franchised Units: 36
Number of Company-Owned Units: 14
Number of Total Operating Units: 50

In Business Since: 1959   **Franchising Since:** 1979

Description of Operation: Sales, service and warranty work (authorized) for over 20 leading names in electrical shavers, personal care and small kitchen appliances.

Equity Capital Needed: $65,000 - $75,000

Franchise Fee: $30,000

Royalty Fee: 3%

Financial Assistance: We provide assistance in arranging government loans and grants and preparing business plan for the bank.

Managerial Assistance: A complete turn-key operation and 5 weeks of training are provided.

Training Provided: We offer 5 weeks of complete training - sales, service, merchandising and administration.

Information Submitted: January 1994

SHOE FIXERS
15965 Jeanette
Southfield, MI 48075
Telephone: (313) 557-2784
Fax: (313) 557-7931
Ms. Colleen McGaffey

Number of Franchised Units: 36
Number of Company-Owned Units: 64
Number of Total Operating Units: 100

In Business Since: 1987   **Franchising Since:** 1987

Description of Operation: Shoe Fixers stores appeal to today's massive market of up-scale consumers - positioned as quality, high-profile retailing environments, while providing the quick service and convenience demanded in today's service-oriented marketplace.

Equity Capital Needed: $45,000 - $102,500

Franchise Fee: $12,500

Royalty Fee: 5%

Financial Assistance: Yes, indirect.

Managerial Assistance: Our franchise development and support team possesses years of experience in the shoe care industry, retail management, franchise operations and marketing. You receive expert guidance from business planning to personnel management.

Training Provided: We provide 14 days at the franchise training center and 5 days on-site.

Information Submitted: December 1993

SHOECRAFTERS
2310 W. Bell Rd., # 8
Phoenix, AZ 85023
Telephone: (602) 863-6985
Fax: (602) 863-6985
Ms. Pamela Lampert, President

Number of Franchised Units: 2
Number of Company-Owned Units: 1
Number of Total Operating Units: 3

In Business Since: 1991   **Franchising Since:** 1992

Description of Operation: Mobile shoe retail and service franchise in a service route format, calling on professionals in their work place. Complete training (technical and marketing) is provided.

Equity Capital Needed: $9,000 - $10,000 total investment.

Franchise Fee: $4,995

Royalty Fee: $100 per month.

Financial Assistance: Some is available - negotiable.

Managerial Assistance: Route planning, marketing, customer set-up, bookkeeping and records maintenance.

Training Provided: Comprehensive program, including 5 days of hands-on training, training manuals and on-going support.

Information Submitted: December 1993

SILKCORP
779 Church Rd.
Elmhurst, IL 60126
Telephone: (800) THE-SILK (708) 833-5500
Fax: (708) 833-5572
Mr. Ed Clamage, President

Number of Franchised Units: 1
Number of Company-Owned Units: 41
Number of Total Operating Units: 42

In Business Since: 1991   **Franchising Since:** 1992

Description of Operation: Retail outlet of silk trees and plants.

Equity Capital Needed: $50,000 - $100,000

Franchise Fee: $25,000

Royalty Fee: 6.5%

Financial Assistance: Not available.

Managerial Assistance: Site selection and financial assistance.

Training Provided: 4 - 6 week training period.

Information Submitted: January 1994

SOAPBERRY SHOP
50 Galaxy Blvd., # 12
Rexdale, ON M9W 4Y5 CAN
Telephone: (800) 387-4818 (416) 674-0248
Fax: (416) 674-0249
Ms. Susan Whyte, Director of Marketing

Number of Franchised Units: 36
Number of Company-Owned Units: 6
Number of Total Operating Units: 42

In Business Since: 1983   **Franchising Since:** 1987

Description of Operation: Specialty retail organization, offering earth-friendly, herbal skin, hair and bath preparations.

Equity Capital Needed: $60,000 - $200,000

Franchise Fee: $27,000

Royalty Fee: 0%

Financial Assistance: None.

Managerial Assistance: We provide site selection, lease negotiations, opening marketing and public relations.

Training Provided: Franchisees must train for 4 weeks at head office, 2 weeks in class and 2 weeks in a shop. Training includes all aspects of owning and managing a Soapberry Shop.

Information Submitted: December 1993

SPORT IT
4196 Corporate Square
Naples, FL 33942
Telephone: (800) 762-6869 (813) 643-6811
Fax: (813) 643-6811
Mr. Rick Hartman, Marketing Director

Number of Franchised Units: 456
Number of Company-Owned Units: 0
Number of Total Operating Units: 456

In Business Since: 1984   **Franchising Since:** 1984

Description of Operation: Dealers sell competitively-priced, brand-name athletic equipment from their homes. The home office offers training, central order processing and free consultation. Dealers can choose from six different selling opportunities: outside sales, fund raising, mail order, home party plan, rep group and catalog retail store.

Equity Capital Needed: $1,500

Franchise Fee: $1,500

Royalty Fee: $25 per month.

Financial Assistance: None.

Managerial Assistance: We provide newsletters, free consultation, service training seminars, conventions, product knowledge, market analysis, competitive pricing, business management, introduction of special programs, etc.

Training Provided: Same as above.

Information Submitted: January 1994

SPORTS SECTION, THE
3120 Medlock Bridge Rd., Bldg. A
Norcross, GA 30071
Telephone: (800) 321-9127 (404) 416-6604
Fax: (404) 416-8302
Mr. Gary Hoyle, Franchise Director

Number of Franchised Units: 74
Number of Company-Owned Units: 2
Number of Total Operating Units: 76

In Business Since: 1983   **Franchising Since:** 1985

Description of Operation: A home-based franchise in youth sports photography, offering over 100 keepsakes with a child's individual and team picture. On-site sales and marketing training, as well as on-site photography training. Franchisees photograph youth groups from pre-schools to soccer, basketball, baseball, etc. - over 200 groups listed.

Equity Capital Needed: $14,900 - $31,500

Franchise Fee: $14,900 - $31,500

Royalty Fee: 0%

Financial Assistance: Financing is available on Plan C. $19,500 is required down with the remainder financed over 1 year.

Managerial Assistance: The franchise development department provides initial business start-up, market development and on-going support in all areas of their operation. Seminars are held twice a year, along with quarterly, 3-day management classes.

Training Provided: Franchisees are provided 3 days of sales and marketing training by the national marketing director. When the first shoot is set up, the franchisee is provided photography training (a 3-day session). Both trainings are provided at the franchisee's location.

Information Submitted: March 1994

STARLOG
80 East Route 4, # 200
Paramus, NJ 07652
Telephone: (516) 759-3380
Fax: (516) 671-1989
Mr. Robert Kushell, Director of Sales

Number of Franchised Units: 1
Number of Company-Owned Units: 2
Number of Total Operating Units: 3

In Business Since: 1992   **Franchising Since:** 1993

Description of Operation: Starlog is a science fiction superstore, with over 6,000 items associated with the world of sci-fi - books, toys, games, videos, apparel, collectibles - special Star Trek section which is designed like a spaceship. It has an attractive comic book section with about 500 magazines. A unique computer program monitors your inventory and sales. Starlog Franchise Corporation is a public company listed under NASDAQ. Outstanding support services are offered to franchisees.

Equity Capital Needed: $196,000 - $266,000, depending on site.

Franchise Fee: $30,000

Royalty Fee: 6% - 4.5% - 3%. First year - $400,000; Second year - $400,000; Third year - $400,000 +.

Financial Assistance: In order to obtain franchise assistance, one should have about 30% cash, plus some type of collateral.

Managerial Assistance: The corporate staff includes site and construction specialists, as well as full franchise training and field servicing support.

Training Provided: We offer 1 week of training at the corporate training center. This will cover all operational and business aspects of managing a Starlog franchise. This is followed by training in your store. Our staff will follow your progress and assist you in "growing" your business.

Information Submitted: January 1994

STRICTLY SHOOTING
25702 Pinewood Dr.
Monee, IL 60449
Telephone: (708) 499-4420
Fax: (708) 499-4421
Mr. Jay Pfeilsticker, Owner

Number of Franchised Units: 2
Number of Company-Owned Units: 1
Number of Total Operating Units: 3

In Business Since: 1988   **Franchising Since:** 1992

Description of Operation: Strictly Shooting offers franchises for the establishment, development and operation of businesses for the retail sale of a wide assortment of high-quality new and used handguns, rifles and shotguns, as well as ammunition and accessories.

Equity Capital Needed: $225,000 - $325,000

Franchise Fee: $20,000

Royalty Fee: 4%

Financial Assistance: We will assist the franchisee in obtaining financing.

Managerial Assistance: We assist the franchisee in all aspects of opening and running his/her business. We help with site location, lease negotiations, store layout and design, stocking and pricing inventory, personnel policies and sales and advertising.

Training Provided: The franchisee will be trained for up to 2 weeks in all aspects of firearms retailing.

Information Submitted: November 1993

SUCCESSORIES
919 Springer Dr.
Lombard, IL 60148
Telephone: (800) 621-1423 (708) 953-8440
Fax: (708) 953-2110
Mr. Terry Keenan, Director of Franchise Development

Number of Franchised Units: 20
Number of Company-Owned Units: 42
Number of Total Operating Units: 62

In Business Since: 1988   **Franchising Since:** 1992

Description of Operation: Successories retail stores sell proprietary products for business and personal motivation. These products include high-quality lithographs, posters, books, cards, apparel and awards.

Equity Capital Needed: $65,000 - $170,000

Franchise Fee: $25,000

Royalty Fee: 2%

Financial Assistance: No.

Managerial Assistance: Successories provides franchisees with a complete operations manual, a weekly newsletter and constant feed-back via periodic visits by corporate representatives.

Training Provided: We offer week-long training seminars near the Company headquarters. Training includes sessions on retailing, visual merchandising, direct marketing, outside sales, computers and accounting, site selection and store operations.

Information Submitted: January 1994

SUNGLASS BOUTIQUE
P. O. Box 21023
Columbia, SC 29221
Telephone: (803) 781-5033
Fax: (803) 781-5033
Mr. Dean Faulkenberry, President

Number of Franchised Units: 0
Number of Company-Owned Units: 8
Number of Total Operating Units: 8

In Business Since: 1984   **Franchising Since:** 1994

Description of Operation: Retail sunglass stores, located in enclosed malls an/or high-traffic tourist locations to sell sunglasses in the $20 - $200 price range. In addition, low-priced sunglasses, readers and assorted accessories are offered.

Equity Capital Needed: $35,000 - $75,000

Franchise Fee: $4,000

Royalty Fee: $10,400 per year.

Financial Assistance: None.

Managerial Assistance: Operations manuals, forms and sales aids are provided, along with on-going assistance, as well as regular promotions, contests and newsletters to provide motivation for all employees.

Training Provided: An extensive 1-week training program is given in one of the Company-owned stores and 1 week of training is provided before and during the store's grand opening.

Information Submitted: March 1994

SWISS COLONY, THE
1 Alpine Ln.
Monroe, WI 53566
Telephone: (800) 356-8119 (608) 328-8803
Fax: (608) 328-8457
Mr. Eugene A. Curran, Executive Director

Number of Franchised Units: 135
Number of Company-Owned Units: 7
Number of Total Operating Units: 142

In Business Since: 1926   Franchising Since: 1963

Description of Operation: Seasonal specialty food and gift shops in shopping malls around the country.

Equity Capital Needed: $15,000 - $60,000

Franchise Fee: $500 per seasonal unit.

Royalty Fee: 4%

Financial Assistance: Not available.

Managerial Assistance: Data not available.

Training Provided: We provide an intensive and all-inclusive 3-day session which covers the seasonal operation from start to finish. Included are sessions on sales training, operations, merchandising and business functions, to name a few.

Information Submitted: January 1994

TOP FORTY
10333 - 174 St.
Edmonton, AB T6K OK4 CAN
Telephone: (800) 661-9931 (403) 489-2324
Fax: (403) 486-7528
Mr. Al J. Herfst, Vice President

Number of Franchised Units: 18
Number of Company-Owned Units: 20
Number of Total Operating Units: 38

In Business Since: 1977   Franchising Since: 1980

Description of Operation: Retailer of pre-recorded music products, such as compact discs, cassettes, videos and other such paraphernalia.

Equity Capital Needed: $120,000 - $200,000

Franchise Fee: $15,000

Royalty Fee: 5%

Financial Assistance: A franchise financing package has been developed with the cooperation of a major chartered bank. Assistance in preparing all of the necessary information and applications is provided.

Managerial Assistance: In addition to the new franchise start-up training, on-going managerial training is provided through regular field visits, counseling from the head office, financial statement review and annual franchise seminars.

Training Provided: Initial training consists of 2 weeks - 1 week at the head office and 1 week at a store location. Upon opening a new store, further assistance and training in starting up a store is provided on-site. An extensive and constantly updated systems manual is provided. Regular operational memoranda are also provided.

Information Submitted: March 1994

TREASURE CACHE, THE
44-F Jefryn Blvd. W.
Deer Park, NY 11729
Telephone: (800) 969-5969 (516) 243-5029
Fax: (516) 243-5908
Mr. Randy G. Romano, Vice President

Number of Franchised Units: 6
Number of Company-Owned Units: 1
Number of Total Operating Units: 7

In Business Since: 1992   Franchising Since: 1992

Description of Operation: Arts and crafts retail stores located in indoor malls. Local and national artisans and crafters rent space in our professionally-designed showrooms and provide all inventory. Turn-key operation provides an excellent return on investment in an enjoyable business.

Equity Capital Needed: $40,000 - $50,000

Franchise Fee: $15,000

Royalty Fee: 6% - 2%

Financial Assistance: Data not available.

Managerial Assistance: Managerial assistance is available in all phases of the operation.

Training Provided: Both initial and on-going training is available. Initial training consists of 1 week of home office and in-store operation and practical application. Follow up is 3 days on-site. On-going 800# assistance line and periodic operational visits, newsletter and updates.

Information Submitted: January 1994

VIDEO DATA SERVICES
30 Grove St.
Pittsford, NY 14534
Telephone: (800) 836-9461 (716) 385-4773
Mr. Stuart J. Dizak, President

Number of Franchised Units: 236
Number of Company-Owned Units: 0
Number of Total Operating Units: 236

In Business Since: 1981   Franchising Since: 1982

Description of Operation: Video, photography and film-to-tape transfers, weddings, other social occasions, promotional and training videos, legal depositions, video editing and special effects. We are the only franchisor to offer a 100% money-back guarantee, even after training.

Equity Capital Needed: $20,000

Franchise Fee: $17,950

Royalty Fee: $500 annually.

Financial Assistance: None.

Managerial Assistance: We provide advertising, marketing, public relations and management consulting via newsletters, phone and an annual convention.

Training Provided: We offer 2 weeks of pre-classroom training and 3 days of classroom training in Rochester, NY or San Diego, CA.

Information Submitted: March 1994

VIDEO QUIKLAB
2121 W. Oakland Park Blvd.
Ft. Lauderdale, FL 33311
Telephone: (800) 225-0005 (305) 735-2300
Fax: (305) 730-0477
Mr. David Bawarsky, Franchise Director

Number of Franchised Units: 0
Number of Company-Owned Units: 1
Number of Total Operating Units: 1

In Business Since: 1993   Franchising Since: 1993

Description of Operation: A retail, multimedia service facility, offering hundreds of video and multimedia services, products and training.

Equity Capital Needed: $475,000 - $550,000

Franchise Fee: $40,000

Royalty Fee: 5% - 7%

Financial Assistance: We will assist in obtaining equipment financing, but we do not provide direct financing.

Managerial Assistance: We offer a turn-key, computerized operation. On-going support through on-line computer and video conferencing.

Training Provided: We provide a pre-training program - 4 weeks at corporate training center and 1 week at the franchisee's location.

Information Submitted: December 1993

VIDEO UPDATE
287 East 6th St., # 615
St. Paul, MN 55101
Telephone: (800) 433-1195 (612) 222-0006
Fax: (612) 297-6629
Mr. John Bedard, President

Number of Franchised Units: 28
Number of Company-Owned Units: 14
Number of Total Operating Units: 42

In Business Since: 1983   **Franchising Since:** 1984

Description of Operation: Franchisor of video superstores. 10 years of experience has resulted in the development of a superior management plan and site selection ability. Video Update promotes the knowledge and material for a turn-key operation.

Equity Capital Needed: $125,000 - $270,000

Franchise Fee: $19,500

Royalty Fee: 5%

Financial Assistance: We will assemble a business plan designed specifically for each prospective location. An in-house CPA will work with candidates and bankers, answering questions and providing information.

Managerial Assistance: A complete and comprehensive operations manual is provided. This material is used in conjunction with our on-site training program. Updates and on-going assistance with store operations are provided on a scheduled basis.

Training Provided: The franchise training program includes 1 week of pre-opening assistance and post-opening training, as well as 24-hour access to toll-free assistance, structured corporate visits, newsletters and an annual meeting.

Information Submitted: January 1994

WEST COAST VIDEO
9990 Global Rd.
Philadelphia, PA 19115
Telephone: (800) 433-5171 (215) 677-1000
Fax: (215) 677-5804
Mr. Mike T. Flannery, Director of Franchise Sales

Number of Franchised Units: 522
Number of Company-Owned Units: 0
Number of Total Operating Units: 522

In Business Since: 1983   **Franchising Since:** 1985

Description of Operation: West Coast Video offers full-service video specialty stores.

Equity Capital Needed: $225,000 - $350,000

Franchise Fee: $25,000

Royalty Fee: 5%

Financial Assistance: Third-party financing.

Managerial Assistance: We provide a formal training program at corporate headquarters, as well as site selection assistance, on-going training and seminars for you and your staff.

Training Provided: Same as above.

Information Submitted: November 1993

WICKS 'N' STICKS
16825 Northchase Dr., # 900
Houston, TX 77060

Telephone: (800) 231-6337 (713) 874-3686
Fax: (713) 874-3655
Ms. Denise Hudson, Franchise Development Assistant

Number of Franchised Units: 197
Number of Company-Owned Units: 0
Number of Total Operating Units: 197

In Business Since: 1968   **Franchising Since:** 1968

Description of Operation: The nation's largest retailer of quality candles, fragrances and related home decorative products. We offer outstanding name recognition, comprehensive training and extensive merchandise support.

Equity Capital Needed: Total investment of $110,000 - $183,000 includes franchise fee.

Franchise Fee: $15,000 - $25,000

Royalty Fee: 6%

Financial Assistance: We provide a finance package in the form of assistance with preparing the proposal for the bank or SBA. We participate in the VetFran program (finance up to 50% of franchise fee).

Managerial Assistance: 2 exclusive buying shows yearly. On-going merchandising support. On-going store visits by operations field managers. Free lease negotiations, legal comments, mall problems (i. e. kiosks, carts, rent reductions), site selection.

Training Provided: We offer 1 week of comprehensive training at the corporate office, 1 - 2 weeks or more in store prior to and during the opening of the store. On-going training/support by field managers and area and regional seminars, etc.

Information Submitted: December 1993

WILD BIRD CENTERS OF AMERICA
7687 MacArthur Blvd.
Cabin John, MD 20818
Telephone: (800) WILDBIRD (301) 229-9585
Fax: (301) 320-6154
Ms. Jane Crowley, Director of Marketing

Number of Franchised Units: 47
Number of Company-Owned Units: 1
Number of Total Operating Units: 48

In Business Since: 1985   **Franchising Since:** 1989

Description of Operation: Supply and educate consumers who enjoy feeding and watching wild birds.

Equity Capital Needed: $35,000 - $49,000 or $52,000 - $73,000.

Franchise Fee: $9,500 or $18,500.

Royalty Fee: 3% first year; 4.5% thereafter.

Financial Assistance: Wild Bird Centers of America provides indirect financing with a business plan kit, including a hard copy business plan, business plan on disk, site selection and lease analysis workbooks.

Managerial Assistance: All aspects of operating Wild Bird Centers and Wild Bird Crossings franchises are supported by an experienced staff, a bi-monthly customer newsletter and advertising support.

Training Provided: The initial training for Wild Bird Centers is 2 weeks long at Company headquarters and emphasizes practical, hands-on activities. On-going activities are conducted through staff visits, regional meetings and annual national meetings. Training for Wild Bird Crossings is 5 days. For an additional fee, Wild Bird Crossing owners can receive additional training days and staff visits.

Information Submitted: November 1993

WILD BIRD MARKETPLACE
710 W. Main St., P. O. Box 1184
New Holland, PA 17557

Telephone: (800) 851-2711 (717) 354-2841
Fax: (717) 355-0425
Mr. John F. Gardner, President

Number of Franchised Units: 17
Number of Company-Owned Units: 0
Number of Total Operating Units: 17

In Business Since: 1988   Franchising Since: 1989

Description of Operation: Wild Bird Marketplace offers a range of products for the birders, gardeners and naturalists interested in their immediate environment. Our primary focus is on birding activities. Our stores are bright, modern and inviting to today's shopper. Located in retail centers, they draw on the booming interest in backyard birding and in bird-related gifts and supplies.

Equity Capital Needed: $50,000 - $75,000

Franchise Fee: $12,500

Royalty Fee: 4%

Financial Assistance: Extended terms are available on some inventory items during the first year of operation.

Managerial Assistance: At present, we have 3 regional representatives working with our franchisees who provide managerial, marketing and other assistance to the franchisees.

Training Provided: Wild Bird Marketplace provides comprehensive training in all areas of operations and management, plus full advertising and marketing support. In addition, we train you in the basics of bird feeding and watching. Training is comprehensive and on-going.

Information Submitted: January 1994

WILD BIRDS UNLIMITED
3003 E. 96th St., # 201
Indianapolis, IN 46240
Telephone: (800) 326-4928 (317) 571-7100
Fax: (317) 571-7110
Mr. Paul E. Pickett, Director of Franchise Development

Number of Franchised Units: 152
Number of Company-Owned Units: 0
Number of Total Operating Units: 152

In Business Since: 1981   Franchising Since: 1983

Description of Operation: Wild Birds Unlimited is North America's original and largest group of retail stores catering to the backyard birdfeeding and nature enthusiast. We have over 150 stores in the US and Canada. Stores provide birdseed, feeders, houses, optics and nature-related gifts. Additionally, stores provide extensive educational programs to the public on backyard birdfeeding. Franchisees are provided with a full support system.

Equity Capital Needed: $60,000 - $90,000

Franchise Fee: $15,000

Royalty Fee: 3%

Financial Assistance: No.

Managerial Assistance: Wild Birds Unlimited provides site selection and lease negotiation assistance. Franchisees attend an initial training session and are then given field training at their store. Support is given in all operational areas, including vendor discounts, business planning, marketing and advertising.

Training Provided: The franchisor provides a 5-day initial training session, covering assorted topics, including customer service, employee training, store build-out, inventory and suppliers, marketing and advertising and detailed business operations. On-going training is given in the form of monthly newsletters, quarterly marketing guides, visits by field representatives and annual and regional meetings.

Information Submitted: January 1994

ZELLERS PORTRAIT STUDIO
3 Picardie St., # 202
Gatineau, PQ J8T 1N8 CAN
Telephone: (819) 561-7113
Fax: (819) 561-2747
Mr. Luc St. Amour, President

Number of Franchised Units: 32
Number of Company-Owned Units: 6
Number of Total Operating Units: 38

In Business Since: 1988   Franchising Since: 1990

Description of Operation: Full professional portrait studio for the family, children, weddings, school and sports photography.

Equity Capital Needed: $25,000 - $35,000

Franchise Fee: $25,000

Royalty Fee: 7%

Financial Assistance: A pre-approved package for leasehold improvements, equipment and inventory is provided.

Managerial Assistance: We provide a full training program on management, marketing, photography and sales.

Training Provided: We offer full accounting, accounts payable, payroll and accounts receivable training. Marketing program on acquisition and special participation in Zellers' flyer.

Information Submitted: January 1994

SECURITY SYSTEMS

ALLIANCE SECURITY SYSTEMS
5 - 140 McGovern Dr.
Cambridge, ON N3H 4R7 CAN
Telephone: (519) 650-5353
Fax: (519) 650-1704
Mr. Brien Welwood, President

Number of Franchised Units: 47
Number of Company-Owned Units: 1
Number of Total Operating Units: 48

In Business Since: 1970   Franchising Since: 1972

Description of Operation: Alliance franchises security alarm dealers.

Equity Capital Needed: $20,000 - $25,000

Franchise Fee: $17,900

Royalty Fee: $100 per month.

Financial Assistance: Assistance on franchise fee and financial package for dealers sales.

Managerial Assistance: Classroom training. On-going sales and technical field support.

Training Provided: Same as above.

Information Submitted: December 1993

CHECKROOM SERVICES
1350 E. 4th Ave.
Vancouver, BC V5N 1J5 CAN
Telephone: (604) 251-1000
Fax: (604) 254-2575
Mr. Don Garden, General Manager

Number of Franchised Units: 2
Number of Company-Owned Units: 1
Number of Total Operating Units: 3

In Business Since: 1993   Franchising Since: 1993

Description of Operation: Manufacture and distribute the unique lock "n" leave coin-operated coat checking machine and associated systems. Providers of in-house/contract coat-check room services.

Equity Capital Needed: $10,000

Franchise Fee: $10,000

Royalty Fee: Included in initial fee.

Financial Assistance: Due to the low initial costs, no financing is available through headquarters. On-going lease and rental options available.

Managerial Assistance: Perpetual assistance as required.

Training Provided: Initial 3 days of training at headquarters in Vancouver, BC, encompassing sales and service of equipment and long-term and short-term marketing strategies. On-site product awareness coupled with live situation solutions.

Information Submitted: January 1994

CUSTOM HOME WATCH INTERNATIONAL
2094 Tomat Ave.
Kelowna, BC V1Z 3C5 CAN
Telephone: (604) 769-4329
Fax: (604) 769-4329
Mr. Terry Bates, President

Number of Franchised Units: 38
Number of Company-Owned Units: 0
Number of Total Operating Units: 38

In Business Since: 1988   **Franchising Since:** 1989

Description of Operation: House-sitting and pet care services. We provide daily house checks for homeowners who are away on vacation or business.

Equity Capital Needed: $5,000 - $10,000

Franchise Fee: $3,950 - $6,950

Royalty Fee: 3%, plus 2% for national advertising.

Financial Assistance: None.

Managerial Assistance: Regular newsletter. Support and marketing ideas as incorporated by head office. A detailed operations manual is available. An 8-hour training course is included in the franchise fee.

Training Provided: Data not available.

Information Submitted: January 1994

FIRE DEFENSE CENTERS
3919 Morton St.
Jacksonville, FL 32217
Telephone: (800) 554-3028 (904) 731-0244
Mr. I. A. La Russo, President

Number of Franchised Units: 25
Number of Company-Owned Units: 1
Number of Total Operating Units: 26

In Business Since: 1973   **Franchising Since:** 1988

Description of Operation: Servicing of fire and safety equipment, such as fire extinguishers, municipal supplies and restaurant fire suppression systems.

Equity Capital Needed: $25,000 - $33,000

Franchise Fee: $15,500

Royalty Fee: 7%

Financial Assistance: We can finance up to $7,000 for qualified applicants.

Managerial Assistance: All training provided in marketing, servicing, warehousing, bookkeeping and site selection.

Training Provided: 2 weeks of initial training provided. All future training provided at franchisor's cost.

Information Submitted: November 1993

FIREMASTER
520 Broadway, # 650
Santa Monica, CA 90401
Telephone: (800) 944-3473 (310) 451-8888
Fax: (310) 395-7048
Mr. Ed Wilmoski, Vice President of Corporate Development

Number of Franchised Units: 436
Number of Company-Owned Units: 0
Number of Total Operating Units: 436

In Business Since: 1962   **Franchising Since:** 1985

Description of Operation: Sales and service of fire extinguishing devices, systems and appurtenances relating to fire protection and suppression.

Equity Capital Needed: Varies.

Franchise Fee: $10,000

Royalty Fee: Data not available.

Financial Assistance: The requirements of an initial fee and a primary fee may be financed by execution of promissory notes which are repaid by semi-monthly deductions from the franchisee's account over a period not to exceed 10 years or less and under the express terms and conditions of the franchise agreement.

Managerial Assistance: FireMaster provides general services, including, but not limited to, telephone answering service for customer calls, mail, accounting for the franchisee's accounts with FireMaster and aid in acquiring certain insurance information, products, etc., along with technical expertise and sales aids.

Training Provided: The following enrichment is available - lectures, seminars, business and procedures, hands-on technical advice, fire protection equipment and service methodology, which includes the use of equipment and required supplies, codes and standards.

Information Submitted: March 1994

INTERNATIONAL LOSS PREVENTION SYSTEMS
1350 E. 4th Ave.
Vancouver, BC V5N 1J5 CAN
Telephone: (604) 255-5000
Fax: (604) 254-2575
Mr. Ian J. Abramson, President

Number of Franchised Units: 28
Number of Company-Owned Units: 2
Number of Total Operating Units: 30

In Business Since: 1987   **Franchising Since:** 1988

Description of Operation: Manufacturer and exporter of shoplifting and employee theft prevention systems.

Equity Capital Needed: $25,000

Franchise Fee: $5,000

Royalty Fee: 1%

Financial Assistance: Up to 50% of start up costs can be financed. The Company will carry these costs.

Managerial Assistance: The Company supports the franchisees in the field and with regular on-site visits.

Training Provided: Training for the new franchisee is approximately 1 week in the head office in Vancouver, BC.

Information Submitted: March 1994

PROFILES - SECURITY & PERSONNEL ASSESSMENTS
P. O. Box 880461
San Diego, CA 92168

Telephone: (619) 280-3486
Fax: (619) 234-9340
Mr. Phil Sprague, President

Number of Franchised Units: 7
Number of Company-Owned Units: 1
Number of Total Operating Units: 8

In Business Since: 1980   Franchising Since: 1983

Description of Operation: Accurate assessments about an applicant's or employee's past and their potential capabilities - attitudes, security risk, alcohol or drug abuse, violence, psychological adjustment and theft investigations. Evaluations of clerks, vehicle drivers, supervisors, managers and executives. No one can match our price or provide employers with as many methods for answering this very important question - Asset or Liability? Make money by providing this valuable answer!

Equity Capital Needed: $2,000 - $15,000

Franchise Fee: $1,000

Royalty Fee: 0%; $3.50 - $5.00 per analysis.

Financial Assistance: $1,000.

Managerial Assistance: Data not available.

Training Provided: 5 days at headquarters in San Diego, CA.

Information Submitted: December 1993

PROSHRED SECURITY
2200 Lakeshore W., # 102
Toronto, ON M8V 1A4 CAN
Telephone: (800) 461-9760 (416) 251-4272
Fax: (416) 251-7121
Ms. Margaret Graham, Franchise Development

Number of Franchised Units: 15
Number of Company-Owned Units: 1
Number of Total Operating Units: 16

In Business Since: 1985   Franchising Since: 1990

Description of Operation: Mobile document destruction business. A business-to-business service with the franchisor supporting the marketing program and handling all telephone inquiries. The franchisee is responsible for customer follow-up, service and managing the shredding operation.

Equity Capital Needed: $100,000

Franchise Fee: $35,000

Royalty Fee: 8%

Financial Assistance: Assistance in arranging leasing options on equipment.

Managerial Assistance: We provide a complete operations manual and 2 weeks of training. On-going support through a central service bureau that handles telephone inquiries, customer database, management, accounting and marketing.

Training Provided: We offer 2 weeks of training with the franchisor, consisting of on-the-job and classroom-style sessions. The franchisee will graduate with an operations manual, maintenance manual and computer software manual. The franchisee will be competent in all aspects of marketing, accounting and customer service.

Information Submitted: January 1994

270

SWIMMING POOLS

CARIBBEAN CLEAR USA
101 Waters Edge
Hilton Head Island, SC 29928
Telephone: (803) 686-5888
Fax: (803) 686-3454
Mr. Jerry Minchey, President

Number of Franchised Units: 200
Number of Company-Owned Units: 0
Number of Total Operating Units: 200

In Business Since: 1977   Franchising Since: 1985

Description of Operation: Caribbean Clear offers a revolutionary new method of purifying swimming pools without chlorine, using technology developed by NASA. Franchisee sells units directly to pool owners in his/her exclusive area.

Equity Capital Needed: $9,760 for initial inventory.

Franchise Fee: $9,760

Royalty Fee: None.

Financial Assistance: No financing is provided at this time.

Managerial Assistance: Caribbean Clear provides on-going management and technical consulting. A staff of engineers, chemist and managers are available to work directly with the franchisee as needed.

Training Provided: An intensive 2-day, mandatory training course is provided for all new franchisees.

Information Submitted: March 1994

PINCH-A-PENNY
14480 62nd St., N.
Clearwater, FL 34620
Telephone: (813) 531-8913
Fax: (813) 536-8066
Mr. John C. Thomas, Vice President of Marketing

Number of Franchised Units: 92
Number of Company-Owned Units: 6
Number of Total Operating Units: 98

In Business Since: 1974   Franchising Since: 1976

Description of Operation: Retail swimming pool supply and patio furniture stores.

Equity Capital Needed: $80,000 - $300,000

Franchise Fee: $15,000 - $200,000

Royalty Fee: 10% (6% royalty and 4% advertising).

Financial Assistance: Data not available.

Managerial Assistance: Managerial assistance is provided.

Training Provided: Initial and on-going training are provided.

Information Submitted: November 1993

TOOLS AND HARDWARE

JUNIOR'S TOOLS INTERNATIONAL
2200 S. Ritchey
Santa Ana, CA 92705
Telephone: (714) 641-8798
Fax: (714) 641-9139
Mr. Mark Skolnick, President

Number of Franchised Units: 3
Number of Company-Owned Units: 3
Number of Total Operating Units: 6

In Business Since: 1985   **Franchising Since:** 1992

Description of Operation: Sales, rental and repair of professional-quality hand and electric tools.

Equity Capital Needed: $75,000 - $200,000

Franchise Fee: $8,500 - $195,000

Royalty Fee: 3%

Financial Assistance: The franchisor will introduce franchisees to potential lenders familiar with Junior's Tools.

Managerial Assistance: We provide 30 days of pre-opening training with management in all facets of the business - accounting, sales, marketing, etc. and an additional 30 days of training with management.

Training Provided: We offer on-site training after opening.

Information Submitted: January 1994

MATCO TOOLS
4403 Allen Rd.
Stow, OH 44224
Telephone: (800) 368-6651 (216) 929-4949
Fax: (216) 929-5008
Mr. Earl W. Farr, Director of Distribution Development

Number of Franchised Units: 853
Number of Company-Owned Units: 0
Number of Total Operating Units: 853

In Business Since: 1979   **Franchising Since:** 1993

Description of Operation: Franchise owners operate a mobile tool truck, calling on professional mechanics and automotive technicians at their place of employment, selling professional-quality tools, diagnostic equipment and service equipment.

Equity Capital Needed: $42,500

Franchise Fee: $0

Royalty Fee: 0%

Financial Assistance: Our in-house finance company will finance up to $27,500 of the initial investment, plus we provide inventory financing for the franchisee and retail financing for his customers.

Managerial Assistance: 46 separate programs aid our franchisees in the operation of their business. Among them are in-house designed corporate business management systems, advertising and sales promotion, field managers (1 per 12 franchisees), training seminars, 40 800# help-lines, etc.

Training Provided: 6 days of classroom training at our offices. 2 weeks of on-truck training with professional trainer. 1 week of on-truck training with district manager.

Information Submitted: November 1993

SERVISTAR HARDWARE
P. O. Box 1510
Butler, PA 16003
Telephone: (412) 283-4567
Fax: (412) 284-1771
Mr. Doug Murdoch, Manager

Number of Franchised Units: 3200
Number of Company-Owned Units: 3
Number of Total Operating Units: 3203

In Business Since: 1908   **Franchising Since:** 1908

Description of Operation: Retail hardware, home center, lumber stores or any combination, catering to contractors, "do-it-yourselfers" and commercial and industrial customers.

Equity Capital Needed: $50,000 minimum.

Franchise Fee: $1,300

Royalty Fee: $2,400.

Financial Assistance: SBA and National Co-operative Bank.

Managerial Assistance: We provide store design, layout, set-up, ordering, advertising, supplies and agricultural guidance.

Training Provided: We offer owner clinics, along with field sales support.

Information Submitted: March 1994

SNAP-ON TOOLS
2801 80th St.
Kenosha, WI 53141
Telephone: (414) 656-4784
Fax: (414) 656-5088
Mr. Tommy Clark, Director of Franchising

Number of Franchised Units: 2630
Number of Company-Owned Units: 820
Number of Total Operating Units: 3450

In Business Since: 1920   **Franchising Since:** 1999

Description of Operation: Mobile franchise, offering high-quality tools and equipment to professional tool-users at their places of business.

Equity Capital Needed: $18,335 - $165,000

Franchise Fee: $3,000

Royalty Fee: $50 per month.

Financial Assistance: Snap-On financing is offered for the total investment, except for the (normally) leased van. A net worth of $30,000 and a 17.5% down payment is needed to qualify. The Sales Rep Apprentice Program allows the candidate to work as an employee for up to 1 year and qualify for franchise financing on more favorable terms.

Managerial Assistance: Data not available.

Training Provided: Training is usually 4 weeks - 2 weeks in a branch and 2 weeks in the field. 1 field manager for each 7 - 10 franchisees provides assistance on an on-going basis.

Information Submitted: November 1993

VENDING

INEDA FRANCHISE SYSTEMS
1045 Palms Airport Dr.
Las Vegas, NV 89119
Telephone: (800) 994-6332 (702) 897-9900
Fax: (702) 897-0276
Mr. Benjamin C. Litalien, Vice President Franchise Development

Number of Franchised Units: 0
Number of Company-Owned Units: 0
Number of Total Operating Units: 0

In Business Since: 1989   **Franchising Since:** 1993

Description of Operation: Ice cream vending system, utilizing an automated merchandiser to distribute premium ice cream novelty products. Includes a delivery vehicle and a minimum of 20 merchandisers.

Equity Capital Needed: $50,000 - $70,000

Franchise Fee: $25,000

Royalty Fee: 0%

Financial Assistance: None; however, the franchisor assists franchisees in applying for leases and/or financing through various sources.

Managerial Assistance: The franchisor locates the sites for each merchandiser, actually installs each merchandiser and readies them for the franchisee.

Training Provided: An extensive 1-week "event" in Las Vegas at corporate headquarters, covering all aspects of operating the franchise.

Information Submitted: December 1993

SUGARLOAF CREATIONS
4870 Sterling Dr.
Boulder, CO 80301
Telephone: (303) 444-2559
Fax: (303) 443-2264
Mr. Randall Fagundo, Vice President

Number of Franchised Units: 40
Number of Company-Owned Units: 2
Number of Total Operating Units: 42

In Business Since: 1987   **Franchising Since:** 1990

Description of Operation: A franchisee granted a franchise to operate a Sugarloaf business shall have the right to conduct a business under the trademark "Sugarloaf" and other trademarks, service marks, logos and identifying features and franchisor's distinctive methods for establishing and operating a Sugarloaf business. A Sugarloaf business places and maintains 1 or more types of coin-operated amusement devices, skill crane amusement devices, vending machines or other dispensing machines.

Equity Capital Needed: $32,000 - $200,000

Franchise Fee: $5,000 - $55,000

Royalty Fee: 2.5%

Financial Assistance: None.

Managerial Assistance: We provide on-site operational training, manuals, video training tapes, group purchasing and annual session and semi-annual owners' and mangers' meetings.

Training Provided: The franchisor offers an initial training program to the franchisee. The training for the Sugarloaf Toy Shoppe business lasts up to 5 days at the franchisor's office in Boulder, CO. Although no tuition or fee is charged, the franchisee will be responsible for travel and lodging expenses associated with attendance at the training. The franchisor provides up to 3 days of on-site assistance for both the Sugarloaf Fun Shoppe business and the Sugarloaf Toy Shoppe business.

Information Submitted: March 1994

UNITED SNACK GROUP
1600 Broadway, NE
Minneapolis, MN 55413
Telephone: (800) 535-9977 (612) 379-7768
Fax: (612) 379-7895
Mr. Edward Klein, President

Number of Franchised Units: 20
Number of Company-Owned Units: 1
Number of Total Operating Units: 21

In Business Since: 1984   **Franchising Since:** 1988

Description of Operation: Snack food services to small businesses with less than 50 employees. Exclusive territory, daily cash flow service business. Customer menus of packaged snack foods and pastries. Company sells all new accounts for owner.

Equity Capital Needed: $75,000 (includes franchise fee).

Franchise Fee: $20,000

Royalty Fee: 5% - first year; $200 per month - second year and thereafter.

Financial Assistance: Up to $20,000 may be financed for qualified individuals.

Managerial Assistance: We provide 10 days of initial home office training, followed by 1 week on-site with the owner. Monthly tele-conferences, annual on-site reviews, monthly research and development newsletter, 800# hotline for advice or help and sales training.

Training Provided: We provide 10 days of home office training, plus 5 days on-site with the owner, as well as an operations manual, training manuals, videos and audio tapes.

Information Submitted: January 1994

WATER CONDITIONING

BYOB WATER STORE
1288 W. Main., # 103
Lewisville, TX 75067
Telephone: (214) 219-1551
Mr. Richard L. Cure, President

Number of Franchised Units: 9
Number of Company-Owned Units: 0
Number of Total Operating Units: 9

In Business Since: 1987   **Franchising Since:** 1991

Description of Operation: A retail operation which manufactures its main product - "water," which is sold to the consumer in his/her own bottle. Other items sold are bottles, crocks, coolers and ice made from the store's water.

Equity Capital Needed: $45,000 - $55,000

Franchise Fee: $10,000

Royalty Fee: 6%

Financial Assistance: Negotiable franchise payments.

Managerial Assistance: Forms, training and an operator's manual, for a simple, low-inventory business.

Training Provided: 1 week of on-the-job training at a Company-controlled store, plus 1 week of training and overseeing the operation.

Information Submitted: November 1993

CULLIGAN INTERNATIONAL
One Culligan Pkwy.
Northbrook, IL 60062
Telephone: (708) 205-5823 (708) 205-6000
Fax: (708) 205-6030
Mr. Kenneth E. Wood, Director of Market Development

Number of Franchised Units: 750
Number of Company-Owned Units: 23
Number of Total Operating Units: 773

In Business Since: 1936   **Franchising Since:** 1938

Description of Operation: Water treatment devices, softeners, filters, drinking water units and bottled water.

Equity Capital Needed: $104,000 - $154,000

Franchise Fee: $5,000

Royalty Fee: 5%

Financial Assistance: A certain amount of inventory can be financed.

Managerial Assistance: Field supervision and conventions.

Training Provided: Extensive training after awarding franchises. On-going training.

Information Submitted: December 1993

WATER MART
33 W. Boxelder Pl., # 105
Chandler, AZ 85224
Telephone: (800) 800-8580 (602) 926-6383
Fax: (602) 926-6463
Mr. Harry McKee, President

Number of Franchised Units: 27
Number of Company-Owned Units: 1
Number of Total Operating Units: 28

In Business Since: 1990   **Franchising Since:** 1991

Description of Operation: Water Mart retail water stores sell purified water that is processed on-site using the very latest in water purification technology. In addition to purified water, each retail store also manufactures purified ice and provides beverages made with purified water.

Each store also carries over 300 water-related products and the list of available products is growing at the rate of about 1 product per week. Territorial development is available in certain markets to qualified individuals or organizations.

Equity Capital Needed: $60,000 - $80,000 (including fees).

Franchise Fee: $10,000

Royalty Fee: 5%

Financial Assistance: Financing of water treatment equipment and ice equipment is available to qualified applicants. This financing is with third-party leasing companies that are familiar with our operations and usually is between $10,000 - $25,000. Pre-qualification is available.

Managerial Assistance: Water Mart provides complete operations packages, including retail signs, forms, testing requirements, etc. We also provide on-going, comprehensive advertising design, expertise and evaluation and are usually able to negotiate better advertising rates via our in-house agency. Each franchisee is assigned a toll-free voice mail box where they receive messages from headquarters on new announcements, products and business-related topics. We also provide comprehensive real estate negotiations.

Training Provided: Water Mart provides a comprehensive, 1 week in-house training program, both in the classroom and hands-on. An additional week of training is provided upon the opening of the franchisee's store. There is also a training class once a month on many topics. The class and hand-outs are also available on video. An experienced staff member visits each store at least once a month.

Information Submitted: February 1994

WATER RESOURCES INTERNATIONAL
2800 E. Chambers St.
Phoenix, AZ 85040
Telephone: (800) 788-4420 (602) 268-2580
Fax: (602) 268-8080
Mr. Chris J. Bower, Executive Vice President

Number of Franchised Units: 34
Number of Company-Owned Units: 1
Number of Total Operating Units: 35

In Business Since: 1966   **Franchising Since:** 1990

Description of Operation: Manufacturing and distribution of residential water treatment equipment.

Equity Capital Needed: $30,000 - $50,000

Franchise Fee: $15,000

Royalty Fee: 1%

Financial Assistance: The franchisor will finance the training fees or equipment purchases.

Managerial Assistance: The franchisor will provide training at corporate headquarters and at the franchisee's location. Training available in all departments.

Training Provided: Up to 13 weeks of training is available in tele-marketing, sales, finance and service departments.

Information Submitted: January 1994

WHOLESALE NOT ELSEWHERE CLASSIFIED

ADVANCED TECHNOLOGY SPECIALISTS
Rte. 9, Box 534, Hi-Tech Center
Crossville, TN 38555
Telephone: (800) 548-5927 (615) 484-5577
Mr. Richard Ordway, Owner

Number of Franchised Units: 0
Number of Company-Owned Units: 1
Number of Total Operating Units: 1

In Business Since: 1986   **Franchising Since:** 1990

Description of Operation: Hi-tech cleaning supplies with video.

Equity Capital Needed: $25,000 - $30,000

Franchise Fee: $9,900

Royalty Fee: 3%

Financial Assistance: None.

Managerial Assistance: Complete training.

Training Provided: 3 days +.

Information Submitted: November 1993

AGWAY
P. O. Box 4746
Syracuse, NY 13212
Telephone: (315) 449-7649
Fax: (315) 449-7260
Mr. Richard L. Kennedy, Manager of Market Development

Number of Franchised Units: 361
Number of Company-Owned Units: 185
Number of Total Operating Units: 546

In Business Since: 1964   **Franchising Since:** 1964

Description of Operation: Agway is a co-operative owned by farmer members in 12 Northeastern states. Agway produces and markets crop needs and services, dairy and livestock feeds, farm related products, pet foods and supplies and yard and garden products. Its internal and external subsidiaries are involved in food processing and marketing, energy products and lease financing.

Equity Capital Needed: Varies.

Franchise Fee: $15,000

Royalty Fee: 0%

Financial Assistance: Financing of a new building through leasing from an affiliated company. Up to 50% of the start-up inventory.

Managerial Assistance: A 4-week training program includes managerial assistance, as well as training from a district manager.

Training Provided: A 4-day operational and product knowledge training program. Set up training and other training programs are on-going.

Information Submitted: January 1994

AIR BROOK LIMOUSINE
115 W. Passaic St., P. O. Box 123
Rochelle Park, NJ 07662
Telephone: (201) 368-3974
Fax: (201) 368-2247
Mr. Ben Zuckerman, Franchise Director

Number of Franchised Units: 150
Number of Company-Owned Units: 0
Number of Total Operating Units: 150

In Business Since: 1969   **Franchising Since:** 1979

Description of Operation: Air Brook is recognized for a standard of service, punctuality and safety second to none. A fleet of immaculate sedans provide ground transportation to and from the metropolitan airports where our firm is an authorized carrier. 160 brand new sedans and limousines offer luxurious ride-with-pride service to special people for every occasion. Air Brook provides group rides, private rides, formal limousine and private mini-buses.

Equity Capital Needed: $12,000 - $18,000 (local franchise).

Franchise Fee: $7,500 - $12,500

Royalty Fee: 60% to franchisee; 40% to Air Brook.

Financial Assistance: Partial interest-free financing for qualified applicants.

Managerial Assistance: Air Brook maintains complete sales, reservation and dispatch departments. The Company provides all customers. The Company also provides all accounting functions, all collections on credit card and charge accounts.

Training Provided: Air Brook maintains training facilities. New franchisees and franchisee's hired drivers are required to attend. Instruction includes forms, daily log records, map reading and customer relations.

Information Submitted: January 1994

ALCOTECH BAR SYSTEMS USA
145 Traders Blvd., # 21/22
Mississauga, ON L4Z 3L3 CAN
Telephone: (800) 565-8129 (905) 568-8556
Fax: (905) 568-9290
Mr. Gordon Brown, President

Number of Franchised Units: 24
Number of Company-Owned Units: 6
Number of Total Operating Units: 30

In Business Since: 1991   **Franchising Since:** 1992

Description of Operation: Area development territory franchise of unsupervised, self-testing breathalizer computers installed in bars and clubs for public use. All bar locations provided with package. Operational time requirement by franchisees is only 1 day per month! Part-time franchise - full-time revenue!

Equity Capital Needed: $25,000 - $70,000

Franchise Fee: $5,000

Royalty Fee: 5%

Financial Assistance: Loan packages available through several banks and trust companies.

Managerial Assistance: On-going assistance, as required. Bar locations provided with franchise package. Monthly updates provided. Yearly software updates.

Training Provided: 3 days of operational on-site training. Monthly update newsletter. On-going video modules. On-going assistance and training, as required.

Information Submitted: December 1993

ARMOLOY CORPORATION, THE
1325 Sycamore Rd.
DeKalb, IL 60115
Telephone: (815) 758-6657
Fax: (815) 758-0268
Mr. Jerome F. Bejbl, President

Number of Franchised Units: 10
Number of Company-Owned Units: 2
Number of Total Operating Units: 12

In Business Since: 1957   **Franchising Since:** 1978

Description of Operation: License of precision, proprietary chromium alloy coating for industry. The Armoloy process creates a thin dense modular chromium (NTDC) coating with a 72Rc surface hardness; excellent friction-reduction lubricity characteristics; superior corrosion-resistant properties; virtually no size changes to coated parts.

Equity Capital Needed: $300,000 - $400,000

Franchise Fee: $50,000 minimum.

Royalty Fee: 7%

Financial Assistance: No direct financing. We will work to create payment schedules where required.

Managerial Assistance: All training provided to key personnel. The sales training program takes 2 - 4 weeks. Processing training takes 4 - 6 weeks. All training is done in the Dekalb, IL corporate facility. The Armoloy Corporation works directly with the licensee during the plant development and the first operating year.

Training Provided: Same as above.

Information Submitted: January 1994

ATLANTIC MOWER PARTS SUPPLY
15965 Jeanette
Southfield, MI 48075
Telephone: (810) 559-1415
Fax: (810) 557-7931
Ms. Colleen McGaffey

Number of Franchised Units: 12
Number of Company-Owned Units: 1
Number of Total Operating Units: 13

In Business Since: 1978   **Franchising Since:** 1991

Description of Operation: Outdoor power equipment after-market parts (small engine, chain saw, lawn mower, snow blower and more).

Equity Capital Needed: $45,000 +

Franchise Fee: $15,900

Royalty Fee: 5%

Financial Assistance: None.

Managerial Assistance: General construction plans, site plans, on-going consultation, pre-opening training in corporate office and on-site training.

Training Provided: One week at corporate office. One week on site.

Information Submitted: January 1994

BEVINCO BAR SYSTEMS
33 Isabella St., # 102
Toronto, ON M4Y 2P7 CAN
Telephone: (800) 665-1743 (416) 960-2195
Fax: (416) 960-1854
Mr. Barry Driedger, President

Number of Franchised Units: 20
Number of Company-Owned Units: 1
Number of Total Operating Units: 21

In Business Since: 1987   **Franchising Since:** 1990

Description of Operation: Liquor inventory control service for licensed bars and restaurants. Inventory stock-taking is done by weighing the open bottles and kegs on our computerized system and counting all full bottles. Sales from the cash register are then entered into the system, producing detailed reports highlighting any and all shrinkage problems to the owner. The service is done on an on-going, weekly basis, creating a terrific cash flow with only a few accounts.

Equity Capital Needed: $20,000 - $30,000

Franchise Fee: $15,000

Royalty Fee: $10 per audit.

Financial Assistance: Third-party leasing on the equipment is available.

Managerial Assistance: Area master franchisees and franchisor are available for on-going hotline support, seminars and training sessions. Quarterly software enhancement updates are provided at no additional cost.

Training Provided: Classroom training and on-site training are provided - typically 3 - 7 days, as required.

Information Submitted: December 1993

BIRDS OVER AMERICA
3926 Innsbrook Dr.
Memphis, TN 38115
Telephone: (901) 797-9897
Mr. Ron Brasfield, President

Number of Franchised Units: 2
Number of Company-Owned Units: 0
Number of Total Operating Units: 2

In Business Since: 1989   Franchising Since: 1990

Description of Operation: Beautiful white birds taking to air, circling the event and flying back to their owner's home or headquarters. Dramatic, spectacular to see and not forgotten. The fee is from $75 to $1,000. Environmentally safe. Growing clients.

Equity Capital Needed: $3,500

Franchise Fee: $10,000

Royalty Fee: 7%

Financial Assistance: $10,000 per area of 1,000,000 population. Smaller area fee can be cut. $25,000 down and 0%. Financial assistance by franchisor, if needed.

Managerial Assistance: Video and print material. Training provided.

Training Provided: 1 week at the franchise site or at headquarters.

Information Submitted: March 1994

CROWN TROPHY
1 Odell Plaza
Yonkers, NY 10701
Telephone: (800) 227-1557 (914) 963-0005
Fax: (914) 963-0181
Mr. Chuck Weisenfeld, Vice President

Number of Franchised Units: 22
Number of Company-Owned Units: 2
Number of Total Operating Units: 24

In Business Since: 1978   Franchising Since: 1986

Description of Operation: Crown Trophy is a rapidly-growing awards business. You assemble, engrave and mass produce awards, selling at discounted prices to many different markets - schools, organizations, businesses, leagues, etc.

Equity Capital Needed: $50,000 - $75,000

Franchise Fee: $15,000

Royalty Fee: 4%

Financial Assistance: Data not available.

Managerial Assistance: The average training program includes at least 2 weeks of on-site training at the franchisee's Crown Trophy store. The contents of training will include instruction in the use of equipment, sales techniques and ordering techniques.

Training Provided: Data not available.

Information Submitted: November 1993

DELINTZ DRYER VENT CLEANING SERVICE
6722 Ralston Beach Circle
Tampa, FL 33614
Telephone: (800) 382-4680 (813) 931-5065
Fax: (813) 932-7175
Mr. Daniel Welhouse, Vice President

Number of Franchised Units: 4
Number of Company-Owned Units: 0
Number of Total Operating Units: 4

In Business Since: 1992   Franchising Since: 1992

Description of Operation: Delintz provides dryer vent cleaning service to commercial and residential customers at their location. Franchisees need service vehicle (truck) and the equipment package is supplied by franchisor. Marketing materials, operations manual and 800# technical support included.

Equity Capital Needed: $17,500 - $30,000

Franchise Fee: $13,900 - $19,900

Royalty Fee: 6%

Financial Assistance: Up to 50% financing to qualified applicants.

Managerial Assistance: Complete office set-up and assistance in organizing business. Accounting and bookkeeping system provided. On-going assistance in establishing business.

Training Provided: Franchisees receive 1 - 2 of days training in all aspects of this business. On-the-job training and 800# support.

Information Submitted: January 1994

DIAL-A-GIFT
2265 E. 4800 South
Salt Lake City, UT 84117
Telephone: (800) 453-0428 (801) 278-0413
Fax: (801) 278-0449
Mr. Clarence L. Jolley, President

Number of Franchised Units: 30
Number of Company-Owned Units: 1
Number of Total Operating Units: 31

In Business Since: 1980   Franchising Since: 1984

Description of Operation: International gift wire network of over 4,000 franchise and dealer locations. Delivery of gifts and gift baskets throughout the US and Canada within 24 hours. The system functions are similar to floral wire services.

Equity Capital Needed: $25,000 - $50,000

Franchise Fee: $10,000

Royalty Fee: 4%

Financial Assistance: Lease available for equipment and fixtures

Managerial Assistance: Initial training newsletters and continual contact from home office.

Training Provided: Initial 3 days of training at home office and 1 - 3 weeks in-store.

Information Submitted: November 1993

FILTERFRESH COFFEE
Trimex Bldg., Route 11
Mooers, NY 12958
Telephone: (800) 463-9754 (514) 676-3819
Fax: (514) 676-1210
Mr. Steve Smith, Franchise Sales

Number of Franchised Units: 32
Number of Company-Owned Units: 3
Number of Total Operating Units: 35

In Business Since: 1984   Franchising Since: 1987

Description of Operation: High-tech gourmet coffee service, using patented, computerized equipment designed exclusively for franchisees.

Equity Capital Needed: $250,000

Franchise Fee: $24,500

Royalty Fee: 5% of gross sales.

Financial Assistance: Financing is available for franchisees with $200,000 in equity in the business and a $500,000 net worth.

Managerial Assistance: Full training provided, including sales, marketing, office management, computerized accounting, asset management/tracking and technical updates.

275

Training Provided: Same as above.

Information Submitted: January 1994

FORCE ONE INTERNATIONAL
333 N. Rancho, # 625
Las Vegas, NV 89106
Telephone: (800) 758-7777 (702) 631-5000
Fax: (702) 631-0565
Mr. Thomas A. Wells, President

Number of Franchised Units: 27
Number of Company-Owned Units: 0
Number of Total Operating Units: 27

In Business Since: 1993   **Franchising Since:** 1993

Description of Operation: Membership organization, providing benefits and services, a discount buying service and business opportunity for all members. Marketing is accomplished through networking. Force One is a unique combination of 2 proven methods of marketing - franchising and networking.

Equity Capital Needed: $1,500 - $4,500

Franchise Fee: $5,000

Royalty Fee: 0%

Financial Assistance: No formal financing; however, in specific situations, where the potential franchisee can demonstrate a commitment to succeed, partial in-house financing can be provided.

Managerial Assistance: Force One International will provide on-site assistance, sales aids, promotional material, local advertising and literature. Force One International is committed to its franchisees.

Training Provided: 3 days of intensive training is conducted in the Las Vegas, NV home office. Complete educational seminars, workshops, videos, tapes, etc.

Information Submitted: January 1994

GLASS MAGNUM
5855 SW 152nd
Beaverton, OR 97007
Telephone: (800) 642-1141 (503) 641-6926
Fax: (503) 641-9393
Mr. John N. Podpah, President

Number of Franchised Units: 11
Number of Company-Owned Units: 0
Number of Total Operating Units: 11

In Business Since: 1982   **Franchising Since:** 1991

Description of Operation: We have developed 8 different glass repair systems. Windshield chip repair, crack repair up to 24" long, plate glass repair, store BB holes, crack-tempered and safety glass repair, graffiti removal, scratch removal, foreign matter removal and antique glass and crystal reconstruction and restoration.

Equity Capital Needed: $10,000 - $11,500; Master program $30,000 - $32,000.

Franchise Fee: $10,000

Royalty Fee: 6%

Financial Assistance: Not available.

Managerial Assistance: Corporate support - Mon. - Sat., 8 AM - 5 PM, as long as part of team. Our concept for success is based on local support by a team facilitator. All supplies and equipment kept in full supply locally. Team support and communication, jointly developing accounts in the local community and being supportive of each other. Quarterly sales meeting and monthly newsletter.

Training Provided: 2 programs: 1) As a master franchisor, you receive 100 hours of classroom training in glass, sales, marketing and enhanced communication skills. Another 50 hours of hands-on, in the field, practical experience. 12-hour test. Free help & refresher courses. 2) As

a franchisee, you receive 80 hours of glass repair training, along with sales/marketing; 50 hours hands-on training in the field. To be certified, you must pass a test. The only complete training program in glass repair industry. Extensive manuals.

Information Submitted: December 1993

HEELMOBILE, THE / HEELS ON WHEELS
3617 E. Oraibi Dr.
Phoenix, AZ 85024
Telephone: (602) 992-2253
Mr. Bruce Lee Baker, President

Number of Franchised Units: 5
Number of Company-Owned Units: 1
Number of Total Operating Units: 6

In Business Since: 1984   **Franchising Since:** 1989

Description of Operation: Assembly of mobile heel repair vans and trucks. Technical training in heel repair. Training in how to set up and maintain a mobile heel repair vehicle.

Equity Capital Needed: $25,000 - $50,000

Franchise Fee: $10,000 - $20,000

Royalty Fee: $100 per month.

Financial Assistance: Financing is available on about 50% of initial investment.

Managerial Assistance: Complete turn-key operation. Van, equipment installed, van painted, materials, operations manual, marketing and training. A technical school is available. On-going support by phone. 24-hour assistance from manager via pager.

Training Provided: Data not available.

Information Submitted: March 1994

HISTORICAL RESEARCH CENTER INTERNATIONAL, THE
632 S. Military Trail
Deerfield Beach, FL 33442
Telephone: (800) 940-7991 (305) 421-8713
Fax: (305) 360-9005
Mr. John Driedger

Number of Franchised Units: 400
Number of Company-Owned Units: 10
Number of Total Operating Units: 410

In Business Since: 1988   **Franchising Since:** 1992

Description of Operation: Specialty retailer of family name histories and coats-of-arms. Hundreds of other heritage-related products are also part of the business.

Equity Capital Needed: $15,000 - $35,000

Franchise Fee: $7,000

Royalty Fee: Key fee.

Financial Assistance: Yes.

Managerial Assistance: Perpetual consultation when needed.

Training Provided: 1 week of on-site training. On-going support.

Information Submitted: December 1993

INDEPENDENT LIGHTING FRANCHISE
873 Seahawk Circle
Virginia Beach, VA 23452
Telephone: (800) 637-5483 (804) 468-5448
Fax: (804) 468-1514
Mr. Chris E. Carpenter, President

Number of Franchised Units: 0
Number of Company-Owned Units: 10
Number of Total Operating Units: 10

In Business Since: 1983 **Franchising Since:** 1992

Description of Operation: Wholesale light bulb supply company. Franchisee calls on local businesses (commercial, industrial and institutional) to supply all their lighting needs. All products are long-life, energy savers. Manufactured to Independent Lighting Corp. standards of quality. All orders are processed through ILFC's headquarters. Low-overhead, high-profit business for sales-oriented people.

Equity Capital Needed: $50,000

Franchise Fee: $24,500

Royalty Fee: 7.5%

Financial Assistance: Yes, 50% down with no-interest financing for 1 year.

Managerial Assistance: The franchisor produces a complete training operations manual and sales aides. Continued market support with updated sales and marketing techniques, plus new product development.

Training Provided: 2 weeks of initial training in franchisee's territory, plus visits on a periodic basis. Home office visits minimum once a year.

Information Submitted: January 1994

K & N MOBILE DISTRIBUTION SYSTEMS
4909 Rondo Dr.
Fort Worth, TX 76016
Telephone: (800) 433-2170 (817) 626-2885
Fax: (817) 624-3721
Mr. Curtis L. Nelson, President/Chief Executive Officer

Number of Franchised Units: 22
Number of Company-Owned Units: 9
Number of Total Operating Units: 31

In Business Since: 1972 **Franchising Since:** 1987

Description of Operation: Distribution and sale of electrical products and fasteners from a "mobile warehouse." 6-month, money-back guarantee in applicable states.

Equity Capital Needed: $25,000 - $85,000

Franchise Fee: $23,500

Royalty Fee: 13%

Financial Assistance: Instead of paying the franchise fee, the franchisee may elect to pay an additional 3% royalty for 5 years. Also, with strong credit the franchisee may sub-lease the "mobile warehouse" from the franchisor. We also offer an unconditional, 6-month money-back guarantee in most states.

Managerial Assistance: We totally manage the franchisee's accounts receivables; we manage their inventory by automatically re-stocking the parts they have sold during the previous week; we also provide several computer-generated reports each month that help the franchisee manage his/her business.

Training Provided: The initial 10-day training course is conducted at corporate headquarters. During the franchisee's first 3 - 10 days in the field, there is a trainer with him/her. During the first year, a trainer rides with the franchisee at least 2 days per quarter. After the franchisee has been in business for 1 year, a corporate representative will spend 4 or more days with a franchisee each year.

Information Submitted: December 1993

KNOCKOUT PEST CONTROL
1009 Front St.
Uniondale, NY 11553
Telephone: (800) 244-PEST (516) 489-7817
Fax: (516) 489-4348
Mr. Arthur M. Katz, President

Number of Franchised Units: 2
Number of Company-Owned Units: 1
Number of Total Operating Units: 3

In Business Since: 1975 **Franchising Since:** 1993

Description of Operation: Pest control services.

Equity Capital Needed: $25,000

Franchise Fee: $15,000

Royalty Fee: 10%

Financial Assistance: None.

Managerial Assistance: Complete marketing and management assistance.

Training Provided: Initial and on-going training on a regular basis.

Information Submitted: January 1994

MAGIS FUND RAISING SPECIALISTS
845 Heathermoor Ln., # 961
Perrysburg, OH 43551
Telephone: (419) 244-6711
Fax: (419) 244-4791
Dr. Richard W. Waring, President

Number of Franchised Units: 1
Number of Company-Owned Units: 1
Number of Total Operating Units: 2

In Business Since: 1991 **Franchising Since:** 1991

Description of Operation: Magis provides full-service fund raising, financial development, marketing and public relations services to all non-profit organizations. Magis conducts major pledge campaigns for new facilities, increases annual giving by 20% or more, builds endowments of $1 million or more, conducts feasibility studies, fundraising audits, personnel searches, writes grant proposals, trains leadership, conducts seminars and workshops, strategic planning, video presentations and newsletters.

Equity Capital Needed: $28,500 - $52,500

Franchise Fee: $7,500

Royalty Fee: 8% or $200 per month minimum.

Financial Assistance: Leased computer hardware, software and office equipment may be financed over 60 payments. Very little capital is needed, as the business can be conducted from your home or added to an existing business with an office already established.

Managerial Assistance: Daily back-up and support. A sales and marketing system. Expertise in all areas of fundraising and development. Whether $5,000 or $50 million is needed, the Magis network can meet the client's fundraising needs. New products and services are constantly tested and offered.

Training Provided: 1 week of correspondence of preliminary materials provided for at-home study. A second week at Magis' headquarters, where all systems are taught. A third week at your location. On-going contact by phone, fax and regular regional seminars. We are looking for people who wish to serve local non-profit community groups and organizations.

Information Submitted: November 1993

MICROTECH
P. O. Box 466
Livingston, MT 59047
Telephone: (800) 354-0371 (406) 222-8102
Mr. Lloyd Black, Secretary

Number of Franchised Units: 0
Number of Company-Owned Units: 4
Number of Total Operating Units: 4

In Business Since: 1986 **Franchising Since:** 1992

Description of Operation: Microtech services and sells microscopes.

Equity Capital Needed: $35,000

Franchise Fee: $15,000 - $30,000

Royalty Fee: 7%

Financial Assistance: None.

Managerial Assistance: We provide 2 weeks of training in the franchisee's exclusive territory, an 800#, mailers twice a year, tools, equipment and supplies. The franchisee does not need a location or office.

Training Provided: We offer 2 weeks of training in the franchisee's exclusive territory.

Information Submitted: January 1994

MR. WIZARD GLASS TINTING
3368 Tennyson Ave.
Victoria, BC V8Z 3P6 CAN
Telephone: (604) 475-2404
Fax: (604) 475-2405
Mr. Wayne H. Good, Assistant Franchise Manager

Number of Franchised Units: 7
Number of Company-Owned Units: 2
Number of Total Operating Units: 9

In Business Since: 1987   **Franchising Since:** 1989

Description of Operation: Commercial and residential and vehicle window tinting. Supply and install Mr. Wizard solar and safety films for 7 key benefits.

Equity Capital Needed: $20,000 - $30,000

Franchise Fee: $25,000 (Canadian).

Royalty Fee: 7%

Financial Assistance: Up to 50% financing is available to qualified franchisees.

Managerial Assistance: Operations manual and training sessions - initial and on-going.

Training Provided: Full initial training with on-site training. Continually up-dated courses. Hotline and newsletters.

Information Submitted: December 1993

NATGO
15965 Jeanette
Southfield, MI 48075
Telephone: (313) 557-2784
Fax: (313) 557-7931
Ms. Colleen McGaffey

Number of Franchised Units: 1
Number of Company-Owned Units: 0
Number of Total Operating Units: 1

In Business Since: 1993   **Franchising Since:** 1993

Description of Operation: If you are a marina or current business owner, and you are looking for an extra product line, NATGO invites you to join them in an exciting new adventure as natural gas, the fuel of the future, is introduced into American boats and automobiles through innovative technology.

Equity Capital Needed: $120,000

Franchise Fee: $40,000

Royalty Fee: 7%

Financial Assistance: Data not available.

Managerial Assistance: Data not available.

Training Provided: 1 week of on-site training.

Information Submitted: December 1993

ORIGINAL BASKET BOUTIQUE
4200 Fairway Place
N. Vancouver, BC V7H 2V3 CAN
Telephone: (604) 929-8552
Fax: (604) 929-8552
Ms. Stella Chandler, President

Number of Franchised Units: 13
Number of Company-Owned Units: 0
Number of Total Operating Units: 13

In Business Since: 1989   **Franchising Since:** 1993

Description of Operation: We are a franchise company with 13 home-based outlets throughout B.C. and the Yukon. We offer unique custom gift baskets, using a wide variety of quality products for every occasion. At present, however, franchises are only available in Canada, as we are not yet licensed in the USA.

Equity Capital Needed: $2,000

Franchise Fee: $6,500 - $9,500

Royalty Fee: 7%

Financial Assistance: None.

Managerial Assistance: We provide start-up training in Vancouver and on-going support.

Training Provided: Training includes full training in basket construction, bow making and wrapping, as well as bookkeeping and office management.

Information Submitted: March 1994

ORTHWEIN WINE CONSULTANTS
1 Walter Ct.
Lake in the Hills, IL 60102
Telephone: (708) 658-1680
Mr. John P. Ruf, President

Number of Franchised Units: 0
Number of Company-Owned Units: 1
Number of Total Operating Units: 1

In Business Since: 1974   **Franchising Since:** 1991

Description of Operation: We specialize in the sale and marketing of exclusive single vineyard premium imported wines. We use the traditional European method of bringing these wines to our customers by arranging a wine tasting in their home or business. We also offer custom-made corporate gifts of wine, champagne, glasses and gourmet foods in stunning gift boxes and wicker baskets. The wine tasting is conducted for an individual or a couple and/or for a small group that have expressed an interest.

Equity Capital Needed: $23,200 - $35,000

Franchise Fee: $10,000

Royalty Fee: 10%

Financial Assistance: None.

Managerial Assistance: 2 weeks of comprehensive training, classroom and in-field, covering marketing, sales, management, product line, personnel management and bookkeeping. 2 months of on-going training at the franchisee's business.

Training Provided: 2 weeks at the home office, plus 2 months on-going at the franchisee's place of business.

Information Submitted: November 1993

PYTHON'S
P. O. Box 6025
St. Cloud, MN 56362
Telephone: (612) 253-9553
Fax: (612) 253-9314
Mr. Daniel H. Huschke, President

Number of Franchised Units: 10
Number of Company-Owned Units: 0
Number of Total Operating Units: 10

In Business Since: 1976   **Franchising Since:** 1989

Description of Operation: A recyclable redemption or buy-back center which handles the widest range of recyclables in the entire industry.

Equity Capital Needed: $80,000

Franchise Fee: $15,000

Royalty Fee: Varies.

Financial Assistance: None.

Managerial Assistance: Each new location will receive assistance regarding office location, procedures, advertisement, equipment and accounting. A manual of instructions is available covering all aspects of the operation.

Training Provided: Initial 3-day session in St. Cloud, MN, with on-site training available at franchisee's location.

Information Submitted: November 1993

RICH PLAN CORPORATION
4981 Commercial Dr.
Yorkville, NY 13495
Telephone: (800) 243-1358 (315) 736-0851
Fax: (315) 736-7597
Mr. W. Randy Wilson, Manager

Number of Franchised Units: 22
Number of Company-Owned Units: 0
Number of Total Operating Units: 22

In Business Since: 1946   **Franchising Since:** 1952

Description of Operation: Franchised dealers operate a direct-to-the-home food service and appliance sales franchise under the name of Rich Plan. Each franchisee provides customers with various food analysis services and offers a line of high-quality, pre-packaged, frozen food. Items are ordered from a price list, food guide or menu planner and are delivered directly to the customer's home. Each franchisee also markets freezers and other appliances for use by its customers. Advertising is mainly direct referrals.

Equity Capital Needed: $50,000

Franchise Fee: $10,000

Royalty Fee: Data not available.

Financial Assistance: None.

Managerial Assistance: Direct on-site managerial assistance is not provided. New franchisees are provided with monthly sales reports, a bi-monthly newsletter and a toll-free 800# telephone access to staff for specific questions.

Training Provided: New franchisees are encouraged to visit the national office in Utica, NY for dealer training with respect to operating a home food service business, sales techniques, dealership organization and financing practices. Training is also available at the other existing franchisee locations.

Information Submitted: November 1993

SCREEN PRINTING USA
534 W. Shawnee Ave.
Plymouth, PA 18651
Telephone: (717) 779-5175
Mr. Russell Owens, President

Number of Franchised Units: 26
Number of Company-Owned Units: 0
Number of Total Operating Units: 26

In Business Since: 1988   **Franchising Since:** 1988

Description of Operation: Full-service silk screen printing franchise - hats, t-shirts, jackets, signs, posters and labels, using ASI full-service computer graphics.

Equity Capital Needed: $60,000

Franchise Fee: $25,000

Royalty Fee: 6%

Financial Assistance: 50% of franchise fee.

Managerial Assistance: 2 weeks of training. On-going phone support, on-site visits and on-line computer help.

Training Provided: 2 weeks of training.

Information Submitted: November 1993

SHOPPING DELIVERY SERVICE OF AMERICA
2 Halsey Dr.
Greenville, DE 19807
Telephone: (302) 429-6985
Fax: (302) 429-6985
Mr. Marc A. Falcone, President/Chief Executive Officer

Number of Franchised Units: 3
Number of Company-Owned Units: 1
Number of Total Operating Units: 4

In Business Since: 1990   **Franchising Since:** 1992

Description of Operation: SDS provides guaranteed contracts with a variety of nationwide companies in the franchisee's immediate area. Advertising support is provided by SDS. Earning potential is limited only by the individual's motivation.

Equity Capital Needed: $15,000 - $20,000

Franchise Fee: $10,000 - $15,000

Royalty Fee: 5%

Financial Assistance: Data not available.

Managerial Assistance: Data not available.

Training Provided: We train our potential franchisees to be very successful in the business. This plan will increase profits and pave the way for new markets to capitalize on.

Information Submitted: November 1993

SPEEDY KEYS
560 Ninth St. S.
Naples, FL 33940
Telephone: (813) 262-7311
Mr. Richard Paganes, President

Number of Franchised Units: 0
Number of Company-Owned Units: 1
Number of Total Operating Units: 1

In Business Since: 1980   **Franchising Since:** 1993

Description of Operation: Mobile locksmith franchise, specializing in auto, residential and commercial accounts.

Equity Capital Needed: $7,500 - $20,000

Franchise Fee: $12,500

Royalty Fee: 5%

Financial Assistance: Financing of the franchise fee is possible. GMAC lease available on van.

Managerial Assistance: We provide a bi-monthly magazine with new products and tips and a hotline to headquarters to help with technical problems.

Training Provided: We offer a home study course, plus 2 weeks of training at corporate headquarters.

Information Submitted: January 1994

SPORTS RECRUITS INTERNATIONAL
3532 Commerce Court
Burlington, ON L7N 3L7 CAN
Telephone: (905) 632-0056
Fax: (903) 847-8108
Mr. Harvey Sullivan, President

Number of Franchised Units: 10
Number of Company-Owned Units: 0
Number of Total Operating Units: 10

In Business Since: 1990   **Franchising Since:** 1990

Description of Operation: International recruiting organization which provides exposure of above-average student-athletes to US and Canadian colleges and universities for the purpose of obtaining a funded college or university education.

Equity Capital Needed: $10,000 - $20,000

Franchise Fee: $10,000 - $20,000

Royalty Fee: Equitable sharing of revenues from profile fees.

Financial Assistance: No financing is available, as the franchise fee is a minimal amount.

Managerial Assistance: The role of a franchisee is principally that of a marketing agent, with all operations support provided by SRI's head office.

Training Provided: We offer a 2-day training seminar at the corporate head office or other suitable locations.

Information Submitted: March 1994

TEMPACO
P. O. Box 54-7667
Orlando, FL 32854
Telephone: (800) 868-7226 (407) 898-3456
Fax: (407) 898-7316
Mr. Charles T. Clark, President

Number of Franchised Units: 16
Number of Company-Owned Units: 4
Number of Total Operating Units: 20

In Business Since: 1946   **Franchising Since:** 1971

Description of Operation: Wholesale and distribution franchise for controls and instrumentation. Protected territories in Florida, Georgia, Texas, Missouri, Mississippi, Alabama, North Carolina, South Carolina, Louisiana, Arkansas, Tennessee and Kentucky.

Equity Capital Needed: $25,000 - $30,000

Franchise Fee: $20,000

Royalty Fee: 50%/50% split of gross margin.

Financial Assistance: We finance half of the licensed franchise fee for the VetFran program. No financing other than that program.

Managerial Assistance: Part of initial training in on-going evaluations and feedback. Also, video and audio tape training on managing and general business.

Training Provided: Initially, 2 weeks in Orlando, FL and 2 weeks in field. On-going in field. Home office training by franchisor and vendor personnel. Occasional regional training as needed. Extensive audio and video technical tapes.

Information Submitted: November 1993

TRUCKSTOPS OF AMERICA
200 Public Square, # 12-5850-0
Cleveland, OH 44114
Telephone: (800) 872-7496 (216) 586-4693
Fax: (216) 586-4706
Mr. Charles H. Gregory, Franchise Development Manager

Number of Franchised Units: 6
Number of Company-Owned Units: 38
Number of Total Operating Units: 44

In Business Since: 1965   **Franchising Since:** 1980

Description of Operation: Full-service interstate highway truckstop and travel plazas.

Equity Capital Needed: Total investment $250,000 - $9,000,000.

Franchise Fee: New building $150,000; conversion $100,000.

Royalty Fee: 4% of non-fuel sales; $.004 per gallon of fuel sales.

Financial Assistance: No direct financing is provided; however, we will assist in developing lender presentations and making presentations for approved projects.

Managerial Assistance: We provide classroom and on-site training. An experienced manager is at new franchised site during opening and for up to 30 - 60 days after opening.

Training Provided: Training consists of on-site training at other established locations, classroom training at our dedicated training center and training at the new franchisee's site.

Information Submitted: December 1993

TWO MEN AND A TRUCK/USA
1915 E. Michigan Ave.
Lansing, MI 48912
Telephone: (800) 345-1070 (517) 482-MOVE
Fax: (517) 482-5070
Ms. Mary Ellen Sheets, President

Number of Franchised Units: 30
Number of Company-Owned Units: 1
Number of Total Operating Units: 31

In Business Since: 1985   **Franchising Since:** 1989

Description of Operation: Local moving company franchise. Trained, polite and humorous movers; clean, new radio-dispatched trucks and equipment; residential and commercial. We sell boxes and packing supplies. "Two Men and a Truck Company Store" - over 40 advertising items for the franchisees.

Equity Capital Needed: $25,000 - $35,000

Franchise Fee: $17,950

Royalty Fee: 4%

Financial Assistance: We will hold a note for $5,000, if necessary. We will help prospective franchisees with bank plans.

Managerial Assistance: A manager of an operating company unit will explain all forms. You will spend a day in the office for on-site training. Toll-free, dedicated line available after training to answer any questions.

Training Provided: A minimum of 5 days is spent in our office in Lansing, MI. Training covers advertising, management, truck maintenance, dispatching and actual packing and moving. We will also train your movers at new location if requested.

Information Submitted: November 1993

UNITED CONSUMERS CLUB
8450 S. Broadway
Merrillville, IN 46410
Telephone: (800) 827-6400 (219) 736-1100
Fax: (219) 755-6279
Mr. Henry Gross, Director of Franchise Development

Number of Franchised Units: 81
Number of Company-Owned Units: 8
Number of Total Operating Units: 89

In Business Since: 1971   **Franchising Since:** 1972

Description of Operation: Private consumer buying service. Members buy at a franchised showroom, directly from the manufacturers, without any retail profit mark-up, saving up to 50% compared to store sales prices. UCC is one of America's most profitable franchises and offers an excellent return on investment.

Equity Capital Needed: $65,000 - $118,500

Franchise Fee: $55,000

Royalty Fee: 22%

Financial Assistance: Financing for $40,000 of the initial franchise fee. Financing for up to 80% of the membership selling price.

Managerial Assistance: We provide regularly updated, comprehensive operations manual, telephone access to 130 specialists at home office. 10-person field staff, monthly newsletters, customized audio and video tapes, quarterly meetings and awards programs.

Training Provided: Training consists of an intensive 4-week training program at the home office, followed by on-the-job training at an established club. Additional training at new franchisee's location for entire staff when club opens.

Information Submitted: November 1993

GROCERY AND SPECIALTY STORES

BENNY'S BAGELS, INC.
2750 Northaven Road, Suite 302
Dallas, Texas 75229
Telephone: (214) 243-1699
Fax: (214) 243-1698
Andrea Dickson, Director of Franchise Development

Number of Franchised Units: 6
Number of Company-Owned Units: 0
Number of Total Operating Units: 6

In Business Since: 1994   **Franchising Since:** 1994

Description of Operation: Bagel bakery specializing in hearth baked bagels. 14 varieties of bagels are baked fresh daily. Benny's offers cream cheeses, gourmet coffees, and specialty sandwiches. Unique store concept with hardwood floors, pine tables and chairs, brick decor, and open baking theater creates a relaxed and warm atmosphere.

Equity Capital Needed: $135,000 to $215,000

Francise Fee: 0

Royalty Fee: 0

Financial Assistance: No.

Managerial Assistance: Evaluations of sites, adaptation of site to standard specifications, marketing and advertising, and continual operational support. Manual for operations, marketing, employee training, and catering are provided.

Training Provided: Comprehensive 2 week training program at corporate stores and headquarters. On-site grand opening assistance for 5 days.

Information Submitted: July 1995

APPENDIX A
Small Business Administration

The SBA has a number of programs and services available. They include training and educational programs, advisory services, publications, financial programs, and contract assistance. The agency also offers specialized programs for women business owners, minorities, veterans, international trade, and rural development.

What Is SBA?

The U.S. Small Business Administration (SBA) was created by Congress in 1953 to help America's entrepreneurs form successful small enterprises. Today, SBA's program offices in every state offer financing, training, and advocacy for small firms. These programs are delivered by SBA offices in every state, the District of Columbia, the Virgin Islands, and Puerto Rico. In addition, the SBA works with thousands of lending, educational, and training institutions nationwide.

Why Are Small Businesses Important?

Small businesses are the backbone of the American economy. They create two of every three new jobs, produce 39 percent of the gross national product, and invent more than half the nation's technological innovation. Our 20 million small companies provide dynamic opportunities for all Americans.

Can SBA Help Me?

If your business is independently owned and operated, not dominant within its field, and falls within size standards met by the SBA, we can help you.

Managing Your Business

Through workshops, individual counseling, publications, and videotapes, the SBA helps entrepreneurs understand and meet the challenges of operating businesses—challenges like financing, marketing, and management. The SBA has business development specialists stationed in more than 100 field offices nationwide. Technical assistance, training, and counseling also are offered by three partner organizations.

- More than 13,000 volunteers in the Service Corps of Retired Executives (SCORE) provide training and one-on-one counseling at no charge.
- Small Business Development Centers provide training, counseling, research, and other specialized assistance at more than 600 locations nationwide.
- Small Busines Institutes at more than 500 universities provide free management studies performed by advanced business students under faculty direction.

Financing Your Business

SBA opens doors of opportunity for small businesses by helping them secure capital. We back eligible small businesses that are having trouble securing conventional financing by offering loan guarantees on loans made by private lenders. We also offer a full range of specialized financing:

- International Trade Loan Guarantees—to finance U.S.-based facilities or equipment for producing goods or services for export.
- Export Revolving Line of Credit Guarantees—to help firms penetrate foreign markets.
- Small Loan Guarantees—to help businesses needing capital of $50,000 or less.
- Small General Contractor Loan Guarantees—for small construction businesses.
- Seasonal Line of Credit Guarantees—for firms facing seasonal business increases.
- Energy Loan Guarantees—for firms that make, install, sell, or service energy equipment and technology.
- Handicapped Assistance Loans—for businesses owned by physically handicapped persons and private nonprofit organizations that employ handicapped persons and operate in their interest.
- Pollution Control Loan Guarantees—for firms involved in pollution control and reduction.
- Loans to Disabled and Vietnam Veterans—to start, operate, or expand a small business.

SBA provides small businesses with long-term loans and venture capital by licensing, regulating, and investing in privately owned and managed Small Business Investment Companies across the country. The agency fosters rural and urban economic development and Development Company Loans, geared to create and retain jobs. It expands access to surety bonds through guarantees on bonding for small and emerging contractors, including minorities, who otherwise cannot secure bid, payment, or performance bonds.

Expanding Your Business

SBA helps small businesses enter and succeed in the global marketplace through counseling by international trade experts, training sessions, publications, and Matchmaker Trade Missions (co-sponsored with the U.S. Department of Commerce to link U.S. firms with potential foreign buyers). The SBA helps small businesses secure their fair share of the billions of dollars in federal contracts awarded each year.

Working closely with all federal agencies, we monitor and help increase both the dollar value and percentage or prime, and subcontract awards to small firms. Through the Procurement Automated Source System (PASS) we electronically bring resumes of qualified small businesses to the desks of thousands of government procurement officials and large government prime contractors throughout the U.S.

The Small Business Innovation Research (SBIR) Program is a competitive three-phase award system that provides qualified small business concerns with opportunities to propose innovative ideas that meet the specific research and R&D needs of the Federal Government as stated in each of the SBIR Program solicitations.

The SBA has offices located throughout the country. For the one nearest you, consult the telephone directory under "U.S. Government", or call the Small Business Answer Desk at 1-800-8-ASK-SBA or (202) 205-7064 (fax). For the hearing impaired, the TDD number is (202) 205-7333.

All of SBA's programs and services are extended to the public on a nondiscriminatory basis.

Small Business Administration Offices

Type	City	State	Zip Code	Address	Phone Number
DO	Anchorage	AK	99501-7559	222 West 8th Avenue, #67	(907)271-4022
DO	Birmingham	AL	35203-2398	2121 8th Ave. N., #200	(205)731-1338
DO	Little Rock	AR	72202	2120 Riverfront Drive, Ste. 100	(501)324-5813
DO	Phoenix	AZ	85004-4599	2005 N. Central Avenue	(602)640-2316
POD	Tucson	AZ	85701-1319	300 West Congress Street, #7H	(602)670-4759
DO	Fresno	CA	93727-1547	2719 N. Air Fresno Drive	(209)487-5605
DO	Glendale	CA	91203-2304	330 N. Brand Boulevard, Ste. 1200	(213)894-7173
BO	Sacramento	CA	95814-2413	660 J Street, Ste. #215	(916)551-1445
DO	San Diego	CA	92188-0270	880 Front Street, Ste. 4-S-29	(619)557-7269
DO	San Francisco	CA	94105-1988	211 Main Street	(415)744-8941
RO	San Francisco	CA	94105	71 Stevenson Street	(415)744-6408
DO	Santa Ana	CA	92703-2352	200 W. Civic Center Dr., #106	(714)836-2494
POD	Ventura	CA	93003-4459	6477 Telephone Road, Ste. 10	(805)642-1866
DO	Denver	CO	80201-0660	721 19th Street, #454	(303)844-3984
RO	Denver	CO	80202	999 18th Street, Ste. 701	(303)294-7116
DO	Hartford	CT	06106	330 Main Street	(203)240-4700
DO	Washington	DC	20036	1111 18th Street, N.W.	(202)634-1500
BO	Wilmington	DE	19801	920 N. King Street, #412	(302)573-6295
DO	Coral Gables	FL	33146-2911	1320 S. Dixie Highway, Ste. 501	(305)536-5521
DO	Jacksonville	FL	32256-7504	7825 Baymeadows Way, Ste. 100B	(904)443-1914
POD	Tampa	FL	33602-3945	501 E. Polk Street, #104	(813)228-2594
POD	West Palm Beach	FL	33407-2044	5601 Corporate Way, Ste. 402	(407)689-3922
DO	Atlanta	GA	30367	1720 Peachtree Road, NW, #600	(404)347-2441
RO	Atlanta	GA	30367-8102	1375 Peachtree Road, NE, 5th Fl.	(404)347-4048
POD	Statesboro	GA	30458	52 N. Main Street, #225	(912)489-8719
DO	Honolulu	HI	96850-4981	300 Ala Moana Boulevard, #2213	(808)541-2990
DO	Cedar Rapids	IA	52401-1806	215 4th Avenue, Ste. 200	(319)362-6405
DO	Des Moines	IA	50309	210 Walnut Street, #749	(515)284-4422
DO	Boise	ID	83702-5745	1020 Main Street, #290	(208)334-9365
DO	Chicago	IL	60661-9987	500 W. Madison Street, Ste. 1250	(312)353-5429
RO	Chicago	IL	60606-6611	300 S. Riverside Plaza, Ste. 1975S	(312)353-4252
BO	Springfield	IL	62704	511 W. Capitol St., Ste. 302	(217)492-4416
DO	Indianapolis	IN	46204-1873	429 N. Pennsylvania, Ste. 100	(317)226-7269
DO	Wichita	KS	67202	100 East English Street, Ste. 510	(316)269-6616
DO	Louisville	KY	40202	600 Dr. M.L. King Jr. PL	(502)582-5971
DO	New Orleans	LA	70130	365 Canal Street	(504)589-6685
POD	Shreveport	LA	71101-5523	401 Edwards Street	(318)676-3196
DO	Augusta	ME	04330	40 Western Avenue	(207)622-8371
DO	Baltimore	MD	21201-2525	10 N. Calvert Street	(410)962-4392
DO	Boston	MA	01111-1093	10 Causeway Street, #265	(617)565-5584
RO	Boston	MA	02110	155 Federal Street	(617)451-2047
BO	Springfield	MA	01103	1550 Main Street, #212	(413)785-0268
DO	Detroit	MI	48226-2573	477 Michigan Avenue, Ste. 515	(313)226-6075
BO	Marquette	MI	49885	300 S. Front Street	(906)225-1108
DO	Minneapolis	MN	55403-1563	100 N. 6th Street	(612)370-2324
DO	Kansas City	MO	64105	323 West 8th Street	(816-374-6708
RO	Kansas City	MO	64105	323 West 8th Street	(816)374-6380
BO	Springfield	MO	65802-3200	620 S. Glenstone Street, Ste. 110	(417)864-7670
DO	St. Louis	MO	63101	815 Olive Street	(314)539-6600
BO	Gulfport	MS	39501-7758	1 Hancock Plaza, Ste. 1001	(601)863-4449
DO	Jackson	MS	39201	101 W. Capitol Street, Ste. 400	(601)965-5825
DO	Helena	MT	59626	301 South Park, #528	(406)449-5381

DO = District Office / RO = Regional Office / BO = Branch Office / POD = Post of Duty

Type	City	State	Zip Code	Address	Phone Number
DO	Omaha	NE	68154	11145 Mill Valley Road	(402)221-4691
DO	Las Vegas	NV	89125-2527	301 East Steward Street	(702)388-6611
POD	Reno	NV	89505-3216	50 South Virginia Street, #238	(702)784-5268
DO	Concord	NH	03301-1257	55 Pleasant Street, #210	(603)225-1400
POD	Camden	NJ	08104	2600 Mt. Ephraim Ave.	(609)757-5183
DO	Newark	NJ	07102	60 Park Place	(201)645-2434
DO	Albuquerque	NM	87102	625 Silver Avenue, SW, Ste. 320	(505)766-1870
POD	Albany	NY	12207	Leo O'Brian Bldg., Rm. 815	(518)472-6300
DO	Buffalo	NY	14202	111 West Huron Street, #1311	(716)846-4301
BO	Elmira	NY	14901	333 East Water Street	(607)734-8130
BO	Melville	NY	11747	35 Pinelawn Road, #102E	(516)454-0750
DO	New York	NY	10278	26 Federal Plaza, #3100	(212)264-9487
RO	New York	NY	10278	26 Federal Plaza, #31-08	(212)264-4480
BO	Rochester	NY	14614	100 State Street, #410	(716)263-6700
DO	Syracuse	NY	13260-7317	100 S. Clinton Street, #1071	(315)423-5377
DO	Charlotte	NC	28202-2313	200 S. Church Street, #300	(704)344-6587
DO	Fargo	ND	58108-3086	657 2nd Avenue North, #218	(701)239-5131
BO	Cincinnati	OH	45202	525 Vine Street, Ste. 850	(513)684-2814
DO	Cleveland	OH	44144-2507	1111 Superior Avenue	(216)522-4180
DO	Columbus	OH	43215-2592	2 Nationwide Plaza, Ste. 1400	(614)469-6860
DO	Oklahoma City	OK	73102	210 Park Avenue, Ste. 1300	(405)231-5521
DO	Portland	OR	97201-6605	222 S.W. Columbia St., Ste. 500	(503)326-5203
BO	Harrisburg	PA	17101	100 Chestnut Street, Ste. 309	(717)782-4405
DO	King of Prussia	PA	19406	475 Allendale Road, Ste. 201	(610)962-3815
RO	King of Prussia	PA	19406	475 Allendale Road, Ste. 201	(215)962-3755
DO	Pittsburgh	PA	15222	960 Penn Avenue	(412)644-2780
BO	Wilkes-Barre	PA	18701	20 N. Pennsylvania Avenue, #2327	(717)826-6497
DO	Providence	RI	02903	380 Westminister Mall	(401)528-4584
DO	Columbia	SC	29202	1835 Assembly Street, #358	(803)765-5376
DO	Sioux Falls	SD	57102	110 South Main Avenue, Ste. 101	(605)330-4231
DO	Nashville	TN	37228-1500	50 Vantage Way, Ste. 201	(615)736-5887
POD	Austin	TX	78701	300 East 8th Street, #520	(512)482-5288
BO	Corpus Christi	TX	78476	606 North Carancahua, Ste. 1200	(512)888-3301
DO	Dallas	TX	76155	4300 Amon Carter Blvd., Ste. 114	(817)885-6504
RO	Dallas	TX	75235-3391	8625 King George Drive, Bldg. C	(214)767-7659
DO	El Paso	TX	79935	10737 Gateway West	(915)540-5676
BO	Ft. Worth	TX	76102	819 Taylor Street, #8A27	(817)334-3777
DO	Harlingen	TX	78550	222 East Van Buren, Ste. 550	(512)427-8533
DO	Houston	TX	77074-1591	9301 S.W. Freeway, Ste. 550	(713)733-6579
DO	Lubbock	TX	79401-2693	1611 Tenth Street	(806)743-7462
POD	Marshall	TX	75670	505 East Travis, #103	(214)935-5257
DO	San Antonio	TX	78206	727 E. Durango, #A527	(210)229-5900
DO	Salt Lake City	UT	84138-1195	125 South State Street, #2237	(801)524-3209
DO	Richmond	VA	23240	400 N. 8th Street	(804)771-2400
DO	Montpelier	VT	05602	87 State Street, #205	(802)828-4422
DO	Seattle	WA	98174-1088	915 2nd Ave., #1792	(206)553-8405
RO	Seattle	WA	98121	2615 4th Ave., #440	(206)553-1456
DO	Spokane	WA	99204	West 601 First Avenue	(509)353-2809
DO	Madison	WI	53703	212 E. Washington Avenue, #213	(608)264-5518
BO	Milwaukee	WI	53203	310 W. Wisconsin Avenue, Ste. 400	(414)297-3941
BO	Charleston	WV	25301	550 Eagan Street, #309	(304)347-5220
DO	Clarksburg	WV	26301	168 W. Main Street	(304)623-5631
DO	Casper	WY	82602-2839	100 East B Street	(307)261-5761

DO = District Office   /   RO = Regional Office   /   BO = Branch Office   /   POD = Post of Duty

Small Business Administration Offices
Outside the Continental United States

Type	City	Country	Zip Code	Address	Phone Number
BO	Agana	Guam	96910	238 Archbishop F.C. Flores St., #508	(671)472-7277
DO	Hato Rey	Puerto Rico	00918	Carlos Chardon Ave., #691	(809)766-5002
POD	Christiansted	U.S. Virgin Islands	00820	4C & 4D Este Sion Farm, #7	(809)778-5380
POD	St. Thomas	U.S. Virgin Islands	00801	Veterans Drive, #283	(809)774-8530

Thirty-One Most Frequently Asked Questions of the SBA

1. Do I have what it takes to own/manage a small business?

You will be your own most important employee, so an objective appraisal of your strengths and weaknesses is essential. Some questions to ask yourself are: Am I a self-starter? How well do I get along with a variety of personalities? How good am I at making decisions? Do I have the physical and emotional stamina to run a business? How well do I plan and organize? Are my attitudes and drive strong enough to maintain motivation? How will the business affect my family?

2. What business should I choose?

Usually, the best business for you is the one in which you are most skilled and interested. As you review your options, you may wish to consult local experts and businesspersons about the growth potential of various businesses in your area. Matching your background with the local market will increase your chance of success.

3. What is a business plan and why do I need one?

A business plan precisely defines your business, identifies your goals and serves as your firm's resume. Its basic components include a current and performance balance sheets, an income statement, and a cash flow analysis. It helps you allocate resources properly, handle unforeseen complications, and make the right decisions. Because it provides specific and organized information about your company and how you will repay borrowed money, a good business plan is a crucial part of any loan package. Additionally, it can tell your sales personnel, suppliers, and others about your operations and goals.

4. Why do I need to define my business in detail?

It may seem silly to ask yourself, "What business am I really in?", but some owner-managers have gone broke because they never answered that question. One watch store owner realized that most of his time was spent repairing watches while most of his money was spent selling them. He finally decided he was in the repair business and discontinued the sales operations. His profits improved dramatically.

5. What legal aspects do I need to consider?

Licenses required, zoning laws, and other regulations vary from business to business and from state to state. Your local Small Business Administration (SBA) office and/or chamber of commerce will provide you with general information, but you will need to consult your attorney for advice specific to your enterprise and area. You also must decide about your form of organization (corporation, partnership, or sole proprietorship) or tax status (e.g., should you opt for a Subchapter S status?).

6. What do I need to succeed in a business?

There are four basics of success in small business:

- Sound management practices
- Industry experience
- Technical support
- Planning ability

Few people start a business with all of these bases covered. Honestly assess your own experience and skills; then look for partners or key employees to compensate for your deficiencies.

7. Would a partner(s) make it easier to be successful?

A business partner does not guarantee success. If you require additional management skills or start-up capital, engaging a partner may be your best decision. Personality and character, as well as ability to give technical or financial assistance, determine the ultimate success of a partnership.

8. How can I find qualified employees?

Choose your employees carefully. Decide beforehand what you want them to do. Be specific. You may need flexible employees who can shift from task to task as required. Interview and screen applicants with care. Remember, good questions lead to good answers—the more you learn about each applicant's experience and skills, the better prepared you are to make your decision.

9. How do I set wage levels?

Wage levels are calculated using position importance and skill required as criteria. Consult your trade association and accountant to learn the most current practices, cost ratios, and profit margins in your business field. While there is a minimum wage set by federal law for most jobs, the actual wage paid is entirely between you and your prospective employee.

10. What other financial responsibilities do I have for employees?

You must withhold federal and state income taxes, contribute to unemployment and workers compensation systems, and match Social Security contributions. You may also wish to inquire about key employee life or disability insurance. Because laws on these matters vary from state to state, you probably should consult local information sources and/or SBA offices.

11. What kind of security measures must I take?

Crimes ranging from armed robbery to embezzlement can destroy even the best businesses. You should install a good physical security system. Just as important, you must establish policies and safeguards to ensure awareness and honesty among your personnel. Because computer systems can be used to defraud as well as keep records, you should check into a computer security program. Consider taking seminars on how to spot and deter shoplifting and how to handle cash and merchandise; it is time and money well spent. Finally, careful screening when hiring can be your best ally against crime.

12. Should I hire family members to work for me?

Frequently, family members of the owner "help out in the business." For some small business owners it is a rewarding experience; for others it can cause irreparable damage. Carefully consider their loyalty and respect for you as the owner-manager. Can you keep your family and business decisions separate?

13. Do I need a computer?

Small business today faces growing inventory requirements, increased customer expectations, rising costs, and intense competition. Computers can provide information that leads to better returns on investment. At the same time, they help you cope with the many other pressures of your business. Computers are not cure-alls, however, and considerable care should be given to (1) deciding if you need one, and (2) selecting the best system (or personal computer) for your business.

14. What about telecommunications?

All small businesses share some common functions: sales, purchasing, financing, operations, and administration. Depending on your individual business, telecommunications can support your objectives in any or all of these areas. In its basic form, the telephone (the terminal) and the network (local or long distance) make up the basic components of telecommunications. It is an effective tool that can easily change with seasonality and growth. How you use telecommunications can affect how efficiently and profitably your company grows in the future.

15. How much money do I need to get started?

Once you have taken care of your building and equipment needs you also must have enough money on hand to cover operating expenses for at least a year. These expenses include your salary as the owner and money to repay your loans. One of the leading causes of business failure is insufficient start-up capital. Consequently, you should work closely with your accountant to estimate your cash flow needs.

16. What are the alternatives in financing a business?

Committing your own funds is often the first financing step. It is certainly the best indicator of how serious you are about your business. Risking your own money gives confidence for others to invest in your business. You may want to consider family members or a partner for additional financing. Banks are an obvious source of funds. Other loan sources include commercial finance companies, venture capital firms, local development companies, and life insurance companies. Trade credit, selling stock, and equipment leasing offer alternatives to borrowing. Leasing, for example, can be an advantage because it does not tie up your cash. Ask your local SBA office for information about these various sources as well as materials produced by SBA including publications such as "Focus on the Facts."

17. What do I have to do to get a loan?

Initially, the lender will ask three questions: How will you use the loan? How much do you need to borrow? How will you repay the loan? When you apply for the loan, you must provide projected financial statements and a cohesive, clear business plan which supplies the name of the firm, location, production facilities, legal structure, and business goals. A clear description of your experience and management capabilities, as well as the expertise of other key personnel, will also be needed.

18. What kind of profits can I expect?

Not an easy question. However, there are standards of comparison called "industry ratios" which can help you estimate your profits. Return on Investment (ROI), for example, estimates the amount of profit gained on a given number of dollars invested in the business. These ratios are broken down by Standard Industrial Classification (SIC) code and size so you can look up your type of business to see what the industry averages are. These figures are published by several groups and can be found at your library. Help is also available through the SBA and the trade associations that serve your industry.

19. What should I know about accounting and bookkeeping?

The importance of keeping adequate records cannot be stressed too much. Without records, you cannot see how well your business is doing and where it is going. At a minimum, records are needed to substantiate:

1. Your tax returns under Federal and State laws including income tax and Social Security laws
2. Your request for credit from vendors or a loan from a bank
3. Your claims about the business, should you wish to sell it

But most important, you need them to run your business successfully and to increase your profits.

20. How do I set up the right record keeping system for my business?

The kind of records and how many you need depend on your particular operation. The SBA's resources and an accountant can provide you with many options. When deciding what is and is not necessary, keep in mind the following questions:

1. How will this record be used?
2. How important is this information likely to be?
3. Is the information available elsewhere in an equally accessible form?

21. What financial statements will I need?

You should prepare and understand two basic financial statements:

1. The balance sheet, which is a record of assets, liabilities and capital
2. The income (profit and loss) statement, a summary of your earnings and expenses over a given period of time

22. What does marketing involve?

Marketing is your most important organizing tool. There are four basic aspects of marketing, often called the "4 P's":

1. **Product:** The item or service you sell.
2. **Price:** The amount you charge for your product or service.
3. **Promote:** The ways you inform your market as to who, what, and where you are.
4. **Provide:** The channels you use to take the product to the customer.

As you can see, marketing encompasses much more than just advertising or selling. For example, a major part of marketing involves researching your customers: What do they want? What can they afford? What do they think? Your understanding and application of the answers to such questions will help guarantee success.

23. What is my market potential?

The principles of determining market share and market potential are the same for all geographic areas. Determine a customer profile (who) and the geographic size of the market (how many). This is the general market potential. Knowing the number and strength of your competitors (and then estimating the share of business you will take from them) will give you the market potential specific to your enterprise.

24. What about advertising?

Your business growth will be influenced by how well you plan and execute an advertising program. Because it is one of the main creators of your business' image, it must be well planned and well budgeted. Contact local advertising agencies or a local SBA office to assist you in devising an effective advertising strategy.

25. How do I set price levels?

The price of a service or item is based on three basic production costs: direct materials, labor, and overhead. After these costs are determined, a price is then selected that will be both profitable and competitive. Because pricing can be a complicated process, you may wish to seek help from an expert.

26. Are some locations better than others?

Time and effort devoted to selecting where to locate your business can mean the difference between success and failure. The kind of business you are in, the potential market, availability of employees, and the number of competitive establishments all determine where you should put your business.

27. Is it better to lease or buy the store (plant) and equipment?

This is a good question and needs to be considered carefully. Leasing does not tie up your cash; a disadvantage is that the item then has no resale or salvage value since you do not own it. Careful weighing of alternatives and a cost analysis will help you make the best decision.

28. Can I operate a business from my home?

Yes. In fact, experts estimate that as many as 20 percent of new small business enterprises are operated out of the owner's home. Local SBA offices and state chambers of commerce can provide pertinent information on how to manage a home-based business.

29. How do I find out about suppliers/manufacturers/ distributors?

Most suppliers want new accounts. A prime source for finding suppliers is the *Thomas Register,* which lists manufacturers by categories and geographic area. Most libraries have a directory of manufacturers listed by state. If you know the product line manufacturers, a letter or phone call to the companies will get you the local distributor-wholesaler. In some lines, trade shows are good sources of getting suppliers and looking over competing products.

30. Where can I go for help?

The U.S. Small Business Administration has offices in nearly every major city in the country. SBA's Office of Business Initiatives operates the toll-free "Answer Desk" at 1-800-8-ASK-SBA, to give callers direct referral to appropriate sources of information. Sponsored by SBA are a variety of counselling, training, and information services including the Service Corps of Retired Executives (SCORE), Small Business Institutes (SBI), and Small Business Development Centers (SBDC). In addition, procurement center representatives can be found at each major military installation. More than 2,700 chambers of commerce are located throughout the country to provide additional assistance.

31. What do I do when I'm ready?

You have done your homework: you have a complete business plan; you know where you want to operate; you know how much cash you will need; and you have specific information on employee, vendor, and market possibilities. You now may want someone to look over your plans objectively. Contact the business department at a local college for another opinion. A SCORE representative at the Small Business Administration can also review your work and help with the fine-tuning. Then, when you have made the final decision to go ahead, it is time to call the bank and get going. Good luck!

APPENDIX B
Small Business Development Center Program

The U.S. Small Business Administration (SBA) organized the Small Business Development Center (SBDC) Program to make management assistance and counseling widely available to present and prospective small business owners. SBDCs offer "one-stop" assistance to small businesses providing a wide variety of information and guidance in central and easily accessible locations.

The program is a cooperative effort of the private sector, the educational community, and federal, state and local governments. It enhances economic development by providing small businesses with management and technical assistance.

There are now 56 small business development centers—one in every state (Texas has four), the District of Columbia, Puerto Rico, and the U.S. Virgin Islands—with a network of more than 950 service locations. In each state there is a lead organization which sponsors the SBDC and manages the program. The lead organization coordinates program services offered to small businesses through a network of subcenters and satellite locations in each state. Subcenters are located at colleges, universities, community colleges, vocational scoools, chambers of commerce, and economic development corporations.

SBDC assistance is tailored to the local community and the needs of individual clients. Each center develops services in cooperation with local SBA district offices to ensure statewide coordination with other available resources.

Each center has a director, staff members, volunteers, and part-time personnel. Qualified individuals recruited from professional and trade associations, the legal and banking community, academia, chambers of commerce, and SCORE (the Service Corps of Retired Executives) are among those who donate their services. SBDCs also use paid consultants, consulting engineers, and testing laboratories from the private sector to help clients who need specialized expertise.

The SBA provides 50 percent or less of the operating funds for each state SBDC; one or more sponsors provide the rest. These matching fund contributions are provided by state legislatures, private sector foundations and grants, state and local chambers of commerce, state-chartered economic development corporations, public and private universities, vocational and technical schools, community colleges, etc. Increasingly, sponsors' contributions exceed the minimum 50 percent matching share.

The SBDC Program is designed to deliver up-to-date counseling, training, and technical assistance in all aspects of small business management. SBDC services include, but are not limited to, assisting small businesses with financial, marketing, production, organization, engineering and technical problems, and feasibility studies. Special SBDC programs and economic development activities include international trade assistance, technical assistance, procurement assistance, venture capital formation, and rural development.

The SBDCs also make special efforts to reach minority members of socially and economically disadvantaged groups, veterans, women, and the disabled. Assistance is provided to both current or potential small business owners. They also provide assistance to small businesses applying for Small Business Innovation and Research (SBIR) grants from federal agencies.

Assistance from an SBDC is available to anyone interested in beginning a small business for the first time or improving or expanding an existing small business, who cannot afford the services of a private consultant.

In addition to the SBDC Program, the SBA has a variety of other programs and services available. They include training and educational programs, advisory services, publications, financial programs, and contract assistance. The agency also offers specialized programs for women business owners, minorities, veterans, international trade, and rural development.

Small Business Development Centers

ALABAMA SMALL BUSINESS DEVELOPMENT CENTERS

John Sandefur, State Director
Alabama SBDC Consortium
Univ. of Alabama at Birmingham
Medical Towers Building
1717 11th Ave. South, Suite 419
Birmingham, AL 35294-4410
(205)934-7260 / Fax:(205)934-7645

Harry Burdg, Acting Director
Small Business Development Center
Auburn University
108 College of Business
Auburn, AL 36849-5243
(205)844-4220 / Fax:(205)844-4268

Vernon Nabors
Small Business Development Center
Univ. of Alabama at Birmingham
1601 11th Avenue South
Birmingham, AL 35294-2180
(205)934-6760 / Fax:(205)934-0538

Joseph Richardson
Alabama Small Business Procurement
Univ. of Alabama at Birmingham
1717 11th Ave. South, Suite 419
Birmingham, AL 35294-4410
(205)934-7260 / Fax:(205)934-7645

David Day
AL Technology Assist. Program
Univ. of Alabama at Birmingham
1717 11th Ave. South, Suite 419
Birmingham, AL 35294-4410
(205)934-7260 / Fax:(205)934-7645

Dr. Kerry Gatlin
Small Business Development Center
Univeristy of North Alabama
Box 5248, Keller Hall
Florence, AL 35632-0001
(205)760-4629 / Fax:(205)760-4813

Jeff Thompson
Small Business Development Center
Northeast Alabama Regional
Alabama A&M and UAH
P.O. Box 168
225 Church St. N.W.
Huntsville, AL 35804-0343
(205)535-2061 / Fax:(205)535-2050

Pat W. Shaddix
Small Business Development Center
Jacksonville State University
700 Pelham Road North
114 Merrill Hall
Jacksonville, AL 36265
(205)782-5271 / Fax:(205)782-5124

Charlie Cook
Small Business Development Center
Livingston University
Station 35
Livingston, AL 35470
(205)652-9661 / Fax:(205)652-9318

Cheryl Coleman
Small Business Development Center
University of South Alabama
College of Business
Mobile, AL 36688
(205)460-6004 / Fax:(205)460-6246

Kenneth Walker, Acting Director
Small Business Development Center
Alabama State University
915 South Jackson Street
Montgomery, AL 36195
(205)269-1102 / Fax:(205)265-9144

Janet Kervin
Small Business Development Center
Troy State University
102 Bibb Graves
Troy, AL 36082-0001
(205)670-3771 / Fax:(205)670-3636

Paavo Hanninen
Small Business Development Center
University of Alabama
Box 870397
Bighood Hall, Room 250
Tuscaloosa, AL 35487-0397
(205)348-7011 / Fax:(205)348-9644

Brian Davis
University of Alabama
International Trade Center
Box 870396
Bighood Hall, Room 250
Tuscaloosa, AL 35487-0397
(205)348-7621 / Fax:(205)348-6974

ALASKA SMALL BUSINESS DEVELOPMENT CENTERS

Jan Fredericks, State Director
Small Business Development Center
University of Alaska
430 West Seventh Ave., Ste. 110
Anchorage, AK 99501
(907)274-7232 / Fax:(907)274-9524

Craig Renkert, Director
Small Business Development Center
University of Alaska Anchorage
430 West Seventh Ave, Suite 110
Anchorage, AK 99501
(907)274-7232 / Fax:(907)274-9524

Theresa Proenza, Director
Small Business Development Center
University of Alaska Fairbanks
510 Second Avenue, Suite 101
Fairbanks, AK 99701
(907)456-1701 / Fax:(907)456-1873

Charles Northrip
JEDC SBDC
124 West Fifth Street
Juneau, AK 99801
(907)463-3789 / Fax:(907)463-5670

Marian Romano, Director
Mat-Su Borough SBDC
1801 Parks Highway, Suite C-18
Wasilla, AK 99654
(907)373-7232 / Fax:(907)373-2560

Vern Craig, Director
Rural Outreach Program
Small Business Development Center
University of Alaska
430 West Seventh Ave., Ste 110
Anchorage, AK 99501
(907)274-7232 / Fax:(907)274-9524

ARIZONA SMALL BUSINESS DEVELOPMENT CENTERS

Mike York, State Director
Arizona SBDC Network
2411 West 14th St., Suite 132
Tempe, AZ 85281
(602)731-8720 / Fax:(602)731-8729

MaryAnn Stanton
Coconina Cty. Community College
3000 N. 4th St., Suite 25
Flagstaff, AZ 86004
(602)526-5072 / Fax:(602)526-8693

Joel Eittreim
Small Business Development Center
Northland Pioneer College
P.O. Box 610
Holbrook, AZ 86025
(602)537-2976 / Fax:(602)524-2227

Jennee Miles
Small Business Development Center
Mohave Community College
1971 Jagerson Avenue
Kingman, AZ 86401
(602)757-0894 / Fax:(602)757-0836

Kathy Evans
Small Business Development Center
Gateway Community College
108 N. 40th St.
Phoenix, AZ 85034-1795
(602)392-5220 / Fax:(602)392-5329

Marti McCorkindale
Small Business Development Center
Rio Salado Community College
301 W. Roosevelt, Suite B
Phoenix, AZ 85003
(602)238-9603 / Fax:(602)340-1627

Richard Senopole
Small Business Development Center
Yavapai College
117 E. Gurley St., Suite 206
Prescott, AZ 86301
(602)778-3088 / Fax:(602)778-3109

Greg Roers
Small Business Development Center
Eastern Arizona College
622 College Avuenue
Thatcher, AZ 85552-0769
(602)428-8590 / Fax:(602)428-8462

Debbie Elver
Small Business Development Center
Cochise College
901 N. Colombo, Room 411
Sierra Vista, AZ 85635
(602)459-9778 / Fax:(602)459-9737

Linda Andrews
Small Business Development Center
Pima Community College
4907 East Broadway
Tuscon, AZ 85709-1250
(602)748-4906 / Fax:(602)748-4585

Hank Pinto
Small Business Development Center
Arizona Western College
281 W. 24 St. #152 Century Plz.
Yuma, AZ 85364
(602)341-1650 / Fax:(602)726-2636

ARKANSAS SMALL BUSINESS DEVELOPMENT CENTER

Janet Nye, State Director
Small Business Development Center
Univ. of Arkansas - Little Rock
100 S. Main, Suite 401
Little Rock, AR 72201
(501)324-9043 / Fax:(501)324-9049

Bill Akin, Director
Small Business Development Center
Henderson State University
P.O. Box 7624
Arkadelphia, AR 71923
(501) 246-5511

Jim Buckner, Director
Small Business Development Center
Univ. of AR at Fayetteville
College of Business, BA 117
Fayetteville, AR 72701
(501) 575-5148

Twig Branch
Regional Office - UALR
1109 S. 16th Street
P.O. Box 2067
Fort Smith, AR 72901
(501) 785-1376

Bob Penquite
Regional Office - UALR
1313 Highway 62-65-412 North
P.O. Box 190
Harrison, AR 72601
(501)741-8009

Richard Evans
Regional Office - UALR
835 Central Avenue, Box 402D
Hot Springs, AR 71901
(501) 624-5448

Stephen Bryant
Regional Office - UALR
1801 Stadium Boulevard
P.O. Box 1403
Jonesboro, AR 72403
(501) 932-3957

John Harrison
State Office - UALR
100 S. Main, Suite 401
Little Rock, AR 72201
(501) 324-9043

Lairie Kincaid
Regional Office - UALR
600 Bessie, P.O. Box 767
Magnolia, AR 71753
(501) 234-4030

Mike Brewer
Regional Office - UALR
The Enterprise Center III
400 Main, Suite 117
Pine Bluff, AR 71601
(501) 536-0654

Gerald Jones, Director
Small Business Development Center
Arkansas State University
Drawer 2650
St. University, AR 72467
(501) 972-3517

Ronny Brothers
Regional Office - UALR
301 S. Grand, Suite 101
Stuttgart, AR 72160
(501) 673-8707

CALIFORNIA SMALL BUSINESS DEVELOPMENT CENTER

Maria Morris, State Director
California SBDC Program
Department of Commerece
801 K Street, Ste. 1700
Sacramento, CA 95815
(916)322-2259 / Fax:(916)322-5084

Elza Minor, Director
Central Coast SBDC
6500 Soquel Dr.
Aptos, CA 95003
(408)479-6138 / Fax:(408)479-5743

Mary Wollesen, Director
Sierra College SBDC
560 Wall Street, Suite J
Auburn, CA 95603
(916)885-5488 / Fax:(916)823-4704

Jeffrey Johnson, Director
Weill Institute SBDC
1330 22nd Street, Suite B
Bakersfield, CA 93301
(805)322-5881 / Fax:(805)322-5663

Kay Zimmerlee, Director
Butte College
Tri-County SBDC
260 Cohasset Road, Suite A
Chico, CA 95926
(916)895-9017 / Fax:(916)895-9099

Mary Wylie, Director
Small Business Development & Intl. Trade Ctr.
Southwestern College
900 Otay Lakes Road, Bldg. 1600
Chula Vista, CA 91910
(619)482-6393 / Fax:(619)482-6402

Fran Clark, Director
North Coast SBDC
779 9th Street
Cresent City, CA 95531
(707)464-2168 / Fax:(707)465-6008

Duff Heuttner
North Coast Satellite Center
408 7th Street, Suite "E"
Eureka, CA 95501
(707)445-9720 / Fax:(707)445-9652

Dennis Winans, Director
Central California SBDC
1999 Tuolumne Street,Suite 650
Fresno, CA 93731
(209)237-0660 / Fax:(209)237-1417

Director
Central California Satellite
P.O. Box 927
Visalia, CA 93279

Peter Graff, Director
Gavilan College SBDC
7436 Monterey Street
Gilroy, CA 95020
(408)847-0373 / Fax:(408)847-0393

Tiffany Haugen, Director
Accelerate Technology SBDC
4199 Campus Drive, Ste. 240
Irvine, CA 92715
(714)509-2715 / Fax:(714)509-2997

Lisa Hasler, Director
Greater San Diego Chamber of Commerce SBDC
4275 Executive Sq., Suite 920
La Jolla, CA 92037
(619)453-9386 / Fax:(619)450-1997

Gladys Moreau, Director
Export SBDC of Southern CA
110 E. 9th, Suite A669
Los Angeles, CA 90079
(213)892-1111 / Fax:(213)892-8232

Director
Merced Satellite Center
1632 "N" Street
Merced, CA 95340
(209)385-7312 / Fax:(209)383-4959

Kelly Bearden, Director
Valley Sierra SBDC
1012 Eleventh Street, Suite 300
Modesto, CA 95354
(209)521-6177 / Fax:(209)521-9373

Michael Kauffman, Director
Napa Valley College SBDC
1556 First Street, Suite 103
Napa, CA 94559
(707) 253-3210 / Fax: (707) 253-3068

Selma Taylor, Director
East Bay SBDC
2201 Broadway, Suite 701
Oakland, CA 94612
(510) 893-4114 / Fax: (510) 893-5532

Heather Wicka, Director
Export Satellite Center
300 Esplanade Drive, Suite 1010
Oxnard, CA 93030
(805) 981-4633 / Fax: (805) 988-1862

Toni Valdez, Director
East Los Angeles County SBDC
363 S. Park Avenue, Suite 100
Pomona, CA 91766
(909) 629-2247 / Fax: (909) 629-8310

Teri Corrazini Ooms, Director
Inland Empire SBDC
2002 Iowa Ave., Ste. 110
Riverside, CA 92507
(909) 781-2345 / Fax: (909) 781-2353

Jeannie Smelser, Director
Greater Sacramento SBDC
1787 Tribute Road, Suite A
Sacramento, CA 95815
(916) 263-6580 / Fax: (916) 263-6571

Gregory Kishel, Director
Orange County SBDC
901 East Santa Ana Blvd., Suite 101
Santa Ana, CA 92701
(714) 647-1172 / Fax: (714) 835-9008

Charles Robins, Director
Redwood Empire SBDC
520 Menocino Avenue, Suite 210
Santa Rosa, CA 95401
(707) 524-1770 / Fax: (707) 524-1772

Gillian Murphy, Director
San Joaquin Delta College SBDC
814 N. Hunter
Stockton, CA 95202
(209) 474-5089 / Fax: (209) 474-5605

Edward Schlenker, Director
Solano County SBDC
320 Campus Lane
Suisan, CA 94585
(707) 864-3382 / Fax: (707) 864-3386

Bart Hoffman, Interim Director
Southwest Los Angeles County SBDC
21221 Western Avenue, Suite 110
Torrance, CA 90501
(310) 782-3861 / Fax: (310) 782-8607

Lance Stevenson, Director
Northern Los Angeles SBDC
14540 Victory Boulevard, Suite #206
Van Nuys, CA 91411
(818) 373-7092 / Fax: (818) 373-7740

Dana Parker, Secretary
Lake County SBDC Satellite
P.O. Box 4550
15322 Lakeshore Drive
Hilltop Professional Ctr, Ste. 205
Clearlake, CA 95422
(707) 995-3440 / Fax: (707) 995-3605

COLORADO SMALL BUSINESS DEVELOPMENT CENTERS

Rick Garcia, State Director
Small Business Development Center
Office of Business Development
1625 Broadway, Suite 1710
Denver, CO 80202
(303) 892-3809 / Fax: (303) 892-3848

Patricia Skroch
Small Business Development Center
Adams State College
Alamosa, CO 81102
(719) 589-7372 / Fax: (719) 589-7522

Kathy Scott
Small Business Development Center
Community College of Aurora
9905 E. Colfax
Aurora, CO 80010-2119
(303) 341-4849 / Fax: (303) 361-2953

Lewis Hagler
Small Business & International Development Center
Front Range Community College\
Boulder Chamber of Commerce
2440 Pearl Street
Boulder, CO 80302
(303) 442-1475 / Fax: (303) 938-8837

Rita Friberg
Small Business Development Center
Pueblo Community College
402 Valley Road
Canon City, CO 81212
(719) 275-5335 / Fax: (719) 275-4400

Harry Martinez
Small Business Development Center
Pikes Peak Community College/
CO Springs Chamber of Commerce
P.O. Drawer B
Colorado Springs, CO 80901-3002
(719) 471-4836 / Fax: (719) 635-1571

Ken Farmer
Small Business Development Center
Colorado Northwestern Comm. College
50 Spruce Dr.
Craig, CO 81625
(303) 824-7078 / Fax: (303) 824-3527

Steve Schrock
Small Business Development Center
Delta Montrose Vocational School
1765 US Highway 50
Delta, CO 81416
(303) 874-8772 / Fax: (303) 874-8796

Carolyn Love
Small Business Development Center
Community College of Denver/
Greater Denver Chamber of Commerce
1445 Market St.
Denver, CO 80202
(303) 620-8076 / Fax: (303) 534-3200

Bard Heroy
Small Business Development Center
Fort Lewis College
484 Turner Dr., Bldg. B
Durango, CO 81301
(303) 247-9634 / Fax: (303) 247-9513

Small Business Development Center
Front Range Community College
1609 Oakridge Drive
P.O. Box 270490
Fort Collins, CO 80527
(303) 226-0881 / Fax: (303) 825-6819

Randy Johnson
Small Business Development Center
Morgan Community College
300 Main St.
Fort Morgan, CO 80701
(303) 867-4424 / Fax: (303) 867-3352

Director
Western Colorado Business Development Center/
Mesa State College
304 W. Main St.
Grand Junction, CO 81505-1606
(303) 243-5242 / Fax: (303) 241-0771

David Sanchez
Small Business Development Center
Aims Community College
Greeley/Weld Chamber of Commerce
1407 8th Ave.
Greeley, CO 80631
(303) 352-3661 / Fax: (303) 352-3572

Jim Hudson
Small Business Development Center
Red Rocks Community College
13300 W. 6th Ave.
Lakewood, CO 80401-5398
(303) 987-0710 / Fax: (303) 969-8039

Elwood Gillis
Small Business Development Center
Lamar Community College
2400 S. Main
Lamar, CO 81052
(719) 336-8141 / Fax: (719) 336-2448

Selma Kristel
Small Business Development Center
Arapahoe Community College/
South Metro Chamber of Commerce
7901 SouthPark Plaza, Suite 110
Littleton, CO 80120
(303) 795-5855 / Fax: (303) 795-7520

Shirley Ortega
Small Business Development Center
Pueblo Community College
900 W. Orman Ave.
Pueblo, CO 81004
(719) 549-3224 / Fax: (719) 546-2413

Roni Carr
Small Business Development Center
Morgan Community College
P.O. Box 28
Stratton, CO 80836
(719) 348-5596 / Fax: (719) 348-5887

Dennis O'Connor
Small Business Development Center
Trinidad State Junior College
600 Prospect St., Davis Bldg.
Trinidad, CO 81082
(719) 846-5645 Fax: (719) 846-5667

Russell Disberger
Small Business Development Center
Colorado Mountain College
215 9th Street
Glenwood Springs, CO 81601
(303) 945-8691 / Fax: (303) 945-7279
1-800-621-1647

Michael Lenzini
Small Business & International Development
Center
Front Range Community College
3645 W. 112th Ave.
Westminster, CO 80030
(303) 460-1032 / Fax: (303) 466-1623

CONNECTICUT SMALL BUSINESS DEVELOPMENT CENTERS

John O'Connor, State Director
Small Business Development Center
University of Connecticut
Box U-41, Rm 422
368 Fairfield Rd.
Storrs, CT 06269-2041
(203) 486-4135 / Fax: (203) 486-1576

John (Jack) Lewis
Associate State Director
Small Business Development Center
University of Connecticut
U-119, Longley Building
Storrs, CT 06269-5119
(203) 486-1826

Juan Scott
Small Business Development Center
Bridgeport Regional Business Council
10 Middle St.
Bridgeport, CT 06604-4229
(203) 335-3800

Roger Doty
Small Business Development Center
Quinebaug Valley Comm. College
742 Upper Maple Street, P.O. Box 59
Danielson, CT 06239-1440
(203) 774-1133 309

William Lockwood
Small Business Development Center
University of Connecticut
1084 Shennecossett Rd.
Administration Bldg. Rm 300
Groton, CT 06340-6097
(203) 449-1188

Neal Wehr
Small Business Development Center
Greater New Haven Cham. of Comm.
195 Church Street
New Haven, CT 06506
(203) 773-0782

George Ahl
Small Business Development Center
SW Area Comm. & Industry Assc. (SACIA)
One Landmark Square
Stamford, CT 06901
(203) 359-3220 ext. 315

Ilene Oppenheim
Small Business Outreach Center
101 South Main Street
Waterbury, CT 06702
(203) 757-8937 / Fax: (203) 756-9077

Richard Rogers
Small Business Development Center
University of Connecticut
1800 Asylum Avenue
West Hartford, CT 06117
(203) 241-4986

Bob Suchy
University of Connecticut
1800 Asylum Avenue
West Hartford, CT 06117
(203) 241-4986

Roger Doty
Small Business Development Center
Eastern CT State University
83 Windham Street
Willimantic, CT 06226-2295
(203) 456-5349

Small Business Development Ctr.
University of Connecticut
Thames River Campus
Unit 1102, (Stone House)
401 West Thames Street
Norwich, CT 06360-7137
(203) 886-1188

DELAWARE SMALL BUSINESS DEVELOPMENT CENTERS

Clinton Tymes, State Director
Small Business Development Center
University of Delaware
Purnell Hall, Suite 005
Newark, DE 19716-2711
(302) 831-1555 / Fax: (302) 831-1423

Jim Crisfield, Director
Small Business Development Center
Delaware State University
School of Business Economics
1200 N. Dupont Highway
Dover, DE 19901
(302) 678-1555

William F. Pfaff, Director
Small Business Development Center
Delaware Technical and Comm. College
P.O. Box 610
Industrial Training Building
Georgetown, DE 19947
(302) 856-1555

DISTRICT OF COLUMBIA SMALL BUSINESS DEVELOPMENT CENTERS

Levi Lipscomb, Acting Director
Metropolitan Washington D.C.
Small Business Development Center Network
Howard University Small Business Development
Center
2600 Sixth Street, Room #128
Washington, DC 20059
(202) 806-1550 / Fax: (202) 806-1777

Susan Jones, Director
Small Business Development Center
George Washington University Small Business
Clinic
720 20th St., N.W.
Washington, DC 20052
(202) 994-7463 / Fax: (202) 994-4946

FLORIDA SMALL BUSINESS DEVELOPMENT CENTERS

Jerry Cartwright, State Director
Florida SBDC Network
19 West Garden Street
Pensacola, FL 32501
(904) 444-2066 / Fax: (904) 474-2030

Mark Hosang, Director
Small Business Development Center
Florida Atlantic University
P.O. Box 3091
Boca Raton, FL 33431
(407) 367-2273 / Fax: (407) 367-2272

Linda Krepel, Associate Director
Office of International Trade
Florida Atlantic University
P.O. Box 3091
Boca Raton, FL 33431
(407) 367-2271 / Fax: (407) 367-2272

Glen Morgan, Regional Manager
Small Business Development Center
Seminole Community College
4590 South Highway 17-92
Casselberry, FL 32707
(407) 834-4404

Anita Moore
Small Business Development Center
Brevard Community College
1519 Clearlake Road
Cocoa, FL 32922
(407) 951-1060 Ext. 2045

William Healy, Regional Manager
Small Business Development Center
46 S.W. 1st Avenue
Dania, FL 33304
(305) 987-0100

John Duizen, Regional Manager
Small Business Development Center
Stetson University
School of Business Administration
P.O. Box 8417
DeLand, FL 32720
(904) 822-7326 / Fax: (904) 822-8832

John Hudson, Regional Manager
Small Business Development Center
Florida Atlantic University
Commercial Campus
1515 West Commercial Blvd., Room 11
Fort Lauderdale, FL 33309
(305) 771-6520 / Fax: (305) 776-6645

Bill Roshon
Small Business Development Center
Edison Community College
8099 College Parkway, SW
Fort Myers, FL 33906-6210
(813) 489-9200

Don Bell, Regional Manager
Small Business Development Center
Indian River Community College
3209 Virginia Avenue, Room 114
Ft. Pierce, FL 34981-5599
(407) 468-4756

Walter Craft, Manager
Small Business Development Center
University of West Florida
1170 MLK Jr. Blvd, Bldg 2/250
Fort Walton Beach, FL 32547
(904) 863-6543 / Fax: (904) 863-6564

William Stensgaard, Regional Manager
Small Business Development Center
University of North Florida
214 W. University Ave., PO Box 2518
Gainesville, FL 32601
(904) 377-5621

Pam Riddle, Director
Florida Product Innovation Center
2622 N.W. 43rd Street, Suite B-3
Gainesville, FL 32606
(904) 334-1680 / Fax: (904) 334-1682

Lowell Salter, Director
Small Business Development Center
University of North Florida
College of Business
Building 11, Room 2163
4567 St. John's Bluff Road, South
Jacksonville, FL 32216
(904) 646-2476 / Fax: (904) 646-2594

Royland Jarrett, Regional Manager
Small Business Development Center
Florida International University
North Miami Campus
NE 151 & Biscayne Blvd.
Academic Bldg. #1, Room 350
Miami, FL 33181
(305) 940-5790

Marvin Nesbit, Director
Small Business Development Center
Florida International College
University Park MO1
Miami, FL 33199
(305) 348-2272 / Fax: (305) 348-2965

Frederick Bonneau
Small Business Development Center
Miami Dade Community College
NW 27th Avenue
Miami, FL 33150
(305) 237-1900

Small Business Development Center
110 E. Silver Springs Blvd.
P.O. Box 1210
Ocala, FL 32670
(904) 629-8051

Al Polfer, Director
Small Business Development Center
University of Central Florida
BA Suite 309, P.O. Box 161530
Orlando, FL 32816-1530
(407) 823-5554 / Fax: (407) 823-3073

Donald Clause, Director
Small Business Development Center
University of West Florida
Building 8
11000 University Parkway
Pensacola, FL 32514
(904) 474-2908 / Fax: (904) 474-2126

Pete Singletary, Dir. of Procurement
Small Business Development Center
UWF Downtown Center
19 West Garden Street
Pensacola, FL 32501
(904) 444-2066 / Fax: (904) 444-2070

Small Business Development Center
St. Petersburg Community College
3200 34th Street, South
St. Petersburg, FL 33711
(813) 341-4414

Patricia McGowan, Director
Small Business Development Center
Florida A & M University
1715-B South Gadsden Street
Tallahassee, FL 32301
(904) 599-3407 / Fax: (904) 561-2395

Scott Faris, Director
Small Business Development Center
University of South Florida
College of Business Administration
4202 E. Fowler Avenue, BSN 3403
Tampa, FL 33620
(813) 974-4274

Bobbie McGee, Regional Manager
Small Business Development Center
Florida Atlantic University
Prospect Place, Suite 123
3111 South Dixie Highway
West Palm Beach, FL 33405
(407) 837-5311

Jamie Shepard, Director
Small Business Development Center
Gulf Coast Community College
2500 Minnesota Avenue
Lynn Haven, FL 32444
(904) 271-1108 / Fax: (904) 271-1100

GEORGIA SMALL BUSINESS DEVELOPMENT CENTERS

Henry Logan, State Director
Small Business Development Center
University of Georgia
Chicopee Complex
1180 East Broad St.
Athens, GA 30602-5412
(706) 542-5760 / Fax: (706) 542-6776

Sue Ford, District Director
Southwest Georgia District SBDC
Business & Technology Center
230 S. Jackson St., Suite 333
Albany, GA 31701-2885
(912) 430-4303 / Fax: (912) 430-3933

Gary Selden, District Director
Kennesaw State College SBDC
P.O. Box 444
Marietta, GA 30061
(404) 499-3191 / Fax: (404) 423-6564

Harold Roberts, District Director
Northeast Georgia District SBDC
University of Georgia
Chicopee Complex
1180 E. Broad St.
Athens, GA 30602-5412
(706) 542-7436 / Fax: (706) 542-6776

Lee Quarterman
Georgia State University SBDC
University Plaza, Box 874
Atlanta, GA 30303-3083
(404) 651-3550 / Fax: (404) 651-1035

Morris Brown College SBDC
643 Martin Luther King, Jr., Dr., NW
Atlanta, GA 30314
(404) 220-0201 / Fax: (404) 220-0236

Augusta SBDC
1061 Katherine St.
Augusta, GA 30910-6105
(706) 737-1790 / Fax: (706) 731-7937

Brunswick SBDC
1107 Fountain Lake Dr.
Brunswick, GA 31525-3039
(912) 264-7343 / Fax: (912) 262-3095

B. Rothschild, Director
Small Business Development Center
West Central Regional Service Center
928 45th St., North Bldg., Room 523
Columbus, GA 31904-6572
(706) 649-7433 / Fax: (404) 649-1928

DeKalb SBDC
DeKalb Chamber of Commerce
750 Commerce Dr.
Decatur, GA 30030-2622
(404) 378-8000 / Fax: (404) 378-3397

James C. Smith
Gainesville SBDC
455 Jesse Jewel Parkway, Suite 302
Gainesville, GA 30501-4203
(706) 531-5681 / Fax: (706) 531-5684

Gwinnett SBDC
Gwinnet Technical Institute
1250 Atkinson Rd.
Lawrenceville, GA 30246
(404) 339-2287 / Fax: (404) 339-2329

David Mills, District Director
Central Georgia District SBDC
P.O. Box 13212
Macon, GA 31208-3212
(912) 751-6592 / Fax: (912) 751-6661

Carlotta Roberts
Kennesaw State College SBDC
P.O. Box 444
Marietta, GA 30061
(404) 423-6450 / Fax: (404) 423-6564

Clayton State College SBDC
P.O. Box 285
Morrow, GA 30260
(404) 961-3440 / Fax: (404) 961-3428

Harry O'Brien, District Director
Southeast Georgia District SBDC
450 Mall Blvd., Suite H
Savannah, GA 31406-4824
(912) 356-2755 / Fax: (912) 353-3033

Statesboro SBDC
Landrum Center, Box 8156
Statesboro, GA 30460
(912) 681-5194 / Fax: (912) 681-0648

Valdosta SBDC
Baytree Office Park, Suite 9
Baytree Rd.
Valdosta, GA 31601
(912) 245-3738 / Fax: (912) 245-3741

Warner Robins SBDC
151 Osigian Blvd.
Warner Robins, GA 31088
(912) 953-9356 / Fax: (912) 953-9376

Beth Fletcher, Center Director
Floyd College SBDC
P.O. Box 1864
Rome, GA 30162-1864
(404) 295-6326 / Fax: (404) 295-6732

HAWAII SMALL BUSINESS DEVELOPMENT CENTERS

Darryll Mlyneck
Acting State Director
Hawaii SBDC Network
University of Hawaii at Hilo
200 West Kawili Street
Hilo, HI 96720-4091
(808) 933-3515 / Fax: (808) 933-3683

Francis A. Hatstat
Associate State Director
Small Business Development Center
University of Hawaii at Hilo
200 West Kawili Street
Hilo, HI 96720-4091
(808) 933-3515 / Fax: (808) 933-3683

Randy Gringas, Business Analyst
Small Business Development Center
Kauai Community College
3-1901 Kaumualii Highway
Lihue, HI 96766
(808) 246-1748 / Fax: (808) 245-5102

David Fisher, Center Director
Small Business Development Center
Maui Community College
Maui Research & Technology Center
590 Lipoa Parkway
Kihei, HI 96753
(808) 875-2402 / Fax:(808) 875-2452

Darryl Mleynek, Business Analyst
Small Business Development Center
University of Hawaii at Hilo
200 W. Kawili
Hilo, HI 96720
(808) 933-3515

University of Hawaii at West Oahu
2800 Woodlawn Drive, #238
Honolulu, HI 96822-1843
(808) 539-3800 / Fax: (808) 539-3799

IDAHO SMALL BUSINESS DEVELOPMENT CENTERS

James Hogge, Acting State Director
Small Business Development Center
Boise State University
1910 University Drive
Boise, ID 83725
(208) 385-1640 / Fax: (208) 385-3877

Robert Shepard, Regional Director
Small Business Development Center
Boise State University
1910 University Drive
Boise, ID 83725
(208) 385-3875

John Lynn, Regional Director
Small Business Development Center
North Idaho College
1000 W. Garden Avenue
Coeur d'Alene, ID 83814
(208) 773-9807

Betty Capps, Regional Director
Small Business Development Center
Idaho State University
2300 N. Yellowstone
Idaho Falls, ID 83401
(208) 523-1087

Helen Le Boeuf-Binninger
Regional Director
Small Business Development Center
Lewis Clark State College
8th Avenue & 6th Street
Lewiston, ID 83501
(208) 799-2465

Paul Cox, Regional Director
Small Business Development Center
Idaho State University
1651 Alvin Ricken Drive
Pocatello, ID 83201
(208) 232-4921

Cindy Bond, Regional Director
Small Business Development Center
College of Southern Idaho
315 Falls Avenue
Twin Falls, ID 83303
(208) 733-9554

ILLINOIS SMALL BUSINESS DEVELOPMENT CENTERS

Jeff Mitchell, Statewide Admin.
Small Business Development Center
Dept. of Commerce & Comm. Affairs
620 East Adams St., 3rd Floor
Springfield, IL 62701
(217) 524-5856 / Fax: (217) 785-6328

Mike O'Kelley, Director
Small Business Development Center
Waubonsee Community College
Aurora Campus, 5 East Galena Blvd.
Aurora, IL 60506
(708) 892-3334 139 / Fax: (708) 892-3374

Dennis Cody, Director
Small Business Development Center
Southern Illinois Univ. - Carbondale
Carbondale, IL 62901-6702
(618) 536-2424 / Fax: (618) 453-5040

Richard Fyke, Director
Small Business Development Center
John A. Logan College
RR 2
Carterville, IL 62918
(618) 985-6506 / Fax: (618) 985-2248

Small Business Development Center
Kaskaskia College
Shattuc Road
Centralia, IL 62801
(618) 532-2049 / Fax: (618) 532-4983

Paul Ladniak, Director
Small Business Development Center
Back of the Yards Neighborhood Council
1751 West 47th Street
Chicago, IL 60609
(312) 523-4419 / Fax: (312) 254-3525

Maria Munoz, Director
Eighteenth Street Develomment Corporation
1839 South Carpenter
Chicago, IL 60608
(312) 733-2287 / Fax: (312) 733-7315

Paul Peterson, Director
Small Business Development Center
Greater North Pulaski Devel. Corp.
4054 West North Avenue
Chicago, IL 60639
(312) 384-2262 / Fax: (312) 384-3850

Alex Viorst, Director
Small Business Development Center
Industrial Council of NW Chicago
2023 West Carroll
Chicago, IL 60612
(312) 421-3941 / Fax: (312) 421-1871

Martin Sandoval, Director
Small Business Development Center
Latin American Chamber of Commerce
2539 North Kedzie, Suite 11
Chicago, IL 60647
(312) 252-5211 / Fax: (312) 252-7065

Carson Gallagher, Director
Chicago SBDC
DCCA - James R. Thompson Center
100 West Randolph, Suite 3-400
Chicago, IL 60601
(312) 814-6111 / Fax: (312) 814-2807

Jerry Chambers, Director
Small Business Development Center
Olive-Harvey Community College
Heritage Pullman Bank
1000 East 111th St., 7th Floor
Chicago, IL 60628
(312) 468-8700 / Fax: (312) 660-4847

Paula Carlin, Director
Small Business Development Center
Women's Business Development Center
8 South Michigan, Suite 400
Chicago, IL 60603
(312) 853-3477 / Fax: (312) 853-0145

Don Glaze, Director
Small Business Development Center
McHenry County College
8900 U.S. Highway 14
Crystal Lake, IL 60012-2761
(815) 455-6098 / Fax: (815) 455-3999

Kim Webster, Director
Small Business Development Center
Danville Area Community College
28 West North Street
Danville, IL 61832
(217) 442-7232 / Fax: (217) 442-6228

Joanne Rouse, Acting Director
Small Business Development Center
Northern Illinois University
Department of Management
305 East Locust
Dekalb, IL 60115
(815) 753-1403 / Fax: (815) 753-1631

Tom Gospodarczyk, Director
Small Business Development Center
Sauk Valley Community College
173 Illinois Route #2
Dixon, IL 61021-9110
(815) 288-5605 / Fax: (815) 288-5958

Donna Scalf, Director
Small Business Development Center
Black Hawk College
301 42nd Avenue
East Moline, IL 61244
(309) 752-9759 / Fax: (309) 755-9847

Karen Pinkston, Director
Small Business Development Center
DCCA, State Office Building
10 Collinsville
East St. Louis, IL 62201
(618) 583-2272 / Fax: (618) 583-2274

Jim Mager, Director
Small Business Development Center
Southern Illinois Univ.-Edwardsville
Campus Box 1107
Edwardsville, IL 62026
(618) 692-2929 / Fax: (618) 692-2647

Craig Fowler, Director
Small Business Development Center
Elgin Community College
1700 Spartan Drive
Elgin, IL 60123
(708) 697-1000 7923 / Fax: (708) 888-7995

Tom Parkinson, Director
Small Business Development Center
Evanston Business and Technology Center
1840 Oak Avenue
Evanston, IL 60201
(708) 866-1841 / Fax: (708) 866-1808

Chuck Mufich, Director
Small Business Development Center
Highland Community College
206 South Galena
Freeport, IL 61032
(815) 232-1366 / Fax: (815) 235-1366

David Gay
Small Business Development Center
College of DuPage
22nd and Lambert Road
Glen Ellyn, IL 60137
(708) 858-2800 ext. 2771 / Fax: (708) 790-1197

Arthur Cobb, Jr., Director
Small Business Development Center
College of Lake County
19351 West Washington Street
Grayslake, IL 60030
(708) 223-3633 / Fax: (708) 223-9371

Becky Williams, Director
Small Business Development Center
Southeastern Illinois College
325 East Poplar, Suite A
Harrisburg, IL 62946-1528
(618) 252-8528 / Fax: (618) 252-0210

Lisa Payne, Director
Small Business Development Center
Rend Lake College
Route #1
Ina, IL 62846
(618) 437-5321 267 / Fax: (618) 437-5321 385

Denise Mikulski, Director
Small Business Development Center
Joliet Junior College
Renaissance Center, Room 319
214 North Ottawa Street
Joliet, IL 60431
(815) 727-6544 1313 / Fax: (815) 722-1895

JoAnn Seggebruch, Director
Small Business Development Center
Kankakee Community College
4 Dearborn Square
Kankakee, IL 60901
(815) 933-0376 / Fax: (815) 933-0380

Dan Voorhis, Director
Small Business Development Center
Western Illinois University
216 Seal Hall
Macomb, IL 61455
(309) 298-1128 / Fax: (309) 298-2520

Daniel Sulsberger, Director
Small Business Development Center
Lake Land College
South Route #45
Mattoon, IL 61938-9366
(217) 235-3131 / Fax: (217) 258-6459

Carol Cook, Director
Small Business Development Center
Maple City Business and
Technology Center
620 South Main St.
Monmouth, IL 61462
(309) 734-4664 / Fax: (309) 734-8579

Maureen Ruski, Director
Small Business Development Center
Heartland Community College
1226 Towanda Plaza
Normal, IL 61761
(217) 875-7200 / Fax: (217) 875-6965

Boyd Palmer, Director
Small Business Development Center
Illinois Valley Community College
Bldg. 11, Route 1
Oglesby, IL 61348
(815) 223-1740 / Fax: (815) 224-3033

John Spitz, Director
Small Business Development Center
Illinois Eastern Communtiy College
401 E. Main Street
Olney, IL 62450
(618) 395-3011 / Fax: (618) 392-2773

Tom Parkinson, Director
Small Business Development Center
William Rainey-Harper College
1200 West Algonquin Road
Palatine, IL 60067
(708) 397-3000 ext. 2804 / Fax: (708) 866-1841

Hilary Gereg, Director
Small Business Development Center
Moraine Valley College
10900 South 88th Avenue
Palos Hills, IL 60465
(708) 974-5468 / Fax: (708) 974-0078

Roger Luman, Director
Small Business Development Center
Bradley University
141 North Jobst Hall, 1st Floor
Peoria, IL 61625
(309) 677-2992 / Fax: (309) 677-3386

Susan Gorman, Director
Small Business Development Center
Illinois Central College
124 S.W. Adams Street, Suite 300
Peoria, IL 61602
(309) 676-7500 / Fax: (309) 676-7534

Meredith Jaszczek, Director
Small Business Development Center
Triton College
2000 Fifth Avenue
River Grove, IL 60171
(708) 456-0300 246 / Fax: (708) 456-0049

Beverley Kingsley, Director
Small Business Development Center
Rock Valley College
1220 Rock Street
Rockford, IL 61102
(815) 968-4087 / Fax: (815) 968-4157

Freida Schreck, Director
Small Business Development Center
Lincoln Land Community College
200 West Washington
Springfield, IL 62701
(217) 524-3060 / Fax: (217) 782-1106

Donald Denny, Director
Small Business Development Center
Shawnee Community College
Shawnee College Road
Ullin, IL 62992
(618) 634-9618 / Fax: (618) 634-9028

Christine Cochrane, Director
Small Business Development Center
Governors State University
University Park, IL 60466
(708) 534-4929 / Fax: (708) 534-8457

INDIANA SMALL BUSINESS DEVELOPMENT CENTERS

Stephen G. Thrash, Exe. Director
Indiana SBDC
One North Capitol, Suite 420
Indianapolis, IN 46204
(317) 264-6871 / Fax: (317) 264-3102

David Miller
Bloomington Area SBDC
116 West 6th Street
Bloomington, IN 47404
(812) 339-8937 / Fax: (812) 336-0651

Glenn Dunlap
Columbus SBDC
4920 North Warren Drive
Columbus, IN 47203
(812) 372-6480 / Fax: (812) 372-0228

Jeff Lake
Southwestern Indiana SBDC
100 N.W. Second Street, Suite 200
Evansville, IN 47708
(812) 425-7232 / Fax: (812) 421-5883

A. V. Fleming
Northeast Indiana SBDC
1830 Wayne Trace
Fort Wayne, IN 46803
(219) 426-0040 / Fax: (219) 424-0024

Patricia Stroud
Southern Indiana SBDC
1613 E. Eighth Street
Jeffersonville, IN 47130
(812) 288-6451 / Fax: (812) 284-8314

Tim Tichenar
Indianapolis Regional SDBC
342 North Senate Avenue
Indianapolis, IN 46204
(317) 261-3030 / Fax: (317) 261-3053

Todd Moser
Kokomo/Howard County SBDC
106 North Washington
Kokomo, IN 46901
(317) 457-5301 / Fax: (317) 452-4564

Susan Davis
Greater Lafayette Area SBDC
122 N. Third
Lafayette, IN 47901
(317) 742-2394 Fax: (317) 742-6276

Rose Marie Roberts
Southeastern Indiana SBDC
301 East Main Street
Madison, IN 47250
(812) 265-3127 / Fax: (812) 265-2923

Jeanenne Holcomb
Northwest Indiana SBDC
8002 Utah Street
Merrillville, IN 46410
(219) 942-3496 / Fax: (219) 942-5806

Barbara Armstrong
East Central Indiana SBDC
401 South High Street
Muncie, IN 47308
(317) 284-8144 / Fax: (317) 741-5489

Doug Peters
Richmond-Wayne County SBDC
33 South 7th Street
Richmond, IN 47374
(317) 962-2887 Fax: (317) 966-0882

Carolyn Anderson
South Bend SBDC
300 North Michigan
South Bend, IN 46601
(219) 282-4350 / Fax: (219) 282-4344

Williams Minnis
Terre Haute Area SBDC
Indiana State University
School of Business, Room 510
Terre Haute, IN 47809
(812) 237-7676 / Fax: (812) 237-7675

IOWA SMALL BUSINESS DEVELOPMENT CENTERS

Ronald Manning, State Director
Iowa SBDC
State Administrative Office
Iowa State University
137 Lynn Avenue
Ames, IA 50014
(515) 292-6351 / Fax: (515) 292-0020
(800) 373-7232

Steve Carter, Director
Iowa State University SBDC
137 Lynn Avenue
Ames, IA 50014
(515) 292-6351 / Fax: (515) 292-0020

Sherry Shafer, Branch Manager
Iowa State University SBDC
111 Lynn Avenue, Suite 1
Ames, IA 50014
(515) 292-6355 / Fax: (515) 292-0020
(800) 373-7232

Lori Harmening-Webb, Manager
DMACC SBDC
Circle West Incubator
P.O. Box 204
Audubon, IA 50025
(712) 563-2623 / Fax: (712) 563-2301

Lyle Bowlin, Director
University of Northern Iowa SBDC
University of Northern Iowa
Suite 5, Business Bldg.
Cedar Falls, IA 50614-0120
(319) 273-2696 / Fax: (319) 273-6830

Ronald Helms, Director
Iowa Western SBDC
Iowa Western Community College
2700 College Road, Box 4C
Council Bluffs, IA 51502
(712) 325-3260 / Fax: (712) 325-0189

Paul Havick, Director
Southwestern SBDC
Southwestern Community College
1501 West Townline Road
Creston, IA 50801
(515) 782-4161 / Fax: (515) 782-3312

Jon Ryan, Director
Eastern Iowa SBDC
Eastern Iowa Comm. Coll. District
304 West Second Street
Davenport, IA 52801
(319) 322-4499 / Fax: (319) 322-8241

Benjamin Swartz, Director
Drake University SBDC
Drake University
Drake Business Center
Des Moines, IA 50311-4505
(515) 271-2655 / Fax: (515) 271-4540

Charles Tonn, Director
Northeast Iowa SBDC
Dubuque Area Chamber of Commerce
770 Town Clock Plaza
Dubuque, IA 52001
(319) 588-3350 / Fax:(319) 557-1591

Todd Madson, Director
Iowa Central SBDC
Iowa Central Community College
330 Ave. M
Fort Dodge, IA 50501
(515) 576-7201 2365 / Fax: (515) 576-7206

Paul Heath, Director
University of Iowa SBDC
University of Iowa
108 Pappajohn
Business Administration Bldg., Ste S160
Iowa City, IA 52242-1000
(319) 335-3742 / Fax: (319) 335-1956
(800) 253-7232

Carol Thompson, Director
Kirkwood SBDC
Kirkwood Community College
2901 10th Avenue
Marion, IA 52302
(319) 377-8256 / Fax: (319) 377-5667

Richard Petersen, Director
North Iowa Area SBDC
North Iowa Area Community College
500 College Drive
Mason City, IA 50401
(515) 421-4342 / Fax: (515) 423-0931

Bryan Ziegler, Director
Indian Hills SBDC
Indian Hills Community College
525 Grandview Avenue
Ottumwa, IA 52501
(515) 683-5127 / Fax: (515) 683-5263

Dennis Bogenrief, Director
Western Iowa Tech SBDC
Western Iowa Tech. Community College
4647 Stone Ave., Box 265
Sioux City, IA 51102-0265
(712) 274-6418 / Fax: (712) 274-6429
(800) 352-4649

John Beneke, Director
Iowa Lakes SBDC
Iowa Lakes Community College
Gateway North Shopping Center
Highway 71 North
Spencer, IA 51301
(712) 262-4213 / Fax: (712) 262-4047

Deb Dalziel, Director
Southeastern SBDC
Southeastern Community College
Drawer F
West Burlington, IA 52655
(319) 752-2731 103 / Fax: (319) 752-3407
(800) 828-7322

KANSAS SMALL BUSINESS DEVELOPMENT CENTERS

Tom Hull, State Director
Kansas Small Bus. Development Centers
Wichita State University
1845 Fairmount
Wichita, KS 67260-0148
(316) 689-3193 / Fax: (316) 689-3647

Dorinda Rolle, Director
Small Business Development Center
Butler County Community College
600 Walnut
Augusta, KS 67010
(316) 775-1124 / Fax: (316) 775-1370

Duane Clum, Director
Small Business Development Center
Neosho County Comm College
1000 S. Allen
Chanute, KS 66720
(316) 431-2820 219 / Fax: (316) 431-0082

Robert Selby, Director
Small Business Development Center
Colby Community College
1255 South Range
Colby, KS 67701
(913) 462-3984 239 / Fax: (913) 462-8315

Wayne E. Shiplet, Director
Small Business Development Center
Dodge City Community College
2501 N. 14th Ave.
Dodge City, KS 67801
(316) 227-9247 / Fax: (316) 227-9200

Lisa Brumbaugh, Regional Director
Small Business Development Center
Emporia State University
207 Cremer Hall
Emporia, KS 66801
(316) 342-7162 / Fax: (316) 341-5418

Dr. Steve Hoyle, Director
Small Business Development Center
Fort Scott Community College
2108 S. Horton
Fort Scott, KS 66701
(316) 223-2700 / Fax: (316) 223-6530

Vern Kinderknecht, Regional Director
Small Business Development Center
Garden City Community College
801 Campus Drive
Garden City, KS 67846
(316) 276-9632 / Fax: (316) 276-9630

Clark Jacobs, Director
Small Business Development Center
Hutchinson Community College
815 No Walnut, #225
Hutchinson, KS 67501
(316) 665-4950 / Fax: (316) 665-7619

Clare Gustin, Regional Director
Small Business Development Center
Fort Hays State University
1301 Pine Street
Hays, KS 67601
(913) 628-5340 / Fax: (913) 628-1471

Preston Haddan, Director
Small Business Development Center
Independence Community College
College Ave. & Brookside
(P.O. Box 708)
Independence, KS 67301
(316) 331-4100 / Fax: (316) 331-5344

Sue Courtney, Director
Small Business Development Center
Kansas City Kansas Comm. College
7250 State Ave.
Kansas City, KS 66112
(913) 596-9660 / Fax: (913) 596-9606

Mike O'Donnell, Regional Director
Small Business Development Center
University of Kansas
734 Vermont, Suite 104
Lawrence, KS 66044
(913) 843-8844 / Fax: (913) 865-4400

Fred Rice, Regional Director
Small Business Development Center
Kansas State University
2323 Anderson Ave., Suite 100
Manhattan, KS 66502-2947
(913) 532-5529 / Fax: (913) 532-7800

Lori Kravets, Director
Small Business Development Center
Ottawa University
College Ave., Box 70
Ottawa, KS 66067
(913) 242-5200 5457 / Fax: (913) 242-7429

Glenda Sapp, Regional Director
Small Business Development Center
Johnson County Comm. College
CEC Bldg., Room 223
Overland Park, KS 66210-1299
(913) 469-3878 / Fax: (913) 469-4415

Mark Turnbull, Director
Small Business Development Center
Labette Community College
200 S. 14th
Parsons, KS 67357
(316) 421-6700 / Fax: (316) 421-0921

Kathryn Richard, Regional Director
Small Business Development Center
Pittsburg State University
Shirk Hall
Pittsburg, KS 66762
(316) 235-4920 Fax: (316) 232-6440

Pat Gordon, Director
Small Business Development Center
Pratt Community College
Highway 61
Pratt, KS 67124
(316) 672-5641 / Fax: (316) 672-5288

Pat Mills, Regional Director
Small Business Development Center
KSU - Salina College of Technology
2409 Scanlan Ave.
Salina, KS 67401
(913) 826-2622 / Fax: (913) 826-2936

Wayne Glass, Regional Director
Small Business Development Center
Washburn University
101 Henderson Learning Ctr.
Topeka, KS 66621
(913) 231-1010 Ext. 1305 / Fax: (913) 231-1063

Chip Paul, Regional Director
Small Business Development Center
Wichita State University
1845 Fairmount
Wichita, KS 67208-0148
(316) 689-3193 / Fax: (316) 689-3647

Tony Foster, Director
Small Business Development Center
Cloud County Community College
2221 Campus Dr. (P.O. Box 1002)
Concordia, KS 66901
(913) 243-1435 / Fax: (913) 243-1459

Bob Carder, Director
Small Business Development Center
Seward County Comm. College
1801 N. Kansas
Liberal, KS 67901
(316) 624-1951 Ext. 150 / Fax: (316) 624-0637

David Allen, Director
Small Business Development Center
Allen County Community College
1801 N. Cottonwood
Iola, KS 66749
(316) 365-5116 / Fax: (316) 365-3284

Mark Eldridge, Director
Small Business Development Center
Coffeyville Community College
11th & Willow Streets
Coffeyville, KS 67337-5064
(316) 252-7007 / Fax: (316) 252-7098

KENTUCKY SMALL BUSINESS DEVELOPMENT CENTERS

Janet Holloway, State Director
Kentucky Small Bus. Development Center
Center for Business Development
225 Business & Economics Building
University of Kentucky
Lexington, KY 40506-0034
(606) 257-7668 / Fax: (606) 258-1907

Kimberly A. Jenkins, Director
Ashland SBDC
Morehead State University
Boyd-Greenup County Chamber of Commerce
P.O. Box 830, 207 15th Street
Ashland, KY 41105-0830
(606) 329-8011 / Fax: (606) 325-4607

Rick Horn, Director
Bowling Green SBDC
Western Kentucky University
245 Grise Hall
Bowling Green, KY 42101
(502) 745-2901 / Fax: (502) 745-2902

Cortez Davis, Director
Southeast SBDC
Southeast Community College
Room 113, Chrisman Hall
Cumberland, KY 40823
(606) 589-4514 Fax: (606) 589-4941

Denver Woodring, Director
Elizabethtown SBDC
University of Kentucky
238 West Dixie Avenue
Elizabethtown, KY 42701
(502) 765-6737 / Fax: (502) 769-5095

Sutton Landry, Director
Northern Kentucky SBDC
Northern Kentucky University
BEP Center 468
Highland Heights, KY 41099-0506
(606) 572-6524 / Fax: (606) 572-5566

Mike Cartner, Director
Hopkinsville SBDC
Murray State University
300 Hammond Drive
Hopkinsville, KY 42240
(502) 886-8666 / Fax: (502) 886-321

William Morley, Director
Lexington Area SBDC
University of Kentucky
227 Business and Economics Building
Lexington, KY 40506-0034
(606) 257-7666 / Fax: (606) 258-1907

Thomas G. Daley, Director
Bellarmine College SBDC
Bellarmine College, School of Business
2001 Newburg Road
Louisville, KY 40205-0671
(502) 452-8282 / Fax: (502) 452-8288

Lou Dickie, Director
University of Louisville SBDC (Technology)
University of Louisville, Center for
Entrepreneurship and Technology
Room 122 Burhans Hall, Shelby Campus
Louisville, KY 40292
(502) 588-7854 / Fax: (502) 588-8573

Wilson Grier, District Director
Morehead SBDC
Morehead State University
207 Downing Hall
Morehead, KY 40351
(606) 783-2895 / Fax: (606) 783-5020

Rosemary Miller, Director
Murray State University
College of Bus. and Public Affairs
Murray, KY 42071
(502) 762-2856 / Fax: (502) 762-3049

Mickey Johnson, District Director
Owensboro SBDC
Murray State University
3860 U.S. Highway 60 West
Owensboro, KY 42301
(502) 926-8085 / Fax: (502) 684-0714

Mike Morley, Director
Pikeville SBDC
Morehead State University
Justice Office B
Rt. 7, 110 Village
Pikeville, KY 41501
(606) 432-5848

Donald R. Snyder, Director
South Central SBDC
Eastern Kentucky University
107 W Mt. Vernon St.
Somerset, KY 42501
(606) 678-5520 / Fax: (606) 678-8349

LOUISIANA SMALL BUSINESS DEVELOPMENT CENTERS

Dr. John Baker, State Director
Louisiana SBDC
Northeast Louisiana University
College of Business Administration
700 University Avenue, Adm 2-57
Monroe, LA 71209-6435
(318) 342-5506 / Fax: (318) 342-5510

Mr. Greg Spann, Director
Capital SBDC
Southern University
9613 Interline Ave.
Baton Rouge, LA 70809
(504) 922-0998

Mr. William Joubert, Director
SBDC
Southeastern LA University
College of Business Administration
SLU Station, Box 522
Hammond, LA 70402
(504) 549-3831

Mr. Dan Lavergne, Interim Director
Acadiana SBDC
College of Business Administration
Box 43732
Lafayette, LA 70504
(318) 262-5344

Mr. Paul Arnold, Director
SBDC
McNeese State University
College of Business Administration
Lake Charles, LA 70609
(318) 475-5529

Mr. Chad J. Acosta, Operations Mgr.
SBDC
Northeast LA University
Admin. 2-57
Monroe, LA 71209
(318) 342-5506

Dr. Paul Dunn, Director
SBDC
Northeast Louisiana University
College of Business Administration
Monroe, LA 71209
(318) 342-1224

Dr. Lesa Lawrence, Associate State Director
SBDC
Northeast Louisiana University Admin. 2-57
Monroe, LA 71209
(318) 342-5506

Dr. Jerry Wall, Consultant
Special Project Director
LA Electronic Assist. Program
College of Business Administration
Northeast Louisiana University
Monroe, LA 71209
(318) 342-1215

Ms. Mary Lynn Wilkerson, Director
SBDC
Northwestern State University
College of Business Administration
Natchitoches, LA 71497
(318) 357-5611

Mr. Ruperto Chavarri, Coordinator
International Trade Center
2926 World Trade Center
2 Canal Street
New Orleans, LA 70130
(504) 568-8222 / Fax:(504) 568-8228

Dr. Ivan Miestchovich, Director
SBDC
University of New Orleans
College of Business Administration
Lakefront Campus
New Orleans, LA 70148
(504) 286-6978

Dr. Ronald H. Schroeder, Director
SBDC
Loyola University
Box 134
New Orleans, LA 70118
(504) 865-3474

Jon Johnson, Director
SBDC
Southern University
College of Business Administration
New Orleans, LA 70126
(504) 286-5308

Mr. Mike Matthews, Director
SBDC
Louisiana Tech University
Box 10318, Tech Station
Ruston, LA 71272-0046
(318) 257-3538

Mr. Jim Hicks, Director
SBDC
LSU-Shreveport
College of Business Administration
1 University Place
Shreveport, LA 71115
(318) 797-5144

Director
SBDC
Nicholls State University
P.O. Box 2015
Thibodaux, LA 70310
(504) 448-4242

MAINE SMALL BUSINESS DEVELOPMENT CENTERS

Charles Davis, State Director
Small Business Development Center
University of Southern Maine
96 Falmouth St.
Portland, ME 04103
(207) 780-4420 / Fax: (207) 780-4810

John Jaworski
Small Business Development Center
Androscoggin Valley Council of Government
125 Manley Rd.
Auburn, ME 04210
(207) 783-9186

Michael Aube
Small Business Development Center
Eastern Maine Development Corp.
1 Cumberland Place, Suite 300
P.O. Box 2579
Bangor, ME 04401-8520
(207) 942-6389

Robert P. Clark
Small Business Development Center
Northern Maine Regional Planning Commission
P.O. Box 779
2 Main Street
Caribou, ME 04736
(207) 498-8736

Dr. William Little
Small Business Development Center
University of Maine at Machias
Math and Science Bldg.
Machias, ME 04654
(207) 255-3313

Madge Baker
Small Business Development Center
Southern Maine Regional Planning Commission
Box Q, 255 Main Street
Sanford, ME 04073
(207) 324-0316

W. Elery Keene
Small Business Development Center
N. Kennebec Regional Planning Commission
7 Benton Ave.
Winslow, ME 04901
(207) 873-0711

Ron Phillips
Small Business Development Center
Coastal Enterprises Incorporated
Middle Street, Box 268
Wiscasset, ME 04578
(207) 882-7552

MARYLAND SMALL BUSINESS DEVELOPMENT CENTERS

Woodrow McCutchen, State Director
Maryland SBDC Network
State Administrative Office
Department of Economic & Employment
Development
217 East Redwood St., Suite 936
Baltimore, MD 21202
(410) 333-6995 / Fax: (410) 333-4460

Dr. Richard Palmer
Central Region SBDC
1414 Key Highway, Suite 310
Baltimore, MD 21230
(410) 234-0505

Robert Douglas (Robin), Exec. Dir.
Western Region SBDC
Three Commerce Drive
Cumberland, MD 21502
1-800-457-7233 / (301) 724-6716

Thomas McLamore (Tom), Exec. Dir.
Suburban Washington Region SBDC
9201 Basil Court, Room 115
Landover, MD 20785
(301) 925-5032

Mr. John Dillard (Kip), Exec. Dir.
Eastern Shore Region SBDC
1101 Camden Avenue
Salisbury, MD 21801
1-800-999-SBDC / (410) 546-4325

Ms. Betsy Cooksey
Southern Region SBDC
235 Smallwood Village Center
Waldorf, MD 20602-1852
1-800-762-SBDC / (301) 932-4155

Ms. Susan Green Simpson, Director
Maryland Manufacturing and Tech. SBDC
Dingman Center for Entrepreneurship
College of Business Management
University of Maryland
College Park, MD 20742-1815
(301) 405-2144

MASSACHUSETTS SMALL BUSINESS DEVELOPMENT CENTERS

John Ciccarelli, State Director
MSBDC Network, State Office
University of Massachusetts
205 School of Management
Amherst, MA 01003
(413) 545-6301 / Fax: (413) 545-1273

Joseph France
Minority Business Assistance Center
P.O. Box 3437
Boston, MA 02101
(617) 457-4444

John McKiernan, Regional Director
Metro Boston MA Regional Office SBDC
Boston College
Rahner House
96 College Road
Chestnut Hill, MA 02167
(617) 552-4091 / Fax: (617) 552-2730

Don Rielly, Director
Capital Formation Service
Boston College
Rahner House
96 College Road
Chestnut Hill, MA 02167
(617) 552-4091 / Fax: (617) 552-2730

Clyde Mitchell, Regional Director
Southeastern MA Regional Office SBDC
Univ. of Massachusetts/Dartmouth
P.O. Box 2785
200 Pocasset Street
Fall River, MA 02722
(508) 673-9783 / Fax: (508) 674-1929

Dianne Fuller Doherty, Regional Director
Western MA Regional Office SBDC
Univ. of Massachusetts/Amherst
101 State St., Suite 424
Springfield, MA 01103
(413) 737-6712 / Fax: (413) 737-2312

Laurence Marsh
Central MA Regional Office SBDC
Clark University
950 Main Street, Dana Commons
Worcester, MA 01610
(617) 793-7615 / Fax: (617) 793-8890

Frederick Young
North Shore Regional Office SBDC
Salem State College
197 Essex Street
Salem, MA 01970
(508) 741-6343 / Fax: (508) 741-6345

MICHIGAN SMALL BUSINESS DEVELOPMENT CENTERS

Ronald R. Hall, State Director
Michigan SBDC
2727 Second Ave.
Detroit, MI 48201
(313) 964-1798 / Fax: (313) 577-4222

Kenneth Rizzio, Executive Director
Michigan SBDC
Ottawa County Economic Development Office, Inc.
6676 Lake Michigan Drive
Allendale, MI 49401
(616) 892-4120 / Fax: (616) 895-6670

Carl Osentoski, Director
Michigan SBDC
Huron County Economic Development Corp.
Huron County Building, Room 303
Bad Axe, MI 48413
(517) 269-6431 / Fax: (517) 269-7221

Mark Clevey, SBDC Director
MERRA Speciality Bus. Devel. Center
2901 Hubbard Road, Suite 106
Ann Arbor, MI 48105
(313) 930-0034 / Fax: (313) 663-6622

Mark O'Connel, Director
Kellogg Community College SBDC
450 North Avenue
Battle Creek, MI 49017-3397
(616) 965-3023 / Fax: (616) 965-4133
1-800 955-4KCC

James Converse, Director
Lake Michigan SBDC
Corporation and Comm. Development
2755 E. Napier
Benton Harbor, MI 49022-1899
(616) 927-3571 Ext. 247 / Fax: (616) 927-4491

Lora Swenson, Director
Ferris State University SBDC
Alumni 226
901 S. State Street
Big Rapids, MI 49307
(616) 592-3553 / Fax: (616) 592-3539

Ronald Andrews, Director
Wexford-Missaukee BDC
117 W. Cass Street, Suite 1
Cadillac, MI 49601-0026
(616) 775-9776 / Fax: (616) 775-1440

James McLoskey, Director
Michigan SBDC
Tuscola County Economic Development Corp.
1184 Cleaver Road, Suite 800
Caro, MI 48723
(517) 673-2849 / Fax: (517) 673-2517

Gary Shields, Director
Wayne State University Lead SBDC
Center for Urban Studies
3043 Faculty/Administration Bldg.
Detroit, MI 48202
(313)577-8339 / Fax: (313) 577-1274

Raymond Genick, Director
Wayne State University SBDC
School of Business Administration
2727 Second Avenue
Detroit, MI 48201
(313) 577-4850 / Fax: (313) 577-8933

Dorothy Benedict, Director
Comerica SBDC
8300 Van Dyke
Detroit, MI 48213
(313) 571-1040

Mark Carley, Director
NILAC-Marygrove College SBDC
8425 W. McNichols
Detroit, MI 48221
(313) 345-2159 / Fax: (313) 864-6670

David Zischke, Director
International Business Development Center
Michigan State University
6 Kellogg Center
East Lansing, MI 48824-1022
(517) 353-4336 / Fax: (517) 336-1009

David Gillis, Director
1st Step, Inc. Business Development Center
2415 14th Avenue, S.
Escanaba, MI 49829
(906) 786-9234 / Fax: (906) 786-4442

Mark Davis, Director
Genesee Economic Area
Revitalization, Inc. SBDC
412 S. Saginaw Street
Flint, MI 48502
(313) 238-7803 / Fax: (313) 238-7866

Bobby Wells, Director
Flint Community College Development Corp.
877 East Fifth Ave., Bldg. C-1
Flint, MI 48503
(810) 239-5847 / Fax: (810) 239-5575

Karen K. Benson, Director
Association of Commerce and Industry
1 S. Harbor Avenue, P.O. Box 509
Grand Haven, MI 49417
(616) 846-3153

Raymond De Winkle, Director
Grand Rapids Community College SBDC
Grand Rapids Community College
Applied Technology Center
151 Fountain N. E.
Grand Rapids, MI 49503
(616) 771-3600 / Fax: (616) 771-3605

Charles Persenaire, Executive Director
Michigan SBDC
Oceana Economic Development Corporation
P.O. Box 168
Hart, MI 49420-0168
(616) 873-7141 / Fax: (616) 873-3710

James Hainault, Program Manager
Michigan Technological Univ. SBDC
Bureau of Industrial Development
1400 Townsend Drive
Houghton, MI 49931
(906) 487-2470 / Fax: (906) 487-2858

Elsie White, Manager
MTU Technology Transfer SBDC
1400 Townsend Drive
Houghton, MI 49931
(906) 487-1245 / Fax: (906) 487-2463

Dennis Whitney, Director
Livingston County BDC
404 E. Grand River
Howell, MI 48843
(517) 546-4020 / Fax: (517) 546-4115

Carl R. Shook, SBDC Director
Kalamazoo College SBDC
Stryker Center for Mgmt. Studies
1327 Academy Street
Kalamazoo, MI 49007
(616) 383-8602 / Fax: (616) 383-5663

Deleski Smith, Director
Lansing Community College SBDC
P.O. Box 40010
Lansing, MI 48901
(517) 483-1921 / Fax: (517) 483-9616

Deleski Smith, Director
Handicapper Business Speciality Center
Lansing Community College, HBSC-63
P.O. Box 40010
Lansing, MI 48910
(517) 483-9948 / Fax: (517) 483-9740

Patricia Crawford-Lucas, Director
Michigan SBDC
Lapeer Development Corporation
449 McCormick Drive
Lapeer, MI 48446
(313) 667-0080 / Fax: (313) 667-3541

Chris Rector, Director
Northern Economic Initiative
Corportation SBDC
1009 West Ridge Street
Marqette, MI 49855
(517) 635-3561 / Fax: (517) 635-2230

Donald Morandini, Director
Michigan SBDC
Macomb County Business
Assistance Network
115 South Groesbeck Hwy.
Mt. Clemens, MI 48043
(313) 469-5118 / Fax: (313) 469-6787

Charles Fitzpatrick, Director
Central Michigan University SBC
256 Applied Business Studies Complex
Mt. Pleasant, MI 48859
(517) 774-3270 / Fax: (517) 774-2372

Mert Johnson, Director
Muskegon Econ. Growth Alliance BDC
349 W. Webster Avenue, Suite 104
P.O. Box 1087
Muskegon, MI 49443-1087
(616) 722-3751 / Fax: (616) 728-7251

Laurie Garvey, Director
Michigan SBDC
Sanilac County Economic Growth
175 East Aitken Road
Peck, MI 48466
(313) 648-4311 / Fax: (616) 648-4617

Robert F. Stevens, Director
St. Clair County Community BDC
323 Erie Street
P.O. Box 5015
Port Huron, MI 48061-5015
(313) 984-3881 Ext. 457 / Fax: (313) 984-2852

JoAnn Crary, Director
Saginaw Future Inc. SBDC
301 E. Genesee, 4th Floor
Saginaw, MI 48607
(517) 754-8222 / Fax: (517) 754-1715

Mark Bergstrom, Director
Michigan SBDC
West Shore Community College
Business and Industrial Development Institute
3000 North Stiles Road
Scottville, MI 49454-0277
(616) 845-6211 / Fax: (616) 845-0207

Phil Lund, Montcalm Tomorrow Director
Michigan SBDC
Montcalm Community College
2800 College Drive SW
Sidney, MI 48885
(517) 328-2111 / Fax: (517) 328-2950

Lillian Adams-Yanssens, Executive Director
Michigan SBDC
Sterling Heights Area Chamber of Commerce
12900 Paul, Suite 110
Sterling Heights, MI 48313
(313) 731-5400

Janet Masi, Vice President, Economic Development
Michigan SBDC
Warren, Center Line, Sterling Heights Chamber of Commerce
30500 Van Dyke, #118
Warren, MI 48093
(313) 751-3939 / Fax: (313) 751-3995

Charles Blankenship, President
Traverse City SBDC
Traverse Bay Economic Development Corp.
202 E. Grandview Parkway
P.O. Box 387
Traverse City, MI 49685-0387
(616) 946-1596 / Fax: (616) 946-2565

Richard Beldin, Chief Admin. Officer
Greater Northwest Regional CDC
2200 Dendrinos Drive
Traverse City, MI 49685-0506
(616) 929-5000

Cheryl Throop, Director
Michigan SBDC
Northwest Michigan College
Center for Business & Industry
1701 E. Front Street
Traverse City, MI 49685-0387
(616) 922-1105

Matthew Meadors, Manager
Traverse City Area Chamber of Commerce BDC
202 E. Grandview Parkway
P.O. Box 387
Traverse City, MI 49685-0387
(616) 947-5075

Dorothy Heyart, Executive Director
Business Enterprise Development Center
Long Lake Crossing
1301 West Long Lake Road, Suite 150
Troy, MI 48098
(313) 952-5800 / Fax: (313) 952-1875

Jo Ann Peterson, Director
Michigan SBDC
Saginaw Valley State University
Business and Industrial Development Institute
2250 Pierce Road
University Center, MI 48710
(517) 790-4000 / Fax: (517) 790-1314

MINNESOTA SMALL BUSINESS DEVELOPMENT CENTERS

Mary Kruger, State Director
Minnesota SBDC
500 Metro Square
121 7th Place East
St. Paul, MN 55101-2146
(612) 297-5770 / Fax: (612) 296-1290

Susan Kozojed
Small Business Development Center
Northwest Technical College
905 Grand Ave., SE
Bemidji, MN 56601
(218) 755-4286 / Fax: (218) 755-4289

Betty Walton
Small Business Development Center
Normandale Community College
9700 France Ave., South
Bloomington, MN 55431
(612) 832-6560 / Fax: (612) 832-6352

Pam Thomson
Small Business Development Center
Brainerd Technical College
300 Quince St.
Brainerd, MN 56401
(218) 828-5302 / Fax: (218) 828-5340

Lee Jensen
Small Business Development Center
University of Minnesota - Duluth
10 University Dr., 150 SBE
Duluth, MN 55811
(218) 726-8758 / Fax: (218) 726-6338

John Damjanovich
Small Business Development Center
Itasca Development Corporation
19 N.E. Third St.
Grand Rapids, MN 55744
(218) 327-2241 / Fax: (218) 327-2242

Allen Jackson
Small Business Development Center
Hibbing Community College
1515 East 25th St.
Hibbing, MN 55746
(218) 262-6703 / Fax: (218) 282-6717

Duane F. Ommen
Small Business Development Center
Rainy River Community College
1501 Highway 71
International Falls, MN 56649
(218) 285-2255 / Fax: (218) 285-2239

Wes Judkins
Small Business Development Center
Region Nine Development Commission
410 South Fifth St., P.O. Box 3367
Mankato, MN 56002-3367
(507) 387-5643 / Fax: (507) 387-7105

Jack Hawk
Small Business Development Center
Southwest State University
Suite #105
Marshall, MN 56258
(507) 537-7386 / Fax: (507) 537-6094

Randall D. Olson
Small Business Development Center
Minnesota Project Innovation
111 Third Avenue South, Ste. 100
Minneapolis, MN 55401
(612) 338-3280 / Fax: (612) 338-3483

Greg Schneider
Small Business Development Center
University of St. Thomas
1000 LaSalle Ave., Ste. MPL100
Minneapolis, MN 55403
(612) 962-4500 / Fax: (612) 962-4410

Len Silwoski
Small Business Development Center
Moorhead State University
Box 303
Moorhead, MN 56563
(218) 236-2289 / Fax: (218) 236-2280

John Sparling
Small Business Development Center
Pine Technical College
1100 Fourth Street
Pine City, MN 55063
(612) 629-7340 / Fax: (612) 629-7603

Danelle Wolf
Small Business Development Center
Hennepin Technical College
1820 North Xenium Lane
Plymouth, MN 55441
(612) 550-7218 / Fax: (612) 550-7272

Ellen Nelson
Small Business Development Center
Univeristy Center - Rochester
Highway 14 East
851 30th Ave., S.E.
Rochester, MN 55904
(507) 285-7536 / Fax: (507) 280-5502

Tom Trutna
Small Business Development Center
Dakota County Technical Institute
1300 145th Steet, East
Rosemount, MN 55068
(612) 423-8262 / Fax: (612) 423-7025

Dawn Jensen-Ragnier
St. Cloud Small Business Development Center
400 S. 1st St., Ste. 430
St. Cloud, MN 56301
(612) 255-4842 / Fax: (612) 255-4957

John Freeland
Small Business Development Center
Minnasota Technology, Inc.
Olcott Plz., 820 N. 9th St.
Virginia, MN 55792
(218) 741-4251 / Fax: (218) 741-4249

Paul Kinn
Small Business Development Center
Wadena Chamber of Commerce
222 Second Street, SE
Wadena, MN 56482
(218) 631-1502 / Fax: (218) 631-3296

Bob Rodine
Small Business Development Center
Northeast Metro Technical College
3300 Century Avenue, N., Ste. 200D
White Bear Lake, MN 55110-1894
(612) 779-5764 / Fax: (612) 779-5802

Tracy Troke-Thompson
Small Business Development Center
Winona State University
P.O. Box 5838
Winona, MN 55987
(507) 457-5088 / Fax: (507) 457-5179

MISSISSIPPI SMALL BUSINESS DEVELOPMENT CENTERS

Raleigh Byars, Executive Director
Small Business Development Center
Old Chemistry Bldg. Suite 216
University, MS 38677
(601) 232-5001 / Fax: (601) 232-5650

John Brandon
Small Business Development Center
Delta State University
P.O. Box 3235 DSU
Cleveland, MS 38733
(601) 846-4236 / Fax: (601) 846-4443

Martha Heffner
Small Business Development Center
Mississippi Delta Community College
1656 East Union Street
Greenville, MS 38702
(601) 378-8183

Heidi McDuffie
Small Business Development Center
Pearl River Community College
Route 9, Box 1325
Hattiesburg, MS 39401
(601) 544-0030 / Fax: (601) 544-0032

Van Evans
Small Business Development Center
MS Dept. of Economic & Comm. Devel.
P.O. Box 849
Jackson, MS 39205
(601) 359-3179 / Fax: (601) 359-2832

Marvel Turner
Small Business Development Center
Jackson State University
Suite A1, Jackson Enterprise Ctr.
931 Highway 80 West
Jackson, MS 39204
(601) 968-2795 / Fax: (601) 968-2358

Rebecca Montgomery, Director
Small Business Development Center
University of Southern Mississippi
USM Gulf Park Campus
730 East Beach Blvd
Long Beach, MS 39560
(601) 865-4578 / Fax: (601) 865-4544

J.W. (Bill) Lang, Director
Small Business Development Center
Meridian Community College
5500 Highway 19 North
Meridian, MS 39307
(601) 482-7445 / Fax: (601) 482-5803

Estel Wilson, Director
Small Business Development Center
Mississippi State University
P.O. Box 5288
McCool Hall, Room 229
Mississippi State, MS 39762
(601) 325-8684 / Fax: (601) 325-8686

Robert D. Russ
Small Business Development Center
Copiah-Lincoln Community College
Natchez Campus
Natchez, MS 39120
(601) 445-5254 / Fax: (601) 446-9967

Marguerite Wall
SBDC/International Trade Center
Hinds Community College
P.O. Box 1170
Raymond, MS 39154
(601) 857-3537 / Fax: (601) 857-3535

Bobby Wilson
Small Business Development Center
Itawamba Community College
653 Eason Boulevard
Tupelo, MS 38801
(601) 842-5621 515

Jeffrey Van Terry
Small Business Development Center
University of Mississippi
Suite 216, Old Chemistry Bldg.
University, MS 38677
(601) 234-2120 / Fax: (601) 232-5650

MISSOURI SMALL BUSINESS DEVELOPMENT CENTERS

Max E. Summers, State Director
Missouri SBDC (State Office)
University of Missouri
300 University Place
Columbia, MO 65211
(314) 882-0344 / Fax: (314) 884-4297

Frank "Buz" Sutherland, Director
Small Business Development Center
Southeast Missouri State University
222 North Pacific
Cape Girardeau, MO 63701
(314) 290-5965 / Fax: (314) 651-5005 (call before)

Nanette Anderjaska, Director
Chillicothe City Hall
715 Washington
Chillicothe, MO 64601
(816) 646-6920 / Fax: (816) 646-6811

Frank Siebert, Director
Small Business Development Center
University of Missouri - Columbia
1800 University Place
Columbia, MO 65211
(314) 882-7096 / Fax: (314) 882-6156

Bruce Epps, Director
Small Business Development Center
Mineral Area College
P.O. Box 1000
Park Hills, MO 63601
(314) 431-4593 Ext. 283 / Fax:(314) 431-6807

Dr. Tom Buchanan, Director
Small Business Development Center
Business and Industrial Specialists
University Extension
2507 Industrial Drive
Jefferson City, MO 65101
(314) 634-2824

Jim Krudwig, Director
Small Business Development Center
Missouri Southern State College
3950 Newman Rd, #107 Matthews Hall
Joplin, MO 64801-1595
(417) 625-9313 / Fax: (816) 926-4588

Judith Burngen, Director
Small Business Development Center
Rockhurst College
1100 Rockhurst Road
Kansas City, MO 64110-2599
(816) 926-4572 / Fax: (816) 926-4588

Glen Giboney, Director
Small Business Development Center
Northeast Missouri State University
207 East Patterson
Kirksville, MO 63501
(816) 785-4307 / Fax: (816) 785-4181

Brad Anderson, Director
Small Business Development Center
Northwest Missouri State University
127 South Buchanan
Maryville, MO 64468
(816) 562-1701 / Fax: (816) 562-1900

John Bonifield, Director
Small Business Development Center
Three Rivers Community College
Business Incubator Bldg.
3019 Fair Street
Poplar Bluff, MO 63901
(314) 686-3499 / Fax: (314) 686-5467

Bob Laney, Director
Small Business Development Center
University of Missouri - Rolla
223 Engineering Management Building
Rolla, MO 65401-0249
(314) 341-4561 / Fax: (314) 341-2071

Don Myers, Director
Ctr. for Tech. Trans. & Econ. Devel.
Univ. of Missouri - Rolla
Rm 104, Bldg. 1, Nagogami Terrace
Rolla, MO 65401-0249
(314) 341-4559 / Fax: (314) 341-4992

Virginia Campbell, Director
Small Business Development Center
Saint Louis University
3642 Lindell Boulevard
St. Louis, MO 63108
(314) 534-7232 / Fax: (314) 836-6337

Jane Peterson, Director
Small Business Development Center
Center for Business Research
S.W. Missouri State University
Box 88, 901 South National
Springfield, MO 65804-0089
(417) 836-5685 / Fax: (417) 836-6337

Cindy Tanck, Coordinator
Small Business Development Center
Central Missouri State University
Grinstead #75
Warrensburg, MO 64093-5037
(816) 543-4402 / Fax: (816) 747-1653

Bernie Sarbaugh, Coordinator
Center for Technology
Central Missouri State University
Grinstead #75
Warrensburg, MO 64093-5037
(816) 543-4402 / Fax: (816) 747-1653

MONTANA SMALL BUSINESS DEVELOPMENT CENTERS

Gene Marcille, State Director
Montana SBDC
Montana Department of Commerce
1424 Ninth Avenue
Helena, MT 59620
(406) 444-4780 / Fax: (406) 444-1872

Jerry Thomas
Billings SBDC
Montana Tradepost Authority
115 N. Broadway, 2nd Floor
Billings, MT 59101
(406) 256-6875 / Fax: (406) 256-6877

Darrell Berger
Bozeman SBDC
Gailatin Development Corp.
321 East Main, Suite 413
Bozeman, MT 59715
(406) 587-3113 / Fax: (406) 587-9565

Ralph Kloser
Butte SBDC
REDI
305 West Mercury, Suite 211
Butte, MT 59701
(406) 782-7333 / Fax: (406) 782-9675

Randy Hanson
Havre SBDC
Bear Paw Development Corporation
P.O. Box 1549
Havre, MT 59501
(406) 265-9226 / Fax: (406) 265-3777

Dan Manning
Kalispell SBDC
Flathead Valley Community College
777 Grandview Drive
Kalispell, MT 59901
(406) 756-8333 / Fax: (406) 756-3815

Leslie Jensen
Missoula SBDC
Missoula Business Incubator
127 N. Higgins, 3rd Floor
Missoula, MT 59802
(406) 728-9234 / Fax: (406) 721-4584

Dwayne Heintz
Sidney SBDC
Edstein Montana RC&D
123 West Main
Sidney, MT 59270
(406) 482-5024 / Fax: (406) 482-5306

NEBRASKA SMALL BUSINESS DEVELOPMENT CENTERS

Robert Bernier, State Director
University of Nebraska at Omaha
60th & Dodge Streets
CBA Room 407
Omaha, NE 68182
(402) 554-2521 / Fax: (402) 554-3747

Cliff Hanson, Center Director
NBDC - Chadron
Chadron State College
Administration Bldg.
Chadron, NE 69337
(308) 432-6282 / Fax: (308) 432-6430

Kay Payne, Center Director
NBDC - Kearney
University of Nebraska at Kearney
Welch Hall, 19th & College Dr.
Kearney, NE 68849-3035
(308) 234-8344

Larry Cox, Center Director
NBDC - Lincoln
University of Nebraska - Lincoln
Cornhusker Bank Bldg.
11th & Cornhusker Hwy., Suite 302
Lincoln, NE 68521
(402) 472-3358

Dean Kurth, Center Director
NBDC - North Platte
Mid Plains Community College
416 N. Jeffers, Room 26
North Platte, NE 69101
(308) 534-5115

Bob Toth, Center Director
NBDC - Omaha
University of Nebraska at Omaha
Peter Kiewit Conference Center
1313 Farnam-on-the-Mall, Suite 132
Omaha, NE 68182-0248
(402) 595-2381 / Fax: (402) 595-2385

Tom McCabe, Center Director
NBDC - OBTC
Omaha Business & Technology Center
2505 North 24 St., Suite 101
Omaha, NE 68110
(402) 595-3511 or 595-3524

David Ruenholl, Center Director
NBDC - Peru
Peru State College
T.J. Majors Hall, Room 248
Peru, NE 68421
(402) 872-2274

Ingrid Battershell, Center Director
NBDC - Scottsbluff
Nebraska Public Power Building
1721 Broadway, Room 408
Scottsbluff, NE 69361
(308) 635-7513

Loren Kucera, Center Director
NBDC - Wayne
Wayne State College
Connell Hall
Wayne, NE 68787
(402) 375-7575

NEVADA SMALL BUSINESS DEVELOPMENT CENTERS

Sam Males, State Director
Small Business Development Center
University of Nevada, Reno
College of Business Administration-032
Room 411
Reno, NV 89557-0100
(702) 784-1717 / Fax: (702) 784-4337

John Pryor, Director
Small Business Development Center
Northern Nevada Community College
901 Elm Street
Elko, NV 89801
(702) 738-8493

Sharolyn Craft, Director
Small Business Development Center
University of Nevada at Las Vegas
College of Business & Economics
4505 Maryland Parkway
Las Vegas, NV 89154
(702) 895-0852 / Fax: (702) 895-4095

Larry Osborne, Executive Director
Small Business Development Center
Carson City Chamber of Commerce
1900 South Carson Street, #100
Carson City, NV 89702
(702) 882-1565

Teri Williams, Director
Small Business Development Center
Tri-County Development Authority
50 West Fourth Street
P.O. Box 820
Winnemucca, NV 89446
(702) 623-5777

Janise Stevenson
Small Business Development Center
19 West Brooks Avenue
North Las Vegas, NV 89030
(702) 399-6300 / Fax: (702) 399-6301

Robert Holland, Business Development Spec.
Small Business Development Center
Foreign Trade Zone Office
1111 Grier Drive
Las Vegas, NV 89119
(702) 896-4496 / Fax: (702) 896-8351

NEW HAMPSHIRE SMALL BUSINESS DEVELOPMENT CENTERS

Liz Mattot, State Director
SBDC
15 Colllege Road, 108 McConnell Hall
University of New Hampshire
Durham, NH 03824-3593
(603) 862-2200 / Fax: (603) 862-4876

Kit McCormick, Regional Manager   SBDC
Heidelberg-Harris Bldg.
Durham, NH 03824
(603) 862-0710 / Fax: (603) 862-0701

Michelle Emig, Director
Office of Economic Initiatives
Heidelberg-Harris Bldg. 108
Durham, NH 03824
(603) 862-0710 / Fax: (603) 862-0701

Gary Cloutier, Regional Manager
SBDC
Keene State College
Blake House
Keene, NH 03431
(603) 358-2602 / Fax: (603) 756-4878

Liz Matott, Regional Manager
SBDC
P.O. Box 786
Littleton, NH 03561
(603) 444-1053

Bob Ebberson, Regional Manager
SBDC
1001 Elm Street
Manchester, NH 03101
(603) 624-2000 / Fax: (603) 623-3972

Bob Wilburn, Regional Manager
SBDC
c/o Center for Economic Development
188 Main Street
Nashua, NH 03060
(603) 881-8333 / Fax: (603) 881-7323

Janice Kitchen, Regional Manager
SBDC
Plymouth State College
Hyde Hall
Plymouth, NH 03264
(603) 535-2523 / Fax: (603) 535-2526

NEW JERSEY SMALL BUSINESS DEVELOPMENT CENTERS

Brenda Hopper, State Director
Small Business Development Center
Rutgers University
180 University Ave.
3rd Floor- Ackerson Hall
Newark, NJ 07102
(201) 648-5950 / Fax: (201) 648-1110

William McGinley, Director
Small Business Development Center
Greater Atlantic City
Chamber of Commerce
1301 Atlantic Ave.
Atlantic City, NJ 08401
(609) 345-5600 / Fax: (609) 345-4524

Patricia Peacock, Ed.D.
Small Business Development Center
Rutgers Univ. Schools of Business
Business & Science Bldg., 2nd Fl.
Camden, NJ 08102
(609) 225-6221 / Fax: (609) 225-6231

Bill Nunnally, Director
Small Business Development Center
Brookdale Community College
Newman Springs Road
Lincroft, NJ 07738
(201) 842-1900 Ext. 751 / Fax: (908) 842-0203

Leroy Johnson, Director
Rutgers Small Business Development Center
3rd Floor - Ackerson Hall
180 University Avenue
Newark, NJ 07102
(201) 648-5950 / Fax: (201) 648-1110

Herbert Spiegel
Small Business Development Center
Mercer County Community College
1200 Old Trenton Road
Trenton, NJ 08690
(609) 586-4800 469

Mira Kostak, Director
Small Business Development Center
Kean College
Morris Ave. and Conant
Union, NJ 07083
(908) 527-2946 / Fax: (908) 527-2960

Jonathan Andrews, Acting Director
Small Business Development Center
Warren County Community College
Route 57 West, Rd #1 Box 55A
Washington, NJ 07882
(908) 689-7613 / Fax: (908) 689-7488

Melody Irvin, Director
Bergen County Community College
400 Paramus Road
Paramus, NJ 07552
(201) 447-7841 / Fax: (201) 447-7495

NEW MEXICO SMALL BUSINESS DEVELOPMENT CENTERS

Frank Hatstat, State Director
NMSBDC Lead Center
Santa Fe Community College
P.O. Box 4187
Santa Fe, NM 87502-4187
(505) 438-1362 / Fax: (505) 438-1237

Dwight Harp
Small Business Development Center
New Mexico State Univ. at Alamogordo
1000 Madison
Alamogordo, NM 88310
(505) 434-5272

Roslyn Block
Small Business Development Center
Albuquerque Tech.-Vocational Inst.
525 Buena Vista SE
Albuquerque, NM 87106
(505) 224-4246

Larry Coalson
Small Business Development Center
New Mexico State Univ. at Carlsbad
P.O. Box 1090
Carlsbad, NM 88220
(505) 887-6562

Roy Miller
Small Business Development Center
Clovis Community College
417 Schepps Blvd.
Clovis, NM 88101-8345
(505) 769-4136

Darien Cabral
Small Business Development Center
Northern New Mexico Comm. College
1002 N. Onate Street
Espanola, NM 87532
(505) 474-2236

Brad Ryan
Small Business Development Center
San Juan College
203 W. Main Street, Suite 201
Farmington, NM 87401
(505) 326-4321

Barbara Stanley
Small Business Development Center
University of New Mexico-Gallup
P.O. Box 1395
Gallup, NM 87305
(505) 722-2220

Clemente Sanchez
Small Business Development Center
New Mexico State Univ. at Grants
709 E. Roosevelt Ave.
Grants, NM 87020
(505) 287-8221

Don Leach
Small Business Development Center
New Mexico Junior College
5317 Lovington Highway
Hobbs, NM 88240
(505) 392-4510

Terry Sullivan
Small Business Development Center
NM State Univ. - Dona Ana Branch
Box 30001, Dept. 3DA
Las Cruces, NM 88003-0001
(505) 527-7601

Michael Rivera
Small Business Development Center
Luna Vocational-Technical Institute
P.O. Drawer K
Las Vegas, NM 87701
(505) 454-2595

Jim Greenwood
Small Business Development Center
Univ. of New Mexico at Los Alamos
P.O. Box 715
Los Alamos, NM 87544
(505) 662-0001

Small Business Development Center
Univ. of New Mexico at Valencia
280 La Entrada
Los Lunas, NM 87031
(505) 865-9596, Ext. 317

Eugene Simmons
Small Business Development Center
Eastern New Mexico Univ. at Roswell
P.O. Box 6000
Roswell, NM 88201-6000
(505) 624-7133

Emily Miller
Small Business Development Center
Santa Fe Community College
P.O. Box 4187
Santa Fe, NM 87502-4187
(505) 438-1343

Linda Kay Jones
Small Business Development Center
Western New Mexico University
P.O. Box 2672
Silver City, NM 88062
(505) 538-6320

Richard Spooner
Small Business Development Center
Tucumcari Area Vocational School
P.O. Box 1143
Tucumcari, NM 88401
(505) 461-4413

NEW YORK SMALL BUSINESS DEVELOPMENT CENTERS

James L. King, State Director
Small Business Development Center
State University of New York
SUNY Central Plaza S-523
Albany, NY 12246
(518) 443-5398 / Fax: (518) 465-4992

Peter George
Small Business Development Center
SUNY at Albany
Draper Hall, 107
135 Western Ave.
Albany, NY 12222
(518) 442-5577

Joanne Bauman
Small Business Development Center
SUNY at Binghamton
P.O. Box 6000
Binghamton, NY 13902-6000
(607) 777-4024

Terrence Clark, Director
Small Business Development Center
Bronx Community College
McCracken Hall, Room 14
W. 181 St. & University Ave.
Bronx, NY 10453
(718) 220-6464

Edward O'Brien
Small Business Development Center
Kingsborough Community College
2001 Oriental Blvd.
Bldg. T4, Room 4204
Brooklyn, NY 11235
(718) 368-4619

Susan McCartney
Small Business Development Center
State University College at Buffalo - BA 117
1300 Elmwood Ave.
Buffalo, NY 14222
(716) 878-4030

Bonnie Gestwicki
Small Business Development Center
Corning Community College
24 Denison Parkway West
Corning, NY 14830
(607) 962-9461

Joseph Schwartz
Small Business Development Center
SUNY of Technology at Farmingdale
Campus Commons
Farmingdale, NY 11735
(516) 420-2765

Celeste Glenn
Small Business Development Center
York College, Science Bldg, Rm 107
The City University of New York
Jamaica, NY 11451
(718) 262-2880

Irene Dobies
Jamestown Communtiy College SBDC
P.O. Box 20
Jamestown, NY 14702-0020
(716) 665-5754

Small Business Development Center
Pace University, Pace Plaza
New York, NY 10038
(212) 346-1899

Small Business Development Center
Clinton Community College
Alpert Bldg., Rt. 9
Plattsburgh, NY 12901
(518) 564-4260

Richard Gorko
Small Business Development Center
Niagara County Community College
3111 Saunders Settlement Road
Sanborn, NY 14132
(716) 693-1910

Loretta DiCamillo, Director
Small Business Development Center
The College of Stanton Island
Sunnyside Campus, Rm. B140
715 Ocean Terrace
Stanton Island, NY 10301
(718) 390-7645

Judith McEvoy
Small Business Development Center
State University at Stony Brook
Harriman Hall, Rm 109
Stony Brook, NY 11794
(516) 632-9070

Jean Morris
Small Business Development Center
Ulster County Community College
Stone Ridge, NY 12484
(914) 687-5272

Thomas J. Morley
Small Business Development Center
Rockland Community College
145 College Road
Suffern, NY 10901
(914) 356-0370

Robert Varney
Small Business Development Center
Onondaga Community College
Excell Building, Route 173
Syracuse, NY 13215
(315) 492-3029

Thomas Reynolds
Small Business Development Center
SUNY Institute of Tech. Utica/Rome
P.O. Box 3050
Utica, NY 13504-3050
(315) 792-7546

John F. Tanner
Small Business Development Center
Jefferson Community College at Watertown
Watertown, NY 13601
(315) 782-9262

Wilfred Bordeau
SBDC
State University of New York
College at Brockport
74 North Main Street
Brockport, NY 14420
(716) 395-2755

NORTH CAROLINA SMALL BUSINESS AND TECHNOLOGY DEVELOPMENT CENTERS

Scott Daugherty, Executive Director
NC SBDC Headquarters Office
Univ. of N. Carolina at Chapel Hill
4509 Creedmoor Road, Suite 201
Raleigh, NC 27612
(919) 571-4154 / Fax: (919) 571-4161
1-800-2580-UNC

Bill Parrish, Director
Northwestern Regional Center
Appalachian State University
Walker College of Business
Boone, NC 28608
(704) 262-2095

George McAllister, Director
Southern Piedmont Regional Center
Univ. of North Carolina at Charlotte
The Ben Craig Center
8701 Mallard Creek Road
Charlotte, NC 28262
(704) 548-1090

R. Daniel Parks, Director
Central Carolina Regional Center
Univ. of N. Carolina at Chapel Hill
608 Airport Road, Suite B
Chapel Hill, NC 27514
(919) 962-0389

Tim Richards, Director
Western Regional Center
Western Carolina University
Center for Improving Mountain Living
Cullowhee, NC 28723
(704) 227-7494

Wauna Dooms, Director
Northeastern Regional Center
Elizabeth City State University
Weeksville Road, P.O. Box 874
K.E. White Graduate Center
Elizabeth City, NC 27909
(919) 335-3247

Dr. Sid Gautam, Director
Cape Fear Area Center
Fayetteville State University
P.O. Box 1334
Fayetteville, NC 28302
(919) 486-1727

Walter Fitts, Director
Eastern Regional Center
East Carolina University
Corner 1st and Reade Streets
Greenville, NC 27858-4353
(919) 757-6157

Cynthia Clemons, Director
Northeast Piedmont Regional Center
NC State
P.O. Box D-22
Greensboro, NC 27411
(919) 334-7005

Nat James, Director
Capital Regional Center
North Carolina State University
4509 Creedmoor Rd, Suite 201
Raleigh, NC 27612
(919) 571-4154

Ted Jans, Director
Southeastern Regional Center
Univ. of N. Carolina at Wilmington
601 South College Road
Room 131, Cameron Hall
Wilmington, NC 28403
(919) 395-3744

Bill Dowe, Director
Northern Piedmont Regional Center
Winston-Salem State University
P.O. Box 13025
Winston-Salem, NC 27110
(919) 750-2030

Rand Riedrich, Director
Catawba Valley Regional Center
840 Second Street NE
Hickory, NC 28601
(704) 345-1110

NORTH DAKOTA SMALL BUSINESS DEVELOPMENT CENTERS

Walter (Wally) Kearns, State Director
State Center/Grand Forks
118 Gamble Hall, UND
University Station Box 7308
Grand Forks, ND 58202-7308
(701) 777-3700 / Fax: (701) 777-3225

Jan Peterson, Regional Director
Bismark Regional Center
Small Business Development Center
400 E. Broadway, Suite 416
Bismarck, ND 58501
(701) 223-8583 / Fax: (701) 222-3843

Bryan Vendsel, Regional Director
Dickinson Regional Center
Small Business Development Center
314 3rd Ave., West, Drawer L
Dickinson, ND 58602
(701) 227-2096 / Fax: (701) 225-5116

Gordon Snyder, Regional Director
Grand Forks Regional Center
Small Business Development Center
The Hemmp Center
1407 24th Avenue S., Suite 201
Grand Forks, ND 58201
(701) 772-8502 / Fax: (701) 775-2772

Jon Grinager, Regional Director
Fargo Regional Center
Small Business Development Center
417 Main Avenue
Fargo, ND 58103
(701) 237-0986 / Fax: (701) 235-6706

Brian Hrgabright, Regional Center
Minot Regional Center
Small Business Development Center
1020 20th Ave. SW
P.O. Box 940
Minot, ND 58702
(701) 852-8861 / Fax: (701) 838-2488

OHIO SMALL BUSINESS DEVELOPMENT CENTERS 4/95

Holly Schick, State Director
Small Business Development Center
77 South High St., 28th Floor
P.O. Box 1001
Columbus, OH 43266-0101
(614) 466-2711 / Fax: (614) 466-0829

Barbara Honthumb
Women's Entrepreneurial Growth Organization
58 W. Center St./P.O. Box 544
Akron, OH 44309
(216) 535-9346 / Fax: (216) 535-4523

Charles Smith
Small Business Development Center
Akron Regional Development Board
One Cascade Plaza, 8th Floor
Akron, OH 44308
(216) 379-3170 / Fax: (216) 379-3164

Don Wright
Small Business Development Center
Northwest Technical College
State Route 34, Box 246-A
Archbold, OH 43502
(419) 267-5511 / Fax: (419) 267-5233

Richard Knight
Kent Stark Small Business Development Center
Kent State University
Stark Campus
6000 Frank Ave., N.W.
Canton, OH 44720
(216) 499-9600 / Fax: (216) 494-6121

Dr. Tom Knapke
Small Business Development Center
Wright State Branch Campus
7600 State Route 703
Celina, OH 45882
(419) 586-2365 / Fax: (419) 586-0358

William A. Fioretti
Cincinnati SBDC
IAMS Research Park
1111 Edison Drive
Cincinnati, OH 45216-2265
(513) 948-2082 / Fax: (513) 948-2007

Linda Stewart, Director
Small Business Development Center
37 North High Street
Columbus, OH 43216
(614) 221-1321 / Fax: (614) 469-8250

Joe Wilson, Director
Small Business Development Center
Terra Technical College
1220 Cedar Street
Fremont, OH 43420
(419) 332-1002 / Fax: (419) 334-2300

Douglas Born, Director
Wood County SBDC
WSOS Community Action Comm., Inc.
P.O. Box 48\121 E. Wooster St.
Bowling Green, OH 43402
(419) 352-7469 / Fax: (419) 353-3291

Harry Bumgarner, Director
Dayton SBDC
Dayton Area Chamber of Commerce
Chamber Plaza - 5th and Main Sts.
Dayton, OH 45402-2400
(513) 226-8230 / Fax: (513) 226-8254

Jeanette Davy, Director
Center for Small Business Assistance
Wright State University
310 Rike Hall
Dayton, OH 45433
(513) 873-3503 / Fax: (513) 837-3545

Rosann Miller-Wethington, Executive Director
Women's Economic Assistance Ventures
100 Corry Street, P.O. Box 512
Yellow Springs, OH 45387
(513) 767-2667 / Fax: (513) 767-8652

Jack Harris, Executive Director
Springfield SBDC, Inc.
300 E. Auburn Ave.
Springfield, OH 45505
(513) 322-7821 / Fax: (513) 322-7874

Dennis Begue, Director
Clermont County Area SBDC
Clermont County Chamber of Commerce
4440 Glen Este-Withamsville Rd.
Cincinnati, OH 45245
(513) 753-7141 / Fax: (513) 753-7146

Renee Keener, Director
Ashtabula County Economic Development
Council, Inc.
36 West Walnut Street
Jefferson, OH 44047
(216) 576-9134 / Fax: (216) 576-5003

Gerald J. Biedenharn, Director
Small Business Development Center
Lima Technical College
545 West Market St., Suite 305
Lima, OH 45801-4717
(419) 229-5320 / Fax: (419) 229-5424

Dennis Jones, Director
Lorain SBDC
Lorain County Chamber of Commerce
6100 S. Broadway
Lorain, OH 44053
(216) 246-2833 / Fax: (216) 246-4050

Tim Bowersock, Administrator
Small Business Development Center
Mid-Ohio
P.O. Box 1208
Mansfield, OH 44901
(800) 366-7232 / Fax: (419) 522-6811

Dr. Michael Broida, Director
Small Business Development Center
Miami University
Dept. of Decision Sciences
336 Upham Hall
Oxford, OH 45056
(513) 529-4841 / Fax: (513) 948-2007

James Ackley, Director
Small Business Development Center
Upper Valley Joint Vocational School
8811 Career Dr., No. County Rd. 25A
Piqua, OH 45356
(513) 778-8419 / Fax: (513) 778-9237

Mike Campbell, Director
Small Business Development Center
Department of Development of CIC
100 E. Main Street
St. Clairsville, OH 43950
(614) 695-9678 / Fax: (614) 695-1536

Robert Proy, Director
Small Business Development Center
Sandusky City Schools
407 Decatur Street
Sandusky, OH 44870
1-800-548-6507 / Fax: (419) 626-9176

Lou-Ann Walden, Director
Small Business Development Center
Lawrence County Chamber of Commerce
US Rte 52 & Solida Rd.\P.O. Box 488
Southpoint, OH 45680
(614) 894-3838 / Fax: (614) 894-3836

Jeff Castner, Director
SBDC of Jefferson County
Greater Steubenville Chamber of Commerce
630 Market St.\P.O. Box 278
Steubenville, OH 43952
(614) 282-6226 / Fax: (614) 282-6285

Deb Campbell, Director
Small Business Development Center
300 Madison Avenue
Toledo, OH 43604
(419) 243-8191 / Fax: (419) 241-8302

Patricia Veisz
Small Business Development Center
Youngstown State University
Cushwa Center for Industrial Devel.
Youngstown, OH 44555
(216) 742-3495 / Fax: (216) 742-3784

Bonnie J. Winnett, Director
Small Business Development Center
Zanesville Area Chamber of Commerce
217 North Fifth Street
Zanesville, OH 43701
(614) 452-4868 / Fax: (614) 454-2963

Marianne Vermeer, Director
Small Business Development Center
Ohio University - Innovation Center
One President Street, Suite 104
Athens, OH 45701
(614) 593-1797 / Fax: (614) 593-1795

Lynn Lovell
Heart of Ohio SBDC Satellite
Marion Area Chamber of Commerce
206 S. Prospect Street
Marion, OH 43302
(614) 387-0188 / Fax: (614) 387-7722

Dan DeSantis, Director
Southeast SBDC: Portsmouth Satellite
Portsmouth Area Chamber of Commerce
1020 Seventh St.\P.O. Box 509
Portsmouth, OH 45662
(614) 353-1116 / Fax: (614) 353-5824

Janet Haar, Director
Cleveland SBDC
Greater Cleveland Growth Association
200 Tower City Center
50 Public Square
Cleveland, OH 44113-2291
(216) 621-3300 / Fax: (216) 621-6013

Jerry Loth, Director
Lake County SBDC
Lakeland Community College
Lake County Econ. Development Center
7750 Clocktower Drive
Mentor, OH 44080
(216) 951-1290 / Fax: (216) 953-4413

Linda Yost, Director
Kent SBDC
277 Martinet Drive
Kent, OH 44240
(216) 673-1640 / Fax: (216) 673-1640

Blanche Tyree, Director
Coshocton SBDC
Coshocton County Chamber of Commerce
124 Chestnut Street
Cosocton, OH 43812
(614) 622-5411 / Fax:(614) 622-9902

Tom Farbizo, Director
Tuscarawas SBDC
Tuscarawas Chamber of Commerce
1323 Fourth Street, N.W.
P.O. Box 232
New Philadelphia, OH 44663
(216) 343-4474 / Fax: (216) 343-6526

Karen Patton, Director
SBDC of Athens
Athens Small Business Center, Inc.
900 E. State Street
Athens, OH 45701
(614) 592-1188 / Fax: (614) 593-8283

Emerson Shimp, Director
Marietta SBDC
Marietta College
213 Fourth Street
Marietta, OH 45750
(614) 376-4832 / Fax: (614) 376-4901

James Ackley, Director
SAM SBDC
EMTEC-Research Park
3171 Research Blvd.
Kettering, OH 45420-4006
(513) 259-1387 / Fax: (513) 259-1303

OKLAHOMA SMALL BUSINESS DEVELOPMENT CENTERS

Grady Pennington, State Director
Small Business Development Center
Southeastern Oklahoma State Univ.
P.O. Box 2584, Station A
Durant, OK 74701
(405) 924-0277 / Fax: (405) 924-7071

Tom Beebe
Small Business Development Center
East Central University
1036 East 10th
Ada, OK 74820
(405) 436-3190

Connie Murrell
Small Business Development Center
Northwesten Oklahoma State Univ.
Alva, OK 73717
(405) 327-5883

Herb Manning
Small Business Development Center
Southeastern State Univ.
517 University Blvd.
Durant, OK 74701
(405) 924-0277

Susan Urbach
Small Business Development Center
University of Central Oklahoma
621 N. Robinson, Suite 372
Oklahoma City, OK 73102
(405) 232-1968

Enid Satellite Center
Small Business Development Center
Phillips University
100 South University Ave
Enid, OK 73701
(405) 242-7989

Robert Allen
Small Business Development Center
Langston University Center
P.O. Box 667
Langston, OK 73050
(405) 466-3256

Lawton Satellite Center
Small Business Development Center
601 SW "D", Suite 209
Lawton, OK 73501
(405) 248-4946

Judy Robbins
Procurement Specialty Center
Rose State College
6420 Southeast 15th
Midwest City, OK 73110
(405) 733-7348

Poteau Satellite Center
Small Business Development Center
Carl Albert College
1507 South McKenna
Poteau, OK 74953
(918) 647-4019

Jeff Horuath/John Maloy
Small Business Development Center
N.E. State University
Tahlequah, OK 74464
(918) 458-0802

Tulsa Satellite Center
Small Business Development Center
440 So Houston St, Suite 507
Tulsa, OK 74127
(918) 581-2502

Chuck Felz
Small Business Development Center
S.W. Oklahoma State University
100 Campus Drive
Weatherford, OK 73096
(405) 774-1040

Miami Satellite Center
215 "I" Street N.E.
Miami, OK 74354
(918) 540-0575

OREGON SMALL BUSINESS DEVELOPMENT CENTERS

Edward Cutler, Ph.D., State Director
Oregon Small Business Development Center
Network
Lane Community College
44 W. Broadway, Suite 501
Eugene, OR 97401-3021
(503) 726-2250 / Fax: (503) 345-6006

Dennis Sargent, Director
Small Business Development Center
Linn-Benton Community College
6500 S.W. Pacific Boulevard
Albany, OR 97321
(503) 967-6112 / Fax: (503) 967-6550

Small Business Development Center
Southern Oregon State College
Regional Services Institute
Ashland, OR 97520
(503) 482-5838 / Fax: (503) 482-1115

Bob Newhart, Director
Small Business Development Center
Central Oregon Community College
2600 N.W. College Way
Bend, OR 97701
(503) 383-7290 / Fax: (503) 383-7503

Jon Richards, Director
Small Business Development Center
Southwestern Oregon Comm. College
340 Central
Coos Bay, OR 97420
(503) 269-0123 / Fax: (503) 269-0323

Bob Cole, Director
Small Business Development Center
Columbia Gorge Community College
212 Washington
The Dalles, OR 97058
(503) 296-1173 / Fax: (503) 298-4973

Jane Scheidecker, Director
Small Business Development Center
Lane Community College
1059 Willamette Street
Eugene, OR 97401
(503) 726-2255 / Fax: (503) 686-0096

Lee Merritt, Director
Small Business Development Center
Rogue Comm. College
290 N.E. "C" St.
Grants Pass, OR 97526
(503) 471-3515 / Fax: (503) 471-3589

Don King, Director
Small Business Development Center
Mount Hood Community College
323 NE Roberts Street
Gresham, OR 97030
(503) 667-7658 / Fax: (503) 666-1140

Jamie Albert, Director
Small Business Development Center
Oregon Institute of Technology
3201 Campus Drive South 314
Klamath Falls, OR 97601
(503) 885-1760 / Fax: (503) 885-1855

Joni Gibbens, Counselor
Eastern Oregon State College
Regional Services Institute
Lagrande, OR 97850
(503) 962-3391 Fax: (503) 962-3668

Mike Lainoff, Director
Small Business Development Center
Oregon Coast Community College
4157 NW Highway 101, Suite 123
P.O. Box 419
Lincoln City, OR 97367
(503) 994-4166 / Fax: (503) 996-4958

Liz Shelby, Director
Small Business Development Center
S. Oregon State College/Medford
Regional Service Institute
229 N. Barlett
Medford, OR 97501
(503) 772-3478 / Fax: (503) 776-2224

Jan Stennick, Director
Small Business Development Center
Clackamas Community College
7616 SE Harmony Road
Milwaukee, OR 97222
(503) 656-4447 / Fax: (503) 652-0389

Kathy Simko, Director
Small Business Development Center
Treasure Valley Community College
88 SW Third Ave
Ontario, OR 97914
(503) 889-2617 / Fax: (503) 889-8331

Garth Davis, Director
Small Business Development Center
Blue Mountain Community College
37 SE Dorion
Pendleton, OR 97801
(503) 276-6233 / Fax: (503) 276-6819

Robert Keyser, Director
Small Business Development Center
Portland Community College
123 NW Second Ave., Suite 321
Portland, OR 97209
(503) 414-2828 / Fax: (503) 294-0725

Tom Niland, Director
Small Business Development Center
International Trade Program
121 SW Salmon Street, Suite 210
Portland, OR 97204
(503) 274-7482 / Fax: (503) 228-6350

Terry Swagerty, Director
Small Business Development Center
Umpqua Community College
744 SE Rose
Roseburg, OR 97470
(503) 672-2535 / Fax: (503) 672-3679

Bobbie Clyde, Director
Small Business Development Center
Chemeketa Community College
365 Ferry St. SE
Salem, OR 97301
(503) 399-5181 / Fax: (503) 581-6017

Kenneth McCune, Director
Small Business Development Center
Clatstop Community College
1240 South Holladay
Seaside, OR 97138
(503) 738-3347 / Fax: (503) 738-7843

Mike Harris, Director
Small Business Development Center
Tillamook Bay Community College
401 B Main Street
Tillamook, OR 97141
(503) 842-2551 / Fax: (503) 842-2555

PENNSYLVANIA SMALL BUSINESS DEVELOPMENT CENTERS

Gregory L. Higgins, State Director
Small Business Development Center
Univ. of PA, The Wharton School
423 Vance Hall, 3733 Spruce Street
Philadelphia, PA 19104-6374
(215) 898-1219 / Fax: (215) 573-2135

Dr. John Bonge
Small Business Development Center
Lehigh Univ., Rauch Business Center #37
Bethlehem, PA 18015
(215) 758-3980

Dr. Woodrow Yeaney
Small Business Development Center
Clarion University of Pennsylvania
Dana Still Building
Clarion, PA 16214
(814) 226-2060

Ernie Post
Small Business Development Center
Gannon Univ, Carlisle Bldg, 3rd Flr.
Erie, PA 16541
(814) 871-7714

Jack Fabean
Small Business Development Center
St. Vincent College, Alfred Hall
Fourth Floor
Latrobe, PA 15650
(412) 537-4572

Dr. Charles Coder
Small Business Development Center
Bucknell University
Dana Engineering Bldg., 1st Floor
Lewisburg, PA 17837
(717) 524-1249

John A. Palko
Small Business Development Center
St. Francis College, Business Resource Center
Loretto, PA 15940
(814) 472-3200

Dr. Keith Yackee
Small Business Development Center
Kutztown University
2986 No. 2nd St.
Harrisburg, PA 17110
(717) 233-3120

Small Business Development Center
LaSalle University
Box 365, 1900 W. Olney Ave.
Philadelphia, PA 19141
(215) 951-1416

Geraldine Perkins
Small Business Development Center
Temple University
Room 6 - Speakman Hall-006-00
Philadelphia, PA 19122
(215) 204-7282

David B. Thornburgh
Small Business Development Center
University of Pennsylvania
The Wharton School
409 Vance Hall
Philadelphia, PA 19104
(215) 898-4861

Ann Dugan
Small Business Development Center
University of Pittsburgh
208 Bellefield Hall
315 S. Bellefield Ave.
Pittsburgh, PA 15213
(412) 648-1544

Dr. Mary T. McKinney
Small Business Development Center
Duquesne University
Rockwell Hall Room 10 Concourse
600 Forbes Ave
Pittsburgh, PA 15282
(412) 396-6233

Elaine M. Tweedy
Small Business Development Center
University of Scranton
St. Thomas Hall, Room 588
Scranton, PA 18510
(717) 941-7588

Kostas Mallios
Small Business Development Center
Wilkes University
192 South Franklin Street
Wilkes-Barre, PA 18766-0001
(717) 831-4340 Fax: (717) 824-2245

PUERTO RICO SMALL BUSINESS DEVELOPMENT CENTERS

Jose M. Romaguera, State Director
Small Business Development Center
University of Puerto Rico
P.O. Box 5253 College Station
Mayaguez, PR 00681
(809) 833-5822/833-5556 / Fax: (809) 832-5550

Small Business Development Center
University of Puerto Rico at Humacao
Box 10226, CUH Station
Humacao, PR 00661
(809) 850-2500/850-9144 / Fax: (809) 850-2335

Marian Diaz, Director
Small Business Development Center
Univ. of Puerto Rico at Mayaguez
P.O. Box 5253, College Station
Mayaguez, PR 00681
(809) 834-3590 / Fax: (809) 834-3790

Elma Santiago, Director
Small Business Development Center
University of Puerto Rico at Ponce
P.O. Box 7186
Ponce, PR 00732
(809) 841-2641 / Fax: (809) 844-0883

Carlos Perez
Small Business Development Center
Univ. of Puerto Rico at Rio Piedras
P.O. Box 21417, UPR Station
Rio Piedras, PR 00931
(809) 763-5933/763-5880 / Fax: (809) 763-5745

Small Business Development Center
Interamerican University
P.O. Box 191293
San Juan, PR 00919-1293
(809) 765-2335 / Fax: (809) 756-6929

RHODE ISLAND SMALL BUSINESS DEVELOPMENT CENTERS

Douglas Jobling, State Director
State Administrative Office
Bryant College RISBDC
1150 Douglas Pike
Smithfield, RI 02917
(401) 232-6111 / Fax: (401) 232-6416

Sam Carr, Case Manager
Aquidneck Island RISBDC
28 Jacome Way
Middletown, RI 02840
(401) 849-6900 / Fax: (401) 849-0815

Erwin Robinson, Program Manager
Bryant College RISBDC
Downtown Providence Office
7 Jackson Walkway
Providence, RI 02903
(401) 831-1330 / Fax: (401) 454-2819

Manager, RISBDC
Community College of RI
Providence Campus
One Hilton Street
Providence, RI 02905
(401) 455-6042 / Fax: (401) 455-6047

Sue Barker, Assistant Director
Quonset P/D Industrial Park
35 Belver Ave., Room 217
North Kingstown, RI 02852
(401) 294-1227 / Fax: (401) 294-6897

Michael Franklin
Financial/Case Manager
Bryant College RISBDC
1150 Douglas Pike
Smithfield, RI 02917
(401) 232-6351 / Fax: (401) 232-6416

O.J. Silas, Program Manager
RIDOT Program
Community College of Rhode Island
Providence Campus
One Hilton Street
Providence, RI 02905
(401) 455-6088 / Fax: (508) 872-7620

Cheryl Faria
Entrepreunership Training Program
Northern RI Private Industry Council
650 George Washington Hwy
P.O. Box 2
Lincoln, RI 02865
(401) 334-1171 / Fax: (401) 334-0585

Raymond Fogarty, Director
Export Assistance Center
Bryant College
1150 Douglas Pike
Smithfield, RI 02917
(401) 232-6407 / Fax: (401) 232-6416

Dennis McCarthy, Entrepreneurship
Training Program
Bryant College RISBDC
1150 Douglas Pike
Smithfield, RI 02917
(401) 232-6115 / Fax: (401) 232-6416

SOUTH CAROLINA SMALL BUSINESS DEVELOPMENT CENTERS

John Lenti, State Director
The Frank L. Roddey
Small Business Development Center
College of Business Administration
University of South Carolina
Columbia, SC 29201-9980
(803) 777-4907 / Fax: (803) 777-4403

Martin Goodman, Area Manager
USC Beaufort SBDC
800 Carteret Street
Beaufort, SC 29902
(803) 521-4143 / Fax: (803) 521-4198

Merry Boone, Area Manager
Charleston SBDC
P.O. Box 20339
Charleston, SC 29413-0339
(803) 727-2020 / Fax: (803) 727-2013

Rebecca Hobart, Regional Director
Clemson Regional SBDC
425 Sirrine Hall
Clemson University
Clemson, SC 29634-1392
(803) 656-3227 / Fax: (803) 656-4869

Russ Madray, Area Manager
Clemson Regional SBDC
425 Sirrine Hall
Clemson University
Clemson, SC 29634-1392
(803) 656-3227 / Fax: (803) 656-4869

Shawn Mewborn, Area Manager
USC Regional SBDC
University of South Carolina
College of Business Administration
Columbia, SC 29201-9980
(803) 777-5118 / Fax: (803) 777-4403

Jim Brazell, Regional Director
USC Regional SBDC
University of South Carolina
College of Business Administration
Columbia, SC 29201-9980
(803) 777-5118 / Fax: (803) 777-4403

Tim Lowery, Area Manager
Coastal Carolina SBDC
School of Business Administration
Coastal Carolina
Conway, SC 29526
(803) 349-2169 / Fax: (803) 349-2990

Area Manager
Clemson SBDC
c/o Greenville Chamber of Commerce
P.O. Box 10048
Greenville, SC 29603
(803) 271-4259 / Fax: (803) 250-8514

David Raines, Area Manager
Florence Darlington Tech, SBDC
P.O. Box 100548
Florence, SC 29501-0548
(803) 661-8324 / (803) 661-8041

George Long, Area Manager
Upper Savannah Council of Government
SBDC Exchange Building
222 Phoenix Street, Suite 200
P.O. Box 1366
Greenwood, SC 29648
(803) 227-6110 / Fax: (803) 229-1869

Jim DeMartin, Consultant
USC Hilton Head SBDC
Suite 300, Kiawah Building
10 Office Park Road
Hilton Head, SC 29928
(308) 785-3995 / Fax: (803) 777-0333

Jackie Moore, Area Manager
Aiken/North Augusta SBDC
171 University Parkway, Ste. 100
Aiken, SC 29801
(803) 442-3670 / Fax: (803) 641-3445

John Gadson, Regional Director
SC State Regional SBDC
School of Business Administration
South Carolina State University
Orangeburg, SC 29117
(803) 536-8445 / Fax: (803) 536-8066

Francis Heape, Area Manager
School of Business Administration
SC State University
Orangeburg, SC 29117
(803) 536-8445 / Fax: (803) 536-8066

Nate Barber, Regional Director
Winthrop Regional SBDC
Winthrop University
119 Thurmond Building
Rock Hill, SC 29733
(803) 323-2283 / Fax: (803) 323-4281

Dianne Hockett, Area Manager
Winthrop Regional SBDC
Winthrop University
119 Thurmond Bldg.
Rock Hill, SC 29733
(803) 323-2283 / Fax: (803) 323-4281

Robert Grooms, Area Manager
Spartanburg Chamber of Commerce/SBDC
P.O. Box 1636
Spartanburg, SC 29304
(803) 594-5080 / Fax: (803) 594-5055

SOUTH DAKOTA SMALL BUSINESS DEVELOPMENT CENTERS

Robert E. Ashley, State Director
Small Business Development Center
University of South Dakota
414 East Clark
Vermillion, SD 57069
(605) 677-5498 / Fax: (605) 677-5272

Ron Kolbeck, Area Director
Small Business Development Center
226 Citizens Bldg.
Aberdeen, SD 57401
(605) 622-2252

Wade Druin, Area Director
Small Business Development Center
105 South Euclid, Suite C
Pierre, SD 57501
(605) 773-5941

Matthew Johnson, Area Director
Small Business Development Center
444 No Mount Rushmore Road, #208
Rapid City, SD 57701
(605) 394-5311

Wayne Flemmer, Area Director
Small Business Development Center
200 North Phillips, L103
Sioux Falls, SD 57102
(605) 330-6008

Jeffrey Heisinger, Business Consultant
Small Business Development Center
University of South Dakota
414 East Clark
Vermillion, SD 57069
(605) 677-5498

TENNESSEE SMALL BUSINESS DEVELOPMENT CENTERS

Kenneth J. Burns, State Director
Small Business Development Center
Memphis State University
Bldg. 1, South Campus
Memphis, TN 38152
(901) 678-2500 / Fax: (901) 678-4072

Bob Flude
Small Business Development Center
Southeast Tennessee Development District
P O Box 4757
Chattanooga, TN 37405
(615) 266-5781

Alan Artress, Director
Tennessee SBDC
Chattamooga State Tech C.C.
4501 Amnicola Highway
Chattanooga, TN 37406-1097
(615) 697-4410 / Fax: (615) 698-5653

John Volker
Small Business Development Center
Austin Peay St. Univ, College of Business
Clarksville, TN 37044
(615) 648-7674

Don Green
Small Business Development Center
Cleveland State Community College
Adkisson Drive, P.O. Box 3570
Cleveland, TN 37320
(615) 478-6247

Richard Prince, Senior Specialist
Tennesse SBDC
Memorial Building, Room 205
308 West 7th Street
Columbia, TN 38401
(615) 388-5674 / Fax: (615) 388-5474

Harold Holloway
Small Business Development Center
Tennessee Technological University
College of Business Administration
P.O. Box 5023
Cookeville, TN 38505
(615) 372-3648

Bob Wylie
Small Business Development Center
Dyersburg State Community College
Office of Extension Services
P.O. Box 648
Dyersburg, TN 38024
(901) 286-3267

Dorthy Vaden, Specialist
Tennessee SBDC
Four Lakes Regional Industrial
Development Authority
P.O. Box 63
Hartsville, TN 37074-0063
(901) 678-4174 / Fax: (901) 678-4072

Phillip Ramsey, Business Counselor
Tennessee SBDC
Lambuth University
705 Lambuth Blvd.
Jackson, TN 38301
(901) 425-3327 / Fax: (901) 421-1990

David Brown
Small Business Development Center
Jackson State Community College
2046 North Parkway Street
Jackson, TN 38305
(901) 424-5389

Robert Justice
Small Business Development Center
East Tennessee State University
College of Business
Johnson City, TN 37614
(615) 929-5630

Rob Lyle, Business Conselor
Tennessee SBDC
Kingsport University
East Tennessee State University
1501 University Blvd.
Kingsport, TN 37660
(615) 392-8017 / Fax: (615) 392-8017

Joe Andrews
Small Business Development Center
Pellissippi State Tech. Comm.
P.O. Box 22990, 3435 Division St.
Knoxville, TN 37933
(615) 694-6661

Richard Volger
Internat'l Trade Specialist
301 E. Church Ave.
Knoxville, TN 37915
(615) 637-4283

Dr. Carl Savage
Small Business Development Center
University of Tennessee at Martin
Pepsi Building, 402 Elm St.
Martin, TN 38238
(901) 587-7236

Earnest Lacey
Small Business Development Center
Memphis St University
320 S. Dudley St.
Memphis, TN 38104
(901) 527-1041

Jack Tucker
Small Business Development Center
Walters State Community College
500 S. Davy Crockett Parkway
Morristown, TN 37813
(615) 587-9722 447

Dr. Jack Forrest
Small Business Development Center
Middle Tennessee State University
School of Bus., 1417 East Main St.
Murfreesboro, TN 37132
(615) 898-2745

Billy Lowe
Small Business Development Center
Tennessee State University
School of Business
330 10th Ave. North
Nashville, TN 37203
(615) 251-1178

TEXAS-DALLAS SMALL BUSINESS DEVELOPMENT CENTERS

Elizabeth Klimback, Regional Dir.
North Texas SBDC
Bill J. Priest Institute
for Economic Development
1402 Corinth St.
Dallas, TX 75215
(214) 565-5835 / Fax: (214) 565-5813

Judy Loden, Director
Small Business Development Center
Trinity Valley Community College
500 South Prairieville
Athens, TX 75751
(903) 675-7403 / Fax: (903) 675-5199

Cynthia Flower-Whitfield, Director
Satellite:Bonham SBDC
Sam Rayburn Library
Bonham, TX 75418
(903) 583-4811

Satellite: Midlothian SDBC
330 N. 8th Street, Suite 203
Midlothian, TX 76065-0609
(214) 775-8500 / Fax: (214) 775-8008

Leon Allard, Director
Navarro SBDC
120 North 12th Street
Corsicana, TX 75110
(903) 874-0658 / Fax: (903) 874-4187

Vera Tanner, Director
Small Business Development Center
Ctr. for Gov't. Contracting
1402 Corinth
Dallas, TX 75215
(214) 565-5842 / Fax: (214) 565-5857

Elizabeth Huddleston, Director
International Business Center SBDC
2050 Stemmons Frwy, Suite #150
World Trade Ctr, P.O. Box 58299
Dallas, TX 75258
(214) 747-1300 Fax: (214) 748-5774

Al Salgado, Director
Small Business Development Center
Dallas County Comm. College
1402 Corinth
Dallas, TX 75215
(214) 565-5879 / Fax: (214) 565-5857

Cynthia Flowers-Whitfield
Small Business Development Center
Grayson County College
6101 Grayson Dr.
Denison, TX 75020
(903) 786-3551 / Fax: (903) 786-6284

Carolyn Birkhead, Coordinator
Small Business Development Center
P.O. Box P
Denton, TX 76201
(817) 382-7151 / Fax: (817) 382-0040

Herb Kamm, Director
Best Southwest SBDC
214 South Main, Ste. 101D
Duncanville, TX 75116
(214) 709-5878 / Fax: (214) 709-6089

Truitt Leake, Director
Tarrant SBDC
1500 Houston Street, Room 163
Ft. Worth, TX 76102
(817) 244-7158 / Fax: (817) 560-6929

Cathy Keeler, Director
Cooke SBDC
1525 West California
Gainesville, TX 76240
(817) 665-4220 / Fax: (817) 668-6049

Lu Billings, Director
Hillsboro SBDC
SOS Building
P.O. Box 619
Hillsboro, TX 76645
(817) 582-2555 Ext. 282

Brad Bunt, Director
Kilgore SBDC
Triple Creek Shopping Plaza
110 Triple Creek Dr., Suite 70
Longview, TX 75601
(903) 757-5857 / Fax: (903) 753-7920

Robert Wall, Director
Northeast/Texarkana SBDC
P.O. Box 1307
Mt. Pleasant, TX 75455
(903) 572-1911 / Fax: (903) 572-0598

Pat Bell, Director
Small Business Development Center
 Paris Jr College
2400 Clarksville St.
Paris, TX 75460
(903) 784-1802 / Fax: (903) 784-1801

Chris Jones, Director
Small Business Development Center
The Courtyard Ctr. for Professional and Economic
Development
4800 Preston Park Blvd., Suite 102
Plano, TX 75093
(214) 985-3770 / Fax: (214) 985-3775

Glenn Galiga, Director
Tyler SBDC
1530 South S.W. Loop 323, Suite 100
Tyler, TX 75701
(903) 510-2975 / Fax: (903) 510-2978

Lu Billings, Director
McLennan SBDC
4601 North 19th Street
Waco, TX 76708
(817) 750-3600 Fax: (817) 750-3620

Pamela Speraw, Coord. of Training
Technology Assistance Center SBDC
Bill J. Priest Institute for Economic Development
1402 Corinth Street
Dallas, TX 75215

TEXAS-HOUSTON SMALL BUSINESS DEVELOPMENT CENTERS

Dr. Elizabeth Gatewood
Regional Director
Small Business Development Center
University of Houston
1100 Louisiana, Suite 500
Houston, TX 77002
(713) 752-8444 / Fax: (713) 756-1500

Gina Mattei, Director
Small Business Development Center
Alvin Community College
3110 Mustang Rd.
Alvin, TX 77511-4898
(713) 388-4686

Kenneth Voytek, Director
Small Business Development Center
Lee College, Rundell Hall
P.O. Box 818
Baytown, TX 77522-0818
(713) 425-6309 / Fax: (713) 425-6307

Roy Huckaby, Director
Small Business Development Center
John Gray Institute/Lamar University
855 Florida Ave.
Beaumont, TX 77705
(409) 880-2367 / Fax: (409) 880-2201
or 1-800-722-3443

Phillis Nelson, Director
Small Business Development Center
Blinn College
902 College Ave.
Brenham, TX 77833
(409) 830-4137 / Fax: (409) 830-4116

Sam Harwell, Director
Small Business Development Center
Bryan/College Station
Chamber of Commerce
P.O. Box 3695
Bryan, TX 77805
(409) 823-3034 / Fax: (409) 822-4818

Joe Harper, Director
Small Business Development Center
Galveston College
4015 Avenue Q
Galveston, TX 77550
(409) 740-7380 / Fax: (409) 740-7381

Mike Young, Director
Small Business Development Center
Houston Lead Center SBDC
1100 Louisiana, Suite 500
Houston, TX 77002
(713) 752-8400 / Fax: (713) 752-8484

Jack Ruoff, Director
Small Business Development Center
Texas Info. Procurement Service
1100 Louisiana, Suite 500
Houston, TX 77002
(713) 752-8477 / Fax: (713) 756-1515

Luis Saldarriaga, Director
International Trade Center
1100 Louisiana, Suite 500
Houston, TX 77002
(713) 752-8404

Bob Barragan, Director
Small Business Development Center
Sam Houston State University
P.O. Box 2058
Huntsville, TX 77341-2058
(409) 294-3737 / Fax: (409) 294-3612

Ray Laughter, Director
North Harris Montgomery County SBDC
N. Harris Montgomery CC District
250 N. Sam Houston Parkway
Houston, TX 77060
(713) 359-1677 / Fax: (713) 359-1612

Patricia Leyendecker, Director
Small Business Development Center
Brazosport College
500 College Dr.
Lake Jackson, TX 77566
(409) 265-7208 / Fax: (409) 265-2944

Chuck Stemple, Director
Small Business Development Center
Angelina College, P.O. Box 1768
Lufkin, TX 75902-1768
(409) 639-1887 / Fax: (409) 634-8726

John Fishero, Director
Small Business Development Center
Houston Community College System
13600 Murphy Road
Stafford, TX 77477
(713) 499-4870 / Fax: (713) 499-8194

Ed Socha
Small Business Development Center
College of the Mainland
8419 Emmett F. Lowry Expressway
Texas City, TX 77591
(713) 499-4870 / Fax: (713) 499-8194

Lynn Polson, Director
Small Business Development Center
Wharton County Jr. College
Admin. Bldg. Room 102
911 Boling Hwy.
Wharton, TX 77488-0080
(409) 532-4560 246 / Fax:(409)532-2201

Susan Macy
Small Business Development Center
Texas Product Development Center
1100 Louisiana, Suite 500
Houston, TX 77002
(713) 752-8440 / Fax: (713) 756-1515

TEXAS-LUBBOCK SMALL BUSINESS DEVELOPMENT CENTERS

Craig Bean, Region Director
Northwest Texas SBDC
Center for Innovation
2579 South Loop 289, Suite 114
Lubbock, TX 79423
(806) 745-3973 / Fax: (806) 745-6207

Judy Wilhelm
Caruth SBDC
Abilene Christian University
ACU Station, Box 8307
Abilene, TX 79699
(915) 674-2776 / Fax: (915) 674-2507

Don Taylor
Panhandle SBDC
1800 S. Washington, Suite 110
Amarillo, Texas 79102
(806) 372-5151 / Fax: (806) 372-5261

David Montgomery
Texas Tech University
Small Business Development Center
Center for Innovation
2579 South Loop 289, Suite 210
Lubbock, Texas 79423
(806) 745-1637 / Fax: (806) 745-6207

Karl Painter
Small Business Development Center
4901 E. University
Odessa, TX 79762
(915) 567-5502 / Fax: (915) 561-5534

Rusty Freed
Small Business Development Center
Tarleton State University
College of Business Administration
Box T-158
Stephenville, TX 76402
(817) 968-9330 / Fax: (817) 968-9329

Tim Thomas
Small Business Development Center
Midwestern State University
3400 Taft Blvd.
Wichita Falls, TX 76308
(817) 696-6738 / Fax: (817) 689-4374

TEXAS-SAN ANTONIO SMALL BUSINESS DEVELOPMENT CENTERS

Robert M. McKinley, Reg. Director
San Antonio Regional
UTSA South Texas Border SBDC
1222 N. Main Street, Suite 450
San Antonio, TX 78212
(210) 558-2450 / Fax: (210) 558-2464

Larry Lucero, Director
Austin SBDC
2211 South IH 35, Suite 103
Austin, TX 78741
(512) 326-2256 / Fax: (512) 447-9825

John Rising, Director
Corpus Christi Chamber of Comm. SBDC
1201 North Shoreline
Corpus Christi, TX 78403
(512) 882-6161 / Fax: (512) 888-5627

Irene Sanchez-Casas, Director
Univ. of Texas-Pan American SBDC
1201 West University
Edinburg, TX 78539-2999
(512) 381-3361 / Fax: (512) 381-2322

Roque Segura, Director
El Paso Community College SBDC
103 Montana Ave., Suite 202
El Paso, TX 79902-3929
(915) 534-3410 / Fax: (915) 534-9834

Gilbert Soliz, Director
Kingsville Chamber of Commerce SBDC
635 E. King
Kingsville, TX 78363
(512) 595-5088 / Fax: (512) 592-0866

David Pulg, Director
Laredo Development Foundation SBDC
616 Leal Street
Laredo, TX 78041
(210) 722-0563 / Fax: (210) 722-6247

Harlan Bruha, Director
Angelo State University SBDC
2601 West Avenue N
Campus Box 10910
San Angelo, TX 76909
(915) 942-2098 / Fax: (915) 942-2038

Morrison Woods, Director
UTSA Downtown SBDC
801 S. Bowie Street
San Antonio, TX 78205-3296
(210) 224-0791 / Fax: (512) 222-9834

Judith Ingalls, Director
UTSA Technology Center
UTSA Downtown
1222 N. Main Ave., Ste. 450
San Antonio, TX 78212
(210) 558-2458 / Fax: (210) 558-2465

Sara Jackson, Director
UTSA International Trade SBDC
801 S. Bowie Street
San Antonio, TX 78205-3296
(210) 227-2997 / Fax: (512) 222-9834

Brenda Blackwood, Director
Middle Rio Grande Development
Council SBDC
209 North Getty St.
Uvalde, TX 78801
(512) 278-2527 / Fax: (512) 278-2929

Carole Parks, Director
University of Houston-Victoria SBDC
700 Main Center, Suite 102
Victoria, TX 77901
(512) 575-8944 / Fax: (512) 575-8852

UTAH SMALL BUSINESS DEVELOPMENT CENTERS

David A. Nimkin, Executive Director
Utah SBDC
University of Utah
102 West 500 South #315
Salt Lake City, UT 84101
(801) 581-7905 / Fax: (801) 581-7814

Ed Harris, Director
Utah SBDC
Southern Utah University
351 West Center
Cedar City, UT 84720
(801) 586-5400 / Fax: (801) 586-5493

Lynn Schiffman, Director
Utah SBDC
Snow College
345 West 1st North
Ephraim, UT 84627
(801) 283-4021 / Fax: (801) 283-6913

Franklin C. Prante, Director
Utah SBDC
Utah State University
East Campus Building
Logan, UT 84322-8330
(801) 750-2277 / Fax: (801) 750-3317

Bruce Davis, Director
Utah SBDC
Weber State University
College of Business & Economics
Ogden, UT 84408-3806
(801) 626-7232 / Fax: (801) 626-7423

Nate McBride, Director
Utah SBDC
College of Eastern Utah
451 East 400 North
Price, UT 84501
(801) 637-1995 / Fax: (801) 637-4102

Kathy Buckner, Director
Utah SBDC
Brigham Young University
School of Management
790 Tanner Building
Provo, UT 84602
(801) 378-4022 / Fax: (801) 378-4501

Scott Bigler, Director
Uintah Basin Applied Technology Ctr.
Utah SBDC
1100 East Lagoon
P.O. Box 124-5
Roosevelt, UT 84066
(801) 722-4523 / Fax: (801) 722-5804

Kathy J. Ricci, Director
Utah SBDC
University of Utah
102 West 500 Sout #315
Salt Lake City, UT 84101
(801) 581-7905 / Fax: (801) 581-7814

Eric Pederson, Director
Utah SBDC
Dixie College
225 South 700 East
St. George, UT 84770
(801) 673-4811 Ext. 455 / Fax: (801) 673-8552

VERMONT SMALL BUSINESS DEVELOPMENT CENTERS

Donald L. Kelpinski, State Director
Vermont SBDC
Vermont Technical College
P.O. Box 422
Randolph, VT 05060
(802) 728-9101 / Fax: (802) 728-3026

William A. Farr, SBDC Specialist
Northwestern Vermont SBDC
Greater Burlington Industrial Corp.
P.O. Box 786
Burlington, VT 05402-0786
(802) 862-5726 / Fax: (802) 860-1899

James B. Stewart, SBDC Specialist
Southwestern Vermont SBDC
Rutland Industrial Development Corp.
P.O. Box 39
Rutland, VT 05701-0039
(802) 773-9147 / Fax: (802) 773-2772

Joseph P. Wynne, SBDC Specialist
Northeastern Vermont SBDC
Northeastern Vermont Development Assoc.
P.O. Box 640
St. Johnsbury, VT 05819-0640
(802) 748-1014 / Fax: (802) 748-1223

Norbert B. Johnston, SBDC Specialist
Southeastern Vermont SBDC
Springfield Regional Development Corp.
P.O. Box 58
Springfield, VT 05156-0058
(802) 885-2071 / Fax: (802) 885-3027

VIRGINIA SMALL BUSINESS DEVELOPMENT CENTERS

Dr. Robert Smith, State Director
Virginia SBDC
1021 East Cary Street, 11th Floor
Richmond, VA 23219
(804) 371-8253 / Fax: (804) 225-3384

Paul Hall, Director
Arlington SBDC
GMU Arlington Campus
3401 N. Fairfax Drive
Arlington, VA 22201
(703) 993-8128 / Fax: (703) 993-8130

Tim Blankenbeder, Director
Southwest SBDC
Mt. Empire Community College
Drawer 700, Route 23 South
Big Stone Gap, VA 24219
(703) 523-6529 / Fax: (703) 523-4130

Dave Shanks, Director
New River Valley SBDC
Virginia Tech
Blacksburg, VA 24061-0548
(703) 231-4004 / Fax: (703) 552-0047

Charles Kulp, Director
Central Virginia SBDC
918 Emmet Street North, Suite 200
Charlottesville, VA 22903-4878
(804) 295-8198 / Fax: (804) 295-7066

Jerry L. Hughes, Director
Longwood SBDC
Longwood College, 515 Main Street
Farmville, VA 23901
(804) 395-2086 / Fax: (804) 395-2359

Michael Kehoe, Director
Northern Virginia SBDC
4260 Chainbridge Road, Suite B-1
Fairfax, VA 22030
(703) 993-2131 / Fax: (703) 993-2126

Jeff Sneddon, Director
Rappahannock Region SBDC
1301 College Ave., Seacobeck Hall
Fredricksburg, VA 22401
(703) 899-4076 / Fax: (SCATS)899-4373

Karen Wigginton, Director
James Madison University SBDC
JMU College of Business
Zane Showker Hall, Rm. 523
Harrisonburg, VA 22807
(703) 568-3227 / Fax: (703) 568-3299

Barry Lyons, Director
Lynchburg Regional SBDC
147 Mill Ridge Road
Lynchburg, VA 24502
(804) 582-6100 / Fax: (804) 582-6106

Linda Decker, Director
Dr. William E.S. Flory SBDC
10311 Sudley Manor Drive
Manassas, VA 22110
(703) 335-2500 / Fax: (703) 335-1700

Bill Holloran, Jr., Director
SBDC of Hampton Roads, Inc.
P.O. Box 327, 420 Bank Street
Norfolk, VA 23501
(804) 825-2957 / Fax: (804) 825-3552

Southwest SBDC
SW VA Community College
P.O. Box SVCC
Richlands, VA 24641
(703) 964-7345 / Fax: (703) 964-9307

Taylor Cousins, Director
Capital Area SBDC
403 East Grace Street
Richmond, VA 23219
(804) 648-7838 / Fax: (804) 648-7849

John Jennings, Director
Western VA SBDC Consortium
The Blue Ridge SBDC
310 First St., S.W. Mezzanine
Roanoke, VA 24011
(703) 983-0717 / Fax: (703) 983-0723

Joe Messina, Director
Loudoun County SBDC
One Steeplechase at Dulles
21736 Atlantic Blvd., Suite 100
Sterling, VA 22170
(703) 430-7222 / Fax: (703) 430-9562

John Clickener, Director
Warsaw SBDC
P.O. Box 490
106 West Richmond Rd.
Warsaw, VA 22572
(804) 333-0286 / Fax: (804) 333-0187

Rob Edwards, Director
Wytheville SBDC
Wytheville Community College
1000 E. Main Street
Wytheville, VA 24382
(703) 228-5541 Ext. 314 / Fax: (703) 228-2542

Jim Tilley, Director
Virginia Highlands SBDC
P.O. Box 828
Abingdon, VA 24210-0828
(703) 676-5615 / Fax: (703) 628-7576

Robert Crosen
Lord Fairfax SBDC
Lord Fairfax Community College
P.O. Box 47
Middletown, VA 22645

VIRGIN ISLANDS SMALL BUSINESS DEVELOPMENT CENTERS

Chester Williams, State Director
Small Business Development Center
University of the Virgin Islands
Sunshine Mall #1, Estate Cane, Suite 104
Frederiksted, VI 00840
(809) 776-3206 / Fax: (809) 775-3756

R. Ian Hodge
Small Business Development Center
University of the Virgin Islands
4200 United Plaza Shopping Center
Suite 5, Sion Farm
St. Croix, VI 00820-4487
(809) 778-8270

WASHINGTON SMALL BUSINESS DEVELOPMENT CENTERS

Lyle M. Anderson, State Director
Small Business Development Center
Washington State University
245 Todd Hall
Pullman, WA 99164-4727
(509) 335-1576 / Fax: (509) 335-0949

Bill Huenefeld
Small Business Development Center
Bellevue Community College
3000 Landerholm Circle S.E.
Bellevue, WA 98007-6484
(206) 643-2888 / Fax: (206) 649-3113

Lynn Trzynka
Small Business Development Center
Western Washington University
College of Business & Economics
308 Parks Hall
Bellingham, WA 98225
(206) 650-3899 / Fax: (206) 650-4844

Don Hays
Small Business Development Center
Centralia College
600 West Locust Street
Centralia, WA 98531
(206) 736-9391 330 / Fax: (206) 753-3404

Jack Wicks
Small Business Development Center
20000 -68th Ave. W.
Lynnwood, WA 98036
(206) 640-1430 2270 / Fax: (206) 640-1532

Glynn Lamberson
Small Business Development Center
Columbia Basin College
TRIDEC, 901 North Colorado
Kennewick, WA 99336
(509) 735-6222 / Fax: (509) 735-6609

Ed Baroch
Small Business Development Center
Big Bend Community College
7662 Chanute Street, Bldg 1500
Moses Lake, WA 98837-3299
(509) 762-6289 / Fax: (509) 762-6329

Peter Stroosma
Small Business Development Center
Skagit Valley College
2405 College Way
Mt. Vernon, WA 98273
(206) 428-1282 / Fax: (206) 336-6116

Douglas Hammel
Small Business Development Center
South Puget Sound Community College
721 Columbia St. S.W.
Olympia, WA 98501
(206) 753-5616 / Fax: (206) 586-5493

Ron Nielsen
Small Business Development Center
Wenatchee Valley College
P.O. Box 741
Okanogan, WA 98841
(509) 826-5107 / Fax: (509) 826-1812

Ann Tamura
Small Business Development Center
North Seattle Community College
International Trade Institute
9600 College Way North
Seattle, WA 98103-3599
(206) 527-3733

Bill Jacobs
Small Business Development Center
180 Nickerson, Suite 207
Seattle, WA 98109
(206) 464-5450 / Fax: (206) 464-6357

Ruth Ann Halford
Small Business Development Center
South Seattle Community College
Duwamish Ind. Educational Center
6770 East Marginal Way South
Seattle, WA 98108-1499
(206) 764-5375 / Fax: (206) 764-5838

Terry Chambers
Small Business Development Center
WSU-Spokane
West 601 1st Street
Spokane, WA 99204-0399
(509) 456-2781

Neil Delisanti
Small Business Development Center
950 Pacific Ave., Suite 300
P.O. Box 1933
Tacoma, WA 98401
(206) 272-7232 / Fax: (206) 597-7305

Dennis Hanslits
Small Business Development Center
Columbia River EDC
100 East Columbia Way
Vancouver, WA 98660-3156
(206) 693-2555 / Fax: (206) 694-9927

Charles DeJong
Small Business Development Center
Grand Central Building
25 North Wenatchee Ave.
Wenatchee, WA 98801
(509) 662-8016 / Fax: (509) 663-0455

Corey Hansen
Small Business Development Center
Yakima Valley College
P.O. Box 1647
Yakima, WA 98907
(509) 575-2284 / Fax: (509) 248-4979

Rich Monacelli
Port of Walla Walla
P.O. Box 1077
Walla Walla, WA 99362
(509) 525-3100 / Fax: (509) 525-3101

WEST VIRGINIA SMALL BUSINESS DEVELOPMENT CENTERS

Dr. Hazel Kroesser, State Director
Small Business Development Center
Governor's Office of Comm. & Ind.
950 Kanawha Blvd. E.
Charleston, WV 25301
(304) 558-2960 / Fax: (304) 558-0127

Tim Oxley
Small Business Development Center
Concord College
Center for Economic Action
Box D-125
Athens, WV 24712
(304) 384-5103

Keith Zinn
Small Business Development Center
Bluefield State College
Bluefield, WV 24701
(304) 327-4107

Wanda Chenoweth
Small Business Development Center
Governor's Office of Community
and Industrial Development
1115 Virginia St., East
Charleston, WV 25301
(304) 348-2960

James Martin
Elkins Satellite SBDC
10 11th St., Ste. 1
Elkins, WV 26241
(304) 637-7205

Dale Bradley
Small Business Development Center
Fairmont State College
Fairmont, WV 26554
(304) 367-4125

Edna McClain
Small Business Development Center
Marshall University
1050 Fourth Ave.
Huntington, WV 25701
(304) 696-6789

Sharon Butner
Small Business Development Center
Potomac State College
Keyser, WV 26726
(304) 788-3011

James Epling
Small Business Development Center
West Virginia Inst. of Technology
Room 102, Engineering Bldg.
Montgomery, WV 25136
(304) 442-5501

Stan Kloc
Small Business Development Center
West Virginia University
P.O. Box 6025
Morgantown, WV 26506
(304) 293-5839

Greg Hill
Small Business Development Center
West VA Univ. at Parkersburg
Route 5, Box 167-A
Parkersburg, WV 26101
(304) 424-8277

Fred Baer
Small Business Development Center
Shepherd College
White Hall - Room 101
Shepherdstown, WV 25443
1-800-344-5231 Ext. 261

Ed Hunttenhower
Small Business Development Center
est Virginia Northern Comm. College
College Square
Wheeling, WV 26003
(304) 233-5900

WISCONSIN SMALL BUSINESS DEVELOPMENT CENTERS

William H. Pinkovitz, State Dir.
Small Business Development Center
University of Wisconsin
432 North Lake Street, Room 423
Madison, WI 53706
(608) 263-7794 / Fax: (608) 262-3878

Fred Waedt
Small Business Development Center
University of Wisconsin- Eau Claire
Schneider Hall #113
Eau Claire, WI 54701
(715) 836-5811

Jim Holly
Small Business Development Center
University of Wisconsin at Green Bay
Wood Hall, Suite 460
Green Bay, WI 54301
(414) 465-2089

Patricia Duetsch
Small Business Development Center
University of Wisconsin at Parkside
234 Tallent Hall
Kenosha, WI 53141
(414) 595-2189

Jan Gaugher
Small Business Development Center
University of Wisconsin at La Crosse
323 N. Hall
La Crosse, WI 54601
(608) 785-8782

Joan Gillman
Small Business Development Center
University of Wisconsin at Madison
975 University Ave.
Madison, WI 53706
(608) 263-2221

Patrick Milne
Small Business Development Center
University of Wisconsin at Milwaukee
929 North Sixth Street
Milwaukee, WI 53203
(414) 227-3226

John Mozingo
Small Business Development Center
University of Wisconsin at Oshkosh
Clow Faculty Building - Rm 157
Oshkosh, WI 54901
(414) 424-1453

Mark Stover
Small Business Development Center
Univ. of Wisconsin, Stevens Point
Lower Level, Main Building
Stevens Point, WI 54481
(715) 346-2004

Neil Hensrvd
Small Business Development Center
University of Wisconsin at Superior
29 Sundquist Hall
Superior, WI 54880
(715) 394-8352

Carla Lenk
Small Business Development Center
Univ. of Wisconsin at Whitewater
2000 Carlson Bldg.
Whitewater, WI 53190
(414) 472-3217

Dave Buchen
Wisconsin Innovation Service Center
402 McCutchan Hall
Whitewater, WI 53190
(414) 472-1365

Debra Malewicki
Wisconsin Technology Access Center
416 McCutchen Hall
Whitewater, WI 53190
(414) 472-1365

WYOMING SMALL BUSINESS DEVELOPMENT CENTERS

Wyoming Small Business Development Center
Mr. Dave Mosley
(307) 766-3505 / FAX: (307) 766-4028
State Director
UNIVERSITY OF WYOMING
P.O. Box 3275
Laramie, Wyoming 82071

SBDC Region One (Southwest Wyoming)
Ms. Diane Wolverton
(307) 352-6894 / FAX: (307) 352-6876
Regional Director
P.O. Box 1168
Rock Springs, WY 82902

SBDC Region Two (Northwest Wyoming)
Mr. Dwane Heintz
(307) 754-6067 / FAX: (307) 754-6069
Regional Director
John DeWitt Student Center
Northwest College
Powell, WY 82435

SBDC Region Three (Northeast Wyoming)
Mr. Leonard Holler
(307) 234-6683 / FAX: (307) 577-7014
Regional Director
111 West 2nd Street, Suite 615
Casper, WY 82601

SBDC Region Four (Southeast Wyoming)
Ms. Arlene Soto
(307) 632-6141 / FAX: (307) 632-6061
Regional Director
1400 East College Drive
Cheyenne, WY 82007-3298

APPENDIX C
Small Business Institute Program

The Small Business Institute (SBI) Program gives small business owners an opportunity to receive intensive management counseling from qualified graduate and undergraduate business students working under expert faculty guidance.

The SBI Program was established in 1972 by the U.S. Small Business Administration (SBA) in cooperation with 36 colleges and universities. Today, more than 500 schools of business participate in the SBI Program.

Every year, about 18,500 SBI students provide assistance to approximately 7,500 businesses. SBI teams have counseled approximately 150,000 businesses to date, provided 370,000 students with real world experience in applying business skills, and involved 6,000 professors in local economic development efforts. Over the course of an academic term, the SBI students meet frequently with the small business owner to solve specific management problems. Business clients receive a detailed report and an oral presentation on the actions needed to improve their business operations.

SBI counseling studies focus on the full range of management problems and solutions including market studies, accounting systems, personnel policies, production design, exporting, expansion feasibility, and strategic planning.

Also, SBI teams occasionally engage in community development projects which involve other SBA business development resources such as Small Business Development Centers (SBDCs). The program also involves SCORE, the Service Corps of Retired Executives, whose volunteers frequently advise SBI teams and offer follow-up counseling to clients.

The emphasis of the program is on practical, realistic, and affordable solutions to problems confronting individual small businesses. Students who best achieve these goals receive national awards each year.

All small business owners/managers are eligible to participate. The business must be independently owned and operated, not dominant in its field, and must conform to SBA business size standards. Interested business people should call their local SBA district office to learn how to contact the nearest SBI school. Any accredited four-year college or university can contact the SBA about becoming an SBI school.

Student teams counsel their small business clients under the supervision of a faculty adviser. Small business institute directors work closely with the SBA, which, along with the Small Business Institute Directors Association (SBIDA), shares responsibility for direction and administration of the SBI Program. Both SBA and the National SBIDA negotiate the statement of work document that defines the SBI contract performance. This activity is authorized under the Small Business Act of 1953, Section 2, as amended, Public Law 95-510, U.S.C. 637, and appears in the Catalog of Federal Domestic Assistance in section 59.005, Business Development Assistance to Small business.

Total annual funding for the SBI Program is allocated to 10 SBA regional offices for distribution to local SBI schools at the rate of $500 (as of FY 1992) per successfully completed case.

Small Business Institutes

SMALL BUSINESS INSTITUTES IN ALABAMA

Pat W. Shaddix
Jacksonville State University
700 Pelham Road, N.
Merrill Hall - Room 114
Jacksonville, AL 36265
(205) 782-5271 / (205) 782-5124 FAX

Charlie T. Cook, Jr.
Livingston University
Coll. of Business & Com., Station 21
Livingston, AL 35470
(205) 652-9661 / (205) 652-9318 FAX

Janet W. Kervin
Troy State University
Sorrell College of Business
Bibbs Graves - Room 102
Troy, AL 36082
(205) 670-3524 / (205) 670-3636 FAX

Sylvanus S. Ogburia
Alabama A & M University
P.O. Box 429
Normal, AL 35762
(205) 851-5685 / (205) 851-5683 FAX

K. Mark Weaver
Univ. of Alabama - Tuscaloosa
Dept. of Marketing
P.O. Box 870225
Tuscaloosa, AL 35487-0397
(205) 348-8947 / (205) 348-6695 FAX

Cheryl S. Coleman
Univ. of South Alabama
College of Bus. & Mgmt.
Mobile, AL 36688
(205) 460-6004 / (205) 460-6246 FAX

Gary Hannem
Auburn University
School of Business, Room 108
Auburn, AL 36830
(205) 844-4220 / (205) 844-4268 FAX

M. Vernon Nabors
Univ. of Alabama - Birmingham
1601 - 11th Ave., So.
Birmingham, AL 35294
(205) 934-6760 / (205) 934-0538 FAX

William S. Stewart
Univ. of North Alabama
Management & Mktg., Box 5013
Florence, AL 35632-0001
(205) 760-4261 / (205) 760-4813 FAX

SMALL BUSINESS INSTITUTES IN ALASKA

William L. Blachman
Univ. of Alaska - Anchorage
School of Business
3211 Providence Dr.
Anchorage, AK 99508-8244
(907) 786-4121 / (907) 786-4119 FAX

L. A. Wilson II
Univ. of Alaska - Southeast
Sch. of Business & Public Admin.
11120 Glacier Highway
Juneau, AK 99801-8672
(907) 789-6402 / (907) 790-5217 FAX

David Porter
Univ. of Alaska - Fairbanks
School of Management
P.O. Box 756080
Fairbanks, AK 99775-6080
(907) 474-7461 / (907) 474-5219 FAX

SMALL BUSINESS INSTITUTES IN ARIZONA

Diane R. Geshwind
Arizona State Univ. - West
4701 W. Thunderbird Road
P.O. Box 37100
Phoenix, AZ 85069-7100
(602) 543-6225 / (602) 543-6220 FAX

George T. Doran
Arizona State University
College of Business
Dept. of Management
Tempe, AZ 85287-4006
(602) 965-7411 / (602) 965-8314 FAX

Wayne Fox
Northern Arizona University
P.O. Box 15066
Flagstaff, AZ 86011
(602) 523-2358 / (602) 523-5990 FAX

SMALL BUSINESS INSTITUTES IN ARKANSAS

Robert Edwards
Arkansas Tech University
Dept. of Bus. Admin. & Econ.
Russellville, AR 72801
(501) 968-0673 / (501) 968-0677 FAX

Don B. Bradley III
Univ. of Central Arkansas
UCA Box 5018
Donaghey Ave.
Conway, AR 72035-0001
(501) 450-5345 / (501) 450-5360 FAX

Bill Akin
Henderson State University
School of Business Admin.
Arkadelphia, AR 71923
(501) 230-5224 / (501) 230-5236 FAX

Harry Kolb
Southern Arkansas University
School of Business Admin.
Magnolia, AR 71753
(501) 235-4305 / (501) 235-5005 FAX

Robert L. Wofford
Univ. of the Ozarks
Div. of Business Admin.

Clarksville, AR 72801
(501) 754-3839 / (501) 754-3839 FAX

John Todd
Univ. of Arkansas - Fayetteville
School of Business Admin.
Fayetteville, AR 72701
(501) 575-4059 / (501) 575-7687 FAX

Melodie Philhours
Arkansas State University
Dept. of Marketing
School of Business Admin.
State University, AR 72467
(501) 972-3430 / (501) 972-3868 FAX

William Rucker
Univ. of Arkansas - Pine Bluff
School of Bus. & Mgmt.
Pine Bluff, AR 71601
(501) 543-8590 / (501) 543-8032 FAX

Michael Epping
Ark. State Univ.-Univ. Ctr. (Ft. Smith)
Westark Community College
Box 3649
Fort Smith, AR 72913
(501) 788-7932 / (501) 788-7914 FAX

Frank Hall
Univ. of Arkansas - Little Rock
School of Business Admin.
2801 So. University
Little Rock, AR 72205
(501) 569-3353 / (501) 569-3588 FAX

Mike McGregor
Univ. of Arkansas - Monticello
School of Business Admin.
Monticello, AR 71655
(501) 460-1041 / (501) 460-1922 FAX

Bill Hemphill
Harding University
School of Business Admin.
Searcy, AR 72143
(501) 279-4075 / (501) 279-4665 FAX

James A. Butch Kelley
Lyon College
Business Program
Batesville, AR 72501
(501) 793-9813 / (501) 698-4622 FAX

SMALL BUSINESS INSTITUTES IN CALIFORNIA

John F. Hulpke
Cal. State Univ. - Bakersfield
9001 Stockdale Hwy.
Bakersfield, CA 93311
(805) 664-2175 / (805) 664-2438 FAX

Marcella McGee
Cal. Lutheran University
School of Business
60 W. Olsen Road
Thousand Oaks, CA 91360
(805) 493-3360 / (805) 493-3179 FAX

William H. Crookston
Univ. of Southern California - LA
Bridge Hall 6 - Entrep. Program
Los Angeles, CA 90089-1421
(213) 740-0649 / (213) 740-2976 FAX

Richardo L. Singson
Cal. State Univ. - Hayward
School of Business & Econ., Marketing Dept.
Hayward, CA 94542
(510) 881-3557 / (510) 727-2039 FAX

Florence Stickney
San Francisco State University
School of Business - Bus. 349
1600 Holloway Ave.
San Francisco, CA 94132
(415) 338-2397

Rudolph I. Estrada
Cal. State Univ. - Dominquez Hills
School of Management
1000 E. Victoria St.
Carson, CA 90747
(310) 516-3551 / (310) 516-3664 FAX

Filemon Campo-Flores
Cal. State Univ. - Long Beach
Dept. of Management/HRM
1250 Bellflower
Long Beach, CA 90840
(310) 985-4579 / (310) 985-5543 FAX

Howard R. Toole
San Diego State University
School of Accountancy
College of Business Admin.
San Diego, CA 92182-0092
(619) 594-5328 / (619) 594-1573 FAX

Joseph B. Lovell
Cal. State Univ. - San Bernardino
5500 University Parkway
San Bernardino, CA 92407
(909) 880-5740 / (909) 880-5994 FAX

Nancy M. Hardison
Point Loma Nazarene College
3900 Lomaland Dr.
San Diego, CA 92106
(619) 221-2328 / (619) 221-2691 FAX

William A. Cohen
Cal. State Univ. - Los Angeles
Sch. of Business & Econ.
Los Angeles, CA 90032
(213) 343-2972 / (213) 343-2813 FAX

George Hess
Loyola Marymount University
College of Business
7101 W. 80th St.
Los Angeles, CA 90045
(310) 338-7409 / (310) 338-5187 FAX

Marshall Burak
San Jose State University
One Washington Square
San Jose, CA 95192-0065
(408) 924-3400 / (408) 924-3400 FAX

Roy J. Millender, Jr.
Westmont College
955 La Paza Road
Santa Barbara, CA 93108
(805) 969-5051

Walter W. Perlick
Cal. Poly. State Univ.
School of Business
Dept. of Business Admin.
San Luis Obispo, CA 93401
(805) 756-1757 / (805) 756-1473 FAX

Max Lupul
Cal. State Univ. - Northridge
School of Business Admin. & Econ.
18111 Nordhoff St.
Northridge, CA 91330
(818) 885-2458 / (818) 885-4306 FAX

David Roberts
Monterey Institute of Intern. Studies
425 Van Buren
Monterey, CA 93940
(408) 647-4149 / (408) 647-3505 FAX

John Berry
Antelope Valley College
3041 W. Avenue K
Lancaster, CA 93536
(805) 943-3241 / (805) 943-5573 FAX

Mary T. Curren
Cal. State Univ. - Northridge
Dept. of Marketing
18111 Nordhoff St.
Northridge, CA 91330
(818) 885-2070 / (818) 885-2458 FAX

Consuelo M. Meux
Fresno Pacific College
1717 So. Chestnut
Fresno, CA 93702
(209) 453-2000 / (209) 453-207 FAX

Hans Schollhammer
Univ. of California - Los Angeles
Grad. School of Management
405 Hilgard
Los Angeles, CA 90024
(310) 825-3045 / (310) 206-2002 FAX

Peter B. Kenyon
Humboldt State University
School of Business & Econ.
Arcata, CA 95521
(707) 826-4762 / (707) 826-6666 FAX

Michael D. Ames
Cal. State Univ. - Fullerton
Management Department
800 No. State College Blvd.
Fullerton, CA 92634
(714) 773-2251 / (714) 449-7101 FAX

Dennis H. Tootelian
Cal. State Univ. - Sacramento
School of Business
Sacramento, CA 95819-6088
(916) 278-6203 / (916) 278-7690 FAX

Dewey E. Johnson
Cal. State Univ. - Fresno
Sch. of Business Admin.
Dept. of Management & Mktg.
Fresno, CA 93740
(209) 278-2496 / (209) 436-4866 FAX

SMALL BUSINESS INSTITUTES IN COLORADO

Maclyn L. Clouse
Univ. of Denver
College of Business Admin.
2020 So. Race St.
Denver, CO 80208
(303) 871-3322 / (303) 871-4850 FAX

Thomas J. Liesz
Western State College
College of Buisness
Gunnison, CO 81230
(303) 943-3055 / (303) 943-7069 FAX

Donna M. Watkins
Univ. of Southern Colorado
School of Business
2200 Bonforte Blvd.
Pueblo, CO 81001
(719) 549-2317 / (719) 549-2909 FAX

Kenneth M. Huggins
Metropolitan State College of Denver
Campus Box 13
P.O. Box 173362
Denver, CO 80217-3362
(303) 556-8312 / (303) 556-6173 FAX

Robert Knapp
Univ. of Colorado - Colorado Spgs.
College of Business
P.O. Box 7150
Colorado Springs, CO 80933-7150
(719) 593-3404 / (719) 593-3494 FAX

D. Lynn Hoffman
Univ. of Northern Colorado
College of Business Admin.
Dept. of Management
Greeley, CO 80639-0002
(303) 351-2088 / (303) 351-1097 FAX

Dale Dickson
Mesa State College
School of Business
Grand Junction, CO 81502
(303) 248-1213 / (303) 248-1730 FAX

Richard Podlesnik
Fort Lewis College
Sch. of Business Admin.
Durango, CO 81301
(303) 247-7296

J. Thomas Gilmore
Adams State College
School of Business
Alamosa, CO 81102
(719) 589-7161 / (719) 589-7522 FAX

SMALL BUSINESS INSTITUTES IN CONNECTICUT

Gene C. Baten
Central Connecticut State Univ.
Entrep. Support Ctr. - MS303
1615 Stanley Street
New Britian, CT 06050
(203) 827-7239 / (203) 827-7120 FAX

SMALL BUSINESS INSTITUTES IN DELAWARE

Tim Bristow
Univ. of Delaware
005 Purnell Hall
Newark, DE 19716
(302) 831-2747 / (302) 831-1423 FAX

SMALL BUSINESS INSTITUTES IN THE DISTRICT OF COLUMBIA

Barbara Bird
American University
Management Dept.
4400 Massachusetts Ave., NW
Washington, DC 20016
(202) 885-1924 / (202) 885-1992 FAX

Michael Ostrow
Howard University
Sch. of Business & Public Admin.
Georgia Ave. & Fairmont St., NW
Washington, DC 20059
(202) 806-1537

SMALL BUSINESS INSTITUTES IN FLORIDA

Donald M. Clause
Univ. of West Florida
College of Business
11000 University Parkway, Bldg. 8
Pensacola, FL 32514-5757
(904) 474-2908 / (904) 474-2126 FAX

Marvin Nesbitt
Florida International University
School of Business/Org. Sciences
Trailer MO-1, Tamiami Trail
Miami, FL 33199
(305) 348-2272 / (305) 348-2965 FAX

Lawrence A. Klatt
Florida Atlantic University
Coll. of Business & Public Admin.
P.O. Box 3091
Boca Raton, FL 33431-0991
(407) 367-3656 / (407) 367-3978 FAX

Eddie Daghestani
Barry University
Andreas School of Business
11300 NE 2nd Ave.
Miami Shores, FL 33161
(305) 899-3502 / (305) 892-6412 FAX

Carl E.B. McHenry
Univ. of Miami
Dept. of Business Mgmt. & Organ.
P.O. Box 24915
Coral Gables, FL 33124
(305) 284-5846 / (305) 284-3655 FAX

Lowell M. Salter
Univ. of North Florida
College of Business
4567 St. John Bluff Road
Jacksonville, FL 32216
(904) 646-2476 / (904) 646-2476 FAX

George Puia
Univ. of Tampa
401 W. Kennedy Blvd.
Box F-148
Tampa, FL 33606
(813) 253-3333 / (813) 258-7408 FAX
Michael L. Avery
Stetson University
School of Business Admin.
P.O. Box 8417
DeLand, FL 32720-3774
(904) 822-7325 / (904) 822-7430 FAX

Ernest P. Boger
Bethune-Cookman College
640 Mary McLeod Bethune Blvd.
Daytona Beach, FL 32114-3099
(904) 255-1401 / (904) 257-5960 FAX

Kenneth Van Voorhis
Univ. of South Florida
College of Business Admin., Room 468
Tampa, FL 33620
(813) 974-2960

Ronald S. Rubin
Univ. of Central Florida
College of Business Admin.
4000 Central Florida Blvd.
Orlando, FL 32816-1400
(407) 823-2682 / (407) 823-5741 FAX

John R. Kerr
Florida State University
College of Business
Business Building - Room 426
Tallahassee, FL 32313
(904) 644-6524 / (904) 644-4098 FAX

SMALL BUSINESS INSTITUTES IN GEORGIA

Sally A. Charles
Kennesaw State College
College of Business
P.O. Box 444
Marietta, GA 30061
(404) 423-6450 / (404) 423-6564 FAX

John R. Wells
West Georgia College
School of Business
1600 Maple St.
Carrollton, GA 30118
(404) 836-6467 / (404)836-6720 FAX

Phil Rutsohn
Augusta College
School of Business
2500 Walton Way
Augusta, GA 30910
(706) 737-1560

Alice M. Ford
Mercer University
3001 Mercer University Dr.
Atlanta, GA 30341-4155
(404) 986-3362 / (404) 986-3337 FAX

Arthur L. Yehle
Georgia College
School of Business
Milledgeville, GA 31061
(912) 453-5772 / (912) 453-5249 FAX

E. Walter Wilson
Univ. of Georgia
Terry College of Business
419 Brooks Halls
Athens, GA 30602
(706) 542-3742 / (706) 542-3743 FAX

Clyde T. Conine, Jr.
Macon College
100 College Station Dr.
Macon, GA 31297
(912) 471-2724 / (912) 471-2846 FAX

Richard J. Stapleton
Georgia Southern University
Dept. of Management
Statesboro, GA 30460-8152
(912) 681-5216

Robert L. Stephens
Georgia Southwestern College
Div. of Business Admin.
Americus, GA 31709
(912) 931-2090

Lee Quarterman
Georgia State University
SBDC
University Plaza
Atlanta, GA 30303-3083
(404) 651-3550 / (404) 651-1035 FAX

SMALL BUSINESS INSTITUTES IN HAWAII

Roland Stiller
Univ. of Hawaii - West Oahu
96-043 Ala Ike Road
Pearl City, HI 96782
(808) 456-4718 / (808) 456-5208 FAX

John Steelquist
Chaminade Univ. of Honolulu
3140 Waialae Ave.
Honolulu, HI 96816
(808) 739-4603

Robert Stack
Univ. of Hawaii - Hilo
200 West Kawili St.
Hilo, HI 96720-4091
(808) 933-3432 / (808) 933-3685 FAX

SMALL BUSINESS INSTITUTES IN IDAHO

Helen M. LeBoeuf
Lewis - Clark State College
500 8th Ave.
Lewiston, ID 83501
(208) 799-2465 / (208) 799-2878 FAX

Cindy Bond
College of Southern Idaho
P.O. Box 1238
Twin Falls, ID 83303
(208) 733-9554 / (208) 733-9316 FAX

Dick Miller
Boise State University
1910 University Dr.
Boise, ID 83725
(208) 385-1511 / (208) 385-3877 FAX

Joe Geiger
Univ. of Idaho
College of Business & Econ.
Moscow, ID 83843-3178
(208) 885-6295 / (208) 885-8939 FAX

Ronald Salazar
Idaho State University
College of Business
Campus Box 8020
Pocatello, ID 83209-8020
(208) 236-3597 / (208) 236-3585 FAX

SMALL BUSINESS INSTITUTES IN ILLINOIS

Chem Narayana
Univ. of Illinois - Chicago
Marketing Department
601 So. Morgan, Room 2329 - M/C 243
Chicago, IL 60607-7123
(312) 996-2680 / (312) 996-3559 FAX

Thomas N. Trone
Univ. of Illinois - Urbana
Dept. of Business Admin.
1206 So. 6th - 339 Commerce West
Champaign, IL 61821
(217) 333-4241 / (217) 244-7969 FAX

Daniel V. Lemanski
Northern Illinois University
College of Business
Williston Hall A313
DeKalb, IL 60115
(815) 753-0779 / (815) 753-0785 FAX

George Harris
Chicago State University
College of Business Admin.
9501 So. King Drive, BHS-435
Chicago, IL 60628
(312) 995-3952

Harold P. Welsch
DePaul University
College of Commerce
One E. Jackson Boulevard, Room 7014
Chicago, IL 60604
(312) 362-8471 / (312) 362-6973 FAX

Christine Cochrane
Governor State University
College of Bus. & Public Admin.
University Parkway
University Park, IL 60466
(708) 534-5000 / (708) 534-8457 FAX

Bruce S. Buchowicz
Illinois Benedictine College
MBA Program
5700 College Road
Lisle, IL 60532
(708) 960-1500 / (708) 960-1126 FAX

Donald E. Strickland
Southern Illinois Univ. - Edwardsville
School of Business Admin.
Campus Box 1100 - Room 2125
Edwardsville, IL 62026
(618) 692-2750 / (618) 692-3979 FAX

Sharon Taylor-Alpi
Millikin University
Tabor School of Business
1184 W. Main
Decatur, IL 62522
(217) 424-6298 / (217) 424-3993 FAX

Jeffrey Fahrenwald
Rockford College
Dept. of Economics & Business
5050 East State St.
Rockford, IL 61108-2393
(815) 226-4178 / (815) 226-4119 FAX

Aaron A. Buchko
Bradley University
Business Management Admin.
327 Baker Hall
Peoria, IL 61625
(309) 677-2273 / (309) 677-3374 FAX

Ramin C. Maysami
Sangamon State University
School of Business & Mgmt.
Dept. of Economics - Bldg. L-99
Springfield, IL 62794-9243
(217) 786-7174 / (217) 786-7188 FAX

Stuart L. Meyer
Northwestern University
Kellogg Grad. School of Management
Room 6-200 LeVerone Hall
Evanston, IL 60208
(708) 491-8688 / (708) 467-1777 FAX

Fred E. Smith
Western Illinois University
College of Business
Seal Hall 212
Macomb, IL 61455
(309) 298-1625

Hamid Akbari
Northeastern Illinois University
College of Business & Mgmt.
5500 No. St. Louis Ave.
Chicago, IL 60625
(312) 794-2896 / (312) 794-6288 FAX

Jerry Fields
Roosevelt University
College of Business
430 So. Michigan
Chicago, IL 60605
(312) 341-3716

Marilyn K. DeRuiter
Eastern Illinois University
Lumpkin College of Business
Charleston, IL 61920
(217) 581-2913 / (217) 581-6642 FAX

Michael Bochenek
Elmhurst College
Business Administration
190 Prospect St., Box 20
Elmhurst, IL 60126
(708) 617-3119

Rodney Lemon
Monmouth College
700 E. Broadway
Monmouth, IL 61462
(309) 457-2181

Marjorie Meier
Illinois College
Economics & Business Admin.
1101 W. College Ave.
Jacksonville, IL 62650
(217) 245-3420 / (217) 245-3034 FAX

John W. Kooyenga
Trinity Christian College
Business Administration
6601 W. College Dr., Groot Hall
Palos Heights, IL 60463
(708) 597-3000 / (708) 385-5665 FAX

Michael W. Winchell
Illinois State University
College of Business Admin.
345 Williams Hall
Normal, IL 61761-6901
(309) 438-7932 / (309) 438-5510 FAX

Dennis D. Cody
Southern Illinois Univ. - Carbondale
Dept. of Management
College of Business Admin.
Carbondale, IL 62901
(618) 536-2424 / (618) 453-5040 FAX

SMALL BUSINESS INSTITUTES IN INDIANA

C.L. Scott III
Indiana University - Northwest
Division of Bus. & Econ.
3400 Broadway
Gary, IN 46408
(219) 980-6912 / (219) 980-6579 FAX

Richard Magjuka
Indiana University/Purdue Univ.
School of Business
801 W. Michigan
Indianapolis, IN 46204
(317) 274-0874

Anthony J. Avallone, Jr.
Grace College
200 Seminary Dr.
Winona Lake, IN 46590
(219) 372-5200 / (219) 372-5265 FAX

John J. Withey
Indiana University - South Bend
School of Business
1700 Mishawaka Ave.
South Bend, IN 46634
(219) 237-4310 / (219) 237-4866 FAX

Patricia Gervais Jacoby
Purdue University North Central
1401 So. U.S.
Route 421
Westville, IN 46391-9528
(219) 785-5392 / (219) 875-5355 FAX

Arnold C. Cooper
Purdue University
Krannert School of Management
West Lafayette, IN 47906
(317) 494-4401 / (317) 494-9658 FAX

William C. Minnis
Indiana State University
School of Business
Terre Haute, IN 47809
(812) 237-3232 / (812) 237-7675 FAX

Michael D. Wiese
Anderson University
1100 E. 5th St.
Anderson, IN 46012
(317) 641-4365 / (317) 641-3851 FAX

Jamaluddin H. Husain
Purdue University - Calumet
Dept. of Management
2273 171st St.
Hammond, IN 46323
(219) 989-2746 / (219) 989-2750 FAX

Ernest H. Hall, Jr.
Univ. of Southern Indiana
School of Business
8600 University Blvd.
Evansville, IN 47712
(812) 465-7038 / (812) 464-1960 FAX

William Shannon
St. Mary's College
Business Admin. & Economics
Notre Dame, IN 46556
(219) 284-4508

Thomas J. Von der Embse
Indiana University - Kokomo
P.O. Box 9003
Kokomo, IN 46904-9003
(317) 455-9275 / (317) 455-9475 FAX

Edward M. Hufft, Jr.
Indiana University - Southeast
School of Business
4201 Grant Line Road
New Albany, IN 47150
(812) 945-2643 / (812) 941-2672 FAX

Laurence R. Steenberg
Univ. of Evansville
School of Nusiness Admin.
1800 Lincoln Ave.
Evansville, IN 47722
(812) 479-2850 / (812) 479-2370 FAX

Douglas Naffziger
Ball State University
WB226 College of Business
Muncie, IN 47306
(317) 285-5312 / (317) 285-8024 FAX

SMALL BUSINESS INSTITUTES IN IOWA

Jarjisu Sa-Aadu
Univ. of Iowa
College of Business Admin.
108 PapaJohn, Bldg. 5252
Iowa City, IA 52242
(319) 335-0930 / (319) 335-1956 FAX

Marilyn Mueller
Simpson College
701 North C Street
McNeil Hall #20
Indianola, IA 50125
(515) 961-1574 / (515) 961-1498 FAX

Delaney J. Kirk
Drake University
313 Aliber Hall
Des Moines, IA 50311
(515) 271-3724 / (515) 271-4518 FAX

Gary Aitchison
Iowa State University
College of Business
300 Carver Hall
Ames, IA 50010
(515) 294-8107 / (515) 294-6060 FAX

Dennis P. Heaton
Maharishi International University
1000 No. 4th St.
DB 1126
Fairfield, IA 52557-1126
(515) 472-1191 / (515) 472-1189 FAX

Robert E. Galligan
Grand View College
1200 Grandview Ave.
Des Moines, IA 50316
(515) 263-2970 / (515) 263-2998 FAX

Pam Carstens
Coe College
Dept. of Business Admin.
1220 First Ave., NE
Cedar Rapids, IA 52402
(319) 399-8690 / Cedar Rapids FAX

Pamela L. Mickelson
Morningside College
1501 Morningside Dr.
Sioux City, IA 51106
(712) 274-5473 / (712) 274-5101 FAX

Alice Griswold
Univ. of Dubuque
2000 University
Dubuque, IA 52001
(319) 589-3193

Artegal Camburn
Buena Vista College
610 W. Fourth St.
Storm Lakes, IA 50588
(712) 749-2416 / (712) 749-1462 FAX

SMALL BUSINESS INSTITUTES IN KANSAS

Lisa Brumbaugh
Emporia State University
Campus Box 4046
1200 Commercial
Emporia, KS 66801
(316) 341-5308 / (316) 341-5418 FAX

Michael O'Donnell
Univ. of Kansas
734 Vermont
Suite 104
Lawrence, KS 66047
(913) 864-7556 / (913) 864-5328 FAX

Don F. Laney
Benedictine College
1020 No. 2nd
Atchison, KS 66002
(913) 367-5340 / (913) 367-6102 FAX

David Wegley
MidAmerica Nazarene College
Metz Building
P.O. Box 1776
Olathe, KS 66061
(913) 782-3750 / (913) 791-3290 FAX

Lewis Paul, Jr.
Wichita State University
1845 Fairmount
Wichita, KS 67260-0148
(316) 689-3193 / (316) 689-3647 FAX

Bruce E. Texley
Bethany College
421 No. First
Lindsborg, KS 67456-1897
(913) 227-3311 / (913) 227-2860 FAX

Jerrold Stark
Fort Hays State University
600 Park St.
Hays, KS 67601
(913) 628-5336 / (913) 628-5398 FAX

Frederick H. Rice
Kansas State University
2323 Anderson Ave.
Suite 100
Manhattan, KS 66502
(913) 532-5529 / (913) 532-7800 FAX

Thomas M. Box
Pittsburg State University
110 Kelce
Pittsburg, KS 66762
(316) 235-4582 / (316) 232-7515 FAX

Lewis Paul, Jr.
Wichita State University
1845 Fairmount
Wichita, KS 67260-0148
(316) 689-3193 / (316) 689-3647 FAX

Bruce E. Texley
Bethany College
421 No. First
Lindsborg, KS 67456-1897
(913) 227-3311 / (913) 227-2860 FAX

Wayne R. Glass
Washburn University
School of Business
101 Henderson Learning Center
Topeka, KS 66621
(913) 231-1010 / (913) 231-1063 FAX

Leah Barnhard
Kansas Newman College
3100 McCormick
Wichita, KS 67213
(316) 942-4291

SMALL BUSINESS INSTITUTES IN KENTUCKY

Larry W. Raybon
Western Kentucky University
2385 Nashville Road
Bowling Green, KY 42101
(502) 745-1900 / (502) 745-1093 FAX

Stephen Brown
Eastern Kentucky University
College of Business
215 Combs
Richmond, KY 40475
(606) 622-1377 / (606) 622-2359 FAX

Robert E. Meadows
Morehead State University
School of Business
UPO 964
Morehead, KY 40351
(606) 783-2475 / (606) 783-5025 FAX

John T. Byrd
Bellarmine College
School of Business
2001 Newburg Road
Louisville, KY 40205
(502) 452-8473 / (502) 452-8288 FAX

James L. Gibson
Univ. of Kentucky - Lexington
355 Business & Econonics Bldg.
Lexington, KY 40506
(606) 257-2961 / (606) 257-3577 FAX

Bruce H. Kemelgor
Univ. of Louisville
College of Business
Dept. of Management
Louisville, KY 40292-0001
(502) 582-4788 / (502) 588-7557 FAX

Peter C. Thornton
Thomas More College
Box 85
Crestview Hill, KY 41017
(606) 341-5800

SMALL BUSINESS INSTITUTES IN LOUISIANA

Robert S. Franz
Univ. of Southwestern Louisiana
Dept. of Mgmt. & Mktg.
P.O. Box 4-3470, USL Station
Lafayette, LA 70501
(318) 231-6347 / (318) 231-6195 FAX

Kenneth J. Lacho
Univ. of New Orleans
Dept. of Management
College of Business
New Orleans, LA 70148
(504) 286-6481 / (504) 286-6481 FAX

Paul R. Arnold
McNeese University
Dept. of Mgmt. & Mktg.
School of Business
Lake Charles, LA 70601
(318) 475-5529 / (318) 475-5012 FAX

Ronald Schroeder
Loyola University
Dept. of Mgmt. & Mktg.
P.O. Box 78
New Orleans, LA 70118
(504) 865-2788 / (504) 865-3496 FAX

Paul Dunn
Northeast Louisiana University
Dept. of Mgmt. & Mktg.
College of Business, ADM 2-104
Monroe, LA 71209
(318) 342-1224 / (318) 342-1209 FAX

Charles D'Agostino
Louisiana State Univ. - Baton Rouge
Dept. of Mgmt. & Mktg.
College of Business
Baton Rouge, LA 70803
(504) 334-5555 / (504) 388-3975 FAX

Charles Chekwa
Xavier University
Dept. of Mktg. & Mgmt.
7325 Pametto St.
New Orleans, LA 70125
(504) 483-7505

Mary Lynn Wilkerson
Northwestern State University
Dept. of Business
College of Business
Natchitoches, LA 71497
(318) 357-5611 / (318) 352-6810 FAX

Teri Root Shaffer
Southeastern Louisiana University
Dept. of Marketing & Finance
SLU 844
Hammond, LA 70402
(504) 549-2277 / (504) 549-5038 FAX

Mike Matthews
Louisiana Tech University
Box 10318, Tech Station
Ruston, LA 71272
(318) 257-3537 / (318) 257-4265 FAX

SMALL BUSINESS INSTITUTES IN MAINE

Larry S. Potter
Univ. of Maine - Presque Isle
181 Main
Presque Isle, ME 04769
(207) 764-0311 / (207) 764-0311 FAX

Warren Purdy
Univ. of Southern Maine
15 Surrenden St.
Portland, ME 04103
(207) 780-4886 / (207) 780-4810 FAX

Roderick A. Forsgren
Univ. of Maine - Orono
209 Donald P. Corbett Hall
College of Business
Orono, ME 04469
(207) 581-1971 / (207) 581-1973 FAX

Martin S. Bressler
Thomas College
West River Road
Waterville, ME 04901
(207) 873-0771 / (207) 877-0114 FAX

Jesse Baker
Husson College
One College Circle
Peabody Hall
Bangor, ME 04401
(207) 941-7060 / (207) 941-7084 FAX

SMALL BUSINESS INSTITUTES IN MARYLAND

Lanny Herron
Univ. of Baltimore
Merrick School of Business
1420 N. Charles St.
Baltimore, MD 21201
(410) 837-5069 / (410) 837-4899 FAX

C. M. (Marty) Green
Salisbury State University
Perdue School of Business
Power Professional Bldg. - Room 165
Salisbury, MD 21801-6860
(410) 546-3679 / (410) 548-5389 FAX

Jonathan Clark
Univ. of Maryland
Dingman Center for Entrep.
College of Business & Mgmt.
College Park, MD 20742-7215
(301) 405-2153 / (301) 314-9152 FAX

Harsha B. Desai
Loyola College
Selling School of Business
4501 N. Charles Street
Baltimore, MD 21210
(410) 617-2395 / (410) 617-2117 FAX

SMALL BUSINESS INSTITUTES IN MASSACHUSETTS

Marilyn Bachelder
Babson College
MFCE Office
Babson Park, MA 02157
(617) 239-4501 / (617) 239-4194 FAX

Robert Stuart
Northeastern University
214 Hayden Hall
Boston, MA 02115
(617) 373-5206 / (617) 373-2056 FAX

Nancy Kotzen
Westfield State College
Westfield Ave.
Westfield, MA 01086
(413) 572-5313 / (413) 562-3613 FAX

Louis J. Zivic
Fitchburg State College
Montachusett Economic Center
Fitchburg, MA 01420
(508) 345-2151 / (508) 343-8603 FAX

Joel Corman
Suffolk University
8 Ashburton Place
Boston, MA 02108
(617) 723-4700 / (617) 573-8395 FAX

Lynne Kendall
Western New England College
1215 Wilbraham
Springfield, MA 01119
(413) 737-6712 / (413) 737-2312 FAX

Robert Hopley
Univ. of Massachusetts - Amherst
School of Management
Amherst, MA 01003
(413) 545-3927 / (413) 545-3858 FAX

Lal C. Chugh
Univ. of Massachusetts - Boston
Dept. of Management
100 Morrissey Blvd.
Boston, MA 02125
(617) 287-7671 / (617) 265-7725 FAX

Kino Ruth
Brandeis University
Dept. of Economics
P.O. Box 9110
Waltham, MA 02254-9110
(617) 736-2250 / (617) 736-2263 FAX

Joseph Stasio, Jr.
Merrimack College
315 Turnpike Road
North Andover, MA 01845
(508) 837-4412 / (508) 837-5013 FAX

Gregory P. O'Connor
North Adams State College
Dept. of Business Admin./Econ.
Murdock Hall
North Adams, MA 01247
(413) 664-4511 / (413) 663-3033 FAX

Peter B. Hodges
Univ. of Massachusetts - Dartmouth
Dept. of Management/HRM
Coll. of Business & Industry
North Dartmouth, MA 02747
(508) 999-8326 / (508) 758-2460 FAX

Michael Peters
Boston College
Marketing Department
St. Clements Hall, Room 301
Chestnut Hill, MA 02167
(617) 552-0421 / (617) 552-0433 FAX

Barbara Bigelow
Clark University
950 Main St.
Worchester, MA 01610
(508) 793-7103 / (508) 793-8827 FAX

SMALL BUSINESS INSTITUTES IN MICHIGAN

Donald Condit
Lawrence Technological University
School of Management
21000 W. 10 Mile Road
Southfield , MI 48075
(313) 356-0200 Ext. 3059

Dale Monson
Ferris State University
College of Business
Business Building, Room 214-A
119 So. St.
Big Rapids, MI 49307-2284
(616) 592-2395 or 2435 (Secretary)
(616) 592-3521 FAX

Debora A. Kiekover
Calvin College
Econ. & Business Dept.
3201 Burton, SE
183 North Hall
Grand Rapids, MI 49546
(616) 957-6190 / (616) 957-8551 FAX

Henry H. Beam
Western Michigan University
Dept. of Management
Haworth College of Business
Kalamazoo, MI 49008
(616) 387-5986 / (616) 387-5710 FAX

Charles J. Fitzpatrick
Central Michigan University
Applied Business Studies Complex
Room 256 AB
Mt. Pleasant, MI 48859
(517) 774-3270 / (517) 774-2372 FAX

Thomas C. Breznau
Kalamazoo College
Business Administration
1327 Academy St.
Kalamazoo, MI 49007
(616) 337-7031 / (616) 337-7352 FAX

Bruce Sherony
Northern Michigan University
Dept. of Marketing & Mgmt.
318 Majors Hall
Marquette, MI 49855
(906) 227-1236 / (906) 227-2930 FAX

Dorothy Heyart
Walsh College
Business Enterprise Development Center
1301 W. Long Lake Road
Suite 150
Troy, MI 48098
(313) 952-5800

James Kadlecek
Grand Valley State University
Office for Economic Expansion
Eberhard Center, Room 718-S
301 W. Fulton St.
Grand Rapids, MI 49504-6495
(616) 771-6770

William B. Nichols, Jr.
Spring Arbor College
Dept. of Business & Econ.
Spring Arbor, MI 49283
(517) 750-1200 / (517) 750-2108 FAX

James Jim M. Hainault
Michigan Technological University
Office of Technology Transfer
1400 Townsend Dr.
Houghton, MI 49931-1295
(906) 487-1245 / (906) 487-2463 FAX

John G. Maurer
Wayne State University
School of Business Admin.
Detroit, MI 48202
(313) 577-4517 / (313) 993-7664 FAX

Kimberly Pichot
Andrews University
Management and Marketing Dept.
Berrien Springs, MI 49103
(616) 471-3116

Raymond Schmidgall
Michigan State University
School of Hotel, Restaurant and
Institutional Management
231 Eppley Center
East Lansing, MI 48824-1121
(517) 353-9211

SMALL BUSINESS INSTITUTES IN MINNESOTA

Leonard Sliwoski
Moorhead State University
Box 303
Moorhead, MN 56563
(218) 236-2289 / (218) 236-2280 FAX

David P. Brennan
Univ. of St. Thomas
Mail #32F-2
2115 Summit Ave.
St. Paul, MN 55105
(612) 962-5077 / (612) 962-5093 FAX

Rod Henry
Bemidji State University
Dept. of Business Admin.
1500 Birchmont Dr., NE
Bemidji, MN 56601
(218) 755-2752

James Bedtke
St. Mary's College
Dept. of Business Admin.
P.O. Box 77
Winona, MN 55987
(507) 457-1458 / (507) 457-1633 FAX

Dawn Jensen-Regnier
St. Cloud State University
720 Fourth Ave., S.
St. Cloud, MN 56301
(612) 255-3215 / (612) 255-3986 FAX

Ken Anglin
Mankato State University
College of Business
Box 14
Mankato, MN 56002
(507) 389-2713 / (507) 389-5497 FAX

M. Lee Jensen
Univ. of Minnesota - Duluth
150 School of Business & Econ.
Duluth, MN 55812-2496
(218) 726-8758 / (218) 726-6338 FAX

James G. Ashman
St. Olaf College
1520 St. Olaf Ave.
Northfield, MN 55057-1098
(507) 646-3432 / (507) 646-3523 FAX

Robert T. Weaver
Bethel College
3900 Bethel Dr.
St. Paul, MN 55112
(612) 638-6400 / (612) 638-6001 FAX

Mark R. Young
Winona State University
Dept. of Marketing
Winona, MN 55987
(507) 457-5671 / (507) 457-5586 FAX

SMALL BUSINESS INSTITUTES IN MISSISSIPPI

M. Elise Dreaden
Delta State University
P.O. Box 3275
Cleveland, MS 38733
(601) 846-4210 / (601) 846-4235 FAX

Hugh J. Sloan III
Univ. of Mississippi
Management & Marketing
Conner Hall, Room 19
University, MS 38677
(601) 232-7414 / (601) 232-5821 FAX

J. William Rush
Mississippi State University
P.O. Box 5288
McCool Hall, Room 5288
Mississippi State, MS 39762
(601) 325-3817 / (601) 325-8686 FAX

SMALL BUSINESS INSTITUTES IN MISSOURI

Anthony S. Marshall
Columbia College
1001 Rogers
Columbia, MO 65216
(314) 875-7558 / (314) 875-7660 FAX

Kevin Riley
College of the Ozarks
Dept. of Business
Point Lookout, MO 65726
(417) 334-6411

Glen Giboney
Northeast Missouri State
207 E. Patterson
Kirksville, MO 63501
(816) 785-4307 / (816) 785-4357 FAX

Wayne Clark
Southwest Baptist University
School of Business
1600 University Ave.
Bolivar, MO 65613
(417) 326-1951 / (417) 326-1887 FAX

Joseph F. Singer
Univ. of Missouri - Kansas City
Henry Bloch School of Business
5100 Rockhill Road
Kansas City, MO 64110-2499
(816) 235-2320 / (816) 235-2947 FAX

Scott Safranski
St. Louis University
3674 Lindell Boulevard
St. Louis, MO 63108-3397
(314) 658-2476 / (314) 658-3897 FAX

Paul F. Jenner
Missouri Western State College
Dept. of Business
4525 Downs Dr., A 309K
St. Joseph, MO 64507
(816) 271-4278 / (816) 271-4508 FAX

John W. Baker, Jr.
Northwest Missouri State University
Sch. of Business & Government
Maryville, MO 64468
(816) 562-1699 / (816) 562-1484 FAX

Wendy Acker
Avila College
School of Business - Whitfield Ctr.
11901 Wornal Road
Kansas City, MO 64145
(816) 942-8600 / (816) 942-3362 FAX

Donald D. Myers
Univ. of Missouri - Rolla
215 Engineering Management
Rolla, MO 65401 / (314) 341-6152

Dennis Wubbena
Evangel College
Business Department
1111 No. Glenstone
Springfield, MO 65802
(417) 865-2815 / (417) 869-9599 FAX

Rodney C. Sherman
Central Missouri State University
Dept. of Business Admin.
105 Dockery Hall
Warrensburg, MO 64093
(816) 543-4026 / (816) 543-8885 FAX

Steve Byrd
Southeast Missouri State University
Dempster Hall of Business
Cape Girardeau, MO 63701
(314) 651-2851 / (314) 651-2909 FAX

Peggy Lambing
Univ. of Missouri - St. Louis
8001 Natural Bridge
St. Louis, MO 63121
(314) 553-6294 / (314) 553-6420 FAX

Bernie Johnson
Missouri Southern State College
School of Business
Mewman & Duquene Roads
Joplin, MO 64801
(417) 625-9339 / (417) 623-8512 FAX

Richard E. Hunt
Rockhurst College
1100 Rockhurst Road
224 Mass Hall
Kansas City, MO 64110
(816) 926-4086 / (816) 926-4614 FAX

Donald Shifter
Fontbonne College
6800 Wydown Blvd.
Clayton, MO 63105
(314) 862-3456 / (314) 889-1451 FAX

SMALL BUSINESS INSTITUTES IN MONTANA

Richard T. Dailey
Univ. of Montana
School of Business Admin.
Dept. of Management
Missoula, MT 59812-1216
(406) 243-6644 / (406) 243-2086 FAX

Linda Kaufman Grimm
Montana Tech
Business Division
Butte, MT 59701
(406) 496-4443 / (406) 496-4133 FAX

William M. Metheny
Eastern Montana College
Dept. of Management
1500 No. 30th St.
Billings, MT 59101-0298
(406) 657-1609 / (406) 657-2327 FAX

Nancy Dodd
Montana State University
College of Business
407 Reid Hall
Bozeman, MT 59717-0306
(406) 994-6206 / (406) 994-6206 FAX

SMALL BUSINESS INSTITUTES IN NEBRASKA

Larry W. Cox
Univ. of Nebraska - Lincoln
11th & Cornhusker Hwy
Cornhusker Bank - Suite 302
Lincoln, NE 68521
(402) 472-3358

Carol A. Myers
Hastings College
Dept. of Business
Hastings, NE 68901
(402) 463-2402 / (402) 463-3002 FAX

Clifford Hanson
Chadron State College
100 Main St.
Chadron, NE 69337
(308) 432-6282 / (308) 432-6430 FAX

David Ruenholl
Peru State College
T.J. Majors Building, Room 248
Peru, NE 68421
(402) 872-2274 / (402)872-2422 FAX

Bob Toth
Univ. of Nebraska
1313 Peter Kiewit Conference Center
Suite 132
Omaha, NE 68182
(402) 595-2381 / (402) 595-2385 FAX

Laurie Johnson
Wayne State College
WSC Connell Hall
Wayne, NE 68787
(402) 375-7575

Silvija Purkalitis
Doane College
1014 Boswell
Crete, NE 68333
(402) 826-2161 / (402) 826-8600 FAX

Kathleen C. Brannen
Creighton University
2500 California Plaza
Omaha, NE 68178
(402) 280-2129 / (402) 280-2172 FAX

Kay Payne
Univ. of Nebraska - Kearney
19th & University Dr.
Welch Hall
Kearney, NE 68849-3035
(308) 234-8344 / (308) 234-8153 FAX

SMALL BUSINESS INSTITUTES IN NEVADA

Sharolyn Craft
Univ. of Nevada - Las Vegas
4505 Maryland Parkway
P.O. Box 456011
Las Vegas, NV 89154-6011
(702) 895-0852 / (702) 597-4095 FAX

Sam Males
Univ. of Nevada - Reno
Business Building
Room 411, Mail Stop 132
Reno, NV 89557-0100
(702) 784-1717

SMALL BUSINESS INSTITUTES IN NEW HAMPSHIRE

Thomas P. McGrevey
New Hampshire College
2500 No. River Road
Manchester, NH 03106-1045
(603) 644-3164 / (603) 644-3150 FAX

Raymond T. Hubbard
Rivier College
420 So. Main St.
Nashua, NH 03060
(603) 888-1311

Frank J. Kopczynski
Plymouth State College
Business Department
Plymouth, NH 03264
(603) 535-2318 / (603) 535-2611 FAX

Keith Moon
Daniel Webster College
20 University Drive
Nashua, NH 03063
(603) 883-3556 / (603) 882-8505 FAX

Neal Pruchansky
Keene State College
Management Department
Keene, NH 03431
(603) 358-2624 / (603) 358-2612 FAX

SMALL BUSINESS INSTITUTES IN NEW JERSEY

Steve M. Fulda
Fairleigh Dickinson University
Rothman Institute of Entrep.
285 Madison Ave.
Madison, NJ 07940
(201) 593-8842 / (201) 593-8847 FAX

Bruce A. Kirchhoff
New Jersey Institute of Technology
University Heights
Newark, NJ 07102
(201) 596-5658 / (201) 596-3074 FAX

Robert D. Lynch
Rowan State College
The Management Institute
201 Mullica Hall Road
Glassboro, NJ 08028
(609) 863-5392 / (609) 881-7951 FAX

Edward D. Bewayo
Montclair State University
Normal and Valley Road
Upper Montclair, NJ 07043
(201) 655-7419 / (201) 655-5312 FAX

Ron Cook
Rider University
2083 Lawrenceville Road
Lawrenceville, NJ 08648
(609) 895-5522 / (609) 896-5304 FAX

SMALL BUSINESS INSTITUTES IN NEW MEXICO

John E. Young
Univ. of New Mexico
Anderson School of Mgmt.
Albuquerque, NM 87131
(505) 277-8869 / (505) 277-7108 FAX

Manuel A. Ferran
New Mexico Highlands University
dept. of Business & Econ.
Las Vegas, NM 87701
(505) 425-7511 / (505) 454-0026 FAX

Peter Anselmo
New Mexico Institute of Mining & Tech.
Dept. of Business Admin., Campus Station
Socorro, NM 87801
(505) 835-5440

J. Stuart Devlin
New Mexico State University
Coll. of Business Admin. & Econ.
Box 3GBE
Las Cruces, NM 88003
(505) 646-6029 / (505) 646-6155 FAX

SMALL BUSINESS INSTITUTES IN NEW YORK

Michael J. Mooney
Dowling College
School of Business
Oakdale, NY 11769-1999
(516) 244-3355 / (516) 589-6644 FAX

Frances Engel
Niagara University
College of Business Admin.
New York, NY 14109
(716) 286-8164 / (716) 282-6884 FAX

Martin J. Canavan
Skidmore College, Business Department
815 No. Broadway
Saratoga Springs, NY 12866
(518) 584-5000 / (518) 584-3023 FAX

Franklin B. Krohn
SUNY College - Fredonia
Dept. of Business Admin.
Fredonia, NY 14063
(716) 673-3504 / (716) 673-3175 FAX

Michael A. Hudson
Cornell University
Entrep. & Personal Enterprise
305 Warren Hall
Ithaca, NY 14853-7801
(607) 255-1576 / (607) 255-9330 FAX

Narendra C. Bhandari
Pace University
Lubin School of Business
Dept. of Management
New York, NY 10038
(212) 346-1877

Herbert Sherman
Marist College
Division of Mgmt. Studies
Dyson Center, Room 374
Poughkeepsie, NY 12601
(914) 575-3000 / (914) 575-3640 FAX

Brian H. Perry
SUNY College - Binghamton
P.O. Box 6000
School of Management
Binghamton, NY 13902-6000
(607) 777-2912 / (607) 777-4422 FAX

Donald Borbee
St. John Fisher College
3690 East Ave.
Rochester, NY 14618
(716) 385-8000 / (716) 385-8094 FAX

Peter Rainsford
Cornell University
School of Hotel Administration
540 Statler Hall
Ithaca, NY 14853-7001
(607) 255-8748 / (607) 255-4179 FAX

Thomas C. Dandridge
SUNY College - Albany
School of Business
1400 Washington Ave.
Albany, NY 12222
(518) 442-4914 / (518) 442-3560 FAX

Frederick D. Greene
Manhattan College
School of Business
Bronx, NY 10471
(718) 920-0455

George J. Petrello
Long Island University
School of Business
1 University Plaza
Brooklyn, NY 11201
(718) 488-1126 / (718) 488-1125 FAX

John P. Burke
SUNY College - Buffalo
1300 Elmwood Ave.
Bacon 117
Buffalo, NY 14222
(716) 878-4030 / (716) 878-4067 FAX

Al Kanters
Clarkson University
CITTEC Business Assistance Center
Peyton Hall-Main St., Box 8561
Potsdam, NY 13699-8561
(315) 268-2304 / (315) 268-4432 FAX

Gregory Wood
Canisius College
Dept. of Management
Buffalo, NY 14208
(716) 888-2645 / (716) 888-2525 FAX

Benjamin Weishan
Mercy College
Dept. of Business Admin.
555 Broadway
Dobbs Ferry, NY 10522
(914) 693-4500

Matthew C. Sonfield
Hofstra University
Management Department
134 Hofstra University
Hempstead, NY 11550-1090
(516) 463-5728 / (516) 564-4296 FAX

Abderrahman Robana
Alfred University
College of Business
Alfred, NY 14802
(607) 871-2226 / (607) 871-2114 FAX

Allan Young
Syracuse University
School of Management
Syracuse, NY 13244
(315) 443-2807 / (315) 443-9361 FAX

Albert Mario
SUNY College - Utica/Rome
Upper Division College
P.O. Box 3050
Utica, NY 13504
(315) 792-7556 / (315) 792-7803 FAX

Robert Barbato
Rochester Institute of Technology
College of Business
Rochester, NY 14623
(716) 475-2350 / (716) 475-5989 FAX

Peter M. Markulis
SUNY College - Geneseo
1 College Circle
Geneseo, NY 14454
(716) 245-5367 / (716) 245-5467 FAX

SMALL BUSINESS INSTITUTES IN NORTH CAROLINA

John P. Workman
Univ. of North Carolina - Chapel Hill
College of Business
Campus Box 3490, Carroll Hall
Chapel Hill, NC 27599
(919) 962-3143 / (919) 962-0054 FAX

Benton Bud Miles
Univ. of North Carolina - Greensboro
Dept. of Mgmt. & Mktg.
366 Bryan Building
Greensboro, NC 27412-5001
(910) 334-5691 / (910) 334-5580 FAX

Stephen C. Harper
Univ. of North Carolina - Wilmington
Cameron School of Business
601 So. College Road
Wilmington, NC 28403
(910) 395-3517 / (919) 395-3815 FAX

James W. Carland
Western Carolina University
School of Business
Cullowhee, NC 28723
(704) 227-7401 / (704) 227-7414 FAX

Assad Tavakoli
Fayetteville State University
School of Business
1200 Murchison Road
Fayetteville, NC 28301-4298
(910) 486-1197

Joyce M. Beggs
Univ. of North Carolina - Charlotte
College of Business Admin.
Dept. of Marketing
Charlotte, NC 28223
(704) 547-2736 / (704) 547-3123 FAX

William A. Sax
Duke University
Fuqua School of Business
Box 90120
Durham, NC 27707
(919) 660-7741 / (919) 684-2818 FAX

Pamela M. Hart
East Carolina University
3015 General Classroom Bldg.
Greenville, NC 27858-4353
(919) 757-6063

John W. Ray
Appalachian State University
College of Business
Boone, NC 28607
(704) 262-6236 / (704) 262-2094 FAX

SMALL BUSINESS INSTITUTES IN NORTH DAKOTA

Dale Zetocha
North Dakota State University
Institute for Busin. & Indus. Dev.
1712 Main Ave.- Suite 202
Fargo, ND 58103
(701) 237-7502 / (701) 298-1007 FAX

Dennis J. Elbert
Univ. of North Dakota - Grand Forks
Marketing Department, Box 8366
Grand Forks, ND 58202
(701) 777-2224 / (701) 777-5099 FAX

Keith L. Witwer
Minot State University
Dept. of Business Admin.
Minot, ND 58701
(701) 857-3313 / (701) 857-3111 FAX

Debora M. Dragseth
Dickinson State University
291 Campus Dr.
Dickinson, ND 58601
(701) 227-2696 / (701) 227-2006 FAX

Tom Dilocker
Jamestown College
Box 6049, Jamestown College
Jamestown, ND 58405
(701) 252-3467 / (701) 253-4318 FAX

SMALL BUSINESS INSTITUTES IN OHIO

Dwight A. Pugh
Ohio University
230 Haning Hall
Athens, OH 45701
(614) 593-2057

Lowell E. Stockstill
Wittenberg University
Ward St. @ No. Wittenberg Ave.
P.O. Box 720
Springfield, OH 45501
(513) 327-7902 / (513) 327-6340 FAX

Joseph K. Ladd
Xavier University
3800 Victory Parkway
Cincinnati, OH 45207-5163
(513) 745-2927 / (513) 745-4383 FAX

Randall Ewing
Ohio Northern University
114 Huber Building
Ada, OH 45810
(419) 772-2070 / (419) 772-1498 FAX

Krishna L. Kool
Univ. of Rio Grande
Box 777
Evans College of Business
Rio Grande, OH 45674
(614) 245-7267 / (614) 245-7123 FAX

E. Terry Deiderick
Youngstown State University
Williamson College of Business
Youngstown, OH 44555
(216) 742-3082 / (216) 742-1459 FAX

Kristen B. Hovsepian
Ashland University
Business Administration
Miller Hall
Ashland, OH 44805
(419) 289-5228

William Lyons
Bluffton College
Business Studies Center
280 W. College Ave.
Bluffton, OH 45817
(419) 358-3427

Edward H. Osborne
Marietta College
Dept. of Economics, Mgmt. & Acctg.
Thomas Hall
Marietta, OH 45750-3031
(614) 374-4632 / (614) 376-7501 FAX

Alvin Kayloe
Lake Erie College
391 W. Washington St.
Painesville, OH 44077
(216) 639-4748 / (216) 352-3533 FAX

Henry Rennie
Heidelberg College
310 E. Market St.
Tiffin, OH 44883-2462
(419) 448-2221 / (419) 448-2124 FAX

Jeff Dilts
Univ. of Akron
College of Business
Dept. of Marketing - CBA 319
Akron, OH 44325-4804
(216) 972-5136

Jeanette Davy
Wright State University
Ctr. for Small Business Assistance
260 Q Rike Hall
Dayton, OH 45435
(513) 873-2290 / (513) 873-3545 FAX

Thomas E. Grove
Kent State University
Grad. School of Management, A 310 Baker
Kent, OH 44242-0001
(216) 672-3586 / (216) 672-2448 FAX

Mary L. Nicastro
Capital University - Columbus
2199 E. Main St.
234 Renner Hall
Columbus, OH 43209-2394
(614) 236-6134 / (614) 236-6540 FAX

Jeffrey C. Susbauer
Cleveland State University
UC 528 College of Business
Cleveland, OH 44115
(216) 687-4747 / (216) 687-9354 FAX

Thomas Monroy
Baldwin-Wallace College
Family/Small Business Institute
275 Eastland Road
Berea, OH 44017-2088
(216) 826-5927 / (216) 826-3868 FAX

Sonny S. Ariss
Univ. of Toledo
College of Business Admin.
2801 W. Bancroft Ave.
Toledo, OH 43606
(419) 537-4060 / (419) 537-7744 FAX

Michael S. Broida
Miami University
Dept. of Decision Sciences
330 Upham Hall
Oxford, OH 45056
(513) 529-4841 / (513) 529-1469 FAX

Paul F. DuMont
Walsh University
Graduate Studies
2020 Easton Road, NW
North Canton, OH 44720
(216) 499-7090 / (216) 499-8518 FAX

Charles H. Matthews
Univ. of Cincinnati
College of Business Admin.
Dept. of Management
Cincinnati, OH 45221-0165
(513) 556-7123 / (513) 556-4891 FAX

SMALL BUSINESS INSTITUTES IN OKLAHOMA

Harry Nowka
Southwestern Oklahoma State University
School of Business
100 Campus Dr.
Weatherford, OK 73096
(405) 774-3754 / (405) 774-3795 FAX

Walter Buddy Gaster
East Central University
Dept. of Business Admin.
Ada, OK 74820
(405) 332-8000 / (405) 332-1623 FAX

George Gillen
Oral Roberts University School of Business
7777 So. Lewis
Tulsa, OK 74136
(918) 495-6555 / (918) 495-6500 FAX

Jeff Seyfert
Southern Nazarene University
6729 39th Expressway
Bethany, OK 73008
(405) 789-6400 / (405) 491-6384 FAX

Robert W. Smith
Oklahoma Christian University
College of Business
P.O. Box 11000
Oklahoma City, OK 73136-1100
(405) 425-5566 / (405) 425-5585 FAX

Richard Buckles
Southeastern Oklahoma State University
School of Business
Station A, Box 4176
Durant, OK 74701
(405) 924-0121 / (405) 924-7313 FAX

E. Scott Henley
Oklahoma City University
Eddie Busin. Research & Coun. Ctr.
2501 No. Blackwelder
Oklahoma City, OK 73106
(405) 521-5104 / (405) 521-5098 FAX

Vance H. Fried
Oklahoma State University
College of Business
Stillwater, OK 74078-0555
(405) 744-8633 / (405) 744-5180 FAX

Herbert O. Giles
Univ. of Central Oklahoma
100 No. University Ave.
Edmond, OK 73034-0108
(405) 341-2980 / (405) 330-3821 FAX

Ron Jacob
Northeastern State University
College of Business
Tahlequah, OK 74464-7098
(918) 456-5511 / (918) 458-2193 FAX

Worth Hadley
Langston University School of Business
P.O. Box 339
Langston, OK 73050
(405) 466-3263 / (405) 466-3498 FAX

R.E. Evans
Univ. of Oklahoma
307 W. Brooks
College of Business Admin.
Norman, OK 73019
(405) 325-2656 / (405) 325-2096 FAX

SMALL BUSINESS INSTITUTES IN OREGON

Martha Sargent
Western Oregon State College School of Business
Monmouth, OR 97361
(503) 838-8350 / (503) 838-8723 FAX

David Gobeli
Oregon State University College of Business
Bexell Hall
Corvallis, OR 97331
(503) 737-6007 / (503) 639-8990 FAX

Dean W. Bishoprick
Portland State University
School of Business Admin.
P.O. Box 751
Portland, OR 97207
(503) 725-3698 / (503) 725-5850 FAX

Randy W. Swangard
Univ. of Oregon College of Business
271 Gilbert
Eugene, OR 97403
(503) 346-3349 / (503) 346-3341 FAX

Verona Kay Beguin
Eastern Oregon State College
1410 L Avenue
La Grande, OR 97850-2899
(503) 962-3428 / (503) 962-3428 FAX

Terry L. Gaston
Southern Oregon State College
School of Business
1250 Siskiyou Blvd.
Ashland, OR 97520
(503) 552-6713 / (503) 552-6715 FAX

Bruce Gates
Willamette University
Atkinson School of Management
900 State St.
Salem, OR 97301
(503) 370-6444 / (503) 370-3011 FAX

SMALL BUSINESS INSTITUTES IN PENNSYLVANIA

Tom E. Rosengarth
Westminster College
P.O. Box 141
New Wilmington, PA 16172
(412) 946-7169 / (412) 946-7171 FAX

Mary T. McKinney
Duquesne University, SBDC - Rockwell Hall
600 Forbes Ave.
Pittsburgh, PA 15282
(412) 396-6233 / (412) 396-5884 FAX

Woodrow W. Yeaney, Jr.
Clarion Univ. of Pennsylvania
101 Business Admin. Building
Clarion, PA 16214
(814) 226-2060 / (814) 226-2636 FAX

Merle Peper
Wilkes University
Sch. of Bus. Society & Pub. Policy
Wilkes-Barre, PA 18766
(717) 831-4706 / (717) 831-4917 FAX

Thomas N. Canfield
Carnegie-Mellon University
Grad. School of Industrial Admin.
Pittsburgh, PA 15213
(412) 578-3481 / (412) 682-7076 FAX

Royce A. Lorentz
Slippery Rock University
Dept. of Mgmt. & Mktg.
Slippery Rock, PA 16057-1326
(412) 738-2592 / (412) 738-2959 FAX

David A. Yingling
Shippensburg University
1871 Old Main Dr.
Shippensburg, PA 17870
(717) 532-1430 / (717) 530-4003 FAX

Hung Mang Chu
West Chester University
801 Roslyn Ave.
West Chester, PA 19383
(215) 436-2649

Clarence F. Curry
Univ. of Pittsburgh
Small Business Development Center
208 Bellefield Ave.
Pittsburg, PA 15213
(412) 648-1544 / (412) 648-1636 FAX

Albert Kowalewski
Point Park College
School of Business
201 Wood St.
Pittsburgh, PA 15222
(412) 392-3943 / (412) 391-1980 FAX

James W. Klingler
Villanova University
Bartley Hall
800 Lancaster Ave.
Villanova, PA 19085-1678
(610) 519-6443 / (610) 519-7864 FAX

Robert J. Chalfin
Univ. of Pennsylvania
Wharton School SBI
428 Vance Hall
Philadelphia, PA 19104
(215) 898-4856

J. Douglas Frazer
Millersville University
Small Business Institute
Millersville, PA 17551
(717) 872-3574 / (717) 871-2003 FAX

Kermit W. Kuehn
King's College
William McGowen Sch. of Business
133 No. Rivwe St.
Wilkes-Barre, PA 18711
(717) 826-5900 / (717) 826-5989 FAX

John E. Stevens
Lehigh University
Rauch Business Center
621 Taylor St.
Bethlehem, PA 18015
(610) 758-3980 / (610) 758-5205 FAX

John W. Bonge
Lehigh University
Rauch Business Center
621 Taylor St.
Bethlehem, PA 18015
(610) 758-3980 / (610) 758-5205 FAX

Timothy W. Sweeney
Bucknell University
Management Department
Lewisburg, PA 17837
(717) 524-3386 / (717) 524-1338 FAX

Solon D. Morgan
Drexel University
Dept. of Business Mgmt.
32nd & Chestnut Sts.
Philadelphia, PA 19104
(215) 895-2122 / (215) 895-2891 FAX

William J. Sauer
Susquehanna University
Weis School of Business
Management Department
Selinsgrove, PA 17870
(717) 372-4436 / (717) 372-4491 FAX

Len Tischler
Univ. of Scranton
School of Management
Scranton, PA 18510-4602
(717) 941-7782 / (717) 941-4201 FAX

Thomas Falcone
Indiana University of Pennsylvania
McElhaney Hall, Room 107
Indiana, PA 15705
(412) 357-2535 / (412) 357-5743 FAX

SMALL BUSINESS INSTITUTES IN RHODE ISLAND

Anthony V. Iannucelli
Roger Williams University
One Old Briston Ferry Road
Bristol, RI 02809-2921
(401) 254-3101 / (401) 254-3545 FAX

Sue Barker
Bryant College
1150 Douglas Pike
Smithfield, RI 02917
(401) 232-6111

Irving Schneider
Johnson & Wales University
8 Abbott Park Place
Providence, RI 02903
(401) 498-4645 / (401) 598-1142 FAX

SMALL BUSINESS INSTITUTES IN SOUTH CAROLINA

Robert L. Anderson
College of Charleston
School of Busin. & Econ.
Charleston, SC 29424
(803) 792-8108 / (803) 792-5697 FAX

Donald E. Kelley
Francis Marion University
301 Highway
Florence, SC 29501
(803) 661-1419 / (803) 661-1219 FAX

Nathaniel A. Barber
Winthrop University
Small Business Development Ctr.
118 Thurmond Building
Rock Hill, SC 29733
(803) 323-2283 / (803) 323-4281 FAX

William Sandberg
Univ. of South Carolina
College of Business Admin.
Columbia, SC 29208
(803) 777-5980 / (803) 777-6876 FAX

Janis L. Miller
Clemson University
Dept. of Management
101 Sirrine Hall, Box 341305
Clemson, SC 29634-1305
(803) 656-3757 / (803) 656-2015 FAX

SMALL BUSINESS INSTITUTES IN SOUTH DAKOTA

Timothy Donahue
Sioux Falls College
1501 So. Prairie
Sioux Falls, SD 57105-1699
(605) 331-6756 / (605) 331-6615 FAX

Bruce Hanson
Augustana College
Business Admin. & Econ.
29th & South Summit
Sioux Falls, SD 57197
(605) 336-5327 / (605) 336-5447 FAX

Scott Peterson
Northern State University School of Business
P.O.Box 627
Aberdeen, SD 57401
(605) 622-2469

Cecelia Wittmayer
Dakota State University
Kennedy Center
Room 136
Madison, SD 57042
(605) 256-5165 / (605) 256-5316 FAX

Chris Carlsen
Univ. of South Dakota
School of Business
414 East Clark
Vermillion, SD 57069-2390
(605) 677-5287 / (605) 677-5427 FAX

Richard Shane
South Dakota State University
Economics Department, Scobey Hall #136
Brookings, SD 57007
(605) 688-4862 / (605) 688-6386 FAX

Randalei Ellis
Black Hills State University
1200 University
Spearfish, SD 57799-9006
(605) 642-6091 / (605) 642-6273 FAX

SMALL BUSINESS INSTITUTES IN TENNESSEE

Dennis Buss
Tennessee State University
College of Business
330 10th Ave., No.
Nashville, TN 37203
(615) 251-1178 / (615) 251-1178 FAX

Donald Clark
Carson Newman College
School of Business
Jefferson City, TN 37760
(615) 471-3417 / (615) 471-3502 FAX

Virginia Moore
Tennessee Technological University
College of Business
Box 5023
Cookeville, TN 38505
(615) 372-3600 / (615) 372-6249 FAX

Robert Wyatt
Union University School of Business
2447 Hwy 45 Bypass
Jackson, TN 30305
(901) 661-5360

H.B. Rajendra
Le Moyne-Owen College
School of Business
809 Waller Ave.
Memphis, TN 38126
(901) 942-7320

Steven Jay Anderson
Austin Peay State University College of Business
P.O. Box 4416
Clarksville, TN 37044
(615) 648-7746 / (615) 648-5985 FAX

John Fulmer
Univ. of Tennessee - Chattanooga
615 McCallie Ave.
Chattanooga, TN 37403
(615) 755-4101 / (615) 755-5255 FAX

SMALL BUSINESS INSTITUTES IN TEXAS

Ray M. Ayres
Univ. of Texas - Arlington
College of Business Admin.
Management Dept.
Arlington, TX 76019-0467
(817) 273-3868 / (817) 273-3122 FAX

Allen F. Ketcham
Texas A & M University
College of Business Admin.
Campus Box 182
Kingsville, TX 78363
(512) 595-2147

Edward R. Marcin
Sul Ross State Univ. - Alpine
Dept. of Business
Box C-35
Alpine, TX 79832
(915) 837-8066 / (915) 837-8046 FAX

Betsy Gelb
Univ. of Houston
Dept. of Marketing
Houston, TX 77204-6283
(713) 743-4558 / (713) 743-4572 FAX

Jude Valdez
Univ. of Texas - San Antonio
Downtown Operations
1222 No. Main
San Antonio, TX 78212
(210) 558-2401 / (210) 558-2405 FAX

Edward G. Cole
St. Mary's University
School of Business Admin.
One Camino Santa Maria
San Antonio, TX 78228-8607
(210) 431-2039 / (210) 431-2115 FAX

Ron M. Sardessai
Univ. of Houston - Victoria
Business Administration
2302-C Red River
Victoria, TX 77901
(512) 576-3151 / (512) 572-8463 FAX

Sam Bruno
Univ. of Houston - Clear Lake
2700 Bay Area Blvd.
Houston, TX 77058
(713) 283-3122 / (713) 283-3163 FAX

Thomas Schaffer
Univ. of Texas - Permian Basin
College of Management
4901 E. University Blvd.
Odessa, TX 79762
(915) 552-2206 / (915) 552-2374 FAX

Mark S. Poulos
St. Edwards University Center for Business
3001 S. Congress Ave.
Austin, TX 78704
(512) 448-8608 / (512) 448-8492 FAX

William T. Jackson
Stephen F. Austin State University
Dept. of Mgmt. & Mktg.
P.O. Box 9070
Nacogdoches, TX 75962-9070
(409) 568-4103 / (409) 568-1600 FAX

Robert Jones
Baylor University
P.O. Box 98011
Waco, TX 76798-8011
(817) 755-2265 / (817) 755-2271 FAX

Charles D. Ramser
Midwestern State University
3410 Taft Blvd.
Wichita Falls, TX 76308
(817) 689-4362 / (817) 696-8303 FAX

Marilyn Young
Univ. of Texas - Tyler
3900 University Blvd.
Tyler, TX 75799
(903) 566-7273 / (903) 561-4738 FAX

R. Ben Neely
West Texas A & M University School of Business
Box 785 - W.T. Station
Canyon, TX 79016-0001
(806) 656-2495 / (806) 656-2927 FAX

Larry R. Davis
East Texas State Univ. - Texarkana
P.O. Box 5518
Texarkana, TX 75505
(903) 838-6514 / (903) 832-8890 FAX

Louis D. Ponthieu
Univ. of North Texas
Box 12345
Denton, TX 76203
(817) 565-3155 / (817) 565-4394 FAX

Sherrill Taylor
Texas Woman's University
Dept. of Business & Econ.
Box 23805 - TWU Station
Denton, TX 76204
(817) 898-2111 / (817) 898-2120 FAX

Frank Hoy
Univ. of Texas - El Paso
College of Business Admin.
El Paso, TX 79968-0545
(915) 747-5241 / (915) 747-5147 FAX

Margaret F. Shipley
Univ. of Houston - Downtown
Business Mgmt. & Admin. Services
One Main St.
Houston, TX 77002
(713) 221-8571 / (713) 221-8632 FAX

Anne Davis
Univ. of St. Thomas
Cameron School of Business
3800 Montrose Boulevard
Houston, TX 77006-4696
(713) 525-2124 / (713) 525-2110 FAX

Rusty Freed
Tarleton State University
Dept. of Management
P.O. Box T-2001
Stephenville, TX 76402
(817) 968-9098 / (817) 968-9329 FAX

Robert A. Berg
Texas A & M University - Corpus Christi
College of Business Admin.
6300 Ocean Dr.
Corpus Christi, TX 78412
(512) 994-5829 / (512) 994-2725 FAX

Brad Reid
Abilene Christian University
ACU Box 8335
Abilene, TX 79699
(915) 674-2053 / (915) 674-2507 FAX

Henry Alton Bridges
Univ. of Texas - Pan American
Ctr. for Entrep. & Econ. Devep.
1201 W. University Dr.
Edinburg, TX 78539-2999
(210) 381-3361 / (210) 381-2322 FAX

Roy Huckabey
GGmar University
855 E. Florida Ave.
Beaumont, TX 77705
(409) 880-2367 / (409) 880-2201 FAX

Michael Bolin
Abilene Christian University
Box 8318 ACU Station
Abilene, TX 79699
(915) 674-2048 / (915) 674-2507 FAX

Thomas M. Moran
Prairie View A & M University College of Business
Rm. 1B 118 Hobart Taylor Bldg.
Prairie View, TX 77446-0638
(409) 857-4010 / (409) 448-1267 FAX

Allen H. Bizzell
Univ. of Texas - Austin
Graduate School of Business
P.O. Box 7726
Austin, TX 78712
(512) 471-5921 / (512) 471-3034 FAX

Roger D. Scow
Southwest Texas State University
School of Business
601 University Dr.
San Marcos, TX 78666-4616
(512) 245-3183 / (512) 245-3089 FAX

Emlyn A. Norman
Texas Southern University
3100 Cleburne Ave.
Houston, TX 77004
(713) 527-7892 / (713) 527-7701 FAX

Harlan L. Bruha
Angelo State University
Dept. of Business Admin.
P.O. Box 10891
San Angelo, TX 76909
(915) 942-2098 / (915) 942-2038 FAX

Robert M. Noe
East Texas State Univ. - Commerce
Dept. of Mktg. & Mgmt.
Commerce, TX 75429
(903) 886-5695 / (903) 886-5702 FAX

Alex Stewart
Texas Tech University Coll. of Business Admin.
Lubbock, TX 79409-2101
(806) 742-2133 / (806) 742-2099 FAX

George Flowers
Houston Baptist University
Business & Economics
7502 Fondren Road
Houston, TX 77054
(713) 774-7661 / (713) 995-3408 FAX

SMALL BUSINESS INSTITUTES IN UTAH

Ed Harris
Southern Utah University
Business Building - 303C
Cedar City, UT 84720
(801) 586-5403 / (801) 586-5493 FAX

H. Keith Hunt
Brigham Young University
Grad. School of Business
660 Tanner Building
Provo, UT 84602
(801) 378-2080 / (801) 378-5984 FAX

Roger H. Nelson
Univ. of Utah
College of Business
Salt Lake City, UT 84112
(801) 581-7458 / (801) 581-7214 FAX

Steven H. Hanks
Utah State University
College of Business
UMC 35
Logan, UT 84322-3555
(801) 750-2373 / (801) 570-1091 FAX

Brian Davis
Weber State College
College of Business & Econ.
Ogden, UT 84408-3802
(801) 626-7947 / (801) 626-7423 FAX

SMALL BUSINESS INSTITUTES IN VERMONT

James M.Kraushaar
Univ. of Vermont School of Business
320 Kalkin Hall
Burlington, VT 05405
(802) 656-0498 / (802) 656-8279 FAX

Kenneth Copp
Green Mountain College
16 College St.
Poultney, VT 05764
(802) 287-9313 / (802) 287-9313 FAX

Henry Ingraham
Lyndon State College
Vail Hill
Lyndonville, VT 05851
(802) 626-9371 / (802) 626-9770 FAX

Genie K. Williams
Johnson State College
Clay Hill Road
Johnson, VT 05656
(802) 636-2356 / (802) 635-9745 FAX

SMALL BUSINESS INSTITUTES IN VIRGINIA

William Schulte
George Mason University
Dept. of Management
Fairfax, VA 22030
(703) 993-1823 / (703) 993-1809 FAX

George W. Rimler
Virginia Commonwealth University
Dept. of Mgmt. - School of Business
1015 Floyd Ave.
Richmond, VA 23284-4000
(804) 828-1487 / (804) 367-8884 FAX

Karen W. Wigginton
James Madison University College of Business
Center for Entrepreneurship
Harrisonburg, VA 22807
(703) 568-3227 / (703) 568-3299 FAX

Jerry Kopf
Radford University, Dept. of Management
College of Business & Econ.
Radford, VA 24142-5765
(703) 831-5481 / (703) 721-3329 FAX

Kermit C. Zieg, Jr.
Florida Institute of Technology
4875 Eisenhower Ave., Suite 200
Alexandria, VA 22304-7304
(703) 751-1060 / (703) 848-1889 FAX

Chris Achua
Clinch Valley College
Dept. of Business & Econ.
College Ave.
Wise, VA 24293
(703) 328-0276

Herbert V. Cork
Virginia Poly. Institute of State Univ.
Dept. of Management
Pamplin College of Business
Blacksburg, VA 24061-0249
(703) 231-7903 / (703) 231-4487 FAX

Lisa D. Spiller
Christopher Newport College
Dept. of Management
50 Shoe Lane
Newport News, VA 23606-2998
(804) 594-7215 / (804) 594-7215 FAX

SMALL BUSINESS INSTITUTES IN WASHINGTON

Harriet Stephenson
Seattle University
Albers School of Business & Econ.
Broadway & Madison
Seattle, WA 98122
(206) 296-5702 / (206) 296-5795 FAX

Willbann Terpening
Gonzaga University, School of Business Admin.
Spokane, WA 99258
(509) 328-4220 / (509) 484-5811 FAX

Thomas Schillar
Univ. of Puget Sound
School of Bus. & Pub. Admin.
1500 No. Warner
Tacoma, WA 98416
(206) 756-3499

Leo R. Simpson
Eastern Washington University
Coll. of Business Admin., MS 182
Cheney, WA 99004
(509) 359-2474 / (509) 359-6649 FAX

Charles Russell
Seattle Pacific University
School of Bus. & Econ.
Seattle, WA 98119
(206) 281-2243

James Bradley
Central Washington University School of Business
Ellensburg, WA 98926
(509) 963-2915 / (509) 963-3042 FAX

David Rasmussen
St. Martin's College
5300 Pacific Ave., SE
Lacey, WA 98503
(206) 438-4331

Karl H. Vesper
Univ. of Washington
School of Business
Mail Stop DJ-10
Seattle, WA 98195
(206) 543-6737 / (206) 685-9392 FAX

Stephen E. Barndt
Pacific Lutheran University
School of Business Admin.
Tacoma, WA 98447
(206) 535-7255 / (206) 535-8723 FAX

Fred C. Lewis
Western Washington University
College of Business & Econ.
Parks Hall, Room 351
Bellingham, WA 98225-9075
(206) 650-3091 / (206) 650-4844 FAX

Jerman Rose
Washington State University
Dept. of Marketing
Pullman, WA 99164-4730
(509) 335-7703 / (509) 335-3868 FAX

SMALL BUSINESS INSTITUTES IN WEST VIRGINIA

Cindy Lee Martinec-Ponte
West Virginia University, 106 BAE Building
P.O. Box 6025
Morgantown, WV 26506-6025
(304) 293-7940 / (304) 293-7061 FAX

Kenneth A. Juul
Shepherd College, Division of Business Admin.
White Hall
Shepherdstown, WV 25443
(304) 876-2511 / (304) 876-3101 FAX

John P. McCullough
West Liberty State College
School of Business Admin.
West Liberty, WV 26074
(304) 336-8053 / (304) 336-8285 FAX

Smiley Weatherford
Concord College, Div. of Business & Econ.
Athens, WV 24712
(304) 384-3115 / (304) 384-9044 FAX

Ronald J. Collins
West Virginia State College
Campus Box 42, Box 1000
Institute, WV 25112
(304) 766-3098 / (304) 766-4127 FAX

John B. Wallace
Marshall University, College of Business
400 Hal Greer Blvd.
Huntington, WV 25755
(304) 522-3806 / (304) 696-4344 FAX

SMALL BUSINESS INSTITUTES IN WISCONSIN

James N. Holly
Univ. of Wisconsin - Green Bay
Wood Hall
2420 Nicolet Dr.
Green Bay, WI 54301
(414) 465-2167

Patricia M. Duetsch
Univ. of Wisconsin - Parkside
School of Business
P.O. Box 2000
Kenosha, WI 53141
(414) 595-2620 / (414) 595-2513 FAX

Neil Hensrud
Univ. of Wisconsin - Superior
School of Business
1800 Grand Ave.
Superior, WI 54880
(715) 394-8352 / (715) 394-8454 FAX

Robert W. Pricer
Univ. of Wisconsin - Madison
School of Business
975 University Ave.
Madison, WI 53715
(608) 263-3464 / (608) 263-0477 FAX

Richard D. Lorentz
Univ. of Wisconsin - Eau Claire
College of Business Admin.
SSS 443
Eau Claire, WI 54701-4004
(715) 836-5829 / (715) 836-5263 FAX

Richard B. Judy
Univ. of Wisconsin - Stevens Point
Div. of Bus. & Econ.
Stevens Point, WI 54481
(715) 346-3770 / (715) 341-6599 FAX

Pravin Kamdar
Cardinal Stritch College
Dept. of Business & Econ.
6801 No. Yates Road
Milwaukee, WI 53217
(414) 352-5400 / (414) 351-7516 FAX

Janice Gallagher
Univ. of Wisconsin - LaCrosse
Business Assistance Programs
323 No. Hall
LaCrosse, WI 54601
(608) 785-8782 / (608) 785-6700 FAX

Paul Reynolds
Marquette University
College of Business Admin.
606 No. 13th St.
Milwaukee, WI 53233
(414) 288-7238

C. Burk Tower
Univ. of Wisconsin - Oshkosh
College of Business
Oshkosh, WI 54901
(414) 424-0351 / (414) 424-7414 FAX

Ann F. Kates
Univ. of Wisconsin - Milwaukee
School of Business
929 No. 6th St.
Milwaukee, WI 53203
(414) 227-3241 / (414) 227-3142 FAX

SMALL BUSINESS INSTITUTES IN WYOMING

Gail M. Gordon
Univ. of Wyoming, Business Assistance Center
P.O. Box 3275
Laramie, WY 82071
(307) 766-2363 / (307) 766-4028 FAX

SMALL BUSINESS INSTITUTES IN PUERTO RICO

Hector I. Zayas-Ortiz
Univ. of Puerto Rico - Ponce Campus
College of Business Admin.
P.O. Box 7186
Ponce, PR 00732
(809) 844-8181 / (809) 840-8108 FAX

Ramachandra K. Asundi
Univ. of Puerto Rico - Mayaguez #1
College of Business Admin.
P.O. Box 5000
Mayaguez, PR 00681
(809) 832-4055 / (809) 832-5320 FAX

Pedro Nelson Gonzalez
Univ. of Puerto Rico - Aguadilla
College of Business Admin.
G.P.O. Box 160
Aquadilla, PR 00604
(809) 890-2681 / (809) 890-4543 FAX

Praxedes Rodriguez
Univ. of Phoenix
Grad. Program of Business Admin.
P.O. Box 3870
Guaynabo, PR 00970-0965
(809) 731-5400 / (809) 731-1510 FAX

Nilda M. Seda
Pontifical Catholic University of P.R.
College of Business Admin.
Postal Station 6
Ponce, PR 007312
(809) 841-2000 / (809) 840-4295 FAX

Jose L. Zayas-Castro
Univ. of Puerto Rico - Mayaguez #2
Industrial Engineering Dept.
P.O. Box 5000
Mayaguez, PR 00681-5000
(809) 265-3819 / (809) 265-3820 FAX

Nancy Acevedo
Interamerican Univ. - Aquadilla
P.O. Box 20,000
Coll. of Business Admin.
Aquadilla, PR 00605
(809) 891-0925 / (809) 882-3020 FAX

Albert Calem
Interamerican Univ. - Puerto Rico
P.O. Box 191293
San Juan, PR 00919-1293
(809) 250-1912

APPENDIX D
The Service Corps of Retired Executives

SCORE, the Service Corps of Retired Executives, is a 13,000-member volunteer program sponsored by the U.S. Small Business Administration (SBA). The program matches volunteers with small businesses that need expert advice. These men and women business executives, whose collective experience spans the full range of American enterprise, share their management and technical expertise with present and prospective owners/managers of small businesses.

Most SCORE volunteers are retired; however, full-time, employed executives are also eligible for membership. About 20 percent of SCORE's membership is still employed. Helping American small businesses to prosper has been SCORE's goal since the program began in 1964. SCORE volunteers are members of 383 locally organized, self-administered chapters offering services in more than 800 locations throughout the United States, Puerto Rico, and the U.S. Virgin Islands.

Members work in or near their home communities to provide management counseling and training to small businesses and to those considering going into business. Every effort is made to match a client's needs with a counselor experienced in a comparable line of business. SCORE counseling is provided without charge; there is a nominal fee for training programs.

Through in-depth counseling and training, SCORE volunteers help small business owners and managers identify basic management problems, determine the causes, and become better managers. SCORE counseling also can help successful firms review their distribution channels, evaluate expansion, modify products, and meet other business challenges.

Management counseling takes place either at a client's business, at an SBA field office, or at a SCORE chapter location. Counselors analyze each business and its operations, and offer suggestions, ways, and means whereby a client can successfully correct problems or institute changes to the business.

SCORE also offers nationwide pre-business workshops as well as a variety of other workshops to current and prospective small business entrepreneurs. These workshops take place in local communities and provide a general overview of what it takes to start a business.

Almost any small, independent business not dominant in its field can get help from SCORE. The approach is confidential and person-to-person. Business clients don't need to have an SBA loan to participate. In fact, they don't even need to have a business. Consultation and counseling before a business start-up is an important part of the service.

To locate the SCORE office nearest you, call (202) 205-6762 or contact your nearest SBA office.

Directory of Offices for
Service Corps of Retired Executives

ALABAMA SCORE CHAPTERS

North Alabama   205-934-6868
1601 - 11th Avenue, South
Birmingham, AL 35294-4552
Mon-Fri, 8:00am-4:30pm

Tuscaloosa   205-758-7588
2200 University Blvd.
P.O. Box 430
Mon-Fri 8:30-5:00
Tuscaloosa, AL 35402

Mobile
205-433-6951
c/o Mobile Area C of C
P.O. Box 2187
Mobile, AL 36652
Mon-Fri, 9-12 Noon

Alabama Capitol City   205-834-5200
c/o Montgomery Area C of C
41 Commerce St., Box 79
Montgomery, AL 36101-1114
By Appt.

Baldwin County   205-928-8799
327 Fairhope Avenue
Fairhope, AL 36532

ALASKA SCORE CHAPTERS

Anchorage   907-271-4022
c/o il SBA/#67
222 W. 8th Avenue
Anchorage, AK 99513-7559
Mon-Fri 8-4:30

ARIZONA SCORE CHAPTERS

Phoenix
602-640-2329
2828 N. Central Ave., #800
Central & One Thomas
Phoenix, AZ 85004
M-F 9-12 & 1-4

Tucson
602-670-4761
300 W. Congress Street
Room 7H
Tucson, AZ 85701
M-F 9-12 & 1-4

East Valley   602-379-3100
Federal Bldg., Room #104
26 N. MacDonald
Mesa, AZ 85201
Mon-Fri, 9:00am-3:00pm

Northern Arizona   602-778-7438
101 W. Goodwin Street
P.O. Bldg., Suite 307
Prescott, AZ 86303
Monday-Friday 10-2

Lake Havasu   602-855-7812-x 3346
1977 W. Acoma Boulevard
Mohave Community College
Lake Havasu, AZ 86403
Mon., Wed., Fri., 9-12

ARKANSAS SCORE CHAPTERS

Little Rock   501-324-5893
2120 Riverfront Drive
SBA/Room 100
Little Rock, AR 72202-1747
M-F/9-11:45am & 1:15-4:14 pm
Not open Fri afternoon

Northwest Arkansas   501-783-3556
#4 Glenn Haven Drive
Fort Smith, AR 72901

Ozark   501-442-7619
c/o Margaret B. Parrish
1141 Eastwood Drive
Fayetteville, AR 72701
No regular schedule

Garland County   501-922-0020
1 Telde Circle
Hot Spgs. Village, AR 71909
No regular schedule

South Central   501-863-6113
P.O. Box 1271
El Dorado, AR 71731
M-Th 8:30-5:00
Fri 8:30-4:30

Southeast Arkansas   501-535-7189
P.O. Box 6866
Pine Bluff, AR 71611
Mon-Fri 8:30-5:00

CALIFORNIA SCORE CHAPTERS

Los Angeles   818-552-3206
330 North Brand Boulevard
Suite 190
Glendale, CA 91203-2304
Mon-Fri, 9:30am-2:00pm

San Francisco   415-744-6827
211 Main Street
4th Floor
San Francisco, CA 94105
Mon-Fri 9-2

Orange County   714-836-2709
901 W. Civic Center Drive
Suite 160
Santa Ana, CA 92703
Mon-Fri, 9:00am-2:00pm

San Diego   619-557-7272
550 West C Street
Suite 550
San Diego, CA 92101-3540
Mon-Fri, 9:00am-2:30pm

Santa Barbara   805-563-0084
P.O. Box 30291
Santa Barbara, CA 93130
Wed. 8:30am-11:30am

Inland Empire   909-386-8278
777 E. Rialto Avenue
Purchasing
San Bernadino, CA 92415-0760

Ventura   805-642-1866
c/o SBA, Suite 10, Bldg. C-1
6477 Telephone Road
Ventura, CA 93003-4459
Wed 9:00am-11:30am

Pomona   909-622-1256
c/o Pomona C of C
485 North Garey Ave.
P.O. Box 1457
Pomona, CA 91769-1457
Wednesday 9-3

Palm Springs   619-320-6682
555 South Palm Canyon
Room A206
Palm Springs, CA 92264
Monday-Friday 9-12 & 1-3

Central California   209-487-5605 x 726
2719 N. Air Fresno Drive
Suite 107
Fresno, CA 93727-1547
Tuesday-Thursday 9-3

Santa Clara County   408-288-8479
96 North 3rd Street
Suite No. 260
San Jose, CA 95112
Mon-Fri 10-1

Sacramento   916-498-6420
660 J Street
Suite 215
Sacramento, CA 95814-2413
Tues, Wed, Thurs, 10-3

Santa Rosa   707-571-8342
777 Sonoma Avenue
Room 115E
Santa Rosa, CA 95404
Monday-Thursday 9-4

Stockton   209-946-6293
401 N. San Joaquin Street
Room 215
Stockton, CA 95202
Mon-Thurs 9-12 Noon

Central Coast   805-934-2620
1650 East Clark Avenue
#252
Santa Maria, CA 93455
No regular schedule

Hemet 909-652-4390
1700 E. Florida Avenue
Hemet, CA 92544
Thur 9-3

East Bay 510-273-6611
2201 Broadway #701
Oakland, CA 94612

Shasta 916-224-4543x508
c/o C of C or 916-225-4433
747 Auditorium Drive
Redding, CA 96099
Tuesdays, 9am-5pm

Yosemite 209-521-9333
c/o SCEDCO
1012 - 11th Street, Suite 300
Modesto, CA 95354

Golden Empire 805-327-4421
1033 Truxton Avenue
P.O. Box 1947
Bakersfield, CA 93301
Wednesdays 9-12

Steinbeck-Roecker 408-649-1770
Monterey Penninsula C of C
380 Alvarado
Monterey, CA 93940-1770
Tues, 10-4, Thurs, 10-1

Greater Chico Area 916-342-8932
1324 Mangrove Street
Suite 114
Chico, CA 95926
Tues. 9-12, Thurs., 9-12

Antelope Valley 805-948-4518
c/o Bruce Finlayson, Chair
747 East Avenue K-7
Lancaster, CA 93535
Thursday only

Tuolumne County 209-532-4212
222 S. Shepherd Street
Sonora, CA 95370
By appt only

San Luis Obispo 805-547-0779
3566 So Hiquera
San Luis Obispo, CA 93401
Mon-Fri 8-5

COLORADO SCORE CHAPTERS

Denver 303-844-3985
US Custom's House, 4th Floor
721 19th Street
Denver, CO 80201-0660
Mon-Fri, 8-4:30pm

Pueblo 719-542-1704
c/o Chamber of Commerce
302 N. Santa Fe
Pueblo, CO 81003

Grand Junction 303-242-3214
360 Grand Avenue
c/o Chamber of Commerce
Grand Junction, CO 81501
Tues-Thurs, 9:00am-12 Noon

Colorado Springs 719-636-3074
332 E. Willamette Ave., Room 208
Colorado Springs, CO 80903

CONNECTICUT SCORE CHAPTERS

Fairfield County 203-847-7348
24 Belden Avenue
5th Floor
Norwalk, CT 06850
Mon-Fri-9:30am-3:30pm

Greater Hartford Co. 203-240-4640
330 Main Street
Hartford, CT 06106
Mon-Fri 9am-4pm

New Haven 203-865-7645
25 Science Park
Bldg 25/Rm 366
New Haven, CT 06511
Mon-Fri 10-12pm, 1-3 pm

Greater Bridgeport 203-335-3800
10 Middle St., 14th Floor
P.O. Box 999
Bridgeport, CT 06601-0999
Mon-Fri 9-12pm

Old Saybrook 203-388-9508
Old Saybrook C of C
P.O. Box 625, 146 Main St
Old Saybrook, CT 06475
Mon-Fri 10-12pm, 1-3pm

Greater Danbury 203-791-3804
100 Mill Plain road
Danbury, CT 06811
Wed only 8:30-5:30

DELAWARE SCORE CHAPTERS

Wilmington 302-573-6552
920 North King Street
One Rodney Sq., Suite 410
Wilmington, DE 19801
Open daily

WASHINGTON, D.C. SCORE CHAPTERS

Washington DC 202-606-4000x287
1110 Vermont Ave., NW, 9th Floor
P. O. Box 34500
Washington, DC 20043-4500
Mon-Friday, 9:00am-3:00pm

FLORIDA SCORE CHAPTERS

Ft. Lauderdale 305-356-7263
299 East Broward Blvd.
Fed. Bldg., Suite 123
Ft. Lauderdale FL 33301
Open daily

Jacksonville 904-443-1911
7825 Baymeadows Way, 100-B
Jacksonville, FL 32256
3rd Fri, 2:00 pm

Daytona Beach 904-255-6889
444 Seabreeze Blvd
First Union Bldg., Ste 365
Daytona Beach, FL 32118
Monday-Friday 10-3

Dade 305-536-5521
1320 South Dixie Hwy.
Suite 501
Coral Gables, FL 33146
M-F/10:00am-3:00pm

Suncoast/Pinellas 813-532-6800
Airport Business Ctr.
4707 - 140th Ave. North #311
Clearwater, FL 34622
Monday-Friday 10-3

Manasota 813-955-1029
2801 Fruitville Road
Suite 280
Sarasota, FL 34237
9:30am-12:30pm (daily)

Central Florida 813-688-4060
404 North Ingraham Avenue
Lakeland, FL 33801

Orlando 407-648-6476
80 N. Hughey Avenue
Room 455, Federal Bldg
Orlando FL 32801
Monday-Friday, 9am-4pm

Hillsborough 813-225-7047
Timberlake Fed. Bldg. RM 104
501 East Polk Street
Tampa FL 33602-3945
Mon-Fri, 10-12 & 1-3

Southwest Florida
The Renaissance 813-489-2935
8695 College Parkway
Suites 345 & 346
Fort Myers, FL 33919
Mon thru Fri, 8am-3pm

Palm Beach 407-833-1672
500 Australian Avenue, South
Suite 100
West Palm Beach, FL 33401
Monday-Friday, 9:am-1:pm

South Broward 305-966-8415
3475 Sheridian Street
Suite 203
Hollywood, FL 33021
Monday-Friday, 9:30-2:30

Treasure Coast 407-489-0548
Professional Ctr. Suite 2
3220 South U.S. #1
Ft. Pierce, FL 34982
Monday-Friday 9-12

Charlotte County 813-575-1818
Punta Gorda Prof. Center
201 W. Marion Ave., #211
Punta Gorda, FL 33950
Monday-Friday 9:30-2:30

Space Coast 407-254-2288
Melbourne Professional Complex
1600 Sarno, Suite 205
Melbourne, FL 32935
No regular schedule

Gainesville 904-375-8278
101 SE 2nd Place
Suite #104
Gainesville, FL 32601
Monday-Friday 9-Noon

South Palm Beach 407-278-7752
1050 S. Federal Highway
Suite 132
Delray Beach, FL 33483
Win., 9:30-1, Sum. 10-2

Lake Sumter 904-365-3556
First Union Nat'l Bank
122 East Main Street
Tavares, FL 32778
Thursday 1:30-4pm

Pasco County 813-842-4638
6014 U.S. Highway 19
Suite 302
New Port Richey, FL 34652
Monday-Friday 10-3

Ocala 904-629-5959
P.O. Box 1210
Ocala, FL 32678

Emerald Coast 904-444-2060
19 West Garden Street #325
Pensacola, FL 32501
Thursday, 9:00-12 Noon

Naples of Collier 813-643-0333
Sun Bank Naples/3301 Danis Blvd
P.O. Box 413002
Naples, FL 33941-3002
Mon-Fri, 9-12 Noon

Tallahassee 904-487-2665
c/o Leon County Library
200 W. Park Avenue
Tallahassee, FL 32301

GEORGIA SCORE CHAPTERS

Atlanta 404-347-2442
1720 Peachtree Road, NW
6th Floor
Atlanta, GA 30309
Monday-Friday/9:30-3:30

Savannah 912-652-4335
Trust Co. Bank Bldg
33 Bull St., Suite 580
Savannah, GA 31401
M-W-F 10am-2pm

Dalton-Whitfield 706-278-7373
c/o Dalton Chamber of Commerce
524 Holiday Avenue
Dalton, GA 30720
Monday-Friday 8:30-5

HAWAII SCORE CHAPTERS

SCORE of Hawaii Inc. 808-541-2977
300 Ala Moana Blvd. #2213
P.O. Box 50207
Honolulu, HI 96850-3212
Mon-Fri, 8:00am - 5:00pm

Score of Maui, Inc. 808-871-7711
26 N. Puunene
Kahului, Maui, HI 96732

IDAHO SCORE CHAPTERS

Treasure Valley 208-334-1780
1020 Main Street, #290
Boise, ID 83702

Eastern Idaho 208-523-1022
2300 N. Yellowstone, Suite 119
Idaho Falls, ID 83401

ILLINOIS SCORE CHAPTERS

Chicago 312-353-7724
Northwest Atrium Center
500 W. Madison St., #1250
Chicago, IL 60661
Mon-Fri, 9:am-2:30pm

Peoria 309-676-0755
c/o Peoria Chamber
124 SW Adams, Suite 300
Peoria, IL 61602
Tu-Wed-Thurs 9am-Noon

Fox Valley 708-897-9214
40 W. Downer Place
P.O. Box 277
Aurora, IL 60507
Wed/Thurs 9-12/Tues 1-4

Decatur 217-424-6297
Millikin University
1184 W. Main Street
Decatur, IL 62522
Monday-Friday 9:00am-12 Noon

Southern Illinois 618-453-6654
150 E. Pleasant Hill Road
Box 1
Carbondale, IL 62901
No regular schedule

Greater Alton 618-467-2280
5800 Godfrey Road
Alden Hall
Godfrey, IL 62035-2466

Quad Cities 309-797-0082
c/o Chamber of Commerce
622 - 19th Street
Moline, IL 61265
Tue & Thu and by appointment

Quincy Tri-State 217-222-8093
c/o Chamber of Commerce
314 Maine Street
Quincy, IL 62301
No regular schedule

Springfield 217-492-4416
511 West Capitol Avenue
Suite 302
Springfield, IL 62704
Mon., Tues., 9-12

Northern Illinois 815-962-0122
515 North Court Street
Rockford, IL 61103

INDIANA SCORE CHAPTERS

Indianapolis 317-226-7264
429 N. Pennsylvania Street
Suite 100
Indianapolis, IN 46204-1873
Mon-Fri, 9-4pm.

Fort Wayne 219-422-2601
1300 S. Harrison St.
Fort Wayne, IN 46802
Mon-Fri, 9-12 Noon

South Bend 219-282-4350
300 N. Michigan Street
South Bend, IN 46601
Mon-Fri, 8-5pm

Evansville 812-421-5879
Old Post Office Place
100 NW 2nd St., #300
Evansville, IN 47708
Tuesday & Wednesday

Gary 219-882-3918
973 West 6th Avenue
Room 326
Gary, IN 46402
3 days a week 9-12

South East Indiana 812-379-4457
C/O Chamber of Commerce
500 Franklin St, Box 29
Columbus, IN 47201
No regular schedule

Anderson 317-642-0264
c/o Chamber of Commerce
205 W. 11th, P.O. Box 469
Anderson, IN 46015
No regular schedule

South Central Ind. 812-945-0054
1702 East Spring Street
P.O. Box 653
New Albany, IN 47150
Monday-Friday 9-5

Bloomington 812-336-6381
c/o Chamber of Commerce
116 W 6th St, Suite 100
Bloomington, IN 47402

Kokomo/Howard Co. 317-457-5301
106 N. Washington
P.O. Box 731
Kokomo, IN 46903-0731
Monday-Friday 8:30-5

Marion/Grant Co. 317-664-5107
215 S. Adams
Marion, IN 46952

Elkhart 219-293-1531
418 S. Main Street
P.O. Box 428
Elkhart, IN 46515

Logansport 219-753-6388
Logansport/County C of C
300 East Broadway, Suite #103
Logansport, IN 46947

IOWA SCORE CHAPTERS

Des Moines   515-284-4760
Federal Building/Room 749
210 Walnut Street
Des Moines, IA 50309-2186
M-F, 10:00am-3:00pm

Sioux City   712-277-2324/2325
Federal Bldg.
320 6th Street
Sioux City, IA 51101
Open daily

Council Bluffs   712-325-1000
Chamber of Commerce
P.O. Box 1565
Council Bluffs, IA 51502-1565

Cedar Rapids   319-362-6405
Lattner Building   319-362-7861 (Fax)
215 - 4th Avenue, SE, #200
Cedar Rapids, IA 52401-1806

River City   515-423-5724
15 West State Street
P.O. Box 1128
Mason City IA 50401

Waterloo   319-233-8431
Chamber of Commerce
215 E. 4th
Waterloo, IA 50703
Thurs/1-5 except holiday

Burlington   319-752-2967
Federal Building
300 N. Main Street
Burlington, IA 52601
Tues & Thurs/1:00-3:00pm

Dubuque   319-556-5110
c/o Northeast Iowa Comm Coll
10250 Sundown Road
Peosta IA 52068

Fort Dodge   515-955-2622
Federal Building, Rm 436
205 S. 8th Street
Fort Dodge, IA 50501
No regular schedule

Iowa Lakes   712-262-3059
P.O. Box 7026
21 West 5th St., Room #5
Spencer, IA 51301-3059
Wednesday, 1-4 pm

South Central   515-683-5127
SBDC, Indian Hills Comm Coll
525 Grandview Avenue
Ottumwa, IA 52501

Iowa City   319-338-1662
210 Federal Building
P.O. Box 1853
Iowa City, IA 52240-1853
Tu 10am-Noon & Th 1-3PM

Central Iowa   515-752-0008
Fisher Community Center
507 N 17th St. Pl.
Marshalltown, IA 50158

Southwest Iowa   712-542-2906
Chamber of Commerce
403 West Sheridan
Shenandoah, IA 51601
No regular schedule

Illowa   319-242-5702
333-4th Avenue South
Clinton, IA 52732

Northeast Iowa   319-547-3970
703 Second Street E.
Cresco, IA 52136

Keokuk   319-524-5055
c/o Keokuk Area C of C
401 Main St., Pierce Bldg, #1
Keokuk, IA 52632

Vista   712-732-4511
Storm Lake Chamber of Comm
620 Michigan
Storm Lake, IA 50588

KANSAS SCORE CHAPTERS

Wichita   316-269-6273
SBA/100 East English, Ste. 510
Wichita, KS 67202

Salina   913-827-9301
P.O. Box 586
Salina, KS 67401

Emporia   316-342-1600
Chamber of Commerce
427 Commercial
Emporia, KS 66801

Ark Valley   316-221-1617
Box 314
Winfield, KS 67156
Open daily

Topeka   913-231-1010x1305
1700 College
Topeka, KS 66621

Hays   913-628-8201
2910 Walnut
Hays, KS 67601
Open daily

Hutchinson   316-665-8468
One East 9th
Hutchinson, KS 67501

Southwest Kansas   316-227-3119
Dodge City Chamber of Commerce
P.O. Box 939
Dodge City, KS 67801

Golden Belt   316-792-2401
1307 Williams
Chamber of Commerce
Great Bend, KS 67530

Southeast Kansas   316-331-4741
P.O. Box 886
404 Westminster Place
Independence, KS 67301-0886

McPherson   316-241-3303
Chamber of Commerce
306 N. Main
McPherson, KS 67460
Open daily

KENTUCKY SCORE CHAPTERS

Louisville   502-582-5976
600 Dr Martin L. King Jr. Pl.
188 Federal Office Bldg.
Louisville, KY 40202
Open daily

Paducah   502-442-5685
Federal Office Building
501 Broadway, Room B-36
Paducah, KY 42001
9 am-12pm/Tues. & Thurs.

Lexington   606-231-9902
1460 Newton Pike
Suite A
Lexington, KY 40511
Monday-Friday, 9am-1pm

LOUISIANA SCORE CHAPTERS

New Orleans   504-589-2356
365 Canal Street
Suite 3100
New Orleans, LA 70130
Mon-Fri/8:00am to 4:30pm

Baton Rouge   504-381-7125
564 Laurel Street
P.O. Box 3217
Baton Rouge, LA 70801
Tues-Wed-Thurs 9am-Noon

Lake Charles   318-433-3632
120 W. Pujo
Lake Charles, LA 70601
Mon-Fri, 8:30-3:30pm

Shreveport   318-677-2509
400 Edwards Street
Shreveport LA 71101
Thursdays 9am-4pm

Lafayette   318-233-2705
804 St. Mary Boulevard
Laf. C of C/PO Drawer 51307
Lafayette, LA 70505-1307
Open daily

Central Louisiana   318-442-6671
802 Third Street
Alexandria, LA 71301
P.O. Box 992
Alexandria, LA 71309

NorthShore   504-345-4457
P.O. Box 1458
Hammond, LA 70404

MAINE SCORE CHAPTERS

Portland   207-772-1147
66 Pearl Street
Room 210
Portland, ME 04101
Mon-Fri 8-12 Noon

Augusta   207-622-8509
40 Western Avenue
Augusta, ME 04330
Tue, Wed, Thu 10-2pm

Cen. & No. Arrostock 207-498-6156
111 High Street
P.O. Box 357
Caribou, ME 04736

Bangor 207-941-9707
Husson Coll, One College Cir
Peabody Hall, Rm 229
Tues & Thursday 10am-2pm
Bangor, ME 04401

Lewiston-Auburn 207-782-3708
c/o Chamber of Commerce
179 Lisbon Street
Lewiston, ME 04240
Tues. & Thurs. 9-12

Maine Coastal 207-667-5800
Box 1105, Main & Water Street
Federal Building
Ellsworth, ME 04605
Wednesday 9-12 Noon

Oxford Hills 207-743-0499
166 Main Street
South Paris, ME 04281
Mon-Fri 8:30-Noon

Penquis 207-564-7201
Chamber of Commerce
South Street
Dover-Foxcroft, ME 04426

Western Mountains 207-364-3733
c/o Fleet Bank
P.O. Box 400, 108 Congress St.
Rumford, ME 04276

MARYLAND SCORE CHAPTERS

Baltimore 410-962-2233
The City Cresent Bldg., 6th Floor
10 South Howard Street
Baltimore, MD 21201
Open daily

Salisbury 410-749-0185
c/o Chamber of Commerce
300 E. Main Street
Salisbury, MD 21801
Wed-Thu, 9-12 Noon

Southern Maryland 410-267-6206
c/o Chamber of Commerce
1 Annapolis Street
Annapolis, MD 21401
Open daily

Hagerstown 301-739-2015
111 W. Washington Street
Hagerstown, MD 21740
Mon-Fri, 9-5pm

Upper Shore 410-822-4606
c/o Talbot County C of C 410-822-7922 (Fax)
P.O. Box 1366
Easton, MD 21601
Wed, 9:15-3:00pm

MASSACHUSETTS SCORE CHAPTERS

Boston 617-565-5591
10 Causeway Street
Room 265
Boston, MA 02222
Monday-Friday 10 to 3

Worcester 508-753-2924
33 Waldo Street
Worcester, MA 01608

Cape Cod 508-775-4884
270 Communications Way
Independence Park, Suite 5B
Hyannis, MA 02601
Mon-Fri, 9-1pm

Springfield 413-785-0314
1550 Main Street
Suite 212
Springfield, MA 01103
Tu-W-Th 9:30-Noon

Northeastern Mass. 508-777-2200
Danvers Savings Bank
1 Conant Street
Danvers, MA 01923
Wednesdays 10-2

Southeastern Mass. 508-587-2673
60 School Street
Brockton, MA 02401
Mon-Th 9-12

Bristol/Plymouth Cos. 508-676-8226
c/o Fall River C of C
P.O. Box 1871
Fall River, MA 02722-1871
Monday-Friday 8-3

MICHIGAN SCORE CHAPTERS

Detroit 313-226-7947
477 Michigan Avenue
Room 515
Detroit, MI 48226
Monday-Friday/5 hours day

Upper Pennisula 906-632-3301
c/o Chamber of Commerce
2581 I-75 Business Spur
Sault Ste. Marie, MI 49783
Mon-Fri, 9:00am-5:00pm

Kalamazoo 616-381-5382
128 North Kalamazoo Mall
Kalamazoo, MI 49007
Tue & Th 9-5pm; Wed. 8-12 Noon

Traverse City 616-947-5075
P.O. Box 387
202 East Grandview Pkwy.
Traverse City, MI 49685
Wednesday 9:30-4:30

Petoskey 616-347-4150/526-5360
401 E. Mitchell
Petoskey, MI 49770
1st. & 3rd. Tue

MINNESOTA SCORE CHAPTERS

Minneapolis 612-591-0539
5217 Wayzata Blvd.
North Plaza Bldg., Suite 51
Minneapolis, MN 55416
Mon-Fri, 9:00am-2:00pm

Southwest Minnesota 507-345-4519
Box 999, 112 Riverfront Street
Mankato, MN 56001

St. Paul 612-223-5010
St. Paul Chamber of Commerce
55 5th Street, E #101
St. Paul, MN 55101-1713
Mon-Fri, 9-1pm

Southeastern Minn. 507-288-1122
Rochester Chamber of Comm
220 S. Broadway, Ste. 100
Rochester, MN 55904
M-T 8-5; Wed-Fri 8-12

Central Area 612-255-4955
4191 Second Street, South
St. Cloud, MN 56301-3600
Tues, & Wed, 10-12

South Metro 612-435-6000/898-5645
Burnsville C of C
101 West Burnsville Pkwy #150
Burnsville, MN 55337
Mon-Fri, 8:30am-5:30pm

MISSISSIPPI SCORE CHAPTERS

Gulfcoast 601-863-4449
c/o SBA, One Hancock Plaza
Suite 1001
Gulfport MS 39501-7758
Monday thru Friday 8-4:30

Jackson 601-965-4378/5333
First Jackson Ctr, Ste. 400
101 W. Capitol Street
Jackson, MS 39201
Tues/Wed, 10:00am-2:00pm

Meridian 601-482-7297
5220 16th Avenue
Meridian, MS 39305

Delta 601-378-3141
Greenville Chamber/915 Wash Ave
P.O. Box 933
Greenville, MS 38701
No regular schedule

MISSOURI SCORE CHAPTERS

Kansas City 816-374-6675
323 W. 8th St., Suite 104
Kansas City, MO 64105

St. Louis 314-539-6600
815 Olive Street
Room 242
St. Louis, MO 63101-1569
Mon-Fri, 9:30am-2:30pm

Springfield 417-864-7670
620 S. Glenstone, #110
Springfield MO 65802-3200

Tri-Lakes 417-858-6798
HCRI Box 85
Lampe, MO 65681

South East Missouri 314-471-2106
423 W. Salcedo Road
Sikeston, MO 63801

Mexico 314-581-2765
Mexico Chamber of Commerce
111 North Washington St.
Mexico, MO 65265
Mon-Fri, 9-5pm

Mid-Missouri 314-256-3331
c/o Carl Trautmann
505 Lalor Drive
Manchester, MO 63011
No regular schedule

St. Joseph 816-232-9793
3418 W. Colony Square
St. Joseph, MO 64506
No regular schedule

Ozark-Gateway 314-885-4954
101 E. Washington Street
Cuba, MO 65453-1826

Lewis & Clark 314-928-2900
425 Spencer Road
St. Peters, MO 63376

Poplar Bluff Area 314-785-4727
c/o James W. Carson, Chair
Route 1, Box 280
Neelyville, MO 63954
No regular schedule

Lake Ozark 314-346-2644
Univ. Extension/P.O. Box 1405
113 Kansas Street
Camdenton, MO 65020
Mon-Fri 8-12 & 1-4:30

MONTANA SCORE CHAPTERS

Great Falls 406-761-4434
815 2nd Street So.
Great Falls, MT 59405
Fridays, 10-12 Noon & 1-3pm

Missoula 406-543-7568
421 Agnes Street
Missoula, MT 59840

Butte 406-494-5595/8165
2950 Harrison Ave.
Butte, MT 59701

Bozeman 406-586-5421
1205 East Main Street
Bozeman, MT 59715

Helena 406-449-5381
301 South Park/Fed. Bldg
Helena, MT 59626-0054

Billings 406-245-4111
815 S. 27th Street
Billings, MT 59101
Mon-Fri, 1-3pm

Kalispell 406-756-5271
2 Main Street
Kalispell, MT 59901
Fri 1:30-4:30pm

NEBRASKA SCORE CHAPTERS

Lincoln 402-437-2409
8800 East "O" Street
Lincoln, NE 68520
Tue & Th 1-3pm

Omaha 402-221-3604
11145 Mill Valley Road
Omaha, NE 68154
Mon-Fri, 8-4:30pm

Norfolk 402-371-0940
504 Pierce Street
Norfolk, NE 68701

Columbus 402-564-2769
Chair's address 402-564-5379/0401
1823 27th Street
Columbus, NE 68601
Mon-Fri, 7:30-4:30pm

North Platte 308-784-2690
414 E. 16th Street
Cozad, NE 69130

Hastings 308-234-9647
Box 42
Kearney, NE 68848

Panhandle 402-221-3604
11145 Mill Valley Road
Omaha, NE 68154

Fremont 402-721-2641
P.O. Box 325
5th Street, Chamber
Fremont, NE 68025
No regular schedule

NEW MEXICO SCORE CHAPTERS

Las Vegas 702-388-6104
301 E. Stewart
Box 7527
Las Vegas, NV 89125
Mon-Fri, 9:00am-3:00pm

Northern Nevada 702-784-5477
P.O. Box 3216
50 South Virginia St. #233
Reno, NV 89505-3216
Mon, Thurs, Fri-10am-2pm

NEW HAMPSHIRE SCORE CHAPTERS

Lakes Region 603-524-9168
67 Water St., Ste. 105
Laconia, NH 03246

Upper Valley 603-448-3491
First NH Bank Bldg.
316 First
Lebanon, NH 03766
Mon-Th 10-3pm

Seacoast 603-433-0575/76
195 Commerce Way, Unit A
Portsmouth, NH 03801-3251

Merrimack Valley 603-666-7561
275 Chestnut St., Room 618
Manchester, NH 03103
Mon-Tue & Th-Fri, 9-1pm

Monadnock 603-352-0320
34 Mechanic Street
Keene, NH 03431-3421

Concord 603-225-7763
P.O. Box 1258
Concord, NH 03302-1258
No regular schedule

North Country 603-752-1090
P.O. Box 34
Berlin, NH 03570
Tue-Wed 1-3pm.

NEW JERSEY SCORE CHAPTERS

Somerset 908-218-8874
Paritan Valley Comm Coll
Box 3300
Somerville, NJ 08876
Wed/1:00-3:00/Thurs 10-12

Newark 201-645-3982
60 Park Place, 4th Floor
Newark, NJ 07102

North West 908-879-7080
c/o John C. Apelian, Chair
5 Old Mill Road
Chester Twp., NJ 07930

Monmouth 908-224-2573
Brookdale Comm Coll Career Svcs
765 Newman Springs Road
Lincroft, NJ 07738
M-Th 2-4pm;Tu 7-9pm; appt

Bergen County 201-599-6090
327 E. Ridgewood Avenue
Paramus, NJ 07652
Fri 9-12 Noon

Ocean County 908-505-6033
33 Washington Street
Toms River, NJ 08754

Southern New Jersey 609-757-5183
2600 Mt. Ephraim Avenue
Camden, NJ 08104
Mon-Th, 9:30-12:30 & 4:30-6:30

NEW MEXICO SCORE CHAPTERS

Albuquerque 505-766-1900
Silver Square, Suite 330
5 Silver Avenue, SW
Albuquerque, NM 87102
Mon-Fri/9:00am-4:00pm

Roswell 505-625-2112
Federal Building, Rm 237
Roswell, NM 88201

Sante Fe 505-988-6302
Montoya Federal Bldg
Room 307
Santa Fe, NM 87501
Mon-Fri, 9-12 Noon

Las Cruces 505-523-5627
Loretto Towne Center
505 So. Main St., Ste. 125
Las Cruces, NM 88001
Mon-Fri, 9-12 Noon

NEW YORK SCORE CHAPTERS 2/95

Rochester 716-263-6473
601 Keating Fed. Bldg.
100 State St., Room 410
Rochester, NY 14614
Mon-Fri 9-Noon; 1-4pm

Buffalo 716-846-4301
Fed. Bldg., Room 1311
111 West Huron St.
Buffalo, NY 14202
M-F, 9:30am-3:30pm

Dutchess
c/o Chamber of Commerce
110 Main Street
Poughkeepsie, NY 12601
Thursdays, 10-12 Noon
914-454-1700

Syracuse
100 S. Clinton St., RM 1073
Syracuse, NY 13260
315-423-5382

Northeast
Leo O'Brien Office Bldg., RM 815
Pearl & Clinton Avenues
Albany, NY 12207
Mon & Wed-Th 9-12pm
518-472-6300

Watertown
CAPC Office, POB 899
518 Davidson Street
Watertown, NY 13601
Open daily
315-788-1200

Utica
SUNY Institute of Technology
P.O. Box 3050
Utica, NY 13504-3050
315-792-7553

Auburn
c/o Chamber of Commerce
30 South St. POB 675
Auburn, NY 13021
Monday thru Friday 8:00-5
315-252-7291

So. Tier Binghamton
49 Court St., P.O. Box 995
Metro Center/2nd Floor
Binghamton, NY 13902
607-772-8860

Brookhaven
Dept. of Economic Dev.
3233 Route 112
Medford, NY 11763
Fridays, 10am-1pm
516-451-6563
516-751-3886

Chatauqua
c/o Chamber of Commerce
101 W. 5th
Jamestown, NY 14701
Open daily
716-484-1103

Westchester
222 Mamaroneck Avenue
White Plains, NY 10605
Mon-Fri 9-2pm
914-948-3907

Chemung
c/o Elmira Savings Bank
333 East Water Street
Elmira, NY 14901
607-734-3358

Huntington Area
c/o Chamber of Commerce
151 W. Carver Street
Tue 9:00-12:00
Huntington, NY 11743
516-423-6100

Tompkins County
c/o Tompkins C of C.
904 E. Shore Drive
Ithaca, NY 14850
607-273-7080

Orange County
Orange County C of C
40 Matthews Street
Goshen, NY 10924
Tues-Wed 3 hours each
914-294-8080

Staten Island
c/o Chamber of Commerce
130 Bay Street
Staten Island, NY 10301
Tue & Wed, 9-12 Noon
718-727-1221

Ulster
Ulster County Comm. Coll.
Clinton Bldg, Rm 107
Stone Ridge, NY 12484
Wed. 9-Noon
914-687-5035

Queens County City
120-55 Queens Blvd., Room 333
Queens Borough Hall
Kew Gardens, NY 11424
Mon-Fri 10-2pm
718-263-8961

New York
26 Federal Plaza
Room 3100
New York, NY 10278
Mon-Fri 10-2pm
212-264-4507

Nassau County   516-571-3303/3304/3341
Dept. of Commerce & Ind.
400 County Seat Dr., #140
Mineola, NY 11501

NORTH CAROLINA SCORE CHAPTERS

Charlotte
200 N. College St., Ste A2015
Charlotte, NC 28202
704-344-6576

Raleigh
Century PO Bldg, Suite 306
P.O. Box 406
Raleigh, NC 27602
Mon-Fri 9-12 Noon
919-856-4739

Asheville
Federal Bldg., Room 259
151 Patton
Asheville, NC 28801
T,W,Th, 10-2pm
704-271-4786

Hendersonville
Federal Bldg., Room 108
West 4th Ave & Church St
Hendersonville, NC 28792
M-W-F 10am-1pm
704-693-8702

Greensboro
400 W. Market Street
Suite 410
Greensboro, NC 27401-2241
Tue & Thurs/by appt. 10-1
919-333-5399

Wilmington
Alton Lennon Fed Bldg.
2 Princess St., Suite 103
Wilmington, NC 28401-3958
M-W-F 1-3pm;T-Th 11am-1pm
919-343-4576

High Point
High Point C of C/300 S. Main St.
P.O. Box 5025
High Point, NC 27262
Monday-Friday 8:30-5
910-882-8625

Unifour
c/o Catawba County C of C
P.O. Box 1828
No regular schedule
Hickory, NC 28603
704-328-6111

Durham
Duke Forest Place, Room 128
3308 Chapel Hill Blvd.
Durham, NC 27707
M-W-F 9am-Noon
919-541-2171

Sandhills Area
c/o Sands Hills Area C of C
1480 Hwy. 15-501/P.O. Box 458
Southern Pines, NC 28387
Mon-Fri, 9:00am-5:00pm
910-692-3926

Chapel Hill
c/o Chapel Hill/Carrboro C of C
104 S. Estes Dr/POB 2897
Chapel Hill, NC 27514
Mon-Fri, 9:00-5:00pm
919-967-7075

Outer Banks
c/o Outer Banks Chamber of Comerce
P.O. Box 1757
Kill Devil Hills, NC 27948
Tuesday 11-2
919-441-8144

Down East
c/o Neuse River Council of Govts.
P.O. Box 334/233 Middle Street
New Bern, NC 28563
Tue-Th, 9am-12 noon
919-633-6688

NORTH DAKOTA SCORE CHAPTERS

Fargo
P.O. Box 3086
657 2nd Ave., Rm. 225
Fargo, ND 58108-3083
Mon-Fri, 9-4pm
701-239-5677

Minot
P.O. Box 507
Minot, ND 58701-0507
701-852-6883

Upper Red River
202 North 3rd Street
Grand Forks, ND 58203
Th 9-4pm
701-772-7271

Bismarck-Mandan
P.O. Box 1912
Bismarck, ND 58502-1912
Wednesday 1-4:30
701-250-4303

OHIO SCORE CHAPTERS

Columbus
2 Nationwide Plaza
Suite 1400
Columbus, OH 43215-2542
Monday-Friday 9am-4pm
614-469-2357

Cleveland 216-522-4194
1100 Superior Avenue
Suite 620, Eaton Center
Cleveland, OH 44114-2507
Mon-Fri, 8:30am-5:00pm

Cincinnati 513-684-2812
525 Vine Street
Ameritrust Bldg., RM 850
Cincinnati, OH 45202
Mon-Fri/9-1:00pm

Toledo 419-259-7598
1946 North 13th Street
Room 352
Toledo, OH 43624
Mon-Fri/9-3:30pm

Akron 216-379-3163
c/o Regional Dev. Board
One Cascade Plaza, 7th Floor
Akron, OH 44308
Mon-Fri/9-3:00pm

Dayton 513-225-2887
Federal Building, Rm. 505
200 W. 2nd Stret
Dayton, OH 45402-1430
Mon-Fri/9-3pm

Youngstown 216-746-2687
306 Williamson Hall
Youngstown University
Youngstown, OH 44555
9-12 Mon-Fri & Mon 1-3pm

Marietta 614-373-0268
Marietta College
Thomas Hall
Marietta, OH 45750
Mon, Wed, Fri 10-12

Mansfield 419-522-3211
Chamber of Commerce
55 N. Mulberry Street
Mansfield OH 44902
Mondays & Wednesday 1-4

Licking County 614-345-7458
50 West Locust Street
P.O. Box 702
Newark, OH 43055
Tu 1:30-2:30; Th 10-11

Zanesville/Muskingum 614-455-3111
Adult Ed., Att: Tessie Wilson
400 Richard Road
Zanesville, OH 43701

Canton 216-453-6047
116 Cleveland Ave., N.W.
Suite 601
Canton OH 44702-1720

OKLAHOMA SCORE CHAPTERS

Tulsa 918-581-7462
Chamber of Commerce
616 S. Boston, Suite 406
Tulsa, OK 74119
Mon-Fri/10:am-2:00pm

Oklahoma City 405-231-5163
c/o SBA, Oklahoma Tower Bldg.
210 Park Avenue, #1300
Oklahoma, City OK 73102
Mon-Fri/10:am-3:pm

Lawton 405-353-8726
Federal Building, Rm 107
431 E. Avenue
Lawton, OK 73501
Monday-Friday 10-3

Northeast Oklahoma 918-786-4729
210 S. Main
Grove, OK 74344

OREGON SCORE CHAPTERS

Portland 503-326-3441
222 S. W. Columbia
Suite 500
Portland, OR 97201
Mon-Fri, 8:00am-4:30pm

Southern Oregon 503-776-4220
132 West Main St.
Midford, OR 97501

Willamette 503-484-5485
1401 Willamette Street
P.O. Box 1107
Eugene, OR 97401-4003

Salem 503-370-2896
P.O. Box 4024
Salem, OR 97302-1024
No regular schedule

Bend 503-382-3221
c/o Bend Chamber of Comm.
63085 North Highway 97
Bend, OR 97701
Mon-Fri, 8:00am-4:30pm

PENNSYLVANIA SCORE CHAPTERS

Pittsburgh 412-644-5447
960 Penn Avenue, 5th Flr.
Pittsburgh, PA 15222

Reading 215-376-6766
c/o Chamber of Commerce
645 Penn Street
Reading, PA 19601
Mon/10-3; 3rd Wed 10-Noon

Lancaster 717-397-3092
118 West Chestnut Street
Lancaster, PA 17603
Open daily 9-4

Harrisburg 717-782-3874
100 Chestnut, Suite 309
Harrisburg, PA 17101
Mon & Fri 9-12, T-W-Th 9-4pm

Philadelphia 215-596-5077
3535 Market Street, Room 4480
Philadelphia, PA 19104
Open daily/10:am-2:00pm

Lehigh Valley 215-758-4496/3980
Rauch Bldg 37/Lehigh Univ.
621 Taylor Street
Bethlehem, PA 18015
Mon-Fri 9am-5pm

Erie 814-833-7540
3532 West 12th Street
Erie, PA 16505
Open daily

N. Central Penn. 717-322-3720
Federal Building
240 W. Third St., Room 304
P.O. Box 725
Williamsport, PA 17703
Open daily

Scranton 717-347-4611
Federal Bldg., Room 104
Washington Ave. & Linden
Scranton, PA 18503
Mon-Fri/9:30am-1:30pm

Wilkes-Barre 717-826-6502
20 N. Pennsylvania Ave.
Wilkes-Barre, PA 18702
Mon-Fri, 8-12pm

York 717-845-8830
Cyber Center
1600 Pennsylvania Avenue
York, PA 17404
Mon-Fri, 9-12pm

Uniontown 412-437-4222
POB 2065 DTS, Pittsburg St.
Federal Building
Uniontown, PA 15401
Mon-Wed-Fri

Mon-Valley 412-684-4277
435 Donner Avenue
Monessen, PA 15062
Mon-Fri, 1-3pm

Eastern Montgomery County 215-885-3027
Baederwood Shopping Center
1653 The Fairways, Suite 204
Jenkintown, PA 19046
Mon-Fri, 9-1pm

Cumberland Valley 717-264-2935/4496
Chambersburg C of C
75 S. Second St.
Chambersburg, PA 17201
Tue-Thur mornings

Monroe County-Stroudsburg 717-421-4433
556 Main Street
Stroudsburg, PA 18301

Chester County 215-344-6910
Gov't Svc Ctr., Suite 281
601 Westtown Road
West Chester, PA 19382-4538
Mon-Fri, 9-3pm & 7-9pm

Westmoreland Co. 412-539-7505
St. Vincent College
Latrobe, PA 15650
Mon-Fri, 8-5pm

Bucks County 215-943-8850
c/o Chamber of Commerce
409 Hood Boulevard
Fairless Hills, PA 19030
Monday-Friday 9-12 Noon

Altoona-Blair   814-943-8151
c/o Altoona-Blair Chamber
1212 12th Avenue
Altoona, PA 16601-3493
Monday-Friday, 9am-5pm

Warren County   814-723-9017
Warren County C of C
P.O. Box 942/315 Second Avenue
Warren, PA 16365

Tri-County   215-32-SCORE
238 High Street
Pottstown, PA 19464

Central Pennsylvania   814-234-9415
200 Innovation Blvd., #242-B
State College, PA 16803

RHODE ISLAND SCORE CHAPTERS

J.G.E. Knight   401-528-4571/4589
380 Westminster Street
Providence RI 02903

SOUTH CAROLINA SCORE CHAPTERS

Midlands   803-765-5131
Strom Thurmond Bldg.
1835 Assembly St., Room 358
Columbia, SC 29201
Monday-Friday 9:00-4:00

Piedmont   803-271-3638
Federal Bldg., Room B-02
300 E. Washington Street
Greenville, SC 29601
Monday-Friday, 9:00-12:00

Coastal   803-727-4778
Federal Bldg., Room 126
334 Meeting Street
Charleston, SC 29403
Monday-Friday, 10am-2pm

Grand Strand   803-449-8538
48th Executive Ct, Suite 211
1109 - 48th Avenue North
Myrtle Beach, SC 29577
Open daily

SOUTH DAKOTA SCORE CHAPTERS

Sioux Falls   605-330-4231
First Financial Center
110 South Phillips Ave., Ste 200
Sioux Falls, SD 57102-1109
Tues & Thurs 1:30-4

Rapid City   605-394-5311
444 Mt. Rushmore Road, #209
Rapid City, SD 57701
Tues. & Thurs. 1-4

TENNESSEE SCORE CHAPTERS

Memphis   901-544-3588
Fed. Bldg., Suite 148
167 North Main Street
Memphis, TN 38103
M-F 9am-Noon

Nashville   615-736-7621
50 Vantage Way, Suite 201
Nashville, TN 37228-1500

Chattanooga   615-752-5190
Federal Bldg., Room 26
900 Georgia Avenue
Chattanooga, TN 37402
Mon-Fri 9am-1pm

Greater Knoxville   615-545-4203
530 South Gay Street
Farragot Bldg, suite 224
Knoxville, TN 37902
Monday-Friday 10-2

Jackson   901-423-2200
c/o CofC, P. O. Box 1904
197 Auditorium Street
Jackson, TN 38302
Mon-Fri/9:00am-1:00pm

Kingsport   615-392-8805
151 East Main Street
c/o Chamber of Commerce
Kingsport, TN 37662
Thursday 11am-1pm

Northeast Tennessee   615-929-7686
c/o Chamber of Commerce
P.O. Box 190
Elizabethton, TN 37643
Mon-Fri 10am-12pm

TEXAS SCORE CHAPTERS

Dallas   214-733-0189/3953
Equitable Bank Bldg.
17218 Preston Road #3202
Dallas, TX 75252

Houston   713-773-6565
9301 Southwest Freeway, Suite 550
Houston, TX 77074
Mon-Fri, 9-3pm

Fort Worth   817-885-6520
100 E. 15th Street #24
Ft. Worth, TX 76102
Mon thru Fri/9:00-4:00pm

San Antonio   210-229-5931/5900
c/o SBA, Federal Bldg. Rm #A527
727 E. Durango
San Antonio, TX 78206
Open daily

Lower Rio Grande Valley   210-427-8533
222 E. Van Buren
Suite 500
Harlingen, TX 78550
Mon-Fri, 9:00am-12 Noon

Corpus Christi   512-888-3306
606 N. Carancahua
Suite 1200
Corpus Christi, TX 78476
9:00am-12:00 pm/M-F

El Paso   915-540-5155
10737 Gateway West
Suite 320
El Paso, TX 79935
Mon thru Fri/8-4:30

Lubbock   806-743-7462
1611 10th Street
Suite 200
Lubbock, TX 79401
Mon-Fri, 9:00am-1:00pm

Abilene   915-677-1857
2106 Federal Post Office &
Court Building
Abilene, TX 79601
Tues, Wed, Thu, 9am-2pm

Austin   512-482-5112
300 E. 8th St., Room 572
Austin, TX 78701

East Texas   903-595-0091
414 First Place
Tyler, TX 75702
M-F, 9:00am-2:00pm

Texarkana   903-792-7191
Texarkana Chamber of Commerce
819 State Line Avenue
Texarkana, TX 75501
Daily

Waco   817-754-8898
Business Resource Center
4601 North 19th Street
Waco, TX 76708
Open daily

Brownsville   210-541-4508
3505 Boca Chica Blvd, #305
Brownsville, TX 78521
Mon-Fri 9-12, Th 1pm-4:30pm

Brazos Valley   409-776-8876
3000 Briarcrest, Suite 302
Victoria Bank & Trust
Bryan, TX 77802
Monday-Friday 9-12

Wichita Falls   817-766-1602
Hamilton Building
P.O. Box 1860
Wichita Falls, TX 76307
Thurs. 8-12 (counseling)

Golden Triangle   409-838-6581
Community Bank
700 Calder, Suite 101
Beaumont, TX 77701
Tuesdays 9-Noon

Midland   915-687-2649
200 East Wall St., RM P121
Post Office Annex
Midland, TX 79701

Amarillo   806-352-3616
5309 W 21st
Amarillo, TX 79106

UTAH SCORE CHAPTERS

Salt Lake   801-524-3211
125 S. State St., Room 2237
Salt Lake City, UT 84138

Ogden   801-625-5712
324 25th Street 6104
Ogden, UT 84401

Central Utah   801-377-8401
1041 East North Temple
Provo, UT 84604

Southern Utah   801-673-4811x353
c/o Dixie College
225 S. 700 East
St. George, UT 84770

VERMONT SCORE CHAPTERS

Montpelier 802-828-4422
c/o SBA/P.O. Box 605
Room 205, 87 State Street
Montpelier, VT 05601
Open daily

Champlain Valley 802-951-6764/62
11 Lincoln St., Room 106
Winston Prouty Fed Bldg
Essex Junction, VT 05452
Mon-Fri 9-12pm

Northeast Kingdom 802-748-5101
c/o NCIC/20 Main Street
P.O. Box 904
St. Johnsbury, VT 05819
Mon-Fri 8-4pm

Marble Valley 802-773-9147
256 No. Main St.,
Rutland, VT 05701-2413
Mon-Fri 8-4pm

VIRGINIA SCORE CHAPTERS

Richmond 804-771-2400x131
1504 Santa Rosa Road
Dale Building, Suite 200
Richmond, VA 23229
Tue-Fri/8:00-12:00 Noon

Roanoke 703-857-2834
Fed. Bldg., POB 1366 703-857-2043 (Fax)
Room 716
Roanoke, VA 24011
Open daily/10:00-4:00pm

Norfolk 804-441-3733
Federal Bldg., Room 737
200 Granby Street
Norfolk, VA 23510
Tu 9-12:30;
M-W-Th-Fri 9:30-11:30

Peninsula 804-766-2000
c/o Peninsula C of C
P.O. Box 7269, 6 Manhattan Sq.
Hampton, VA 23666
Tues-Thurs

Bristol 615-989-4850
20 Volunteer Parkway
P.O. Box 519
Bristol, VA 24203

Northern Virginia 703-662-4118
c/o Winchester-Frederick C of C
1360 S. Pleasant Valley Road
Winchester, VA 22601
Monday-Friday, 9:00-5:00pm

Shenandoah Valley 703-949-8203
c/o Waynesboro C of C
301 W. Main Street
Waynesboro, VA 22980
Monday, 9:00-11:00

Central Virginia 804-295-6712
918 Emmet Street North
Suite 200
Charlottesville, VA 22903-4878
Monday & Wednesday 9:00-4:00pm

Greater Lynchburg 804-846-3235
Federal Building
1100 Main Street
Lynchburg, VA 24504-1714
Monday-Friday 10-1

Martinsville 703-632-6401
115 Broad Street
P.O. Box 709
Martinsville, VA 24112-0709
Thursday 12 Noon-2:00pm

Williamsburg 804-229-6511
c/o Chamber of Commerce
P.O. Drawer HQ
Williamsburg, VA 23185

Tri-Cities 804-458-5536
c/o Chamber of Commerce
P.O. Drawer 1297
Hopewell, VA 23860
Mon., Wed., Fri., 9-5

WASHINGTON SCORE CHAPTERS

Seattle 206-220-6530
915 2nd Avenue, Room 1792
Seattle, WA 98174

Spokane 509-353-2820
West 601 First Avenue
10th Floor, East
Spokane, WA 99204-0317
M-F, 9-12 & 1-4pm

Tacoma 206-627-2175
950 Pacific Ave., #300
Tacoma, WA 98402
Monday-Friday 8:30-5

Ft. Vancouver 206-699-3241
1200 Fort Vancouver Way
P.O.Box 8900
Vancouver, WA 98668

Mid-Columbia 509-965-2021/2502
c/o Greater Yakima C of C
P.O. Box 1490
Yakima, WA 98907

Bellingham 206-676-0367/734-1330
Fourth Corner, Economic Dev. Group
P.O. Box 2803, 1203 Cornwall Avenue
Bellingham, WA 98227

WISCONSIN SCORE CHAPTERS

Milwaukee 414-297-3942
310 W. Wisconsin Ave, #425
Milwaukee, WI 53203
Mon-Fri 8:30-12pm & 1-3pm

Madison 608-264-5117
670 S. Whitney Way
Madison, WI 53711
Mon-Fri, 9am-12noon

Eau Claire 715-834-1573
Federal Building, Rm B11
510 South Barstow Street
Eau Claire, WI 54701
Tue-Th, 9:30-12

Fox Cities 414-734-7101 x 24
227 S. Walnut Street
P.O. Box 1855
Appleton, WI 54915
Open Daily

Lacrosse 608-784-4880
712 Main Street
P.O. Box 219
Lacrosse, WI 54602-0219
Mondays 1-4pm

Wausau 715-845-6231
300 Third St, POB 6190
Wausau, WI 54402-6190

Green Bay 414-437-8704
P.O. Box 1660
Green Bay, WI 54305

Central Wisconsin 715-421-3900
2240 Kingston Road
Wisconsin Rapids, WI 54494
No regular schedule

Superior 715-394-7716
305 Harborview Parkway
Superior, WI 54880

WYOMING SCORE CHAPTERS

Casper 307-261-5860
Federal Bldg. #2215
100 East "B" Street
Casper, WY 82602
Mon-Wed, 9:30-11:30

GUAM SCORE CHAPTERS

Guam 671-472-7308
Pacific News Bldg. Rm 103
238 Archbishop Flores St.
Agana, GU 96910-5188
Monday-Friday 8-5

PUERTO RICO SCORE CHAPTERS

Puerto Rico & Virgin Islands 809-766-5001
Citibank Towers Plaza 2nd Floor
252 Ponce de Leon Avenue
San Juan, PR 00918-2041
Open daily

APPENDIX E
Small Business Association

The resources in this appendix are all available from the Small Business Association. The products are grouped into various categories such as Financial Management, Marketing, and Personnel Management. to order any of these materials, contact the Small Business answer Desk at 1-800-827-5722. All of the SBA's programs and services are extended to the public on a nondiscriminatory basis. For more information about SBA economic development programs and services, or for a free copy of *The Small Business Directory*, consult the BA office nearest you.

Resources Available from the Small Business Association

EMERGING BUSINESS SERIES

Transferring Management/Family Businesses
Help your family business successfully survive the transfer of ownership from generation to generation. Proper planning is the key.
Item # EB02 $3.00

Marketing Strategies for Growing Businesses
Unravel the mystery of marketing—putting the customer first—and discover practical marketing approaches to budgeting, layout and design, copy-writing, media analysis, and more.
Item # EB02 $3.00

Management Issues for Growing Businesses
Learn to examine the marketplace environment and create employment and profit opportunities that provide growth and financial viability to your business through effective management.
Item #EB03 $3.00

Human Resource Management for Growing Businesses
Uncover the characteristics of an effective personnel system and training program. Learn how these functions come together to build employee trust and productivity.
Item #EB04 $3.00

Audit Checklist for Growing Businesses
Designed with the small business in mind, this audit checklist helps the entrepreneur conduct a comprehensive search for existing and potential problems and opportunities.
Item #EB05 $3.00

Strategic Planning for Growing Businesses
Stragetic planning is not just for big business. Learn to effectively match your business' strengths to available opportunities by developing a clear mission statement, goals, and objectives.
Item # EB06 $3.00

Financial Management for Growing Businesses
Develop a comprehensive financial plan outlining the assets, debts, and current and future profit potential of your business through effective financial management.
Item #EB07 $3.00

FINANCIAL MANAGEMENT

ABC's of Borrowing
This best-seller tells you what lenders look for and what to expect when borrowing money for your small business.
Item #FM01 $2.00

Eiementos Basicos Para Pedir Dinero Prestado
Esta publicacion le da a conocer lo que los prestatarios buscan y lo que esperan de usted cuando pide dinero prestado para su pequeno negocio.
Item #FM01s $2.00

Understanding Cash Flow
The owner/manager is shown how to plan for the movement of cash through the business and thus plan for future requirements.
Item #FM04 $2.00

A Venture Capital Primer for Small Business
Learn what venture capital resources are available and how to develop a proposal for obtaining these funds.
Item #FM05 $2.00

Budgeting in a Small Service Firm
Learn how to set up and keep sound financial records. Study how to effectively use journals, ledgers, and charts to increase profit.
Item #FM08 $2.00

Recordkeeping in a Small Business
Need some basic advice on setting up a useful record keeping system? This publication describes how.
Item #FM10 $2.00

Pricing Your Products and Services Profitably
Discusses how to price your products profitably, plus various pricing techniques and when to use them.
Item #13 $2.00

Financing for Small Business
Learn how, when, and where to find capital for business needs including ste-by-step instructions.
Item #FM14 $2.00

MANAGEMENT AND PLANNING

Problems in Managing a Family-Owned Business
Specific problems exist when attempting to make a family-owned business successful. This publication offers suggestions on how to overcome these difficulties.
Item #MP3 $2.00

Business Plan for Small Manufacturers
Designed to help an owner/manager of a small manufacturing firm, this publication covers all the basic information necessary to develop an effective business plan.
Item #MP04 $2.00

Business Plan for Small Construction Firms

This publication is designed to help an owner/manager of a small construction company pull together the resources to develop a business plan.

Item #MP05 $2.00

Planning and Goal Setting for Small Business

Learn proven management techniques to help you plan for sucdcess.

Item #MP06 $2.00

Business Plan for Retailers

Business plans are essential road maps for success. Learn how to develop a business plan for a retail business.

Item #MP09 $2.00

Business Plan for Small Service Firms

Outlines the key points to be included in the business plan of a small service firm.

Item #MP11 $2.00

Checklist for Going into Business

This is a must if you're thinking about starting a business. It highlights the important factors you should know in reaching a decision to start your own business.

Item #MP12 $2.00

Lista Para Comenzar Su Negocio

Esta publicacion es necesaria si usted esta pensando en comenzar un negocio. Demuestra los factores importantes que usted debebe de conocer antes de tomar la decision de comenzar su propio negocio.

Item #MP12s $2.00

How to Get Started with a Small Business Computer

Helps you forecast your computer needs, evaluate the alternatives, and select the right computer system for your business.

Item #MP14 $2.00

Business Plan for Home-Based Business

Provides a comprehensive approach to developing a business plan for a home-based business.

Item #MP15 $2.00

How to Buy or Sell a Business

Learn several techniques for determining the best price to buy or sell a small business.

Item #MP16 $2.00

Developing a Strategic Business Plan

This best-seller helps you develop a strategic action plan for your small business.

Item #MP21 $2.00

Inventory Management

Discusses the purpose of inventory management, types of inventories, record keeping, and forecasting inventory levels.

Item #MP22 $2.00

Selecting the Legal Structure for Your Business

Discusses the various legal structures that a small business can use in setting up operations. It identifies types of legal structures and the advantages and disadvantages of each.

Item #MP25 $2.00

Evaluating Franchise Opportunities

Evaluate franchise opportunities and select the business that's right for you.

Item #MP26 $2.00

Small Business Risk Management Guide

This guide can help you strengthen your insurance program by identifying, minimizing, and eliminating business risks.

Item #MP28 $2.00

Child Day-Care Services

An overview of the industry, including models of day-care operations.

Item #MP30 $3.00

Handbook for Small Business

Handy information for getting started. A new publication developed by the SBA's Service Corps of Retired Executives (SCORE).

Item #MP31 $3.00

How to Write a Business Plan

What you need to know to write a good plan at the start. It can save your business dow the line.

Item #MP32 $3.00

MARKETING

Creative Selling: The Competitive Edge

Explains how to use creative selling techniques to increase profits.

Item #MT01 $2.00

Marketing for Small Business: An Overview

Provides an overview of marketing concepts and contains an extensive bibliography of sources covering the subject of marketing.

Item #MT02 $2.00

Researching Your Market

Learn inexpensive techniques that you can apply to gather facts about your customer base and how to expand it.

Item #MT08 $2.00

Selling by Mail Order

Provides basic information on how to run a successful mail-order business. Includes information on product selection, pricing, testing, and writing effective advertisements.

Item #MP09 $2.00

Advertising

Advertising is critical to the success of any small business. Learn how you can effectively advertise your products and services.

Item #MT11 $2.00

PRODUCTS/IDEAS/INVENTIONS

Ideas into Dollars

This publication identifies the main challenges in product development and provides a list of resources to help inventors and innovators take their ideas into the marketplace.

Item #PI01 $2.00

Avoiding Patent, Trademark and Copyright Problems

Learn how to avoid infringing the rights of others and the importance of protecting your own rights.

Item #MI02 $2.00

PERSONNEL MANAGEMENT

Employees: How to Find and Pay Them

A business is only as good as the people in it. Learn how to find and hire the right employees.

Item #PM02 $2.00

VIDEOTAPES

Each VHS videotape below comes complete with a workbook.

Marketing: Winning Customers with a Workable Plan

Take advantage of this easy-to-follow course and develop the marketing plan designed to meet your goals. Developed by two of the country's leading small business marketing experts, this hands-on program offers a step-by-step approach to writing the best possible marketing plan for your business.

Item #VT01 $30.00

The Business Plan: Your Road Map to Success

Learn the essentials of developing a business plan that will lead you to capital, growth, and profitability. This video teaches you what to include, what to omit, and how to get free help from qualified consultants when developing your business plan.

Item #VT02 $30.00

Promotion Solving the Puzzle

Master the components that make a successful promotional campaign—advertising, public relations, direct mail and trade shows. This video-tape shows you how to put the pieces together. Learn how to choose the best advertising medium for your needs, and much more.

Item #VT03 $30.00

Home-Based Business: A Winning Blueprint

This practical program examines the essentials of operating within a productive and profitable home-based business—from designing your home office and avoiding isolation to networking strategies and building an image that gets you taken seriously.

Item #VT05 $30.00

Basics of Exporting

This videotape shows you how to open the doors to international markets. This tape provides information on: getting your goods overseas, payment mechanisms, selling and distributing overseas, international marketing, and sources of financial assistance.

Item #VT05 $30.00

For more information about SBA economic development programs and services or for a free copy of the "The Small Business Directory," consult the U.S. government section in your telephone directory for the SBA office nearest you.

Small Business Answer Desk
1-800-827-5722

APPENDIX F
Sources of Franchising Information
(Books, Directories, Newsletters, Services, Etc.)

THE BEST HOME-BASED FRANCHISES, Gregory Matusky and The Philip Lief Group, Doubleday, New York, NY. 1992. 307 pp. $15.00.

This book provides prospective franchisees with an overview of the rewards and challenges of home-based franchises. In addition to the fundamentals of operating a business at home, the book provides a fairly detailed profile of some 97 franchising opportunities.

BLUEPRINT FOR FRANCHISING A BUSINESS, Steven S. Raab with Gregory Matusky, John Wiley & Sons, New York, NY. 1987. 244 pp. $24.95.

This book discusses how franchising works, its advantages and disadvantages (including legal, business, marketing and sales issues) and the crucial steps required to launch a successful franchise program. The book is interspersed with "nuggets"—insightful summaries of the author's experience in various facets of franchising. The appeal is for potential and actual franchisors rather than franchisees. Understanding the mechanics, however, better prepares the franchisee for a knowledgeable investment decision.

THE COMPLETE GUIDE TO FRANCHISING IN CANADA, Ted LeValliant, Macmillan Canada, 29 Birch Avenue, Toronto, ON M4V 1E2 Canada. 1993. 245 pp. $34.95.

This guide explains the franchising world from both the franchisee's and the franchisor's point of view. No matter which side of the fence the reader is on, it's important to know how things look from the other side. The primary topics include: how franchising works, assessing a franchise program, choosing a location, contract essentials and international opportunities. In addition to LeValliant's observations, the book includes chapters by other industry professionals.

THE CONTINENTAL FRANCHISE REVIEW, Sparks Publishing Co., Inc., P.O. Box 3283, Englewood, CO 80155; (800) 938-1044, (303) 470-7744; FAX (303) 470-7745. Subscription fees: $155 per year US, $175 per year outside US. 26 issues annually, plus four special reports.

This 8-page, bi-weekly analytical newsletter keeps readers updated on franchising, state legislation, FTC investigations, court decisions, tax issues, operations and environmental issues. The format is broken down into: Bulletins, Trends, Finance, Legal and Editorial. All subjects covered are indexed annually. (Sample copies are provided.)

FINANCING YOUR FRANCHISE, Meg Whittemore, Andrew Sherman and Ripley Hotch, Whittemore & Associates, P.O. Box 322, Lewes, DE 19958; (202) 463-5662; FAX (202) 463-3102. 1993. 275 pp. $20.95.

This book is a guide on how to locate money for a franchise. It offers information on steps and techniques for raising capital, including how to write a loan proposal, how to deal with bankers, what is in a purchasing agreement, financing tips for women and minorities, interpreting disclosure documents and how to cut through the sales hype. In addition, the book provides directories of franchise lenders, sample forms, checklists and business plans. Lists of franchisors who offer financing assistance, those who target women and minorities and helpful federal agencies are also included.

FRANCHISE BIBLE: A COMPREHENSIVE GUIDE, Erwin J. Keup, Oasis Press/PSI Research, 300 N. Valley Drive, Grants Pass, OR 97526. 1994. 311 pp. $19.95.

This guide is useful to prospective franchisees and franchisors alike. The comprehensive guide and workbook explain in detail what the franchise system entails and the precise benefits it offers. The book contains an actual offering circular to familiarize the reader with its terms and conditions and what must be included in the circular if you are a franchisor. To assist the prospective franchisee in rating a potential franchisor, the guide provides check lists and forms. Also noted are the franchisor's contractual obligations to the franchisee and what the franchisee should expect from the franchisor in the way of services and support.

A FRANCHISE CONTRACT, Jerrold G. Van Cise, International Franchise Association (IFA), 1350 New York Avenue, NW, Suite 900, Washington, DC 20005; (202) 628-8000; FAX (202) 628-0812. $4.95.

A legal examination of the proper elements of a contract to protect both franchisor and franchisee.

THE FRANCHISE FRAUD: HOW TO PROTECT YOURSELF BEFORE AND AFTER YOU INVEST, Robert L. Purvin, Jr., American Association of Franchisees and Dealers, P.O. Box 81887, San Diego, CA 92138; (619) 235-2556; FAX (619) 235-2565. 1994. 275 pp. $27.95.

This new book challenges industry claims that franchising per se is a safe and secure path to business ownership. More than an expose of the franchise industry, the book provides a blueprint for selecting, negotiating and maintaining a successful franchise relationship.

THE FRANCHISE GAME, (RULES AND PLAYERS), Harold Needle, Olempco, Dept. C, P.O. Box 27963, Houston, TX 77027. $8.00.

The Franchise Game deals with the potential physical, emotional and mental traumas experienced by franchisees and provides insight from the point of view of both franchisors and franchisees.

THE FRANCHISE HANDBOOK, Edited by Andrew Sherman, American Management Association, 135 W. 50th Street, New York, NY 10020; (800) 538-4761. 1993. 510 pp. $75.00.

The Handbook is a collaborative effort providing advice from over 25 professionals, executives and advisors in the franchising community. Together, the contributors discuss pragmatic solutions to day-to-day issues involved in starting up or running an established franchise program. It reflects approaches to the management, operations, marketing, financial and legal issues that can bolster the success of every franchising company. The seven primary chapters deal with: developing an effective management structure, operational issues, dynamics in the franchisor/franchisee relationship, marketing advertising and PR, legal and regulatory issues, financial issues and current trends.

FRANCHISE IT! Hans Yeager, Positive Software Solutions, 7765 W. 91st, F-3107, Playa del Rey, CA 90293; (310) 301-8446. 1993. $49.95.

This is a windows-based software guide to evaluate franchises and to plan new businesses. It contains information on more than 1,400 franchises for the user to investigate. The potential franchisee can look up franchises based upon user-specified criteria—type of business, equity capital required, minimum number of operating units, etc. Once sorted, the information can be saved to file and/or to print. Various checklists and guidelines are also included. The planning menu provides complete, step-by-step instructions on how to prepare a financial plan for your business.

FRANCHISE OPPORTUNITIES GUIDE, IFA. 1994. 300 pp. $15.00.

A comprehensive listing of the world's leading franchise companies grouped by product or service with an alphabetical index, plus sources of legal advice, financial assistance and more. The Guide deals primarily with members of the IFA.

THE FRANCHISE OPTION, EXPANDING YOUR BUSINESS THROUGH FRANCHISING, DeBanks M. Henward, III and William Ginalski, Franchise Group Publishers, IFA. 1985. 179 pp. $25.95.

This is an excellent overview of the interworkings of the industry from the franchisee's standpoint. Basically, the book offers a do-it-yourself approach to successful franchise development and in so doing discusses what franchising is, how it works, what it takes to be a successful franchisor and how to undertake the development of a franchise system. There is an in-depth discussion of planning for a franchise system, test-marketing the franchise concept, system implementation, prohibitions and liabilities and when and how to terminate a franchise relationship. This book is addressed to the sophisticated potential franchisee/franchisor.

FRANCHISE SELECTION: SEPARATING FACT FROM FICTION, Raymond Munna, Granite Publishers, 80 Granada Drive, Kenner, LA 70065. 1986. 215 pp. $19.95.

This is a valuable source of checklists for the franchisee who is unaware of the potential pitfalls that clearly exist. Especially helpful are the sections on analyzing the franchise contract, laws affecting franchising and the critical, but hard to find, information on a franchisor and how to obtain it.

THE FRANCHISE SURVIVAL GUIDE, Carol B. Green, Probus Publishing, 51 Beaver Creek Place, Box 19-413, Avon, CO 81620. 1944. 225 pp. $22.95.

Green provides a detailed guide to selecting and operating a profitable business, using case studies to illustrate key points. Areas covered include: objective guidelines to selecting the right franchise, marketing an already-known product, access to capital, competitive analysis and management and operational issues in franchising.

FRANCHISE UPDATE PUBLICATIONS, P.O. Box 20547, San Jose, CA 95160; (408) 997-7795; FAX (408) 997-9377.

Franchise UPDATE Publications is a leading publisher of franchise information, serving both the existing franchisor marketplace and those considering the business of franchising. Its specialized publications include: 1) Franchise UPDATE Magazine, which focuses on the issues, research and data that are critical to franchise professionals; 2) The Directory of Franchise Attorneys, a source of franchise legal professionals, referenced both al-

phabetically and geographically; and 3) The Executives' Guide to Franchise Opportunities, a publication designed for individuals thinking about going into business for themselves. Over 100 franchise companies actively seeking qualified franchise candidates are included. It is also complete with franchise statistics, franchise evaluation tips and financing options.

FRANCHISING AND LICENSING: TWO WAYS TO BUILD YOUR BUSINESS, Andrew J. Sherman, Amacom Press, 135 W. 50th Street, New York, NY 10020. 1991. 250 pp. $27.95.

This book covers the "how to's" of creating a franchise program. In no-nonsense language, it covers all the management, operational and legal issues that must be faced. With check lists, case studies and sample contracts, this guidebook makes otherwise illusive concepts easy to grasp. The author notes how 1) to raise capital, 2) create and test a prototype, 3) structure franchise agreements, 4) develop operations manuals and 5) market the franchise.

FRANCHISING IN THE ECONOMY, 1991-1993, University of Louisville, College of Business and Public Administration and IFA Educational Foundation, Inc. IFA. 1994. Price not set.

Based on information supplied by 297 U.S.-based IFA franchisor member companies, this statistical analysis breaks down the industry into 65 business types divided into 18 categories. This is a source book for potential franchisees, who can subsequently ask franchisors hard questions as to how their franchise compares with industry averages. This is the only readily available source of reliable industry statistics.

FRANCHISING: A PLANNING AND SALES COMPLIANCE GUIDE, Norman D. Axelrod and Lewis G. Rudnick, IFA. $35.00

A discussion of the industry and the legal and procedural considerations of a franchise program. Divided into two sections, this guide addresses the major business decisions and typical management problems, as well as state and federal regulations of franchise and business opportunity sales.

FRANCHISING: THE BOTTOM LINE, Robert Bond, Source Book Publications, P.O. Box 12488, Oakland, CA 94604; (510) 839-5471; FAX (510) 547-3245. 1994. 420 pp. $34.95.

This book provides (as of May 1994) actual sales, costs and profits for some 150 broad-based franchise systems. In addition to the actual earnings claims, a profile is provided on each company, general information about the firm and the assumptions used in arriving at the projections. Most major industry categories are covered. In addition, the author provides detailed worksheets and his own insights into making meaningful projections.

FRANCHISING: THE HOW-TO BOOK, Lloyd T. Tarbutton, Prentice-Hall, Englewood Cliffs, NJ. 1986. 226 pp. $17.95.

This guide provides a soup-to-nuts action plan for building and expanding a successful franchising operation. In addition to valuable checklists, the book answers critical questions on franchise marketing and sales, fee structures, franchise agreements, franchisee training programs and various assistance programs. Worthwhile reading for franchisor and franchisee alike.

FRANCHISING WORLD, IFA. $12.00 per year.

This trade magazine is published 6 times per year by the International Franchising Association and gives current news on what's happening in franchising in a news magazine format. The key elements covered are franchise operations, franchisee relationships, legislative information, marketing and industry developments. While intended for franchisors, the publication is of interest to prospective franchisees in terms of staying abreast of the industry.

FRANDATA, 1155 Connecticut Ave., NW, Suite 275, Washington, DC, 20036; (202) 659-8640; FAX (202) 457-0618.

The 1,000 or more current Uniform Franchise Offering Circulars in FranData's library contain vital information on most franchise companies, including their histories, fee structures, initial investment ranges, earnings claims and system growth information, as well as complete copies of financial statements, franchise agreements and franchisee lists. FranData offers the following unique services: 1) document retrieval at approximately $.80/page; 2) research at $50/hour; and 3) financial statements and SEC filings.

HOW TO BE A FRANCHISOR, Robert E. Kushell and Carl E. Zwisler, III, IFA. $5.00.

This booklet describes step-by-step details about how to launch a franchise program. Written from both the operational and legal perspectives, this is excellent reading for all potential franchisors.

HOW TO SELECT A FRANCHISE, Robert McIntosh, IFA. $10.00.

A workbook and cassette tape designed to help individuals decide whether and how to become a franchisee.

INTRODUCTION TO FRANCHISING, Calvin B. Haskell, Jr., Franchise Solutions, P.O. Box 5178, Portsmouth, NH 03802; (800) 898-4455. 1993. 72 pp. $39.95.

This 3-part manual assists the prospective franchisee in making an informed business decision through evaluation, investigation and negotiation. The first part evaluates one's skills, aptitudes, goals and attitudes and is essentially a personal profile or assessment of the franchisee's suitability for franchising. The second part is a step-by-step process for investigating, evaluating and negotiating an optimal franchise opportunity. The third part allows the company, through a telephone interview, to match the background, interests and abilities of the prospective franchisee with several franchises that match the profile. Data sheets on various companies will be forwarded.

IS FRANCHISING FOR YOU?, Robert K. McIntosh, IFA. $3.95.

Basic primer for prospective franchisees with emphasis on self-evaluation to determine whether the opportunities and challenges offered by a franchise system meet the ambitions and abilities of a prospective franchisee.

ROADSIDE EMPIRES—HOW THE CHAINS FRANCHISED AMERICA, Stan Luxenberg, Viking Penguin Press, New York, NY. 1985. 295 pp. $17.95.

A readable history of how franchising has transformed the American landscape, diet and economy. Includes folklore on advertising and marketing techniques, the attention to detail displayed by certain franchisors, and profiles on franchising legends Ray Kroc, Colonel Sanders, Howard Johnson and others. Most informative, however, is the critical look that Luxenberg takes at the real effect of franchising on the economy.

RUNNING A SUCCESSFUL FRANCHISE, Kirk Shivell and Kent Banning, McGraw-Hill, Blue Ridge Summit, PA 17294; (717) 794-5461; FAX (717) 794-2080. 1993. 320 pp. $29.95.

This book focuses on the special issues and day-to-day operational problems involved in actually running a franchise. Coverage includes the transition from corporate life, real world "do's" and "don'ts," setting up and implementing management and reporting procedures, developing sales and marketing programs, creating purchasing and inventory control procedures and recruiting. In addition, there is timely coverage on common areas of conflict between franchisees and franchisors.

THE SOURCE BOOK OF FRANCHISE OPPORTUNITIES, Robert and Jeffrey Bond, Source Book Publications, P.O. Box 12488, Oakland, CA 94604; (510) 839-5471; FAX (510) 547-3245. 1994. 550 pp. $34.95.

A comprehensive directory of franchise offerings, now in its 7th edition, covers some 2,450 franchisors in 47 business categories. Over 1,100 detailed franchisor profiles of leading franchisors in the industry. Its advantage is that its graphic format allows for easy comparison between various franchises. In addition to the profiles, the author provides a statistical overview of the industry and insights into the mechanics of analyzing and investigating various franchises.

TIPS AND TRAPS WHEN BUYING A FRANCHISE, Mary E. Tomzack, McGraw-Hill, New York, NY. 1994. 256 pp. $14.95.

This book steers potential franchisees around the pitfalls and guides them in making a smart, lucrative purchase. Topics include: matching a franchise with personal finances and lifestyle, avoiding the 5 most common pitfalls, choosing a prime location, asking the right questions, etc.

THE 50 BEST LOW-INVESTMENT, HIGH-PROFIT FRANCHISES, Robert L. Perry, 5111 Berwyn Road, # 204, College Park, MD 20740; (301) 441-9424. 1994. 348 pp. $15.95.

This handbook selects and evaluates what it considers to be 50 of the best franchises from among the 2,500 available. It also gives step-by-step instructions on how to choose the best franchise that matches your personal interests and financial resources. It reveals hidden costs and warning signs and how to find them in an offering circular. It describes in detail the pros and cons of 50 proven leaders in franchising.

Nongovernment Assistance
Programs and Information

Better Business Bureaus

Files on many firms that distribute their goods/services through the franchise method are maintained by Better Business Bureaus. A summary report for a specific company on which a Bureau has a record can be obtained free of charge from the Better Business Bureau in the area where the franchising company is headquartered.

If the address of the local Bureau is not known, send a postage paid, self-addressed envelope with the complete name and address of the company on which information is desired to the Council of Better Business Bureaus, Inc., 1515 Wilson Boulevard, Arlington, VA 22209. The Council will either refer your request to, or provide the address of, the appropriate Bureau.

International Franchise Association

The International Franchise Association (IFA) is a non-profit trade association representing more than 680 franchising companies in the U.S. and around the world. It is recognized as a spokesman for responsible franchising. Information on its services and membership requirements may be obtained from the Association's executive offices at 1350 New York Avenue, Northwest, Suite 900, Washington, DC 20005. The IFA's telephone number is (202) 628-8000.

American Association of Franchisees and Dealers

The American Association of Franchisees and Dealers (AAFD) is a multi-faceted, direct member, franchisee trade association. AAFD is dedicated to promoting market and negotiating power and leverage for franchise business owners; educating franchisees and the public to franchising practices; and, providing fair and equitable solutions to problems in the industry. For more information about AAFD, contact:

AAFD
P.O. Box 81887
San Diego, CA 92138-1887
(619) 235-2556

American Franchisee Association

The American Franchisee Association (AFA) is an organization of franchise owners and represents franchisees in 27 industry areas. AFA works to protect the economic investment of franchisees and provides a wide range of services to its members. For more information about AFA, contact:

AFA
53 W. Jackson Boulevard, Suite 205
Chicago, IL 60604
1-800-334-4AFA

Franchise Fact Sheet

International Franchise Association
The Voice of Franchising®
1350 New York Avenue, N.W., Suite 900, Washington, D.C. 20005-4709
Telephone: 202/628-8000 • Fax: 202/628-0812 • Fax On Demand: 202/628-3IFA • IFA's PRODIGY®ID No.: RXNS90C
NOTE: ALL FACTS AND FIGURES ARE FOR U.S. MARKET ONLY.

INTERNATIONAL **Franchise** *Expo*
Washington, D.C. Convention Center
March 8, 9, 10, 1996

SALES:

• $803.2 billion sales estimated in 1992.

• 40.9% of all retail sales.

• Total franchise sales could reach $1 trillion by the year 2000.

• 1 of every 12 business establishments is a franchised business.

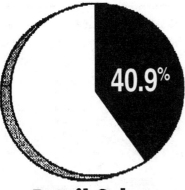

40.9%

Retail Sales

ESTABLISHMENTS:

Growth

• A new franchise opens every 8 minutes of each business day.
• There were 542,496 franchises in 1991, which was estimated to grow to approximately 558,123 by the end of 1992.

25.9%
Product/Trade Name Franchises →

74.1%
← Business Format Franchises

1990: 521,215 Total Franchises
Business format franchises accounted for 48.5% of all establishments in 1975, by 1990 they accounted for 74.1%.

• In 1992, franchise chains created approximately 21,000 new business format franchises. In contrast, more than 220,000 new businesses failed last year, resulting in over 400,000 job losses.

EMPLOYMENT:

• Today, more than 8 million people are employed by franchise establishments, with an average of 8 to 14 employees per establishment.

Jobs
8 Million

• From 1975 to 1988, the total number of people employed in franchising nearly doubled from 3.5 million to 7 million. The number of persons employed per establishment increased 80% from 1975 to 1988, from 8.1 to 14.6 per establishment.

• In the last 12 months, franchise establishments have created more than 170,000 new jobs.

SATISFACTION:

• According to studies conducted by the U.S. Commerce Department from 1971 to 1987, less than 5% of franchises were terminated on an annual basis.

• A 1991 study by Arthur Andersen & Company of 366 franchise companies in 60 industries reported that nearly 86% of all franchise operations opened in the previous five years were still under the same ownership, only 3% of these businesses were no longer in business.

• In contrast, a study by the U.S. Small Business Administration from 1978 to 1988 revealed that 62.2% of all new businesses were dissolved within the first six years of their operation, due to failure, bankruptcy, retirement, or other reasons.

Franchising In The Economy, 1991-1993

Results from *Franchising in the Economy, 1991-1993*, indicate that franchising is not only participating in, but helping to lead America out of its recent economic downturn. The study found that the total number of business format franchises increased 5.36 percent from 1991 to 1992, and 6.95 percent from 1992 to 1993. For 1994, the number of units is expected to increase 8.5 percent. Total sales by franchises increased 4.7 percent from 1991 to 1992 and 8.3 percent from 1992 to 1993. Sales for 1994 are projected to increase 12.9 percent in 1994.

This study, conducted by the University of Louisville, surveyed IFA member companies based in the United States. Usable responses were received from 297 companies (46.8 percent of companies surveyed), representing 65 percent of all business format franchise establishments.

Franchising In The Economy, 1989 to 1992

($ In Billions)	1989	1990	1991	1992	% Change 91-92 (est.)
Total Franchising	$677.9	$713.8	$757.8	$803.2	5.9%
Total Franchises	492,498	521,215	542,496	558,125	2.9%
Business Format Franchising	$192.9	$213.2	$232.2	$249	7.2%
Business Format Franchises	353,253	386,118	408,217	429,217	5.1%
Product & Name Franchising	$484.9	$500.7	$525.6	$554.2	5.4%
Product & Name Franchises	139,245	135,097	134,279	128,908	(.04)%

Business Format Franchise Sales
By Business Category

	1989	1990	1991
Restaurants	70.1	77.8	85.5
Retailing, Non-Food	26.7	29.2	31.4
Hotels/Motels	21.6	23.8	26.0
Business Aids/Services	16.9	18.6	20.8
Automotive Products/Services	12.5	13.8	15.4
Convenience Stores	14.3	14.3	15.0
Retail Food, Non-Convenience	10.0	11.7	12.1
Auto/Truck Rental	6.9	7.3	8.0
Construction, Home Improvement	5.8	6.4	7.1
Recreation	3.5	4.8	4.81
Miscellaneous	2.0	2.3	2.6
Educational Products/Services	1.6	2.03	2.3
Rental Equipment	0.69	0.75	0.77
Laundry & Dry Cleaning	0.36	0.40	0.45
Total	**192.95**	**213.18**	**232.23**

Business Format Franchising

Business format franchises offer the franchise owner not only a trademark and logo but a complete system of doing business. The franchisee receives assistance with site selection, personnel training, business set-up, advertising and marketing, and product supply. For these services the franchisee pays an up-front franchisee fee and agrees to pay on-going royalties which allows the franchisor to provide training, research, development and support for the entire franchise system.

Investigate Before Investing

Franchising is an excellent way to be in business for yourself but not by yourself. While there are thousands of excellent and exciting franchise opportunities, IFA encourages prospective franchisees to investigate before investing. There is no such thing as a guaranteed success in any business venture, including franchising. IFA encourages prospective franchisees to consult with a qualified franchise attorney prior to signing any franchise agreement. IFA provides many educational publications about franchising, including the *Franchise Opportunities Guide*, ($15.00 plus $6.00 for shipping and handling), which includes a list of all IFA members.

International Franchise Association

The mission of the International Franchise Association, founded in 1960, is to enhance and to safeguard the business environment for franchisees and franchisors worldwide. IFA serves as a resource center for curre   nt and prospective franchisees and franchisors, the media, and the government. IFA has been instrumental in devleoping legislation that safeguards franchising from abuse by fraudulent operators. The Association has testified on behalf of programs that expand opportunities for women and minorities in franchising.

IFA represents 27,644 members worldwide, including franchisors, franchisees, the Council of Franchise Suppliers, educational institutions, and sister franchise associations.

FOOTNOTES— Statistics used in this fact sheet are based on numerous studies including *Franchising in the Economy, 1991* (Horwath International and the IFA Educational Foundation), *Franchising in the Economy 1989-1992* (Arthur Andersen & Co. And the IFA Educational Foundation), *Franchising's Growing Role in the U.S. Economy, 1975-2000* (U.S. Small Business Administration), and *State of Small Business, 1989* (U.S. Small Business Administration).

INDEX OF FRANCHISING PARTICIPANTS

Alphabetical

INDEX OF FRANCHISING PARTICIPANTS

By Category

378